Minimal Theologies

Critiques of Secular Reason
in Adorno and Levinas

Hent de Vries

Translated by Geoffrey Hale

The Johns Hopkins University Press
Baltimore and London

An earlier version of this work was published in a German-language
edition as *Theologie im pianissimo: Zur Aktualität der Denkfiguren Adornos
und Levinas'* (Kampen, Neth.: J. H. Kok, 1989).

The Johns Hopkins University Press
2715 North Charles Street
Baltimore, Maryland 21218-4363
www.press.jhu.edu

Library of Congress Cataloging-in-Publication Data
Vries, Hent de.
[Theologie im pianissimo & zwischen Rationalität und Dekonstruktion.
English.]
Minimal theologies : critiques of secular reason in Adorno and Levinas /
Hent de Vries ; translated by Geoffrey Hale.
    p.   cm.
Includes bibliographical references and index.
ISBN 0-8018-8016-5 (hardcover : alk. paper) — ISBN 0-8018-8017-3 (pbk. :
alk. paper)
    1. Philosophical theology. 2. Rationalism. 3. Deconstruction.
4. Dialectic. 5. Transcendence (Philosophy) 6. Adorno, Theodor W.,
1903–1969. 7. Levinas, Emmanuel. I. Title.
BT40.V7513   2004
230'.01—dc22   2004005543

A catalog record for this book is available from the British Library.

For my parents

One who believes in God therefore cannot believe in Him. The possibility for which the divine name stands is maintained by whoever does not believe. [*Wer an Gott glaubt, kann deshalb an ihn nicht glauben. Die Möglichkeit, für welche der göttliche Name steht, wird festgehalten von dem, der nicht glaubt.*]
THEODOR W. ADORNO, *Negative Dialectics*

To bear witness to God is precisely not to state this extraordinary word. [*Témoigner de Dieu, ce n'est précisément pas énoncer ce mot extra-ordinaire.*]
EMMANUEL LEVINAS, *Otherwise than Being or Beyond Essence*

Contents

Preface and Acknowledgments

True thoughts are those alone which do not understand themselves
[*Wahr sind nur die Gedanken, die sich selber nicht verstehen*].
— THEODOR W. ADORNO, *Minima Moralia*

INTRODUCING AND REVISING a book first drafted more than fifteen years earlier — given that one has thought about and studied its topic and wider implications somewhat more in the interim — is surely a risky undertaking. To pretend to have reviewed and mastered the immense corpus of scholarly literature and primary texts published since the book's initial appearance would be even riskier. One soon realizes that one is torn between two contradictory impulses, without any hope of resolution.

On the one hand, there is the painful awareness that in the earlier book so many gaps remain to be filled in, lacunae that could be addressed far better now that new materials have become available. For Adorno there are the lecture courses published as part of the *Nachgelassene Schriften* (*The Posthumous Works*): in particular, *Probleme der Moralphilosophie* (*Problems of Moral Philosophy*), *Kants 'Kritik der reinen Vernunft'* (*Kant's "Critique of Pure Reason"*), *Metaphysik: Begriff und Probleme* (*Metaphysics: Concept and Problems*), *Zur Lehre von der Geschichte und von der Freiheit* (*On the Doctrine of History and of Freedom*), and *Ontologie und Dialektik* (*Ontology and Dialectics*).[1] For Levinas we now have his students' transcription of his final seminar, *Dieu, le temps et la mort* (*God, Death, and Time*), the essays he collected shortly before his death, some of them diffi-

---

1. Theodor W. Adorno, *Probleme der Moralphilosophie*, ed. Thomas Schröder (Frankfurt a.M.: Suhrkamp, 1996) / *Problems of Moral Philosophy*, trans. Rodney Livingstone (Stanford: Stanford University Press, 2000); *Metaphysik: Begriff und Probleme*, ed. Rolf Tiedemann (Frankfurt a.M.: Suhrkamp, 1998) / *Metaphysics: Concept and Problems*, trans. Edmund Jephcott (Stanford: Stanford University Press, 2000); *Kants 'Kritik der reinen Vernunft,'* ed. Rolf Tiedemann (Frankfurt a.M.: Suhrkamp, 1995) / *Kant's "Critique of Pure Reason,"* trans. Rodney Livingstone (Stanford: Stanford University Press, 2001); *Zur Lehre von der Geschichte und von der Freiheit*, ed. Rolf Tiedemann (Frankfurt a.M.: Suhrkamp, 2001); *Ontologie und Dialektik*, ed. Rolf Tiedemann (Frankfurt a.M.: Suhrkamp, 2002).

cult to locate before, and others that have appeared posthumously.[2] Then there is the flood of studies on each of these authors, on those who influenced them, and on those they influenced in turn. And, of course, there is the correspondence of Adorno, as well as, for both authors, biographical accounts.

On the other hand, despite this intimidating wealth of new information, on top of an ever more voluminous and diverse reception, there remains the stubborn but unshakable conviction that one's own earlier interpretation, whatever its many flaws or inevitable omissions, must and can stand as it is. If the comparison were not immodest, one could feel encouraged by words Adorno added in an editorial note to the republication, some thirty years later, of his own *Habilitationsschrift*, entitled *Kierkegaard: Konstruktion des Ästhetischen* (*Kierkegaard: Construction of the Aesthetic*):

> That much . . . no longer satisfies the author is understandable; . . . he would no longer declare metaphysical intentions in such an affirmative way; and the tone strikes him as often more celebratory and idealistic than is warranted. . . . Nevertheless, the author has altered none of the text. . . . He disdains the typical and feeble declaration that the book ought to have been completely revised and that there was not enough time. From early on, he harbored a mistrust of those who deny the writings of their youth, burn manuscripts, and vehemently enlist their own integrity against themselves. His deep aversion to ever beginning a new life extends also to the relationship to his own book. He suspects that, behind the modest self-criticism for which nothing can ever be good enough, there lies the hidden hubris of one who imagines later to have achieved it; a faith in maturity fed by bourgeois prejudice, behind which gerontocracy entrenches itself. Strange to him is also the position, so happily exemplified precisely in Kierkegaard, of the supposed struggle with oneself; one should do as well as possible at a particular time and then leave it at that, and not confuse the compulsion to tinker with the idea of completion. (*K* 262)

This insight emboldens me to present these pages in a slightly revised form after more than a decade has elapsed. True, Adorno based this remark on a different historical experience and distance from the one I allude to here. Having lived through the worst times (as Adorno and his

2. Emmanuel Levinas, *Dieu, la mort et le temps* (Paris: Grasset & Fasquelle, 1993) / *God, Death, and Time*, trans. Bettina Bergo (Stanford: Stanford University Press, 2000).

generation did) is, of course, different from having read and written a few more books under the best of circumstances (as I was privileged to do), in a world in which many things — though not all — have changed for the better. But, when Adorno adds that what has "happened since 1933 ought ultimately to affect a philosophy that always understood itself to be opposed to the equation of metaphysics and a doctrine of eternal constancy," then this conclusion holds true in a more general sense as well (*K* 262).

Having reviewed some of the most significant writings that have appeared since *Theologie im pianissimo*, the original title of this work, was first published in German in 1989,[3] I am still confident that it succeeds in presenting some valid and productive insights that so far have not been formulated by others in these terms or with similar aims and consequences. These insights, I believe, are not refuted but, on the contrary, are confirmed by the newly published sources.

Granted, an impressive body of scholarship on both Adorno and Levinas has appeared since *Theologie im pianissimo* was conceived and written, during my formative years at the University of Leiden from 1984 through 1989. But this literature pays no attention to a systematic confrontation between their respective philosophical projects, if it mentions their names in conjunction at all. There are a few exceptions to this — in my view surprising — situation, but they tend to limit themselves to painting a similarity in existential concerns in all too quick strokes or to stressing comparisons between the intellectual legacies and heirs of these respective authors (e.g., by focusing on parallels between Habermas and Levinas or between Adorno and Derrida).[4] To my knowledge, no single author has analyzed the works of Adorno and Levinas as being invested in a parallel and comparable, if not common, systematic theoretical project, namely, that of exploring — and often dramatically, rhetorically exploiting — alter-

---

3. Hent de Vries, *Theologie im pianissimo: Zur Aktualität der Denkfiguren Adornos und Levinas'* (Kampen, Neth.: J. H. Kok, 1989). Two small sections of the original version of chapters 4–5 appeared as "Die *Dialektik der Aufklärung* und die Tugenden der 'Vernunftskepsis': Versuch einer dekonstruktiven Lektüre ihrer subjektphilosophischen Züge," in *Die Aktualität der "Dialektik der Aufklärung": Zwischen Moderne und Postmoderne*, ed. Harry Kunneman and Hent de Vries (Frankfurt a.M.: Campus, 1989), 183–209; and as "Moralität und Sittlichkeit: Zu Adornos Hegelkritik," in *Hegel-Jahrbuch 1988*, ed. H. Kimmerle, W. Lefèvre, and R. W. Meyer, 300–307.

4. See, e.g., Axel Honneth, "The Other of Justice: Habermas and the Ethical Challenge of Postmodernism," in *The Cambridge Companion to Habermas*, ed. Stephen K. White (Cambridge: Cambridge University Press, 1995), 289–323; and Christoph Menke, *Die Souveränität der Kunst: Ästhetische Erfahrung nach Adorno und Derrida* (Frankfurt a.M.: Suhrkamp, 1991).

native modalities of the *performative contradiction* of argumentative discourse as it seeks to come to terms with *its* other (the nonidentical, Nature, the other, the face, the infinite, the trace, all notions that touch upon, but are not necessarily synonymous with, the religious and the theological). Furthermore, no one has *contrasted* and *confronted,* rather than assimilated, their similar endeavors and the positions taken by the later Habermas and early Derrida, respectively.

In addition to contributions of a more philological, historical, and biographical — or sometimes merely anecdotal — nature, there have been useful thematic explorations of Adorno's relationship to social and political theory, psychoanalysis, philosophy of music, and aesthetics.[5] These studies are of great importance in the further reception and critical reassessment of his thought, as are the numerous studies that have engaged the interdisciplinary features of so-called Frankfurt School Critical Theory, its demarcation from alternative methodologies, its institutional strategies and alliances, and the like. Yet, for all their importance, these inquiries into the intellectual genealogy of this body of work and its socioinstitutional ramifications (aptly investigated by Martin Jay, Rolf Wiggershaus, Helmut Dubiel, Hans-Joachim Dahms, and Alex Demirovic, to name just a few) do not directly address the issue that *Minimal Theologies* engages. Here I am interested in what is first of all (although not exclusively) a *philosophical* argument, one less obsessed with empirical impasses or pitfalls (and, in Adorno's diagnosis of the contemporary social and political world, there were many indeed) than with the *systematic* and *analytical* force of what is an admittedly deeply paradoxical or aporetic thought: Adorno's dialectical critique of dialectics. This dialectics — its concept and categories, like the metaphysics, moral philosophy, and aesthetics that it takes as its model and which it, in turn, implies — is a procedure and practice that remains negative (hence, a *negative dialec-*

5. See, e.g., the various contributions to Nigel Gibson and Andrew Rubin, eds., *Adorno: A Critical Reader* (Oxford: Blackwell, 2002). For more anecdotal details, see Hartmut Scheible, *Theodor W. Adorno* (Reinbek bei Hamburg: Rowohlt, 1989); and Josef Früchtl and Maria Calloni, eds., *Gegen den Zeitgeist: Erinnern an Adorno* (Frankfurt a.M.: Suhrkamp, 1991). Some very informative biographies have been published on the occasion of commemorating Adorno's one hundredth anniversary: Stefan Müller-Doohm, *Adorno: Eine Biographie* (Frankfurt a.M.: Suhrkamp, 2003); Detlev Clausen, *Theodor W. Adorno: Ein Letztes Genie* (Frankfurt a.M.: S. Fischer, 2003); Wolfram Schütte, ed., *Adorno in Frankfurt: Ein Kaleidoskop mit Texten und Bildern* (Frankfurt a.M.: Suhrkamp, 2003); Theodor W. Adorno Archiv, Gabriele Ewenz, Christoph Gödde, Henri Lonitz, and Michael Schwartz, eds., *Adorno: Eine Bildmonographie* (Frankfurt a.M.: Suhrkamp, 2003).

tics) in a sense to be determined. Yet its negativity and the performative contradictions that it deploys or suggests contain a certain — albeit *minimal* — promise as well. To this argumentative, rhetorical, conceptual, and imaginative potential — which, far from creating a deadlock, contains an enormous resource for contemporary philosophizing and theorizing (and not just about religion) — this book is devoted. I locate it in an unmistakable logic and rhetoric of exaggeration, hyperbole, and excess, each of which seeks to convey the smallest thinkable difference, the near indifference that makes all the difference in the world.

Many authors share my interest in the philosophical promise of the immanent critique of dialectics which goes under the name of negative dialectics. Seyla Benhabib, Susan Buck-Morss, Judith Butler, Jay M. Bernstein, Peter Dews, Alessandro Ferrara, Nancy Fraser, Peter Uwe Hohendahl, Axel Honneth, Andreas Huyssen, Fredric Jameson, Martin Jay, Hans Joas, Heinz Kimmerle, Klaus-M. Kodalle, Thomas McCarthy, Christoph Menke, Anson Rabinbach, Martin Seel, Ruth Sonderegger, Anke Thyen, Albrecht Wellmer, and others have all explored the paths set out by the tradition of Critical Theory with an eye to its parallels and contrasts with the philosophy that originated in France during the second half of the twentieth century (which, for reasons that will become clear, I am reluctant to describe in terms of neo- or even poststructuralism). These concerns have found an echo in the most recent work of Habermas, published after 1989 and hence not consulted for the first publication of this study: in particular, *Faktizität und Geltung* (*Between Facts and Norms*), *Nachmetaphysisches Denken* (*Postmetaphysical Thinking*), and *Die Einbeziehung des Anderen* (*The Inclusion of the Other*), and the many essays in his volumes of political writings.

Would these writings, I have each time asked myself, have made it more difficult to play Adorno against Habermas in the way I had proposed in my opening chapter? Do they substantially modify Habermas's somewhat unfortunate polemic against recent French thought as it took shape in *Der philosophische Diskurs der Moderne* (*The Philosophical Discourse of Modernity*), which, like parts of Adorno's *Negative Dialektik* (*Negative Dialectics*), was first presented at the Collège de France? Moreover, would his recently collected essays, statements, and interviews on the subject of religion and rationality or faith and knowledge not ultimately force me radically to revise my overall claims concerning his all too limited treatment of the minimal theological implications of his attempts to "include the other"?[6] Not necessarily. In this book I argue not against Habermas's concrete sociological, juridical, and political insights and engagements—which, by contrast to Adorno's and especially Max Horkheimer's views on the postwar "administered world [*verwaltete Welt*]" have seemed to me always sound and prudent—but against the philosophical premises of his theory of modernization, differentiation, and secularization, in short, against the formalism and supposedly postmetaphysical stance on which his project as a whole relies. So far as I can see, these premises have not been revoked in the later work, in which, as in the earlier writings, they fail to provide necessary or sufficient ground for the analyses based upon them. There is, I argue, a lack of (and perhaps in) *justification* that no formal, let alone transcendental, pragmatic theory of communication can recuperate so long as it claims consistency, generality, universality, and, indeed, formality. Extrapolating my alternative reading, I would also claim that the current tendencies to espouse alternative models of intersubjective justification based on the model of—and struggle for—"recognition [*Anerkennung*]" must founder on the structural deficiency of both the theoretical paradigm in question and, perhaps, the theoretical or any concept of justification as such. By contrast I suggest that, by *showing* an alternative route, Adorno's "solidarity with metaphysics in its downfall" has, for all its paradox, aporia, and seeming abstractness, lost nothing of its topicality. It thus remains far more compelling than his "material" contributions to an interdisciplinary critique of society and culture ever were.

What good would it do to point this out? What difference in contemporary debates could such a negative metaphysics—a minimal and, in Adorno's words, "other" or "inverse" theology—make (theoretically, practically, aesthetically, experientially, and even "spiritually")? What, in other words, would be the major contours of a *minimal metaphysics* in relation to—or as it takes the shapes of—*minimal moralia* but also *minimal politics, minimal expression* (whether in art or life), and so on? Adorno, whose title *Minima Moralia* I have mimicked and varied, adopted the term *micrology* to capture the philosophical logic[7]—the *critical models*

6. See Jürgen Habermas, *Religion and Rationality: Essays on Reason, God, and Modernity,* ed. and intro. Eduardo Mendieta (Cambridge: Polity Press, 2002); and *Glauben und Wissen: Friedenspreis des deutschen Buchhandels 2001* (Frankfurt a.M.: Suhrkamp, 2001).

7. Interestingly, the term *micrologist* is also used by Leo Strauss in *Persecution and the Art of Writing* (Chicago: University of Chicago Press, 1952), 43. For a subtle study of the many meanings of the "minimal" in the history of thought and contemporary philosophy, see Rodolphe Gasché, *Of Minimal Things: Studies on the Notion of Relation* (Stanford: Stanford University Press, 1999).

and *catchwords* (*Stichworte*) — inherent in all genuine thought and praxis, experience and art. What forms could these suggestive figures take under the conditions of present debate? These are the questions this book seeks to raise and to answer, however tentatively.

As with Adorno, many recent thematic, systematic, and biographical studies devoted to Levinas have opened new avenues of research.[8] I discuss some of the most relevant in my *Philosophy and the Turn to Religion* and its companion volume, *Religion and Violence*, especially Jacques Derrida's pivotal essays "Donner la mort" (*The Gift of Death*) and *Adieu à Emmanuel Levinas* (*Adieu to Emmanuel Levinas*).[9] I will therefore not comment upon them further here. Others focus on important thematic and analytical issues that, rightly or wrongly, have not been central to my concerns (e.g., discussions of sexual difference, as in the work of Catherine Chalier, Tina Chanter, Sabine Gürtler, Paulette Kayser, and Ewa Ziarek; engagements with psychoanalysis, as in the work of Elisabeth Weber; the encounter with literary studies and aesthetics, as in the work of Jill Robbins) or opt for a systematic approach of which I am quite frankly somewhat critical: specifically, attempts to appropriate Levinas within the context of Jewish philosophy or, worse still, of a Judeo-Christian theological perspective (which one sees, here and there, in the studies of Richard Cohen, once again Catherine Chalier, Robert Gibbs, Adriaan Peperzak, Josef Wohlmut, and others). I do not deny the tremendous importance of Franz Rosenzweig's *Der Stern der Erlösung* (*The Star of Redemption*) as a source of inspiration for Levinas, as Stéphane Mosès and Dana Hollander have forcefully demonstrated, nor the significance of the biblical and rabbinical tradition, whose reading can, in Levinas, hardly be reduced to

---

8. For an overview, see the special issue *Levinas's Contribution to Contemporary Philosophy*, ed. Bettina Bergo and Diane Perpich, *Graduate Faculty Philosophy Journal* 20, no. 2, and 21, no. 1 (1998). Two informative biographies are Marie-Anne Lescourret, *Emmanuel Levinas* (Paris: Flammarion, 1994); and Salomon Malka, *Emmanuel Lévinas: La Vie et la trace* (Paris: Jean-Claude Lattès, 2002). See also Emmanuel Levinas, *Is It Righteous to Be? Interviews with Emmanuel Levinas*, ed. Jill Robbins (Stanford: Stanford University Press, 2001).

9. Hent de Vries, *Philosophy and the Turn to Religion* (Baltimore: Johns Hopkins University Press, 1999); Hent de Vries, *Religion and Violence: Philosophical Perspectives from Kant to Derrida* (Baltimore: Johns Hopkins University Press, 2001); Jacques Derrida, "Donner la mort," in *L'Éthique du don: Jacques Derrida et la pensée du don*, ed. Jean-Michel Rabaté and Michael Wenzel (Paris: Métailié, Transition, 1992), 11–108 / *The Gift of Death*, trans. David Wills (Chicago: University of Chicago Press, 1995); Jacques Derrida, *Adieu à Emmanuel Levinas* (Paris: Galilée, 1997) / *Adieu to Emmanuel Levinas*, trans. Pascale-Anne Brault and Michael Naas (Stanford: Stanford University Press, 1999).

the confessional genre or to talmudic exegesis or hermeneutics. But Levinas's more overtly "theological" writings, in my view, do not diminish the academic, cultural, and democratic-republican privileging of philosophical reason and universality in his work as a whole.[10] A few authors have been willing to respect this nuance and analyze the fine balancing act it requires: I think in particular of Howard Caygill, Jean-Luc Marion, Hilary Putnam, and Paul Ricoeur.

My greatest disagreement is with readings that attempt to reduce Levinas's radical project to a rehabilitation of ethics or of the primacy of practical philosophy per se. To suggest that Levinas's ethical first — or transcendental — philosophy salvages the task of metaphysics in a new, practical instead of theoretical, guise is, I argue, to underestimate its relentless modernism, not only in its relatively few but remarkable dealings with questions of art but also, and more importantly, in its indefatigable antimoralism. Some critics who have read Levinas coming from (or to) Derrida or Foucault have made similar observations, albeit with other ac-

10. To read Levinas as a representative of Jewish philosophy, let alone in Judeo-Christian fashion, surely cannot mean reading him from an assumed or ascribed subject position that would be Jewish, Christian, or Judeo-Christian. The very act of reading, interpreting, discussing, and philosophizing in a scholarly and responsible fashion ipso facto excludes assuming for oneself — or ascribing to an other — a fixed or supposedly determinable identity as a Jew, Christian, or Judeo-Christian (even if one identifies oneself or the other as such on different, say, empirical, biographical, or confessional grounds). Indeed, despite a marked asymmetry between Levinas's critique and affirmation of certain essential aspects of Christian dogma (to say nothing of liturgy, prayer, and practices in the largest sense), both oblique and explicit references to Christian figures of thought recur throughout his texts. More than interpretive — and, one should add, historically undeserved — generosity is at work here. Invocations of the Christian, of Christianity and Christianicity (or *Christlichkeit*, to cite Overbeck and Heidegger), punctuate his writing at argumentatively crucial points. Reading Levinas in a philosophically responsible and Judeo-Christian way means being sensitive to the isolated yet systematic Christian motifs (theologemes, tropes, and much more) with which Levinas engages throughout his writings and in more than a simply polemical way. True, "Polémiques" ("Polemics") is the title of one of the sections of *Difficile liberté* (*Difficult Freedom*). Yet any careful reading of the essays this book collects must soon complicate the assumption that Levinas's distance from Christianity is easy to determine, let alone purely negative. In what follows I suggest a reading that complicates facile distinctions and thus remains external to any attempt to read Levinas in either Christian or Jewish terms, external even to the *amitié judéo-chrétienne* which Levinas appreciates in the Rosenzweig of the *Star of Redemption*. Here I do not, as in *Philosophy and the Turn to Religion*, take my lead from the figure of *kenosis*, nor do I propose inscribing Levinas into the tradition of "political theology," spelling out its implicit dialogue with a tradition that runs from Augustine to Kant and beyond, as I suggest in the final chapter of *Religion and Violence*. The logic of "theology in pianissimo" suggests yet another possible approach to the recurrent motif of *sans identité* (without identity), which I take to be the core of Levinas's thought.

cents and different lines of approach and argument: Robert Bernasconi, Judith Butler, Fabio Ciaramelli, Simon Critchley, Paul Davies, John Llewelyn, Paola Marrati, Jean-Luc Nancy, Silvano Petrosino, François-David Sebbah, Bernhard Waldenfels, and others. Along these lines Levinas is at once inscribed into the phenomenological tradition and acknowledged as its most subtle deconstructionist *avant la lettre;* one can thus also read him as *l'anti-Heidegger* and, even more forcefully, *l'anti-Hegel,* which he undoubtedly was as well. To this last assessment my book brings a minor—indeed, minimal—qualification, whose consequences, however, are far-reaching (and not just in view of the necessity of rewriting the intellectual history of postwar French thought, its internal demarcations and legacies):[11] Levinas's thought, even though it remains in sync with the general indictment of dialectics (and hence of negativity) in postwar French intellectual life and although it eschews Adornian and, perhaps somewhat more surprisingly, Benjaminian terminology, sketches a *dialectical and negative metaphysics* of sorts. Moreover, just as Adorno's relationship to the tradition of dialectics touches upon this concept's structural limitations, Levinas's solidarity with the method and implied ontology of Husserlian phenomenology goes only that far. In this he does not stand alone, but his articulation of these limitations resembles certain Adornian procedures and themes more than it resonates with the phenomenologies of his day.[12]

WHILE I BELIEVE that the general thrust of my argument is still valid and largely absent from the current philosophical and more largely critical theoretical, cultural, and political debate, I wish I had developed some further points of intersection between the writings and intellectual development of Adorno and Levinas, one of which—the analytical connection, so to speak—would seem somewhat external to my whole undertaking at first glance but, as I have slowly learned, is not. Lack of space and, I

11. For an overview and assessment of the critical engagements with Hegel in twentieth-century French thought, see Vincent Descombes, *Le Même et l'autre: Quarante-cinq ans de philosophie française (1933–1978)* (Paris: Minuit, 1979) / *Modern French Philosophy,* trans. L. Scott-Fox and J. M. Harding (Cambridge: Cambridge University Press, 1982); and esp. Judith Butler, *Subjects of Desire: Hegelian Reflections in Twentieth-Century France* (New York: Columbia University Press, 1987).

12. See François-David Sebbah, *L'Epreuve de la limite: Derrida, Henry, Levinas et la phénoménologie* (Paris: Presses Universitaires de France, 2001); and Agata Zielinski, *Lecture de Merleau-Ponty et Levinas: Le Corps, le monde, l'autre* (Paris: Presses Universitaires de France, 2002).

should add, lack of intellectual resources and strength at the time of completing the earlier project prevented me from elaborating these points in all necessary detail. In this preface and in the revisions and additions to the original text I can scarcely make good on these consecutive challenges.

First, I wish I had even more strongly emphasized the interrogation of phenomenology which Adorno undertakes, starting with his dissertation, through his studies in Oxford from 1934 through 1937, up to the publication of *Zur Metakritik der Erkenntnistheorie* (*Against Epistemology*) in 1956, parallel to his more extensive endeavors to rethink the premises, the scope, and the limits of dialectics in a nonidealist, nonorthodox, materialist sense of the term. Adorno considered *Against Epistemology*, which he had originally intended to entitle *Die phänomenologische Antinomien* (*Phenomenological Antinomies*), to be one of his most important publications, next only to *Negative Dialectics*. Especially in its introduction, it is at least as programmatic as the pivotal essay "Der Essay als Form" ("The Essay as Form"), which was republished in *Noten zur Literatur* (*Notes on Literature*).[13] Although I suggest throughout that one can and must read Adorno *phenomenologically* no less than dialectically — just as, I claim, one must read Levinas *dialectically* no less than phenomenologically — I failed to detail the extent to which Adorno himself prepares for this reading. A more sustained confrontation of Adorno's and Levinas's arguments with the deconstructive readings Jacques Derrida has proposed from early on of the writings of Husserl and Heidegger could have made that even clearer and would have further supported my conclusion that the *dialectical critique of dialectics* (Adorno) and the *phenomenological critique of phenomenology* (Levinas) resemble each other formally, to the point of becoming *almost* interchangeable and collapsing into each other.[14]

Indeed, it is no accident that Bernhard Waldenfels, resuming his many studies on the genealogy of French phenomenology and its contrasts with the tradition of Marxism, systems theory, and discourse theory, observes that "phenomenology entertains with the older Critical Theory — in terms of its content and personal influences — a much more intensive relation-

13. See the editorial afterword to *GS* 5.

14. See Sabine Wilke, "Adornos und Derridas Husserllektüre: Ein Annäherungsversuch," *Husserl Studies* 5 (1988): 41–68; and Rolf Wiggershaus, *Die Frankfurter Schule: Geschichte, theoretische Entwicklung, politische Bedeutung* (Munich: Carl Hanser, 1986), 590 ff. / *The Frankfurt School: Its History, Theories, and Political Significance,* trans. Michael Robertson (Cambridge: MIT Press, 1994), 531 ff. See also Fred. R. Dallmayr, "Phenomenology and Critical Theory: Adorno," *Cultural Hermeneutics* 3 (1976): 367–405.

ship than everything which came later,"[15] in particular, Habermas's pragmatics of language (*Sprachpragmatik*) and the outspoken "normativism [*Normalismus*],"[16] on which it seems premised. One important element in this relationship between phenomenology and Critical Theory, Waldenfels notes, was the "strong concept of experience" which Adorno in particular shares with Edmund Husserl (and Henri Bergson).[17] In consequence it is hardly surprising that Waldenfels should characterize his own early dialogical corrections of the egological features of classical phenomenology (in its orthodox reading) with the Adorno-inspired expression of an "open dialectics."[18] Much less convincing is his suggestion that these corrections of "egology" could only have come from a rethinking that draws on "Foucault and *then* Levinas, since it will not do to follow the reverse route, beginning from an immediate Thou."[19] With this claim Waldenfels endorses the overly naive reading of Levinas which my own reconstruction, with the help of Adorno, seeks to correct. That the immediate yet symmetrical relationship with the "Thou" has never sufficed to articulate our desire for—and exposure to—the other is precisely what Levinas, in his critical departure from Martin Buber's *Ich und Du* (*I and Thou*) and *Das dialogische Prinzip* (*The Dialogical Principle*), stresses from early on. In his own later writings Levinas analyzes this "interpellation" of the other in terms that are indeed reminiscent of Foucault. A common source of inspiration—namely, the work of Maurice Blanchot—may have counted for something here. But, then, some philosophical themes—the interpellation by the other among them—resonate with the whole intellectual climate of postwar French thought.

Second, I should have pursued my insistence on the question of aesthetics—not just literature but also visual arts and music—for Levinas even farther than I do in the present study. I proposed unwrapping Levi-

15. "Gespräch mit Bernhard Waldenfels: '. . . jeder philosophische Satz ist eigentlich in Unordnung, in Bewegung,'" in *Vernunft im Zeichen des Fremden: Zur Philosophie Bernhard Waldenfels*, ed. Matthias Fischer, Hans-Dieter Gondek, and Burkhard Liebsch (Frankfurt a.M: Suhrkamp, 2001), 411.

16. Ibid., 438.

17. Ibid.; see also 457: "Phenomenology is a philosophy of experience or is nothing at all. As is the case in Adorno—albeit in a different way. However, experience does not exhaust itself in there being simply something there. Already in the early *Logische Untersuchungen* (*Logical Investigations*), Husserl notes: to have an experience means to experience something as something [*etwas als etwas*]. And this 'something as something' cannot be located in things."

18. "Gespräch mit Bernhard Waldenfels," 433.

19. Ibid., 434.

nas's intellectual development from its germ cell (*Urzelle*), the pre-ethical and almost surrealist 1935 essay *De l'évasion* (*On Escape*). I also stressed the influence of Maurice Blanchot in the early work, just as I highlighted the presence of rhetoric and poetics in the later. Originally, it sufficed to tease out the implications of the pathbreaking study by Thomas Wiemer, *Passion des Sagens* (*Passion of Saying*). But I should have shown in far more detail just how Levinas adopts an aesthetic mode of presentation and a certain performativity that never intends to substitute for the ethico-religious or, rather, saintly gesture of the Saying (though it can hardly avoid doing so) yet supplements and almost inverts it in surprising and unsettling ways. Mutatis mutandis, the same could have been demonstrated of the motifs of the image, rhythm, eroticism, femininity, caress, and even fecundity, which likewise present philosophy with an otherness (with an other or Other) it can neither comprehend nor exclude but must presuppose or, rather, assume and affirm as a condition of its possibility and its impossibility. Here, from the other side of the spectrum—and from the other end of the book—as it were, it would be necessary to force Levinas and Adorno even closer together. This would have been a promising avenue of research, not least because, although Adorno's engagement with questions of aesthetics appears to be more sustained and straightforward, the comparison with Levinas's—indeed, quite minimal—aesthetic theory allows one to complicate things a bit more.

Third, I ought to have drawn out certain consequences whose logic I was able to formulate only afterward, in *Philosophy and the Turn to Religion* and *Religion and Violence*. With the benefit of hindsight, it now strikes me as an inescapable consequence that both Adorno and Levinas investigate a paradoxical structure of reason in relation to revelation—beyond secularism and beyond fideism—whose implications we have not yet begun to understand in full measure. A reconsideration of Adorno's debate with Eugon Kogon, published under the title "Vernunft und Offenbarung" ("Reason and Revelation"), would have allowed an interesting confrontation with Levinas's "Dieu et la philosophie" ("God and Philosophy"). Both texts leave the task of thinking stretched out, indeed, suspended between identity and difference—or moving in a pendular, alternating, oscillating, and elliptical fashion between these two poles, in the trace of the other (*Spur des Anderen* or *l'Autre, autrui*)—leading to a mode of philosophizing and experiencing which situates itself beyond classical metaphysics, traditional theology, and the modern schools of thought (including the methodological atheism of higher, i.e., historical and textual, criticism; hermeneutic and existential theology; religious studies; etc.).

These authors thus take dialectics and phenomenology to be not ends in themselves but—as Heidegger would have said—*formally indicative modes* of revealing the singular structure of singularity (not *Besonderheit* but *Besonderes;* not alterity or *l'autre* but *l'Autre, autrui*). Dialectics and phenomenology form the *terminus a quo* of the analysis, not the telos of Adorno's and Levinas's thinking as such. The other is not to be had or captured. On the contrary, the paradoxical or, rather, aporetic structure of all discourse about the other necessitates the betrayal of what it "is" which is thus conveyed. Philosophy thus ends up in a continual *performative contradiction.*[20] Testimony, moreover, is structurally insufficient here. *Good conscience is bad conscience.*

Fourth, I should have confronted more centrally some insights from the tradition of analytic or, rather, postanalytic philosophy. Adorno relentlessly criticizes the paradigms of logical positivism, pragmatism, and critical rationalism—all of which he amalgamates and collapses into a single syndrome of supposedly empiricist phenomenalism, undialectical immediacy—for falling victim to the "myth of the given," as Wilfred Sellars phrases it in his classic study *Empiricism and the Philosophy of Mind* and as Richard Rorty canonizes it in *Philosophy and the Mirror of Nature.* There seems not much hope, then, for a fruitful confrontation between negative dialectics, with its meditations on—and solidarity with—metaphysics "in its downfall," on the one hand, and at least a certain phase of analytic thought, on the other. Yet it is surely no accident that such interpreters as Albrecht Wellmer, Rolf Wiggershaus, and Marjorie Perloff have suggested interesting parallels between Adorno's procedures and the later work of Ludwig Wittgenstein,[21] just as Jay M. Bernstein finds ele-

20. See Martin Jay, "The Debate over Performative Contradiction: Habermas vs. the Post-Structuralists," in *Zwischenbetrachtungen: Im Prozess der Aufklärung, Jürgen Habermas zum 60. Geburtstag,* ed. Axel Honneth, Thomas McCarthy, Claus Offe, and Albrecht Wellmer (Frankfurt a.M.: Suhrkamp, 1989), 171–89.

21. See Albrecht Wellmer, "Ludwig Wittgenstein: Über die Schwierigkeiten einer Rezeption seiner Philosophie und ihre Stellung zur Philosophie Adornos," in Brian McGuinness and others, *"Der Löwe spricht . . . und wir können ihn nicht verstehen": Ein Symposium an der Universität Frankfurt anlässlich des hundersten Geburtstages von Ludwig Wittgenstein* (Frankfurt a.M.: Suhrkamp, 1991), 138–48; also in Wellmer, *Endspiele: Die unversöhnliche Moderne, Essays und Vorträge* (Frankfurt a.M.: Suhrkamp, 1993), 239–49 / *Endgames: The Irreconcilable Nature of Modernity, Essays and Lectures,* trans. David Midgley (Cambridge: MIT Press, 1998), 239–49; and Rolf Wiggershaus, *Wittgenstein und Adorno: Zwei Spielarten modernen Philosophierens*

ments of comparison between Adorno's critique of epistemology and John McDowell's *Mind and World*.[22] Furthermore, Habermasian thinkers are greatly interested in the concept of the "normative" as it has been developed by Robert Brandom, Christine Korsgaard, Sabina Lovibond, and others. Still other parallels have in the meantime been observed between the early and later writings of Derrida and those of Wittgenstein, J. L. Austin, Stanley Cavell, and Donald Davidson.[23]

Likewise, although Levinas remains completely silent about these contemporary analytic positions, which he seems simply to ignore, there are good reasons for not taking things at face value here. Not only have attempts been made to explicate Levinas's discourse in terms of speech-act theory, especially the performative, but it is no coincidence that Cavell (after having discussed Walter Benjamin on more than one occasion) has recently found good reason to address the resonance between his own — post-Wittgensteinean and post-Austinean — philosophy of the ordinary in its dealing with the skepticism concerning other minds, on the one hand, and some central issues in the philosophy of Levinas, on the other.[24] Moreover, the theme of Nature, in its Emersonian variety, so central to Cavell's concerns, would again seem to reveal some interesting parallels with the work of Adorno.

Two further points of comparison and confrontation would have been in order, which I will mention here only in passing. First is the question of the nature of Eros, so central to Adorno's understanding of material-

---

(Göttingen: Wallstein, 2000). For a critical account of Adorno's severe judgments concerning Wittgenstein's work, see Marjorie Perloff, *Wittgenstein's Ladder: Poetic Language and the Strangeness of the Ordinary* (Chicago: University of Chicago Press, 1996), 12.

22. See J. M. Bernstein, "Re-enchanting Nature," in *Reading McDowell: On Mind and World,* ed. Nicholas H. Smith (London: Routledge, 2002), 217–45. Yet a further interesting parallel and contrast to be explored would be between Adorno's thinking and the philosophy of Alain Badiou. See Peter Hallward, *Badiou: A Subject to Truth* (Minneapolis: University of Minnesota Press, 2003), 387–88 n. 2.

23. See Ludwig Nagl and Chantal Mouffe, eds., *The Legacy of Wittgenstein: Pragmatism or Deconstruction* (Frankfurt a.M.: Peter Lang, 2001); Samuel C. Wheeler III, *Deconstruction as Analytic Philosophy* (Stanford: Stanford University Press, 2000); Martin Stone, "Wittgenstein on Deconstruction," in *The New Wittgenstein,* ed. Alice Crary and Rupert Read (London: Routledge, 2000), 83–117.

24. See Stanley Cavell, "Benjamin and Wittgenstein: Signals and Affinities," in *Philosophie in synthetischer Absicht / Synthesis in Mind,* ed. Marcelo Stamm (Stuttgart: Klett-Cotta, 1998), 565–82; and Cavell, "What Is the Scandal of Skepticism?" in *ASCA Report 2000,* 22–47; and in *Skepticism in Context,* ed. James Conant and Andrea Kern, forthcoming. On Levinas and the performative, see Jan de Greef, "Skepticism and Reason," in *Face to Face with Levinas,* ed. Richard A. Cohen (New York: State University of New York Press, 1986), 159–79.

ism and to Levinas's phenomenology of femininity and fecundity. I am not convinced that the actuality of their thought resides in these motifs, caught up in part in residual naturalism and the most traditional sexism.[25] By now Levinas has become a point of reference in Anglo-American feminism, gender studies, and queer theory, as in the recent writings of Judith Butler, Seyla Benhabib, Iris Marion Young, and others. Second, I ought to have addressed the critical appreciation of certain psychoanalytic insights, the different ways in which especially Freud and (more obliquely), for Levinas, Lacan are at once a constant point of reference and a locus of contestation. These remain important themes to be developed further.

FOR THE PRESENT EDITION I have corrected obvious errors and updated references and notes where possible and relevant. In addition to this new preface, I have also included an excursus on Adorno's treatment of conceptual idolatry and a discussion of Levinas's engagement with aesthetics as well as a few explanatory notes and paragraphs that draw together some of the main conclusions and outline avenues for further research, some of them linked with the past and ongoing collective projects that culminated in the two volumes *Violence, Identity, and Self-Determination* and *Religion and Media*, and aim to result in a third, *Political Theologies*.[26] I have also added an appendix on Derrida's early conception of the theological and its interpretation by Habermas. This chapter fills in some all too elliptical references in the earlier edition and enables me to circle back to the central considerations from which this book sets out: the difficulty of demarcating the difference between the philosophical and the theological on the basis of the premises of the theory of modernization, rationalization, differentiation, and secularization of the Weberian and Habermasian variety. This chapter also prepares the ground for my more detailed expositions of Derrida's subsequent arguments in *Philosophy and the Turn to Religion* and *Religion and Violence*.

An earlier version of the section on Levinas's *Urzelle*, translated by Dana Hollander, appeared as "Levinas," in Simon Critchley and William R. Schroeder, eds., *A Companion to Continental Philosophy* (Oxford: Blackwell, 1998), 245–55; a version of the appendix was published in Ilse N. Bul-

---

25. For a different recent assessment, see the informative study by Paulette Kayser, *Emmanuel Levinas: La Trace du féminin* (Paris: Presses Universitaires de France, 2000).

26. Hent de Vries and Samuel Weber, eds., *Violence, Identity, and Self-Determination* (Stanford: Stanford University Press, 1997); and de Vries and Weber, eds., *Religion and Media* (Stanford: Stanford University Press, 2001).

hof and Laurens ten Kate, eds., *Flight of the Gods: Philosophical Perspectives on Negative Theology* (New York: Fordham University Press, 2000), 166–94; a shorter version in German of chapter 8 came out in Matthias Fischer, Hans-Dieter Gondek, and Burkhard Liebsch, eds., *Vernunft im Zeichen des Fremden: Zur Philosophie von Bernhard Waldenfels* (Frankfurt a.M.: Suhrkamp, 2001), 99–129; and J. Hackett and J. Wallulis, eds., *Philosophy of Religion for a New Century: Essays in Honor of Eugene Thomas Long* (Dordrecht: Kluwer Academic Publishers, 2004), 187–210; and an early version of the final chapter, "The Other Theology," was published in *Archivio di Filosofia*. All these texts were considerably rewritten for the present publication.

IN WRITING THE ORIGINAL version of this, my first book, I incurred many debts, which I would like to acknowledge here. First of all, I want to express my gratitude to my teacher, Han Adriaanse, whose scholarly integrity and erudition have remained an example long after my years at the University of Leiden were over. With Harry Kunneman I have shared an undiminished passion for the inspiring program of the first and second generation of the so-called Frankfurt School, which dates from the moment when we jointly organized an international workshop in Amsterdam on the fortieth anniversary of the publication of the *Dialektik der Aufklärung* (*Dialectic of Enlightenment*), which appeared in 1947 from Querido in Amsterdam, as well as during the conference that we convened in 1991, which resulted in the volume *Enlightenments: Encounters between Critical Theory and Contemporary French Thought*.[27] Wouter Oudemans and Jean Greisch were among the first to confront me with critical and helpful feedback. Without the initiative and encouragement of Rainer Nägele, my first chair, Bill Regier, my first editor, and Rodolphe Gasché, my first external reader, the English translation and re-edition of my first book would never have been undertaken. Furthermore, without the generous support of Sijbolt Noorda, then provost and now president of the University of Amsterdam, and Pieter de Meijer, its former Rector Magnificus, it would not have gotten started and financed. None of this would have come about, however, were it not for the intervention of Hotze Mulder, secretary of the board of the Faculty of Humanities, whose gracious support

27. Kunneman and de Vries, *Die Aktualität der 'Dialektik der Aufklärung': Zwischen Moderne und Postmoderne;* and *Enlightenments: Encounters between Critical Theory and Contemporary French Thought* (Kampen, Neth.: Kok Pharos, 1993).

over the years I hereby wish to acknowledge. I am also grateful for the conscientious and persistent labor with which Geoffrey Hale has brought this translation to a conclusion. As so often, Helen Tartar, my other editor, was a truly wonderfully engaged reader of the manuscript in its penultimate stage.

Finally, I feel privileged to have had the chance to discuss the book with Emmanuel Levinas, who kindly invited me to his home on two occasions, in 1989 and 1991, to examine its central theses. These meetings, as well as three others at international conferences devoted to his work, in Roermond and Wahlwiller, in the south of The Netherlands, offered a model of relentless and disinterested philosophizing which I shall not easily forget. Not only was Levinas keen to point out the two major lacunae in this work—the relative absence of a discussion of Heidegger and a largely implicit indebtedness to Derrida, whom I had then insufficiently read—he was also extremely generous in encouraging a young, enthusiastic reader to go his own way without any concern for the directions his reception might take. His own intellectual encounter with Adorno had consisted in no more than a cursory reading of Adorno's anti-Heideggerian pamphlet *Jargon der Eigentlichkeit* (*Jargon of Authenticity*), by which he was clearly—and rightly—not greatly impressed. And my attempt to steer the discussion in the direction of Walter Benjamin, a seemingly more promising venue, incited even less enthusiasm. What remained was his hospitality to my modest attempts to formalize the logic of his argument in philosophical terms and with systematic concerns at times quite different from his own. That the confrontation with Adorno's dialectical critique of dialectics, with its obsessive treatment of the "other" and even the "totally other," could lead one to broaden, generalize, universalize, and thereby—inevitably—trivialize his own concern with the "ethical Other" (the other as *autrui*, in the trace of God) as it takes shape in his no less radical phenomenological critique of phenomenology, was clearly not an avenue of thought he could have himself imagined pursuing. But an important thesis of my book is that this remains a possible result of the—as Adorno would say—immanent critique of his work.

With the publication of this volume, I conclude what I have come to think of as a trilogy. Ironically, this translation forms an extended prolegomenon, after the fact, to my *Philosophy and the Turn to Religion* and *Religion and Violence*, even though it can be read independently and, I hope and trust, on its own merits. I thank the staff of the Johns Hopkins University Press, especially Henry Tom, Michael Lonegro, Carol

Zimmerman, Claire McCabe, Casey Schmidt, Andre Barnett, and Karen Willmes, for the great care with which they have consistently supported the production of these three long volumes. Paola Marrati shared and inspired many moments of final work on the manuscript, as did my other wonderful colleagues at the Humanities Center of Johns Hopkins University — Michael Fried, Ruth Reys, Neil Hertz, and Richard Mecksey. All of them, together with our group of excellent graduate students, created a truly exceptional and hospitable intellectual climate in which one can only feel very privileged to teach and write.

Like its German original, this concluding work — the trilogy's first and last word — is dedicated to my parents. Their undiminished moral example and intellectual interest over all these years, often at moments when I myself had all but given up, has meant more to me than any formal acknowledgment could express. Without their calm insistence and trust I would not have completed this study or, for that matter, the ones to follow. They taught me that, in writing a book like this one, one must give all. But also that this — writing a book — is not all there is, or even the most and best there is to give.

Abbreviations

APh   Theodor W. Adorno. "Die Aktualität der Philosophie." *GS* 1, *Philoso-phische Frühschriften* (1973): 325–44. Trans. Benjamin Snow under the title "The Actuality of Philosophy," *Telos*, no. 31 (Spring 1977): 120–33.

AT   Theodor W. Adorno. *Ästhetische Theorie. GS* 7 (1972). Trans. Robert Hullot-Kentor under the title *Aesthetic Theory* (Minneapolis: University of Minnesota Press, 1997).

CPP   Emmanuel Levinas. *Collected Philosophical Papers.* Trans. Alphonso Lingis. Dordrecht: Martinus Nijhoff, 1986.

DE   Max Horkheimer and Theodor W. Adorno. *Dialektik der Aufklä-rung: Philosophische Fragmente. GS* 3 (1981). Trans. Edmund Jephcott under the title *Dialectic of Enlightenment* (Stanford: Stanford University Press, 2002).

DEHH   Emmanuel Levinas. *En découvrant l'existence avec Husserl et Heidegger.* 2d ed. Paris: Vrin, 1967.

DF   Emmanuel Levinas. *Difficile liberté: Essais sur le Judaïsme.* Paris: Albin Michel, 1976. Trans. Seán Hand under the title *Difficult Freedom: Essays on Judaism* (Baltimore: Johns Hopkins University Press, 1990).

Drei Stud   Theodor W. Adorno. *Drei Studien zu Hegel. GS* 5 (1970): 247–375.

EE   Emmanuel Levinas, *De l'existence à l'existant.* Paris: Vrin, 1978. Trans. Alphonso Lingis under the title *Existence and Existents* (Dordrecht: Kluwer, 1988).

EI   Emmanuel Levinas, *Ethique et infini: Dialogues avec Philippe Nemo.* Paris: Arthème Fayard and Radio France, 1982. Trans. Richard A.

Cohen under the title *Ethics and Infinity: Conversations with Philippe Nemo* (Pittsburgh: Duquesne University Press, 1985).

EN Emmanuel Levinas. *Entre nous: Essais sur le penser-à-l'autre.* Grasset & Fasquelle, 1991. Trans. Michael B. Smith and Barbara Harshav under the title *Entre Nous: Thinking-of-the-Other* (New York: Columbia University Press, 1998).

GCM Emmanuel Levinas. *De Dieu qui vient à l'idée.* Paris: Vrin, 1982. Trans. Bettina Bergo under the title *Of God Who Comes to Mind* (Stanford: Stanford University Press, 1998).

GS Theodor W. Adorno. *Gesammelte Schriften.* Ed. Rolf Tiedemann. Frankfurt a.M.: Suhrkamp, 1970–86.

HAH Emmanuel Levinas. *Humanisme de l'autre homme.* Montepellier: Fata Morgana, 1972.

Idee Theodor W. Adorno, "Die Idee der Naturgeschichte." *GS* 1, *Philosophische Frühschriften* (1973): 345–65.

K Theodor W. Adorno. *Kierkegaard: Konstruktion des Ästhetischen. GS* 2 (1997). Trans. Robert Hullot-Kentor under the title *Kierkegaard: Construction of the Aesthetic* (Minneapolis: University of Minnesota Press, 1989).

MM Theodor W. Adorno. *Minima Moralia: Reflexionen aus dem beschädigten Leben. GS* 4 (1980). Trans. E. F. N. Jephcott under the title *Minima Moralia: Reflections from Damaged Life* (London: Verso, 1974).

ND Theodor W. Adorno. *Negative Dialektik. GS* 6 (1973): 9–412. Trans. E. B. Ashton under the title *Negative Dialectics* (London: Routledge and Kegan Paul, 1973).

NL Theodor W. Adorno. *Noten zur Literatur. GS* 11 (1974). Trans. Shierry Weber Nicholsen under the title *Notes to Literature,* 2 vols. (New York: Columbia University Press, 1991–92).

OB   Emmanuel Levinas. *Autrement qu'être ou au-delà de l'essence.* The Hague: Martinus Nijhoff, 1974. Trans. Alphonso Lingis under the title *Otherwise than Being, or Beyond Essence* (The Hague: Martinus Nijhoff, 1981).

OE   Emmanuel Levinas. *De l'évasion.* Ed. and intro. Jacques Rolland. Montpellier: Fata Morgana, 1982. Trans. Bettina Bergo under the title *On Escape* (Palo Alto: Stanford University Press, 2003).

OMB   Emmanuel Levinas. *Sur Maurice Blanchot.* Montpellier: Fata Morgana, 1975. Trans. Michael B. Smith under the title "On Maurice Blanchot," in Levinas, *Proper Names* (Stanford: Stanford University Press, 1996), 127–70.

OS   *Hors sujet.* Montpellier: Fata Morgana, 1987. Trans. Michael B. Smith under the title *Outside the Subject* (Stanford: Stanford University Press, 1994).

P   Theodor W. Adorno. "Fortschritt." In *Stichworte, GS* 10.2 (1977): 617–38. Trans. Henry W. Pickford under the title "Progress," in Adorno, *Critical Models: Interventions and Catchwords* (New York: Columbia University Press, 1998), 143–60.

PN   Emmanuel Levinas. *Noms propres.* Montpellier: Fata Morgana, 1976. Trans. Michael B. Smith under the title "Proper Names," in Levinas, *Proper Names* (Stanford: Stanford University Press, 1996), 1–123.

RS   "La Réalité et son ombre." *Les Temps Modernes* 38 (1948): 771–89. Trans. Alphonso Lingis under the title "Reality and Its Shadow," in *Collected Philosophical Papers* (Dordrecht: M. Nijhoff, 1987), 1–13; reprinted in Seán Hand, ed., *The Levinas Reader* (Oxford: Basil Blackwell, 1989), 129–43.

TI   Emmanuel Levinas. *Totalité et Infini: Essai sur l'extériorité.* The Hague: Martinus Nijhoff, 1961. Trans. Alphonso Lingis under the title *Totality and Infinity: An Essay on Exteriority* (Pittsburgh: Duquesne University Press, 1969).

TIH   Emmanuel Levinas. *Théorie de l'intuition dans la phénoménologie de Husserl.* 1930. Reprint. Paris: Vrin, 1978. Trans. André Orianne under the title *The Theory of Intuition in Husserl's Phenomenology* (Evanston, Ill.: Northwestern University Press, 1973, 1995).

TO   Emmanuel Levinas. *Le Temps et l'autre.* Paris: Presses Universitaires de France, 1979. Trans. Richard A. Cohen under the title *Time and the Other and Additional Essays* (Pittsburgh: Dusquesne University Press, 1987).

In all abbreviations and short-form citations in which dual page numbers are given, the first page refers to the English translation, the second to the text in its original language. If only one page number is given, no published English translation of the text or portion of a text exists or was consulted.

Minimal Theologies

Introduction: Tertium Datur

The history of philosophy is probably nothing but a
growing awareness of the difficulty of thinking.

In the meantime, we tread a *no-man's land,* an
in-between that is uncertain even of the uncertainties
that flicker everywhere. Suspension of truths! Unusual
times!

— *PN* 55 / 81–82

IN THE MODERN AGE thought increasingly must do without a substantial and fundamentally onto-theological determination of philosophical reason and rationality. No longer can modern thinkers reconcile the concept of theoretical reason with the idea of an all-encompassing speculation on metaphysical grounds, establishing a "mirror of nature," as Richard Rorty succinctly puts it, a reflection on (and of) being, including, ultimately, the highest Being, the One and All, traditionally called "God." Similarly, modern thought has ceaselessly stripped practical reason of its basis and its confidence in concrete communal conceptions of the forms in which the good life (*das gute Leben*) might be available, whether historically or in the present. The texts that will interest us here explore *and* avoid — or, more carefully, bracket — such possibilities for life as one of their central themes. Finally, modern thinking has relentlessly severed the making of aesthetic judgments from the imitation (*mimesis*) or figural representation of the natural object, from the expression of moral imperatives and the dictates of political engagement, as well as from preestablished identities and fixed determinations of the self. Kant's Copernican turn effected a reversal of perspective which located knowledge, action, and judgment squarely within the constructive and synthetic faculty of the individual human intellect and its freedom. But the erosion of metaphysics didn't stop there.

As the tradition of Frankfurt School Critical Theory from Theodor W. Adorno to Jürgen Habermas reminds us, it would nevertheless be overhasty to reduce the concept of reason — in the wake of naturalism and culturalism, relativism and hermeneutical skepticism[1] — to an exclusively subjective, even instrumentalist disposition, whose generality and ultimate universality is mere illusion, indeed, no more than a fundamentally fictional narrative on a grand scale. As Habermas rightly claims in *Der philosophische Diskurs der Moderne* (*The Philosophical Discourse of Modernity*): "Reason is valid neither as something ready-made, as an objective teleology that is manifested in nature or history, nor as a mere subjective faculty."[2] In his intellectual project Habermas attempts to persuade us that, in a modern theory of rationality, although the universal conditions of possibility for reasonable thought and action, like those for aesthetic judgment and expression, are not a given, written in Nature, one can at least reconstruct them in a formal — more precisely, formally pragmatic — way. In marked contrast to the Husserlian and Heideggerian concern with the "transcendental historicity" and "formal indication" of idealizations and all other essential linguistic, practical, and imaginative features of human existence — and still farther from Foucault's archaeology of the "historical a priori" (to which some critical chapters of *The Philosophical Discourse of Modernity* are devoted) — Habermas's inquiries retain a notion of reason and rationality which is at once more emphatic, proleptic, and fragile. In his view a philosophically and empirically informed critical theory that could have relevance for social, legal, and political questions (and be in tune with the sensibility of modern subjects) should not search for transcendental essences, categories, existentials, paradigms, or even epistemes but should limit its ambition to capturing more elusive motifs and motivations. Yet Habermas is convinced that the "reproduction of life forms and life histories leaves behind impressions in the soft medium of history which, under the strained gaze of those seeking traces

1. Jennifer Hornsby notes that the term *naturalism* "is commonly used nowadays for the position that the mind's place is *in* nature, that conscious purposive subjects are simply elements of the natural world. The presumed alternative to naturalism in this sense, branded Cartesian Dualism, holds that minds are unnatural things — that conscious purposive subjects are not through and through a part of the natural world" (*Simple Mindedness: In Defense of Naïve Naturalism in the Philosophy of Mind* [Cambridge: Harvard University Press, 1997], 2). We will come to the terms *culturalism, relativism,* and *skepticism* later.

2. Jürgen Habermas, *Der philosophische Diskurs der Moderne: Zwölf Vorlesungen* (Frankfurt a.M.: Suhrkamp, 1985), 69 n. 4 / *The Philosophical Discourse of Modernity: Twelve Lectures,* trans. Frederick G. Lawrence (Cambridge: MIT Press, 1987), 392 n. 4. In the following references to this work, as well as to all other cited texts for which a translation is available, page references to the English translation will precede references to the German (or French) original, either parenthetically in the text or in the footnotes.

[*Spurensuchern*], solidify into sketches [*Zeichnungen*] and structures,"[3] whose minimal traits are far from irrelevant. It is from these, he believes, that the philosophical and empirically oriented discourse of modernity, with its agenda of personal and political emancipation—that is to say, of individual and collective learning processes—should take its lead.

Of course, the formal theory of communicative rationality, as Habermas will come to call it, can always err in its reconstruction of these fundamentally contingent, unstable, and fragile "configurations."[4] It can grasp the "encoded [*verschlüsselte*] indications in the trace of unfinished, interrupted, and misguided processes of self-formation [*Bildungsprozesse*] that transcend the subjective consciousness of the individual"[5] only as hypothetical and counterfactual clues to what constitutes reason and reasonableness in their formal (i.e., rational) feature.[6] It lacks the competence to determine the temporally and culturally—indeed, ethically and politically—variable content (*Substanz, Gehalt*) which would translate, incarnate, yet also distort these formal features. Hence, it must suspend—or, in phenomenological parlance, bracket—all philosophical judgment concerning concrete and singular matters of fact and value. Its naturalism and cognitivism goes only so far and avoids determining the good life in empirical or conceptual terms. In teasing out merely the structural or formal features of reason, the theory of communicative action (as Habermas will come to say) professes its postmetaphysical, antiontological, and ultimately antiutopian stance. It assumes that there are no further principles or foundations whose substance or essence (origin, idea, or telos) could be theoretically reconstructed, practically justified, or aesthetically validated. Without these traditional ambitions and warrants, the "philosophical discourse of modernity" acknowledges the limited and provisional character of all its intuitions as well as the intrinsic fallibility of each of its individual statements. It thereby relies on purely formal and structural—and, in Habermas's reading, this means procedural and discursive—criteria alone. By means of these criteria the theory of rationality, after Kant and in the wake of the hermeneutic sociology of Max Weber,

3. Ibid., trans. modified.

4. Ibid.

5. Ibid.

6. The challenge and difficulty of Habermas's project is, in my reading, not so much the determination of the "reasonableness of the rational" but of the "rationality of reason and the reasonable." The latter, I will argue, presupposes a certain limitation of the concept of reason as well as rationality.

becomes an intersubjectively transformed "first philosophy" that is no longer substantialist, objectivist, egological, or monological: this time in the guise of a "de-transcendentalized" and, at best, *quasi*-transcendental pragmatics.[7]

Freed from all "substance" and "content," even from the atemporal and immutable transcendental conditions of possibility for experience as they have been traditionally and, in the Kantian idiom, critically defined, the philosophical discourse of modernity draws from this a remarkable consequence. It places "the sphere of nonbeing and the mutable under the determinations of insight and error; it transports reason into a realm that was held to be simply meaningless and unsusceptible to theory by Greek ontology as well as by the modern philosophy of the subject."[8] This ambition of Habermas, together with his indefatigable reception of the most challenging (and diverse) schools of twentieth-century thought — Freudian psychoanalysis, Western neo-Marxism, American pragmatism, post-analytic philosophy of language, speech-act theory, generative grammar, developmental psychology, ethno-methodology, and systems theory — in addition to a permanent reflection on the classic authors of social thought and anthropology (Marx, Weber, Durkheim, Mead, and Parsons), is sufficient reason to admire the theoretical span of his theory.

One cannot help wondering, however, whether a theory so firmly oriented to systematic integration and, finally, empirical anchoring can adequately reconstruct and interpret the instances (or, as Habermas puts it, "traces") of a postmetaphysical and emphatic-proleptic concept of reason — that is, an idea of reason in the mode of the counterfactual and the nonexistent. Given its preoccupation with the formal, the procedural, the discursive, the finite, and the fallible, can the theory of rationality and communicative action Habermas proposes convincingly claim to have confronted the "sphere of nonbeing and the mutable," from which it claims to take its leading, and perhaps most fundamental, inspiration? Won't, to cite Max Horkheimer's famous distinction, *Critical* Theory find this "sphere" (which is neither the ancient *topos noētos* nor the modern realm of the noumenal, or intelligible) just as "meaningless and unsusceptible" as did *traditional* theory, which discarded it as too ephemeral and singular to be worthy of philosophical attention, let alone of being cap-

---

7. For a more recent restatement of this position, see Jürgen Habermas, *Kommunikatives Handeln und detranszendentalisierte Vernunft* (Stuttgart: Reclam, 2001).

8. Habermas, *Philosophical Discourse of Modernity*, 392 n. 4.

tured by scientific reasoning?[9] Does reason not touch here upon a dimension or an element directly opposed to itself, upon an otherness standing at its opposite pole, an "other" of reason, the nonrational par excellence? Should it, then, consider this otherness, this other of reason, to be the fully irrational, that is to say, the mere privation of rationality, the not yet fully rational or the beyond of the rational? Or, rather, is this other dimension or element of otherness, like discursive rationality itself, somehow a constitutive moment in the emphatic, communicative idea of reason, whose concept and multiple features (and, as we shall see, "voices") form the core of Habermas's own theory in its most articulate and subtle formulations?

How might one — philosophically, practically, aesthetically, and, if need be, theologically — grasp conceptually or otherwise express such an "other of reason" (*ein Anderes der Vernunft*, in all the ambiguity of this double genitive, that is, as *genitivus objectivus* and *subjectivus*, as the other compared with, indeed, well beyond, reason or as reason's own other dimension and element)? Can one articulate the diffuse and singular traces and configurations of the good or just life (rather than its "substance" or "content," origin and telos) in a general framework of discourse? (Even if this discourse has been communicatively transformed and now defines itself — after yet another Copernican, this time linguistic-pragmatic turn — as in principle open, that is to say, endless, if not infinite, without any preconceived opinions or prejudice, indeed, as nonviolent.) Does the diffuse and singular, however formally captured, not do violence to reason; or, conversely, does reason not — inevitably — do violence to it?

To avoid this consequence, should one not return to the age-old idea of the Absolute, now as an "absolute" that, under "postmetaphysical" conditions, must be marked as a nonbeing, that is to say, as a hypothetical, a counterfactual *instance,* a nonverifiable yet falsifiable hypothesis, a *trace,* even if nothing more than the always precarious and effaceable "trace of the other," in Levinas's words? Such an absolute, which no longer either can or should resemble or represent the highest being — indeed, in a certain sense, which no longer even "is" — might, I would suggest, best be called an *ab-solute,* in the etymological sense of the word (i.e., from the Latin *absolvere,* "to set free"). Its "encoded indications," hinting at the "sphere of nonbeing and the mutable" — that is, at that which, at least for

9. Max Horkheimer, "Traditionelle und kritische Theorie," in *Gesammelte Schriften,* vol. 4, ed. Alfred Schmidt and Gunzelin Schmid Noerr (Frankfurt a.M.: S. Fischer, 1988), 162–216; see also Alfred Schmidt, *Zur Idee der kritischen Theorie* (Regensburg: Carl Hanser, 1974), 7–35.

traditional reason and critique, must remain (almost) meaningless and unsusceptible—would thus stand for that which incessantly breaks away from any solid or definite context of meaning and action, judgment and expression.

Yet did Habermas not aim to reconstruct the solid and definite contexts that would enable the regulative idea of an ideal speech situation, wherein equals converse without coercion—that is to say, with appropriate transparency and, hence, without idiosyncrasy or violence? Can his project allow us to think, reconstruct, and act upon the "absolute" as at once minimally and, I would venture to say, globally conceived?

Emmanuel Levinas's philosophy can help us to describe this idea of the absolute in what seems an at once structural *and* singular, formal *and* indicative, as opposed to merely demonstrative or indexical, way. The absolute—the idea of the "infinite" or "in-finite," in his idiom—is a signification or sense without (fixed) context, without (given) horizon, without (ultimate) referent.[10] Nonetheless, this motif—presented in philosophical terms but not without important biblical, talmudic, and literary antecedents—will help us to pair a certain operation of abstraction with a no less interesting procedure of phenomenological concretization. The absolute and the infinite are not mere ideas; they are equally intelligible in their embodied (if not, strictly speaking, corporeal, material, or incarnate) forms. Their paradoxical phenomenality escapes the grasp of the empirical categories with which the different naturalisms (whether biological, psychological, or cultural) by definition operate. By contrast, the absolute—and in Levinas's reading this means the ethical, the saintly—can emerge only where all such categories, concepts, or forms of perception, experience, language, and life have, as it were, not yet appeared and dictated their rule or, conversely, where they are already too late to register what has passed them by: the trace of the other/Other, which never enters our horizon but comes to us, as Levinas says, from a dimension of height.[11]

10. See Emmanuel Levinas, "Infini," in *Encyclopaedia Universalis* (Paris: Presses Universitaires de France, 1976), 8:991–94; rpt. in Emmanuel Levinas, *Altérité et transcendence* (Montpellier: Fata Morgana, 1995), 69–89 / *Alterity and Transcendence*, trans. Michael B. Smith (New York: Columbia University Press, 1999), 53–76. On the historical and systematic ramifications of the notion of the infinite, see also A. W. Moore, *The Infinite* (London: Routledge, 1990).

11. A different question concerns whether or to what extent Levinas's conception of the infinite—the infinity of being or the infinity beyond being and beings (fundamentally, the difference between the two alternatives matters little here)—resembles the later Maurice Merleau-Ponty's notion of "the flesh [*la chair*]." See Agata Zielinski, *Lecture de Merleau-Ponty et Levinas: Le Corps, le monde, l'autre* (Paris: Presses Universitaires de France, 2002).

The central features of this Levinasian motif of the absolute and the infinite, I claim, can also be distilled from a careful reinterpretation of Adorno's central texts. His negative dialectics is premised on a similar oscillation between formalization and abstraction, on the one hand, and materialization qua singularization, on the other.[12] The two central parts of my study will be devoted to these authors. As we shall see, their procedures do not involve a hermeneutically understood process of interpretation, translation, transposition, and application of the absolute and infinite in determinable and finite ethical, political, cultural, and juridical contexts, whose meanings would somehow be given with human existence, history, and sociality as such. Rather, each of these determinants (the ethical, the political, the cultural, the juridical, etc.) is put under erasure and reconfigured from the ground up with the help both of newly coined concepts and of traditional — religious, theological, and metaphysical — ideas, which have been radically recast, in a manner (and often, in both authors, with a certain textual mannerism and monomania) which exceeds the alternative between orthodoxy and heterodoxy and which is at once infinitely close to and at an infinite remove from the dogmas, rhetorical strategies, and imagery of Judeo-Christian religion, including the mystical, negative, affirmative, and superlative modes of its discourse (apophatic and kataphatic theology, *via eminentiae,* etc.). Interestingly, such an intermediary position — a position beyond known and mutually exclusive alternatives, a *tertium datur* — can also be discerned in some, albeit largely implicit, elements of Habermas's later writings.

It might seem exaggerated to suggest that the motivation for Habermas's major work lies in what he once attributed to Michael Theunissen, the author not only of numerous studies on Hegel's *Logic,* Kierkegaard, and Adorno but also of *Der Andere* (*The Other*) and essays collected under the title *Negative Theologie der Zeit* (*Negative Theology of Time*), namely: "seizing at least a tip of the absolute — even if in concepts of inter-

---

12. Adorno's thinking in these matters is continually entwined with the quasi-messianic and quasi-theological thought of Kierkegaard and Walter Benjamin (whose writings I shall discuss only indirectly). By the same token Levinas, in his "confessional" and talmudic writings, repeatedly draws on the tradition of rabbinical thought, its hermeneutics, conception of the relationship between Israel and the nations, and understanding of the politics of everyday life. For a more extensive treatment, see my book *Religion and Violence: Philosophical Perspectives from Kant to Derrida* (Baltimore: Johns Hopkins University Press, 2001), chaps. 3–4. For the motif of "everyday life," found in Freud, Wittgenstein, and Cavell as well as in Levinas, see Eric L. Santer, *On the Psychotheology of Everyday Life: Reflections on Freud and Rosenzweig* (Chicago: University of Chicago Press, 2001), esp. 14 n. 3.

subjectivity—after a long journey through the ruins [*Trümmer*] of negative theology."[13] References to the theological heritage, in particular, to
the mystical tradition, are not absent from Habermas's writing. Indeed,
they remind us of his early concern—in his dissertation, "Das Absolute in
der Geschichte" ("The Absolute in History")—with the philosophy of the
Weltalter (*The Ages of the World*) of the later Schelling,[14] which also deeply
influenced Franz Rosenzweig and, via him, Levinas. The difficulty is to determine the exact role they play in Habermas's overall argumentation. Do
they indicate a religious legacy that forms part and parcel of his intellectual biography and thus constitutes a central element in the genealogy and
general orientation of his work? Are they a merely a point of departure
which was subsequently left behind, reduced to invisibility, inaudibility,
or near insignificance? Are they metaphors and tropes that have gradually
become concepts, or are they original motifs and motivations reinforced
by fundamental philosophical intuitions, based on concerns of a more
existential nature that, under modern conditions, could not be expressed
or articulated without recourse to the realm of intersubjectivity—that is
to say, interaction, discourse, and communicative action? Some of Habermas's statements, which claim a dual source of inspiration in religion and
in the quotidian experience of conversing with others, made explicit by
rational reconstruction, seem to point in that direction:

> I have a conceptual motive [*Gedankenmotiv*] and a fundamental intuition.
> This, by the way, refers back to religious traditions such as those of the Prot-
> estant or Jewish mystics, also to Schelling. The motivating [*motivbildende*]
> thought concerns the reconciliation of a modernity which has fallen apart, the
> idea that without surrendering the differentiation that modernity has made
> possible in the cultural, the social and economic spheres, one can find forms

13. Jürgen Habermas, *Nachmetaphysisches Denken: Philosophische Aufsätze* (Frankfurt
a.M.: Suhrkamp, 1988), 278. The appendix from which the quote is taken is not included in
the English translation, *Postmetaphysical Thinking: Philosophical Essays,* trans. William Mark
Hohengarten (Cambridge: MIT Press, 1993). Habermas refers to Michael Theunissen's article
"Negativität bei Adorno," in *Adorno-Konferenz 1983,* ed. Ludwig von Friedenburg and Jürgen
Habermas (Frankfurt a.M.: Suhrkamp, 1983), 41–65; and to Michael Theunissen, *Selbstverwirklichung und Allgemeinheit: Zur Kritik des gegenwärtigen Bewußtseins* (Berlin: Walter de Gruyter,
1982). Since then Theunissen has published *Negative Theologie der Zeit* (Frankfurt a.M.: Suhrkamp, 1991).

14. Jürgen Habermas, "Das Absolute in der Geschichte: Von der Zwiespältigkeit in Schellings Denken" (Ph.D. diss., Bonn, 1954). See also the chapter devoted to Schelling and the kabbalistic motif of the contraction of God in the German version of *Theorie und Praxis: Sozialphilosophische Studien* (Frankfurt a.M.: Suhrkamp, 1978), 172–227.

of living together in which autonomy and dependency can truly enter into a non-antagonistic [better, a peaceful, *befriedetes*] relation, that one can walk tall [*aufrecht gehen*] in a collectivity that does not have the dubious quality of backward-looking substantial forms of community [*Gemeinschaftlichkeiten*].

The intuition springs from the sphere of relations with others; it aims at experiences of undisturbed intersubjectivity. These are more fragile than anything that history has up till now brought forth in the way of structures of communication — an ever more dense and finely woven web of intersubjective relations that nevertheless make possible a relation between freedom and dependency that can only be imagined with interactive models. Wherever these ideals appear, whether in Adorno, when he quotes Eichendorff, in Schelling's *Weltalter,* in the young Hegel, or in Jakob Böhme, they are always ideas of felicitous interaction, of reciprocity and distance, of separation and of successful, unspoiled nearness, of vulnerability and complimentary caution. All of these images of protection, openness, and compassion, of submission and resistance, rise out of a horizon of experience, of what Brecht would have termed "friendly living together." *This* kind of friendliness does not exclude conflict, rather it implies those human forms through which one can survive conflicts.[15]

These structures of communication are "fragile" because they are the ever-contested product of a long process of differentiation, which decenters all worldviews and can no longer be warranted by (or gathered into) some original (or ultimate) meaningful whole or substance — the absolute in history, the totality of all forms of life.

Habermas leaves no doubt that the contexts in which this intuition first made itself known — tradition and the everyday, the theological legacy and ordinary language — do not (or do no longer) by themselves provide a necessary, let alone sufficient, context of *justification:* "Once religion had been the unbreakable seal upon this totality; it is not by chance that this seal has been broken."[16] Conversely, the experience of the ordinary, of the small and grand narratives whose succession delimits human practices and life forms, cannot be reconstructed on its own terms. Although they do not demand full justification per se, the central intuition's original contexts (the everyday and tradition) point beyond themselves. Their

---

15. Jürgen Habermas, *Die neue Unübersichtlichkeit: Kleine politische Schriften V* (Frankfurt a.M.: Suhrkamp, 1985), 202–3 / trans. in idem, *Autonomy and Solidarity: Interviews,* ed. and intro. Peter Dews (London: Verso, 1986), 125–26.

16. Habermas, *Philosophical Discourse of Modernity,* 83–84 / 104.

inevitable particularisms contain — or at least presuppose, rely on, and enable — an equally irreducible universality, whose structural and formal-pragmatic features can be reconstructed with some success and whose "necessary idealizations" (to borrow a term from Hilary Putnam) cannot be easily dismissed. Hence come Habermas's strong reservations about skeptical and fundamentally historicist or culturalist forms of hermeneutics, pragmatism, deconstructionism, and so on — reservations that form the flip side of his critique of religio-mythical or theologico-metaphysical totalities, that is to say, all the postulated absolutes whose progressive corrosion throughout history is, in his eyes, inevitable as well as irreversible and the very price of not only our "self-determination," "freedom," and "autonomy" (as he will say with Kant and Adorno) but also our "separation" and "interiority" (as Levinas will add).

Let me begin to clarify this point, before turning, in the next chapter, to Habermas's critical engagement with the modern conceptions of historicism, culturalism, hermeneutics, pragmatism (a critique he shares with some of the very "neo-" and "poststructuralists" — "young conservatives," in his idiom — from whom he sets himself apart in the polemical lectures of *The Philosophical Discourse of Modernity*). Habermas sees the transition to modernity, for all its agonistic tendencies — and, at times, near agony — as being an irreversible, if not directly linear, development: a metaphysically contingent unfolding of linguistic, practical, and expressive potentialities with inevitable, even necessary effects — in other words, as an unforgettable learning process "in which there remains out of the universalistic religions [*Universalreligionen*], the more so the purer their structures stood out, not much beyond the core of a universalistic morality [*in der von den Universalreligionen, je reiner ihre Strukturen hervortreten, nicht viel mehr als der Kernbestand einer universalistischen Moral übrigbleibt*]."[17]

Habermas leaves no doubt that the material substance and content of the historical, "positive," monotheistic religions has evaporated, almost without remainder, leaving merely the formal framing — in his words, the core, or *Kernbestand* — of our moral intuitions as its sole legacy, to be salvaged under modern conditions of intellectual and social differentiation, that is to say, of modernization, rationalization, privatization, and secularization.[18] Nothing more of "religion" remains, but also nothing less

17. Jürgen Habermas, *Zur Rekonstruktion des historischen Materialismus* (Frankfurt a.M.: Suhrkamp, 1976), 109.

18. Jose Casanova convincingly argues in *Public Religions in the Modern World* (Chicago: University of Chicago Press, 1994) that this version of the "secularization thesis" is vulnerable

than a genealogy of the modern and secular is thus — and increasingly — affirmed. The *minimal* (and ever changing) dissymmetry between this "nothing more" and "nothing less" is the main source of our interest in these and other revealing passages in Habermas's writings.

The reasoning behind Habermas's view seems clear. He locates the medium of cognition — and, hence, of a decidedly cognitivist morality or "discursive ethics [*Diskursethik*]" — in a language oriented toward mutual understanding (*Verständigung*), a language that, in the wake of the linguistico-pragmatic turn, comes to replace the paradigmatic status of the cosmos, nature, the subject, history, and spirit, as mirrored in the traditional metaphysical thinking that culminated in Hegel. Not only does the medium of language, in Habermas's view, offer, methodologically speaking, a more tangible and solid basis for reconstructing universalistic, especially moral, intuitions (whose formalization strips them of unnecessary ambiguity and potential violence), but in genealogical and comparative perspective the linguistico-pragmatic turn also expresses an outspoken modern insight: namely, that finitude and contingency — a certain non-naturalness, if not necessarily arbitrariness (as Saussure would say), let alone undecidability (as Derrida would add) — forms the very condition of possibility for human cognition, action, judgment, and expression. Nevertheless, Habermas insists on the formal, if not, strictly speaking, logical, "impossibility of circumventing the symmetrical structure of perspectives built into every speech situation, a structure that makes possible the intersubjectivity that permits reaching understanding in language."[19] Distancing himself from Karl-Otto Apel's foundationalist project of the reflective "transformation of philosophy" and its ambition to provide a rationally grounded "first philosophy" based on the possibility of ultimate justification (*Letztbegründung*), Habermas affirms that a *"weak and transitory unity of reason,* which does not fall under the idealistic spell of a universality that triumphs over the particular and the singular, asserts itself in the medium of language."[20] One of the major presuppositions of the linguistic turn thus remains "the conviction that language forms the medium for the historical and cultural embodiments of the human mind, and that a methodologically reliable analysis of mental activity must therefore begin with the linguistic expressions of intentional phenomena, instead of im-

---

to critique. For attempts to substantiate and modify his thesis, see the contributions to de Vries and Weber, *Religion and Media.*

19. Habermas, *Postmetaphysical Thinking,* 117 / 155.

20. Ibid., my emph.

mediately with the latter."[21] But on what grounds can the linguistic—or, for that matter, pragmatic—turn be taken to be a more reliable point of departure for the philosophical and, fundamentally, reconstructive analysis than cosmos, nature, the subject, history, or even spirit ever were? In order to answer that question, we need to look more closely at the premises of Habermas's argument.

Following the historical schema of Karl Löwith's classic *Von Hegel bis Nietzsche* (*From Hegel to Nietzsche*), which greatly impressed him in his formative years, Habermas assumes that, with Hegel's death and the breakup of his system, the *Philosophie des Geistes* (*Philosophy of Spirit*), into the many *Geisteswissenschaften* (the "human" or, as John Stuart Mill would have said, "moral" sciences), the philosophical discourse of modernity could begin its flight into the dusk of traditional, substantialist metaphysics. For Hegel, he writes,

> the synthetic labor of spirit is supposed to be performed through the medium of history and assimilated to the progressive form of the latter. Along with history, however, contingencies and uncertainties break into the circular, closed-off structure of unifying reason, and in the end these contingencies and uncertainties cannot be absorbed, even by a supple dialectic of reconciliation. With historical consciousness Hegel brought a force [*ein Instanz*] into play whose subversive power also set his own construction teetering. A history that takes the self-formative processes [*Bildungsprozess*] of nature and spirit up into itself, and that has to obey the logical forms of the self-explication of this spirit, sublimates [*sublimiert*] itself into the opposite of history. To bring it to a simple point that had already irritated Hegel's contemporaries: a history with an established past, a predecided future, and a condemned present, is no longer *history*.[22]

It is, of course, not hard to see how this critique could be leveled at the Hegelian legacy of orthodox Marxism, since the supposed dialectics of history (and, in some cases, also of nature) relies on the same conceptual schema, reverting idealistic referents to materialist (or even mechanistic and social Darwinist) terms. Indeed, the studies collected in Habermas's *Theorie und Praxis: Sozialphilosophische Studien* and *Zur Rekonstruktion des historischen Materialismus* (*Theory and Practice: Studies in Social Philosophy* and "Reconstructing Historical Materialism") demon-

21. Ibid., 134 / 174.
22. Ibid., 130 / 169.

strate to what extent this reversal (altogether an "abstract negation," in Adorno's terminology) rendered the paradigm of orthodox Marxism — or at least its material substance, its ontological and scientific claims, if not its most profound impetus, inspiration, or even "spirit" — obsolete, unable to cope with the new realities of postindustrial societies and their corresponding theoretical and technological matrices. The grounds Habermas provides for this analysis are in part similar to those given by the earliest generation of the Frankfurt School. But, whereas both Horkheimer and Adorno remained deeply steeped in some of Marxism's most questionable economic assumptions and, like the Lukács of *Geschichte und Klassenbewusstsein* (*History and Class Consciousness*), continued to share some of its most tenacious metaphysical presuppositions — not least that of the *isomorphism,* the "elective affinity" if not the mono-causal link, between social and intellectual trends — Habermas moves a step farther. An additional criticism of the paradigm of historical and dialectical materialism in his texts concerns the "production paradigm" and "model of societal control [*Verfügungsmodell*]" which he addresses in *The Philosophical Discourse of Modernity* and *Faktizität und Geltung* (*Between Facts and Norms*)[23] and of which he finds fatal reminiscences throughout the writings of Adorno and Horkheimer.

Habermas's reassessment of historical and dialectical materialism should be distinguished from those in Jean-François Lyotard's *Le Différend* (*The Differend*) and Derrida's *Spectres de Marx* (*Specters of Marx*). Both these authors likewise distinguish between the "differend" (Lyotard) or the "spirit" (Derrida) of Marxism, on the one hand, and its positive — indeed, positivistic, scientistic, empirical, and ontological — doctrines, on the other. But their premises and arguments differ from those guiding Habermas. These differences have to do with two alternative conceptions of the *strategic* (rather than methodological) privilege of language, in the wake of Saussure, Wittgenstein, and Austin. In Habermas's discussion Humboldt, Chomsky, Davidson, and Searle lead the way. By contrast, Derrida and the early Lyotard work out a radicalized and radically transformed semiotics, which Lyotard later presents as an ontology of "language games."

---

23. See the excursus in Habermas, *Philosophical Discourse of Modernity,* 75–82, 341 ff. / 95–103, 396 ff.; and Habermas, *Faktizität und Geltung: Beiträge zur Diskurstheorie des Rechts und des demokratischen Rechtsstaats* (Frankfurt a.M.: Suhrkamp, 1992), 393 n. 56 / *Between Facts and Norms: Contributions to a Discourse Theory of Law and Democracy,* trans. William Rehg (Cambridge: MIT Press, 1996), 552 n. 56.

Unlike Habermas, Derrida and Lyotard—despite fundamental differences in point of departure, argumentative strategy, and overall philosophical aims (which in both thinkers intersect at crucial moments with the thought of Adorno and Levinas)—draw a further consequence from the self-undermining, indeed, the auto-deconstruction, of the Hegelian system. This is the fundamental instability of language. Habermas attempts to develop a concept of language oriented toward the "weak and transitory unity of reason," one that "does not fall under the idealistic spell of a universality that triumphs over the particular and the singular" but, rather, is conceived as a "medium" for communicative understanding, identifiable ascription (as Habermas will say, "meaning-identity" or "unequivocal meaning [*Eindeutigkeit*]"), "linguistic competence," "sincerity," and "accountability"—in short, a language with formal features that could in principle be adequately reconstructed in the theoretical framework of a formal, universal pragmatics, that is, a theory of communicative action and its implied procedural discourse ethics. But in the view of Derrida and Lyotard such a "language" hardly seems language in the quotidian, theoretical and practical, not to mention rhetorical or poetic, uses of the word. A "language" with a structurally established or formally determinable past, anticipated future, and known present is, they claim, no longer language as a living, innovative reality, premised on the possibility, perhaps the necessity, of misunderstanding, misdirection, limited translatability, polysemy, dissemination, difference, and differend. This dramatic consequence—the instability of the very idea of language's conceptual schemes and, hence, of linguistic interaction and communicative understanding—betrays itself on numerous occasions throughout Habermas's own texts, above all in his use of striking metaphors, whose theological overtones are hardly accidental and are difficult to ignore.

References to religion or theologemes appear in the overall theoretical formulation of Habermas's project in yet another way. They are cited, time and again, not just as witnesses to the particular intellectual historical (or autobiographical) origin or motivational resource for intuiting a morality and concept or representation of justice (*Gerechtigkeit*) which could in principle be adequately, if not fully, formalized and universalized but as tropes for the very mode in which the differentiated and decentered forms and pragmatic structures of cognition, action, judgment, and expression are said to *inter-act,* that is to say, interrelate and resonate with one another. In the first chapter of this book I spell out this transposition of the religious and the theological onto some of the nodal points and most suggestive insights of Habermas's theory. These motifs, I will argue, are not mere ornaments, not pedagogic or rhetorical devices, aesthetic modes of presentation or *parerga* (as Kant would say),[24] which one could in principle do without. On the contrary, they reveal an internal, systematic lacuna and hence indicate the need for some conceptual and figural supplements. In order to be consistent and coherent, Habermas's theory must, paradoxically, at once acknowledge *and* seek to deny this lack. In a word these motifs contaminate his theory's formal, finite, and even discursive features, from within and without. These motifs and motivations— from which a certain reference to tradition (if not necessarily to myth, archaism, dogmatics, or onto-theology, though often to tradition in its most heterodox and even antinomian theological varieties) cannot be effaced— challenge the very construction and reconstruction of the philosophical discourse of modernity as Habermas envisions it. They gently force it in the direction of an alternative modernity, whose contours have not yet fully been sketched out, let alone thoroughly assessed. To essay such a sketch is the task I have set myself in this study. I suspect that Habermas's theory of rationality only reluctantly, and often unexpectedly, encounters such nodal points and the neuralgic issues they imply: questions of autonomy and heteronomy, self- and, if we can say so, other-determination, modernity and religion, secularism and the postsecular, and so forth. For the sake of its theoretical integrity and consequence, it must extricate itself from them, but it cannot actually do so at each step or with full rigor.

IN HIS "Open Letter to Max Horkheimer" of 1965 Adorno praises his longtime friend and colleague for having "absorbed the utopian impulse without compromise into the spirit of critique, without affirmative consolation, even without the consolation of trust in a future that could not redress past suffering."[25] Benjamin contrasts to this view his concept of "anamnesis [*Eingedenken*]," a notion that is decidedly and deeply paradoxical.[26] But Adorno's praise for and Benjamin's corrective of Horkheimer's view also have implications for the presuppositions and possible

24. For a more sustained analysis of the question of the *parerga* in Kant's moral philosophy and his philosophy of history and religion, see my book *Philosophy and the Turn to Religion* (Baltimore: Johns Hopkins University Press, 1999), chap. 6; and *Religion and Violence*, chap. 1.

25. Adorno, *GS* 20.1:161.

26. See Walter Benjamin, *Das Passagenwerk*, ed. Rolf Tiedemann (Frankfurt a.M.: Suhrkamp, 1983), N 8,1, 1:588–89 / *The Arcades Project*, trans. Howard Eiland and Kevin McLaughlin (Cambridge: Harvard University Press, 1999), 471.

reception of Habermas's work. Indeed, Adorno acknowledges having "never been able to oppose [Horkheimer's pessimistic position] with anything other than the question of whether the inexorability [*Unerbittlichkeit*] that carries . . . in such a direction does not receive its content from what it excludes."[27] This question, he added, had no definitive answer: having "absorbed the utopian impulse without compromise into the spirit of critique, without affirmative consolation, even without the consolation of trust in a future that could not redress past suffering" does not preclude the possibility, perhaps even the necessity, of drawing on sources, motivations, and inspirations whose empirical reality and practical validity — in short, whose "content" — one must nonetheless "exclude." Perhaps the "inexorability" of having to think, act, judge, and express oneself under modern conditions carried "critique" in this paradoxical, indeed, aporetic "direction." But this impasse, I will argue, was typical not only of Horkheimer's later work and of the somewhat enigmatic reading Adorno gives it in his "Open Letter." Nor can the hesitant and contradictory — indeed, minimal — theological consequences that Benjamin drew from his "corrective [*Korrektiv*]" of Horkheimer's course of thinking be avoided, as if we were dealing with the idiosyncrasies of one thinker.

We touch on a similar motif and, perhaps, motivation in analyzing the intrinsic limit (and, I will argue, the inevitable paradox and aporia) of the conceptual scheme and argumentative layout of the theory of communicative action (indeed, of any theory, any practice, any judgment, any expression), which cannot easily be cast aside and for which even the linguistic and pragmatic turn — away from the limited conceptual apparatus and vocabulary of the philosophy of the subject and of consciousness as well as from the instrumentalist, monological understanding of rationality on which it relies — has, for all its intellectual span and subtlety, no ready interpretation. Hence, despite the transformation or paradigm shift proposed by the philosophical discourse of modernity as reconstructed by Habermas (needless to say, alternative readings of this discourse, as of "modernity" and "modernism," remain possible, even necessary),[28] certain tantalizing questions, together with their deeply paradoxical — to be precise, aporetic — responses reappear at every step. If the psychoanalytic schema were not vulnerable to the same logic, we could say that the re-

---

27. Adorno, *GS* 20.1:161.

28. I am thinking of the writings of Albrecht Wellmer, Seyla Benhabib, Nancy Fraser, Axel Honneth, Martin Seel, Christoph Menke, Alessandro Ferrara, and others.

emergence of the theological argument, vocabulary, and imaginary—in other words, of an at least minimal theology, whose "global religion" extends virtually everywhere—resembles nothing less than a "return of the repressed" at the very heart of Enlightenment rationality, in one of its fullest and most differentiated articulations: the theory of communicative action.

The central thesis of my first chapter is, therefore, that the modern theory of rationality and formal pragmatics must always already, however provisionally and unwittingly (surreptitiously, as Kant would say), have taken into account such theological motifs and their consequence. Where it represses, glosses over, or renders secondary these motifs and motivations (that is to say, secularizes, translates, and transforms them), it indirectly acknowledges them, *e silentio* and *ex negativo,* as it were. The theory remains essentially incomplete for the simple reason that it must bring into play concerns (tropes and metaphors) which it ultimately neither can thematize, as such or on their own terms, nor reduce to mere accidentals and ornaments. To rationalize, formalize, and thereby bring into language "a tip of the absolute"—albeit it a "transcendence from within," a "transcendence in immanence"[29]—goes only that far.

As Adorno remarked in his essay "Fortschritt" ("Progress"), to which I will return in the fifth chapter, recourse to conceptions of the "immanent-transcendent" (or "transcendent-immanent"), which seek to avoid (or mask) this circumstance—for example, by introducing some middle ground (*tertium datur* once again, though this time with a bent toward harmonization, the cardinal sin of dialectics in its modern idealist and materialist varieties)—"pass sentence on themselves by their very nomenclature."[30] They betray a paradox, an aporia, which ought to be not obscured but addressed and, if possible, formalized—indeed, universalized, even exacerbated and dramatized—in the most straightforward and rigorous

29. Jürgen Habermas, *Die Einbeziehung des Anderen: Studien zur politischen Theorie* (Frankfurt a.M.: Suhrkamp, 1996), 16 / *The Inclusion of the Other: Studies in Political Theory,* ed. Ciaran Cronin and Pablo de Greiff, trans. Ciaran Cronin (Cambridge: MIT Press, 1998); "Transzendenz von innen, Transzendenz im Diesseits," *Texte und Kontexte* (Frankfurt a.M.: Suhrkamp, 1991), 127–56; "Transcendence from Within, Transcendence in This World," in Habermas, *Religion and Rationality: Essays on Reason, God, and Modernity,* ed. Eduardo Mendieta (Cambridge: Polity Press, 2002), 67–94; and T. M. Schmidt, "Immanente Transzendenz," in *Im Netz der Begriffe: Religionsphilosophische Analysen,* ed. Linus Hauser and Eckhard Nordhofen (Freiburg: Oros, 1994), 78–96.

30. "Expedient expositions [*Hilfskonstruktionen*] of an immanent-transcendent concept of progress pass sentence on themselves by their very nomenclature" (P 147 / 621).

fashion. I take this to be the task undertaken in Adorno's dialectical critique of dialectics and Levinas's phenomenological critique of phenomenology, two exemplary philosophical modes (though not the only and, perhaps, not even most tenable or promising ones) of analyzing and, as it were, enacting the performative contradiction Habermas thinks one can and ought to avoid.[31]

Habermas approvingly cites Hilary Putnam, who, in "Why Reasons Can't Be Naturalized," states that reason is "both immanent (not to be found outside of concrete language games and institutions) and transcendent (a regulative idea that we use to criticize the conduct of all activities and institutions)."[32] Although these words—"both immanent . . . and transcendent"—would at first glance seem to reiterate the appeals to the immanent-transcendent whose "nomenclature," as Adorno succinctly puts it, condemns itself, upon closer scrutiny it becomes clear that, in Putnam's reconstruction of Habermas's thought, they underline the Kantian duality of these (inside and outside) perspectives while affirming their mutual implication and, as it were, co-originariness. As Putnam argues in greater detail in *Renewing Philosophy*, this double focus enables one to steer clear of the false alternative between scientistically oriented versions of "analytic metaphysics," on the one hand, and a host of philosophical skepticisms and relativisms, on the other.[33] Habermas, in turn, reformulates the double focus of the Kantian conception of reason in his "own words" by stating that "the validity claimed for propositions and norms transcends spaces and times, but in each actual case the claim is raised here and now, in a specific context, and accepted or rejected with real implications for social interaction."[34] Leaving both Hegel's philosophy of spirit and orthodox dialectical materialism—and their functional equivalents—behind, he offers the following statement of the "necessary idealization" given with any claim: "The transcendental gap [*Gefälle*] between the intelligible and the empirical worlds no longer has to be over-

31. See Martin Jay, "The Debate over Performative Contradiction: Habermas vs. the Post-Structuralists," in *Zwischenbetrachtungen: Im Prozess der Aufklärung: Jürgen Habermas zum 60. Geburtstag*, ed. Axel Honneth, Thomas McCarthy, Claus Offe, and Albrecht Wellmer (Frankfurt a.M.: Suhrkamp, 1989), 171–89.

32. Hilary Putnam, "Why Reasons Can't Be Naturalized," *Realism and Reason, Philosophical Papers* (Cambridge: Cambridge University Press, 1983), 3:229–47, cited after Habermas, *Postmetaphysical Thinking*, 139 / 179.

33. See Hilary Putnam, *Renewing Philosophy* (Cambridge: Harvard University Press, 1992), 141.

34. Habermas, *Postmetaphysical Thinking*, 139 / 179.

come through the philosophy of nature and the philosophy of history. It has instead been reduced to a tension [*Spannung*] between the unconditional character of context-bursting, transcendent validity claims, on the one hand, and, on the other hand, the factual character [*Faktizität*] of the context-dependent "yes" and "no" positions that create social facts *in situ*."[35]

What would seem a radical duality—an elliptical figure with two foci, mutually excluding yet constantly referring to each other, in endless oscillation[36]—is thus mitigated, harmonized, and reduced to a productive tension whose creative force, as it traverses "everyday practice" and opens up the very possibility of "social facts," is that of a minimal "mark," a "heuristic idea": "everyday practice becomes permeated with idealizations that nevertheless set the stage for social facts. The ideas of meaning-identity [or unequivocal meaning, *Eindeutigkeit*], truth, justice, sincerity, and accountability leave their mark [or, rather, traces, *Spuren*]. Yet they retain world-constituting power only as heuristic ideas of reason; they lend unity and organization [or, rather, coherence, *Zusammenhang*] to the situation interpretations that participants negotiate [*aushandeln*] with each other."[37]

But how, exactly, can the "tension" between the unconditional and the conditional—or, put otherwise, the immanent transcendence of the "traces," that is to say, the situated and local incarnations of the ideas of reason—ever lend "unity" and "coherence" to interpretation and negotiation? How, moreover, can counterfactual, idealized presuppositions hope to acquire factual (i.e., empirical) force without betraying themselves on every count?[38]

35. Ibid., 142 / 182.

36. I analyze the contours and implications of such a figure in the concluding chapter of *Philosophy and the Turn to Religion*.

37. Habermas, *Postmetaphysical Thinking*, 143 / 183.

38. See also Hilary Putnam, *The Collapse of the Act/Value Dichotomy and Other Essays* (Cambridge: Harvard University Press, 2002), chap. 7, first published as "Werte und Normen," in *Die Öffentlichkeit der Vernunft und die Vernunft der Öffentlichkeit: Festschrift für Jürgen Habermas*, ed. Lutz Wingert and Klaus Günther (Frankfurt a.M.: Suhrkamp, 2001), 280–313; Jürgen Habermas, "Werte und Normen: Ein Kommentar zu Hilary Putnams Kantischen Pragmatismus"; and Hilary Putnam, "Antwort auf Habermas," in *Hilary Putnam und die Tradition des Pragmatismus*, ed. Marie-Luise Raters and Marcus Willaschek (Frankfurt a.M.: Suhrkamp, 2002), 280–305 and 306–21, respectively. For a restatement of Habermas's views in terms of Putnam's philosophical project, in particular his "internal realism," see Cristina Lafont, *The Linguistic Turn in Hermeneutic Philosophy*, trans. José Medina (Cambridge: MIT Press, 1999), 283 ff.

Surely the recourse to modifiers such as *regulative* and *heuristic* does not suffice to spell out the modes in which ideas—in post-Kantian parlance, "idealizations" or "idealized presuppositions"—are normally (and normatively) put to work. Does not the very concept of "negotiation," as Derrida has taught us, presuppose an element of the nonnegotiable which no constructive or reconstructive analysis, however differentiated, and no pragmatics, however formal, hence no communicative action and understanding—albeit under the most ideal speech conditions—could ignore or smooth out?[39] Is this not, precisely, what critique and fallibilism, finitude and anti-utopianism, not least in Habermas's own definition of these terms, amount to?

At times Habermas seems to acknowledge as much and to concede that the theory of communicative action presupposes at once too much and not enough, but also that this noncoincidence of the theory with itself is unavoidable, the necessary tension, if not contradiction, in which (and from which) it lives. Interestingly, also by his own admission (expressed mostly in anecdotal and dispersed statements concerning his intellectual biography, of which we have seen an example here), it would seem that no better terms for this circumstance could be found than in the religious tradition of mystical theology, Protestantism, messianism, and antinomianism from which the theory of rationality departs, without (apparently) ever being able to step completely out of its shadow. A longer passage confirms this suspicion:

> The concept of communicative reason is still accompanied by the shadow of a transcendental illusion. Because the idealizing presuppositions of communicative action must not be hypostatized into the ideal of a future condition in which a definitive understanding has been reached, this concept must be approached in a sufficiently skeptical manner. A theory that leads us to believe in the attainability of a rational ideal would fall back behind the level of argumentation reached by Kant. It would also abandon the materialistic legacy of the critique of metaphysics. The moment of unconditionality that is preserved in the discursive concepts of a fallibilistic truth and morality is not an absolute, or it is at most an absolute that has become fluid as a critical procedure [*ein zum kritischen Verfahren verflüssigtes Absolutes*]. Only with this residue of metaphysics can we do battle against the transfiguration of the world through metaphysical truths—the last trace of "*Nihil contra Deum nisi*

39. See, most recently, Jacques Derrida, *Negotiations: Interventions and Interviews, 1971–2001*, ed., trans., and intro. Elizabeth Rottenberg (Stanford: Stanford University Press, 2002).

Deus ipse." Communicative reason is of course a rocking hull [*schwankende Schaale*] — but it does not go under in the sea of contingencies, even if shuddering [*Erzittern*] in high seas is the only mode in which it "copes" [*bewältigt*] with these contingencies.[40]

The formula *Nihil contra Deum nisi Deus ipse* (nothing can stand against God but God Himself) should, of course, give one pause (as should the interpretation that its use is "not to appeal to some sort of deified reason, but on the contrary to say that it is only through reason that we can determine the limits of our own rationality. *This* is the fundamental figure of Kantian thought that was definitive for modernity").[41] So should reference to the Kierkegaardian motif of "shuddering," the fear and trembling, indeed, the *horror religiosus* that would seem to characterize the existential — and, however de-dramatized, individual — "mode [*Modus*]" with which human agency must engage its frailty, that is to say, the provisional nature and fallibility of all its projects, constructs, and reconstructions. Precisely because the idea of an absolute is linguistically liquefied, if not liquidated, into a critical procedure (*ein zum kritischen Verfahren verflüssigtes Absolutes*) whose outcome (and, I should add, formal schema) is always hypothetical, by invoking it we cannot retheologize a pragmatically and intersubjectively transformed — and thus no longer "first" — philosophy. Nor does its cautious ("sufficiently skeptical," that is to say, provisional, hypothetical, fallible, and materialist) reformulation take the form of a "negative metaphysics," in the definition Adorno gives to this term. Significantly, Habermas demarcates his project from Adorno's negative metaphysics (as formulated in "Meditations on Metaphysics," at the end of *Negative Dialectics*) even more sharply than he distinguishes between his central intuitions and those animating the historical, that is to say, the positive and revealed religions. Indeed, although he retains the central Hegelian-Adornian motif of "determinate negation" (which he reduces to determinate negations of "discursive language"), Habermas hastens to add that the formally and pragmatically revised concept of reason is

not even stable enough for a negative metaphysics [in Adorno's sense]. The latter after all continues to offer an equivalent for the extramundane perspective of a God's-eye view: a perspective radically different from the lines of sight

40. Habermas, *Postmetaphysical Thinking*, 144 / 184–85.
41. Jürgen Habermas, *Vergangenheit als Zukunft* (Zurich: Pendo, 1990), 94 / *The Past as Future*, trans. and ed. Max Pensky (Lincoln: University of Nebraska Press, 1994), 125.

belonging to innerworldly participants and observers. That is, negative metaphysics uses the perspective of a radical outsider, in which one who is mad,
existentially isolated, or aesthetically enraptured distances himself from the
world, and indeed from the life-world as a whole. These outsiders no longer
have a language, at least no speech based on reasons, for spreading the message of that which they have seen. Their speechlessness finds words only in
the empty negation of everything that metaphysics once affirmed with the
concept of the universal One. In contrast, communicative reason cannot withdraw from the determinate negations in language [*bestimmten Negationen
der Sprache*], discursive as linguistic communication in fact is. It must therefore refrain from the paradoxical statements of negative metaphysics: that the
whole is the false [*das Ganze das Unwahre*], that everything is contingent,
that there is no consolation whatsoever. Communicative reason does not stage
[*inszeniert*] itself in an aestheticized theory as the colorless negation of a religion that provides consolation. It neither announces the absence of consolation in a world forsaken by God, nor does it take upon itself to provide any
consolation. It does without [*verzichtet auf*] exclusivity as well. As long as no
better words for what religion can say are found in the medium of rational
discourse, it will even coexist abstemiously [*enthaltsam koexistieren*] with the
former, neither supporting it nor combating it.[42]

These words draw a fine but unmistakable line between the critical
perspective of formal pragmatics and its concept of communicative reason, on the one hand, and the one implied by Adorno—for example, in
the concluding aphorism of *Minima Moralia* (which claims that the "only
philosophy which can be responsibly practiced in the face of despair is the
attempt to contemplate all things as they would present themselves from
the standpoint of redemption . . . as it will appear one day in the messianic light" [MM 247 / 283]) — on the other. Habermas similarly wishes to
distinguish his position from that of the later Horkheimer, most provocatively expressed in "Die Sehnsucht nach dem ganz Anderen" ("The Desire
for the Totally Other"),[43] just as no less decisive reservation is expressed
with respect to Benjamin's notion of anamnestic solidarity and its concept of redemptive critique. All these positions and reservations should,

42. Ibid., 144–45 / 185, trans. modified.
43. Max Horkheimer, "Die Sehnsucht nach dem ganz Anderen," in Horkheimer, *Gesammelte Schriften*, ed. Gunzelin Schmid Noerr (Frankfurt a.M.: S. Fischer, 1985), 7:385–404. See
also Jürgen Habermas, "Zu Max Horkheimers Satz: 'Einen unbedingten Sinn zu retten ohne
Gott, ist eitel,'" *Texte und Kontexte*, 110–26.

of course, be carefully differentiated and cannot be reduced to a single stance, whether to be advocated or refuted.

This being said, the whole difficulty, for Habermas, lies in articulating and analyzing "transcendence" ("transcendence from within" or "transcendence in immanence") *without* succumbing to classical-metaphysical thinking—or, what amounts to the same, the "ethnocentrism" of a particular language-game or form of life[44]—which does not live up to the rational potential and formal criteria of the philosophical discourse of modernity delineated by the theory of communicative action. But many postmythical yet, in Habermas's own terms, nonetheless traditional systems of thought—the historical religions, to name just the most prominent example—preempt, more precisely anticipate, this theory's most basic intuitions, in particular its moral universalism, which they interpret and present in all too concrete and substantialist (as Rawls would

---

44. At times the difference between these two complementary yet mutually dependent extremes of classical-metaphysical thinking and the singular will seem almost imperceptible: "the nuanced debate surrounding the one and the many cannot be reduced to a simple for or against. The picture is even made more complex by latent elective affinities. The protest against the overpowering argument made today in the name of an oppressed plurality allows at least a sympathetic detachment vis-à-vis the appearance of unitary thinking in renewed metaphysical form. In fact, radical contextualism thrives on a negative metaphysics, which ceaselessly circles around that which metaphysical idealism had always intended by the unconditioned but which it had always failed to achieve" (Habermas, *Texte und Kontexte*, 116 / 154). Yet Habermas contrasts to these two extremes—which are mutually exclusive but nonetheless touch upon (or revert to) each other and which seem to exhaust all possible options for philosophical thought— an alternative, a *tertium datur,* which cannot be formulated in their terms. Presenting it as "a skeptical and postmetaphysical yet not defeatist" humanism of Kantian origin, Habermas agrees that it cannot but be perceived as either too "weak" (in the eyes of transcendental[ist] philosophers) or too "strong" (in the eyes of radical skeptics):

As seen by the unitary thinking of metaphysics, the procedural concept of communicative reason is too weak because it discharges everything that has to do with content into the realm of the contingent and even allows one to think of reason itself as having contingently arisen. Yet, as seen by contextualism, this concept is too strong because even the borders of allegedly incommensurable worlds prove to be penetrable in the empirical medium of mutual understanding. The metaphysical priority of unity above plurality and the contextualistic priority of plurality above unity are secret accomplices. My reflections point toward the thesis that the unity of reason only remains perceptible in the plurality of its voices—as the possibility in principle of passing from one language into another—a passage that, no matter how occasional, is still comprehensible. This possibility of mutual understanding, which is now guaranteed only procedurally and is realized only transitorily, forms the background for the actual diversity of what encounters each other—even where understanding fails [*die aktuelle Vielheit des einander—auch verständnislos—Begegnenden*]. (Habermas, *Texte und Kontexte*, 116–17 / 154–55, trans. modified)

say, "comprehensive") terms.[45] Nor should one overly formalize—indeed, empty out—transcendence, reducing it to a mere idea, a mere trace, leaving nothing but how (or so Habermas thinks) a metaphysics turned negative abstractly negates itself in a performative self-contradiction that leaves no claim (concerning objective truth, social validity, sincerity, or expressiveness) intact.

The question, therefore—after Habermas—is not to rehabilitate the substantial concept of theoretical reason, however constructed (as in monism and dualism; idealism and materialism; realism, naturalism, and irrealism), nor is it to inflate the formal core of the age-old epistemological claims of classical theology or the all too affirmative conceptions of the ethically good life, the aesthetically beautiful, and their supposed ultimate unity and harmony. There can be no metaphysics, no onto-theology, ethics, or aesthetics in the no-man's-land between modernity and "postmodernity" except in pianissimo: that is to say, in the infinitely small—and infinitely distanced, couched in language, liquefied, and nearly liquidated—dimension of the absolute (more precisely, the ab-solute) and the infinite (as Levinas says, in-finite), whose minimal theology nonetheless steers clear of the (supposed) total negativism and inverted absolutism that Habermas (as we shall see, wrongly) ascribes to the first generation of the Frankfurt School in general and to Adorno in particular.

In this investigation I will attempt systematically to clarify this idea of a minimal theology and to demonstrate that its central features are anticipated—and, I would add, rigorously systematized and formalized—in the writings of Adorno, notably in his departure from a certain eschatologico-apocalyptic messianism suspected in Benjamin and Ernst Bloch as well as from the Schopenhauerian metaphysical and cultural pessimism of Horkheimer. I also claim that these traits find an even more consequential expression in Levinas's philosophy of the trace of the absolutely other, especially as systematized—formalized, and, as it were, generalized, even radicalized and dramatized—in the studies Derrida has devoted to this author, from his 1963 "Violence and Metaphysics" on. His discussion forms both a watershed in the reception of Levinas's work and

---

45. See Jürgen Habermas, "Ein Gespräch über Gott und die Welt," *Zeit der Ubergänge* (Frankfurt a.M.: Suhrkamp, 2001), 173–96; and Habermas, *Glauben und Wissen: Friedenspreis des Deutschen Buchhandels 2001* (Frankfurt a.M.: Suhrkamp, 2001). In both texts Habermas points repeatedly to the "semantic potential" and "resources of meaning" of the historical, revealed, monotheistic religions.

a matrix for my interpretation, even though I seek to tease out some consequences and to establish some connections that might seem to diverge from the philosophy of deconstruction, at least in some of its influential receptions.

I believe that Habermas's reconstruction of historical materialism can only measure up to its ambitions and, to cite Benjamin, "easily be a match for anyone if it enlists the services of theology, which today is wizened [*klein und hässlich*] and has to keep out of sight."[46] Such an alliance differs from the fundamentally ascetic relationship and mutual indifference of theory and the theological, "neither supporting it nor combating it," at least so long as "no better words for what religion can say are found in the medium of rational discourse." This ascesis, Habermas suggests, is the logical consequence of the procedure of *determinate negation*, Adorno's most cherished Hegelian *terminus technicus*, which for Habermas can only indicate a determinate negation in and of language, not of the materiality of (external) nature or the contingent, transient empiricity of history, let alone their tangential encounter in the concept of "natural history" (*Naturgeschichte*), from which Adorno's thinking takes its point of departure. I will argue that if one focuses on the latter motifs — without denying the importance of language, including the "language of philosophers" for Adorno's own account — a more compelling reading of the motif of determinate negation results: one whose "method" is no longer (or not yet or in any case not primarily) *procedural*, in the sense Habermas himself gives to the term.[47]

In lieu of any ecumenical cohabitation of theory and religion or any reduction of one to the other (whether deductively, analytically, causally, genealogically, hermeneutically, or structurally) my alternative reading will demonstrate (and, as does Adorno himself, dramatize or exaggerate) their mutual contamination and undecidability, especially at the systematic and nodal points that matter most.

A further consideration will make that clear. In *Die Einbeziehung des Anderen* (*The Inclusion of the Other*) Habermas reiterates his position with formulations that seem to echo the terminology and arguments that we

46. Walter Benjamin, "Über den Begriff der Geschichte," *Gesammelte Schriften* (Frankfurt a.M.: Suhrkamp, 1980), 1.2:693 / "Theses on the Philosophy of History," in *Illuminations*, ed. Hannah Arendt, trans. Harry Zohn (New York: Harcourt, Brace and World, 1955), 255.

47. See Theodor W. Adorno, "Thesen über die Sprache des Philosophen," *GS* 1:366–71.

will find in Adorno and Levinas without, however, endorsing the full consequences that these views entail. Habermas insists here on the "relational
structure of alterity [*Andersheit*] and difference [*Differenz*]" which would
be realized, validated, or expressed by any universalism worthy of the
name. This "universalism that is highly sensitive to differences," he suggests, finds its articulation only in a moral and legal theory—a Kantian
cognitivism and republicanism, of sorts—based on the following premises:

> Equal respect for *everyone* is not limited to those who are like us; it extends to
> the person of the other in his or her otherness. And solidarity with the other
> *as one of us* refers to the flexible "we" of a community that resists all substan-
> tive determinations and extends its permeable boundaries ever further. This
> moral community constitutes itself solely by way of the negative idea of abol-
> ishing discrimination and harm and of extending relations of mutual recog-
> nition to include marginalized men and women. . . . Here inclusion does not
> imply locking members into a community that closes itself off from others.
> The "inclusion of the other" means rather that the boundaries of the commu-
> nity are open for all, also and most especially for those who are strangers to
> one another and want to remain strangers.[48]

Paradoxically, such distancing and, simultaneously, formalization,
guided by a counter-factual and quasi-transcendental idea, a "glimmer
[*Vorschein*]" of sorts,[49] allow communicative understanding to operate
without force, independent of any utopian—read messianic or redemptive—aspirations toward concrete forms of the good life. Or at least this
is what a formally and universally oriented theory of rationality under
modern conditions would make us believe. As a matter of fact, Habermas
writes:

> No prospect of such forms of life can be given to us, this side of prophetic
> teachings, not even in the abstract [*in abstracto*]. All we know of them is that
> if they could be realized at all, they would have to be produced through our
> own combined effort and be marked by solidarity, though they need not nec-
> essarily be free of conflict. Of course, "producing" does not mean manufac-
> turing according to the model of realizing intended ends. Rather, it signifies a
> type of emergence that cannot be intended, an emergence out of a cooperative

48. Habermas, *Inclusion of the Other*, xxxv–xxxvi / 7–8.
49. Habermas, *Postmetaphysical Thinking*, 145 / 185.

endeavor to moderate, abolish, or prevent the suffering of vulnerable creatures. This endeavor is fallible, and it does fail over and over again. This type of producing or self-bringing-forth places the responsibility on our shoulders without making us less dependent upon "the luck of the moment [*Gunst der Stunde*]." Connected with this is the modern meaning of humanism, long expressed in the ideas of a self-conscious life, of authentic self-realization, and of autonomy—a humanism that is not bent [*versteift*] on self-assertion [*Selbstbehauptung*]. This project, like the communicative reason that inspires it, is historically situated. It has not been made, it has formed itself [*es hat sich gebildet*]—and it can be pursued further, or be abandoned out of discouragement. Above all, the project is not the property of philosophy. Philosophy, working together with the reconstructive sciences, can only throw light on the situations in which we already find ourselves [*vorfinden*]. It can contribute to our learning to understand the ambivalences [*Ambivalenzen*] that we come up against as just so many appeals [*Appelle*] to increasing responsibilities within a diminishing range of options.[50]

This being said, Habermas does not carry the "ambivalences"—and hence the "appeals to increasing responsibilities"—to their logical and axiological, let alone rhetorical or aesthetic, extreme. Far from seeing them as impediments—that is to say, unintelligible antinomies, irrevocable paradoxes, and hence aporias—he views these ambivalences as the relatively unproblematic, indeed simple, conditions of possibility for any conceptual determination, identifying ascription, intersubjective agreement, or subjective expression in general.

I will argue that Adorno and Levinas, in parallel formalizations and concretizations of the performative contradiction inherent in all thought and in every single action or judgment, demonstrate this assumption to be false, irresponsible, and insufficiently expressive. False consciousness and reification, idolatry and blasphemy, the good conscience that is the bad conscience, stupidity and insincerity—all have the same basis: namely, securing grounds where this is, in principle, impossible and indeed undesirable epistemologically, linguistically, morally, politically, and aesthetically speaking. In Habermas's reading, which chooses to ignore the logic of extremes, excess, and exaggeration which my own—as it were, rhetori-

50. Ibid., 146 / 186, trans. modified. See Habermas's excursus on the obsolescence of the "production-paradigm" (*Philosophical Discourse of Modernity*, 75–82, 341 ff. / 95–103, 396 ff.); and, from a different perspective, Donald Davidson, "The Emergence of Thought," *Subjective, Intersubjective, Objective* (Oxford: Oxford University Press, 2001), 123–34.

cal—interpretation of these authors will emphasize, such a view merely dramatizes things in a way that is unnecessary, dangerous, and stereotypical:

> Repulsion [*Perhorreszierung*] towards the One and veneration of difference and the Other obscures the dialectical connection between them [but what, precisely, would *dialectical* mean here?]. For the transitory unity that is generated in the porous and refracted intersubjectivity of a linguistically mediated consensus not only supports but furthers and accelerates the pluralization of forms of life and the individualization of lifestyles. More discourse means more contradiction and difference. The more abstract agreements become, the more diverse the disagreements with which we can *nonviolently* live. And yet in public consciousness the idea of unity is still linked to the consequence of a forced integration of the many. Moral universalism is still treated as the enemy of individualism, not as what makes it possible. The attribution of identical meanings is still treated as the injury of metaphorical multivalence, not as its necessary condition. The unity of reason is still treated as repression, not as the source of the diversity of its voices.[51]

Following several of Habermas's more subtle critics, I will begin by addressing the question of the traces (of the other) of reason, including the conditions of possibility for formal rationality, by analyzing the concept of negative metaphysics. This concept, I suggest, finds its most powerful articulation in Adorno and must be carefully distinguished not only from the positive, substantialist grand designs in the philosophical tradition but also from the classical-dogmatic and modern-scientific conceptions of theology, that is to say, from onto-theology, philosophical theology, the study of divinity, and the scholarly study of religion. Negative metaphysics is, so to speak, the theoretical component of a well-tempered, indeed minimal, theology that steers clear of all confessional forms and commitments of biblical or practical theology as well as from their secularist—and necessarily reductionist—counterparts. One can understand the practical-institutional and aesthetic connotations (broadly defined) of negative metaphysics by returning to the Kantian *terminus technicus* of "judgment [*Urteilskraft*]"[52] (reflective and other) as well as by refer-

---

51. Habermas, *Postmetaphysical Thinking*, 140 / 180, trans. modified.

52. A minimal theology (metaphysics, ethics, or aesthetics) which operates *in pianissimo* appeals not least to the "matured judgment [*Urteilskraft*] of the age, which refuses to be any longer put off with illusory knowledge [*Scheinwissen*]" (Immanuel Kant, *Kritik der reinen Vernunft*, ed. Wilhelm Weischedel [Darmstadt: Wissenschaftliche Buchgesellschaft, 1983], 3:13 /

ring to the significance of comparative cultural analysis in contemporary religious studies.[53] Following the critique of classical and modern
theology elaborated in the opening chapter, I will address the speculative question of negative metaphysics in its theoretical and more abstract
guises, then pause to elaborate this practical-aesthetic or hermeneutical-
rhetorical problem of judgment and comparative analysis in the chapters
that make up part 1. All these qualifications ("theoretical," "speculative,"
"practical," "aesthetic," and "hermeneutical-rhetorical") will, I trust, become clearer as we proceed.

Although negative metaphysics is just as incapable of constructing,
reconstructing, analyzing, and incorporating the traces of reason (and
its other) as is Habermas's theory of rationality, it more decidedly — indeed, unapologetically — assumes the form of a paradoxical or even aporetic figure of speculative thought. Its consequences, as Benjamin wrote
Adorno in 1937, after having read the manuscript of the final part of *Zur
Metakritik der Erkenntnistheorie* (*Against Epistemology*), lead it into and
through a virtual desert and force it to "cross the frozen waste of abstraction to arrive at concise, concrete philosophizing [*man müsse durch die
Eiswüsste der Abstraktion hindurch, um zu konkretem Philosophieren bün-
dig zu gelangen*]" (*ND* xix / 9). This is not to imply that the abstractions
of negative metaphysics do not entail a formal pragmatics and moral philosophy — a negative aesthetics and even negative political theology — of
their own. The concrete philosophical thinking in question is, on the contrary, directed toward an absolute, infinite, and infinitizing idea (of reason, justice, and aesthetic expression), which can be circumscribed only
in endlessly expanded and condensed concentric circles, constellations,
epicycles, ellipses, and similar figures and configurations of thought —
Denkfiguren — whose linguistic expression (including rhetorical hyperbole, parataxis, condensation, etc.) is never accidental but leads into the
very materiality and singularity of the "concrete," which Adorno strips of
all the organico-idealist and totalizing connotations implied by Latin *concrescere* in Hegelian dialectics.[54] What is more, here performative contradiction is taken to be not an avoidable and corrigible flaw in reasoning but

---

Critique of Pure Reason, trans. Norman Kemp Smith [New York: St. Martin's Press, 1965], A
xii, 9).

53. On the qualifier *comparative,* see my introduction to de Vries and Weber, *Religion and
Media,* 29 ff.

54. On the notion "figure of thought," see Pierre Fontanier, *Les Figures du discours,* intro.
Gérard Genette (Paris: Flammarion, 1977).

a matter of principle, the very modus operandi of any principle, concept, argument, judgment, or expression, rather than an alibi for its irrelevance or demise.

Adorno's *negative dialectics,* both in solidarity with and opposed to the legacy of idealist and materialist dialectics (to which pt. 2 of this book is devoted), and Levinas's idea of an *alternating reflection* within and opposed to the more recent tradition of Husserlian and Heideggerian phenomenology (which forms the central subject of pt. 3) serve as instructive models of such a negative metaphysics, whose peculiar modernity, contemporary relevance, or (what comes down to same thing) both timelessness and untimeliness interests me most. As we shall see, the "actuality" of this philosophy resides not least in the fact that it escapes the vague characterizations and genealogies of present-day thought in terms of traditional and posttraditional, metaphysical and postmetaphysical, modern and postmodern. But Adorno's and Levinas's negative metaphysical, that is to say, *theoretical,* models and motifs do not stand on their own; I will further ask how these authors' descriptive and conceptual strategies connect with the model and motif of *judgment* — in particular, of reflective judgment — as well as with those of comparison and nonsynonymous substitution, stemming from traditions of practical wisdom, rhetoric, hermeneutics, and deconstruction.

Negative dialectics reveals a figure of thought whose categories, models, and examples correspond to the demands of an "inverse theology [*inverse Theologie*]." Adorno once described it, in the wake of Benjamin's dispersed allusions to "profane illumination" and the theological, though with greater rigor and consequence, as "the position against natural and supra-natural interpretation" at once.[55] Neither affirmative (kataphatic or dogmatic) nor simply negative (apophatic or mystical), this alternative theology — more precisely, "the other theology [*die andere Theologie*]" (as if other options were not available) — in his view consists in the paradoxical endeavor to circle around natural history's "secret" in as rational as possible a way. As he wrote in a letter to Max Horkheimer in 1941:

> I have a weak, infinitely weak, feeling that that is possible and in which way, but I am honestly not yet in a position today to formulate it. The premise that *theology is shrinking and becoming invisible* is one motif, while another is the conviction that, from the most central point of view, there is no difference

55. Theodor W. Adorno, *Über Walter Benjamin,* ed. Rolf Tiedemann (Frankfurt a.M.: Suhrkamp, 1970), 103.

between theology's relation to the negative and its relation to the positive [or that "the difference between the negative and the positive doesn't matter to theology"; *der Unterschied des Negativen und des Positiven zur Theologie nichts besagt*]. . . . But above all I think that everything we experience as true — not blindly, but as in the movement of the concept [*in der Bewegung des Begriffs*] — and what presents itself to us really *to be read* as the *index sui et falsi*, only conveys this light as a reflection of that other light.[56]

By the same token Adorno is concerned with a "theology in parentheses [*in Klammern*],"[57] whose methodological bracketing of the original, canonized, and dogmatic presupposition of historical belief, as well as its ultimate Referent, resembles the Husserlian procedure of phenomenological *epochē* and leaves uncertain — in suspension, indeed undecided — the speculative or neuralgic point from which thought and experience were once thought to gain their meaning and intensity. And yet, for all its indeterminacy, abstraction, and minimalism, the figure or trace of the other — like the figure-beyond-figure of the other of (every) other, and the other of "this" other (but which "one," exactly?), the best and the worst — remains a *moment* (as Adorno would say, a "truth-moment [*Wahrheitsmoment*]") whose theological overtones (or, in psychoanalytic parlance, overdetermination), like a riddle, remain discernible or, rather, legible, decipherable.

In roughly this sense Adorno would probably agree with Derrida's programmatic statement, in the opening section of *De la grammatologie* (*Of Grammatology*), that "the 'theological' is a determined moment in the total movement of the trace."[58] This statement could very well serve as the epigraph of my study, and it will help me explain what it means when Adorno, in a lecture entitled "Vernunft und Offenbarung" ("Reason and Revelation"), refusing the alternative between theism and atheism, claims to see "no other possibility than an extreme ascesis toward any type of revealed faith, an extreme loyalty to the prohibition of images [*äusserste Treue zum Bilderverbot*], far beyond what this once originally meant."[59]

56. Adorno to Horkheimer, 4 September 1941; cited in Rolf Wiggershaus, *Die Frankfurter Schule: Geschichte, theoretische Entwicklung, politische Bedeutung* (Munich: Carl Hanser, 1986), 561 / *The Frankfurt School: Its History, Theories, and Political Significance*, trans. Michael Robertson (Cambridge: MIT Press, 1994), 503, trans. modified.

57. I borrow this expression from Wiggershaus, *Frankfurt School*, 504; cf. 507 / 562; cf. 565.

58. Jacques Derrida, *De la grammatologie* (Paris: Minuit, 1967), 69 / *Of Grammatology*, trans. Gayatri Chakravorty Spivak (Baltimore: Johns Hopkins University Press, 1976), 47.

59. Theodor W. Adorno, "Vernunft und Offenbarung," *GS* 10.2:616 / "Reason and Reve-

In his later work, in the spirit of a radically enlightened critique of Enlightenment, Adorno no longer explicitly speaks of a transformed concept of theology ("inverse theology," "the other theology") but replaces it with a figure of metaphysical and even spiritual (*geistige*) experience. Such experience is an instance of a "thinking [*Denken*]" — beyond classical and modern metaphysics, without being thereby postmetaphysical but, rather, "solidary [*solidarisch*] with metaphysics in the moment [*Augenblick*] of its downfall" (*ND* 408 / 400, trans. modified) — which Adorno will come to call the "secularization" of the theological in the concept. It exemplifies an experiential mode of the practice of thought, an examined life, whose parallels with the tradition of "spiritual exercises," from antiquity up to Wittgenstein and Foucault, would require a more detailed study than I can undertake in these pages, which I reserve for a different context.[60]

The models that Adorno adopts in his later work, I will demonstrate, are not fundamentally different in their intellectual genesis, argumentative structure, rhetorical contours, and overall aim from those he employs earlier. They indicate the same phenomenon — the same limit of phenomenality, the trace of the other, the absolute, the infinite, but also the nonidentical, nature, natural history (*Naturgeschichte*) — in virtually the same formal and figural way. What is more, both approaches, the "inverted" and "parenthetical" theological approach as well as the negative metaphysical and "experiential" one, touch upon a certain materialism whose nonnaturalistic (and, hence, nonsociologistic, antipsychologistic, indeed antireductionist) features will become clear as we proceed.

ESPECIALLY IN HIS EARLIEST and late work, Levinas presents the essential ambiguity of the absolute and the infinite as the other (aspect, element, dimension, or horizon) of reason, that is to say, of its very concept, but also as reason's "life" and "spirituality"; simultaneously, he introduces it as the beyond (*au-delà* or, on this side, *en-deçà*) of reason, in an equally

---

lation," *Critical Models: Interventions and Catchwords,* trans. Henry W. Pickford (New York: Columbia University Press, 1998), 142. The text was first presented in 1957 in Münster, at a roundtable with Eugen Kogon, author of *Der SS-Staat;* see Theodor W. Adorno and Eugen Kogon, "Offenbarung oder autonome Vernunft," *Frankfurter Hefte* 6 (1958): 392–402; and 7 (1958): 484–98.

60. The opening chapter of my forthcoming *Instances,* devoted to the work of Pierre Hadot, will discuss the concept of "spiritual exercises." Incidentally, Levinas's early work *De l'existence à l'existant* (Paris: Fontaine, 1947) was first published in a collection, ed. Georges Blin, entitled "Exercise de la pensée."

exemplary manner. Like Adorno, he does not strive to overcome the language of classical metaphysics and onto-theology from an extraterritorial, Archimedean point, since that would merely lead to abstractly negating all that has ever been said, done, or expressed in the past and present and anything that could still be said, done, or expressed in the future. On the contrary, he shows how, often with the most traditional means, that very tradition (just like the present and future) can be radically opened up in an alternating, oscillating, and almost dialectical movement of thought, whose metaphysical and experiential features betray a remarkable similarity to the thrust of Adorno's lifelong project—which, as we have seen, was partly phenomenological. This last observation may sound surprising and will need some clarification, not least because Levinas, like so many other postwar French thinkers (including Derrida), indefatigably repudiated the concept of "dialectics," which he consistently associated with the speculative idealism and objectivism of Hegelian logic.[61]

Infinity and transcendence, exteriority and the other (*l'Autre, Autrui*), of which *Totalité et Infini* (*Totality and Infinity*), in particular, speaks with such fervor, are not only reason's immemorial "origin" or unattainable "beyond" but also its very condition, albeit it one that is integral to reason. In the words of *Autrement qu'être ou au-delà de l'essence* (*Otherwise than Being or beyond Essence*), these motifs are not determinable, let alone fixed referents, but relational terms that hint at "a movement going from said to unsaid in which the meaning shows itself, eclipses and shows itself." In this "navigation," Levinas continues suggestively, "the element that bears the embarkation is also the element that submerges it and threatens to sink it. Philosophy is perhaps but this exaltation of language in which the words, after the event, find for themselves a condition in which religions, sciences and technologies owe their equilibrium of meaning" (*OB* 181 / 228).

Like Adorno, Habermas, and Derrida, Levinas engages in an almost transcendental—one might say quasi-, ultra-, or simili-transcendental—mode of thinking, in which the hypothetical condition of possibility assumed for all thought, agency, judgment, and expression simultaneously threatens the possibility of this very thinking (and thus of autonomous action, appropriate judgment, and even sincere expression). Following a classic deconstructive formula: the condition of possibility for reason in its threefold faculty is at the same time the condition of its impossibility.

61. See studies by Vincent Descombes, Manfred Frank, and esp. Judith Butler.

It must presuppose what it cannot account for, justify, and convey in any adequate, that is to say, intelligible, appropriate, or authentic manner. But the "logic of presupposition" (to cite Derrida's formula, relentlessly analyzed in *Apories* [*Aporias*]) and its contemporary modifications remain of limited value for understanding the projects — and, indeed, performative contradictions — which interest us here.

Access to the characteristic figures of thought in Adorno and Levinas — the dialectical critique of dialectics and the phenomenological critique of phenomenology — and their manner of concrete unfolding are quite different, of course. So far as we know, these two authors never met or exchanged their views in writing. Yet a *lectio difficilior* and imagined confrontation of their work reveals how their respective procedures can be brought to a "point of indifference" where — as in a chiasmus (*PN* 62 / 89) — they momentarily connect, intersect, and then part ways again. Such a comparative analysis yields the following dilemma: either Adorno's negative dialectics is, in the strict (i.e., idealist-Hegelian or materialist-Marxist) sense, not dialectical at all (and how, exactly, could we ever determine this?), or the work of the apparent anti-dialectician Levinas might just as well be read as thoroughly "dialectical" (in the alternative, consequent, and immanently critical — that is to say, the negative — meaning Adorno gives to this term). But also either the method of phenomenological concretion developed by Levinas is, in the strict (i.e., Husserlian and Heideggerian) sense, not phenomenological at all (and, again, how could we ever be sure that this is the case?), or the work of the apparent antiphenomenologist Adorno can be understood as "phenomenological" through and through (or at least phenomenological in the meaning Levinas has given to this term, a meaning that could also be said to be alternative, immanently critical, and consequent). The radical formalism and singular concreteness of their respective analyses, the paradoxical and aporetic relationship of their writings to the philosophical tradition as a whole, the interchangeability of certain motifs, argumentative procedures, and rhetorical strategies — all epitomized by the proliferation and exaggeration of performative contradiction as a challenge, task, and style of modern philosophizing — permit one, in principle, to translate the thought of the one into the terms of the other, and vice versa.

This is not a trivial observation. From this perspective the structural insights derived from the work of these authors — to the extent that such insights can be distinguished or separated from the particular idiom of each — can be analyzed more distinctly, more freely, and in terms other than those possible within the boundaries of their respective (equally consistent and heterodox) dialectical or phenomenological approaches. I believe such a formal translation, transformation, and (as Derrida would say) nonsynonymous substitution of their concerns (if not necessarily vocabularies) should begin by exploring the at times orthodox, at times unorthodox hermeneutics of the trace of the other of reason as variously intoned, though often *pianissimo* and hence almost inaudibly, in their work.

The figure of the trace hovers between a fractured, paradoxical, or aporetic *idea* (in all the emphatic Platonic, Cartesian, and Kantian connotations of this term) and a practical-aesthetic *motif* or *figure* (in all the post-Romantic and, in Levinas's case, biblical-hermeneutical or exegetical overdeterminations of these words). This ambiguity is no sign of these authors' lack of conceptual precision. On the contrary, in this structural indeterminacy, I suggest, lies their greatest analytical, moral, imaginative, and expressive strength. It has repercussions for religious and existential questions concerning the good life which have concerned all previous ages (and which, in light of the horrors of the twentieth century, have crystallized in the Adornian maxim "to try to live so that one may believe oneself to have been a good animal [*versuchen, so zu leben, dass man glauben darf, ein gutes Tier gewesen zu sein*]" (*ND* 299 / 294, trans. modified); in other words, in the "new categorical imperative . . . imposed by Hitler upon humans in the state of unfreedom: to arrange their thoughts and actions so that Auschwitz will not repeat itself, so that nothing similar will happen" [365 / 358, trans. modified]).[62] Indeterminacy on the conceptual level (and between the conceptual and the practical or aesthetic) leads us to the very heart of the political — more precisely, theologico-political — matters that increasingly concern us: religious violence, nationalism, ethnic strife, genocide, technological warfare, terror, global capitalism, the power of the new media, international relations, and the limits of sovereignty, of the human, of human rights, of the boundaries of life, and of the animal.

If one holds that the content and modality of an unconditional, absolute, and infinite appeal to truthfulness, moral obligation, justice, sincerity, and to "the other" — including the other, the *ipseity*, in and of me

---

62. See Rolf Tiedemann, intro., "Nicht die Erste Philosophie sondern eine letzte," in his selection of Adorno's writings entitled *Ob nach Auschwitz noch sich leben lässe: Ein philosophisches Lesebuch*, ed. Rolf Tiedemann (Leipzig: Suhrkamp, 1997), 7–27 / "Introduction: Not the First Philosophy but a Last One," in Adorno, *Can One Live after Auschwitz? A Philosophical Reader*, trans. Rodney Livingstone and others (Stanford: Stanford University Press, 2003), xi–xxvii.

—must necessarily be kept open, at least so long as one philosophizes (without knowing, acting, or judging in a determinate way or according to fixed and preestablished rules); moreover, if this appeal remains by definition exposed to an, in principle, endlessly variable intonation and dimensionality of meaning and sense; finally, if one does not want surreptitiously to incorporate or reify the trace (whether naturalistically or religiously, by reducing it to a biological, sociological, psychological, or spiritual given, the "myth of the Given" criticized by Wilfrid Sellars, Richard Rorty, and John McDowell, rather than seeing it as the "originary donation" of which phenomenology, from Husserl to Marion, speaks); one must carefully examine how these ideas, motifs, or motivations can be put to work. Adorno (and, more incidentally, Horkheimer, Benjamin, and Habermas) and Levinas (and, more directly, Derrida) are witnesses to another type of thought and to an altogether different version of praxis, action, judgment, and expression, whose central tenet is the indeterminacy of the other, the enigma of signifyingness, the performative contradiction of the Said (*le Dit,* in Levinas's words) in its intrinsic relationship with all Saying (*le Dire*).

THIS OSCILLATION OR ALTERNATION between immanence and transcendence—"transcendence in immanence" or "immanence in transcendence," if we care to insist on this "nomenclature"—like the (more or less consequent) adoption of the figure of the trace in the writings of Adorno and Levinas, suggests a remarkable parallel with Derrida's strategy of philosophical and rhetorical deconstruction. The rigor of Derrida's inquiry into the presuppositions of metaphysical language—"our language," he writes in *Of Grammatology*—leads to the extreme point of a "strange non-order of the excluded middle, in which the disjunction of the yes and no, the imperious alternative, thanks to which computers decide about the universe, is challenged" (*PN* 60 / 87). Derrida's consequentialism or *jusqu'au boutisme,* to cite an insightful formulation from Levinas's essay on Derrida, entitled "Tout autrement" ("Wholly Otherwise"), seems to formalize one step further the critiques that Adorno and Levinas put forward with the help of dialectical and phenomenological idioms and methods and to draw out their implications and consequences even more consistently than they dared to do.

Admittedly, Derrida attempts to transform the philosophy of dialectical, ontological, and ethical difference into what seems an altogether different philosophy of the trace of the other, namely, that of "general difference," "Difference," or, as he will come to name it, *différance*. He thus seems to remove himself from the singular — read sensualist, materialist, and utopian — stances taken by Adorno, for whom the nonidentical stands for "nature" and the transience (*Vergänglichkeit*) of "natural history." By the same token he seems to distance himself from the ethical and religious sensibility of Levinas, for whom the other (*l'Autre*) evokes above all the "idea of the Infinite" and the other human being (*Autrui*), in whose face God leaves his trace, thereby signaling being par excellence or, as Levinas will come to say, the otherwise than being, beyond all essence. Although, as I will show, Derrida desubstantializes, deformalizes, and phenomeno-logically — or is it dialectically? — analyzes these notions in a different and ever-expanding idiom, the "theoretical matrix" of his general difference or *différance* allows us to reinscribe such central motifs and their accom-panying movement of thought in a more consistent and consequential logic of the same and the other: via a seriality (*sériature*) for which the early *terminus technicus* "nonsynonymous substitution," borrowed from the essay "La Différance" ("Difference"), still forms one of the most com-pelling descriptions.[63]

In place of the formal determination of the symmetrical conditions of rational thought and action with which Habermas works in his discursive model of a theory of rationality, the deconstructive analysis — here appar-ently still captive to the metaphysics of a "temporalized philosophy of ori-gins," as *The Philosophical Discourse of Modernity* suspects — would seem to consider the formal yet asymmetrical structures of every constitution of meaning, for any decision, judgment, or expression. If one must, with Habermas, attribute a quasi-, ultra-, or simili-transcendental mode of in-quiry to such deconstructive thought, does this inquiry not then secretly assume much more than it may think or imagine? Does Derrida's writ-ing about these matters not betray (i.e., intentionally ignore and unwit-tingly signal) an all too easily unheard minimal tonality — *in pianissimo*, as it were, and irretrievable by formalizations, whether oriented symmet-rically or asymmetrically, pragmatically or pragrammatologically, semi-otically or semiologically, or, some would say, neostructurally and "tex-tually"? Does not deconstruction entail more than it claims (or is willing to acknowledge)? And are not the philosophies of Adorno and Levinas, *pace* Habermas and Derrida, at least in part correct in their more explicit, performative, yet also contradictory presentation of ethical-metaphysical,

63. See chap. 4, "Hospitable Thought," in my book *Religion and Violence*.

utopian-messianic, and religious premises and aims (i.e., motifs and motivations), which are at once immemorial and unforgettable? Or is this
impression simply based on a limited reception of Habermas's and Derrida's more recent writings, which have increasingly sought to address the
legacies of Adorno and Levinas, respectively, while engaging in an increasingly polite intellectual dialogue both with these teachers and with
each other?[64] Finally, do we have at our disposal the necessary conceptual
tools to decide this matter unambiguously, given that the confrontation
between the different methodologies, implications, and overall ambitions
of these thinkers has only just begun to emerge?

However one responds to these questions, it seems clear that the minimal theology I suspect at the heart of their philosophical endeavors must
be located in the seemingly irresolvable tension *and* intersection—once
again, the chiasmic crossing—between the (modern) theory of rationality
and the (supposedly postmodern, post- or neostructuralist)[65] philosophical strategy of deconstruction. If I am not mistaken, it can be rigorously
articulated with most profit in a systematic reconstruction and analysis of the no less tense proximity of—and distance between—Adorno's
and Levinas's philosophies of the nonidentical and the other, that is to
say, of the trace, the strange, and the stranger.[66] Although these philosophers stem from different intellectual backgrounds and draw on different traditions, Adorno's figures of thought—his models, indeed, micrologies, of a dialectics turned negative yet no less consequential, though it
is often mistakenly depicted as neo-Hegelian—are in surprising accord
with the concretizations of intentional analysis by the phenomenologically trained Levinas, whose relationship to the Husserlian legacy, dialectics, and dialogue is hardly less complicated than that of his counterpart
with the Hegelian. Both indulge in argumentative procedures and rhetorical exaggerations, allowing paradoxes, performative contradictions,

64. I am thinking of Habermas's interventions at the conference "Judéités" ("Comment
répondre à la question éthique?" in *Judéités: Questions pour Jacques Derrida*, ed. Joseph Cohen
and Raphaël Zagury-Orly [Paris: Galilée, 2003], 181–96); and of Derrida's elliptical remarks
on Frankfurt School thought throughout his writings, notably in the afterword to the English
edition of *Limited Inc*, "Toward an Ethic of Discussion," trans. Samuel Weber (Evanston, Ill.:
Northwestern University Press, 1988), 111–60; and, more recently, in the lecture with which he
accepted the Adorno prize (Jacques Derrida, *Fichus* [Paris: Galilée, 2002]).

65. I will seek to justify my dissatisfaction with these ascriptions (post-this and post-that)
as we proceed.

66. See the double connotation of the German *fremd* in Bernhard Waldenfels's multi-
volume *Phänomenologie des Fremden* (Frankfurt a.M.: Suhrkamp, 1997–99).

aporias, oscillations, and alternations that have to do not with the idio-syncrasies of their respective idioms or the pitfalls of their respective itin-eraries but with a more general — and, I would claim, continuing — task, challenge, and, as it were, *spiritual exercise,* of contemporary philosophical thinking.

Again, these two thinkers never met, and neither mentions nor ap-pears ever to have taken notice of the other's work.[67] Yet, from the very beginning of their careers, both independently made an "idea of the other" — in forms that are figuratively comparable and structurally indistinguish-able, if in part incommunicable — an integral part of their intellectual projects. This idea, sufficiently analyzed, systematized, and formalized, will prove essential to what I term a "minimal theology," that is to say, a theology stripped its lofty pretensions and attuned to singular aspira-tions that, in modernity (as Max Weber knew), only resonate — and con-trast — *in pianissimo.* Both see a "noetical" ferment (or, again, idea) of the ab-solute or the infinite, together with "dia-noetical-discursive" ratio-nality and judgment, as being necessary for the constitution and regula-tion of reasoned and responsible thought, action, and "spiritual experi-ence [*geistige Erfahrung*]," of expressiveness and passivity, without which no human life (or, indeed, life as such) would seem worth living.

The idea of "transcendence" continues to play a key role in the strik-ing passages in which Adorno displays a qualified "solidarity with meta-physics in its downfall" (*ND* 408 / 400, trans. modified); indeed, with-out this idea, he says, "truth would be unthinkable" (*ND* 246 / 244). For Levinas the historical idea of the infinite, as held by Plato, Plotinus, or Descartes, remains no less pertinent. Beginning with his first indepen-dent philosophical texts, published after (and, in part, parallel to) his early commentaries on Husserl and Heidegger in the 1930s and 1940s — in ex-plicit solidarity with their respective *Abbau* and *Destruktion* of the natur-alisms, psychologisms, and ontologisms of metaphysics, its logic, and its humanism — he interprets the idea of the infinite as the inexhaustible yet

---

67. As I indicate in the preface, Levinas was familiar with Adorno's *Jargon der Eigentlich-keit* (*Jargon of Authenticity*), a book he did not admire. Adorno for his part knew of Levi-nas's translation of Husserl's *Cartesianische Meditationen* and refers to it in *Zur Metakritik der Erkenntnistheorie* (cf. *GS* 5:25). In a letter to Horkheimer, written in October 1936, he further once mentions the name of Levinas as a possible — but, in his view, unsuitable — contributor (suggested to him by Raymond Aron) to the projects of the Institute for Social Research (see Theodor W. Adorno and Max Horkheimer, *Briefwechsel*, vol. 1: *1927–1937,* ed. Christoph Gödde and Henri Lonitz [Frankfurt a.M.: Suhrkamp, 2003], 184). Horkheimer responded, "Levinas I don't know" (ibid., 193).

forgotten source of the *philosophia perennis,* and thus of the "essentially hypocritical civilization" of the West, in its double allegiance to philosophers and prophets, Athens and Jerusalem, "attached both to the True and to the Good, henceforth antagonistic" (*TI* 24 / xii). That this "hypocrisy" is not an individual moral flaw to be perfected in human nature but a condition of culture as such, that the painful awareness of its presence is the sure sign of a learning process of sorts, contributes to Levinas's understanding of the drama, the divine comedy, of existence.

As we will see, Adorno and Levinas both attempt, within their own idioms and frames of reference, to circumscribe and transcribe the traces of reason's other or Other (again in the subjective and objective senses of this genitive), whether they proceed dialectically and, in a sense to be determined, negatively or via a series of phenomenological descriptions and intentional analyses. In their view irruptions of the other (*das Andere; l'Autre* or *Autrui*) into the order of the same (*das Identische, das Gleiche,* or *das Immergleiche; le Même* or *le Neutre*) illumine and reveal a kind of alterity which cannot be said actually to exist anywhere as present (or as presence). In their eyes it would be equally misguided to hold this heterogeneous element—a "curvature of social space," as Levinas will come to call it—to be devoid of all reality, of all concreteness, as if it concerned a pure nonbeing, an abstract possibility, an empty construct, an actual nothingness, the mere negation and flip side of presence. For these authors the radical nature of the idea of the ab-solute or the infinite does not lie in the need to define it by contrast to the traditional-metaphysical philosophy of origin, with its substantialized (idealized or naturalized) foundations and its teleological and—theologically speaking—eschatological, if not necessarily messianic or apocalyptic, orientation.

Moreover, the notions of the ab-solute and the infinite are incompatible with the logical law of the excluded third (*tertium non datur,* i.e., either p or $\sim p$), which in the Western tradition stands as the Archimedean point of logos, reason, rationality, and discourse, granting coherence and consistency to all philosophical knowledge, indeed, to all meaningful speech that has wrested itself from opinion and confusion or which escapes the essential muteness of a *flatus vocis.* Adorno and Levinas exasperate and confound their interpreters with their tireless attempts to investigate the presuppositions, consequences, and margins of this regime of the excluded middle. They undermine its generally acknowledged centrality in order to create a conceptual (or merely figural, rhetorical?) space for their suggestive idea of the other beyond—or on this side of—being and nonbeing, traversing the very distinction between being and nonbeing, affirmation and negation, and, again, p and $\sim p$. However differently their philosophical points of departure may appear and however differently their intellectual, sociopolitical, and religious horizons might determine the substance (if we can still call it that) of their thought, their independently articulated ideas of the ab-solute can be viewed formally as figures of thought which, in parallel and complementary ways, provoke both a delimitation and a displacement of the philosophical tradition as a whole, including its modern equivalents and transformations.[68] In their common critique of totality they therefore, somewhat paradoxically and ironically, share an almost totalizing depiction of this tradition's most general and tenacious intellectual traits, ethical implications, political ramifications, and aesthetic limitations. Not all of their assumptions and suggestions are prima facie convincing, unless one reads them, as I will attempt to do, against the grain and interprets them in light of their specific argumentative and rhetorical strategy, that is to say, as deliberate exaggerations and performative contradictions. One notorious example of this strategy would be Adorno's dictum *Das Ganze ist das Unwahre* (The whole is the untrue), which, for all its paradoxical and aporetic nature, both hides an almost irrefutable conceptual truth, indeed a truism, and conveys an unmistakable moral appeal. Such phrases often reflect a provocative modernist aesthetic sensibility and its predilection for fragment, aphorism, and parataxis.

Adorno and Levinas consider the Western tradition to descend primarily through the works of Kant, Hegel, Husserl, and Heidegger, though in part by way of Marx, Nietzsche, and Kierkegaard, although references to other thinkers — Plato, Aristotle, Plotinus, Augustine, Aquinas, and (for Levinas) Descartes — abound in their writings. The pre-Socratics, the Hellenistic schools (Stoicism, Skepticism, Epicureanism, and Cynicism), Scholasticism, and Renaissance thought, let alone empiricist, logical positivist, or contemporary analytical and American pragmatist thought, are largely absent or appear only in brief allusions and schematic or pejorative presentations. In both, the philosophical legacy is thus not eliminated or destructed but, rather, in a subtle way opened up from within and without — displaced and deconstructed, almost in Derrida's use of

---

68. See the powerful account of the linguistic, pragmatic, hermeneutic, and semiotic turns in twentieth-century European and Anglo-American thought given by Karl-Otto Apel in the two volumes of *Transformation der Philosophie* (Frankfurt a.M.: Suhrkamp, 1973).

these terms. In their derangement of and disengagement from the Western heritage, Adorno and Levinas legitimate (or should we say *justify*?) their projects by suggesting that neither traditional metaphysical speculation nor modern subjective, let alone scientific or scientistic, models of experience and experiment are capable of grasping and conveying the "experience" — within quotation marks — of extreme negativity and absurdity which marks life "after Auschwitz." The title "Nach Auschwitz" ("After Auschwitz") introduces "Meditationen zur Metaphysik" ("Meditations on Metaphysics"), the final section of *Negative Dialektik* (*Negative Dialectics*), and that proper name stands for a radical caesura in Levinas's texts as well, as the dedication of *Otherwise than Being* testifies.

These thinkers rely on the uncanny appeal with which the rarefied and seemingly obsolete traces of the good and just life which remain — as instances of "spiritual experience" (Adorno) and "the spiritual life" (Levinas) — signal themselves here and now, under the conditions of modernity. The question of the meaning of truth, justice (for Adorno), the beautiful, or (more rarely, in Levinas) the sublime must, in their view, henceforth be thought without any reference to substantial guarantees immanent in some actual — or even possible, that is to say, potential and actualizable — reality, whether material or ideal, phenomenal or noumenal, profane or holy. The universalism of past philosophical systems of thought, they hold, was based on the illusion of being able to navigate stoically between the extremes of an ambivalent "experience" of the horrible and the no less ambivalent "experience" of the good, both of which — precisely because they are extremes (extremes that touch upon each other) — could be successfully forgotten, ignored, or repressed. Moreover, the traditional and modern philosophies of the same (of identity, totality, and the neuter), Adorno and Levinas claim, already founder on the attempt to convey any particular suffering or happiness through concepts of general or universal relevance or meaning. The inevitable deficit of Western philosophy, thus conceived, lies in this lapse — in short, in the space or interval that opens between the singular and the general or universal, that is to say, between the particular and particularity, between what is without concept (*das Begriffslose*) and the concept, between the nonpropositional Saying (*le Dire*) and the performative Said (*le Dit*) — though philosophy, by and large, acknowledges nothing of the sort.

Nevertheless, such singular "experiences" and particulars — before and beyond the categories of empirical or scientific experience as defined by Kant and expressed in concepts, statements, experiential judgments

(*Erfahrungsurteile*), and the like—must receive some kind of philosophical articulation if they are not to be dismissed as irrational outbursts or the convulsions of a tortured corporeality or a naively desiring spirituality, two contrasting figures of structurally similar manifestations of the ab-solute, the worst and the best, of which we find compelling instances in both Adorno and Levinas. Where these "experiences"—sometimes treated as nonexperiences, as not yet or no longer experienced, or as experiences par excellence, that is, as absolute experiences, experiences of the ab-solute—are forgotten, ignored, or repressed, philosophy is reduced to a kind of shadow play, becoming irresponsible, indeed irrelevant. Where it does not model its categories and concepts on a singular materiality or, rather, *matter*—evoked by Adorno's constellations of dialectical concretion no less than by Levinas's method of phenomenological deformalization—philosophy renders itself obsolete by betraying the very task and "honor of thinking."[69]

That is where the "substance" of these writings lies, a substance that is quite different from—and often diametrically opposed to—the meaning traditionally granted to this term. Adorno and Levinas broach "experiences" that traverse and exceed the order and history of being as well as the schemes of thought, concepts of normativity, and canons of taste which correspond to it. They hint at the less than heroic and more than tragic "experiences" of recent modernity which have set the negative standard (and, as Adorno says, "categorical imperative") for all history and responsibilities to come. Living "after Auschwitz," they suggest, one can no longer assume the presence of a divinity originating and directing the course of the world, though one must at the same time doubt the real or genuine—that is, conceptual or existential—possibility of rigid nihilism, consequent skepticism, lax relativism, and the like. "After Auschwitz" any appeal to a common cause and course of humankind, any eulogy to "culture," should be regarded with the deepest suspicion. What remains shows itself elsewhere, not in life—pure life—as such but in the minimal traits and instances of the other, whatever its nature.

IN THIS BOOK I attempt to illustrate the paradoxical and aporetic figure of these philosophically diffused differences, which are simultaneously sig-

69. I borrow this phrase from Jean-François Lyotard, *Le Différend* (Paris: Minuit, 1983), 10 / *The Differend: Phrases in Dispute*, trans. Georges Van Den Abbeele (Minneapolis: University of Minnesota Press, 1988), xii. See my essay "On Obligation: Lyotard and Levinas," *Graduate Faculty Philosophy Journal* 20–21, nos. 1–2 (1998): 83–112.

naled and betrayed within the limits of reason, for good and for ill. In such an ambiguous figure of thought, the contours of a minimal theology can clearly be recognized. This philosophical discipline — a "spiritual exercise" in a new guise — corresponds both to our modern or modernist (some would say postmodern) sensibilities and to a plausible, emphatic, and hyperbolic idea of reason, rationality, agency, and expressiveness. As I have suggested, we can formalize this intuition by examining the conceptual idiom, argumentation, rhetoric, and images employed by Adorno and Levinas throughout their long philosophical careers. Whereas part 1 analyzes the modern critique of, and remaining possibilities for, theology against the background of Habermas's theory of rationality, parts 2 and 3 of the book describe the intellectual backgrounds, methodological procedures, and conceptual and figural innovations of Adorno's and Levinas's writings while indicating some major systematic problems in interpretation which must be elaborated in an attempt at an immanent critique and *lectio difficilior* which would be faithful to the most rigorous principles of textual critique as well as of historical and conceptual analysis. I cannot presume to offer a *total* interpretation (a horrifying *contradictio in terminis!*) or an exhaustive reconstruction that would locate all the challenges and difficulties posed by their work. Still, I attempt a certain philosophical "appropriation from a distance"[70] and would suggest that whoever wants to investigate the possibility or impossibility of a philosophical theology — or, for that matter, any other thought, action, judgment, or expression — "after Auschwitz" must come to terms with the lessons of these formidable teachers. The comparison and confrontation of motifs and turns of thought or phrase which results from this apprenticeship does not consist in a problem-oriented "history of ideas," however interesting (and necessary) that might be, but, rather, in an attempt to read and analyze a certain "history of theory" with what Habermas rightly calls a "systematic purpose."[71]

In part 4, chapter 11 sums up the general argument of my comparative analysis and confrontation. It sets out, from yet another perspective, how a critical reception of Adorno's and Levinas's most important insights must be differentiated not only from classical, dogmatic, and confessional

---

70. Habermas's phrase, in von Friedeburg and Habermas, *Adorno-Konferenz 1983*, 351.

71. Jürgen Habermas, *Theorie des kommunikativen Handelns* (Frankfurt a.M: Suhrkamp, 1981), 1:201 / *Theory of Communicative Action*, trans. Thomas McCarthy (Boston: Beacon Press, 1984) 1:140.

theology (in addition to being liberated from the modern theory of rationality and the historicist and culturalist conception of the study of religion that accompanies it) but also from the postmodern interpretation of the philosophical strategy and ambition of "deconstruction." Chapter 12, finally, consists in an exposition of the problem of conceptual idolatry and blasphemy, which enables me to circle back to the questions from which I set out. The appendix clarifies some misinterpretations in the earlier reception of "deconstruction" as "poststructuralism."

PART ONE

Antiprolegomena

Chapter One
Toward a Critique of Theology

THE THEOLOGIAN FRANZ OVERBECK once remarked that modern Christianity tends to embrace the thinkers farthest removed from positive religion. The works of Goethe, Feuerbach, Schopenhauer, and Nietzsche, for example, have thus been viewed not as fatal attacks on Christianity but, above all, as prolegomena to the proper understanding of faith.[1] The skeptical philosopher Odo Marquard explains this phenomenon by suggesting that in modernity the notion of transcendence has become increasingly—and inescapably—*ethereal*. In modernity, we might add, drawing on the distinctions Habermas borrows from Max Weber, the unity of traditional orientations that once determined the integrity and intelligibility of life (of the cosmos, nature, society, and the self) seems to have irrevocably been lost. Through the disclosures of the critique of the Enlightenment, and in terms of their intellectual history, such traditional orientations stand revealed to be giants with feet of clay. Or, rather, sociohistorically and sociologically speaking, they have lost their material foundation, their anchor in life, and are left hanging in the air. "All that is solid melts into air," to cite Marx's famous words.

Ever since the "reform in ways of thinking [*Reform der Denkungsart*]" of the European Enlightenment,[2] both theologians and philosophers have

---

1. Overbeck writes:

It is the fashion for contemporary Christianity to give itself to the world in its own way, in the world of today no man of importance can behave in anti-Christian fashion without being claimed by Christianity with special preference. Among the Christians of modern observance, Goethe and Schiller, Feuerbach, Schopenhauer, Wagner, Nietzsche, and, naturally, their successors, must be content with this. . . . In actuality, we will soon be at the point with Christianity that all those great men will be much more familiar to us as devout Christians than as apostates from Christianity. If nothing more were needed for evidence of such an estimation than to pluck out of their writings the raisins of "warm" tones, approving of Christianity, who would hesitate long before joining himself wholeheartedly to modern Christianity? (Cited in Karl Löwith, *Von Hegel zu Nietzsche: Der revolutionäre Bruch im Denken des 19. Jahrhunderts* [Hamburg: Meiner, 1981], 39 / *From Hegel to Nietzsche: The Revolution in Nineteenth-Century Thought*, trans. David E. Green [New York: Holt, Rinehart and Winston, 1964], 24–25)

2. Immanuel Kant, "Was ist Aufklärung?" in Weischedel, *Werke*, 9:55 / "What Is Enlight-

shared the opinion that the existence of God must be affirmed, even if, upon closer examination, it could only be figured as a kind of "postulate," an "idea," or "the absolute other" — even if, that is, it could be revealed only in the distant future of the end of all things, the *eschaton*.[3] Yet the strategies that corresponded to the retreat and increasing abstraction of the divine and its substance — interpreting modern history as the emancipation of humanity, understanding its open-ended future as the play of the perfectibility of mankind, and viewing freedom as the ultimate goal or merely regulative concept of historical possibility — have shown their own fallibility and neither remove the seemingly senseless negativity that, so long as things have not come to a close, increasingly marks individual and collective historical experiences nor allow one to ignore it. "God" (and everything for which the concept stands) must logically assume a progressively "unreal" place. Through a "theodicy in a new guise," as Marquard calls it, "He" is increasingly relieved of His ever more fragmented creation. The sensibility of this modern theodicy inspires the discourses of the anti-Christian thinkers mentioned here but, understandably, also allows a revitalization of whatever had remained of theological interest.

Philosophically speaking, the modality of God's transcendence has thus seemed less and less capable of finding, let alone securing, a certain presence, a hold in existence. And yet it does not allow itself simply to be reduced, falsified, naturalized, or secularized, once and for all. In this paradoxical phenomenon, a distinctive mark of the (post)modern — the undecided (and fundamentally undecidable) transition and transformation taking place, not just between the modern and the so-called postmodern but already between the mythical, the traditional, the classical, and the modern — the notion of God, the very word *God*, is not ignored but redefined, infinitely refined, to the point of becoming ethereal, without extension, and almost inaudible. This development, which seems both irreversible and inconclusive — as well as in a sense to be determined, *dialectical*, a dialectic of *Enlightenment* in every meaning of the word — also affects the question of the relationship between the concept and theory of Western rationality and the domain and practice of theology. The paradox, which everyone already senses physically in daily existence, is that one can speak of the absolute only if one thinks its "reality" or "possi-

---

enment?" trans. Lewis White Beck, in *Philosophical Writings*, ed. Ernst Behler (New York: Continuum, 1986), 264.

3. Odo Marquard, *Schwierigkeiten mit der Geschichtsphilosophie: Aufsätze* (Frankfurt a.M.: Suhrkamp, 1973), 63; see also 68 ff.

bility" primarily as a certain absence, a certain negativity, a trace: in short, as the *ab-solute* in the etymological sense of the word (from Latin *absolvere*, "to loosen, detach, set free"). Yet that absence and negativity are never total but remain premised upon and continue to refer to an irreducible element or dimension of the other for which the theological archive — the name and names of the divine — still contains the most pertinent (and most provocative) designations and figures of thought.

This paradox, I will claim, reproduces itself at the reflexive meta-level where theology functions either as scholarly discipline — whether as the empirical study of the cultural phenomenon of religion (within the parameters of Western scientific, humanistic, historical, and exegetico-philological methodologies) or as the interpretation and self-explication of dogma (within the limits set by the study of "Divinity" and by biblical, practical, and systematic theology) — or as philosophical theology and the philosophy of religion (from which the minimal theology that we pursue here must finally be distinguished as well).[4]

Minimal Theology: Neither the "Science" of God nor the Science of "God"

Only a theology that addresses the problem of the infinite reduction and recession of the infinite, while still accounting for the remaining — and, perhaps, increasing — worthiness of its very question (its *Fragwürdigkeit*, in the double sense of the word, of which Heidegger has reminded us), is capable of conveying the simultaneously diminishing and abiding intelligibility that, especially in our time, characterizes the notion (i.e., the word, reality, and actuality) of "God." Such a theology could scarcely be furthered by up-to-date versions of the classical *prolegomena*, in which a number of philosophical, anthropological, or linguistic givens, or "grounds,"[5] form the ontological or pragmatic basis for the variable "categorical leap [*Sprungvariation*]"[6] which constitutes the supposed novelty and specificity of Judeo-Christian faith. On the contrary, a theology

4. The question of "dogmatics," of course, is not limited to the discipline of theology. See Pierre Legendre, *Sur la question dogmatique en Occident: Aspects théoriques* (Paris: Fayard, 1999). On the theological concept of "dogma," see Adolph von Harnack, *Lehrbuch der Dogmengeschichte* (Tübingen: J. C. B. Mohr, 1909), 3 vols.; and Karl Barth, *Die Lehre vom Wort Gottes: Prolegomena zur kirchlichen Dogmatik*, vol. 1 of *Die kirchliche Dogmatik* (Zurich: EVZ, 1964).

5. See Harry M. Kuitert, *Wat heet geloven? Structuur en herkomst van de christelijke geloofsuitspraken* (Baarn: Ten Have, 1977), 74 ff.

6. Hendrikus Berkhof, *Christelijk Geloof: Een inleiding tot de geloofsleer* (Nijkerk: Callenbach, 1975), 13.

that traces the ab-solution of the infinite under the successive onslaughts of modern critical reflection (and its historical antecedents: reason in all its guises) can be maintained only in the thorough, consistent discipline and exercise of what one might ironically call "antiprolegomena." By this I mean the correction, undoing, and unsaying of the presuppositions of theological thought, which restrict its discourse and imagination, confining it within the limits of "natural" theology, onto-theology, and their secularist equivalents. The latter, I claim, fulfill—indeed, sublate—some of the deepest aspirations of classical theological thinking. In fact, they come down to (more of) the same. This being said, two observations impose themselves.

(1) To sidestep or bracket the question of the ab-solute and retreat into the camp of the modern empirical scholarly study of religion (*Religionswissenschaft*), however respectable the reasons for doing so, is to offer only half an answer to the paradox of the progressively reduced yet increasingly poignant notion of "God." From the empirical, sociohistorical, or culturalist perspective—studying religion as a "fact of civilization" among others, as an "object of culture," not an "object of cult" (I will return to this terminology later)—one could at most stoically maintain the principles of a *methodological atheism,* an atheism that one might then, in turn, interpret subjectively as a form of intellectual ascesis *ad maiorem gloriam Dei.*[7] Admittedly, the central premise of classical theology—namely, that it is possible to *know* and *demonstrate* at least something concerning God's existence, essence, and predicates (if not necessarily concerning his creation ex nihilo, his providence, his divine names, and the "mysteries" of faith, incarnation, the trinity, and the Eucharist)—has lost its validity in the modern scholarly study and concept of religion. By and large such study assumes that nothing about God can be asserted scientifically: that is to say, in any verifiable or falsifiable way, or at least in statements and claims that could be subject to rational critique. According to this doctrine—and, for our purposes, it can claim no other status than that of one opinion among others, being merely a half-truth at that—one can only have faith in God.

This attitude is not just a response to Karl Barth's dialectical theology, his attack on the natural theology against which he claimed the cultural Protestantism of liberal theology had sinned in the late nineteenth and early twentieth centuries. Barth based his critique on a radical reinterpre-

---

7. Marquard, *Schwierigkeiten mit der Geschichtsphilosophie,* 65, 70, 71.

tation of St. Paul's Letter to the Romans and of church dogma as it was established in later ages. Inspired by Kierkegaard and with explicit reference to Overbeck, he sought to reestablish an Anselmian *fides quaerens intellectum* that would not conceptually and argumentatively rely on the onto-theological presupposition of the *analogia entis* in its classical and modern guises.

More decisive for the appeal of methodological atheism in the scholarly study of religion are considerations of a strictly philosophical—of a skeptical, ironic, often melancholic, and even somewhat resigned—nature. If one conforms to the reigning scientific model, and there may be perfectly legitimate reasons to do so, then every personal agreement with the content of faith, every response to its singular (and singularizing) appeal, must remain suspended—ad infinitum, as it were—subject to a phenomenological *epochē*.[8] Accordingly, the theological referent can be hinted at only *in obliquo,* with a certain reticence, in *disciplina arcani.*[9] What is considered most important—especially by those who adopt this methodological strategy or who want to prevent scientific methodology from taking possession of the divine subject—cannot appear discursively

8. By this Husserl means not a bracketing of our belief in the world, the self, and others (including the Other named God) but the cessation of the naturalist *interpretation* of these intentional objects. In an essay on Bataille, Derrida has shown how such an *epochē* could still remain bound to the metaphysical tradition. The methodological procedure of *epochē* distinguishes in vain between our apparent dependency on unwarranted—naturalist, psychologistic—assumptions, on the one hand, and the apparently much less metaphysical assertion of a scientifically determinable identity of meaning, on the other. By contrast, the transgression of (mythically or empirically given) meaning, as Bataille attempts to discover, breaks with both classical and modern ideas concerning the givenness and determinacy of meaning: "we would have to speak of an *epochē* of the epoch of meaning, of a—written—putting between brackets that suspends the epoch of meaning: the opposite of a phenomenological *epochē*, for this latter is carried out *in the name and in the sight of* meaning. The phenomenological *epochē* is a reduction that pushes us back toward meaning. Sovereign transgression is a reduction of this reduction: not a reduction to meaning, but a reduction of meaning. Thus, while exceeding the *Phenomenology of Mind*, this transgression at the same time exceeds phenomenology in general, in its most modern developments" (Jacques Derrida, *L'Écriture et la différence* [Paris: Seuil, 1967], 393–94 / *Writing and Difference*, trans. Alan Bass [Chicago: University of Chicago Press, 1978], 268). A similar transgression of meaning as affirmed, negated, or described in Hegelian and Husserlian phenomenology is thematized in the discussions of Adorno and Levinas which follow (pts. 2–3).

9. Hendrik Johan Adriaanse, *Het specifiek theologische aan een rijksuniversiteit: De verborgenheid der godgeleerdheid* (The Hague: Universitaire Pers Leiden, 1979), 20; Hendrik Johan Adriaanse, Henry A. Krop, and Lammert Leertouwer, *Het verschijnsel theologie: Over de wetenschappelijke status van de theologie* (Amsterdam: Boom, 1987), 133. See also Adriaanse, "After Theism," in *Posttheism: Reframing the Judeo-Christian Tradition,* ed. Henri Krop, Arie L. Molendijk, and Hent de Vries (Leuven: Peeters, 2000), 33–61.

at all. At best it shows itself, reveals itself, or leaves its traces elsewhere, otherwise. It does not enter intact into the concept of reason and the procedures of rationality without idolatry, without blasphemy. Reason is thus left to itself, as is the theological—that is, the concept of God, the idea of the infinite, and everything for which it stands. But is it thus respected, lived up to, and—ultimately—*itself*? Is preventing the divine and the infinite from being absorbed into and presented in an idolatrous and blasphemous manner not, paradoxically, idolatrous and blasphemous in turn? Does this not condemn the ab-solute to remaining a merely ineffable—and hence ineffective—nothingness, an unsayable, unexpressible, and unexpressive "I know not what" which is not only "not of this world" but which cannot enter into and engage (e.g., create, love, or redeem) it? On both counts, it seems, reason and rationality are halfway thought, halfheartedly acted upon, only partly represented.

(2) Likewise, one only halfway answers the paradox of the fading yet simultaneously growing pertinence of "God" by simply ignoring the wisdom of the world, which knows about His retreat, and thereby adhering, whether on second thought or stubbornly, to the classical, biblical, systematic, practical—in short, confessional—theology of the church. This would imply a similar and complementary ascesis, resignation, and often melancholy (hardly a joy or, in principle, a freedom of thought). The reigning dogmatic, constructive, and edifying discourse in classical theology (its exegesis and homiletics, its ecclesial formation and ecumenicalism) remains impossible without a *sacrificium intellectus,* however minimal.[10] In other words, classical theology in all its differentiated guises is fundamentally unthinkable without particularistic moments of "having" and "belonging" at odds with the formal—and in principle universalistic—disengagement of "knowing" and "responsibility." Kant means just this when he introduces the concept—or is it a practice or judgment?—of "reflective faith," in *Religion innerhalb der Grenzen der blossen Vernunft* (*Religion within the Boundaries of Mere Reason*). Classical theology, by definition, given its primary allegiance, cannot live up to this elementary requirement of reason (as Kant would say) and of rationality (as Habermas has it).

---

10. Max Weber, "Wissenschaft als Beruf," *Gesammelte Aufsätze zur Wissenschaftslehre* (Tübingen: J. C. B. Mohr, 1973), 553–54 / "Science as a Vocation," in *From Max Weber: Essays in Sociology,* ed. and trans. H. H. Gerth and C. Wright Mills (New York: Oxford University Press, 1946), 154.

In consequence classical and modern theologies—together with the concepts of their object and the methodologies that they imply—*bisect* reason and rationality. This will be my most important claim.[11] An undivided rationality, by contrast—here, a *minimal theology*—would have to do justice both to the accumulated wisdom of the world *and* to the ever weaker, yet ever more demanding, appeal of the infinite. The range of such a critical perspective in view of the ab-solute, spanning from *micrology* (Adorno) to *intentional analysis* (Levinas), can only become visible, however, when we are prepared to notice its blind spots. These aporias are not necessarily a conceptual deficit but, rather, the very rhetorical and argumentative mode of the philosophical discourse that will interest us here. Here resides the contemporary relevance of the writings of Adorno and Levinas—and, indeed, their virtual dialogue, whose implications we have scarcely begun to realize.

Could one imagine a (post)modern theology that would outline the contours of such a concept of rationality and, in so doing, claim a general relevance extending far beyond the narrow confines of classical theological discourse and its scientific scholarly counterparts? As I have argued, the latter are formally equivalent in that they both, each in its own way, bisect what remains of reason in the very concept of rationality. What would the structural features and exemplary idioms of such a theology,

---

11. The metaphor of the "bisection" of rationality is borrowed from Habermas's contribution to the somewhat confusing discussion surrounding what has been called the "positivist dispute." See Jürgen Habermas, "Gegen einen positivistisch halbierten Rationalismus," in Theodor W. Adorno and others, *Der Positivismusstreit in der deutschen Soziologie* (Darmstadt: Luchterhand, 1972), 235–66 / "A Positivistically Bisected Rationalism," in Adorno and others, *The Positivist Dispute in German Sociology* (New York: Harper & Row, 1976), 198–225. Yet, as will become apparent in the following section of this chapter, this concept of "bisection" can be worked out in a way different from Habermas's account. It should be noted, moreover, that the demarcation between "Frankfurt School" Critical Theory and competing paradigms in the philosophy of science, the social sciences, and the humanities was historically and systematically more complex than has long been assumed. See Hans-Joachim Dahms, *Positivismusstreit: Die Auseinandersetzungen der Frankfurter Schule mit dem logischen Positivismus, dem amerikanischen Pragmatismus und den kritischen Rationalismus* (Frankfurt a.M.: Suhrkamp, 1994), who rightly criticizes the somewhat "static" features of Adorno's (and, to a lesser extent, Horkheimer's) critique of positivism, even as logical-positivist thinking was evolving to the point at which C. I. Lewis, in another critique, could call it a "moving target" (402). On Habermas's contribution to the second round of the "Positivism Dispute," including his "changing sides" by developing a conception of language and truth which draws heavily on the writings of the American pragmatists (and their successors), whose position had been condemned by the older generation of the Frankfurt School as "positivist," see ibid., 361–400, 403; see also Wiggershaus, *Frankfurt School*, 566–82 / 628–46.

given its assumed minimalism, look like? Could it circumvent the all too abstract opposition between "cult" and "culture" and their more sophisticated analogues?[12]

The complex and often antagonistic interplay between theology and reason or rationality constitutes only the point of departure, not the ultimate goal, of my investigation. Its aim, as will become apparent, concerns the entwining — or interchangeability — of the theories of rationality, dialectics, phenomenology, and deconstruction in their dealings with "metaphysical," even "spiritual," experience, with the experiment, trial, and exercise of, or meditation on, the ab-solute, all of which complement and substitute for one another when read against the grain and in view of what I (for lack of better terminology) have called here a "hermeneutica sacra sive profana." By this I mean an interpretive concern with the other in its most general and singular features, for which the religious tradition and its intellectual archives still offer the most promising concepts, arguments, rhetorical figures, and stock images. Yet the passage through religion — in solidarity, as it were, with dogmatic and scholarly theology in their obsolescence (or downfall) — can be only provisional and strategic, though thus also eminently philosophical. Reconsidering religion and the theological in that sense (and with that aim) implies supplementing the classical notion of divine speech (or, subsequently, "godtalk"), the modern practice of science, and the contemporary concept of discourse, including the theories of rationality upon which all these are based.

Adorno puts the problem thus: "Seen from the point of view of science and scholarship [*Wissenschaft*], an element of the irrational enters, as a moment, into philosophical rationality itself, and it is up to philosophy to

---

12. On the distinction between *cult* and *culture*, see Jakob Taubes, *Vom Kult zur Kultur: Bausteine zu einer Kritik der historischen Vernunft, Gesammelte Aufsätze zur Religions-und Geistesgeschichte*, ed. Aleida and Jan Assmann, Wolf-Daniel Hartwich, and Winfried Menninghaus (Munich: Wilhelm Fink, 1996); as well as Régis Debray, *L'Enseignement du fait religieux dans l'école laïque*, intro. Jack Lang (Paris: Odile Jacob, 2002), 28. On the "putting in brackets of personal convictions" that would mark the "optics of knowledge," as opposed to the "optics of faith," and which should govern the "deontology of teaching" in a public, laicized, or republican institution of secondary education or higher learning, see ibid., 28–29. Debray insists: "the teaching *of* the religious *is not* a religious teaching" and, a little farther on, "Learning to know [*Donner à connaître*] a reality or doctrine is one thing; promoting a norm or an ideal is another" (23, 29). Analytically, pragmatically, and institutionally distinct, the two contradictory perspectives might well coincide in one person. Debray has elaborated his views on the "religious fact" in several other publications, the most relevant here being *Dieu: Un Itinéraire* (Paris: Odile Jacob, 2001). The expression *fait religieux* is also used by Claude Lévi-Strauss; see Claude Lévi-Strauss and Didier Éribon, *De près et de loin* (Paris: Odile Jacob, 2001), 114.

absorb this moment without thereby subscribing to irrationalism" (*Drei Stud* 108 / 342, trans. modified). Of course, what is absorbed in this movement of thought is negated in a determinate way and, if not sublated, then at least transformed and displaced. Theology, however, whether as traditionally conceived or as modeled on the modern conception of science and disciplinary scholarship, must guard against such a possibility. By definition it can neither accept the transformation and displacement of its dogmatic core (a displacement that it must finally identify with heterodoxy, idolatry, or blasphemy, in short with sin) nor acknowledge the absorption of some irrationality — albeit the most sublime — into rationality, a situation it must immediately condemn as a paradox or, worse still, a performative contradiction. Perhaps the first leg of this dilemma is why Adorno denied (classical) theology any place in the emphatic construction of the rational, favoring instead the term *metaphysics* or *metaphysical experience*: "Vis-à-vis theology, metaphysics is not just a historically later stage, as it is according to positivistic doctrine. It is not only theology secularized into a concept. It preserves theology in its critique, by uncovering the possibility of what theology forces upon men and thus desecrates [*schändet*]" (*ND* 397 / 389, trans. modified). Yet, as we shall see, *secularization into the concept* does not equal scholarly integration and reduction according to scientific procedures. The *preservation of theology in its critique* is not less speculative about or faithful to the religious legacy. In a paradoxical way it is more so: it maintains the "possibility" of the theological by freeing it from its imposture, that is to say, from being violated by preconceptions, reification, or, what comes down to the same, idolatry and blasphemy. This is "the other theology [*die andere Theologie*]" whose contours — and systematic parallels in later or alternative avenues of thought (the theory of communicative action, the phenomenology of the trace of the other, and the deconstruction of every other as totally other) — I seek to formalize in these pages, drawing out its critical, analytical, disciplinary, and interdisciplinary consequences without forgetting its original impetus, its heterodoxy, and, perhaps, its *untimeliness*. But the latter, I suggest, involves the relevance of this Adornian motif.

The problems sketched here point toward larger questions than those concerning the possibilities for legitimating theology, whether classical, modern, or postmodern. What is at issue exceeds the ongoing debate about the status of this discipline in its academic — whether confessional or scholarly — guises. Attempts to legitimate both the ecclesial study of Divinity at denominational and public universities (in the European context, both usually publicly funded) and the conglomeration of fields which makes up programs of religious studies have provoked debates that apply not to this topic alone. These debates seem to have arrived at a stalemate, however, and so we will need to explore an alternative approach to the questions that orient them and a revision of their underlying presuppositions, if the theological and the religious continue to guide us (as they will no doubt for some time still to come).

The stalemate has taken the form of the following dilemma: (a) if theology is still to follow the classical "science of God," it is difficult to see how it could satisfy scientific standards of public availability and verifiability in anything but a trivial way (e.g., by giving its propositions a certain coherence and intelligibility, nothing more); (b) by contrast, if theology, in the guise of the modern science and study of religion (*Religionswissenschaft*), limits itself to discussing the cultural phenomenon or historical fact of "religion," that is to say, of a "God" or of "gods" — whose existence is discretely set in quotation marks and thus bracketed, suspended, reduced — then it can no longer claim to have its own specific subject matter. Neither its approach nor its contributions could in principle distinguish it from other empirical disciplines. In its concentration on myth, ritual practices, and figural representations or images, its mode of investigation is indistinguishable from the general humanistic approaches to the cultural object in literary history, psychology, sociology, anthropology, and, more recently, studies in visual culture and media. Theology as the sum total of religious studies appears to be superfluous, given that it lacks an object, indeed a *figure d'existence,* of its own. The reigning concept of academic scholarship and its division of labor would simply forbid it to assume proper disciplinary status.[13]

13. In a reconstruction of the historical, archaeological, philological, and comparative study of religion in the "fifth section" of the École Pratique des Hautes Études, where scholars such as Marcel Mauss, Henri Hubert, André-Jean Festugière, Georges Dumézil, and Claude Lévi-Strauss taught at some point during their careers, Jean-Pierre Vernant notes two difficulties that resulted from the tendency, formulated most explicitly by Mauss in his inaugural lecture, to view religion no longer as "a more or less autonomous spiritual universe, a sort of lived philosophy, a metaphysics *en acte*" but, rather, as "a social dimension," "religious fact," and "phenomenon" whose meaning and function must be related to other elements in the "social morphology." The difficulty of focusing on the *fait social total,* according to Mauss, lies less in methodology (which had been enriched to include empirical observation of contemporary religious practices as well as the study of different genres of texts, such as ethnological field reports) than in the questions it leaves open: "First question: If religion is a dimension of the social, in what respect does it distinguish itself from the other constituents of the collective life — that is, how does the sphere of the religious trace itself [or "design itself," *se dessine*] and demar-

Theology, apparently, must be one or the other: either it must be the science of God or the science of "God." Neither pole of the dilemma, however, could by itself justify the existence of an independent faculty or discipline of theology within the context of the modern secular university.[14]

Although many rearguard actions somewhat desperately assert the contrary, the critique of all scientific truth claims made by classical biblical and dogmatic theology — however bound up with confession and tradition — is essentially irrefutable. One might, at best, dispute the sort of argument such a critique might assume. That is not my purpose here; rather, I will address the shadowy character of such debates, taking up, on the one hand, a more pragmatic argument (a), and, on the other, one of *principle* (b). Both illustrate why the dispute in question could never be resolved, whether institutionally or conceptually, and why a change of terrain is necessary — and possible — for us today.

(a) The principle objections to the autonomy of the modern science

cate itself within society? Second question: Is the place of religion, of its finalities and definition, the same in civilizations in which the religious is organized and institutionalized, where the cut [*coupure*] between the profane and the sacred is by and large firmly established, and in civilizations in which the religious appears, on the contrary, either as diffused throughout the whole of the social fabric or as narrowly intertwined — and solidary — with political organization?" A first consequence of these questions, Vernant says, would be to ask, "About what are we speaking when we speak about religion, and are we speaking of the same thing when we are dealing with Australian aboriginals, the civic religion of fifth-century Greeks, medieval Christianity, and our contemporary Western societies [*notre Occident*]?" (Jean-Pierre Vernant, "La Religion objet de science," *Entre mythe et politique* [Paris: Seuil, 1996], 98). A further result of this development in the scholarly study of religion becomes clear when we realize the full implications of the term *comparatism*, as indicated in both the method and the "general conception of the *sciences religieuses*" 99), which Vernant links to the establishment in 1934 of Georges Dumézil's fifth section chair "comparative mythology," which was to become in 1945 a chair in the "comparative study of the religions of the Indo-European peoples." Operating on the same terrain as a linguist (of Indo-European languages), a comparatist then asks, "What is the conceptual architecture that presides over the grouping and distribution of the divinities that are addressed by rites, myths, and images?" It then becomes necessary to "disentangle the structures of the pantheon with regard to both an intellectual order — an ideological field — and a social order: the forms of collective organization known from the history of the Indo-European peoples." In doing so, a comparatist must engage different disciplinary fields, all of which add up to a single inquiry: "The hierarchized equilibrium of powers in the divine world, different types of human activities and behaviors, and forms of social life — these different, intertwined domains [*plans*] are traversed in a single movement of inquiry. . . . The frontiers of the religious become incertain [*floues*] from the moment the intellectual framework of a religious system is taken into account, in addition to its social context [*cadre*]" (100).

14. Herman Philipse, "Theologie: Een wetenschap? Beschouwingen naar aanleiding van drie redes gehouden aan de Theologische Faculteit van de Rijksuniversiteit te Leiden," *Nederlands Theologisch Tijdschrift* 38 (1984): 45–66.

of religion, to the academic programs of religious studies—that they lack thematic unity and exhibit disciplinary overlap and reduplication—might appear trivial at first glance. What would prevent one from saying about the scholarly study of theology what Gilbert Ryle says about the discipline of psychology in *The Concept of Mind*? After psychology was deprived of the spiritualist assumption of a Cartesian soul, a "ghost in the machine," and was then also freed from its reflex to move in the opposite, materialist direction toward *l'homme machine* (to cite De la Mettrie's well-known title), Ryle claims that it became a more or less random accumulation of inquiries and methods.[15] Similarly, theology has had to relinquish the pretense of offering a phenomenology of the "essence" of religion (as claimed by such authors as Adolph von Harnack, Leo Baeck, Rudolf Otto, Gerardus van der Leeuw, and Heiko Miskotte). Minus that claim, it can be concerned only with what other cultural sciences and humanities can study equally well. Yet from a *pragmatic* perspective it makes as little sense to require theology to concern itself with a clearly delineated subject, ignored or neglected by other disciplines, as it would to demand this of psychology.

What determines the status of theology at the modern secular (or, in the European context, usually public) university is the reigning array of social powers, in which arguments *pro domo* stand under the suspicion of ideology from the moment they are put forward. Whoever is irritated by this might and "right of the factual"[16]—by the influence, that is, of extrascientific factors, such as the piety of secular states in the face of the heritage of Christian culture or simple fear of the continuing social weight of communities of faith—would be attempting to summon cultural facts before the tribunal of reason,[17] on the supposition that only reason (but whose reason exactly?) could and should guarantee their legitimacy. The various arguments for and against theology, which seek to elucidate the social, cultural, and personal relevance of the scientific, scholarly study of religion in a particular historical and political context, are largely concerned with an empirical question, which I will not address here. This does not mean that a more philosophical approach to this question could not play a heuristic role in such empirical inquiry—could not, so to speak,

15. Gilbert Ryle, *The Concept of Mind* (Harmondsworth, Middlesex: Penguin, 1978), 301 ff.

16. Wolfhart Pannenberg, *Wissenschaftstheorie und Theologie* (Frankfurt a.M.: Suhrkamp, 1977), 8.

17. See Immanuel Kant, "Vorrede zur ersten Auflage der *Kritik der reinen Vernunft*," A xii, in Weischedel, *Werke*, 3:13n / preface to the first edition of the *Critique of Pure Reason*, trans. Norman Kemp Smith (New York: St. Martin's Press, 1965), xii.

have the provocative effect of a determinate move in what seems ultimately to be an institutional game of chess. (We are reminded here of
Benjamin's automaton.) I hope one might understand my philosophical
arguments concerning the status of theology (or lack thereof) in just this
way.

(b) The *systematic* question about the conditions under which theology might still claim a certain right to existence, under which, in any
guise (or, indeed, *figure d'existence*) it might still be possible, even irre-
placeable, before the forum of reason and in the whole of science and
culture—albeit as the hidden dwarf in the machine of historical materialist critique (and all its naturalistic, communicative, systems-theoretical,
structuralist, and pragmatist successor forms)—has not yet, I believe, been
sufficiently fathomed. Indeed, in debates about the status of theology the
proverbial baby seems to have been thrown out with the bathwater. With
the loss of its original subject, theology runs the risk of losing its innovative strength in the perennial "conflict of the faculties"—and what could
legitimate it more than its transformation into the heuristic, hermeneutic,
or comparative analysis of the controversial semantic potential of a "religion" whose archive, arguments, figures of speech, and imagery are, more
than ever before, in need of being rediscovered and, perhaps, *reclaimed*?

One might, perhaps a tad wickedly, articulate the stalemate between
the two opposing theoretical camps of classical-confessional and modern-
academic theology with the parable that Ryle ironically uses to illuminate
the similar and equally unproductive conflict between classical-spiritual
and modern-materialist psychologies. He ends *The Concept of Mind* with
the following narrative:

> One company of a country's defenders installs itself in a fortress. The soldiers
> of the second company notice that the moat is dry, the gates are missing, and
> the walls are in collapse. Scorning the protection of such a rickety fort, yet still
> ridden by the idea that only from forts like this can the country be defended,
> they take up their stand in the most fortlike thing they can see, namely, the
> shadow of the decrepit fort. Neither position is defensible; and obviously the
> shadow stronghold has all the vulnerability of the stone fort, with some extra
> vulnerabilities of its own. Yet in one respect the occupants of the shadow-fort
> have shown themselves the better soldiers, since they have seen the weakness
> of the stone fort, even if they are silly to fancy themselves secure in a fort made
> of no stones at all. The omens are not good for their victory, but they have
> given some evidence of teachability. They have exercised some vicarious stra-

tegic sense; they have realized that a stone fort whose walls are broken is not a stronghold. That the shadow of such a fort is not a stronghold either is the next lesson that they may come to learn.[18]

If theology is to remain innovative and demonstrate its willingness to learn, then, in terms of Ryle's metaphor, it must recognize the crumbling foundations of a ruinous fort, without settling down in what is merely its shadow. It should not embrace empty form, stripped of all determinate content, but neither should it shun the remnants of the former stronghold, which offer ample opportunities for strategic bricolage. For all its skepticism, then, it should not choose a nomadic existence that, in continually renewed figures, leaves its traces in the wilderness of our culture — a culture that continually erases them.[19] On the contrary, it should negotiate with the ruins, even be "solidary" with the stronghold — including its decrepit building blocks, weakened foundations, and porous walls — in the very hour of its disintegration: "in the very moment of its downfall [*im Augenblickes ihres Sturzes*]," as Adorno said of metaphysics in the closing words of *Negative Dialectics*.

Of course, this viewpoint, which perhaps may seem nostalgic, cannot easily be assimilated to the sobriety and mildly ironic character of Ryle's pragmatism. In this investigation, therefore, we will have to rely on other witnesses.

As the (legitimate?) heir of its philosophical or systematic predecessors — in sympathy more with heterodoxies and nominalism than with onto-theologies and realism — minimal theology must tack between the Scylla of classical theology (which in its biblical, dogmatic, or confessional guises, i.e., as bound by the authority of some "cult," falls short on rational grounds and remains merely a science of God) and the Charybdis of the modern empirical science of religion (i.e., of "God" as a substitutable object of "culture"). In the archipelago of the sciences and other forms of rationality a minimal theology will be able to demonstrate its nautical skill only if it neither resorts to the dogmatic positions of classical theology nor steers toward the latent dispositions that threaten to turn the modern academic study of religion into a scholarly Procrustean bed. If it wants to mark its difference otherwise — that is to say, signal its proper expressivity or express its signifyingness in alternative ways — its only chance lies with

18. Ryle, *Concept of Mind*, 311.
19. "Sceptics, a species of nomads despising all settled modes of life [*Anbau des Bodens*]" (Kant, preface to the first edition of the *Critique of Pure Reason*, ix / 12).

what we might call a (post)modern reason or a nonscientific rationality, which avoids the extremes of relapsing into a fallback theology, on the one hand, and celebrating mere bricolage, on the other.

Such a nonbisected rationality can, strictly speaking, no longer be that of a *science* for the simple reason that science—with its criteria of inductive verifiability, critical rational falsifiability, corroboration according to a given paradigm, episteme, or practice, and also its empiricisms, positivisms, naturalism, reductionism, and the correspondence or coherence theories of truth all these involve—is fundamentally incapable of addressing, let alone thematizing, the ab-solute as such or on its own terms. But what, exactly, would such address or such terms entail? Before answering that question, suffice it to note that the minimal and philosophically oriented theology that interests us here appears neither as a positive, disciplinary, or regional science nor as a general or fundamental ontology (to say nothing of their merely abstract and relativistic negations) but, rather, as a *(post)modern reprise of the metaphysica specialis,* that is to say, as a radical transformation of natural theology, albeit one that avoids the latter's sins as much as possible. I shall argue that this reprise must consist in a de-transcendentalization of the central presuppositions of philosophical theology in its traditional formulation, with the aim of giving them not a merely historicized or narrativized but a *quasi-transcendental* status.

In its traditional form as a mode of cultural expression, philosophical theology shared with mythology, religion, and art the tendency toward exhaustively interpreting all of reality, while it shared with unfolding disciplinary scientific knowledge—directed toward particular segments of reality—faith in human reason as its proper and exclusive element. Although this demarcation may have been arbitrary, that does not eliminate the task of understanding it for heuristic purposes. The concepts of totality and reason have themselves become extremely problematic, of course. This has drastic repercussions, because precisely the concepts of totality and reason allowed philosophy—and, hence, philosophical theology—to situate itself in the no-man's-land between opposed poles of thought. Speaking of philosophy—and, by analogy, this holds for philosophical theology as well—Bertrand Russell, in his *History of Western Philosophy,* expresses this in-between-ness as follows:

> Philosophy is something intermediate between theology and science. Like theology, it consists of speculations on matters as to which definite knowledge

has, so far, been unascertainable; but like science, it appeals to human reason rather than to authority, whether that of tradition or that of revelation. All *definite* knowledge . . . belongs to science; all *dogma* as to what surpasses definite knowledge belongs to theology. But between theology and science there is a No Man's Land, exposed to attack from both sides; this No Man's Land is philosophy. Almost all the questions of most interest to speculative minds are such as science cannot answer, and the confident answers of theologians no longer seem so convincing as they did in former centuries.[20]

What traits, then, would a *philosophical* theology have to exhibit in order to guard against the suspicion that its figures of thought are merely irrational testimonies, senseless expressions condemned to go up in smoke? Its fate appears to be bound up with that of the entire metaphysical tradition. Perhaps one could understand the "broken relationship between the philosophy of religion and metaphysics" along these lines.[21] Philosophical theology takes shape as a discourse (perhaps a figure of thought, nothing more or less) about an *element* or *dimension* of our most quotidian, elevated, and banal experiences; an element and dimension that tradition — including classical theology in its revealed, positive, and imposed or onto-theologically constituted varieties — somewhat prematurely indicates as *God*, without quotation marks. It no longer approaches its subject, the ab-solute and its singular forms, directly but, rather, comes at it indirectly, through endless detours and false starts that, taken together, make up the laborious task of the *hermeneutica sacra sive profana.*

Adorno captures this relationship between philosophy — including "the other theology," the "spiritual" experiment (or exercise?) and "metaphysical experience" still open to us — and the historical weight of the canon in almost programmatic fashion: "Philosophy's methexis in tradition would only be a *definite* denial of tradition. Philosophy is founded by [*wird gestiftet von*] the texts it criticizes. They are brought to it by the tradition they embody, and it is in dealing with them that the conduct of philosophy becomes commensurable with tradition. This justifies the

20. Bertrand Russell, *The History of Western Philosophy: and Its Connection with Political and Social Circumstances from the Earliest Times to the Present Day* (London: George Allen & Unwin, 1975), 13.

21. Adriaanse, Krop, and Leertouwer, *Het verschijnsel theologie,* 94. See also Hent de Vries, "Theologie en moderniteit, rationaliteit en skepsis," *Nederlands Theologisch Tijdschrift* 42 (1988): 21–41.

move from philosophy to exegesis [or interpretation, *Deutung*], which exalts neither the interpretation nor the symbol into an absolute but seeks the truth where thinking secularizes the *irretrievable* archetype [*Urbild*] of sacred texts" (*ND* 55 / 64, my emph.). In all of these interpretations in which it submerges itself, philosophy necessarily subjects itself (and this is its universalist regime) to discourse concerning transcendence in the broadest sense, although for all its generality it remains inextricably bound to an acknowledgment of and respect for the particular. Its rationality resides in this ambivalence—that is to say, the hesitation, indecision, oscillation, and alternation—between universality and singularity. The rationality of religious and theological language is intelligible only to the extent that it may be interpreted in terms of a *general* concept of transcendence. Yet this conceptual necessity does not form a sufficient condition for rationality.

One objection is immediately apparent. Doesn't such a more or less formal interpretation threaten the exceptionally concrete phenomena of religious experience and religious meaning, as witnessed in divine speech, prophecy, speaking in tongues, the *confessio fidei*, the mysteries of faith, the sacraments, and the original theologies that remained closest to them? In a certain sense it does. My intent, however, will be to show that a plausible, rational, philosophical, minimal theology—and vice versa, every bona fide theory of rationality on which theology could draw or, for its part, illuminate—must always allude to some singular incarnation, materialization, phenomenologization, or concretization of transcendence in general. This can only proceed "indirectly."[22] Theology cannot itself produce or reconstruct this *concretissimum* through its arguments[23]—though this does not imply that the *concretissimum* is therefore the irrational par excellence. It is, rather, the flip side of every possibility of speculation, interpretation, conceptualization, argumentation, delibera-

22. Arnold Burms and Herman de Dijn, *De rationaliteit en haar grenzen* (Assen: Van Gorcum, 1986).

23. This term is taken from Johan F. Goud, *Levinas en Barth: Een godsdienstwijsgerige en ethische vergelijking* (Amsterdam: Rodopi, 1984), 152. It suggests the unexpected, contingent, and fully singular revelation of the "absolute Other" in Barth's late work, which crosses all a priori structures of being or of consciousness (180, 362 n. 703). According to Goud, the term can also articulate the "statute" of the other in Levinas (348–49 n. 553). I will also relate it here to the "nonidentical" in Adorno's work. I must investigate more closely, however, whether, for Adorno and Levinas, this idea is or should be lacking in all "meta-phorical possibilities," as Goud maintains. Our rhetorical reading of at least certain elements in their work suggests the contrary.

tion, action, judgment, and expression and, as such, one of the foci that constitute the elliptical figure of rationality.

The question of the contours of and conditions of possibility for a rational, philosophical—and, under present conditions, minimal—theology is relevant beyond the philosophy of religion in the narrow sense, even if the academic discipline of the philosophy of religion is often the institutional place where this question is most explicitly thematized. The term *systematic theology*[24] or the modifier *comparative* in the expression *comparative religious studies* can also refer, more generally, to a philosophical, interpretive, or hermeneutical ferment in the exegetical, historical, or sociological procedures of theology (here the science of religion) and thus also in the study of cults and culture broadly defined. Because of what one might call the increasingly philosophical nature of the study of culture (*Kulturwissenschaften,* cultural studies, cultural analysis), these borderlines cannot be precisely drawn. Likewise, one cannot attribute a foundational or overarching role to philosophical theology in order to create an exclusionary division between the normal, scientific questions of truth, on the one hand, and some alternative "discourse" (*Diskurs, discours*) concerning questions of meaning—and the extra-ordinary—on the other. If we are to avoid the pitfalls of the complementary constructs of modern "scientism" and classical-modern "existentialism,"[25] then we

24. For a discussion of the history of this concept, see Pannenberg, *Wissenschaftstheorie und Theologie,* 406–25.

25. See Jürgen Habermas, "Die Philosophie als Platzhalter und Interpret," *Moralbewusstsein und kommunikatives Handeln* (Frankfurt a.M.: Suhrkamp, 1983), 21 / "Philosophy as Stand-In and Interpreter," trans. Christian Lenhardt and Shierry Weber Nicholsen, in Habermas, *Moral Consciousness and Communicative Action* (Cambridge: MIT Press, 1991), 13–14. There Habermas criticizes Richard Rorty's distinction between discourses concerning "representations" and those concerning "edification." The difference between these two perspectives would be that between epistemology and its successor disciplines, on the one hand, and hermeneutics, on the other:

> Hermeneutics sees the relations between various discourses as those of strands in a possible conversation, a conversation which presupposes no disciplinary matrix which unites the speakers but where the hope of agreement is never lost so long as the conversation lasts. This hope is not a hope for the discovery of antecedently existing common ground, but *simply* hope for agreement, or, at least, exciting and fruitful disagreement. Epistemology sees the hope of agreement as a token of the existing common ground which, perhaps unbeknown to the speakers, unites them in a common rationality. For hermeneutics, to be rational is to be willing to refrain from epistemology—from thinking that there is a special set of terms in which all contributions to the conversation should be put—and to be willing to pick up the jargon of the interlocutor rather than translating it into one's own. For epistemology, to be rational is to find the proper set of terms into which all contributions

must address the gradual, implacable difference always already apparent *within* the corpus of the individual sciences of culture, rather than between them. Individual disciplines, it has been claimed, are best able to question their fundamental concepts at times of "scientific revolution"; philosophy, by contrast, is permanently in a condition of self-contradiction—both as an intellectual discipline and perhaps even as a "way of life." But scholarly disciplines—and perhaps even personal scholarly discipline as a way of life—have their philosophical moments or momentum as well. They enable us to interpret reality from continually shifting perspectives that, if they are to avoid lapsing into mere perspectivism, must at the same time retain a view toward the ab-solute, whose place—that is to say, whose "structure," "form," and (if one can still say so) "content"—it keeps, in principle, open.

"The Actuality of Philosophy"

The "actuality [*Aktualität*] of philosophy," to borrow a phrase from Adorno's inaugural address, presented in Frankfurt am Main in 1931, depends upon its ability to articulate its intertwining with the most advanced positions and epistemologies of science and with experience—including the moral intuitions and aesthetic expressions of the different modernities and modernisms—in general. It is, Adorno makes clear, capable of a *second-order reflection* if (and only if) its guiding principle is one of "interpretation [*Deutung*]," which undermines rules, by contrast to science, which is more rigidly rule bound and guided by the pathos of "re-

---

should be translated if agreement is to become possible. For epistemology, conversation is implicit inquiry. For hermeneutics, inquiry is routine conversation. (Richard Rorty, *Philosophy and the Mirror of Nature* [Oxford: Blackwell, 1980], 318)

One is reminded of the terms proposed in Adorno's early essay "The Actuality of Philosophy," especially between "research [*Forschung*]" and "interpretation [*Deutung*]." In Rorty's view, only open societal conversation rather than universalizing—and, one might add, normativizing—"routine conversation" or "inquiry" is hospitable to what Thomas Kuhn calls "abnormal" discourse. In Rorty's words: "The production of abnormal discourse can be anything from nonsense to intellectual revolution, and there is no discipline which describes it, any more than there is a discipline devoted to the study of the unpredictable, or of 'creativity.' But hermeneutics is the study of abnormal discourse—the attempt to make some sense of what is going on at a stage where we are still too unsure about it to describe it, and thereby to begin an epistemological account of it" (ibid., 320–21). Habermas offers a different interpretation of the possibilities of the "philosophization of the sciences of man" (*Moral Consciousness and Communicative Action*, 15 / 22). See also Karl-Otto Apel, "Types of Rationality Today: The Continuum of Reason between Science and Ethics," in *Rationality Today*, ed. Thomas Geraets (Ottawa: University of Ottawa Press, 1979), 307–40.

search [*Forschung*]." Philosophy neither views phenomena as facts nor
contains them within preexisting structures. On the contrary, from the
very beginning it views all phenomena as signs that must be deciphered.
Nevertheless, philosophy gains its "material content [*materiale Fülle*]"
not by revisiting and intuiting some intelligible realm (or *topos noetos*) of
ideal forms but from the empirical, social, historical, and cultural sciences
(as well as from the more elusive aesthetic, moral, and metaphysical experiences that individuals continuously—and, perhaps, increasingly?—
undergo) (APh 126 / 333). As Adorno suggests, philosophy thus defined
is able neither *analytically* to subdivide this "material content" into its
isolated constitutive elements nor *synthetically* to produce and reconstruct it. Although the very structure of such a philosophy, its internal
composition, differs from the more or less organically figured concretion (*Konkretion,* from Latin *concrescere*) of Hegelian thought, it can decipher this material content only *dialectically*—which for Adorno always
means paradoxically and only through the "juxtaposition of what is smallest [or most insignificant, *Zusammenstellung des Kleinsten*]" (APh 127 /
336, trans. modified). It must decode "truth" without ever possessing a
key to unlocking it—which accordingly means that it must always remain without definitive results, inconclusive. It has nothing at its disposal
other than "fleeting, disappearing traces within the riddle figures of what
exists [*Rätselfiguren des Seienden*] and their astonishing [*wunderlichen*]
entwinings" (APh 126 / 334).

I will return later to these enigmatic formulations, which draw heavily
on what Benjamin, in the notes for *Das Passagen-Werk* (*The Arcades Project*) called "interpretation in detail [*Ausdeutung in den Einzelheiten*]," a
method anticipated by the *Ursprung des deutschen Trauerspiels* (*The Origin
of the German Tragic Drama*) and "Einbahnstrasse" ("One-Way Street").[26]
By this Benjamin means not only the ambition "of interpolating into the
infinitely small [*im unendlich Kleinen zu interpolieren*]"[27] but also the

26. The questions of Benjamin's influence on the inaugural lecture and of whether Adorno
should have publicly acknowledged it haunt the opening exchanges of their correspondence
(Theodor W. Adorno and Walter Benjamin, *The Complete Correspondence, 1928–1940,* ed. Henri
Lonitz, trans. Nicholas Walker [Cambridge: Harvard University Press, 1999], 8–13). The debt is
stated explicitly in the lecture "Die Idee der Naturgeschichte" ("The Idea of a Natural History").
On the notion of "interpretation in detail [*Ausdeutung in den Einzelheiten*]," see Benjamin,
Arcades Project, N2, 1, 460 / 5.1:574.

27. Benjamin, "One-Way Street," in *Walter Benjamin, 1913–1926,* ed. Marcus Bullock and
Michael Jennings, vol. 1 of *Selected Writings,* ed. Michael Jennings (Cambridge: Harvard University Press, 1996), 466 / *Gesammelte Schriften,* 4:117.

"commentary on a reality [or actuality, *Kommentar zu einer Wirklichkeit*]" which requires "theology" as its method (and which is thus to be distinguished from commentary on a "text," which requires "philology" as its "foundational discipline [*Grundwissenschaft*]").[28] Likewise, in a letter to Hugo von Hofmannsthal in 1928 Benjamin characterizes his "One-Way Street" as the documentation of an "internal struggle" whose object is: "To grasp reality [or actuality, *Aktualität*] as the reverse of what is eternal in history and to take an impression from the side of the medal thus uncovered."[29] Likewise, the *Arcades Project* was conceived as an "attempt at an example . . . of how far one can go in making historico-philosophical connections 'concrete,'"[30] while never giving up the historical materialist — but also almost inverted, interpolated, Hegelian — ambition "to discover in the analysis of the small individual moment the crystal of the total event."[31] Adorno shares this interest both in "concretion" and in a peculiar temporality and historicity: no longer that of linear progression, let alone "progress," but an "actualization [*Aktualisierung*],"[32] an anamnestic reenactment (and, hence, salvaging or redemption) of the past in and for the present.

Adorno lacks, however, the fascination with surrealist dream theory and the reenactment of dreamlike states which formed another constitutive element in the conception of "profane illumination [*profane Erleuchtung*]" in Benjamin's middle phase. Needless to say, this extends to experiments with narcotics, which — like the surrealist dream — had for Benjamin merely preparatory, propaedeutic value in view of a secularized or, rather, inverted theology: "But the true, creative overcoming of religious illumination certainly does not lie in narcotics. It resides in a *profane illumination*, a materialistic, anthropological inspiration, to which hashish, opium, or whatever else can give an introductory lesson").[33] For Benjamin, as for Adorno, the aim was to wake up from the dream — the nightmare — of myth. The mystical and materialist conceptions with which he approached it coincided in "the new, the dialectical method of doing his-

---

28. Benjamin, *Arcades Project*, N2, 1, 460 / 5.1:574.

29. Cited after Rolf Tiedemann, editor's notes, *Gesammelte Schriften*, 5.2:1083.

30. Ibid., 5.2:1086.

31. Ibid., N2, 6, 461 / 5.1:575.

32. Ibid., N2, 2 460 / 5.1:574.

33. Benjamin, "Surrealism: The Last Snapshot of the European Intelligentsia," in Walter Benjamin, *1927–1934*, ed. Michael W. Jennings, Howard Eiland, and Gary Smith, trans. Rodney Livingstone and others, vol. 2 of *Selected Writings*, ed. Michael Jennings (Cambridge: Harvard University Press, 1999), 209 / *Gesammelte Schriften*, 2:297.

tory: with the intensity of a dream, to pass through what has been, in order to experience the present as the waking world to which the dream refers."[34] Both mystical and material, positive and negative, resemble and touch upon each other in the methodology Benjamin proposes to apply "until the entire past is brought into the present in a historical apocatastasis."[35]

For the moment suffice it to say that, in Adorno's early conception, philosophical interpretations are not characterized by a high degree of abstraction or generality or by a specific domain of reality, let alone by the classically dualistic supposition of a metaphysical "secret world [or afterworld, *Hinterwelt*]," behind or beyond the actual world of phenomena (APh 126 / 335). Such a philosophy—in the wake of the dissolution of all notions of totality as well as all idealistically postulated autonomy—cannot fully return to the rational prerequisites, the categories, transcendentals, or transcendental conditions of possibility which once had seemed to support such notions or assign them their limits. It must contend with the intrusions of an "irreducible reality [*Wirklichkeit*]," which always take place "concrete-historically" and for which its concepts are from the outset inadequate. If, at this point, philosophy stubbornly examines its own enabling conditions still further, "it will be able to reach them only formally and at the price of that reality [*Wirklichkeit*] in which its actual tasks are laid" (APh 132 / 343).

A postclassical and (post)modern philosophical—a *minimal*—theology that neither aspires toward the apologetic assumption of some organic totality nor reduces itself to conceptual analysis of isolated terms (and their correlated sense data, protocol statements, and the like) embarks on uncharted territory, of which Adorno's enigmatic and often apodictic formulations speak in exemplary ways. Perhaps we should begin, then, by formulating a simple working hypothesis. In the peculiar amalgam of classical and modern, ecclesiastical and nonconfessional theological disciplines—of biblical or dogmatic theology, on the one hand, and the scientific study of religion as empirical, historical, anthropological, and cultural phenomenon, on the other—a philosophical, minimal, and, in Adorno's terms, *micrological* theology can present itself as a *placeholder* for rationality in an emphatic sense. Borrowing a suggestive phrase from Habermas—who, in turn, may have borrowed the metaphor, if not its interpretation, from Adorno[36]—I would suggest that we could con-

---

34. Benjamin, *Arcades Project*, 838 / 5.1:20.
35. Ibid., N1a, 3, 459 / *GS* 5.1:573.
36. See Adorno's essay on Paul Valéry, "Der Artist als Statthalter" ("The Artist as Deputy

ceive of philosophical theology as the touchstone and guardian of universality, truth, veracity, intersubjective validity, even authentic expressivity
in all matters concerning (the study of) religion and, perhaps, not religion
alone. Philosophical theology, thus defined, would be the very *instance*
of all theological critique, of idolatry, blasphemy, reification — but also of
the critique of religion and traditional-classical theology as such; it would,
further, be the *hermeneutic ferment* in the academic discipline of religious
studies.

Philosophical theology, thus defined, should also assume the role of
an *interpreter*. That is, it should *mediate* and *negotiate* between the results
of scientific inquiry while incessantly oscillating between these insights
and the quotidian life-world (*Lebenswelt*) outside the walls of the university. Although every scientist and believer intuitively senses these separa-
tions and the tension they imply, philosophical analysis consists in making
them explicit.[37]

Such a philosophical theology must operate like a (not strictly scientific) stowaway in the realm of science. It must secretly, invisibly, inaudibly, express the movement of transcendence which we typically connect to the more than simply regulative idea of the ab-solute — in other
words, to that which paradoxically sustains, motivates, inspires, and yet
also eludes our investigation. Or, in Habermas's words, it must express "*an
element of unconditionality* [ein Moment des Unbedingten]" in the wake of
the destruction of traditional metaphysics and theology[38] — or, perhaps,
in solidarity with thought in the very moment of its downfall, as Adorno
would add. Only where it might succeed in making the indispensability
of such an idea apparent could philosophical theology claim to open up
(*entgrenzen*) the modern science of religion and culture to its beyond, to
what lies before it, surrounds and accompanies it, carries or traverses it.

Does philosophical theology have sufficiently precise criteria of rationality at its disposal to express such presumptuous ambitions? How fine is

---

[or, literally, Placeholder]"): "Valéry's whole conception is directed against . . . the enthroning
of genius that has been so deeply entrenched especially in German aesthetics since Kant and
Schelling. What he demands of the artist, technical self-restriction, subjection to the subject
matter, is aimed not at limitation but at expansion. The artist who is the bearer of the work of
art is not the individual who produces it; rather, through his work, through passive activity,
he becomes the representative [placeholder, *Statthalter*] of the total social subject" (*NL* 1:107 /
126). Adorno also uses the term *Stellvertretung* ("representation" [*NL* 1:108 / 126]).

37. On all the implications of this agenda, see Robert Brandom, *Making It Explicit: Reasoning, Representing, and Discursive Commitment* (Cambridge: Harvard University Press, 1994).

38. Habermas, *Moral Consciousness and Communicative Action*, 19 / 27, my emph.

the weave of the net thus thrown over real, existing theological discourses, scholarly and other? In a certain sense it must be too crude, too imprecise, as we have verified. On the one hand, nothing less than the *proprium* of former theology—God without quotation marks, as the sum total of all experience—seems to fall through the cracks in this philosophical theology, just as it does in the empirical study of religion as a cultural object among others. On the other hand, without a minimal formal measure and a specific perspective, we would be groping in the dark. Not everything that presents itself as theological discourse *de Deo* can, upon closer inspection, carry the predicate *rational*. If it could, then the very question concerning the relationship between theology (however defined) and rationality (whether as commonly accepted or in a more emphatic sense of the word) would lose all legitimacy; each narrative would claim equal rights.

My thesis is that, in our modern or postmodern epoch, philosophical theology, viewed *formally* (systematically) and perhaps even *substantively* (empirically),[39] is condemned to a certain marginality. The expression *minimal theology* or even *theology in pianissimo,* loosely modeled after Max Weber's terminology, alludes to this position at the fringes of discourse. In his essay "Science as a Vocation" Weber suggests that it is "today only within the smallest and intimate circles, in personal human situations [*von Mensch zu Mensch*], in *pianissimo* [*im* pianissimo], that something [*jenes Etwas*] is pulsating that corresponds to the prophetic *pneuma,* which in former times swept through the great communities like a firebrand, welding them together."[40]

Only a minimal theology warrants, in my opinion, the predicate *rational* or is "rational" in an emphatic (and, hence, no longer bisected) sense. Yet, before I can present such a conception of theology in sufficient detail, I must first delineate the contours of a—halfway plausible—theory of rationality through which the conceptual necessity of such a theology might become apparent.

---

39. This cannot be established by means of theoretical argument alone, as I shall demonstrate.

40. Weber, "Science as Vocation," 155 / 554. If it seems justified to draw on Max Weber's *pianissimo* motif in the attempt to liberate Adorno from a certain Hegelian and Marxist legacy, then this strategy finds further support in *Negative Dialectics'*s praise for Weber's ability, in *Die protestantische Ethik und der "Geist" des Kapitalismus* (*The Protestant Ethic and the "Spirit" of Capitalism*) and in *Wirtschaft und Gesellschaft* (*Economy and Society*), to think in "constellations" and thereby to situate himself within a "third possibility beyond the alternative of positivism and idealism" (*ND* 166 / 168).

Klaus-M. Kodalle maintains that the philosophy of religion — in light of the decreasing intelligibility of all divine speech and godtalk — deserves rehabilitation only if it makes apparent that its modality is to be found in indirect discourse. It must demonstrate "that and how the subject of the truly absolute enters into the concepts of rationality that play an undisputed and indispensable role in the current philosophical discourse and that of themselves — to judge from their superficial structure — pretend to have absolutely no relevance in the philosophy of religion."[41] My task in the methodological detour that follows is to adopt this strategy. But can one do so without succumbing to identification with the aggressor, which Overbeck rightly condemned?

The Diminishing Intelligibility of the Discourse on (and of) God

Jürgen Habermas's work is arguably one of the best places to begin investigating the complex antagonism and interplay between theology and rationality in modernity. In his formal, pragmatic theory of rationality, which finds its most extensive formulation in *Theorie des kommunikativen Handelns* (*Theory of Communicative Action*), he attempts to do justice to the double challenge emerging from the increasingly differentiated discussions over the past few decades concerning the question of rationality. Harry Kunneman offers a comprehensive interpretation of this "cultural learning step," as he calls it, in *De waarheidstrechter* (*The Funnel of Truth*). In his estimation there was first a paradigm shift that subverted the subject-object schema in modern, postempiricist, postanalytical, and pragmatist thought concerning the structure of scientific knowledge, a turn away from the "philosophy of consciousness." Following the "lin-

41. Klaus-M. Kodalle, "Gott," in *Philosophie: Ein Grundkurs*, ed. E. Matens and H. Schnädelbach (Reinbeck bei Hamburg: Rowohlt, 1985), 396. Kodalle remarks, "The evidence of philosophical assertions, which attempt to establish an absolute ground in finite events, must come out of constellations of finite reason itself" (400). With this programmatic statement Kodalle situates himself in "closest proximity to Adorno" (418), despite his claim elsewhere that Adorno's *Negative Dialectics* is shot through with distorted premises and false alternatives. With Traugott Koch, Kodalle maintains that transcendence need not be interpreted as the absolute other; its "traces" can already be discerned in Adorno's texts, even if his caricatural rendering of traditional and modern forms of theology, together with what is simply bad theological practice ("nature" as deus ex machina), prohibits him from expressing these thoughts unambiguously. See Traugott Koch, Klaus-M. Kodalle, and Hermann Schweppenhäuser, *Negative Dialektik und die Idee der Versöhnung* (Stuttgart: W. Kohlhammer, 1973), 23, 26 ff., 50 ff. See also Klaus-M. Kodalle, *Die Eroberung des Nutzlosen: Kritik des Wunschdenkens und der Zweckrationalität im Anschluss an Kierkegaard* (Paderborn: F. Schöningh, 1988), 42–44.

guistic turn,"[42] to use the title of Richard Rorty's famous selection of representative writings in the philosophy of language (semantics, ordinary language philosophy, speech-act theory, etc.), a *communis opinio* grew up about the untenability of this modern schema. Yet this consensus, Kunneman continues, has now in turn been variously criticized by "postmodern" or "poststructuralist" authors, whose work consists in the subtle "articulation of the internal connection between truth and power."[43] Within these centrifugal forces, Habermas indefatigably insists that even a philosophy that would follow both these recent "linguistic" and "poststructuralist" turns need not abandon its position as the guardian—that is to say, the judge of, stand-in for, and navigator of—rationality. Adhering without reservation to the demand for universality given, though too often merely implicitly, in the self-understanding of Western rationality, philosophy can show how opinion and superstition can be argumentatively transformed into "knowledge [*Wissen*]" as well as how free and argumentatively justified assent based on "insight [*Einsicht*]" can substitute for expressions of power or arbitrariness.[44] Philosophy would thus appropriate the intentions of the tradition of critical (i.e., Kantian) transcendental thinking, even if, as Habermas paradoxically suggests, under the proviso of a "simultaneous detranscendentalization [*Detranszendentalisierung*] of its procedures and demonstrative aims."[45] Its status is that of *quasi*-transcendental argument alone. But where exactly does the "quasi"

42. Richard Rorty, ed., *The Linguistic Turn*, 2d ed. (Chicago: University of Chicago Press, 1992). See also Habermas, intro., entitled "Realismus nach der sprachpragmatischen Wende," and opening chapter, "Hermeneutische und analytische Philosophie: Zwei komplementäre Spielarten der linguistischen Wende," *Wahrheit und Rechtfertigung: Philosophische Aufsätze* (Frankfurt a.M.: Suhrkamp, 1999). See also Habermas, *Between Facts and Norms*, 9 ff. / 24 ff.

43. See Harry Kunneman, *De waarheidstrechter: Een communicatietheoretisch perspectief op wetenschap en samenleving* (Amsterdam: Boom, 1986), 411.

44. Habermas, *Theory of Communicative Action*, 1:44, 53 ff.; cf. 25, 38 / 1:73, 85ff.; cf. 48, 65.

45. Jürgen Habermas, *Vorstudien und Ergänzungen zur Theorie des kommunikativen Handelns* (Frankfurt a.M.: Suhrkamp, 1984), 505. Interestingly, in the same context Habermas cites approvingly a passage by Joel Whitebook indicating that the way toward this "*quasi*- transcendental" perspective is more consonant with "Aristotelian *phronesis*" and "aesthetic taste" than with the purportedly more rigorous argument of the *prima philosophia* (505–6). Mutatis mutandis, this is what I will suggest in the following pages, adding different theological and metaphysical notions to these concepts, which are central to the ancient tradition of practical reason (*phroneses*) and the modern understanding of aesthetic rationality (taste). What, I will ask, are their theologico-metaphysical equivalents and counterparts? On the meaning of "detranscendentalization," see also Jürgen Habermas, "Wege der Detranszendentalisierung: Von Kant zu Hegel und zurück," *Wahrheit und Rechtfertigung*, 186–229; and Habermas, *Kommunikatives Handeln und detranszendentalisierte Vernunft* (Stuttgart: Reklam, 2001).

reside, if not in some narrative, some fictionality (though clearly it does not)?

In a preliminary definition Habermas understands rationality in fundamentally fallibilistic terms as *the possibility of initiating, founding, and criticizing thought, speech, and action.*[46] He is primarily concerned with justifying—and doing justice to—the widest possible spectrum of forms of rationality, which he believes are constituted and invested with meaning *intersubjectively* (not monologically, as the historical specters would have it: from Protagoras to Hume, psychological phenomenalism; from Descartes to Husserl, mentalism and egology; and from Fichte to Stirner, solipsism). In addition to the concepts of cognitive and instrumental rationality favored by the Western logos, there are equally valid media in which human interaction (or communicative action) can be *reflexively* pursued. Habermas thus grants practical-moral and aesthetic-expressive rationality almost equal significance. He diagnoses and radicalizes a "break with the 'logos-characterization [*Logosauszeichnung*] of language,' that is, with privileging its representational function" (a change of paradigm, he notes, which was initiated by J. L. Austin and researched in its historical dimension by Karl-Otto Apel).[47] Rationality concerns *normativity* in the broadest sense and pertains to cognitive claims, moral arguments, aesthetic judgments, and, to some extent, authentic expressions alike. Objective nature, social commerce, and subjective expressiveness form three differentiated domains on which modern reason can still—or once again?—be brought to bear.

This approach claims to steer clear of naive historical-philosophical (speculative-idealist or naturalist, e.g., historical-materialist) premises. Habermas takes as the point of departure for every relevant philosophy in our age the fundamental insight that it is no longer possible (or necessary) to propose a substantially articulated world picture (*Weltbild*). Modern rationality distances itself from worldviews (i.e., from *Weltanschauung*) and is increasingly suspicious of the contents and images with which the world—including the "good life"—has been depicted in the past. Reason is no longer capable of speculatively or even critically employing concepts concerning the "whole of the world, of nature, of history, of society, in the sense of a totalizing knowledge."[48] According to Habermas, this does not only result from the fact that advanced *empirical* knowledge has

46. Habermas, *Theory of Communicative Action*, 1:8–22, esp. 10 / 1:25–44, esp. 27.
47. Ibid., 1:278 / 1:375.
48. Ibid., 1:1 / 1:15.

robbed various mythologies and religious-metaphysical cosmologies of their plausibility. The *reflexivity* of the consciousness that anticipated and resulted from this development is at least as responsible for the inability of idealized projections of totality to remain convincing in today's multi-faceted—that is, sociopolitically differentiated and intellectually decen-tered—world. Accordingly, the "substantial" concept of reason, on which classical metaphysics was once based, has gradually—or now and then abruptly—been replaced by a more modest concept of rationality, at least insofar as its epistemological (i.e., cognitive) claims are concerned.

The philosophical project of modernity redirects the interest of rea-son (more precisely, the interest it always associated with reason) away from essences or metaphysical substances and turns, instead, to the dif-ferent *formal* structures that function as quasi-transcendental—that is, linguistic, pragmatic, in short, *enabling*—conditions for human cogni-tion, agency, interaction, judgment, and expression. In the absence of any claim to totality, philosophy loses the possibility of self-sufficiency, com-placency, or even autonomy and thus no longer finds its ultimate ground-ing in itself. In fact, under modern conditions, speaking of firm grounds or absolute grounding has lost all relevance. In Habermas's words: "To the goal of formally analyzing the conditions of rationality, we can tie neither ontological hopes for substantive theories of nature, history, society, and so forth, nor transcendental-philosophical hopes for an aprioristic re-construction of the equipment of a nonempirical species subject, of con-sciousness in general. All attempts at discovering ultimate foundations, in which the intentions of First Philosophy live on, have broken down."[49] For this reason Habermas's decidedly universalistic position can no longer be based on hypostasizing specific cultural contents but only on the pre-supposition of specific structural features. These formal—linguistic and pragmatic—elements must be apparent in the life-world if one is to speak of rationally motivated thought and action at all.[50] Because these are not

---

49. Ibid., 1:2 / 1:16. Habermas bases this last comment, not without reason, on Adorno's *Zur Metakritik der Erkenntnistheorie* (*Against Epistemology: A Metacritique*). Adorno writes in the programmatic introduction to his text: "The process of demythologization . . . reveals the untruth of the very idea of the first. The first must become ever more abstract to the philoso-phy of origin. The more abstract it becomes, the less it comes to explain and the less fitting it is as a foundation" (*Zur Metakritik der Erkenntnistheorie: Studien über Husserl und die phä-nomenologische Antinomien, GS*, 5:9–245, 22 / *Against Epistemology: A Metacritique, Studies in Husserl and the Phenomenological Antinomies*, trans. Willis Domingo [Cambridge: MIT Press, 1983], 14).

50. Habermas, *Theory of Communicative Action*, 1:179–81 / 1:254–55.

ontological or ideal conditions, traditionally and transcendentally conceived, how are we to understand these presuppositions, their nature and
function, *concretely*? What, in other words, do Habermas's "weak naturalism" (or detranscendentalized realism) in issues of theoretical philosophy
and his cognitivism in matters of practical philosophy (as well as philosophical aesthetics?) amount to?

Following Max Weber's sociological studies of cultural and religious
history, notably the preface ("Vorbemerkung") to his collected essays on
the sociology of religion and his magnum opus, *Wirtschaft und Gesellschaft* (*Economy and Society*), Habermas's theory presumes that the progression of modernity in the West can, in retrospect, be viewed as a process
of rationalization, differentiation, and secularization. In this process the
cultural potential of the postclassical structures of consciousness formed
a necessary, if also insufficient, condition of possibility for the societal
counterparts in which modernity—following a selective and restrictive
pattern—was both articulated and solidified, not to say reified. As he
writes: "A selective pattern of rationalization occurs when (at least) one
of the three constitutive components of the cultural tradition is not systematically worked up, or when (at least) one cultural value sphere is
insufficiently institutionalized, that is, is without any structure-forming
effect on society as a whole, or when (at least) one sphere predominates
to such an extent that it subjects other ordered realms of life [*Lebens-
ordnungen*] to a form of rationality that is alien to them."[51] In Habermas's view the disenchantment (*Entzauberung*) or de-mythologization
of the world, beginning with the rationalization to which the mythical
image of the world was subjected through Greek enlightenment and the
Judeo-Christian tradition, resulted in a differentiation and pluralization
of worlds into the formal concepts of three different (objective, social, and
subjective) "worlds" out of the originally closed, totalizing worldviews
that dominated premodern societies. From this perspective myths constituted the most extreme contrast to modern consciousness, which first
becomes historically possible when the authority of collectively held traditional beliefs can, in principle, be unmasked without remainder through
the force of the better argument of autonomous individuals, who establish their claims in intersubjective discourse alone. Habermas thus seems
to share the ambition—ensuring a position beyond myth, if not in all respects beyond tradition—of most of the other authors who will interest

---

51. Ibid., 1:240 / 1:329, trans. modified.

us throughout this investigation, even though there are reasons to believe that his view (like theirs) must necessarily (and, as one says, performatively) contradict itself in asserting this position in full rigor, or in a single step.[52]

The mythical worldview of "heroic" societies,[53] Habermas demonstrates with specific anthropological examples, does not yet differentiate between objective nature, social norms, and subjective experiences. In such societies a person receives his or her identity from the role he or she plays in the cosmic whole and the social hierarchy that it reflects. A rationalization and modernization of worldview, however, causes certain displacements to occur. Humans begin to master surrounding reality, external nature, the social life-world, and—constricted within an unholy dialectic—themselves. Nature is no longer perceived as an animate, teleological, and organic order but increasingly as something dead, mechanical, and controllable; culture is no longer understood as a naturally given, necessary, and divine order but, rather, as the contingent creation of humanity, which is therefore open to criticism. De-mythologization here means the disentangling of a double illusion: the *de-socialization of nature* and a *de-naturalization of society and culture*.[54] The human subject, finally, no longer has to be given over to its natural circumstances or its social role; it gains, in an initially minimal autonomy, the possibility of distance and critique. Individual identity can thus, at least in principle, be continually reshaped in the process of modernization, for "it attaches to structures that are increasingly disengaged from contents that are open to revision."[55]

By analogy with Jean Piaget's concept of developmental psychology,

---

52. See ibid., 1:44 ff. / 1:73 ff.; and, for a contrasting view, Odo Marquard, "Lob des Polytheismus, über Monomythie und Polymythie," in *Abschied vom Prinzipiellen: Philosophische Studien* (Stuttgart: Reklam, 1981), 91–116. Later I will take up the question of how the dialectic of enlightenment, in the eyes of Adorno and Horkheimer, can be read and deciphered, if not reconstructed, as the secret, uncomfortable relationship between myth and Enlightenment. Their view, which complicates the Weberian-Habermasian schema, is largely indebted to Benjamin's work on myth and capitalist modernity, even though their respective philosophies of history, I will argue, remain fundamentally different in orientation as regards their epistemology and politics.

53. This term is borrowed from Alasdair MacIntyre, *After Virtue: A Study in Moral Theory* (London: Duckworth, 1981), 114 ff. See also the opening chapter of his book *A Short History of Ethics: A History of Moral Philosophy from the Homeric Age to the Twentieth Century* (Notre Dame, Ind.: University of Notre Dame Press, 1998).

54. Habermas, *Theory of Communicative Action*, 1:47–49 / 1:78–80.

55. Ibid., 1:64 / 1:100.

Habermas identifies his notion of the *irreversible* extraction of modern individual consciousness from mythical collective consciousness — and from the collective unconscious — as a kind of *decentering of worldview*.[56] Like the cognitive development of the child (*ontogenesis*), the progressive rationalization of culture as a whole (*phylogenesis*) concerns not so much an increase in the content of knowledge as the acquisition of ever more formal, abstract, and general patterns of thought or paradigms. Just as the child develops a capacity to overcome its egocentrism, so too can humanity learn to think and act under increasingly universalistic perspectives. This universalism in Habermas's theory of rationality — a retranslation of Weber's "occidental rationalism," not to be confused with simple Eurocentrism[57] — is as intriguing as it is untimely, especially for the contemporary reader, who, in uncritical reaction to the Western colonial heritage, may be more inclined to adopt some form of naive, resigned, or cynical cultural relativism. Analytic theories of radical interpretation and translation, from W. V. O. Quine to Donald Davidson, have persuasively established, using arguments from Wittgenstein and others, that such relativism is untenable on semantic grounds, and Richard Rorty has subsequently taken up those arguments. But this is not Habermas's strategy.[58] In fact, so Habermas's counterfactual claim goes, the communicative presuppositions on which the universalist, especially moral, perspective relies cannot be the "privilege" of any culture because they are "anchored" much "deeper" — namely, in the "symmetries" of the in principle unlimited mutual recognition of free and autonomous subjects under idealized conditions.[59]

Modernity, understood as a form of continual enlightenment (*Aufklärung*), has, in Habermas's view, progressively led to a differentiation and secularization of the former mythical, sacral-religious, theological, and

56. Ibid., 1:69 / 1:106. Within this perspective there is not much use for the Benjaminian *Urgeschichte* of the nineteenth-century dreamworld or for Jameson's notion of the "political unconscious." Habermas construes — or, in his idiom, "reconstructs" — a radical break between the mythical world of "participation" and its *mentalité primitive* (see the reference to Lévy-Bruhl, ibid., 1:74 / 1:113), on the one hand, and the unforgettable learning steps of modern thought, on the other. He shares this polarity of concepts — but not their possible, indeed inevitable, contamination — with the authors I will study in later pages.

57. Habermas, *Theory of Communicative Action*, 1:66, 196–97 / 1:102, 274–75.

58. Habermas mentions Donald Davidson's work only in passing in ibid., 1:276 / 1:373; there he passes over Quine in silence. These authors are extensively discussed in the *Vorstudien* and in *Wahrheit und Rechtfertigung*.

59. Habermas, *Between Facts and Norms*, 63 / 86.

metaphysical worldviews. It has brought about a plurality of objective, social, and subjective worlds. The various elements of "reason," which still formed a diffuse, illusory, and substantial unity in mythical and religious-metaphysical worldviews,[60] became irrevocably dispersed. The objectification of nature in modern science and its explication in terms of causal, mechanical connections has forever eradicated the possibility of returning to an interpretation of the external, objective world through natural philosophy (*Naturphilosophie,* hylozoism, organicism), as if this world were a purposive, teleological, and properly ordered cosmos or creation. The rationalization of right and morality has also freed the understandings governing social and practical life from the mythical and religious-metaphysical order in which they were formerly embedded. Norms that had been legitimated through a particular and concrete tradition—for example, through a particular revelation with its authoritative interpretation, practices, and institutions—have been replaced by universal, abstract, profane principles of natural right. As such, they now constitute a purely formal morality, based on intersubjectively constituted rules and procedures—in short, on *normativity.* In the social world consensus can, so the argument goes, be established and justified through conformity with conventional agreements, which are now no longer seen as written in stone (dictated by nature or divinely ordained) but as always open to question and potentially subject to dismissal.

The autonomy of art and literature, finally, makes it possible (especially in the aesthetic of the avant-gardes) to articulate subjective experience, the meaning of which no longer depends upon a cult function, a realistic image and mimesis of objective reality, or a moral purpose. Art is now seen as following its own particular logic concerning both its material development and the (self-)expression of the artist. The only criteria still applicable, then, would be those of beauty and authenticity. According to Max Weber, who is careful not to project a unilinear and one-dimensional development but, rather, builds his diagnosis on an uncanny déjà vu, this perspective—and its inevitable perspectivalism—presents itself as follows:

> If anything, we realize again today that something can be sacred not only
> in spite of its not being beautiful, but rather *because* and *insofar* as it is not

---

60. Habermas, *Zur Kritik der funktionalistischen Vernunft,* vol. 2 of *Theorie des kommunikativen Handelns* (Frankfurt a.M.: Suhrkamp, 1981), 487 / *Lifeworld and System,* vol. 2 of *The Theory of Communicative Action,* trans. Thomas McCarthy (Boston: Beacon Press, 1987), 330.

beautiful. You will find this documented in the fifty-third chapter of the book of Isaiah and in the twenty-first Psalm. And, since Nietzsche, we realize that something can be beautiful, not only in spite of the aspect in which it is not good, but rather in that very aspect. You will find this expressed earlier in the *Fleurs du mal*, as Baudelaire named his volume of poems. It is commonplace [*Alltagsweisheit*] to observe that something may be true although it is not beautiful and not holy and not good.[61]

With the loss of traditional worldviews, meaning no longer depends upon the unity of the true, the good, and the beautiful—or, to the extent that meaning and meaningfulness, together with their supposed referents (truth, the good, the beautiful) require such intrinsic unity, no meaning or meaningfulness can still be found. No comprehensive, cosmological, divine, or moral perspective could reunify these disentangled dimensions of modernity in a substantial way or determine how the theoretical, the practical, and the aesthetic might still—or once again—relate to one another. Worse yet, the spheres of autonomy, which certainly widened the possible range and playing field (*Spielraum*) of human freedom, come, according to Weber, into irreconcilable and thus unending conflict with one another.[62] In consequence, the rationalized world is in permanent— and increasing—danger of becoming both meaningless and directionless. An ever more intense conflict between reified orientations of life, a *new polytheism*, has been breached: "Many old gods ascend from their graves;

61. Weber, "Science as a Vocation," 147–48 / 545–46. Needless to say, Weber's view of Baudelaire is something of a caricature. For a concise and informative exposition of the intellectual background and overall aim of Weber's lecture, see Friedrich Tenbruck, "Nachwort," in Max Weber, *Wissenschaft als Beruf* (Stuttgart: Reklam, 1995), 47–77; see also Raymond Aron's preface to the French translation of Weber's text in *Le Savant et le politique*, trans. Julien Freund, rev. E. Fleischmann and Éric de Dampierre (Paris: Plon, 1959), 9–69.

62. It is interesting to compare this view with Adorno's "Theses upon Art and Religion Today," written in English and first published in the *Kenyon Review* 7 (1945): 677–87, rpt. in *NL* 2:292–98 / 647–53. There Adorno claims: "The lost unity between art and religion, be it regarded as wholesome or as hampering, cannot be regained at will. This unity was not a matter of purposeful cooperation, but resulted from the whole objective structure of society during certain periods of history, so the break is objectively conditioned and irreversible" (2:292 / 647). In modern poetic technique, for example, religious motifs are reduced to being an "ornamental" and "decorative" aspect, becoming "a metaphorical circumscription for mundane, mostly psychological experiences of the individual," so that religious symbolism "deteriorates into an unctuous expression of a substance which is actually of this world" (2:293–94 / 648). Yet this deterioration does not have the last word. Adorno concludes his essay on a quite different note, stating, "As firmly as I am convinced that the dichotomy between art and religion is irreversible, as firmly do I believe that it cannot be naively regarded as something final and ultimate" (2:297 / 652).

they are disenchanted and hence take the form of impersonal forces. They strive to gain power over our lives and again they resume their eternal struggle with one another. What is hard for modern man, and especially for the younger generation, is to measure up to such *everydayness* [Alltag]. The ubiquitous chase after 'experience [*Erlebnis*]' stems from this weakness; for it is weakness not to be able to countenance the stern seriousness of our fateful times [*Schicksal der Zeit*]."[63]

Habermas hears in this passage unmistakable echoes of the nihilism that indelibly marked the generation of World War I. Weber describes that atmosphere as almost the logical result and inevitable outcome of an *internal dialectic* of Western rationalization: in the process of de-mythologization, reason dismantles both the world and itself into a multitude of moments, each of which follows its own particular logic, undermining its own universality in the process. From such a disintegration of individuals and society into an at once atomized and totally administered world, we can, in the end, expect only an "unbearable lightness of being."[64] In the private sphere it produces a loss of meaning and a loss of orientation. In the public sphere it implies a loss of legitimacy: culture itself, in Weber's view, destroys its own former integrative force.

Weber's ambivalent reaction to the diagnosis of this nihilism of the era vacillates between criticism and skepticism, on the one hand, and heroic affirmation, on the other. This ambivalence already anticipates the dialectic of Enlightenment, which, as we shall see, forms one of the leitmotifs in Adorno's work and has continued to inspire philosophers to this day. Alasdair MacIntyre, to mention just one example from a different tradition of thought, rightly insists in *After Virtue* that our contemporary situation is still somehow Weberian.[65]

Habermas also agrees with Weber that there can no longer be any connection between the substance and content of what he identifies as

63. Weber, "Science as a Vocation," 149 / 547, trans. modified.
64. Milan Kundera succinctly describes this condition in *The Art of the Novel*: "Having brought off miracles in science and technology, this 'master and proprietor' [man] is suddenly realizing that he owns nothing and is master neither of nature (it is vanishing, little by little, from the planet), nor of History (it has escaped him), nor of himself (he is led by the irrational forces of his soul). But if God is gone and man is no longer master, then who is master? The planet is moving through the void without any master. There it is, the unbearable lightness of being" (*The Art of the Novel*, trans. Linda Asher [New York: Grove Press, 1986], 41). See also Kundera, *The Unbearable Lightness of Being*, trans. Michael Henry Heim (New York: Harper & Row, 1984).
65. MacIntyre, *After Virtue*, 103.

the three independent modern dimensions: the objective world, the social realm, and subjective experience. The objectifying tendencies of the sciences, the universalization of concepts of right and morality, and the autonomization of art, in the process of solidifying their respective interests, standards, and institutions, have separated themselves from all original unifying practices of life. There can be no more *"integration of contents* a posteriori."[66] Nevertheless, there is, Habermas claims, still a *formal* connection between them because the conditions of possibility for argumentation, critical learning processes, and "reaching understanding [*Verständigung*]"[67] — of rationality, in short — are only now built into each of these three areas, in distinctive yet parallel ways. It is possible to reconstruct, therefore, the internal dynamic of scientific knowledge. In the institutions of science and technology, which are concerned with the — in Habermas's terminology, cognitive-instrumental — question of the truth and manipulation of the objective world or nature, it is possible to show how the positivist fixation on the purely technical mastery of reality can always be empirically corrected and opened up to nonreductionist approaches. Likewise, there is a potential for practical justification of universal juridical and moral principles in the social world, which simultaneously find a certain embodiment in the acts and institutions of modern citizens, states, and supranational federations. Finally, art and art criticism, in which the authenticity of the individual is expressed and translated in an exemplary fashion, create free spaces for the enrichment of subjective experience. It is here — again, especially in the artistic currents of the avant-gardes — that subjects are shaken out of the purposive and conventional patterns of their everyday perceptions.

Following Weber's example, Habermas defines the forms assumed by these worlds as "value spheres [*Wertsphären*]" — that is, realms of reality in which different sorts of "claims of legitimacy [*Geltungsansprüche*]" can be made.[68] At the same time, Habermas assumes that differing claims of legitimacy can be articulated and *in principle* resolved — or decided —

---

66. Jürgen Habermas, "Entgegnung," in *Kommunikatives Handeln: Beiträge zu Jürgen Habermas's "Theorie des kommunikativen Handelns,"* ed. Axel Honneth and Hans Joas (Frankfurt a.M.: Suhrkamp, 1986), 340 / "A Reply," in *Communicative Action: Essays on Jürgen Habermas's "The Theory of Communicative Action,"* trans. Jeremy Gaines and Doris L. Jones (Cambridge: MIT Press, 1991), 224.

67. On the concept of "reaching understanding [*Verständigung*]," see Habermas, *Theory of Communicative Action,* 1:69–71, 100 / 1:107–8, 150.

68. Ibid., 1:164 / 1:234.

in *analogous* ways through a symmetrical and reciprocal discursive process, "if only the argumentation could be conducted openly enough and
continued long enough."[69] Here he clearly departs from Weber's more
pessimistic and downright skeptical interpretation of the "new polytheism" of the age. For him the different claims of legitimacy concern
what he calls "equi-primordial reference points of a process of differentiation that moves outward radially [read: centrifugally] in three directions [*gleichursprüngliche Bezugspunkte eines dreistahligen Differen-
zierungsprozesses*],"[70] each bound to its own mode of rationality and each
endowed "with different degrees of discursive binding force [*Verbindlichkeit*]."[71]

Habermas acknowledges that there is to date no adequate—let alone
comprehensive—pragmatic "logic" of argumentation which could show
us what constitutes the precise "internal connections" between the different "*forms* of speech acts" governing the different claims of legitimacy
and their respective modes of rationality.[72] But should one not perhaps
view the possibility and prospects of such a general theory of discourse,
guaranteeing the "unity of argumentation"—and, thereby, the very concept of "procedural rationality" after the fatal critique and demise of all
"substantial concepts of reason"[73]—with a bit of skepticism? Are there
parallel routes in the archipelago for transporting concepts, imperatives,
images, and gestures? Or, to remain with a metaphor used by Kant, Habermas, and Lyotard, are its isles (in other words, its genres and regimes of
discourse) fundamentally isomorphic, despite all their external and internal differentiation? Lyotard, who uses this terminology of "genres" and
"regimes of discourse," demonstrates in *The Differend* that this cannot be
the case.[74] And the assumption fares no better in an altogether different
line of thought and an alternative tradition of scholarship, Robert Brandom's *Making It Explicit*.

---

69. Ibid., 1:42 / 1:71. The aesthetic-expressive form of rationality as a possible form for "critique" rather than a "discourse" takes up a somewhat ambiguous position. See also Kunneman's
comments about the "discourse of identity" (*De waarheidstrechter*, 232–35). On the concept of
aesthetic rationality, see Habermas, *Theory of Communicative Action*, 1:19, 41 / 1:41, 70; and,
more extensively, Martin Seel, *Die Kunst der Entzweiung: Zum Begriff der ästhetischen Rationalität* (Frankfurt a.M.: Suhrkamp, 1985).

70. Habermas, "Reply," in Honneth and Joas, *Communicative Action: Essays on Jürgen
Habermas's "The Theory of Communicative Action,"* 219 / 334.

71. Habermas, *Theory of Communicative Action*, 1:249 / 1:339–40.

72. Ibid., 1:249 / 1:340.

73. Ibid.

74. See my essay "On Obligation: Lyotard and Levinas."

Nevertheless, this avowed lacuna in the theory of communicative action does not prevent Habermas from postulating that, contrary to Weber's interpretation, consensus cannot be excluded a priori. Weber and, to the extent that they adopt his premises, Adorno and Horkheimer in *Dialektik der Aufklärung* (*Dialectic of Enlightenment*) tend, in Habermas's reading, to restrict rationality to self-assertion and purpose-oriented engagement with nature. Thus, they never really free themselves from fixation on the empiricist and utilitarian self-interpretations of the modern age, with its cognitive-instrumental orientation toward subjectivity and toward the objective and social world in which it is situated. Habermas, by contrast, sets out to reconstruct a broader concept of rationality more appropriate to the modern life-world (*Lebenswelt*), that is to say, the realm in which the measure of efficient action cannot necessarily claim validity. He considers the concept of "communication" or "communicative action" to be better suited for analyzing the interaction, reciprocal agreement, and solidarity that form the organizing principle (i.e., counterfactual assumption and regulative idea) here. The material production of life, in relation to the system of market and power,[75] is not what is most important in this life-world but, rather, the cultural reproduction of the symbolic universe through the reinterpretation of traditions, social integration, and education. This reservoir, with which the functional, economic, and bureaucratic rationality governing social systems in today's Western world must ultimately collide, contains unrecognized possibilities and unused resources. Its realm, regulated by and oriented toward linguistic communication, presupposes, according to Habermas, that *consensus* is the—often unspoken and rarely attained—goal given with the gift of human language. Before even a single word is spoken, consensus inhabits linguistic competence as its very heart, its intrinsic aim: "Reaching understanding is the inherent telos of human speech [*Verständigung wohnt als Telos der menschlichen Sprache inner*]."[76]

Appropriately enough, Habermas adopts Kant's concept of a formal and self-differentiated reason. Like Weber's view of Western rationalism, Kant's concept is modern because it consciously displaces the scientifically

---

75. Interestingly, the Foucauldian question of bio-power seems largely absent from this perspective. On the reproduction of life, *stricto sensu*, see the essays on cloning in Habermas, *Die postnationale Konstellation: Politische Essays* (Frankfurt a.M.: Suhrkamp, 1998), 243–56; and Habermas, *Die Zukunft der menschlichen Natur: Auf dem Weg zu einer liberalen Eugenik?* (Frankfurt a.M.: Suhrkamp, 2001).

76. Habermas, *Theory of Communicative Action*, 1:287 / 1:387.

and philosophically untenable truth claims of substantialist, religious-metaphysical worldviews and replaces them with the idea of "procedural rationality," in the phrase Habermas coins. As we have already seen, this idea allows us not only to distinguish different possible forms of modern rationality internally but externally constitutes the—again, *formal*—bond, the "unity of reason in the diversity of its voices." But are theoretical and practical discourses, together with the identity discourse of aesthetic rationality (following roughly the tripartition of Kant's major critiques), the *only* possible forms conceivable? Are there just three "forms" or "value spheres"—each with its own internal procedures yet also somehow formally, again procedurally, related to the two others—to which all human utterances and expressions can be reduced, at least for analytical (and, in Kant's sense, critical) purposes? Do our statements, value claims, and judgments, to say nothing of all other speech-acts and intentions, nonverbal acts and gestures, amount to three categorically distinguished yet structurally related parallel universes alone? Does rationality take merely three forms, all of which, moreover, are comparable, if not computable, in light of one single form or discursive procedure? Finally, is the nonhuman world of animals and angels, the nonliving and the artificial, devoid of reason and rationality thus—or otherwise—defined?

Habermas has some outspoken answers to most of these questions, and we will turn to them later. For now suffice it to note that in his exposition it remains unclear just *how* the idea of procedural rationality would mediate, negotiate, or navigate among them. This, as we shall see, is a fundamental problem in the architecture of the theory of communicative action. The differentiation and inevitable solidification of the cognitive, practical, and aesthetic domains, like their de facto overlap and potential imperialism with respect to one another, is not only the distinctive mark but also the stigma and scar that modernity (and its philosophical discourse) bears. While modern thinkers have explored and expanded the imaginative space (*Spielraum*) of human freedom, an abyss (or, in the metaphor of the archipelago, an ocean) has increasingly opened between the specialized regime of "experts" and an impoverished life-world, which can hardly keep up with the increasing independence of these social and cultural forms of rationality.

In his early Jena writings Hegel had anticipated this situation: "When the power of unification [*Vereinigung*] disappears from human life, and antitheses lose their lively relationship [*lebendige Beziehung*] and alternation [*Wechselwirkung*] and gain independence, the need [*Bedürfnis*] for philosophy arises."[77] Habermas borrows from these writings some of his earliest intuitions, in *Technik und Wissenschaft als "Ideologie"* (*Technology and Science as "Ideology"*), concerning "interaction." From that concept his subsequent attempts to expand and modify his paradigm via "recognition" (*Anerkennung*) take their lead, thus multiplying and diversifying the forms rationality and normativity can assume.[78] Habermas comes to ascribe a double role to philosophy in the delicately articulated nervous system of modern rational competence. Its universalistic intentions and hermeneutic capacity should prove fruitful both (1) *within* the specialized corpus of the natural, social, and human sciences, and (2) *directed outward* at the cross-section between modern sociocultural institutions — including the "system" of state and market — and the life-world. Because the task of the minimal theology I propose must be interpreted in a roughly analogous way, I must both examine more closely Habermas's specific formulations of philosophy's double task, given his remarkable use of metaphor and figures of thought, and analyze the (often unacknowledged) consequences of such wording for the systematics and architecture of his theory as a whole.

(*ad 1*) *Within the realm of the sciences,* with their different disciplines, Habermas argues, philosophy cannot claim the role Kant intended in *Der Streit der Fakultäten* (*The Conflict of the Faculties*): it can no longer function as the arbiter, let alone the tribunal, of reason.[79] It can only assume the role of a kind of stowaway, indeed, as Benjamin suggested, that of a dwarf plotting grand schemes in an unobtrusive, a largely invisible or inaudible way. Philosophy appears only as the placeholder for the emphatic universalist demands of the most advanced (empirical) theories. Referring to Sigmund Freud, Émile Durkheim, George Herbert Mead, Max Weber, Jean Piaget, and Noam Chomsky, Habermas names various universalist motifs that, reformulated in philosophical terms and in their empirical applicability, are also central to his own theory: "Symptom forma-

77. Cited in Habermas, *Zur Rekonstruktion des historischen Materialismus*, 102–3. Lyotard speaks in (an other?) connection of philosophy's finest hour in *The Differend*, xii / 11: "The time has come to philosophize."

78. See Axel Honneth, *Kampf um Anerkennung: Zur moralischen Grammatik sozialer Konflikte* (Frankfurt a.M.: Suhrkamp, 1992), chap. 1.

79. That Kant's view on these matters is deeply ambiguous — steeped in an irresolvable performative contradiction — I have argued in detail in *Religion and Violence*, 18–122. See also my book *Philosophy and the Turn to Religion*, 359–430.

tion through repression, the creation of solidarity through the sacred, the identity-forming function of role taking, modernization as rationalization of society, decentering [*Dezentrierung*] as an outgrowth of reflective abstraction from actions [*Handlungen*], language acquisition as an activity of hypothesis testing—these key phrases stand for so many paradigms in which a philosophical idea is present in embryo while at the same time empirical, yet universal, questions are being posed."[80]

Habermas thus endows philosophy with the capacity to combine the various fragments of scientific progress into a kind of puzzle, just as it does the upsurges and learning processes in moral consciousness or the revolts in artistic experience. At best, then, philosophy, as a *theoretical* exercise (and academic discipline), might arrive not at scientific or otherwise warranted knowledge (as Russell believed) but at a meaningful and illuminating *constellation* of insights. Because it can only help establish a theory of rationality without any absolutist claims, it must find its way "with a fallibilistic consciousness, which rejects the dubious faith in philosophy's ability to do things single-handedly, hoping instead that the success that has for so long eluded it might come from an auspicious matching [*glücklichen Kohärenz*] of different theoretical fragments."[81]

(*ad 2*) *In the whole of culture,* directed outwardly or toward the lifeworld, philosophy likewise can no longer function as a kind of judge. Culture is in as little need of "justification," let alone evaluative "classification [*Einstufung*]," as is science. Certainly, philosophy can satisfy the unmistakable desire for an interpretive mediation or negotiation of the disintegrated moments (the "great lop-sided multiplicities") of modernity. Further, it can oscillate between the general and abstract perspectives of the "expert cultures" in which specializations are crystallized, on the one hand, and the concrete but fragmentary consciousness of "everyday practice,"[82] on the other. This task of "translating" specialist alternative interpretations in order to make them accessible and available to the larger public has an eminently political component. Habermas puts it succinctly: "In democracy there can be no political privilege of expertise [*Privileg des Sachverstandes*]."[83] Finally, the tendency toward mediation, to which

---

80. Habermas, *Moral Consciousness and Communicative Action*, 15 / 22.

81. Ibid., 16 / 23, trans. modified. For the "happy coherence of different theoretical fragments," see also Habermas, *Theory of Communicative Action*, 2:400 / 2:588.

82. Habermas, *Moral Consciousness and Communicative Action*, 17–18 / 25, trans. modified.

83. Jürgen Habermas, *Die Normalität einer Berliner Republik: Kleine Politische Schriften VIII* (Frankfurt a.M.: Suhrkamp, 1995), 143.

art criticism notably contributes,[84] already becomes apparent within the boundaries of these increasingly independent regions.

Yet, in its role as interpreter, philosophy can aspire only to a limited and paradoxical status. Just as we have available no adequate, comprehensive, pragmatic logic of argumentation which could demonstrate the internal connection between forms of speech-acts governing claims of legitimacy and modes of rationality, Habermas acknowledges a similar lacuna — indeed, a structural incompleteness — in his considerations concerning the task of philosophy. Indeed, the intended logic of a reasonable (if not strictly reasoned) symbiosis of specialized knowledge or professional know-how, on the one hand, and the "hermeneutics of everyday life," on the other, is insufficiently worked out.[85] This should hardly surprise us, because it is in the realm of the quotidian, the life-world, that the three analytically distinguished spheres of (cognitive, practical, and aesthetic) validity claims originally intertwine. They do so in varying degrees and constellations, whose patterns are not easily formalized by a logic of any kind — pragmatic, material, informal, or even "fuzzy" — given that each of these must necessarily be specialized.

Under the conditions of modernity, a negotiated "unity" that would be neither naive (i.e., substantial) nor diffuse (i.e., undifferentiated) but philosophically sound can be achieved only "this side of expert culture." Only "in everyday life" and not "beyond, in the grounds and abysses of the classical philosophy of reason,"[86] can a reasonable, if not fully reasoned, mediation take place without regression, that is to say, without ignoring or violating the properly differentiated argumentative structures and internal logic of science, morality, and art. As we will later verify, the perspective of reasonable mediation can only be that of a perspectivism in view of — or in tune with — the unconditional, the absolute, the infinite, the trace. This, I argue, is already suggested by Habermas's choice of metaphors or images, by what I call the figure of rationality, which enables and destabilizes his theory *from within*. In proposing this admittedly deconstructive reading, I am not opting for an aestheticization of theory, nor do I think that "aesthetic assimilations" are ever at issue in Derrida's writings, as Habermas suggests in the unnecessarily polemical pages of *The*

84. See Habermas, *Philosophical Discourse of Modernity*, 181 ff. / 243 ff.

85. Habermas, "Reply," in Honneth and Joas, *Communicative Action*, 224–25 / 341.

86. Habermas, *Moral Consciousness and Communicative Action*, 18 / 26. See also his book *The Theory of Communicative Action*, 2:398 / 2:586: "in a nonreified communicative everyday practice."

Philosophical Discourse of Modernity and reiterates in the preface to *Between Facts and Norms*. Aestheticization as a pejorative category is also out of place with regard to Adorno's negative dialectic of the nonidentical (including its parallel elaboration in *Aesthetic Theory*) and Levinas's phenomenology of the other (including its incursions into the theory of art).

To a certain extent—and despite the prominence of Kant and neo-Kantian elements in Weber's thought—Habermas's proposal of an interpretive and integrative task for philosophy as the "placeholder" of reason is still strangely reminiscent of at least the formal schema of Hegel's dream. Spirit or reason manifests itself, according to Hegel, in a dialectical process of differentiation whose moments, along with emancipation, symbolize a loss that, in the progression of the consciousness of freedom, can finally be restored—negated, elevated, and sublated—in the absolute knowledge of the philosopher. For Habermas mediation and hermeneutic feedback (*Rückkoppelung*), with far more fissures, are to be found in the everyday practice of modern citizens, competent in speech and action. Only in the practical wisdom of a "hermeneutics of everyday life [*Alltagshermeneutik*]"[87] does the possibility of "leveling" the abyss between theory and practice, abstract moral principles and concrete ethical [*sittlich*] forms, art and life, still exist.[88] The modest role that philosophy might play in view of the life-world would be to set "the petrified interplay [*das stillgelegte Zusammenspiel*]" of the three encapsulated forms of rationality in motion again. Thus, a "new balance [*ein neues Gleichgewicht*]" could be formed in the rationalized life-world, as in a "tangled mobile [*Mobile, das sich hartnäckig verhakt hat*]." These strikingly metaphorical formulations of Habermas's central assertions—while they certainly attest to the theory's inventiveness and heuristic capacity—also indicate that some figural aspects and elusive traits of his theory of rationality cannot be expressed in strictly discursive, formal-pragmatic terms and therefore ought to be brought under greater scrutiny.

87. Habermas, "Reply," in Honneth and Joas, *Communicative Action*, 225 / 341.

88. See also the opening lines of Habermas's *Between Facts and Norms*, xxxix / 9, in which he states with reference to Hegel's *Grundlinien der Philosophie des Rechts:* "If I scarcely mention the name of Hegel and rely more on the Kantian theory of law, this also expresses my desire to avoid a model that sets unattainable standards for us. . . . What could once be coherently embraced in the concepts of Hegelian philosophy now demands a pluralistic approach that combines the perspectives of moral theory, social theory, legal theory, and the sociology and history of law."

Because of the ambivalence in the term *communicative action*[89] — which refers both to intersubjective understanding *within* discourse and to the interplay *between* different discourses — this scrutiny should operate on two different levels. First, one ought to question the *internal* differentiation (and perhaps number) of the manifold aspects of rationality as well as the characterization of their "proper meaning and autonomy [*Eigensinn*]," especially in its moral-practical and aesthetic-expressive forms (a). Beyond that, one ought to examine Habermas's subsequent emphasis on the *external* connections between these areas of rationality, which suggest consequences incompatible with the conceptual framework of his theory (b). These two areas of inquiry require, I will argue, at least one further internal differentiation of aspects of rationality which Habermas does not provide. In addition, one would need to present a more explicit account of the way in which these various aspects (unintentionally) hang together or might be (consciously, responsibly) connected externally. Both sets of problems emerge from the immanent critical — and, as we have said, deconstructive — observation that one can hardly articulate the specific intentions upon which Habermas bases his theory within the theoretical construct he proposes. They raise the question not so much of a comprehensive theoretical alternative but of how to comprehend the metaphysical and hermeneutic supplement at once required and denied by his theoretical matrix. Neither the metaphysical nor the hermeneutic "supplement" should be considered irrational or unreasonable, even in terms of Habermas's own theory.[90] Such a supplement refers, rather, to a *figure of thought* and a *faculty of judgment* which both, finally, resist the simple equation of rationality with discursiveness, with the decidability of sharply delineated (cognitive, practical, and aesthetically expressive) validity claims, and with the force of the better argument alone. In this sense my attempt to supplement the theory under consideration requires a radi-

89. Martin Seel, "Die zwei Bedeutungen 'kommunikativer Rationalität': Bemerkungen zu Habermas's 'Kritik der pluralen Vernunft,'" in Honneth and Joas, *Kommunikatives Handeln*, 53–72 / "The Two Meanings of 'Communicative' Rationality: Remarks on Habermas's Critique of a Plural Concept of Reason," in Honneth and Joas, *Communicative Action*, 36–48.

90. In this context Derrida's term *supplement* (see *Writing and Difference*, 211–12, 289 ff. / 314, 423 ff.; and *Of Grammatology*, 144–45, 163–64 / 207–8, 234) marks both a problem and an open question. An attempt to bridge the gap in a comprehensive theory of rationality it opens in a way that would do justice both to the heuristic and social-critical strength of Habermas's work and to the quasi-theological concerns on which I intend to focus seems premature. At the moment I can at least explore, in a preliminary manner, motifs and dimensions that do not seem to fit Habermas's theory (or which do not seem to fit well together within it).

cal modification, not just a reinterpretation, of its paradigm of rationality; in other words, it demands an extension of its scope—even an extrapolation and extension of some of its central intuitions—that, I suspect, goes far beyond the limits Habermas himself would accept.

(*ad a*) The first question concerns the internal grounds of the different forms of rationality. It concerns, that is, an intra-discursive problem, most apparent in (but not limited to) practical discourse and aesthetic critique. We will approach objections to Habermas's analysis both directly, through Klaus M. Kodalle's critique of *The Theory of Communicative Action* from the perspective of the philosophy of religion, and indirectly, by drawing on Derrida's critique of John Searle, the chief proponent of the philosophy of language on which the theory of communicative action is largely, if not exclusively, based. The two objections at issue are Habermas's theory of culture, of the rationalization of the life-world, and the conception of the differentiated linguistic utterances, the "speech-acts" in terms of which it operates. Most questionable in all these theorems is, perhaps, the supposition of a continual—or even completed?—rationalization of the life-world, which, at least potentially, would make it so transparent that "structural violence could no longer be concealed in the pores of communicative action."[91] According to Habermas, in modern Western societies no validity claim can *systematically* immunize itself against critique. It is difficult not to feel challenged by this strongly counterintuitive and—technically speaking—counterfactual claim. Wouldn't it be far more convincing to insist, as Kodalle does, that the modern life-world must be understood first of all as structurally diffuse and, hence, we should add, systematically and potentially open to—even responsible for—violence? Concerning the observation of an ineradicable lack of transcendence (or, conversely, of irreducible opacity and remaining obscurity), Habermas himself, Kodalle claims, suggested as much on several occasions and would thus himself have contributed to the falsification of the general thesis of a progressive—and ultimately exhaustive, if not complete—"linguistification of the sacred [*Versprachlichung des Sakralen*]."[92] The sacred would not only fail to disappear as an empirical presence; it

91. Kunneman, *De waarheidstrechter*, 279; cf. 241, 242, 256 ff.

92. Klaus-M. Kodalle, "Versprachlichung des Sakralen? Zur religionsphilosophischen Auseinandersetzung mit Jürgen Habermas's *Theorie des kommunikativen Handelns*," *Allgemeine Zeitschrift für Philosophie* 12 (1987): 39–66. See also Kodalle, *Die Eroberung des Nutzlosen*, 45–51. From a different, phenomenological, perspective this has been systematically argued by Bernhard Waldenfels, esp. in *In den Netzen der Lebenswelt* (Frankfurt a.M.: Suhrkamp, 1985).

would also systematically retain some of its systemic secrecy. Not merely a relict of the life-world, it would pervade the system of state and market, for good and for ill.[93]

Furthermore, the structurally diffuse character of the life-world (and the system) is apparent not only in the global sphere, in which moral and subjective-expressive utterances (or any other, e.g., propositional attitudes) are put forward and, as it were, play themselves out. Within the necessary differentiation — and, hence, analytical distinction — of the three (cognitive, practical, and aesthetic) aspects of rationality which Habermas emphasizes, each of them (without, strictly speaking, presupposing the others but insofar as each is faithful to its own particular logic) always already brings the others back into play.[94] This paradoxical circumstance — an aporia and a performative contradiction in its own right — brings the question of *intra*- as well as *inter*-discursive judgment (as well as the question of how to decide between the two) to the fore. Habermas's theory, above all where it addresses the moral and aesthetic-practical dimensions that regulate human agency and constitute individual meaningfulness, already inadvertently conjures up a *metaphysical supplement* that it ought to preclude and that cannot (yet?) be fully formalized or otherwise formulated in its terms. Such a supplement, I suggest, does not affect the overall heuristic value of Habermas's conception of rationality, especially in its sociopolitical diagnostics. Yet its heuristics lacks the firm foundation it claims to need. But does it? Adorno and Horkheimer seem to suggest otherwise when, in *Dialectic of Enlightenment,* they make the following almost Wittgensteinean observation: "Whereas the rules do not arise from rational reflection, rationality arises from the rules" (*DE* 178 / 202).

(*ad b*) The second problem concerns the external connection between the different forms of rationality. As indicated, this interdiscursive problem affects not only practical deliberation and aesthetic criticism but also theoretical discourse in its relation to the two other forms of rationality. If this problematic suggests (perhaps too strongly?) a continuity or formal analogy between the different forms of rationality as Habermas reconstructs them, then we confront here the strong discontinuity between

---

93. Drawing on the work of many scholars, I have sought to demonstrate and theorize the continuous interference among the religious, states, and markets in my introduction to de Vries and Weber, *Religion and Media,* as well as in an ongoing project on "Political Theologies."

94. For an elaboration of this point, see Seel, "The Two Meanings of 'Communicative' Rationality: Remarks on Habermas's Critique of a Plural Concept of Reason," in Honneth and Joas, *Communicative Action,* esp. 43 ff. / 60 ff.

these discourses, which contradicts their supposed structural affinity. At times overtly and at times inadvertently, Habermas's texts show that the "interaction" or the "communicative action" between the various modes of rationality can only be described *metaphorically* (hence, the invocation of "play," the "mobile," or, in theoretical discourse, the "happy coherence," of fragments). Neither are the various discourses immediately connected to one another, nor can any comprehensive metatheoretical discourse be constructed to relate the various forms of rationality to one another. There is a simple reason why only supplementary metaphors can help to clarify this necessary yet impossible mediation, which can take place only in the concrete exercise and experiment of life, that is to say, in a historically situated and specifically — singularly — contextual way.

At times Habermas goes so far as to maintain, with a clear echo of Ranke and, as we will see, Adorno as well: "There are in fact no metadiscourses whatsoever; every discourse is, so to speak, equally close to God [*unmittelbar zu Gott*]."[95] But he also maintains, on more than one occasion, that the idea of communicative rationality is itself a model for an argumentative and procedural connection between the value spheres and their forms of discourse. A question remains: How can we "switch [*umschalten*]" in a reasonable and meaningful way from one form of rationality to another? In other words, this is where, as Habermas himself puts it, "in the communicative practice of everyday life, 'switching stations [*Schaltstellen*]' have to be brought into operation so that individuals can shift their action orientations from one complex to another."[96] This, again, would imply that the connectivity and mediation of the various aspects of rationality is no less important — or imperative — than the difference, differentiation, and differentiality between moments of reason emphasized here. "The only protection against an empiricist abridgment of the rationality problematic," Habermas says, invoking yet another metaphor, "is a steadfast pursuit of the tortuous routes [*verschlungenen Pfade*] along which science, morality and art communicate with one another."[97] His theory thereby once more relies upon a hermeneutical supplement that it itself cannot provide within the parameters of the formal pragmatic concept of rationality it proposes. But, again, this hermeneutic supplement leaves the overall *heuristic* — and thus pragmatic — value of his theory untouched.

95. Habermas, "Reply," in Honneth and Joas, *Communicative Action*, 226 / 343.
96. Habermas, *Theory of Communicative Action*, 1:250 / 1:341.
97. Ibid. 2:398 / 2:585.

The Abiding Intelligibility of the Discourse on (and of) God

Klaus M. Kodalle's "Linguistification of the Sacred? Toward an Examination of Jürgen Habermas's *Theory of Communicative Action* from the Perspective of the Philosophy of Religion" ("Versprachlichung des Sakralen? Zur religionsphilosophischen Auseinandersetzung mit Jürgen Habermas's *Theorie des kommunikativen Handelns*") can help us begin to rehearse some common criticisms of the fundamental assumptions in Habermas's theory. Building on the hypothesis that Habermas's theory takes the form of a "funnel of rationality,"[98] Kodalle's critique comes close to expressing my central intuition: the notion that a plausible postclassical and postmodern philosophy or comparative study of religion should operate both *beyond* historicist or cultural relativism and *on this side of* the traditional need for redemption. According to Kodalle, such a posttraditional philosophy of religion should start out from the principle that the absolute recedes from any teleology immanent to nature and life as well as from all societal—that is to say, all goal- and system-oriented or functional—rationality: "the absolute is purpose- or aimless [*zwecklos*]."[99] Following Benjamin, Kodalle insists that consciousness of the absolute must be *without intention* (*intentionslos*).[100] Freed from all classical metaphysical ballast, the absolute would prove dysfunctional wherever it might be employed and exploited as a "resource of meaning" for "mastering contingency."[101] The "desire for the totally Other," if one might extend Kodalle's conceptualization in the direction of the formulations of the later Horkheimer and the writings of Levinas's middle period—does not concern a

98. In this expression I am adapting Kunneman's ironic metaphor in *De waarheidstrechter,* in which he uses "funnel of truth" to convey the way in which Habermas criticizes the restriction of the registers of rational communication to the realm of cognition, propositional truth, veracity, etc., but does not fully escape that limitation himself. Habermas thereby fails, Kunneman argues, to expand upon and explore the implications of the concept of rationality intrinsic to the other two domains, those of the practical-normative and the aesthetic-expressive. Roughly the same reservations about Habermas's theory, elaborated in the following section, can be found in the writings of Friedrich Dallmayr, Dieter Henrich, and Bernhard Waldenfels. See Kodalle, "Versprachlichung des Sakralen?" 62–63 n. 19.

99. Kodalle, "Versprachlichung des Sakralen?" 40. See also Kodalle, "Gott," 404 ff.; and Kodalle, *Die Eroberung des Nutzlosen,* 15.

100. Kodalle, "Versprachlichung des Sakralen?" 40. See also Kodalle, "Gott," 420–21; and Kodalle, "Walter Benjamins politischer Dezisionismus im theologischen Kontext: Der 'Kierkegaard' unter den spekulativen Materialisten," in *Spiegel und Gleichnis,* ed. Norbert W. Bolz and Wolfgang Hübner (Würzburg: Königshausen & Neumann, 1983), 301–17, esp. 309 ff.

101. On this motif, see also Marquard, *Abschied vom Prinzipiellen.*

need that could be assuaged but, rather, a longing that cannot, in principle, be satisfied and is, strictly speaking, useless and good for nothing
(or in any case not a means to some ulterior, however superior, end).

I will follow a few steps down the trail Kodalle has blazed, without
entering onto the existentialist terrain toward which he is drawn and
whose horizon motivates his question. One can bring out the motif of "intentionlessness [*Intentionslosigkeit*]" in Benjamin — and give it a certain
primacy over and against the premises of the modern theory of rationality — without Kodalle's recourse to the "position and effective history
[*wirkungsgeschichte Position*] of the 'Kierkegaard paradigm.'" [102] To be successful, however, such a counterpoint to the paradigm of communicative
action (and its existentialist alternatives) must be posited both more systematically and less disjointedly than the views articulated by either Benjamin or Kodalle. This is not the least reason for taking my lead from the
writings of Adorno, Levinas, and Derrida.

To the extent that Habermas establishes an attempt to understand
"the structure of linguistic communication without reference to structures
of purposive activity [*Zwecktätigkeit*]" as the goal of his theory of rationality,[103] his project could be welcomed by the philosophy of religion
— or minimal theology — outlined here. When examined in that light,
however, his theory of communication clearly remains captive to commonplaces in the traditional critique of religion. Moreover, the categories
of Habermas's formal concept of rationality are too large — and thus too
imprecise — to express an intention-free and nonteleological concept of
the absolute. Where he does speak of motifs that might seem to transcend
the formally circumscribed conditions and limits — or "grids" — of communication (*Kommunikationsgitter*),[104] they remain "unmediated," that is
to say, merely abstractly posited or metaphorically evoked and, hence,
inconsequential for the theory as a whole. Such is, in essence, Kodalle's
critique.

Kodalle further emphasizes a motif in Habermas's work that will occupy me in the pages that follow, namely, his insight into the differ-

102. For an alternative reading of the systematic of the Kierkegaardian paradigm, as articulated by Heidegger, Patočka, Levinas, and Derrida — and, hence, relatively independent of
its existentalist reception — see my books *Philosophy and the Turn to Religion*, chap. 3; and *Religion and Violence*, chap. 2. For an extensive discussion of Adorno's reading of Kierkegaard, see
"The *Urzelle*," in chap. 3.

103. Habermas, *Theory of Communicative Action*, 1:293 / 1:394; see also 2:87 / 2:133.

104. The term is Kunneman's, from *De waarheidstrechter*, 251. See also Habermas's diagram
in *Theory of Communicative Action*, 2:192 / 2:286.

entiation of and remaining discrepancy between the life-world and communicative action. Even though it becomes ever smaller, this diminishing yet abiding difference cannot be removed or sublated, however much elements of the life-world are subjected to rational critique:[105] "in opposition to every altered or even only consciously accepted element, also in a life-world that has, so to speak, been fully reconnoitered, tried, and tested, stands the immense mass of elements that have not even crossed the threshold of thematization, even in the most radical alternative representations."[106] Since the whole life-world cannot be problematized all at once, or in toto, we are always left with an "impure reason [*verunreinigten Vernunft*]."[107] The life-world seems to be marked by a structurally diffuse remainder that can never reach the level of articulation — the principal possibility of "making it explicit" (as Brandom would say) or seeing it enter the "space of reasons" (as John McDowell would add) — stipulated by Habermas's formal pragmatic concept of rationality.[108] In his words: "The life-world is a curious thing, which falls apart and disappears before our eyes as soon as we want to bring it piece by piece before us. With respect to processes of communication, the life-world functions as a resource for what is contained in explicit utterances; but the moment this background knowledge enters into communicative utterances, the moment it becomes explicit and thus open to criticism, it loses the certainty, background character, and unquestionability [*Nichthintergehbarkeitscharakter*] which the structures of the life-world have for its inhabitants."[109] Ironically, the life-world would be just what "is not thematized and not criticized."[110]

This reduces the life-world to a counterfactual postulation, neither empirically given nor adequately, let alone fully, analyzable or intelligible at the level of discursive thought. The life-world remains merely "a totality that is implicit and that comes along prereflectively — one that crumbles the moment it is thematized; it remains a totality only in the form of im-

105. Habermas, *Philosophical Discourse of Modernity*, 342–43 / 397.

106. Habermas, *Die neue Unübersichtlichkeit*, 186–87.

107. Habermas, *Philosophical Discourse of Modernity*, 323 / 376.

108. Interesting in this context is Habermas's recent discussion of the work of Robert Brandom, esp. *Making It Explicit*. See Habermas, *Wahrheit und Rechtfertigung*, 138 ff., as well as *Zeit der Übergänge*, 166–70. See also the more incidental discussion of John McDowell's *Mind and World* (Cambridge: Harvard University Press, 1994), in Habermas, *Wahrheit und Rechtfertigung*, esp. 169 ff.

109. Habermas, *Philosophical Discourse of Modernity*, 157 / 186.

110. Ibid.

plicit, intuitively presupposed background knowledge."[111] Far from representing a knowledge that would be up to rational standards—albeit one that is somewhat more explicit than the diffuse background "knowledge" of the life-world—mythical, religious, and metaphysical worldviews, Habermas claims, asserted themselves by "taking the unity of the life-world, which is only known subconsciously, and projecting it in an objectifying manner onto the level of explicit knowledge."[112] But, if the transition from the resources of the life-world and explicit communicative utterances is categorical, not gradual, then this hypostatization could never be successful or even get started in the first place. Moreover, the more differentiated and rational forms of articulation (in cognition and science, practical wisdom and morality, aesthetic judgment and criticism) would hardly be in a better position to undertake the task of making the life-world resources explicit than the mythical, religious, and metaphysical worldviews Habermas sets aside. In both—and by Habermas's own account—there is an irreducible element of hypostatization, of projection, a categorical leap from the implicit to the explicit, the obscure to the transparent, the diffusive to the articulated, intuition to the concept. When Habermas writes, "The moment one of its elements is seized, criticized, and opened to discussion, this element no longer belongs to the life-world,"[113] this means that no element—not even the intuitive background knowledge of some inexpressible totality accompanying all utterances as an inescapable shadow that somehow enables all visibility, all communicability[114]—can be projected, made explicit, or enter the space of reasons *at all*. However it would be articulated, it would no longer be "itself," no longer be "it." Speaking of it (*Es, Ça, das Ding, la Chose,* but also the nonidentical, the other, etc.), one would be speaking of something else.

Habermas's idea of the rationalization of the life-world, taken at its word, seems thus finally to rest on an internal antinomy. Not only would a fully rationalized life-world be no life-world at all, but also, to the very extent that the life-world is rationalized, it loses its character of being a life-world in any strict sense. Further, not only could a rationality fully caught up in life-worlds never be pure, formal, or explicit; to the very extent that rationality is embedded in life-worlds, it cannot be rationality in

111. Habermas, *Postmetaphysical Thinking*, 142 / 183.

112. Ibid., 142–83.

113. Habermas, *Philosophical Discourse of Modernity*, 157 / 186.

114. See Charles Travis, *Unshadowed Thought: Representation in Thought and Language* (Cambridge: Harvard University Press, 2000).

the reconstructed or normative sense that Habermas proposes. And, since neither life-world nor rationality can exist in isolation—as abstractions, mere concepts, or ideas, separated from each other—neither of them ever comes into its own, ever coincides with itself. Life-world and rationality, we are thus forced to conclude, are merely differential concepts, whose meaning and polarity absolve them from all determination—including all self-determination—and each is supplemented only by its other. Constituted and negated by each other, these central notions of the theory of communicative action are therefore deeply paradoxical—indeed, as aporetic as they remain indispensable to any analysis of modernity in post-classical, even postmodern, terms.

Kodalle seeks to strengthen his critique by pointing out a further unwarranted hypothesis in the theory of modernization and rationalization: he calls into question Habermas's insistence that the "linguistification [*Versprachlichung*]" of the sacred does not necessarily lead to a significant loss of meaning and meaningfulness within the life-world (and in what makes up its grammar). He thereby reveals a remarkable ambiguity in the theory of communicative action. Although Habermas claims in passing that we ought to hold in memory the "semantic energy" that animated myths, rituals, and religious-metaphysical worldviews (we will return to the meaning of such *eingedenk sein*),[115] he leaves no doubt that its irrevocable loss is the price of humanity's entrance into modernity. His work might thus be understood as the cautious, sometimes hesitant diagnosis of an oscillating cultural equilibrium. In this calculation of gains and losses, emancipation—that is, the weight of formal (universalistic) *possibilities* of thought and action—can increase only at the expense of the richness and, as it were, the density of the particular contents of past, present, and future ideas. Habermas's ambivalent description of this development and the wager or choice it implies cannot obscure the supposition that guides his work from the outset:

> the socially integrative and expressive functions that were at first fulfilled by ritual practice pass over to communicative action; the authority of the holy is gradually replaced by the authority of an achieved consensus. This means a freeing of communicative action from sacrally protected normative contexts. The disenchantment and disempowering of the domain of the sacred takes place by way of a *linguistification of the ritually secured, basic normative agreement;* going along with this is a release of the rationality potential in commu-

115. Habermas, *Theory of Communicative Action*, 1:65–66 / 1:101.

nicative action. The aura of rapture and terror that emanates from the sacred, the *spellbinding* [bannende] power of the holy, is sublimated into the *binding/bonding* [bindenden] force of criticizable validity claims and at the same time turned into an everyday occurrence [*veralltäglicht*].[116]

In other words, the "linguistification of the sacred" of which Kodalle speaks comes down to what Habermas calls a "liquefaction [*Verflüssigung*] of the basic religious consensus,"[117] given that he holds the rationalization of worldviews to be marked by an irreversible development "in which the more purely the structures of universal religions [*Universalreligionen*] emerge, merely the kernel [*Kernbestand*] of a universalistic morality remains."[118] That is to say, a certain *globalization*—an expansion, generalization, and universalization—of the religious goes hand in hand with a formalization of its historical, positive, and ontic content. A procedure of reconstruction and quasi-transcendental reduction empties or thins out the original referents of religion and reveals its "kernel" to be morality. The result, as in Kant, is a purely moral religion but one whose features are now naturalized, reformulated in formal pragmatic terms. Interestingly, such a transposition and translation of the religious into the secular, the profane, the exoteric, and the public constitutes at once a purification and intensification of its supposedly ultimate concern *and* its trivialization or profanation: a global or globalized religion but a merely global—that is, minimally theological—sense of what "religion" once meant. But there are no historical or conceptual means for deciding whether this "secularization" does not, by minimizing religion, *realize* it in a more fundamental and promising way—that is to say, whether profanation and heterodoxy are not, rather, the kernel and final consequence of orthodoxy. Conversely, there are no historical or conceptual means for deciding whether this process—by merely repeating the same, in a seemingly senseless, nonformal tautology—does not produce something radically new as well: the heterology of some undeterminable, indeed undecidable—now religious, then nonreligious—other.[119]

Regardless of the necessary and historically irrevocable linguistification, liquefaction, and virtual liquidation of the sacred, we must never-

---

116. Ibid., 2:77 / 2:118–19.
117. Ibid., 2:82, trans. modified / 2:126; see 2:140.
118. Habermas, *Zur Rekonstruktion des historischen Materialismus*, 109.
119. One could, I would suggest, read in a similar vein Gerschom Scholem's inquiries into the historical phenomenon of antinomianism in chiliastic and other movements.

theless, Habermas says, "guard against the danger . . . of completely losing sight of the light of the semantic potential once preserved in myth."[120] Yet such a formulation cannot in itself lead to a reconsideration of the verdict passed on mythology, classical theology, and metaphysics. Only a minimal theology (a negative metaphysics, ethics, and aesthetics, in Adorno's sense) which would not uncritically resort to the premodern (or, in Kantian parlance, dogmatic) assumptions rightfully addressed by Habermas's theory of rationality might—perhaps—succeed in compellingly reassessing these semantic, rhetorical, and figural resources. Such a prospect, however, lies beyond the spirit, if not always beyond the letter, of Habermas's text.

Habermas convincingly argues that the decentering of worldviews and the rationalization of the life-world form the necessary, if not always sufficient, conditions for emancipation.[121] No normative consensus that could once again be formulated in the symbolic medium of religious language could, in his terms, be ascribed *intentionality,* the central category of any theory of action:[122] being based on "archaic" forms of interpretation, it would—by definition—lack communicative rationality.[123] According to Kodalle, this conclusion (correct in itself) ought not to embarrass philosophers of religion, provided they keep in mind the *intentionless* character of the absolute. Benjamin was aware of this feature, whose singular formality of increasing abstractness combined with intensified concreteness enables some analytical and existential possibilities of its own. The absolute, as Levinas argues, leaves its traces not in intentionality, phenomenologically defined, but in an almost traumatic passivity of the subject, in a radical subjectivation and singularization that—paradoxically— makes all intersubjectivity possible, although it will always elude the grasp of theories of action, regardless of their universal intent. Even from a purely etymological perspective—and in spite of any definitional clauses, which should prevent us from equating action all too quickly with communication and communication with "reaching understanding [*Verstän-*

120. Habermas, *Nachmetaphysisches Denken,* 275. (This appendix is not included in the English trans.)

121. Habermas, *Theory of Communicative Action,* 1:74 / 1:113.

122. For the connotations of the concept of intentionality, from Aristotle up to twentieth-century notions of human agency, see G. E. M. Anscombe, *Intention,* 2d ed. (1957; rpt. Cambridge: Harvard University Press, 2000).

123. See also Habermas, *Theory of Communicative Action,* 2:54 / 2:87, on the "archaic" character of religious interpretations.

digung]"[124]—a theory of action would seem to preclude the experiential dimensions of "receptivity, passivity, suffering, silence, and aesthetic perception."[125] Would it not, then, be better to explore a "theory of passion [*Leidenstheorie*],"[126] a methodological "agonistics,"[127] or a concept of *mésentente* ("disagreement"),[128] all of which would allow us to express heterogeneity, antagonism, and unresolved disputes in cognition, action, and judgment much better than the theories oriented toward action and interaction, consensus and universality?

In Habermas the hypothesis of the linguistification, liquefaction, and (eventual?) liquidation of the sacred forms part of a constellation of thought in which the renewed insistence upon a certain passivity, let alone *Gelassenheit*, of subjectivity—including its historical and functional equivalents in the tradition of "spiritual exercises"—might seem antimodern, reactionary, or simply ideological. Given the dispersal and disappearance of the "auratic traces of the sacred" caused by the irrevocable differentiation of the three irreducible spheres of validity,[129] one might from now on feel justified, he suggests, in postulating a potential transparency in the practice of everyday life. Henceforth, it would be impossible to speak of permanent places of refuge from which a structural, unjustified, and ideological violence could still make itself felt. Our intellectual,

124. Ibid., 1:100–101 / 1:150–51.

125. Helmut Peukert, *Wissenschaftstheorie, Handlungstheorie, Fundamentale Theologie: Analysen zu Ansatz und Status theologischer Theoriebildung* (Dusseldorf: Patmos, 1978), 260 / *Science, Action, and Fundamental Theology: Toward a Theology of Communicative Action*, trans. James Bohman (Cambridge: MIT Press, 1984), 170. Peukert believes that it is possible to relativize this objection on the basis of methodological considerations. We seem to be dealing here merely with a self-imposed ascetic restriction on the part of a formal-pragmatic theory whose reconstruction of the conditions of human interaction abstracts from all nonuniversalizable contents and features that inform or instantiate each singular speech and each individual action.

126. The term is taken from a comment by Hans Georg Gadamer during a seminar in Heidelberg, June 1986.

127. Compare Jean-François Lyotard's *La Condition postmoderne: Rapport sur le savoir* (Paris: Minuit, 1979), 23, 33, 36 / *The Postmodern Condition: A Report on Knowledge*, trans. Geoffrey Bennington and Brian Massumi (Minneapolis: University of Minnesota Press, 1984), 10, 16, 25. See also the demarcation of the "cynical [*kynischen*]" alternative with respect to the work of Apel and Habermas in Peter Sloterdijk, *Kritik der zynischen Vernunft*, 2 vols. (Frankfurt a.M.: Suhrkamp, 1983), 2:652 ff. / *Critique of Cynical Reason*, trans. Michael Eldred (Minneapolis: University of Minnesota Press, 1987), 357 ff.

128. Jacques Rancière, *La Mésentente: Politique et philosophie* (Paris: Galilée, 1995), 12 / *Disagreement: Politics and Philosophy*, trans. Julie Rose (Minneapolis: University of Minnesota Press, 1999), x.

129. Habermas, *Theory of Communicative Action*, 2:354 / 2:520.

political, cultural, and personal histories are no longer premised upon a mythical totality that must in principle remain opaque to us; the totalitarianisms that punctuated (modern) history need no longer be seen as endemic to the unfolding of its processes. As Habermas says: "Once religion had been the unbreakable seal upon this totality; it is not by chance that this seal has been broken."[130] The substantial, religious, metaphysical, and theologico-political concepts of totality have been "critically dissolved" or have "evaporated."[131] For this reason there is no well-founded or argumentatively justifiable alternative to the project of modernity and its philosophical discourse.

Habermas considers neither the critical possibility of contemporary functional equivalents to the semantic dimension of classical metaphysical worldviews nor the contemporary confessional theologies — secular theologies, God-is-dead theologies, a-theologies, and radical orthodoxies — based upon them.[132] It would be a mistake to view this as mere oversight on his part, for at least two reasons.

First, the success of any postmetaphysical metaphysics, postethical ethics, or posttheological theology will be limited unless it has at least some recourse to traditions that have remained largely esoteric or unexplored. One should think here not only of the traditions of apophatic, negative, and mystical theology but also of contemporary religious expressions and forms of faith linked to recent developments in the new technological media, the societal and cultural transformations signaled by globalization, and so on.[133] That Habermas's theory of rationality seizes upon the mainstream metaphysical — that is, onto-theological — tradition of the *Universalreligionen* is no argument for giving the contemporary philosophical theologian free rein, if what is at stake is to make the rationality of discourse on (and of) God conceivable in a postclassical and postmodern world. This is the element and task of minimal theology and its central theme: the diminishing and abiding intelligibility of the discourse on (and of) God which reveals itself as the trace of the ab-solute, in its very indeterminacy signaling now the Other, then the other (but also the

130. Habermas, *Philosophical Discourse of Modernity*, 83–84 / 104.

131. Habermas, *Theory of Communicative Action*, 1:249 / 1:340; 2:353 / 2:519.

132. I am thinking here of the early writings of Paul van Buuren, Harvey Cox, Thomas Altizer, and Mark C. Taylor, as well as the current work being published and edited by John Milbank, Catherine Pickstock, Graham Ward, and others.

133. See de Vries and Weber, *Religion and Media*.

Other as other and the other as Other as well as the "other" of this no longer simply oppositional pair of concepts or names). By contrast, dogmatic, biblical, systematic, confessional, even emancipatory or "genitive" theologies of all varieties (liberation theology, feminist theology, black theology, etc.), fall short of the minimal—the necessary but not sufficient—criteria for rationality stipulated by Habermas's theory, which we are trying to make our own while expanding its scope and range of application. Although one might question whether the concept of rationality has been exhaustively characterized when it is identified with emancipation (in Kant's sense of *Mündigkeit*), more precisely, with the possibility of providing reasons where needed (*Argumentierbarkeit*), this much at least is clear: a return to substantialist styles of philosophical reasoning, based on the (ontological, axiological, aesthetic, or theological) privileging of a particular and, hence, particularist content is, after Habermas, no longer an option for "us."

The second, more important argument is a logical consequence of the first. *From a formal, rational perspective, a plausible religious answer to the question of the ab-solute—a discourse on (and of) God, without quotation marks—could never be sharply distinguished from its possible nonreligious counterpart.* The reverse would be equally true. Formally, structurally, and analytically speaking, in dealing with the ab-solute—indeed, in any genuine discourse on (and of) God—we are dealing with an alterity, a transcendence, a relation to some fundamentally indeterminate other that always lets itself be translated and transposed into its supposed (immanent, mundane) opposite. And vice versa. A minimal theology that consists in nothing other than taking this insight to its logical, practical, and expressive extreme would thus subvert every historical, systematic, or conceptual distinction between theism and atheism, belief and unbelief, respect for law and antinomianism, prayer and blasphemy, iconology and idolatry. In so doing, its project would explore and perhaps exploit an intrinsic possibility—a *risk* and a *chance*—of reason and rationality which Habermas's thought touches upon, if only indirectly and obliquely. To bring out this possibility, multiplying its examples (not just in formal pragmatics but also in post-Hegelian dialectics, post-Husserlian phenomenology, and post-Heideggerian deconstruction) and assessing its consequences, pitfalls, and opportunities, while avoiding obscurantism, is the task I have set for myself here.

In connection with his critical observations (and with a twist of argument which echoes both Kierkegaard and Adorno), Kodalle accuses

Habermas of "leveling symbolically mediated, nonidentical meanings."[134] Habermas, he says, ignores the possibility of—and conditions of possibility for—discourses that lie outside established codes and systems of signification and communication yet nonetheless (or for that very reason) express an "indeterminate freedom."[135] With respect to prereflexive but indispensably valid forms of life, Kodalle continues, one should bear in mind that there are also "limits to the requirement to found the imperative to universalize demanded by morality [*Grenzen der Begründungsforderung des Universalisierungsprinzips der Moral*]."[136] Neither the impetus toward nor the desire for interaction, nor the *quality* of these, emerges from universalistic reason itself. They are too fragile and simply too corruptible to be gauged by the standard of communicative rationality.[137] To do justice, then, to the religious, ethical, aesthetic, and other elements and dimensions of meaning, including the utterances and gestures in which they are phrased or expressed, would amount to "qualitative *intervention* in the fundamental philosophical traits [*Grundzug*] of the whole" of the theory of rationality rather than a mere "*extension*" of its intention and general scope.[138]

Kodalle's assertion, I would claim, is only partly correct. Habermas does grant a certain right to metaphysical notions, "at least as limit concepts,"[139] although he insists that they do not add up to "problems that could be worked through cognitively,"[140] with the help of the necessary

134. Kodalle, "Versprachlichung des Sakralen?" 49.

135. Ibid., 59, 63. See also Habermas, *Philosophical Discourse of Modernity*, 309 / 360.

136. Kodalle, "Versprachlichung des Sakralen?" 65. This a tricky point for Habermas: nowhere does he offer a satisfying answer to the question, posed by Perry Anderson and Peter Dews of the *New Left Review*, of how the connection between discourse ethics and the question of happiness, justice, and the good life—in Hegelian parlance, "morality [*Moralität*]" and the "ethical life [*Sittlichkeit*]"—can possibly be thought. At one point, in his essay on Benjamin in *Philosophisch-politische Profile*, Habermas claims that a rationalized society, free of unequal power relations but nonetheless without meaning (*ohne Sinn*), is entirely thinkable. Does such a pure possibility of a form of rationality without a corresponding notion of the successful life not implicitly contradict Habermas's tirelessly varied argument that each consensus-oriented speech act is, as such, an (admittedly formal) "anticipation of the good life"? See his books *Die neue Unübersichtlichkeit*, 236; and *Vorstudien und Ergänzungen*, 490.

137. Kodalle, "Versprachlichung des Sakralen?" 64, 52. Kodalle acknowledges that Habermas is in no way blind to the dimension of meaning, though Kodalle views it as a weakness that these "existential" motifs, in Habermas's terminology, have no consequences for the formal, universalist theory.

138. Ibid., 59.

139. Habermas, *Vorstudien und Ergänzungen*, 515.

140. Ibid., 519.

standards of, in this case, theoretical rationality. In his view whoever would contest this postmetaphysical stance only applauds the subliminal yet ever-present tendency toward *dedifferentiation* or "re-enchantment [*Wiederverzauberung*]" which threatens the life-world from within and without; more specifically, such denegation would risk forgetting and conflating the (ideal-typical) distinction between the worlds of objective nature, social interaction, and subjective expression, plus their respective — merely formally analogous — validity claims and modes of argumentation, discourse, judgment, and expression. In other words, to resort to religious and metaphysical *truths* — whether as truth contents or as truth moments (as Adorno would say) — is ipso facto to depart from the philosophical discourse that accompanies and in part establishes modernity.[141]

Habermas's theory of rationality thus rightly acknowledges its debt to a certain cultural modernity, calling it at the same time, less convincingly, the "only source [*Fundus*] from which we can draw our creative force [*aus dem wir schöpfen können*]."[142] This historical and systematic claim seems surprising, even more so the pathos of autonomy, self-determination, and even self-generation with which Habermas backs it up: "Modernity *has to create its normativity out of itself* [die Moderne . . . muss ihre Normativität aus sich selber schöpfen]"; or, again: "Just as it always has, philosophy understands itself as the defender [*Hüterin*] of rationality in the sense of a claim of reason *endogenous to our form of life*."[143] Does modern reason actually see itself, as Habermas believes, "cast back upon itself without any possibility of escape [*Ausflucht*]"?[144]

Kodalle limits himself to the *programmatic* formulation of the desirability of qualitative interventions in Habermas's framework. Such a program could probably not successfully be worked out, however, without drawing on the impressive breadth of the very theory it seeks to criticize. Certainly, there are many occasions on which Habermas himself is pressed to formulate — or at least implicitly to acknowledge — what I would like to call a *negative metaphysical supplement* to the theory of rationality. Such an addendum ought to insist, with Habermas, on the *cognitively* speaking *aporetic* character of the traces of the other (or Other) of reason. Contrary to Habermas's own understanding, however, it could only confirm the in-

---

141. Habermas, *Philosophical Discourse of Modernity*, 59–60 / 74.

142. Habermas, *Die neue Unübersichtlichkeit*, 183.

143. Habermas, *Philosophical Discourse of Modernity*, 7 / 16 and 409 n. 28 / 246–47n, respectively, trans. modified; my emph.

144. Ibid., 7 / 16.

valuable but restricted *heuristic* function of the rest of his theory's most fundamental presuppositions. Accordingly, the elaboration of a negative metaphysical supplement to Habermas's project would have to limit the range of the discourse-theoretical account of rationality (in cognition, ethics, law, and aesthetics) while keeping in view what draws us either *beyond* or back to *this side* of its most general categories.

Herbert Schnädelbach advocated the articulation of such a figure of negative metaphysical thought precisely with reference to Adorno's conception of negative dialectics and its solidarity, not with metaphysics in its classical or modern systems, but in its very "downfall." I will take up this suggestion later.

Chapter Two

A Possible Internal and External Differentiation of Habermas's Theory of Rationality

HABERMAS'S FORMAL-PRAGMATIC reconstruction of the conditions of possibility which constitute rationality can be questioned from a number of perspectives. They all converge in the suspicion that rationality necessarily alludes to nonformal, prereflexive, and even metacommunicative elements and dimensions in the life-world and its differentiated value spheres as well as in specialized systems of economic market exchange or administrative-juridical and political power. How, then, could one do justice to these elements and dimensions — as so many traces or instances of the ab-solute, as we shall see — without relapsing into a classical, substantialist-metaphysical, and onto-theological understanding of reason, on the one hand, or into the subjectivist, monological, and egological conception of its modern flip side, on the other? How, in other words, could one avoid both traditional utopianism — that is to say, presentism — and the wishful appeal to regulative ideas, constitutive fictions, perspectivism, projection, empty referents, metaphors we live by, narratives that are better for us to believe, and so on and so forth? What, in other words, is the *minimal, albeit nonnaturalist, realism* of the ab-solute — of ab-solutes, since we must think of the singularity in question as inherently plural — whose traces we follow here?

As we have observed, one already runs up against such elements and dimensions *within* the three realms of validity claims and their respective discourses which Habermas, in the wake of Kant and Weber, distinguishes. One can also track them by looking at how the various domains of rationality thus established — that is to say, not transcendentally deduced but postulated as ideal types — hold together *externally*. I shall argue that the traces and instances of the ab-solute — that is, of the other (or Other?) of reason — cannot be fully reconstructed in formal-pragmatic terms; they allow for at least two different interpretations, whose precise (complementary, supplementary, contradictory?) relationship needs to be clarified.

First, we should submit these notions — again, elements and dimensions of the ab-solute and of the concept and structure of the elemental and of dimensionality altogether — to an interpretation that draws on Adorno's interrupted program of *negative metaphysics*. This program, we will demonstrate, reveals remarkable parallels to the procedure of phenomenological concretion to which Levinas exposes classical metaphysics — and everyday experience. Second, we must raise the question of the historically situated or hermeneutic relationship between all these notions individually (the intradiscursive inquiry) and between their respective value spheres and genres of discourse as they engage, overlap, or interpenetrate one another as relative wholes in the life-world as well as between the life-world and the system of market and power (the interdiscursive inquiry).

Both these aspects and inquiries concern the same difficulty and involve the nonbisected concept of rationality introduced earlier. The first, negative-metaphysical part of my analysis concerns a critical idea, an idea of transcendence whose paradoxical or aporetic status forms the very crux of minimal theology: the internal connection between extreme abstraction, formalization, and openness, on the one hand, and extreme materialization and concretion, on the other. This crux, properly elucidated, helps explain why we are dealing here not with an idealism or mere negativism but with a nonnaturalistic realism whose contours can take different forms (of incarnation, sensualism, eroticism, etc.).

The second part of my analysis involves a faculty of judgment with which tactfully to approach empirical contingencies (i.e., spatiotemporal occurrences, actions, and events), if not discursively, then at least more prosaically than the more elusive (if not poetic) idea of negative metaphysics would seem to allow. Judgment — Kant would say reflective judgment — is the disposition and experiment upon which we must rely whenever in our practices we bring together the unmistakably and beneficially disparate aspects of rationality in a configuration or constellation within which an actual figure of the good life could possibly shine forth. The reality or actualization — and thus, in another sense, the materialization or concretization — of such figures never, of course, depends upon (inter)subjectively formed representations or competences alone. Habermas acknowledges as much: "Happiness can never be brought about intentionally and can only be fostered very indirectly."[1] But what does *in-*

---

1. Habermas, *Die neue Unübersichtlichkeit*, 237.

directly mean here? We need only recall aphoristic phrases evoking the other states of happiness found in Adorno's *Minima Moralia* ("We can tell whether we are happy by the sound of the wind" / "Ob einer glücklich ist, kann er dem Winde abhören" [*MM* 49 / 54]) or in Wittgenstein's *Tractatus Logico-Philosophicus* ("The world of the happy is quite another than that of the unhappy" [6.43]) — in order to realize that happiness, to judge from these negative-metaphysical ideas, cannot be conceived as a determinable state of affairs, an action, an event, or even a mind-set within the world (of nature, sociality, psychological interiority), which one could somehow, somewhere, plan or anticipate, let alone bring about (albeit "indirectly").

Negative metaphysics prevents us from positively or affirmatively anticipating, articulating, imagining, visualizing, or narrating such a figure of the successful life, prohibiting its conceptualization or figuration in theoretical, practical, or aesthetic terms alone. Yet we cannot consistently intuit — let alone maintain — a merely prohibitive idea of transcendence whose empty referent and ascetic strategy could never stand on its own or have the last word. Judgment, therefore, realizes the inevitable, necessary, and imperative instantiation of the other by way of an act or acknowledgment of concretization which signals incarnation and betrayal (divine speech and blasphemy, iconology and idolatry) at once.

The negative metaphysical idea and the hermeneutic judgment are thus complementary or supplementary. Both together constitute what reason — or, more precisely, a nonbisected rationality — might mean in the present day and age. Broadly defined, the faculty of judgment (as Kant and, in his wake, at opposite extremes of the philosophical spectrum, Gadamer, Habermas, and Lyotard insist, on alternative grounds and with different purposes) designates our critical, selective use of a certain concept, figure, or gesture: both by identifying it as such and by putting it to work at a certain moment, in a given context, and in a certain way. Formally defined, the idea of negative metaphysics enables us to keep options open and explains how we can return to earlier steps; it is the very principle of fallibility, of counterfactuality, and hence the necessary reminder that *this* particular use we have for concepts, figures, or gestures is not all or not-yet-it (i.e., true, adequate, good, just, beautiful, or sublime) when compared to the immeasurable standard that makes up the emphatic idea of reason: the infinite, the ab-solute, the other (or Other), for which the theologico-religious tradition has thus far provided the most provocative and richest vocabulary.

One remark is in order, however. The terminology we have chosen to indicate these two procedures may seem misleading. Surely, the negative metaphysical idea that stands (in) for the transcendence and constitutive lack in *each* of the three genres of discourse somehow remains associated with one of them. Being an idea, it seems located in the domain of theory rather than in those of practical discourse or of aesthetic experience and subjective expression. Likewise, the figure of judgment which stands (in) for the modes of relationship between the three genres of discourse seems to draw on the value sphere of the aesthetic-expressive more than on theory and practical moral reasoning. Although they cannot be understood in terms of any of the three discourses alone, our negative idea and our specific judgment betray, at least terminologically, a residual impurity, a certain inconsistency. Two responses to this possible objection can be given. First, the terminological choice imposed upon us makes it clear that there cannot be an overarching instance — a meta-discourse — to capture what internally escapes the differentiated discourses that we know (or may one day come to know), nor could such an instance be envisioned as a regulatory repository for the external relationship between them. The relationship between the theoretical, the practical, and the aesthetic-expressive is neither theoretical, practical, nor aesthetic-expressive, nor all of them at once. The negative metaphysical idea is solidary with traditional metaphysics "in its downfall"; the term *judgment* traverses questions of practical reason as well.[2]

We might stress the point further by surmising that what orients the relationship between the negative metaphysical idea, on the one hand, and the appeal to judgment, on the other, is less a quasi-theoretical idea or an act of judgment than a quasi-moral concern, whose "normativity" is not governed by criteria, norms, imperatives, or rules and whose "moral point of view," far from being disincarnated, touches upon the amorality of the other domains.

The Philosophy of Difference and the Motif of Intradiscursive Structural Asymmetry

We can corroborate and further substantiate Kodalle's critique by focusing on the smallest element in the communicative process, the speech-act. Noting that contingencies necessarily cling to every speech-act, Kodalle points out that Habermas ultimately has to deny any such

---

2. See Howard Caygill, *Art of Judgement* (Oxford: Blackwell, 1989); and Manfred Riedel, *Norm und Werturteil: Grundprobleme der Ethik* (Stuttgart: Reklam, 1979).

dependency in order to support his idealizing premise.[3] Although Kodalle does not pursue the point much further—which he could have done by mobilizing Kierkegaard's view of the linguistic strategy of indirect communication and his anticipation of Heidegger's phenomenology of *das Gerede* (chatter)[4]—one could elaborate it more closely via Derrida's deconstruction of some of the central presuppositions of speech-act theory as inaugurated by Austin and appropriated then systematized (or domesticated?) by Searle.[5] Derrida's discussion applies not only to Austin and Searle but also to Habermas, insofar as the latter, with few reservations, incorporates their linguistic model into his own analyses of the structure of validity claims, yes-no positions, performative contradiction, intentionality, the sensitivity of all meaning to context, and the distinctions between the serious and the nonserious, between philosophy and literature, and so on.

The philosophy of speech-act theory marks for Habermas "the first step toward a formal pragmatics that extends to non-cognitive modes of employment."[6] Expanding on the agenda sketched out in *Erkenntnis und Interesse* (*Knowledge and Human Interest*), he uses speech-act theory to develop and refine what he calls a "universal pragmatics."[7] Although we

3. Kodalle, "Versprachlichung des Sakralen?" 53; see also Habermas, *Theory of Communicative Action*, 1:335 / 1:450.

4. See Peter Fenves, *"Chatter": Language and History in Kierkegaard* (Stanford: Stanford University Press, 1993).

5. See Jacques Derrida, "Signature, événement, contexte," *Marges de la philosophie* (Paris: Minuit, 1972), 367–93 / "Signature, Event, Context," in *Margins of Philosophy*, trans. Alan Bass (Chicago: University of Chicago Press, 1982), 307–30; as well as John Searle's critique in "Reiterating the Differences: A Reply to Derrida," *Glyph*, no. 1 (1977): 198–208; and "The Word Upside Down," *New York Review of Books*, 27 October 1983, 74–77. For a response to Searle, see Derrida, *Limited Inc.* Cf. also Manfred Frank, "Die Entropie der Sprache: Überlegungen zur Debatte Searle-Derrida," *Das Sagbare und das Unsagbare* (Frankfurt a.M.: Suhrkamp, 1980), 141–210 / "The Entropy of Language: Reflections on the Searle-Derrida Debate," in *The Subject and the Text: Essays on Literary Theory and Philosophy*, trans. Helen Atkins, ed. and intro. Andrew Bowie (Cambridge: Cambridge University Press, 1997); as well as Frank, *Was ist Neustrukturalismus?* (Frankfurt a.M.: Suhrkamp, 1984), 286 ff., 497–98, 504 ff. / *What Is Neostructuralism?* trans. Sabine Wilke and Richard Gray (Minneapolis: University of Minnesota Press, 1989), 392 ff., 404–8, 413 ff. See Habermas, *Philosophical Discourse of Modernity*, 194 ff. / 228 ff.

6. Habermas, *Theory of Communicative Action*, 1:277 / 1:374–75. Habermas's claim that speech-act theory neglects certain functions of speech, programmatically alluded to by Bühler and Jakobson, lies outside my present scope. See Habermas's comments about Humboldt in "Reply," in Honneth and Joas, *Communicative Action*, 216 ff. / 329 ff.

7. Habermas, "Was heisst Universalpragmatik?" *Vorstudien und Ergänzungen*, 353–440 / "What Is Universal Pragmatics?" in *Communication and the Evolution of Society*, trans. Thomas McCarthy (Boston: Beacon Press, 1979), 1–68.

are not concerned here with the details of this project, its central motive is important for our purposes: namely, the ambition to avoid pitting points of reference (supposedly clearly delineated) against the illocutionary force of utterances, which forms an impenetrable remainder that cannot enter into the intentionality of speech and action, strictly defined, and therefore tends to resist it. In other words, universal pragmatics — like speech-act theory, by which it largely lets itself be guided — does not "set illocutionary role over against propositional content as an *irrational* force, but conceive[s] of it as a component that specifies *which* validity claim a speaker is raising with his utterance, *how* he is raising it, and *for what*."[8]

The philosophy of language which founds Habermas's theory, insofar as it is based upon Austin's intuitions as rendered and systematized by Searle, thus depends upon the presupposition of a narrow and, in principle, transparent connection between intentionality and the linguistic expression of validity claims, whether cognitive, practical, or aesthetic. Intentionality is defined as the determinable and hence communicable or translatable "component" of utterances. If the minimal formal or procedural conditions of symmetrical communication — that is to say, of nonhierarchical interaction without violence, strategy, power, unjustified force, deception, or hegemony — are satisfied, these validity claims can be specified, repeatedly identified, and recognized by others (and ourselves) and thus, in principle, contribute to the leveling of conflict in a dialogue oriented toward consensus. Their normative (rather than merely factual) persuasion is contingent upon an open and, in principle, unending discourse that permits no other force than the "force of the better argument." This and nothing else constitutes the "conversation of mankind."

Habermas combines these motifs in the postulation of an *ideal speech situation* — a "formal anticipation of the correct or just [*richtigen*] life"[9] — presupposed ipso facto by every communicative act that deserves the name. Its hypothetical character, based upon a counterfactual assumption and an ideal or idealized presupposition, is at once unreal and necessary; its intelligibility is that of a paradoxical (or aporetic?) idea of transcendence — an immanent transcendence or transcendent immanence — which *regulates* and *orients*, as Kant would say, cognition, rational agency, and judgment in the widest possible sense.

<hr/>

8. Habermas, *Theory of Communicative Action*, 1:278 / 1:375–76.
9. Habermas, "Der Universalitätsanspruch der Hermeneutik," in *Hermeneutik und Ideologiekritik*, ed. Karl-Otto Apel and others (Frankfurt a.M: Suhrkamp, 1971), 154.

Helmut Peukert describes the paradoxical status of this counterfactual idea: "As a historical [or historial] anticipation [*geschichtlicher Vorgriff*], it is a factical performance [*faktische Leistung*] of free subjects that is transcendentally constitutive."[10] His formulation reveals that the concept "transcendental" can, in this context, no longer be understood in its Kantian sense.[11] Given the finite, sociopolitical beings that we are, the possibility of "explicitness" (as in Brandom) or the "space of reasons" (as in McDowell) which rules and criteria provide is not, above all, that of "intelligible characters," as Kant had thought.[12] Hence comes the need to de-transcendentalize and relatively naturalize them, in a weak or minimal way. This inevitably entails a de-formalization and, as it were, re-concretization of its own.

Because it is a *quasi*-transcendental idea, the ideal speech situation need not be conceived as being an anthropological constant, the a priori of value spheres per se (as in neo-Kantianism), an existential of *Dasein* or epochal sending in the history of Being (in Heidegger's sense), a historical a priori or episteme (as in Foucault), or even a rule in the language game of dialogue and discourse (as Wittgenstein and, to some extent, Lyotard might have said). On the contrary, because it is a formal-pragmatic idea, it is conceived as being a feature of linguistic competence and the ability to act on the basis of reasons. Hence, Habermas's striking statement: "An 'ideal speech situation' is a somewhat too concretistic expression for the many general and unavoidable presuppositions of communication that every subject capable of speech and action must make in order seriously [*ernsthaft*] to take part in argumentation."[13]

Clearly, the rules that govern any such argumentation do not possess the same directive force as those of, say, the moves in a game of chess; more generally, their rigor is not of the same order as that stipulated by mathematically oriented, game-theoretical approaches. In contradistinction to certain contemporary theories of argumentation and in tune with ancient conceptions of rhetoric—including their modern successors in textual hermeneutics, jurisprudence, the art of judgment, and so on—the rules of discourse are, in Habermas's eyes, not merely subject to restric-

---

10. Peukert, *Wissenschaftstheorie, Handlungstheorie, Fundamentale Theologie*, 286.
11. Ibid., 284–85.
12. See Habermas, *Moral Consciousness and Communicative Action*, 82 ff., esp. 86–87 / 97 ff., esp. 101–2; see also his book *Vorstudien und Ergänzungen*, 397–85.
13. Habermas, *Die neue Unübersichtlichkeit*, 229.

tions of time, space, situation, and context but bound to specific practices of institutionalization, to inscription and archivization.

If this is so, why does Habermas term the very idea of the "ideal speech situation"—or the "ideal community of communication [*Kommunikationsgemeinschaft*]," as Apel, following Peirce, calls it—"a fallacy of misplaced concreteness"[14] or "a somewhat too concretistic expression" for the numerous inevitable presuppositions in serious communication? Is it too concretistic because it reduces an apparent multiplicity of conditions to a single image, a single "expression"? Indeed, is a condition—even a virtual infinity of conditions—not given with every utterance, with each act, with any judgment? Or does the problem lie in the image—indeed, any image, the given "expression," or any expression—as such? Why restrict the conditions of communication, even serious communication, to such images and expressions as "speech" and "situation," however ideally, quasi-transcendentally, formally, counterfactually, hypothetically, or fallibilistically conceived? The reservation about the "all too concretistic" presentation of the "many" conditions of all serious utterance, of all communicative action, in the name of whatever ideality, not only prohibits the invocation of alternative images and other expressions, it also places "speech" and "communication"—and all the concepts they entail (intentionality, action, understanding, etc.)—on the same level as a potentially infinite number of terms that could be substituted for them. Compared to the ideal, no single image, no single expression, it would seem, is adequate, responsible, proportionate, or fitting. Nor could we reasonably—even physically—embrace all as equally pertinent here and now. Our reasons for privileging one inevitably "too concretistic" figure over and against others (and perhaps our good judgment in doing so) thus cannot result from a reconstruction of the many discourses and their implied assumptions.

Distancing himself somewhat from the idea of the ideal speech situation and the ideal community of communication, Habermas notes: "Images are concretistic because they suggest a final state that could be reached within time, but which cannot be intended. I insist, however, on the idealizing content of the inevitable, pragmatic presuppositions of a practice in which only the better argument could get a chance. After abandoning the concept of truth as correspondence, one can explain the

14. Habermas, *Die Normalität einer Berliner Republik*, 153.

unconditional meaning of truth claims only by reference to 'justification under ideal conditions.'"[15]

A citation from *Between Facts and Norms* further illustrates this point, stressing that the expressions "ideal community of communication" and, to a lesser extent, "ideal speech situation" could easily lead to the "misunderstanding" and "hypostatization [*Hypostasierung*]" of an ideal that can be "realized in an approximate manner":

> The counterfactual presuppositions assumed by participants in argumentation indeed open up a perspective allowing them to go beyond local practices of justification and to transcend the provinciality of their spatiotemporal contexts that are inescapable in action and experience. This perspective thus enables them to do justice to the meaning of *context-transcending* validity claims. But with context-transcending validity claims, they are not themselves transported into the beyond of an ideal realm of noumenal beings. In contrast to the projection of ideals, in the light of which we can identify *deviations*, "the idealizing presuppositions we always already have to adopt whenever we want to reach mutual understanding do not involve any kind of correspondence or comparison between idea and reality."[16]

The only remaining option, therefore, would be to mitigate the "essentialist misunderstanding" to a merely "methodical fiction."[17]

At this point Derrida's deconstruction of speech-act theory becomes relevant. I will limit myself to a few objections that his main argument, most clearly expounded in *Limited Inc, La Carte postale* (*The Post Card*), and *Papier machine* (*Typing Paper*), enables us to formulate.[18] One consequence of Derrida's analysis of the constative-performative distinction in Austin is that at least "normative" (read practical) and expressive (or aesthetic) validity claims cannot be strictly isolated from each other. They cannot be specified and, hence, repeatedly identified or recognized in all purity *as such*. Utterances in which they occur, though they are singular events, can never be grasped directly, let alone intuitively, without further interpretation, translation, and, hence, transformation—operations

---

15. Ibid.

16. Habermas, *Between Facts and Norms,* 323 / 392. Habermas quotes Hauke Brunkhorst, "Zur Dialektik von realer und idealer Kommunikationsgemeinschaft," in *Transzendentalpragmatik,* ed. A. Dorschel et al. (Frankfurt a.M.: Suhrkamp, 1993), 345.

17. Ibid.

18. See also some of the arguments developed in my book *Philosophy and the Turn to Religion,* under the heading "Speech Tact," 404–18.

that carry with them the inevitable risk of misunderstanding, distortion, or *infelicity* (to use Austin's term).

This is similarly true for the seemingly more straightforward cognitive validity claims. Their propositional (descriptive or constative) character has a certain standing with the prescriptive and evaluative modalities of the normative (in the more restrictive, i.e., practical, sense of the term) and the aesthetic and thus, despite all analytical distinction, contaminates them from within and without. In other words, theoretical, practical, and expressive utterances are *always already* inextricably bound up with one another in the contingent contexts in which they make their appearance. The different "situations" that govern their uses as distinguished are—by definition, as already implied by the very concept of "situation"—never ideal or, as Austin would have it, "total." Nor can "intentionality," however conceived, ever master their meaning or intervene in them in a controlled, let alone calculable, way.

Similar objections might be raised when we move from the central assumption of speech-act theory to the attempt to ground a communicative ethics (an ethics of discussion, a discourse ethics, or *Diskursethik*), once again based on strong presuppositions. In problematic—and repeatedly qualified—proximity to Apel's transformation of the program of transcendental philosophy in its quest for ultimate foundations, Habermas defends a cautious *cognitivist* position within ethics, "according to which practical questions can in principle be decided by way of argumentation."[19] Again, an almost innocuous observation leads to an idealized assumption, which, in turn, is ultimately based on what seems an almost analytical truth: "In everyday life . . . no one would enter into moral argumentation who did not intuitively start from the strong presupposition that a grounded consensus could in principle be achieved among those involved. . . . [T]his follows with conceptual necessity from the *meaning* [Sinn] of normative validity claims."[20]

From this quotidian intuition and its necessary implication, Habermas draws two related consequences. First, he infers that the—in principle unlimited—possibility of intersubjective acknowledgment *and* critique of norms is constitutive of the rationality of the actions directed by these

19. Habermas, *Theory of Communicative Action*, 1:19 / 1:40, trans. modified. Karl-Otto Apel formulates his position in *Das Apriori der Kommunkationsgemeinschaft*, vol. 2 of *Transformation der Philosophie*, 358–435; and Apel, *Diskurs und Verantwortung: Das Problem des Übergangs zur postkonventionellen Moral* (Frankfurt a.M.: Suhrkamp, 1988).

20. Habermas, *Theory of Communicative Action*, 1:19 / 1:39, trans. modified.

very norms. Second, he asserts that the rationality of communicative practice, although it takes place against the backdrop of a life-world that can never be thematized—let alone problematized—in its totality, is directed toward establishing, maintaining, and renewing consensus. Given with the possibility of speech and, broadly defined, of action and interaction *as such*—somehow *called for* by any single word, utterance, expression, or gesture—consensus forms the *archē*, the medium, and the telos of language, of all linguistically mediated experience. For all its methodological precautions and proper accents, formal pragmatics is thus in essential agreement with the basic assumption of the linguistic turn and even shares some of the most speculative doctrines of philosophical hermeneutics, in its "urbanization of the Heideggerian province": namely, the ontological thesis that "Being," insofar as it can be understood, is made up of language ("Sein, das verstanden werden kann, ist Sprache," "Being that can be understood is language," as Hans-Georg Gadamer puts it in *Wahrheit und Methode* [*Truth and Method*]).[21] A further consequence of this presupposition emerges in the form of a curious, nonformal tautology: phenomenologically speaking—that is to say, insofar as things appear for "us"—rationality is an option, but only "for us." Only linguistically endowed and competent subjects—constituted interactively, dialogically, and intersubjectively, and thus socialized and disciplined—can be the agents and addressees of rationality. Not only does the human animal form the ultimate referent of this and every discourse, it implies that, within humanity, some animals are potentially more rational than others and thus more worthy of our consideration as agents, addressees, *face-to-face*.

A "communicatively achieved agreement" is judged rational only when it, "*in the end* [letzlich],"[22] rests on well-grounded reasons (*Gründe*). Such reasons are validity claims that are acceptable to or acknowledged yet at any time subject to refutation by all relevant others. But who exactly is included and excluded in this set? Who judges whom as fit for inclusion and on what "grounds"? The answer is as simple as it is mind-boggling: *all* relevant others, the omni-inclusive community of autonomous humans, capable of speech and communication.

21. Hans Georg Gadamer, *Wahrheit und Methode: Grundzüge einer philosophischen Hermeneutik* (Tübingen: J. C. B. Mohr, 1965), xxii / *Truth and Method* (New York: Crossroad, 1982), xii. The expression "urbanization of the Heideggerian province" is Habermas's somewhat unkind characterization of Gadamer's work; see Habermas, *Philosophisch-politische Profile* (Frankfurt a.M.: Suhrkamp, 1984).

22. Habermas, *Theory of Communicative Action*, 1:17 / 1:37.

Unlike Kant, whose intelligible realm hosted angels and "us" as intelligible entities even after our own deaths, and unlike Adorno and Levinas, whose reflections on animality (indeed, on the morality of dogs) have gained new prominence, not least because of the scrutiny Derrida has recently given these motifs in "L'Animal que donc je suis" and *Fichus*), Habermas excludes all other others—and, hence, all other incarnations of otherness—from the horizon of reason and rationality as presumably irrelevant: all living and nonliving nature that is not human, but also all humans who are no longer or not yet among the living, and, finally, all humans to whom, if only for a moment, we deny linguistic competence and autonomy (as in cases of immaturity, senility, psychiatric illness, delinquency within a given system of law, or supranational, war-related crimes). All these would require and merit a different consideration, for which the formal-pragmatic concept and procedure of rationality would merely constitute an *analogon*.

Unlike Levinas and Derrida, within the realm of relevant human others Habermas further seems to discount all relationships that are based on asymmetry, nonreciprocity, or misrecognition. He does not ignore or trivialize these relationships, but where they blatantly manifest themselves, he sees interaction, communication, discourse, and argumentation become interrupted or even terminated.

Habermas's outspokenly universalistic account is thus premised on a double exclusion that should give us pause: not only are not all others considered relevant, but, within the community of (potentially) relevant others, only symmetrical relationships are considered fit to exemplify— that is to say, initiate, establish, justify, and uphold—theoretical propositions, moral justifications, aesthetic judgments, and individual expressions whose communicative quality is deemed worthy of being called rational, reasonable, normative, authentic, and so on. All other relationships to the other, to others, indeed, to all other others—not least the one addressing the absolute Other, God—are bracketed for methodological reasons. Supposedly, we would not be able to say much about them in merely formal, rational, and universal terms.

There is a further, related difficulty. Surely the question of what is (to be) accepted or acknowledged as a "ground" or "reason" among relevant others solicits the problem of "criteria," as introduced by Wittgenstein in *Philosophical Investigations* and as analyzed at length in Stanley Cavell's *The Claim of Reason*. The question of finding grounds and giving reasons thus touches upon a certain indeterminacy and thus even ultimate undecidability, whose consequences for Habermas's analysis we should ponder. For one thing these consequences would seem to delimit the range not only of theoretical reason and propositional knowledge but also of moral reason and its practical discourse (to say nothing of aesthetic judgment, art being arguably the weakest point in Habermas's overall account of value spheres and value claims).

To limit ourselves to the second aspect of the double exclusion upon which Habermas bases the methodological, scholarly, and ascetic reconstruction and exposition of his universalism: could human morality (but also cognition, judgment, and expression) be plausibly characterized in Habermas's terms? Isn't there always a certain asymmetry and groundlessness in these (and all) value claims, for which reciprocal recognition, that is to say, understanding discursively mediated and produced, let alone consensus (whether provisional or final), cannot account? Should one not speak, with Levinas, of an irreducible "'curvature' of social space" which is — perhaps — "the very presence of God" (*TI* 291 / 267), or at least formally indistinguishable from the more religiously and ethically inflected interpretations of this transcendence in (and of?) immanence? By the same token should we not agree with Adorno when he stresses the unfathomable and nonetheless compelling character of ethical life (the *uneinsichtige Verbindlichkeit des Sittlichen*) and takes it as a model for "spiritual [*geistige*]" but also metaphysical, moral, and aesthetic experience (so that it affects cognition, deliberation, and perception from within)?

In an amendment to Habermas's construction of theoretical discourse, Kunneman suggests including at least a minimal reference to objective reality in the otherwise consensual and coherentist cognitive concept of reality.[23] If the concept of truth on which theories rely is to hook onto the world of things, actions, and events, it must point beyond its reconstruction in merely formal-pragmatic terms, without thereby being definable in terms of some *adaequatio rei et intellectus* or correspondence.

Similarly, we would suggest that there is a certain necessity for simultaneous lack and excess in practical discourse as well as in aesthetic and therapeutic critique. At issue here is a remainder and surplus of a minimal asymmetry, which can perhaps only be linguistically articulated or otherwise presented outside the medium and criteria that the theory of rationality (in its formal-pragmatic reconstruction) has available: discursive reasoning and the force of the better argument as pursued and ac-

23. Kunneman, *De waarheidstrechter*, 229.

knowledged by present, relevant human others. A negative metaphysical figure of thinking the ab-solute and a hermeneutic sensibility to singular instances might serve as alternatives to this discursive medium and these criteria—more precisely, as alternative models for analyzing what this medium and its standards entail and imply. Here we find ourselves at the core of a minimal theology, understood as a postmodern theology that resonates *in pianissimo* rather than in the propositions, that is to say, the dogmas and empirical hypotheses, employed by the classical study of divinity and the modern science of religion as cultural object, respectively.

The fact that, according to Habermas, consensus based on *symmetrical* intersubjective relationships finds its origin and even model in the *asymmetrical* order of the prelinguistic dimension of the divine and the sacred "originary consensus [*Urkonsens*],"[24] as analyzed by Durkheim and others, should not mislead us into understanding the structural asymmetry, the inevitable meta-communicative remainder and surplus, in a mythical or classical metaphysical sense. Nor should we hear in it the echoes of some lost organic or social totality in which ancient communities revered and retrospectively projected themselves or of what grounded, oriented, and exceeded them.

The analysis of structurally different validity claims ultimately touches upon a lack of foundation, or "anarchy,"[25] in every possible dimension of meaning. Yet the "force" expressed by the very concept of "validity" ought not necessarily to be understood as sacred, as Levinas has shown, or as mythical, as Adorno explains, or, I would add, as religious or even *normative,* in the general sense Habermas and others give to this word.[26] Although the meaning and weight of validity might be characterized in these historically variable ways, depending on how terms are defined at a given time and place, such characterizations can never be exclusive; nothing definitive can be said about them in any *strict* philosophical sense. This, and nothing else, is what the notion "ab-solute" and its nonsynonymous substitutes (transcendence, the infinite, the other, the trace, etc.) seek to convey. The utterance of and response to value claims are not governed by ontological, axiological, or evaluative codes in advance or once

---

24. The term comes from Kunneman, *De waarheidstrechter,* 257 ff. See also Habermas, *Theory of Communicative Action,* 2:48 ff. / 2:77 ff.

25. *OB* 198 n. 28 / 158–59 n. 28.

26. See Christine Korsgaard, *The Sources of Normativity,* with G. A. Cohen, Raymond Geuss, Thomas Nagel, and Bernard Williams, ed. Onora O'Neill (Cambridge: Cambridge University Press, 1996).

and for all. The task of elucidating this original or residual indeterminacy, which Levinas ascribes to philosophers, aptly illustrates this point: in his view philosophers are, traditionally, "not called to ascribe scientific certainty to the *essential* uncertainty of paths opened by the Revelation that must be sought out at one's own risk and peril. They came to make audible a voice whose tone must have been retained before hearing the Revelation, a tone familiar or a priori, a tone that, once heard, one must recognize in order to dare to trust spoken words." [27]

Neither appeal to some prior connection of moral ideas with the sacred in a postulated originary consensus, nor reference to an anamnestic solidarity with the dead, nor the hope of an eschatological sublation of suffering, nor the groundlessness of validity claims can connect Habermas's theory to theological ambitions of a classical, confessional, let alone apologetic nature. Nor does his theory fully justify the limitation of the theological to the empirical and historical study of religion as a cultural object. After Habermas, neither the ecclesial nor the modern academic study of the religious exhausts the place and unexplored possibilities of the religious. The minimal theologies that we sound out here—albeit *in pianissimo* and in the realm of the *pianissimo* which Weber diagnosed—signal in a different, if not directly opposite, direction. They allow us to read the same *otherwise*.

In so doing, given the decision to take Habermas's work as my point of departure, I must begin by observing not only the lacunae and surpluses revealed by ab-solute(s) within and between the value spheres and the "pores" of the life-world but also the minimal attention—especially in the emphasis on the "truth-analogous character" and, hence, moderately cognitive nature of normative validity claims—given to the relatively "strong incarnation" [28] of the evocative, poetic, or sacred meanings around which issues of sense in general and moral questions in particular circle. These questions cannot be resolved into a situation from which one could answer yes or no (*Ja/Nein Stellungnahme*), and, hence, they elude unambiguous, clear-cut, or consistently argued decision concerning their acceptability. Instead, they are bound up with undecidability, incalculability, and uncontrollability—which explains the residual decisionism, and hence the leaps of faith, in the theory of rationality as it concerns cognition, agency, expression, and judgment. Habermas, then, has

27. Emmanuel Levinas, *Transcendance et intelligibilité* (Geneva: Labor & Fides, 1984), 9.
28. See Burms and de Dijn, *De rationaliteit en haar grenzen*, 34.

to admit that formal-pragmatic analyses, as they have been carried out so far, "neglect the dimension of time and thus do not take into account phenomena of creative speech, the creative use of language."[29]

Indeed, neither the original motivating power that characterizes validity claims within the three different modalities nor the presumed possibility of eventually grounding them (if necessary or when asked) in a reasonable or otherwise acceptable way can be fully articulated at the explicit level of argument and discourse. Seel rightly points out that Habermas's indefatigable emphasis on "the central experience of the unconstrained, unifying, consensus-bringing force of argumentative speech [*die zentrale Erfahrung der zwanglos, einigenden, konsenstiftender Kraft argumentativer Rede*]"[30] cannot itself be theoretically—that is, argumentatively—articulated at all.[31] Within both theoretical and practical discourses, as well as within theoretical and therapeutic critique, the motivation and ultimate grounds for argumentation cannot be conceived as argumentation.[32]

29. Habermas, *Vorstudien und Ergänzungen*, 553.

30. Habermas, *Theory of Communicative Action*, 1:10 / 1:28.

31. See Martin Seel, "The Two Meanings of 'Communicative' Rationality," in Honneth and Joas, *Communicative Action*, 268 n. 17 / 70 n. 17. According to Seel, this experience, upon closer investigation, can only be thematized "without reduction [*unreduziert*]" in the interpretation of aesthetic phenomena (268 n. 17 / 71 n. 17). His book *Die Kunst der Entzweiung* offers a nuanced explication of this point of view by examining the aesthetic aspects that are constitutive of rationality from the very outset, as its necessary, albeit insufficient, conditions (9). In terms drawn from the Frankfurt School tradition of critical theory, he opposes both a "postmodern," aestheticizing critique of reason and the complementary, nondialectical "de-rationalizing [*Entrationalisierung*] of the aesthetic" (10). He holds aesthetic rationality to be one of the constitutive factors of "reason," but, unlike the author of the *Ältesten Systemprogramm*, he writes: "'The highest act of reason' is not 'an aesthetic act.'" According to Seel, (the concept of) reason which "is not aesthetic is not yet reason, and reason that becomes aesthetic is no longer reason." To emphasize that, in this quasi-differential description of the concept of reason in "second modernity," aesthetics is not a privileged center for the critique of reason, he adds: "Reason that is not moral, political, expressive, reflexive, or communicative, that is not habituated or institutionalized, not negative and playful . . . would not yet or not rightly be reason: however, if it were *only* or *primarily* this—mutual obligation, regulation of interests, ecstasy of revelation, excess of doubt, communion of those taking part, a habit, an ironic discharge, a game . . . then it would not or no longer be reason" (29). See also Seel, "Plädoyer für die zweite Moderne," in Kunneman and de Vries, *Die Aktualität der "Dialektik der Aufklärung,"* 36–66. Similarly, minimal theologies attempt to revive or interpolate an aesthetic portion of philosophical theology while seeking to avoid the complete dispersal of the theological into some artistic form or other, to say nothing of a lax aestheticism. Johan Huizinga's inaugural lecture, "Het aesthetisch bestanddeel van geschiedkundige voorstellingen [The Aesthetic Component in Historical Representations]," in his book *Verzamelde Werken* (Haarlem: H. D. Tjeenk Willink,1948–55), 7:3–28, can serve as a model here.

32. One is reminded of the difficulty Lyotard recalls in *The Postmodern Condition* when he writes that for the Wittgenstein of *Philosophical Investigations,* sec. 65–84, "the concept of the

Habermas himself inadvertently betrays the existence of this predicament by calling various metaphors—which, by his own definition, are hardly arguments—to his aid. They secretly draw on dimensions of the other (or Other) unearthed by the philosophy of the trace that I will reconstruct in Adorno and Levinas and whose method and implications no one has formalized more consistently than Derrida.

At crucial moments Habermas speaks of the "factual force of the counterfactual" or of the "must" of a weak "transcendental solicitation [*Nötigung*]"[33] validated in every—successful?—interaction. Furthermore, his texts themselves demonstrate that, in the "game of argumentation [*Argumentationsspiel*],"[34] we (can) never ascertain the decisive criteria that could distinguish the often conflicting appeals and demands of normative and aesthetic validity claims (and of these two from cognitive ones), nor, in different contexts, do we have any rule or certainty concerning how to apply them in appropriate, just, or elegant ways. The hermeneutic problem of application (*Applikation* or *Anwendung*) must be relegated to the faculty of judgment, reflexive and other, whose range and competence exceeds the parameters set by the theory of communicative reason, including its procedural ethics and, more rudimentarily, its conception of aesthetic critique.

In describing the postmetaphysical unity of modern moments of reason—while lacking, as we have seen, precise formal criteria for singling out value claims or governing their implementation—Habermas invokes the delicate balance of a "mobile." This figure implies, as do the other images cited earlier, an implicit acknowledgment of the irrevocable meta-

---

game cannot be mastered by a definition, since definition is already a language game" (*Postmodern Condition*, 8 n. 33 / 23 n.33). This is not to say, of course, that there could be a metalanguage—or a language game of some second order—from which the meaning of the term (*game* or, for that matter, *rule*) could be inferred or distilled. Following Wittgenstein, Lyotard notes "that if there are no rules, there is no game, that even an infinitesimal modification of one rule alters the nature of the game, that a 'move' or utterance that does not satisfy the rules does not belong to the game they define." And yet "every utterance should be thought of as a 'move' in a game" (19 / 23). Likewise, the game or the mobile of the forms of rational discourse (or the discursive forms of rationality) cannot be interpreted rationally, discursively, formally.

33. Habermas, *Philosophical Discourse of Modernity*, 206, 325 / 242, 378. See also Habermas, *Between Facts and Norms*, 4–5 / 18. Marquard notes with irony that we here encounter an abyss that must be bridged: "as a rule, one can maintain a greater distance from transcendental responsibilities than from empirical ones" (*Schwierigkeiten mit der Geschichtsphilosophie*, 73).

34. Habermas, *Die neue Unübersichtlichkeit*, 227. For the metaphor of the game, see Habermas, *Theory of Communicative Action*, 1:3, 363 / 1:112, 485; as well as Habermas, *Vorstudien und Ergänzungen*, 521, 539, 559.

phorization of philosophical concepts (and vice versa). Nietzsche, in "Über Wahrheit und Lüge in einem aussermoralischen Sinne" ("On Truth and Lying in an Extra-Moral Sense"), was the first to put forward this insight; Heidegger further amplified it in light of the history of Being, and Derrida and others (Davidson and Ricoeur being the most relevant, in our context) have systematized it. Although Habermas would in principle like to banish metaphor from questions of philosophical justification and from "reconstruction" in the empirical and sociocultural sciences — considering, like Kant, all illustrative or evocative figures to be so many parergonal forms of "aesthetic presentation," whose function is at best didactic — he apparently remains incapable of doing so and draws on figural representation where conceptual analysis, the appeal to criteria, and argumentative procedures fall short.

It comes as no surprise, therefore, that Habermas accuses Derrida of "aesthetic contextualism," that is to say, of blurring the boundaries between philosophy and literature,[35] and claims that Derrida, like Rorty, misses both the essential differences and the — intrinsic? — relationship between the "capacities for world-disclosure" of language, on the one hand, and its "problem-solving capacities," on the other.[36] Even more strongly, Habermas condemns Derrida's differential approach, claiming that he "holistically levels these complicated relationships,"[37] whereas Rorty's insistence on the incommensurability of the genres of discourse is taken to task on methodological grounds for being entrapped in an "objectivistic fallacy," that is to say, for objectifying Western rationality as a whole from without, from the perspective of a "fictive ethnology."[38]

Needless to say, the assertions that a deconstructive philosophy of difference and the trace could be understood "holistically" and that a pragmatist undoing of realist and representationalist knowledge claims is guilty of an "objectivist fallacy" might already indicate a misunderstanding of the philosophical positions in question. First, what Derrida would have us consider is merely that the distinction between a conceptual and a rhetorical use of language — a distinction Habermas both exploits

35. Habermas, *Philosophical Discourse of Modernity*, 205 / 241.

36. Ibid., 206, 207 / 241, 243. Habermas objects to Heidegger and Castoriadis on similar grounds (154 ff., 318 ff. / 182 ff., 370 ff.).

37. Ibid., 207 / 243.

38. See Habermas, "Questions and Counterquestions" in *Habermas and Modernity*, ed. Richard J. Bernstein (Cambridge: MIT Press, 1985), 194; and Habermas, *Philosophical Discourse of Modernity*, 59 / 74.

and ignores while failing to acknowledge his slippage from one register
into the other and leaving the consequences unanalyzed — is ultimately
arbitrary, undecidable. Whenever, like Habermas, one substitutes quasi-
transcendental, hypothetical, and fallible reconstructions — idealizations
and abstractions of the concrete occurrences of language and action —
for "ultimate foundations" (stating, e.g., that "theoretical truths exist in
actuality only in the form of plausibilities"),[39] whenever one captures their
meaning and effect with the help of metaphor or other figures of thought,
one has already admitted this seemingly trivial truth of deconstructive
philosophy. At times Habermas's own texts would seem to state as much —
for example, when he writes: "Stability and absence of ambiguity are rather
the exception in the communicative practice of everyday life. A more
realistic picture is that . . . of a diffuse, fragile, continuously revised and
only momentarily successful communication in which participants rely
on problematic and unclarified presuppositions and feel their way from
one occasional commonality to the next."[40] But, then, this observation
could serve as a counterpoint alone and does not dispense with the need
of human reason for successive idealizations. The counterpoint, therefore,
merits relativization in its turn.

Second, the debate between Habermas and Rorty should have made
it clear that pragmatism hardly relies on the "objectivistic" assumption —
or, worse, "fallacy" — of which it stands accused. Rorty merely insists on a
practically relevant distinction between a residually Platonic conception
of Truth and a merely pragmatic notion of justification which seems hard
to refute or ignore. But his appeal to the merely "cautionary" use of the
term *Truth* as a reminder of insights and agreements that occur in the presence of future — or other — audiences who may come along and challenge
what were until then held to be justified beliefs does not fully rid discourse
of its transcending moment. The very caution of such "truth" potentially
infinitizes discourse, rather than grounding it in some — definite or indefinite — unconditionality. From here on discourse keeps itself, if not principally then at least practically (morally and politically), open toward being
contested, indeed, contradicted, and must do so consciously, deliberately,
and performatively (which is precisely the attitude required and expressed
by a genuine concept and experience of democratic citizenship, societal

39. Habermas, *Die neue Unübersichtlichkeit,* 207.
40. Habermas, *Theory of Communicative Action,* 1:100–1 / 1:150; and Habermas, *Philosophical Discourse of Modernity,* 209–10 / 245–46.

solidarity, etc.). One could thus think of unconditionality, like truth, in a "cautionary" — Adorno would say negative or negative metaphysical — way. Conversely, wherever unconditionality would give itself *more* positively — as the "fugitive" and "ephemeral" experience on which Adorno's "ethical modernism" relies, according to the suggestion of J. M. Bernstein — it would resist at least a certain naturalization. *Naturalistic* would now come to mean merely that "nothing supports the practice other than the practice itself."[41]

The Task of Extradiscursive and Interdiscursive Judgment

Can an *external* connection between the aspects of rationality be produced or guaranteed by means of an "orderly, rationally controlled" transition among objectifying, normative, and expressive attitudes,[42] or by means of "a new step in the rationalization of the life-world"?[43] Does Habermas's analysis not once more bring into play a host of metaphors, together with an appeal to the practical capacity for judgment (both reflexive and other), because the external — that is to say, nonsubstantial and formal — unity of modern reason cannot be articulated within the theory of rationality itself? Were its presuppositions too ascetic, that is to say, not strong enough?

Let us recall Habermas's basic intuition, formulated in the context of his considerations concerning the discourse-theoretical reconstruction of the philosophy of law in its intrinsic relation to the concept of radical democracy:

> Moreover, a moral-practical self-understanding of modernity as a whole is articulated in the controversies we have carried on since the seventeenth

41. Bernstein, *Adorno*, 450. For a more sustained discussion by Habermas of Rorty's views, see the title essay of *Wahrheit und Rechtfertigung*, 230–70, trans. as "Richard Rorty's Pragmatic Turn," in *Rorty and His Critics*, ed. Robert B. Brandom (Oxford: Blackwell, 2000), 31–55. The same volume contains Rorty's detailed response (56–64), as well as his essay "Universality and Truth" (1–30), which incisively discusses Habermas's (and Albrecht Wellmer's) views. Here Rorty summarizes their agreement and (more fundamental) disagreement about the nature and ideal of reason: "Although I think Habermas is absolutely right that we need to *socialize* and *linguistify* the notion of 'reason' by viewing it as communicative, I also think that we should go further: we need to *naturalize* reason by dropping his claim that 'a moment of *unconditionality* is built into *factual processes* of mutual understanding'" (2; the quote is from Habermas, *Philosophical Discourse of Modernity*, 322–23 / 375).

42. Habermas, *Theory of Communicative Action*, 1:444 n. 84 / 1:442 n. 84.

43. Kunneman, *De Waarheidstrechter*, 280.

century about the best constitution of the political community. This self-understanding is attested to both by a universalistic moral consciousness and by the liberal design of the constitutional state. Discourse theory attempts to reconstruct this normative self-understanding in a way that resists both scientistic reductions [read Luhmann] and aesthetic assimilations [read Derrida]. The three dimensions of cognitive, evaluative, and normative validity that have been differentiated within the self-understanding of modernity must not be collapsed. After a century that, more than any other, has taught us the horror of existing unreason, the last remains of an essentialist trust in reason have been destroyed. Yet modernity, now aware of its contingencies, depends all the more on a procedural reason, that is, on a reason that puts itself on trial. The critique of reason is its own work: this double meaning, first displayed by Immanuel Kant, is due to the radically anti-Platonic insight that there is neither a higher nor a deeper reality to which we could appeal — we who find ourselves already situated in our linguistically structured forms of life.[44]

According to Seel, Habermas suggests that reason is not the same as argumentation — the latter is the possibility, in principle, of providing articulate reasons when necessary or if challenged. Reason, Seel contends, resides by contrast in the "capacity for an *interrational* judgment which itself cannot in turn be explained as a form of an excessive logic of argumentation."[45] The reasonable and critical character of this faculty of judgment depends upon the possibility of appropriating an "excessive association with the *immanent* other of each and every form of rationality."[46] That is something other than the metaphysical delimitation of modes of thought and experience "in the name of an *extraterritorial* Other of reason."[47] The thesis, articulated differently in the work of Adorno and of Levinas, that there could also be a *postclassical* metaphysical dimension of exteriority, of the nonidentical or the wholly Other, even if only in a fragmentary and aporetic way, yet which would nonetheless be constitutive of

44. Habermas, *Between Facts and Norms*, xl–xli / 11.

45. Seel, "Two Meanings of 'Communicative' Rationality," 46 / 67. Seel assumes, following Habermas, that theoretical, practical, and aesthetic judgment can in principle be founded (41; cf. 42 / 60; cf. 62) and speaks of the "wisdom [*Klugheit*] of the *problematization* which has to link the tact of transitions with the courage to interrupt" (47 / 67, trans. modified). Such a view remains polemically opposed to the French philosophy of absolute difference in general (47 / 68) and Derrida's supposed "totalization" of play in particular (45 / 66).

46. Ibid., 47 /68, my emph.

47. Ibid., my emph.

every conceivable concept of rationality or reason, will form the burden of my investigation.

The idea of a reasonable judgment that would oscillate (navigate rather than mediate, alternate rather than negotiate) between the forms of rationality draws its critical potential exclusively from an *openness* that is never sufficiently guaranteed by any one of the differentiated genres of discourse and their different criteria or regimens alone. The external connection between the forms of discourse is conceivable—without substantialist regression or uncritical affirmation of what merely positively exists—only through this oscillation between the (seemingly practical-aesthetic) capacity of judgment and the (seemingly theoretical or formal) idea of metaphysics in its novel, negative-critical guise.

An important question remains, however. How does this openness manifest or reveal itself? Does it manifest itself through detours into the natural or natural-historical features of human life in its transience and animality (Adorno), or does it reveal itself in the intersubjective realm of the ethical relationship, which produces itself as the infinite and in which God is said to leave His trace (Levinas)? Do these two possibilities constitute a genuine alternative?

Seel's observation that dealings with the alterity that permeates forms of rationality presuppose dealings with concrete—perhaps even all—*human* others seems to confirm the second reading: "This relationship with *the* other [dem *anderen*] of each and every justifiable orientation is . . . visibly related to our dealings with the *others* [*den* anderen]. . . . The constitutive perspectival character of reason cannot be thought of without at the same time conceiving of a plurality of subjects who depend on coordinating their actions in language."[48] But, then, is a given plurality of subjects ipso facto—or by its very nature—ethical, religious, or even spiritual in Levinas's sense, regardless of how it coordinates its actions, in language or otherwise? Moreover, would further qualifications or modifications of that plurality—say, in terms of unity, community, commonality, being-with, people, nation, democracy, but also love, friendship, brotherhood, mortality, and so forth—be equally open to and respectful of the alterity whose infinity or absoluteness we seek to convey? Could a genuine plurality of human subjects be thought and lived responsibly without addressing the other that is not of the order of the human: animality, the living in general, the artificial, the technological, and so on; or without addressing the

48. Ibid., 45 and 47 / 66 and 68, respectively.

others (human and other) who are not here and now present (dead, not yet living, not quite living, etc.)? What would, in principle, keep open the plurality in question? And on the ground of what judgment could we present—that is to say, instantiate and figure—it in a plausible, responsible, and prudent manner, depending on the plurality of situations (and hence the variety of contexts) which mark every here and now?

As we have seen, Habermas's analysis of each of the three value spheres and respective types of value claims touches upon a "moment of unconditionality" whose transcendence—albeit a "transcendence in immanence"—it can no longer articulate in theoretical, practical, or aesthetic terms. Hence, his recourse to metaphor, to figural presentation of the ab-solute *internal* to each discourse. Negative metaphysics, we indicated, formalizes this inevitable appeal at the heart of all idealization, exceeding any presupposition, and keeps it open for an illimitable series of non-synonymous substitutions, each of which instantiates and betrays the idea in question.

Conversely, Habermas's metaphorical description of communicative rationality indicates just how indispensable an *inter*discursive capacity for judgment is. The metaphor of *"uninhibited and balanced"* interplay between aspects of rationality does not emerge from one of the discourses out of which the structure of communicative rationality is supposedly constituted.[49] Rather, it alludes to something that always precedes and exceeds the triadic structure of world, social realm, and self, whose complex relation of *triangulation* (to cite Donald Davidson) apparently cannot fully—at least not consistently—be described in formal-pragmatic or discourse-theoretical terms.

This is no less true of the manner in which we assess the theoretical, practical, and aesthetic-subjective problems that confront us. They cannot be anticipated within the sphere of communicative reason and action as Habermas defines them or even with their aid. Instead, they impose themselves upon us empirically: "The life-world is so unproblematic for us that we cannot bring any part of it to consciousness at will, as a free-standing portion. That certain elements of the life-world become problematic for us is an objective process and depends on problems imposing themselves on us objectively from without, indicating that something has become problematic behind our backs."[50] Only retrospectively, Haber-

---

49. Habermas, "Reply," in Honneth and Joas, *Communicative Action,* 225 / 342.
50. Habermas, *Die neue Unübersichtlichkeit,* 187.

mas concedes, can they be argumentatively reconstructed and evaluated within the terms of a specific discourse, assessed in terms of their propositional truth, normative propriety (*Richtigkeit*), and subjective veracity (*Wahrhaftigkeit*), all of which owe their validity to an emphatic notion of formal, procedural reason and each of which can be brought into play — into constellation, as in a mobile — in the dynamic that holds the value spheres together, despite (or thanks to) their differentiation and which interprets and mediates their results in light of the general culture, at the crystallized edges of the system (state, market, power, and money) and at the very heart of the quotidian, that is to say, the life-world.[51]

Yet is there not reason to be skeptical about this all too harmonious perspective and the regulative idea upon which it is based? Is it still possible to hope for a correct, appropriate, genuine, even just balance between forms of rationality and forms of life in "postmodernity"? Can judgment, held in check by nonessentialist, formal, procedural justice — and, as I have suggested, by the ultimately negative metaphysical idea of absolute justice — bring this constellation about? Under present conditions can this pathos still be sustained?

According to Jean-François Lyotard, in *La Condition postmoderne* (*The Postmodern Condition*), the idea of justice remains determinant for any discourse, any philosophy, deserving of the name. If one thinks the idea through to its end, however, it turns out to be incompatible with any anticipated, actual, or future consensus, even (or especially?) those established under postulated, counterfactual, and idealized conditions. Somewhat bluntly and programmatically, Lyotard states: "Consensus has become an outmoded and suspect value [*valeur*]. But this does not apply to justice. We must thus arrive at an idea and practice of justice that is not linked to those of consensus."[52] This, however, cannot be done in a discursive, procedural, formal, and argumentative way, even though a certain notion of the pragmatic and of language games is crucial here. Moral obligation, Lyotard impresses upon his readers, does not belong to the order of dialogue.[53] Moreover, in light of the absolute heterogeneity of and irre-

---

51. Habermas, "Reply," in Honneth and Joas, *Communicative Action*, 227; cf. 225 / 345; cf. 343.

52. Lyotard, *Postmodern Condition*, 66 / 106, trans modified.

53. See Lyotard, *Differend*, 107 ff. / 159 ff. For reference to Levinas, see also Lyotard, *Postmodern Condition*, 40 / 66. For a more detailed analysis, see my essays "On Obligation"; and "*Sei gerecht!* Lyotard over de verplichting," in *Lyotard lezen: Ethiek, onmenselijkheid en sensibiliteit*, ed. H. Kunneman and R. Brons (Amsterdam: Boom, 1995), 32–49.

solvable conflict (or differend) between different genres of discourse and the regimes of their phrases, justice is, as Wolfgang Welsch aptly summarizes, "impossible as a real and positive form . . . and, in this sense, precisely, binding as an idea. The real implanting of this idea in this or that form would necessarily turn into its opposite, since it would have to occur in a specific form and thus dominate the heterogeneous. Only as long as one does not take this dialectic seriously or does not understand its unsublatable ground can one systematically install injustice in the name of justice and thus accuse the critics of this movement of defeatism."[54]

The task of judgment thus becomes problematic and paradoxical. It cannot refrain from establishing a "unity" that has become not only factically impossible because of the differentiation—Lyotard would say, the incommensurability—of language games but morally unjust as well. It thus ends up testifying to these aporias, that is to say, to the differend: postmodern knowledge, *The Postmodern Condition* claims in its opening pages, "refines our sensitivity to differences and reinforces our ability to tolerate the incommensurable."[55] For that reason Welsch is correct to assume that Lyotard's increasingly elaborate reprise of linguistic pragmatics establishes a "moralia linguistica."[56]

Lyotard, probably the most distinguished representative of philosophical postmodernism, for all his subsequent skepticism about this problematic term,[57] attempts to work out these thoughts in his magnum opus, *The Differend*, by outlining an "honorable postmodernity" and undertaking a radical correction of prior ideals of reason.[58] In the earlier, more circumstantial work *The Postmodern Condition,* Lyotard precisely and innocuously defines *postmodernity* (with reference to American sociologists and critics) as "the state of our culture following the transformations which, since the end of the nineteenth century, have altered the game rules for science, literature, and the arts,"[59] further as "incredulity" concerning the

54. Wolfgang Welsch, "Heterogenität, Widerstreit und Vernunft: Zu Jean-François Lyotards philosophischer Konzeption von Postmoderne," *Philosophische Rundschau* (1987): 170.

55. Lyotard, *Postmodern Condition,* xxv / 8–9.

56. Welsch, "Heterogenität, Widerstreit und Vernunft," 169.

57. On the determination of Lyotard's position within the literature of and about postmodernism, see Wolfgang Welsch, "Vielheit ohne Einheit? Zum gegenwärtigen Spektrum der philosophischen Diskussion um die 'Postmoderne': Französische, italienische, amerikanische, deutsche Aspekte," *Philosophisches Jahrbuch* 1 (1987): 111–41, esp. 112, 121, 135.

58. Lyotard, *Differend,* xiii, 11.

59. Lyotard, *Postmodern Condition,* xxiii / 7.

"grand narratives [*méta-récits*]" which had formed the driving force behind modernity: the Enlightenment ideal of an emancipation of humanity
within the confines of mere reason, in view of the establishment of a
"kingdom of ends" and an "eternal peace"; the organic teleology and dialectic of the spirit elaborated within German Idealism and continued in
another form in Marxism;[60] the program offered by a historical hermeneutics of the ultimate reconstruction of meaning; and, finally, the growth of
wealth within the confines of the market. Not only substantively but formally—that is, as the implicit assumption of a totality of sense, mediated
by thought, action, aesthetic experience, and expression—these specifically modern frames of thought have lost their credibility. This incredulity
toward metanarratives, Lyotard notes, giving his diagnosis an interesting twist, "is undoubtedly a product of progress in the sciences: but that
progress in turn presupposes it."[61]

Referring less to Kant here than to the tradition of modern sociology,
as well as, centrally, to the Wittgenstein of the *Philosophical Investigations,*
Lyotard starts from the assumption that classical and modern totalities
of meaning have disintegrated, dispersing into "clouds of narrative language elements—narrative, but also denotative, prescriptive, descriptive,
and so on. Conveyed within each cloud are pragmatic valences specific to
its kind."[62] These language games, made up of different types of enunciation or categories of utterance, which can no longer be reduced to a common denominator from any unifying perspective, are "clouds of sociality"
as well, albeit not in transparent ways, since the linguistically defined pragmatic elements cannot (easily) be translated into one another: "Each of us
lives at the intersection of many of these. However, we do not necessarily
establish stable language combinations, and the properties of the ones we
do establish are not necessarily communicable."[63] Lyotard thus disagrees
with the privilege that Habermas gives to the paradigm of communication, which he contests throughout *The Postmodern Condition,* stating that
"to speak is to fight, in the sake of playing,"[64] and recalling the meaning
of the *agōn* in Heraclitus, the first tragedies, the Sophists, Aristotle, and

60. Ibid., 12–13/ 28–29; and Lyotard, *Differend,* 171 / 246. Here Lyotard contends that Marxism can only continue as a "feeling of the differend."
61. Lyotard, *Postmodern Condition,* xxiv / 7.
62. Ibid., xxiv / 8.
63. Ibid.
64. Ibid., 10 / 23.

Nietzsche. Yet he affirms, with Habermas, that "the observable social bond is composed of language 'moves.'"[65] In consequence, does not a certain *methodological linguisticism*—whether established in view of the principal possibility, if not the ultimate horizon, of consensus or in the name of inevitable dissensus and differend—form the starting point for both these authors, at least in the writings that concern us here? Would not our proposed turn to the "curvature of social space" (Levinas) or to the concept of "natural history" (Adorno) gesture in an altogether different direction, namely, toward elements and motifs whose medium is not limited to language, not articulated in light of its discursive value claims, simple yes-and-no positions, and more inventive "blows"? Lyotard, at least, seems more cautious here:

> I am not claiming that the *entirety* of social relations is of this nature—that will remain an open question. But there is no need to resort to some fiction of social origins to establish that language games are the minimum relation required for society to exist: even before he is born, if only by virtue of the name he is given, the human child is already positioned as the referent in the story recounted by those around him, in relation to which he will inevitably chart his course. Or more simply still, the question of the social bond, insofar as it is a question, is itself a language game, the game of inquiry. It immedi-

65. Ibid., 11 / 24. There would perhaps be a further parallel when Lyotard notes: "there is a strict interlinkage between the kind of language called science and the kind called ethics and politics: they both stem from the same perspective, the same 'choice,' if you will—the choice called the Occident" (8 / 20). Later he writes: "what is meant by the term *knowledge* is not only a set of denotative statements, far from it. It also includes notions of 'know-how,' 'knowing how to live,' 'how to listen' [*savoir-faire, savoir-vivre, savoir-écouter*], etc. Knowledge, then, is a question of competence that goes beyond the simple determination and application of the criterion of truth, extending to the determination and application of criteria of efficiency (technical qualification), of justice and/or happiness (ethical wisdom), of the beauty of a sound or color (auditory and visual sensibility), etc." (18 / 36).

There is thus a formal resemblance and affiliation between, on the one hand, the pragmatic rules to which the language game of cognition is subject—namely, enunciations that are "true of . . . ," as Lyotard, following Quine's *Word and Object,* identifies them (ibid., 88, n. 29 / 21 n. 19)—and the regime to which prescriptives and directives concerning morality and legal, administrative, and political authority pertain, on the other. Mutatis mutandis, the same holds for utterances and expressions that belong within the domain of the aesthetic. For Habermas this structural analogy and filiation is not a "choice" but the sign of the "unity of reason in the multiplicity of its voices." What is more, it is a quasi-transcendental necessity and solicitation (*Nötigung*), albeit one whose appeal we can choose to follow up on, to live up to, or not. To ignore it is be far from easy, however, not only because of the dire consequences said to result from doing so but also because one cannot simply "choose" to forget or undo "learning processes," whether ontogenetic or phylogenetic.

ately positions the person who asks, as well as the addressee and the referent asked about: it is already the social bond.[66]

Rather than understanding postmodernity to be a departure from a distinctly demarcated era of modernity, we should see it as the "fulfilled format [*Einlösungsform*] of specifically modern contents."[67] Thus defined, the term need not allude to any form of "transmodernity"; instead, it signals the becoming exoteric of experiences that had previously been expressed esoterically, especially in avant-garde art, namely, experiences of the increasingly and irrevocably pluriform or even heterogeneous character of the modern life-world. Like *modernity*, the term *postmodernity* denotes an undelimitable, undecidable, open time span.[68]

According to Lyotard, the differences between language games and their agonistics, which constitute the postmodern polymorphy or heteromorphy, contain no credible, counterfactual allusion to consensus. Incommensurable disparities occur not only within certain genres of discourse (as my insistence on the negative metaphysical trace internal to Habermas's value spheres and their respective claims and modes of argumentation pointed out) but also, and especially, between divergent forms of speech and action, leading inevitably to conflict and dissent. Consensus is a regulative idea in some language games, Lyotard concedes, but certainly not in all of them. The discourse theories of consensus (read Apel and Habermas) rest, in his eyes, on at least two inadmissible premises: "The first is that it is possible for all speakers [*locuteurs*] to come to agreement on which rules or metaprescriptions are universally valid for language games, when it is clear that language games are heteromorphous, subject to heterogeneous sets of pragmatic rules. The second assumption is that the goal [*finalité*] of dialogue is consensus. But ... consensus is only a particular state of discussions, not their end. Their end, on the contrary,

66. Ibid., 15 / 32.

67. Welsch, "Vielheit ohne Einheit?" 111. See also M. Köhler, "'Postmodernismus': Ein begriffsgeschichtlicher Überblick," *Amerikastudien* 22 (1977): 8–18; H. Bertens, "Die Postmoderne und ihr Verhältnis zum Modernismus: Ein Überblick," in *Die unvollendete Vernunft: Moderne versus Postmoderne*, ed. D. Kamper and W. van Reijen (Frankfurt a.M.: Suhrkamp, 1987), 46–98; and W. Hudson, "Zur Frage postmoderner Philosophie," in Kamper and van Reijen, *Die unvollendete Vernunft: Moderne versus Postmoderne*, 122–56.

68. For Lyotard's own comments on the *post* of postmodernity, see Jean-François Lyotard, *Le Postmoderne expliqué aux enfants* (Paris: Galilée, 1988), 126 / *The Postmodern Explained*, trans. Julian Pefanis and Morgan Thomas (Minneapolis: University of Minnesota Press, 1993), 80.

is paralogy."[69] A more adequate description of postmodern reality, therefore, would aim toward a "general" or "linguistic agonistics" rather than
a theory of communication.[70] The philosopher, Lyotard says, must bear
witness to conflict, because only conflict poses a singular, insurmountable obstacle to the hegemony of the economic rationality of ends and
means.[71] Systemic rationality, to use one of Habermas's terms (adopted
from "systems theory," i.e., from Talcott Parsons and Luhmann), threatens increasingly to eliminate "the occurrence, the event, the wonder, the
expectation of a community of sentiments [*l'attente d'une communauté
de sentiments*]."[72] Lyotard agrees with Adorno that such testimony makes
necessary a strategy of "micrologies." Micrology implies abandoning the
Archimedean point — the "observatory"[73] — of the critique of ideology, on
whose basis the classical intellectual always imagined himself to be the
representative of universality.[74]

For Habermas, as for Lyotard, acknowledging the differentiation of
genres of discourse with their respective value claims, types of enunciation, and pragmatic rules or criteria is the *conditio sine qua non* of every
relevant modern or postmodern philosophical thought, action, expression, and judgment. Yet they encounter the biases and contradictions that
mark the "new obscurity [*neue Unübersichtlichkeit*]" in seemingly opposite ways.[75] Habermas hopes to reconstruct a non-Hegelian mediation between discourses that could function as a therapy for social and individual
pathologies and paradoxes. To this end he expands his diagnosis of the age
with a comprehensive theory of rationality aimed at making feasible the
formal or procedural unification of disparate moments of reason. More
precisely, he seeks to liberate their interplay, as in a disentangled, freely
moving mobile. Lyotard, by contrast, defends — and starts out from — the
radical heterogeneity of different language games. Not only does he assume that the essentially ambivalent character of modern reality creates
or expresses a loss of meaning and orientation, but he also expects the

69. Lyotard, *Postmodern Condition*, 65–66 / 106, trans. modified; see also Lyotard, *Postmodern Explained*, 3 / 16.

70. Lyotard, *Postmodern Condition*, 88 n. 35 / 23 n. 35.

71. Lyotard, *Differend*, 181 / 260.

72. Ibid., 178 / 255.

73. Lyotard, *Postmodern Condition*, 12 / 27.

74. See Jean-François Lyotard, *Tombeau de l'intellectuel et autres papiers* (Paris: Galilée,
1984), 85. On Adorno, see Lyotard, *Postmodern Explained*, 96 / 115.

75. See Richard Rorty, "Habermas and Lyotard on Postmodernity," in *Habermas and Modernity*, ed. Richard J. Bernstein (Cambridge: MIT Press), 161–75.

undeniable incredulity concerning the grand metanarratives, which once sought to counter or gloss over this tendency, to increase our capacities and opportunities for thought, action, expression, and judgment. How should we evaluate this difference, this differend, if it is one?

Welsch maintains that Lyotard's critique of Habermas is justified, but only in part. Habermas's "catalogue of the forms of reason"[76] seems to him too narrow, leaving no room, for example, for a particularly religious form of rationality. Welsch offers no suggestion, not even approximately, concerning what such a religious form of rationality might look like. Yet this should not surprise us: could the specifically religious ever be adequately described through a particular, let alone unique, form of rationality? In addition, Welsch finds Habermas's theory too formalistic, inasmuch as it overhastily identifies attempts to decipher philosophically intra- and interdiscursive incommensurabilities with a tendency toward irrationality. Yet Lyotard's position, he thinks, leads to consequences that are simply absurd. If the heterogeneity between the different kinds of discourse and between the differences that play themselves out among phrases within them is made *absolute,* then it is difficult to see how he can still speak of the *suppression* of the internal or external other.[77] Even the mutual delimitation of forms of discourse would then be inexplicable. Thus, the "general" or "linguistic agonistics" and the "honorable post-modernity" testified to by the philosophy of *The Differend* could, in this reading, only be carried out in a limited, or mitigated, way. If one ignores the merely relative nature of the separation between the genres of discourse and their respective pragmatic rules and criteria, then one must view the former interweaving of value spheres and value claims in the diffuse totalities of myth or in the imaginary of historical religion only as a "category mistake" that could always have been avoided. One would then lose sight of the fact that even the "separation between *is* and *ought*" is in all probability less an anthropological or linguistic constant than the product of a historical, even specifically modern, constellation. As Alisdair MacIntyre observes, "Moral incommensurability is itself the product of a particular historical conjunction."[78]

76. Welsch, "Hetergenität, Widerstreit und Vernunft," 185.

77. Welsch, "Vielheit oder Einheit?" 139; and Welsch, "Heterogenität, Widerstreit und Vernunft," 178.

78. MacIntyre, *After Virtue,* 69. But some caution is needed here. Lyotard is careful to distinguish his position from the one ascribed to Baudrillard, which takes the "breaking up of the grand narratives" to imply the almost complete "dissolution of the social bond and the dis-

In the reading of Welsch (like those of Habermas and Seel), the idea of the absolute heterogeneity or incommensurability of discourse inadvertently brings into play an assumption that Lyotard plainly mistrusts: namely, the comprehensive view "from nowhere" of an ideal observer not caught up in discursive practices. Such a position, however, when taken literally, performatively contradicts itself. As a theoretical, practical, or aesthetic *position*, it states, acts out, or presents as a universal and intelligible claim what from its own perspective it cannot uphold in full rigor or seriousness. In other words, the postmodern skeptic cannot disguise the fact that absolute heterogeneity or radical incommensurability can only be thought, lived, and expressed as a counterpoint, of sorts. Nothing more, nothing less.

Neither the postulating of philosophical historical (quasi-Hegelian) total syntheses, which would appear in the form of idealist or materialist dialectical mediation and reconciliation, nor the complementary hypos-

---

integration of social aggregates into a mass of individual atoms thrown into the absurdity of Brownian motion." Rebutting this position, Lyotard writes, "Nothing of the kind is happening: this point of view, it seems to me, is haunted by the paradisaic representation of a lost 'organic' society" (*Postmodern Condition,* 15 / 31). Referring to Robert Musil's *Der Mann ohne Eigenschaften* (*The Man without Qualities*), he summarizes its perspective as: "Each individual is referred to himself. And each of us knows that our *self* does not amount to much" (15 / 30). He continues: "A *self* does not amount to much, but no self is an island; each exists in a fabric of relations that is now more complex and mobile than ever before. Young or old, man or woman, rich or poor, a person is always located at 'nodal points' of specific communication circuits, however tiny these may be" (15 / 31). Interestingly, though it points beyond my present scope, he then characterizes these "circuits" in postal terms, as Derrida had earlier in *The Post Card* (*La Carte postale: De Socrate à Freud et au-delà* [Paris: Flammarion, 1980] / *The Postcard: From Socrates to Freud and Beyond,* trans. Alan Bass [Chicago: University of Chicago Press, 1987]).

Lyotard continues his critique of Baudrillard in his discussion of the concept of progress and of "development," an idea that founds the evolutionary assumptions in theories of modernization from Kant and especially Hegel onward and which motivates Derrida to distinguish sharply between differentiality—in terms of the displacement and temporalization of *différance*—and the idealist-organicist understanding of dialectical differentiation (see "Difference," in *Margins of Philosophy*). He argues that the concept of development permeates the Western understanding of "formation [*Bildung*]," indeed, of "culture" generally speaking. He writes: "The very idea of development presupposes a horizon of nondevelopment where, it is assumed, the various areas of competence remain enveloped in the unity of a tradition and are not differentiated according to separate qualifications subject to specific innovations, debates, and inquiries. This opposition does not necessarily imply a difference in nature between 'primitive' and 'civilized' man [referring to Lucien Lévy-Bruhl's *La Mentalité primitive*], but is compatible with the premise of a formal identity between 'the savage mind' and scientific thought [referring to Claude Lévi-Strauss, *La Pensée sauvage* (*The Savage Mind*)]; it is even compatible with the (apparently contrary) premise of the superiority of customary knowledge over the contemporary dispersion of competence" (19 / 37–38).

tasis of the separation of aspects of rationality stressed by a radical philosophy of the differend seems capable of plausibly describing the regime
that governs language games and forms of life in postmodernity. At best
they can—rhetorically, *cum grano salis*—indicate the logical extremes and
potential risks of common experiences and, hence, carry within themselves the possibility of a critical counterpoint as well as its (perhaps unavoidable) perversion or, rather, "pervertibility" (Derrida).

One might suspect, therefore, that a philosophy of difference and of
the differend which could mitigate the ambition and scope of a comprehensive theory of rationality is itself, in turn, subject to further qualification, which restricts, modifies, or displaces its supposed radicality (in its
ontology, epistemology, ethics, and aesthetics). In this respect it resembles
the radical Pyrrhonism whose temptation David Hume knew only too
well. Its apparently invulnerable arguments may make this version of
skepticism seem unavoidable, and yet it can be sustained—and lived—
only in tempered form: "Nature is always too strong for principle."[79] That
does not eliminate the fact that it can have an equally sobering and intoxi-
cating therapeutic—or, better, heuristic—effect, especially if one employs
it to confront presumptuous theoretical assertions, moralism, and kitsch.

To make ab-solute differences theoretically absolute could result in
only a new terror or a petrified silence. Reason and reasonableness are,
by contrast, always dependent upon connections, oscillations, and the
crossing of demarcations. In order to elucidate this point, Welsch introduces a concept of "transverse reason,"[80] which, in his opinion, better
accounts for the legitimate efforts he recognizes in Lyotard's postmodernism. Welsch understands this idea of reason to be primarily aesthetic,
although it could just as well be seen in light of the transcending gesture
of the metaphysical, which the classical tradition cut short (and liberated
in its semantic and figural potential only in "solidarity with metaphysics
in its downfall").[81] Nonetheless, neither "transverse reason" nor judgment
nor a paradoxical or even aporetic idea of absolute justice that has been
de-transcendentalized into a critical corrective can suffice to determine
the idea of a nonbisected rationality. For that, a metaphysical supplement

---

79. David Hume, *Enquiries concerning Human Understanding and concerning the Principles
of Morals*, ed. L. A. Selby-Bigge and P. H. Nidditch (Oxford: Oxford University Press, 1975),
160.

80. Welsch, "Vielheit ohne Einheit?" 139–41; Welsch, "Heterogenität, Widerstreit und Vernunft," 180 ff.; and Welsch, *Unsere postmoderne Moderne*, 2d ed. (Weinheim: VCH, 1988), 294 ff.

81. Welsch, "Heterogenität, Widerstreit und Vernunft," 180–81.

remains necessary, though such an idea can be realized only if classical-modern metaphysics no longer leads the way.

Such "perspectivism," free from the deceptive dogma of the philosophy of origins as well as from a radical utopianism and God's-eye point of view, need not operate as Nietzsche envisioned. Adorno's and Levinas's figures of thought, which likewise touch upon — and reach beyond — the limits of "modernity" and its grand narratives, indicate a more promising alternative. Before turning to the details of their respective itineraries, central arguments, conceptual strategies, and rhetorical devices, however, it seems useful to summarize what I have established thus far.

Negative Metaphysics

My discussion thus far confirms Schnädelbach's assessment of the "impossibility of completely representing rationality in principles, rules, or norms."[82] The fact that rationality is in principle an "open concept" inevitably leads, according to him, to an examination of the *historicity of reason* and the acknowledgment of an irrevocable *residual decisionism in ethics*. Reason can never sufficiently be explicated because it can "never arrive at a totalizing theory of rationality in the sense that would make it possible fully to internalize its external conditions."[83] Of Apel's transformation of philosophy, with its ideal of "ultimate foundation [*Letztbegründung*]" and its strong assumption of the "ideal of a community of communication" — the two central constituents of his "transcendental pragmatics" — Schnädelbach says, "There is no transcendental-pragmatic 'first philosophy' and thus also no discourse-ethical [*kommunikationsethisches*] equivalent to Kant's 'fact of pure practical reason.'"[84] The objection, especially its second part, seems fatal to Habermas's undertaking as well.

As I have established, Habermas distances himself not only from any substantial metaphysical backing for the theory of communicative action and the discourse ethics it proposes but also from Apel's ambition to offer a *transcendental*-pragmatic "*ultimate* foundation" of reason and

82. Herbert Schnädelbach, "Bemerkungen über Rationalität und Sprache," *Vernunft und Geschichte: Vorträge und Abhandlungen* (Frankfurt a.M.: Suhrkamp, 1987), 76.

83. Ibid., 167.

84. Ibid. On the motif of the historicity of reason, see also 88 ff.; and Schnädelbach, "Zur Dialektik der historischen Vernunft," also in *Vernunft und Geschichte*, 47–63. See also Albrecht Wellmer, *Ethik und Dialog: Elemente des moralischen Urteils bei Kant und in der Diskursethik* (Frankfurt a.M.: Suhrkamp, 1986), 82–85 / *The Persistence of Modernity: Essays on Aesthetics, Ethics, and Postmodernism*, trans. David Midgley (Cambridge: MIT Press, 1991), 168–70.

morality:[85] no "first philosophy" could replace or transform the age-old drive toward grounds that would in principle be of an essentialist nature, namely, a *fundamentum in re*. By the same token a reconstructive appropriation of objective, let alone subjective, idealism—whether resituated with the aid of Peirce (a constant reference for Apel) or reformulated in a critical reassessment of Hegel's and Fichte's systems (as undertaken by Vittorio Hösle)[86]—is no longer available to "us."

Yet shifting toward a formal, universal, yet fallible and *quasi*-transcendental reconstruction of counterfactual presuppositions hardly protects Habermas's program from Schnädelbach's objection that, in comparison with Apel's version, his pragmatic reconstruction of the ideal speech situation only displaces the "sizable burden of proof" requisite to establish it as a general theory worthy of the name.[87] Not only must the attempt to explicate the concept of rationality remain far more hypothetical than Habermas intends, but to be comprehensive, coherent, and explanatory the theory must somehow point—and be carried—beyond itself. Its success would imply its failure, and yet, paradoxically (extending Schnädelbach's suggestion a bit further), this failure implies a certain success as well. Precisely in its aporias and performative contradictions—and there are more than one—the theory of communicative action and discourse ethics, together with its discursive theory of rights, democracy, law, and sovereignty, reveals its greatest insights.

Schnädelbach's point of departure is the question of post-Hegelian historicism and historical situatedness as it affects philosophical concepts and theories. From a different perspective Albrecht Wellmer observes that the central premise of both transcendental (Apel) and formal (Habermas) pragmatics—namely, the possibility of eventual consensus as the telos of all mutual understanding (*Verständigung*)—is fundamentally flawed: "If . . . we transfer the function of guaranteeing truth to an infinite rational consensus, then it is strictly speaking no longer possible to speak of *redemption* [or resolution, *Einlösung*] of validity claims."[88] This being said, the question remains what the "unconditionality built into factual processes of mutual understanding" and "resolution"—or, in the unmistak-

85. Habermas, *Theory of Communicative Action,* 1:137 / 1: 198.

86. See Vittorio Hösle, *Hegels System: Der Idealismus der Subjektivität* (Hamburg: F. Meiner, 1987); and his contribution to Wolfgang Kuhlmann, ed., *Moralität und Sittlichkeit: Das Problem Hegels und die Diskursethik* (Frankfurt a.M.: Suhrkamp, 1986).

87. Habermas, *Theory of Communicative Action,* 1:138 / 1:198.

88. Wellmer, *Persistence of Modernity,* 166 / *Ethik und Dialog,*79.

ably religious and theological idiom of which Wellmer is suspicious, "redemption"—might then mean. Maybe "unconditionality" would, from now on, signal *nothing in this world,* nothing attainable here, even given endless time and space—that is to say, the possibility of infinite approximation, albeit under the most ideal communicative conditions. But if this is so—and if we must avoid theological language, as Wellmer, who is especially critical of Adorno, claims—how can we *naturalize* reason, the unconditional, or the ab-solute *without* absolutizing, indeed rationalizing, nature, as opposing schools of metaphysics and materialism, or philosophies of nature and scientism, have always pretended to do?

Schnädelbach notes that the quasi-transcendental rules we attribute to rationality can never be reconstructed independently of their empirical use: "Language is *impure* reason—that is, reason influenced by empiricism and marked with contingency."[89] The theory of rationality and discourse ethics cannot, therefore, guarantee its own rationality—that is to say, its (motif of and motivation for) unconditionality. For all the theory's insistence on the embodiment or incarnation (*Verkörperung*) of reason, this irreducible empiricity—and, hence, always already naturalistically reduced "unconditionality"—is not permissible or justifiable on the basis of premises within the theory itself. From this Schnädelbach draws the lesson that "a discourse theory becomes philosophical only when, beyond the phenomenology and classification of types of discourse, it reflects upon the conditions of possibility of the *adequacy* and *relevance* [*Sachangemessenheit*] of such discourses."[90] This typically philosophical reflection, he claims, requires reference to *extra*discursive elements and dimensions.

Schnädelbach describes such reference as metaphysical—more precisely, with reference to Adorno, as the very task of negative metaphysics. Implying neither an ontology nor a doctrine of value, as does classical and modern "positive" metaphysics, it recalls only that the true and the good (and, we should add, the beautiful) concern something that can never be expressed or even anticipated in discourse "but must, rather, show [*zeigen*] itself and be experienced."[91] The true, the good, and the beautiful concern more than consensus alone. And they do not correspond to some preceding reality or set of principles and rules: "In this understanding,

89. Schnädelbach, *Vernunft und Geschichte,* 85; see also 89. In precisely this sense we could once again agree with Marquard: "The factical is the a priori of the principal" (*Abschied vom · Prinzipiellen,* 17).

90. Ibid., 168, my emph.

91. Ibid., 171–72.

the term *negative metaphysics* does not point in the direction of prior constitutive conditions of knowledge independent of the subject, but rather to something which must *be supplemented* [*hinzutreten*] if our knowledge is to be true and our lives good."[92] This motif of the supplement—in Adorno's words, that which adds on, adds up, *das Hinzutretende*—will concern us extensively in the next chapter.

In practical and theoretical philosophy Kant's limit concepts of the "thing in itself" and the "highest good" are important examples of this supplement to the formal concept and differentiation of rationality—that is, of communicative action and the entire spectrum of its validity claims (propositional truth, normative rightness, and sincerity or expressiveness). But the crowning witness is, Schnädelbach argues, Adorno's negative dialectics, with its invocation of metaphysical, spiritual (*geistige*) experience. When Adorno closes *Negative Dialectics* with the paradoxical claim that thought should be "in solidarity with metaphysics at the moment of its downfall" (*ND* 408 / 400), he hints at a negative metaphysics. That is, in metaphysical thought we should seize the momentum revealed whenever its Icarus flight turns into free fall. Metaphysical ideas, Adorno seems to suggest, neither reflect some positive presence nor stand in for mere absence; they signal something in between, whose modality (if we can still call it that) forms the condition of possibility for and the very element of thought, experience, agency, and judgment under modern conditions, especially "after Auschwitz."

There exists, Adorno says, an unheard and undiminished relevance of metaphysics which—with respect to dogmatic theology as well as the scientific discovery of whatever is the case—represents "the moment [*das Moment*] of free, unguided, and unregimented thought."[93] It is in this speculative gesture and freedom that, he writes, "in a motivated way we exceed what is the case, because what confronts us demands as much."[94] Yet this metaphysical speculation remains negative because it does not employ dogmatic suppositions nor allow definitive conclusions. Echoing,

92. Schnädelbach, "Dialektik und Diskurs," in *Vernunft und Geschichte*, 172, my emph. See also Anke Thyen, *Negative Dialektik und Erfahrung: Zur Rationalität des Nichtidentischen* (Frankfurt a.M.: Suhrkamp, 1989), 281–88.

93. Theodor W. Adorno, *Philosophische Terminologie*, ed. R. zur Lippe, 2 vols. (Frankfurt a.M.: Suhrkamp, 1974), 2:168. The study of these texts should now be supplemented with Adorno, *Metaphysik: Begriff und Probleme*, ed. Rolf Tiedemann (Frankfurt a.M.: Suhrkamp, 1998) / *Metaphysics: Concept and Problems*, trans. Edmund Jephcott (Stanford: Stanford University Press, 2000).

94. Adorno, *Philosophische Terminologie*, 2:168.

as it were, Russell's demarcation between the criteria for theological and
scientific inquiry, Adorno's characterization of speculation's openness and
freedom in principle turns philosophy into a peculiar activity or exercise. Far from formulating hypotheses, let alone theses, which could be
deduced from simple axioms and related ideas or which could be verified, falsified, corroborated, or demonstrated by equally simple matters of
fact, speculation consists in a tireless questioning or in a reticent, skeptical exercise of the dialectic of question and answer which, following a
well-known hermeneutic topos (spelled out in detail by Gadamer in his
monumental *Truth and Method*), characterizes all true philosophizing.
Although such thinking must be distinguished from what Adorno understands as classical theology, the lines of demarcation between speculative solidarity with metaphysics in its downfall and the theological remain
essentially unclear. At times Adorno suggests that theology is classical —
that is to say, dogmatic and an imposition, *by definition* — thus leaving philosophy no other possibility than to demand its "secularization into the
concept," namely, into metaphysics (associated first with its classical systems, then, now that these have become untenable, with metaphysics in
its downfall). At other times he suggests that "theology properly speaking [*die eigentliche Theologie*] is, rather, a postmetaphysical phase of consciousness,"[95] thereby implying that theology *strictu sensu* — and not just
"the other theology [*die andere Theologie*]" (unless this term indicates the
original intent and strength of theology all along) — is, in fact, nothing
other than the postmetaphysical metaphysics that we have called "negative." Negative metaphysics thus locates itself at once squarely *within* the
theological tradition and well *beyond* it; by the same token it seems to
transcend the given without being able to do so. The difference would be
impossible to tell.

> Metaphysics opposes the totality [*Inbegriff*] of facts with which we concern
> ourselves in science with a fundamental otherness [*ein prinzipiell Anderes*],
> without requiring of this other that it exist, as theologies tend to do with

95. Ibid., 2:164; cf. 2:167. In a letter to Scholem Adorno equates the "primacy [or preva-
lence, *Vorrang*] of the object" with the very meaning of materialism. Yet this materialism, he
goes on to say, should not be misunderstood as "conclusive [*abschlusshaft*]," as a "worldview
[*Weltanschauung*]," or as something "fixed [*Fixiertes*]." On the contrary, at issue is a version
of materialism which is no longer tied backwards to idealism but is liberated from "dogma
[*Dogma*]" and, thereby, reveals striking affinities with metaphysics — indeed, Adorno cautiously adds, with theology ("I would almost have said: with theology [*beinahe hätte ich gesagt:
zur Theologie*]" (cited after Müller-Doohm, *Adorno*, 662–63).

their divinities [*Gottheiten*]; for the existence of divinities belongs to them in a much different sense from what can be claimed, for example, of concepts. From this arises the idea of metaphysics as a kind of no-man's-land, a castle in Cloudcuckooland — that is to say, a realm in which things take on a nebulous quality [or take a nebulous turn, *in dem es nebulös zugeht*]. What exists is not enough for this thought; but it does not, in turn, acknowledge the existence of what is more than merely being [*dem, was mehr ist, als bloss zu sein spricht es nicht selber zu, dass es sei*].[96]

Curiously, Schnädelbach does not mention the passages in these lectures, concluding, instead, that "Adorno does not himself speak of negative metaphysics, because he has in mind [*ins Auge fasst*] a metaphysics beyond or after the end of dialectics, including that of negative dialectics" and indicating that, in his (and Adorno's) view, this is also "why negative dialectics cannot be the organon of negative metaphysics."[97] To be more than a silent and powerless figure or gesture of thinking, a negative metaphysics, Schnädelbach argues, must be integrated into a "critical discourse."[98] To do so would mean dissociating the two connotations of dialectics which Adorno seems to conflate: the Platonic notion of dialectics as *dialegēsthai* and the Hegelian (and vulgar Marxist) definition of dialectics as a process and force in reality — that is, in nature and history — which, according to Schnädelbach, Adorno inverts into what *Negative Dialectics* calls an "ontology of the false situation [*Ontologie des falschen Zustandes*]."[99]

Freed from every positive (ontologized) feature, negative metaphysics, in Schnädelbach's reading, does not formalize or metaphorically evoke the intra- or interdiscursive modalities of asymmetry and interplay but, rather, continually recalls the extradiscursive (i.e., historically situated and indeterminate or contingent) conditions of every discourse that has come about. Being a critical corrective, it simultaneously acknowledges that rationality must be thought of as an *open concept* and protects the theory of rationality from once more locking itself into a Hegelian circle: "Dialectics as negative must take care that our theory of rationality remains rational."[100]

96. Adorno, *Philosophische Terminologie*, 2:163.
97. Schnädelbach, *Vernunft und Geschichte*, 176 n. 37.
98. Ibid.
99. Ibid.
100. Adorno, *Philosophische Terminologie*, 2:163.

How, then, can we refer to the extradiscursive conditions of discourse — that is, the true, the good, the beautiful or sublime, which cannot simply be reduced to conversational, dialogical, and communicative qualities nor be identified with states of affairs which could be described — in an *open,* more Platonic than Hegelian, dialectic without ipso facto concurring with the classical metaphysical tradition and its substantial (idealist, materialist, realist, or naturalist) presuppositions?[101] By contrast to the reception of Adorno's negative dialectics in debates concerning aesthetics (in particular, the philosophy of "new music"), in which its specific contribution has been well established, Schnädelbach suggests that the translation of negative dialectics into present-day theoretical and practical philosophical terms remains an open question.

At this juncture, I would claim, the question of a minimal theology, operating *in pianissimo* — almost invisibly, *klein und hässlich,* as Benjamin suggested — opens up. Its agenda could be formulated as a modest and provisional response to the challenge that Schnädelbach formulates in almost programmatic terms. So far, he notes, the "task of actually combining the theory of negative dialectics with the theory of rationality has not yet been accomplished: no one has unfolded the implications of negative dialectics for practical philosophy."[102] What would it mean to take on this double challenge?

To begin with, one should avoid the pitfalls of either theologizing or secularizing Adorno's work, if these terms are understood in their accepted classical and modern definition (which I consider to be one-dimensional). Neither the simple affirmation nor the all-out negation and discrediting of Adorno's quasi-theological motives will help us understand to what strategic and innovative use these figures of thought can be put. Negative metaphysics — theology properly speaking (*die eigentliche Theologie*), the other theology (*die andere Theologie*), the difference matters little — undercuts and circumvents the alternative between classical, dogmatic theology, on the one hand, and modern, scientist materialism or methodological atheism, on the other. These alternatives, Adorno suggests, are tied to an unproblematic (Horkheimer would say "traditional") notion of theory, just as they are premised upon a naive understanding of the corresponding relationship between theory and praxis. The open-

---

101. See ibid., 2:169.
102. Schnädelbach, *Vernunft und Geschichte,* 174.

ing words of *Negative Dialectics* set the stage for a radical interrogation—indeed, deconstruction—of their respective presuppositions:

> Philosophy, which once seemed obsolete, lives on because the moment [*Augenblick*] to realize it was missed. The summary judgment that it had merely interpreted the world, that resignation in the face of reality had crippled it in itself, becomes a defeatism of reason after the attempt to change the world miscarried. Philosophy offers no place from which theory as such might be concretely convicted of the anachronisms it is suspected of, now as before. Perhaps it was an inadequate interpretation which promised that it would be put into practice. Theory cannot prolong the moment its critique depended on. A practice indefinitely delayed is no longer the forum of appeals [*Einspruchsinstanz*] against self-satisfied speculation; it is mostly the pretext used by executive authorities to choke, as vain, whatever critical thoughts the practical change would require. Having broken its pledge to be as one with reality or at the point of realization, philosophy is obliged ruthlessly to criticize itself. (*ND* 3 / 15)

A second requirement for accepting Schnädelbach's challenge is to acknowledge that Adorno's negative metaphysics does not present us with a coherent position per se; more precisely, that it analyzes and even rhetorically dramatizes the inevitability of incoherence—and does so systematically, consistently. It must be stressed, therefore, that Adorno's negative metaphysics does not ignore or gloss over the cognitive and practical aporia of the motif of nonidentity (in other words, of transcendence, the other, the absolute, the infinite, the divine name, the messianic, immortality, all nonsynonymous substitutions queried in subtle "models" and "micrologies" whose internal, not entirely discursive, logic and interrelationship—which is one of interplay, resonance, and constellation—I will study in depth in the following chapter).

Negative metaphysics, as it emerges in the quotations that I have analyzed here, concerns a purely *formal*, abstract, differential idea whose paradox and aporia are from the outset acknowledged and exemplified as such. Accusing Adorno of ending up in performative contradiction is therefore, quite simply, to miss the point: namely, that *that*—philosophy's inevitable encounter with aporia, as its starting point, element, and result—is precisely the point his finely wrought texts indefatigably seek to make.

This is not to deny that both in Adorno's negative dialectics and the minimal theology that follows in its track we must distinguish yet another, and seemingly far more concrete, motif and motivation. This aspect of his writing finds expression in the various sensuous-materialist, moralizing, and modernist aesthetic concerns and is summed up in the imperative to signal then dispel horror (*das Grauen*) and suffering (*das Leiden*). Unlike the negative metaphysical idea of transcendence, this motif and motivation cannot be formalized or paraphrased (*referiert,* Adorno would say); it is not easily grasped by dialectical mediation, nor does it have the format of phenomenological description and intentional analysis. Such moments must, as it were, be *quoted,* as no one saw more clearly than Adorno's teacher in these matters, Benjamin, who wanted to compose the *Arcades Project* as purely a collection of citations. In words that now echo Habermas and Wittgenstein, these moments cannot be reconstructed by argument but can only be *shown.*

Indeed, Adorno's citation of these instances of the nonidentical refers indirectly to a praxis or passivity (as Levinas would say, a patience) of the subject, dependent upon the historical situation and political-cultural context in which it finds itself. Paradoxically, this more concrete strand of thought and agency in his philosophy, which supplements his more abstract negative-dialectical theoretical speculation, bracketing or postponing the immediate transition to praxis which traditional Marxism had promised, might show us that the range of possibility within which minimal theologies must operate and orient themselves (metaphysically, morally and politically, aesthetically and expressively) is limited not only formally but in matters of enabling context and relevant content as well.

If this interpretation is correct, a further differentiation imposes itself. Only formal features can be made philosophically and rationally plausible as the structural margins within which the minimally theological reveals itself in its diminishing yet abiding intelligibility. Whether, beyond that, there might still remain room for qualitative motifs and motivations of thought, agency, judgment, and experience is a question that must remain suspended, depending on the good fortune or ill fate of past, present, and future context. Philosophically and rationally speaking, this question cannot be answered in general terms; it remains imponderable, indeed, undecidable. No one could tell in advance or once and for all.

This does not mean that we cannot form certain rules of thumb. Marquard, for example, suggests always prioritizing a pluralizing hermeneutics over a singularizing one.[103] Such rules, however, are a matter of judgment and even of commonplaces, not the result of metaphysical speculation or rational argument.

The *ambiguity between the most abstract and the most concrete* in Adorno's philosophy forces us to postulate a duality or double focus in his concept of reason and at the core of the minimal theology (theology "properly speaking," "the other theology") which we associate with it. For the sake of simplicity these two poles of a concept of rationality that is pluridimensional rather than bisected and one-dimensional could be described, in a felicitous distinction drawn by Schnädelbach, as *dianoetical* and *noetical* moments.[104] The first names the discursive, argumentative, and, in Platonic parlance, dialectical trajectory of philosophical reason, whereas the second points to the silent—that is, nondiscursive and unutterable—vigilance and prudence that lies at its root and accompanies, inspires, and interrupts it along the way. The latter, Adorno insists, should not be understood idealistically, as if we were dealing with a merely intuitive quality, an a priori value, or *Wesenschau,* to cite some of the historical examples of immediacy against which he positions himself throughout his writings.

The categorical difference between—yet mutual conditioning of—discursivity and nondiscursive intelligibility have long been hidden in an unbroken (supposedly god-given, natural, organic, or substantial) relationship under the mantle of a singular concept in the history of reason. In postmodernity they have been torn apart like the fragments of a broken grail or the pieces of a shattered mosaic which we can no longer fit together by reflecting upon the alleged fundamentals of the universe (Nature, God, Spirit, the subject, sociality, even language). Such is the *broken complementarity*—and, hence, the need for supplementarity—discussed earlier. If one accepts this duality in principle of (at least) two traces in Adorno's use of the term *rationality,* what, then, would remain irrational? That could only be the belief that one might be able to think, act, judge, or experience on the basis of one pole without at least implicit reference to the other.[105]

103. Marquard, "Frage nach der Frage, auf die die Hermeneutik die Antwort ist," *Abschied vom Prinzipiellen,* 117–46.

104. See Schnädelbach, "Dialektik als Vernunftkritik: Zur Konstruktion des Rationalen bei Adorno," *Vernunft und Geschichte,* 185 ff.; and in von Friedeburg and Habermas, *Adorno-Konferenz 1983,* 72ff.

105. I am fully aware of the conceptual and historical limitations of this proposal. For a

Adorno's thought remains undeniably modern in that he subscribes to the continuing claims of reason and rationality. Almost every aspect of his oeuvre confirms this fact. Yet the double-edged interpretation of the variously discursive and intelligible poles of reason, in figures of thought which allow for no synthesis, mediation, or coherence, suggests an equally strong postmodern motif. His thinking is not postmodern in its original intention but in the fact that its two moments of reason — one of which is based upon a nearly empty idea, whereas the other is reduced to an almost improbable *concretissimum* — neither necessarily imply each other nor refer to each other in ways that could be reconstructed by philosophical argument.

For this reason a postmodern philosophizing that could do justice to both these points of view cannot rest with the formulation or dianoetic presentation of a negative metaphysical supplement to the theory of rationality which takes the form of an emphatic idea. Like the theory of rationality, it requires a hermeneutic supplement — a quasi-immediate noetic moment — whose pièce de résistance is the concept of judgment traditionally associated with practical philosophy and aesthetics. Yet the faculty of judgment at stake here can no more be understood in an exclusively moral-juridical or aesthetic sense than the negative metaphysical idea can be fully mediated through theoretical reason. Neither practical wisdom or prudence in the classical Aristotelian and Stoic sense, nor a matter of taste, as in the modern reflection on art natural beauty from Kant and the Romantics on, the faculty of judgment which interests us here would need to be thought and exercised completely otherwise. The specific competence upon which one must rely in responding *responsibly* to the question opened up by the negative presentation of the metaphysical in its paradoxical-aporetic idea is, in the final analysis, nothing but the *tact* of judgment which makes reason and rationality sensitive to singular cases.[106]

Negative metaphysics concerns an abstract, though universalist, idea; judgment, by contrast, is concrete, particular, and specific to context. Whereas negative metaphysics can be situated "beyond" our discourses (whose internal logic and external differentiation are articulated by Kant, Weber, Habermas, and Lyotard), judgment lies, as it were, "on this side" of

---

systematic analysis of the concept of the irrational in philosophy, the history of logic and mathematics, perspective in painting, and contemporary cosmology, see Gilles Gaston Granger, *L'Irrationnel* (Paris: Odile Jacob, 1998).

106. See the section "Speech Tact" in my book *Philosophy and the Turn to Religion,* 404–18.

them. Yet the concrete engagement of judgment can stand on its own no more than the disengagement of negative metaphysics. It is always provisional and subject to interruption and contradiction, not only in the light of endless other contexts — or due to the impossibility of demarcating any given (concept of) context in full rigor — but especially with regard to the horizons and dimensions (the "curvature of social space") opened up by the idea of negative metaphysics. Judgment and negative metaphysics are related to each other as inner and outer perspectives that mutually correct each other, as in a tension between concretization and retraction or as in the dialectic or oscillation between a sense for the broken forms of the good life and the emphatic idea of justice. The practical, aesthetic, religious, or materialist-sensuous forms that judgment assumes therefore remain philosophically (even if not always subjectively, existentially) arbitrary. From a truly rational optic, judgment should always remain open and vulnerable to the possibility of theoretical critique. Only the improbable conjunction of a fleeting idea and an almost leaden responsibility seems capable of countering the resignation and cynicism that characterize "Enlightenment's wake."[107] Although the appeal to these motifs and motivations does not exclude daring theoretical formulation and tough societal practice, these remain open to revision only if theory is mindful (*eingedenk*) of the continual alternation between their polar extremes.

The Rationality and Irrationality of Classical and Modern Theology: The Two Traces of Minimal Theology

The question of whether theology can be established as a modern empirical science of religion — considered as a historical and cultural fact — within "theoretical" discourse from Kant through Weber and Habermas through Lyotard needs no further consideration here. Yet my analyses make clear why any attempt to render plausible the *cognitive* rationality of classical theology is condemned to failure. One cannot, of course, deny the cognitive intentions and truth claims inherent in questions of meaning, in general, and in religious discussions (or so-called godtalk), in particular. The problem is that such confessional discourse, regardless of its universalistic aspirations, *per definitionem* cannot be made scientifically and rationally true.[108] In concluding this chapter, I would like to explore

107. See John Gray, *Enlightenment's Wake: Politics and Culture at the Close of the Modern Age* (London: Routledge, 1995).

108. See Adriaanse, Krop, and Leertouwer, *Het verschijnsel theologie*, 121–22.

the extent to which Habermas's (a) external and (b) internal differentiations of a modern, supposedly postmetaphysical concept of reason and rationality can elucidate this issue.

(*ad a*) Because classical theology or dogmatics (as well as biblical and systematic theology, etc.) can be viewed as a *discours mixte*, consisting of both cognitive and other kinds of validity claims or argumentative strategies, it runs up against not only the analytical force of the modern theory of rationality but also the dilemmas that characterize it. The consequences of the restricted scope of the theory of rationality—namely, its inability to generate a second-order or meta-theoretical description of the *external* connections between different rational discourses, in particular, a description that could dispense with metaphor—redounds upon dogmatics, which intends to be a theoretical discourse, even though its statements cover the whole spectrum of past, present, and future human experience. In consequence its assertions refer simultaneously to the three worlds I have distinguished. It not only proposes a theory concerning origination, causality, and factual matters within the cosmos but entails generalization about the symbolically, normatively, and existentially structured domains of sociality and subjectivity. Yet the external connection in dogmatics between the created cosmos, the community of believers, and the individual human soul—one recognizes the three worlds formally described by Habermas—can, once again, be described only metaphorically. Hence, for dogmatics the way back to a total theoretical—that is to say, substantial or ontological—interpretation of reality is finally also blocked. This means that the persuasive power of dogmatic discourse—indeed, its very criteria for acceptability and success—cannot be distinguished in full rigor from those of other genres, such as moral edification, narrative, historiography, literature, and the like. Viewed systematically, far from delivering empirical or formal proof—if one ignores the internal aspects of rationality, to which it may live up by respecting a minimal coherence, consistency, and precision in the definition of its terms, and so on—dogmatics appeals in the end not to theoretical critique, moral reasoning, or aesthetic taste but to our general capacity for judging the singular in singular cases.

(*ad b*) Another, more pressing problem remains, however. This second difficulty in ascertaining the academic status of dogmatic discourse follows from Habermas's characterization of *intradiscursive* rationality. In the sciences as in ethics (or any other scholarly discipline), modernity, he notes, accepts no mental, conceptual, or normative reservations, that is to say, no "exemptions from the critical power of *hypothetical thought.*"[109] Dogmatics, however, knows no *formal* concept of the objective world, sociality, and subjectivity which can be isolated and within which an in principle unlimited number of interpretations that differ in content but have equal claims to justification can be offered. From the perspective of the general theory of rationality, not just from that of the theoretical (scientific) discourse that makes up one world, this constitutes both the argumentative weakness—and, in the long run, the ill-fated destiny—of all dogmatics and, paradoxically, its historical tenacity in acquiring intellectual hegemony while promising personal, existential strength.

The classical theological exposition of dogmatic discourse by its very definition cannot view all its contents as possible, variable options that one might eventually weigh against one another, depending on context and will. That could happen only if dogmatics or biblical and systematic theology were prepared not only to consider other interpretations of Scripture and tradition but also to leave open in principle frames of reference other than the canon or church doctrine. This requirement forms the *conditio sine qua non* for the formal and procedural concept of rationality and also remains in place in the supplements to its general theory that we propose.

Indeed, for all Jewish, Christian, or Islamic theology, as for every concrete, particular answer to the "question of meaning," there must *per definitionem* emerge a moment at which the process of argumentation comes to an end and, as Weber already knew, a *sacrificium intellectus* becomes inevitable. Thus, religion, in its cultural formations, is, indeed, a "conversation stopper."[110] Anyone who would maintain even a minimal discrepancy between belief in revelation—or any grappling with existence (*Existenzergreifung*)—on the one hand, and the break with a "natural attitude" (Husserl), on the other, has already confirmed ipso facto an analytical distinction between concrete life forms and the primarily formal conceptions of rationality. There remains a categorical difference between the conversion of faith and the *conversio* of the philosophical gaze, which from the earliest interpretations of philosophy as "a way of life" (Hadot) and a spiritual exercise up to how Husserl's use of *Konversion* as a figure for the phenomenological *epochē* and transcendental reduction, in the *Krisis*

---

109. Habermas, *Theory of Communicative Action,* 1:214 / 1:297, my emph.

110. Richard Rorty, "Religion as Conversation-stopper," in *Philosophy and Social Hope* (Harmondsworth, Middlesex: Penguin, 1999), 168–74.

der europäischen Wissenschaften und die transzendentale Phänomenologie (*The Crisis of the European Sciences and Transcendental Phenomenology*), defines turning the intellectual gaze away from dogmatic slumber. Even though the terminological continuity between these tropes for the activity of spiritual life and philosophical examination is significant (and risks contaminating the distinction, whose analytic and categorical nature must nonetheless be affirmed), the difference between the two levels of experience and thought seems clear.

As has been observed by several authors: "Classical theology moves from faith to faith. While it can problematize parts of the content of faith, it can never problematize its core." Furthermore: "Classical theology can assume or negate this or that article of faith, but it cannot eliminate talk about God."[111] Given this silent premise, one cannot see how dogmatics could ever satisfy the minimal standard of procedural rationality or, for that matter, of any other formally defined concept of reason.[112] It then follows — and here I would draw the distinction somewhat more sharply — that any accounting of one's views to outsiders who express doubts that are not merely partial but "objections in principle that jeopardize the entire content of faith" can no longer take place rationally, that is to say, with reference to argumentative grounds.[113]

One dramatic consequence of Habermas's theory of rationality would, therefore, be that the historically prominent, if contemporarily dormant, disciplines of "apologetic" and "fundamental" theology, which traditionally concerned the external foundations of theological discourse as a whole, could, under modern premises, be interpreted only as a form of expressivity or, worse, as "strategic" behavior, unless their spokespersons might assume a completely hypothetical attitude about faith (and the sum of its doctrine: sacraments, rituals, etc.).[114] Otherwise, only the expressive rationality of the discourse evoking God remains available as a final resort, that is to say, as the sole chance for dogmatics and confessional theology to salvage their authority and plausibility, not in terms of theoretical truth or normative rightness but in light of the value claims of existential authenticity and testimonial exemplariness. Here Habermas offers a criterion as

---

111. Adriaanse, Krop, and Leertouwer, *Het verschijnsel theologie,* 127.

112. Adriaanse, Krop, and Leertouwer claim this only implicitly in *Het verschijnsel theologie* (see, e.g., 121, 123).

113. Ibid., 126.

114. See, e.g., the critique of neo-Thomism which Habermas sketches in connection with Horkheimer (*Theory of Communicative Action,* 1:374 / 1:501).

simple as it is convincing: "That a speaker means what he says can be made credible only in the consistency of what he does and not through providing grounds."[115] This implies that nothing can be done with this possible subjective form of rationality on a theoretical or normative meta-level, and that is where classical (dogmatic, biblical, systematic) and "practical" theology pretend to operate primarily, if not exclusively.

Once we have arrived at this point, it is of little use to gesture toward the limits of rationality and emphasize that religion can be described in terms of supposedly nonrational quests for "meaning" and "meaningfulness" better than in terms of cognitive-manipulative interest.[116] Not only does such an assertion miss the cognitive as well as practical-normative intention of religion; more important, although religion may express "the moment of the nonavailability of meaning,"[117] it can never advance this expression to a privileged position in the "total" field of meaning, to say nothing of offering rational grounds to support that claim. Yet, in moral, aesthetic, and erotic experiences of meaning, meaningfulness, and the "nonavailability" of meaning, a movement of transcendence can be carried out or observed which is, philosophically speaking, similar in its structure or figure. Telling examples of this analogy and a frequent confusion of and interchangeability between the religious and its competing modes of transgression abound in the writings of Adorno, Benjamin, Levinas, and Derrida.

One could, of course, object that the critique of the *intra*discursive aspects of Habermas's theory of rationality counters my assessment of whether or not a minimal rationality—that is to say, a form of rationality that is nontheoretical, nonnormative, and subjective-expressive—should be granted to religious and dogmatic theological discourse. As I have stated, there are at least two forms of rationality, which inadvertently come up against elements and dimensions whose incommensurability calls for supplementary notions, given that they cannot, using the terminology and criteria of the three discourses themselves. Furthermore, in Habermas's symmetrically structured theory of cognitive, normative, and aesthetic rationality, not only does the dimension of reference in the concept of truth need to be revised, but there is an asymmetrical or even heteronomous dimension in the idea of normative correctness as well as

---

115. Ibid., 1:303 / 1:408.

116. One is reminded of a whole tradition of thought which spans, at least, from David Friedrich Schleiermacher up to Rudolf Otto.

117. Adriaanse, Krop, and Leertouwer, *Het verschijnsel theologie*, 123.

in those of aesthetic expressivity and subjective authenticity. But would this structure of asymmetrical referral, which takes different, incompatible forms in each of the three discourses and their respective value claims, have no consequences for the status of religious speech, if only to let it in again by the back door, offering it a theoretical, practical, and aesthetic niche in modernity, after all? Would this not explain the diminishing yet abiding intelligibility I noted earlier?

Such a conclusion would be overhasty. The dimension of the heteronomous cannot philosophically or comprehensibly be described as *specifically* or *primarily* religious. In assuming an unsublatable remainder, a more or less ab-solute difference, dogmatics, viewed formally and structurally, is no different from other interpretations of experience, whose format and structure reveal similar features of transcendence.

What is specific to dogmatics lies in its nondiscursive commitment and its concerns with a *particular* content—and, ultimately, a particularistic praxis—regardless of the universality of its overall intent. This is why its degree of rationality is weak in comparison to that of the generalized philosophy of difference, of the ab-solute, whose minimal theology I seek to spell out. Dogmatics knows no formal concept of transcendence which would allow an *in principle* infinite range of changing interpretations of *in principle* equal theoretical and normative validity to be put forward in the conversation of humankind.

Accordingly, when the dimension of difference is brought to bear on Habermas's construction, we do not arrive at the gate—or the *parvis*—of dogmatics, to say nothing of God, even if this dimension explains the abiding intelligibility of the ongoing talk about and discussion of God. Godtalk and divine speech are just two among many individual colorations and intonations of ab-solute difference, whose ultimate validity must philosophically remain in suspense. In the face of this *individuum ineffabile,* as Dilthey once called it,[118] philosophy cannot but become aporetic.

This does not necessarily deny every aspect of rationality to talk about God, without quotation marks—hence, as something, someone, more and other than a "cultural fact." We have denied it most rational formats but not all. One could still attribute to dogmatics, roughly following Max Weber, a value-bound rationality. Weber discusses rationalization in the sense of "a disenchantment" of worldview and a "dogmatization" of the

118. See Wilhelm Dilthey, "Die Entstehung der Hermeneutik," *Gesammelte Schriften* (Stuttgart: B. G. Teubner, 1964), 5:330.

contents of faith. He writes: "To judge the level of rationalization a religion represents there are two principle yardsticks, which are in many ways interrelated. One is the degree to which the religion has divested itself of magic; the other is the degree of systematic unity it gives to the relation between God and the world and correspondingly to its own ethical relation to the world."[119] Value-bound rational action, which, according to Weber, is situated on the scale of increasingly diminished rationality after purposeful rational action and before affective and traditional action, is distinguished "through conscious belief in the (ethical, aesthetic, religious or however interpreted) unconditional, *intrinsic* value [Eigenwert] of a certain mode of behavior, purely as such and independently of success."[120]

Drawing on Karl Barth and Husserl, one could further grant dogmatics, as Adriaanse demonstrates, a certain phenomenological rationality.[121] In the terms of Habermas and Schnädelbach one could perhaps even attribute to it the rationality of explicative discourse,[122] which explicitly takes into account the symbols already in use by human beings. Such explicative discourses, which depend upon situation, have "much in common with the 'piecemeal engineering' on a ship at sea, which must make do with what is on board, for one cannot sail on a ship and have it in dock at the same time."[123]

Following yet another suggestion, we could borrow from the work of Paul Tillich (one of Adorno's teachers) several other necessary conditions for rationality, which would suffice for classical theological discourse, at least internally. So-called semantic, logical, and methodological rationality would guarantee that "great care is taken in the use of concepts to avoid contradictions and [that] the path once followed . . . is consequently pursued further."[124] Yet whether these conditions are also sufficient remains a question. From the perspective of Habermas's theory of rationality, the answer can only be negative. Thus, Adriaanse, Krop, and Leertouwer, recalling Tillich, can hardly be basing themselves on Habermas's text (though it is a central reference in their work) when they characterize rationality as a "value on a scale," so that (a) it is not an "issue of whether

119. Qtd. in Habermas, *Theory of Communicative Action*, 1:205 / 1:285.

120. Qtd. in ibid., 1:281 / 1:380.

121. Hendrik Johan Adriaanse, *Zu den Sachen selbst: Versuch einer Konfrontation der Theologie Karl Barths mit der phänomenologischen Philosophie Edmund Husserls* (The Hague: Mouton, 1974).

122. See Habermas, *Theory of Communicative Action*, 1:21–22 / 1:43–44.

123. Schnädelbach, *Vernunft und Geschichte*, 166. The image comes from Otto Neurath.

124. Adriaanse, Krop, and Leertouwer, *Het verschijnsel theologie*, 130.

or not, but rather of more or less,"[125] and (b) they can conclude that "irrationality or a-rationality" can be attributed only to "strictly naïve forms
of religion."[126]

For Habermas, by contrast, the question of the lower or upper boundaries of rationality can, it seems, be decided philosophically or even empirically. As an ideal and conceptual lower limit, for him rationality presupposes at least a differentiation (*Ausdifferenzierung*) of the diffuse and
illusionary unity of the objective, social, and subjective worlds bound
together in myth and religious-metaphysical worldviews. At the philosophically and empirically determined upper limit, rationality assumes
that there can be no total *dis*integration of value spheres, in which a meaningful connection among (or within) the three worlds would give way to a
fragmentation of consciousness, ethical skepticism, and pressure imposed
by the system (of state, market, power, and money) on the resources of
the life-world. Both the lower and the upper boundaries are reconstructed
in formal pragmatic terms according to a logic of development, but they
nonetheless remain dependent on investigations into the precise dynamics of their respective developments. Nonetheless, it is clear that the motifs of differentiation and integration in Habermas are not symmetrical
but incongruent and that he is, in this respect, more of a Kantian than a
Hegelian.[127]

Yet, if my arguments for the necessity of a (negative) metaphysical supplement are sufficiently sound, these considerations need not be the final
word. According to my initial thesis, a rational philosophical theology — a
minimal theology, a theology *in pianissimo* — should not cut rationality in
two. The minimal theology I seek cannot be satisfied with the claustropho-
bia, reductionism, and methodological atheism of the modern science of
religion, which limits its object to one — admittedly multifaceted — sociohistorical, psychological, and cultural "fact" to be studied using a pragmatically motivated assemblage of already-existing philological and empirical scholarly disciplines. Nor is it in a position to acknowledge, let
alone corroborate, the free-floating existence or the normative and truth
claims of classical, confessional theology, whose existence in the Western
academy is largely a fruit of the past and present hegemony of Christian

---

125. Adriaanse, Krop, and Leertouwer, *Het verschijnsel theologie*, 120; see also 99.
126. Ibid., 122.
127. On the difference between the logic and dynamics of development, see Habermas,
Theory of Communicative Action, 1:194–200 / 1:272–77.

communities and their respective traditions. Nor can it compensate for the fact that the theory of rationality resulting from Habermas's systematization and formal-pragmatic reconstruction of the philosophical and sociological discourse of modernity (from Kant to Hegel and Husserl and from Marx to Durkheim and Weber) is incapable of thinking an important internal and external aspect of the reasonable as it reveals itself within its three discourses and conditions their interrelation—the noetical.

This structurally asymmetrical and aporetic "moment" cannot be "linguistified" with the sacred, nor can it be reduced to an element within intersubjective communication; it is, on the contrary, constitutive of the abiding intelligibility of all talk concerning God, although not unambiguously so. "*We can, from the perspective of the philosophy of history, catch sight of this absolute sense of freedom,*" says Kodalle, following the model of Kierkegaard, "*only because we stand on the ground of the powerful historical differentiation of a thoroughly rationalized form of life*";[128] and "only now are we free to develop again a sufficient understanding of the absolute."[129] Yet in postmodernity the timbre or tonality of transcendence always sounds differently, *in pianissimo,* and can at any time fade away. This is probably the most important reason for the decreasing intelligibility of the discussion of God. If philosophers and theologians refuse to attend to this retreat but continue to start out by assuming (or denying) the continuing intelligibility of godtalk, as if nothing had happened— as if the modes of revelation were not always already (to be) thought and experienced completely differently—they will become unintelligible. Whether they do so by becoming reductionist or dogmatic matters little. Both positions are secret allies in the ongoing bisection of reason.

Minimal theologies find themselves, like Adorno's negative metaphysics and Levinas's philosophy of the other, on the far side of the rationality assumed by the modern science of religion, although it wisely situates itself, like those figures of thought, on this side of classical theological dogmatics. One might suspect, then, that in between these apparent antipodes, which halve rationality from opposing directions, minimal theology can exist only in a figurative, metaphorical, rhetorical, or even allegorical, and, hence, *improper* sense. Yet could a minimal theology claim to do anything else? What, by contrast, would theology *properly* speaking mean: a theology that would live up to its concept (but which one?), to its

128. Kodalle, "Versprachlichung des Sakralen?" 41. See also his essay "Gott," 432.
129. Kodalle, *Die Eroberung des Nutzlosen,* 17.

etymology (but why should it?), to its common — classical and modern, confessional and secularist — understanding?

In the outlaw standing it has chosen for itself, minimal theology is exposed on both flanks to attack by an unholy alliance it has aligned against itself. The precarious situation in which it maneuvers might plead against it. Yet in the following pages I will observe the concept of minimal theology in various authors and reconstruct it from them, in sufficient detail to make (and thereby rest) our case. Rather than articulating minimal theology directly, systematically, or conceptually, however, we can better illustrate it indirectly via detours and errant paths that lead through singular motifs that are simultaneously abstract and concrete: for example, Adorno's idea of an inverse theology, Benjamin's and Schopenhauer's notion of an allegorical theology,[130] Levinas's concept of a thinking of the infinite, and, finally, Derrida's insistence on the theological as a "determinate moment in the total movement of the trace" and, consequently, the unavoidability of its neither negative nor affirmative apophatics.

Due to my methodological strategy, only during the course of these investigations will it be possible to explicate fully what I mean in saying that theology can and must be set upon the narrow trace of difference. Beyond the horizon of the spaces and niches for thought contained within the theory of rationality, minimal theologies attempt to pave the necessarily circuitous way toward a thought that is capable of explicating its fragile and transient conditions of possibility, that is neither classical nor modern, let alone "postmetaphysical," but, instead, expresses "solidarity with metaphysics in the moment of its downfall."

Minimal theology, therefore, has little in common with Peukert's notion of fundamental theology, developed in close connection with Habermas and Kant.[131] Peukert describes this as a kind of "basic theory [*Basis-*

130. See my essays "Theologie als allegorie: Over de status van de joodse gedachtenmotieven in het werk van Walter Benjamin," in *Vier joodse denkers in de twintigste eeuw: Rosenzweig, Benjamin, Levinas, Fackenheim,* ed. H. J. Heering and others (Kampen, Neth.: J. H. Kok, 1987), 22–51; *Religion and Violence,* chap. 3; and "Zum Begriff der Allegorie in Schopenhauers Religionsphilosopie," in *Schopenhauer, Nietzsche und die Kunst,* ed. Wolfgang Schirmacher, *Schopenhauer-Studien* 4 (Vienna: Passagen, 1991), 187–97.

131. Peukert reformulates Kant's well-known third question (see the *Critique of Pure Reason,* B 833) according to the postulates of the theory of communicative action, whose central motivation he gives a decidedly Benjaminian twist: "It ought no longer to read: What may I hope — for myself? But: What may I hope — for the other — in his death?" See Peukert, *Wissenschaftstheorie, Handlungstheorie, Fundamentale Theologie,* 312 n. 1, 316 n. 8, and 342–43 n. 13. We will return to the Benjaminian motif. See also R. J. Siebert, *The Critical Theory of Religion:*

theorie]" and a philosophical theory of science (*Wissenschaftstheorie*) which can provide theology with methodological foundations and which, furthermore, ought to be of hermeneutic value in practical theological, ecclesial practice. He identifies this fundamental theology as a "formal dogmatics," whereas the discipline of dogmatics appears in his account as a "material fundamental theology."[132] His main claim is that, in the twentieth-century linguistic turn toward formal pragmatics, as represented primarily by Habermas—notably in the "dialectical limit reflections [*Grenzreflektionen*]" to which Peukert feels one should subject his work[133]—the implicit theological dimensions of communicative action manifest themselves. Especially in "anamnestic solidarity," in responsibility for the lot of past generations, we encounter an experience that, in its asymmetrical structure, puts into question the central premises of the theory of action. While this raises an important issue, one might ask whether fundamental theology, as Peukert thinks, could be the discipline that can enable one to identify, name, and, hence, somehow communicate this experience as it reveals itself at the fringes of (the paradigm of) communicative action. In his view fundamental theology could subject the "origin of a possible language [or discourse, *Rede*] concerning God," in its "originary access [*originären Zugang*]" as well as in its "fundamental structures [*Grundstrukturen*]," to a "reflexive theoretical presentation [*Vergegenwärtigung*]."[134] Such formulations make clear that his approach is unlike the one on which I will focus here. "Solidarity with metaphysics in the moment of its downfall" is not exactly anamnestic solidarity with the victims of past generations, as Peukert (and Benjamin) defines it.

The program of a philosophy in the trace of ab-solute difference "experienced" theologically, metaphysically, ethically, or aesthetically, which I have roughly outlined, might be viewed as a sort of hermeneutics, providing that one does not exaggerate the horizon and applicability of this concept. As no one has indicated more convincingly than Gadamer, in his magnum opus, *Truth and Method*, tradition must come "into question [*fragwürdig*]"—which implies becoming "worthy of a question"—before

---

The Frankfurt School, from Universal Pragmatic to Political Theology (Berlin: Mouton, 1985); and my review in *Bijdragen* 49 (1988): 468–70.

132. Peukert, *Wissenschaftstheorie, Handlungstheorie, Fundamentale Theologie*, 17.

133. Ibid.

134. Ibid., 342; also 316–17.

hermeneutical consciousness can establish itself.[135] Gadamer's philosophical hermeneutics, which inscribes itself in the legacy of practical philosophy, jurisprudence, and ancient and Humanist rhetoric, attempts to uncover the boundaries that limit the power of reflection. It impresses upon thought the consciousness of its own finitude and offers an account of the twilight in which reason shows its most suspect and corruptible sides.[136] Outside the alternatives of classical-modern transcendental reflection and empirical-pragmatic forms of knowledge, it seeks a third way.[137] For it the familiar Archimedean standpoints from which ideology critique and psychoanalysis once struggled to find an ultimate transparency of society and individuality have fallen away. Even the perspective toward transcendence, which might still be open to us, can, in the wake of hermeneutics, appear only as ephemeral. Contra Hegel, Gadamer skeptically emphasizes the "absoluteness [or unsublatability] of the border that separates [us] from the divine [*Unaufhebarkeit der Grenze zum Göttlichen*]."[138] By the same token he states that within the tradition of transmitting ideas, vocabularies, and cultural goods we always remain outside of the latest truths imagined as "presence" because "every assimilation of tradition is historically different . . . every one is the experience of a 'view [*Ansicht*]' of the object itself [*Sache selbst*]."[139]

Perspectivism and participation in "truth" are paradoxically intertwined here. That has, in turn, given rise to the impression, aptly formulated by Marquard, that "skepticism is the core of hermeneutics and hermeneutics is the actual form of skepticism."[140] Above all else, skepticism makes clear that philosophy has no access to any extraterritorial position and is not capable of "absolute communication [*Mitteilung*]"; on the contrary, it is, from the very beginning, "entangled in a life that is always too difficult and too short to reach absolute clarity about itself."[141] But could that be its last word?

Like the general theory of rationality and communicative action, with

135. Gadamer, *Truth and Method*, xxi / xxi; see also Habermas, *Theory of Communicative Action*, 1:130–31 / 1:188–89.

136. See Hans Georg Gadamer, *Hermeneutik II: Wahrheit und Methode, Ergänzungen, Gesammelte Werke* (Tübingen: J. C. B. Mohr, 1986), 2:42.

137. See Hans Georg Gadamer, "Das Erbe Hegels," in Gadamer and Jürgen Habermas, *Das Erbe Hegels: Zwei Reden* (Frankfurt a.M: Suhrkamp, 1979), 35–94.

138. Gadamer, *Truth and Method*, 320 / 339.

139. Ibid., 430 / 448.

140. Marquard, *Abschied vom Prinzipiellen*, 138; also 20.

141. Ibid., 20.

which it is in continuous dialogue, a truly consequential philosophical hermeneutics must leave some space for a metaphysical supplement, which at first allows itself to be outlined only negatively. Then, however, it leaves its indelible trace of difference. In this chapter I have established the reasons why one can limit the contours of this trace neither to those of the Christian (or Jewish or Muslim) God nor rely for its interpretation on the general criteria for a scientific discipline, which, viewed from this metaphysical perspective, turn out to be as arbitrary—that is, as provisional and fallible—as those of any other mode of discourse.

Consequential skepticism, whose precise meaning remains to be specified more closely, could be called the actual form of hermeneutics. It can and must contend with alterity in the only sense in which meanings, signs, and gestures might be called "ab-solute": that is, by withdrawing themselves from every narrowly delineated context and every definitive interpretation. In precisely this sense Marquard rightly says: "Skeptics are thus not those who know nothing in principle; they only know nothing of principle [*nichts Prinzipielles*]; skepticism is not the apotheosis of perplexity [or despair, *Ratlosigkeit*], but rather the *departure from principle*."[142]

The irreducible "being-other" of our metaphysical tradition, like that of contemporary reality, can be convincingly, indeed rationally, demonstrated in a transcending and, as Habermas formulates it, quasi-transcendental, if not necessarily reconstructive, movement of thought. This being-other is at once internal and external to the tradition in question; the formulation "the other of metaphysics," like the expression "the other of reason"—read likewise as *genitivus subjectivus* and *objectivus* both—indicates as much.

Metaphysics, as Kant already knew, even though traditionally cast in a questionable manner via positive concepts, still remains the unavoidable horizon of all our thought, action, judgment, and experience, for good and for ill and for some time to come: "That the human mind will ever give up metaphysical researches is as little to be expected as that we, to avoid inhaling impure air, should prefer to give up breathing altogether. There will, therefore, always be metaphysics in the world; nay, everyone, especially every reflective man, will have it and, for want of a recognized standard, will shape it for himself after his own pattern. What has hitherto been called metaphysics cannot satisfy any critical mind, but to forgo it

142. Ibid., 17.

entirely is impossible."[143] With this diagnosis we find ourselves in the element of minimal theology. Apparently, whatever traditional metaphysics and classical theology—as well as their mirror images in modern science, modernism, secularism, and humanism, including the scholarly study of religion as an empirical or cultural fact—have understood to be transcendent (or, in methodological ascesis and atheism, deemed reducible to some external or ulterior cause) is only one of the possible interpretations of the infinite work of distinction called for by the ab-solute difference in (every) question. Certainly, it is not the interpretation that would most extensively and intensively account for—and thereby do justice to—the experience of the postmodern, let alone be strong or subtle enough to measure up to it.[144]

143. Immanuel Kant, *Prolegomena*, A 192–93, *Werke*, 5:245 / Kant, *Prolegomena to Any Future Metaphysics*, trans. P. Carus, rev. and intro. Lewis White Beck (Indianapolis: Bobbs-Merrill, 1950), 116.

144. Concluding this chapter with these formulations, I am paying homage to a teacher, Professor Herman J. Heering of the University of Leiden, according to whom philosophy strives for "the systematic interpretation of reality that would most extensively and intensively do justice to reality." See his book *Inleiding tot de godsdienstwijsbegeerte* (Amsterdam: Boom, 1976), 28.

PART TWO
Dialectica

Chapter Three

Paradox and Aporia in Adorno's
Philosophy of Nonidentity

A FUNDAMENTAL PROBLEM facing any interpretation of Adorno announces itself in his oft-cited dictum that every true philosophy is "essentially not expoundable [*referierbar*]" (*ND* 33 / 44). A philosophy understood as continually renewed articulation rather than the one-track development of a single line of thought cannot be summed up in a few thematic or systematic paragraphs. Because of the nonsystematic or, better, *antisystematic* character of Adorno's philosophy, it can best be approached via its historical development and the problems it has successively encountered and addressed. In what follows, I will attempt to sketch the basic contours of this development, paying special attention to aspects relevant to the systematic perspective of the present study.

Adorno's program for an interpretive (*deutenden*) philosophy is *in nuce* already present in his habilitation on Kierkegaard and in three posthumously published lectures from the early 1930s. Thereafter, his thought develops with impressive continuity and consequence. Nonetheless, one can easily detect differing layers within it, involving the introduction of new philosophical interlocutors and perspectives as well as the articulation of the "nonidentical," or "other," in varying vocabularies, such as those of the philosophy of history, epistemology, the philosophy of science, psychoanalysis, moral philosophy, aesthetics, and so on. Furthermore, one can speak of an expanding analytical scope in Adorno's thought, within which his original insight becomes increasingly radicalized, deepened, and concretized and within which, in a certain sense, his late work returns to and draws on his earliest designs and first intuitions. By contrast, in the middle period, which includes his closest collaboration with Max Horkheimer and their common authorship of *Dialectic of Enlightenment* (published in 1947), Adorno's position is less clearly defined. As we shall see, Adorno, rather lamely, relies on two thoughts during this time. On the one hand, he develops a broad and *negativistic* philosophy of history, which can be approached and expressed only through ephemeral yet emphatic traces of the nonidentical, or other. On the other hand,

Dialectic of Enlightenment anxiously adheres to the hope of eventually formulating a *positive* concept of "Enlightenment." The traces of the other-than-whatever-exists are—to echo a metaphor from Walter Benjamin—irrevocably scattered in the storm that drove mankind from Paradise.[1] Yet Horkheimer and Adorno maintain that a positive concept might nonetheless be prepared and then indicate how, in better times and under more auspicious circumstances, the foregoing history—or, rather, prehistory (*Vorgeschichte*)—of humanity could be turned on end. The last period of Adorno's work, during which he wrote *Negative Dialectics* (1966) as well as *Aesthetic Theory* (his final text, which was never fully completed and was published only posthumously, in 1970), no longer seems to share in this messianic pathos and drops the central hope on which the philosophies of redemption are premised. Here he radicalizes the "prohibition of images," already mentioned in *Dialectic of Enlightenment,* which should guarantee respect for the fragile other of reason, to the point where a renewed inquiry into the question of conceptual and nonconceptual forms of expression, to whatever extent they might still be available to philosophy and art, becomes unavoidable. The answer offered in his late work suggests that the unruly other resounds only in a dissonant composition in which philosophy and art silently refer to each other.

This leads to difficult questions, however. Must philosophy finally give up the task heretofore set it, namely, to receive the nonidentical into thought and help cast it into words? Does philosophy—as this term, in the later phases of Adorno's work, is bestowed on an emphatic "spiritual experience [*geistige Erfahrung*]"—finally transfer its banner to nonconceptual art? Adorno does not *intend* this to be so. In what follows, we shall see that, de facto, in his writings philosophy is neither rendered obsolete nor fully aestheticized, as has often been claimed. On the contrary, at decisive moments Adorno brings philosophy and art into a subtle, *fragmentary-complementary* or, better, *alternating* relationship. My claim in the previous chapter—that minimal theologies can inherit an important legacy from Adorno's figures of thought—stands or falls on establishing this thesis.

---

1. Benjamin, *Gesammelte Schriften,* 1.2:697–98.

The Early Reorientation of the Institute for Social Research toward the Philosophy of History: The "Critique of Instrumental Reason"

Here I will focus on a relatively small though essential part of the more than twenty volumes of Adorno's collected writings, namely, his philosophical texts. Except for a close reading of his earliest independent work, I will be interested primarily in the phase of his involvement with the Frankfurt School which begins with the "critique of instrumental reason," as Helmut Dubiel terms the historico-philosophical turn of about 1940 which displaces — not least through the increasing influence of Adorno — the predominant social-theoretical orientation of the Frankfurt School's previous "materialist" (1930–37) and "Critical Theory" (1937–40) phases.[2]

The neo-Marxist empirical and philosophical studies of the Frank-

2. Dubiel, *Wissenschaftsorganisation und politische Erfahrung*, 24; see also Martin Jay, *The Dialectical Imagination: A History of the Frankfurt School and the Institute of Social Research, 1923–1950* (Berkeley: University of California Press, 1973), 253 ff. Jay describes the radical critique of Western thought in this period as the final step away from orthodox Marxism. In his postscript to the new edition of *Dialektik der Aufklärung* (Frankfurt a.M.: Fischer Verlag, 1986), 277–94, Habermas suggests that this development goes along with Horkheimer's increasing attention to various motifs in Benjamin's philosophy of history, which also strongly influenced Adorno's early writings (281 ff.). See also Gunzelin Schmid Noerr, editor's afterword, in Max Horkheimer, *Gesammelte Schriften*, vol. 5, ed. Alfred Schmidt and Gunzelin Schmid Noerr (Frankfurt a.M.: S. Fischer, 1985), 432–34; and *DE* 217–47.

For the development of the Frankfurt School and the Institute for Social Research starting from its early origins, as well as a detailed discussion of the phenomenon of Critical Theory, reconstructed in part through the unpublished correspondence of its participants, see Wiggershaus, *Frankfurt School*. For its intellectual and philosophical premises, see Seyla Benhabib, *Critique, Norm, and Utopia: A Study of the Foundations of Critical Theory* (New York: Columbia University Press, 1986); and Seyla Benhabib, Wolfgang Bonss, and John McCole, eds., *On Max Horkheimer: New Perspectives* (Cambridge: MIT Press, 1993). For its institutional and reception history after Horkheimer and Adorno's return from the United States, see Alex Demirović, *Der nonkonformistische Intellektuelle: Die Entwicklung der Kritischen Theorie zur Frankfurter Schule* (Frankfurt a.M.: Suhrkamp, 1999). See Dahm, *Positivismusstreit,* for the unfortunate encounters, but also convergences and divergences, between the representatives of the first- and second-generation Frankfurt School and the logical positivists of the Vienna Circle in the 1930s; the critical rationalists, notably Karl Popper and Hans Albert; and the tradition of American pragmatism. That the demarcations "Critical Theory" and "Frankfurt School" contain only the *"suggestive fiction of a unified school"* is emphasized by Habermas in "Drei Thesen zur Wirkungsgeschichte der Frankfurter Schule," 11. See also Albrecht Wellmer, "Die Bedeutung der Frankfurter Schule heute: Fünf Thesen," *Endspiele: Die unversöhnliche Moderne: Essays und Vorträge* (Frankfurt a.M.: Suhrkamp, 1993), 224–35 / "The Significance of the Frankfurt School Today: Five Theses," *Endgames: The Irreconcilable Nature of Modernity: Essays and Lectures,* trans. David Midgley (Cambridge: MIT Press, 1998), 251–62.

furt School can, on the whole, be read as a "reflective expression of historical experience."[3] They underlie an extension and radicalization of the
historical-materialist critique of ideology toward a philosophy of history
of *seemingly* unbridled pessimism—accompanied by a further departure
from the economic determinism of the orthodoxy of the Second International—which characterizes the studies of the 1940s, to which the writings
of what we have called Adorno's middle period belong. In the writings of
this period the question of the causes and effects of the "dialectic of rationality" take center stage. Adorno and Horkheimer combine many elements
into a historical-philosophical critique of modern, subjective forms of reason: Max Weber's theory of Occidental rationalization, its reprise in Georg
Lukács's Hegelian-Marxist doctrine of reification, formulated in the central chapter of his epochal *Geschichte und Klassenbewußtsein* (*History and
Class Consciousness*), a distancing of themselves from the self-evidence of
the project of Enlightenment via Nietzsche[4] and the transformation of the
conservative cultural critique,[5] and an empirical explanation for the development of Stalinism and for the defenselessness of the working-class
and bourgeois culture against both fascism and the integrative power of
mass culture. "Interdisciplinary materialism" and a variety of "Freudo-
Marxism" are among the tools used to establish why the Marxist dual
analysis of society in terms of material base (of production) and ideal
superstructure does not suffice to explain why the masses, classes, and
individuals do not perceive or pursue their "objective interests" but are
caught in psychological mechanisms and repressions of which these are
just the most significant forms.[6] Moreover, they trace these elements back
to material reported from the earliest history of humankind. The interests

3. Dubiel, *Wissenschaftsorganisation und politische Erfahrung*, 17.

4. See Peter Pütz, "Nietzsche im Lichte der Kritischen Theorie," *Nietzsche-Studien* 3 (1974):
175–91; and Habermas, "Die Verschlingung von Mythos und Aufklärung: Bermerkungen zur
'Dialektik der Aufklärung' nach einer erneutern Lektüre," in *Mythos und Moderne: Begriff und
Bild einer Rekonstruktion,* ed. Karl-Heinz Bohrer (Frankfurt a.M.: Suhrkamp, 1983), 405–31, rpt.
in *Der philosophische Diskurs der Moderne,* 130–57 / "The Entwinement of Myth and Enlightenment: Max Horkheimer and Theodor Adorno," *Philosophical Discourse of Modernity,* 106–30.
See also how this motif is delineated in Norbert Rath, "Zur Nietzsche-Rezeption Horkheimers
und Adornos," in *Vierzig Jahre Flaschenpost: "Dialektik der Aufklärung" 1947–1987,* ed. Willem
van Reijen and Gunzelin Schmid Noerr (Frankfurt a.M.: S. Fischer, 1987), 73–110.

5. Herbert Schnädelbach indicates the possible influence of philosophies of life in *Phi-
losophie in Deutschland, 1831–1933* (Frankfurt a.M.: Suhrkamp, 1983), 172–73, 317–18 nn. 505–6.
See also Axel Honneth, *Kritik der Macht: Reflexionsstufen einer kritischen Gesellschaftstheorie*
(Frankfurt a.M.: Suhrkamp, 1985), 54, 339–40 n. 25.

6. See Dahm, *Positivismusstreit,* 45.

of both authors thus shift at this time from historical materialism and the affirmation of class struggle to the *apparently* irreconcilable entanglement and mutual oppression of nature and humanity. They situate the main problem of Western thought and the larger culture, indeed, of its modern economic and political institutions, in the broken relationship of the subject to both *external* nature and its own *internal* nature. For them the experience of the mid-twentieth century is that of being inundated, as in a second, inverse Flood, by totalitarian traits that have lain hidden under the surface throughout the entire Western tradition, from early myth and magic onward.

Such a *generalization* and *intensification* of traditional ideology critique well beyond its Marxist parameters threatens the Archimedean point upon which that critique once relied. It risks, that is, a *trivialization* of critique in the very moment when it expands its (intellectual and cultural) domain and extends its reach back to the origins of thought, agency, morality, and judgment. Reason itself becomes suspect or, better, nearly every trace of reason *seems* to have disappeared from historical reality as such — and not just modernity, bourgeois society, and capitalist forms of production. The almost archaeological critique of ideology must, from here on, as Dubiel notes, articulate nothing less than "the world-historical drama of the human altercation with nature [*Naturauseinandersetzung*]."[7] Summarizing the development outlined here, he claims: "The theoretical development of the group began with the (ideology) critique of the prefascist ideologies of the Weimar Republic. In 1937 the critique of 'Critical Theory' was directed against the 'traditional,' i.e., theoretical, ideal of all of bourgeois science. By 1944, however, the theory was directed against nothing more and nothing less than the Western tradition of reason as such."[8]

Dubiel and Martin Jay correctly point out the modification that the Hegelian concept of totality and its Marxist inversion undergo in this critique of "universal history." The consequences of the pessimism of the philosophy of history now reach farther than a simple rejection or affirmation of an already existing, realized, *positive,* and *concrete totality* in Hegel's and, say, Lukács's sense of this concept. Nonetheless, Adorno and Horkheimer hardly defend the contrary hypothesis of an *inverse, negative totality,* as if history were a web of purely hermetic connections, in which

---

7. Dubiel, *Wissenschaftsorganisation und politische Erfahrung,* 124.
8. Ibid., 129.

cause determines effect and force calls forth counterforce.[9] As I shall propose, a *rhetorical* and *hyperbolic* interpretation of their invective is more appropriate. Jay suggests as much when he writes: "Adorno . . . seemed to be open to the charge of inconsistency because he combined an increasingly gloomy analysis of the totality on the macrological level with a call for theoretical and artistic resistance to it on the micrological. Either the totality was completely watertight in its reifying power . . . or the totality still contained negations and Adorno's descriptions of its Satanic 'falseness' were exaggerations."[10] The question of how to understand this paradox, aporia, or performative contradiction will form the central concern of this chapter.

For Marx science and technology still possessed an unambiguously emancipatory potential. Horkheimer and Adorno, however, are more skeptical about the ideal of objectivity in the positive—in their eyes, mainly positivistic—sciences. They emphasize further that the formalization of morality and right in the establishment of universal principles and laws threatens to render *indifferent* to reason all factors relating to empirical content, experience, and affect. Modern mass culture, they suggest, shows that the innovative power of art has become increasingly feeble, at best hibernating in avant-garde and esoteric works of art.

The more universal history fails to live up to the emancipatory promise of the reasonable control of the forces of—objective and human—nature; further, to the extent that the aspiration to natural law and the meaning of art to life become forgotten and nineteenth- and mid-twentieth-century bourgeois capitalist society distances itself from the slogans of freedom and equality, the less it becomes possible to describe *positively* a rational arrangement of public and private life. Apparently, the alternative to history as we know it can now be "thought" or "expressed" only *ex negativo,* as utopia and, therefore, *nowhere-near-place,* in the literal sense of the word. If the cynical views expressed by de Sade, Nietzsche, Goethe's Mephistopheles, and Dostoevsky's Grand Inquisitor speak the truth about modern culture,[11] then there is something absurd about adhering to an idea or postulate of the good life, just as it has become impossible to affirm or positively describe the unity of truth, morality, and beauty, their respective value spheres, claims, and discourses.

9. But see ibid., 128, 122.

10. Martin Jay, *Marxism and Totality: The Adventures of a Concept from Lukács to Habermas* (Berkeley: University of California Press, 1984), 264–65.

11. See Sloterdijk, *Kritik der zynischen Vernunft,* 1:330–69.

It would seem, then, that we ought to attempt only *quasi-theologically,* like Benjamin, to hold open a small gap in our world pictures through which the Messiah, at any moment, might still come.[12] In a fully administered world, in which a nearly irreconcilable contradiction between freedom and equality, between erotic life and the pill,[13] has become the rule, only a seemingly *unfulfillable longing* for the wholly other—a *Sehnsucht nach dem ganz Anderen,* as Horkheimer said, or an *unhappy consciousness,* as Hegel put it earlier—is possible. In this view marginalized and politically isolated individuals are the ones most capable of holding open any perspective toward general interests. Autonomy and maturity—*Mündigkeit,* as Kant said—is merely the ability to be alone. If one does not want silently and inadvertently to support the inhuman and, moreover, wants to preserve solidarity with the suffering that has occurred across the whole course of history, one should distance oneself from any overly enthusiastic praxis or immersion in "participation [*Mitmachen*]" (*MM* 26 / 27).[14]

Such an interpretation, however, implies a dramatic change in the conception of the breadth of Critical—or any other—Theory and its possible addressees. Theory and the philosophy that spells out its guiding idea, coins its concepts, formalizes its arguments, and produces its examples can from now on *appeal only to singular instances, not even given individuals,* without being able to expect any echo in the foreseeable future: it lies dormant like a "message in a bottle [*Flaschenpost*],"[15] because "true resistance" opposes the means and media of all propaganda and, ultimately, all communication, all summary paraphrase (*DE* 212 / 293). In a telling passage Adorno and Horkheimer draw the full consequences of this predicament: "What is suspect is not . . . the depiction of reality as hell but the routine invitation to break out of it. If discourse [*die Rede*] can be addressed to anyone today, it is neither to the so-called masses nor to the individual, who is powerless, but rather to an imaginary [*eingebildeter*] witness, to whom we bequeath it so that it is not entirely lost with us" (*DE* 213 / 294).

In this "moral pragmaticization [*Pragmatisierung*] of philosophy,"[16]

---

12. See Benjamin, *Gesammelte Schriften,* 1.2:704.

13. See Max Horkheimer, "Die Sehnsucht nach dem ganz Anderen," *Gesammelte Schriften,* vol. 7, ed. Gunzelin Schmid Noerr (Frankfurt a.M.: S. Fischer, 1985), 396.

14. See also the self-characterization of Leo Löwenthal in his book *Mitmachen wollte ich nie: Ein autobiographisches Gespräch mit Helmut Dubiel* (Frankfurt a.M.: Suhrkamp, 1980).

15. On Adorno's frequent use of this metaphor, see Wiggershaus, *Frankfurt School,* 279 / 313.

16. Dubiel, *Wissenschaftsorganisation und politische Erfahrung,* 130.

as Dubiel calls it, Critical Theory evolves from an interdisciplinary program of empirical and analytical research to a "comportment [or form of agency, *Verhalten*]" which can be expressed only in fragments: utopia can now only be "philosophized [*philosophiert*]," even "transcendentalized."[17] But this also holds for the subject whom it addresses, to whose "imagination [*Einbildungskraft*]"[18] or "exact fantasy [*exakte Phantasie*]"—two instances or instantiations of the need for "judgment" which I established in the previous chapter—one must now appeal.

This theoretical restriction of the competency of knowledge and coordinated—indeed, communicative—action has been interpreted as outright *resignation* about the possibilities of empirical and theoretical work, as the result of a mind-set completely given over to a *particular* historical constellation, in which what is most important can apparently no longer be grasped by scholarly, even rational, means.[19] Where in such an explanation the reception of Adorno's work oriented by social theory leaves off,[20] those interested in negative metaphysical elements and alternative models of agency and judgment are likely to prick up their ears. That is not necessarily a betrayal of Adorno and Horkheimer's original intentions. After all, they never believed that "the theory of society could account for the whole [*die Theorie der Gesellschaft sei das Ganze*]."[21]

This alleged attitude of resignation in the late work of the Frankfurt School has been the object of criticism not only because it deviates from the mainstream of Western Marxism but also because it increases skepticism about its own former ambitious program for an interdisciplinary social science or emancipatory theory. This skepticism marks the central turning point in the history of Critical Theory and provides the point of departure for our investigation. Here, too, we shall find numerous salient parallels with the thought of Levinas (or Lyotard and Derrida).[22]

17. Ibid., 126.

18. Ibid., 85, 126.

19. Wiggershaus, *Frankfurt School*, 496 / 553.

20. See representative essays by Helmut Dubiel, "Die Aktualität der Gesellschaftstheorie Adornos"; and Wolfgang Bonss, "Empirie und Dechiffrierung von Wirklichkeit: Zur Methodologie bei Adorno," both in von Friedeburg and Habermas, *Adorno-Konferenz 1983*, 293–313 and 201–25, respectively. See also the concluding section of Habermas, *Theory of Communicative Action;* and Honneth, *Kritik der Macht.*

21. Adorno, "Offener Brief an Max Horkheimer," *GS,* 20.1:158. On Adorno's increasing skepticism about and distancing from the potential of empirical social research in the course of the 1950s, see Dahms, *Positivismusstreit,* 285–319.

22. The much less controversial reference to methodological and thematic parallels in twentieth-century French thought is to Michel Foucault. See Kunneman, *De Waarheidstrechter;* Ha-

Of course, a question still remains: how is it possible to think or express the "increased abstraction [*Abstraktifizierung*] of the utopian frame of reference" at which Adorno hints[23]—and which for him, paradoxically, is often accompanied by a concretization of philosophical procedure—without immediately discrediting such abstraction in the name of a reinvigorated critical social theory or relegating it, in antiquarian fashion, to a bygone past? An answer to that question, I suggest, can be found in the fact that its argumentative scheme or nucleus—the relentless demonstration of the perils *and* chances of traditional and modern philosophy's inevitable aporias, as laid bare by and echoed in a procedure of calculated rhetorical exaggeration and intentional performative contradiction—cannot be reduced to the personal idiosyncrasy of these authors, has lost nothing of its systematic appeal, and could be reformulated in other philosophical idioms (nondialectical ones, e.g., phenomenological, analytical, pragmatist, or deconstructive). In order to make this clear we should take a step back, however, for the critical hermeneutics that resulted from the reorientation of Critical Theory in the 1940s, conceived via the traces and remnants of metaphysics, is not merely a reflection of the cruel realities of its time.[24] Its beginnings can be traced back to Adorno's earliest independent texts.

The *Urzelle*

As C. Petazzi rightly notes, the roots of Adorno's later thought extend far beyond the field marked out by the first members of the Frankfurt Institute. Adorno's thinking draws on eccentric philosophical and artistic sources, whose streams would suffuse the early formulation and subsequent modification of Critical Theory and, much later, negative dialectics, until the Frankfurt program, in its paradigm transformation after the linguistic and pragmatic turns, seemingly inevitably let them dry up again.[25] The "linguistification of the sacred" of which we spoke in the previous

bermas, *The Philosophical Discourse of Modernity;* and Honneth, *Kritik der Macht.* See also Michael Kelly, ed., *Critique and Power* (Cambridge: MIT Press, 1994). Foucault himself acknowledged analogies between his interests and those of Horkheimer and Adorno.

23. Dubiel, *Wissenschaftsorganisation und politische Erfahrung,* 84.

24. A fine sketch of the intellectual atmosphere in question can be found in Anson Rabinbach, *In the Shadow of Catastrophe: German Intellectuals between Apocalypse and Enlightenment* (Berkeley: University of California Press, 1997), esp. intro. and chap. 1.

25. C. Petazzi, "Studien zu Leben und Werk Adornos bis 1938," in *Theodor W. Adorno: Text und Kritik,* ed. Heinz Ludwig Arnold (Munich: Edition Text + Kritik, 1977), 23; see also Peter von Haselberg, "Wiesengrund-Adorno," in Arnold, *Theodor W. Adorno,* 7–21.

chapter resulted not only in the "liquefaction" of essentialist and reified forms of thought—a strategy Adorno might have approved, even though "solidarity with metaphysics in the moment of its downfall" would hardly welcome the destruction of metaphysics and the inauguration of a "post-metaphysical thinking"—but also in the virtual liquidation of some of his earliest and most persistent (indeed, for us most valuable) concerns. In this chapter I will revisit these original motifs, to track their subsequent and ever more subtle formalization and concretization in Adorno's writings of the middle and final period of his career, to evaluate their systematic—or antisystematic—claims systematically, and to investigate the possibility of translating and transcribing them into a logic and vocabulary other than his own.

An analysis of the influences that contributed to the formation of Adorno's complex and at times idiosyncratic intellectual horizon ought at the very least to note the importance of Siegfried Kracauer's stubbornly concrete sociological reading of Kant as well as Hans Cornelius's epistemological research, with its tendency toward "empirio-criticism" (the philosophical position of Ernst Mach and Richard Avenarius, with which W. I. Lenin would take issue in 1909 in his *Materialismus und Empiriokritizismus* [*Materialism and Empirical Criticism*], accusing it of subjective idealism, solipsism, and fideism, and Husserl would relentlessly criticize for its psychologism in *Logische Untersuchungen* [*Logical Investigations*]).[26] They helped Adorno early on to distinguish his own philosophical intuitions from the conceptual frameworks of neo-Kantianism and phenomenology. Between these two contrasting poles he discovered that "among the tensions that are the lifeblood of philosophy the tension between expression and rigor [or, rather, required acceptability, i.e., a certain imperative nature of things, or *Verbindlichkeit*] is perhaps the most central."[27]

In addition, one ought to note his musical studies under Alban Berg in Vienna in 1925 and, somewhat less directly, the charisma he experienced emanating from Arnold Schönberg and Karl Kraus.[28] My goal here, however, is not to discuss each and every influence on his development. It is

26. On the relationship between Horkheimer, Adorno, Benjamin, and Löwenthal, on the one hand, and Hans Cornelius, on the other, see Dahm, *Positivismusstreit*, 22 ff.

27. Adorno, "Der wunderliche Realist: Über Siegfried Kracauer," *NL* 389 / "The Curious Realist: On Siegfried Kracauer," *NL* 2:59.

28. See V. Zmegac, "Adorno und die Wiener Moderne der Jahrhundertwende," in Honneth and Wellmer, *Die Frankfurter Schule und die Folgen*, 321–38.

sufficient, as Jay remarks, to avoid "reducing Adorno to any particular star in his constellation."[29]

I take the period from 1927 to 1931 as terminus a quo for my investigation. During this time Adorno, strongly influenced by the early Benjamin of the *Ursprung des deutschen Trauerspiels* (*Origin of the German Mourning Play*), Lukács's *History and Class Consciousness*, and, to a somewhat lesser extent, Ernst Bloch's *Geist der Utopie* (*The Spirit of Utopia*), transformed the transcendental idealism of his teacher Cornelius into his own version of materialism. This metamorphosis is apparent already in his habilitation, which was accepted in 1931 by Paul Tillich, who replaced Cornelius and Max Scheler as chair of philosophy in Frankfurt,[30] and published in 1933 under the title *Kierkegaard: Konstruktion des Ästhetischen* (*Kierkegaard: Construction of the Aesthetic*). Its program is most cogently formulated, however, in the lecture "Die Aktualität der Philosophie" ("The Actuality of Philosophy"), with which Adorno assumed his position as lecturer at the same university in 1931.[31]

29. Martin Jay, "Adorno in Amerika," in von Friedeburg and Habermas, *Adorno-Konferenz 1983*, 358.

30. Not only was Tillich, after Hans Cornelius, Adorno's supervisor; he also instigated from early on a conversation on theological matters, to which the protocol of the dialogue that took place in Frankfurt in 1931, in which Adorno and Horkheimer participated, testifies. See Paul Tillich, "Das Frankfurter Gespräch," in Tillich, *Briefwechsel und Streitschriften: Theologische, philosophische und politische Stellungnahmen und Gespräche,* ed. Renate Albrecht and Rene Tautmann (Frankfurt a.M.: Evangelisches Verlagswerk, 1983), 314–69. Much later Adorno asked Paul Tillich to lend him (the third volume of) his *Systematic Theology* while he was composing the "Meditations on Metaphysics." See the editorial afterword to Adorno's lecture course *Metaphysics*, 194 / 298–99.

31. I will not consider *in extenso* Adorno's dissertation, *Die Transzendenz des Dinglichen und Noematischen in Husserls Phänomenologie,* written under the supervision of Hans Cornelius in 1924, or his habilitation, *Der Begriff des Unbewußten in der transzendentalen Seelenlehre* (1927), rescinded at Cornelius's request, although these, too, contain traces of Adorno's later development. The preface to the second book opens with an emphatic declaration that the aim of its epistemological, not historical, investigations is no other than *Aufklärung* in the double meaning of the word: namely, as the explication of a problem and in the much broader, modern sense of a "destruction of dogmatic theories and in their place the formation of theories that are grounded in experience and are, for this experience, beyond doubt." In addition to Cornelius, Adorno also credits "Dr. Max Horkheimer," Cornelius's assistant, for having helped him think through the dissolution of Kant's antinomies of unconsciousness, which had resulted from their "hypostatization [*Hypostasierungen*]" of Kantian limit concepts and, further, for having helped Adorno understand that the unconscious must be seen as a "task [*Aufgabe*]" (*GS* 1:81–82).

For a more extensive discussion, see G. Arlt, "Erkenntnistheorie und Gesellschaftskritik: Zur Möglichkeit einer transzendentalpsychologischen Analyse des Begriffs des Unbewußten in den Frühschriften Theodor W. Adornos," *Philosophisches Jahrbuch* 90 (1983): 129–45. See also Fred R. Dallmayr, "Phenomenology and Critical Theory: Adorno," *Cultural Hermeneutics* 3

THE KIERKEGAARD BOOK, to which, in a 1962 letter to Bloch, Adorno attributed "the character of a dreamlike anticipation,"[32] contains the actual
beginnings of his philosophy. As Benjamin observed in his review: "In
this book much is contained in little space. Very possible that the author's
later books will spring from this one. In any case the book belongs to that
class of rare and peculiar first works in which a winged thought appears
in the pupation of critique."[33]

The Kierkegaard study, however, scarcely presents itself as a systematic
treatise *in nuce*. Nor does it aim to contribute to the history of philosophical ideas. Instead, it takes the form of a collage of quotations, chosen in
such a way as to allow Kierkegaard's declared intentions to founder when
confronted with the actual manner — and mannerisms — in which they are
expressed. Although this montage of citation echoes and anticipates one
of Benjamin's favorite methods (which Adorno would have known from
conversations with Benjamin; the latter would most fully adopt it in the
Arcades Project), Adorno's reading also presages "deconstructive" reading
strategies. The two procedures are combined in an attempt to read Kierkegaard's texts against the grain precisely in order to *save* their "utopian" —
as it were, nondeconstructible — moment.

(1976): 367–405. Arlt shows the importance of this early study primarily by highlighting the
final section of Adorno's *Der Begriff des Unbewußten*, which relates Cornelius's transcendental analysis, as explicated (Adorno announces from the outset) in *Transcendentale Systematik:
Untersuchungen zur Begründung der Erkenntnistheorie* (Munich: E. Reinhardt, 1916), to Freudian psychoanalysis. For philosophical reasons and with a certain gusto for the critique of ideology, Adorno rejects vitalistic philosophies of the unconscious, which metaphysically reify this
concept and base it on an ideal of knowledge as intuition. Freudian psychoanalysis provides a
weapon against the "metaphysics of drives [*Triebmetaphysik*] and the idolization [*Vergottung*]
of mere, numb [*dumpf*] organic life" (*GS* 1:320), by showing that the unconscious can be pene-
trated by reflection. Thus, in Adorno's earliest work there already appears a line of defense
against the conservative critique of reason, even though in his late work he will no longer appeal to the transparency and reunification of conscious and unconscious being. Relevant in this
context are also Adorno's "Zur Philosophie Husserls," refused by Horkheimer for inclusion in
the *Zeitschrift für Sozialforschung* and first published in *GS* 20.1:46–118, as well as the text of a
lecture given at Columbia University and first published in the *Journal of Philosophy* 37, no. 1
(1940): 5–18. This text, entitled "Husserl and the Problem of Idealism," was republished in *GS*
20.1:119–34.

    32. Cited in Rolf Tiedemann, "Editorische Nachbemerkung," *GS* 1:384.

    33. Benjamin, "Kierkegaard: Das Ende des philosophischen Idealismus," *Gesammelte
Schriften*, 5.3:383, cited after the translation by Robert Hullot-Kentor in his foreword to *K*, xii–
xiii. See also Pettazzi, "Studien zu Leben und Werk Adornos bis 1938," 28–33; and the preface
of Éliane Escoubas to the French translation: "Adorno, Benjamin et Kierkegaard," in Adorno,
Kierkegaard: Construction de l'esthétique, trans. Éliane Escoubas (Paris: Payot & Rivages, 1995),
i–xvii.

In his review of Adorno's first philosophical publication, Benjamin correctly notes that Kierkegaard is not "continued [*fortgeführt*]" here, as he is in Karl Barth's dialectical theology. Instead, he is turned around, set back, and relegated "to the core of philosophical idealism, under whose spell [*Bannkreis*] the thinker's intentions, which are in fact theological, remain condemned to languish."[34] Whether or not Adorno's reading actually does justice to the whole of Kierkegaard's work or to its fundamental intent and style is of little concern here.[35] Instead, I am interested in the degree to which this first of Adorno's philosophical publications prepares the way for his distinctive figures of thought.

As Adorno retrospectively noted in 1966, his interpretation of Kierkegaard already announces a critique of "existential ontology" (K 262), in particular of Heidegger's thought, which will later be taken up explicitly in a central chapter of *Negative Dialectics* and in the pamphlet *Jargon der Eigentlichkeit* (*Jargon of Authenticity*). He also criticizes the antagonism toward nature apparent in Kierkegaard's description of subjective existence as an "objectless interiority" (K 53 / 78). This inwardness, which Kierkegaard believes to be removed from the vortex of determinations envisaged by the Hegelian philosophy of history, thus lacks any real *con-*

---

34. Benjamin, *Gesammelte Schriften*, 3:381.

35. This question plays an important role in the controversies between Kodalle and Hermann Deuser. See Klaus-M. Kodalle, "Adornos Kierkegaard — Ein kritischer Kommentar," in *Die Rezeption S. Kierkegaards in der deutschen und dänischen Philosophie und Theologie: Vorträge des Kolloquiums am 22. und 23. März 1982*, ed. Heinrich Anz, Poul Lübke, and Friedrich Schmöe (Copenhagen: W. Fink, 1983), 70–100; and the companion article by Hermann Deuser, "Kierkegaard in der Kritischen Theorie," 101–13. See also Kodalle, *Die Eroberung des Nutzlosen*, 195–214, 223–33; and Hermann Deuser, *Dialektische Theologie: Studien zu Adornos Metaphysik und zum Spätwerk Kierkegaards* (Munich: Kaiser, 1980). Kodalle maintains that Adorno "continually — as in a diversionary tactic — compiles arguments against Kierkegaard that remain adequate solely to his own position" (80). Adorno overlooks, he says, the fact that Kierkegaard thinks the incommensurability of inwardness and meaning in relation to exteriority primarily as a "corrective" (78). Such a figure of thought, he believes, could safeguard Adorno's own negative dialectic. One can, however, find this motif of a corrective in Adorno as well, in addition to a more subtle description than Kodalle suggests of the negativity of history and of the other. The decisive point seems to be that Adorno distances himself from a pathos that sees "in the highest tension [*Anspannung*] of existence" a possibility for the subject to project itself into the "space in which the absolute exists" (79). Adorno alludes far more ambivalently and in a less subject-centered way than Kierkegaard to the disruption of the autonomy and sovereignty of the ego by an other, which cannot be identified without ipso facto being betrayed. Precisely this increased ambivalence and antisubjectivism forms the basis of Adorno's repeated critique of existentialism and personalism, as the introductory section of *Negative Dialectics* testifies. A similar rejection can be found in Levinas, whose relation to Kierkegaard is at least as complex. See chap. 2, "Kierkegaardian Meditations," in my book *Religion and Violence*.

cretization and is therefore unthinkable "in its fullness" (*K* 51 / 76). In 1969
Adorno described his book as a departure from Kierkegaard.[36] He would
return to Kierkegaard on two other occasions (in 1940 and 1963), and references to this author are interspersed throughout his other major writings. But he would never revoke his early assessment—so different in tone
and argument from those of his contemporaries (the dialectical theologians, especially Karl Barth in the second edition of *Der Römerbrief* [*The
Epistle to the Romans*], but also Heidegger's early writings).[37]

Adorno's rejection of Kierkegaardian "spiritualism" contains the beginnings of a subtle critique of Hegel. In effect, Adorno plays Kierkegaard
and Hegel against each other. With Kierkegaard he denies, on the one
hand, the actuality and possibility that the contradictions between reality
and philosophical discourse concerning the "concept" can be reconciled,
while, on the other, with Hegel he dismisses a transcendence that cannot
be mediated in any way:

> Kierkegaard, in contrast to Hegel, failed to achieve historical concretion—
> the only authentic concretion; he absorbed it into the blind self, volatilized
> it in the empty spheres: he thereby surrendered philosophy's central claim to
> truth—the interpretation of reality. . . . More emphatically than all previous
> philosophers, Hegel posited the question of concretion, but succumbed help-
> lessly to it by believing that he had produced it; succumbed to a reality that
> is not rational [*vernünftig*] vis-à-vis a "meaning [*Sinn*]" that escaped from
> it. Both philosophers remain idealists: Hegel by the concluding conceptual
> definition of existence [*Dasein*] as meaningful, "rational"; Kierkegaard by ne-
> gating Hegel's claim and tearing "meaning" away from existence with the
> same insistence that Hegel forces them together. (*K* 93 / 133–34)

Kierkegaard's idea of individual existence, Adorno suggests, merely
internalizes Hegelian world history: his concept of the self inadvertently
amounts to that discredited system, this time, however, "dimensionlessly
concentrated in the 'point'" (*K* 80 / 116, see 32–33 / 49). His "negative philosophy of history" (*K* 36 / 55) discards the exteriority of nature, together
with that of history, while secretly being subjected to them. One can escape from the despair to which this immanence of the "eviscerated self
[*entselbsteten Selbst*]" (*K* 56 / 82) unavoidably leads only via a paradoxi-

36. Jay, *Dialectical Imagination*, 68, 313 n. 118.
37. See Theodor W. Adorno, "Kierkegaards Lehre von der Liebe" ("Kierkegaard's Doctrine of Love"), in *GS* 2:217–36; and Adorno, "Kierkegaard noch einmal" ("Kierkegaard Once
More"), in *GS* 2:239–58.

cal leap into transcendence. This radically heteronomous gesture takes on the character of a *salto mortale,* because in the same moment it crosses out subjectivity itself. Paradoxically, any such escape thereby lapses even more forcefully into mythical nature, which in its absolute freedom it imagined itself to have fled. How, then, would it be possible to avoid nature and history in their petrified form as myth(s), whose presence or perpetual recurrence Adorno in no way denies? How could one criticize this constant sameness—in Adorno's idiom, *das Immergleiche*—without, *nolens volens,* remaining trapped within it? In this difficulty of thinking, living, and acting upon some *ontological escape* we touch upon a theme that inaugurates Levinas's independent thought—and, indeed, upon his intellectual germ *Urzelle,* the essay *De l'évasion* (*On Escape*).

Adorno subjects Kierkegaard to a double reading, one that simultaneously is deconstructive and follows the lines of ideology critique. First, according to his analysis, an insufficiently reflected upon, Left-Hegelian reaction to the reified world of commodities is mirrored in Kierkegaard's notion of an isolated inwardness (*K* 38–40, 48 / 59–61, 71). Second, the metaphors Kierkegaard uses to describe this inwardness are, in Adorno's eyes, taken from the bourgeois *intérieur* (*K* 40 ff. / 61 ff.). Third, Kierkegaard's allusions to spirituality, despite all appearances, have physicality and embodiment at their core (*K* 54 / 77). Through his interpretation Adorno thus relativizes the idealistic dualisms of inner and outer, spirit and nature, freedom and necessity. He suggests—both directly, by way of explicit theses, and indirectly, by presenting Kierkegaard's conflicting moments, thus playing out this author's intent against the letter of his text—that these oppositions ought not to be isolated in an abstract fashion that would forgo their dialectical mediation or prematurely identified in "dialectical sublation."

Here Adorno touches on a point that will remain important for the later development and deepening of his critique of Hegel. At the same time, he paves the way for *a third way between the metaphysics of absolute reason and the decisionism that pervades every existential, ethical allegiance (Observanz) or leap of faith.* The purported controversy between these opposing positions, Adorno concludes, "cannot be concluded on idealistic terrain" (*K* 93 / 133). In consequence, the customary interpretation—namely, that Adorno, in his materialist and, as we shall see, *infinitist* revision of dialectical thought, merely projects the Hegelian synthesis "into time"—becomes highly questionable. We will see why Adorno does *not* situate a Hegelian telos in a messianic (as opposed to historical) time, in another time, albeit the time of the other. Nor does he simply place it beyond time, in an ethereal atemporality, let alone a *nunc stans,* of sorts. For Adorno the idea of utopia is not—primarily—about a future dimension in the sense "in which the certainty of its occurrence is bound up with uncertainty about its content and the manner in which it will realize itself."[38] Although much in *Kierkegaard* and his other texts might suggest such an interpretation, there are no less essential passages in which reconciliation— *Versöhnung* being a concept or term Adorno refuses to drop— is no longer thought of as arriving in any future time (or futurity, historicity) whatsoever. The *appearance* of a positive eschatology, which shines out "in reverse [*in Verkehrung*]" (K 140 / 198, trans. modified) in the sorrowing gaze, can, upon closer examination, never fulfill but only *intensify* and *increase* desire, to borrow a motif from Levinas. Perhaps that is why at the end of his book Adorno no longer speaks of a desire or longing for transcendence but, rather, of the *transcendence of longing:* "Longing [*Sehnsucht*] is not extinguished in the images [*Bildern*], but survives in them just as it emanates from them. By the strength of the immanence of their content, the transcendence of longing is achieved" (K 140 / 199).

Perhaps Adorno's comment, in the "Note" added to the 1966 edition, that after so many years there were many things in the text he no longer approved of concerns the contrasting "positive" formulations, which are hardly commensurable with the open-ended gesture of thought expressed in the formula the "transcendence of longing."

The metaphysical tone of the work seemed to him in retrospect more affirmative, "more celebratory, more idealistic than it should have been," on grounds that, he acknowledged, were related to historical experiences no less than to structural and analytical necessities (two conditions of philosophical discourse which, in any post-Hegelian dialectical view, however "negative"—as in Adorno's own "negative dialectics"—remain deeply intertwined): "What has transpired since 1933 ought least of all [*am letzten*] to leave undisturbed a philosophy that always knew to resist equating metaphysics with a doctrine of ahistorical unchangingness" (K 261). But moments in this early text on Kierkegaard—conceived and written well before the events that "transpired since 1933"—already suggest the later articulation and modification of a *metaphysical experience* still possible (or, perhaps, for the first time possible) "after Auschwitz."

---

38. Petazzi, "Studien zu Leben und Werk Adornos bis 1938," 35.

Adorno speaks, for example, of a "secret writing [*Geheimschrift*]," in which the divine truth of the "invariable meaning [*konstante Sinn*] of the invariable text" for Kierkegaard is simultaneously hidden or "displaced," and alludes to Kafka — "a late pupil of Kierkegaard" — whose parables express this motif in the most exemplary way (*K* 25 / 39).

Likewise, Adorno uses the concept of allegory to present the *ambiguity of the ethical and the aesthetic* and to illustrate the paradox of the *hidden and indirect communication* (*Mitteilung*) of the religious in Kierkegaard. Both modalities, he suggests, involve a dimension of reality that is neither ontologically given in advance nor capable of being captured in intersubjective categories but points toward a "realm in between [*Zwischenreich*]," which appears in "affect." According to Adorno, Benjamin's concept of allegory as "not merely a sign but an expression" illuminates this idea (*K* 26 / 40). In such a framework, *unlike any conventional theological symbolism,* there is an unbridgeable abyss between the sphere of immanence and that of lost "meaning," which supposedly remains valid and effective only as an "abstract desideratum" (*K* 26–27 / 41). This could be gleaned from Kierkegaard's concept of dialectics as well as from the general proximity to the baroque in his work, which Adorno, following Benjamin, underscores. Kierkegaard shares with the baroque an emphasis on closed immanence and a creaturely desolation as well as the "the conjuration through allegory of fallen contents of being [*Beschwörung entsunkener Seinsgehalte durch Allegorie*]" (*K* 62 / 91, trans. modified). Adorno's interpretation of Kierkegaardian "melancholy [or depression, *Schwermut*]" (*K* 59–62 / 90–91) also belongs in this context. "Dialectical in itself" and exposed as "semblance" where it remains condemned to inwardness, this affect finally is also the "image of an other [*Bild eines Anderen*]" (*K* 61/ 90). It pursues the "deliverance of lost 'meaning'" and knows no other way to grasp truth than in the form of "imagination" (*K* 60–61/89). These and other motifs in Kierkegaard's work lead Adorno to suspect that *utter despair is inconceivable* (*K* 139 / 196). We will return later to this motif in his thought, which is one of the most difficult to interpret and in which much that remains unarticulated nonetheless resonates.

Strikingly, Adorno's critique of Kierkegaard is triggered above all by the privileged position of *subjectivity* as the scene of transcendence. On similar grounds, from his earliest writings onward, Adorno distrusts Heidegger, whose "existential ontology" he sees as hovering in the vicinity

of Kierkegaard's "existential dialectics." Heidegger, too, he suggests, resorts to substantive determinations (imbued with empirical or ontic content despite their formally indicative function),[39] which he places deep
within the structures of subjectivity because he does not succeed in disclosing them "in the open fullness [*in der offenen Fülle*]" of nature and
society (APh 123 / 329). The very idea of being, toward which Adorno already directs his fire, is, according to him, only "an empty form-principle
[*Formalprinzip*] whose archaic dignity helps to cover any content whatsoever" (APh 120 / 325). Such stark formulations say nothing about Adorno's
undeniable proximity to Heidegger on many other points, and Adorno's
characterization of Heidegger's philosophy violates, more than once, the
standards of immanent critique he himself developed, as one can learn
from the work of Hermann Mörchen.[40] Here, however, we are interested
in the reasons that lead Adorno to regard every program of a subjective ontology, including its anticipation in the work of Kierkegaard, as
condemned to failure. Kierkegaard's goal of newly grounding ontology
in existence is, according to Adorno, "irreparably shattered" because his
"restless dialectic" can never get firm ground under its feet, never arrive at
a single, "firmly grounded being" (APh 123 / 329). Precisely in the foundering and abandonment of such designs begin to emerge the contours that
a truly interpretive philosophy must assume.

The Hermeneutics of the Riddle

Adorno's inaugural address, "The Actuality of Philosophy" (which he
intended to dedicate to Benjamin but then never published),[41] presents the
first explicit formulation of such a fragmented hermeneutics. The text is of
interest not least because of the subtle ways in which, in this outline for a
philosophical program, he distinguishes his approach, guiding concepts,
and central methodology from those of his contemporaries. Here Adorno
describes philosophy as the *activity of solving riddles,* a position that not
only indicates the influence of Benjamin's early work but also suggests
close proximity to the antimetaphysical pathos of the Vienna Circle. An-

39. See the chapter "Formal Indication," in my book *Philosophy and the Turn to Religion.*
40. See Hermann Mörchen, *Macht und Herrschaft im Denken von Heidegger und Adorno*
(Stuttgart: Klett-Cotta, 1980); and Mörchen, *Adorno und Heidegger: Untersuchung einer philosophischen Kommunikationsverweigerung* (Stuttgart: Klett-Cotta, 1981); as well as the critical
review by Hans Ebeling, "Adornos Heidegger und die Zeit der Schuldlosen," *Philosophische
Rundschau* 29 (1982): 188–96.
41. Tiedemann, "Editorische Nachbemerkung," *GS* 1:383.

ticipating some of the arguments formulated by Horkheimer in his 1937 article "Der neueste Angriff auf die Metaphysik" ("The Latest Attack on Metaphysics"), which effectively terminated the chances for cooperation between the two groups, he counters the works of logical positivism with a series of fatal objections that have since become commonly accepted in the postempiricist philosophy of science.[42] Ironically and, as we shall see, unjustly, almost all representatives of the second (and third) generation of the Frankfurt School tradition in Critical Theory, with its program now shifted toward the paradigm of transcendental or formal pragmatics following the linguistic turn in (post)analytic philosophy, continue to make just these objections against the purportedly subjectivist and monological presuppositions in Adorno's own work. Yet the problematic aspect of his thought hardly lies in inattention to language or in ignoring the differences between the philosophy of the subject, with its intrinsic idealism and atomism, and the complexities of intersubjectivity. It is just that all paradoxes and aporias diagnosed in the domain of subjective interiority simply reappear, albeit in different guises, in the realm of exteriority in which subjects interact and converse with one another. No general theory of rationality and communicative action, no matter how provisional and hypothetical—how fallibilistic and counterfactual—its presuppositions, can ignore or gloss over this fact (which is, as Adorno will come to suggest, a fact of reason in its own right).

According to Adorno, the epistemological criterion applied by the (logical) empiricist critique is too rigid, both in its purported departure from tradition and in its reduction of philosophy to scientific methodology. This supposed "turn" in philosophy ignores at least two problems.[43] First, Adorno stresses a post-Kantian insight belonging to the philosophy of history, if not the historicism that followed in Hegel's wake: "the subject of the given [*Gegebenheit*] is not ahistorically identical and transcenden-

42. Horkeimer's attempt to situate "materialism" in relation to "positivism" is interesting in this context. Dahm demonstrates that, although before attacking the Vienna Circle in 1937 Horkheimer positioned himself in close proximity to the logical-empiricist or neopositivist criterion of taking sensible "experience" and controllability to be touchstones for the establishment and justification of knowledge and meaningfulness (of propositional content, concepts, and terms), he nonetheless defined experience in much broader terms than they did. He thereby also anticipated some of the later insights concerning the theory-laden character of experience. (See Dahm, *Positivismusstreit*, 53–58.)

43. See Moritz Schlick, "Die Wende der Philosophie," in *Logischer Empirismus—Der Wiener Kreis: Ausgewählte Texte mit einer Einleitung*, ed. H. Schleichert (Munich: Wilhelm Fink, 1975), 12–19.

tal, but rather assumes a changing and historically comprehensible form" (APh 125 / 333). Second, in a pragmatist insight *avant la lettre*,[44] Adorno indicates that a radical and ultimately subjectivist philosophy of empiricism can never account for intersubjectivity. This second point concerns the problem that would (later) come to be known, in phenomenology, as that of the *alter ego* (as developed by Husserl in the fifth of his *Cartesianische Meditationen* [*Cartesian Meditations*]) and, in the analytic tradition, as that of *other minds* (to cite Austin's terminology). Adorno accuses the empiricist critique of attempting to resolve this problem starting out from the supposed analogy of our own psychological ideas, distilled from sensible impressions, to the experience of other subjects. By contrast, he insists that the simple given of linguistic capabilities, which obviously is also constitutive of the verification postulates of empiricism, already assumes others and thus intersubjectivity.

In spite of these two shortcomings, logical positivism has, Adorno acknowledges, contributed to a more precise assessment of the task of philosophy. It has cleared out a host of surreptitious metaphysical presuppositions in several complex questions of theoretical formation, not least by demonstrating that some issues should be relegated to the disciplinary sciences, whereas others require a mode of inquiry proper to the conceptual analysis and *inter*disciplinary activity of philosophy. If philosophy is not to succumb to dogmatism, it must, paradoxically, enter into a symbiosis with science, which can never be free of tension, and simultaneously give voice to what is *forgotten* in the systematic division of labor between the disciplines, however advanced.

In his discussion of the "saving of the phenomena" (to cite an age-old dictum) which he thus attributes to philosophy, Adorno attends, above all, to Benjamin's theory of epistemology as set out in the preface to the *Trauerspielbuch*. In understanding reality as a text to be deciphered, he follows in Benjamin's footsteps. According to Adorno, no positive meaning, substance, or essence lies hidden in or behind such "writing [*Schrift*]." The "fragmentation [*Brüchigkeit*] in being itself" makes it impossible to assume that there could be a full meaning — or meaningfulness — of reality (APh 125 / 334). In this sense truth can no longer be understood as the fulfillment, confirmation, or corroboration of one's anticipations (or, as Heidegger would say, *Vorgriffe*) and expectations but occurs, rather, in

---

44. On the debates between Critical Theory and American pragmatism, see Dahms, *Positivismusstreit*, 191 ff.

the "death of intention [*Tod der Intention*]," to borrow Benjamin's central phrase. In Adorno's words:

> He who interprets by searching behind the phenomenal world for a world-in-itself which forms its foundation and support acts mistakenly, like someone who wants to find in the riddle the reflection [*Abbild*] of a being which lies behind it, a being mirrored in the riddle, by which it lets itself be carried. Instead, the function of riddle-solving is to light up the riddle-*Gestalt* like lightning [*blitzhaft*] and to negate [and sublate, *aufheben*] it, not to persist behind the riddle and imitate it. Authentic [*Echte*] philosophic interpretation does not meet up with a fixed meaning that already lies, immobile, behind the question, but lights it up suddenly and momentarily [*augenblicklich*], and consumes it at the same time. Just as riddle-solving is constituted, in that the singular and dispersed elements of the question are brought into various groupings long enough for them to close together in a figure [*Figur*] out of which the solution springs forth, while the question disappears — so philosophy has to bring its elements, which it receives from the sciences, into changing constellations, or, to say it with less astrological and scientifically more current expression, into changing trial combinations [*Versuchsanordnungen*], until they fall into a figure which becomes readable [*lesbar*] as an answer, while at the same time the question disappears. The task of philosophy is not to search for concealed and manifest [or present at hand, *vorhandene*] intentions of reality, but to interpret an intentionless reality. (APh 127 /335, trans. modified)

If thinking cannot reduce things to (one) implicit meaning — as, for example, a religious one — then it must separate itself from a philosophy of *symbols*. The idealist tradition used the symbol to ground the particular, allowing it to be illuminated by the universal, which it in turn reflected or represented. By contrast, via an *allegory* of fragmented, nonsymbolic phenomena, philosophy as practiced by Benjamin and Adorno allows the *concrete* to be retrieved, indeed saved, and respected.

Adorno's further formulation of a philosophy that would abandon the spirit of traditional philosophies of identity and totality and follow only the *byways of interpretation* thus cannot be understood outside the stamp impressed upon it by the work of Benjamin. This is equally true for the concepts he uses to delineate the hermeneutical figures of thought still available to philosophy after the collapse of the great philosophical systems: *configuration, constellation, mosaic,* and *micrology,* though the list is far from complete.

Philosophy, Adorno writes, "cannot do without the least thread [*des geringsten Fadens*] which earlier times [*die Vorzeit*] have spun and through which the lineature is perhaps completed which could transform ciphers into a text." The ephemeral traits in the present and the past which philosophy tries to retrace and convey do not of themselves guarantee the good, the true, and the beautiful, let alone their supposed traditional unity; the traits in question are in various ways entangled with "demonic forces [or powers, *Gewalten*]" (APh 126 / 334). For all their "absolution" — that is to say, while being absolved from every text or context, which only philosophical reading or interpretation can establish — they are in no way innocent. A careful reading of these "remains of the world of appearance" (APh 128 / 336, trans. modified), however, promises to turn the mythical powers upside down or at least to strip them of their (thus far or once again) uncontested validity.

Nevertheless, and in unmistakable contrast to some aspirations of early Critical Theory and its later transformations into the theory of communicative action, the discursive theory of ethics and right, the struggle for recognition, and the like, Adorno leaves no misunderstanding that his program, "precisely as a program . . . does not allow itself to be worked out in completeness and generality" (APh 129 / 339). Its potential fruitfulness appears in the striking development of detail, which requires what Adorno calls "exact fantasy." By this he understands an imagination that, regarding the questions forced upon it by reality, "rearranges the elements of the question without going beyond the circumference of the elements, the exactitude of which has its control in the disappearance of the question" (APh 131 / 342).

This last phrase, however, betrays an almost logical empiricist or neopositivist pathos — in a sense, even a deconstructive affirmation — which disappears in the most rigorous articulations of his late work. Helping the question dissolve and making it lose its very meaning, hinting at the beyond or the before of the question and the questioning attitude that Derrida invokes in his discussion of Heidegger: these motifs are at odds with others that, in the later Adorno, tend to make the riddle and riddle solving *even more enigmatic*. In *Aesthetic Theory*, for example, we read that the solution to the riddle consists in indicating the very reason for the impossibility of its resolution. Adorno thereby replaces the image of the Gordian knot to be cut through with the figure of an intrigue that cannot be unraveled or, more cautiously, a permanent — yet ultimately unsustainable — oscillation and dialectic between the riddling character of reality and the misleading unambiguousness of philosophical concepts.

The early essay is also informative for the way in which Adorno believes he can connect the figure of the riddle to *materialism*. Materialism, according to Adorno, completes "in *earnest*" the gesture attributed to the *play* in solving riddles. The philosophical interpretation of reality and its sublation are mutually related, each implicating the other: "The interpretation of given reality and its abolition are connected to each other, not, of course, in the sense that reality is negated [or sublated, *aufgehoben*] in the concept, but that out of the construction of a configuration of reality [*Figur des Wirklichen*] the demand for its [reality's] real change always follows promptly." It is not clear, however, how such a transition is possible *without* presupposing once again the metaphysical premises of identity philosophy—which ought to be avoided on the grounds of Adorno's own argument in this early lecture. In the sentence immediately following, Adorno therefore modifies somewhat the intended unification of theory and practice: "The change-causing gesture of the riddle game [*Rätsel-spiels*]—not its mere resolution as such—provides the originary image [*Urbild*] of resolutions to which materialist praxis alone has access" (APh 129 / 338, trans. modified). This gesture is nothing other than what has been expressed, at its core, by the word *dialectics*, a concept that Adorno will increasingly attempt to free from its connotations and implications in the service of philosophies of identity and totality and turn into an open concept (while, in the process, remaining continually aware of the long shadows cast over his own—or any dialectician's—work by the remnants of metaphysical presuppositions). His notion of practice also is clarified in the course of this development. It betrays increasing ambivalence—increasing "patience," as Levinas would say, which should be distinguished from any quietism or resignation—and thereby a shift of emphasis which seems hardly compatible with the original, somewhat activist and engaged (if not interventionist or anarchist, let alone decisionist and spontanist) intentions of the Frankfurt School and assumes its proper place only in his later work.

In his "Offener Brief an Max Horkheimer" ("Open Letter to Max Horkheimer") Adorno notes retrospectively, "The tension upon which we work throughout our life is, I may be so bold as to say, inexhaustible in that it is itself the vacillating [*schwebende*] and fragile [*zerbrechliche*] reality that we try in vain to articulate."[45] If this is the upshot of Adorno's early program, progressively realized in the later work—precisely in ex-

45. Adorno, *GS* 20.1:159.

ploring increasing ambivalence—then what is problematic in Adorno's thought is not so much the purported traits of subjectivism (as Habermas and others have repeatedly suggested) but, rather, the (indeed, undeniable) reminiscences and metaphysical remains of the illusion of a messianic overcoming of such ambivalence, failure, and vanity of articulation. A truly open-ended dialectics, living up to Adorno's earliest aspirations, would be situated *between the philosophy of origins and quasi-theological eschatology,* granting these concepts only the limited value of a critical corrective, not the status of the beginning, end, or center of thought. It is worth noting that Adorno almost never draws this inevitable consequence of his dialectical critique of ontology and idealism without hesitation, that is to say, without ambivalence. The ambiguity persists—and increases—throughout the various themes and stages of his later thinking, to which I will now turn.

Chapter Four

The Construction of Occidental Subjectivism

Reductio ad hominem versus
Remembrance of Nature in the Subject

IN *DIALECTIC OF ENLIGHTENMENT* Horkheimer and Adorno weigh up the entire Western process of rationalization and modernization. *Enlightenment,* in their sense, no longer exclusively refers to the cultural correlatives of the societal development of the middle class in eighteenth-century Europe. Instead, it serves to label a phenomenon that encompasses a number of aspects of Western thinking as a whole. In their view "enlightenment" already exists in the earliest Greek myths and in the biblical passages of Genesis which crown man lord of creation (*DE* 5 / 24). Yet in these earliest accounts the paradox or even internal contradiction of such enlightenment makes its first appearance as well: if one can be set free from nature, one can never entirely escape—reinforcing, displacing, interiorizing—its power. Myth, in spite (or because?) of its attempt to *master* human destiny, makes that clear.

Every mythological representation is formed, according to Horkheimer and Adorno, in imitation (mimesis) of nature. Myths describe, on closer scrutiny, nothing but "natural conditions [or relations, *Naturverhältnisse*]" or "nature as self-repetition" (*DE* 12 / 33), and through them thought brings itself into line with the world. Thus, initially "mimesis" is merely a *terminus technicus* for the primary movement of all workings of thought, though it often suggests something more: "Mimesis is the name for the sensuously receptive, expressive, and communicative modes of behavior by which living beings nestle themselves [into their world and with respect to one another]."[1] This initial and no longer purely instinc-

---

1. Albrecht Wellmer, *Zur Dialektik von Moderne und Postmoderne: Vernunftkritik nach Adorno* (Frankfurt a.M.: Suhrkamp, 1985), 12. On this concept, see also Habermas, *Philosophisch-politische Profile,* 362–63; Habermas, *Theory of Communicative Action,* 1:453 n. 52 / 1:512 n. 111; Josef F. Schmucker, *Adorno: Logik des Zerfalls* (Stuttgart: Frommann-Holzboog, 1977),

tual gesture of unfolding human thought and experience already encompasses a moment of enlightenment. It attempts to rid natural phenomena of their immediacy, although, lacking as yet any explanatory instance, it can only appeal to demonic or divine powers. This "ruse" of the mythological worldview and of ritual action casts a long shadow, however. The more fully explicated modern forms of knowledge which we are accustomed to describe as "enlightened" must also follow this primary—even primordial—movement of mimesis. Bacon's well-known dictum *natura non nisi parendo vincitur* has forever documented our repressed memory of this fact. That in order to master nature one must first obey it is no new insight. *Dialectic of Enlightenment* proclaims, with unprecedented severity and dramatic effect, the suffering with which both mankind and nature must pay for this.

Myth and science, in the judgment of the authors, both derive from human anxiety and are therefore an "echo of the real preponderance [*Übermacht*] of nature" (*DE* 10–11 / 31; cf. *ND* 172 / 174). Enlightenment is the attempt to correct this distorted relationship—though it inadvertently misses the correct equilibrium—via a comprehension that, in principle, leaves nothing out. Yet this "outside" (the nonidentical, as Adorno calls it; exteriority, as Levinas will say) is precisely the source and sum of all fears.

In its demythologizing and unmasking, reason contains a gesture toward conceptual totalization and therein, Horkheimer and Adorno suggest—as if this inference and apparent isomorphy were not deeply questionable and could be assumed without further demonstration—an initial susceptibility to and intellectual justification for totalitarianism in the political sense of the word. Indeed, if power and knowledge seem to have become synonymous in the process of disenchantment and the mastery of both internal and external nature (see *DE* 2 / 20), then the historical and moral consequences can only be catastrophic.

The upshot of the universal historical analyses presented by the authors of *Dialectic of Enlightenment* is an almost despairing attempt to understand "why humanity, instead of entering a truly human state, is sinking into a new kind of barbarism" (*DE* xiv / 11). In search of a plausible explanation for this unmistakable shadow side or even "self-destruction"

29 n. 63; and Josef Früchtl, *Mimesis: Konstellation eines Zentralbegriffs bei Adorno* (Würzburg: Köningshausen & Neumann, 1986).

of enlightenment, Horkheimer and Adorno find themselves from the very beginning in a dire and paradoxical situation, which they formulate in unmistakable terms, putting all their cards on the table yet avowing the performative contradiction of this very gesture: "We have no doubt—and herein lies our *petitio principii*—that freedom in society is inseparable from enlightenment thinking. We believe we have perceived with equal clarity, however, that the very concept of that thinking, no less than the concrete historical forms, the institutions of society with which it is intertwined, already contains the germ of the regression which is taking place everywhere today" (*DE* xvi / 13).

Enlightenment inscribes on its banner the disenchantment of the world and wishes to destroy opinion and myth in order to ground the authority of knowledge. Yet what Horkheimer and Adorno *retrospectively* observe or, better, *construct* is the reversal of this potential for critique into an affirmation of whatever is. The perspective of freedom, which was once brought to bear against older forms and modes of thought, results in a new domination: "What freedom produced reverses into unfreedom" (*ND* 262 / 259, trans. modified). Yet the structural ambiguity and aporia of enlightenment is not completely thought through in the fragments that make up *Dialectic of Enlightenment*. Moreover, the tone Adorno and Horkheimer adopt is strikingly different from the one that interests us both in the earliest writings (the book on Kierkegaard and the inaugural lecture on the actuality of philosophy) and in the later, more consistent and consequential work that leads up to and culminates in *Negative Dialectics*.

The critique of enlightenment has two aspects. The authors disclose the repressive moment of enlightenment which, as Adorno will later express it, "hides in the principle of rationality itself" (*ND* 214 / 213), while rejecting every affirmative discourse concerning an other of reason as well as every direct reference to an originary and diffuse unity with nature or among individuals. Yet, whereas *Dialectic of Enlightenment* likewise states that the "not merely theoretical but practical tendency toward self-destruction has been inherent in rationality from the first, not only in the present phase when it is emerging nakedly" (*DE* xix / 17), the analysis of the destructive aspects of progress is never about a "conservation of the past" but, rather, about a "fulfillment of past hope [*Einlösung der vergangenen Hoffnung*]" (*DE* xvii / 15, trans. modified; see also 60–61 / 97). The structural resemblance between this *resolution of a hope that no longer is*

(or that *no longer is ours*) with the "solidarity with metaphysics in the moment of its downfall" will occupy me later. Suffice it to note that both
formulations retain, in the very mode of their *forlornness* or *transience*, the
impetus — one is tempted to say, the formal schema — of traditional hope
and the substance of metaphysical ideas. This and nothing else we will discover to be the modality of transcendence and the infinite that can — still,
once again, or for the first time? — mean something to us under modern
or postmodern conditions of thought and experience.

It is therefore questionable to interpret *Dialectic of Enlightenment* and
Adorno's later work as the reprise of an archaic, romantic, or nostalgic critique of culture, however much some of what he says might suggest that.[2]
Motifs of this sort suffer the same fate as the religious Judeo-Christian
topoi in Critical Theory: the figures of thought in which they are cited
work ipso facto, a transformation *beyond recognition.* Such topoi thus take
on a meaning that they neither possess in themselves nor receive from
an earlier context. But how, in fact, could we understand any meaning
kath'auto, any meaning "without context," as Levinas will say? This question will concern me throughout the following chapters.

Horkheimer and Adorno mistrust every reference to a kind of irrationalism concerning the *ratio* of enlightenment, its concept and its historical
practice. They refuse any invocation of forms of knowledge or experience which purport to be simply other than modern, rational knowledge
or modes of experience: "Thought therefore becomes illusory whenever
it seeks to deny its function of separating, distancing, and objectifying"
(*DE* 31 / 57, trans. modified; see also *Drei Stud* 311). Like the *Habilitationsschrift* and the inaugural lecture, the critique of instrumental reason formulated in the *Dialectic of Enlightenment* echoes the pathos that Weber
formulated in "Science as a Vocation" and can thus be understood as a
reaction against the interest in irrationalist philosophical movements during the 1920s, such as the philosophies of life and vitalism and certain
aspects of the renaissance of Kierkegaard's work. Adorno explicitly states
that the "attempts at escape [*Ausbruchsversuche*]" (supposedly in Bergson
and Husserl) intended to break through to a new kind of intuitive knowledge are condemned to failure (*ND* 8–10, 14–15, 157–58, 167–68, 333–34 /
20, 21, 26, 160, 170, 327). Knowledge and science, moral deliberation and

---

2. See Günther Rohrmoser, *Das Elend der kritischen Theorie: Theodor W. Adorno, Herbert
Marcuse, Jürgen Habermas* (Freiburg i.B.: Rombach, 1970), 27, 32–35; L. Kolakowski, *Main Currents of Marxism: Its Rise, Growth and Dissolution,* 3 vols. (Oxford: Oxford University Press,
1978), 3:376.

action, and aesthetic expression and judgment require conceptual mediation, although they never exhaust themselves within it.

Adorno is therefore, perhaps, even more ambivalent than many of his interpreters, such as Kodalle and Schnädelbach, who are, in principle, sympathetic to his negative metaphysics about the question of whether, within the broad range of the aspects of the reasonable, some determined place must not also be made for the "noetic," or intelligible, dimension of the other, as it has been both preserved and mutilated by the philosophical tradition. After the fall of classical metaphysics, such a perspective on the nonidentical, he seems to suggest, cannot be rescued without thoroughgoing transformation, no more than could its complementary "dianoetic," discursive-rational moment of reason.

From this precarious position Adorno time and again rejects any premature, false reconciliation of the poles of knowledge and experience (or the complex processes by which they are differently constituted). He honors the idea of reconciliation only if its advent is perpetually *deferred*, or if its coming about implies a *noncoincidence* of reconciliation with itself, and hence a nonarrival, of sorts. Indeed, we read: "All mystical union remains a deception" (*DE* 31 / 57). That is one of the most important starting points for the interpretation I will pursue. One might legitimately object that it hardly applies in the same degree to *all* modes of expression Adorno uses, but no interpretation can entirely avoid this fate, certainly not the *lectio difficilior* that I will—somewhat counterintuitively—risk here.

Enlightenment undermines myths bound up in nature (or extending nature, reifying themselves as "second nature") by unmasking them as sheer projection. In consequence, enlightenment inadvertently propels life, narrative, and meaning back into the subjectivity that had constructed them. Adorno's complex assessment of the philosophy of the subject takes off from this assumption of the projective mechanism in reflex to the forces of nature, whose overwhelming character it seeks to control by subjecting itself to its—again, projected—regularities, its repetition of the same. His prime target is the mode of Western thinking which, through the mouth of a Descartes, Kant, or Husserl, elevates the *ego cogito* or transcendental consciousness to the staging ground or foundation of phenomena, thus lowering itself to a "peephole metaphysics [*Guckkastenmetaphysik*]" (*ND* 138–40 / 142–44). There the subject is constituted and self-conceived only in a distorted form, with a dismal outlook: "As through the crenels of a parapet [or tower, *Turm*], the subject gazes upon a black sky in which the star of the idea, or of Being, is said to rise. And yet it is the very wall around the subject that casts its shadow on whatever the subject conjures: the shadow of reification [*des Dinghaften*], which a subjective philosophy will then helplessly fight again" (*ND* 139–40 / 143).

When reason is rendered subjective and the age of the world picture (the *Zeit des Weltbildes,* as Heidegger will say) becomes scientific and mechanistic,[3] the *qualitative* aspects of outer and inner nature — in other words, the semantic wealth earlier guaranteed by religion and other embodiments of objective spirit — are increasingly removed from the sphere of thought, agency, experience, and judgment. The program of enlightenment prohibits any speculation about the *auratic* dimensions of the regions that it *must* unearth in its desire for total mastery. This results not only in a theoretical and imaginative poverty but also in devastating social consequences: "Just as prohibition has always ensured the admission of the more poisonous product, the blocking of the theoretical imagination [*Einbildungskraft*] has paved the way for political delusion [*Wahne*]" (*DE* xvi / 13).

Enlightenment deduces its distancing power — as well as its doubling, mirroring, and therefore alienating effects — from the *dualistic* character of its fundamental presuppositions. In its schemata nature disintegrates into "mere nature," and, conversely, the power of humanity over *external* nature comes at the expense of the regulation of one's own *inner* nature. In order successfully to divide up the world, the subject must objectify itself and thus itself become increasingly *schematic.* Yet the thinking that thus separates itself from sensuous experience will inevitably become impoverished: "the separation of the two realms leaves both damaged" (*DE* 28 / 53). The subject, which this development helps put into effect yet which then becomes increasingly reified within it, apparently can identify itself only through the desire for self-preservation. Horkheimer and Adorno thus find the maxim of Western civilization pointedly expressed in the well-known dictum in Spinoza's *Ethics:* "conatus sese conservandi primum et unicum virtutis est fundamentum [the endeavor to preserve oneself is the first and only basis of virtue],"[4] which will likewise sum up the basic tenet of the history of ontology since Parmenides in Levinas's later thought, notably in *Otherwise than Being.* Adorno later succinctly summarizes this entire tendency as a generalized *reductio ad hominem*

3. The term comes from E. J. Dijksterhuis's *De mechanisering van het wereldbeeld* (Amsterdam: H. M. Meulenhoff, 1950) / *The Mechanization of the World Picture,* trans. C. Dikshoorn (Oxford: Oxford University Press, 1961).

4. Spinoza, *Ethica,* bk. 4, prop. 22 coroll.; see also *DE* 22, 53 / 46, 105; *ND* 349 / 342.

(*ND* 387 / 380), that is, as the *nonformal tautology* of the identification or, rather, self-identification and self-determination of the self, whose moral and political consequences—premised on the silent axiom "what ought to be is what is anyway [*sein soll, was ohnehin schon ist*]" (*ND* 349 / 342) — are devastating: the ontologization of conformity by way of a repetition of the self-same.

Dialectic of Enlightenment demonstrates, through its virtually deconstructive reading of the founding documents of two privileged episodes in the genealogy of Occidental rationalization, how the subject must involuntarily become entangled in the enchantment brought about by a renewed and reiterated mythology. Odysseus, as *homo economicus* and "enlightener" *avant la lettre,* in the long and detailed excursus to the book drafted by Adorno, only appears to break through myth; the works of de Sade, Kant, and Nietzsche, as is suggested by the next excursus, sketched out by Horkheimer, make it crystal clear that a fully thought through, enlightened subject turns out to be defenseless against the accusation of complete immorality.

Guided by a principle of *immanence,* enlightenment clarifies everything in terms of repetition and returns everything to the same, to an (abstract) identity. It contents itself with a subject that "cannot lose itself in identification with the other [or otherness, *mit anderem*]" (*DE* 6 / 16, trans. modified). Therefore, it must also disavow *in advance* what is qualitatively new—the singular or an unanticipated and unpredictable event—and sanction anew what myth once termed "fate": "Whatever might be different [or other, *anders*] is made the same" (*DE* 8 / 28). In other words: "In the terseness of the mythical image, as in the clarity of the scientific formula, the eternity of the factual [*des Tatsächlichen*] is confirmed and mere existence [*Dasein*] is pronounced as the meaning it obstructs" (*DE* 20 / 44, trans. modified). Although the immediate effects of the force of nature may diminish under the onslaughts of reason, within the progress of enlightenment, paradoxically, lodges a regressive element insofar as the power of nature reproduces itself ever more subtly within every conscious subject in search of self-preservation and the domination of (its) nature.

In his studies of the philosophy of the subject and of consciousness, ego, and existence (or *Dasein*) in Kierkegaard and Husserl, Adorno therefore stresses the significance of the "remembrance [*Eingedenken*] of nature in the subject" (*DE* 32 / 58). Although mastery over nature is the *conditio sine qua non* for the emergence of a certain minimum of civilization, to the extent that spirit can recall, remain aware of, and project or re-establish its affinity with (its) nature, it will no longer (be able and willing to) appropriate this nature *without remainder* (see *ND* 268, 396–98 / 266, 389–90).

All reification is a "forgetting," and in the undoing and working through of this *quasi-therapeutical* motif—through an *anamnesis* that, in Adorno, combines Platonic-noetic, dialectical-dianoetic, and materi-alist-sensualist elements—all past hopes seem to concentrate themselves. Hope, in other words, resides solely in the possibility that reason, through self-consciousness, through the *recollection* of (its) oppressed creatureli-ness, might prepare a "positive concept" of enlightenment after all. With that hope Adorno and Horkheimer point to what in reason is *more* than a pure drive—or pure *organon*—for self-preservation and self-determina-tion: that is, they aim at the possibility of a *self-reflection* that is at once emphatic and susceptible, a singular capacity for thinking, judging, ex-periencing, and acting upon the singular (*das Besondere*) as it absolves itself from all preestablished concepts and categories (or, in Husserlian-Levinasian parlance, from all presentation, retention, or protention).

One ought not to be misled here by the evident influence on *Dialectic of Enlightenment* of the psychoanalytic concept of emancipation. The idea that human beings do not just remember nature but are also capable of internalizing it scarcely seems—however much Horkheimer and Adorno at times seem to suggest the contrary—to be taken as a serious possibility. If this assumption is correct, then nature would be thinkable (judged, re-sponded to, experienced, and expressed) only as a *cipher* or, more pre-cisely, as the *trace* of what could be other than being (i.e., other than Being and beings, other than whatever is ready-at-hand or even authentically exists, as Heidegger would have it).

A closer consideration of Adorno's early philosophical-historical con-cept of "natural history [*Naturgeschichte*]," introduced in an unpublished lecture in 1932 to which I will return at some length, confirms the im-pression that nature and subjectivity stand in an *open* dialectical or alter-nating relationship. The crux of this idea lies in the demise of the fixed, traditional and modern significance of the constitutive concepts of both "nature" and "history." Nature, for Adorno, can stand as a *metaphor* for generally threatening natural forces, yet it can also *allegorize* the concrete-particular and transitory or corporeal aspect of creatureliness. History, by contrast, can indicate both the static reproduction of the "always the same" (*das Immergleiche*) and the free space in which innovative human action comes into play. The concept "natural history" sets all these mobile elements in relation to one another for strategic purposes and with *critical* intent: "It would be up to thought to see all nature, and whatever would install itself as such, as history, and all history as nature" (*ND* 359 / 353). Rather than suggesting that both poles "are not yet themselves,"[5] as one commentator thinks, this polarity indicates that both could *never*— or only *falsely*— come into their own in a thinking (a moral sensibility and judgment) from which every inclination toward ontologization of the real has been removed.

The fact that in their later work Horkheimer and Adorno speak of a reconciliation with nature, and reconciliation in general, in *transcendent* figures of thought such as "desire," "hope," "utopia," and "metaphysical and spiritual experience" might, at one level, be understood as a modification or revision of the views professed in *Dialectic of Enlightenment*. For both authors, however, such revision involves a return to earlier impulses. Further, one need not interpret this development as a symptom of increasing or returning resignation at all. An alternative methodological and interpretive approach, informed by the work of Levinas and Derrida, as well as drawing on Adorno's own principle of "immanent critique," may enable us to see the much-decried dead end of Critical Theory as a step ahead, that is to say, an advancement in learning, speculative and imaginative force, analytical rigor and moral reasoning, expressive sensibility and sound judgment, all of which enables us most *extensively* and *intensively* to account for—and do justice to—the experience of the (post)modern. Such an interpretation—which, admittedly, requires a *lectio difficilior* of sorts—appears to be more promising than the various reductionistic attempts of external critique.

Lectio difficilior

In their "*rhetorical* presentation"[6] of the horrifying reality and prehistory of what they term "subjectless" capitalism (*DE* 89 / 134), Horkheimer and Adorno offer, almost in passing, a methodological tip for the reader seeking to understand the general argument of *Dialectic of Enlightenment*. In what is clearly a "philosophically intended" statement,[7] they formulate, in almost programmatic fashion, the methodological outlook

5. Friedemann Grenz, *Adornos Philosophie in Grundbegriffen: Auflösung einiger Deutungsprobleme* (Frankfurt a.M.: Suhrkamp, 1974), 164–65.

6. Habermas, *Philosophical Discourse of Modernity*, 110 / 134, my emph.

7. Ibid., 111 / 135, my emph.

of their work, guided as it is by a certain rhetorical excess in its diagnoses not only of their times but of history—in fact, "prehistory—so far: "only exaggeration is true. The essential character of prehistory is the appearance of utmost horror in the individual detail. A statistical compilation of those slaughtered in a pogrom . . . conceals the essence [*das Wesen*], which emerges only in an exact description of the exception, the most hideous torture. A happy life in a world of horror is ignominiously refuted by the mere existence of that world. The latter therefore becomes the essence, the former negligible [*zum Nichtigen*]" (*DE* 92–93 / 139, trans. modified).

In contrast to the expectation—before the appearance of Adorno's *Negative Dialectics*—which ties the term *dialectic* to a type of argumentation which proceeds by drawing on concepts of totality, mediation, and resolution (or redemption, *Versöhnung*), this passage shows that the method or model of philosophical reflection, at least in its open-ended and, in that sense, negative dialectical form, is also capable of the exact opposite philosophical aim. Precise immersion in the details of a historical negativity that has been stylized in the extreme, the exception becoming the rule, now seems to become the leitmotif not for a metaphysics with *infinitist* aspirations but for an *unending* (again, open-ended) thought that can scarcely promise anything, least of all firm results. One could—perhaps—call this dialectical figure of thought one of *phenomenological concretion,* to use the terminology Levinas will favor. In doing so, one should not take "concrete" in its Hegelian usage, in which *concrete*—derived philologically from Latin *concrescere* or *concretum,* namely, what has grown together—is understood as the whole, in opposition to the individual, abstract element, and as signifying something positive, even what is true.[8] In the most polemical and rhetorical moments of Adorno's philosophy, the whole is, by contrast, identified as the "untrue." ("Das Ganze ist das Unwahre," we read in *Minima Moralia*.) Phenomenological concretion might better be understood as the description of the *trace of the other,* which cannot be contained and examined within the space of concepts and reasons and which has always already implanted and insinuated itself in the intentionless *passivity of the subject* and become audible only there (and not in, say, the cosmos and living nature, history and its institutions, "second nature" and culture). True, in *Aesthetic Theory* Adorno claims: "Even by artworks the concrete is scarcely to be named other than negatively" (135 / 203). Moreover, in *Three Studies on Hegel* he signifi-

8. See Adorno, *Philosophische Terminologie,* 1:31.

cantly comments that "Hegel imported infinitely more of the concrete into philosophical thinking than any of the movements to which his idealism was opposed, namely, the concretion of the phenomenological, anthropological, and ontological schools" (*Drei Stud* 306–7). That ought not to mislead us, however, about Adorno's strong anti-Hegelianism or about the radical modifications of the phenomenological method in Levinas which resonate with it. Later we will develop these parallels further.

Wellmer aptly characterizes Horkheimer and Adorno's description of the dialectic of enlightenment as the "phenomenology of a reifying rationality"; in particular, he speaks of Adorno's thought as the "phenomenology of a post-rationalist rationality and its de-centered subject."[9] This figure of thought is of interest because it relies on a position that is neither relativistic nor that of the philosophy of subjectivity in the narrow sense. Moreover, it does not assume the possibility of either a positive or a negative theory of totality. The historico-philosophical and anthropological critique of the lost foundations of *their present,* generalized and amplified by Horkheimer and Adorno into nothing less than the course of *universal history,* vacillates "ceaselessly [or tirelessly, *ruhelos*]"[10] back and forth between the forms of subjective and objective reason, which, in their view, have become equally untenable. Precisely this makes *Dialectic of Enlightenment* into an "ironic affair,"[11] while implying that redemption can enter *at any moment* through a "keyhole,"[12] to cite the Benjaminian topos, while it may *in the very same instant* definitively fail to appear. In the following analysis, which will engage the central figures of thought in *Dialectic of Enlightenment,* I will substantiate this understanding of the *ambiguity in principle* of philosophical discourse in its pursuit of the other, that is, of what might be otherwise than — more precisely, slightly but nonetheless radically different from — whatever exists (namely, the order of nature, mythological fate, the apparent necessities and supposedly progressive determination of history, the capitalist mode of production, bourgeois aestheticism, the industrial exploitation of culture, self-mastery and its price, etc.).

Philosophy, if one might paraphrase the passages that formed our initial point of departure, is fundamentally possible only as lament, in which the "stigma [*Wundmal*] of civilization," namely, "mourning" (*DE* 179 /

9. Wellmer, *Zur Dialektik von Moderne und Postmoderne,* 147 and 162, respectively.
10. Habermas, *Theory of Communicative Action,* 1:383 / 1:513.
11. Ibid.
12. Benjamin, *Gesammelte Schriften,* 1.2:704.

244), achieves undiminished expression. Therein and thereby philosophy can salvage the *possibility of utopia*. That is to say, only thus can it succeed in holding open the prospect of experiencing and expressing the trace of something else, of something better: "expression is the painful echo of overwhelming power, violence which finds utterance in complaint [*Klage*]. It is always overdone [*übertrieben*], no matter how heartfelt it may be, because, as in each work of art, the whole world seems contained in every plaintive sound" (*DE* 150 / 207). In this light one can understand dialectic as attempting "a critical rescue of the rhetorical element, a mutual approximation of a thing and expression, to the point where the difference fades" (*ND* 56 / 66).

In *Minima Moralia* philosophy is succinctly characterized as the gesture of thinking "arrested [or maintained, *festgehaltene*] difference": what is essential, Adorno stresses once again, is "an element of exaggeration [*Übertreibung*], of over-shooting the object, of self-detachment from the factual, so that instead of merely reproducing being it can, at once rigorous and free, determine it. Thus every thought resembles play, with which Hegel no less than Nietzsche compared the work of the mind" (*MM* 126–127 / 144). Such a gesture appeals to a philosophical experience in which the few who can sustain it "make the moral and, as it were, representative [or substituting, *stellvertretend*] effort to say what most of those for whom they say it cannot see or, to do justice to reality, will not allow themselves to see." Only those who presuppose "direct communicability [*Kommunizierbarkeit*] to everyone" as a criterion for true philosophical insight could find in this a disqualification of that peculiar dialectic (*ND* 41 / 50–51).

Söllner portrays the intentional figures of thought in *Dialectic of Enlightenment* and Adorno's late work as *subjectivism raised to the level of method*, which, he adds, "seeks the totality [*Totale*], which resides negatively, in the experience of the historical individual, without ever being actually able to find it." Söllner adds: "the complete view [or the total, *Totale*] of society aimed at in the concepts of 'spell,' 'bloc,' 'total integration,' etc., either contradicts the methodological program of negativism or concerns mere metaphors, images which serve the escaped victim as a mirror, in order to guarantee the continuity history of his own thought, and all of which we might now, perhaps, put aside."[13] This diagnosis is linked

---

13. A. Söllner, "Angst und Politik: Zu Aktualität Adornos im Spannungsfeld von Politikwissenschaft und Sozialpsychologie," in von Friedeburg and Habermas, *Adorno-Konferenz 1983*, 340.

to a description that would see Adorno's thinking as a circular movement around the empty pole of a disappearing yet still abiding subject or individual.

Here we can pursue only indirectly the question of whether or not this figure of thought protects Adorno from relapsing into the modern philosophy of the subject or the philosophy of consciousness. Our first concern will be the *halfway* realized theoretical and practical skepticism concerning the status of cognition, moral principle, and aesthetic judgment that emerges across the darkest pages of *Dialectic of Enlightenment*. I will ask only in passing whether their critique of the modern subject approximates the purported all-out postmodern rejection of that concept. Our authors distance themselves from any "fabulous invention [*Fabulieren*] of a 'new subject,'"[14] but they nonetheless describe the dissolving contours of a self that is conceived and situated *beyond* the undifferentiated, amorphous realm of nature, yet *this side* of its socialization within a totally integrated collective. Various elements of a hesitant antisubjectivism can nevertheless be detected in *Dialectic of Enlightenment*. Not only does this antisubjectivism affect Horkheimer and Adorno's diagnosis and negative image of their time; it extends equally to the description of the qualities of the subject which they aspire to salvage against all odds.

Horkheimer and Adorno try to uncover the *ambiguous* relationship between enlightenment and historical domination because, in their view, world history can be "equated [or postulated as being one, *in eins gesetzt*]" with enlightenment almost to the point of indifference (*DE* 37 / 63). Its ambiguity resides in the fact that, on the one hand, in every period enlightenment served to expose relationships of domination; on the other, it has always been used to manipulate people, regardless of their emancipation — or even by means of it. Horkheimer and Adorno demonstrate this double character of enlightenment — that is, its potential for improvement as well as its purportedly universal-historical connection with domination or blindness — by reconstructing the prehistorical adventures of the modern subject. They argue that, whereas enlightenment is originally opposed to myth, once enlightenment achieves universal mastery, it reverts to mythology again.

In retrospect "self-preservation," "the introversion of sacrifice," or "renunciation" — in short, human self-mastery, through which the self and selfhood are constituted — "practically [or virtually, *virtuell*] always in-

14. Habermas, *Philosophisch-politische Profile*, 172.

volves the annihilation of the subject in whose service that mastery is maintained" (*DE* 43 / 73; see 22 ff. / 46 ff.). Ultimately, in this seemingly inevitable process "even the human being becomes an anthropomorphism for human beings" (*DE* 45 / 76). This anthropomorphism, which is a projection of the subjective onto nature, has been the "basis of myth" ever since Xenophanes (*DE* 4 / 22).

Thus, for Horkheimer and Adorno the subject turns out to be nothing but "an imaginary meeting point of the impersonal [*ein imaginärer Treffpunkt des Unpersönlichen*]," [15] as Robert Musil puts it in *Der Man ohne Eigenschaften* (*The Man without Qualities*). Ever since Shakespeare's Hamlet (see *DE* 126 / 179), Horkheimer and Adorno suggest, the unity of the person has been unveiled as mere illusion. In the epoch of late capitalism suffering resides in the "nothing" of the false reconciliation of subject and society, "the horror of which is still just fleetingly visible in the vacuous semblance of the tragic." Indeed, the foreseeable full eclipse of the tragic confirms this "abolition of the individual" (*DE* 124 / 177). But this development does not complete itself in a single stroke or without ambiguity. In historical objectivity the subject is grasped in a process of dissolution "without yet giving rise to a new one, individual experience necessarily bases itself on the old subject, now historically condemned, which is still for-itself [*für sich*], but no longer in-itself [*an sich*]" (*MM* 16 / 14).

According to Adorno, it is therefore no longer possible to speak of the self in simple empirical or ontologizing terms. In order truly to keep one's distance from the affirmation of the "devilishly positive" and "barren interest" in subjectivity, one can philosophize about the self "at the most theologically, in the name of its likeness to God [*Gottesebenbildlichkeit*]" (*MM* 154 / 176). But speaking of the concept of theology — of "anthropomorphism" and "likeness to God" — in this context is somewhat misleading. As indicated earlier, its precise meaning resembles at best the *quasi*-theological interpretation given of such notions by Derrida, for whom, as we have seen, "the theological" is nothing more (and nothing less) than "a determinate movement in the total movement of the trace." [16]

Given the primarily rhetorical formulas and strategies of exaggeration through which Horkheimer and Adorno depict the negativity of history and the emergence and disappearance of the modern subject, it is, at first

15. Robert Musil, *Der Mann ohne Eigenschaften*, ed. A. Frisé (Hamburg: Rowohlt, 1978), 474 / *The Man without Qualities*, trans. Sophie Wilkins (New York: Alfred A. Knopf, 1995), 1:444.

16. Derrida, *Of Grammatology,* 47 / 69.

glance, surprising that throughout *Dialectic of Enlightenment* they occasionally allude, although *in reverse* — obliquely, as if in *mirror writing* — to the conditions of possibility for hope (see *DE* 61–62, 172 / 98–99, 234), utopia (see *DE* 69, 71, 93, 170 / 108, 110, 140, 231), and, finally, reconciliation. This becomes understandable if one recognizes their view that it is not so much "existence that is without hope, but knowledge which appropriates and perpetuates existence [*Dasein*] as a schema in the pictorial or mathematical symbol" (*DE* 21 / 44). In their eyes false reality testifies not only to a "meagre residue [*Rest*]" but also to a "last thought of resisting that [same] reality" (*DE* 43, 116 / 73, 167); moreover, it can, in its form as "the history of thought as an instrument of power" (*DE* 92 / 138, trans. modified), summon rescue in the very moment of ultimate danger. The well-known Hölderlin quotation is clear evidence of this assumption, which guides Horkheimer and Adorno throughout in the *Dialectic of Enlightenment* and forms a necessary — a deeply paradoxical and, indeed, metaphysical — condition for maintaining at the least the theoretical (or should we say virtual?) possibility of a positive concept of enlightenment: "But where danger threatens / That which saves from it also grows" (*DE* 38 / 65). That is to say, Critical Theory not only sings the proper melody to liberate society's repressed or not yet fully mobilized potential (as Marx had suggested in his early writings, notably *Die deutsche Ideologie* [*The German Ideology*] and then executed in *Das Kapital* [*Capital*]), but also that reality — almost miraculously — produces its proper remedy as its pathology grows ever more desperate.

True, the horror of fascism admits no truth by which its own reality could be "measured," but "its absurdity is so monstrous as to bring truth *negatively* within reach [*zum Greifen nahe*]" (*DE* 172 / 234, my emph.). The age of Enlightenment, "in taking fright at the image in its own mirror" — for example, in Sade's "*chronique scandaleuse*," in which "the Homeric epic after it has discarded its last mythological veil" is thought through to its end — may nonetheless open (indeed, may necessitate as well as demand) a view toward "what lies beyond it" (*DE* 92 / 138). In such passages Horkheimer and Adorno maintain, more than would be entirely justifiable in terms of the modern and subject-centered form of reason, an almost effusive idea of a "true universality [*Allgemeinheit*]," a "secret utopia" which can be discovered (*DE* 65, 66 / 102, 103), "if only subterraneously" (*DE* 73 / 112), in the philosophical tradition. Subterraneously — because the modern, formal understanding of reason not only passes over "*who* is applying reason" (*DE* 68 / 106, trans. modified, my emph.), it also stifles the possibilities for its own gradual and progressive realization. So long as substantive goals and qualitative impulses are denounced as merely the unauthorized, mystified force of nature, reason must become, paradoxically, *indifferent* to every natural—even reasonable—interest: "depending on the situation of individuals and groups, it presents either peace or war, tolerance or repression, as the given state of affairs" (*DE* 68 / 106).

To understand these paradoxes of reason's principle indifference as well as of its possible turning around (itself) for good and for ill, Horkheimer and Adorno use the concept of enlightenment *equivocally,* in both negative and positive senses of the term. A comparison of various passages brings out this ambiguity quite clearly. On the one hand, they write, "Human beings have always had to choose between their subjugation to nature and its subjugation to the self" (*DE* 25 / 49), thereby suggesting that the difference between these two—negative—options mattered (or matters) little in the end. Yet, on the other hand, they also emphatically claim, "Enlightenment is more than enlightenment [*Aufklärung ist mehr als Aufklärung*], it is nature made audible [or become perceptible, *vernehmbar wird*] in its estrangement [*Entfremdung*]" (*DE* 31 / 57). If at first sight the mere hopelessness of a modernity already positioned via its prehistory seems to shine through—and we should not underestimate the grimness of the diagnosis[17]—in a second instance *Dialectic of Enlightenment* seems to promise a bit more than pure bleakness and horror. Although Horkheimer and Adorno clearly emphasize that the "metamorphoses of critique into affirmation" do not leave the *theoretical* content of enlightenment untouched, to the extent that "its truth evaporates [*verflüchtigt*]" (*DE* xv / 12), they also insist that enlightenment can and should "reflect on itself [*sich auf sich selbst besinnen*]" in order to fulfill the hopes of the past (*DE* xvii / 15). The proficient critique of enlightenment should prepare a *positive* concept of it, as a propaedeutic that "liberates it from its entanglement in blind domination [*Herrschaft*]" (*DE* xviii / 16). This positive turn of reason can be summed up in catchwords scattered throughout the text, such as: "mind's self-recognition as nature divided from itself [*Selbsterkenntnis des Geistes als mit sich entzweiter Natur*]" (*DE* 31 / 57),

17. As is clear from passages such as these: "With the spread of the bourgeois commodity economy the dark horizon of myth is illumined by the sun of calculating reason, beneath whose icy rays the seeds of the new barbarism are germinating. Under the compulsion of power [*Herrschaft*], human labor has always led away from myth and, under power, has always fallen back under its spell" (*DE* 25 / 49).

"remembrance of nature within the subject [*Eingedenken der Natur im Subjekt*]" (*DE* 32 / 58), and "the self-conscious work of thought [*die ihrer selbst bewusste Arbeit des Gedankens*]" (*DE* 160 / 219). Nonetheless, in a paradoxical manner these motifs of the apparently *possible positivity* of enlightenment must go hand in hand with the repeated requirement of "determinate negation" (*DE* 18, 20 / 40, 43) and, ultimately, with the Judaic *prohibition of images,* both of which are to be distinguished from mere abstract negation but which prevent thought from succumbing to the false affirmation of whatever exists.

Contrary to these enlightening intentions of both the authors of *Dialectic of Enlightenment,* which, as Habermas opines, "are in no way seamlessly woven together,"[18] one might, as some have pointed out, see in their argumentative strategy a "totalizing" or "self-surpassing [*Selbstüberbietung*]" of ideology critique, which at the same time threatens to rock its own foundations and, hence, the conditions of its very possibility. Such a strategy is even said to be accompanied by the "inability to analyze society" and by an "ultimate repression of the social,"[19] at least in Axel Honneth's assessment of the historical-philosophical and anthropological approach of Critical Theory, especially in Adorno's late work.

Habermas likewise diagnoses and criticizes the paradoxical figures of thought in Horkheimer and Adorno as a "skepticism regarding reason [*Vernunftskepsis*]" and accuses them of "sarcastic agreement with ethical skepticism."[20] According to him, these authors perceive modernity from an "experiential horizon" comparable to that of Nietzsche — that is, "with the same heightened sensibility, and even with the same cramped optics that render one insensible to the traces [*Spuren*] and the existing forms of communicative rationality."[21] He believes that Horkheimer and Adorno give themselves over to a "limitless [or unrestrained, *hemmungslosen*]" skepticism about reason "instead of weighing the grounds that cast doubt on this skepticism itself"; to do so means "setting the normative foun-

18. Jürgen Habermas, "Bemerkungen zur Entwicklungsgeschichte des Horkheimerschen Werkes," in *Max Horkheimer heute: Werk und Wirkung,* ed. Norbert Altwicker and Alfred Schmidt (Frankfurt a.M.: S. Fischer, 1986), 166. See also his afterword in Horkheimer and Adorno, *Dialektik der Aufklärung,* 277–94.

19. Honneth, *Kritik und Macht,* 9 ff., 70 ff. Yet see also Axel Honneth, "Über die Möglichkeiten einer erschliessenden Kritik: Die *Dialektik der Aufklärung* im Horizont gegenwärtiger Debatten über Sozialkritik," *Das Andere der Gerechtigkeit: Aufsätze zur praktischen Philosophie* (Frankfurt a.M.: Suhrkamp, 2000), 70–87.

20. Habermas, *Philosophical Discourse of Modernity,* 119 / 136.

21. Ibid., 129 / 155.

dations of critical social theory so deep that they would not have been disturbed by the decomposition of bourgeois culture."[22] Habermas proposes an alternative reconstructive strategy in *The Theory of Communicative Action,* in which, ironically, the contrary accusation is voiced, as if Horkheimer and Adorno, in the wake of Lukács, carried out their critique of reason rather *too deeply* and did so by means of a double generalization of the concept of reification which the latter had expounded in the central essay of *History and Class Consciousness.*[23]

Such an interpretation, I will argue, does not do justice to the analytic strength — and, perhaps, the ethical virtues — of this "skepticism regarding reason." Whereas the authors of *Dialectic of Enlightenment* seem to deny that there exist postulates, ideas, and possible forms of communicative rationality which are given positively and unambiguously, even if counterfactually, they in no way deny that there are traces of the o/Other, reminiscences, musings, or announcements of the "other state [*des anderen Zustandes*]," to which Musil alludes in his explorations of the mystical in *The Man without Qualities.* In their opinion, however, the condition of possibility for these traces of the other (state) does not consist in the fundamental — that is, *phylo- and ontogenetically based* — competences of a subject capable of thought, action, and judgment, competences that are rational, mediated by the fact of language, and capable of being theoretically, that is to say, formally and discursively, reconstructed. The "condition" of its "possibility," if these words are still of use, gains in their reading a quasi-transcendental and counterfactual status that must be thought completely otherwise and reveals itself, rather, in the *unsublatable ambiguity* or (as Derrida would say) *undecidability* of the (not exclusively linguistic) experience of the traces of the "nonidentical." As I have argued in the previous chapters, such a lack of directionality [*Richtungslosigkeit*] is at odds with Habermas's paradigmatic reformulation of the intentions of early Critical Theory and his attempt to premise the triadic articulation of the different value claims on what he calls elementary "yes/no positions."

I hope cautiously to propose a plausible model for interpreting precisely those philosophical elements and fragments of *Dialectic of Enlightenment* which do *not* fit the defined standards of procedural and communicative rationality but nonetheless reveal significant virtues of the supposed "skepticism with respect to reason" of its authors. This method

22. Ibid., 129 / 156.
23. Habermas, *Theory of Communicative Action,* 1:379 / 1:508.

seems more promising than any attempt to transform — to reduce and distort — Horkheimer's and Adorno's critical intent so that it could be unambiguously expressed within the terms of the theory of rationality and communicative action.

First, however, I must examine — briefly and without any claim to address all implications exhaustively — the way in which Horkheimer and Adorno pursue their enlightened *intent* in this book and, further, evaluate whether and how they fulfill it (or, rather, might possibly have redeemed it had they only pushed their pivotal argumentation to its logical extreme or inevitable consequence). Perhaps — and this will be my working hypothesis — it would be more reasonable to regard the concepts of hope and redemption which always reemerge in their discussions not merely as *unredeemed promises* but, rather, simultaneously or ultimately as something thought as *unredeemable in principle*. To do so we need — seemingly contrary to the authors' own self-understanding — to see the greatest achievement of their book in the ultimate *foundering* of its claims and of the conscious and relentlessly honest exposition by way of *performative contradiction* of this at once disturbing and promising fact.

In their perspective on the other of reason (but also of nature, history, culture, the subject), Horkheimer and Adorno hardly insist on a — Kantian — regulative idea that could, in principle, be approximated asymptotically but, rather, on a differential notion of the trace which is deeply paradoxical, indeed aporetic. Precisely this self-contradictory character of the utopian, I would suggest, allows them not to affirm but to *keep open* this impossible "possibility" for thought and agency, expression and judgment: not so much the potentiality or mere chance that things might turn around as the hope against hope that the riddle of reality — that is, of natural history and transience — might be resolved, that is to say, redeemed against all odds, at any given moment, or when all is said and done. Praxis, life, happiness, and justice can meaningfully entail nothing else. Wherever and whenever this comes to pass, philosophy comes to an end, rendering itself unnecessary, that is to say, *free*. To believe otherwise would be to neutralize the essential uncertainty of experience. To hope against hope, without hope, for hope, for lack of any real or even possible hope — all this would come down to an altogether different logic of the "messianic," one that Jakob Taubes, somewhat unjustly, saw betrayed in Adorno's invocation of the "as if" in the concluding lines of *Minima Moralia*.

To bring to light the virtues of "skepticism regarding reason" and their relevance for the question of minimal theology, we must read the text of *Dialectic of Enlightenment* against the grain. Admittedly, Horkheimer and Adorno, like Hegel before them, contest skepticism as an acceptable figure of philosophical thought but only by declaring that one precept of determinate negation is to be "not exempted from the enticements of intuition by the sovereignty of the abstract concept, as is skepticism, for which falsehood and truth are equally void" (*DE* 18 / 40–41). In their dialectical rejection of philosophical skepticism they simultaneously renounce Hegel's idealist inheritance, to which the path still lay open as a way to overcome the "emptiness" of skepticism in the "progression through the complete series of forms" in the phenomenology of spirit, as if it came about "of itself."[24]

Notwithstanding this ambivalent relationship to the concept of skepticism (a concept still untouched by its subsequent — and far more convincing — rearticulation by other thinkers such as Stanley Cavell, Odo Marquard, and, I would add, Levinas), precisely the least apparent and most recalcitrant traits in *Dialectic of Enlightenment* — that is, those that fall somewhat short of the authors' explicit intentions — most clearly reveal the virtues of their "skepticism regarding reason." We must, therefore, be on the lookout for such spots in the text. Theology has always had a name for this sort of procedure in textual criticism, namely, *lectio difficilior*. Freely translated, this names a method according to which the scattered, dissonant, and least articulated motifs and layers of a text express what is most plausible within it.

Nature and Subjectivity: Reminiscences of Ideology Critique and Psychoanalysis, Alienation and Reconciliation, Forgetting and Recollection

Dialectic of Enlightenment contains various indications that Horkheimer and Adorno follow an argumentative structure borrowed in part from the chapter on lordship and bondage in Hegel's *Phänomenologie des Geistes* (*Phenomenology of Spirit*), in part from Nietzsche's *Zur Genealogie der Moral* (*On the Genealogy of Morals*).[25] Likewise, reminiscences of the

24. G. W. F. Hegel, *Phänomenologie des Geistes*, vol. 3 of *Theorie-Werkausgabe* (Frankfurt a.M.: Suhrkamp, 1969–71), 3:74 / trans. A. V. Miller under the title *Phenomenology of Spirit*, with analysis of the text and foreword by J. N. Findlay (Oxford: Oxford University Press, 1977).

25. Referring to the section on the Enlightenment in Hegel's *Phenomenology of Spirit* (398 ff.), Horkheimer and Adorno remark, "Any intellectual resistance [Enlightenment] encounters merely increases its strength" (*DE* 3 / 22). By contrast, they observe that in their time

application of Marx's ideology critique in Adorno's early writings abound. Moreover, their book cannot be correctly understood without reference to the heritage of Freudian psychoanalysis, especially Freud's studies of culture. Yet in the end a picture of it based on these influences alone is deceptive.

Horkheimer and Adorno's more original approaches to a "dialectical anthropology" (*DE* xix / 17) — whose intelligibility stands or falls according to whether one can allocate to the enlightening procedure they identify a constitutive role in the diagnosis and cure of the pre- and early history of modern subjectivity — must, upon closer inspection, draw our attention to something else. The terms *alienation* and *reconciliation, forgetting,* and *recollection,* apparently taken from ideology critique and psychoanalysis, can at decisive moments in their work be seen as figures of thought, metaphors, or, more precisely, ciphers for what *always already* eludes these modern patterns of signification and interpretation. I would argue that they serve merely as rhetorical formulas for a consciously excessive — indeed, exaggerated and dramatized — diagnosis of the time and never *adequately* describe or indicate what could be otherwise than whatever exists.

Take their idiosyncratic use of the psychoanalytic model: according to Adorno, psychoanalysis "brought a piece of Hegelian speculation home to roost."[26] He emphasizes the significance of Freudian psychoanalytic theory for the collective project *The Authoritarian Personality,* which sought neither to bind itself rigidly to Freudian theory nor "to water it down," as psychoanalytic "revisionism" apparently had done. Adorno recognizes that Freud could have understood the sociological perspective only as applied psychology and that quantitative analysis thus had little relevance for him in comparison with its qualitative counterpart. Nonetheless, Adorno underscores the social-psychological significance of

---

the ongoing process between subject and reality occurs as "one of liquidation [*Liquidation*] instead of sublation, of formal instead of specific [or determinate, *bestimmten*] negation" (*DE* 170 / 231). They further maintain that the distance between subject and object — that is, "the instrument of enlightenment," namely, abstraction — finds its origin and model in "the distance from things which the ruler [*der Herr*] attains by means of the ruled [*Beherrschten*]" (*DE* 9 / 29–30). Again referring to Hegel, the authors go on to claim: "The servant [*Knecht*] is subjugated in body and soul; the master [*Herr*] regresses. No system of domination [*Herrschaft*] has so far been able to escape this price, and the circularity [more precisely, semblance or resemblance of circularity, *Kreisähnlichkeit*] of history in its progress is explained in part by this debilitation, which is the concomitant [*Äquivalent*] of power" (*DE* 27 / 52). Yet one also reads: "Thought, however, has always been equal to the task of concretely demonstrating its own equivocal nature [*Fragwürdigkeit*]. It is the servant whom the master cannot control at will" (*DE* 29 / 54).

26. *Drei Stud* 291. See also *ND* 351–52 / 344–45.

central psychoanalytic notions such as the death drive, which Freud set forth in *Das Unbehagen in der Kultur* (*Civilization and Its Discontents*) and which seems to Adorno "the most dangerous subjective mass potential in the contemporary political situation."[27] By the same token in *Dialectic of Enlightenment* the "urge to destroy" is repeatedly mentioned (see *DE* 139 / 194 and 137 / 192). Yet various passages in *Dialectic of Enlightenment* reveal the fundamental distance from Freud at which Critical Theory — or at least Adorno — finally arrived.

According to Söllner, "the ominous contrary" to a merely instrumental reason appears in Adorno as a "nature conceived as more hypothetical than ontological, which is split by the historical process of rationalization (read: civilization) into a repressed inner part and a technological, dominated exterior one."[28] In Söllner's presentation it remains unclear, however, how "the repressed side of the rationalization process" could be brought home after the model of psychoanalysis and, at the same time, integrated in a "restorative [or redemptive, *rettender*] appropriation."[29] Recognition of and reconciliation with an *inner* nature characterizes the program of *Dialectic of Enlightenment,* although, as Söllner rightly adds, "its obviousness naturally stands or falls on whether one finds Freudian psychoanalysis promising for social theory or research at all."[30] Although this supposition (i.e., this "promise") is hard put to find grounds within the book itself, Söllner believes one can see it explored at least implicitly in "Elements of Anti-Semitism," which contains *in nuce* Adorno's later social psychology. Here his phenomenological strength shows itself for the first time.[31]

How, then, is it possible to imagine in a distinctively *psychoanalytic* model the recollection of a "nature conceived as more hypothetical than ontological"? Söllner's formulation needs to apply not only to a detached, *exterior* or *second,* and hence "objective" nature but also to an *inner,* as it were subjective, nature. If this is so, should one not interpret this repressed inner nature in line with Lacanian psychoanalysis, oriented to the philosophy of language, and conceive its "hypothetical" nature as meaning something (some Thing, *la Chose*) that "*is*" *conceptually ungraspable, per-*

27. Theodor W. Adorno, "Wissenschaftliche Erfahrungen in Amerika," *GS* 10.2:702–38, 733.
28. Söllner, "Angst und Politik," 342, my emph.
29. Ibid., 341 and 342, respectively.
30. Ibid., 342.
31. According to Söllner, these fragments have received too little attention in the interpretations of authors such as Habermas and Helmut Dubiel.

haps no longer in need of conceptual or discursive clarification or philosophical interpretation, but — simply, ordinarily, almost naturally — *lived* (i.e., felt as well as shown)?[32] The error and ideology of all so-called philosophies of life would be that they hold this relation to nature (one's own and that of others) as realized or possible under past and present historical conditions.

How should we understand this relationship between consciousness and (its) nature, especially when the latter becomes what seems a merely idealized or virtualized object, absolving itself in a singular structure of at once sensualist and almost metaphysical — that is, transcending — desire? Wiggershaus suggests the following solution: "The proximity to nature produced through consciousness out of distance could first be realized retrospectively as an imaginary lost happiness, namely, a 'properly mimetic behavior,' the 'organic amalgamation with the other [*Anschmiegung ans Andere*],' as sublated."[33] But this assertion that the relationship to nature in *Dialectic of Enlightenment* can be thought in terms of "sublation" finds no support in the text. Its model, therefore, can hardly be understood in terms of the classical-modern frame of reference which interprets Freud in either biological materialistic — that is to say, ontological, mechanistic, and scientistic — terms or in view of speculative-dialectical or hermeneutic motifs and motivations.[34]

Freudian psychoanalysis is certainly present in *Dialectic of Enlightenment* as a materialistic motif but only *polemically* and *rhetorically,* like Adorno's use of the concept of totality and the falsity or even horror it harbors. These excessive, exaggerated expressions and their analogues

32. See Manfred Frank, "Das 'wahre Subjekt' und sein Doppel: Jacques Lacans Hermeneutik," *Das Sagbare und das Unsagbare,* 114 ff.; as well as his reference to *MM* in *Was ist Neostrukturalismus?* (Frankfurt a.M.: Suhrkamp, 1984), 495. Frank also stresses the divergences between the reception of psychoanalysis "by the second Frankfurt School" and Lacanian psychoanalysis (370). Lacan's concepts of the *sujet véritable,* the *sujet de l'inconscient,* and the *sujet de l'Autre* are separate from the self-reflection of the subject. Thus, Lacan would give the famous sentence from Freud's *Neue Vorlesungen zur Einführung in die Psychoanalyse* (New Lectures in Psychoanalysis), namely, "where Id was, there shall Ego be [*wo Es was, soll Ich werden*]," the following meaning: its point is "that from the Id should develop, not merely consciousness or self-consciousness (in the sense of reflection), as in Hegel, Ricoeur, or Lorenzer, but rather a subject other than the reflective subject" (Frank, 373). This true subject loses itself in reflection, although it is simultaneously the very ontological ground [*Seinsgrund*] for reflection, and hence necessarily becomes 'an appearance, an image, in short: something *imaginary*'" (381, my emph.).

33. Cf. Wiggershaus, *Frankfurt School,* 343 / 382.

34. For a discussion of these tensions within the Freudian corpus, see Paul Ricoeur's *De l'interprétation: Essai sur Freud* (Paris: Seuil, 1965).

never have the last word; instead — paradoxically, aporetically, almost miraculously — they point beyond themselves. A quotation can illustrate this point: "The chaotically regular flight reactions of the lower animals, the patterns of swarming crowds, the convulsive gestures of the tortured — all these express what wretched life can never quite control: the mimetic impulse. In the death throes of the creature, at the furthest extreme from freedom, freedom itself irresistibly shines forth as the thwarted destiny of matter" (*DE* 150–51 / 208).

In Adorno's most lapidary comment on the Freudian legacy, in psychoanalysis "nothing is true except the exaggerations" (*MM* 49 / 54). Its diagnoses are at once less and more pessimistic than it would seem at first glance: less pessimistic because its propositions are not so much ontological — or, more precisely, psycho- and phylogenetic or pathological — claims per se but performative utterances with a strategic, indeed, emancipatory aim; more pessimistic because even its most powerful reflection on and negation of whatever exists seem outweighed by the powers that be, by "positivity." As Adorno writes: "reflection, which in the healthy subject breaks the power of immediacy, is never as compelling as the illusion it dispels. As a negative, reflective movement not directed straight ahead, it lacks the brutality inherent in the positive" (*DE* 161 / 220).

One might, then, wonder whether the Freudian motifs in *Dialectic of Enlightenment* have the same status as they do in the work of Herbert Marcuse, for example. Referring to *Eros and Civilization,* Marcuse's counterpart to *Dialectic of Enlightenment,*[35] Wiggershaus at one point asks rhetorically, "Does not Marcuse finally expose in his book what nourished the work of Horkheimer and Adorno?" He further questions: does not his insistence on a "reason embedded in the 'good' drive-structure, in Eros, not bluntly bring to the fore what Horkheimer and Adorno (only indirectly, abashedly, aphoristically) support: namely, that there is a positive version [*Spielart*] — ultimately grounded in a spontaneous and therefore natural feeling for the correct, the good, and the true — that extends from nature through myth up to the Enlightenment and to reason?"[36] Such rhetorical questioning (for Wiggershaus does not doubt the answer) seems more convincing than it in fact is. It ignores the unmistakable cri-

35. Herbert Marcuse, *Eros and Civilization: A Philosophical Inquiry into Freud* (Boston: Beacon Press, 1966).

36. Wiggershaus, *Frankfurt School,* 501 / 559; see also the conversation on this subject between Habermas and Marcuse in Habermas, *Philosophisch-politische Profile,* 265 ff.; and Habermas, *Theory of Communicative Action,* 1:385 / 1:514.

tique of Freud—or the playing out of Freud against Freud—in *Dialectic of Enlightenment,* which only intensifies in Adorno's later work.[37] Wellmer seems more correct, therefore, in stressing the opposition of central motifs in *Dialectic of Enlightenment* to the enlightened "realism" of Freudian psychoanalysis: "From the perspective of *Dialectic of Enlightenment,* within psychoanalysis there appears a piece of precisely the rationalism whose idealistic form as reflection Freud had so persistently destroyed."[38]

Without a doubt, Freud plays an important role in the interpretation of anti-Semitism as a "rage against difference [*Wut auf die Differenz*]" (*DE* 172 / 233). Horkheimer and Adorno explain this violence as anxiety about the uncanniness of the foreign, which (or who) "is all too familiar" (*DE* 149 / 206). Anti-Semitism is a "false projection" that does not, like mimesis, amalgamate with its environment but attempts to make the other resemble itself, drawing and absorbing it into the orbit of the self-same through identification (*DE* 154 / 211–12). Yet how, then, against the background of this psychoanalytic topos, is one to interpret the authors' lapidary assertion that "psychology used to explain the other [*den anderen*] is impertinent [or outrageous, *unverschämt*], and to explain one's own motives sentimental" (*DE* 204 / 284, trans. modified)? Or, again, how should we understand their repeated emphasis that psychoanalysis reduces meaning "to the monotony of sexual symbolism" (*DE* 110 / 160), in addition to the earlier explicit critique of Freud's *Totem and Taboo* (*DE* xiv / 11)?

Horkheimer and Adorno likewise tend to be skeptical about Freudian categories when it comes to naming or determining what would be other than (or different from) the mere forgetting of nature—all too often a "forgetting rationalized as tact" (*DE* 178 / 243)—or of the dead. Although they stress that nature, "in being presented by society's control mechanism as the healing antithesis of society, is itself absorbed into that incurable society and sold off" (*DE* 119 / 171), they nonetheless make "good"—that is to say, neither first nor second—nature into something of a cipher for an always elusive and, in an etymological sense, *ab-solute* difference: that is, a difference that disengages itself from everything and, hence, is no longer "mere nature [*blosse Natur*]" (*DE* 153 / 210). Their text thus does not amount to the "positing and positive valuation [*Positivierung*]

37. See *ND* 272–73 / 269; *AT* 8 ff. / 20 ff.; as well as Wiggershaus, *Frankfurt School,* 266–67 / 299–300.

38. Wellmer, *Zur Dialektik von Moderne und Postmoderne,* 76.

of untouched nature"[39] attributed to the tradition of Rousseau and the romantics, nor can it simply be interpreted along the lines of a "quasi-Hegelian dialectical anthropology."[40] For Adorno not only is there no dialectic of nature in Friedrich Engels's sense of the terms—and its later Stalinist abuse[41]—but nature cannot be intended as the goal of philosophically articulated experience or a phenomenology of nature.[42] In this Adorno stays close to the negative-ontological concept of nature found in the early Marx.[43] With a Benjaminian reversal of a line from Karl Kraus, "the origin is the goal [*Ursprung ist das Ziel*]," Adorno can thus ultimately claim that the direction of critical thinking is oriented not backward but forward, albeit in view of a telos—a "life," including a "life of concepts [*Leben der Begriffe*]" (*GS* 5: 35/42)—which is largely elusive, ephemeral, and, in that sense, once more ab-solute: "The goal would not be found back in the origin, in the phantasm of 'good' nature; on the contrary, the origin falls to the goal alone [*Ursprung fiele allein dem Ziel zu*], that it is only from the goal that the origin will constitute itself. There is no origin save in ephemeral life [*Kein Ursprung ausser im Leben des Ephemeren*]" (*ND* 155–56 / 158).

If one reads *Dialectic of Enlightenment* retrospectively, with the benefit of hindsight and with an eye to such traces of (in this case natural) difference, it can no longer be understood as "a chapter in speculative naturalism" but should be seen as a philosophy of the ab-soluteness—and absolution?—of a "good nature" whose referent and telos are never given or attainable as such, in their purity, that is to say, as "mere nature." In such a *lectio difficilior* Horkheimer and Adorno's perspective can hardly be described as "a position that naturalistically turns on the speculative fundamental figure of a self-dividing totality, and relegates it instead to a concept of nature."[44] True, various seemingly classically dialectical formulations might seem to support this interpretation. Adorno writes, for example: "Physical work . . . necessarily depends upon what it itself is not,

---

39. The phrase is taken from a reference to Rousseau's *Confessions* in Marquard's *Abschied vom Prinzipiellen*, 52. I will return to the possible parallels between Rousseau and Adorno.

40. Marquard, *Schwierigkeiten mit der Geschichtsphilosophie*, 140 ff.

41. See Grenz, *Adornos Philosophie in Grundbegriffen*, 122.

42. See Gernot Böhme and Gregor Schiemann, eds., *Phänomenologie der Natur* (Frankfurt a.M.: Suhrkamp, 1997).

43. See Alfred Schmidt, *Der Begriff der Natur in der Lehre von Marx Überarbeitete, ergänzte und mit einem Postscriptum versehene Neuausgabe* (1962; rpt., Frankfurt a.M.: Europäische Verlagsanstalt, 1971).

44. Schnädelbach, *Vernunft und Geschichte*, 160.

upon nature. Without the concept of nature, work — and finally also its reflected form as spirit — is as unimaginable as nature without work: both are at once distinct and mediated via one another" (*Drei Stud* 270). But we can also read this against the grain and maintain that in these dialectically intended sentences, which also intend their contrary, "nature" is not a fixed referent but always already refers to the other of itself (here human labor).

"Enlightenment is more than enlightenment, it is nature made audible [*vernehmbar*] in its estrangement" (*DE* 31 / 57): one would not go wrong to see in this paradoxical sentence the crystallized core of the disparate fragments of *Dialectic of Enlightenment*. A topos shared by Benjamin, Scholem, Bloch, and Marcuse remains determinant for Horkheimer and Adorno. On the one hand, they articulate how "people cannot hope for their own emancipation without the return to and resurrection of fallen and exiled nature."[45] On the other hand, they show that the opposite also holds because, as Benjamin notes in "Über Sprache überhaupt und über die Sprache des Menschen" ("On Language as Such and on Human Language"), they see it as "a metaphysical truth that all nature would begin to lament if it were granted language," and, a little farther: "Speechlessness: that is the great sorrow of nature (and for the sake of its redemption, human life and language is in nature)."[46]

What, however, could fallenness and a hope for the realization of the human mean here? Moreover, what could Habermas's allusion to the resurrection imply in the context of Horkheimer and Adorno's statement that "abolishing death is the innermost cell of all antimythological thought" (*DE* 60 / 96)?

As we have seen in part 1, Habermas seeks to replace the idea of a universal, post-Hegelian reconciliation of reason and nature, society and the individual, with the ideas of autonomy and linguistic competence. The "powerless rage of nature in revolt [*ohnmächtige Wut der revoltierenden Natur*]"[47] and the concept of "nature in itself [*Natur an sich*]," he maintains, have no place in either theoretical or moral-practical discourse, since they could be expressed in these discourses only "at the expense of de-differentiation, that is, of a re-enchantment of the world."[48] Although

45. Habermas, *Philosophisch-politische Profile*, 164.
46. Benjamin, *Gesammelte Schriften*, 2.1:140–57, 155.
47. Habermas, *Theory of Communicative Action*, 2:333 / 2:491, trans. modified.
48. Habermas, *Vorstudien und Ergänzungen*, 519–20. On the problematic of disenchantment and reenchantment in the context of Adorno's philosophy as it relates, in part, to that of

he acknowledges that the idea of nature as it is in itself "inevitably ends up in the aporetic double role of an epistemological *boundary concept* and a *basal concept* supporting evolutionary materialism,"[49] he is nonetheless reluctant to give it a function within the matrix of his theory as a whole. This rather Kantian postulate of a nature "in itself," which one must somehow construct if one is to understand as "originating under contingent circumstances"[50] reality's resistance to one's own attempted interpretations (and, more generally, one's subjective nature), in a single stroke pens reason up within insurmountable barriers.

In Habermas's view one cannot treat the "experiential potential" of nonobjectivist dealings with external nature theoretically or make them fruitful for the "accumulation of knowledge," nor, conversely, can one expect to learn something about inner nature "qua subjectivity"[51] through an objectifying lens. The attempt *"to restore the unity of reason in the theoretical"* fails to reach the level of learning, differentiation, and rationalization established by modernity and lapses into substantialist metaphysics, dogmatic theology, and the like. (As we have seen, Habermas's quick verdict on alternative types of negative metaphysics, attributed to Adorno and others, is no less devastating.) By contrast, an *expressive* or *performative* attitude to both our inner and outer natures (which, incidentally, in Habermas' s eyes can be distinguished via "sensations analogous to morality")[52] must be reserved for aesthetic-practical rationality, that is, for the realms of art and the erotic.[53]

Helga Gripp has questioned Habermas's assertion "that only a paradigm shift to the theory of communication could save any of the contents for which Adorno's thought stands but whose grounding could be achieved within his philosophy."[54] Gripp believes that the linguistic-and formal-pragmatic conceptions of second-generation Critical Theorists create a "lacuna [*Leerstelle*],"[55] by contrast to earlier approaches in the

---

John McDowell's *Mind and World,* see Bernstein, "Re-enchanting Nature," in Smith, *Reading McDowell,* as well as McDowell's response (ibid., 297–300).

49. Habermas, Vorstudien und Ergänzungen, 510.

50. Ibid.

51. Ibid., 514, 520.

52. Ibid., 512.

53. Ibid., 520. See also Habermas, *Theory of Communicative Action,* 1:237–39, 382 / 1:324–27, 512.

54. H. Gripp, *Theodor W. Adorno: Erkenntnisdimensionen negativer Dialektik* (Paderborn: F. Schöningh, 1986), 11.

55. Ibid., 17.

Frankfurt School. The replacement of the subject-object relation as philosophical point of departure and the transition to the paradigm of intersubjective understanding certainly cuts through "the Gordian knot" of the philosophy of consciousness, but only "at the expense of ultimately destroying the 'in itself' of appearances, which Kant not only thought through but understood to be the impetus [*Stimulus*] for all thought."[56]

One might, however, ask whether nature in Adorno's sense corresponds to the concept of a "nature in itself" which could serve the role of placeholder in the empty space that Gripp detects. One cannot help feeling that the idea of the trace of the other of nature in Adorno's presentation is scarcely intended to be a *philosophy of nature* which retreats beyond the level of differentiation and rationalization—and, hence, critique of substantialism—which Habermas presupposes, and instead might direct our attention toward a conceptuality less tied to the remnants of metaphysics, invoking at most a negative metaphysical orientation. Suffice it to maintain, with Gripp, that for Adorno the price of the linguistic-pragmatic paradigm shift—that is, the *philosophical* abandonment of the nonidentical "in" nature—would have been far too great.

Of course, Habermas himself acknowledges this indirectly when he writes: "If the idea of reconciliation could be 'absorbed [*aufginge*]' into the idea of autonomy [or maturity, *Mündigkeit*], of living together via forceless [*zwangloser*] communication, and could unfold in the form of the ever-pending logic of everyday speech, then this reconciliation would not be universal. It would not contain the demand that nature open its eyes—that in the state of reconciliation we speak with animals, plants, and stones."[57] But, ironically, for the authors of *Dialectic of Enlightenment* "discussion [*Diskussion*]," however widened its circle of interlocutors, is deeply suspicious. They describe it as "the medium of traditional bourgeois intelligence" (*DE* 174 / 236). Indeed, they comment with equal cynicism on "the dialectic of eloquence" (*DE* 53 / 87) and on the overestimation of language in general (*DE* 133 ff. / 187 ff.). Does this mean that they advocate an altogether different concept of reason and rationality, indeed, of science and technology? Not quite, but Habermas intimates as much when, regarding the motif of "hope" in *Dialectic of Enlightenment*, he asserts: "The concept of a categorically different science and technology is just as empty as the idea of universal reconciliation is groundless. This has

56. Ibid., 146.
57. Habermas, *Philosophisch-politische Profile*, 176.

its ground rather in something else: the need for consolation and confidence in the face of death, which even the most urgent critique cannot fulfill. This pain is inconsolable without theology."[58] However "unmistakably
atheistic" Adorno may be, he cannot, according to Habermas, do without
this deeply theological idea, even though he would certainly have resisted
contracting the idea of universal reconciliation into the idea of autonomy
and maturity.

But, as indicated, in *Dialectic of Enlightenment* Horkheimer and
Adorno never support a categorically different concept of reason and
rationality, science and technology. Still more important, one should be
careful not to draw confusing consequences from Habermas's discussion
of consolation as a theological motif in their work. Are Adorno's early
"inverse theology," as well as his conception of a "melancholy [*traurige*]
science" (*MM* 15 / 13), and the "desire for the wholly other [*Sehnsucht nach
dem ganz Anderen*]" in the late Horkheimer simply a *consoling* gesture of
thought, or do they not, rather, indicate upon closer examination another
structure, which the text announces in various spots?

Furthermore, one can read in Habermas himself that *Dialectic of Enlightenment* "remains, in its depths, *undecided* [*unentschieden*] about
whether or not a sympathetic connection is torn apart with that first act
of violent self-assertion — simultaneously the technological control of external nature and the repression of one's own internal nature — which
reconciliation must then restore, or whether universal reconciliation is
not, rather, an unattainable idea."[59] If this is true, one should recognize
in this indecision and unattainability — more precisely, *undecidability* —
the book's ultimate *achievement*, rather than its theoretically avoidable
failure. In their failure to offer or even to formulate a positive concept
of enlightenment lies precisely the success of the authors of *Dialectic of
Enlightenment*, namely, in having pointed or at least alluded, *nolens volens*, to the ambiguity of the dimension of the other, of the nonidentical and whatever comes in its trace. Perhaps this idea of the apparently unsublatable ambivalence of the process of Western rationalization
is, in the end, more accurate than Habermas's version of the text, however carefully articulated, namely, that it is an "incomplete *project* — dis-

58. In almost the spirit of the late Horkheimer in the interview "Die Sehnsucht nach dem
ganz Anderen," Habermas observes, "although not even it [this pain] can be indifferent when
pitted against a society whose reproduction no longer needs to exploit our repressed fears"
(ibid., 177).

59. Ibid., my emph.

tracted from its goal, garbled in its intents, often indecipherably worded, indeed in parts wrongheaded—of modernity, albeit one that is at odds with itself."[60] Such an analysis bespeaks "an understanding of modernity obligated to or 'trapped in [*verhafteten*]' Enlightenment."[61] Paradoxically, aporetically, attaining the idea of Enlightenment (somehow, sometime, somewhere) would be no longer (to have) to think it, but to practice, to experience spiritually—in other words, to *live* it. Here, critical reflection and philosophy come to their end (their telos and ending). Only then can one tell whether, when, where—or how—this could come about, if at all. Chances are that such "realization"—indeed, the suspension and aim of all interpretation—does not inaugurate a new era or *posthistoire* but, instead, intermittently punctuates the pace and flow of all times and spaces. No grand eschatological scheme, beyond prehistory, contemporaneity, and even futurity, is aimed at, let alone intuited, here—merely an *instant* of otherness and othering whose occurrence and modality lacks any certainty, determination, and decisiveness and yet in this near indifference makes all the difference in the world. The concluding paragraph of Adorno's programmatic introduction to *Zur Metakritik der Erkenntnistheorie* (*Against Epistemology*) alludes to this intrinsic limit—that is, telos and ending—of philosophical discursiveness: "If the age of interpreting the world is over and the point is now to change it, then philosophy bids farewell, and in its farewell concepts leave off and yet persist [*innehalten*] and become images" (*Against Epistemology*, 39–40 / 47). Adorno comes close to the Heideggerian understanding of *krinein*, namely, knowing where to pause, and hence dismisses the—ultimate, if not principal or provisional—pertinence of *criteriological* knowledge and action, judgment and experience.

Traces of Difference

According to Hans Robert Jauss, Rousseau can be seen as the "crowning witness" for Horkheimer and Adorno's diagnosis of modernity, although they almost never mention him.[62] If this is so, Derrida's remarkable commentary on Rousseau is relevant to my theme, more precisely to my

---

60. Habermas, *Vorstudien und Ergänzungen*, 507.

61. Ibid.

62. Hans Robert Jauss, "Der literarische Prozess des Modernismus von Rousseau bis Adorno," in von Friedeburg and Habermas, *Adorno-Konferenz 1983*, 101. He also identifies Rousseau as Adorno's "most significant unnamed precursor" (107). Rousseau is mentioned once indirectly in *Dialectic of Enlightenment* (*DE* 62 / 99).

attempt to read Horkheimer's and, more strongly, Adorno's concept of
nature ("good nature" and also "natural history") not as a postulated or
imagined reality per se — in or for itself, the difference matters little — but
as ab-solute, in the sense I have given to this term: that is to say, as a trace
of an other whose existence can be neither positively stated nor denied
and "is," therefore, ambiguous, undecided, indeed, undecidable.

In the second part of *Of Grammatology,* under the title "Nature, Culture, Writing," Derrida attempts to show that there is a problematic relationship to nature in Rousseau. This author, Derrida suggests, thinks of
nature as a presence, as a "transcendental signified," in short, as a secret
and uncanny metaphysical remainder.[63] If this judgment is pertinent, does
it have repercussions for the concept of nature in *Dialectic of Enlightenment*? Several places in this text support such a supposition. Yet that
should not blind us to the fact that equally decisive passages describe nature as a *trace,* almost in Derrida's (and, as we shall see, Levinas's) sense
of the term.

As Horkheimer and Adorno formulate this concept: "Novalis's definition according to which all philosophy is homesickness [*Heimweh*] holds
good only if this longing is not dissipated in the phantasm of a lost original
state, but homeland [*Heimat*], and nature itself, are pictured as something
that have had first to be wrested from myth. Homeland is a state of having
escaped [*Entronnensein*]." They continue: "For this reason the criticism
that the Homeric legends 'withdraw from the earth [*die der Erde sich ent-
fernen*]' is a warranty of their truth. They 'turn to men [*Sie kehren zu der
Menschheit sich*]'" (*DE* 61 / 97).[64] Nature is thus severed from an archaic-
mythical, if not romantic, understanding, is de-substantialized and de-
ontologized, and is conceived as resisting all attempts to reduce its meaning along historicist, culturalist, or narrativist paradigms. Moreover, its

---

63. See Derrida, *Of Grammatology:* "But Rousseau *describes what he does not wish to say:*
that 'progress' takes place *both* for the worse *and* for the better. At the same time. Which annuls
eschatology and teleology, just as difference — or originary articulation — annuls archeology"
(229 / 326). Paul de Man claims, however, "Contrary to Derrida's assertion, Rousseau's theory of
representation is not directed toward meaning as presence and plenitude but toward meaning
as void" (*Blindness and Insight: Essays in the Rhetoric of Contemporary Criticism* [Minneapolis:
University of Minnesota Press, 1983], 127). He quotes *La Nouvelle Héloïse:* "tel est le néant des
choses humaines qu'hors l'Etre existant par lui-même, il n'y a rien de beau que ce qui n'est pas"
(131).

64. The quotes are from Hölderlin's poem "Der Herbst" ("Autumn"). On these topological
motifs, see also my essay "Winke: Divine Topoi in Nancy, Hölderlin, Heidegger," in *The Solid
Letter: New Readings of Friedrich Hölderlin,* ed. Aris Fioretos (Stanford: Stanford University
Press, 1999), 94–120.

ancient materialistic and modern naturalistic-scientistic determinations are portrayed as inadequate to its very concept.

The "loneliness [*Einsamkeit*] which ails the whole of nature" (*DE* 156 / 214, trans. modified) — so long as nature is understood, according to modern physics "before and after quantum theory," as *per definitionem* "what can be registered mathematically" (*DE* 18 / 41)[65] — can, it seems, only be overcome by the "mind's self-recognition as nature divided from itself." Yet — and this is crucial for my interpretation — that overcoming can happen only insofar as nature is thought of as "blind and mutilated," that is, insofar as nature is thought of as neither "omnipotence," "*mana*" (*DE* 31 / 57), nor "mere nature," into which civilization as "the triumph of society over nature" tends to transform everything (*DE* 153 / 211). In short, the concept of nature does not stand for a positive presence, let alone for a deplorable absence, but, as Adorno later puts it, for "the trace of the nonidentical [*Spur des Nichtidentischen*]." Still later, in *Aesthetic Theory,* Adorno reiterates this central figure: "Natural beauty is the trace of the nonidentical in things [*die Spur des Nichtidentischen an den Dingen*] under the spell of universal identity" (73 / 114).

Early on, Habermas points out that nature has two sides in Adorno's writings. Like the concept of enlightenment, it presents both a friendly and a terrifying face: "over the friendly and enticing face of nature there lies, however, a peculiar shadow of ambivalence. This is the *unrest* in the clockwork of Adorno's opus"; only occasionally, Habermas goes on to say, does the image of a "*devotion* [or giving oneself, *Hingabe*] entirely removed from the desire to possess"[66] break through, most often in the tenderness of erotic love. In the text of *Dialectic of Enlightenment* this ambivalence about nature, which also concerns its terrible side, never really resolves itself. Under the conditions of modernity "any devotion [*Hingabe*] which believed itself objective, grounded in the matter at hand, was dispelled as mythological" (*DE* 73 / 112), so that one can give oneself to the other, to nature, only ironically, hence, only in the modality of the "as if" (*Als ob*). This modality differs in many respects from the as if that Kant and the neo-Kantians develop — notably Hans Vaihinger, in *Philosophie des Als-ob*

---

65. Referring to Husserl's *Die Krisis der europäischen Wissenschaften und die transzendentale Phänomenologie* (*The Crisis of European Sciences and Transcendental Phenomenology*), Horkheimer and Adorno claim that, in modern science — and, in its wake, phenomenology — "even what cannot be assimilated, the insoluble and irrational, is fenced in by mathematical theorems" (*DE* 18 / 41).

66. Habermas, *Philosophisch-politische Profile,* 164–65.

(*Philosophy of the As-if*). Horkheimer and Adorno's understanding of the irony of devotion and giving oneself over to, into the hands of, nature does not take the form of a regulative idea to be pursued in an intellectual or moral process of infinite approximation or, as in Vaihinger, through a life-affirming perspectivism of sorts. The modality of *Hingabe* is, quite literally, broken and, in that sense, irreparably and tragically ironic from the outset.

Not by chance, in the situation of bourgeois mastery, which extends back into the prehistory of subjectivity, the song of the Sirens (which is, in Horkheimer and Adorno's reading of the *Odyssey,* the call of amorphous nature) is *always already* "neutralized as the yearning [*Sehnsucht*] of those who pass it by" (*DE* 46–47 / 78). Ambiguity is the signature of the courtesan Circe's promiscuity. She grants a "trace of pleasure [*Spur der Lust*]," "in however delusive a form, a semblance of reconciliation" and happiness (*DE* 55 / 89), which then endangers the autonomy of the self, whose identity has been constituted through the repression of drives. Civilization, at least up until now, *Dialectic of Enlightenment* suggests, has defamed sex, and in consequence the Homeric epic can conceive of Circe in no other way than as weak—just as, later, developed bourgeois society attributes to women the status of the second sex. As "a representative of nature," woman thus becomes "an enigma [*Rätselbild*] of irresistibility and powerlessness." Because of her historical position in the patriarchal order, she negatively conveys—like every victim of history (e.g., of anti-Semitism) does or could do—the idea of the alterity of nature: "she reflects back the vain lie of power, which substitutes the mastery over nature for reconciliation with it" (*DE* 56 / 91).

Nature can appear only brokenly and speculatively, as tender reflection. This is confirmed in "the gravity of the lover, who presciently pins his whole life to the fleeting moment [*entrinnenden Augenblick*]" (*DE* 112 / 163; see also 111 / 162). To those who attempt to control it through denial and resignation, repressed nature "provocatively reflects back the appearance of a powerless happiness." Yet this powerless reflection is anything but nature's defeat and consciousness's triumph, rather the reverse, not least because "the idea of happiness without power is unendurable because it alone would be happiness" (*DE* 141 / 196).

Thus viewed, happiness, as Freud states in *Civilization and Its Discontents,* seems no longer to have any cultural value.[67] More precisely, it is nec-

---

67. Sigmund Freud, "Das Unbehagen in der Kultur," *Kulturtheoretische Schriften* (Frankfurt a.M.: S. Fischer, 1974), 197–270 / *Civilization and Its Discontents* (New York: Norton, 1961).

essarily maimed in the "indissoluble contradiction of order, which, when it sanctions happiness, turns it into self-parody and creates it only through proscribing it" (*DE* 89 / 134). Modernity apparently tends to freeze into a world in which every pointless expression can appear only as a "grimace" in which "the rage of the tormentor and of the tormented" always already shines forth "indistinguishably [*unentschieden*]" (*DE* 150 / 207). The works of Sade and Nietzsche betray such a contradiction insofar as they put it into words, make it explicit, and at the same time perpetuate it by fictionalizing, literalizing, or eternally willing what remains in fact a historical contingency or, more fundamentally, what for all its historical necessity remains metaphysically arbitrary and, therefore, "ain't necessarily so."

Yet we should not understand these and similar characterizations in Horkheimer and Adorno as if a sublation of the ambiguity they sketch were theoretically *conceivable, close at hand,* or even *desirable,* although they often suggest as much (and thereby expose themselves to the very critique whose principle and method they devise). Indeed, we find quasi-affirmative allusions to happiness as if it were "in essence a result," confirmed only in the sublation of suffering, that is to say, by "the realization of utopia" through historical work, thus opposed to the subject's "simply abiding within an image of bliss [*Verweilen im Bild der Seligkeit*]" (*DE* 49 / 81, 82). Yet no less important passages make clear that not for any price would these authors relinquish the openness that characterizes every *ab-solute*—and, in that sense, unattainable in principle—utopian perspective. It is difficult to see how this perspective on the absolute, if thought through to the end, could be represented in philosophical discourse in anything other than an *aporetic* and *infinitizing* way—and not only in theoretical argument, for the "secret of aesthetic sublimation," Horkheimer and Adorno write, is also "to present fulfillment in its brokenness" (*DE* 111 / 162). Aesthetic expression and experience stand under the same regime as theoretical and practical reason.

The concept of the trace of nature's alterity thus resists the putative problems of a "restoration of the unity of reason in the theoretical"[68] or in morality in the name of an external or internal "nature in itself." In a more elusive and paradoxical figure of thought Horkheimer and Adorno's tracings of nature point to a *third way*—*tertium datur*—leading beyond the fruitless alternatives of naturalism and cynicism, on the one hand, and theology and idealism, on the other.[69] They allude to a dimension that can

68. Habermas, *Vorstudien und Ergänzungen,* 514.
69. See Wellmer, *Zur Dialektik von Moderne und Postmoderne,* 76–77: "The critique of rea-

be seen as neither present nor absent, that is neither the unattainable limit of our finite thought nor the symbol of a quasi-religious hinterworld.[70] The trace of nature always already *traverses, permeates,* and *relativizes* the boundaries of our discourse without thereby rendering it fully obsolete.

Modern subjects, it would seem, can most easily sense this trace of nature in the relationship of the self to itself—that is, in the way the self relates to its own inner nature—and in the relationship of the self to another self, to the naturalness of other selves. As Weber knew, the trace belongs not to the visible and deafening spaces of the public and of publicity but to the realm of the *pianissimo.* But this does not make the languages of intersubjective communication, expressivity, eroticism, and art the exclusive medium of the experience of the other of nature, no matter how much one might agree with Habermas's "skepticism about the possibility of *rationalizing* fraternal dealings with a nonobjectified nature,"[71] that is, of integrating it into theoretical or practical discourse. The formal question of the asymmetrical structure of the trace of nature (or of anything whatsoever) belongs to a different type of inquiry, which one might be tempted to call "negative metaphysics" and which can be concretely determined only on the basis of singular instances of *judgment* (see chap. 1).

ACCORDING TO HORKHEIMER AND ADORNO, starting early on civilization replaces an "organic adaptation to otherness [*Anschmiegung ans andere*]," that is, "mimetic behavior properly speaking," with rationality interpreted as domination and work: "The angel which, with fiery sword, drove humans out of paradise and onto the path of technical progress, is itself the symbol [*Sinnbild*] of that progress"; and, if for humans any return to the prehistorical must remain forever closed, the prospect of immediate and undominated mimesis is also—starting with "the religious ban on graven images [*Bilderverbot*]" (*DE* 148 / 205)—destroyed or broken. Precisely here lies the condition of possibility for civilization.

The power of nature is reproduced in enlightened bourgeois "sobriety" and "factuality [*Tatsachensinn*]," now in the form of a conscious conformity to its imperatives: "The reason that represses mimesis is not merely

son in terms of the logic of identity seems to empty itself into the alternatives of cynicism or theology, even if doing so would make one into the advocate of either a joyful resignation or a disintegration of the self, with no consideration for the consequences."

70. On the concept of the trace, see *OB* 100–101 / 126–27; and Levinas, "La Trace de l'autre," *DEHH* 187–202.

71. Habermas, *Vorstudien und Ergänzungen,* 521, my emph.

its opposite. It is itself mimesis: of death. The subjective mind which disintegrates the spiritualization of nature masters spiritless nature only by imitating its rigidity" (*DE* 44–45 / 75–76). Viewed thus, the inevitably doomed yet unavoidable attempt to overhear the temptation of nature in oneself and in others is evidence of an unsuccessful civilization and, as such, *the reverse side of culture* (see *DE* 87–88 / 132).

In attempting to answer the question of the place of *Dialectic of Enlightenment* in today's discussion between the two supposed extremes of modernism and postmodernism by designating it a *midpoint* between the theory of rationality and the strategies of deconstruction,[72] it cannot suffice to point out and extrapolate the various motifs that would speak for one or the other position or disposition. Likewise, it would be misguided to view the critique of the limitation of the modern Western concept of the subject as anticipating a subversion of reason as such. First, and above all, that would necessarily deny the explicit intention of the book's authors: *Dialectic of Enlightenment* is meant to be a "construction of rationality."[73] Second, the discussion of forerunners and followers presupposes, at least implicitly, a universal-historical assumption or an intellectual teleology that contemporary conceptions of "multiversal history" have rendered suspect.[74] Perhaps it might be better to speak of a *mirror relationship* between *Dialectic of Enlightenment* and the disparate approaches of "postmodernism."[75] This implies a secret *elective affinity,* or "happy coherence,"[76] between figures of thought and themes that cannot be reduced to each other.

Thus, for example, both the emphasis on seriousness in *Dialectic of Enlightenment* and the stress on play in "postmodern" texts allude—again, as if in a kind of mirror writing—to a parallel ambiguous structure. Likewise, *Dialectic of Enlightenment* brings out the *amor intellectualis diaboli* its authors attribute to enlightenment: the "pleasure," if not of "defeating

72. See Harry Kunneman and Hent de Vries, intro., Kunneman and de Vries, *Die Aktualität der "Dialektik der Aufklärung,"* 9–14.

73. See Schnädelbach, "Dialektik als Vernunftkritik: Zur Konstruktion des Rationalen bei Adorno," in von Friedeburg and Habermas, *Adorno-Konferenz 1983,* 67; and Schnädelbach, *Vernunft und Geschichte,* 180.

74. On this terminology, see Odo Marquard, "Universalgeschichte und Multiversalgeschichte," *Apologie des Zufälligen: Philosophische Studien* (Stuttgart: Reclam, 1986), 54–75.

75. Wellmer also emphasizes that Adorno's philosophy could be read as a philosophy of the postmodern. See *Zur Dialektik von Moderne und Postmoderne,* 160. For another assessment, see Axel Honneth's subtle essay on *Dialectic of Enlightenment* in *Das Andere der Gerechtigkeit: Aufsätze zur praktischen Philosophie* (Frankfurt a.M.: Suhrkamp, 2000).

76. On this term, see Habermas, *Moral Consciousness and Communicative Action,* 11.

civilization with its own weapons" (*DE* 74 / 114), at least of unmasking it. Their book lacks any explicit appreciation of humor, for which they can claim precedents in Baudelaire and Hölderlin (*DE* 112 / 163). Yet they insist upon the "ambivalence [*Doppelsinn*] of laughter" (*DE* 60 / 97) as both the terrible sign of violence or the conventional (see *ND* 334 / 327–28) and the "echo of escape [*Echo des Entronnenseins*] from power" (*DE* 112 / 160).

By the same token "traces of something better [*Spuren des Besseren*]," according to Horkheimer and Adorno, lodge even in the culture industry, most likely in "those features . . . by which it resembles the circus": in the "stubbornly purposeless expertise [*eigensinnig-sinnverlassenen Könner-schaft*] of riders, acrobats, and clowns." These are being rendered obsolete by "organizational reason," which is "causing meaninglessness to disappear at the lowest level of art just as radically as meaning is disappearing at the highest" (*DE* 114 / 165). Seen thus, seriousness and play seem peculiarly intertwined in *Dialectic of Enlightenment,* which thus—if one really wants to insist on this—resonates with a distinctive motif in postmodern sensibility.

We might even go a step farther by showing, through a closer reading of these leitmotifs in *Dialectic of Enlightenment,* how the text subverts the intentions of its authors precisely with regard to the question of the subject and its nature and how, in this failure, their most illuminating insights break through. To the extent that this is so, one ought, with an ironic glance at the clear-sighted interpretation of Habermas, to speak once more of the virtues of the "skepticism regarding reason" to which he seems blind. Such a reading might be called, once more with reference to Derrida, "deconstructive," because we are basically concerned here with a *consistently hermeneutic* mode of reading, which is also *rhetorical* and moderately though effectively *skeptical.* Using the term *deconstruction* in this context highlights certain elements in my account and brings this possible intellectual lineage of *Dialectic of Enlightenment* into a bit more balance with the one advocated (although not always consistently) by Habermas and his pupils. Gripp has already suggested that Derrida "thinks Adorno's philosophy radically to the end."[77] She supports this claim with reflections on the philosophy of language. One can, I have been suggesting, arrive at a similar assessment in light of the concepts of nature and subjectivity in *Dialectic of Enlightenment.*

It therefore seems less fruitful to explicate the *spirit* of *Dialectic of En-*

77. Gripp, *Adorno,* 144, 176n.

lightenment, as Habermas claims to do (although he neither does nor can), than to follow the *letter* of the text, as Derrida in no way pretends to do (although he both can and in fact does) — so extensively are blindness and insight intertwined.[78]

If one wants to pursue the analogy with Derrida's deconstruction of the metaphysical tradition, the authors of *Dialectic of Enlightenment* can be seen as pointing toward the concept of nature as trace, although they do so *unintentionally* and *without saying as much,* since one finds this motif only sporadically in their text. Yet, as the comparison to Derrida also brings out, like him they forcefully read the fundamental literary and philosophical texts of European civilization in terms of what these texts express (see *DE* 37 / 63), at least implicitly, without having intended it. Anyone who subscribes to Adorno's model of immanent critique owes it to the authors of *Dialectic of Enlightenment* to subject this text to their own form of reading. Thus, for example, they do not regard the legacy of Greek or modern enlightenment as a historical or social source but, rather, as a collection of foreboding "allegories of ruin [or perversion and decay, *Allegorien des Verderbens*]" (*DE* 158 / 217). In this they join a rhetorical tradition of narration which one could best describe as a *philosophia narrativa* composed with *critical* intent.[79] Self-reflection and the memory of disastrous and unsalutary history, they write, have a chance but only "at the moment of narrating [*im Augenblick der Erzählung*]" and when these are distinguished from "mythic song." Finally, however, like the victim's lament, these, too, must end in silence: in a silence whose "numb pause [or petrifaction, *Erstarrung*]" is "the rest of all genuine speech [*der wahre Rest aller Rede*]" (*DE* 61 / 98, trans. modified).

The Virtues of the "Skepticism regarding Reason"

I can now comment on the question of whether Horkheimer and Adorno actually reach the zero degree of reflection and hope in *Dialectic of Enlightenment,* their "blackest book."[80] Habermas argues that in this text the authors have extended their ambivalence about the self-destructive process of progressive thinking so far that, "on their own analysis,"[81] they can no longer maintain any hope of its emancipatory and integrative, let alone redemptive, power. The conceptuality of instrumental reason

78. See Paul de Man, *Blindness and Insight.*
79. See Marquard, *Abschied vom Prinzipiellen,* 110–11.
80. Habermas, *Philosophical Discourse of Modernity,* 106 / 130.
81. Ibid.

stemming from the tradition of the philosophy of the subject shows that, though in thinking and acting, science and praxis, a subject can make nature available and control it, reason is not capable of saying "*to an objectified nature what is to be done to it.*"[82]

Habermas thinks that this makes Horkheimer and Adorno's *Dialectic of Enlightenment* particularly "ironic."[83] He sees the fact that its authors nevertheless will not dispense with the work of the concept as proof of the somewhat unproductive paradox and aporia of a critique of reason become "subjectless, as it were."[84] Such a critique, for all its insistence on the demise of the subject, cannot but remain chained to the conceptual framework of subjectivity. And, where it points elsewhere, the remembrance of nature in the subject turns out to be "shockingly close" to the Heideggerian reminiscence of Being (*Andenken des Seins*),[85] whose associations both authors profoundly despise. Moreover, Habermas continues, Horkheimer and Adorno's insistence on the usefulness of mimesis can appear only as an irrational impulse, that is, as "the sheer opposite of reason."[86]

This being said, there are good reasons why Horkheimer and Adorno's remarks about the question of the subject and the diminishing yet persistent meaning of individuality cannot be translated into a theory of communicative action, at least not without substantial reduction. They lead, rather, toward an enlightened tradition of *hermeneutics*—as I indicated earlier, a radical perspectivism in name and in view of the ab-solute— which has succeeded in unmasking the dogmatism of enlightenment, in its ancient Greek and modern European articulations. With this intellectual orientation, perhaps, Horkheimer and Adorno's *unintentional affinity* with the most significant aspects of contemporary French philosophy, as represented in the thought of Levinas and Derrida, becomes apparent.

Seen in this light, the concept of communicative action, as postulated in Habermas's magnum opus, is perhaps not yet "sufficiently skeptical" in every necessary respect.[87] Perhaps a philosophy of the subject developed via a thoroughgoing skepticism, like the one that shines through in many passages of *Dialectic of Enlightenment*—often unintentionally, as we have seen—finally would burst open or, rather, enlarge and supplement the

82. Habermas, *Theory of Communicative Action*, 1:389 / 1:522.
83. Ibid., 1:383 / 1:513.
84. Habermas, *Die neue Unübersichtlichkeit*, 219.
85. Habermas, *Theory of Communicative Action*, 1:390 / 1:516.
86. Ibid., 1:390 / 1:522.
87. Ibid., 1:xlii / 1:8.

framework of a formal-pragmatic theory of intersubjectivity. Whatever the result of such exposure, one could, of course, still ask whether rationality can ever be thought without some — however minimal — concept of subjectivity.[88] This line of questioning would not imply a clear theoretical alternative to Habermas's version of the linguistico-pragmatic turn but only open up an account of the price it has to pay for its systematic theoretical span.[89] Every serious reading of *Dialectic of Enlightenment* is bound to spell out at least the "negativity" inherent in any such project.

Horkheimer and Adorno seek to make a virtue of the apparent impasse of the skepticism regarding reason by practicing philosophy as a *topology,* or rather topography, *of the good life* while continuing to observe the tradition of the Jewish prohibition of images and its modern analogues. In their work this concerns a negative dialectical circumscription and *micrology* of what might be other than whatever exists. It therefore gestures toward nothing less than a *utopia* and exemplifies a *minima moralia* that takes the place of the *magna moralia* of Aristotelian practical philosophy.

Yet Horkheimer and Adorno are either unwilling or, at least in *Dialectic of Enlightenment,* unable to take a further step in the direction of

---

88. See Manfred Frank, *Die Unhintergehbarkeit von Individualität: Reflexionen über Subjekt, Person und Individuum aus Anlaß ihrer 'postmodernen' Toterklärung* (Frankfurt a.M.: Suhrkamp, 1986), 13.

89. One must then wonder whether or not Habermas is correct about Adorno's attempt "to break through the fallacy of constitutive subjectivity with the strength of the subject" (*ND* xx / 10). In his view Adorno's appropriation of neo-Hegelian motives "puts into question the concept of sensible identity itself, though without relinquishing the intention it should express" (Habermas, *Zur Rekonstruktion des Historischen Materialismus,* 123 n. 16). But this leaves undisturbed the concept of identity proposed by the theory of communication: "The ideas of reconciliation and freedom, which Adorno encircles negatively dialectically, ultimately only trapping him in the circle of Hegelianism, are in need of some explication; and they can also be unfolded with the aid of the concept of communicative rationality, which they already indicate with Adorno" (Habermas, *Theory of Communicative Action,* 2:8 / 2:9). See also Wellmer, *Zur Dialektik von Moderne und Postmoderne:* "The 'remembrance of nature in the subject' demanded by *Dialectic of Enlightenment* cannot demythologize the idealistic philosophy of the subject. Only the remembrance of *language* in the subject leads beyond the confines of the philosophy of the subject; it makes visible the communicative practice that founds the life of linguistic meaning, of which the subject who 'imagines' and 'judges,' 'identifies' conceptually and acts instrumentally, is merely the silhouette. Of course, this removes the foundation of the critique *of* the 'identifying' concept" (88). Rolf Tiedemann, however, emphasizes: "Adorno would have accepted that the truth of utterances is bound to the intention of a true life as unquestioningly as he would have refused to recognize this intention in the structures of everyday speech, however it might be idealized" ("Begriff Bild Name: Über Adornos Utopie von Erkenntnis," in *Hamburger Adorno-Symposion,* ed. Michael Löbig and Gerhard Schweppenhäuser [Lüneburg: D. zu Klampen, 1984], 70).

thinking what might be other than whatever exists as something different *in principle* or for formal-structural reasons. They do not yet explore "difference" and the "trace" along the lines that will emerge, with far greater consistency and rigor, in the writings of first Levinas and then Derrida. Although Adorno's negative dialectic will eventually tend toward the "idea of a 'transdiscursive' philosophy,"[90] *Dialectic of Enlightenment* still bears witness to the overly naive assumption that "enlightenment itself, having mastered itself and assumed its own power, could break through the limits of enlightenment" (*DE* 172 / 234). Nevertheless, as we have seen, at isolated moments their text also points toward the limit of this philosophical intention. Thus, whenever Horkheimer and Adorno find themselves forced to speak of a "hypocritical [more precisely, one-dimensional, *gleisnerischen*] identity of truth and sophistry," they must also confess in the same breath that the separation between truth and sophistry is "as uncompelling as it nevertheless is strict" (*DE* 160 / 219). They suggest as much when they speak about the virtual disappearance of the ever so slight opposition between the culture industry and the avant-garde (see *DE* 102 / 150). Might this not suggest, at least implicitly, that the question of truth in relation to sophistry is *philosophically* (though not necessarily practically or, rather, existentially) undecidable from the very beginning? What Horkheimer and Adorno add to this seems merely to affirm the opposite (see *DE* 160–61 / 219–20). Does not this paradoxical motif suggest a remainder of bad metaphysics, even more than do the openly aporetic and performatively contradictory formulations that Adorno will explore with ever greater consequence?

Negative dialectics (Adorno) and the desire for the wholly other (Horkheimer) can perhaps be understood as the final implications of what in *Dialectic of Enlightenment* still lies diffusely hidden behind the "skepticism regarding reason." Seen thus, the late philosophy of Horkheimer and Adorno no longer winds up in the much-maligned dead end of a totalizing anthropology and philosophy of history but is, rather, a possible and plausible modification of a philosophy of ab-solute difference, indeed, of a difference that cannot be sought or brought out within philosophical reflection. Of course, in so doing they are not concerned with "an always *other* 'Other of reason [*ein jeweils* anderes *'Anderes der Vernunft,'*"[91] as Derrida seems to be, but, rather, with a nature always already conceived in

---

90. Wellmer, *Zur Dialektik von Moderne und Postmoderne*, 75.
91. Ibid., 80.

a moral, metaphysical light. Their method of phenomenological concretion, however, promises precisely, though micrologically and aporetically, an incarnation of the scattered traces of a different meaning, one formally articulated by Derrida. (I will address this in chap. 11).

Insofar as Horkheimer and Adorno often present this *materialized difference* garbed in rhetorical figures of language and thought, it traverses the perhaps false and premature alternative between a modern "construction of the rational," on the one hand, and the "aesthetic play of a postmodern way of dealing with the world," on the other.[92] In this context one might, once more, agree with Marquard, who claims that "the aesthetic play of composition and formulation . . . is not the contrary of seriousness, but rather one of its states of aggregation: that of someone who takes seriousness so seriously that he considers play necessary to make that state endurable."[93]

92. Schnädelbach, "Dialektik als Vernunftkritik," in von Friedeburg and Habermas, *Adorno-Konferenz 1983*, 67; and Schnädelbach, *Vernunft und Geschichte*, 180.
93. Marquard, *Abschied vom Prinzipiellen*, 9.

Chapter Five

The Breaking Apart of Western Objectivism and the Resurrection of the Particular and the Ephemeral in the Philosophy of History

IN THE RATIONAL PRINCIPLE of enlightenment, according to Adorno, lies hidden a violence comparable to the diffuse power of myth: "Ideology's power of resistance to enlightenment is owed to its complicity with identifying thought, or indeed with thought at large [*Denken überhaupt*]" (*ND* 148 / 151). In general we can characterize the Western philosophical tradition as the thinking of identity and totality, in whose terms all that is not identical is forced into line with the unambiguous meaning of the Cartesian *clare et distincte percipere*. Adorno rejects any such *prima philosophia,* philosophy of origin, philosophy of consciousness, or transcendental philosophy. In his eyes these modes of thinking ontologically and epistemologically reduce the "nonidentical" to the self-same.

This criticism applies to classical and modern-subjective forms of reason as well as to the *objective,* speculative idealism of Hegel and its naturalist reversal in Marx. Adorno's unique position, which in a first argumentative step we might describe as a *dialectical critique of dialectics,* is characterized by his separation from Hegel and his proximity to Kant. Schnädelbach has aptly described this peculiar, intermediary position: "Negative dialectics is supposed, in confrontation with Kant, to rehabilitate reason as a capacity for knowledge and at the same time to protect it from Hegelian speculative hubris. . . . Adorno's negative dialectics is thus the difficult task of criticizing Hegel by Hegelian means."[1]

One must therefore correct one important avenue in the reception of Adorno's work, which continues to portray him as, above all, a neo-

---

1. Schnädelbach, "Dialektik als Vernunftkritik," in von Friedeburg and Habermas, *Adorno-Konferenz 1983,* 67; and Schnädelbach, *Vernunft und Geschichte,* 180.

Hegelian.[2] Precisely Adorno's skeptically aggravated *anti-Hegelian* "inversion of the philosophy of history"[3] and the reversal of the perspectives of classical-modern philosophies of totality and identity which he proposes make it possible to compare his work with that of Levinas. Despite his emphasis on "mediation," of which subjective forms of reason lose sight, in his later writings, even where he probingly and critically adapts the work of Hegel, Adorno emphatically rejects every "reconciliation" of contradictions, whether put forward as *real* or merely as *realizable.*

My account of the most significant traits of Adorno's philosophy of history has a dual goal. First, I am interested in delineating an idea of the *historically ephemeral* in Adorno's work which would enable his hermeneutics of the particular to resist Levinas's critique of *history as such.* That another (concept of) history is thinkable is not without interest because, as I shall verify in part 3, Levinas's own critique of the metaphysical tradition, of totality and identity, in short, of the "same," would be impossible without reference to concrete historical "experience." Second, I will, conversely, find some lack of consequence in Adorno's characterization of the mode of transcendence that can be "experienced" *within* history. Although he breaks free of the shadow of determinism in the philosophy of history, he does, perhaps, not resist with sufficient decisiveness a no less false alternative: namely, the assumption of an eventual abstract other *beyond* history (and not just history as we know it, epochs of Being as revealed and sent to us or still to come, but history *tout court*). A more plausible idea concerning the occurrence of—an encounter with—a *concrete* other of history (in both subjective and objective senses of the genitive), one that could be clarified by the concept of the *trace,* announces itself in various strong formulations in Adorno's late work, though they leave intact his less convincing utopian affirmations concerning either the past and present absence or the possible future presence of the other. This concept of the trace (*Spur des Anderen, Spur von Nichtidentität, Spur von Affirmation*), which, I shall argue, plays an even more central role in Levinas's late work—even though he often fails to admit its repercussions for rethinking the premises of the philosophy of language or of history (in-

2. Hegel may have influenced the Frankfurt School insofar as its members' work presents a dialectical thinking. For them, however, his philosophy is scarcely the "decisive point of reference for the critique of bourgeois thought and for the reformulation of dialectics as a critical theory of reason, history, and society." See Schmidt, "Hegel in der Kritischen Theorie der Frankfurter Schule," 17.

3. See Geyer, *Aporien des Metaphysik-und Geschichtsbegriff der Kritischen Theorie,* 133.

cluding his own) — can enable us to articulate better the pièce de résistance of Adorno's critique. Neither the current concept of a deterministic pessimism concerning history (along the lines of the early and later Horkheimer) nor its counterpart in a utopian messianism (in the spirit of Benjamin) can do justice to the *double meaning* of alterity in Adorno's most astute interpretations. And the same holds true for the transformation of its critical potential into a formal conceptual — indeed, pragmatic — frame with the help of categories of intersubjectivity and communicative action.

Philosophy, Adorno claims, if it is not to forget its utopia, faces a paradoxical task: "to unseal [or open up, *aufzutun*] the non-conceptual with concepts, without making it their equal" (*ND* 10 / 21). In other words, if "thinking without a concept is not thinking at all" (*ND* 98 / 105), philosophical thought must "strive, by way of the concept, to transcend the concept [*über den Begriff durch den Begriff hinauszugelangen*]" (*ND* 15 / 27). Adorno attempts to show that what exists and all thinking that reflects upon it leave no place for what could be otherwise without doing violence to this other. Existence and existing thought distort whatever exceeds them.

As I have shown, every path of thought directed toward sublation — whether in the sense of subjective, objective, or speculative idealism, of materialist or reductionist naturalism, of psychoanalysis or ideology critique — is thereby closed off a priori as a possible route toward naming and respecting the nonidentical. Of course, it would be equally misguided to attempt to rectify this embarrassment for thought through the naive "avowal of a being-in-itself outside the totality of cogitative definitions" (*ND* 5 / 17). To do so would mean to espouse a magical understanding of things or to presuppose what Kant called a dogmatic notion of "intellectual intuition," in short: exaltation, or *Schwärmerei*.

This dilemma of false identification and equally false immediacy — indeed, of thinking reduced to a nonformal tautology, on the one hand, or to free-floating heterology, on the other — is perhaps the main reason why Adorno repeatedly confirms his solidarity with the prohibition of images while acknowledging that there is no alternative to its predicament.

Dialectics can and should be only negative. This position is foreshadowed in *Dialectic of Enlightenment*. In his late work Adorno takes it up and — drawing upon his earliest beginnings, which are stamped by the influence of Benjamin — develops it into a thought of *constellations* or *configurations*. Adorno's unique position might best be discussed in light of

the classical-modern, Kantian-Hegelian question concerning the relationship between *morality* (*Moralität*) and *ethical life* (*Sittlichkeit*), which has
been resuscitated in debates about the status of "discourse ethics" or the
"ethics of discussion," and the critical difference between the "normative point of view," on the one hand, and different articulations of "Neo-
Aristotelianism" and communitarianism, on the other.

Adorno's critique of the (inter)subjective-formalist and objective-
substantialist concept of reason, like his critique of utopianism, allows us
to differentiate his thinking from various angles: first, as we have seen, in
confronting any subjectivist philosophy of existence of whatever origin;
second, in confronting objectivist traits in the philosophies of history of
Hegel, Marx, Engels, Lukács, and Bloch; and, finally, in light of the messianic thinking of discontinuity in Rosenzweig and Benjamin. This last
demarcation runs into the greatest difficulties, since its points of connection are often quite fluid. This holds especially for the link to Benjamin.
Notwithstanding their unmistakable differences in emphasis, one might
characterize Adorno's negative dialectics as a systematization of motifs
in Benjamin's seemingly *un*systematic thought. Adorno, more than anyone else, took it upon himself to smuggle Benjaminian explosives into
philosophical discourse, often leaving the misleading impression that the
concept of negative dialectics could not, finally, be thought without the
messianic irruption of what is absolutely other. Eventually, he came to see
that one ought to articulate the other and the same in a different fashion.
For this to happen, however, the subtle interplay of identity and difference
designated by the concept of the trace needed to displace the notion of a
sudden flash of discontinuity.

Of course, the question remains *whether* and, if so, *how* such an enriched and rectified philosophy of negative dialectics and trace could ever
enter into alliance with the programs of formal pragmatics or discourse
ethics. How can negative dialectics and the thinking of the trace toward
which it works its way vouch for the undeniable negative-metaphysical aspects of dissymmetry in thought, praxis, and judgment, which one tends
to neglect when transforming philosophy into a quasi-transcendental
theory of rationality and communicative action? How can they be put
into words without obscuring the high level of differentiation and de-
mythologization—even secularization or profanization—achieved in the
"cultural learning step" for which the project of modernity, at least in
Habermas's reading, must stand?

Adorno's Dialectical Critique of Dialectics

Adorno's departure from Hegel is based on the insight that only what does not fit into the world as it exists can exhibit a trace of truth, and it can never adequately be described in terms borrowed from this world's present state and direction. From this Adorno draws the most extreme consequence: "The idea of reconcilement forbids its positive positing [*Setzung*] with the help of the concept [more precisely, *in* the concept, or *in view of* a concept, its concept, *im Begriff*]" (*ND* 145, trans. modified / 148-49; see 6-7, 20 / 18-19, 31). He therefore feels impelled toward the scarcely interpretable model of a dialectical critique of dialectics, toward a thinking that oscillates between the extremes of an aporetic — and, systematically and historically speaking, Kantian — motivation, on the one hand, and a paradoxical Hegelian dialectical logic, on the other. In so doing, Adorno moves toward a figure of thought which seeks to respect the transcendence of the nonidentical at all costs while remaining shaped by the awareness that all thought and speech must necessarily betray what is other than itself. In other words: alterity can only be detected, indeed retraced, by allowing itself — halfway and necessarily unsuccessfully — to be usurped by its other, that is to say, by the mediation and discursiveness of language and thought, praxis and representation.

In his philosophical masterwork, *Negative Dialectics*, Adorno thus remains faithful to the program of his early inaugural address: he searches for the model of a nonaffirmative philosophy, which — following the collapse of the great philosophical systems and any claim to totality — strives to interpret the singular concreteness of the extreme experiences of horror [*das Grauen*] and of the good. Like skepticism, dismissed by Hegel as excessively abstract and presumably overcome by objective and speculative idealism, which had become questionable in Adorno's eyes, the conceptual, argumentative, and even speculative path of dialectics ought to remain negative, to the point of refusing to turn even this sustained negativity into a principle or thesis (as Schopenhauer and, ultimately, Horkheimer, like so many others, did).

Philosophy, Adorno claims, should investigate and present a "binding [or obligation, *Verbindlichkeit*] without system" (*ND* 29 / 39). At first sight his thinking seems to draw on the legacy of romanticism. The young Friedrich Schlegel, for example, notes in one of the aphorisms in *Athenäum-Fragmente* (*Athenaeum Fragments*), "It is equally deadly for the spirit to have a system and not to have one. It must therefore, perhaps, decide to combine both."[4] The challenge of Adorno's philosophy, however, is that, although it exhibits romantic traits, it undermines them at the same time; its mode of presentation thus seems shaped by "romanticism with the bad conscience of reflection."[5]

Whereas *Dialectic of Enlightenment* holds fast to the intention,[6] to the possibility, that its disparate philosophical fragments might pave the way—however obscurely—toward a positive concept of "enlightenment," *Negative Dialectics* sloughs off this classical-modern reminiscence of the unity of reason, pregnant with hope. Adorno does so without exchanging his critical sense of the ab-solute for a cheerful affirmation regarding the radical heterogeneity of the forms of thought, on the one hand, and those of action, on the other. This refusal distinguishes negative dialectics from less rigorous variants of postmodern thought and its intellectual precursors in the tradition of ancient and modern skepticism, nineteenth-century nihilism, and the Nietzschean attempts first to dramatize and then to overcome its impasse.

In his late work Adorno pushes underlying questions concerning the anthropological, philosophical-historical—in short, *ontological*—forms of the thinking of identity and totality to vertiginous heights. These questions are given focus by a logical, epistemological, and philosophical-linguistic critique of one-dimensional reason. This contraction and deepening of Adorno's perspective does not prevent the overall endeavor of his heuristic and rhetorical analyses or formulations from remaining radically *enlightened* [*aufklärerisch*]. Yet, apparently, under late-twentieth-century (post)modern conditions, in which Archimedean points to ground theoretical, moral, and aesthetic judgments seem to be lacking, one can prac-

---

4. Cited in Rüdiger Bubner, "Adornos Negative Dialektik," in von Friedeburg and Habermas, *Adorno-Konferenz 1983*, 35. Adorno's claim in *Minima Moralia* that art is now obliged "to introduce chaos into order" might also seem derived from romanticism. Novalis writes, for example, "Chaos must shine forth in every poem" (cited in Hugo, *The Structure of Modern Poetry: From the Mid-Nineteenth to the Mid-Twentieth Century*, 14 / 29).

5. Thomas Baumeister and Jens Kulenkampff, "Geschichtsphilosophie und philosophische Ästhetik," *Neue Hefte für Philosophie* 5 (1973): 102. For Adorno's critique of romanticism, see *DE* 33 / 59. In the intentional double meaning of this statement, Adorno is, once again, in unacknowledged proximity to Musil's novel *The Man without Qualities*. Musil summarizes the tragic paradox of modernity: "without spirit there can be no proper human life, yet with too much spirit, there also can be none. Our culture rests entirely on this conviction" (Musil, *Der Mann ohne Eigenschaften*, 1:521).

6. Or, more cautiously, formulations that can plausibly be attributed to Horkheimer appear to have this intent. See Habermas, afterword to Max Horkheimer and Theodor W. Adorno, *Dialektik der Aufklärung: Philosophische Fragmente* (Frankfurt a.M.: S. Fischer, 1986), 277–94.

tice critique only as a paradoxical — and, ultimately, aporetic — procedure or even spiritual exercise of sorts.[7]

True, knowledge and truth require rationality, conceptual mediation, and argumentation, but Adorno also suspects that there remains a contradiction between everything toward which thought is thus directed and the possibility of grasping this subject matter (*Objekt, Gegenstand, Sache*) in concepts. In his view the concept is an "organon of thinking, and yet the wall between thinking and the thought" (*ND* 15 / 27). Because singular objects must already be caught up in contradiction with the norm of *adaequatio,* it is difficult to see how that contradiction, that "index of the untruth of identity, the fact that the concept does not exhaust the thing conceived" (*ND* 5 / 17), might ever be overcome. Behind Adorno's intensification of the motif of contradiction lies, most likely, the assumption that every predication, every collection of judgments, and every chain of argumentation demands in advance the production of identity. Yet precisely this goal of thinking (i.e., identity) is in conflict with actual experience of the factual content that any determination within thought pretends — must pretend or, indeed, ought to pretend — to grasp.

From other angles, with different argumentation, it has been suggested that Adorno thereby assumes a scarcely tenable and, historically speaking, extreme nominalistic position, which can be justified only via an exaggerated, emphatic concept of the singular (*Besonderes, das Nicht-Identische*) or, conversely, with the aid of a one-dimensional stylization and, indeed, caricature of our conceptual and linguistic apparatus. No doubt, as one commentator notes, "the realm of substantive speech without contradiction is far greater than Adorno granted," and, perhaps, there is therefore "no need for dialectics to the extent that he assumed."[8] But, given that Adorno on occasion also rejects the thought of a *prima dialectica* and in other contexts sees in the model of language a privileged framework for the articulation of the experience and expression of otherness, one might argue that his conception of contradiction in speech is more nuanced than has often been claimed.

As we shall see, the systematic-philosophical Achilles' heel in Adorno's

7. This does not characterize the tradition of Critical Theory alone. According to Habermas, Karl Popper's critical rationalism is, ironically, also connected to Adorno's "negativism" in that both authors "reject transcendental and dialectical knowledge by paradoxically making use of it" (*Moral Consciousness and Communicative Action,* 15–16).

8. Schnädelbach, "Dialektik als Vernunftkritik," in von Friedeburg and Habermas, *Adorno-Konferenz 1983,* 88; and Schnädelbach, *Vernunft und Geschichte,* 201.

paradoxical and aporetic mode of proceeding is the secret power of his rhetorical style of writing, with its tendency toward exaggeration and excess. Although his critique of the thinking of identity seems unacceptable as a simple thesis, its actual articulation proves surprisingly productive. Precisely its character of exaggeration and excess should prevent us from too quickly viewing Adorno's philosophical-historical and logical dialectic in the ontological light that it criticizes. Thus, in typical fashion he writes: "Dialectical contradiction 'is' not simply; it means—it has as its subjective moment—that it cannot be talked out of this. In this meaning, this intention, dialectics aims at what is different" (*ND* 153 / 156, trans. modified). That means, however, that the *objective* contradiction between thinking and reality—quite controversial and questionable in the wake of Hegel's ontological dialectics and its Marxist heirs—the "inadequacy [*Inadäquanz*]" of thought to things, is grounded primarily in *subjective experience* (see *ND* 153, 204 / 156, 205–6). In other words: "Experience forbids the resolution in the unity of consciousness of whatever appears contradictory. For instance, a contradiction like the one between the definition which an individual knows as his own and his 'role,' the definition forced upon him by society when he would make his living—such a contradiction cannot be brought under any unity without manipulation, without the insertion of some wretched cover concepts that will make the crucial differences vanish" (*ND* 152 / 155).

Dialectics thus is not an ontological principle or a mere methodological procedure, a heuristic principle, a "point of view" (*ND* 5 / 17). It is, with allusion to Gadamer, less a doctrine of art (*Kunstlehre*) than a *passion* of sorts. It is not a "metaphysics running amuck" (*ND* 152 / 155), which imagines that it can overstep the resistance of concrete-material and intellectual reality. Instead, Adorno's emphasis on the motif of objective contradiction serves to limit the ontologization and naturalization of dialectics which constituted the most significant principle of construction in both Hegelian and Marxist philosophies of totality: "Once a vehicle of total identification, it [namely, dialectics] has become the organon of its impossibility" (*ND* 153 / 156).[9]

For Adorno, as for Gadamer, the truly dialectical method is "the doing

---

9. The contrast with Hegel could not be greater: "This *dialectical* movement, which consciousness practices on itself, both on its knowledge and on its contents, *insofar as new true content* emerges from it, is what can actually be called *experience*" (Hegel, *Phenomenology of Spirit*, 55 / 78, trans. modified).

[*das Tun*] of the thing itself."[10] Yet, notwithstanding the similarity to Gadamer's hermeneutics, Adorno's reticence about the "neo-Aristotelian" rehabilitation of the tradition of practical reason remains intact.[11] According to Adorno, the contradiction to be grasped remains first of all a "category of reflection [*Reflexionskategorie*]," brought into play for the purpose of critique. The term *dialectics* thus indicates a *modality of experience*. It means, furthermore, "the cogitative [*denkende*] confrontation of concept and thing" (*ND* 144 / 148). These two perspectives on dialectics, according to Adorno, ought to be inextricably joined in an *irreversible* and *infinite* movement.

From early on, dialectics was seen as bringing about something positive by negating the supposedly immediate. Already in Plato's dialogical dialectics and the art of speaking portrayed therein, the image of truth is elicited by unmasking false opinions.[12] With merely apparent consequence, as Adorno demonstrates, Hegel elevated this dialogical procedure into the ontological principle of how being itself appears in its historical movement and the progression of its objective forms. In the negation of its negations, something positive supposedly results, as if of itself in the fullness of its concretion — even, finally, the absolute, which is initially posited only abstractly. Adorno's proposal of a different, negative, or *open* form of dialectics frees the concept "from such affirmative traits" (*ND* xix / 9). The moment of truth in the traditional concept of dialectics lies only in its correspondence to the subjective experience of philosophical formation, culture, or *Bildung*. In Adorno's words: "If the knower knows precisely enough what an insight lacks or where it goes wrong, he will, by virtue of such definiteness, usually already have what he has missed." Adorno adds, however, a limitation — diametrically opposed to Hegelianism — according to which "this moment of definite negation on its part is subjective and must thus not be credited to objective logic, let alone to metaphysics." Such an insight *ex negativo* seems for Adorno capable only of being a placeholder for the idea of "emphatic [*emphatischer*] knowledge": it guarantees, as he paradoxically notes, the "possibility of metaphysics beyond Hegelianism" (*ND* 159n / 161n). One might suspect, however, that such an intellectual effort — which, on the one hand, would withdraw itself from

10. Gadamer, *Truth and Method*, 420–21 / 439.

11. See Herbert Schnädelbach, "Was ist Neoaristotelismus?" in *Moralität und Sittlichkeit: Das Problem Hegels und die Diskursethik*, ed. W. Kuhlmann (Frankfurt a.M.: Suhrkamp, 1986), 38–63.

12. See Gadamer, *Truth and Method*, 316–17 / 320–21 / 336, 440.

traditional and modern-subjective forms of knowledge and, on the other, would refuse the alternative of a mystical silence or a stark nihilism — will find it difficult to pave a sure path to knowledge.

Negative and Speculative Dialectics

Adorno's negative dialectics attempts, like the Hegelian dialectic and in opposition to Kant, to expand thinking beyond its formal domain while, with Kant and opposed to Hegel, insisting on "the highest critical moment, the critique of totality, of any ultimately [or conclusively, *abschlusshaft*] given infinity" (*Drei Stud* 323). The negative *and* speculative figure of thought which results from Adorno's reading of idealist, ontological, and logical dialectics cannot simply be understood as a reprise of former Left-Hegelian attacks on the system of absolute idealism. Upon closer examination, the obstinacy of negative dialectics as a figure of thought proves, instead, to be a kind of *critical hermeneutic,* or "deciphering of the phenomenon [*Dechiffrierung des Phänomens*]" (*MM* 69 / 77).

I will support this thesis via an interpretation of the moral-philosophical dimensions of negative dialectics. Precisely there, according to Adorno, one can show how philosophy is able "in the opposition between feeling [*Gefühl*] and understanding [*Verstand*] to seek their unification: that is to say, in morality" (*MM* 198 / 225). This theme will help to focus the metaphysics in Adorno's negative dialectics and to emphasize the way it confronts the particular nature of the aesthetic, contrary to many accepted interpretations of his work. As I tackle this problematic, it is useful to keep in mind what Benjamin once insightfully commented about Adorno's *Zur Metakritik der Erkenntnistheorie* (somewhat unfortunately translated under the title *Against Epistemology*): "one must cross the frozen waste of abstraction to arrive at concise, concrete philosophizing" (*ND* xix / 9).

Morality and Ethical Life:
Adorno's Ambivalence toward Hegel

According to Adorno, Hegel is correct to say "that morality is in no way capable of understanding itself by itself, that conscience does not guarantee correct action, and that the pure self-absorption of the self in what is to be done or not to be done gets entangled in nonsense [*Widersinn*] and vanity." Hegel would take an impulse of radical enlightenment a step farther not by opposing the good as an "abstract principle" and "a self-satisfying idea" to empirical life but, rather, by connecting the good through its own content to "the establishment of a correct whole [*eines richtigen Ganzen]"* (*Drei Stud* 291). In this judgment Adorno seems to subscribe to Hegel's critique of every "philosophy of ought," especially his critique of Kant's formal determination of the will in practical reason, of the dualism of pure duty and natural-sensuous reality, and of the absolute moral autonomy of the individual which occurs in the separation of morality and legality. True, Kant understands the law of the subject's particularity and subjective freedom, which entered the world with Christianity, and grasps it most deeply as "the turning and mid point between *antiquity* and *modernity*,"[13] but he immediately limits subjectivity to interiority. Kant, in Hegel's and Adorno's view, thus never overcomes the duality of interior and exterior reality. In agreement with Hegel, Adorno seems to hold that morality according to Kant lacks concrete implication and implementation: it remains mere obligation [*blosses Sollen*]. It is thus unclear how practical reason could come into existence or even touch upon the existent.

Likewise, in the section "Freedom" in *Negative Dialectics,* under the subtitle "On the Metacritique of Practical Reason," Adorno seemingly remains close to Hegel's critique of Kant. Thus, he speaks of the "absurdity" of a "monadological construction of morals" (*ND* 236 / 234). At first glance his own concept of morality seems opposed to Kant's, in whose conception, he writes, all "conceivable definitions of the moral aspect down to the most formal, the unity of self-consciousness *qua* reason, were squeezed out of that matter [*Materie*] with which moral philosophy did not want to dirty its hands" (*ND* 243 / 241). Whereas Kant upholds freedom via the pure law of reason, Adorno, in Hegelian fashion, notes, "Freedom would need something of what Kant calls the heteronomous." Significantly, he immediately adds, "There would be no more freedom without some element of chance, according to the criterion of pure reason, than there would be without rational judgment" (*ND* 237 / 236, trans. modified).

Indeed, according to Hegelian phenomenology, the subject initially forms the concepts of freedom and unfreedom in relation to what is exterior and opposed to oneself: "In ourselves, by introspection, we discover neither a positive freedom nor a positive unfreedom" (*ND* 223 / 222). In the impulse to betterment, in the transition from will to practice, "freedom extends to the realm of experience; this animates the concept of free-

13. Georg Wilhelm Friedrich Hegel, *Grundlinien der Philosophie des Rechts,* ed. J. von Hoffmeister (Hamburg: F. Meiner, 1955), 122.

dom as a state that would be blind nature no more than it would be oppressed nature. Its *phantasm* [*Phantasma*] — which reason will not allow
to be withered by any proof of causal interdependence — is that of reconciling nature and the mind." For Kantian reflection, which abstractly
conceives the will to betterment as pure practical reason, that necessarily
always remains only "otherness pure and simple [*ein schlechthin Anderes*]"
(*ND* 229 / 228, trans. modified; my emph.).

One might ask whether and how this "phantasm" could ever be incorporated into Adorno's negative dialectics, which consciously seeks to
free itself from the affirmation of the speculative, idealist synthesis of
Hegelian dialectics — notably, however, *without* "reducing any of its conceptual determinacy" (*ND* xix / 9, trans. modified) — and, hence, steers
clear of any involvement with phantasmatic *Schwärmerei*. If Adorno says
that the "*ephemeral traces* [*ephemeren Spuren*] of freedom which herald its
possibility to ephemeral life tend to grow more rare"; if, indeed, freedom
shrinks into a "borderline value [*Grenzwert*]" and is no longer anywhere
"positively given or ready at hand [*positiv vorhanden*]" (*ND* 274, 239 / 271,
238, my emph.), or is condensed "to pure negativity" (*MM* 38 / 41); if the
concept of a positive freedom has thus become an aporia (see *ND* 251 /
249), then an unsettling question becomes unavoidable: *does Adorno himself live up to the demand that moral philosophy avoid the empty and abstract
idea of a mere other without shoring itself up via affirmation?*

The modern bourgeois enlightenment diagnosed and criticized by
Adorno and Horkheimer in *Dialectic of Enlightenment* did not bring the
freedom and redemption it had promised but, rather, lapsed into the
opposite, a subjectification of reason molded by self-preservation and
the control of nature. This corresponds to the dualism of a merely internal
morality and an opposing external reality, which by its externality condemns every moral perspective to powerlessness, thereby leaving things
just as they are. Adorno sums up this nondialectical constellation of the
concepts of freedom, history, and morality: "Not the least of the reasons
why the idea of freedom lost its power over people is that from the outset it was conceived so abstractly and subjectively that the objective social
trends found it easy to bury. . . . Indifference to freedom, to the concept and
to the thing itself is caused by the integration of society, which happens to
the subjects *as if it were irresistible* [*als wäre sie unwiderstehlich*]" (*ND* 215–
16 / 215, my emph.). Hegel's significance lies, according to Adorno, in the
attempt to transcend the bourgeois separation of a moral sentiment that
pertains only to the subject from a social objectivity — and ethos — appar-

ently given as an insurmountable fact. Kant, he suggests, did not realize that freedom is "essentially historic" and not an "eternal idea" (*ND* 218 / 217). On the contrary: "Freedom is a moment, rather in a twofold sense: it is entwined [*verflochten*], not to be isolated; and for the time being it is never more than an instant [*Augenblick*] of spontaneity, a historical node [*Knotenpunkt*], the road to which is blocked under present conditions" (*ND* 219 / 218). That also means that the domain of objective spirit cannot be misconstrued as a simple progress in the consciousness of freedom (as Hegel mistakenly assumed).

In what follows I will seek to determine Adorno's position in the Hegelian debate about the relative weight of subjective morality and objective forms of ethical life (in Hegel's terminology: *Sittlichkeit*). The strongest motifs in Adorno's *negative-ethical* argument can be summarized as follows. Given that freedom can never entirely dispense, either externally or internally, with the controlling forces that make up society and the subject and is always already in part betrayed as soon as it "enters into history,"[14] it contains an ineradicable double meaning: as "the deputy [*Statthalter*] of better things," the practice and very concept of freedom "is always an accomplice of worse ones" (*ND* 297 / 292). That Adorno often seems to counter this ambivalence with a new — still utopian — understanding of freedom's possible unequivocal meaning and value in different contexts might appear to contradict this assessment. But only it, I will argue, can save Adorno's philosophies of history and morality from the untenable construction of a history of disaster [*Unheilsgeschichte*], on the one hand, and a complementary, this time messianistic, construction of history in terms of its discontinuity, on the other.

In the section on morality in *Dialectic of Enlightenment* Horkheimer and Adorno argue that the "dark [*dunklen*]" writers of the Enlightenment, the Marquis de Sade and Nietzsche, no longer pretended "that formalistic reason had a closer affinity to morality than to immorality" (*DE* 92 / 139). In that, they merely express an inner consequence that also applies to Kant's practical philosophy: "The work of the Marquis de Sade exhibits 'understanding without direction from another [*Verstand ohne Leitung eines anderen*]' — that is to say, the bourgeois subject freed from all tutelage" (*DE* 68 / 106). Because the reason of this modern subject unmasks

14. The formulation comes from a letter by Franz Rosenzweig, in which he claims, "Every act becomes sinful as soon as it enters into history" (cited in Stéphane Moshès, "Hegel beim Wort genommen: Geschichtskritik bei Franz Rosenzweig," in *Zeitgewinn: Messianisches Denken nach Franz Rosenzweig*, ed. G. Fuchs and H. H. Henrix [Frankfurt a.M.: J. Knecht, 1987], 67).

all substantive goals as being a restriction on its autonomy, in the end it comes to be the most extreme instance of a "purposiveness without purpose" (*DE* 69 / 108): in other words, "all affects are equally remote to it" (*DE* 70 / 108–9). In consequence, this modern stylization of the reasonable not only implicitly contains the inevitable and conclusive "destruction of romantic love" (*DE* 85 / 128) but also, when thought to its conclusion, implies the "impossibility of deriving from reason a fundamental argument against murder" (*DE* 93 / 140). Herein, among other things, lies its "indifference [*Indifferenz*]" (*ND* 237 / 236). It is no wonder that an "alliance of libertarian doctrine and repressive practice" appears so readily in history (*ND* 215 / 214). One can recognize in Sade and Nietzsche that in the process of the apparently unavoidable increasing formalization of subjectivized reason, only compassion is left to serve as a "naturalized mediation" between extremes (*DE* 79 / 121). This situation does not, however, lead the authors of *Dialectic of Enlightenment* to propose an ethics of compassion [*Mitleidsethik*], along the lines propounded by, say, Max Scheler. Measured against the idea of universal justice, compassion will always fall short (see *DE* 80–81 / 123).[15]

Adorno defends the legitimacy of a *dialectical* philosophy against these exponents of the failure of enlightenment in its illusory victory over mythology and its successful destruction of traditional religious-metaphysical worldviews.[16] Only the procedure of *reflecting upon reflection once again* seems capable of opposing every form of subjective or transcendental idealism, positivism, and fundamental ontology. Further, only the thought-figure of an "organized spirit of opposition [*Widerspruchsgeist*]" (*Drei Stud* 287), as Hegel once called it, is able "to think against itself without abandoning itself" (*ND* 141 / 144), for only with the aid of dialectics can it be shown that subject-centered opinion "posits as true what has never been entirely true" (*Drei Stud* 282).

Moreover, classical-modern *prima philosophia* is always already accompanied by dualism (*ND* 138 / 142; see also 202 / 202). By contrast, the "brilliance [*Glanz*]" (*ND* 384 / 377) of the German idealist philosophy of identity is to maintain the *thought of a possible reciprocal and nonallergic*

---

15. Here we recognize a distance from Schopenhauer, which extends into Adorno's late work and distinguishes him from Horkheimer, whose late work is molded around a resumption of Schopenhauer's pessimistic metaphysics, already a decisive strain in his early writings. Adorno's derogatory remark about Scheler in *Minima Moralia*—"Scheler: le boudoir dans la philosophie"—leaves nothing to be guessed about his opinion of this author.

16. On the critique of the concept of empirical experience, see *Drei Stud* 296–97, 299, 304.

relationship between subject and object. "If there were no *similarity* [*Ähn-liches*] between subject and object, both would stand, as positivism wishes, absolutely and irreconcilably in opposition; there would be, therefore, not only no truth, but no reason" (*Drei Stud* 285, my emph.). So long as the singular and the universal are simply *heterogeneous* or *radically* "diverge" (*AT* 42 / 69), there is scarcely any chance for freedom. The dialectical tra- dition is therefore ruled by an equally *consequent* and *futile* effort to over- come the insufficiency of the always concrete singular and individual (see *ND* 389–90 / 382).

Unlike the modern Cartesian ideal of knowledge, based upon clear and distinct ideas, dialectics would have us believe that the subject does not find itself opposed to a static, mathematically structured reality. Sub- jective idealism betrays a "reified [*dinghaftes*] consciousness" of the real, whereas the latter must be thought as "moved within itself" (*Drei Stud* 334). Hegel's concept of reason could thus be positively distinguished from Heidegger's concept of Being in that Hegel presents reality as "mediated in itself" (*Drei Stud* 282). Hegel "dismissed the equation of philosophical content, of truth, with the highest abstraction and posited truth precisely in that determination with which traditional metaphysics was too noble to dirty its hands. Not least in this intention, which holds primarily in the close connection of the levels of consciousness to social historical levels in the *Phenomenology of Spirit*, idealism transcends itself in Hegel" (*Drei Stud* 280; see 253, 255, and 281). This observation, however, ought not to obscure the fact that, according to Adorno, Hegelian mediation rests on the assumption of a "problematic totality" (*Drei Stud* 336). This means that, whereas Hegel emphasizes that totality, as a whole toward which one strives [*erstrebtes Ganzes*], can and should be realized, he claims, in oppo- sition to the romantic longing for harmony, this can come about only "through rupture, alienation, and reflection" (*Drei Stud* 253). The totality aimed at cannot, therefore, be situated outside its constitutive moments, even if Hegel may "subjectively" have harbored such illusions in his later work (*Drei Stud* 254; see 168).

Adorno's dialectical delimitation and transgression of limits probably offers the best argument for describing him as "Hegelian,"[17] since dia- lectics, as he himself says, is "the quintessence of Hegelian philosophy" (*Drei Stud* 258). One could even say that the "motif of contradiction,"

---

17. See Henning Ottmann, *Hegel im Spiegel der Interpretationen*, vol. 1 of *Individuum und Gemeinschaft bei Hegel* (Berlin: Walter de Gruyter, 1977), 121.

which Adorno's negative dialectics consistently maintains and extends, is the "entire principle" of Hegelian philosophy in general (*Drei Stud* 313). Until Adorno's break with Hegelian dialectics and the implications of his concept of a *negative* dialectics are sufficiently worked out, however, such suggestions are of little value. More precisely, a Hegelian interpretation of Adorno's work misconstrues the specific difference inherent in the gestures of his thought, one that, thought through to the end, betrays more Kantian than Hegelian characteristics.

We still need to understand why, according to Adorno, Hegel's objective idealism has actuality only "against an other, not in itself [*gegen ein Anderes, nicht an sich*]" (*Drei Stud* 302). Adorno once referred to Hegel's doctrine of absolute spirit as "a wholesome [*heilsames*] corrective" to the resignation of modern consciousness (*Drei Stud* 286) — no less and no more! To understand what it could mean for the claims of Hegelian thought to be both "accurate [*triftig*]" and "questionable [or worth questioning, *fragwürdig*]" (*Drei Stud* 311), we need to contrast negative and idealist dialectics more rigorously. Upon closer examination, it will become apparent that, finally, *the speculative and philosophical-historical moments of truth Adorno notes in Hegel's philosophy, on the one hand, and their emphatic untruth, on the other, do not balance out.*[18] Even a brief summary account of Adorno's paradoxical movement of thought supports this supposition: "It is a *reflection on the difference*, not its extirpation, that would help to reconcile the universal and the singular" (*ND* 347 / 341, trans. modified; my emph.). He continually emphasizes, in debate with Hegel, that "none of the reconcilements claimed by absolute idealism — and no other kind remained consistent — has stood up, whether in logic or in politics" (*ND* 7 / 19). But, then, what would dialectics look like if it aimed to put into words an experience of transcending the singular, *without*, however, rashly in advance identifying any one such singularity in particular? Conversely, what could negative dialectics, determinate negation, or even speculation promise to critical thought under the conditions of an unmasked subjective and objective idealism alike?

IN A RETURN TO THE tradition of Aristotelian practical philosophy, Hegel had attempted to dissolve the separation of morality and reality and to sublate it into the ethical life (*Sittlichkeit*) of social and political institu-

---

18. As, for example, Ottmann claims: "By equating identity and nonidentity, Adorno remains within the circle of Hegelian thought" (ibid., 119).

tions, that is, into "a sublime existence beyond subjective opinion and
desire [*Meinen und Belieben*],"[19] made concrete in the institutions of family, bourgeois society, and state. According to Hegel, this objective, ethical
being, this *whole*, is not alien to the subject but, rather, is *"evidence of spirit
. . . as of its own essence."*[20] Ethical life would be the unity of subjective
and objective good existing in and for itself: "Subjectivity, which constitutes the grounds for the existence of the concept of freedom and which
from the moral perspective is still different from its concept, is from the
perspective of ethical life its proper existence."[21] Adorno, however, objects
vehemently to this assertion: "The claim to force open the singular via the
whole becomes illegitimate, because any whole is not itself the true, as is
famously claimed in the *Phenomenology,* given that any affirmative and
self-aware reference to that whole, as if one might with certainty grasp it,
is *fictive*" (*Drei Stud* 324, my emph.). This brings out Adorno's deep ambivalence toward Hegel. It concerns more than the relationship between
morality and ethical life, given his paradoxical idea that to the philosophy
of morals "it is essential that the individual and society should be neither
reconciled nor divided by a simple difference [*einfache Differenz*]" (*ND*
282 / 278).

That Adorno both criticizes Hegel's concept of totality and uses it
negatively in the oft-cited phrase that the whole is the untrue has led to
the assumption that he is fundamentally a *negative Hegelian.*[22] Much in
his texts would seem to support this conclusion. Perhaps, however, his
use of concepts of totality could be interpreted in a different way, namely,
rhetorically (or, as we will show, as *a critical hermeneutics*). Perhaps his
philosophy might best be understood as the attempt to overcome subjectivist reason and its moral limitations or abstractions *without* taking refuge
in Hegel's objectivist philosophy of history, with its logic of the absolute.
This suspicion finds its source, above all, in Adorno's grappling with the
philosophy of morals, for "it was in the philosophy of law that Hegel, following *Phenomenology* and *Logic,* carried the cult of the world's course
to extremes" (*ND* 309 / 303). Adorno accepts the aspiration of Hegel's

19. Hegel, *Grundlinien der Philosophie des Rechts,* 142. See Joachim Ritter, "Moralität und
Sittlichkeit: Zu Hegels Auseinandersetzung mit der kantischen Ethik," *Metaphysik und Politik:
Studien zu Aristoteles und Hegel* (Frankfurt a.M.: Suhrkamp, 1977), 281–309.
20. Hegel, *Grundlinien der Philosophie des Rechts,* 143.
21. Ibid., 147.
22. See Schnädelbach, "Dialektik als Vernunftkritik," in von Friedeburg and Habermas,
Adorno-Konferenz 1983, 90; and Schnädelbach, *Vernunft und Geschichte,* 203.

"substantiation [*Verinhaltlichung*]" (*Drei Stud* 305) of thought to mediate between the poles of an empty formalism and an arbitrary worldview—or better, Hegel's reference to a third possibility beyond both of these alternatives—but he decisively refuses the construction of a philosophy of identity which would make the Hegelian interpretation of this substantiation possible. Ultimately, the reason for this distance from Hegel's ambition is a moral one, for, as Adorno notes: "The *smallest trace* [*kleinste Spur*] of senseless suffering in the empirical world belies all the identitarian philosophy that would talk us out of that suffering: 'As long as there exists a beggar, there is a myth'" (*ND* 203 / 203, trans. modified; my emph.).[23]

Adorno's negative dialectics, in its advocacy of the singular, might thus better be described as a vehemently philosophical-historical *and* speculative *anti-Hegelianism*, broadly comparable to the radicalness of Levinas's antihistoricism and antilogocentrism, though not completely to be identified with it. In what follows I will pursue these parallels.

Not only does Adorno's critique of Hegel proceed, "in opposition to Hegel's method and at the same time in consequence of his thinking about negativity" (*MM* 16 / 15, trans. modified), but in the end he also transgresses the bounds of immanent critique, which he otherwise claims to respect. Even Adorno remains faithful to the thought of an absolute, if not in a traditional—or objective-idealist, speculative—sense. Schweppenhäuser puts it concisely: "If speculative dialectics is the negation of the finite in the absolute, then negative dialectics wants to be the negation of the absolute for the sake of the finite and its rescue, while still keeping the absolute."[24] The question then becomes: whether and in what way does Adorno, in his critique of Hegel, slip back into a new, unmediated philosophy of the ought [*Sollensphilosophie*] which, whether he wants to or not, approaches the Kantian position he has criticized in Hegelian terms? Whether he wants to or not, because there seems to be a certain ambiguity in his position here. In fact, the repeatedly discussed problem of Adorno's paradoxes and aporias might very well result not from too much Hegel (as is often suggested) but from too little Hegel, at least if we subject the latter to a "*minimal* interpretation," that is, if we read his philosophy as nothing

---

23. The quotation comes from Benjamin, *Arcades Project*, 400 / 5.1:505.

24. Hermann Schweppenhäuser, "Spekulative und negative Dialektik," in *Aktualität und Folgen der Philosophie Hegels*, ed. Oskar Negt (Frankfurt a.M.: Suhrkamp, 1970), 93. See also Schweppenhäuser, "Negativität und Intransigenz: Wider eine Reidealisierung Adornos," in Koch, Kodalle, and Schweppenhäuser, *Negative Dialektik und die Idee der Versöhnung*, esp. 99–100.

other than relentless "research into mediation [*Vermittlungsforschung*],"[25] something Adorno would perhaps not entirely have contradicted.

A second and final reflection concerning my suspicion about Adorno's positioning vis-à-vis Hegel, seen from this modest — that is to say, minimal — hermeneutical view, supports these claims. Perhaps in this purported *weakness* of Adorno's negativism, that is, in his inability to mediate conceptually his concerns about morality and ethical life, lies, once again, a *secret success*. Yet this highly consequential claim becomes convincing only through a *lectio difficilior* of Adorno's texts and their critique or deconstruction of historical reason.

On the Critique of the Philosophical-Historical Primacy of the Universal in the Philosophies of Totality and Identity

In the *Three Studies on Hegel* and in the excursus on Hegel in *Negative Dialectics,* entitled "World Spirit and Natural History," Adorno argues that the moment of truth in Hegel's doctrine of objective spirit resides in its experiential content. Its value for knowledge consists in bringing to light the "preponderance of anything objective over the individuals, in their consciousness as well as in their coexistence" (*ND* 300 / 295), that is, in the "ultra-condensed web of a universally socialized society" (*ND* 267 / 264). In Hegel's words, the world spirit, as explicated in human consciousness, is the substance of the individual. For Adorno, by contrast, therein lies "the distorted sense" of the real power of the social universal (*ND* 304 / 299). Social reality is what might "essentially" be described as the "substance of the individual" (*MM* 17 / 16). This presupposition, based on Adorno's diagnosis of a modernity that reaches back into prehistory and implying an "isomorphy of social domination and domination by 'identifying' thought,"[26] is open to question. The abstract universal of the thinking of unity "since the Eleatics" (*ND* 314 / 309), that is to say, since Parmenides, according to Adorno, has an affinity with the coercive character of the objective's power to predetermine individual consciousness; this is "akin to the universality of thought, the spirit" (*ND* 316 / 310). What does one gain by using this Hegelian conceptuality — probably used here more provocatively and heuristically than as part of an ontological claim — for a

25. Marquard, "Hegel und das Sollen," *Schwierigkeiten mit der Geschichtsphilosophie,* 166 n. 60, 42.

26. Michael Theunissen, "Negativität bei Adorno," in von Friedeburg and Habermas, *Adorno-Konferenz 1983,* 42.

philosophical investigation that remains attuned to the givens and "truth moments" of history in the broadest sense of the term?

Adorno believes that in the "nondialectical constants" of a Hegelian philosophy of history (such as the world spirit, totality, universal history, progress, second nature, and natural history) one can read the degree to which history threatens to become fixed as an "immutable, *a bad infinity of guilt and atonement*" (*ND* 339 / 332, my emph.). Yet, within the reconstruction and decomposition of the history of Western culture, concepts of totality can, upon closer investigation, only *critically* have a potential for meaning. In those concepts it shimmers through that the seemingly isolated fate of individuals "reflects the whole" (*ND* 319 / 313). Conversely, however, the sign of their untruth is also written on their brows. It therefore can and should be shown that the unclouded mirror relationship of the universal and the singular is finally an illusion. In consequence the constructive use and apparent reversal of Hegelian concepts in Adorno resists every assumption of a social-historical totality in itself, whether positive or negative.

Insofar as Hegel's metaphysics reproduces in itself the principle of expansion of bourgeois society, it mirrors "how the world actually is" (*Drei Stud* 274). To this extent it is, in Adorno's eyes, *true to reality*. In Hegel's deification of history, however — that is to say, in his "theodicy of 'this world'" (*ND* 305 / 300)[27] — the suffering or the negative in history is both in advance and belatedly trivialized as well as idealistically anchored. Adorno notes that, although Hegel makes transparent the totality to which society apparently is united, he incorrectly describes it as reasonable and inevitable, as if it were a positive totality. In light of the disasters it causes, it is, in Adorno's words, rather "unreason: the totality of the negative" (*Drei Stud* 324), for "it is the negative objectivity that is a system, not the positive subject" (*ND* 20 / 31). The identity of reason and reality, subject and object, presupposed by Hegel's system is finally only "mere assertion" (*Drei Stud* 273; see 315–16). Even if the Hegelian concept of an "organic" system had positively distinguished itself from the deductive concept of system in positive science — because it attempts to think an "intertwining and integration of all its constitutive parts on the basis of a whole which already resides within each of them" — its *speculative* anticipation of reconciliation loses credibility for its lack of anticipation *in*

---

27. On the concept of modern theodicy, see Marquard, *Schwierigkeiten mit der Geschichtsphilosophie*, 52–65; and his *Abschied vom Prinzipiellen*, 38 ff., 72 ff.

reality. Reconciliation, according to Adorno, could never be accomplished as a "comprehensive system" (*Drei Stud* 273).[28]

Adorno believes that Hegel's metaphysics secularizes archaic, mythic, and divine omnipotence: "What the mythological name of fate used to stand for is no less mythical when it has been demythologized into a secular 'logic of things.' It is burned into the individual as the figure of his particularization. Objectively, this motivated Hegel's construction of the world spirit" (*ND* 319 / 313). No longer expressing a divine plan, Hegelianism presents only the inexorability of what exists. Hegel combines both these motifs in his statement that "world history presents nothing but the plan of Providence. God rules the world; the content of his rule, the execution of his plan, is world history; to comprehend this plan is the philosophy of history; and its premise is that the ideal is accomplished, that only that which corresponds to the idea has reality."[29] Our age seems to have "satanically proven" this philosophy of history (*Drei Stud* 273); it is "the horror that verifies Hegel and stands him on his head" (*ND* 320 / 314). By this Adorno means that the ontic and moral negativity of the historical dialectic cannot be newly interpreted as the movement of an absolute that is realizing itself positively but, instead, must be denounced as a teleology of absolute suffering. The Hegelian, idealistic construction of the world spirit can thus be unmasked as hypostasis and "mystification" (*ND* 304 / 299). Of course, the doctrine of objective spirit only makes explicit "what has always been teleologically inherent in the emphatic concept of society," but Hegel reinforces this irrefutable tendency "*as if it were ontological;* it thus reinforces antagonism and the foreseeable calamity" (*ND* 316–17 / 311, my emph.).

Thus, polemically, strategically, and rhetorically—given that every "drastic thesis" is false (*ND* 264 / 261)—Adorno can define the concept of the world spirit as the absolute opposite of justice and as "permanent catastrophe" (*ND* 320 / 314), thus inverting Hegel's notorious dictum into: "The whole is the false [*Das Ganze ist das Unwahre*]" (*MM* 50 / 55; *Drei*

---

28. Although the concept of system first finds favor in conjunction with the modern concept of natural science (see Georg Lukács, *Geschichte und Klassenbewußtsein: Studien zur marxistischen Dialektik* [Darmstadt: Luchterhand, 1968], 218 n. 52 / *History and Class Consciousness: Studies in Marxist Dialectics*, trans. Rodney Livingstone [Cambridge: MIT Press, 1972], 211 n. 11; Gadamer, *Truth and Method*, 515 n. 5 / 164 n. 2), Adorno speaks of its "primal history in the pre-spiritual." He has a suspicion that the idea of a system rationalizes "rage at the victim" (*ND* 22 / 33).

29. G. W. F. Hegel, *Die Vernunft in der Geschichte* (Hamburg: F. Meiner, 1955), 77; cited in *ND* 324 / 318.

Stud 324–25).[30] In a further external, transcendent, and *emphatic* sense, the social and historical connection is also mere semblance—not totality or identity but, rather, the singular. The whole cannot be equated any longer with the "pressing" and "struggling" of the ultimately divine absolute fabricated by Goethe and speculatively surmised by Hegel. Not its "play within itself" but, rather, its "opposite rendered unfamiliar by thought" is intended by this concept, which has been censured and, so to speak, turned inside out to become negative (P 149 / 624).

Adorno attempts to show how the universal undermines itself. Because it must have its "substance" in the life of singular moments, without them it would wither "to an abstract, separate and eradicable form." Thus, "total socialization" paradoxically creates its own tendency toward "disintegration"; it "objectively hatches its opposite, and there is no telling yet whether it will be a disaster or a liberation" (*ND* 346 / 340).

This insight results from a deconstruction, as it were, of the Hegelian concept of spirit. Adorno's reading of Hegel's doctrine of objective spirit as the paradigm for the connection between history and society, which finally returns to an understanding of labor, adapts in part Marx's *Ökonomisch-philosophische Manuskripte* (*Economic and Philosophic Manuscripts of 1844*)[31] and Lukács's epochal *Geschichte und Klassenbewußtsein* (*History and Class Consciousness*), although it goes beyond them both. Suffice it to say that the concept of labor, the thesis of reification, and the relation in practice between historical and dialectical materialism also can form no central part of ideology critique in Adorno's work. Neither physical nor intellectual production can be made absolute, as Marx realized, in accordance with a fictive "predominance of the productive principle" (*ND* 178 / 179). And only "a humanity free of work would be free of domination" (*Drei Stud* 272).

30. See also Theunissen, "Negativität bei Adorno," 49: "If the negative is the whole only by being dominant, then its universality does not mean that there is nothing positive. It means only that the negative *over-forms* everything else in the existing world. The negative can be recognized from within, since it conceals within itself the positive. . . . If one wishes to conceive a totality under negativity, then Adorno's philosophy is not such a conception." Theunissen also adds, "It is one thing simply to insist on a 'dislocated trace in the negative whole,' and another to secure it" (50). Were one to subtract from Adorno's concepts of totality the polemical point that constitutes their core, one would be justified in complaining that his mode of writing indulges in "anti-intellectualism" (see *Drei Stud* 302).

31. See Herbert Marcuse, "Neue Quellen zur Grundlegung des Historischen Materialismus," *Ideen zu einer kritischen Theorie der Gesellschaft* (Frankfurt a.M.: Suhrkamp, 1969), 7–54; Habermas, *Theorie und Praxis*, 387 ff.

The reference to Hegel's "metaphorics of labor [*Arbeitsmetaphorik*]"[32] makes possible an internal critique of idealism, following which the reduction of all beings to the concept of totality can *in principle* never succeed. As a first step, one might show that the "absoluteness of spirit cannot be immanently carried through by Hegel" (*Drei Stud* 266). In Hegel himself, as Adorno notes in the wake of Marx and Lukács, the breakthrough to materialism is already apparent, though he disguises it again. Especially in the *Phenomenology of Spirit,* Hegel recognizes the reference of spirit to work, the "archetype [*Urbild*]" of negation (*ND* 19 / 30): "The way of natural consciousness to the identity of absolute knowledge is itself work" (*Drei Stud* 268; see also 307–8). The concepts of self-consciousness and of spirit are finally derived from the individual subject's finite experience of itself. The "indissolubility" of the trace of empiricism secretly attached to Hegel's analysis can neither deny nor acknowledge his philosophy of identity, even following the "criterion of its own concept" (*Drei Stud* 264).

In the famous section "Lordship and Bondage" Hegel develops self-consciousness out of the relationship to work, the origin of the ego out of what is other than itself. When he thereafter makes spirit into the absolute subject, he betrays his own conception, Adorno feels: "At the time he wrote the *Phenomenology of Spirit,* Hegel would hardly have hesitated to designate the concept of spirit as mediated in itself, as both spirit and not spirit; he would not have followed up by casting off the chains of absolute identity." Thus, the absoluteness of spirit remains, again, "mere assertion": "To succeed somehow, he must blow it up into a whole," to which Adorno unambiguously adds, "A spirit that is to be a totality is nonsense" (*ND* 199 / 199, trans. modified). And again: "That identity exists no more than do freedom, individuality, and whatever Hegel identifies with the universal. The totality of the universal expresses its own failure. What tolerates nothing particular thus reveals itself as particularly dominant" (*ND* 317 / 311). Adorno can then maintain that, "notably by the Hegel of *Philosophy of History* and *Philosophy of Law,* the historical objectivity that happened to come about is exalted into transcendence" (*ND* 323 / 317).

Yet, where idealism reinforces spirit as a metaphysical principle, as in-itself, and "transfigures into eternity and law" (*Drei Stud* 269), the frailty

---

32. See Marquard, *Schwirigkeiten mit der Geschichtsphilosophie,* 161 n. 25. Adorno ignores the juridical metaphors stressed by Marquard. According to Adorno, the concept of universality in Hegel's philosophy is "the simultaneously precise and, for the sake of the general thesis of idealism, hidden expression of the social essence of work" (*Drei Stud* 265).

of human aspiration and suffering, the sympathy of *materialistically* inflected negative dialectics with nominalism begins.[33] This consonance is nuanced, of course, because "what nominalism clings to as its most assured possession is utopia" (*ND* 313 / 308). Philosophical interpretation finds itself exposed to the moment of universality at least "in the necessity of transition" (APh 129 / 338). For various reasons that moment can be dismissed neither as a "soap bubble" (*ND* 199 / 199) nor via a theory that would intervene and opt for the singular: "Such a treatment would let the theory grasp neither the universal's pernicious supremacy in the status quo nor the idea of conditions which in giving individuals their due would rid the universal of its wretched particularity" (*ND* 199 / 200).

The first motif in this quotation can be explained most simply through a closer explication of Adorno's philosophical procedure, which, as we have seen, attempts to construct "keys, before which reality springs open." According to Adorno, the keys selected by German idealism were so large that they "did not even come close to fitting the keyhole." By contrast, the nominalistic narrowing of "pure philosophical sociologism" made keys so small that they lack any heuristic strength: they fit the lock, but "the door doesn't open" (APh 129–30 / 340). As examples, Adorno offers the failure of a less than distinct concept of class, whose point of reference is replaced by independent social groups that are interchangeable with one another, and of the concept of ideology, whose relativistic and merely formal use in the sense of the "arrangement of contents of consciousness in regard to particular groups" has rendered obsolete the question of truth content (APh 131 / 341).

The second aspect of the earlier quote, which suggests that no idea of the true and the good can be grasped without a concept of the universal, is stylistically somewhat misleading. One might certainly ask whether such an idea of a correct condition, in Adorno, can still be conceived in a Hegelian fashion in the sense of a true universality or a reconciled totality.

---

33. One must stress here that the concept of materialism in Adorno in no way indicates a form of naturalism: "By no means will ideology always resemble the explicit idealistic philosophy. Ideology lies in the substraction of something primary, the content of which hardly matters; it lies in the implicit identity of concept and thing, an identity justified by the world even when a doctrine summarily teaches that consciousness depends on being" (*ND* 40 / 50). Furthermore: "If matter were total, undifferentiated, and flatly singular, there would be no dialectics in it" (*ND* 205 / 205). On the term's various layers of meaning, see A. Schmidt, "Begriff des Materialismus bei Adorno," in von Friedeburg and Habermas, *Adorno-Konferenz 1983*, 14–31.

Does Adorno's position here not also imply a difference in the *speculative* sense with respect to absolute idealism and the whole tradition of Western Marxism?

If this question is answered in the affirmative, Schnädelbach's objection to Adorno's negative dialectical philosophy of history can, in part, be refuted. In his view, in the materialist application of negative dialectics to an "ontology of the false condition" Adorno does not "problematize the totalizing anticipation of the whole" and thus remains Hegelian despite his critique of Hegel.[34] In his theory of universal social mediation Adorno, so to speak, refers to the position of a negatively applied holistic ontology, which is still formally consonant with Hegel and thus can neither speculatively nor empirically be established: "Whether the power of the absolute idea enters into everything ephemeral or the 'spell' [*Bann*], the 'context of delusion' [*Verblendungszusammenhang*], into 'exchange society' [*Tauschgesellschaft*] — in both models, the plausibility of positive or negative ontology depends upon a totalizing anticipation that Adorno, no more than Hegel, cannot attain in the execution of dialectics."[35]

Adorno would not entirely disagree with this criticism, because dialectics is ultimately "the self-consciousness of the objective context of delusion; it does not mean to have escaped from that context" (*ND* 406 / 398; see 159 / 160), so that "it too remains false according to identitarian

34. Schnädelbach, "Dialektik als Vernunftkritik," in von Friedeburg and Habermas, *Adorno-Konferenz 1983*, 89; and Schnädelbach, *Vernunft und Geschichte*, 202.

35. Schnädelbach, "Dialektik als Vernunftkritik," in von Friedeburg and Habermas, *Adorno-Konferenz 1983*, 87; and Schnädelbach, *Vernunft und Geschichte*, 200. By contrast, elsewhere Schnädelbach argues that Adorno — as opposed to Hegel, Lukács, and Sartre — makes no *constitutive* use of the perspective of totality but, instead, uses it *critically*. See Schnädelbach, "Sartre und die Frankfurter Schule," in *Sartre: Ein Kongreß*, ed. Traugott König (Reinbek bei Hamburg: Rowohlt, 1988), 13 ff. The accusation of a "totalizing view" can be found in Christel Beir, *Zum Verhältnis von Gesellschaftstheorie und Erkenntnistheorie: Untersuchungen zum Totalitätsbegriff in der kritischen Theorie Adornos* (Frankfurt a.M.: Suhrkamp, 1977); Honneth, *Kritik der Macht*, 49; Gernot Böhme and Hartmut Böhme, *Das Andere der Vernunft: Zur Entwicklung von Rationalitätsstrukturen am Beispiel Kants* (Frankfurt a.M.: Suhrkamp, 1983), 18; and Habermas, *Theory of Communicative Action*, 2:378 ff / 2:555 ff. The last of these voices the suspicion that there are totalizing traits in Adorno's reconstruction of exchange society. Jan Baars speaks of a "negative deification: a diabolization of history" in *De mythe van de totale beheersing: Adorno, Horkheimer en de dialectiek van de vooruitgang* (Amsterdam: SUA, 1987), 77, 96, 237 ff. According to Söllner, a motif of totality in Adorno's work would be "theoretically aporetic, since it resists empirical historical confirmation, and . . . fatal in practice" ("Angst und Politik," 343). Jay offers a more plausible, if less consequent, metaphorical or rhetorical interpretation of concepts of totality in Adorno's texts: "Like Foucault, Adorno uses 'totality' as an insult to designate the omnipresent domination of power structures that can only be challenged locally and particularly" ("Adorno in Amerika," 374).

logic" (*ND* 147 / 150). Yet numerous motifs in his work, upon closer examination, run counter to a holistic interpretation of his philosophy of history, as if it were a Hegelianism or "a Leibnizean monadology that is negatively determined."[36] One could, instead, agree with Schnädelbach that Adorno's *logical* dialectics, perhaps more than his more ontologically pointed dialectics, must be designated a dimension of his thought "that not only deserves, but is urgently in demand of further work."[37] The question still remains whether the various recalcitrant traits of his philosophical-historical observations can be reconstructed in such a way that they could result in a less aporetic or untenable image.

As already intimated, much in Adorno's use of concepts of totality (as well as his utopian counter-concepts) argues for seeking a *rhetorical* factor in his philosophy. The end of the introduction to the *Negative Dialectics* already suggests as much. Adorno's formulations possess a character of exaggeration, motivated by historical experience and occasioned by his rejection of every *prima philosophia*. As Adorno puts it, in typically lapidary fashion: "Total determinism is no less mythical than are the totalities of Hegel's logic. . . . The *totum* is the totem. Grayness could not fill us with despair if our minds did not harbor the concept of different colors, a scattered *trace* [*Spur*] of which is not absent from the negative whole" (*ND* 377–78 / 370, trans. modified; my emph.). Although one cannot deny that there are contexts in which Adorno's categories appear to betray their heuristic quality and wrap themselves in the aura of the remains of metaphysics, it is precisely there that they open themselves up to critique. One should therefore, *against Adorno,* remove their mythical shells and, *with Adorno,* bring them philosophically into balance. Only thus can his thinking be freed from being seen as the useless construction of a dramatized history of disaster, on the one hand, and, on the other, a messianic leap into an as yet unrevealed salvation whose prospect grows dimmer by the day. Only by extending Adorno's thought, both against and with him, can one account for one of the strongest motifs in *Negative Dialectics*. As if referring to a scarcely articulated philosophy of the trace of the other of reason, Adorno insists insightfully that the "world's course is not absolutely conclusive, nor is absolute despair; rather, despair is its conclusiveness. However frail every *trace* of the other [*Spuren des Anderen*] in it,

36. Schnädelbach, "Dialektik als Vernunftkritik," in von Friedeburg and Habermas, *Adorno-Konferenz 1983,* 87; and Schnädelbach, *Vernunft und Geschichte,* 200.

37. Schnädelbach, "Dialektik als Vernunftkritik," in von Friedeburg and Habermas, *Adorno-Konferenz 1983,* 86; and Schnädelbach, *Vernunft und Geschichte,* 199.

however much all happiness is displaced by its *revocability:* in the breaks
that belie identity, existence is still pervaded by the *ever-broken promises
of that other"* (*ND* 404 / 396, trans. modified; my emph.). The intention re-
sounding in this claim both testifies to a perspective different from that of
total negativism and opposes the no less fatal — and futile — heterological
affirmation of a pure, unmediated positivity.

This ambiguity is worth examining further, not least with the aid of
core elements in the philosophy of Levinas, as we will see. In doing so,
one would need to examine the contexts in which the articulation of the
negativity of history brings Adorno to the point of postulating an irrational catastrophe in human prehistory — that is, in which he prompts his
readers to see historical determination *as if* it were ultimately contingent
and metaphysically fortuitous: "Only if things might have gone differently; if the totality is recognized as a socially necessary semblance, as the
hypostasis of the universal pressed out of individual human beings; if its
claim to be absolute is broken — only then will a critical social consciousness retain its freedom to think that things might be different some day"
(*ND* 323 / 317).

Some scholars believe Adorno inherited this motif of irrational catastrophe from romanticism,[38] but a more appropriate reference might be to
the notion of the contraction of God stemming from the Jewish tradition
of the Kabbalah. This idea, as Habermas has shown, strongly influenced
the German idealist philosophy of history and the reactions it evoked,
from the late Schelling to the most important work of Franz Rosenzweig.[39]
It also left traces in the work of Benjamin, Bloch, and Adorno.

The idea of the beginning of a movement of God's retreat, which
is profanized in Adorno's melancholy glance at the critical postulate —
rather than the ontological or theological affirmation — of an originary
catastrophe, establishes a radical break with *every* philosophy of history
in the spirit of either Hegelianism or orthodox Marxism. "Not only Hegel,
but Marx and Engels — whose idealism was hardly anywhere as pro-

38. See Rohrmoser, *Das Elend der kritischen Theorie,* 43–44.
39. See Habermas, "Dialektischer Idealismus im Übergang zum Materialismus — Ge-
schichtsphilosophische Folgerungen aus Schellings Idee einer Contraction Gottes," *Theorie und
Praxis,* 172–227; Gershom Scholem, "Schöpfung aus Nichts und Selbstverschränkung Gottes,"
Über einige Grundbegriffe des Judentums (Frankfurt a.M.: Suhrkamp, 1970), 53–89; and Stéphane
Mosès, *Système et révélation: La Philosophie de Franz Rosenzweig* (Paris: Seuil, 1982) / Mosès,
System and Revelation: The Philosophy of Franz Rosenzweig, trans Catherine Tihanyi (Detroit:
Wayne State University Press, 1992).

nounced as in relation to totality—would have rejected all doubts of the inevitability of totality. No one who means to change the world can help feeling such doubts, but Marx and Engels would have warded them off like fatal attacks on their own system rather than upon the ruling system" (*ND* 321 / 315; see also 248 / 248).

On the one hand, Adorno does follow the classical Marxist schema of the diagnosis and sublation of the delusional "commodity character" of modern modes of thinking.[40] On the other, his distance from Marxist categories is unmistakable. In the critique of reification and alienation, in particular, a gulf opens between Adorno and orthodox Marxism in Lukács's sense.[41] This dual quality of Marxist conceptuality and structures of argumentation in Adorno's philosophy of history deserves a brief explanation.

Like the Marxists, Adorno holds that the basic mistake of classical-modern thinking concerning the philosophy of history lies in its conception of social reality as a "subject in general" or a "macroconsciousness."[42] The irrationality of the concept of world spirit, as well as its materialist inversion, was borrowed from that of the course of the world, yet the equation of a total subject, however constructed, with the substance of history in an emphatic sense remains untrue or "fetishistic." It can only be derived from the subjective form assumed by the world spirit in individual consciousness: "To that consciousness nothing more appears that would be outside; *in a certain sense* there actually is nothing outside any more, nothing *unaffected* by total mediation" (*ND* 357 / 351, trans. modified; my emph.). At first Adorno sweepingly designates this phenomenon as "spell," "ideology," "reification," and "alienation," as if it were equivalent to the fetishistic character of the commodity as deciphered by Marx and Lukács. In a second step, however, these common terms are put into question, despite the fact that they hold in common a certain experiential

40. Although early on Adorno was deeply influenced by Lukács's *Die Theorie des Romans: Ein geschichtsphilosophischer Versuch über die Formen der grossen Epik* (*The Theory of the Novel: A Historico-Philosophical Essay on the Forms of Great Epic Literature*), from the beginning his studies of Marxist dialectics are marked by certain reservations. He criticizes the solution to the problem of the thing-in-itself which Lukács presents in *History and Class Consciousness* (see APh 128 / 337).

41. See Lukács, "Was ist orthodoxer Marxismus?" in *Geschichte und Klassenbewußtsein*, 58–93 / "What Is Orthodox Marxism?" in *History and Class Consciousness*.

42. Habermas, "Moralität und Sittlichkeit: Treffen Hegels Einwände gegen Kant auch auf die Diskursethik zu?" in Kuhlmann, *Moralität und Sittlichkeit*, 29. For Habermas's critique of the Hegelian philosophy of consciousness, see *Philosophical Discourse of Modernity*; for the term *macroconsciousness*, with reference to Foucault, see ibid., 251 / 295.

content, in that they appear adequately to express the subjective corre-
late of the historical delusional context: "The self-made thing becomes a
thing-in-itself" (*ND* 436 / 339).

According to the theory of reification, to which Lukács devotes a famous chapter in his dialectical investigations in *History and Class Consciousness,* things in the world of commodities take on a phantasmagori-
cal form. Inversely, one might say that human interaction as well as the
dealings of every individual with himself underlie the world of things,
which has now become foreign, because, as Habermas explains, "social actions are no longer coordinated through values, norms or linguistic understanding, but through the medium of exchange value."[43] In this Habermas
suggests that Horkheimer and Adorno, in their conception of a critique of
instrumental reason, subject the concept of reification to a "double generalization."[44] Insofar as they trace the tendencies toward reification not
only in capitalism but in history in general—and not only in the functional connections between people but even in individual corporeality—
they advance Marx's and Lukács's perspective both with regard to *time*
and in *substance.*[45] At first glance the figure of argumentation appears the
same.

The "phenomenology of the anti-spirit" (*ND* 356 / 349), as Marx depicts it in the famous chapter on fetishism in *Das Kapital* (*Capital*)—
"truly a piece from the heritages of classic German philosophy" (*ND* 190 /
190)[46]—makes apparent, according to Adorno, that social totality can also
be revealed to be mere semblance. Here lies the *ambivalence*—read dialectic—of Marxist social philosophy:[47] it both ties the concrete subject to
the wheel of an unbroken systemic functionalism yet, conversely, sets up
the conditions of possibility for escape into freedom. Adorno recapitu-
lates this paradox, at which his own negative dialectics seems all too often
to be working away, and interprets it in an interesting rhetorical way: "It
is only in a *sardonic* sense that the natural growth of exchange society is
a law of nature" (*ND* 190 / 190, trans. modified; my emph.). Moreover:
"That the assumption of natural laws is not *to be taken à la lettre* . . . is con-

43. Habermas, *Theory of Communicative Action,* 1:379 / 1:508.

44. Ibid., 1:379–80 / 1:508.

45. "The meaningful times for whose return the early Lukács yearned were due as much
to reification, to inhuman institutions, as to the bourgeois age, to which he would later only
attribute it" (*ND* 191 / 192, trans. modified).

46. See also Löwith, *From Hegel to Nietzsche,* 129–35 / 168–75.

47. Sloterdijk, *Kritik der zynischen Vernunft,* 91.

firmed by the strongest motive behind all Marxist theory: that those laws can be abolished" (*ND* 355 / 348). Viewed thus, Marx was a social Darwinist only "*ironically*" (*ND* 356 / 349). "Diamat" (i.e., dialectical materialism) uncoupled the Marxist mode of discourse—which, finally, can be understood or applied only *polemically*—from its natural historical "construction" with critical intent, and wrongly converted it into a "scientific doctrine of invariants" (*ND* 355 / 348) or even a "confession of faith [*Glaubenkenntnis*]" (*Drei Stud* 314).

With this interpretation of Marx's polemically accentuated diagnoses of the times, as in his negative transcription of utopia, Adorno merely touches on what is at the heart of his own conception. He never completely shifts over from a deconstruction of the idealist or materialist-determinist worldview to a quasi-anarchistic "*retour à la nature*" (*ND* 147 / 150). Were this so, we could speak only of a destruction of tradition. Instead, Adorno presents a reading of classical-modern conceptuality in which familiar concepts gain in significance or betray their underlying meaning.

Thus, one should not imagine that insight into the possibility of a limitless "dissolution" of reification grants possession of the "philosophers' stone." Not only is reification, viewed in light of real suffering and the "possibility of total disaster," a kind of "epiphenomenon" (*ND* 190 / 191),[48] but the "*total* liquefaction of everything thinglike," the "wishful image of unbroken subjective immediacy" (*ND* 374 / 367, my emph.), can no longer be decisive for critique. To be sure, fetishism and "pure" immediacy are complementary, and both are untruth. According to Adorno, the "mature" Marx would therefore have avoided depicting freedom in terms of "original immediacy." He adds: "If a man looks upon thingness as a radical evil, if he would like to dynamize all entity into pure actuality, he tends to be hostile to the other, to the alien thing that has lent its name to alienation, and not in vain" (*ND* 191 / 192, trans. modified). Deviating from romantic *Weltschmerz*, Eichendorf's discussion of the "beautiful strangeness [*schöne Fremde*]" (*ND* 191 / 192, not included in the English trans.) uncovers according to Adorno, the perspective of an experience that can be designated *metaphysical*.[49] But how might such strangeness

48. Likewise, the concepts of infrastructure and superstructure seem almost "innocent" in an apparently completely socialized society because there all relationships are "inextricably interwoven" (*ND* 267 / 264) and "equidistant from the center" (268 / 265).

49. See Adorno's essay "In Memory of Eichendorf" ("Zum Gedächtnis Eichendorf"), *NL* 1:55–79 / 69–94.

be understood or expressed without being immediately posited as pure immediacy?

Adorno nevertheless attempts, as we have seen, to critique the modern philosophy of the subject without unreservedly concurring with objective idealism or orthodox Marxism. At the same time, he seeks to critique philosophical-historical objectivism without immediately—in a bad-utopian inversion—speaking of a shutdown of or indifference to the historical event. This impression of Adorno's pointed critique of every sort of philosophy of identity and totality, even where it assumes a negative form in nihilism in the vulgar sense, is decisive for my interpretation. It is strengthened if one takes his early texts as a kind of hermeneutical key. Both his inaugural lecture, "The Actuality of Philosophy," and his first conception of a thinking of the philosophy of history, which is centrally presented in "The Idea of Natural History" and will remain at issue up through his late work, offer rich material for this particular aspect of our investigation.

In "The Actuality of Philosophy," like Benjamin, he forbids the philosophical assumption "that the power of thought is sufficient to grasp the totality of the real" (APh 120 / 325). This limitation of the epistemological claims of idealism is crystallized, Adorno goes on to suggest, in the crisis of philosophical claims of totality which assume reality to be grounded in reason. Instead of this antiquated pretension, one should identify philosophy as the activity that "assumes always and forever that the law-giving of autonomous reason pierces through a being which is not adequate to it and cannot be laid out rationally as a totality" (APh 132 / 343). This does not yet speak emphatically of the irruption of sheer immediacy, but at least it opens an anti-Hegelian perspective that will become increasingly pronounced in Adorno's work.

The Benjaminian tenor of his presentation is unmistakable from the very beginning. It comes through unmistakably when Adorno describes his approach: "No justifying reason could rediscover itself in a reality whose order and form suppresses every claim to reason; *only polemically does reason present itself to the knower as total reality, while only in traces [Spuren] and ruins [Trümmern] is it prepared to hope that it will ever come across correct and just reality*" (APh 120 / 325, my emph.; see also 121, 132–33 / 326, 343–44; *ND* 136 / 140).

When such presentation is analyzed in terms of the philosophy of history, what results is an optic molded by the world of Benjamin's thought. The historical "images" that philosophy, in Adorno's view, must employ can no longer be regarded as "organic" entities laid out ready to hand in historical reality. History, according to Adorno, "would no more be the place from which ideas arise, stand out independently and disappear again. On the contrary, the historical images would at the same time be themselves ideas, the configuration of which constituted unintentional truth, rather than that truth appeared in history as intention" (APh 128–29 / 338). They are not granted in unmediated vision to the human spirit or intuitively grasped but, rather, "must be produced by human beings and are legitimated in the last analysis alone by the fact that reality crystallizes about them in striking conclusiveness." Therefore, Adorno can designate them *constellations* and *constructions,* the *instruments* and *models* with which thought can seek to unlock reality by testing and probing it. This, of course, goes against quasi-scientific lawfulness per se. Adorno also distinguishes such configurative images "from the archaic, the mythic archetypes which psychoanalysis lights upon, and which Klages hopes to preserve as categories of our knowledge" (APh 131 / 341). Because historical images are constructed and must also disappear, thanks to how they are fitted to the deciphering work of interpretation, they are fundamentally different from their antipodes or distortions in the "philosophies of life."

Although spirit can never encompass the totality of reality in a concept, to say nothing of creating it out of itself, it retains the possibility "to penetrate the detail [*im kleinsten*], to explode in miniature [*im kleinsten*] the mass of merely existing reality" (APh 133 / 344). Adorno does not fail to recognize that the denial of the postulate of a self-sufficient "totality of spirit" equals an inversion of what has always been called "philosophy." His conception not only relinquishes, in more than abstract terms, the claim to totality of a now obsolete absolute idealism but also eliminates all "ontological questions in the traditional sense," "invariant general concepts, also perhaps the concept of man" and "a self-contained history of spirit." Philosophy should concentrate only on "concrete inner-historical complexes" (APh 129 / 339, trans. modified).

We must now first show how closely this perspective is bound up with the quasi-messianic epistemology sketched by Benjamin. Only then will it be possible to embark on a *lectio difficilior* of Adorno's critique of history, in which the core elements of its figure of thought can also be contrasted to Benjamin's overall assumption of a possible radical discontinuity to be absolved from history as a whole.

Transience versus Historicity: The Idea of Natural History
as a Critical Hermeneutics of Historical Contingency

In the posthumously published lecture "The Idea of Natural History" Adorno develops dialectically a concept of nature and history that: (1) avoids an easy synthesis of the ideals of scientific and humanistic methods; (2) "has absolutely nothing to do" with the conventional use of the concept of nature in the modern, mathematical natural sciences (Idee 345); and (3) resists an interpretation of the historical as something ontological,[50] or, indeed, an anticipation of the unification of nature and history or their (transcendental) conditions of possibility (Idee 352–53). By contrast, Adorno is concerned with approaching conceptually the "*concrete* unity of nature and history" (Idee 354) — which, in the wake of subjective idealism, is thought purely antithetically — without, as in objective idealism, taking up a thesis out of the philosophy of identity. With that we arrive at the key concept, the "canon [*Kanon*]" (Idee 353), of Adorno's critique of history.

The concept of nature which Adorno seeks to resolve here and in *Negative Dialectics,* in conjunction with Benjamin, contrasts a mythically suspended, archaic reality. It takes aim at "what has always been there, what carries human history as fatefully constructed, predetermined being, in which what is substantial in it appears within it" (Idee 346). The historical and ontological way of seeing, Adorno suspects, cannot really rid itself of this concept. Thus, for example, Heidegger's fundamental ontology rejects concrete reality in that it prepares to master the unforeseeable of historical contingency with the "subjective" category of "historicity [*Geschichtlichkeit*]" (Idee 353, 350). It betrays a tendency toward tautology when it grants "ontological dignity" to those phenomena that cannot become transparent before the transcendental gaze and "come to a standstill in pure thereness [*Daheit*]" (Idee 351) — such as the diversity of the empirical and the

---

50. Adorno's lecture was presented at the invitation of the local circle of the Kantgesellschaft, presided over first by Cornelius then by Horkheimer until 1933 (see Dahms, *Positivismusstreit,* 64 n. 151). According to Mörchen (*Adorno und Heidegger,* 142; see also 13), Adorno's lecture was, among other things, an answer to Heidegger's "Philosophical Anthropology and the Metaphysics of Existence," which was also delivered in Frankfurt in 1929. The relationship to phenomenology and fundamental ontology in the first section of Adorno's text is reconstructed in Friedemann Grenz, "'Die Idee der Naturgeschichte': Zu einem frühen, unbekannten Text Adornos," in *Natur und Geschichte,* ed. Kurt Hübner and Albert Menne (Hamburg: Meiner, 1973), 344–50. Here I will limit myself to the portion of Adorno's Heidegger critique relevant for this investigation and will therefore focus on the second and third sections of his text.

irruption of death. Heidegger's general concepts of "facticity" and "being unto death" make this tendency as recognizable as does Dilthey's attempt to grasp the dimensions of meaning and the structural totality of an era in disparate "material reality" (Idee 361).

Such "Platonism" (see Idee 363), which Adorno scents not only in Hegel (see *ND* 328 ff., 351 / 322 ff., 357) but, above all, in Heidegger's existential thinking, finally champions little more than an ahistorical and painless concept of history (see *ND* 352 / 358). It expands "the claim of all *prima philosophia* to be a doctrine of invariants . . . to what is variable" and collapses into a justification for what exists (*ND* 129 / 133, trans. modified). Like Platonism, fundamental ontology is of the untenable opinion that "the imperishable must be the good — which is to say no more than that in permanent warfare the stronger is always right" (*ND* 131 / 135). In a different way from Plato, however, what is, according to Heidegger, given because of being is no longer measured in terms of the "*idea of justice*": "In the darkened sky of the existence doctrine, however, no *star* is shining any more" (*ND* 131 / 136, my emph.). Ontology and the "determination which no longer knows wherefore it is determined" which it decrees thus succumb to an "affirmation of what is anyway" and reveal themselves finally to be an "affirmation of power" (ibid.).[51] Therefore, not only is fundamental ontology morally suspect, but it is also in no position ever to gain sight of the *advent of the historically new*, which must mark an emphatic concept of history. These two perspectives are condensed in Adorno's construction of the idea of natural history.

For one thing, he seeks to achieve a concept of historicity in which discontinuity and the other, smuggled in dialectically, so to speak, are given primacy. Of course, history can only be thought and experienced as a movement "that does not take place in pure identity, the pure reproduction of what has always been there, but rather in which something new occurs and that gains its true character through what appears to it as new" (Idee 346). For another, Adorno seeks to clarify what it means that the "expression of what is historical about things . . . is nothing other than *past suffering*" (*MM* 61 / 55, my emph.). Both of these aspects indicate how it would be possible to eliminate the illusion of static history.

A better understanding of our historicity would have to begin with the alienating and shocking experience of a "dead world" (Idee 356). Ac-

---

51. See Karl Löwith, *Heidegger: Denker in dürftiger Zeit* (Frankfurt a.M.: S. Fischer, 1953), 49; cited in *ND* 130n. / 135–36n. See also his book *Mein Leben in Deutschland vor und nach 1933: Ein Bericht* (Stuttgart: J. B. Metzler, 1986), 29.

cording to Adorno, Lukács's *Theorie des Romans* (*Theory of the Novel*) and Benjamin's *Ursprung des deutschen Trauerspiels* (*Origin of the German Tragic Drama*) are exemplary discussions, in aesthetic and philosophical material, of this consciousness of a transience that can be recuperated only with difficulty or not at all. Thus, for example, Adorno adds the concept of "second nature," first taken up by Lukács after Hegel and Marx, to the list of polemical, diagnostic concepts, such as totality, world spirit, universal history, and so on. It indicates that in modernity the totality of human conventions takes on the character of a force of nature, "from whose omnipotence only the innermost part of the soul is withheld."[52] Second nature "is not silent, visible, or foreign to meaning, as the first is: it is an ossified complex of meaning that has become foreign and no longer awakens interiority."[53] According to Lukács, this transformation of historical vitality into dead nature, in a "Golgotha [*Schädelstätte*]" that fades away into ciphers,[54] can only be reversed in a mythical, eschatological "reanimation of the soul."[55] At this point Adorno brings in Benjamin's figure of thought, because Benjamin makes it possible to salvage the question of a possible awakening of second nature "from infinite distance into infinite proximity" and to make it into the object of philosophical interpretation (Idee 357).

According to the complementary perspective offered by Benjamin, nature, now understood as creation (Idee 358–59), bears within it the taint of the historical. Moreover, Benjamin's book on tragic drama makes it possible to grasp the question of the emphatic concept of nature and history more rigorously in words. In the allegories of the baroque poets he studies, nature "flows" before one's eyes as "eternal transience."[56] Furthermore, they interpret transient nature as "writing," a term that, as we have already seen, also found favor with Adorno: "On the face of nature, 'history' is written in the signs of transience."[57] What is, "in principle" (Idee 357),

52. Georg Lukács, *Die Theorie des Romans: Ein geschichtsphilosopher Versuch über die Formen der grossen Epik* (1920; rpt., Darmstadt: Luchterhand, 1971), 53 / *The Theory of the Novel: A Historico-Philosophical Essay on the Forms of Great Epic Literature*, trans. Anna Bostock (London: Merlin, 1971), 000; cited in Idee 356.

53. Lukács, *Theory of the Novel*, 50 / 55; cited in Idee 356-57. On the concept of second nature, see also Lukács, *History and Class Consciousness*, 167, 228, 239 / 174, 235, 246.

54. Ibid.; see also Idee 357.

55. Lukács, *History and Class Consciousness*, 167, 228, 239 / 174, 235, 246.

56. Benjamin, *Ursprung des deutschen Trauerspiels*, *Gesammelte Schriften* 1.1:355; cited in Idee 357; and *ND* 366 / 359.

57. Ibid., 1.1:353; also cited in Idee 357; and *ND* 366 / 359.

new about Benjamin's philosophy of history in comparison with Lukács must presumably be attributed to this double enhancement of the idea of natural history. Nature and history rest upon each other at their deepest point, in the element of transience. This convergence or commensurability is, however, not accessible to a general form of questioning (see Idee 358; *ND* 359 / 353). It *emerges,* according to Benjamin, only in the *allegorical* interpretation of concrete historical signs, which, like crystalline figures, converge in a *unique constellation* (see Idee 359). This development of intentionlessness can be further clarified via a famous quote from Benjamin, which opposes allegorical reading to the concept of the symbol:

> Whereas in the symbol, with the metamorphosis of decline, the transfigured face of nature reveals itself fleetingly in the light of redemption, in allegory the *facies hippocratica* of history lies before the observer's eye as an ossified primal landscape. History — everything in it that from the beginning was untimely, full of suffering, misdirected — manifests itself in a face: no, a death's head. And indeed all "symbolic" freedom of expression, all classical harmony of form, all that is human is lacking to such a one — it voices not the nature of human existence pure and simple, but rather the biographical historicity of the figure of an individual in his natural deterioration, meaningful as a riddle. That is the core of allegorical observation, of the baroque, mundane exposition of history as the history of suffering in the world; it is significant only in the stations of its fall. So much significance, so much ruination into death — because at its deepest death buries the jagged line of demarcation between *physis* and meaning.[58]

In the allegorical-melancholic view historical reality is transformed into "ruins," "fragments." For Benjamin this rehabilitation of allegory should signal at the same time a recovery of "origin" and "originary phenomena [*Urphänomene*]." Adorno would go still farther, claiming paradoxically: "Originary history is absolutely present as transience" (Idee 360). That means that natural disintegration would have to be rewritten as the "sign" of reality as it passes historically, precisely "in its most extreme historical determination, there where it is most historical" (Idee 354; *ND* 364 / 359), whereas, conversely, nature can be comprehended in its historical significance "where it apparently most deeply persists in itself" (Idee 355; *ND* 364 / 359). Thus, he claims: "All being, or at least all that has come into being, all past being is transformed into allegory, and thereby allegory

58. Ibid., 343; also cited in Idee 358–59.

ceases to be merely a category of art history" (Idee 360). The allegorical viewpoint makes it possible to present the world as lost and underscores this again in the awareness that only "subjective intentions" can be projected onto reality (Idee 364). Nevertheless, it does not reduce the character of second nature as appearance to "mere pictoriality" but, rather, perceives it as the "expression" of what "cannot be described independently of it" (Idee 385, 365).

Adorno, of course, does not have in mind an "enchantment" of the horizon of our historical experience. The startling and unsettling insight into the threatening natural character of history should not be convicted of being a "night of indifference" but, rather, should show whether and how into this night a dawn might shine (Idee 361).

The concept of natural history can, according to Adorno, only be deciphered through the detour of a "change in perspective" (Idee 356) or a "differential experience" (Idee 362), without postulating any unity in advance. The two dimensions are neither simply antithetical nor purely identical. That they mutually condition each other implies that neither of them can assume the role of an absolute principle (see *ND* 357–58 / 351–52).

If all this leads to more than just a clever word game, that is perhaps because in his presentation Adorno plays in a double way on a kind of *perspectivism for the sake of the absolute.* The reality of the archaic-mythical as well as of second nature is peculiar to a *transcending* motif that can be read in the "ambivalence" and "counter-sense" of the "originary words," or, like rescue while in gravest danger, results paradoxically in a dialectic of appearances. In tragic myth something redemptive always already shines through: "going beyond, in principle, the natural context" (Idee 363). The later, more daring interpretation of the *Odyssey* demonstrates how such an interlacing of stasis and dynamics might look. In this early lecture Adorno already raises the subtle double meaning of tradition to a quasi-apocalyptic conception, and at one point he claims that the aspect of reconciliation "is above all there where the world most presents itself as semblance; that is where the promise of reconciliation is most thoroughly given, where at the same time the world is most thickly walled off from all 'meaning'" (Idee 365).

One might, of course, ask how, on the one hand, the character of an "immanent interpretation" of various fundamental traits of historical materialism can be attributed to the interpretation of the idea of natural history, while, on the other hand, as Adorno suggests, that interpretation must set itself up as the "judicial instance of materialist dialectics" (Idee 365). To answer, one might examine the Benjaminian qualification of the concept of the historical, as opposed to Adorno's earlier (and also Benjamin's later) interpretation in terms of its *un-Marxist obstinacy*. This duality of a critical hermeneutics of historical contingency positioned both internally *and* externally can, of course, be traced in the tradition of Marxist thought, although this tradition never thinks it through to the end or realizes its aporetics.

On the Alternation of Historical Discontinuity and Continuity: The Question of Progress in Benjamin and Adorno

According to Adorno, Benjamin's "Über den Begriff der Geschichte" ("Theses on the Philosophy of History") constitutes a contribution of the utmost importance to a progressive critique of the familiar concept of progress (P 145 / 619). In that text's "epistemological considerations,"[59] which also appear in the *Arcades* project, both Adorno and Horkheimer see a similarity to their intentions at the time they wrote *Dialectic of Enlightenment*.[60] Benjamin traces the assumption of an inexorable and, in principle, boundless progress of humanity back to the untenable assumption that time is an empty and homogeneous space filled merely by a chain of occurrences. Benjamin counters this basically abstract conception of history with the concept of a concretely instantiated "*now* [*Jetztzeit*]," which, in the "signs" and "fragments" of a "messianic time," introduces a "cessation of happening."[61] He points toward an experience of the present which would fundamentally consist in a "standstill,"[62] rather than a "transition," in the temporal flow.[63]

59. Adorno, *Über Walter Benjamin*, 26.

60. See Adorno's letter to Horkheimer of 6 December 1941, cited in Wiggershaus, *Frankfurt School*, 311 / 348; and Susan Buck-Morss, *The Origin of Negative Dialectics: Th. W. Adorno, Walter Benjamin, and the Frankfurt Institute* (New York: Free Press, 1979), 60.

61. Walter Benjamin, "Über den Begriff der Geschichte," *Gesammelte Schriften*, 1.2:703–4 / "Theses on the Philosophy of History," in *Illuminations*, trans. Harry Zohn, ed. and intro. Hannah Arendt (New York: Schocken, 1969), 261–63.

62. Ibid., 262 / 1.2:702.

63. On the concept of time, see *ND* 331–32 / 325–27. Adorno valued Thomas Mann's *Magic Mountain* for analyzing the duality of the modern experience of time without resorting to simple antithesis. See *ND* 276–77 / 273–74. Benjamin was also impressed by what he recognized as the novel's "unmistakable familiarity"; see Benjamin, *Briefe*, ed. Gershom Scholem and Theodor W. Adorno (Frankfurt a.M.: Suhrkamp, 1978), 1:377–78.

Scholem senses in this the "secularization of a Jewish apocalypse."[64] According to Benjamin's quasi-mystical conception, history marches on in an infinite, linear progression only until, as he puts it, "the whole past is brought into the present in a historical apocatastasis."[65] Only in such an image, which always "*flits*" by, which flashes up quickly and irrevocably "as . . . at a moment of danger," is the past accessible to memory; that is, it is accessible only via constructing a view of history and never in a sympathetic, additive, or reconstructive procedure that could pursue the question of "the way it really was." "Every image of the past that is not recognized by the present as one of its own concerns," however, tends to slip away from this or any other present.[66]

Stéphane Mosès notes parallels with the equally "ahistorical"[67] path of redemption in Rosenzweig's *Star of Redemption*. For both authors the critique of empty, profane temporality is accompanied by the motif of a sudden leap into utopia. In their view every moment is either ripe for the entrance of eternity or houses a revolutionary chance.[68] In Benjamin's thinking of redemption, whose resemblance to the anarchist traits of Surrealism can scarcely be overlooked, the messianic state of exception takes on the character of an other of history.[69] This impression of a radical thinking of historical discontinuity becomes even stronger if one takes the short early text "Theologisch-politisches Fragment" ("Theological-Political Fragment"),[70] influenced by Bloch's *Geist der Utopie* (*Spirit of Utopia*), as a kind of hermeneutical key.

Benjamin connects his concept of the now to a metaphysical, *monadological* recognition of the historical, whose roots reach back into his

64. Gerschom Scholem, "Walter Benjamin," *Judaica 2* (Frankfurt a.M.: Suhrkamp, 1970), 223.

65. Benjamin, *Arcades Project*, 459 / *Gesammelte Schriften*, 5:573.

66. Benjamin, "Theses on the Philosophy of History," 255 / 1.2:695.

67. Stéphane Mosès, "Walter Benjamin und Franz Rosenzweig," *Deutsche Vierteljahrschrift für Literaturwissenschaft und Geistesgeschichte* 56, no. 4 (1982): 638–39. See also Ulrich Hortian, "Zeit und Geschichte bei Franz Rosenzweig und Walter Benjamin," in *Der Philosoph Franz Rosenzweig (1886–1929): Internationaler Kongreß — Kassel 1986*, ed. Wolfdietrich Schmied-Kowarzik (Freiburg: K. Alber, 1988), 2:815–27.

68. In his Kafka essay Benjamin says that, according to a great rabbi, the Messiah "does not want to change the world by force, but rather to set it straight by just a little" (*Gesammelte Schriften*, 2.2:432).

69. See R. Tiedemann, "Historischer Materialismus oder politischer Messianismus? Politische Gehalte der Geschichtsphilosophie Walter Benjamins," in *Materialien zu Benjamins Thesen "Über den Begriff der Geschichte,"* ed. Peter Bulthaup (Frankfurt a.M.: Suhrkamp, 1975), 108.

70. Benjamin, *Gesammelte Schriften*, 2.1:203–4.

Trauerspiel book. In the now, "which, as a model of messianic time, comprises the entire history of mankind in an enormous abridgment,"[71] an inversion of the speculative Hegelian philosophy of history comes to light, and totality then reflects itself or draws itself together in the interior of the constructed monad.[72] The constellation in which historical facts no longer enter as mere facts or moments into a linear series of cause and effect has the result that "the lifework is preserved in this work and at the same time sublated; in the lifework, the era; and in the era, the entire course of history."[73] This motif, which is also apparent in isolated formulations in Adorno (see *ND* 330 / 324), is, in both authors, difficult to reconcile with the ambivalent discussion of the disparate "fragments" of the messianic.

At any rate, as Habermas has shown, in Benjamin's late work the juxtaposition of the concepts of natural history and of an eternity guaranteed by the doctrine of Ideas, in which ephemeral phenomena are to be redeemed, gives way to a different constellation. In the theses on the philosophy of history the bursting apart of the historical continuum in the antithesis between *universal history* and the *now*[74] takes the place of the earlier origin or, rather, upsurging (*Ursprung*) of frail appearances in a chain of emergence and disappearance.[75]

Nevertheless, both interpretations share the allegorical and constructive mode of observing a historical world frozen in myth and an emphasis on the power of the remembrance (*Eingedenken*) of frail phenomena to bring deliverance as well as an anamnestic solidarity with everything violently sacrificed. Such recollection, as Habermas rightly points out, "is supposed not to foster a dissolution of the power of the past over the present, as it was from Hegel down to Freud, but to contribute to the dissolution of a guilt on the part of the present with respect to the past."[76] Thus, Benjamin returns to a famous motif of the mystical tradition, which describes the responsibility of the living generation for both future *and* past generations. In such remembrance resides the chance of restoring or liberating the integrity of creation in the wake of its abandonment to

71. Benjamin, "Theses on the Philosophy of History," 263 / 1.2:703.

72. See Günther Mensching, "Zeit und Fortschritt in den geschichtsphilosophischen Thesen Walter Benjamins," in Bulthaup, *Materialien zu Benjamins Thesen "Über den Begriff der Geschichte,"* 176.

73. Benjamin, "Theses on the Philosophy of History," 263 / 1.2:703, trans. modified.

74. Ibid., 261–62 / 1.2:701–2.

75. See Habermas, "Walter Benjamin: Bewußtmachende oder rettende Kritik," *Philosophisch-politische Profile,* 347–48.

76. Habermas, *Philosophical Discourse of Modernity,* 15 / 25.

human freedom via the contraction of God. In Habermas's account Benjamin transforms this thought into the "supremely profane insight that ethical universalism also has to take seriously the injustice that has already happened and that is seemingly irreversible."[77] This solidarity is possible only in *anamnesis*. Benjamin's consideration of historical discontinuity attests to an unprecedented correction of the "secret narcissism of effective-historical consciousness."[78] Not only is historical tradition never free from the scars of barbarism,[79] but the human past is accessible only from the standpoint of redemption. Nonetheless, it would be inexcusable to overlook the claims of tormented former generations. Thus, Benjamin claims: "The past carries with it a temporal index by which it is referred to redemption. Are we not touched at each breath by air that has passed through those of earlier times? Do not the voices to which we lend our ears carry an echo of ones now silenced? Do not the women whom we court have sisters who can no longer be known? There is a secret appointment between past generations and the present one. Our coming was expected on earth. Like every generation that preceded us, we have been endowed with a *weak* messianic power, a power to which the past has a claim."[80] This thought is associated, in Benjamin, with the almost pragmatic insight that the power necessary for resistance is "nourished by the image of enslaved ancestors rather than that of liberated grandchildren."[81]

I can now make clear in what sense Adorno's analysis both appropriates and modifies motifs from Benjamin's philosophy of history. The conception of a messianic time as a world of "general and integral actuality" hardly forms a leitmotif in his work.[82] But, if the negative power of both negative universality and historical determination are *metaphysically accidental,* the breaking open of prehistory would seem to be random, too. Must not freedom and redemption, for Adorno as well as for Benjamin, be localized in a radical discontinuity of historical occurrences? A truly advanced philosophy, Adorno concedes to Benjamin, would have to unmask the secret complicity of the postulate of universal history—"a concept whose validity inspired Hegelian philosophy in similar fashion as that of the mathematical natural sciences had inspired the Kantian one" (*ND*

77. Ibid., 14 / 25.
78. Ibid., 15 / 25.
79. See Benjamin, "Theses on the Philosophy of History," 255 / 1.2:696.
80. Ibid., 254 / 1.2:693–94, trans. modified.
81. Ibid., 260 / 1.2:700.
82. Benjamin, *Gesammelte Schriften,* 1.3:1285.

319 / 313) — with ideological thinking. Whereas Kant limited the category of necessity to nature, in Hegel every critique of it was "removed by leger-demain [*eskamotiert*]" (*ND* 327 / 321).[83] In answer to the cynical assumption — however carefully formulated — of a historical teleology corrected of all despairing fragmentation, a materialist dialectic must place "*the heaviest accent*" on an opposing perspective (*ND* 320 / 314, my emph.): dialectical knowledge must concentrate on what cannot be aligned with universal history, what is left "by the way-side." It must turn toward the "waste products and blind spots that have escaped the dialectical" (*MM* 151 / 170).[84] But this counterpoint, according to Adorno, should not obscure the fact that history can only be thought of as the "unity of continuity and discontinuity." The concept of universal history must be "*constructed and negated [leugnen]*" accordingly (*ND* 320 / 314, trans. modified; my emph.). In that shines through a more ambivalent relationship to the concept of history, whose alternative can no longer be a "leap in the open air of history [*Sprung unter dem freien Himmel der Geschichte*]."[85]

In a short text that, by his own admission, belongs to a preliminary stage in the thought complex of *Negative Dialectics*,[86] Adorno examines an analogous figure of thought in the notion of progress. Here, as in the idea of natural history, the "impossibility of the unambiguous" appears to be inherent in the thing itself (P 143 / 617). Adorno sketches the *in hoc tempore* irrevocably antinomian character of the idea of progress, which can and must simultaneously be combined, in a peculiar fashion, with the idea of redemption. Historical progress, like its counterpart, decay, cannot be "ontologized, unreflectedly ascribed to Being" (P 147 / 622). Historical negativity is not "a metaphysical substance" (P 154 / 630), and even being itself — to which one is tempted immediately to attribute decay in, as Adorno likes to say, a "falsely resurrected metaphysics" (*ND* 358 / 352) — is only a "cryptogram of myth" (P 153 / 629). Even social institutions and modes of production rigidified into second nature are not "being as such [*Sein schlechtin*]" but only "revocable" (P 156 / 632). Progress, however, cannot be equated with redemption as "transcendental intervention

83. See *ND* 345n / 338–39n; and Dieter Henrich, "Hegels Theorie über den Zufall," *Hegel im Kontext* (Frankfurt a.M.: Suhrkamp, 1981), 157–86.

84. "It is in the nature of the defeated to appear, in their impotence, irrelevant, eccentric, derisory. What transcends the ruling society is not only the potentiality it develops but also all that which did not fit properly into the laws of historical movement. Theory must needs deal with cross-grained, opaque, unassimilated material" (*MM* 151 / 170).

85. Benjamin, "Theses on the Philosophy of History," 261 / 1.2:701.

86. See *GS* 10.2:597.

per se," nor does it possess the character of an immanent teleology. Otherwise, in the first instance, devoid of any temporality and attachment to the
empirical, progress forfeits "its intelligible meaning and evaporates into
ahistorical theology" (P 147 / 621), and, in the second instance, it threatens
to degenerate into ideology, together with its mediatization in historical
reality. Adorno interprets this aporetic relationship as follows: progress
can be posited neither simply as something factual nor as a mere idea;
therefore, it cannot be thought as an abstract negation, as "merely the
other [*einfach bloss das Andere*]" (P 152 / 627). Its contradictory essence is
evident in that the conditions of possibility for reconciliation with nature
and for freedom are in each case codetermined by their opposites. In the
concept of reason, which enlightenment must employ, though in a gesture
of self-limitation, the potential for the control of nature and for reconciliation seem inextricably intertwined: "Not only does the whole demand its
own modification in order not to perish, but by virtue of its antagonistic essence it is also impossible for it to extort that complete identity with
human beings that is relished in negative utopias. For this reason innerworldly progress, adversary of the other progress, at the same time remains open to the possibility of this other, no matter how little it is able to
incorporate this possibility within its own law" (P 156 / 632). Nonetheless,
Adorno lets himself be led astray by *quasi-eschatological* formulations, so
to speak, which betray the need for a sublation of that awkward ambivalence: "redemption and history can exist neither without each other nor
within each other but only in tension, the accumulated energy of which
finally desires nothing less than the sublation of the historical world itself"
(P 147 / 622). If this is so, one would almost have to say that "progress
occurs only where it ends" (P 150 / 625). Or it means that totality without a unity imposed upon it is only thinkable in the sense of an emphatic
concept of a "humanity" that is no longer limited by itself (P 145 / 619). In
other words, it would become "totality," and then there would no longer
be any totality.

    At other moments Adorno respects the duality and Janus face of the
motif of progress. Moreover, he touches briefly on the possibility of a third
way of thought and experience, which would pass between the extremes
of affirmative and negative stylizations of historical reality. From this perspective the world cannot be entirely denied some reason and some good,
but these have become homeless, utopian in the literal sense of the word,
insofar as no presence to which they can undeniably and unambiguously
attach themselves is granted any longer. Conversely, it would be a false

alternative to appeal to the other as to something fully absent. Precisely this ambivalence the concept of the trace brings to expression:

> Too little of what is good has power in the world for progress to be expressed in a predicative judgment about the world, but there can be no good, not a trace of it, without progress. If, according to a mystical doctrine, all inner-worldly events down to the most insignificant happenstance are of momentous consequence for the life of the absolute itself, then certainly something similar is true for progress. Every individual trait in the nexus of deception is nonetheless relevant to its possible end. Good is what wrenches itself free, finds a language, opens its eyes. In its condition of wrestling free, it is interwoven in history that, without being organized unequivocally toward reconciliation, in the course of its movement allows the possibility of redemption to flash up. (P 147–48 / 622)

Seen thus, Adorno's position between the Marxist evolutionist faith in progress and that of the Social Democratic Second International, on the one hand, and the quasi-eschatological messianism of Benjamin, Rosenzweig, and Bloch, on the other, is not so far removed from the position Habermas takes with respect to the question concerning the relationship between historical continuity and discontinuity. Even in Adorno, all this revolves primarily around the *empirical* question—one that appeals to *judgment*—of how to distinguish historical contexts in which we can safely allow ourselves to blend into given traditions and institutions, from moments in which "almost everything must be negated in order to take the smallest step toward emancipation."[87] Yet Adorno holds out no illusion: this question is *undecidable* within any universal theoretical frame, that is to say, a priori, in advance, or even a posteriori, in retrospect.

To summarize our lines of argumentation and delimit them from other, overly harmonizing, optimistic, or negativistic interpretations, Adorno's early work and his later conception of negative dialectics seem also to stand apart from the Hegelian philosophical-historical and speculative telos. "The matters of true philosophical interest at this point in history are those in which Hegel, agreeing with tradition, expressed his disinterest. They are nonconceptuality, individuality, and particularity— things which ever since Plato used to be dismissed as transitory and insignificant, and which Hegel labeled 'lazy existence.' Philosophy's theme

---

87. Habermas, *Die Neue Unübersichtlichkeit*, 178.

would consist of the qualities it downgrades as contingent, as a *quantité négligeable*" (*ND* 8 / 19–20). This change in perspective concerns not just the material aspects of Hegel's system but his method and ultimate aim as well. The critique is articulated with greatest consequence in *Negative Dialectics*, in which Adorno says, for example, "Since the basic character of *every* general concept dissolves in the face of distinct entity, a total philosophy is no longer to be hoped for" (*ND* 136 / 140, my emph.).

Hegel's "logical rigor [*Stringenz*]" is thus finally untruth (*Drei Stud* 323), as compared with and opposed to the no less problematic breaks and aporias in Kantian philosophy. Kant's "incomparable greatness" was to postulate the unification of a theoretical reason that controls nature and a "judgment snuggling up to nature in reconciliation" while making their difference dependent upon a "self-limitation" of one in opposition to the other. In this sense Kantian philosophy might better serve as evidence for a dialectic of enlightenment than does the work of the "dialectician par excellence," Hegel (P 152 / 628). In Hegel the limit of the faculty of reason is effaced in the false light of an imagined reconciliation. Even where experience speaks through him, Adorno says summarily, Hegel betrays in advance the utopia of the singular and unsublatable "difference between the conditioned and the absolute" (*Drei Stud* 324), precisely what Adorno's thought would, in a circular movement, pretend to respect.

The Hegelian conception can only be reconciled with empirical contradictions in the real world, since, as Löwith lucidly observes, "as the last Christian philosopher, he was in the world as though he were not of it."[88] For Adorno, and not just for him, such a mode of existence has become unthinkable and unlivable. For him the idea of the reasonableness of reality in philosophical-historical thinking is only "one of Hegel's most questionable theses" (*Drei Stud* 320), and the speculative figure of thought which makes this assumption possible is fundamentally misguided.

Toward a Critique of the Speculative Primacy of Universality and a New Form of the Unhappy Consciousness

Despite his critique of Hegel, Adorno seems to consider historical universality and objectivity to be constitutive for freedom, happiness, morality, and ethical forms of life: "A true preponderance of the singular would not be attainable except by changing the universal. Installing

---

88. Löwith, *From Hegel to Nietzsche*, 97 / 111.

the singular as purely and simply extant would be a complementary ideology" (*ND* 313 / 307, trans. modified; see 134, 153, 261, 354 / 140, 156, 261, 346). If the subject is itself mediated via objectivity, then moral subjectivity cannot always experience this objectivity as hostile. Adorno writes: "the constellation changes in the dynamics of history," and "however frail, the reconcilement with objectivity transcends the invariable" (*ND* 306 / 300). At first glance Adorno's distance from Hegel thus concerns only his "eschatological design [*endgeschichtliche Konstruktion*]" of reality.[89] In a superficial reading it might appear to resume the Left-Hegelian attack on Hegel. Central to such a position would be the accusation that Hegel postulates his reconciliations prematurely, whereas they have yet to be realized.[90] Such interpretations, as we have seen, are in the end not convincing, even though in all too many of Adorno's formulations they are ready to hand. Thus, for example, when he claims that "because of its immanently critical and theoretical character, the turn to nonidentity is an irrevocable [*unerhebliche*] nuance of New-Hegelianism or of the historically obsolete Hegelian Left" (*ND* 143 / 146, trans. modified), he thereby suggests that, given that this position had scarcely been taken seriously (see *ND* 144 / 147), only now can it offer up its truth, which had been too hastily dismissed. In other words, its insight is that Hegelian theory "must renounce itself in order to remain philosophy" (*Drei Stud* 308).

This should not, of course, blind us to the fact that the point of Adorno's thinking lies elsewhere. Although much in his work would support the conclusion that he remained more faithful to the intention of Hegelian philosophy than Hegel himself,[91] its conception is not without gaps and breaks here. Adorno holds *the Hegelian system to be untrue in an emphatic sense, not only in terms of the philosophy of history but also speculatively, as an idea yet to be realized and as an aspiration toward the true, the good, and the beautiful.* His critique of Hegel therefore goes farther than that of the old Left-Hegelians because for him not only the reasonableness of the real but even the reasonableness of thinking itself has become problematic.

As Löwith demonstrates, the "middle [*Mitte*]" in Goethe's conception of nature and the "mediation" of Hegelian spirit, which guaranteed the

89. The term is taken from Löwith, *From Hegel to Nietzsche*, 31, 36, 52, 125–26, 130–31 / 44, 49, 64, 142, 147.

90. See Ute Guzzoni, "Hegels 'Unwahrheit': Zu Adornos Hegelkritik," *Hegel-Jahrbuch 1975* (Cologne, 1976), 242–46.

91. Schmidt, "Hegel und die Frankfurter Schule," in Negt, *Aktualität und Folgen der Philosophie Hegels,* 31–32.

unity of interiority and exteriority, essence and existence, temporality and eternity, modernity and antiquity around "1800," were rejected in 1840s thought, which is marked by a vehement falling out with what exists. In the postidealist world one pressed for decision without disputing the principle and the goal of mediations.[92] The inaccessibility of these earlier neo-Hegelian fundamental philosophical assumptions and their overall ideal and idealizations make up both the subject matter and the express motivation of *Negative Dialectics:* "Having broken its pledge to be at one with reality *or at the point of realization,* philosophy is obliged ruthlessly to criticize itself" (*ND* 3 / 15, my emph.). We can surmise, therefore, that Adorno's thinking, in the philosophy of history no less than in moral philosophy, can scarcely be aligned with Left or Young Hegelian philosophical activism, which Moses Hess describes as the "party of movement."[93] This suspicion emerges in various leitmotifs in his texts.

Thus, for example, Adorno draws on the ban on graven images to deal with what could be other, writing, "Irreconcilably, the idea of reconcilement bars its affirmation in a concept" (*ND* 160 / 163). Where he cannot avoid alluding to reconciliation, he expresses it only negatively: it "would release the nonidentical, would rid it of coercion, including spiritualized coercion; it would open the road to the multiplicity of different things and strip dialectics of its power over them. Reconcilement would be the *thought [Eingedenken] of the many as no longer inimical,* a thought that is anathema to subjective reason" (*ND* 6 / 18, my emph.). The goal of dialectical thinking, if there is one, according to Adorno and in contrast to the tradition, thus becomes *qualitatively changed reconciliation,* which can no longer be established in an idealistic or materialistically determined yet fundamentally affirmative way. Such reconciliation would respect the singular, the nonidentical, the different, the heterogeneous, the individual as the irretrievable and irrevocable other. Schnädelbach is right, therefore, to describe Adorno as "Platonic" or even as a "theoretician of evidence [*Evidenztheoretiker*]" of the nonidentical, although in the same context he perhaps incorrectly paraphrases the qualitatively changed reconciliation of Adorno's utopia as "an imageless image of the no longer untrue whole [*ein bilderloses Bild des nicht mehr unwahren Ganzen*]."[94] Nor is he right in assuming that the "ambivalence of the concept of totality" in

92. Löwith, *From Hegel to Nietzsche,* 30, 44, 95, 162, 154–55 / 43, 58, 109, 179, 181.
93. This suggestion is taken from Habermas, *Philosophical Discourse of Modernity,* 58 / 73.
94. Schnädelbach, "Dialektik als Vernunftkritik," in von Friedeburg and Habermas, *Adorno-Konferenz 1983,* 73, 91.

Adorno resides in the paradoxical circumstance, indeed, the aporia, that it is "the description of a real but false totality, on the one hand, and, on the other, of the idea of the correct totality."[95] The reasons why this cannot be the case are simple: Adorno no longer thinks of reconciliation as the unity of identity and nonidentity. In his sense utopia "would be *above identity and above contradiction; it would be a togetherness of diversity*" (*ND* 150 / 153, my emph.). Habermas has correctly pointed out that Adorno does not delineate reconciliation conceptually in the Hegelian sense. It remains, he says, "as a cipher, nearly in the manner of the philosophy of life."[96] One might best approach it through various images derived from the heterodox tradition of mysticism, for example, through the metaphor of a circling movement around an "empty" core, or simply ask, with Alfred Schmidt, whether there is not "a Goethean amalgamation of self and things here, an erotic, so to speak, snuggling up to them, a fervent partnership in the romantic sense or that of the philosophy of life," and thereby conclude that, "in any event, Adorno's tentative concepts are closer to such a metaphysics than to a theory of knowledge."[97]

Yet, were one to take the abstract-utopian idea of an "equation of all who have a human shape" as the point of departure for political thought and action (*MM* 102 / 113), one would work against the "realization of universality in the reconciliation of differences." A better world could then be thinkable, formally and negatively, only insofar as one "could be different without fear" (*MM* 103 / 114). Put otherwise and more pointedly: "The reconciled condition would not be the philosophical imperialism of annexing the alien. Instead, its happiness would lie in the fact that the alien, in the proximity it is granted, remains what is distant and different, *beyond the heterogeneous and beyond that which is one's own*" (*ND* 191 / 192, my emph.). Of reconciliation, the just condition, one can speak *philosophically*, therefore, only in the *mode of absence*. The true is "what does not fit into this world" (*AT* 59 / 93), because what would really be different from what exists would have to refuse "a language that bears the stigmata of existence" (*ND* 297 / 293). That, however, pushes the good and the just into the dimension of metaphysical transcendence, that is, more and more into what is *hidden*, "as though concentrating *in an outermost point above*

95. Schnädelbach, *Vernunft und Geschichte*, 186, 204. See also Grenz, *Adornos Philosophie in Grundbegriffen*, 158.

96. Habermas, *Theory of Communicative Action*, 1:382 / 1:512.

97. See also on this complex of ideas the comments of Schmidt, "Begriff des Materialismus bei Adorno," in von Friedeburg and Habermas, *Adorno-Konferenz 1983*, 25–26.

all mediations" (*ND* 402 / 394, my emph.). The question of how such a retreat of meaning could be thought, how it might be brought into language
in whatever fragmented or, rather, minimal way (whether metaphysically,
theologically, ethically, or aesthetically) remains open. But the difference
between these central motifs in Adorno and speculative idealism should
be sufficiently clear by now. If one sets up "minimal interpretation" as a
foil to the Hegelian system, that is, reads it as "research into mediation,"
one can scarcely avoid describing Adorno's figure of thought as a kind of
anti-Hegelianism, even, from a certain perspective, as an "anti-dialectics."

According to Hegel, the process of the spirit is "a self-enfolding circle
that presupposes its beginning and reaches it only in the end,"[98] because
the result of dialectical movement displays only what, in Adorno's words,
in its origin is "a thought already" (*ND* 27 / 38). The foundation and completion of this gesture of thought, as Adorno testifies untiringly, is the
primacy of the subject and of an abstract universal, "the identity of identity and nonidentity" (*ND* 7 / 19). Only these presuppositions allow Hegel
to establish the mediations and reconciliations that singular, emphatic,
subjective experience condemns as lies, because "the *slightest remnant* of
nonidentity sufficed to deny an identity conceived as total" (*ND* 22 / 33,
my emph.). Only because the unity of increasingly isolated moments "is
already thought in advance [*vorgedacht*]" is it possible for Hegel to postulate what pure observation — "the abandonment purely to the thing and
its moments" as promised by his dialectical method, for example, in the
introduction to the *Phenomenology of Spirit* — can of itself never suggest
(*Drei Stud* 329). The demand for an "immersion in detail" is certainly
one side of Hegel (*ND* 303 / 298), although in idealism it finally seems
thinkable as a tautological implementation, that is, in a spirit that has
been misunderstood from the very beginning as being total and absolute.
Against such a *Platonism of the universal* — which renews the contradiction
or Kantian *chorismos* between idea and reality, even if unintentionally (see
ND 334 / 329) — Adorno stresses "that, from the viewpoint of logic as well
as of the philosophy of history, the universal contracts into the singular"
(*ND* 330 / 324). One can thus show that Adorno's emphasis on the primacy of the singular must be seen as more than a redemption of Hegelian
intentions or a quasi-Hegelian and, as it were, postidealist dialectic. As
in the passage cited earlier, it suggests, rather, a kind of Platonism, if no
longer that of good or bad universality, then a *"Platonism" of the singular.*

98. Hegel, *Phenomenology of Spirit,* 488 / 585, trans. modified.

Herein resides the unmistakable modernity of Adorno's writings, namely, their emphasis on "the transitory aspect of the moment, pregnant with meaning, in which the problems of an onrushing future are tangled in knots."[99]

Yet again, an almost Benjaminian metaphorics makes possible Adorno's reversal of the traditional philosophical perspective. Adorno understands Benjamin's metaphysics, as developed in the epistemological preface to *The Origin of German Tragic Drama,* to be an anti-Hegelian attempt "to save inductive reasoning": "When Benjamin writes that the smallest cell of visualized reality outweighs the rest of the world, this line already attests to the self-consciousness of our present state of experience, and it does so with particular authenticity because it was shaped outside the domain of the so-called 'great philosophical issues' which a changed concept of dialectics calls upon us to distrust" (*ND* 303 / 298).

Hegel's doctrine of the reasonableness of reality is "denied [*dementiert*]" by that very reality, according to Adorno, and with this collapses not only the philosophical-historical construction of Hegel's theory but also the conceptual predeterminations that enable his philosophy of identity to remain consistent: "The difference between subject and object cannot be eliminated in theory any more than it has been sloughed off in the experience of reality up till now" (*Drei Stud* 323). Of course, on the one hand, Hegelian dialectics claims to grant singularity a place within the ever expanding boundaries it construes and reconstructs for all meaning and sense, precisely because his logic wants to demonstrate, in place of the abstract separation of substance and individual, the unity and identity of the universal and the singular (see *ND* 320 / 320). From this perspective, however, it exposes itself to immanent critique by failing to realize its own innermost intention: "For all his emphasis on negativity, division, nonidentity, Hegel is actually familiar with this dimension only insofar as it serves identity, only as its instrument" (*Drei Stud* 375). On the other hand, Adorno emphasizes that Hegelian logic is able only to assume "the mediation of the two poles of knowledge" (*ND* 328 / 322, trans. modified), since it never recognizes the singular, only singularity (*Besonderheit*)—that is, what is itself already something conceptual. In this we can see Adorno's separation from Hegel's epistemological and dialectical goal. Hegel's procedure a priori brings into play and makes necessary for speculative thought—if not also for individual experience—the

99. Habermas, *Philosophical Discourse of Modernity,* 53 / 67.

confirmed "logical primacy of the universal," which provides the "funda-ment" for the historical, social, and political primacy of the universal (*ND* 328 / 322). Conversely, one might say that in his thinking Hegel follows the praxis of a history and society which, fundamentally, can tolerate the singular only as a *category* (see *ND* 334 / 328). In Adorno's view, however, neither the philosophical-historical universal nor the logical universal can be construed as primary. Instead, they strengthen each other negatively, in an unholy affinity that, given the quick transitions and dazzling tones with which Adorno portrays them, appears as suggestively salient rather than argumentatively grounded or otherwise demonstrable and, indeed, decidable.

Adorno makes clear that not only the singularity favored by Hegelian logic but also the singular (*Besonderes*) itself must be *dialectically deter-mined.* It would be a mistake to attempt to think the singular directly, im-mediately, without the moment of the universal, "which differentiates the singular, puts its imprint on it, and in a sense is needed to make it singu-lar" (*ND* 328 / 322, trans. modified). Were one to negate pure and simple, abstractly, the unity that Hegel asserts, one would have to imagine that multiplicity can be grasped intuitively, at which point a return to the "gray and diffuse [more precisely, the grayness of the diffuse [*Grauen des Dif-fusen*]" would be inevitable. The self-critique of enlightenment ought to avoid its "retraction [*Widerruf*]" and thus preserve some reference to the work of the concept with its implied tendency, as Adorno believes, toward semantic and mental identities and its ultimately more than merely lin-guistic totality (*ND* 158 / 160). *Polemically,* Adorno underscores this in the rhetorically powerful formulation that "unity [*Einheit*] alone transcends unity." In the dialectical opposition of one moment to its other, however, the one is not separate from the other that appears to be "contradicto-rily" opposed to it. The concept always determines itself through an other, through "what is outside it" (*ND* 157 / 159). This singular other or outside, "even if it were without the barest quality" (*ND* 173 / 175, trans. modi-fied), could never, in effect, be reduced to nothing, "as Hegel knew well but liked to forget on occasion" (*ND* 328 / 322), insofar as it is predicated with the aid of a universal. According to Adorno, however, a potential for order already inheres in the concept itself. In this, at least, it unwittingly promotes the principle of identity and confirms "that what our thinking practice merely postulates is a fact in itself, solid and enduring" (*ND* 154 / 156–57). The concept that bestows identity betrays reality, so to speak, or sublates it. Nonetheless, reality can then once more assert its opposition to the nexus of concepts.

Individual experience attests to this. Aging (a motif to which Levinas also appeals) can provide a demonstration, in that the ego is able at once to recognize itself retrospectively in the various stages of its life course and to perceive this self as another, a stranger. This reveals the fragility of the category of identity, or the "ambivalence of identity and nonidentity" (*ND* 173 / 175).

It can also be proved in another way, by an analysis of judgment. The moment of *"opacity"* to which all predication refers and upon which it depends *"is maintained within the constellation."* The words immediately following are of particular interest: for *"else dialectics would end up hypostasizing mediation without preserving the moments of immediacy, as Hegel prudently wished to do everywhere else"* (*ND* 328–29 / 322, my emph.).

One could demonstrate an *asymmetry* in the central definition of reflection in conceptual mediation that could avert such a hypostasis. As Adorno states it: "Immediacy does not involve being mediated in the same sense in which mediation involves something immediate that would be mediated. Hegel neglected this difference" (*ND* 171 / 173, trans. modified). The assertion that the immediate does not exist without conceptual mediation expresses only *privatively* and epistemologically that the indissoluble something cannot be determined without mediation in thought. It neither means that mediation conceptually exhausts the nonidentical nor precludes that the possibility of conceptually establishing the adequation of thought and thing is denied a priori to conceptual advances:

> Mediation of the immediate refers to its mode: to knowledge of it, and to the limit of such knowledge. Immediacy is not a modality, not a mere determination of the "how" for consciousness. It is objective: its concept points to what cannot be swept away through its concept. Mediation makes no claim whatever to exhaust all things; it postulates, rather, that what it mediates is not thereby exhausted. Immediacy itself, by contrast, stands for a moment that does not require cognition—or mediation—in the same sense in which cognition needs the immediate." (*ND* 171–72 / 173–74, trans. modified)

Where Hegel presupposes "mediation pure and simple" and makes it the telos of thinking, "the singular has to pay the price, down to its authoritarian dismissal in the material parts of the Hegelian system" (*ND* 329 / 322–23, trans. modified). A truly *negative*-dialectical determination of the singular takes place (so I can now summarize Adorno's argumentation) not so much within a dialectical *sublation,* however constituted, but, above all, through the dialectical *encirclement* of the other. The singular can only falsely, and in a basic sense perhaps never in reality, be subsumed under the concept of universality, whether negatively or positively conceived — although, conversely, it cannot easily be made taboo as "uninterpretable," as if it were "another 'last' thing against which cognition knocks its head in vain" (*ND* 161 / 163). It is "something [*Etwas*] — as a cogitatively indispensable substrate of any concept" (*ND* 135 / 139) — and thus, as a nonidentical "*individuum ineffabile*" (*ND* 145 / 148; cf. 11 / 22), it is a permanent dialectical "impetus [or scandal, *Anstoss*]" (*ND* 173 / 175), which, in opposition to the process of conceptual abstraction and the claim to a totality in thought, however it may be implied (see *ND* 162 / 165), appears irreducibly and, indeed, irreconcilably. Adorno attributes the fundamental error of idealism "ever since Fichte" to the contrary assertion: that "the movement of abstraction allows us to get rid of that from which we abstract" (*ND* 135 / 139). This forgetting of its own abstractions causes reason to regress, as Adorno resumes the thesis of *Dialectic of Enlightenment* in *Negative Dialectics* (see *ND* 149 / 152).

Having set out the philosophical-historical dimensions of Adorno's "ontological" negative dialectics, I can now tentatively and abstractly broach the question of the epistemological dimensions of its "logical" side, given that the aforementioned ambivalence of identity and nonidentity "is sustained in the logical problematics of identity" (*ND* 157 / 157). The interpretation proposed here can be confirmed only in an interpretation of the concrete, material aspects of Adorno's metaphysics and aesthetics, something I can pursue here only by retracting a few of his most characteristic assertions.

Hegelian dialectics counts, according to Adorno, as the "'vain attempt' to use philosophical concepts for coping with all that is heterogeneous to those concepts." That becomes especially clear if one takes the "heterogeneous" to be the "ab-solute," though, as I have suggested, that is not always so in Adorno. This thinking of the ab-solute does not cause Adorno to break with philosophy and dialectics tout court. Nevertheless, one must ask "whether and how there can still be a philosophy at all, now that Hegel's has fallen" (*ND* 4 / 16), without, that is, being able to claim or reclaim the status of a *prima philosophia,* however transformed. Philosophy would appear to be thinkable in the present only as the relentless — perhaps, spiritual — exercise of a concept of dialectics which goes "beyond, and to the point of breaking with, the dialectics of Hegel" (*ND* 34 / 44). This cannot be executed as a leap into the realm of the transcendent but must, so long as possible, be achieved through an *immanent critique* of Hegel's model and a distortion of dialectics, because the dialectic of the singular as designed by Hegel "cannot be carried out *idealistically*" (*ND* 329 / 323, trans. modified, my emph.). Whoever follows Hegel's assertions logically, however, arrives at a point where positive speculation extends beyond and leaps over itself, that is to say, turns "into a dialectics that cannot be accounted for, whose solution exceeds its omnipotence" (*Drei Stud* 374–75). At the "extreme" of Hegel's philosophy, Adorno reads "materialist implications" (*Drei Stud* 307) and "hidden motifs" (*Drei Stud* 304), of which speculative dialectics remains nonetheless unconscious, and attempts to demonstrate that in Hegel the peak and "turning point" has been reached (*Drei Stud* 260).

Thus, as we have seen, an "indissoluble objectivity in subjectivity" can be traced even in the construction of the absolute subject (*Drei Stud* 255; cf. 264). In other words, Hegel's principle of total mediation "contradicts itself." In the attempt to determine identity through nonidentity, nonidentity, idealistically speaking, leaves its trace, at least as a "necessary negative," or is "perpetuated" (*ND* 318 / 312), materialistically speaking, as a damaged remainder. But when the difference between the subjective and objective poles of knowledge is sublated in the absolute, the singular also loses its *subaltern* status. Ironically, thought through to its end, identity "inverts into the driving force of the nonidentical" (*Drei Stud* 308). Indeed, Adorno sums up: "Unless the idealistically acquired concept of dialectics harbors experiences contrary to the Hegelian emphasis, experiences independent of the idealistic machinery, philosophy must inevitably do without substantive insight, confine itself to the methodology of science, call that philosophy, and virtually cross itself out" (*ND* 7–8 / 19).

Especially if we assume that all phenomena are in themselves mediated by spirit, we must acknowledge a *passive relationship to whatever appears*. The "mode of conduct through thinking" or "spiritual experience [*geistige Erfahrung*]" of the subject is apparent in its passive submission to the thing, even disappearance into it: "The truth would be its demise." The thing is, of course, neither positively given to thought nor merely the subjective product of thinking. Here one must speak, rather, of the nonidentical in a more emphatic sense: "not an 'idea,' but an adjunct [or supplement, *ein Zugehängtes*]" (*ND* 189 / 189–90).

Accordingly, the nonidentical requires thinking or argumentation less than a mode of conduct which enables one to love things (see *ND* 191 / 191), articulated in "descriptions of sense implications" (*Drei Stud* 370). Adorno finds that, in the introduction to the *Phenomenology of Spirit*, Hegel presents this process as a "pure observation [*das reine Zusehen*],"[100] not of ideal, static essences but of real things moved within themselves. More precisely, the "micro-structure [*Mikrostruktur*]" of Hegel's thinking and writing in the *Phenomenology* appears as "the eye's experience of a drop of water under the microscope at the point it begins to teem; only that which, under a stubborn, enchanted gaze, is not firmly and objectively delimited, but rather is frayed at the edges, so to speak" (*Drei Stud* 364). Such an analysis, according to Adorno, touches in its depths on Husserl's late doctrine of *spontaneous receptivity*, which might still be described as "thoroughly Hegelian" (*Drei Stud* 256; see 369). As we shall see in Levinas's reading of the late Husserl, this figure of interpretation comes close to undermining the priority of spirit or the primacy of the subject (*Drei Stud* 261, 259). In addition, it indicates notable parallels with the juxtaposition of a "general" and a "restricted economy," as Derrida reads them in Bataille.[101]

However that may be, Adorno himself pushes his reading into tense proximity to Benjamin's concept of a *dialectics that has come to a standstill* (*Dialektik im Stillstand*) (see *Drei Stud* 364; *ND* 156 / 159; *AT* 83 / 130).[102] This is, one might say with Wiggershaus, not so much the "coming to a standstill [*Stilstellung*]" of dialectical procedure as a "dialectics that first begins to function by coming to a standstill [*Stillstand*]."[103] Hegel's dialectics, by contrast, is distinguished by an incessant "passing on without being able to linger [*Verweilenkönnen*]" and thus implicitly already attests to the violent primacy of the universal, which levels the singular to a "through-station." The mode of recognizing the ongoing singular conceived by Adorno inverts Hegel's subsumption: it is a "process of resolution [*Auflösungsprozess*] of the concrete in itself." Adorno agrees with the "doubleness" of Hegel's phenomenological procedure, the attempt, in the same breath, to bring the thing itself into language via a pure observation *and* to avoid giving up the medium of reflection altogether. In the wake of objective and absolute idealism (i.e., Hegel) this sole *moral* gesture of

100. Hegel, *Phenomenology of Spirit*, 54 / 77, trans. modified.
101. Derrida, "From Restricted to General Economy: A Hegelianism without Reserve," *Writing and Difference*, 251–77 / 367–407.
102. See Adorno, *Über Walter Benjamin*, 22, 28.
103. Wiggershaus, *Frankfurt School*, 204 / 231.

philosophizing, the demand to be "at *every moment both within things and outside them*" (*MM* 74 / 81–82, my emph.), becomes increasingly awkward. Not surprisingly, Adorno makes Baron von Münchhausen's paradoxical attempt to pull himself out of the bog by his own hair into an exemplary gesture of modern, dialectical cognition.

Idealism can never really be overcome "strictly from within" (*ND* 182 / 183). Like Gadamer, Adorno claims that the Archimedean point from which one might invert the Hegelian figure of thought "can never be found within reflection."[104] Using Hegel's own premises — but without being able to take advantage of his method of speculation — every critique of Hegel ipso facto can, in the end, be shown to depend upon him. Conversely, when Hegel's critics attack him from without, they are exposed to the criticism that they display a predialectical, dogmatic standpoint. Adorno attempts to avoid this fruitless alternative between a continuation of Hegelianism by other means, on the one hand, and naive irrationalism, on the other.

He asserts that idealism can be made to "dance to 'its own' tune" (*ND* 182 / 183), as Marx put it,[105] given that speculation breaks through its own barriers. His program for an immanent critique of Hegel is, however, both implicitly and explicitly crossed out at various decisive moments in his texts, with reference to the immediate, as it were, minimal traces of "the other condition" (as Musil would have said). In Adorno's words: "No immanent critique can serve its purpose wholly outside knowledge, of course — without a moment of immediacy, if you will, a bonus from the subjective thought that looks beyond the dialectical structure. That is the moment of spontaneity, and idealists should be the last to ostracize it, because without it there would be no idealism. . . . it needs an outside impulse [*Anstosses von aussen*]" (*ND* 182 /1 83). An *immanently* motivated and directed critique thus finally always reverses into a *transcending* procedure (see *ND* 145 / 149), without ever being extinguished by this apparently antithetical gesture. Adorno's deciphering of the tradition is woven of this *deconstructive doubleness*, so to speak.

One could nonetheless ask *whether* and *how* one might conceive of a dialectic that sets its sights on the singular without identifying it and without prematurely blending it into a universal but therefore no less false

---

104. Gadamer, *Truth and Method*, 305 / 324 ff.
105. See Karl Marx, "Zur Kritik der Hegelschen Rechtsphilosophie," in *Die Frühschriften*, ed. Siegfried von Landshut (Stuttgart: A Kröner, 1971).

reconciliation. In a further move Adorno underscores that his own conception of a negative dialectic is ultimately no longer compatible with
Hegelian dialectic: "Its idea names the difference from Hegel" (*ND* 141 /
145); it even implies an "abandonment of Hegel" (*ND* 144 / 148). The line
of separation reveals, above all, a difference in "intention" (*ND* 147 / 150),
because Hegel, according to Adorno, lacks "sympathy with the utopian
singular that has been buried underneath the universal" (*ND* 318 / 312,
trans. modified).

In sum Hegel sees identity as coinciding with positivity when he asserts that in "conceptual thinking" the negative belongs "to the content
itself" and is significant "as its *immanent* movement and definition, as its
whole for which it is the *positive.*"[106] Adorno, by contrast, holds that the
power of the whole, which holds sway over every isolated determination of
something nonidentical or objective, is not only its negation but itself the
negative: "To negate a negation does not bring about its reversal; it proves,
rather, that the negation was not negative enough. . . . The thesis that the
negation of negation is something positive can only be upheld by one who
presupposes positivity—as all-conceptuality—from the beginning" (*ND*
159–60 / 162). Positivity thus resides not in the thing itself but, rather, in
a traditional logic that, "*more arithmetico,* takes minus times minus for a
plus." As a result, the conception of negative dialectics is "decisively" severed from Hegelian speculation. The nonidentical, according to Adorno,
is available neither immediately "as something positive" nor in the mael-
strom of the negation of negation (*ND* 158 / 161). Only in a transferred
significance can a "positive" be granted to the third way of *critique* or of
determinate negation.

Hegel's principle of identity "thwarts" reconciliation because it is *aller-
gic* to its other, to what is not itself (*ND* 143 / 146). By contrast, Adorno
insists, a dialectical "procedure [*Verfahren*]" in an emphatic sense would
be "to think in contradictions, for the sake of the contradiction once experienced in the thing, and against that contradiction. A contradiction in
reality, it is a contradiction against reality. . . . Its motion does not tend to
the identity in the difference between each object and its concept; instead,
it is suspicious of all identity. Its logic is one of disintegration" (*ND* 145 /
148).

Can we still speak of a dialectics here? According to Adorno, the bottom drops out of the Hegelian system with the critique of the positive

---

106. Hegel, *Phenomenology of Spirit,* 36 / 57, trans. modified.

negation of dialectics, but the dialectical movement does not take its measure from this otherwise "vital nerve" of Hegelian logic. Instead, its "experiential substance [*Erfahrungsgehalt*]" is to be found in the "resistance
that the other offers to identity" (*ND* 160–61 / 163, trans. modified). In
Hegelian terms Adorno remains caught within the standpoint of *skepticism* (or negative reason), which Hegel famously wants to distinguish from
abstract understanding, on the one hand, and "speculation" (or "positive
reason"), on the other (*ND* 16n / 27n).[107] For Hegel philosophy contains
skepticism as a *dialectical* moment, but the negative-dialectical in itself is
the very core of skepticism. Unlike skepticism, the speculatively dialectical, as "self-fulfilling skepticism,"[108] does not stop at the "merely negative
result of dialectics" (*ND* 16n / 27n). In place of abstract negation it recognizes a third step in the logic: that the negative-dialectical result is the
positive because it contains what is negated as sublated within itself.[109]

Nevertheless, also according to Adorno, a moment of *speculation* cannot be denied to philosophy, "of course, in a broader sense than the overly
positive Hegelian one" (*ND* 15–16 / 27). It should be thought as a *negative-
dialectical speculation*, so to speak. This self-consciousness of reflection
(see *Drei Stud* 358) can initially be represented as the power of negation "to
blast apart the indissoluble [*das Unauflösliche aufzusprengen*]" (*ND* 27 /
38, trans. modified). Then, however, it must be presented, with less ambition and more promise, as a *medium of ambivalence,* because a "character
of being suspended [*Charakter des Schwebenden*] is joined to it" (*Drei Stud*
328). The "skandalon" of Hegelian speculation is that it strives to identify the "unconditional" with the "quintessence of the conditional," even
if in vain. From this classical-modern gesture of transcendence stems the
impression that speculation maintains itself "in the air." As Adorno puts
it, "*the name of the highest speculative concept, even that of the absolute, of
the utterly detached [Losgelösten], is literally the name of that suspension
[Schwebenden]*" (*Drei Stud* 261, my emph.). Here the proximity and distance between Adorno's concept of speculation and that of Hegel appear
to be inextricable. The ab-solute whose traces negative dialectics pursues
into the metaphysical realm is probably less a "quintessence of the conditional," however materially deployed, than its—no longer merely abstract—negation. Hegel, by contrast, abstracted from and "thought away"

---

107. See also Schnädelbach, *Vernunft und Geschichte,* 157.
108. The quotation is taken from ibid.; see also *ND* 16n / 27n.
109. See also Hegel, *Phenomenology of Spirit,* 51 / 74.

the difference between that immanence and the absolute (*Drei Stud* 324), between the conditional and the unconditional. According to Adorno, one can at most say that, where Hegel identifies the life of the absolute with the "totality of the transience of all finite things," something true still resounds. In Adorno's "transmutation of metaphysics into history," the price of redeeming the absolute of *prima philosophia* is a profanization of this metaphysical semantic potential "in the secular category pure and simple, the category of decay." Adorno encapsulates this in a formula that one could take as the motto for all his metaphysical meditations: "No recollection of transcendence is possible any more, save by way of perdition; eternity appears, not as such, but diffracted through what is most perishable" (*ND* 360 / 353, trans. modified).

The thought of the ab-solute which Adorno wishes to redeem is thus a figure that strives to break out of the medium of universality, however conceived. The "nerve" of the methodical-dialectical concept of *determinate negation* refers to this: "It is based on the experience of the powerlessness of critique so long as it stays within universality" (*Drei Stud* 318). Its "paradigm" is *a subtle critique of relativism that avoids the alternatives of absolutism and absolute nihilism* (*ND* 38 / 48), without being able, in turn, itself to contain its other in a concept. Therefore, a quality of being suspended characterizes its movement of thought, and it now and again changes into the speculative, albeit in a novel sense of the term. Gadamer describes this aspect of the speculative figure of thought, which leads to the heart of Adorno's most convincing formulations. Speculation allows "an infinity of meaning to enter into a finite presentation."[110] Of course, one should not interpret this inexhaustibility of meaning in Adorno on the model of the modern philosophical and hermeneutical understanding of human limitation. Adorno's position resembles more the rhetorical-deconstructive idea and device of a *permanent deferral*. Yet for Adorno, as for Gadamer, "the actual mystery of reflection is precisely the ungraspability of the image, the suspension of pure reproduction."[111] Such an idea of the other and the intention of Hegel's philosophy can no longer be reduced to a common denominator.

Adorno's philosophy seems, in Hegelian terms, to be *a new, modern form of the unhappy consciousness,* a description that Adorno would perhaps not entirely have denied, since unhappy consciousness, as he says,

---

110. Gadamer, *Truth and Method,* 422–23 / 441.
111. Ibid.

"is not a delusion of the spirit's vanity but something inherent in spirit, the one authentic dignity it has received in its separation from the body. This dignity is the spirit's negative reminder of its physical aspect; its capability of that aspect is the only source of whatever hope spirit can have" (*ND* 203 / 203, trans. modified). For him, the movement of thinking seems to be, as Hegel phrases it, "a musical thinking that never reaches the concept"; it is like the "movement of infinite *desire*" directed toward "the unattainable *beyond*, which slips away as it is grasped or, rather, has already escaped."[112] In this "*absolute dialectical unrest*"[113] Adorno's figure of thought can bear witness to the "*pain* [Schmerz] of spirit."[114] As remarked earlier, it suggests a quasi-hermeneutical and deconstructive figure of thought which situates itself well beyond the premises of the more activist and affirmative Left-Hegelian or Marxist critiques of Hegel.

According to Gadamer, Heidegger was probably the first to open up new paths outside of the "merely dialectical reversal" of the principle of spirit by the Young Hegelians. He no longer thinks of truth as a "full disclosure, whose ideal accomplishment would ultimately remain the self-presence of absolute spirit":[115] by contrast, for him the thought that truth is to be understood "as simultaneous disclosure [*Entbergung*] and concealment [*Verbergung*]" is fundamental.[116] If one disregards Adorno's ex-aggeratedly (and negatively) formulated expressions of totality and his invocations of what might be otherwise, when heightened to almost utopian intensity, and if one further overlooks Adorno's no less exaggerated critique of the "jargon of authenticity" suspected in Heidegger's prose, then one might note in Adorno's philosophy traces of a nearly analogous understanding of the concept and essence of truth.

The Young Hegelians and their neo-Marxist successors were, like Hegel, able to think of truth only as "the correspondence between concept and reality as a whole."[117] Adorno, however, presents a different herme-(neu)tic perspective. In Hegelian terms it could be described as *a kind of bad infinity.* As in Gadamer, the infinite in Adorno's figure of thought cannot be grasped "as an unending further determination and constitution [*Fortbestimmung*] of the objective world, neither in the neo-Kantian sense

112. Hegel, *Phenomenology of Spirit*, 131 / 168–69, trans. modified.
113. Ibid., 124 / 161.
114. Ibid., 410 / 495, trans. modified.
115. Gadamer, *Ergänzungen*, 504.
116. Ibid.
117. Schnädelbach, *Philosophie in Deutschland, 1831–1933*, 129–30.

of the infinite task nor in the dialectical sense of a thinking beyond-being [*Hinaus-Seins*], across any delimitation."[118] Whenever Adorno adopts the terminology of identity or totality, one must therefore seek to interpret his claims either rhetorically or heuristically. Otherwise, they deteriorate into matter for critique. Only then is totality "not an objectivity that remains to be determined."[119]

Between Morality and Ethics: An Incomprehensible Obligation

The necessary and sufficient condition for a *philosophy of ought* (*Sollensphilosophie*), according to Otto Marquard, is that in such a moral philosophy no observable connection can exist between actual reality and the good.[120] Whether he intends it or not, this condition seems to hold in Adorno, though in a unique manner, as Kantian as it is un-Kantian. Adorno writes, "In the right condition, as in the Jewish *theologoumenon*, all things would differ only a little from the way they are; but not even the least can be conceived now as it would be then" (*ND* 299 / 294). In the "constant feast-day light" of the "sabbatian peace," in which the world will appear when it is capable of throwing over the "law of labor" (*MM* 112 / 125), everything will seem almost unchanged, and yet all will no longer be a lie. Thus, redemption results not from rejecting the world but from regrouping its fragile references to utopia: "The elements of this other are present in reality, and they require only the most minute displacement into a new constellation to find their right position" (*AT* 132 / 199). The result, in Adorno's view, is the impossibility, in the strong sense, of grounding morality: "What will one day be imposed and bestowed upon a better practice can here and now — according to the warning of utopianism — be no more visualized by thought than practice, under its own concept, will ever be completely exhausted by knowledge" (*ND* 245 / 243).

The Kantian undeterminable, aporetic concept of intelligible character thus encounters "something of the truth of the prohibition of images" (*ND* 298 / 293), namely, the *unfathomable, unrationalizable, and unnaturalizable* possibility of the other, of "averting catastrophe in spite of everything" (*ND* 323 / 317). At the end of *Negative Dialectics* Adorno says of the categorical imperative, "A new categorical imperative has been imposed

118. Gadamer, *Ergänzungen*, 505–6.

119. Ibid., 506. But Gadamer's assumption that "totality is not an object, but a world horizon that closes us in and into which we live" would probably be too affirmative for Adorno.

120. Marquard, *Schwierigkeiten mit der Geschichtsphilosophie*, 44–46.

by Hitler upon unfree mankind: to arrange their thoughts and actions so that Auschwitz will not repeat itself, so that nothing similar will happen" (*ND* 365 / 358). Immediately afterward, however, he adds: "When we want to find reasons for it, this imperative is as refractory as the given one of Kant was once upon a time. Dealing *discursively* with it would be an outrage, for the new imperative gives us a bodily sensation of *the moment of the moral addendum* — bodily, because it is now the practical abhorrence of the unbearable physical agony to which individuals are exposed. . . . It is in the unvarnished materialistic motive only that morality survives" (*ND* 365 / 358, trans. modified; my emph.). Whereas Kant allows only formal reason to be a valid "*movens* of practice" (*ND* 229 / 228), for Adorno reason always requires some addendum, something factical.

Not objective spirit — that is to say, ethical life (*Sittlichkeit*) in the Hegelian sense — releases morality from its interiority but, rather, almost the opposite: impulse, spontaneity, corporeality. This is a materialistic moment, which the tradition always incorrectly interpreted only as consciousness. Every impulse toward something better encounters, in Adorno's presentation, *an incomprehensible obligation* (*uneinsichtige Verbindlichkeit*), though he acknowledges that this and the condition of justice which it seemingly anticipates can never be idealistically or subjectively narrowed. This addendum, Adorno further remarks, "has an aspect which under rationalist rules is irrational" (*ND* 228 / 227): "Every impulse in the direction of better things is not only rational, as it is to Kant; before it is rational, it is also stupid [*Dummheit*]" (*ND* 277 / 273–74). The root of the irrational in Kant's moral law is its sheer givenness: "The antinomical character of the Kantian doctrine of freedom is exacerbated to the point where the moral law seems to be regarded as directly rational and as not rational — as rational, because it is reduced to pure logical reason without content, and as not rational because it must be accepted as given and cannot be further analyzed, because every attempt at analysis is anathema" (*ND* 261 / 258). In this contradiction, however, Kantian moral philosophy reveals its truth content. In this way it curbs "the *purely* rational character of the moral law" (*ND* 242 / 240, my emph.). Adorno believes that this ambiguity in the idea of freedom ought to be respected. Its ambivalence confirms Adorno's unavoidable dictum that freedom and reason "are nonsense without each other." Yet it would be difficult to see how reality could ever be "transparent" to that idea (*Drei Stud* 288). The later analyses of the doctrine of freedom in *Negative Dialectics,* which I have discussed earlier, rightly exhibit greater reservations on this point.

Because the connection to the whole and to every universality has become problematic, for Adorno philosophy becomes, as Dubiel says, "emphatically stylized into a rhetorical-moral capability, possible only for 'isolated' intellectual individuals." Indeed, it becomes "itself a kind of moral-political practice,"[121] which, as Habermas reproaches, can no longer account for its own normative foundations.[122] The attempt of Adorno's reflection to remain close to the utterly undiminished experience of damaged life thus seems to proceed, paradoxically, at the expense of communicability and of the ability to mediate to the good or better life. At this point one is tempted to agree, with Marquard, that "the difficulties in the attempt to be Hegelian are exceeded only by the difficulties in attempting not to be Hegelian."[123] But this cannot be the final word.

Perhaps one might lay out Adorno's many mutually exclusive motifs and figures of argumentation in yet another way. Some of his formulations undeniably suggest that he is only a Hegelian under the sign of the negative, a Platonist of the negative universal. Moreover, one finds in him an equally indisputable, a complementary, we might say, eschatological-messianic perspective—a "Platonism" of the singular. This line of interpretation, which has much in its favor, should not obscure the fact that Adorno's texts also investigate a *third* mode of experience, which is not rigidified into a fruitless antithesis at either extreme. His thinking moves like a pendulum, *seeking to sail between the Scylla of the negative philosophy of totality and the Charybdis of messianism.* It betrays the beginnings of a philosophy directed toward the trace of the other of reason. The negative-metaphysical dimensions of negative dialectics, as well as Adorno's concrete, materialist, moral, aesthetic, and quasi-theological motifs, all point, it would seem, beyond the philosophy of ought. Adorno's moral philosophy indicates a third option between the extreme poles of cognitivist ethics and skepticism about value. The formulation of an incomprehensible obligation of morality expresses just this. If idealist dialectics represents homecoming in the odyssey of spirit, then in Adorno's view, by contrast, it behooves the morality of thought and action "not to be at home alone [or, rather, not to be at home in one's own place, *nicht bei sich selber zu Hause zu sein*]" (*MM* 39 / 43), or, conversely—to borrow an expression from Novalis—"to be at home everywhere" (*ND* 172 / 174).

121. Dubiel, *Wissenschaftsorganisation und politische Erfahrung,* 129.
122. See Habermas, *Theory of Communicative Action,* 1:373–74 / 1:500.
123. Marquard, *Schwierigkeiten mit der Geschichtsphilosophie,* 51.

The Metaphysics in Negative Dialectics:
The Structure of "Spiritual Experience"

In place of traditional philosophy's *positive metaphysics of the infinite*, especially that of Hegel, which, by definition, imagines that it possesses its object as infinite and thereby becomes finite, that is, "conclusive [*abschlusshaft*]," negative dialectics appears as an *infinite movement* that no longer believes itself to be open to the fullness of the infinite, let alone to have some conceptual grasp on it. "Instead, if it were delicately understood," as Adorno puts it, it "itself would be infinite in the sense of scorning solidification in a body of enumerable theorems" (*ND* 13 / 25). In a move not unlike Hegel's, it tirelessly recalls that "every single concept, every single conclusion, is false according to an emphatic idea of truth" — that is, according to negative dialectics, what is true "cannot be grasped in any single thesis, in any delimited, positive expression" (*Drei Stud* 328; cf. 339). Idealism, however, in its affirmation of a principle of positive infinity, stylizes the transcendent creation of thinking into the static construction of traditional metaphysics (see *ND* 26 / 37). An altered dialectics, by contrast, should be seen as an *alternation* between identity and difference which cannot be concluded; its goal is *openness,* not the system (see *ND* 20 / 31). Because it recognizes that knowledge can never entirely possess its objects, it no longer attempts to chase after the "phantasm of the whole" in order to bring it into a concept (*ND* 13 / 25).

If the idealist system imagines a totality "to which nothing remains extraneous" (*ND* 24 / 35) and thus anticipates, in the realm of thought, the specter of a totally administered world—strengthening it, moreover, while also calling forth an antagonism that cannot be appeased (see *ND* 24–27, 38–39 / 35–38, 48–49)—then negative dialectics can be described as an "anti-system" whose partiality for the singular and for the residue of freedom is equivalent, so to speak, to a *second Copernican revolution* in the orientation of the entire Western tradition of thought (*ND* xx / 10). Adorno seeks "the reconciling side of the irreconcilable" (*ND* 320 / 314), in that society, in its tendency toward totality, also summons its own dissociation, without its being possible to say whether this heralds liberation or regression. The fact that the universal also works "against itself" (*ND* 346 / 339), however, grants hope to the ripening "potential of an other" (*ND* 349 / 342). Of course, negative dialectics thus conceived salvages certain motifs from classical-modern metaphysics in the broken form of a *post-metaphysical metaphysics,* as it were. "What makes philosophy," in its *meta-critical* turn against the philosophy of origins, "risk the strain of its own infinity is the unwarranted expectation that each individual and particular puzzle it solves will be like Leibniz's monad, the ever-elusive entirety in itself—although, of course, in line with a pre-established disharmony rather than a pre-established harmony" (*ND* 13–14 / 25).

Such a philosophy can only take place in "fragments," as the subtitle to *Dialectic of Enlightenment* says, or in "models," as in the third part of *Negative Dialectics*. It ought to seek an "obligation [*Verbindlichkeit*] without a system" (*ND* 29 / 39), and it should occur as the interpretive construction of constellations, in a "dependence—patent or latent—on texts" (*ND* 55 / 65): "As a constellation, theoretical thought circles the concept it would like to unseal, hoping that it may fly open like the lock of a well-guarded safe-deposit box: in response, not to a single key or a single number, but to a combination of numbers" (*ND* 163 / 166; see APh 130 / 340). Reminiscences of Benjamin are unmistakable in such articulations of the work of deciphering, in a philosophical interpretation concentrated on rhetoric: "Constellation is not a system. It levels nothing, it absorbs nothing, but one thing casts light on others, and the figures that the individual moments collectively form are a determinate sign and a legible *writing* [or scripture, *Schrift*]" (*Drei Stud* 342, my emph.). Philosophy, in Adorno's view, should not reduce reality to specific categories; rather, it should *compose* (see *ND* 164 / 167). It is not distinguished by its supposedly single-track line of argumentation but by its fabric (see *ND* 34 / 44). Such a program, according to Adorno, can be read as the silent, driving force of imagination in every illuminating specialist investigation. Thus, for example, the work of Max Weber, like Adorno's own writings, proves to be "a third possibility beyond the alternatives of positivism and idealism" (*ND* 166 / 168).

One might also describe this procedure as a reprise of Bacon's or Leibniz's earlier doctrine of *ars inveniendi* (APh 131 / 343–44). In such a conception of philosophy, thought approaches a reality that "refuses to submit to law" by "testing [*probierend*]" it (APh 131 / 341). According to Adorno, the "organon" of the *ars inveniendi* must be fantasy because it is capable of establishing a connection between the elements of reality, "*which is the irrevocable source of all judgment*" (*MM* 122 / 137, my emph.; see *ND* 383 / 376). Adorno defines that capability as an "*exact fantasy*," that is, as "fantasy which abides strictly within the material which the sciences present to it, and reaches beyond them only in the smallest aspects of their arrangement" (APh 131 / 342). In Adorno's work it is convincingly carried out as a movement of thought which, like art (*ND* 16 / 28), earns its right to exist "solely in its enactment [*Vollzug*]" (*ND* xix / 9, trans. modified; cf. 29 / 39), in the course of its articulation. Only thus can the object of thought, now encircled, perhaps begin to speak for itself (*ND* 28 / 38).

Chapter Six
Metaphysical Experience

A CONUNDRUM LIES AT THE CORE of negative dialectics: thinking inherently levels the other of reason, yet we have no plausible or responsible means to break through this dead end except by using what is still *philosophical discourse*—that is to say, in a critique of thinking by thinking itself. At times Adorno seems actually to believe that philosophy might be able to carry out this paradoxical task without the result being a performative contradiction of sorts. At others his thinking appears to be characterized by a double strategy, as I have demonstrated in the previous chapter. The attentive reader can detect an unsublatable tension between a strategy of immanent critique and a transcendent demand, which runs counter to the categories of negative dialectics itself. True enough, in his use of various originally religious categories, such as "the absolute," "God," and "meaning [*Sinn*]," Adorno does not fall behind Nietzsche. Yet in his earliest and latest work there is an undeniable ambivalence between, on the one hand, salient passages in which he presumes to follow a path of thinking which is thoroughly or even consistently negative and, on the other hand, less conspicuous fragments in which he condemns the totality of what exists for being wholly untrue, on the nondiscursive grounds of a nearly appellative concept of truth.[1] What is the exact relationship between these two poles around which Adorno's central figure of thought revolves? Can they be clearly distinguished and kept apart? Or does the path of immanent critique, with its internal delineation of identifying thought, and the transcending, breaking open, or surpassing of that very thought prove, on closer examination, to be inextricably intertwined, to the point of being almost interchangeable?

Adorno's critical combination of dialectical and metaphysical meditations strives to establish a "knowledge [*Wissen*]" of the absolute without assuming, like Hegel, the possibility of an absolute knowledge in the clas-

---

1. See Grenz, *Adornos Philosophie in Grundbegriffen*, 116. He notes, "The philosophy of negativity cannot be thought without assuming the potential for something better" (135). See also Schmucker, *Adorno—Logik des Zerfalls*, 137 n. 40. Schmucker summarizes the problem of negative dialectics: "So long as what the nonidentical is cannot be said—or can be said only falsely—what the whole is also cannot be said, or can be said only falsely" (144; see 147, 132).

sical sense (see *ND* 405 / 397). The attempt to determine how it might be
possible to look beyond the constitutive conditions of thought and action
is decidedly *metaphysical,* even though the contours of the metaphysical
are only negatively circumscribed and demarcated from within and without. From this, then, results the paradoxical or even aporetic character of
his philosophy. Adorno is perfectly clear about that: "Is a man who deals
with the absolute not necessarily claiming to be the thinking organ with
the capacity to do so, and thus the absolute himself? And . . . if dialectics
turned into a metaphysics that is not simply like dialectics, would it not
violate its own strict concept of negativity?" (*ND* 405 / 397).

The total identification in which thought continually threatens to become ensnared need not have the final word. Dialectics should be, without reserve, the capability of tracing "the difference that has been spirited
away." It should strive to break through, *from within,* the spell of what
is apparently always the same "without *dogmatically,* from without, contrasting it with an allegedly *realistic* thesis" (*ND* 172 / 174, my emph.).
Thought is able, Adorno further maintains, "to think against itself without
abandoning itself." Dialectics thus can "see through" the deception of its
own inadvertent claims to identity and totality (*ND* 141 / 144): "By means
of logic, dialectics grasps the coercive character of logic, hoping that it
may yield." Of course, this supposed dissolution of logical rules, whose
force even negative dialectics can never entirely elude, also implies a preparedness to take aim against itself "in a final movement" and to evaluate
itself: "It lies in the definition of negative dialectics that it will not come
to rest in itself, as if it were total. This is its form of hope" (*ND* 406 / 398).

Nonetheless, the question of whether philosophy can ultimately succeed in realizing this hope without a *pregiven idea of exteriority* is equally
justified. Of course, "today at least" (*ND* 365 / 358; see 405 / 397), thought
must practice self-reflection as self-critique. But this attempt would be
futile without a speculative moment of freedom and spiritual experience.
The inner and outer perspectives, in the end, thus mutually constitute
each other: "The *immanently argumentative* element is legitimate where
the reality that has been integrated in a system is received in order to oppose it with its own strength. The free part of thought, on the other hand,
represents the authority [or the instance, *Instanz*] which already knows
about the *emphatic* untruth of that real-systematic context. Without this
knowledge there would be no eruption; without adopting the power [or
violence, *Gewalt*] of the system, the outbreak would fail" (*ND* 30 / 40, my
emph.). Over this moment, which lies outside the widespread system of

domination in the world, "which is faulty to the core," dialectical theory has no "jurisdiction." It can only seek to retain some memory of the "inter-action [or interrelation, *Wechselwirkung*]" and alternation or oscillation between philosophy and "experience" in a singular sense of the term (*ND* 141 / 144). Adorno thus speaks to a "mobility" that permeates sensible consciousness at its deepest level: "It means a *doubled mode of conduct:* an inner one, the immanent process which is the properly dialectical one, and a free, unbound one like a stepping out of dialectics. Yet the two are not merely disparate. The unregimented thought has an *elective affinity* to dia-lectics, which as criticism of the system recalls what would be outside the system; and the force that *liberates* the dialectical movement in cognition is the very same that rebels against the system. But altitudes of conscious-ness are linked by criticizing one another, not by compromising" (*ND* 31 / 41–42).

One might ask about the nature of the "*impulse* to transcend that natu-ral context and its delusion [or blinding, *Verblendung*]" which, according to Adorno, dialectics always already "*follows*" (*ND* 141 / 145, my emph.). Dialectics can neither conceptually catch up with this hidden impulse nor recognize it as merely positively given. Moreover, to all appearances one cannot, via dialectics, trace the explosive material that is the secret source of power and even violence for negative-dialectic discussions. This ma-terial, however, is not some symbolization, derived from classical phi-losophy or from the remnants of metaphysics, for something somehow present, here and now or in some distant past, nor even a fleeting refer-ence to a utopian condition *in absentia,* whose conceptual disclosure in a concept would only temporarily have been postponed. Moreover, the *idea of transcendence,* not unlike the Kantian concept of the intelligible, stands for "*something which is not, and yet it is not a pure nonbeing* [*etwas, was nicht ist und doch nicht nur nicht ist*]." Measured against the rules of ontology's game, such fragile — and hardly ideal or idealized — transcen-dence could be apostrophized only as "imaginary [*imaginär*]" (*ND* 393 / 385, my emph.).

Insofar as many of Adorno's formulations do not entirely escape the long shadow of ontologism, with its premises, concepts, and ambitions, a certain taint of nebulosity adheres to his work. As I will attempt to make clear, his concept of philosophical argumentation can only be understood and, indeed, salvaged to the extent that this hint of otherness is inter-preted as ab-solute in the etymological sense of the term, which Levi-nas, in his own way, ascribes to the dimension and height of the (ethical-religious) other. As his thinking develops, Adorno tends to describe the truth and status of that otherness in terms of something virtually *hidden,* even if he never allows it to be entirely absorbed into concealment as such. It would seem that only the concept of the trace — unfortunately only tangentially and not systematically introduced by Adorno — can guard against the danger of a purely negativistic, crudely nihilistic philosophy, on the one hand, and negative theology, on the other.

In modernity, according to Adorno, thought finds itself in the paradoxical position of having to think an idea that it *eo ipso* betrays. Above all, in *Negative Dialectics* and *Aesthetic Theory* seemingly insoluble problems appear whenever Adorno speaks explicitly of the "trace," the "riddle [*Rätselbild*]," or the "appearance" of the other, because these motives threaten to be driven outside discursive thought altogether. In such contexts Adorno addresses metaphysical, moral, aesthetic, and even religious-philosophical aspects of thought and action which seem to contradict the supposedly relentless negativity of his overall intellectual approach. With the aid of concepts that allude to "what is other than being," "the intelligible," "hope," "utopia," "reconciliation," "the absolute," "God," "happiness," and "freedom," he cautiously gropes toward experiences that resist or elude conceptual grasp. What then emerges at least *tends,* at least in its *structure,* to withdraw from the armatures of theory and practice, however formalized:

> The more transcendence crumbles under enlightenment, both in the world and in the spirit, the more hidden will it become, *as though concentrating in an outermost point above all mediations.* In this sense, the anti-historical theology of the utterly different has its historical index. The question of metaphysics is sharpened into the question whether this utter tenuousness, abstractness, indefiniteness is the last, already lost defensive position of metaphysics — or whether metaphysics survives only in the meanest [or smallest, *Geringsten*] and shabbiest, and from a state of consummate insignificance restores reason to the autocratic reason that performs its office without resistance or reflection. (*ND* 402–3 / 394–95, trans. modified, my emph.)

That is why metaphysics must migrate into *micrology.* Metaphysics is no longer thinkable in the sense of a deductive structure of judgments about being or a dogmatic doctrine about a difference made absolute. It can only be conceived as a *broken hermeneutic* process, as a "legible constellation" or the "script [*Schrift*]" of an always concrete, material being (*ND* 407 / 399).

Because, as Adorno notes, "enlightenment leaves practically nothing of the metaphysical content of truth" and *"that which recedes keeps
getting smaller and smaller,"* only a thoroughgoing exegesis of *the most
frail and ephemeral phenomena* can provide a sanctuary for the questions
that classical-modern philosophy once assigned to its doctrine of the unchangeable. But in this process and procedure of enlightenment "almost
nothing [*so gut wie nichts*]" of substance remains. The absolute "flees"
farther and farther from the grip of thought. Thus, any path for approaching the absolute can only be a "mirage [*Spiegelung*]" (*ND* 407 / 399, my
emph.).

I have already examined this speculative side of Adorno's thought. Suffice it to say that philosophical thought, even if it sought to address the
"mystery [*Geheimnis*]" by teasing out of that enigma ever more numerous demystified "chunks [*Brocken*]," would in the end never be able to
"resolve [or loosen and dispel, *lösen*]" its form as enigma (*ND* 407 / 399).
An interesting theme underlies these formulations: Adorno's idea of the
nonidentical cannot be understood according to the pattern of an "infinitesimal principle" that — as in Leibniz and Kant — would be in principle, if
not in fact or in practice, "commensurable" with the idea of science (*ND*
401 / 393). In consequence, however, one can never approach emphatic
transcendence "asymptotically" (*ND* 407 / 398).[2] In every act of identification and reidentification, in every series of conceptual determinations,
the very cognitive process not only pushes ahead of consciousness, as it
were, the consciousness of any outside of consciousness but betrays it ipso
facto in a paradoxical, indeed aporetic, movement.[3]

One might, then, ask whether and in what way the nonidentical, the
other, might not still unintentionally be pushed into an "unattainable distance" (*ND* 394 / 387). Does not this motif of the other of reason culmi-
nate in something "downright" incommensurable with thought? (see *ND*
405 / 397). But thought would then once again be handed over to the pre-
critical, dogmatic tradition, something that, Adorno insists, ought to be
avoided. Adorno sees the possibility of metaphysics after the Enlightenment, therefore, as residing in the attempt to answer the question *whether
and how* "we can get out of this aporia otherwise than by stealth [or surreption, *Erschleichung*]" (*ND* 406 / 397). It nonetheless remains ques-

2. See also Grenz: "Adorno's concept of truth does not function as a regulative idea" (*Adornos Philosophie in Grundbegriffen*, 57).

3. Grenz suggests understanding Adorno's concept of the nonidentical "as the distance that
is intended in Benjamin's definition of 'aura'" (ibid., 204).

tionable in what way the "self-reflection" of negative dialectics (*ND* 407 / 398), to which Adorno owes his primary allegiance, can ever *in itself* suffice. Even if one admits that only the self-questioning of thought — instead of an all-inclusive, irrational attempt at escape — can demarcate the terrain within which a true revolution, a *Revolution der Denkungsart*, in Kant's sense, might manifest itself after all, it remains uncertain whether that reflex could be derived from the conceptual resources of thought alone. The most serious philosophizing is, with respect to its own intentions, necessarily — not only actually but essentially, always already — *belated*. Nevertheless, it would be a mistake to oppose Adorno's critique of the abstract other on the grounds of this uncomfortable circumstance and, instead, grant renewed validity to an *absolutum* derived from the remains of metaphysics as we knew it. The task is, rather, to explore an idea or metaphor of an *ab-solute* alterity that allows itself to be distinguished both from the realm of the self-same and from its radical negation, from a heterogeneity or heterology *made absolute*. When one looks at things in this way, however, one finds oneself caught between two lines of fire.

The nonidentical cannot be conceived as something immediately positive, nor does it result from the negation of negation (see *ND* 159 / 161). Against this backdrop, as Schnädelbach notes, it nearly amounts to a "conceptual symbol [*Begriffssymbol*]."[4] In other words, the core concept of negative dialectics designates, paradoxically, "an empty space for a concept"[5] or even — to borrow Jaspers's famous term — "a cipher." Adorno, according to Schnädelbach, should therefore be seen as fundamentally a "Platonist of the nonidentical,"[6] even as a "theoretician of the evidence [*Evidenztheoretiker*] of truth." Of course, we might ask how such a *"Platonism" of the singular*, which at the same time stubbornly denies itself any recourse to a dogmatic, idealistic intuitionism, is to be understood as well as how it can be reconciled with the concepts of materialism, natural history, and transience.

It is clear from my previous examination of the genesis of Adorno's intellectual approach that his idea of a corrective to universal mediation hardly stems from the Platonic tradition as it has been historically docu-

---

4. Schnädelbach, "Dialektik als Vernunftkritik," in von Friedeburg and Habermas, *Adorno-Konferenz 1983*, 70; and Schnädelbach, *Vernunft und Geschichte*, 183.

5. Schnädelbach, "Dialektik als Vernunftkritik," in von Friedeburg and Habermas, *Adorno-Konferenz 1983*, 70; and Schnädelbach, *Vernunft und Geschichte*, 183.

6. Schnädelbach, "Dialektik als Vernunftkritik," in von Friedeburg and Habermas, *Adorno-Konferenz 1983*, 73; and Schnädelbach, *Vernunft und Geschichte*, 186.

mented and philosophically understood. Where he does not invoke Kant as a source, he instead takes up elements not of Neoplatonism but of a heterodox mystical tradition — mediated through Kafka and later Beckett, Proust, Benjamin, and Scholem — while removing those elements entirely from their former religious horizons of understanding and meaning.[7]

Adorno makes no secret of this: "One of the mystical impulses secularized in dialectics was the doctrine that the intramundane and historic is relevant to what traditional metaphysics distinguished [or set aside, *abhob*] as transcendence" (*ND* 361 / 354; see 364, 372 / 357, 365). The task of the micrological view is to show in what way these "smallest intramundane traits," as Adorno puts it, "would be of relevance to the absolute" (*ND* 408 / 400). The ambition of *Negative Dialectics* to attempt a second Copernican revolution in philosophy enters in here (*ND* xx / 10),[8] as the aspiration to reverse the prejudice — in both Plato *and* Kant — that "the immutable is truth and that the mobile, transitory is appearance" (*ND* 361 / 354; see 372 / 365). As a result, traditional metaphysical ideas can be salvaged only via the complete *abandonment* of their eternal and universal content (see *ND* 364 / 357). This must be effected in a "denial of sacrosanct transcendence" (*ND* 17 / 29), as well as of any kind of spiritualization of any idea of the other, since, as Adorno unwaveringly maintains, "transcendence feeds on nothing but the experiences we have in immanence" (*ND* 398 / 390). Such a view opposes any "hypostasis of a non-corporeal and individualized spirit — and what without it would contain theology" (*ND* 401 / 393). With that, negative dialectics effects a transition to the realm of *materialism* (materiality, sensuality), in opposition to which the venerable Ideas, as well as classical theological dogma, were initially conceived. He even claims: "The category of nonidentity still obeys the measure of identity. Emancipated from that measure, the nonidentical moments *show up*

---

7. As in central moments in Benjamin, in Adorno one finds reference to the claim that Kabbalah, the name of the corpus of Jewish mysticism, means "tradition" (*ND* 372 / 365). For an explication of the claim that tradition is inherent in thought, see *ND* 53 / 63. In the same context Adorno further says that tradition should be described as "opposed to the transcendental moment," even as "quasi-transcendental" (*ND* 55 / 64), and as "unconscious remembrance": "no question could even be posed which would not preserve and extend the knowledge of the past" (*ND* 54 / 63, trans. modified). Husserl sought to grasp this "trace of the historical [*Spur des Geschichtlichen*]" in his concept of "inner historicity [*innere Historizität*]" (*ND* 54 / 64, trans. modified). Benjamin directed his own thinking in accordance with the tradition by preferring to articulate his ideas in terms of canonical texts — though for him this was, as Adorno writes, "a voluntarily installed, subjectively chosen tradition that is as unauthoritative as it accuses the autarkic thought of being" (*ND* 54 / 64).

8. See Kant's introduction to the *Critique of Pure Reason*.

as matter, or as inseparably fused with *material* things" (*ND* 193 / 193, my emph.). This does not exclude the daunting task of reevaluating nothing less than the metaphor of resurrection: "Christian dogmatics, in which the souls were conceived as awakening simultaneously with the resurrection of the flesh, was metaphysically more consistent—more enlightened, if you will—than speculative metaphysics, just as hope means a physical resurrection and feels defrauded of the best part by its spiritualization" (*ND* 401 / 393; see 207, 193 / 207, 193 ff.).

Adorno's brief comment that thinking succeeds in its configurations only when it heeds its own motivating factor—a "wish" or "need" (*ND* 407 / 399)—is noteworthy.[9] Indeed, there is something that "longs," in an "effort" born of a "vital need," for its own disappearance in the thinking of negation. Yet, in the satisfaction of this longing, something "survives" as a ferment within thought, because "*represented* in the inmost cell of thought is *that which is unlike thought*" (*ND* 408 / 400, my emph.). Therein quietly resounds a motif that can be heard more clearly in Levinas, namely, the insatiable (first erotic, then ethical) longing directed in principle toward an other that can never entirely be appropriated. A striking parallel occurs in Adorno's formulation of a "saving desire" (*ND* 253 / 250, trans. modified).

The paradoxical situation into which history forces thought can be distinguished, Adorno asserts, in ever-new attempts to express what cannot escape the logic of identity and totality in a single stroke. On the one hand, we must unflinchingly confront the decline of traditional metaphysical ideas. On the other, consciousness cannot immediately affirm this specifically modern problematic—a twilight in which the owls of Minerva will probably not soon again take flight. To do so, consciousness would need both to renounce itself and to withdraw the possibility of critique as well as of a certain semantic sensitivity (see *ND* 372 / 365).

Adorno prizes Kant for taking his *absoluteness* from the infinite progress of knowledge through the "at least *formal* recognition of the nonidentical" (*ND* 26 / 37, my emph.; see *ND* 246 / 244). In his "*desire*" to salvage metaphysical ideas as well as the sphere of the thing-in-itself (*ND* 384 ff. / 377 ff., my emph.), he maintains the "idea of otherness" without shrinking from the aporias that inevitably result (*ND* 184 / 185; see 26 / 37, 406 / 398). Such aporias of philosophical conceptuality are "marks of what is objec-

9. *Aesthetic Theory* contains an analogous thought. Works of art, Adorno says, attest to more than "mere longing" only because they "retrace" "the neediness inscribed as a figure in the historically existing," which it wants as "the other" (*AT* 132 / 199).

tively, not just cogitatively, unresolved" (*ND* 153 / 156). This is not the only reason that the justified critique of the thing-in-itself becomes a "sabotage of knowledge" (*ND* 313 / 308). The supposed inconsequence of Kant's thought makes apparent an insoluble as well as *quasi-transcendental difference:* "The construction of thing-in-itself and intelligible character is that of a nonidentity as the premise of possible identification; but it is also the construction of that which eludes identification" (*ND* 291n / 286n).

Kant's thought, like every other authentically philosophical thinking, Adorno boldly states, both circles tirelessly around the question of the *ontological proof of God* and prohibits "jumping from thoughts of the absolute which might one day be realized, like eternal peace, to the conclusion that therefore the absolute exists." Adorno's thinking is likewise profoundly motivated by the experience, here and elsewhere attributed to Kant, of having to leave one's own position open "in a magnificent ambiguity [*Zweideutigkeit*]" (*ND* 385 / 378, trans. modified).[10] This openness cannot, of course, be equated with a simple agnosticism, in which thinking would be subjugated to the regime of a logical *epochē.* The "humanly promised other of history [*menschliche verheissene Andere der Geschichte*]," around whose possibility Adorno's figure of thought circles and to whose traces it attests, means, rather, something at once *open* and *concrete.* It "points unswervingly to what ontology illegitimately locates before history, or exempts from history." The place at which what is in many respects utopian can be maintained is thus not just a realm of philosophical reflection on the *as if:* "The concept is not real [*wirklich*], as the ontological argument would have it, but there would be no conceiving it if we were not urged to conceive it by something in the matter" (*ND* 404 / 396).

The aporia of Kant's *mundus intelligibilis* lies in that it intends neither something real nor something imaginary. The displacement into the imaginary of what is meant by the intelligible is, according to Adorno, the "cardinal sin" of neoromanticism, Jugendstil, and . . . phenomenology (*ND* 392 / 384).[11] Ideas neither represent something purely perceptible, nor

10. Gripp rightly claims that Adorno's assurance that the ontological proof of God is the central problem of philosophy is deceptive "because the metaphor 'God' in Adorno becomes a metaphor for the 'nonidentical,' which is not just a terminological change, but a qualitatively new definition of the content subsumed under this concept" (*Theodor Adorno,* 23 n. 2). Nevertheless, Adorno claims, "Is not everything nothing if God is nothing?" (*Philosophische Terminologie,* 1:114–15).

11. This might discredit the concept of the imaginary somewhat overhastily. In the opinion of Proust's biographer G. D. Painter, Proust's novel, which Adorno praises, is an allegory for

can they simply be equated with "mirages." They therefore, Adorno emphasizes (probably in opposition to Kant's understanding), indicate only "negative signs" (*ND* 150 / 153). That is, as Schnädelbach describes them, they resemble "logical metaphors,"[12] which fit neither into philosophical concepts nor into predicative judgments. As such, they can never contain more than *an indirect and broken—that is, refracted and diffused—sign of an other*. In any case they do not indicate something that "exists nowhere but in the postulate," as one commentator suggests.[13] According to Adorno, these ideas cannot, contrary to Kant's view, be readily thought. "The pathos of Kantian intelligibility complements the difficulty of ascertaining it in any way, and if it were only in the medium of the self-sufficient thought designated by the word *intelligible*" (*ND* 391 / 383).

The supposed internal contradiction in the idea of the transcendent is that it cannot be "nailed down [or reified, that is, made *dingfest*]" without being betrayed, while, conversely, "the possibility, however feeble and distant, of redemption in existence" must be upheld, if that thought is not to be reduced to an empty shell (*ND* 400 / 392). In a relatively emphatic concept of transcendence, into which Adorno occasionally intensifies his reflections, the necessary (even if partial) *sensory fulfillment* of transcendence excludes *per definitionem* the no less decisive (permanent) *deferral* of any empirical coloration and solidification of that dimension.

This thesis, however, is fuzzy. More than any other thinker, Adorno drives to its aporetic apex the founding problematic of a postidealist and nonformal reason bound both to critique *and* to the ab-solute. Without wanting to deny this thinking a certain consistency and even justification, we could pose a few questions concerning the conceptual level upon which Adorno constructs that antinomy. This would in no way presume to bring from the outside a ready-made solution to the problem that Adorno's analysis confronts. Mentions of a solution that, though it opens no immediate way out, can at least serve to unravel a few threads in the Gordian knot lie scattered throughout Adorno's and, even more, Levinas's texts.

---

the life of its author, "a work not of fiction but of imagination interpreting reality." He adds further: "His work is an illustration of Wordsworth's distinction between Fancy and Imagination—between the art which invents what has never existed and the art which discovers the inner meanings of what exists" (*Marcel Proust: A Biography,* 2 vols. [Harmondsworth, Middlesex: Penguin, 1977], 1:xiii.

12. Schnädelbach, "Dialektik als Vernunftkritik," in von Friedeburg and Habermas, *Adorno-Konferenz 1983,* 70; and Schnädelbach, *Vernunft und Geschichte,* 183.

13. Werner Post, *Kritische Theorie und metaphysischer Pessimismus: Zum Spätwerk Max Horkheimers* (Munich: Kösel, 1971), 122.

Only *one* thought and *one* procedure among those that could be sifted from their work might be immune to the skeptical consequences sketched earlier. These are the metaphor of the trace of difference and the rhetoric of infinite interpretation.

One might first, in a reading at once weakened and focused, moderate this seemingly hopeless aporia to a "questionable [*fragwürdigen*]" paradox, that is to say, a paradox worthy of further thinking through. Of course, that could succeed only if one could interpret Adorno's and Levinas's presentations in such a way that the ab-solute could never actually be defined or described, whether dialectically or phenomenologically, without having the respective dimensions or motifs of singular concreteness immediately lose their ultimate intractability. If, however, the figure of the trace, which possesses a structural ambiguity in itself, can be used to illustrate the actual modality of all possible transcendence, not the ground on which the antinomy is based but, rather, its fateful nature slips away. Only if one fails to take into account the *one-dimensionality* of certain epistemologies and thus subtracts their "code-model" from necessary examination or critique does the dead end of classical-modern philosophy — often associated with the problem of "skepticism" — leave no room for further thought. Various considerations in Adorno's work, reminiscent of Kafka and Benjamin, suffer from this failing. They attribute the undeniable groundlessness of reason to the hiddenness of an overdue reconciliation, in a situation in which only an absurd leap into messianic redemption can offer salvation. This changes, however, in the no less decisive moments when Adorno adopts a more ambiguous position and relies on the notion of the trace (whose central figure Levinas and, in his footsteps, Derrida will analyze more systematically). In those more isolated instances Adorno concludes — without giving in to the one-sidedness of either affirming or negating a presence or absence of any truth and meaning — that only the experience of an a priori displaced and equivocal fragment of the good life allows one to circumscribe any point of "reference" for the idea of the other. This relationship to the other must be seen not as a blemished and incomplete thought but as a more productive insight into the essentially *uncompletable* quality of our knowledge and experience, of our acts and judgments. Only in this way can one think otherwise of the aporia of the emphatic idea of transcendence — an aporia produced within traditional philosophical conceptuality — and circumvent it in interpretation.

The primacy of practical reason does not ward off the pressing question concerning the absolute within theoretical reason, which, for Adorno, is itself a "mode of relation" (*ND* 383 / 376). Resignation before an absolute cognitive barrier and the putative possession of absolute knowledge are in secret harmony with the renunciation of the transcendence of thought itself. The reason Adorno offers for this is interesting. Absolute idealism, "according to the train of thought of Hegel's *Phenomenology*, comes also to the net result that absolute knowledge is nothing but the train of thought of phenomenology itself, and thus in no way a transcending" (*ND* 386 / 379). Only the *gesture* of these antipodes, therefore, which correct each other, can be followed, not their *position* in isolation. According to one of the most strongly developed claims in *Negative Dialectics,* the intelligible logically, "in the spirit of Kantian delimitation no less than in that of the Hegelian method, would be to transcend the limits drawn by both of these, to think in negations alone. Paradoxically, the intelligible sphere which Kant envisioned would once again be 'appearance': it would be what that which is hidden from the finite mind shows to the mind, what the mind is forced to think and, due to its own finiteness, to disfigure" (*ND* 392 / 384).

Of course, the appropriate skeptical question would be: how, then, can all this be newly described as a "self-negation" (*ND* 392 / 384) or a self-transcending of thought? What does Adorno mean when he writes that the efforts of Kant's idealist followers to establish "spirit as its own union with that which is not identical with it were as consistent as they were futile" (*ND* 389 / 382)? The insight that spirit should think "what would be beyond it" (*ND* 392 / 385) and, further, that it stands or falls by a certain unhappy consciousness, that it does not satisfy (or never satisfies?) itself, lends primacy, rather, to a certain *exteriority* in opposition to thinking. At the core of Adorno's philosophy is, I would claim, a full-scale attempt to account for that asymmetry, without ever dispensing with thought.

Adorno censures Kant's tendency toward resignation; his "block"—according to Lukács's doubtful equation—is basically "one" with the bourgeois principle of work and denial (*ND* 389 / 381). Indeed, Adorno positions his idea of metaphysical experience against Kant: "The naive consciousness, to which Goethe too probably tended—that we do not know yet, but that some day, perhaps, the mystery will be solved after all [*man wisse es noch nicht, aber vielleicht enträtsele es sich doch noch*]—comes closer to metaphysical truth than does Kant's *ignoramus*" (*ND* 386 /

379). Likewise, the question of what a deciphering *in metaphysicis* could actually be called remains open. What would it look like if the idea of transcendence not only, as we have seen, knows no actual life form that corresponds to it but also, as we suspect, contains not an inch of truth that could be actually made real? The character of the variable leap (see Benjamin) and the infinite/infinitizable idea of redemption (see Levinas) appear curiously entwined here. How might we better understand this embrace?

At one point Adorno explains the idea of metaphysical experience — which, he assures us, by no means finds its model in "allegedly primal religious experiences" — via various subtle but decisive flashbacks and experiences of the past in Marcel Proust's *À la recherche du temps perdu* (*In Search of Lost Time*). In childhood memories, formed "in the face of *absolute, indissoluble* individuation" (*ND* 373 / 366, my emph.), one can read how, under modern conditions, metaphysics must shroud itself in a veil of *unrealizability* — that is, both of futility and of infinity or infinitization. The duality of Adorno's perspective on redemption makes clear why this circumstance is at times affirmed but also is often, by contrast, admitted in a melancholic tone.

Metaphysical experience, he says: "makes the promise recede like a rainbow. And yet one is not disappointed; the feeling now is one of being too close, rather, and not seeing for that reason" (*ND* 373 / 366; see *AT* 120 / 185).[14] After the substantial grounds of traditional metaphysics have been weakened, its experiential potential can take refuge only in the negative question "Can this be all? [*Ist das denn alles?*]." It finds its paradigm in the "idle waiting" (*ND* 375 / 368) which is expressed musically, above all, in Berg's *Wozzeck* and *Lulu* and, in literature, is most closely approximated in Beckett's *Waiting for Godot*. Expectation without any confirmation of a future arrival forbids taking "sparse and abrupt living remnants for the phenomenal absolute." At the same time, this ascesis is confined to traits of resignation. Nothing, Adorno says in the same context, could "be experienced as truly alive if something that transcends life were not promised also; no straining of the concept leads beyond that. *The transcendent is, and it is not [Es ist und es ist nicht]*" (*ND* 375 / 368, my emph.). Only in fragile moments of happiness can metaphysical experience appear as more than "impotent longing [*Verlangen*]" (*ND* 374 / 367). Yet in order to participate in truth — an experience that resembles a nonviolent, contem-

14. See, for a historical and systematic analysis of the figure of the rainbow, Philip Fisher, *Wonder, the Rainbow, and the Aesthetics of Rare Experiences* (Cambridge: Harvard University Press, 1998).

plative regard directed toward things—happiness cannot assimilate the disparate fragments.

Metaphysical experience *per definitionem* is maintained in a "field of tension" (*MM* 127 / 142), in a "distanced nearness" in which "the inside of objects" must be thought "as something removed from the objects" (*MM* 90 / 98; *ND* 374 / 367). Such a description can hardly be reduced to a common denominator with definitions of happiness or of truth as a "being encompassed" or even an "original shelter" (*MM* 112 / 124). If it can be understood as copied from the domain of the erotic (as will be the case, at least in part, in Levinas as well), that is only because its guiding idea can no longer be translated in terms of economic exchange or even relationships of possession. Its synthesis, if the word is appropriate here, takes place, as Adorno says (again in striking similarity to Levinas), in "historical negation"; that is, it is "the opposite of slackness, blessed straining" (*MM* 217 / 246). Thus, the singular, authentic inclination of a lover—though bound to the always concretely particular features of the loved one and fully cognizant of love's debt to the contingent, exclusive nature of the lover's experience of that singular person, an experience at once unique and illimitable—does not foreclose openness to the universality of the other; indeed, it "endures [rather than tolerates, *duldet*]" that possibility (*MM* 79 / 89, trans. modified). Adorno thus highlights a paradoxical relationship according to which true universality in knowledge and action, though not grounded in the singular, nonetheless is criticized for how knowledge and action are concretized, without the reverse being equally true. Adorno's philosophy of the nonidentical thereby brings out the constitutive asymmetry in the web of modern conceptuality, agency, and judgment. In other words, in the trace of metaphysical as well as moral and aesthetic experience, an *irrefutable concretion* holds but must at the same time be described as *structurally incapable of being grasped in any argumentatively determinable or normatively decisive way.*

The "polarity" of happiness (*NL* 2:317 / 675), on the one hand, and futility, unattainability, and transience, on the other, bring Proust's category of memory into play. Art, according to Adorno, must follow the "trace of memory" (*AT* 131 / 198) in a mimetic procedure that at base is "not reality." Only this kind of memory can concretize utopia without ceaselessly "betraying it to existence" (*AT* 132 / 200). At one point in his interpretation Adorno claims that the measure of Proust's novel lies in its need for the total recapitulation and complete redemption of what was lost and what was promised (see *NL* 2:317 / 675); then again, he attributes to its author the insight "that even this fullness, the instant saved by remembrance, is not it" (*ND* 378 / 371). Or again: "Being fully oneself, absolutely differentiated, means at the same time isolation and profound alienation. The unfettered potential, and readiness, for happiness hinders one's own fulfillment" (*NL* 2:317 / 675). The quest for a fulfilled life, he now says, is not only suspicious because of its "immeasurable discrepancy with death"; it is also affected by the *violence of desire*. The "quenching" of such desire, until it can be retracted, is caught up in the hopeless "cycle of fulfillment and appropriation" (*ND* 379 / 371). But how could such a retraction be thought: at once *disjointedly* and *in alternation*?

The ambivalent characteristic of metaphysical and spiritual experience thus returns in an analogous way in the experience of the most advanced works of art. Adorno's reference in *Aesthetic Theory* to a modality in which art surpasses existence, even art's "trace of revelation" (*AT* 106 / 162), forms a case in point. The enigmatic character of authentic art, Adorno assures us, is that works of art "say something and in the same breath conceal it" (*AT* 120 / 182). Art's game of hide-and-seek is like the intrigue in Poe's famous story in which the purloined letter "is visible and is, by being visible, hidden" (*AT* 121 / 185).[15] Adorno thus summarizes an important element of the narrative. With inimitable double meaning, Poe first relates how the thief can use the letter to blackmail his victim only so long as he does not actually make the letter public and thus destroy the effect it gains by being hidden; then he shows how the letter being sought cannot be found so long as it lies in plain view, thus, so to speak, eluding its own presence.

Wellmer is certainly correct to establish that, according to Adorno, no concepts "in which we could think the status of reconciliation" can be given (any more) because the idea of reconciliation appears alone "*ex negativo* on the horizon of art and philosophy."[16] The grounds for this insight might, however, be different from the one that he, with Habermas, cites: the overly hasty suspicion that Adorno's idea of a form of life which would no longer be constrained and even reasonable remains stuck in an inadequate conceptual framework, namely, the philosophy of consciousness. If we consider the negativity of the idea of the nonidentical — in philosophical discourse no less than in the conceptless and mimetic

---

15. See Edgar Allan Poe, "The Purloined Letter," in *The Fall of the House of Usher and Other Writings,* ed. and intro. D. Galloway (Harmondsworth, Middlesex: Penguin, 1986), 330–49. See also Jacques Lacan, "Le Séminaire sur 'La Lettre volée,'" *Écrits* (Paris: Seuil, 1966), 11–61.

16. Wellmer, *Zur Dialektik von Moderne und Postmoderne,* 19.

gesture of art — to be its *contrastive value* against the backdrop of a walled-off totality of meaning, then another interpretation becomes possible and, indeed, due. In the metaphor of the trace, the ab-solute singular manifests itself in reality as the "concentration of meaning,"[17] of which Wellmer speaks in other words. But this obviously stands opposed to either purely conceptual, completely moralistic, or even exclusively aesthetic representations. Viewed from each of these separate dimensions of rationality, it appears as *unthinkable, ununderstandable, unspeakable,* and, accordingly, *aporetic.* Adorno thus addresses the circumstance, difficult to interpret, which makes perceptible a constitutive ferment in the medium of metaphysical, moral, and aesthetic experiences yet never allows itself to be grounded or even approximately articulated in the terminology of those individual spheres. Only an *alternating thinking* or a *reflecting judgment* that would no longer be reasonable can illustrate this motif as, in actuality, a paradoxical one. According to Wellmer, the "immeasurability of the separation between reality and utopia" lies in "that reality is, so to speak, transcendentally, before all experience, fixed in negativity."[18]

It is easy to see in what way my outline of an alternative interpretation of Adorno contradicts this. Certainly, the other cannot be grasped anywhere as something present, nor can it be proclaimed and conjured up as something simply absent. Yet neither reality nor the differentiated modes of experience in which we seek to grasp it can dispense with its trace. Its *quasi-transcendental* modality forecloses any *prima philosophia,* any formal transformation of philosophy, as well as any separate theoretical, practical, or expressive mode of experience. As a figure of thinking, alternation means precisely that the metaphor of the trace of the ab-solute implies, above all, a *phenomenon of interference.*

The Permanent Alternation of Philosophical Discourse and Aesthetic Mimesis: A Fractured Complementarity

At first sight philosophy driven into a corner, as presented in *Negative Dialectics* — in Adorno's words, as "full, unreduced experience in the medium of conceptual reflection" (*ND* 13 / 25) — is based upon an unholy inner antinomy. Adorno's philosophy appears to bear witness to an experience that lies both *this side of* and *beyond* its own conceptual frame. Such a seemingly paradoxical endeavor amounts in the worst case to a

17. Ibid., 69.
18. Ibid., 20.

futile *contradictio in adjecto.* As has so frequently been said, *Negative Dialectics* would then amount to scarcely more than a laborious explication of the inability of negative dialectical "categories" to think and articulate the nonidentical.[19] Habermas is not alone in maintaining that Adorno's later texts—despite the often astonishing continuity, unanimity, and consequence in the progression of his thought—merely provide an intensification of the earlier perspective of Critical Theory. Yet at countless moments in *Negative Dialectics,* and likewise in *Aesthetic Theory,* Adorno refuses the ambivalent perspective of *Dialectic of Enlightenment*—its hesitation between a relentless skepticism concerning reason and the anticipation of a positive concept of enlightenment. The critique of the philosophy of identity in his late work is concentrated in a drastic critique of the identifying character of the philosophical concept as such, "which denies to philosophy not only the claim to totality but the hope for a dialectical grasp of the nonidentical."[20] *Negative Dialectics,* according to Habermas, reluctantly abandons the expectation once expressed in "The Actuality of Philosophy": that the connection between the true, the good, and the beautiful could (one day?) be deciphered in the smallest elements of a fragmented reality. Being a theory that attempts to account for the impossibility of theoretical thought, it seeks only to "circumscribe" discursively what can no longer be grasped conceptually or argumentatively.[21] As evidence for this interpretation, one might take this sentence from *Aesthetic Theory:* "A taboo on any possible answer is all that discursive thought can offer" (185 / 193). Philosophy thus strives, as an "exercise in perseverance,"[22] to create at best a free space for the other of reason, insofar as it insists upon the negativity and futility of any emphatic cognitive claim of philosophical discourse. Reason can, as a result, find "only an echo in the powers of a wordless mimesis,"[23] that is, in a mimesis that can be dialectically circumscribed and even encircled but can no longer be "opened up."[24]

Habermas infers from this pattern of interpretation that for Adorno only aesthetic experience or hermetic art can accommodate or express the other. In his view Adorno seeks to restrict philosophy's "cognitive com-

---

19. See Habermas, *Theory of Communicative Action,* 1:373, 384 / 1:498, 514–15.
20. Ibid., 1:452 / 1:499 n. 87.
21. Habermas, *Philosophical Discourse of Modernity,* 68 / 85.
22. Habermas, *Die neue Unübersichtlichkeit,* 219.
23. Ibid.
24. Ibid.

petence"[25] and to grant to art, in a romantic "farewell to philosophy,"[26] the foundational function formerly assigned to critique, namely, the role of a placeholder for a domain of freedom which as yet resides in a distant future.

Although there is much to support such an interpretation, I believe one can find, in relevant passages, equally strong grounds to support the argument that Adorno develops a more careful and ambiguous reading of the tension between the discursive and nondiscursive. One might even assert that Adorno's work allows one to maintain that a *fractured complementary* or, better, a relationship of *alternation* exists between philosophy and aesthetic experience.[27] Only such an interpretation can help us grasp with any precision what it means to say that *Negative Dialectics* and *Aesthetic Theory* can only "refer helplessly to one another."[28] The thesis mutually implied in the thematic domains of the two books seems to be that neither the conceptual work of philosophy nor the concept-free synthesis of artistic mimesis can immediately apprehend the utopian contents scattered throughout history and the tradition. That may further be connected to the fact that Adorno indeed suggests on occasion that the

25. Habermas, *Theory of Communicative Action,* 1:384; see 366–67 / 1:514; see 489–90. See also Habermas, *Philosophical Discourse of Modernity,* 68, 186 / 85, 220; and Theunissen, "Negativität bei Adorno," in von Friedeburg and Habermas, *Adorno-Konferenz 1983,* 54, 56–57.

26. Habermas, *Philosophical Discourse of Modernity,* 52 / 66.

27. Schnädelbach develops the hypothesis that *Negative Dialectics* and *Aesthetic Theory* enhance and correct each other in his essay "Dialektik als Vernunftkritik," in von Friedeburg and Habermas, *Adorno-Konferenz 1983,* 92 n. 1, 93 n. 8. See also Schnädelbach, *Vernunft und Geschichte,* 205 n. 1, 205–6 n. 8; and Wellmer, "Wahrheit, Schein, Versöhnung: Adornos ästhetische Rettung der Modernität," in von Friedeburg and Habermas, *Adorno Konferenz 1983,* 138–76: "Just as a moment of blindness inheres in the immediacy of aesthetic perception, so too a moment of emptiness inheres in the mediation of philosophical thought; only together can they circumscribe a truth that neither alone can express." In the tension between philosophy and art in Adorno, "a theological perspective is sublated" (143), and in the pendular movement of his thought Adorno enters into a *negative* theology. Elsewhere Wellmer alludes to Adorno's "Fragment on Music and Language," in which Adorno says of the "complementary untenability" of conceptual and nonconceptual cognition and experience: "Discursive language wishes to express the absolute in a mediated way, but the absolute eludes its grasp at every turn, leaving each attempt behind in its finitude. Music expresses the absolute directly, but the very moment it does so, the absolute is obscured, just as excessively strong light dazzles the eye so that it can no longer register what is clearly visible" ("Fragment über Musik und Sprache," *GS* 16:254). Wellmer comments: "The language of music and discursive language appear as the separated halves of 'true language,' a language in which 'the content itself would become manifest,' as we read in the same fragment. The idea of this 'true language' is 'the figure of the divine name'" (*Persistence of Modernity,* 7; *Zu Dialektik von Moderne und Postmoderne,* 155, 14).

28. Baumeister and Kulenkampff, "Geschichtsphilosophie und philosophische Ästhetik," 74 ff.; and Habermas, *Theory of Communicative Action,* 1:384–85 / 1:515.

experience of art resembles a *via regia* toward utopia. On closer examination, however, one sees that Adorno never grants to art any romantic
exclusivity. Moral and metaphysical experiences construct a *supplement*
to philosophical discourse as well. They both reflexively indicate a *structural parallel* to the experience of art, as I have previously explained. In
the end it would be altogether incorrect to claim that Adorno's program
for the dialectical grasp of the nonidentical could only be realized aesthetically because one would then completely overlook an important aspect of this aesthetics. Art is no more capable than philosophy of stepping
forward as the *medium* — that is, as the carefree sanctuary, the *organon,*
or an unambiguous presentation — of the other of reason. Neither in philosophy nor in art is the absolute "immediately present" (*AT* 133 / 201).
Philosophy investigates an ab-solute without ever actually approaching
it — more precisely, without ever knowing whether it comes closer to this
nonidentical in its increasingly conceptual determinations and mediations. If this is true, every philosophical interpretation is finally *undecidable;* yet, though its telos is not so much mutual understanding as the point
at which one can leave argumentation (and hence communication, discussion, discourse) behind, this is not to deny that its determinate negations
may nonetheless yield some — nonpropositional, noetic — "truth content
[*Wahrheitsgehalt*]" after all. Art, by contrast, expresses without mediation
an ab-solute that cannot be recognized and thus is given over from the
outset to the interpretive work of philosophy. Both threads combine as
follows: "The truth of discursive knowledge is unshrouded, and thus discursive knowledge does not have it; the knowledge that is art has truth,
but as something incommensurable with art" (*AT* 126 / 191).[29] Thus, in
whatever different ways, in these two spheres transcendence is possible
only as *fractured:* as an always *to be determined* empty space for an other in
philosophy, as an *incomprehensible* sensuous-material appeal in art (and,
as we have seen, in moral, spiritual, and metaphysical experience, etc.).[30]
The metaphor of the trace of the other of reason may help us to approach,
describe, and render plausible the interplay between these two (or three)

29. Art, Adorno claims at another point, depends upon philosophy, "which interprets it,
in order to say what it is unable to say, whereas art is only able to say it by not saying it" (*AT*
72 / 113).

30. Adorno writes: "The opaque particular declares itself as the norm in the beautiful, since
the normal universality has become too transparent" (*MM* 94 / 104, trans. modified). The fact
that "the beautiful," if in a more shocking and uglier form, still exists "attests to the avoidability
of terror" (121 / 135).

aspects. Only thus, it seems, can one find in the waning flip side of the aporetics in Adorno's construction of rationality and mimesis a meaning that could have relevance beyond the domain of the aesthetic, narrowly defined. When one understands it in this way, Adorno's insight that art, and not only that, "works surreptitiously against what it wants to say" can be extended and made more productive (P 157 / 634).

Dialectical philosophy and aesthetic (moral, even metaphysical) experience neither entirely gape asunder nor collapse into each other: all these aspects or dimensions of rationality stand, rather, shimmering in *constellations* that can no longer adequately be described using what are only apparently diametrically opposed twin concepts, such as heterogeneity and totality or identity.

One can never entirely get around or catch up with the obduracy of art (of morals, of metaphysics) through conceptual analysis, whether one seeks to construe an object or to construct an argument. Conversely, philosophy cannot and should not be altogether aesthetically stylized, and what we have termed the *alternation between inside and outside, argument and experience* should not be seen as an *aesthetic* process per se. According to Bubner, Adorno's negative dialectical manner of speaking oscillates ceaselessly "back and forth between assertion and refraction." He considers this mode of experiencing "constitutive undeterminability" to be eminently aesthetic.[31] At best such an ascription helps us only to understand the "What?" — that is, the intellectual historical origin of specific figures of thought. It overlooks the problem of "How?" — the question of the actual modalities and composition of that pendular movement.

Nevertheless, the enigmatic character of art might also be indicative of the tension, the "configuration of mimesis and rationality," which Adorno describes (*AT* 127 / 192). The unavoidable enigmatic modality of the aesthetic does not reside only in its inner composition. Its truth content, which refers to something outside the aesthetic sphere, is finally also enigmatic: "The indefatigably recurring question that every work incites in whoever traverses it — the 'What is it all about?' — becomes 'Is it true?' — the question of the absolute, to which every artwork responds by wresting itself free from the discursive form of answer" (*AT* 127 / 192). Indeed, the

31. Rüdiger Bubner, "Adornos negative Dialektik," in von Friedeburg and Habermas, *Adorno-Konferenz 1983*, 39. See also his essay "Kann Theorie ästhetisch werden? Zum Hauptmotiv der Philosophie Adornos," in *Materialien zur ästhetischen Theorie Th. W. Adornos: Konstruktion der Moderne*, ed. B. Lindner and W. M. Lüdke (Frankfurt a.M.: Suhrkamp, 1980), 108–37.

question of whether art in its seeming truly reflects an objective meaning would be undecidable. There is no "key" to an answer to it (*AT* 127 / 193). One can list a series of observations in which this idea shines through.

Adorno thus confirms the character of semblance in even the most advanced—namely, *hermetic*—works of art. Yet only "what is not semblance," of which semblance is a "promise" (*ND* 404–5 / 396–97), can have imbued them with what is "irresistible" about them. A metaphysical potential resides in the aesthetic salvation of the transcendent's unavoidable character of semblance (see *ND* 394–95 / 386). Art objects to what is the case and in the same breath resists the crudely nihilistic assumption that everything is finally nothing. Yet, because of its enigmatic "structure of reference," aesthetic experience alone can never authenticate the other: "*Whether the promise is a deception, that is the enigma*" (*AT* 127 / 193, my emph.). Art, therefore, is always pursued by its no less enigmatic shadow, the "terror born of the primordial world" (*AT* 127 / 193), the flip side of its alterity.

Understanding, the central category of hermeneutics, takes hold of the *hermetic,* what in authentic works of art cannot fully be grasped or comprehended, either too briefly or too broadly. Only an understanding "in the highest sense," which, while puzzling out the work, can preserve and respect its enigmatic way of appearing, can correspond to the inexhaustible character of true art.[32] Such a *deciphering without end* must proceed by concretizing this enigmatic quality; as Adorno significantly says: "The solution of the enigma amounts to giving the reason for its insolubility, which is the gaze artworks direct at the viewer" (*AT* 122 / 185). This concretization is linked to an *infinitization* (*Verunendlichung*) of aesthetic experience, in which the more understanding of an artwork deepens, "the more obscure its constitutive enigmaticalness becomes." "Every artwork is a 'picture puzzle,' a puzzle to be solved, but this puzzle is constituted in such a fashion that it remains a vexation, the preestablished routing of its observer" (*AT* 121 / 184). What remains decisive for Adorno's thinking, however, is that, in any structurally ambiguous manifestation of the aesthetic, he sees not the blemish of rapturous irrationality but, rather, the sign of its rationality and that without this *counterpoint* there could be no sensible reason, no reason worthy of its name.

Adorno does not intend for philosophy to transfer to art its demand

---

32. This inexhaustibility cannot be equated with the "positive" designation of art's "much touted complexity" (*AT* 127 / 192).

for knowledge. It can never give up in resignation; Adorno recognizes the existence of a *philosophia perennis* as well as not only a difference in degree but a *categorical* distinction between aesthetic and discursive knowledge (see *ND* 296 / 291). Accordingly, philosophy becomes for him a practice of thinking or contemplation that is disturbed and disturbing, *both from within and without,* even if in his presentations he often attributes a provisional quality to this status, implying that it can be justified only on the basis of a — scarcely plausible — messianic interpretation of the "until it has been revoked [*bis auf Widerruf*]." However that may be, until such time as in general (at that time) it could be revoked, philosophy always needs "knowledge from outside," "something other, something new" (*ND* 182-83 / 183–84). Only thanks to each moment when the unforeseen enters, *"as if an other were added to rationality"* (*ND* 229 / 228, trans. modified, my emph.), is philosophy able to tear away the deception of what seems always the same, to which it must always succumb again.

If philosophy wants to account for this alternation or succession in perspectives, it must at once seek to resist its proclivity to one-track developments in thinking by drawing on alternative figures of argumentation and, so to speak, seek to *derail* it, without having recourse to regressive, that is, substantialistic, models of thought. In this connection Adorno offers most often the examples of "constellation," "web," and "play," speaking further of a "clowning" and "foolishness" in philosophy. In other words, he draws on the *speculative, metaphorical,* and *rhetorical* capabilities in our thinking and speaking,[33] that is to say, on *language,* though hardly on the structures that formal and transcendental pragmatics discover in it. Moreover, he exploits an irresistible logic of exaggeration and excess: "The un-naïve thinker knows how far he remains from the object of his thinking, and yet he must always talk as if he had it entirely" (*ND* 14 / 26).

This, of course, leaves open the question of whether such figures of thought ever have the wit to moderate, via a *paradoxical unfolding,* the apparently insoluble aporias of philosophy, as they reveal themselves in metaphysical, moral, and aesthetic dimensions of experience. How could any micrology imply something more than aporia — *within* the spheres of the always-disparate discourses or modes of experience — without shoving aside the medium of argument? Nonetheless, to cast the question of the

33. See *ND* 13–15, 55, 404 / 25–27, 65–66, 396; *MM* 125, 226–27 / 142, 258–59; *AT* 37, 42 / 64, 71.

relationship between philosophy and art (metaphysics and morals) exclusively in terms of an alternative or a dilemma would lead one overhastily to abandon Adorno's thought to irrationalism. To do so would be to misconstrue Adorno's main concern: namely, while keeping an eye open to the other of reason, to avoid, at whatever cost, the *leap* into the other. Therefore, it is important to render productive the tensions to which Adorno's work testifies on virtually every side, without any detrimental reduction. Otherwise, one once more risks approaching his pièce de résistance with models of interpretation which are in equal measure fruitless and glum with regard to the points under dispute in his negative metaphysics, ethics, and aesthetics. For this reason alone, it would be appropriate to understand the frictions in Adorno's discussion in terms of its unsublatable double and even multiple meanings. In a pendular movement between the most extreme poles of the cruel reality of history and the ephemeral traces of the good life, our experience runs up against irritating and intriguing limits. Dialectics can certainly sense them, but it can neither *pass over* them into a speculative idealism nor *break through* them in a dogged materialist practice. Negative dialectics takes this insight as its own.

Between Rationality and Deconstruction

My first chapter began by discussing the transformations effected by attempts to carry out the agenda of early Critical Theory within a paradigm shift from the "philosophy of the subject" to the philosophy of language. In particular, via theories of rationality, several thinkers have proposed new distinctions in the diagnosis, undertaken in a line leading from Weber to Adorno, of a subjective loss of meaning or objective confinement in a thoroughly administered world. The question remains, however, whether Habermas's paradigm shift from the philosophy of the subject to a theory of communicative action actually renders obsolete Adorno's figures of thought.

Wellmer and Schnädelbach, in particular, have pointed the way toward a reception of Adorno's moral and aesthetic or metaphysical "intuitions." Although these motifs cannot really find a place within the realm of formal pragmatics, they unmistakably indicate something that is constitutive of the reasonableness of our thought and action. Habermas subsumes these recalcitrant aspects of Adorno's philosophy consciously, and not without serious social theoretical reasons, under the symmetrical coordinating structure of the ideal of emancipation. In doing so, however, he sacrifices their expressive force. Formal pragmatics grants them only the role of placeholder for problems at the limit of thought that cannot be further worked out. This self-limitation—however justified it may be in the quest for scientific discipline or for the sake of sociological application—is, for a very simple reason, philosophically and experientially untenable. It unavoidably loses sight of a series of necessary suppositions in the in the very structures of communication which it nonetheless prepares to reconstruct. Second-generation Critical Theorists have argued more than once that the connection between negativism and messianism is decisive for Adorno's philosophy. In Adorno's later work, they imply, the subjective working out of a historical experience that is negative in the extreme is anchored in a theory of the concept that a priori ascribes to discursive rationality as such all forms of domination. Adorno's philosophy, they feel, is forced to postulate any reconciliation as *logically*—and not merely empirically—an other *in opposition to* reason and history. For the theologian Adorno reconciliation is said to be "the wholly other of existing reason."[34] Such a perspective of philosophical reconciliation, however, so the argument goes, gets in the way of actually thinking together social complexity, in the form of a (certainly paradoxical) differentiation of modern value spheres, on the one hand, and just forms of the good life, on the other. The development of the economic and political system, together with the consequent problems of the pathological semblance of reification, are—if we take that messianism at its word—not contingent and empirical but grounded in the logic of the conceptual space of modernity itself. The paradoxes of modernity result from an inevitable dialectics anchored in history.

According to Wellmer, Habermas's theory, unlike Adorno's, successfully regains a "historical horizon of possibility," or a "degree of freedom."[35] Habermas proposes that what Adorno attributes to the development of a contradictory quality within modern formal reason itself indicates not too much but *too little* discursive, procedural, that is, communicative, rationality. Adorno, according to this thesis, limited himself to the model of an irreconcilable, identifying thinking because, finally, he could understand discursivity only as monological—and, hence, as con-

34. Wellmer, *Ethik und Dialog,* 93; see also 94–96.
35. Albrecht Wellmer, "Die Bedeutung der Frankfurter Schule heute," in *Die Frankfurter Schule und die Folgen,* ed. Axel Honneth and Albrecht Wellmer (Berlin: Walter de Gruyter, 1986), 30; and Wellmer, *Zur Dialektik von Moderne und Postmoderne,* 23.

ceptually reductive and metaphysically totalizing — and intersubjectivity solely as "extended subjectivity."[36] Given that he defined the relationship between people and their social and natural world, as well as human self-experience, following the one-sided and one-dimensional contour of an "asymmetrical subject-object model of knowledge and action,"[37] in his work the mimetic moment in any interaction tends to be displaced by an other of rationality, "almost extraterritorial to the sphere of conceptual thought."[38] By contrast, Habermas anchors that "resistant structure" in a potential for rationality inherent in language as such. Only in this way, he claims, can language be "apprehended,"[39] so that one need no longer leave it aesthetically undecidable.

As Wellmer pointedly demonstrates, however, any addition to rationality which might lead out of the dead end of modernity can never be grasped exhaustively within a formal pragmatic theory of communication. This inability always concerns a *qualitative* moment that, we learn from Adorno, "is at work in every communication *a tergo*."[40] According to Wellmer, this *how*, rather than a mere *that*, of a no longer reified rationality can be described not as a *form* of communication but, rather, as a kind of nonviolent *synthesis*. Out of the concretion thus presented, in which alone the experience of successful communication can achieve expression, new, nonreified interactions can spring up. He thus suggests at least a direction for the possible reception of Habermas *and* Adorno. I understand it in this way: Adorno's approaches to negative metaphysics, ethics, and aesthetics might — perhaps — be interpreted as phenomenological *concretions* and *delimitations* and thus as *supplements* to the (admittedly, invaluable) heuristic model of interpretation in Habermas's theories of rationality and society, differentiation and modernization.

At the same time, Wellmer agrees to a certain extent with Habermas's critique, holding that Adorno was blind to the idea of a "groundless and yet not helpless reason, a reason without ultimate foundation and without

36. For the former point, see Wellmer, *Zur Dialektik von Moderne und Postmoderne*, 95; and also 96. For the latter, see Schnädelbach, *Vernunft und Geschichte*, 171; and Honneth, *Kritik der Macht*, 55.

37. Wellmer, *Zur Dialektik von Moderne und Postmoderne*, 20; see also 21; and Habermas, *Theory of Communicative Action*, 1:390 / 1:523.

38. Wellmer, *Zur Dialektik von Moderne und Postmoderne*, 21.

39. Habermas, *Die neue Unübersichtlichkeit*, 220. What he means, expressed less daringly, is the "conviction that humane cohabitation depends upon available forms of everyday communication that are innovative, reciprocal, informal, and egalitarian" (223).

40. Ibid., 33.

a view toward ultimate reconciliation."[41] Although this observation seems incontestable, at least in part, I believe that equally decisive figures of argumentation in Adorno's work provide just such an *open* conception of reason. Wellmer speaks at one point of the possibility of reading Adorno "stereoscopically," with the goal "of showing his philosophical insights to best advantage in opposition to his own systematics," adding: "With Adorno, it is as if he projects a three-dimensional system of fundamental categories onto a two-dimensional surface."[42] Perhaps it would even be justified, expanding this metaphor somewhat, to admit the possible significance of a "kaleidoscopic" mode of reading (see *AT* 197 / 294).

As we have seen in the previous chapter, Adorno's intellectual approach passes beyond an outdated preliminary stage in the theory of communication and the discourse ethics that can be formulated according to its premises. Discourse ethics itself points toward various aporias or, better, gaps, which with the help of Adorno's philosophy (and that of Levinas or Derrida) we cannot resolve or simply plug up but, rather, *thematize* — to the extent that the word still makes sense in this context. These would be: the ultimately deceptive self-interpretation of formal pragmatics when it claims to offer more than a plausible heuristic perspective on the paradoxes of modernity and overstates the reconstructive and analytical force and scope of its counterfactual claims; the presence of a secret metaphorics in the determination of the mutual relationship between discourse and practice and between practice and expressiveness; the objections to reservations concerning any doctrine of the good life; and, finally, the absence of a satisfying development of the horizon of reference for formal pragmatics' own, so to speak, implicit idea of an ab-solute, of a transcendent-immanent moment of the unconditional. These areas, each in its own way, obviously indicate a hermeneutic or (negative) metaphysical supplement in need of closer examination. A renewed examination of Adorno's and (Levinas's) texts can, in my opinion, be productive precisely for discussing these knotty points. This implies neither bringing to naught the unmistakable merits of Habermas's social theory nor suggesting that Adorno's philosophy should be protected from incisive reformulation. Yet it seems to me that a relevant and fruitful reconstruction of the most promising traits of Adorno's thought would follow a direction that is the

41. Wellmer, "Die Bedeutung der Frankfurter Schule heute," in Honneth and Wellmer, *Die Frankfurter Schule und die Folgen*, 34.

42. Wellmer, *Zur Dialektik von Moderne und Postmoderne*, 158; see also 44, 157.

inverse of the one Habermas chooses. Unlike the formal pragmatic transformation of earlier Critical Theory, such an approach would develop another mode of argumentation, one that would attempt to (re)construct not the conditions of symmetry between critical thought and action but, rather, if I might put it this way, their *conditions of asymmetry.* Only such a deconstructive reading could—perhaps—avoid the long shadow of classical transcendental First Philosophy.

However that may be, one can object to various details in Habermas's interpretation of Adorno's figure of thought. We have already seen this with regard to his reservations about the historical-philosophical position first assumed in *Dialectic of Enlightenment.* There I singled out, as my first reservation, how "skepticism concerning reason" can be seen only from its darkest angle throughout his reading of Adorno. However justified such an interpretation might appear if one has a certain line of questioning in mind, it largely overlooks a salient point: it is unable to say to what degree the conceptuality of the "philosophy of consciousness" is already broken through *within* Adorno's work. Only with difficulty can one apply the epithet "philosophy of the subject" if one cannot say precisely at what fractures in structures of undamaged intersubjectivity Adorno indirectly takes aim. Second, in offering grounds for a more positive valuation of the reception possibilities for Adorno's late work, I would object to Habermas's devaluation of the "performative contradiction" in the self-referential and apparently total critique of reason.[43] The claim that negative dialectics—being the program that uses the conceptual arsenal of the philosophy of consciousness systematically to undermine that very philosophy of consciousness—necessarily collapses is not only overhasty but also abstract. Like the classical refutation of skepticism, Habermas's reconstruction presents negative dialectics with a formally irrefutable argument, since the negation it puts forward raises the claim of its own truth, which it itself ipso facto denies. But, even if this dilemma holds for Adorno, one might ask whether "anything has been proven" with this in itself irrefutable argument.[44] Here, more than anywhere else, it is im-

43. Habermas, *Philosophical Discourse of Modernity,* 119 / 145; Habermas, *Die neue Unübersichtlichkeit,* 172, 219 ff.

44. Gadamer, *Truth and Method,* 308–9 / 327. Gadamer adds: "It was also he [Plato] who saw clearly that there is no argumentatively adequate criterion to distinguish truly between philosophical and sophistic discourse. In particular, in his seventh Letter, he shows that the formal refutability of a proposition does not necessarily exclude its being true" (309 / 327). See also Heidegger, *Sein und Zeit* (Tübingen: Neomarius, 1979), 229 / *Being and Time,* trans. John MacQuarrie and Edward Robinson (New York: Harper & Row, 1962), 271–72.

portant that the certainly paradoxical attempt at a postclassical limitation and self-surpassing of reason, which, as we have seen, leads to irreconcilable antinomies, can also be changed into a "form for organizing indirect communication."[45] Precisely in this at once concentrated and dispersed micrology, if we might use Habermas's suggestive characterization, negative dialectics conveys insights that unsettle the theory of communication at its deepest levels. We have already touched on this important point in explicating the relationship between negative and speculative dialectics as well as with regard to the challenge Adorno's moral philosophy poses to discourse ethics.

Finally, I would question Habermas's stylization of the relationship between philosophy and art or aesthetics in Adorno. In all three of these areas, which affect the status of the subject, history, and the scope of philosophical discourse, Adorno's position is stronger than Habermas admits.

One central hypothesis of my investigation is that the thought of Levinas and Derrida, each in different ways, provides a better medium for explicating the paradoxical and rhetorical aspects of Adorno's philosophy, which have trouble finding a place in the universal pragmatic reformulation of Critical Theory. The interpretive approach I propose rests on a central intuition—namely, to say that Adorno merely immanently poses a critique of the metaphysical, classical modern tradition does not exhaustively characterize his work. By contrast, instead of fixating on the unmistakable aporias in that work, it would be more valuable to design a model of interpretation which could support both that immanent critique, which finally bogs down, and—dialectically viewed—the *external* or *transcendent* (aesthetic, moral, and metaphysical) motifs that keep it going, like a *philosophia perennis* in a new guise. Such a two-track interpretation of Adorno would have to connect up the two foci of the elliptical concept of reason in a nonregressive way.

In what follows I will pursue the question of whether and to what extent the interference of internal and external perspectives in any critical hermeneutics, to which negative dialectics often only hesitantly alludes, can be clarified with the help of Levinas's concept of the alternation of the self and the other or the intrigue of the other in the self. Furthermore, I will need to discuss whether or to what degree Derrida's rhetorical-hermeneutical and eminently philosophical procedure of deconstruction, which appropriates and modifies elements of Levinas's thought, can help

45. Habermas, *Philosophical Discourse of Modernity*, 185–86 / 219.

further decipher Adorno's figure of thought. If it can—and I will need
to sketch out how one might confirm this suspicion—then it might be
productive to explain these structural parallels via Benjamin's suggestive
philosophy of language, on which Derrida also draws.[46]

Habermas himself has emphasized various resonances between the
mature form of negative dialectics and the strategy of deconstruction. He
even believes that they could be viewed as "different answers to the same
question."[47] Again, he indicates the dead end of the critique of reason as it
is questioned from (at first) within: "The means of thinking that miss the
'nonidentical' and remain bound to the 'metaphysics of presence' are, at
the same time, the only available means of uncovering their own insufficiency."[48] Despite this similarity, according to Habermas, Adorno remains
tied to the model of a modernity radicalized in the avant-garde sense, even
to "the counter-discourse dwelling within [modernity] from its very beginnings."[49] One can demonstrate, however, that this assertion overlooks
decisive nuances. Nevertheless, it points toward the sense in which one
might find in a herme(neu)tic of the absolute possible common ground
in the thought of Adorno, Levinas, and Derrida.

The affinity between Adorno's thought and hermeneutics does not
alter the fact that his work in no way presents a reconstructive or integrative model of interpretation, like that famously to be encountered in the

46. For an extensive analysis, see my *Religion and Violence,* chap. 3.

47. Habermas, *Philosophical Discourse of Modernity,* 185–86 / 219.

48. Ibid. See also Habermas, *Die neue Unübersichtlichkeit,* 172, 184, 222 ff. Further suggestions concerning the similarities between Adorno's work and "poststructuralism" can be found
in H.-T. Lehmann, "Das Subject als Schrift: Hinweise zur französischen Texttheorie," *Merkur*
347 (1979): 665–77; Lindner and Lüdke, *Materialien zur ästhetischen Theorie Th. W. Adornos,*
35–36; J. Hörisch, "Herrscherwort, Geld und geltende Sätze: Adornos Aktualisierung der Frühromantik und ihre Affinität zur poststrukturalistischen Kritik des Subjekts," in Lindner and
Lüdke, *Materialien zur ästhetischen Theorie Th. W. Adornos,* 397–414; Michael Ryan, *Marxism
and Deconstruction: A Critical Articulation* (Baltimore: Johns Hopkins University Press, 1982),
65, 73–80; Jay, "Adorno in Amerika," in von Friedeburg and Habermas, *Adorno-Konferenz 1983,*
357; see also 372, 375; Jay, *Marxism and Totality,* 510 ff.; Martin Jay, *Adorno* (Cambridge: Harvard
University Press, 1984), 21–22, 166 n. 29; Marc Jimenez, *Vers une esthétique négative: Adorno
et la modernité* (Paris: Le Sycomore, 1983), 22, for the definition of *deconstruction* in relation
to Adorno; Rainer Nägele, "The Scene of the Other: Theodor W. Adorno's Negative Dialectic
in the Context of Poststructuralism," in *Postmodernism and Politics,* ed. Jonathan Arac (Minneapolis: University of Minnesota Press, 1986), 91–111, esp. 94 ff.; Peter Dews, *Logics of Disintegration: Post-structuralist Thought and the Claims of Critical Theory* (London: Routledge,
1987), 13 ff., 38 ff.; Sabine Wilke, "Adornos und Derridas Husserllektüre: Ein Annäherungsversuch," *Husserl Studies* 5 (1988): 41–68; Christoph Menke, *Die Souveränität der Kunst: Ästhetische
Erfahrung nach Adorno und Derrida* (Frankfurt a.M.: Suhrkamp, 1991).

49. Habermas, *Die neue Unübersichtlichkeit,* 222.

classical romantic hermeneutics of Schleiermacher or the quasi-Hegelian philosophical hermeneutics of Gadamer.[50] Furthermore, Adorno's "hermeneutics" is scarcely compatible with the version of a pluralizing, skeptical hermeneutics suggestively developed by Marquard. His negative dialectics circles incessantly around an ab-solute that classical hermeneutics, in all of its stages, vainly seeks to comprehend via experience or concept, which philosophical hermeneutics displaces into the always-shifting horizon of a totality of meaning, and which skeptical hermeneutics denies altogether.[51] In seeking to bring Adorno's thought into a meaningful constellation with Levinas, I aim not at some reduction to a single common denominator but to bring into view the *formal*, in part aporetic, in part paradoxical, figures of thought in their work, without ignoring the differences in content, idiom, thematics, methodology, or even overall existential and philosophical concern. That Derrida functions here as *tertium comparationis* does not mean that his philosophy should be seen as a *terminus ad quem*. Such an assumption would not only be contrary to his own program, it would also bypass the critical comments that the philosophy of difference — especially in light of a careful reading of the texts of Adorno and Levinas — might allow one to make. In this sense the interpretation of these thinkers' work proposed here, as well as the theology *in pianissimo* inspired by their figure of thought, moves between the extremes of the theory of rationality and the strategy of deconstruction.

Adorno, Lyotard, and Doctor Faustus

One can sense the climate of Adorno's thought in the atmosphere of a catastrophe at once German *and* European in Thomas Mann's great bildungsroman, *Doctor Faustus* (1947). In direct consultation with Adorno and *The Philosophy of Modern Music*,[52] Mann uses the paradigm of mod-

---

50. See Gadamer, *Truth and Method*, 146 ff. / 157 ff.

51. If skepticism has meaning, it is not to be found in a "complete absence of thesis" but, rather, "as also a part of the forces that convictions are," precisely in an "abundance of theses" (Marquard, *Abschied vom Prinzipiellen*, 138).

52. During his time in California Thomas Mann had access to the manuscripts of Adorno's *Philosophy of Modern Music*, in which Schönberg's atonal music plays a central role. In *The Origin of Doctor Faustus: Novel of a Novel*, Mann remarks of Adorno: "I found a most advanced, subtle, and deep artistic sociological critique, which had the most curious affinity to the idea of my work, to its 'composition,' which I was weaving and in which I lived. It was decided instinctively: 'That is my man'" (*Die Entstehung des "Doktor Faustus": Roman eines Romans* [Frankfurt a.M.: S. Fischer, 1949], 42). See also B. Heimann, "Thomas Manns *Doktor Faustus* und die Musikphilosophie Adornos," *Deutsche Vierteljahrschrift für Literaturwissenschaft und*

ern music to probe the intellectual-historical reasons that culture had become derailed. Music, Adorno claims at one point in *Minima Moralia,* offers a more rigorous concept of the aesthetic than poetry and painting because it does not carry along with it "something substantive that oversteps the confines of the aesthetic and is not dissolved in the autonomy of form." That also implies, however, that it must be removed from the silent language of things, to use Benjamin's words, and can only redeem "the name as pure sound" (*MM* 222 / 252, trans. modified). Mann's novel explores how this reaches its apex in modern music, so that the disintegration of culture unfolds from the highest point in its development— in short, through its *dialectic.* The novel's interweaving of the most extreme abstraction (as expressed in a precise analysis of the twelve-tonal technique of musical composition) and the most extreme concreteness (in the portrayal of the decline of Weimar culture) offers a good view of the doubling of schematism and empiricism which so deeply marks Adorno's work. What the central character in Mann's novel formulates as being most proper to music, the fact that it is "ambiguity as system,"[53] aptly expresses Adorno's own figure of thought. The ironic and humanistic tone of Mann's novel does not allow it to plumb the depths of Adorno's world of thought, however; for that, one would need to turn to the modern, hermetic, and almost absurd works of authors who might with better reason be identified as the crowning witnesses in his work: Kafka and Beckett. I will come to them, but first I will seek to tease several fundamental traits of Adorno's thought out of Mann's text. An early essay by Lyotard with the intriguing title "Adorno come diavolo" will be helpful in this.

Lyotard points out that Adorno's features seem to be hidden behind one of the three masks Mann attributes to the devil in chapter 25 of *Doctor Faustus,* which reports his conversation with the novel's main character, the composer Leverkühn: Mann writes of "the bespectacled musical intellectual," assuming the air of a critic who "himself composes, insofar as thinking allows him to."[54] According to Lyotard, this scene, which

---

Geistesgeschichte 38 (1964): 248–66; and Theodor W. Adorno and Thomas Mann, *Briefwechsel, 1943-1955,* ed. Christoph Gödde and Thomas Sprecher (Frankfurt a.M.: Suhrkamp, 2003).

53. Thomas Mann, *Doktor Faustus: Das Leben des deutschen Tonsetzers Adrian Leverkühn erzählt von einem Freunde* (Frankfurt a.M: S. Fischer, 1982), 50 / *Doctor Faustus: The Life of the German Composer Adrian Leverkühn as Told by a Friend,* trans. H. T. Lowe-Porter (New York: Alfred A. Knopf, 1948), 47. Music thus does nothing less than express the ambiguity of life itself (see 193 / 194).

54. Ibid., 243, 238 / 244–45, 239.

Mann lards (or ironizes?) with Adorno's formulations and diagnoses of alienation in modern art in general and the esoterics of modern music in particular, like the way in which he puts Luther's Old German dialect into the mouths of Leverkühn and various diabolical figures, unconsciously betrays the secret alliance between a negative, nihilistic aesthetics and a "theological" pathos. In modernity, in which the experience of art can no longer be borne along on a cult of rapture and enthusiasm, in the eyes of Adorno (and Mann) aesthetic inspiration and intensity, under penalty of inauthenticity and falsehood, can be upheld only by the isolated artist. In other words, only in forms of art driven to their extreme can the aesthetic be redeemed and sustained. In a godless world art must emit a negative, diabolical aura and thus withdraw into a seeming that tends to become incomprehensible. It thereby comes to be burdened with a deputized guilt.[55] In this most extreme abandonment, in the extraordinary "cold" of pure aestheticism, in a composing determined ultimately only by a devotion to developing the material, there paradoxically exists, according to Adorno, a secret turning point, a view toward reconciliation.[56] In such an ascetic, tragic, and melancholy conception of art, in which a consciousness become unhappy laments the loss of subjective expression and reacts with sudden faith in the power of art — which, in the final instance, turns out still to be redemptive — the potential for meaning in the aesthetic domain comes to depend, according to Lyotard, upon the dialectic of a history of salvation and its opposite. In this, however, Adorno overlooks an important "dispositive" of art in contemporary reality, namely, the fact that it can work as a medium of "anonymous intensities," "intensities beyond intentions."[57] Being a permanent parody that is no longer expected to *represent* truth of any kind, art is able to expand and enrich the dimensions of our thinking and action. Such an "affirmative," postmodern concept of art falls outside of the realm of options and possibilities held open in *Doctor Faustus*.[58] But the diabolical and the reconciliatory, salvific functions of art, which Mann depicts largely in terms borrowed from Adorno, only roughly express, Lyotard continues, the theological roots of a negatively

55. According to the famous claim in the *Philosophy of Modern Music*, music "has taken on itself all the darkness and guilt in the world" (*GS* 12:126).

56. See Mann, *Doctor Faustus*, 248 / 248.

57. Jean-François Lyotard, "Adorno come Diavolo," *Des dispositifs pulsionnels* (Paris: Union Générale d'Éditions, 1973), 115. Other references to this essay will be given by page number parenthetically in the text.

58. For the denial of parody, see Mann, *Doctor Faustus*, 241 / 242.

tinged aesthetics. They demonstrate and unmask in an exemplary way the powerlessness of the pathos of modern "critique," however this shrouds itself in Marxist, Freudian, structuralist, semiological, or hermeneutical garb. For the postmodernist Lyotard, Adorno thus demarcates the boundary beyond which no critique can go: "Adorno is the endpoint of critique, its laurels, its revelation in a burst of fireworks" (121).

Lyotard senses that the considerations concerning the limits of modernity put forward by Adorno take their bearings from (or even are involved in?) the tradition of theological-metaphysical thinking. But his characterization of the philosophical and aesthetic transformations of that tradition in Adorno is seriously distorted. Even the escape that in this early article he holds to be both possible and desirable — the decentered play of an affirmative aesthetics in the general frame of a libidinal economy — is, on closer examination, hardly convincing. It may be true, as Lyotard maintains, that Freud and Marx thought they could still *represent* the essentially arbitrary play of forces in our burdens and desires in a therapeutic ("in verbis") or in a critique of political economy ("in verbis et rebus" [128]), while in Adorno there remains only a fading "theological" mark of these two variants of critique. This interpretation becomes unconvincing, however, when it attributes to negative dialectics and aesthetics the illusion that the utopian dimension could be presented *without* any reference to the corporeal and material "economy" to which, in Lyotard's view, every effective and affirmative strategy of desire is connected (120). If we acknowledge a greater ambiguity in this "utopia" and use the qualification "theological" more carefully, then what Lyotard cites as the weakness in Adorno's figure of thought might, perhaps, turn out to be its strength.

In its strongest formulations, precisely because it understands itself to be an irredeemably fragmented thinking following on the loss of any totality, Adorno's dialectics remains skeptical about every flirtation with a totality of meaning which has vanished or even with what Lyotard calls an unmediatable nature "*in absentia*" (132). This preserves his work from the danger of "political Stravinskyism" (133), against which the philosophy of libidinal desire which Lyotard defends in this early text and its correlative "politica figura" can never really be protected. Unmistakably, both Adorno and Mann have in view the obvious inter-involvement of culture and barbarism, as can be seen most clearly in the extreme of an ambiguous, immoral *and* moral aestheticism. In it theology can tend to be presented merely as myth, as had already been articulated in Wagner's *Par-*

sifal. That tendency does represent a strain in Adorno's work—the naive belief that "only the spear that strikes the wound can heal it" (*Drei Stud* 313; see *ND* 49 / 59; *AT* 194 / 202)—which cannot be salvaged. Yet, if one reads this formula as the program for a *critique that, in its rejection of tradition, still must continually return to tradition,* it becomes acceptable. One can and should no longer summon up a sensuous-utopian or aesthetic teleology that supposedly could renew or produce out of itself a totality of meaning in the life-world. Only the refusal by philosophical thinking and political action to *moralize,* to say nothing of *aestheticize*—only the attempt not to allow the borders between spheres of value to dissolve but, instead, to bring these neither heterogeneous nor analogous but, rather, *differential* aspects of rationality together in a meaningful constellation— can suffice to trace (i.e., mourn, express, if not anticipate) both suffering and its counterpart, the good life. Only an alternating thought can help express these extremes while respecting their *otherness.* The traces of such a micrological perspective, as unmistakably attested in the core elements of Adorno's work, seem to have left their mark in Lyotard's account, even if a different optics prevails in Lyotard's thought overall.

Philosophy "after Auschwitz"

"Meditations on Metaphysics," the concluding movement in Adorno's philosophical magnum opus, *Negative Dialectics,* begins with a section entitled "After Auschwitz." In it Adorno offers a diagnosis of culture and describes the inescapable awareness that, after the horrors that occurred at Auschwitz, any confirmation of a "positivity" in existence (*ND* 361 / 354), any construction of a meaning in history, any affirmative discussion of transcendence, of the absolute, or even of an omnipotent or an infinitely good (but powerless) God, stands as an injustice to those who were slaughtered with unprecedented systematicity. In light of this historical "experience" every design for a positive metaphysics is deserving of scorn from the very outset: "After Auschwitz there is no word tinged from on high, not even a theological one, that has any right unless it has undergone a transformation" (*ND* 367 / 360, trans. modified).

After Auschwitz the historical-philosophical question, rather than the epistemological one in the Kantian spirit, should be posed: *is metaphysical experience possible at all?* (see *ND* 372 / 365). Because the societal catastrophes of the twentieth century have broken any connection between traditional metaphysical ideas and human experience, metaphysics seems to have become a lie: "Our metaphysical faculty is paralyzed because actual events have shattered the basis on which speculative metaphysical thought could be reconciled with experience" (*ND* 362 / 354). After Auschwitz "shame" should prevent us from uttering metaphysical thoughts directly (*NL* 1:111 / 129, trans. modified). *The immediate affirmation of meaning and its absolute negation are equally inappropriate:* "What might not have to be ashamed of the name of meaning lies in candor, not in self-seclusion. As a positive statement, the thesis that life is senseless would be as foolish as it is false to avow the contrary; the thesis is true only as a blow at the high-flown avowal" (*ND* 377 / 370). "Auschwitz," in Adorno's texts, serves as a kind of *cipher,* to borrow Jaspers's term.[59] It is the great question mark behind everything that the Western metaphysical tradition and culture have ever meant and the *terminus a quo,* the *Sitz im Leben,*[60] of Adorno's reflection. Respect prevents us from regarding this occurrence as only the "gradual accumulation" (*MM* 234 / 266) of a catastrophe that has always been latent or from viewing it as a merely temporary derailment from civilization's otherwise straight track, as if it concerned only some sort of traffic accident. Adorno presents "Auschwitz" as an extreme manifestation and culmination, as a return of specific traits that have accompanied the development of the Western tradition of reason from the very beginning as an unavoidable shadow. The cipher "Auschwitz" might therefore be characterized as a point where the reversal of enlightenment into its opposite crystallizes, as if it were the final, dazzling triumph of the Hegelian dialectical motif of the conversion of quantity into quality (*ND* 361–62 / 354–55).[61] One must not insist that history unavoidably led to this, yet the fact that "Auschwitz" actually occurred within the heritage of science, morality, and art already pronounces a negative judgment, which reaches beyond the naive and trivial assertion that "spirit," whose banner was carried by the very cultural phenomena that resulted in "Auschwitz," has not been sufficiently successful in fundamentally changing the consciousness of humanity or human behavior.

The dilemma in Adorno's thesis about the failure of culture is that, although one must recognize that culture has foundered, one cannot write

59. One should perhaps not conflate this term with a *boundary situation,* a term that would allow the despair manifest in Auschwitz to be disclosed as the world's "essential substance" (*NL* 1:111 / 129).

60. Werner Brändle, *Rettung des Hoffnungslosen: Die theologischen Implikationen der Philosophie Theodor W. Adornos* (Göttingen: Vandenhoeck & Ruprecht, 1984), 50 ff.

61. See *MM* 55 / 61.

it off—at least if one does not want, in consequence, to give oneself over directly to barbarism.[62] In culture there emerges the paradox that Adorno had already revealed in the domain of philosophical argumentation, experience, and language in general: the impossibility of still speaking affirmatively of meaning in a time of its *nearly* total negativity, while complete negativism (relativism or, indeed, nihilism) seems secretly to collude in silencing the tormented creature and reinforcing that silence. Adorno defends the integrity of thinking, even at the price of an aporia: "Not even silence gets us out of the circle" (*ND* 367 / 360). This ambivalent situation, in which every sensitive philosophizing finds itself, brings to light one of the hidden and virtually absurd aspects in Adorno's thought: the "unthinkability" of absolute despair (*ND* 385 / 378). Adorno illustrates this motif via a description of the modern experience of death.

It is not a new insight that in modernity death cannot be worked through or integrated, whether individually or culturally.[63] What may once have made it seem possible to reconcile death with life, "the feeling of its epic unity with a full life" (*ND* 369 / 362), is transfixed from the outset by the specifically modern experience of the incongruence of possible and successful deeds and of cessation from action: "As subjects live less, death grows more precipitous, more terrifying" (*ND* 370 / 363, trans. modified). The "illusion" of a "commensurability" of death with life has become less and less available (*ND* 369 / 362). Likewise, the experience of death is hardly something ontologically "ultimate and undoubted" that could constitute as existential the advent of *Dasein* as a totality, according to Heidegger (*ND* 368 / 361). Not only does the modality of the experience of death change across history, but the horrors of the twentieth century cast a dark shadow over the very fact of transience. Therefore, Adorno comments that the "final solution" turned death into a phenomenon that "one had never yet to fear in just this fashion" (*ND* 362 / 355); "since Auschwitz, fearing death means fearing worse than death" (*ND* 371 / 364). The individual has been made exemplary—indeed, "an exemplar"—as never before, and this casts a shadow over the survivors, whose very existence becomes a burden of guilt.

Nevertheless, Adorno claims that it is *unthinkable* "to think of death as the last thing pure and simple" (*ND* 371 / 364). The Kantian postulate of practical reason, that of immortality, helps express this paradox: "That

62. See ibid. and *MM* 55 / 49.
63. See Weber's careful observations on this topic in "Science as a Vocation."

no reforms within the world sufficed to do justice to the dead, that none of them touched upon the wrong of death—that is what moves Kantian reason to hope against reason. The secret of his philosophy is the unthink-ability of despair" (*ND* 385 / 378; see 252 / 250–51). Of course, Adorno's paradoxical formulation does not assert that there is, as Kant claimed, im-mortality in the sense of the infinite duration of some constant core of a human being which would in itself remain unchanging. Adorno's negative paraphrase is more cautious: "If death were that absolute which philoso-phy tried in vain to conjure positively, everything is nothing" (*ND* 371 / 364). It is essential, however, that truth survive the *hic et nunc*,[64] and to that extent it contains an element that does not die (see *ND* 363 / 356). The discussion of immortality should not be taken literally, as Adorno shows with regard to Proust's novel, but, rather, as a metaphor for a split in what intolerably exists, in which the moral and aesthetic power of humanity can be established—as in a "last, pale, secularized and nevertheless inex-tinguishable shadow of the ontological proof of God" (*NL* 1:183 / 214).[65] The "last trace" (*ND* 371 / 364) of such a "truth," if we might put it this way, would give the lie to the supposed absoluteness of death. Not only would a critical observation *as if* counter nihilism in the common sense of the term, what is not utterly wiped out by the process of demythologi-zation "is not an *argument*—the sphere of arguments is antinomical pure and simple—but the *experience* that if thought is not decapitated it will flow into transcendence, down to the idea of a world that would not only abolish extant suffering but revoke the suffering that is irrevocably past" (*ND* 403 / 395, my emph.).

In Adorno's view Kafka and Beckett have, from different directions, given literary, indeed, *allegorical* form to this awareness[66]—perhaps thanks to their "inhuman" intellectual and aesthetic distance, that is, their "spectator's posture" (*ND* 363 / 356). Kafka's striking dictum in *The Castle* might easily serve as the motto for Adorno's metaphysical conclusions in *Negative Dialectics:* "That everything is lost is even more improbable

64. In the late Adorno truth in an emphatic sense would thus not be comparable to a Benjaminian, messianic *Jetztheit* but comes into contact with it only negatively.

65. "The idea of immortality is tolerated only in what is itself . . . transient—in works of art as the last metaphors for revelation in the authentic language" (*NL* 1:184 / 214).

66. Allegorical because Kafka's parables and Beckett's novels and dramatic pieces elude the category of the symbolic: "Because no subject matter is simply what it is, all subject matter appears to be the sign of an inner sphere, but the inner sphere of which it would be a sign no longer exists, and signs do not point to anything else" (*NL* 1:251 / 292).

than the improbable."⁶⁷ Like Kafka's, Adorno's texts inexhaustibly circle around an empty center that eludes both every determination, in the sense of substantive content, and also absolute nihilism. Yet, according to Adorno, that center, whose silence threatens to envelop Kafka's parables, is still shot through with fragments of the other. The absurd idea of a world that is, in a sense, "worse than hell" *negatively* opens out of itself a view toward another one: "As in Kafka's writings, the disturbed and damaged course of the world is *incommensurable* also with the sense of its sheer senselessness and blindness; we cannot stringently construe it according to their principle. It resists all attempts of a desperate consciousness to posit despair as an absolute" (*ND* 403–4 / 395- 96, my emph.). With this first step in a critique of any negative ontology, which holds back from a negation of ontology, Adorno takes a stand, above all, against Schopenhauer's inter- pretation of the world's essence and—at least implicitly—Horkheimer's pessimism.⁶⁸ I will go into Adorno's reading of Kafka in greater detail; first, let us turn our attention to Beckett, Adorno's no less important crowning witness.

Adorno wanted to dedicate his *Aesthetic Theory* to Beckett. Precisely where Beckett's work puts before readers and spectators the fact that abso- lute negativity has entered into the human capacity for action and imagi- nation, it "simultaneously expresses the doubt that this could be all" (*ND* 363 / 356). Beckett, especially in *Endgame,* puts into words the fact that, confronted with the situation in and after Auschwitz—about which he re- mains silent, "as if it were subject to a prohibition of images" (*ND* 380 / 373)—the category of angst is no longer in accord with the experience of reality. Fear can only be attributed to an independent individual (see *ND* 362 / 355), and Beckett describes the liquidation of such an individual, "to the point where it contracts into a here and now" (*NL* 1:246 / 287). More conscientiously and with greater consequence than any existentialism of whatever origin, he strips the subject of every quality and thus conveys the ontological concept of the "I," of existence, reduced "literally . . . *ad absurdum*" (*NL* 1:246 / 287). Whereas existential philosophy still seeks

67. Franz Kafka, *Das Schloß,* in *Gesammelte Werke,* ed. Max Brod (Frankfurt a.M.: Suhr- kamp, 1983), 253 / *The Castle,* trans. Willa and Edwin Muir (New York: Modern Library, 1969), 250. According to Adorno, Kafka's work is the "apotheosis" of the *inversion of metaphysics* (as is evident in its development from Marx's Hegelianism to Benjamin's "salvation by induc- tion"), in which metaphysics is discarded precisely so that it can be retained in a transition to *materialism.*
68. See de Vries, "Zum Begriff der Allegorie in Schopenhauers Religionsphilosophie."

the meaning of being in categories of thrownness or, later, in absurdity, Beckett remains true to concrete experience: "What becomes of the absurd once the characteristics of the meaning of existence have been demolished is not something universal—if it were, the absurd would turn back into an idea. Instead, the absurd turns into forlorn particulars that mock the conceptual" (*NL* 1:251–52 / 293).

Despite (or thanks to?) this *contraction* of Beckett's presentation into a seemingly empirical remainder, Adorno believes one can read out of it a universal content: that is, an established *guilt of subjectivity itself* on *this side* of the ontological order, namely, "merely existing, and thereby already committing an outrage" (*NL* 1:251 / 293). The figures presented in Beckett's art have, of course, basically "done" nothing (*NL* 1:271 / 317). At issue is the circumstance that they *are there* at all: "Heretically, original sin is fused with creation" (*NL* 1:272 / 293). Adorno thus addresses something in Beckett deeply touched by the spiritual experience to which the end of *Negative Dialectics* attests. Adorno speaks there of the "guilt of a life which purely as a fact takes the breath away from other life." Since this guilt can never be entirely "present" to thought, it is bound "incessantly" to existence like a blight (*ND* 364 / 357, trans. modified). In Beckett's drama, according to Adorno, the element of the absurd breaks through this presumed ontological inevitability. The "immanent contradiction" of the absurd is able, beyond that apparently hopeless perspective, to open "the emphatic possibility of something true that cannot even be conceived of anymore." In this *enigmatic reversal*, if I might put it that way, lies the quintessence of Adorno's figure of thought, which pushes its "negative ontology" toward a "negation of ontology" (*NL* 1:273 / 319). The ambiguity of this "nihilism" bears a structural parallel to (indeed, shares a point of indifference with), on the one hand, the virtually absolute mastery of "hell . . . , in which absolutely nothing changes anymore," and, on the other, the "messianic state in which everything would be in its right place" (*NL* 1:274 / 321). Such a seemingly *gnostic* (see *ND* 381 / 374) or *apocalyptic* perspective on reality or redemption—which the anti-Schopenhauerian Adorno attributes to the art of Beckett, who was influenced by Schopenhauer[69]—results in the final absurdity "that the peacefulness of the void and the peacefulness of reconciliation cannot be distinguished from one

---

69. See U. Pothast, *Die eigentlich metaphysische Tätigkeit: Über Schopenhauers Ästhetik und ihre Anwendung durch Samuel Beckett* (Frankfurt a.M.: Suhrkamp, 1982).

another" (*NL* 1:274–75 / 321). *Negative Dialectics* clarifies this enigmatic thought.[70] There Adorno claims that the constitution of the existing world involuntarily brings the image of death into line with that of redemption. One might ask, of course, whether we then can ever hope to remain, so to speak, *eccentrically* or *extraterritorially* opposed to that connection to guilt; whether we can still imagine a place from which self-consciousness would be possible. For the most part Adorno leaves the answer to this question open. The occasional concealed allusion to literal utopia is, I claim, hardly the most fruitful in his work. However that may be, *between nihilism and ontologism there is a third way,* which may be able to track and to redeem the scattered traces of transcendence without reestablishing them in the sense of a substantialist metaphysics: "The *slightest difference* between nothingness and coming to rest would be the haven of hope, *the no man's land between the border posts of being and nothingness.* Rather than overcome that zone [i.e., in nihilism], consciousness would have to extricate from it what is not in the power of the alternative" (*ND* 382 / 374, my emph.).

IN ONE OF THE APHORISMS of *Minima Moralia,* the "Reflections from Damaged Life" written in exile, Adorno recalls a song that had been significant to him from childhood. The song tells the story of two rabbits that were shot by hunters while "regaling themselves on the grass." As soon as they came to their senses and realized that they were still alive, they "made off in haste" (*MM* 200 / 226). The hidden meaning of the song, Adorno says, only occurred to him later. The cunning of the unconscious rabbits signifies that catastrophe finally can also be seen through as semblance and that absolute despair must, perhaps, be unreal: "Reason can only endure in despair and extremity; it needs the absurd in order not to fall victim to objective madness. One ought to follow the example of the two rabbits; when the shot comes, fall down giddily, half-dead with fright, collect one's wits and then, if one still has breath, show a clean pair of heels. The capacity for fear and for happiness are the same, the unrestricted openness to experience amounting to self-abandonment in which the vanquished rediscovers himself. What would happiness be that was not measured by the immeasurable grief at what is?" (*MM* 200 / 226). This aphorism points

70. See Werner Martin Lüdke, *Anmerkungen zu einer "Logik des Zerfalls": Adorno-Beckett* (Frankfurt a.M.: Suhrkamp, 1981).

toward one of the deepest motifs in Adorno's attempt to redeem the possibilities that metaphysical ideas still authenticate, however improbable metaphysical experience may have become "after Auschwitz."

More than any other contemporary author, Lyotard has, in his recent work, attempted, from a different direction, to provide a form of articulation or, better, an idiom for the perspective traumatized by Auschwitz, which formerly had renounced all idiom and which perhaps still must do without "Auschwitz." Because Adorno's negative dialectics and Levinas's description of ethical obligation form the elliptical points around and between which Lyotard's striking observations circle in *The Differend,* these discussions deserve closer examination.[71] Moreover, they suggest a number of essential points for the further course of my investigation. The relative proximity of Lyotard's recent thought to Adorno (and Levinas), as we shall see, does not prevent it from being characterized by a tireless but at the same time futile attempt to avoid any nostalgia and, more strongly, any "nostalgia about nostalgia."[72] This is why, in more closely thinking through the concept of minimal theology and Adorno's and Levinas's figures of thought, only with difficulty could I connect my discussion directly onto that of Lyotard.

Lyotard, departing from Adorno, takes "Auschwitz" to be a unique model, not an example of an anonymity that can no longer be grasped in conceptual or classical speculative terms but a "name for the nameless"[73] and, in this respect, a "para-experience"[74] or, better, a name for the destruction of all experience. No conceptual language is adequate to express what results "after Auschwitz." The void "Auschwitz" leaves behind nevertheless resonates unmistakably in the silence that now seems to be the only thing possible. Adorno emphasizes this insight via the example of Beckett's drama, which reveals that the "violence of the unspeakable" (*NL* 1:245 / 286; see also 1:248–49 / 290), which concerns an incommensurability that goes beyond all experience, can only be enunciated silently or "in euphemisms" (*NL* 1:245 / 286, my emph.). Thus, in the seemingly stoical posture in which, after the world already appears to have come to an

71. See Lyotard, *Differend,* 87–127 / 131–86.

72. A motif that an author such as Derrida, from whom this formulation comes, regards as constitutive for his own work. See Philippe Lacoue-Labarthe and Jean-Luc Nancy, eds., *Les Fins de l'homme: À partir du travail de Jacques Derrida* (Paris: Galilée, 1981), 311.

73. Lyotard, "Discussions: ou, Phraser 'après Auschwitz,'" in Lacoue-Labarthe and Nancy, *Les Fins de l'homme,* 283–315.

74. Lyotard, *Differend,* 88, 97 / 133, 145–46.

end, Beckett's figures (must?) continue their meaningless gestures, there are, in Adorno's interpretation, "inaudible cries that things ought to be different" (*ND* 381 / 374).

Lyotard advocates an analogous insight when he remarks, "The silence imposed by knowledge does not impose the silence of forgetting; it imposes a sensation."[75] Lyotard appositely articulates this awareness in a parable. An earthquake strikes not only people and buildings but also highly sensitive seismographic instruments. The dilemma that ensues for survivors, when they want to ascertain the extent of the catastrophe and determine its measurement on an exact scale, is that such precision cannot eliminate the awareness of catastrophe. In such a situation—one that, as Adorno reminds us, sufficed to cure Voltaire of Leibniz's theodicy (see *ND* 361 / 354)—what matters is, according to Lyotard: "The expert says that he knows nothing, the common people feel a complex sensation which gives rise to the negative presentation of indeterminacy. *Mutatis mutandis* the silence imposed by the crime of Auschwitz for the historian is, for the people, a sign."[76] Lyotard thereby identifies something that, as we have seen, is also determinate for Adorno's observations on moral philosophy. In the final instance, unimaginable terror still corresponds to the ethical impulse to do good, to exercise all one's strength to prevent a recurrence of "Auschwitz." Given that our moral seismography has apparently lost its orientation, finally only a sensitive reflex seems possible, without further (quasi-cognitive) reflection or argumentative justification before and afterward. This much can be derived from Adorno's work at its most extreme.

Yet this sketch of the "Auschwitz" problematic does not concern only Adorno's postwar work.[77] At the time of the Institute for Social Research's empirical studies on the structure of the authoritarian character and totalitarian formations of power, Adorno insisted that the whole endeavor crystallized in an effort to discern the foundations of the phenomenon of anti-Semitism and to combat it. Up to that point anti-Semitism had not been interpreted as a phenomenon sui generis, but, rather, as in Marx's *Zur Judenfrage* (*On the Jewish Question*), it was reduced sociologically to a

75. Ibid., 56 / 91, trans. modified; see also 13, 104 / 29, 155.

76. Ibid., 56 / 91, trans. modified. For different responses to natural and societal-cultural catastrophe, in particular the historical signs of Lisbon and Auschwitz, in Adorno, Levinas, Lyotard, and others, see Susan Neiman, *Evil in Modern Thought: An Alternative History of Philosophy* (Princeton: Princeton University Press, 2002), 192–93, 238, 251, 262, 305–10.

77. As Baars suggests in *De mythe von de totale beheersing;* see 19.

class-specific problem. Only later would it be interpreted psychologically in terms of Freudian psychoanalytic categories.[78]

The point of Adorno's argument concerning the need for a change in perspective is important to my argument. In a letter to Horkheimer of 5 August 1940 he writes, after first expressing his skepticism about the "superstition of the secret otherness of the Jew": "I am beginning to feel, particularly under the influence of the latest news from Germany, that I cannot stop thinking about the fate of the Jews anymore. It often seems to me that everything that we used to see from the point of view of the proletariat has been concentrated today with frightful force upon the Jews. . . . I ask myself whether we should not say what we really want to say in connection with the Jews, who are now at the opposite pole to the construction of power."[79]

Similarly, in connection with Adorno's aversion to Marxist philosophies of totality and identity, what increasingly forces itself on our attention is that Jewish existence, in a certain sense, was paradigmatic of the "enclaves of negation" which might authenticate the integrity of his theory.[80] Anti-Semitism, according to Adorno, could be pointedly interpreted as an exemplary phenomenon of the leveling of all difference: as the focus of every injustice. The Jews, in this interpretation, became victims precisely because they constituted the *prefiguration of a nature that has been respected:* "happiness without power, reward without work, a homeland without frontiers, religion without myth" (*DE* 165 / 225). Adorno appears here to have encountered a figure of thought which might justifiably be described as a form of "phenomenological concretization"—an allusion he himself, however, does not use. According to this methodological principle, one should direct one's attention toward the point where the most extreme negativity appears in reality: "our form of physiognomy must attend to the world where it shows its face at its most gruesome."[81] At various points in Adorno's work it becomes apparent that, in his view, this negativity of the theory forms a necessary, so to speak, though scarcely sufficient, condition for the possibility of retaining a view toward reconciliation or utopia. In this, elements of a Hegelian dialectics stood on its head, though no less idealistic in its structure of thinking, might not be

78. See Martin Jay, "Frankfurter Schule und Judentum: Die Antisemitismusanalyse der Kritischen Theorie," *Geschichte und Gesellschaft* 5 (1979): 439–54.

79. Quoted in Wiggershaus, *Frankfurt School,* 275 / 309; see also 276 / 310–11.

80. Jay, "Frankfurter Schule und Judentum," 453.

81. Quoted in Wiggershaus, *Frankfurt School,* 309 / 346; see also 320, 356 / 358, 397.

entirely out of place, in the form of a supposed conversion of negativity into positivity. Hölderlin's lines "But where danger threatens / That which saves from it also grows" resonate here,[82] and originally Jewish mystical, quasi-eschatological, and apocalyptical motifs work as a further, secret leavening. This says it all and yet still says little that would be decisive. The naming and inheritance of the pièce de résistance in Adorno's work seems to be reserved, rather, for a different, a double-sided, one might say, and deconstructive reading.

82. Friedrich Hölderlin, "Patmos," ll. 3–4, *Poems and Fragments,* trans. Michael Hamburger (Cambridge: Cambridge University Press, 1980), 463. See *DE* 47 / 65.

PART THREE

Phaenomenologica

Chapter Seven

Paradox and Aporia in Levinas's Philosophy of the Ethical-Religious Other

There is neither God nor the Good, but there is goodness.
— VASSILY GROSSMAN, *Life and Fate*

LEVINAS CONFRONTS WESTERN philosophy with a critique that is potentially even more incisive than that of Adorno. He, too, attempts to express transcendence—the nonidentical, the particular, the singular, the other or Other—in a world that, he acknowledges, has become all too familiar with reasonable grounds for atheism (which, he hastens to add, is not the same as adopting nihilism, skepticism, relativism, or even naturalism, in historicist and psychologistic guises). As Levinas says in his own, unmistakable idiom, he wishes to elucidate a "nonallergic" and "nonusurpatory" relationship between the realms of the same and self-same (*le Même*) and the other (*l'autre, l'Autre,* and, specifically, *Autrui,* the neighbor, the other human being). These (opposing, correlative, or alternating?) philosophical concepts and the ontological as well as the axiological, if not juridical-political, orders for which they come to stand in Levinas's reception point toward a classical thematic and modern problematic that recall the central concerns of Plato and Neoplatonism.[1] They have left a lasting mark on the postwar philosophical landscape in France, whose development Levinas influenced in remarkable, if often unnoticed or unacknowledged, ways.[2]

Levinas's investigation of the relationship between the same and the other—between identity and difference, immanence and transcendence,

1. See Werner Beierwaltes, *Identität und Differenz* (Frankfurt a.M.: Klostermann, 1980).

2. See Vincent Descombes, *Le Même et l'autre: Quarante-cinq ans de philosophie française (1933–1978)* (Paris: Minuit, 1979) / *Modern French Philosophy,* trans. L. Scott-Fox and J. M. Harding (Cambridge: Cambridge University Press, 1982); and Judith Butler, *Subjects of Desire: Hegelian Reflections in Twentieth-Century France* (New York: Columbia University Press, 1987).

interiority and exteriority—betrays certain commonalities with the central figure in Adorno's thought as he moves from the cautiously posited positivity of the *Dialectic of Enlightenment* (in its preparation for and anticipation of a "positive concept of *Aufklärung*") to the more sustained negativity and assumed circularity of *Negative Dialectics*. Certain striking structural similarities and formal analogies between these itineraries can be observed, even though, at least at first glance, Levinas's oeuvre seems specifically geared toward an ethical and at times religious tonality, whereas Adorno's primary engagement seems to be with the question of aesthetic and metaphysical experience.

In his writings Levinas, unlike Adorno, tracks the other almost exclusively in the realm of intersubjectivity, in asymmetrical rather than dialogical relations. The Other appears not in any ethereal communion of souls but from a dimension of height in which the down-to-earth matter of "handing the bread from my mouth to the stranger" is at issue. Absolute alterity, Levinas suggests, manifests itself, above all, if not solely, in the countenance of another human being (*TI* 66 / 42–43), to whom I am referred in a manner that is neither dialectical nor dialogical, neither conversational (i.e., in Habermas's idiom, interactive or communicational) nor reciprocal, but premised on a heteronomy that precedes my initiative and, Levinas says, "invests" my freedom with a meaning and responsibility that it cannot dream of or measure up to on its own. In this ethical, though far from moralistic, point of view, he situates himself beyond (and on this side of) the conceptual parameters that frame traditional and modern philosophies of the same and the self-same.

Levinas adopts the position neither of ontological realism nor of its antipode, philosophical idealism. In his own analysis he moves beyond the conventional antithesis between the substantive being-in-itself of the objective world, which scarcely admits a concept of subjectivity, and the being-for-itself of modern philosophies of consciousness and freedom from Descartes through existentialism, which has difficulty situating itself in the world of things and events. His perspective is neither classical nor modern because he emphasizes the singular exposition—indeed, exposure—of "the human," more precisely, the "humanism of the other human being [*humanisme de l'autre homme*]," beyond (or before) any ontological, epistemological, or axiological criterion.

Without pathos but not without the rhetorical exaggeration that is his trademark, Levinas writes: "Beyond the *in-itself* and *for-itself* of the disclosed, there is human nakedness, more exterior than the outside of the world—landscapes, things, institutions—the nakedness that cries out its strangeness to the world, its solitude, death concealed in its being."[3] This exteriority has nothing in common with the naturalness or cultural activity of subjects, let alone with the solidity, the phenomenal appearance, of objects—that is to say, the world of *phusis* and of things. Like history, nature (both in such obvious senses as natural beauty and as human internal or corporeal nature) is, for Levinas, neither a paradigm for alterity nor a medium in which the drama of the absolutely nonidentical—the unique, *das Besondere*, as Adorno would say—can unfold or be mediated, let alone brought to the "Result" that Lyotard, in the central chapter of *The Differend*, takes to be the ultimate ambition and conclusion of both Hegel's and Adorno's projects. Moreover, Levinas takes a general strife within (and for) Being in its presence or absence, fullness and privation—the *conatus essendi*, as Spinoza's *Ethics* has it—to be the central philosophical problem from the perspective of a "recognition of holiness" or "ontological absurdity." In his words: "the fundamental trait of being is the preoccupation that each particular being has with his being. Plants, animals, all living things strive to exist. For each one it is the struggle for life. And is not matter, in its essential hardness, closure and shock? In the human, lo and behold, the possible apparition of an ontological absurdity. The concern for the other breaches concern for self. This is what I call holiness. Our humanity consists in being able to recognize this priority of the other. . . . It is here in this priority of the other man over me that, before my admiration for creation, well before my search for the first cause of the universe, God comes to mind."[4]

A second, structural divergence from Adorno might seem inevitable here. For Levinas the relationship to the other seems to resist description in terms of a Hegelian dialectic or the work of negation—that is, as the consequence of a struggle for recognition, as a telos of history, or as the outcome of conceptual-speculative sublation. Yet it does have a place, Levinas writes in the opening pages of his 1947 essay *Le Temps et l'autre* (*Time and the Other*), as "a category of being" in the "dialectic of being" or

3. Emmanuel Levinas, *Entre nous: Essais sur le penser-à-l'autre* (Paris: Grasset & Fasquelle, 1991), 250 / Levinas, *Entre Nous: Thinking-of-the-Other*, trans. Michael B. Smith and Barbara Harshav (New York: Columbia University Press, 1998), 198 / Levinas, "Vorwort zur deutschen Übersetzung," *Totalität und Unendlichkeit*, trans. W. N. Krewani (Freiburg: Alber, 1987), 9.

4. Emmanuel Levinas, *Les Imprévus de l'histoire* (Montpellier: Fata Morgana, 1994), 201–2 / *Is It Righteous to Be? Interviews with Emmanuel Levinas*, ed. Jill Robbins (Stanford: Stanford University Press, 2001), 235–36.

the "general economy of being" (*TO* 39 / 18). As if to avoid all ambiguity between the terminology of "dialectics" in its open-ended or unending variety (as in Plato, the Romantic thinkers, Gadamer, Adorno, Bataille, and, perhaps, Derrida), on the one hand, and its "more determinate" sense (*TO* 39 / 18), on the other, Levinas adds: "The dialectic that these developments may contain is in any case not Hegelian. It is not a matter of traversing a series of contradictions, or of reconciling them while stopping History. On the contrary, it is toward a pluralism that does not merge into unity that I should like to make my way and, if this can be dared, break with Parmenides" (*TO* 42 / 20).

But does such pluralism escape the model of a negative dialectics developed in Adorno's later work? The cautious answer "No, perhaps not fully" has significant consequences for my evaluation of the formal and substantive differences between these two thinkers. Can the idea of the other or Other be exclusively attributed to the realm of intersubjective relationships, ethics, and saintliness, as distinguished from our relation to nature, animality, history, culture, art, and technology? Or does the structural similarity between Adorno's "idea of transcendence" and Levinas's "idea" of the now "infinite," then "Infinite" — not to mention the conceptual implications of the notion of the "trace" in both authors — imply that the concrete distinctions between "ethics" and its supposed other cannot, in the final analysis, be sustained? Moreover, would this formal and material indeterminacy not constitute the distinct modality of all genuine morality, whose certainty and evidences are never of an epistemic nature, reducible to axiological criteria, norms, and statements of yes or no? Finally, when Levinas writes that the "face to face situation is . . . an impossibility of denying, a negation of negation" (*EN* 34–35 / 48), must we read him dialectically in, perhaps, an Adornian sense of that word?

Bearing in mind the impossibility of disentangling the formal analysis of the modality of the idea of the absolute in philosophical discourse from concrete analysis of the intonation or colorization, however minimal, of its "objectless dimension" (*EE* 35 / 66), in the chapters that follow I will approach Levinas's texts from Adorno's perspective, as I have done the reverse in the preceding pages of this volume.

From within and beyond Metaphysics

Reference to a truly other, Levinas maintains, announces itself only in "ethics" (*TI* 43 / 13). Only in that dimension does the Infinite leave its trace (*TI* 24 / 4). More important, only in its undertow, where the Infinite in a certain sense resides, is the irreducibility or the ab-solute character of alterity—more singularly, this particular and unique otherness or Other—guaranteed: "The other is only other if his alterity is absolutely irreducible, that is, infinitely irreducible; and infinitely Other can only be Infinity."[5] At this point Levinas's approach, as he frequently recalls, touches upon that of monotheistic religion. This echo of—or, better, resonance with—the Jewish religion's central motif in part determines the tone and texture of his philosophical thinking. Yet this should not blind us to the fact that he is in no way constructing, reconstructing, or deconstructing a religious philosophy in the systematic, let alone dogmatic, theological sense. Therefore, religious tradition cannot weigh decisively in an evaluation of the contribution of his figures of thought to a minimal theology whose modus operandi lies in the diminishing yet still remaining dimension of the almost invisible, the nearly untouchable, the scarcely audible, *in pianissimo*. Although for the Jewish philosopher Levinas there is something like an elective affinity between prophetic speech and Greek Logos, between Jerusalem and Athens, here I will mostly leave aside the biographical, if not outright anecdotal, question of the relationship between religious inspiration and philosophical conceptuality or argumentation.

Levinas must interest us, above all, as the philosopher he rightly claimed to be. A comparison and confrontation of Adorno's and Levinas's philosophical approaches must be undertaken relatively independently of "existential" matters in the two authors' lives.[6] Furthermore, the religious heritage is almost completely absent from Levinas's earliest texts, the first

---

5. Derrida, *Writing and Difference*, 104 / 154.

6. One cannot assimilate Levinas's inversion of the tradition of ego-onto-theology to what Heidegger, discussing anxiety and fear, says of Augustine, Luther, and Kierkegaard: namely, that their writings are less *ontologically* than *ontically* edifying. He writes: "This has happened whenever the anthropological problem of man's Being towards God has won priority and when questions have been formulated under the guidance of phenomena like faith, sin, love, and repentence" (Heidegger, *Sein und Zeit* [Tübingen: Neomarius, 1979], 190 n. 1 / *Being and Time*, trans. John MacQuarrie and Edward Robinson [New York: Harper & Row, 1962], 492 n. iv). The introduction to Levinas's *Quatre lectures talmudiques* (Paris: Minuit, 1968) / *Nine Talmudic Readings*, trans. Anne Aronowicz (Bloomington: Indiana University Press, 1990), suggests that the significance of Jewish tradition cannot be thought primarily in such devotional terms, even if one were to attempt to separate, vainly, some confessional dimension in Levinas's writings from a philosophical one. One cannot maintain of Levinas, as Heidegger does of Kierkegaard, that "there is more to be learned philosophically from his 'edifying' [i.e., confessional] writings than from his theoretical ones" (*Being and Time*, 494 n. vi / 235 n. 1), assuming it would be at all meaningful to speak of a narrowly "theoretical" style of writing in Levinas which could be separated out of his mode of expression overall.

in which he finds his distinctive voice. They speak to a specific, almost surrealistically inflected experience of modernity and contain *in nuce* the themes and figures of thought in his later texts. Moreover, as Levinas himself repeatedly stresses, one should not mingle the spheres of philosophy and positive religion.[7] He neither allows them to coincide or fuse nor acquiesces in a simplistic disjunction between them. Gadamer's metaphor of the blurring of horizons (*Horizontverschmelzung*) in *Truth and Method* is out of place here, but so is the radical antithesis between revelation and reason that Levinas condemns in Pascal and Yehuda Halevy at the outset of "God and Philosophy" (*GCM* 57 / 96–97).

Levinas's thought distinguishes itself from any rationalization of religious salvation or any hermeneutics of faith, just as it troubles all facile attempts to keep faith and reason apart. In consequence, his thought is neither the crypto-theological appropriation and adaptation of traditional motifs and motivations in a modern philosophical, phenomenological idiom nor their secularization within its terms. Nor can his work be interpreted as condemning religion to ethnocentrism or parochialism and philosophical reason to its scientist other extreme. One cannot limit the significance of Levinas's work to its contribution to the twentieth-century revival of Jewish philosophical thought (in the lineage of Hermann Cohen, Franz Rosenzweig, and Martin Buber), let alone inscribe it in the nineteenth-century legacy of the *Wissenschaft des Judentums,* of which Levinas nonetheless speaks respectfully, in the essays on Judaism published under the title *Difficile liberté* (*Difficult Freedom*).

Indeed, "to be Jewish," in Levinas's view, is "not a particularity; it is a modality." He immediately adds: "Everyone is a little bit Jewish, and if there are men on Mars, one will find Jews among them. Moreover, Jews are people who doubt themselves, who, in a certain sense, belong to a religion of unbelievers."[8] In other words, the adjective *Jewish* stands for a relationship that is based on a "spiritual" belonging whose "modality" is that of ontological, epistemic, and axiological uncertainty. The question of philosophical skepticism and practical-political disengagement — together with the parallel movement of modernist-aesthetic evasion or es-

---

7. See, e.g., Levinas and R. Kearney, "Dialogue with Emmanuel Levinas," in *Face to Face with Levinas,* ed. R. A. Cohen (Albany: State University of New York Press, 1986), 18; see my review of this book in *Bijdragen* 3 (1988): 348–50; see also *EI* 23–25, 113 ff. / 13–15, 111 ff.

8. Interview with Christian Decamps, in *Philosophies,* vol. 1 of *Entretiens avec "Le Monde,"* ed. Christian Delacampagne (Paris: Découverte / Le Monde, 1984), 147 / *Is It Righteous to Be?* 164.

cape—is never far away. But how, exactly, did we get there? Or were we always already in its proximity, though forgetful of its possibilities and perils?

To suggest this is to note that Levinas's philosophical texts concern an immanent critique of a series of fractures that have constituted then haunted Western discourse from the outset. Neither Bible verses nor excerpts from religious literature are, in his view, entitled to any value as evidence: "The verses of the Bible do not here have as their function to serve as proofs; but they do bear witness to a tradition and an experience. Do they not have a right to be cited at least equal to that of Hölderlin and Trakl? The question has a more general significance: have the Sacred Scriptures read and commented on in the West influenced the Greek scripture of the philosophers, or have they been united to them only teratologically? Is to philosophize to decipher a writing hidden in a palimpsest?" (*CPP* 148 / *HAH* 96). This said, the internal fractures of Western discourse are indelible traces that *betray*, in all the ambiguity of the term—which implies translation and distortion at once—an obdurate transcendence that the religious idiom cannot guard or convey in all purity. That is, transcendence both makes itself apparent in philosophical discourse and at the same time eludes it. Better, it manifests itself and is obliterated in the very same moment. The dilemmas of classical and modern ontology, which reveal an "other" that always already precedes any conceptual appropriation or always already exceeds it, are, in Levinas's view, as many opportunities for a metaphysics, ethics, or philosophy of genuine difference.[9] Levinas's thought thus follows a third way between pure theory of a quasi-scientific or autonomous nature and dogmatic or speculative theology,[10] navigating between—and from within—reason and rationality, on the one hand, and irrational mysticism and intuition, on the other, focusing paradoxically on something that cannot, in principle, be a term of thought while calling thought into its own, from within and afar.

Given his openness toward the nonphilosophical, however, this demarcation does not exclude problematic and often contradictory borrowings from the theological tradition. Thus, Levinas can at times describe his undertaking as a kind of theology, more specifically, as a "theology" that, as he says, "does not proceed from any speculation on the beyond

9. See Theodore de Boer, *Tussen filosofie en profetie: De wijsbegeerte van Emmanuel Levinas* (Baarn: Ambo, 1976), 104.

10. See also Roger Burggraeve, *Mens en medemens, verantwoordelijkheid en God: De metafysische ethiek van Emmanuel Levinas* (Leuven: Acco, 1986), 134–36.

of worlds-behind-the-world, from any knowledge transcending knowledge."[11] Elsewhere, by contrast, he can just as easily maintain that the idea of a good beyond Being does not primarily imply a negative, let alone affirmative, theological insight. In such contexts Levinas insists on "the *philosophical* primacy of the idea of the infinite" (*TI* 26 / xiv, my emph.) and that "the place of the Good above every essence is the most profound teaching, the definitive teaching, not of theology, but of philosophy" (*TI* 103 / 76).

One can avoid this contradiction by distinguishing between various levels of meaning in the term *theology*. Because Levinas refers neither to knowledge nor to revelation in the literal sense, only in a metaphorical, nonliteral sense would a concept of theology seem to be suitable to his thinking. The model of dialectical theology, which Levinas rejects in its Hegelian version (see *GCM* 63 / 105) but values in the form of Kierkegaard's and perhaps Barth's paradoxical method,[12] is hardly compatible with a purportedly rational dogmatic or speculative theology, to say nothing of a modern theology in the sense of the empirical, scholarly study of religion as a historically, philologically, and culturally defined object (as in nineteenth-century *Religionswissenschaft* and the *Wissenschaft des Judentums*). A first glance might indicate, then, that Levinas's figure of thought holds great promise for understanding the contours of a minimal theology, which is the project of this book. He states, for example, that he is "providing a theology without a theodicy," like Kant, who also advocated "a theology without preaching": "one can ask oneself to assume responsibility for oneself—this is very hard—but this request cannot be made of the other. To preach to the other is not allowed."[13]

As Theodor de Boer suggests, one can convey the universe and tonality of Levinas's thought via the legend of the deputized suffering of the just in André Schwarz-Bart's 1959 prize-winning novel, *Le Dernier des justes* (*The Last of the Just*), which concerns several generations of persecuted Jews.[14] In Schwarz-Bart's novel, as in the work of Levinas, both bourgeois idealism and intellectualism as well as a piercing historical look at the subterranean metastases of the shattered European spirit that we encountered in Mann's

11. *EN* 199 / 251 / "Vorwort zur deutschen Übersetzung," 11.

12. See Johan F. Goud, "'Wat men van zichzelf eist, eist men van een heilige': Een gesprek met Emmanuel Levinas," *Ter Herkenning* (1983): 24.

13. Levinas, *Is It Righteous to Be?* 146.

14. See Theodore de Boer, intro. to Levinas, *De plaatsvervanging* (Baarn: Ambo, 1977), 16, 18, 19; André Schwarz-Bart, *Le Dernier des justes* (Paris: Seuil, 1959).

Doctor Faustus, influenced by Adorno and read by Lyotard, give way to an almost inarticulate cry. Rather than a precise and protracted study of the decomposition of high culture, using Schönberg's atonal music as a paradigm, in Schwartz-Bart we find the condensed legend of a seemingly senseless election that, despite or because of an apparently absurd and perverse logic in Western history, opens a chilling perspective on what supports the universe as a whole.

The juxtaposition of these two novels suggests the gap between the intellectual and cultural horizons — the "climate" — of Adorno's and Levinas's worlds as well as the different ways in which their philosophies are haunted by a historical negativity of more than Hegelian proportions, which does not seem able to end or to heal its wounds and in which necessity and contingency revolve around each other in ways that are at once paralyzing and enabling. Yet Adorno and Levinas, Mann and Schwartz-Bart, share a common optics in the theme of "Auschwitz," a point where their divergent universes seem to merge, even to collapse, into each other.[15] After all, Mann, too, remarks that the main character in his novel, the composer Adrian Leverkühn, "bears the suffering of an era."[16] I have analyzed the role of "Auschwitz" in Adorno's thinking, and one hardly needs to point out that the history of anti-Semitism and its culmination in the Shoah deeply mark Levinas's philosophy from beginning to end. In an interview he observed, "The injustice committed against Israel during the war, that one calls the *shoah* — the passion of Israel in the sense in which one speaks of the passion of Christ — is the moment when humanity began to bleed through the wounds of Israel."[17] His second major work, *Otherwise than Being, or Beyond Essence,* first published in 1974, might be read as a search for the answer to the seeming senselessness of the victims' deaths and the guilt and shame it inflicts upon the cultural and political history of the European West and, indeed, of existence and of Being in toto. Its dedication is already a peculiar singular universal (or is it a universalized singular?): "To the memory of those who were closest among the six million assassinated by the National Socialists, and of the millions on millions of all confessions and all nations, victims of the same hatred of the other man, the same anti-Semitism" (*OB,* epigraph). Only rarely has Western

---

15. See Lyotard, "Discussions: ou, Phraser 'après Auschwitz,'" in Lacoue-Labarthe and Nancy, *Les Fins de l'homme,* 283–315. Part of this text is also included in Lyotard, *Différend,* 86 ff. / 130 ff.

16. Mann, *Die Entstehung des "Doktor Faustus,"* 81.

17. Levinas, *Is It Righteous to Be?* 92.

philosophy allowed itself to acknowledge that it is not true that "every-thing wicked forms part of meaning," let alone "that things occur which stand outside of history and therefore have no meaning,"[18] although in isolated passages of the *Lectures on Aesthetics* Hegel himself speaks of what is "merely negative."[19]

At first glance Levinas, unlike Adorno, does not seem to allow the cumulative negativity of history to dictate thinking and future experience once and for all. Despite the mythical fatality and the apparently irrevo-cable power of history, which stigmatize a reality from which all that was meaningful seems relentlessly to have been removed, one can, Levinas believes, still speak of a minimal positive dimension, which could make meaning possible once again. This dimension cannot be philosophically, let alone empirically, confirmed or rediscovered, yet, being a nearly nega-tive positivity, it is the sole instance that testifies or cries out against the positive negativity—as in Adorno, *das Ganze ist das Unwahre*—to which history has come in following its premise and tendency to a logical and horrible extreme. That dimension is the proximity of other people, which makes the relationship to an absolute otherness concrete as an *ethical* one, in which "life is no longer measured by being, and death can no longer introduce the absurd into it" (*OB* 129 / 166). In another context Levinas mentions the possibility of a "suffering 'for God' who suffers from my suf-fering" (*OB* 117 n. 21 / 150 n. 21; 16 / 21). Superficially, it would thus appear that, unlike Adorno, Levinas takes the wind out of the sails of nihilism by pushing it *ad absurdum*, over the top.[20]

Yet things are more complicated because metaphysical and moral traces of the other, whether human or other, are not lacking in Adorno's work. And one should not underestimate the radical ambiguity and ar-bitrariness that in Levinas the ever-diminishing yet still remaining—per-haps ineffacible?—trace of ethical otherness acquires from the weight of history, of Being. Unrepresentable, it is also "indestructible." The latter motif can best be illustrated in the tense proximity of Levinas's work to that of his lifelong friend and intellectual companion, Maurice Blanchot,[21] whose term this is. The steep and narrow path that, after all is said and done, remains open from the near-complete removal or even dissolution

18. Ibid., 146.
19. Ibid.
20. See Goud, *Levinas en Barth*, 28.
21. See Marie-Anne Lescourret, *Emmanuel Levinas* (Paris: Flammarion, 1994), 64–69; Levi-nas, *Is It Righteous to Be?* 29–30.

of meaning to the sudden proximity of a final, quasi-transcendental, ethical orientation seems to be the shortest one, as is so often the way in passing between two extremes. This reversal is impressively described in Blanchot's novels and literary essays, beginning with *Thomas l'obscur* (*Thomas the Obscure*), which deeply influenced the early Levinas.

In Adorno the self-imposed prohibition on images often de facto generalizes and intensifies into the suspicion of not just reification but idolatry and blasphemy in every word, in each concept. By contrast, the idea of transcendence bears traces of an alterity that always already escapes the registers of affirmation or negation, positivity or negativity, and, hence, is other, ab-solute, a trace. Similarly, especially in his later work and with far greater consequence than in Adorno, Levinas presents the manifestation of transcendence as a trace, an ambiguity, an enigma. It thereby "designates" a "reality," if these terms still make any sense here, which no longer has anything to do with one or another "presence" in need of being illuminated by (or via) a concept, a proposition, a discourse. As Levinas writes, "Infinity does not first exist, and *then* reveal itself" (*TI* 26 / xv).

Mutatis mutandis, the same figure of thought can be found in Adorno, especially in his late work. In the middle period of Levinas's development he is sometimes inconsistent in the formulation of this idea, remaining trapped in an optics and conceptuality conditioned by the metaphysics of presence and absence. But, like Adorno, Levinas gradually radicalizes his key motifs and the discursive and rhetorical forms they take in figures of argumentation, persuasion, and testimony, in the process returning to distinctive assertions in his earlier work. In both thinkers this recovery, generalization, and intensification of early intuitions finally arrives at the point of questioning whether the absolute or infinite other can be linguistically communicated or otherwise gestured toward *at all*. Counter to some influential interpretations of Levinas's work,[22] as in Adorno, the earliest and latest phases of his thinking form, as it were, a dialectical span that stretches from the beginning of the 1930s to his death in 1995. We

---

22. See Strasser's division of Levinas's work, which sets out *grosso modo* his philosophical development, even if we might question the common denominator to which he reduces these periods: the *first* phase (*On Escape, Existence and Existents, Time and the Other*), according to Strasser, falls under the heading "critique of ontology"; the second stage, crystallized in *Totality and Infinity,* takes as its slogan "metaphysics instead of fundamental ontology"; and, finally, the third phase, especially in *Otherwise than Being,* is characterized by a climate in which "ethics" might serve as "First Philosophy." See Stephan Strasser, "Ethik als Erste Philosophie," in *Phänomenologie in Frankreich,* ed. Bernard Waldenfels (Frankfurt a.M.: Suhrkamp, 1987), 220–22.

should therefore resist the tendency to view *Totality and Infinity*, published in 1961 and undeniably the most systematically worked-out text of his middle period, as the culmination of his thinking, to which everything else leads up or serves as mere addenda and minor *retractationes*. To see Levinas's contribution as a new foundation or transformation of Western philosophy, in which ethics replaces an earlier First Philosophy and assumes the role of transcendental philosophy — one that "integrates phenomenological ontology into dialogical thinking" by postulating dialogue (in the sense Buber and Rosenzweig give the term) as the "transcendental framework for the intentional relation to the world"[23] — however useful this may be for understanding *Totality and Infinity*, is to miss the greatest challenge of his philosophical oeuvre as a whole. Thought through to its end, the philosophy of the trace of the other necessarily breaks open the frame of classical and modern philosophical discourse: its beginnings, methods, and goals. No notion of a paradigm shift from the philosophy of the subject, by way of the phenomenological turn and hermeneutic understanding, toward a pragmatically defined concept of dialogue and communication can capture the "spirituality" and "difficult freedom" whose leads Levinas follows with ever-increasing rigor. Not much room for philosophical articulation is left, then, where terms such as the *trace* and its synonyms are evoked. But, in interpreting the body of his work, should we not continue to follow the method of *lectio difficilior*?

Might the line from *Totality and Infinity* to *Otherwise than Being* (and, to a lesser extent, *De Dieu qui vient à l'idée* [*Of God Who Comes to Mind*]) not reveal a structural parallel to the oscillating movement of Adorno's thought from *Dialectic of Enlightenment* to the complex of *Negative Dialectics* and *Aesthetic Theory*? In such a progression toward a dialectics open to the other of reason — a dialectical critique of dialectics which in Levinas takes the parallel form of a phenomenological critique of phenomenology — the perspective of Levinas's middle work (from the publication of "La Philosophie et l'idée de l'infini" ["Philosophy and the Idea of the Infinite"] in 1957 to "La Trace de l'autre" ["The Trace of the Other"] in 1963)[24] — constitutes just one moment, albeit an important one. Did not

23. Theodore de Boer, "An Ethical Transcendental Philosophy," in *Face to Face with Levinas*, ed. R. Cohen (Albany: State University of New York Press, 1986), 83–84.
24. Emmanuel Levinas, "La Philosophie et l'idée de l'infini," *Revue de Métaphysique et de Morale*, no. 3 (1957): 241–53; rpt. in *DEHH* 165–78 / "Philosophy and the Idea of Infinity," trans. Alphonso Lingis, in *CPP* 47–59; "La Trace et l'autre," *Tijdschrift voor Filosofie*, no. 3 (1963): 605–23, rpt. in *DEHH* 187–202 / "The Trace of the Other," trans. Alphonso Lingis, in *Deconstruction*

Levinas himself emphasize that his whole undertaking was marked by a relative continuity, that it had "remained faithful to its purpose [or finality, *finalité*], even though it . . . varied in its terminology, its formulas, its operative concepts, and certain of its theses"?[25]

Nonetheless, Levinas had serious conceptual grounds for modifying, radicalizing, generalizing, and intensifying his approach in his late work, moving from an ethically transformed First Philosophy, whose central axioms are the intelligibility and unequivocal positivity of the exterior Other and the idea of the infinite, toward the enigmatic and haunting an-archy of the Other in the deepest interiority of the self. In these writings he strives to come to terms with problems that immanently emerge within his thinking by returning to his oldest intuitions as an original philosophical author.[26] He does so because a philosophy that would take an ab-solute other or Other as the basis of or aim for its conceptual system, yet still employ the methods of classical modern metaphysics as the ultimate stakes of thought, seems condemned to failure, despite the transcendental, linguistic, and pragmatic transformations and alterations of the classical modern paradigm. In thinking through this consequence, the course of Levinas's work might seem to have something in common with that of Heidegger. As Otto Pöggeler claims, referring to Heidegger's path of thinking (*Denkweg*): "All attempts to carry out in the language of metaphysics its proper, quite different concerns must . . . succumb to the force that emanates from this language."[27] Heidegger was incapable of undoing the predicament that the tradition thinks Being as a constant being at hand, and thus cannot catch sight of the temporality of the enactment of factual life. For similar reasons, in the philosophy of the nonidentical or the infinite other in Adorno and Levinas, the need to direct thought toward a *meta-ontology* (*OB* 100 / 129), *meta-logic* (*OB* 101 / 130), *meta-*

in Context, ed. Mark Taylor (Chicago: University of Chicago Press, 1986), 345–59. For useful bibliographical details, see Roger Burggraeve, *Emmanuel Levinas: Une Bibliographie primaire et secondaire (1929–1985)* (Leuven: Peeters, 1986).

25. *EE*, preface to the 2d ed., 13.

26. See Silvano Petrosino's assessment in *La Vérité nomade: Introduction à Emmanuel Lévinas* (Paris: Découverte, 1984); trans. of *La Verità nomade* (Milan: Editoriale Jaca Book, 1984), according to which a curious circularity is characteristic of Levinas's thought: "Levinas's text *repeats itself,* but it is precisely in this repetition that it must be read. In this repetition, the writing does not progress, it deepens" (quoted in Rolland, notes to *OE*, 97 n. 4 / 54 n. 4).

27. Otto Pöggeler, *Der Denkweg Martin Heideggers* (Pfullingen: Neske, 1983), 41 / *Martin Heidegger's Path of Thinking,* trans. Daniel Magurshak and Sigmund Barber (Atlantic Highlands, N.J.: Humanities Press, 1987), 28–29.

ethics,[28] *meta-phenomenology*, and in particular *meta-theology*[29] (in contrast to a fundamental ontology, a material moral philosophy, or a fundamental theology) is imposed from the very outset.

The direction of such ever more radical questioning might account for the haunted, hyperbolical, and indeed circular style of writing Levinas develops over the years. Increasingly, he shifts from the conceptuality of the ethical First Philosophy to a kind of rhetoric — a *poetics of the good* — without, in doing so, switching from philosophy to the aesthetic, the literary, and the lyrical. The term *alternation* indicates this rhythm between philosophical reason and *its* other, following an oscillation for which *skepticism* stands as the primary model in both ancient and modern thinking. Skepticism, in Levinas's reading, is less an epistemological or practical problem — the question of realism, of the existence of objects, or of "other minds" — than the temporality and modality of our relationship to a world inhabited by neighbors and strangers, whose claims on us precede and exceed the ones we can make on them. Here Levinas's line of questioning crosses — then parts ways with — the powerful rethinking of the whole problematic of philosophical skepticism developed by Stanley Cavell.

Philosophical Beginnings

In his youth Levinas studied the Bible and traditional rabbinical commentaries, in the tradition of the rational Mithnague Judaism of Rabbi Haim Voloziner, and he read the classics of Russian and Western European literature (Pushkin, Lermontov, Gogol, Turgenev, Chekhov, Dostoyevsky, and Tolstoy, among the former; among the latter, Shakespeare in particular).[30] In retrospect he saw all this not as identical with but as "preparation for" philosophy.[31] His introduction to major works in the tradition of

28. On this term, see Goud, *Levinas und Barth*, 192 ff.

29. See Derrida, *Writing and Difference*, 85 /127.

30. See *EI*, chap. 1, and esp. the 1986 interview with François Poirié, in Poirié, *Emmanuel Levinas: Qui êtes-vous?* (Lyon: La Manufacture, 1987), 63–136; rpt. in Poirié, *Emmanuel Levinas: Essai et entretiens* (Arles: Actes Sud, 1996), 61–169 (in subsequent references page numbers will be to the Actes Sud edition) / "Interview with François Poirié," trans. Jill Robbins, Marcus Coelen, and Thomas Loebel, in *Is It Righteous to Be?* 23–83. See also Lescourret, *Emmanuel Levinas;* Salomon Malka, *Emmanuel Lévinas: La Vie et la trace* (Paris: Jean-Claude Lattès, 2002); and Emmanuel Levinas, preface to Rabbi Hayyim de Volozhyn, *L'Âme de la vie (nefesh hahayyim),* trans. Benjamin Gross (Paris: Verdier, 1986), vii–x. See also Alan Nadler, *The Faith of the Mithnagdim: Rabbinic Responses to Hasidic Rapture* (Baltimore: Johns Hopkins University Press, 1997).

31. Levinas, "Interview with Myriam Anissimov," *Is It Righteous to Be?* 89. There Levinas is

Western philosophy followed, beginning in 1923 in Strasbourg. The philosophical climate in which he found himself there was deeply influenced by the sociological work of Émile Durkheim and stamped by the philosophy of Henri Bergson, both of whom had "incontestably been the professors of our masters" (*EI* 26 / 16). Those masters were Charles Blondel, a psychologist who had studied with Bergson and Lévy-Bruhl, who considered himself an anti-Freudian and who, Levinas says, kept him "outside of psychoanalysis to this day";[32] Maurice Halbwachs, a professor of sociology who had studied with Durkheim and Lévy-Bruhl and who was named to the Collège de France just before his deportation to and death in Buchenwald; Maurice Pradines, a philosopher who in his course on ethics impressed the young Levinas by citing the Dreyfus affair — a cause that, like all these teachers, he vehemently supported — as an example of primacy of the ethical over the political; and Henri Carteron, a Catholic professor of ancient philosophy who acquainted Levinas with the teachings of Christianity and to whom he would dedicate his first book, on Husserl.[33] In Durkheim and Bergson, Levinas came across scattered philosophical intuitions, motifs, and motivations in which one easily finds convergences and parallels with his own subsequent concerns without having recourse to simplistic genealogical narratives of influence and reception.

Such parallels include Durkheim's emphasis on the *irreducibility of the social* to the sum of individual psyches. He claimed, rather, that sociality constitutes the moral aspect and spiritual element that enable individual existence. In Levinas's metaphysically oriented interpretation — "Durkheim, a *metaphysician!*" — this founding father of empirical sociology established an "eidetic of society," which implies the "idea that the social is the very order of the spiritual, a new plot [*intrigue*] in being above the animal and human psychism; the level of 'collective representations' defined with rigor and which opens up the dimension of spirit in the individual life itself, where the individual comes to be recognized and even redeemed [or disengaged, *dégagé*]." In Durkheim, he felt, there is in a sense "a theory of 'levels of being,' of the irreducibility of these levels to one another, an idea which acquires its full meaning within the Husserlian and Heideggerian context" (*EE* 26–27 / 17).

---

speaking explicitly of Russian novels, but elsewhere he uses similar wording in a context that also includes Western national literatures and the Bible (*EI* 22 / 12).

32. Levinas, "Interview with Myriam Anissimov," 86.

33. Ibid.; also see 91. See also Lescourret, *Emmanuel Lévinas,* 51–62; Malka, *Emmanuel Lévinas,* 41–42.

Then there is Bergson's doctrine of a *temporal duration* that cannot be conceived as a cosmological-physical, homogeneous, and linear time but which makes possible a future and new perspectives for action, thus undermining the constancy of fate (see *EI* 27–28 / 16–18). In spite of a sustained polemic against "Bergsonism" in his early and late writings (a polemic we also find in the writings of Adorno and Horkheimer, who never acknowledge the full importance of this author), Levinas insists that, apart from the classical ancient and modern philosophers who impressed him from early on (Plato, Aristotle, Descartes, Malebranche, Kant, and Maine de Biran), "the first contemporary influence" on his own thinking was Bergson.[34] It was fundamentally Bergson's notion of temporality as concrete duration (*la durée concrète*), long ignored in postwar philosophy, which, in retrospect, "prepared the soil for the subsequent implantation of Heideggerian phenomenology into France"; indeed, this circumstance, Levinas concludes, should modify our view of Heidegger's own self-image: "It is all the more ironic, therefore, that in *Being and Time* Heidegger unjustly accuses Bergson of reducing time to space." Levinas continues: "in Bergson's *Creative Evolution,* one finds the whole notion of technology as the destiny of the Western philosophy of reason. Bergson was the first to contrast technology, as a logical and necessary expression of scientific rationality, with an alternative form of human expression that he called creative intuition or impulse — the *élan vital.* All of Heidegger's celebrated analyses of our technological era as the logical culmination of Western metaphysics and its forgetfulness of being came after Bergson's reflections on the subject."[35]

After citing his primary "inspiration" by the phenomenological and dialogical schools of thought — Husserl and Heidegger but also Rosenzweig, Buber, and Gabriel Marcel — in the preface to the German edition of *Totality and Infinity* Levinas makes good on his omission of Bergson from the initial edition's list of explicitly mentioned influences by acknowledging that the book "also claims, in contemporary thought, a faithfulness to the innovative work of Henri Bergson, who made many of the essential positions of the masters of phenomenology possible." Again, Levinas credits Bergson with two central philosophical intuitions: "With his notion of duration, he freed time from its obedience to astron-

---

34. See esp. Howard Caygill, *Levinas and the Political* (London: Routledge, 2002), 9 ff.
35. Levinas and R. Kearney, "Dialogue with Emmanuel Levinas," in Cohen, *Face to Face with Levinas,* 13–33.

omy, and thought from its attachment to the spatial and the solid, and to its technological ramifications and even its theoretical exclusivism" (*EN* 197 / 249).

Bergson's *L'Évolution créatrice* (*Creative Evolution*) and *Les Deux sources de la moral et de la religion* (*The Two Sources of Morality and Religion*) thus prefigured Levinas's own understanding of a "spirituality freeing itself from a mechanistic humanism" and of temporal duration as the very "relationship with the other and with God." Here, for the first time, we encounter the idea of a "proximity that cannot be reduced to spatial categories or to modes of objectivation and thematization" (*EN* 224 / 253–54). In an interview with François Poirié we find Levinas paying homage to the legacy of this "new philosophy" by stating that, despite the reservations he subsequently formulated, he "remained very faithful to this sensation of novelty." The reasons he gives serve almost as a summary of his own thought:

> in the notion of duration, in the notion of invention, in all the putting into question of substantiality and of solidity; in the putting into question of the notion of being, a little bit beyond being and otherwise than being, the whole marvel of diachrony; in the manner in which, for the man of our time, time is no longer simply a broken eternity or the missed eternal that always refers to something solid, but on the contrary, the very event of infinity in us, the very excellence of the good. Plenty of technical moments in the Bergsonian discourse. His quarrel with associationism or with mechanistic biology concerns me less than temporality, its superiority over the "absolute" of the eternal. The humanity of man is not just the contingent product of temporality but its original effectuation or the initial articulation.[36]

This temporality, Levinas says elsewhere, stands on a par with two later major sources of inspiration, to which I will come. Moreover, it forms the *via regia* to the conception of ethics and religion — indeed, of a minimal theology — which interests me in his oeuvre:

> I have sought for time as the deformalization of the most formal form that is, the unity of the *I think*. Deformalization is that with which Bergson, Rosenzweig, and Heidegger, each in his own way, have opened the problematic of modern thought, by starting from a concreteness "older" than the pure form of time: the freedom of invention and novelty (despite the persistence of the

---

36. Levinas, *Is It Righteous to Be?* 31 / Poirié, *Emmanuel Levinas*, 75.

kinetic image of a *flow*) in Bergson; the biblical conjunction of "Creation, Revelation, and Redemption," in Rosenzweig; and the "nearness to things," *Geworfenheit,* and *Sein-zum-Tode* (despite the still kinetic *ex* of the *extases*) in Heidegger. Is it forbidden to also recall that in *The Two Sources of Morality and Religion,* the duration of *Time and Free Will* [*Essai sur la données immédiates de la conscience*] and *Matter and Memory* [*Matière et mémoire*], thought as *élan vital* in *Creative Evolution,* signifies love of the neighbor and what I have called "to-God"? But do I have the right to make this comparison, notwithstanding all the teachings of the half-century that separates us from the publication of *The Two Sources of Morality and Religion?*[37]

This does not map out the whole terrain, however. The teachings of Léon Brunschvicg, whose seminars at the Sorbonne Levinas attended,[38] together with the famous lecture courses of Alexandre Kojève in the 1930s, the renaissance of Hegelianism and, in its wake, the ascent of Marxism, the introduction of Husserl's phenomenology and its singular reception in existential phenomenology, as well as the "poststructuralist" reaction to all of these intellectual approaches—all contributed to the philosophical horizon against which Levinas's most innovative thoughts took shape. These intellectual currents—to the most vocal of which Levinas responded, in his own words, primarily as "reader and spectator rather than *engagé*"[39]—fed into to the specifically French impression of a heterodox and complex reception history of phenomenology, at whose origin and in whose vanguard Levinas stood and under whose aegis both the methodological and the thematic elements of his work would develop.

As Adorno arrived at his dialectical critique of dialectics only after first laboring over "phenomenological antinomies" and Kierkegaardian "aesthetics," Levinas came "by a pure accident" (*EI* 29 / 19) to be in touch with the philosophical school whose methodological discipline—albeit it from a certain distance—he would come to appreciate as the "undoubtedly most important" contemporary source of orientation:[40] Husserl's theory of intuition and the procedure of intentional analysis. But from the outset, as in Adorno's reception of Hegel, Levinas's reception of Husserl's phenomenology is valid less for its truth per se than as a refutation and

37. Levinas, "Diachrony and Representation," *TO* 119–20 / 98.

38. See Emmanuel Levinas, "L'Agenda de Léon Brunschvicg" ("The Diary of Léon Brunschvicg"), *DF* 38–45 / 63–71.

39. Levinas, *Is It Righteous to Be?* 80 / Poirié, *Emmanuel Lévinas,* 164.

40. Levinas and Kearney, "Dialogue with Emmanuel Levinas," in Cohen, *Face to Face with Levinas,* 14.

correction of opposing views: naturalism, psychologism, naive realism, idealism, historicism, relativism, scientism, and skepticism.

Levinas studied with Husserl in Freiburg during the master's two final semesters in 1928 and 1929. In the same period, which inaugurated a path of thinking which Levinas in retrospect designates *"incontournable,* necessary, that which one cannot get around,"[41] he also attended seminars with Husserl's successor, Heidegger. Whereas the work of the first struck him as "somewhat pat, despite his emphasis on research" — "There was also something pat [or completed, *achevé*] about his oral teaching"[42] — the courses and writings of the latter, by contrast, impressed Levinas as totally "unexpected."[43]

Levinas's systematic studies of the major works of Husserl, documented in several expository early essays, not to mention his involvement, together with Gabrielle Pfeiffer and Alexandre Koyré, in the translation into French of Husserl's *Cartesian Meditations,* published in 1931,[44] served an important mediating function for the reception of Husserl in the subsequent *via regia* of existential phenomenology.[45] Levinas's prize-winning 1930 dissertation, *Théorie de l'intuition dans la phénoménologie de Husserl* (*The Theory of Intuition in Husserl's Phenomenology*), was the first significant monograph in France on this mode of thought, dedicated to the "lasting kernel of what is popularly known as a pathic form of existentialism,"[46] a movement addressed only marginally — and then often critically — in his own writing. In a reasoned departure from existentialism's doctrine of subjective freedom, including its Kierkegaardian Christian premises, and at a distance from the false alternative of Hegelian-Kantian objectivism, which he detected first in Marxism and then in structuralism, lies one of

41. Levinas, *Is It Righteous to Be?* 31 / Poirié, *Emmanuel Lévinas,* 76.

42. Ibid., 33 / 78–79.

43. Ibid., 33 / 79.

44. Levinas's first publication was the review article "Sur les *Ideen* de M. E. Husserl," *Revue Philosophique de la France et de l'Étranger,* nos. 3–4 (1929): 230–65; rpt. in *Les Imprévus de l'histoire,* 45–93 / "On Ideas," trans. Richard A. Cohen and Michael B. Smith, in Emmanuel Levinas, *Discovering Existence with Husserl,* trans. Richard A. Cohen and Michael B. Smith (Evanston, Ill.: Northwestern University Press, 1998), 3–31. For an analysis of this early, largely receptive phase, see Jean-François Lavigne, "Lévinas avant Lévinas: L'Introducteur et le traducteur de Husserl," in Emmanuel Lévinas, *Positivité et transcendance,* ed. Jean-Luc Marion (Paris: Presses Universitaires de France, 2000), 49–72. On Levinas's role in the reception of Heidegger's work in France, see Dominique Janicaud, *Récit,* vol. 1 of *Heidegger en France* (Paris: Albin Michel, 2001), 30 ff.

45. Bernhard Waldenfels, *Phänomenologie in Frankreich* (Frankfurt a.M.: Suhrkamp, 1987), 50.

46. Waldenfels, *Phänomenologie in Frankreich,* 15; cf. 35.

the most original contributions of Levinas's philosophy to contemporary moral and political thought, as well as to our reinterpretation of such age-old metaphysical categories as God, self, history, event, language, expression, art, truth, mind, and world.

The Identity Philosophy of the Same and the Absolute Alterity of the Other

Although Levinas discerns five "crossroads [*carrefours*]" in the history of thinking ("ontotheology, transcendental philosophy, reason as history, pure duration, and the phenomenology of Being as distinguished from beings"),[47] he describes Western philosophy in Husserl's terms as, above all, a philosophy of the self-same, an *egology* (*Egologie*). Ever since Socrates, he suggests, the model of one's capacity to learn has been *maieutic* and *anamnestic:* "to receive nothing of the Other but what is in me, as though from all eternity I was in possession of what comes to me from the outside—to receive nothing, or to be free" (*TI* 43 / 13–14). Philosophical thought, in this view, receives, experiences, encounters, and recognizes nothing really new. Levinas interprets this self-sufficiency of the "I," in identifying with everything other than itself, incorporating and introjecting it into its own orbit, as power, violence, and injustice. In relation to the other, within the conceptual framework of the Western tradition it is impossible to speak of peace, only of overcoming and possession: "'I think' comes down to 'I can'—to an appropriation of what is, to an exploitation of reality" (*TI* 46 / 16). The "*idée fixe*" of contemporary philosophy (*HAH* 29), reaching back through Hegel and Cartesian dualism to the principle of Christian individuality and freedom, is to break through the subject-object structure.

This narcissistic dream of Western *theoria,* Levinas suggests, in a sweeping gesture typical of his historical analysis, still haunts the modern philosophies of the subject articulated by Husserl and Heidegger. In a second set of essays on these two thinkers, which are less expository than exploratory—indeed, which are remarkable in their immanent critique (as Adorno would say) or deconstruction (as Derrida would add) of texts that were relatively unknown at the time—Levinas shows how a dimension of otherness irrupts into the spheres of phenomenology and ontology. Constitutive consciousness and even *Dasein,* in which Heidegger, appealing to an anti-intellectual affect—indeed, to a "new pathos [*pathétique*] of

47. Levinas, *Is It Righteous to Be?* 32 / Poirié, *Emmanuel Lévinas,* 78, trans. modified.

thinking"[48] — roots the Husserlian transcendental ego, are not sufficient to account for this *ethical* dimension, which Levinas terms "metaphysical" and "eschatological" and which, in a certain sense, makes phenomenological or fundamental-ontological instances possible in the first place.

From Kant, Hegel, and phenomenology on, Levinas suggests, modern idealism enriched Western ontology with the insight that the manifest appearance of Being is expressed by a consciousness that discloses its intelligibility: "Nothing is more characteristic of phenomenological reflection than the idea of intentional relations maintained with correlates that are not representations and do not exist as substances. . . . There is truth without there being representation."[49] In other words, the appearance of things before (i.e., in and through) consciousness in its broadest possible sense belongs to the course of Being itself, to the "intentional life" of which subject and object are "only the poles." Hence, Levinas can write: "The phenomenological reduction has never seemed to me to justify itself by the apodicticity of the immanent sphere, but by the opening of this play [*jeu*] of intentionality, by the renouncing of the fixed object that is the simple result and the dissimulation of this play. Intentionality means that all consciousness is consciousness of something, but above all that *every object calls forth and as it were gives rise to the consciousness through which its being shines and, in doing so, appears.*"[50] Nevertheless, in the horizon in which what appears is thus situated, "the existent has a silhouette, but has lost its face" (*TI* 45 / 15; see *OB* 131 / 169). The intentionality of theoretical consciousness, or *noesis*, which, according to a certain strain of Husserlian thought, must be adequate to the intended object, or *noema*, does not, in Levinas's view, characterize human "conscience" at its deepest. Conscience, animated — as Descartes already knew — by the idea of the infinite and bearing both knowledge and freedom, is made possible and characterized by an *inadequacy par excellence* (see *TI* 26 / xv). Levinas writes of this "exemplary" interpretation of intelligibility:

> Every experience opens up new contexts which are not given by the experience of perception. . . . Idealism has always wanted to interpret experience.

48. Ibid., 35 / 83.

49. Levinas, "Réflexions sur la 'technique phénoménologique,'" *DEHH* 122 / "Reflections on Phenomenological 'Technique,'" trans. Richard A. Cohen and Michael B. Smith, in Levinas, *Discovering Existence with Husserl*, 101–2. (This essay was first published in French in *Husserl*, Cahiers de Royaumont, Philosophie, no. 3 [Paris: Minuit, 1959].)

50. Levinas, *Discovering Existence with Husserl*, 119 / *DEHH* 134, trans. modified. Interestingly, this view is not so different from the one articulated by McDowell in *Mind and World*.

In a sense, it wanted to think that the real was absolutely equal to conscious-ness, that there was no overflowing, no deficit, no surplus. However, Descartes shows clearly that the form of God is greater than psychological meaning. From the outset, we think more than we can think. . . . The things that we have within our horizon always overflow their context. . . . Idealism always imagined that reality was only representation; phenomenology teaches us that reality constitutes more than what captures our gaze. Reality has weight.[51]

Later developments in phenomenological thought—Husserl in *The Crisis of the European Sciences and Transcendental Phenomenology,* Merleau-Ponty in *Le Visible et l'invisible (The Visible and the Invisible)*—stress this beyond of representation through which "reality" gains its "weight." When asked whether Merleau-Ponty's notion of "la chair du monde [the flesh of the world]" conveys the meaning of this "weight," as opposed to the mere "unbearable lightness" or "shadow" of "reality," Levinas agreed, "That is an excellent formula."[52]

Levinas recognizes these motifs—which extend and express them-selves beyond the structure of intention and intentionality in its classi-cal, Scholastic, modern, and twentieth-century uses—in the letter (rather than the spirit) of Husserl's texts. Thus, although in the *Cartesian Medita-tions* Husserl presents the other as an "analogy" of myself,[53] we nonetheless find in his work consequent articulation of the philosophical prominence of the intersubjective, of the structure of inner time consciousness, of cor-poreality, and of the life-world, all of which implicate the transcenden-tal ego in realms that exceed the confines of representation and present experience, alluding to a dimension of passivity—indeed, a passive gene-sis—whose contours Levinas will draw with relentless consequence in his later essays devoted to phenomenological "technique," in the opening chapters of *Otherwise than Being,* and in central passages in *Of God Who Comes to Mind.*

Yet Husserl's conception of "vision" already implies a reductive form

---

51. Levinas, *Is It Righteous to Be?* 159–60 / Delacampagne, *Entretiens avec "Le Monde,"* 139.

52. Ibid. See also, to give just an example, the oblique reference to Merleau-Ponty's ter-minology in *OB* 196 n. 21 / 150 n. 21, in which Levinas speaks of the passivity on this side of all passivity which insinuates itself at the very bottom of materiality as it turns into "flesh" (*"passivité en-deçà de toute passivité au fond de la matière se faisant chair"*).

53. Edmund Husserl, *Cartesianische Meditatione: Eine Einleitung in die Phänomenologie,* ed. and intro. Elisabeth Ströker (Hamburg: F. Meiner, 1977), 96 / *Cartesian Meditations: An Introduction to Phenomenology,* trans. Dorion Cairns (Dordrecht: Martinus Nijhoff, 1960), 111. See *DEHH* 45 ff.

of "intelligibility": "To see is already to render the encountered object one's own, as drawn from one's own ground. In this sense, 'transcendental constitution' is but a way of seeing in full clarity. It is a completion of vision" (*TO* 64 n. 39 / 92 n. 4). Levinas, by contrast, opposes Descartes's "Third Meditation" to Husserl's "Fifth Cartesian Meditation."[54] There Descartes encounters the idea of the infinite (indeed, the invisible) as presupposed and implanted in finite thought. Among all other mathematical and moral ideas (*TI* 49 / 19), it alone cannot stem from consciousness itself. Thought, Descartes demonstrates, cannot account for its *ideatum* because the idea of the infinite—more precisely, of fallibility, imperfection, and the notion of perfection it implies—concerns "a noesis, which was not on the scale of its noema, its cogitatum. An idea which gave the philosopher *bedazzlement* instead of accommodating itself within the *self-evidence* of intuition."[55]

Interestingly, Levinas takes up only the "formal structure" (*dessin formel* [*DEHH* 171]) of this idea. He accepts neither its supposed value as evidence for the existence of God, nor the substantialist language Descartes uses to model His infinite Being.[56] There remains only the paradoxical figure of a not purely theoretical orientation toward something incommensurable, so that "the actuality of the *cogito* is thus interrupted by the unencompassable," to the extent that it is not so much "thought but undergone, carrying in a second moment of consciousness that which in a first moment claimed to carry it" (*GCM* 64 / 106).

Levinas thus opposes to maieutics and anamnesis, reflection and recognition, the instruction that the Other offers the ego concerning what

54. See Derrida, *Writing and Difference*, 106, 132 ff. / 156–57, 180 ff. As Derrida notes, Levinas would concur with Sartre's claim that "one *encounters* the Other, one does not constitute it" (quoted in *Writing and Difference*, 315 n. 44 / 181 n. 1). On the division of labor between G. Pfeiffer, A. Koyré, and Levinas in the translation of Husserl's work, see Lescourret, *Emmanuel Levinas*, 72.

55. Levinas, "Preface to the German Edition," *EN* 200 / 252 / *Totalität und Unendlichkeit*, 11.

56. In his dissertation Levinas already presents a critique of such substantialist language, which he also recognizes in the determination of the cogito (an area examined more deeply by Husserl). See esp. *TIH* 59. Later he writes of Descartes's conception of divine being: "While thinking of God as a being, Descartes thinks of him nevertheless as an eminent being, or he thinks of him as a being who *is* eminently. Before this *rapprochement* between the idea of God and the idea of being, we must certainly ask ourselves whether the adjective *eminent* and the adverb *eminently* do not refer to the height of the sky over our heads and thus overflow ontology. Be that as it may, Descartes maintains a substantialist language here, interpreting the immeasurableness of God as a superlative way of existing" (*GCM* 62 / 104; see also 63–65, 119 / 105–7, 185).

the ego cannot of itself know, construct, experience, or receive: "The idea of infinity implies a soul capable of containing more than it can draw from itself. It designates an interior being that is capable of a relation with the exterior, and does not take its own interiority for the totality of being." In other words, in the history of Western thought the idea of infinity concerns a "Cartesian order, prior to the Socratic order," and the reason is, once again, only formal in its design. The Socratic order cannot come first on the simple ground that its "dialogue already presupposes beings who have decided for discourse, who consequently have accepted its rules" (*TI* 180 / 155).

Yet the primary confrontation or encounter with another person is of another order than what could be grasped by modern, Cartesian criteria, that is to say, in terms of "clear and distinct ideas" (*OB* 133 / 170). Absolute alterity, the idea of the infinite, reveals itself in the nakedness of the face, which, being quasi-abstract, is neither a phenomenon of this world nor an idealized intentional object. The face has no physiognomy and no portrait. Levinas can therefore observe: "The best way of encountering the Other is not even to notice the color of his eyes!" (*EI* 85 / 79). Levinas insists that the notion of the face ought not to be taken "in a narrow way":

> This possibility for the human of signifying in its uniqueness, in the humility of its nakedness and mortality, the Lordship of its reminder — word of God — of my accountability for him, and of my chosenness qua unique to this responsibility, can come from a bare arm sculpted by Rodin.
>
> In *Life and Fate,* Grossman tells how in Lubyanka, in Moscow, before the infamous gate where one could convey letters or packages to friends and relatives arrested for "political crimes" or get news from them, people formed a line, each reading on the nape of the person in front of him the feelings and hopes of his misery. . . .
>
> Grossman isn't saying that the nape is a face, but that all the weakness, all the mortality, all the naked and disarmed mortality of the other can be read from it. He doesn't say it that way, but the face can assume meaning on what is the "opposite" of the face! The face, then, is not the color of the eyes, the shape of the nose, the ruddiness of the cheeks, etc.[57]

But is the "face," then, exclusively human, not to be ascribed to nonhuman living beings, to nature, to the artificial, the technological?

It is easy to see why Heidegger's renewal of phenomenology and its

---

57. Levinas, *Is It Righteous to Be?* 208.

existential phenomenological reception, which no longer takes the transcendental ego to be the absolute ground of being but, rather, makes *Dasein* or (as with Merleau-Ponty)[58] the *corps-sujet* its point of departure, is finally of little benefit for Levinas's ethical perspective. In his dissertation Levinas already indicates that the analytic of *Dasein* and the existential phenomenology of the *corps-sujet* transport classical intellectualism and objectivizing knowledge back to the context of prereflexive life (see *OB* 65 / 83), but he increasingly comes to see that they remain stuck in an *ethical indifference,* in a self-seeking doctrine of being-for-itself and freedom which falls short of the description of ipseity and its opening toward others which genuine experience requires. The insight that consciousness forms a derivative mode of *Dasein,* that the understanding of Being is less a theoretical issue than a specific, truth-disclosing event that can be attributed to the entire spectrum of human behavior, to academic endeavor, to work, and to the satisfaction of desire[59] — all this may have contributed a new dimension to ontological thinking, but it hardly touches the ethical point of Levinas's thought, which can be summarized in the dictum "Signification precedes essence" (*OB* 13 / 16), or that a human being is not *Dasein,* that is to say, "being there," but, precisely, "utopia," that is, in a sense, "being nowhere."[60] Invoking an almost Durkheimian critique of Heidegger — in addition to undercutting Hegelian dialectics, modern utilitarianism, empathy, and epistemology — he attempts to see

> in justice and injustice a primordial access to the Other beyond all ontology. The existence of the Other does not concern us in the collectivity by reason of his participation in the being that is already familiar to us all, nor by reason of his power and freedom which we should have to subjugate and utilize for ourselves, nor by virtue of the difference of his attributes which we would have to surmount in the process of cognition or in a movement of sympathy merging us with him, as though his existence were an embarrassment. The Other does not affect us as what must be surmounted, enveloped, dominated, but as other, independent of us: behind every relation we could sustain with him, an absolute upsurge. (*TI* 89 / 61–62)

58. See Bernhard Waldenfels, *Deutsch-Französische Gedankengänge* (Frankfurt a.M.: Suhrkamp, 1995), 346–82; and Agata Zielinski, *Lecture de Merleau-Ponty et Levinas.*

59. See *DEHH* 57, 59, 67, 68; as well as the essay "L'Ontologie est-elle fondamentale?" *Revue de Métaphysique et de Morale* 56 (1951): 88–98, trans. as "Is Ontology Fundamental?" in *Emmanuel Levinas: Basic Philosophical Writings,* ed. Adriaan T. Peperzak, Simon Critchley, and Robert Bernasconi (Bloomington: Indiana University Press, 1996), 1–10.

60. Goud, "Wat men van zichzelf eist," 85–86.

Therefore Levinas tirelessly investigates the possibilities and the conditions of possibility for a "tearing of this equality to self which is always being" (*GCM* 82 / 133). His phenomenological philosophy revolves around the question of the thinkability and sayability of a virtually unthinkable and unsayable ab-solute alterity that *structurally* eludes all immanent — that is, ontological, existential, epistemological, historical-philosophical, and linguistic-philosophical — definitions or categories but which nonetheless can express, gesture, signal, or, rather, trace itself *as other* and does so, as he says, ab-solutely, in-finitely.

It comes as no surprise, then, that Levinas's texts, like Adorno's, employ in part paradoxical, in part openly aporetic figures of argumentation and persuasion. Like the range of rhetorical procedures he draws upon, these figures of argumentation are out of step with the tendency toward unilinear discursivity and unambiguous intelligibility to which the Western philosophical tradition most often adheres. Yet Levinas never intends to break with this tradition. Whether or not such a break occurs de facto remains open to argument. Perhaps his thought fascinates us because it succeeds in balancing on the very edge of what seems presentable within the conceptual and systematic confines of our tradition. Western theoretical discourse, propelled by the ideals of universality and objectivity, does not, in his view, correspond to its own worthy endeavor. This is not just the result of the tradition's deafness to the sort of wrestling with truth possible in self-critique. And his inspiration (see *TI* 29 / xvii), although it stems from a radical exteriority that philosophical discourse never entirely encompasses, cannot be dismissed as something irrational: "the necessity of thinking is inscribed in the sense of transcendence" (*OB* 187 n. 6 / 9 n. 5).

Ab-solute alterity — however differently it may be motivated in Adorno and Levinas or resound throughout their works — eludes, according to both philosophers, a rational sequential ordering of meanings in a discourse, although it cannot therefore be deemed simply meaningless. The "experience" of the other, the infinite, which Levinas at times apostrophizes as true being extending beyond the limits of the (always) historical totality (see *TI* 23 / xi), at others as the beyond of being (see *TI* 301 / 278), as a "counter-concept,"[61] as "the barbarous expression 'otherwise than being'" (*OB* 178 / 224), is incompatible only with the more restricted historical interpretations of the "Logos." Levinas's central ideas combat the reductive character of what is perhaps the central category of West-

61. Rolland, *OE* 6 / 14.

ern philosophy: the key role played by the concept of *mediation,* which even Adorno maintains is to a certain extent indispensable for thought, experience, language, and action. The Western thinking of identity and totality, which depends on this concept, does not admit actual otherness, that is, transcendence "outside all mediation, all motivation that can be drawn from a generic community—outside all prior relationship and all *a priori* synthesis."[62] The tradition always attempts (in vain) to position transcendence within a conceptual context. The concept, constitutive consciousness, perception, the system, Being and its history are well-known examples of the neutral and neutralizing rubric of a third, medial term under which the beings encountered by the ego are placed, thereby forming the basis for their identification, re-identification, cognition, and recognition (*TI* 42–43 / 12–13). Western ontology thus needs to be exposed, according to Levinas, as being an egology, a philosophy of the neuter (of the "idea," of "Being," of "the concept" [*TI* 115 / 87]), and even as a logocentrism. In it the "concretissimum"[63] of the naked face, in which the infinite leaves its trace, is made into an object or theme for the becoming present of consciousness and thus subjugated to the judgment of history or involuntarily assimilated into a discourse that strives for coherence. In such a context every uncoupled alterity is subordinated under the Cartesian ideal of a rational order of clear and distinct ideas related in an axiomatic fashion (indeed, *more geometrico,* as Spinoza insisted).

The central metaphors that, according to Levinas, characterize Western conceptions of reality and the subject are Odysseus and the Odyssey (*TI* 26, 102, 176, 271 / xv 75, 151, 249; *HAH* 40, 41; *OB* 81 / 102; *DF* 10 / 24; *DEHH* 191). The wandering, loss of self, and cunning of reason which characterize the movement of subjective and objective spirit never mark a conclusive failure but, rather, always only the *preliminary deferral* of a certain homecoming. As Hegel says, "Spirit is the knowledge of itself in its renunciation; essence, which the movement is, in its otherness retains its similarity with itself."[64] By contrast, Levinas describes the ethical, religious—or, as he will also call it, metaphysical and eschatological—rela-

---

62. Levinas, "Preface to the German Edition," *EN* 199 / 251 / *Totalität und Unendlichkeit,* 10.

63. Johan F. Goud, "Über Definition und Infinition: Probleme bei der Interpretation des Denkens des Emmanuel Levinas," *Nederlands Theologisch Tijschrift* 36 (1982): 142.

64. Hegel, *Phenomenology of Spirit,* 459, see also 464 / 522, 557–58. See Henri A. Krop, "Abraham en Odysseus: Een confrontatie van Levinas en Hegel," *Tijdschrift voor Filosofie* 46 (1984): 92–135.

tionship as a relationship to an exteriority that slips away a priori from the process of the subject's coming-to-itself in its consciousness, its history, its discourse, its works and actions: "The exodus of the just is different from the odyssey of a hero; it leads toward a land promised rather than possessed."[65] Prefigured by the emigration of Abraham, its journey leads not to selfhood but to the singular and alienated ipseity and passion that can be discerned in Kafka, in which, Levinas says, "there is no returning; there is a search for a place, *un lieu* somewhere," but this is "a movement to the past," if only because in Kafka "there is, in general, no place."[66]

The ethico-religious relation, Levinas suggests, contains "the bond that is established between the same and the other without constituting a totality" (*TI* 40 / 10); it is "non-integrateable" (*TI* 53 / 24) and concerns neither an intentional object, a historical teleology, nor a communicatively structured a priori. As Levinas puts it: "The first 'vision' of eschatology (hereby distinguished from the revealed opinions of positive religions) reveals the very possibility of eschatology, that is, the breach of the totality, the possibility of a *signification without context*. The experience of morality does not proceed from this vision — it *consummates* this vision; ethics is an optics. But it is a 'vision' without image, bereft of the synoptic and totalizing objectifying virtues of vision, a relation of intentionality of wholly different type" (*TI* 23 / xii).

This conceptual preliminary decision in favor of singularity and concretion, which Levinas himself still attempts to read in the sensuous dimensions of familiar phenomena, makes the category of experience into a problematic concept in his philosophy. On the one hand, the encounter with the other is an *experience par excellence* (see *TI* 25 / xiii); on the other, Levinas maintains that he is concerned only with the attempt *to present experience as such as the source of meaning* (see *HAH* 14). The paradox is resolved if one considers the sui generis character of the ethical relation. One should emphasize that the experience of the moral enigma — like the experience of horror, which can deprive life of any meaning — is incompatible with our a priori or acquired categories of experience, thought, language, and action. But can such an experience — as a metaphor without conceptual focus, so to speak — be *philosophically* articulated outside the

65. Adriaan T. Peperzak, "Une Introduction à la lecture de *Totalité en Infini*, commentaire de 'La philosophie et l'idée de 'infini,'" *Revue des Sciences Philosophiques et Théologiques* 71 (1987): 214; see also Peperzak, *To the Other: An Introduction to the Philosophy of Emmanuel Levinas* (West Lafayette, Ind.: Purdue University Press, 1993), 68.

66. Levinas, *Is It Righteous to Be?* 141.

conceptuality developed by the philosophical tradition, its understanding of the empirical, of intuition, of synthesis? If one follows this radical line of thinking, will one not constantly be forced into argumentation *ex negativo* or—what would amount to the same—into a rhetorical strategy of hyperbole, of excess, as represented historically by the *via eminentiae*? Here reticence about using the concept of a now apophatic (or negative) then kataphatic (or affirmative) theology appears to repeat itself on the level of philosophical discourse. Levinas's work, more emphatically and explicitly than that of Adorno, compels us to consider that such a negative or superlative procedure might not suffice to articulate the *truly* other once and for all. As with Adorno, Levinas's complex mode of thinking does not base itself in common conviction, as if there were only one alternative to unfounded negativism and positivism, as if the single possible answer to the paradoxical situation of thought would consist in either falling back into a classical-metaphysical substantialism or a merely *formal* denial of the capacity of philosophy to convey alterity. In his strongest and most ambiguous formulations Levinas's philosophy, like Adorno's, suggests a third way out of this classical-modern (or is it modern-postmodern?) stalemate.

In Levinas's work philosophy therefore comes to require an alternating movement, though not Adorno's pendular movement of a dialectical critique of dialectics. Briefly put, the revolution in thinking proposed by Levinas can be formulated in a simple paradox. It seeks to be a critique of phenomenology in the doubled sense of the genitive (*genitivus subiectivus* and *obiectivus*). Levinas is concerned, as I have said, with a phenomenological critique of phenomenology,[67] which makes "use of the phenomenological method to disengage from phenomenology itself."[68] Of course, one might ask whether and how such a strategy is possible. Can one truly distinguish or even separate a methodological procedure from the ontology underlying it?

The task of philosophy, according to Levinas, is *indiscretion* in relation to the other(s). It must translate this other and act as its interpreter, which is also, of course, to betray it. Yet Levinas sees a possibility of leading this betrayal of discourse (*OB* 7, 45–46, 137, 152, 156, 161, 164 / 8, 56–58, 175, 194, 198, 206, 209), back to the postmetaphysical "metaphysical" dimen-

---

67. See Stephan Strasser, "Antiphénoménologie et phénoménologie dans la philosophie d'Emmanuel Levinas," *Revue Philosophique de Louvain* 75 (1977): 101–25. Strasser underscores that "Levinas's philosophy differs essentially from everything that, up to now, has been considered phenomenology" (101).

68. Quoted in de Boer, *Tussen filosofie en profetie*, 145 n. 102; see also 108.

sion, if we might put it this way, of the "foreword preceding languages" (*OB* 5 / 6). Such a pendular movement might, he believes, be made plausible by referring to the model of skepticism, which follows philosophical transmission like its inseparable "shadow." Even if skepticism appears to be formally irrefutable, it nevertheless belongs to the legitimate heritage of the most reflective—speculative as well as analytical—thought. (I will return to this in chap. 10.)

Alongside this always possible, quasi-skeptical canceling out or unsaying of thinking, in Levinas's later texts one also encounters an attempt to allow philosophy and language to express themselves to excess. Here he investigates the range and semantic potential of the classical *via eminentiae*, thereby weaving a rhetorical element into his philosophy.

The traits in Levinas's work that suggest parallels to Adorno leave open, of course, many critical questions that are eminently important for our understanding of minimal theologies as they depart from the dogmatic conceptions of philosophical theology, on the one hand, and from empiricist characterizations of the scholarly study of religion, on the other. Here I have attempted to offer answers to the following questions. Does true transcendence, even if one respects its ambiguity with the help of motifs such as the prohibition of images, the trace, and the enigma, not finally end up becoming an unthinkable, unsayable, thoroughly emptied X? Are not negative dialectics and the Levinasian approach of alternation in danger of plunging thought into a joyless and fruitless regression? Finally, does the revaluation of the rhetorical capacity attributed to philosophy— in its tense proximity to and distance from art and aesthetic experience— grant a more direct way to expressing ab-solute otherness than conceptual thought and argumentation? Or does the *via eminentiae* merely constitute an impossible revolt against the necessary discursivity of any *philosophical* language worthy of the name? These questions touch on complexes of problems which deserve thorough investigation and may break open the limits of immanent critique, to which we should feel bound.

Levinas's *Urzelle:* The Structure of Modern and Modernist Experience

Levinas's early independent writings contain, *in nuce,* many of the most interesting themes and figures of thought in his oeuvre as a whole.[69]

69. This section of the book was translated by Dana Hollander; an earlier version appeared as "Levinas," in *A Companion to Continental Philosophy,* ed. Simon Critchley and William R. Schroeder (Oxford: Basil Blackwell, 1998), 245–55.

As we have pointed out, religious inspiration plays a surprisingly minor role in these first, exploratory texts. They are texts that "had no especially Jewish thematic to them but which probably stemmed from that which the Judaic classifies [or accuses of being, *accuse*] or suggests as the human."[70] This is especially so for the *Urzelle* (the "germ cell," in a term inspired by Rosenzweig) of Levinas's oeuvre, the essay *On Escape,* which appeared in 1935 in *Recherches philosophiques,* an avant-garde journal edited by Alexandre Koyré, Gaston Bachelard, and Jean Wahl, among others. In this essay Levinas, referring to modern and contemporary literature from Baudelaire to Céline, evokes the specifically modernist experience of a "disorder of our time [*mal du siècle*]" (*OE* 52 / 70), a "malaise" of existing, the sickness unto being which marks this century. In Levinas's own words we find here "the anxieties of the war to come. And the whole 'fatigue of being,' the spiritual condition [*l'état d'âme*] of that period. Distrust in relation to being (which, in another form, continued in what I was able to do after this date) arose at a time in which the presentiment of the imminent Hitlerism was everywhere. Will my life have been spent between the incessant presentiment of Hitlerism and the Hitlerism that refuses itself to any forgetting?"[71] One therefore finds in *On Escape* an echo of the threat to Jewish existence during the 1930s.[72] In this and other forms of experience Levinas discerns the *horror*—the term is used throughout these early sketches—of living in a world without hope, a world stigmatized by what Benjamin and Adorno called the "ever same of the new [*Immergleiche des Neuen*]," which revives antiquity's obsession with fate (*EI* 28 / 18) and, indeed, with myth and mythology.

In retrospect this critique of the period—which relies heavily on phenomenological analyses of the subject's being thrown back upon itself, the "solitude" of existence, of the "monad" (with whose analysis *Time and the Other* commences)—may be read as a somewhat idiosyncratic reception and implicit critique of Heidegger's existential analytic of *Da-*

---

70. Levinas, *Is It Righteous to Be?* 39 / Poirié, *Emmanuel Levinas,* 90. Fabio Ciaramelli is right to note that Levinas, even before pointing to (Jewish) religion and ethics as the *via regia* to the critique of ontology, sought routes of escape from Being. *On Escape* is the best illustration of this, but the 1947 *Existence and Existents* already contains the "messianic motif" as well. See Ciaramelli, "De l'évasion à l'exode: Subjectivité et existence chez le jeune Levinas," *Revue Philosophique de Louvain* 80 (1982): 554. See also the 1947 essay "Etre juif," first published in *Confluences* 7, nos. 15–17 (1947): 253–64; and recently reprinted in *Cahiers d'Études Lévinassiennes,* no. 1 (2002): 99–106.

71. Levinas, *Is It Righteous to Be?* 39 / Poirié, *Emmanuel Levinas,* 90, trans. modified.

72. See Rolland's annotation, *OE* 74–75 / 103–4.

sein in its "thrownness [*Geworfenheit*]" and "anxiety [*Angst*]." Yet, as
Jacques Rolland makes clear, the "fundamental mood [*Grundstimmung*]"
of "anxiety" in Heidegger's *Was ist Metaphysik?* (*What Is Metaphysics?*) is
to some extent comparable to the "indeterminacy [*Unbestimmtheit*]" in
Levinas's characterizations of malaise and disgust, indeed, of the "horror
[*l'horreur*] of being" (*EE* 20 / 20; see also 60–61 / 97–98). These states and
modes of Being, of existence in the very moment and momentum that
it posits and hypostatizes and diversifies itself into separate existents—
without, therefore, allowing Being to be thought as multiple *in itself* (and,
hence, no longer permitting one to think ontological pluralism radically
enough)—are determined neither by something particular in the world
nor by the subject's psycho-physical state.[73]

Levinas links his interpretation of the oppression of modern existence
to a preliminary outline of a demand that is central to his early and late
work: the call for an escape (*évasion,* or, in a neologism, *excendance* [see
OE 54 / 73]) from Being as such, "getting out of Being by a new path,
at the risk of overturning certain notions that to the common sense and
the wisdom of nations seemed the most evident" (*OE* 73 / 99). This early
motif disproves the view that the question concerning the "otherwise than
Being" is without precedent in the development of Levinas's thought and
merely results from the "turn" that his writing seems to have taken after
1963, following the revision, in the essay "The Trace of the Other," of certain premises upon which *Totality and Infinity* rested and perhaps also
from Derrida's immanent critique in "Violence and Metaphysics."[74]

The desire to break out of Being is, Levinas asserts, most apparent in
modern literature. (Here he still uses the word *besoin,* although later he
will prefer *désir.*) Such an appeal to literature is not unusual in his work.
In *On Escape* he praises the manner in which the merciless fantasy and
brilliant use of language in Louis Ferdinand Céline's *Voyage au bout de la
nuit* (*Journey to the End of Night*), by evoking a "sad and desperate cynicism" that seems to permeate modern experience (*OE* 64 / 86), strips the

73. See Jacques Rolland, "Sortir de l'être par une nouvelle voie," published as an introduction to the re-edition of *De l'évasion;* "Getting Out of Being by a New Path," *OE* 15–16, 102–3,
12 / 23, 57, 20. In his annotation Rolland notes that Levinas is here already interested in a "questioning . . . not of Being in the being-there or *Da-sein* . . . , but rather that of the being-there
in its Being" (*OE* 83 / 111).

74. See, for this view, Stephan Strasser, *Jenseits von Sein und Zeit: Eine Einführung in Emmanuel Levinas' Philosophie* (The Hague: Martinus Nijhoff, 1978), 220, 223. Incidentally, Strasser
also identifies a turn (*Kehre*) in Levinas's later work toward positions whose radicality is comparable to that of the earlier work (225).

world of all ornament — or, rather, liberates it. The weariness in which we want to escape existence itself could, Levinas suggests, be called an escape "without an itinerary and without end," a feeling of indeterminacy which was sounded to its depths by Baudelaire: "Like Baudelaire's true travellers, it is a matter of parting for the sake of parting" (*EE* 25 / 32). Indeed, as if Levinas were anticipating the mood and modality of the idea of messianic redemption which Adorno so poignantly formulates in the final aphorism of *Minima Moralia*, the "need for evasion" is "filled with chimerical hopes or not, no matter!" (*OE* 56 / 74).

Although Levinas scarcely succeeds, in this *Urzelle* essay, in finding a clear point of departure, a point from which the possibility and the modality of a way out of Being can be described "concretely" or "positively," he does so "negatively" by drawing important lines of demarcation between his own concerns and those of both traditional and modern or contemporary philosophy. From Aristotle to Bergson and Heidegger, he suggests, philosophy has always emphasized the finitude of Being, without ever putting Being itself into question. Occidental philosophy has, Levinas goes on to say, couched ontological critique only as the wish for a "better Being," that is, with a view to community and infinite Being, a correspondence between an "I" and the world, and the inner harmony of a subject that realizes itself by resisting oppression and limitation. Yet this pathos of freedom and the longing to be at peace with oneself presuppose a principal — original or ultimate — *self-sufficiency* of Being. Levinas counters this self-sufficiency with the question "Is being sufficient unto itself?" (*OE* 70 / 95)?

Being is not the final ground or the highest limit to our philosophical reflections, Levinas believes (*OE* 56–58 / 74). Indeed, a civilization that puts up with the sheer ineluctable tragedy and despair of Being, as well as with the crimes that Being justifies, deserves to be called "barbarian" (*OE* 73 / 98). He would endorse without hesitation one of idealism's deepest aspirations: the search for ways of surpassing the world of things, on which Being was first modeled. But the course idealism took toward this goal led to a vanishing point at which all its discoveries — the dimensions of the ideal, consciousness, and becoming (*OE* 71 / 96) — quickly fell prey to a renewed ontologization. In *On Escape* Levinas already tries to disrupt this ontological imperialism, this tendency toward a concept of Being which in its very dynamic is rather static and which is no more than a "mark of a certain civilization" (*OE* 56 / 74; see 72–73 / 98): "The insufficiency of the human condition has never been understood otherwise than as a limitation of Being. . . . The transcendence of these limits, [and] communion with the infinite Being remained philosophy's sole preoccupation.... And yet the *modern sensibility* wrestles with problems that indicate, *perhaps for the first time,* the abandonment of this concern with transcendence" (OE 53 / 69, my emph.).

How can the motif of escape—which, according to Levinas, has intermittently punctuated the intellectual and political history of the West, in a rhythm that obeys no determinable law of progress, decline, or cyclical development and "is" in that sense ahistorical, always untimely and out of joint—nonetheless find a certain privilege and elective affinity in the economic and artistic conditions of modernity in which it manifests or reveals itself, "perhaps for the first time"? Levinas observes that neither the classical-modern response to the age-old question of Being nor the romantic revolt against this response ever breaks with a *harmonizing* ideal of being-human, an ideal that reaches its highest expression in the ideology of the late-bourgeois intelligentsia. Levinas's first independent reflection on the problem of subjectivity (apart from his commentaries on Husserl and Heidegger) was thus already prompted by a critique of the self-sufficiency of the bourgeois "I," whose constant striving to enrich and complete itself corresponds to the industriousness that shaped the contours of Western capitalist societies. Here we are already dealing with what Derrida, in "Violence and Metaphysics," describes as a critique of ideology which is other than merely Marxist.[75] In a different context Levinas later adduces this stifling "concept of progress," which poisons the atmosphere of modernity, as the deeper motive behind the 1968 students' and workers' revolt. A closer look reveals that there, too, the conditions of possibility for a society driven by achievement and consumption were subjected to critique. Levinas regards these as an "ontology of the false present," to use an expression of Adorno's, and unmasks the blind, collective striving for individual self-preservation, "which no religious breath any longer renders egalitarian."[76] To put it more succinctly: "Behind the capital of *having* weighed a capital of *being*."[77] This overinvestment in Being inspires, motivates, and necessitates evasion and ethical disinterestedness—a difference that is not ontological, as Heidegger thought, but a *non-indifference* that, according to Levinas's later work, is the condition of possibility for the critique of ideology and ontology as such.

75. See Derrida, *Writing and Difference*, 97 / 145.
76. Levinas, *HAH* 110 n. 9 / "No Identity," in *CPP* 150 n. 9.
77. Ibid.

In the modern epoch no one can remain in the margins of the inscrutable mechanisms that generate the universal (ontological, symbolical, and political) order. Within the churning gears of the modern age, anybody can be mobilized, and no one can withdraw from the game or restore an innocence to things. Modernity thus defines itself in an unrelenting earnestness and a premature adulthood: "Temporal existence takes on the inexpressible flavor of the absolute. The elementary truth *that there is being*—a being that has value and weight—is revealed at a depth that measures its brutality and its seriousness" (*OE* 54 / 70).

The two extremes of modern experience—the experiential mode of naked being, on the one hand, and the desire for escape that this being provokes (but how exactly?), on the other—both exhibit a single structure, which is sui generis. The analogy with which Levinas first describes the burden of naked being and then evokes a flight that can barely hope to effectuate a real break rigidifies these two dimensions into mirror images of each other. If the transitions in Levinas's presentation are not entirely convincing, this *absolutization* of extremes—making them into something more than purely critical or rhetorical motifs—is to blame. The idea of a pure Being of things or the notion of a frightening, neutral dimension that would remain if one were to subtract the world of things and the idea of a possible break with this Being and thus a retreat to an otherwise than Being all risk becoming *abstract.* In particular, these complementary figures signal the limits of their phenomenological description, in a gesture that will be reiterated in Levinas's later analyses of the polarity between the excluded thirds—neither being nor nothingness—of *il y a* (there is) and *illeity* as two different but co-originary modalities and possibilities of one and the same transcendence,[78] as well as of the up-and-down movements *en-deçà* (on the hither side) and *au-delà* (beyond), or, indeed, the movements of *transdescendence* and *transascendence,* to cite notions that *Totality and Infinity* will borrow from the metaphysical treatises of Jean Wahl, which the two terms for escape in the *Urzelle, évasion* and *excendance,* prefigure (*OE* 54 /73).

Whatever difficulties lurk behind these complex notions, one cannot deny the heuristic power of Levinas's findings. The words he chooses in this early essay lay down an explosive charge under the tradition of Western ontology and onto-theology which waits only to be ignited. These

78. See my essay "Adieu, à dieu, a-Dieu," in *Ethics as First Philosophy: The Significance of Emmanuel Levinas for Philosophy, Literature, and Religion,* ed. and intro. Adriaan T. Peperzak (New York: Routledge, 1995), 211–20.

early analyses make clear that the problem he addresses is not simply the question concerning the existence of God, His way of being and essential attributes. Levinas might even be called, as Rolland rightly notes, a thinker of the "death of God" (*OE* 89 / 117), in that he writes: "it is not in view of eternity that escape is made. Eternity is just the intensification, or radicalization, of the fatality of that being, which is riveted to itself. And there is a deep truth in the myth that says that eternity weighs heavily upon the immortal gods" (*OE* 71 / 95). A different, more elusive, and, perhaps, more evasive temporality is at work in the notion of escape.

According to Levinas—who in this respect is in agreement with the early and later Heidegger as well as with the Derrida of "Violence and Metaphysics"—the classical-metaphysical and modern *antithesis of the finite and the infinite,* of permanence and becoming, of nothingness and eternity, can apply only to *that which is,* that is, to the world of things and its natural composition (*OE* 49 / 69). This antithesis operates within a space of reasons, conceptuality, and metaphorics which allows for a certain extension, for certain properties of objects of thought and experience to be determined in a process of mutual comparison, a process finally reflected in the ideal of perfection. But the *Being of things,* the bare fact of the existence of beings, refers only to itself and in doing so takes on the character of a *virtual absolute* (*OE* 56–57 / 76). This Being betrays a "defect still more profound" than mere limitation (*OE* 51 / 69), whether qualitative or quantitative. With this, Levinas announces a decisive break with any philosophy of finitude: "Existence of itself harbors something tragic, something that is not there only because of its finitude and that death cannot resolve" (*EE* 20 / 21, trans. modified).

The malaise of Being is expressed in the desire for a way out. Levinas calls this desire "the fundamental category of existence" (*OE* 65 / 88). The suffering that gives rise to it is the pervasive awareness that it is impossible to let the treadmill stand still. The oppressive feeling associated with the analogous phenomena of shame and disgust, for instance, attacks us from within; it is a "revolting presence of ourselves to ourselves" (*OE* 66 / 89). Shame consists in the impossibility of breaking away from oneself, no matter how much one would like to do so (*OE* 65 / 87). Disgust, repugnance, which Levinas subtly analyzes long before Sartre's *La Nausée* (*Nausea*),[79] corresponds to the impossibility of affirming the being that

---

79. Jean-Paul Sartre, *La Nausée* (Paris: Gallimard, 1938).

one is (*OE* 66 / 90; see also *EE* 17 / 39). The modern experience of permanent affirmation and self-reference of Being, "closed to all the rest, without windows onto other things" (*OE* 68 / 92), which Levinas illustrates in a concentrated form, does not yield a new array of properties in our existence. What is central here is not the fact that in our undertakings we always already leave unrealized a number of possibilities or, better, that we have a need for "innumerable lives." The desire for escape does not attempt, via creative activity, to elude the obstacles that it encounters but, rather, withdraws from the weight of Being by breaking through the prison within itself (see *OE* 55 / 73). No romantic or nihilistic revolt, no nostalgic longing for death, and certainly no desire for a fulfilled Being—in sum, no new founding of the I (see *OE* 53–54, 55 / 71, 73) and no escape from the originary guilt of which Heidegger speaks in *Being and Time*—can adequately express the desire to which Levinas points. These regressive figures of human striving are in search of a secure abode; they are merely a means of evading a forbidding "*definition*" of existence, more precisely, "the horror of a certain *definition* of our being and not of being as such" (*OE* 53 / 71). Levinas does not hesitate to point out that this holds true for Heidegger's (and for Sartre's) philosophy of freedom. The proper escape, in the sense he himself seeks, is not a search for the proper, as these contemporaries thought.

True flight is not directed toward any goal. It prefigures or echoes an exodus, the journey undertaken by Abraham as opposed to that of Odysseus, about whose destination there is never any doubt. The malaise and the desire for a way out concern "an attempt to get out without knowing where one is going" (*OE* 59 / 78; see also *OB* 8 / 9). What is sought is less satisfaction than deliverance (*OE* 59 / 78): "The desire for escape is found to be absolutely identical at every juncture to which its adventure leads it as need; it is as though the path it traveled could not lessen its dissatisfaction" (*OE* 53 / 71–72, trans. modified). The sublimity of this gesture resides in the unsublatable inadequacy of any satisfaction to this desire (*OE* 59–60 / 79). In other words, attempts to quench the desire never remove the restlessness of the malaise. In this we have, in a sense, the *photographic negative* or *formal analogy* of what Levinas will describe as metaphysical-ethical desire—*désir* as opposed to *besoin*—in his later work. This means that at the level of argumentative structure and, perhaps, descriptive content there can be no *conceptually determinable* distinction between the two extremes around which Levinas's reflection incessantly revolves. As Lévi-

Strauss remarked, "a photographic positive and negative contain the same quantity of information."[80]

A description of the supposed satisfaction of desire in pleasure shows that pleasure's (closed) dialectic is, in the final analysis, condemned to failure (*OE* 60–63 / 82–84). Even though its dynamic breaks away from the fixed forms in which beings are placed and even though its affectivity points to a third way between thinking and acting, the path of gratification remains a "deceptive escape" (*OE* 62 / 83). Levinas's later ambivalence toward the erotic as a model of transcendence, his tendency to focus on *agape* and, indeed, on love in general, is already in evidence here.

Psychology, by contrast, misunderstands desire as need in the sense of "privation" (*OE* 54, 56–57 / 73, 76), as a weakness or a defect in the human condition. It therefore rests, according to Levinas, on an untenable metaphysical assumption. It identifies the ground of desire with emptiness, a vacuum, a lack of Being, while interpreting the actual in terms of fullness, of a wholeness of Being. In doing so, it absolutizes a metaphorics that makes sense only in the world of things that exist as a part of nature (*OE* 58–59 / 77–78). Desire seeks to free itself from this assumption (*OE* 61–62 / 83): "Desire expresses the presence of our being and not its deficiency" (*OE* 60 / 81, trans. modified). Desire concerns, in other words, "the purity of the fact of being, which already looks like an escape" (*OE* 57 / 76).

The early text *On Escape,* not unlike the first work of Adorno, thus allows us to read *in nuce* a problematic leitmotif in the development of Levinas's thought. This leitmotif is the aporia that the flight from Being is, on the one hand, conceived as the *internally produced mirror image* of Being, while, on the other hand, it is both *called for* and *impossible.* This impossibility, however, is not simply a failure. It is the structure of the failure of a certain metaphysics, which is reread and made productive here. The impossibility for beings to escape from Being or from being-there corresponds in the later writings to an impossibility for thought, experience, or language to grasp, let alone determine, the Other in its ambiguity as the face of the neighbor and the stranger, as the idea, the trace, or the enigma of the infinite, as the intrigue of the other in the finite totality of the same. Yet, while the formalism of the original structure of escape is thus concretized as an ethical movement toward the Other, this Other "is," paradoxically, that which — or the one who — continues to escape. In Levinas's later work these two moments come to be presented as two aspects of one and the same movement.

In *On Escape* Levinas attempts to understand this flight or evasion in terms of an "inner structure" of Being's own self-positing (57 / 75). In this view Being—which is returned to the phenomena that testify to its ineluctability—produces its own opposite by a contradictory movement, in the "*very experience of pure being.*" In a combined moment of malaise, pleasure, shame, disgust, and horror, it gives rise to an experience of revolt: "This 'nothing-more-to-be-done' is the mark of a limit-situation in which the uselessness of any action is precisely the sign of the supreme instant from which we can only depart. The experience of pure being is at the same time the experience of its internal antagonism and of the escape that foists itself on us" (*OE* 67 / 90).

Powerlessness and the finitude of Being itself thus seem to kindle the desire for flight. In other words, that Being is a burden for itself (see *OE* 65 / 88) is the "source of all desire" (*OE* 69 93, trans. modified). But it is no less obvious that, when one follows the progression of this type of reflection, a real way out of or beyond Being cannot be found. The question of what kind of utopia of happiness and dignity such an escape might promise must remain unanswered (*OE* 55/ 74). The escape remains a possibility internal to Being and thus, in a sense, remains in its very essence tainted by Being, existence, and existents.

Only when, starting in the final sections of *Time and the Other*, Levinas turns to the *concretion* of the ethical dimension and articulates the modality of transcendence with the help of the metaphor or, rather, figure of the trace does he manage to break out of this impasse. Or so it seems at first glance. The trace of the other allows one to think the modality of transcendence otherwise than by an abstract negation that presupposes an identity preceding the very act of this negation.[81] It is not an essential possibility inherent in the structure of Being and existence as such. If anything, the trace "is not"; it signals the impossibility that Being, existence, and existents might come into their own.

Unlike this later thought of the trace, then, Levinas's earliest attempts to put the frightening and oppressive experience of Being into words remain ensnared in irresolvable problems. The same is true for the middle

---

81. See *OB* 195 n. 16 / 142 n. 16: "Every idea or evasion, as every idea of malediction weighing on a destiny, already presupposes the ego constituted on the basis of the self and already free."

period of his oeuvre, which centers on the opposite pole of an ethical *primum intelligibele* and thus on an ethical transcendental philosophy of sorts.[82] In the main work of this middle period, condensed in the thesis submitted at the suggestion of Jean Wahl for the *doctorat d'état*, which was to become *Totality and Infinity*, Levinas rethinks exteriority in terms of an infinity of Being. In a sense he thereby retreats from the position put forward in *On Escape*. The fact that in the later philosophy of the trace of the ethical takes up again the radical critique of ontology contained in this early essay — and, so to speak, turns it against the position consolidated in the middle period — serves once again to emphasize the importance of that short text. Studying it, as Rolland notes, is hardly an exercise in "archaeology" or "paleography,"[83] for the most radical features of Levinas's later writing are anticipated and prefigured in this youthful text. In Levinas's own words: one can discern in *On Escape* a vigilant awareness of the modern experience of the "no way out [*sans-issue*]" which goes hand in hand with a "determined anticipation of impossible new thoughts."[84] Although the later work explicitly keeps its distance from the figure of the evasion or flight that plays such a central role in *On Escape,* it reaffirms the "impossible new thought" of a movement beyond Being's essence which does not know where it is going: "The task is to conceive of the possibility of a break out of essence. To go where? Toward what region? To stay on what ontological plane? But the extraction from essence contests the unconditional privilege of the question 'where?'; it signifies a null-site [*non-lieu*]. The essence claims to recover and cover over every ex-ception — negativity, nihilation, and, already since Plato, non-being, which 'in a certain sense is'" (*OB* 8 / 9). That the exception "is" an ethical one in this passage from *Otherwise than Being,* whereas in *On Escape* the primacy of the other is not yet that of the Other (*autrui*), the infinite, *illeity,* or the "divine comedy" matters little, for the evocation and articulation of these later motifs are bound up — *at least structurally or formally* — with the experiences described earlier. Paradoxically, these experiences in turn serve to concretize, deformalize, and modulate the modality of ethical transcendence in whose shadow they stand (and which they follow, without escape).

---

82. See de Boer, "Ethical Transcendental Philosophy," in Cohen, *Face to Face with Levinas,* 83–115.

83. Rolland, "Getting Out of Being by a New Path," *OE* 4 / 12.

84. The quotation is from Levinas's 1981 letter to Rolland, *OE* 2 / 8.

This Side of Ontological Difference: Descending into the Vanishing Point of All Experience

In presenting the shadow side of our specifically modern experience of anonymity, amorality, and depersonalization, for which the *il y a,* the "there is," stands, Levinas uses the very linguistic figures and formal structures with which he characterizes the positive ethical relationship. How are we to understand this? We have already noted the irony that Levinas attempts to undo "idealism" via a thought experiment that is in many respects analogous to the one with which Husserl attempts to establish transcendental idealism (and in which Descartes finds the indubitable foundation, i.e., the clear and distinct idea, of the *ego cogito,* at the very heart of the experiment of doubting everything else—the external and interior world, all we have learned through the senses and tradition).[85]

Again, for Levinas, as for Adorno, the question or threat of epistemological skepticism is not the issue. In the discussion following his presentation of "Reflections on Phenomenological Technique," Levinas recalls what the problem—and "scandal"—of idealism and, hence, of skepticism entails:

> The question of knowing if the outside world exists or not has no meaning in phenomenology. The refutation of idealism is known: Kant wrote it. In Husserl I believe it goes exactly the same way. But Husserl continues to speak about idealism anyway. He didn't know it would greatly impede his students. In what sense does he speak about it? The meaning of the world is permeable to thought, as if it came from thought. But above all the subject is maintained with a special dignity. In no way is the subject involved with the reality it constitutes. It doesn't identify with its legacy or its work. It always stays behind. And it is for this reason that the subject can always speak: it is the possibility of rupture. What is speech, if not the power of detachment. . . . If the subject didn't have this possibility of standing away from everything that happens to it, it would disappear into a totalitarianism. That's the sense in which idealism is valid in phenomenology—in the moral sense of the term.[86]

In other words, what for Levinas is at stake in phenomenology, both in its Husserlian transcendental idealist and its Heideggerian hermeneutic-

---

85. See de Boer, "Ethical Transcendental Philosophy," in Cohen, *Face to Face with Levinas,* 87. I take the following sketch from this essay.

86. Emmanuel Levinas, *Discovering Existence with Husserl,* trans. Richard A. Cohen and Michael B. Smith (Evanston, Ill.: Northwestern University Press, 1998), 106.

ontological orientation, is the modern philosophical concern with "realism" and its antipodes. The "renewal of ontology" which these thinkers have brought about

> does not presuppose an affirmation of the existence of the external world and of its primacy over consciousness. It affirms that what is essential in human spirituality does not lie in our relationship with the things which make up the world, but is determined by a relationship, effected in our very existence, with the pure fact that there is Being, the nakedness of this bare fact. This relationship, far from covering over nothing but a tautology, constitutes an event, whose reality and somehow surprising character manifest themselves in the disquietude in which that relationship is enacted. The evil in Being, the evil of matter in idealist philosophy becomes the evil of Being. (*EE* 19 / 18–19)

Evoking the (spiritual?) exercise of universal doubt, descending into the vanishing point of all experience, this side of this world and its objects, this side of ontology and the ontological difference, has a more than theoretical aim. It purpose is not to once and for all establish the unshakeable foundation, the *fundamentum inconcussum,* of all metaphysical, physical, and moral thought but, instead, to expose the dimension of—and beyond—Being as such: the "element" of judgment and action which is irreducible to any ontico-ontological situatedness and, in this sense, is this side (*en-deça*) of all experience.

This thought experiment is an imaginary destruction of the world, the mental act—in classical phenomenology the merely theoretical or methodological operation—of subtracting persons and things (see *OE* 7 ff., 52 / 15 ff. 70; *EE* 21, 57, 63, 66 / 25, 93, 103; *TO* 134 ff., 167, / 25 ff., 60; *TI* 141, 143, 150, 190, 258, 281 / 115, 117, 120, 124, 165, 236, 257). According to Husserl, only transcendental consciousness then remains and, for the rest, "a nothing." In a marginal note in his own copy of *Ideen I* (*Ideas 1*) Husserl later changed that expression to "an anti-sense [a nonsense, *Widersinn*]."[87] Levinas, by contrast, moves this limit of our engrained capacity for imagination to the center of philosophical reflection, although he admits that there can be no representation of this dimension, or even a phenomenological description of it in the common sense of the term. That insight makes the question of the conditions of possibility for Levinas's paradoxi-

---

87. See de Boer, "Ethical Transcendental Philosophy," in Cohen, *Face to Face with Levinas,* 88.

cal discourse — in which a place needs to be kept for this shadow side of our existence — so difficult.

In Levinas's view the realm of the absurd, silence, and the void does not concern a nothing: "an analysis which feigns the disappearance of every existent — and even of the *cogito* which thinks it — is overrun by the chaotic rumbling of an anonymous 'to exist,' which is an existence without existents and which no negation manages to overcome. *There is* [il y a] — impersonally — like *it is raining* [il pleut] or *it is night* [il fait nuit]" (*DF* 292 / 407; see also *EE* 52, 53 / 93, 95; *TO* 47 / 26). Or again: "There is not only something that is but '*there is,*' above and through these somethings, an anonymous process of being. Without a bearer, without a subject. As in insomnia, it doesn't stop being — *there is.*"[88] This "impersonal expression," Levinas notes, finds its equivalent in Heidegger's later phrases such as "it worlds [*es weltet*]."[89]

In a similar thought experiment that repeats and modifies the motif of the "evil genius" in Descartes, Levinas seeks to show just the opposite. He believes that, by surpassing Husserl and Descartes in raising the possibility of universal doubt about the "integrity" or reliability of the world — not only of external appearances but also of internal ones and their supposed Archimedean point, the *ego cogito* — he can make plausible an *unavoidable* ethical relation that alone can restore our acknowledgment of and belief in the world, its objects, and persons. Given that the possibility of total doubt is inherent in phenomena as such, objective knowledge is thinkable only if there is (at least) an Other whose (sincere) expression creates meaning in the essential ambiguity of the world, which is silent in and of itself: "But a world absolutely silent that would not come to us from the word, be it mendacious, would be an-archic, without principle, without a beginning. Thought would strike nothing substantial. On first contact the *phenomenon* would degrade into *appearance* and in this sense would remain in equivocation, under suspicion of an evil genius" (*TI* 90 / 63). By contrast, Levinas consistently emphasizes that "the Other is the principle of phenomena." It would be a mistake to have the phenomenon *derived* from the Other in the way Kant sought to base the world of appearances on the thing in itself. Not a causal relationship but, rather, the mutual implication of condition of possibility and reality is at stake here. Even in this context, Levinas avoids the Kantian concept of deduction: "For de-

88. Levinas, *Is It Righteous to Be?* 45/ Poirié, *Emmanuel Levinas,* 101.
89. Levinas, *Is It Righteous to Be?* 147.

duction is a mode of thinking that applies to objects already given." Yet, he concludes, "the interlocutor cannot be deduced, for the relationship between him and me is presupposed by every proof" (*TI* 92 / 65).

Yet must we not question the thought experiment of a *total* doubt about what is given? Even if one takes into consideration that this concerns solely a theoretical abstraction from the quotidian experience of the world as it is lived, one might rightly object that, by appropriating the experiment, Levinas remains ipso facto within the same problematic as Descartes and Husserl, a domain he otherwise attempts to escape. How can Levinas distance himself from the implicit premises he has appropriated from the idealist philosophy of consciousness, which he wants to criticize, while, paradoxically, surpassing it?[90] Might the modification of the Cartesian and Husserlian approach which he performs, in which not the *ego cogito* or transcendental consciousness but the Other appears as the "origin" of true meaning, actually set limits to the thought of a complete reduction of the world of beings, which he had once expressed? Or was Hume correct to note: "But neither is there any such original principle, which has a prerogative above others . . . or if there were, could we advance a step beyond it, but by the use of those very faculties of which we are supposed to be already diffident. The Cartesian doubt, therefore, were it ever possible to be attained by any human creature (as it plainly is not) would be entirely incurable"?[91] Perhaps that thought experiment, which Levinas approaches from two perspectives, can only be salvaged by reinterpreting it *rhetorically* and seeking to understand it as an articulation at the most extreme point of the experience of a difference, whether horrific or ethical, that cannot be grasped conceptually. As I will show, in his later designation of the ethical via the metaphor of anarchy, which he had previously attributed to the unsublatable double meaning of phenomena, Levinas does, in a certain sense, confirm this suggestion.

But there is yet another way in which Levinas reads the Husserlian experiment — indeed, spiritual exercise — of the imaginary destruction of the

---

90. According to the critique of "mentalism" in the later Wittgenstein, Ryle, and Rorty, the Cartesian doubt experiment disavows an intertwining of consciousness, language, and world which it must *always already* presuppose. This critique would seem equally applicable to Levinas's use of the topos of the imaginary destruction of the world. But Wittgenstein's *Philosophical Investigations,* Ryle's *Concept of Mind,* and Rorty's *Philosophy and the Mirror of Nature* also miss some crucial elements in this thought experiment — a "spiritual exercise" of sorts.

91. David Hume, *An Enquiry concerning Human Understanding,* 150. The only result of such an argument would be "that momentary amazement and irresolution and confusion, which is the result of scepticism" (155 n. 1).

world and the *epochē* (or conversion of the intellectual gaze) upon which it is based. This reading makes its appearance in the short and enigmatic essay entitled "La Réalité et son ombre" ("Reality and Its Shadow"), to which the following chapter will be devoted. There we read: "The consciousness of the absence of the object which characterizes an image is not equivalent to a simple neutralization of the thesis, as Husserl would have it, but is equivalent to an alteration of the very being of the object, where its essential forms appear as a garb that it abandons in withdrawing" (RS 7 / 135–36 / 779). Here, as in *On Escape,* we find the hypothesis of an internally produced — indeed, engendered — inversion of Being and beings, of things into images, of faces into caricatures or masks, a reversal that comes about in movements of resemblance and allegorization which both, Levinas suggests, escape our control, although they are at once the very condition for and limitation of philosophical critique, artistic criticism, commerce, and responsibility. The neutralization that Husserl reduced to a mental operation becomes here a general ontological principle, whose temporal structure — or seeming lack thereof — is all that counts: "Being is that which it is, that which reveals itself in its truth, and, at the same time, it resembles itself, is its own image. The original gives itself as though it were at a distance from itself, as though it were withdrawing itself, as though something in being delayed behind being" (RS 6–7 / 134 / 779, trans. modified). The delay or belatedness of Being and beings with respect to themselves is thus based on a coincidence — a simultaneity — whose ontological characteristic is that of an indifference of sorts; more precisely, an absolute difference between Being and its "error," a difference one is not able to tell (i.e., determine in any conceptual or discursive way). In this reading I need no longer resort to a heterological, let alone theological, affirmative, or apophatic, model for interpreting Levinas's most paradoxical statements and aporias; instead, I will restrict myself to an ontological — a negative metaphysical or aphenomenological, as it were — reading alone. Levinas thus presents us with an ontological — an immanent — critique of ontology, a step removed (ahead and beyond) from the phenomenological critique of ontology which we encountered earlier. In the early essays *On Escape, Existence and Existents, Time and the Other,* and "Reality and Its Shadow" this critique digs its way downward, *transdescendance in immanence,* as it were.

In the texts surrounding *Otherwise than Being* it works its way upward, *via eminentiae,* in what constitutes a similar movement or figure of thought, namely, that of a *transascendence in immanence.* But these characterizations (not used by Levinas, who, following Wahl, speaks of "transdescendance" and "transascendance" pure and simple) remain unsatisfactory and deeply problematic as well. Indeed, they serve to indicate a problem: that of the *self-insufficiency* of Being, its noncoincidence with itself here and now, in every instant (or instance) itself:

> These are two contemporary possibilities of being. Alongside of the simultaneity of the idea and the soul [*l'âme*] — that is, of being and its disclosure — which the *Phaedo* teaches, there is the simultaneity of a being and its reflection [*reflet*]. The absolute at the same time reveals itself to reason and lends itself to a sort of erosion, outside of all causality. The non-truth of being is not an obscure residue of being, but is its sensible character itself, by which there are resemblance and images in the world. . . . As a dialectic of being and nothingness, becoming [*le devenir*] does indeed, since the *Parmenides,* make its appearance in the world of Ideas. It is through imitation that participation engenders shadows and cuts through the participation of the Ideas in one another which is revealed to the understanding [*intelligence*]." (RS 7 / 135–36 / 781, trans. modified)

Blanchot says as much when, in his homage to Levinas, entitled "Notre compagnon clandestine" ("Our Clandestine Companion"), he cautions against an approach that would interpret this author's work in terms of a given set of "topics," thereby promoting a "cursory reading" that might "arrest those extreme questions continually being posed to us."[92] Any such approach, Blanchot suggests — for example, the attempt to describe Levinas's work as a "philosophy of transcendence or as a metaphysical ethics," would be "inadequate, if only because we no longer know how to grasp such words, overcharged as they are with traditional meaning. The word *transcendence* is either too strong — it quickly reduces us to silence — or, on the other hand, it keeps both itself and us within the limits of what it should open up."[93] Instead, Blanchot opts for a reading that amplifies the most radical consequences of Levinas's thought, the most important of which was anticipated by Wahl: "In his own unique way, Jean Wahl used to say that the greatest transcendence, the transcendence of transcendence, is ultimately the immanence, or the perpetual referral, of the one to the

---

92. Maurice Blanchot, "Notre compagnon clandestine," in *Textes pour Emmanuel Levinas,* ed. François Laruelle (Paris: Jean-Michel Place, 1980), 84 / "Our Clandestine Companion," in Cohen, *Face to Face with Levinas,* 47.

93. Ibid., 48 / 85.

other. Transcendence with immanence: Levinas is the first to devote himself to this strange structure."[94]

De Boer too quickly, then, concludes that philosophy does not succeed in its attempt to bring the *il y a* into view: Levinas, he writes, "describes it in a suggestive way by drawing on quotations from Racine, Shakespeare, and Blanchot. Here the thinker must make room for the poet."[95] Phenomenology can run up against the boundary of solipsism but can never pass beyond it. The *il y a* can thus never be dissected "objective-analytically."[96] It may also elude every phenomenological intuition and description, even though Levinas seems to introduce it as an extrapolation from them. Upon closer examination, his analyses circumscribe the *il y a* only *"poetically and evocatively."*[97] Levinas, of course, maintains a difference between philosophical discourse in the more narrow sense and poetics, with the latter needing further clarification—although, as with Adorno, the lines of demarcation are (unintentionally) fluid. Because horror and its contrary motif, the transcendence of the good—which are topics for both philosophers—cannot be grasped *per genus proximum et differentiam specificam,* their heterogeneity or incommensurability can only be presented aesthetically, via metaphor and allegory. The metaphor of the trace, as we will show, may, however, prevent Levinas's and Adorno's philosophical discourse from lapsing into the merely aesthetic. Only the ambiguity of that metaphor can provide *philosophical* validity to any difference—motivated from whatever opposed poles.

One might still ask, however, whether the realm of the aesthetic is actually more appropriate to the sphere of the uncanny than is philosophy. Levinas's analyses of the experience of art reveal whether and how art can help express the *il y a.* Before I embark on an aesthetic entry into the *il y a,* however, I should clarify this recalcitrant concept.

Levinas presents us with the *epochē* out of which we might begin to trace the *il y a* as a more than theoretical process. He connects this dimension with the supposedly epochal event of the fate of Being (*Seinsgeschick*), which paradigmatically unveils its hideous face in the experience of war. During World War II there was, especially for Jews, a descent into chaos "as

94. Ibid.

95. De Boer, "Ethical Transcendental Philosophy," in Cohen, *Face to Face with Levinas,* 88.

96. R. Burggraeve, "Het 'il y a' in het heteronomie-denken van Levinas," *Bijdragen* 44 (1983): 275.

97. Ibid.

if being itself had been suspended" (*NP* 119 / 178). That absolute emptiness corresponds to the "biblical 'unformed and void' [*tohuwabohu*]" (*NP* 91 / 135) which might be imagined before creation. This enigmatic pole of Levinas's thought is related to the motif of the mythical prior world in Rosenzweig's *Star of Redemption*. Levinas also alludes to Anaximander's *apeiron*, or "the indefinite" (*TI* 157, 196 / 132, 171), as well as to Pascal's notion of the silence of infinite spaces (*EE* 53 / 95). Yet what Levinas is after cannot be illustrated merely by a problematic thought experiment and various motifs borrowed from the philosophical tradition. He also traces the depersonalizing stream in concrete experiences in which the structures of the natural order, as well as the categories of reflection, become bounded and erased. Burggraeve's designation of these "subjectless procedures" as "limit experiences" may be too strong. Just as "primitive" participation cannot give rise to the thought of an independent subject — but only to an "*impersonal vigilance*" (*EE* 55 ff. / 98 ff.), as Levinas, freely following Lévy-Bruhl, suggests[98] — these prereligious experiences have something in common with what Maurice Blanchot expresses in his novels *Thomas the Obscure* and *Aminadab* in particular (see *TO* 56, 83 / 37, 75): "It is not a matter of 'states of the soul,' but of an end of objectivizing consciousness, a psychological inversion" (*EI* 50 / 40). The result is the wavering situation of a "*without-self* [*sans-soi*]" (*TO* 49 / 27). Levinas explicates this via the phenomena of fatigue, laziness, and exertion, in which the "I" strives in vain to wrest itself from Being in an "evasion," but cannot escape the shadow of the *il y a* (*EI* 51 / 41). Levinas illustrates this further with the impression conveyed by night and sleeplessness, "when silence resounds and the void remains full" (*EE*, preface to the 2d ed.;[99] see also *TO* 48 / 27, *EI* 48 / 38; *OMB* 133 / 17). In all these experiences the *il y a* shows its mask and bears the horrifying traits of the desert and of obsession.

Is the dimension of the *il y a* suggested by Levinas a horrific equiva-

98. See Levinas, "Lévy-Bruhl et la philosophie contemporaine," *Revue Philosophique* 147 (1957): 556–69 / "Lévy-Bruhl and Contemporary Philosophy," *EN* 39–51 / 53–67. See also the special issue *Autour de Lucien Lévy-Bruhl* of *Revue Philosophique de la France et de l'Étranger*, no. 4 (1989). Lévy-Bruhl was the editor of the *Revue Philosophique,* which published Levinas's first essay on Husserl, entitled "Sur les 'Ideen' de M. E. Husserl," *Revue Philosophique de la France et de l'Étranger*, nos. 3–4 (1929): 230–65 / "On *Ideas*," trans. Richard A. Cohen and Michael B. Smith, in Levinas, *Discovering Existence with Husserl*, 3–31.

99. Unfortunately, the important introduction to the second edition of *De l'existence à l'existant*, which was reissued in 1984, some thirty years after its first publication, is lacking from the English translation. Translations of quotes from the preface to the second edition are mine.

lent for Heidegger's Being?[100] This question can be approached from two directions. The first tack would be to emphasize that Levinas rejects the assumption of a parallel between the two motifs. The *il y a* is a term "that is fundamentally distinct from the Heideggerian '*es gibt.*' It has never been either a translation or a rescension [*démarque*] of that German expression, with its connotations of abundance and generosity."[101] Whereas Heidegger's "es gibt" invokes a "diffuse goodness," the Levinasian-Blanchotian sense of the *il y a* is "unbearable in its indifference": "Not anguish but horror, the horror of the unceasing, of a monotony deprived of meaning. Horrible insomnia."[102]

In thus taking his distance from Heidegger, Levinas shows his deep mistrust of the "climate" of Heideggerian thought (and expresses the "need [*besoin*]" to leave it behind while acknowledging that "we cannot leave it for a philosophy that would be pre-Heideggerian" [*EE* 19 / 19]). Yet how is it possible, as Levinas, unlike Adorno, attempts, to avoid falling back into the fundamental traits of Heidegger's doctrine while transferring to another register the basic *tone* that resonates within it and has too long been overlooked?[103] Would that be an issue of philosophical argu-

---

100. Although I basically reject this as a characterization of the *il y a*, at some points it appears justified. See, e.g., *NP* 90–91 / 134–35; and esp. *TI* 298 / 274, in which Levinas speaks of "the philosophy of the Neuter: with the Heideggerian Being of the existent whose impersonal neutrality the critical work of Blanchot has so much contributed to bring out." See, however, Derrida's question in "Violence and Metaphysics": "But is not the 'there is' the totality of inde-terminate being, neutral, anonymous beings rather than Being itself?" (*Writing and Difference*, 89–90 / 133). Perhaps there is a third possible interpretation, according to which the *il y a* is neither Being nor the totality of neutral existents but, rather, the sphere of a difference *this side of* Heideggerian ontological difference.

101. *EE*, preface to the 2d ed. Heidegger, referring not to Levinas but to Sartre's *L'Existential-isme est un humanisme* (*Existentialism Is a Humanism*), remarks in "Brief über den Humanis-mus" ("Letter on 'Humanism'"): "*Il y a* translates 'it gives [*es gibt*]' imprecisely. For the 'it [*es*]' that there 'gives' is being itself. The 'gives' names the essence of being that is giving, granting its truth" (Heidegger, *Wegmarken* [Frankfurt a.M.: Vittorio Klostermann, 1967], 331 / *Pathmarks*, ed. William McNeill [Cambridge: Cambridge University Press, 1998], 254–55). Levinas stresses that when he coined the term he was unaware that Apollinaire had written a book with the title *Il y a*. For Apollinaire the expression indicates joy about what exists, "a little like the Heidegge-rian *es gibt*. For me, to the contrary, the *il y a* is the phenomenon of impersonal being: 'it'" (*EI* 47–48 / 37). Levinas contrasts the "sense of abundance" in Apollinaire's use of the expression with his own "sense of desolation" (Levinas, *Is It Righteous to Be?* 91).

102. Levinas, *Is It Righteous to Be?* 45 / Poirié, *Emmanuel Levinas*, 101.

103. Derrida puts this motif into question from two opposing points of view. First, how can Levinas accord the most important of Heidegger's doctrines, that of ontological difference, a (decisive?) place in his own thought, if he hopes to avoid the climate of Heideggerian thought? Derrida insists that "its climate is never totally exterior to thought itself" (*Writing and Differ-*

mentation or, rather, a question of style, that is, of the development of a new form of rhetoric? Or is such a division of labor not relevant to Levinas's work?

Mentioning the climate of Heidegger's thought thus raises the question of its *ethical indifference* as well as the suspicion, which Levinas articulates from the very beginning, that the existential-analytic concepts of "anxiety [*Angst*]" and "care [*Sorge*]" cannot grasp human existence at its deepest level of concern, that is to say, of its "horror" no less than its "enjoyment [*jouissance*]." Human tragedy is characterized not by the lack of Being and the threat of nothingness, "where evil is always defect, that is, deficiency" (*EE* 20 / 20), but by the almost unavoidable positivity, fullness, infinity, and presence of impersonal Being. The task is to view the shift from the immanence of *Dasein* to the transcendence—that is to say, in the language of *Time and the Other,* the "mystery" or "Mystery" and "event"—of the other or Other as a problem "no less thought-provoking than the being of beings" (*NP* 92 / 135).

Nevertheless, one of the most central of Heideggerian distinctions, if not *the* most important, stands at the beginning of Levinas's analyses. That is the *ontological difference between Being and beings.* The deepest insight of *Being and Time* (see *TO* 44 / 24), as Levinas succinctly puts it, is to indicate a "Being, which at the same time is not (that is, not posited as an existent) and yet corresponds to the work plied by the existent, which is not a nothing. Being, which is without the density of existents, is the light in which existents become intelligible" (*TI* 42 / 13). For Heidegger, as Levinas knows, there can only be an ontological distinction, not a separation; there is no Being without beings.[104] Because Being must be characterized by *Jemeinigkeit,* there is Being only in human *Dasein*'s understanding of Being. Precisely in alluding to a Being without beings,[105] Levinas sur-

---

ence, 145 / 215). Second—asking with and against Levinas—can a philosophy be independent of the conditions of its origin and the history of its reception, and should it not be judged accordingly? As Derrida writes: "But does not the naked truth of the other appear beyond 'need,' 'climate,' and a certain 'history'? And who has taught us better than Levinas?" (148–49 / 220–21). A representative sketch of the alleged climate of Heideggerian thought in Levinas's work can be found in OMB 137–38 / 24.

104. See *TO* 45 / 24; and Heidegger's *Being and Time*: "Of course, only as long as Dasein *is* (that is, only as long as an understanding of Being is ontically possible), 'is there' Being" (*Being and Time,* 255 / 212). Levinas writes: "*Being and Time* has argued perhaps but one sole thesis: Being is inseparable from the comprehension of Being (which unfolds as time); Being is already an appeal to subjectivity" (*TI* 45 / 15).

105. As Annelies Schulte Nordholt reminds us, Blanchot uses the motif of the *il y a* in his narrative *Le Ressassement éternel,* which appeared at the same time as the first publication of

passes (or undercuts) Heidegger's analysis. For Levinas only the common habit of blurring the separation between Being and beings can explain the vertigo that occurs when thought perceives the terrifying fullness in the emptiness of the word *Being*.[106] The desolation and absurdity of the *il y a*, however, apparently lies on this side of ontological difference.[107] Only in an exaggerated sense might one speak here of a "pre-Heideggerian" motif.[108]

By analogy to this widening of the Heideggerian horizon, as I will show, the transcendental dimension of the ethical can in no way proceed simply from a renewal or reinterpretation of the ontic domain (at the expense of Being). It lies, rather, *beyond the ontological difference between Being and beings.* How are we to understand such a descent and ascent in pre- and post-ontological dimensions? How can these simultaneously divergent and parallel movements of thought be reconciled? In which constellation does Levinas include this undoing of our conventional categories of experience after the diabolical and the divine, "the horrible and the sublime" (*CPP* 64 / *DEHH* 206)?

OE ("Langage et négativité: La Poétique de Maurice Blanchot dans son rapport à la pensée hégélienne" [MS., Amsterdam, 1987, 36]). Blanchot also speaks of an "existence without Being" (317) in "La Littérature et le droit à la mort," to the interpretation of which Schulte Nordholt's work is dedicated (Maurice Blanchot, "La Littérature et le droit à la mort," *La Part du feu* [Paris: Gallimard, 1949], 294–331 / "Literature and the Right to Death," trans. Lydia Davis, in *The Work of Fire*, trans. Charlotte Mandell [Stanford: Stanford University Press, 1995], 300–344). See also Schulte Nordholt's reference to Levinas's *EE* ("Langage et négativité," 320 n. 1, 324).

106. See *EE* 17 / 16: "The difficulty of separating Being from beings and the tendency to envisage the one in the other are accidental. They are due to the habit of situating the instant, the atom of time, outside of any event." Levinas adds, "the instant . . . that cannot be decomposed."

107. One probably cannot view the *il y a* in Levinas as "a new ontological notion," as Ciaramelli does ("De l'évasion à l'exode," 565–66). Peperzak sees a "foreshadowing" of it in Hegel's concept of nature: "When Levinas considers 'being' under the name of *il y a*, he does not think of an abstract categorical structure, as thematized in the beginning of Hegel's (onto-)logic, but of the most elementary form of being real or being there, which resembles the lowest level of Hegel's 'nature.' The *il y a* precedes the formation and appearance by which nature organizes and manifests itself" ("Some Remarks on Hegel, Kant and Levinas," in Cohen, *Face to Face with Levinas,* 208).

108. See Burggraeve, "Het 'il y a' in het heteronomie-denken van Emmanuel Levinas," 267–68. This concerns a motif that, according to Levinas, is already present in the concepts of *Geworfenheit* and *Nichtung*. The first concept presupposes a fleeting dimension of reality, which cannot be mastered and in whose being-there a *Verlassenheit* already exists from the beginning (see *TO* 45 / 25). This idiosyncratic interpretation of the Heideggerian concept already occurs in the early essay "Martin Heidegger et l'ontologie" (*DEHH* 53–76). The second concept remains reminiscent of a positive moment: "'nothingness nothings.' It does not keep still. It affirms itself in this production of nothingness" (*TO* 49 / 28).

The Traveling Companion: Maurice Blanchot and the Nocturnal, Obscure Dimension of Art

Blanchot describes the dimension that Levinas designates using the term *il y a* in ways that manifest a remarkable "convergence" and "parallelism."[109] He uses a different vocabulary, however, speaking, among other things, of "the second night" (OMB 133 / 17), "the neuter [*le neutre*]," and the "outside [*le dehors*]," "chaos [*remue-ménage*]," "rumor [*rumeur*]," and "murmur [*murmure*]" of Being—or, finally, its "disaster." The last motif, Levinas explains, "signifies neither death nor an accident, but as a piece of being which would be detached from its fixity of being, from its reference to a star, from all cosmological existence, a *dis-aster*. He gives an almost verbal sense to the substantive *disaster*. It seems that for him it is impossible to escape from this maddening, obsessive situation" (*EI* 50 / 40–41).

Yet both *Existence and Existents* and *Time and the Other* seek to accomplish—or, rather, demand—just this escape. And they do so in vain: "What is presented as an exigency is an attempt to escape the 'there is,' to escape the non-sense" (*EI* 51 / 41), Levinas says in retrospect. As in *On Escape,* the aim is never realized in full or without ambiguity, relapse, and hence return to more of the same or self-same. In retrospect Levinas acknowledges the difficulty of this itinerary, which in its final steps returns to its point of departure and first concern, as if the modality—the experience and the trial (*épreuve*)—of the worst and the best, of the horror of Being as well as the *il y a* and the marvel of the Other, were similar in structure, a similar challenge (as Blanchot has it: a "terror that is not terrorism," or a "fear and trembling," as Kierkegaard already knew):

> My first idea was that perhaps a "being," a "something" one could point at with a finger, corresponds to a mastery over the "there is" which dreads in being. I spoke thus of the determinate being or existent as a dawn of clarity in the horror of the "there is," a moment where the sun rises, where things appear for themselves, where they are not borne by the "there is" but dominate it. Does one not say that the table is, that things are? Then one refastens being to the existent, and already the ego there dominates the existents it possesses. I spoke thus of the "hypostasis" of existents, that is, the passage going from a *being* to a *something,* from the state of verb to the state of thing. Being which is posited, I thought, is "saved." In fact, this idea was only a first stage.

109. Levinas, *Is It Righteous to Be?* 45 / Poirié, *Emmanuel Lévinas,* 101.

> For the ego that exists is encumbered by all these existents it dominates. For me the famous Heideggerian "Care" took the form of the cumbersomeness of existence.
>
> From whence an entirely different movement: to escape the "there is" one must not be posed but deposed; to make an act of deposition, in the sense one speaks of deposed kings. This deposition of sovereignty by the *ego* is the social relationship with the Other, the dis-inter-ested relation. I write it in three words to underline the escape from being it signifies. I distrust the compromised word "love," but the responsibility for the Other, being-for-the-other, seemed to me, as early as that time, to stop the anonymous and senseless rumbling of being. It is in the form of such a relation that the deliverance from the "there is" appeared to me. Since that compelled my recognition and was clarified in my mind, I have hardly spoken again in my books of the "there is" for itself. But the shadow of the "there is," and non-sense, still appeared to me necessary as the very test of dis-inter-estedness. (*EI* 51–52 / 42–43)

For Levinas the *il y a* is an ongoing event that can no longer be ascribed to the diurnal and nocturnal sides of Being, although it is also impossible to call it pure nothingness. This originary or pure form of terror and confusion can only be thought of or described, according to Levinas, in terms of an "excluded middle" (*EI* 48 / 38): "This Neuter, or this Excluded Middle, is neither affirmation nor pure negation of being. For affirmation and negation are in the Order, they are part of it. And yet the insistence of this Neuter bears an exclusively negative quality" (OMB 152 / 48). Such a vacillating definition demonstrates both the vigor and the paradox — the performative contradictoriness or aporetics — of Levinas's thought, which, apart from Derrida, no one observed with more clarity than did Blanchot. These modalities not only concern Levinas's claims about the realm of the *il y a* but also have repercussions for his discussion of ontological difference, alterity, ethical difference, nonindifference, substitution, and holiness. The phrase "excluded middle" already announces a disquieting structural relationship between horror (absurdity, nausea) and ethical transcendence, whose abyssal and infinitizing dimensions and contours seem to mirror and, as it were, presuppose one another. It refers directly to the question of the place of philosophical reason and rationality in Levinas's thought, a question that can be set out via a brief discussion of Georges Bataille's intriguing, yet ultimately flawed, commentary on the ultimate *incommunicability* of the *il y a* within the discourse of philosophy, as Levinas understand it.

According to Bataille, who reviewed *Existence and Existents* in his journal *Critique,* the situation in which the *il y a* becomes noticeable cannot
itself be expressed in terms of cognition or offer itself up to any project
of work or action.[110] Although Levinas repeatedly emphasizes that there
can be no experience, strictly speaking, of the *il y a* (see *EE* 83–83 / 94; *TO*
70 / 57), he believes it is possible to approach the "horror" of Being without beings via the phenomenological description of specific experiences
at the limit of the possible (*EI* 49, 51 / 39, 42). The experience of art leads
up to — and into — this domain.

Bataille accentuates, with some justification, the unsublatable discrepancy between the general procedure of all philosophical interpretation,
on the one hand, and a particular *poetic* articulation of that experience,
on the other. Levinas must, Bataille argues, proceed discursively as a philosopher and accordingly define and generalize "something" that in Blanchot, for example, is audible only literarily, as the isolated cry of existence:
"Levinas says of some pages of *Thomas the Obscure* that they are a description of the *there is.* But this is not entirely correct [or just, *pas tout à fait
juste*]. Levinas describes and Blanchot cries out, as it were, the *il y a.*"[111] By
choosing an approach that is, finally, intellectual, Levinas must do without
the surprise of the mystical abyss, to whose inexpressibility only a poetics might do justice: "The problem introduced by the little work of Levinas is exactly that of the communication of an ineffable experience. The
there is is, apparently, the ineffable of mystics: although Levinas *has spoken*
about it, nevertheless he has expressed it exactly only through the chan-
nel of formal effects (modern painting, surrealist art, Lévy-Bruhl's participation). The rest is intimacy, which cannot be communicated under the
heading of clear knowledge, but solely in the form of poetry."[112] He here
alludes — at least implicitly — to an important problem: the impossibility
of thinking an absolute heterogeneity or negativity. Indeed, as Derrida
has consistently shown: the purely negative and absent, like the purely

110. Georges Bataille, "De l'existentialisme au primat de l'économie," *Critique* 21 (1948):
127–41 / "From Existentialism to the Primacy of Economy," trans. Jill Robbins, in her book
Altered Reading: Levinas and Literature (Chicago: University of Chicago Press, 1999), 155–80. He
speaks here of *ineffability,* not, as Ciaramelli believes, of a situation "at the limit of the *ineffable*"
(Ciaramelli, "De l'évasion à l'exode," 365).

111. Bataille, "From Existentialism to the Primacy of Economy," 168 / 129, trans. modified.
Bataille refers to his quotation from Blanchot's book in *L'Expérience intérieure* (Paris: Galli-
mard, 1954), 158 / *Inner Experience,* trans. Leslie Boldt (Albany: State University of New York
Press, 1988), 101, in which he speaks of the same "experience."

112. Bataille, "From Existentialism to the Primacy of Economy," 171 / 132.

positive and present, is the unthinkable par excellence. But does not something similar also apply to its *ethical* counterpart? Does this still concern
the negative and positive in the conventional sense of the terms? To put
it another way, how might we approach philosophically and/or aesthetically the negative (i.e., amoral) and the positive (i.e., moral) shading of
the certainly "absurd" dimension of the excluded middle?

Because of the radicality in Levinas's doubled approach—the consequence of his attempt to put into words an evil heterogeneity or a
good incommensurability—the border between philosophical discourse,
to which he adheres, and poetics, to which he would at first glance appear
to remain opposed, threatens to become blurred. As Levinas says of Blanchot: "The mode of revelation of what remains *other,* despite its revelation,
is not the thought, but the language, of the poem" (OMB 130 / 14). The
question then arises of where Levinas's approach and procedure stand in
relation to poetics or, more generally, to aesthetics. In his consideration
of art Blanchot is quite close to Levinas, and not primarily from an ethical
perspective. Levinas uses Blanchot's work to articulate forcefully the relationship between philosophy and modern artistic experience. Blanchot,
in turn, increasingly draws on Levinas to think through the "strange relationship which consists in the fact that there is no relationship," since the
terms withdraw to the very degree that they approach one another.[113] The
task in what follows is to ascertain to what degree the critical-essayistic
and literary activity of the former writer illuminates the starting point and
ongoing path of the latter's thought—and finally also bursts them apart.

LIKE ADORNO, LEVINAS RUNS UP against the almost indecipherable
enigma of art, to which conventional hermeneutics apparently cannot
measure up: "Modern art speaks of nothing but the adventure of art itself;
it strives to be pure painting, pure music. No doubt the critical and philosophical work, relating that adventure, is far below art, which is the voyage into the end of the night [again, a reference to Céline's title] itself,
and not merely the travel narrative." But why, one might counter, should
one constantly occupy oneself *philosophically* with the question of art? Immediately after this passage, Levinas writes, "And yet Blanchot's research
brings to the philosopher a 'category' and a new 'way of knowing'" (OMB
133 / 18). How are we to understand this? Does this formulation suggest

---

113. Maurice Blanchot, *L'Entretien infini* (Paris: Gallimard, 1969), 73 / *The Infinite Conversation,* trans. Susan Hanson (Minneapolis: University of Minnesota Press, 1992), 51; see also
Blanchot, "Our Clandestine Companion."

a connection between art and philosophical understanding in the sense of a hierarchy, or does it anticipate a dialectical or — more cautiously — an alternating relationship of sorts?

Levinas offers essentially two definitions of Blanchot's concept of art. With respect to literature, he speaks of a "passage from language to the ineffable that says itself." In addition, he speaks of an equally paradoxical "making visible of the obscurity of the elemental through the work" (OMB 133 / 18). This at first glance altogether contradictory task of art should not be misunderstood as any form of dialectics "because no level of thought emerges at which that alternance is overcome, at which contradiction is reconciled" (OMB 134 / 18). According to Levinas, the essence of dialectics is a "delayed self-evidence" (OMB 127 / 10) — a definition that hardly fits the concept of *negative* dialectics as Adorno introduces it.

Blanchot, like Adorno, subjects Hegel to a thoroughgoing critique by insisting upon the inapplicability of any conceptual thinking to the experience of art. Whereas Hegel believes that art comes to an end after antiquity, after its subordination to religious ideas during the Middle Ages and after the rise of philosophical thought in modernity,[114] Blanchot insists on the *necessary* and peculiar character of the mode of experience of art. In the medium of poetry resides a potential for meaning which is a priori denied to philosophy. Aesthetic "sense," if we might put it this way, does not occur in an order or grammar that can be logically reconstructed but shows itself only in the bursting apart of language, in a "dissemination" (OMB 151 / 46; see also 153–54 / 50–51), for which philosophical interpretation always comes too late. Levinas glosses this point by seeming to agree with both Blanchot and Hegel without wanting (or being able?) to express himself decisively: "And perhaps we are wrong in using the designation art and poetry for that exceptional event, that sovereign forgetting, that liberates language from its servitude with respect to the structures in which the *said* maintains itself. Perhaps Hegel was right as far as art is concerned. What counts — whether it be called poetry or what you will — is that a meaning is able to proffer itself beyond the closed discourse of Hegel; that a meaning that forgets the presuppositions of that discourse becomes *fable*" (OMB 143 / 33).

The fable, which characterizes Blanchot's work, traces the experience of the closure of Being. Levinas reads this in a short text, *La Folie du jour* (*The Madness of the Day*), and emphasizes its infinitizing movement. That

---

114. See Hegel, *Phenomenology of Spirit*, 455–56 / 547–48.

concerns a "strangulation, but in endless agony" (OMB 158 / 57),[115] an un-changeableness in time itself, in which everything is petrified by a threatening recollection, a perpetual repetition of the same: "A movement without outside, ex-pulsion without emptiness to receive the diaspora. . . . The madness of Auschwitz, which does not succeed in passing. . . . The infernal that shows itself in Auschwitz, but that lies hidden in the temporality of time, maintaining it" (OMB 159 / 60). By trying to put such an experience into words, Blanchot, Levinas goes on to suggest, articulates the refusal of onto-theological transcendence as well as insight into an absolute despair or heroic nihilism that cannot be thought or accomplished: "This work, an exacerbation of alterity, impugns the traditional transcendence that, ever recuperable, insures a world even more sure of itself than the world without God" (OMB 153 / 49). And a little earlier: "The idea that God has withdrawn from the world, or that God is dead, may be the expression of that monotony" (OMB 141 / 31).[116]

Although one finds in Levinas's thinking tendencies toward a philosophy of mourning, he nonetheless resists a tragic worldview. For that he relies on Blanchot (see OMB 162–63 / 63–64). (More episodically, there is a reference to Kafka, who describes "a culpability without a crime, a world in which man never gets to know the accusations charged against him," to which Levinas adds: "We see there the genesis of the problem of meaning. It is not only the question 'Is my life righteous?' but rather 'Is it righteous to be?'")[117]

Unlike Blanchot, Levinas views the cipher of the experience of Auschwitz from a moral perspective. No organic-dialectical poetics can correspond to the negative and to moral resistance. The development of thinking and writing, on the contrary, needs to be *suspended* here. Benjamin's expression "dialectics at a standstill"—which otherwise Levinas appears

115. "Death is not the end, it is the never-ending ending. As in certain of Edgar Allan Poe's tales, in which the threat gets closer and closer and the helpless gaze measures that ever still distant approach" (OMB 132 / 16–17).

116. In "Impersonality in the Criticism of Maurice Blanchot," *Blindness and Insight: Essays in the Rhetoric of Contemporary Criticism,* 2d ed., intro. Wlad Godzich (Minneapolis: University of Minnesota Press, 1983), 60–78, Paul de Man refers to this transformation of the classical concept of transcendence when discussing Blanchot's interpretation of Mallarmé: "Criticism . . . becomes a form of demystification on the ontological level that confirms the existence of a fundamental distance at the heart of all human experience." Unlike the late Heidegger, according to de Man: "Blanchot does not seem to believe that the movement of a poetic consciousness could ever lead us to assert our ontological insight in a positive way. The hidden center remains hidden and out of reach; we are separated from it by the very substance of time" (76–77).

117. Levinas, *Is It Righteous to Be?* 163 / Delacampagne, *Entretiens avec "Le Monde,"* 146.

to overlook—fruitfully encapsulates what he has in mind: "There is no progressive dialectic, in which the moments of the story spring up in their newness, before contradicting their freshness by all they conserve. The circular return of the identical does not even follow a long-term cycle. It is a twirling on the spot" (OMB 161 / 63). In the words of Blanchot: "Withdrawal and not expansion. Such would be art, in the manner of the God of Isaac Louria, who creates solely by excluding himself."[118]

This motif explains the disengagement of art only in part, however. Contrary to the classical conception of aesthetics, there is in art, according to Blanchot, no ascent to an ideal world beyond appearances. Art is not the "sensory appearance of the idea," as Hegel claimed. In agreement with Heidegger, Blanchot sees art as more like a "clearing [*Lichtung*]." Yet this proximity to the late Heidegger should not blind us to the fact that for Blanchot the status and the composition of this light, like the actuality that it discloses, are articulated in a way fundamentally different from Heideggerian *Andenken:*

> Art, according to Blanchot, far from elucidating the world, exposes the desolate, lightless substratum underlying it, and restores to our sojourn its exotic essence—and, to the wonders of our architecture, their function of makeshift shelters. Blanchot and Heidegger agree that art does not lead (contrary to classical aesthetics) to a world behind this world, an ideal world behind the real one. Art is light. Light from on high in Heidegger, making the world, founding place. In Blanchot it is a black light, a night coming from below—a light that undoes the world, leading it back to its origin, to the over and over again, the murmur, ceaseless lapping of waves, a "deep past, never long enough ago." The poetic quest for the unreal is the quest for the deepest recess of that real. (OMB 137 / 23)

Whereas for Heidegger art shares with other forms of existence the effect of illuminating Being, Levinas points out that Blanchot attributes such illumination to art as an exclusive calling. Yet for Blanchot art reveals not the truth of Being but its lack or *untruth,* although this "negativity" in the experience of art should not be misunderstood as returning to Hegelian or Marxist positions, as if art were a medium for presenting the transformation of nature or for social or political action.[119] The dark

118. Maurice Blanchot, *L'Écriture du désastre* (Paris: Gallimard, 1980) / *The Writing of the Disaster,* trans. Ann Smock (Lincoln: University of Nebraska Press, 1986), 13 / 27.

119. See Françoise Collin, *Maurice Blanchot et la question de l'écriture* (Paris: Gallimard, 1986), who writes, "Literature requires the imaginary statute of Being, designed as neuter, and

depths to which art descends do not allow its sublation into the realm of truth. Instead, they guarantee an *authenticity this side of Being in truth.* Levinas sees in this central motif in Blanchot's work the (condition of?) possibility for escaping Heideggerian thought. Because Blanchot presents "truth and poetry" (*Wahrheit und Dichtung*) as not peculiarly opposed but, rather, almost *dualistically* separated, one finds in his poetics a clear vision of the uprooting and homelessness of the "human condition." By undermining fixed notions of time and place, his essays and novels sketch the dangers *and* opportunities of a nomadic "existence," in which there can no longer be any fixed abode. "Writing does not lead to the truth of being. One might say that it leads to the errancy of being—to being as a place of going astray, to the uninhabitable. Thus, one would be equally justified in saying that literature does not lead there, since it is impossible to reach a destination" (OMB 134 / 19); it concerns "a sojourn devoid of place" (OMB 136 / 22).

Levinas discerns a minimal moral trait in this (even though ethical considerations are as far from Blanchot's concern as they are from that of the "orthodox Heideggerians" [OMB 136 / 22]), just as Blanchot, in *L'Entretien infini* (*The Infinite Conversation*), will, in turn, reinscribe ethical transcendence into a dimension that, for lack of a better word, he terms the "neuter" (and from which, in Levinas's view, this transcendence seeks to escape). Levinas writes, "If the authenticity Blanchot speaks of is to mean anything other than a consciousness of the lack of seriousness of edification, anything other than derision—the authenticity of art must herald an order of justice, the slave morality that is absent from the Heideggerian city" (OMB 137 / 24). But how, exactly, can it do this? Levinas seems to content himself with rhetorical questions alone, such as the one we find a little farther in the text:

> Does Blanchot not attribute to art the function of uprooting the Heideggerian universe? Does not the poet, before the "eternal streaming of the outside," hear the voices that call away from the Heideggerian world? A world that is not frightening because of its nihilism. It is not nihilistic. But, in it, justice does not condition truth—it remains for ever closed to certain texts, a score of

in its turn the imaginary defines itself as an element of the negative—but not of negation" (23); Collin, "La Peur: Emmanuel Levinas et Maurice Blanchot," in *Emmanuel Levinas*, ed. Catherine Chalier and Miguel Abensour, *Cahier de l'Herne* (Paris: L'Herne, 1991), 334–56. See also Annelies Schulte Nordholt, *Maurice Blanchot: L'Écriture comme expérience du dehors* (Geneva: Droz, 1995); and Marlène Zarader, *L'Être et le neutre: À partir de Maurice Blanchot* (Lagrasse: Verdier, 2001).

centuries old, in which Amalek's existence prevents the integrity of the Divine Name — that is, precisely, the *truth of being*. (OMB 139 / 25-26)

And, again:

> Can we be sure that perception is transcended only by mathematical abstractions — and fallaciously so, since abstractions spring from a place, and no place can be harbored in a geometrical space? Was not perception — long before the gods, landscapes, and Greek or German mathematicians — abandoned as a system of reference in the revelation of the Invisible God which "no sky can contain"? . . . At stake here was — before the stories that religions tell children and women — a new dimension of Height and Ideal. Surely Heidegger knows this. But while Hellenic "truth of being" merits a subtle hermeneutics, the monotheist revelation is always expedited in a few unnuanced theological formulas. (OMB 138 / 25)

In Levinas's reading the (later) Heidegger is, as Adorno might have said, never nihilistic enough. Blanchot, by contrast, is more nihilistic than is warranted by the testimony of minimal things, even in terms of what he himself terms the "indestructible." As in the work of the Russian novelist Vassily Grossman, signs, gestures, or, rather, traces of "goodness" resist the all too bleak — and all too affirmative — postulation of posited negativity, whose totalization founders upon the original affirmation of a negatively circumscribed, yet all too concrete, "positive," if not "positiv*y*," of sorts. Not that "things have really gotten somewhat better" (as Habermas suggested) but because positively asserted positivity and negativity are still too good to be true. Not that where "danger grows, salvation is near" (as Hölderlin thought) but because maximum dereliction and minimal escape — horror and the sublime — inhabit the same space beyond reason.

According to Levinas, therefore, Blanchot's texts "can be interpreted in two directions at the same time" (OMB 154 / 50), in an ambiguity related to the loss of meaning traceable in modernity. (Adorno says something similar of Beckett's *Endgame* and trilogy of novels, in particular *The Unnamable,* and Kafka's work.) On the one hand, Levinas writes, Blanchot's writing is "the announcement of a loss of meaning, a scattering of discourse, as if one were at the extreme pinnacle of nihilism — as if nothingness itself could no longer be thought peacefully, and had become equivocal to the listening ear" (OMB 154 / 51). On the other hand, inextricably intertwined with this lapse in the order of things and in the history of Being, one still can imagine the dimension of some otherness (another other, "the *absolutely other* [*l'absolument autre*]," as Jankelevitch says [OMB 130 /14]) — at least obliquely, *ex negativo,* as a presence *in absentia.* The experience of the Neuter in art — outside of the world and of categories of thinking, communication, work, and action, also outside of every clearing of Being [*Seinslichtung*] — allows one to suspect that no attempt to assimilate alterity (through knowledge, action, or work) can have the final word: "Blanchot reminds that world that its totality is not total" (OMB 154 / 51). "There is [*es gibt*]" properly transcendence only in the cracks in our transparent temporo-spatial world, which solidify as "second nature": "Yet there is in it more transcendence than any world-behind-the-worlds ever gave a glimpse of" (OMB 155 / 52). Hence, Levinas can state that any "Negation of the Order" (OMB 151 / 48) in Blanchot "does not consist in leading us further than knowledge. It is not telepathic: the outside is not the distant. It is what appears — but in a singular fashion — when all the real has been denied: realization of that unreality" (OMB 130–31 / 14). This Neuter, which is "not achieved by simple negation," is "further away than any God" (OMB 152–53 / 49). To use Baudelaire's terms, it is a "departure from Numbers and of Beings" (OMB 151 / 47).[120] Quoting Valéry's "deep past, never long ago enough [*profond jadis, jadis jamais assez*]" (OMB 137 / 23), Levinas thus characterizes the dimension of a "night coming from behind" in a way that corresponds to the motif of ethical transcendence. But, if art descends into the *unthinkable* (see OMB 133–34 / 18–19), how can the ethical experience — characterized in literally the same terms — conceive of itself as something *thinkable* within thought?

One can outline only via paradox the "position of consciousness" which might correspond to this double perspective or, indeed, to the undecidability of modern experience. Levinas articulates this paradox and in the same breath intimates a religious-philosophical perspective that is crucial for him: "Extreme consciousness would seem to be the consciousness of there being no way out; thus it would be not the outside, but the idea of the outside, and, so, obsession. *An outside conceived of in the impossibility of the outside* — thought producing the desire for the impossible outside. In which respect it is *madness, or our religious condition*" (OMB 162 / 63, my emph.). A certain absurdity that one can sense in interpersonal relationships also promises, Levinas points out, to hold out a pos-

---

120. Baudelaire's poem "Le Gouffre" ("The Abyss"), referring to Pascal, reads: " — Ah! ne jamais sortir des Nombres et des Êtres!" (Charles Baudelaire, *Les Fleurs du mal,* vol. 1 of *Oeuvres complètes,* ed. Claude Pichois [Paris: Gallimard, 1975], 142–43; on the difficulty of interpreting the final strophe, which Levinas cites, see 1115–16).

sible escape from the unchangeableness of the occurrence of Being. Typically, Levinas gives an ethical coloring to this gap in Being: "Relation to the Other — a last way out" (OMB 165 / 68). Yet this relation involves no release from the obsession of the neuter; rather, it intensifies that experience and thus turns out to offer no way out, after all: "The Other, the only point of access to an outside, is closed. The Other stabs a knife into my flesh and derives a sense of spirituality from declaring himself guilty" (OMB 169 / 72).[121]

Levinas is certainly aware that in Blanchot such a moral perspective — "at least in explicit form" (OMB 137 / 23) — is bracketed. In that, Blanchot comes close to Heidegger (and Foucault).[122] His discussion of the traumatizing foreignness of the other-worldly and unnatural neuter is, in Levinas's eyes, "a diabolical mockery of the burning bush" (OMB 162 / 64; see also 153 / 50). Yet poetics, which both names and breaks apart the immanence of language in that it attempts to utter what cannot be spoken, cannot be reduced to a purely aesthetic process: "the word *poetry* does not, after all, designate a species, the genus of which would be art. Inseparable from the verb, it overflows with prophetic meaning" (OMB 185 n. 4 / 79 n. 3). Of course, it would be appropriate to ask whether Levinas does not, in this, ipso facto contradict his otherwise tirelessly repeated caesura between ethical and aesthetic perspectives. As we shall find, Levinas's explanation of the relationship between poetry and transcendence lets us glimpse how his otherwise express intention of denying any actual and real alterity to art finally cannot be carried through or maintained. In consequence, literature, to give just one example among the arts, not only expresses a transcendent movement but is itself this occurrence (see OMB 151 / 46). Further, there remains, as in the relationship between ethical saying and the normative (or juridico-political) said, an unsublatable tension between the aesthetic force of expression and its engrained form in cultural production. In Levinas's words: "Into the Trojan horse of the *cultural product,* which belongs to the Order, this 'chaos' is inserted that rocks all the thinkable" (OMB 151–52 / 47; see also 147 / 40). But how, precisely, is this possible? The answer lies, in part, in a better understanding of Levinas's conception of art as well as its critical relation to reason, philosophy, ethics, and responsibility.

---

121. In the same context, Levinas quotes a passage from Paul Celan: "The world is no more, I shall have to carry you" (*Die Welt ist fort, ich muß dich tragen*) (OMB 169 / 72).

122. See the sympathetic presentation in Maurice Blanchot, *Michel Foucault tel que je l'imagine* (Montpellier: Fata Morgana, 1986).

Chapter Eight
Levinas on Art and Truth

ALMOST RELUCTANTLY, IT SEEMED, in 1948 the journal *Les Temps Modernes* published "La Réalité et son ombre" ("Reality and Its Shadow"), an article on art and truth by Emmanuel Levinas, who was then a relatively unknown young philosopher whose dissertation, *The Theory of Intuition in Husserl's Phenomenology,* had, as we now know, inspired Jean-Paul Sartre to go to Germany to study Husserl and Heidegger first-hand.[1] Not only is the essay significant for the reception of phenomenology in postwar France, like *On Escape,* it sheds surprising light on the relentless modernity and aesthetic modernism of Levinas's oeuvre. What is more, I will argue, it has unsurpassed systematic relevance for contemporary debates on the relationship between art and truth, image and concept.

According to Simone de Beauvoir's record in her memoirs, Raymond Aron pointed Sartre toward Levinas's dissertation, which was the first rigorous exposition in French of Husserl's phenomenology, its methodology, and its implied ontology. Aron thought it might match Sartre's interests and thereby initiated an indirect and largely oblique — or downright suppressed — exchange between interlocutors whose actual paths crossed only a few times.[2] In retrospect, however, one can see that Aron misinterpreted two divergent philosophical projects that fundamentally differed in points of departure, sources of inspiration, argumentative styles, philosophical temperament, political preoccupations, and overall theoretical aims. One would eventually develop into a philosophy of freedom in the guise of existential phenomenology, the other into an ethical metaphysics of the Other (*l'Autre, Autrui*), which would end up as a singular testimony to a disinterested, disengaged, and almost maddening saintliness. Even while under the spell of the writings of Husserl and Heidegger, in his dissertation Levinas had already taken steps in a direction of which Sartre, the author of *L'Être et le néant* (*Being and Nothingness*) could never have dreamed. These would lead to positions irreconcilable with the French re-

---

1. See Levinas, *Les Imprévus de l'histoire,* 155.
2. See Annie Cohen-Solal, *Sartre: 1905–1980* (Paris: Gallimard, 1985), 139.

ception of Husserl's phenomenology, both in its earliest existentialist expressions (in *Being and Nothingness, L'Existentialisme est un humanisme* [*Existentialism Is a Humanism*], *Nausea,* and many of Sartre's early plays) and in its later dialectical and uneasily Marxist forms (in particular the ones attempted in *Critique de la raison dialectique* [*Critique of Dialectical Reason*]).³

Levinas never directly took issue with the significant differences between his ethical metaphysics — another humanism of sorts, but this time a humanism of the other person — and the philosophical movement or, rather, intellectual *rage* that flared "avec tant d'éclat" in publications between 1940 and 1945, at a moment when Levinas was himself in captivity, as he wryly notes in the preface to *Existence and Existents,* written during the war but published in 1947, a year before "Reality and Its Shadow." Indeed, in the introductory remark to this small book — one of the texts in which he would first find an independent philosophical voice and no longer limit himself to exposition and interpretation of the basic concepts of phenomenological thought in the writings of Husserl and Heidegger — Levinas almost excuses himself for not referring to the flood of writings by the existential phenomenologists. Although the jacket of the book assured its public that here, for once, one would learn nothing about "anxiety," one need only read between the lines to see what was being prepared: an ethically motivated metaphysics that, rather than returning to traditionally defined concepts of spirituality (as did Vladimir Jankelevitch, Gabriel Marcel, Emmanuel Mounier, and, in part, Jean Wahl), instead radicalized the method of phenomenology by stripping it — more than Sartre and Merleau-Ponty ever would dare — of its final presentist, foundationalist, and subjectivist remnants.⁴ Intentionality and the ontological premises it presupposes, regardless of its nontheoreticist interpretation; authenticity and freedom; the body, whether taken as *corps-sujet,* in the early Merleau-Ponty, or as the privileged figure of the flesh (*la chair*) of *l'Être brut* in that author's later writings: Levinas's writings radically put into question all these philosophemes or revise them beyond recognition.

This is not to say that there are not remarkable parallels between Levi-

3. For an interesting account of Sartre's later development and unhappy engagement with Marxism, see Mark Poster, *Existential Marxism in Postwar France: From Sartre to Althusser* (Princeton: Princeton University Press, 1975).

4. An interesting essay, in this context, is Levinas, "Intervention dans *Petite histoire de l'existentialisme* de Jean Wahl," first published in Jean Wahl, *Petite histoire de "l'existentialisme"* (Paris: Club Maintenant, 1947), 81–87; rpt. in Levinas, *Les Imprévus de l'histoire,* 110–15; see Cohen-Solal, *Sartre,* 342.

nas's analyses of language, meaning, sensation, image, the body, and expression and the role these psychological, phenomenological, and ultimately ontological motifs play in Sartre's and Merleau-Ponty's writings. But, qua philosophical intuition, impetus, and orientation, these authors and Levinas move in almost opposite directions.[5]

Levinas's attempt to situate the ethical relation to the other beyond or before — *au-delà* and *en-deça* — traditional and modern presuppositions in phenomenology qua ontology explains why he could become a point of reference for thinkers as diverse as Bataille, Blanchot, Derrida, Lyotard, Marion, and Ricoeur, all of whose considerations concerning obligation, responsibility, donation, and decision take shape, at least in part, against the foil of Levinas's thought.

Yet "Reality and Its Shadow," in which the critique of existential phenomenology remains as implicit as in *Existence and Existents,* has never had the direct philosophical impact of Levinas's writings on ethics and infinity. This has resulted in a lacuna in the reception of his thought and, coupled with the continuing neglect of *On Escape,* has facilitated a naive and moralistic view of the relation to the Other, in whom God, far from merely being a *grand Autrui,* has left His trace. We have hardly begun to correct this moralistic view in light of the more complex experiences to which the aesthetic — art in its relation to truth — forms a major point of access, opening a more complex understanding of the task of philosophy and criticism, as well as the relation of artistic responsibility to the general culture, and ultimately providing a reminder of some of the central biblical motifs concerning the prohibition of pictorial images and improper language, that is to say, idolatry and blasphemy.[6] An avenue of equal importance in correcting attempts to moralize Levinas's oeuvre would be his phenomenology of eroticism and sexual difference; yet others would be his rethinking of materiality and spatiality and of capitalism, money, Europe, and colonization. But I must leave those for another context.

One reason for this neglect may be a certain obscurity in the essay itself. The editors of *Les Temps Modernes* offered a somewhat reserved ri-

5. Françoise Armengaud, "Éthique et esthétique: De l'ombre à l'oblitération," in Chalier and Abensour, *Cahier de l'Herne: Emmanuel Levinas,* 605–19. Armengaud recalls the important role Merleau-Ponty plays in Levinas's essay "La Signification et le sens," in *HAH* 19–63. See also Levinas's preface to T. F. Geraets, *Vers une nouvelle philosophie transcendentale: La Genèse de la philosophie de Merleau-Ponty jusqu'à la 'Phénoménologie de la perception'* (The Hague: Martinus Nijhoff, 1971), xi–xv.

6. Emmanuel Levinas, "Jean Atlan et la tension de l'art," in Chalier and Abensour, *Cahier de l'Herne: Emmanuel Levinas,* 621.

poste to its outspoken and polemical theses, which seem at once to have struck a chord and to have created an embarrassment. Even the most interesting scholarship often glosses over the basic thrust of its argument and the precise meaning of the central terms it invokes. This reflects the uncertain, seemingly negative position art and aesthetic experience—as well as aesthetics and philosophical criticism—appear to have for Levinas, both in this early essay, as in *On Escape,* and throughout his subsequent philosophical career.

From his earliest writings onward Levinas insists on the curious, in the final analysis nebulous and, as we will see, undecidable position of art in relation to truth, reality, discourse, and action, despite his repeated emphasis on art's secondary or derivative—that is to say, unethical or at best an-ethical, prehuman, inhuman, or a-human—status. It would be facile and even wrong to accuse Levinas of a lack of rigor or consistency here. Rather, an inner logic is at work in these passages, one that is deeply complex, paradoxical, and aporetic and which holds sway in his later, more episodic and dispersed descriptions of art and aesthetic experience, as well. In the latter one can trace clarifications and refinements of the analyses first begun in *On Escape, Existence and Existents, Time and the Other,* and "Reality and Its Shadow."

Moreover, the predicament of the aesthetic as it emerges across Levinas's oeuvre—a predicament that, like skepticism (hardly a fortuitous parallel), follows philosophical thought as an inescapable shadow, an insurmountable reservation and irrepressible laughter that withholds the subject from the being-in-the-world and the being-with-others of which Heidegger and his pupils make so much—reveals the difficulties of demarcating art from truth, life, or politics, but also of establishing demarcations among art, aesthetics, ethics, and politics, not to mention between all these together and magic, mystery, myth, religion, participation and separation, communal fusion and election, the sacred and the holy, and so on. More than interesting documentation of the lively debates concerning art, engagement, literature, and politics in postwar France, Levinas's text offers a remarkable systematic philosophical consideration *in obliquo* which, for all its apparent obscurity, deserves to be examined as such.

We now know that Merleau-Ponty authored the prefatory editorial note, signed "T.M.," to "Reality and Its Shadow."[7] It reminds readers of

---

7. Merleau-Ponty's editorial was reprinted in *Parcours 1935–1951* (Lagrasse: Éditions Verdier, 1997), 121–24.

the sharp contradiction between the theses advocated by the newcomer and those formulated by Sartre in *L'Imaginaire: Psychologie phénoménologique de l'imagination* (*The Imaginary: A Phenomenological Psychology of the Imagination*) and "Qu'est-ce que c'est la littérature?" ("What Is Literature?").[8] Although nothing could have been more obvious to its particular audience, one can see what motivated the editors to introduce Levinas's essay with what is in effect a warning—an *avertissement*—that the presentation and assessment of the aesthetic contained therein signals a radically different universe from the one familiar to the readers of *Les Temps Modernes*.[9]

The distinctive—even, almost literally, iconoclastic—profile of Levinas's alternative views on art, engagement, philosophy, and philosophical criticism stands out against the backdrop of Sartre's conception of a *littérature engagée*. But there is more to this essay than a debate with existential phenomenology's views on literature and the responsibility of the artist in everyday and political struggles, including its rethinking of the relationship between the concept and the image, which Sartre had begun to develop in *The Imaginary*. Like *On Escape*, "Reality and Its Shadow" is a "germ cell" of Levinas's entire philosophical project.

Although in Levinas's later work his concern with art (like his concern with the phenomenology of eros) appears to diminish, wherever, often in passing and indirect statements, art is addressed—or downright dismissed—the tone and fervor of these renewed references remains reminiscent of

---

8. Jean-Paul Sartre, "Qu'est-ce que la littérature?" published in six installments in *Les Temps Modernes* 17–22 (February–July 1947) and reissued in Sartre, *Situations, II* (Paris: Gallimard, 1948) / *"What Is Literature?" and Other Essays*, ed. Steven Ungar (Cambridge: Harvard University Press, 1988), 23–245. Sartre, *L'Imaginaire: Psychologie phénoménologique de l'imagination* (1940; rpt., Paris: Gallimard, 1986) / *The Imaginary: A Phenomenological Psychology of the Imagination*, trans. and intro. Jonathan Webber, rev. Arlette Elkaim-Sartre (London: Routledge, 2004).

9. See also Sartre's "Présentation des *Temps modernes*," published in the inaugural issue of *Les Temps Modernes* (October 1945) / "The Case for Responsible Literature," *Partisan Review* 12 (Summer 1945), and "Introducing *Les Temps modernes*," trans. Jeffrey Mehlman, in Sartre, *"What Is Literature?" and Other Essays*, 249–67.

Levinas would publish a second article on similar matters in this journal. The essay, entitled "La Transcendence des mots," focused on Michel Leiris, *Biffures*. See *Les Temps Modernes* 44 (1949): 1090–95. For background information on this whole period, see Martin Jay, *Downcast Eyes: The Denigration of Vision in Twentieth-Century French Thought* (Berkeley: University of California Press, 1993), chap. 5. For a comprehensive presentation of Levinas's views on art and literature, see Fabio Ciaramelli, "L'Appel infini à l'interprétation: Remarques sur Levinas et l'art," *Revue Philosophique de Louvain* 1 (1994): 32–52. See also Jill Robbins, *Altered Reading: Levinas and Literature* (Chicago: University of Chicago Press, 1999), 75ff.

the early essay. "Reality and Its Shadow" provides the sole elaborated argument underlying these often lapidary and apodictic pronouncements. Moreover, in its own right the essay offers a full meditation on the phenomena comprising art and sociality as well as critique in general. It consists in a concise and concentrated discussion of the complex relationship between the aesthetic and philosophical criticism, the *otherness* of art and the *alterity* of ethics, disengagement and engagement, silence and language (dialogue, communication), play and seriousness, the temporality of the instant — the timelessness of the in-between-time or *entretemps* — and the experience of being in its reality and truth, which is to say, Levinas concludes, its "time."

In what follows, after briefly rehearsing Levinas's basic argument and spelling out some of the most important elements in its intellectual background in traditional metaphysics, Scripture, phenomenology, and modernist aesthetics, I will focus on Levinas's systematic philosophical contribution to the discussion of the relationship between art and truth: namely, his attempt to demarcate the image from the concept and thereby to differentiate aesthetic experience, on the one hand, from criticism — in particular, from philosophical criticism and aesthetics — on the other. I will then quickly recall some alternative responses to the same problematic and conclude by pointing out some consequences of the vulnerability of most, if not all, of the distinctions introduced by "Reality and Its Shadow."

This vulnerability — indeed, deconstructibility — by no means invalidates Levinas's overall philosophical contribution to the debates in question. Rather, it testifies to their inevitable impasse. In addition, it has repercussions for Levinas's perspective on the ethical "optics," which can no longer understand — or present — itself as a *First Philosophy* or even an "ethical transcendental philosophy" and whose "primacy of practical reason" must, hence, be dramatically (perhaps poetically, rhetorically) qualified.

Levinasian Aesthetics: Historical and Philosophical Background

Levinas's main target in the opening pages of "Reality and Its Shadow" is Sartre's conception of an engaged art, a conception that influenced the modernist idea of literature and literary authorship and was extended to all other art forms. This polemic with Sartre's essay on literature finds its full justification only in the subsequent and more far-reaching disagreement with the presupposition that, Levinas assumes, is central to many theories of art: namely, that art embodies a special sort of knowledge concerning reality and truth, which lies beyond the grasp of concepts and categories, that is to say, of empirically based perception and cognition. In this common view, Levinas suggests, aesthetic claims are truth claims of sorts, and art is taken to consist first of all in a mimesis or representation of a pregiven reality, whose deeper structure and essence it may bring to light more effectively than the down-to-earth, quotidian procedures for establishing this reality through psychological introspection and empirical observation, whether or not accompanied by inductive-deductive reasoning (e.g., ideographic or nomothetic description, epistemes, paradigms, etc.).

As Merleau-Ponty reminds us in the editorial note, Sartre's claims are largely the same, and so Levinas has only partially understood him. "Nobody," Merleau-Ponty claims, "has done more for marking the difficulties of literary communication, which threaten at every instant [à chaque instant] to refer the writer back to his solitude." Already in *The Imaginary,* first published in 1940, Merleau-Ponty continues, Sartre interprets the image in terms of a "magical act [une conduite magique]," with which "conscience seeks to fascinate itself, to evoke the thing, irremediably absent, by its physiognomy, its style, its deserted garment [défroque]." According to Sartre, art therefore needs to be defined as the quest for a "pseudo-presence of the world without the means of objective knowledge and with the force of metaphor alone." Consequently, Merleau-Ponty notes, Sartre would acknowledge that a painting does not "signify in the same way as prose" but aims to "unite the minds of people [les esprits] without passing through [or by] the concept [sans passer par le concept]." Poetry searches for the "signifying soil [humus signifiant]" which words carry along with them even when they are transformed into concepts, and even the most realistic or transparent prose, Sartre suggests, contains an element of the poetic which eludes common understanding.

While the "whole enterprise of human expression" thus runs up against an internal limit that prevents it from ever fully inhabiting an "Intelligible World," Merleau-Ponty — still in full agreement with Sartre — stresses that, nonetheless, an "act of signification" enables human beings to communicate with others, to "associate freedoms, each of them in a singular situation." Yet the predicament of literary expression — indeed, of all signification, linguistic or other — Merleau-Ponty goes on to say, should not be exaggerated; it never authorizes the writer to "paint his defeat as victory, to seek refuge, as Mr. Blanchot put it, in the 'petty hell of liter-

ary eternity,' and to turn away from an experience that is his contact with
the world, the avowed or secret theme of everything he says." When Levinas expects philosophical criticism to reestablish the link between art and
reality, expression and truth, he is thus, Merleau-Ponty concludes, from
a Sartrian perspective at once too pessimistic and too optimistic. On the
one hand, he ignores that art and literature can "save themselves if they
rediscover themselves as living word or signification [*comme parole ou signification vivantes*]." On the other hand, he is perhaps too naive in assuming that "the difficulties of action or of philosophical expression are of a
lesser nature than those of literature and art," as well as in believing that
these difficulties are of a completely "different order." This, Merleau-Ponty
once more agrees with Sartre, is not the case; in both artistic and philosophical expression the task (indeed, the imperative) is to save artistic
consciousness and conscience from itself ("Pour l'un comme pour l'autre,
la conscience artiste doit être sauvée d'elle-même").[10] This, at least in part,
Levinas's essay shows in a compelling way.

AGAINST THE FIRST OF THE TWO presuppositions attributed to Sartre —
that is to say, the idea of an engaged, committed art, a *littérature engagée* —
Levinas insists that art and aesthetic experience are, if not disinterested
(this will become the privilege of ethics), then at least instances of disengagement, evasion, escape, and, consequently, irresponsibility, laughter,
and play. Against the second — the assumption that art is knowledge and
truth in disguise, in its very origin or perhaps of a higher, surreal order —
he stresses that art and aesthetic experience transport us into a realm not
of light but of darkness, shadows, silence, insincerity, not-knowing (or,
rather, unknowing), and nontruth. The result is a dissolution of factual
life or, rather, a cessation of its flux and its intrinsic normativity, indeed,
spirituality. Art and aesthetic experience, Levinas holds, interrupt the very
possibility of what seems, at least at first glance, a reality without shadows, seriousness, or weight, a world of faces and words, symbols and signs,
things and objects, movement and novelty, action and light — that is to

---

10. Merleau-Ponty, *Parcours*, 123–24 (my trans.). An implicit discussion between Levinas
and Merleau-Ponty is evident here, well before the latter's own engagement with art. The following remarks, therefore, shed indirect light on the intellectual filiations and differences between
these two authors. See also Waldenfels, *Deutsch-Französische Gedankengänge*, 346–82; and Zielinski, *Lecture de Merleau-Ponty et Levinas*. For an excellent exposition and interpretation of
Merleau-Ponty's own views on art and aesthetics, see Jenny Slatman, *L'Expression au-delà de
la représentation: Sur l'aisthêsis et l'esthétique chez Merleau-Ponty* (Louvain: Peeters, 2003).

say, human existence in its theoretical, practical, volitional, and spiritual aspects: "Art brings into the world the obscurity of fate [*fatum*] but it especially brings the irresponsibility which charms as a lightness and grace. It frees. To make or to appreciate a novel and a picture is to no longer have to conceive, is to renounce the effort of science, philosophy, and of action. . . . Myth takes the place of mystery. The world to be built [*à achever*] is replaced by the essential completion [*achèvement*] of its shadow" (RS 12 / 141 / 787, trans. modified).

For all his implicit and explicit opposition to Heidegger in his early commentaries, *On Escape, Existence and Existents, Time and the Other*, and the major essays and major works, in "Reality and Its Shadow" Levinas comes remarkably close to what the later Heidegger, in "Der Ursprung des Kunstwerkes" ("The Origin of the Work of Art"), calls the "self-sufficient presence [*selbstgenügsames Anwesen*]" or the "self-sufficiency [*Selbstgenügsamkeit*]" of the work of art.[11] Heidegger also stresses that the work of art, in spite of (or thanks to) its self-sufficiency as a crafted thing — indeed, in its very thinglike quality or thingness — speaks to us not as a mere thing but as something else as well. Like Levinas, Heidegger also will come to characterize the artwork in terms of "allegory"; the work of art brings the thing and something else (*etwas Anderes*) together and is, hence, a "symbol," in the etymological sense of the word.[12] Levinas implies as much, even though for him, for reasons that will become clear in a moment, the work of art is, first of all, a "symbol in reverse [*un symbole à rebours*]"; it points elsewhere, away from the light of day, from the unintelligible realm of ideas, reasons, freedom, and acts.

To understand why this is so, we must realize that the origins of Levinas's concept of the aesthetic lie elsewhere, outside the phenomenological project with its existential analytic (Heidegger) and subsequent existentialist or hermeneutic appropriations. In "Reality and Its Shadow" the parallel and contrast with Heidegger (referring, of course, not to "The Origin of the Work of Art," which was not yet published, but to *Being and Time*),

11. Martin Heidegger, *Der Ursprung des Kunstwerkes* (Stuttgart: Reclam, 1988), 21, 22 / "The Origin of the Work of Art," trans. Albert Hofstadter, in Heidegger, *Poetry, Language, Thought* (New York: Harper & Row, 1975), 29. For the origins and presuppositions of Heidegger's essay, see Jacques Taminiaux, "The Origin of 'The Origin of the Work of Art,'" *Reading Heidegger: Commemorations* (Bloomington: Indiana University Press, 1993), 392–404.

12. See Heidegger, "Origin of the Work of Art," 10. In this context, see also the analysis of symbol in Gadamer, *Truth and Method,* 65–67 / 69–70. In partial agreement with Benjamin, Gadamer considers the relationship and contrast between "symbol" and "allegory."

as well as the critical engagement with Sartre, are to some extent secondary to other concerns and an altogether different inspiration.

The obvious source for Levinas's emphasis on the image and the plasticity of all art is the biblical prohibition on graven images, which de facto reduces the work of art to an idol.[13] The two other main sources of inspiration which lead Levinas to his—prima facie somewhat surprising, counterintuitive, and even traditionalist and iconoclastic—observations can be found, I think, in the writings of Blanchot (for "Reality and Its Shadow") and of Franz Rosenzweig (for the "mature" writing that culminates in Totality and Infinity, as well as for the later work, which follows the publication of "The Trace of the Other" and finds its major articulation in Otherwise than Being).[14]

Beyond Levinas's succinct analyses of their statements on literature and art, neither of these authors has figured centrally in more strictly philosophical debates on aesthetics. In Rosenzweig's Star of Redemption, which is close in this respect to the Hegelian system, although Rosenzweig otherwise relentlessly seeks to dismantle it, art and aesthetics seem merely a surpassed and strictly limited stage of human expression, the perspective of the "pagan" self and its "world of silence." This position has led scholars to overlook the quite different picture, testifying to an almost modernist sensibility, which emerges from observations about art and aesthetics dispersed throughout Rosenzweig's letters and diaries and the later essays collected in Zweistromland (The Land of Two Rivers), as has been forcefully argued by Stéphane Mosès.

Outside the canon of "poststructuralist" thought and a substantial body of scholarly secondary literary studies, Blanchot's theoretical writings and récits have likewise been largely neglected in contemporary philosophical debates concerning art, aesthetics, and the question of truth. Yet Blanchot arguably forms the single most important influence on the early

13. Thomas Wiemer, one of the first to offer a succinct analysis of the importance of this early essay for the rest of Levinas's oeuvre, points this out. See Thomas Wiemer, Die Passion des Sagens: Zur Deutung der Sprache bei Emmanuel Levinas und ihrer Realisierung im philosophischen Diskurs (Freiburg: Karl Alber, 1988), 311 ff., 316–17.

14. See, for an excellent analysis of Rosenzweig's work, Système et révélation, 72–74, 249–57. Levinas's preface to this important book is also interesting (7–16). For a discussion of different aspects of the question of language, art, and myth in Rosenzweig's thinking, see Wolfdietrich Schmied-Kowarzik, ed., Der Philosoph Franz Rosenzweig (1886–1929) (Freiburg: Karl Alber, 1988), 2:903 ff.; H. J. Heering, Franz Rosenzweig: Joods denker in de 20e eeuw (The Hague: Martinus Nijhoff, 1974), 66 ff.; and Leora Batnitzky, Idolatry and Representation: The Philosophy of Franz Rosenzweig Reconsidered (Princeton: Princeton University Press, 2000).

Levinas, whereas Rosenzweig—the author whom the preface to *Totality and Infinity* acknowledges as more present than can be indicated by any footnotes—forms a major source of inspiration for Levinas's middle and later period, especially in the episodic instances where the reassessment of art and aesthetics is explicitly at issue. Moreover, the views of these two authors seem almost to blend in some of the most telling statements Levinas makes in "Reality and Its Shadow," for example, in the paragraph that summarizes the theme of its opening section:

> To go beyond is to communicate with ideas, to understand. Does not the function of art lie in not understanding? Does not obscurity provide it with its very element and a completion *sui generis,* foreign to dialectics and the life of ideas? Will we then say that the artist knows and expresses the very obscurity of the real? But that leads to a much more general question, to which this whole discussion of art is subordinate: in what does the *non-truth* of being consist? Is it always to be defined by comparison with truth, as what is left over after *understanding?* Does not the commerce with the obscure, as a totally independent ontological event, describe categories irreducible to those of cognition? We should like to show this event in art. Art does not know a particular type of reality; it contrasts with knowledge. It is the very event of obscuring, a descent of the night, an invasion of shadow. To put it in theological terms, which will enable us to delimit however roughly our ideas by comparison with contemporary notions: art does not belong to the order of revelation. Nor does it belong to that of creation, which moves in just the opposite direction. (RS 3 / 131–32 / 773)

That art and revelation, art and creation, move in opposite directions has to do with the silent axiom, taken from or at least in resonance with Rosenzweig's work, that meaning, responsibility, truth, and freedom can emerge only where a certain destiny, myth, fixity, or supposed completion is interrupted, opened up, and offered up to the other, moving against the philosophical (*in philosophicis*) and the theological (*in theologicis*) in the direction of life (*ins Leben*), in an in principle infinite process of interpretation which is the very realm of intersubjectivity and dialogue, indeed, of being in its very reality, that is to say, its "time" (as the final words of Levinas's essay have it). Virtually every page of *Totality and Infinity* stresses that this realm—even as it exceeds the finite totality of being and, hence, the scope of the philosophies of the Same and the "Neuter" which frame it into ideas, categories, concepts, or any other medial terms—is not identical with that of truth but remains, in a sense, exterior to it (farther out than the most distant telescopic or microscopic object, beyond the "infinite space" within and without which Pascal evokes), its *reverse* side, even its *inversion*.

Unlike "Reality and Its Shadow," *Totality and Infinity* leaves no doubt that even when truth is thought in light of the infinity of being, beyond all finite totality, it must nonetheless presuppose the exteriority of justice, of the transfinite idea of the good, *epekeina tes ousias*. The artwork, by contrast, is defined by its virtual *saturation,* its seeming completion, its substantiality, solidity, solitude, and inaction.

Like the justice and responsibility of which Levinas's later work speaks, the artwork is identified with a sleeplessness of sorts: not the restless vigilance that forms the very modality of uprightness, or *droiture,* but the wakefulness that testifies to a nightmarish fatefulness, leaving at best room for tragic, stoic, or heroic resignation and allowing no genuine escape, novelty, event, or time. Art disengages the artist and the beholder from the light of day, in which ethics, human agency, interiority, and economy are firmly situated. In so doing, it fulfills a peculiar ontological role — that of "a totally independent ontological event" — in what Levinas, with oblique reference to Bataille, will elsewhere call the "general economy of being."

Levinas writes that, in the production of the work of art, the artist stops because the work refuses to accept anything more, "appears saturated." More precisely, the work of art is "completed *in spite of* the social or material causes that interrupt it"; indeed, its very status — and stasis — as a work of art exempts it from the realm of causal determination and purposive effect: "It does not give itself out as the beginning of a dialogue" (RS 2 / 131 / 772–73). Art is not the commencement of an act, the vantage point of judgment. But how, then, could it have come to be seen in that way? Levinas explains:

> Perhaps the tendency to apprehend the aesthetic phenomenon in literature, where speech provides the material for the artist, explains the contemporary dogma of knowledge through art. We are not always attentive to the transformation that speech undergoes in literature. Art as speech, art as knowledge, then brings on the problem of committed art, which is a problem of committed literature. The completion, the indelible seal of artistic production by which the artwork remains essentially disengaged, is underestimated — that supreme moment when the last brush stroke is done, when there is not another word to add or to strike from the text, by virtue of which every artwork is classical. . . . This completion does not necessarily justify the academic aes-

thetics of art for art's sake. The formula is false inasmuch as it situates art *above* reality and recognizes no master for it, and it is immoral inasmuch as it liberates the artist from his duties as a man and assures him a pretentious and facile nobility. But a work would not belong to art if it did not have this formal structure of completion, if at least in this way it were not disengaged. We have to understand the value of this disengagement, and first of all its meaning. (RS 2 / 131 / 772–73)

The disengagement of art as well as of the artist is a fatality, a destiny (*destin*) of sorts. This is not to say that the work of art *represents,* faithfully renders, depicts, or mimics the *fatum* of beings afflicted by their destiny. Rather, it means that, from the moment they are captured in, frozen by, or drawn into the image—by (or into) *their* image, that is; and every single being has, Levinas suggests, at least one—and thus become an "allegory" and "caricature" of themselves, these beings somehow "enter their fate" (RS 9 / 138 / 783). This is what Levinas takes to be the "artistic event as such," namely, the "obscuring of being in images" and the "stopping of being in the meanwhile [*entretemps*]" (RS 13 / 142 / 788), that is to say, in the in-between, in the "interstices" of the world, where no word can resonate and silence reigns, where no light can enter or escape but everything comes to a halt, becomes absorbed or absorbs itself, in the entropy of an infinity of black holes that double up all existing entities, objects, and subjects, and thus constitute the drama of history—and the history of Being—as such.

Of course, many questions could be raised here. Paradoxically, these formulations seem to suggest that Levinas—in an almost Heideggerian fashion—comes to the defense of the translucence and phosphorescence of being, of its movement and illumination, which his own later writings denounce in increasingly violent terms as the very essence, the *essance* and *conatus essendi,* of the self-perseverance of Being and its Truth. The nonbeing and nontruth that Levinas dismisses in art would thus be nothing but the reverse and inverse—indeed, the mirror image, mimicry, allegory, and resemblance—of the ontological dimension that he suspects with growing apprehension in his subsequent work. Clear and dark light would simply be pitted against each other as contrasting symbols—symbols "in reverse"—for the intrinsic duplicity of being and *its* other.

But this is not all there is to it. Although in "Reality and Its Shadow" being and truth, the conceptual and the philosophical—in short, reality and discourse—still form the realm of the relation to self and other (as

well as self to self), they already stand under the aegis of an ethical responsibility that assigns them their proper — that is to say, limited — place.
As we will see, this assigning takes place precisely by contrast with — and
in critical response to — the "totally independent ontological event" of art
and aesthetic experience, which forms the flip side, the Janus face, the intrinsic dimension and standing possibility of *all* phenomena, indeed, of
the world of appearance *as such.* Although the work of art and its experience have a "completion *sui generis,* that precedes dialectics and the life
of ideas," a completion, moreover, that is "different from the simple irruption which limits language and the works of nature and industry," we
may, Levinas says, nonetheless "wonder if we should not recognize an element of art in the work of craftsmen, in all human work, commercial and
diplomatic, in the measure that, in addition to its perfection to its ends,
it bears witness to an accord with some destiny extrinsic to the course of
things, which situates itself outside the world, like the forever bygone past
of ruins, like the elusive strangeness of the exotic" (RS 2 / 131 / 772).

By the same token — and as if already describing the irreducible distinction between the "face" and the sum of all empirical qualities of persons and characters — Levinas writes: "Being is not only itself, it escapes
itself. Here is a person who is what he is; but he does not make us forget,
does not absorb" (RS 5 135 / 778).

Apparently then, like art, reality — including practical engagement,
freedom, and the realm of judgment and critique — also is not all that there
is. More precisely, like art, reality does not represent the ultimate or highest value, which, it would now seem, must lie somewhere "outside the
world," that is to say, in-between — in the "interstices" or *entretemps,* the
in-between-space(s)-and-time(s) — between reality and its shadow, being
and (its?) nonbeing, truth and (its?) nontruth.

It comes as no surprise, then, that the reversal and inversion of being,
truth, and reality — art's substitution for them — *comes about by reality's
own most inner movement,* of which the shadow (the image, the allegory)
is but the necessary and intrinsic possibility: the possibility of its (i.e.,
reality's) impossibility, its being toward a certain death, or, as Levinas will
come to add, with Blanchot and against Heidegger, the "impossibility of
its possibility").[15]

When, throughout the essay, Levinas speaks of a logic of "resem-

---

15. For an interpretation of this formula, see my book *Philosophy and the Turn to Religion,*
esp. the chapter "Formal Indications."

blance," this is what he means. The process of resemblance — that is, the allegorization of reality by the substitution of the concept (or the sign and the symbol) for the image (which is its own?) — cannot simply be defined as resulting from "a comparison between an image and the original." Resemblance, he writes, should rather be seen as "the movement that engenders the image" (RS 6 / 135 / 778). In other words, there are no originals — beings, objects, or subjects — which are then, in a second instance, doubled (represented, substituted for, copied, scanned, cloned, etc.). In other words, the splitting of reality into at least two incommensurable realms — namely, reality and (its?) nonreality, irreality, shadow, or "error" — has *always already happened,* just as it is, happily, *always already overcome, reversed, inverted, and forgotten.* As Thomas Wiemer rightly points out:

> Not as a process that would add something to existing reality after the fact, but as the movement in being that is co-originary with that of reality and accompanies reality from the very beginning: as its shadow, its other possibility, as it were.
>
> Possibility without possibilities, in which being, that is, reality revealed and unconcealed, escapes itself — because this other possibility does not fall into the domain (the event [*Ereignis*]) of the possible unconcealment of being, but rather stays outside the alternative of concealed and unconcealed, of attained or possible knowledge and truth, in the domain of the purely sensible.[16]

What does this mean? As in *Totality and Infinity,* the most challenging claims in "Reality and Its Shadow" seem to be made in the name of a genuine infinity of being and, in the final analysis, on behalf of a *transfinite* being, being beyond Being — the realm of the Other, the existent (*l'existant*), and ultimately *Autrui* — which remains forever exterior to all the finite totalities that populate the history of the Western tradition, its ontology, theology, aesthetics, and politics. In accord with the progressive radicalization and intensification of his overall philosophical inquiry following the publication of *Totality and Infinity,* Levinas later drops this still too metaphysical and affirmative assumption in favor of an otherwise than being or beyond essence that no longer has even a common measure (or, as we have seen, any dispute) with being in its supposed — albeit transfinite — infinity. Infinitism and ontological pluralism thus seem to give way to a heterology of sorts, reliant upon a methodology that stands out not

16. Wiemer, *Die Passion des Sagens,* 321.

via its negativism, its *via negativa,* but via a rhetorical procedure of exaggeration and excessiveness, a poetics of emphasis, and, hence, by a return to the classical motif and motivation of the *via eminentiae.*

This radicalization and intensification of perspective is both consistent with Levinas's previous work, even a de facto return to some of Levinas's earliest aesthetic motifs, especially the desire to escape or evade the dread of being altogether, and an ethico-religious transformation of them. The motif of escape, which involves, well before the publication of Sartre's famous novel, a seemingly unavoidable nausea with respect to being, to its self-sufficiency rather than its lack or privation, finds its most powerful expression in the essay *On Escape.* This essay, I have suggested earlier, provides the first tentative exploration of an evasion or escape from being which will form the matrix for all Levinas's later investigations into the movements of transcendence *au-delà* and *en-deça,* of trans-ascendence and trans-descendence, of which ethics and aesthetics, together with the erotic and materiality, form the primary instantiations.

While in "Reality and Its Shadow" there is as yet no sign of Levinas's later ethical preoccupation in terms of metaphysical desire and the primacy of its intelligibility, where concern with "religion" and "morality" gains prominence, this early essay is shaped around the formal schematics of aesthetics and the attempt to escape. To this degree, ethics and aesthetics resemble each other in their very structure. Both are each other's most extreme and opposite possibility, each at once excluding and presupposing the other.

Systematics: Image and Concept, Art versus Truth

In "Reality and Its Shadow" Levinas's argument hinges on a remarkable — and remarkably traditional — antithesis between image and concept (including image and symbol, image and sign), which he believes founds the distinction between art and philosophy, aesthetic experience and criticism. This opposition, as Merleau-Ponty points out in his editorial note, is played out against certain aspects of Sartre's philosophy. In *L'Imagination* (*The Imagination*) and then in *The Imaginary* Sartre insists that the image should not be confused with sensory perception or sense data,[17] on which so many empiricist and rationalist psychologisms and representationalist theories are built. He pits the phenomenology of

17. Jean-Paul Sartre, *L'Imagination* (Paris: Presses Universitaires de France, 1936).

Husserl—especially the Husserl of *Ideas I*—against the phenomenalism of Hume and, somewhat unjustly, as Merleau-Ponty observed in a review of *The Imagination,* against Bergson.[18]

For Sartre the image not only represents nothing (with which Levinas would agree), it represents—indeed, is the primary form of—the nothingness of human existence and its freedom before and beyond essence. For Levinas, however, this last conclusion is unacceptable. Sartre, Levinas suggests, is right to liberate the image from a long tradition of thinking artistic production—the invention of images—only in terms of mimetic reproduction or representation, thereby ignoring the expression, expressiveness, and "resemblance" to which art testifies in singular ways. He is, moreover, correct in showing that imagination destructs the realism of our natural worldview. For Sartre, who speaks of a *néantissement* of representational consciousness and a *néantissement* of the world, the intentional structure of this experiment in world destruction—and, hence, the discovery of yet another "transcendence of the ego"[19]—is a paradigm of the negativity of human existence, its *être pour soi,* and its agency. For Levinas, on the contrary, the intentionality of artistic expression and aesthetic experience is, first of all, that of a descent—a *transdescendance*—into the depths, into the interstices and in-between times, of that existence and its hinterworld (*Hinterwelt,* or *arrière-monde*), that is to say, into a parallel universe of shadows, night, myth, fate, arbitrariness, and irresponsibility.

The image, he holds, is without concept. Its visuality is, in a sense, blind. The light it diffuses is a dark light; its proper voice is silent. To face it is to face a caricature and a mask. Its temporality is that of an interruption or cessation of all futurity, all pastness, any meaningful present; its spatiality is that of a hole—a black hole, as it were—piercing the ever-moving horizon of our world as the always possible impossibility of its possibilities, the irreality of its reality. But what, exactly, does this mean, especially in light of a long philosophical and religious—an onto-theological—tradition premised upon the constancy and uniqueness of (especially the supreme) Being? Levinas gives the following response, which highlights the artwork's peculiar temporality (or lack thereof): "The insurmount-

18. Merleau-Ponty's short review of Sartre's *L'Imagination,* published in 1936 in the *Journal de Psychologie Normale et Pathologique,* can be found in *Parcours,* 45–54.

19. See Sartre, *La Transcendence de l'ego: Esquisse d'une description phénoménologique* (Paris: J. Vrin, 1978) / *The Transcendence of the Ego: An Existentialist Theory of Consciousness,* trans. Forrest Williams and Robert Kirkpatrick (New York: Hill & Wang, 2001).

able caricature in the most perfect image manifests itself in its stupidness as an idol. The image qua idol leads us to the ontological significance of its unreality. This time the work of being itself, the very *existing* of a being, is doubled up with a semblance of existing. . . . To say that an image is an idol is to affirm that every image is in the last analysis plastic, and that every artwork is in the end a statue — a stoppage of time, or rather its delay behind itself."

A statue realizes the paradox of an instant that endures without a future. Its duration is not really an instant. It does not give itself out here as an infinitesimal element of duration, the instant of a flash; it has in its own way a quasi-eternal duration. I am not thinking just of the duration of an artwork itself as an object, of the permanence of writings in libraries and of statues in museums. Within the life or, rather, the death of a statue, an instant endures infinitely: eternally, Laocoon will be caught up in the grip of the serpents; the Mona Lisa will smile eternally. Eternally the future announced in the strained muscles of Laocoon will be unable to become present; eternally the smile of the Mona Lisa about to broaden will be unable to become present. An eternally suspended future floats around the congealed position of a statue like a future forever to come. The imminence of the future lasts before an instant stripped of the essential characteristic of the present, its evanescence. It will never have completed its task as a present, as though reality withdrew from its own reality and left it powerless. In this situation the present can assume nothing, can take on nothing, and thus is an impersonal and anonymous instant (RS 8–9 / 137–38 / 781–82).

Here the motif of the instant intervenes in a long philosophical tradition of thinking this notion as an element in a continuity or flow. Levinas gives two examples: dialectics in all of its idealist, materialist, and narrativist articulations; and the Bergsonian concept of *durée*. With regard to the first, Levinas develops a *Dialektik im Stillstand,* to quote Benjamin; with regard to the second, he mobilizes the Cartesian understanding of the instant while giving it a different twist.

Levinas characterizes the resemblance — and, hence, the doubling and immobilization — of being in literary narrative, especially in novels, as a "fixity . . . wholly different from that of concepts, which initiates life, offers reality to our powers, to truth, opens a dialectic. By its reflection in a narrative, being has a non-dialectical fixity, stops dialectics and time" (RS 10 / 139 / 784).

Concerning Bergson, he writes:

Since Bergson it has become customary to take the continuity of time to be the very essence of duration. The Cartesian teaching of the discontinuity of duration is at most taken as the illusion of a time grasped in its spatial trace, an origin of false problems for minds incapable of conceiving duration. And a metaphor, one that is eminently spatial, of a cross-section made in duration, a photographic metaphor of a snapshot of movement, is accepted as a truism.

We on the contrary have been sensitive to the paradox that an instant can stop. The fact that humanity could have provided itself with art reveals in time the uncertainty of time's continuation and something like a death doubling the impulse of life. The petrification of the instant in the heart of duration — Niobe's punishment — the insecurity of a being which has a presentiment of fate, is the great obsession of the artist's world, the pagan world. (RS 11 / 140 / 785)

These formulations take aim, through the implicit debate with Sartre with which Levinas's text sets out, at a much longer tradition of thinking the image. He takes issue with the view that the image represents or substitutes for reality as we know it or that it represents reality as we always already know it only in part (albeit in infinite progression and ideal approximation, as Kant claims). The image carries us beyond the conceptual determinations that — as the dictum *omnis determinatio negatio est* reminds us — are in fact as many limitations. For Levinas, moreover, this transportation beyond the confines of empirical cognition, beyond known matters of fact and established (or supposedly fixed) relations between ideas, does not consist in knowledge of a higher or more secure order. Yet the strong noncognitivism he thus defends does not necessarily reduce art and aesthetic experience to subjective emotive expression.

On the contrary, the image comes to stand for the rapture of "participation" in a totality of sorts. This totality is diffuse and not conceptual, and Levinas models it on certain ethnographic findings and their interpretation in the wake of the classical theories of Émile Durkheim and Marcel Mauss, preceding the structuralist anthropology inaugurated by Lévi-Strauss. Indeed, another important subtext for understanding "Reality and Its Shadow" is an early essay devoted to Lucien Lévy-Bruhl, whose — partly Bergsonian — views form a constant point of reference and contrast throughout all of Levinas's later writings.[20]

The image, Levinas states, is fundamentally "magic" and signals a re-

---

20. Emmanuel Levinas, "Lévy-Bruhl et la philosophie contemporaine," *Revue Philosophique* 147 (1957): 556–69, esp. 562.

versal in which reality is no longer grasped and construed (or constructed) but, instead, captures the beholder (and actor). Levinas uses the terms *participation, rhythm,* and *musicality* to characterize this neutralization and depersonalization:

> The idea of rhythm, which art criticism so frequently invokes but leaves in the state of a vague suggestive notion and catch-all, designates not so much an inner law of the poetic order as the way in which the poetic order affects us, closed wholes whose elements call for one another like the syllables of a verse, but do so only insofar as they impose themselves on us, disengaging themselves from reality. *But they impose themselves on us without our assuming them.* Or rather, our consenting to them is inverted into a participation. Their entry into us is one with our entry into them. Rhythm represents a unique situation where we cannot speak of consent, assumption, initiative or freedom, because the subject is caught up and carried away by it. The subject is part of its own representation. It is so not even despite itself, for in rhythm there is no longer oneself, but rather a sort of passage from oneself to anonymity. This is the captivation or incantation of poetry and music. It is a mode of being to which applies neither the form of consciousness, since the I is there stripped of its prerogative to assume its power, nor the form of unconsciousness, since the whole situation and all its articulations are, in a dark light, *present.* (RS 4 / 133-34 / 774-50)

I have spoken of the *otherness* of art and the *alterity* of ethics. In the first the self is absorbed in an anonymous other; in the second the self relates to an other while remaining separate, identical to itself or other (the difference eventually will matter little), becoming other to itself through substitution and subjection yet without participation and without the alienation that excludes uniqueness and election. Absorption by (and participation in) the other and exposure (and relating) to the other represent two distinct yet complementary perspectives on the total drama of human existence: of subjectivation and depersonalization, on the one hand, and responsibility and irresponsibility, on the other, two mutually constitutive yet opposite extremes that Greek philosophy seeks to master—and reconcile—in vain.

The becoming art of reality absorbs the self and the other into an indifferent yet all too present and overwhelming sameness whose shadowy existence—a "being" before Being and subjects—should not lead us to forget its reifying and petrifying effect: art brings movement and time to a standstill in the "statue," in the fixity of forms (albeit those of "rhythm," "dance," "chant," and moving images).

The later Heidegger seems to state as much when, from an altogether different perspective, he observes that in "what the senses of sight, hearing, and touch convey, in the sensations of color, sound, roughness, hardness, things move us bodily, in the literal meaning of the word. The thing is the *aistheton,* that which is perceptible by sensations in the senses belonging to sensibility."[21] But the parallel ends here because, in Levinas's view, art's *counter-creation* and *counter-revelation* result first of all in a de-subjectivation, a loss of self and other, and, hence, of experience and temporality as such. The work of art is the exact contrary of the putting to work of truth (*ins Werk setzen der Wahrheit*) on which Heidegger muses.

Strictly speaking, for Levinas the expression *aesthetic experience,* taken for granted by a whole tradition, is thus almost a contradiction in terms. The whole point of his critical engagement with the aesthetic is to demonstrate that art — including the aesthetic in its broadest, etymological meaning (i.e., in the sense Baumgarten and Kant give to the term) — runs counter to truth and truthfulness and, hence, is at odds with the essence of discourse, freedom, and authenticity. Art and aesthetic experience express a "being *among* things [*être* parmi *les choses;* that is to say, not "with things" or "toward things," as in the *Gelassenheit, Nähe zu den Dingen,* or *Liebe zu den Dingen* on which Heidegger and Adorno muse]" which is no longer a being-in-the-world, a being-among-others, and, strictly speaking, no longer even a being *of* this world (RS 4 / 133 / 775).

Clearly, Heidegger could not have accepted this position. Already in *Being and Time* he makes clear that the concepts of truth and of the aesthetic, taken in their original meaning, are in a sense co-originary and say the same thing.[22] For Levinas, by contrast, art and truth move in altogether different, even opposed directions. Being polar extremes, they do not meet. But is this all there is to say?

Alternative Interpretations: Deconstructing Levinas

Of course, the relationship between art and truth, image and concept, aesthetic experience and criticism, sameness and otherness, participation and distance, the idolatry of masks and the face to face, could be construed in completely different terms, starting from other premises and in

21. Heidegger, "Origin of the Work of Art," 25 / 17.
22. Heidegger, *Being and Time,* 57 / 33.

view of alternative aims. It could be argued, for instance, that the image
cannot be reduced to the imagery that is (rightly?) held suspect by the
long biblical, rabbinic, and critical tradition of the ban on graven images.
Jean-Luc Marion takes this line of argument and, in *L'Idole et la distance*
(*The Idol and Distance*), *Dieu sans être* (*God without Being*), *La Croisée
du visible* (*The Crossing of the Visible*), and *Du surcroît* (*On Excess*), systematically elaborates a radical distinction between two terms, *idol* and
icon, whose relation to some visuality—albeit negatively, in the destruction of all imagery—is exemplary for a rethinking of the multiple ways
in which the given and the originary donation manifest themselves. For
Marion the domain of seeing or visuality and its presentation is not ipso
facto devoid of the alterity—more precisely, the gift—which his heterology seeks to evoke in parallel phenomenological and theological ways.
For Marion the icon gives itself in such dramatic or theatrical liturgical
practices as the Eucharist or in the rhetorical genre of the confession of
faith. Yet the icon's formal description is that of the saturated phenomenon,[23] of which Marion gives compelling examples in his interpretations
of Dürer's *Melancholia* and of Cubist painting.

A full examination of Levinas's position would require extended engagement with this and other alternatives for describing the potential
that the image offers to thought concerning aesthetics and visual culture
today. Marie-José Mondzain, for example, in *Image, icône, économie: Les
Sources byzantines de l'imaginaire contemporain* (*Image, Icon, Economy:
The Byzantine Sources of the Contemporary Imaginary*), invokes the semantic, imaginative, and argumentative potential of earlier clerical debates, whereas W. J. T. Mitchell, in *Iconology: Image, Text, Ideology* and
Picture Theory: Essays on Verbal and Visual Representation, draws from
an examination of images a program for literary and cultural studies. In
the analytical tradition, Avishai Margalit and Moshe Halbertal, in *Idolatry*, differentiate between aspects of—and motivations behind—the prohibition of images and its continuing relevance for questions of semantics
and pragmatics. Gilles Deleuze's *Cinema 1: L'Image-mouvement* (*Cinema
1: The Movement-Image*) and *Cinema 2: L'Image-temps* (*Cinema 2: The
Time-Image*) open with a discussion of Bergson's *Matter and Memory*
and the instant, thus echoing a motif central to Levinas's observations
on aesthetic experience in *Existence and Existents* and "Reality and Its
Shadow." Indeed, Deleuze's entire argument seems built around the oppo-

---

23. I discuss these matters at some length in *Philosophy and the Turn to Religion*, 53ff.

site conviction—to which he comes at a point late in his career—namely, that the image does not (necessarily) immobilize temporality or freeze thought.[24]

To point toward other reservations concerning Levinas's observations on art, in "Reality and Its Shadow" and elsewhere, the Platonic theme of mimesis could be interpreted in quite different terms from those of "resemblance," as Derrida has shown convincingly in *Dissemination* and "Le Retrait de la métaphore" ("The Retreat of Metaphor"). On a different note, at least since Adorno's *Philosophy of Modern Music* we have learned to evaluate musicality in a register different from the one on which Levinas insists when he reduces it to the somewhat diffuse category and supposedly pure mediality of rhythm.

Similar objections can be anticipated from the ever more complex recent reflections on "new media." If Levinas targets classical and modern art and aesthetic experience, does he have something to say about postmodern forms of art? Can they be reduced as easily to the paradigmatic state—and stasis—which Levinas defines as "classical"? Can one blur all distinctions, as he seems to do, not only between different periods and styles but also between Western art forms and effects and non-Western art? Further, does Levinas not locate the aesthetic outside of (or before) the discursive and institutional realms represented by the Western, Greco-European Logos (regardless of struggles between the Ancients, the Moderns, and beyond) and thereby questionably reduce all art and aesthetic experience to primitivism—indeed, to exoticism—regardless of any given work's classical, modernist, or postmodernist sophistication?[25]

All this should restrain somewhat our enthusiasm for Levinas's early meditation. Yet there remain, I would argue, two different but related observations, whose validity seems beyond dispute. That is not to say that they do not stand in need of further elaboration and justification, but each is a sine qua non and even a truism of any convincing philosophical consideration concerning art.

The first is Levinas's insight that art, artistic expression, and aesthetic experience begin where the question of (and the distinction between)

---

24. I rely here on Paola Marrati, "'The Catholicism of Cinema': Gilles Deleuze on Image and Belief," in de Vries and Weber, *Religion and Media*, 227–40; see also Marrati, *Gilles Deleuze: Philosophie et cinéma* (Paris: Presses Universitaires de France, 2003).

25. On primitivism, see Arthur O. Lovejoy and George Boas, *Primitivism and Related Ideas in Antiquity*, with supplementary essays by W. F. Albright and P.-E. Dumont (1935; rpt. Baltimore: Johns Hopkins University Press, 1997).

truth and untruth is not necessarily, not yet, or no longer at issue. Not everything is a mode — albeit a privative one — of truth; the work of art is neither the appearance (the *Schein* or *Scheinen*) of the idea nor a mere epiphenomenon (*blosse Erscheinung*) of, and hence reducible to, something else. In Levinas's account the phenomenon and phenomenality of art and aesthetic experience do not fit the analytical distinctions that Heidegger sketches out in paragraph 7 of the introduction to *Being and Time,* nor do they respect the contours drawn in "The Origin of the Work of Art." Indeed, Levinas's polemic with Sartre in this early essay is exceeded only by the criticism it levels at Heidegger.

As we have seen, Levinas contrasts sensation — the specificity and the very element of the aesthetic, including its proper mode of seeing, the image — to the "being-in-the-world as such" (*In-der-Welt-sein überhaupt*) which Heidegger, in the first division of *Being and Time,* defines as the "basic state," or *Grundverfassung,* of *Dasein.* The aesthetic, therefore, does not constitute a particular ontico-empirical realm — for example, that of subjective or collective sentiment, let alone a world of ideal and beautiful or sublime forms — but a unique and separate "ontological dimension," which can manifest (rather than "reveal") itself anywhere at any time and does so with a temporality of its own. It inaugurates a qualified present as much as a cessation of time as we know it. This proper modality, that of the *entretemps,* the in-between-time or, as the translation has it, the "meanwhile," together with its reference to the "interstices" in the world of being (or within Being itself), merits lengthy analysis in its own right. Suffice it to say that it signals the classical motif of the *nunc stans* as well as the instantaneous "moment" that both Kierkegaard and, in his footsteps, Heidegger (and perhaps Schmitt and Benjamin) define as the *Augenblick,* the decision of human existence, its *kairos* no less than its *parousia.*[26] In Levinas's words:

> It is as though sensation free from all conception, that famous sensation that eludes introspection, appeared with images. Sensation is not a residue of perception, but has a function of its own — the hold an image has over us, a function of rhythm. What today is called being-in-the-world is an existence with concepts. Sensibility takes place as a distinct ontological event, but is realized by the imagination.
>
> If art consists in substituting an image for being, the aesthetic element, as

26. For a fuller discussion, see my book *Philosophy and the Turn to Religion,* 158–243.

its etymology indicates, is sensation. The whole of our world, with its elementary and intellectually elaborated givens, can touch us musically, can become an image. That is why classical art which is so attached to objects—all those paintings, all those statues representing something, all those poems which recognize syntax and punctuation—conforms no less to the true essence of art than the modern works which claim to be pure music, pure painting, pure poetry, because they drive objects out of the world of sounds, colors and words into which those works introduce us—because they break up representation. A represented object, by the simple fact of becoming an image, is converted into a non-object. . . . The disincarnation of reality by an image is not equivalent to a simple diminution in degree. It belongs to an ontological dimension that does not extend between us and a reality to be captured, a dimension where commerce with reality is a rhythm. (RS 5 / 134 / 776-77)

These insights are a potent corrective to representationalist, realist, or cognitivist forms of aesthetics (of "aesthetic ideology," to cite Paul de Man's phrase).[27] At the very least Levinas shows that art, in its "deconceptualization of reality" (RS 6 / 135 / 776), should not—indeed, cannot—serve the pursuit of truth or be reduced to ethics, public spectatorship, or general culture, let alone politics. To insist that art is "not committed by virtue of being art," and that for this very reason art is "not the supreme value of civilization" (RS 12 / 142 / 787-88), is a sound counterpoint at a time when eulogies to cultural production, artistic expression, and their supposed edifying value and effectiveness have become increasingly vain, unreal, and even somewhat immoral. Art, it would seem, contains no clues for ethics, even less so for the more complex life of the polis. Art, in short, is not in its essence part of the movement and the temporality that, in Levinas's view, constitute the very element of the world of action, of the Other (*autrui*) and of the third (*le tiers*), of justice and truth. In other words, Levinas protests the "hypertrophy" of art, which consists in taking its surreal realm of shadows for "spiritual life" itself (RS 2/ 131 / 771, 12 / 141-42 / 788). (Surrealism, Levinas writes, was just a "superlatif," indicating a supposedly "superior realism.") Art, therefore, is in need of being brought back home to this world that it—in its pagan otherwordliness, in its being neither *in* nor *of* this world—evades, escapes, if only intermittently as it situates itself in-between times as well as "among things" (and, hence, on

27. See Rodolphe Gasché, *The Wild Card of Reading: On Paul de Man* (Cambridge: Harvard University Press, 1998).

this side—indeed, in-between, in the interstices of—the specific temporal modes of the Heideggerian *Umwelt, Mitwelt,* and *Selbstwelt).* As idolatry in the most traditional sense of the term, religiously motivated and religiously condemned, art and aesthetic experience stand for a standstill of life and of the flux (*durée*) of time and thus of the agency and responsibility that they make possible and which make them possible in turn. But, being this cessation and petrifaction of the dynamic and its somewhat paradoxical immobilization in rhythm, art and aesthetic experience also become the foil against which "critique" and "criticism" become possible, necessary, and imperative: "One then has the right to ask if the artist really knows and speaks. He does in a preface or a manifesto, certainly; but then he is himself a part of the public. If art originally were neither language nor knowledge, if it were therefore situated outside of 'being in the world' which is coextensive with truth, criticism would be rehabilitated. It would represent the intervention of the understanding necessary for integrating the inhumanity and inversion of art into human life and into the mind" (RS 2 / 131 / 772). Here we find all the elements necessary for the "non-Marxist" critique of ideology (i.e., of reification, alienation, fetishization, and false gods) which Derrida, in "Violence and Metaphysics," rightly discerns in Levinas's work.

Levinas reminds us that truth is not the hidden truth of art, that art is not a half- or half-articulated truth, an image only waiting to be put into words and framed by proper concepts. Nor does art, as common "dogma" has it, extend or supplement truth (ethics, life, philosophy, etc.) in any direct, indirect, or even dialectical way. The work of art, as Levinas conceives it, does not even attain the status of the *parergon,* of which Kant and Derrida make so much. On the contrary, for Levinas art is diametrically opposed to the order of truth and to the light, clarity, and responsibility for which it stands. Art, artistic expression, and aesthetic experience thus seem limit cases of what is humanly possible: "The artist moves in a universe that precedes . . . the world of creation, a universe that the artist has already gone beyond by his thought and his everyday actions" (RS 7 / 136 / 779).

Long before Lyotard, Levinas thinks art—the beautiful *and* the sublime—as the "inhuman" (his word) and its temporality as the "instant,"[28] the less or more than infinitesimal split second of a neither moral nor immoral, thus an-ethical rather than irresponsible, evasion and escape into

---

28. See on this comparison my essay "On Obligation," 112.

a nonpresentist presence and, hence, irreality of sorts: a faint echo of the nonspatial and atemporal "here and now" to which the tradition of "spiritual exercises" aspired from its earliest beginnings and whose proper relationship to philosophy, religion, and ethics remains to be determined.

Conversely, Levinas has shown us that truth should not (and, indeed, cannot) be "presented" or expressed aesthetically (as Kant used to say) without immediately running the risk of becoming a shadow, caricature, or allegory of itself—a "symbol in reverse." To force or gently push truth into the realm of the idols by whatever "aesthetic presentation [*Darstellung*]" is ipso facto to condemn it to ideology; indeed, *in Levinas's view all ideology is aesthetic (and vice versa), just as all aesthetics is idolatrous.* Levinas thus enables one to formulate the kind of critique which Jean-Luc Nancy and Philippe Lacoue-Labarthe, on different grounds and with other arguments, develop in their book *Le Retrait du politique* (*The Retreat of the Political*) and which Lacoue-Labarthe expands in *La Fiction du politique* (*Art and Politics*), in an attempt to uncover the hidden origins and guiding principles of the ill-fated aestheticization of the political, the becoming shadow of the most real, and the becoming real of the most shadowy.[29]

This brings me to my second point. Although the distinction between art and truth, image and concept, play and seriousness, is crucial to Levinas's undertaking, the question of art nonetheless also calls forth, solicits, and provokes the question of truth, albeit a truth solely ascribed to the realm of the other (and via *autrui*, the neighbor, to that of the third, and thereby all others, and via these others to God, who is said to leave His trace in their face and to "come to mind" in this asymmetrical sociality alone). To introduce sociality is not to resort to the arguments of reception theory or to rely on the premises of a transcendental or formal pragmatics of sorts. Instead, Levinas's introduction of the relation to the other—and thus of ethics—into the analysis of how art, artistic expression, and aesthetic experience are brought to light and, hence, returned to the world of truth from which they, by their very exoticism, have exiled themselves resembles a well-known deconstructive argument: what is presupposed in the description—the discussion, judgment, and critique—of the phenomenon of art, namely, the ethical relation, is precisely what art

29. From yet a different perspective Éric Michaud, in *Un Art d'éternité: L'Image et le temps du national-socialisme* (Paris: Gallimard, 1996), has analyzed the relationship between the conception and reception of art, religion, and the political.

excludes. Mutually exclusive, art and ethics — and, more indirectly, art and truth — in this reading at once require and displace or supplement each other.

To speak of "deconstruction" here is not to deny the important differences between Levinas's and Derrida's analyses. For the latter there is a way in which the fictional, fabulous, poetic, or prosthetic *may yet make itself true.* Derrida argues this at length, discussing the relation between *Dichtung* and *Wahrheit,* in *Demeure,* the essay on Blanchot's *L'Instant de ma mort* (*The Instant of My Death*) which opens the collective volume *Passions de la littérature* (*Passions of Literature*).[30] The theme is also developed in the short text "Che cos'è la poesia?" in isolated remarks on "verification" in *Politics of Friendship,* and in the reading of Baudelaire in *Given Time.* It figures prominently in the epigraph taken from Van Gogh which opens the polylogue "Restitutions de la vérité en peinture" in *The Truth in Painting:* "But truth is so dear to me, and so is the *seeking to make true* [*Mais elle m'est si chère, la vérité, le chercher à faire vraie aussi*]."

For Levinas, however, the categorical distinction between the two realms of reality and its shadow seems to allow only an endless pendular movement of alternation or oscillation, an open-ended — Adorno would say negative — dialectical movement, one that resembles the gesture of skepticism, the radical and seemingly self-contradictory interrogation that, like art, follows the philosophical tradition as its inevitable and indispensable shadow. Aesthetics and ethics (meaning here the realm of criticism and truth) thus remain diametrically opposed, unable to signal to, let alone translate, each other.

Yet they also take up a symmetrical or structurally and formally parallel position as the opposite extremes of experience as we know it. In the final analysis aesthetics and ethics come to stand for the contrasting — mutually exclusive yet co-originary and codependent — movements of "trans-descendence" and "trans-ascendence," to cite again terms Levinas borrows from Jean Wahl. They hint at movements that are ultimately modulations — or perhaps "rhythms" — of an immanence unable to coincide with itself, a transcendence in immanence or, what comes down to the same, a transcendence that cannot keep to itself, a *transcendence of transcendence,* an immanence of (or within) transcendence.

But these two distinct movements *en-deça* and *au-delà* cannot be seen

30. See my essay "'Lapsus absolu': Some Remarks on Maurice Blanchot's *L'Instant de ma mort,*" *Yale French Studies* 93 (1998): 30–59.

as a simple or pure opposition between evasion, escape, irreality, and irresponsibility, on the one hand, and truthfulness, engagement, and responsibility, on the other. In his later work Levinas therefore views the movement of descent almost as an integral part—as a "modality" or "trial"—of
the ethical intrigue of the other in the self: ascending to the other now
comes down to descending into the depths of alienating layers of an ipseity
that is presubjective, that is "oneself" but only as "another," without determinable identity yet unique and elected. Here, in the domain of Husserlian *Urimpression* and Freudian trauma, we stand once again face to face
with the *il y a*, whose anonymous reign we seemed to have, well, evaded
and escaped, in the realm of truth and criticism, freedom and responsibility.

This is hardly an inconsistency on Levinas's part. Already the preface to *Totality and Infinity* speaks of "events" of eschatology which do not
manifest themselves in the light of day, of truth and Being, and which
are therefore "nocturnal," in a way. The "production" of infinity, Levinas
suggests there, could be described as a "drama," if only this Nietzschean
terminology were not so ambiguous.

This implication of the realm or shadow of the aesthetic in the ethical
intrigue and divine comedy does not yet appear in the schema by which
"Reality and Its Shadow" differentiates the world of action and intentionality from that of passivity and passion. But it is no accident that in the
later work these characterizations can switch places: passivity becomes
the dimension of the *pour l'autre*, whereas action and intentionality are
now relegated to the regime of the same (and, hence, of fixed identities, finite totalities, and the very *essance* and *conatus* of Being as such). "Reality
and Its Shadow" already develops a striking—and disconcerting—parallel, however: just as there is a "simultaneity of truth and image," two
"possibilities of being" (RS 7 / 136 / 779), so also there is a simultaneity of
ethics and its other, that is to say, in terms of the later work, of illeity and
il y a.

Our text is thus a shadow text, which reveals the photographic negative (indeed, the image) and the formal structure (indeed, the rhythm) of
the "reality" and "truth" of ethics beyond the grip of Being and before and
beyond our being-in-and-of-the-world, our being-with-others, and even
the relation of self to self. It evokes "an event of darkening of being, *parallel
with its revelation*, its truth" (RS 9 / 138 / 781; my emph.); moreover, it suggests this "event" to be that of a "degradation or erosion of the absolute"
(RS 8 / 137 / 780), an inversion whose possibility is intrinsic, necessary,

and a "modality" of the very transcendence called ethical, religious, absolute. In other words, one should not exaggerate the "divergences" between
the early essay and Levinas's "mature ethical philosophy."[31] The "shadow"
and "inversion" in and of Being of which the essay speaks is an immanent feature of (human) existence in general and as such is a condition —
or in-condition — of the ethical conversion that it calls forth: "There is a
duality in existence, an essential lack of simplicity. The ego has a self, in
which it is not only reflected, but with which it is involved like a companion or a partner; this relationship is what is called inwardness. It is never
innocently alone, nor innocently poor. The kingdom of heaven is already
closed to it. Existence casts a shadow, which pursues it tirelessly. It does
not merge with its shadow with the innocence of Narcissus espousing his
own image, but through its shadow learns of its want of innocence."[32]

Art, Aesthetic Experience, and the
Task of Philosophical Criticism

Two concluding observations can sum up what I have suggested thus
far. First, the image perhaps does not simply or primarily belong to the
realm of the same, of participation, silence, and irresponsibility, as Levinas seems to think. For Levinas each image is an idol, a mask, a caricature,
a "symbol in reverse," allegory. Yet there are other possibilities for thinking the image as belonging to — indeed, as the very instantiation of — the
realm of alterity, distance, movement, temporality, responsiveness, and
responsibility. As Marion has shown, the image can be rethought or experienced as an icon. And, as Deleuze has demonstrated, it can take the
form of the "time-image [*image-temps*]."

In a sense Levinas already admits as much when he stresses that *the
whole of reality can, at each single instant, become an allegory of itself* —
that is to say, art. He immediately adds that this shadow of reality can also
always be brought to *reenter* the world of action, judgment, and, therefore,
responsibility. This implies that in a sense — and by its own account? —
each single element of reality can escape, evade evasion, and, if only momentarily, chase the shadow away from reality.

Such transition — indeed, such reversal, a reversal of the "inversion"
and a conversion of sorts — constitutes the moment and momentum of
intersubjectivity, the appearance on the scene of the other. But, since Levi-

---

31. As Robbins seems to do in *Altered Reading*, 83.
32. Levinas, *Existence and Existents*, 16 / 37–38.

nas is far from defending a subjectivist aesthetics (of the sort that Gadamer dismantles in the first part of *Truth and Method*) and steers clear of all evaluation of art in terms of its public reception alone, there must be something in the artwork — that is, in the allegory, idol, mask, image, or sensation itself — which enables or allows this reentry into the orbit of the world, the polis, and so on by which art and the artist are salvaged, justified, corrected, and made responsible, after all.

Although Levinas relies on an outspoken, moralistic condemnation of art — "art, essentially disengaged, constitutes, in a world of initiative and responsibility, a dimension of evasion" (RS 12 / 141 / 787) — the moral judgment that he passes on art, almost without reservation, is, paradoxically, held in check by the fact that ethics is apparently not all there is to human existence, either, nor all that is relevant to its (and, indeed, ethics') phenomenological description. In fact, the order of creation and revelation — the realm of action and speech in which a world remains to be built — receives its distinctive profile and value, its meaning and sense, its ontological weight and seriousness, only against the background of this contrasting ontological dimension — another time, that of the in-stant, the in-between-time or *entretemps* — in which the sensation of rapture and participation, rhythm and silence, play and irresponsibility, holds sway over everything else. This other ontological dimension, the netherworld of untruth and unreality, is not portrayed by Levinas as simply before, behind, or beyond the world of phenomenality. Rather, it is the shadow, the allegory, caricature, and Janus face of itself which the whole of phenomenality can become, at every moment and in each truthful word, in any responsible act — indeed, in even the sincerest gesture. Withdrawn from our being in and of this world, we envision an altogether different modality of existence without (human) existents, a "being among things," in the "interstices" and "in-between-times (*entretemps*)" which open up (and close off) the world as it is, that is to say, as we know it and act upon it.

Second, against the Levinas of "Reality and Its Shadow" I should maintain that the concept is not simply the realm of otherness and freedom, of truth or veracity (*droiture*). The concept can become an idol, too, as Marion has shown in his argument concerning the second, "conceptual" idolatry (in *Idol and Distance, God without Being,* and elsewhere). Again, Levinas admits as much when, in *Otherwise than Being,* he draws a crucial distinction between the saying (*le Dire*) and the said (*le Dit*). There he describes the saying in almost poetical, rhetorical, dramatic, and even musical terms, using it to carry discourse beyond itself in a procedure of emphasis, exaggeration, hyperbole, and excess which constitutes an interesting reprise of the ancient *via eminentiae*. In the later work even truth — the regime of Truth, indeed, the Truth of all truth, its *Wahren, Bewährung*, essence, or, as Levinas now writes, *essance* — is itself described as idolatrous, as a shadow of reality, as reality qua shadow. In the beyond of discourse — Logos, the state, science, distributive justice, and everything they stand for — is to be built the ethical relation, now thought as an ultimate passivity, without initiative or identity. Its disengagement is portrayed as an unreal, almost Shakespearean world of shadows and specters, whose haunting forms the modality of transcendence: a transcendence "to the point of absence," in which extreme materiality and ultimate alienation go hand in hand as the ciphers of the drama — the "divine comedy" — of responsibility.

Paradoxically, in Levinas's late writings art and ethics, aesthetic experience and criticism, thus eventually come to touch upon each other, intersect, revert to and into each other, invert each other, and become virtually interchangeable in the extreme of *un-* or at least *non*truth. Perhaps, in a sense, they always already did. Art and truth, the image and the concept, musical rhythm and philosophy, regardless of their relative (or is it absolute?) specificity and incommensurability, can thus no longer be opposed in a rigorous way or once and for all. That is not to say that the distinction between them should be trivialized or simply done away with. But where they come "truly" into their own, their difference becomes undeterminable — indeed, undecidable — philosophically, aesthetically, if not ethically speaking.

In consequence the "analysis" of philosophy and aesthetics, concept and image, truth and art — of their distinction and mutual exclusion as much as their interdependency and reversibility — can be neither *philosophical* nor *aesthetic* in any consistent and historically or systematically precise meaning of these words. Because the alternative of a more adequate encompassing meta-theoretical or, for that matter, practical discourse seems available neither to Levinas nor to us, we should conclude that the problem of art in relation to truth — and, hence, of aesthetics in relation to philosophy — is resolved not by either one of these disciplines, let alone by their conflation, but in between them, in the interstices of the spaces that they open up and further only instantaneously, in an *entretemps* or in-between-time-and-times of sorts.

Levinas acknowledges as much when he writes, in the final section of "Reality and Its Shadow," that philosophy — more precisely, "philosophical criticism" (as if there were no difference between these two, as if literary criticism, art or cultural criticism, and so forth could not aspire to a distinctive questioning and method of their own) — is in its very pursuit of truth incessantly referred to its other, that is to say, to art and its images:

> The value of images for philosophy lies in their position between two times and their ambiguity. Philosophy discovers, beyond the enchanted rock on which it stands, all its possibles swarming about it. It grasps them by interpretation.[33] This is to say that the artwork can and must be treated as myth: the immobile statue has to be put in movement and made to speak. Such an enterprise is not the same as a simple reconstruction of the original from the copy. Philosophical exegesis will measure the distance that separates myth from real being, and will become conscious of the creative event itself, an event which eludes cognition, which goes from being to being by skipping over the intervals of the meanwhile. *Myth is then at the same time untruth and the source of philosophical truth, if indeed philosophical truth involves a dimension of intelligibility proper to it, not content with laws and causes which connect beings to one another, but searching for the work of being itself.* (RS 13 / 142 / 788, my emph.)

In interpreting the netherworld of aesthetic imagery — the element that surrounds philosophical truth in its very foundation — philosophical criticism will of necessity have to select. But any such selection — criticism "qua choice" (*comme choix*) — risks becoming entrapped on the "hinter side of the world which is fixed in art" or, inversely, risks transporting and reintroducing, Levinas writes, that other world "into the intelligible world in which it [namely, philosophical criticism] stands, and which is the true homeland of the mind" (RS 13 / 142 / 788).

In the terms of Levinas's own analysis this slippage or surreptitious passage of one realm into the other seems the inescapable condition on the basis of which the quest for truth, responsibility, and the pursuit of "the *better* [*le* mieux]" becomes possible, necessary, and imperative in the first place (RS 12 / 141 / 787). Yet this fundamental insight does not prevent him from insisting that the philosophical assessment of art and aesthetic experience can and must resist the temptation of this slippage and surreptitious passage not of the intelligible into the empirical, phenomenal world (which Kant feared but never fully avoided) but of the intelligible

---

33. One is reminded here of the opening chapter of Bergson's *Matter and Memory,* even though the polemic with Bergson is not absent (see RS 11 / 140 / 786).

into the pagan, nightly world that precedes the order of creation, revelation, and light, whose ontological structure is that of a fixation and reification of being, and, hence, of its untruth, its unreality, its deprivation of movement and temporality. Of this, myth and participation, resemblance and rhythm, allegory and silence—in short, "artistic idolatry"—form the proper modes.

To resist them, Levinas concludes, philosophy should find its way back to its own domain, away from the ambiguous space opened up by art between beings and between times. Yet, paradoxically, art forms the very space and movement in relation to which philosophy assigns itself its proper task, to wit: the pursuit of freedom, justice, and truth. Art is thus the *negative foil* against which philosophical inquiry and, hence, truth receive their distinctive profile, but art, I have established, also forms a *positive modality*—and thus an intrinsic possibility—of both. Radically distinct, they evoke fundamentally the same, that is to say, the other.

Chapter Nine

The Dialectics of Subjectivity
and the Critique of Objectivism

LEVINAS'S FIRST INDEPENDENT philosophical publications attempt to find a way out of the anonymity of the *preontological* sphere. They strive to escape the sonorous din of the *il y a*, the dreary dimension behind all experience, indeed, any thing or object in the world. Its —inescapable?—shadow and diffuse senselessness cannot be eliminated and continue to loom beyond both all formal negations of thought (e.g., the Cartesian and Husserlian mental experiments of the imaginary destruction of the world and transcendental reduction) and any concrete negation through work and action (in the Hegelian and Marxist conception of dialectic as objective idealism or historical materialism). In Levinas's view the *il y a* resides in the cleft between Being and nonbeing like an *excluded middle* (EI 48 / 38).

Levinas seeks to explore how we break through the solitude of existence in the experience of temporality, which makes possible our relationship to the Other. He expounds this thesis in contrast to his reconstruction of the Western epistemological and ontological model, in which, because of the fundamentally solipsistic character of its categories of thought and the existential modes it believes define experience, one can never really *get beyond* or examine *critically* Being (or the being of the subject). Idealism's moment of truth lies in its insight into this seemingly inescapable *petitio principii.*

To formulate it in quite general terms, which are therefore to a certain degree devoid of content, Levinas sketches (not "postulates" or even "projects" but, as Cavell would say, "acknowledges" or "attunes to") a goodness beyond Being (or, as he says elsewhere, following Vassily Grossman, the "small goodness [*la petite bonté*]" beyond God and the Good). He summarizes the paradox of this undertaking as follows: "the movement which leads an existent toward the Good is not a transcendence by which that existent raises itself up to a higher existence, but a departure from Being and from the categories which describe it: an *ex-cendence*. But *excendence and the Good necessarily have a foothold in being, and that is why Being is better than non-being"* (*EE* 15 / 18, my emph.; see also 39–40, 68–69 / 28, 58). This movement of thought—first the descent into the preontological dimension and shadow of Being without beings, the *il y a,* then the movement past separate individual beings in the direction of the Other, and finally perhaps even back again—occurs in three stages, whose intrinsic relationship Levinas construes in an almost dialectical (I would venture to say, negative dialectical) fashion.

Levinas describes how the subject can be torn, if not saved, from the meaninglessness and impersonality of the *il y a* and from the passivity of its being before and beyond existence. The main thesis of *Existence and Existents* is that out of an "inversion" or "hypostasis" and "contraction" in Being emerges a being that can, in its autonomy, do without the mythical element. In the course of his development Levinas subjects this assumption to various modifications, and in the end the "I" comes to find its uniqueness when, rather than resist the burden of Being, it is (before the Other or before God) made to carry that burden on its shoulders, and thus elects or is elected to do so. Whereas the initial text of *Existence and Existents* terms the *il y a* "the theme of the present work" (*EE* 15 / 18), the preface to the second edition names opposition to the *il y a* the central "bit of resistance [*le morceau de résistance*]." The "dis-position" and depossession of the subject increasingly take the place of earlier emphasis on "position" and "possession."

The course of subjectivation Levinas discerns—out of mythical violence and anonymity, through individual autonomy and economy, to peace with the Other—can, as I have indicated, be divided into three phases, which correspond to stages in the subject's life, albeit in a very different sense than Kierkegaard assumed. Levinas does not (re)construct this process according to a historical-genealogical or even classical-dialectical scheme of development but, rather, describes it in an undeniably systematic and, I would add, *open* or even *negative dialectical* way. Because certain Hegelian connotations have become almost unavoidable in the very concept of dialectics, Levinas, like so many of his generation, prefers a different articulation of words, things, and events: Bataille's concept of a "general economy of being," for example (see *TO* 39 / 18; or *TI* 39 / 9). But the interpretive model that Levinas follows in his early writings (and not only there) nonetheless looks very much like a non-Hegelian—or even anti-Hegelian—dialectic, of sorts: "It is not a matter of traversing a series of contradictions, or of reconciling them while stopping History. On the contrary, it is toward a pluralism that does not merge into unity that I should like to make my way and, if this can be dared, to break with Parmenides" (*TO* 42 / 20).

(1) As the first stage in the journey to selfhood and then ipseity, we find the situation of undifferentiatedness, or the participation or absorption in (and reduction to) the "other." Here there cannot yet be something like subjectivity, and the I is depersonalized by the "experience" of the anonymous, monotonous, and absurd *il y a*. Of this horrific vanishing point of all possible experience—more precisely, this virtual point from which experience cannot yet emerge—one can speak only retrospectively in terms of the absolute emptiness of the mythical world that preceded creation (*EI* 48 / 38), to borrow Rosenzweig's terminology in *The Star of Redemption*. Or, by extrapolation, one can refer to the virtual emptiness after the imagined end of the world in the mental or spiritual exercise of the phenomenological reduction: "where the continual play of our relations with the world is interrupted we find neither death nor the 'pure ego,' but the anonymous state of being. Existence is not synonymous with the relationship with a world; it is antecedent to the world. In the situation of an end of the world the primary relationship which binds us to being becomes palpable" (*EE* 21 / 26). Although this "experience" can perhaps best be grasped in art, as we have seen, it can also be found elsewhere. Ordinary experiences such as fatigue and sleeplessness bring about the same sentiment of the bareness and insufficiency of Being, which is due not to Being's limitation or finitude but to its fullness and self-perpetuation— the *conatus essendi*.

In his early and middle phases (though less evidently so in the latter) Levinas's thinking is guided by the seemingly unambiguous intention to set out the conditions of possibility for a decisive flight from the horror and disgust of Being. In his late work this pole of experience on this side (*en-deçà*) of the realm of subjectivation and freedom, words and concepts, work and action, plays a more ambivalent role. There he asserts that this being-without-beings should be borne rather than escaped, because it puts our responsibility to the test and co-constitutes the enigmatic character of the dimension of the truly other as the very modality—the risk and trial—of its transcendence.

(2) At the second stage of the analysis Levinas appears, despite his assurances to the contrary, to stand on its head the hierarchical relationship to which Heidegger subjected the terms of ontological difference. Levinas seems to grant primacy to concretely human existents (which should not be understood in terms of Heideggerian *Dasein*) and to ground them

in relation to Being. The French title of his 1947 study *De l'existence à l'existent* (*From Existence to the Existent*) conveys that sense more aptly than the standard English translation, *Existence and Existents,* whose title drops this statement of movement, direction, and aim — namely, ontological pluralization from the one Being to many beings.

Yet, just as the impression of an unproblematic and, so to speak, linear and liberating movement out of the *il y a* is deceptive, so is the hypothesis of a simple reversal of the hegemony of Being over existents: "To glimpse in the 'existent,' in the human *being,* and in what Heidegger will call the 'beingness of the existent,' not an occultation and 'dissimulation' of Being, but a stage [*étape*] on the way toward the Good and toward a relation to God, and, in the relations among beings, to see something other than 'metaphysics drawing to a close' does not signify only that one simply inverts the terms of the famous Heideggerian difference by privileging the being to the detriment of Being."[1] By shifting emphasis onto the establishment of a true ontological pluralism, Levinas prepares — almost in the sense of a deconstructive strategy — a change in perspective in which the concepts of Being *and* of existence can be stripped of their customary value. In Heidegger's fundamental-ontological analytic of *Dasein* or hermeneutics of facticity, Levinas senses a prolongation of the dominant tradition of the philosophy of the same and self-same, if now in an anti-intellectual — that is to say, anti-Cartesian and anti-Husserlian — alignment. Just as Levinas's idea of a threatening heterogeneity (of the *il y a*) cannot correspond entirely to the Heideggerian conception of Being or even to the *es gibt,* so his idea of an intrigue and obsession with the absolute that intervenes in the subject's self-centeredness and natural atheism finally is incompatible with Heidegger's category of human *Dasein* or even the most authentic understanding of this *Dasein*'s "existence [*Existenz*]." Quite the contrary, Levinas insists that in this second instant one "catches sight, in the very hypostasis of a subject, its subjectification, of an ex-ception, a null-site [*non-lieu*] on the hither side [*en-deça*] of the negativity which is always speculatively recuperable, an *outside* [*un* en-dehors] of the absolute which can no longer be stated in terms of being. Nor even in terms of entities, which one would suspect modulate being, and thus heal the break marked by the hypostasis" (*OB* 17–18 / 21). Therefore, Levi-

---

1. *EE,* preface to the 2d ed., my emph. Levinas thus distances himself from the analysis of Jean-Luc Marion in *L'Idole et la distance: Cinq études* (Paris: Grasset, 1977) / *The Idol and Distance: Five Studies,* trans. Thomas A. Carlson (New York: Fordham University Press, 2001).

nas does not so much give a new answer to the honorable old question of (the meaning of) Being. As he contends, the question of (the meaning of) Being is, already beforehand, "without response" (*EE* 22 / 28, trans. modified), just as "death" can be phenomenologically characterized as the "experience" of *sans réponse*. Levinas thus shifts traditional and modern ontological questioning in the direction of a "more" that can no longer be disclosed in terms of—or, better, in the light of—a truth or Truth, however conceived. The surplus of this more resembles the "Good beyond Being," the *epekeina tes ousias* of which Plato speaks in *The Republic,* or the "idea of the Infinite" which Descartes's *Meditations* discover as the ground of our awareness of fallibility and imperfection. More precisely still, it echoes the *minimal* "small goodness [*la petite bonté*]" which Vassily Grossman rescues from the universe in which "God" and "the Good" have lost their force and meaning but reveal themselves as the *proton pseudos* of the very principle of social organization, as well as the totalitarianism and wars to which it must lead.

Within the emptiness of the *il y a*—before and beyond Being and its supposed opposite, nothingness—an "inversion" emerges (*TO* 50 / 31), an "existent contracts its existing" (*TO* 43 / 22; see *DL* 295 / 411). This is the positing of a subject that attempts to overcome the horror of Being without beings. Why or how this posited—and retrospectively hypothesized—position of the subject comes about, Levinas does not say. It proceeds neither from an act of reflection or practical, Fichtean of self-constitution nor from the struggle against mythical fate and blind nature.[2] One cannot explain its appearance but can only describe it or attempt to give it some meaning (*TO* 51 / 31): for example, by way of the metaphor of *creatio ex nihilo.* Levinas does not interpret this monotheistic motif in terms of a postulated first cause of nature and its perpetuation—"God is the other who turns our nature inside out"[3]—indeed, he deprives the doctrine of creation of all its ontological and dogmatic character (see *HAH* 108 n. 17). In sharp contrast to a long tradition beginning with Parmenides, for him the idea of creation presents the possibility of a "multiplicity not united into a totality" (*TI* 104 / 78). Ontological pluralism is no mere appearance or imagination only if one understands that creation can be "neither a negation nor a limitation nor an emanation of the One" (*TI* 292 / 268–69).

The paradox of creative infinity is that its *infinitization* occurs in rela-

---

2. See *EE* 24, 82–83, 97 ff. / 29–30, 140–41, 172 ff.
3. See Levinas and Kearney, "Dialogue," in Cohen, *Face to Face with Levinas,* 25; see also 24.

tion to a Being that it does not contain (and which does not contain it, in turn). By analogy to the idea of creation as a contraction of God, an idea that has left its traces in the Kabbalistic tradition from Isaac Luria up to the late Schelling (whose *Weltalter* deeply influenced Rosenzweig and thus, indirectly, Levinas), the process of subjectivation is conceived as a shrinking and condensation, a "hypostasis" through which separate beings emerge out of the anonymity of the *il y a,* out of the diffuse sensation of the elements, and out of the mythic totality of primitive participation. In addition to this speculative anthropogenesis of the self in its separation and interiority, we find a remarkable parallel in the contraction, if not entropy, which Levinas addresses in his philosophy of language. As I will analyze in the following chapter, there, too, we find a "movement of progressive, ethical-metaphysical *reduction*": "Not unfolding and expansion, but rather shrinking, drawing together, and concentration determine the picture."[4]

In exploring these motifs, from the very beginning Levinas takes up a position counter to existentialism of any origin that would try to grasp the secret of the human through concepts such as "freedom," "project," or "ecstasy": "To the notion of existence—where the emphasis is put on the first syllable, we are opposing the notion of a being whose very advent is a folding back upon itself [*un repli en soi*], a being which, contrary to the ecstaticism [*l'extatisme*] of contemporary thought, is in a certain sense a substance" (*EE* 81 / 138; see also 94, 98–99 / 167–68, 173).

Negatively viewed, this contraction means a first radical break with participation in any magically or mythically devised unity. On the "positive" side it means the beginning of an inexorable appropriation—a possession and enjoyment—of other beings. Again, negatively viewed, the "I" gains this independence in the enclaves of its autonomy, interiority, and economy only at the expense of an allergy to the truly other. Yet, positively viewed, this egoism is also somehow necessary for the relationship to the absolute other to be possible in the first place.[5] Indeed, such a relationship can begin to occur once ostensibly religious or historical totalities are shattered.

Levinas thus esteems the realm of autonomy as a *condition of possibility* for the encounter with true foreignness, one that is forgotten or not yet

---

4. Goud, "Über Definition und Infinition," 141–42.

5. See Peperzak: "Without a certain egoism, the separation between the same and the other would be impossible; the two poles of relation could only decay and merge together" ("Introduction à la lecture de *Totalité et Infini*," 216).

thinkable in mythical and mystical participatory thinking: "The separation is radical only if each being has its own time, that is, its *interiority*, if
each time is not absorbed into the universal time. By virtue of the dimension of interiority each being declines the concept and withstands totalization—a refusal necessary for the idea of Infinity, which does not produce
this separation by its own force" (*TI* 57 / 28). Egoism is evaluated—and
valued—in its own right; it is given a limited privilege over and against
the pejorative characterizations that have punctuated Western philosophy
from Platonism all the way to Heidegger. As Levinas writes:

> in the ontological adventure the world is an episode which, far from deserving
> to be called a fall, has its own equilibrium, harmony and positive ontologi-
> cal function: the possibility of extracting oneself from anonymous being. At
> the very moment when the world seems to break up we still take it seriously
> and still perform reasonable acts and undertakings; the condemned man still
> drinks his glass of rum. To call it everyday and condemn it as inauthentic is to
> fail to recognize the sincerity of hunger and thirst. Under the pretext of saving
> the dignity of man, compromised by things, it is to close one's eyes to the lies
> of capitalist idealism and to the evasions in eloquence and the opiate which
> it offers. The great force of Marxist philosophy, which takes its point of de-
> parture in economic man, lies in its ability to avoid completely the hypocrisy
> of sermons. It situates itself in the perspective of the sincerity of intentions,
> the good will of hunger and thirst, and the ideal of struggle and sacrifice it
> proposes, the culture to which it invites us, is but the prolongation of these
> intentions. What can be captivating in Marxism is not its alleged materialism,
> but the essential sincerity this proposal and invitation maintain. It is beyond
> the always possible suspicion that casts its shadow over every idealism which
> is not rooted in the simplicity and univocity of intentions. One does not at-
> tribute to it the second thoughts of deceivers, dupes, or the sated. (*EE* 37 /
> 69–70)

Levinas is concerned, then, with "two stages" of overcoming the *il y a*
(*EI* 57 / 49), more precisely, of bringing about its convalescence, its *Verwindung*, as Heidegger might have said. In the act of a creative separation
and, hence, in the appearance of existing things (words, objects, acts, and
gestures), as well as in the hypostasis of an autonomous I which accompanies and enables their manifestation and meaning, a possible first step
emerges in (conclusively?) escaping monotonous monism. Out of the act
of creation arises the position of human exception, its separation, its autonomy in the universe. Yet out of this also emerge, paradoxically, ego-

ism and atheism. The human soul is, so to speak, "naturally atheist" (*TI* 58 / 29). Atheism, being a break with mythical participation, is a necessary condition for the ethical-metaphysical relation to the ab-solute. Already in the opening essay of *Difficult Freedom,* "Une Religion d'adultes" ("A Religion for Adults"), Levinas confirms this dialectical role of atheism: "Atheism is worth more than the piety bestowed on mythical gods. . . . Monotheism surpasses and incorporates atheism, but it is impossible unless you attain the age of doubt, solitude and revolt" (*DL* 16 / 31). This dialectics reiterates itself in the intrinsic dynamic of the relation between self and other: "Only an atheist being can relate himself to the other and already *absolve himself* from this relation" (*TI* 77 / 49). The marvel of creation consists in the emergence of a moral being who ("at the same time" [*TI* 89 / 61]) is both atheist *and* able to be ashamed, so to speak, of the arbitrariness of his freedom.[6] Not until the second step—the event of the revelation of the Other and the action corresponding to it or, better, the passive saying of the subject which is its very production[7]—does the exception and separation *in ontologicis* become a being chosen as uniquely responsible *in ethicis.*

Upon closer examination, however, the hypostasis proves to be incapable by itself of completely breaking out of the course of anonymous Being without beings, the *il y a* (see *EE* 79, 84 / 132, 142–43). The independence of the I, accordingly, can indicate only a preliminary approach to a "metamorphosis" of the escape called for in Levinas's early work.[8] Seeking to designate a certain "escape itself" (*EE* 69 / 121), it reaches only a position of the subject in which a closed dialectic—within the constant sameness of Being—inevitably plays itself out: "the subject's mastery over

6. On this complex of problems, see also Herman J. Heering, "Die Idee der Schöpfung im Werk Levinas," *Nederlands Theologisch Tijdschrift* 38 (1984): 298–309.

7. One should say, if one were to follow through Levinas's reading of Rosenzweig with any consequence, that this is also a step toward redemption. Nevertheless, Levinas turns in a different direction. In *Totality and Infinity* only a faint echo of Rosenzweig's central concept, *Erlösung,* can be detected, notably in the idea of eschatology. Redemption in Levinas never assumes cosmic proportions, as it does in Rosenzweig. Its role is to generalize and intensify the scope and weight of my unique responsibility for the well-being of the Other, of all others, of all things. One could, of course, show that, because Levinas's social philosophy is not directed toward the cosmos or history, it encounters problems of mediation which do not seem to occur in Rosenzweig's recapitulation and inversion of Hegelian and, especially, late Schellingian idealism. But there is a sense in which *Otherwise than Being* reintroduces, if not a "cosmic consciousness" (to borrow a term Pierre Hadot uses in his studies of the tradition of spiritual exercises), then at least a cosmic modality of the responsible *sub-jectum* itself.

8. Rolland, "Getting Out of Being by a New Path," *OE* 42 / 48.

existing, the existent's sovereignty, involves a dialectical reversal" (*TO* 55 / 36; see also *EE* 80 / 134–35). As Ciaramelli correctly observes, we are dealing here with a "dialectic of the hypostatic constitution of the existent, a first liberation with regard to being, but at the same time a chaining to the self."[9] As he further notes, modern poetry (from Baudelaire and Rimbaud to Celan) serves Levinas as a sounding board in the attempt to articulate the desire for a way out of Being, out of the *il y a,* and out of the realm governed by the ontico-ontological distinction. Modern tragedy, by contrast, supplies him with an interpretive model for the permanent failure of any such striving.[10]

Subjective existence is, therefore, not a mighty fortress that can shield us from persecution by the meaningless heterogeneity, the *tertium datur,* of the *il y a.* Indeed, one can speak of separation only because that terrifying dimension still retains all its force and validity: "The separation that is accomplished by egoism would be but a word if the ego, the separated and self-sufficient being, did not hear the muffled rustling of nothingness back unto which the elements flow and are lost" (*TI* 146 / 120).

Levinas must therefore insist that only the *asymmetrical*—that is, the irreversible and nondialectical—relationship to the Other can open a breach in the apparently rock-solid neuter: "de-neutralization cannot take hold of its truly human meaning in the *conatus essendi* of the living—of existents—nor in the world where they maintain themselves and where the savagery of their *care for the self* [soucis de soi] becomes civilized, but turns toward the indifference, to the equilibrium of anonymous forces, and hence, if need be, to war. This in-difference maintains itself within the egotism of a salvation sought beyond the world, but without consideration for others" (*EE,* preface to 2d ed.). Only in sociality and the temporality it makes possible does the subject—as if on a higher plane—finally encounter a genuine alterity (see *TO* 39 / 17; *EI* 58 / 48), whose immediacy and uprightness pierces every horizon and all anticipation and thus leaves no room for mediation, negotiation, interpretation, representation, and the like.

In his early work and in his first major work, *Totality and Infinity,* Levinas attempts to elucidate this in terms of the erotic and fecundity. In these figures of an apparently infinitizing, if not necessarily infinite (or, in Levinas's sense, ethico-religious), relation, a structure other than that of

9. Ciaramelli, "De l'évasion à l'exode," 575.
10. Ibid., 557; see *EE* 61, 88 /101, 151; *TO* 50, 72–73 / 29, 60.

knowledge and work, theory and praxis, begins to emerge. Levinas condemns the latter to remain mired in the realm of the self and the same, however much they might be able to penetrate to the farthest depths and distances of the universe and, as Pascal says, to its "infinite spaces" within and without (*EE* 58 / 102). Just as the enthusiasm of magic or the holism of myth always dissolve the order of the self into an (often anonymous) other, knowledge and work set out to appropriate that other into the self, in a converse movement that comes down to the same, that is to say, to a now conceptually articulated rather than diffusely assumed totality. Only a true *alternation* of immanence and transcendence could, in Levinas's eyes, prevent these complementary false sublations and the dialectic of magic, myth, superstition, and enlightenment to which they lead.

After the realm of interiority and its economy separates itself off from the diffuse, anonymous sphere of the *il y a,* a further separation emerges between these preontological and ontological instances, on the one hand, and the ethical-metaphysical "optic," on the other. This second step results in an unsublatable — a nondialectical (or is it an open and negative dialectical?) — tension between the egoistic self and the I rendered responsible, between historical forms of life which abide by normative or juridical rules and ethical consciousness, between the order of the Said (*le Dit*) and the command of pure Saying (*le Dire*). Levinas must account for the circumstance that one can never approach the Other in a linear and unalterable way, to linger there in contemplation, so to speak. A plausible philosophy must set out how all thought, action, experience, and judgment must continually move back and forth between the poles of the preontological and ontology and between the latter and metaphysics (i.e., ethics, religion, eschatology).

(3) In a third moment, for Levinas subjectivity signals passivity and passion, the "ultimate metaphorphosis"[11] of the self into an other and thereby "ethical deliverance" (*OB* 164 / 209) — to be distinguished from ontological separation — from the anonymity of the *il y a.* In it the subject seeks less to escape impersonal Being than to assume and thus "deneutralize"[12] its full and meaningless weight (see *OB* 43 / 56). Levinas's late work testifies to an extremely concrete suffering and, indeed, subjection of the subject. In being given over to the Other, being held hostage in a singular way, the subject, this time in its very interiority, seems to effect, echo,

---

11. Rolland, "Getting Out of Being by a New Path," *OE* 47 / 52.
12. See ibid.

or resonate with a break in Being: subjectivity is "an exception putting out of order the conjunction of essence, entities and the 'difference'" (OB xli / x). In an altogether different way from that envisioned in the middle period and in a remarkable return to the earliest essays, notably On Escape, Levinas again thinks of the I as being itself "ineffable,"[13] in a far more radical sense than the philosophical tradition, from Aristotle through the Scholastics up to Hegel and Dilthey, ever had.

The relationship Levinas now seeks to elucidate concerns not the assimilation of any Other by the I nor the absorption of the latter into the former but, rather, the *intrigue* of "the-Other-in-the-Same" (GCM 80 / 130), to the point of "substitution." The proximity in which the relation to the truly other plays itself out is that of a certain affectivity—Levinas speaks of a "sentiment"—whose "fundamental *tonality [tonalité]*" is desire:[14] "Distinct from tendency or need [*besoin*], desire [*désir*] does not appear in activity, but rather constitutes the intentionality of the affective [*l'affectif*]" (DEHH 205). But, then, what could the expression "the intentionality of the affective" mean? Clearly, it stands for the mode of consciousness and conscience—the wakefulness—which should enable both knowledge directed toward objectivity and universality and action striving toward justice because it arouses the I from its slumber and disquiets it so that it takes leave of its complacency and self-centeredness. Levinas emphasizes that the manner in which the Other(s) break(s) into the I causes an undesired and unchosen passivity and an obsession that appears almost corporeally: an inversion of intentionality (see OB 47, 53 / 60–61, 69), a "passion."

The subject, according to dominant philosophical opinion, is not disturbed from beyond the visible; indeed, subjectivity is customarily considered to be the center around which the actual is rendered present (see OB 165 / 210). The thinking of presence—including presence to oneself—from which this concept of subjectivity stems is based upon the assumption that it is possible to arrive at a privileged point in the flow of time from which everything given can *in principle* be kept in view in its entirety (see DEHH 203). Hegel paradigmatically illustrates this timelessness of traditional philosophy; nonetheless, in his thinking "history" comes into its own (see ND 330 / 324). Löwith encapsulates his "detemporalization" of

13. In "Le Moi et la totalité" Levinas writes, "The I is ineffable" (Revue de Métaphysique et de Morale 59 [1954]: 363).

14. DEHH 205 n. 1, my emph.

subjective and historical time as follows: "According to Hegel, the spirit's relationship to time consists simply in the fact that it must 'expound' itself in time as if in space, but not insofar as it has any innate temporal quality itself, arising from time and falling into its power."[15] In Hegel, as in the metaphysical tradition, fundamentally there is only one modality of time: the present. A brief quotation from Hegel substantiates this: "Only the present [*Gegenwart*] is; before and after are not. The concrete present is the outcome of the past, and is pregnant with the future. The true present is thus eternity."[16]

By contrast, Levinas wants to render plausible the possibility of an interruption of the (historical) order of time, "a lapse of time that does not return, a diachrony refractory to all synchronization" (*OB* 9 / 11; see *TI* 57 / 28). He thus confirms Husserl's view that the subject is not *in* time but must, rather, be thought of as temporalizing.[17] Levinas does not deny the absolute necessity for consciousness to identify meanings and assemble phenomenal actuality in retentions and protentions, recollections and anticipations (see *OB* 39, 50 / 43, 66). Yet, in contrast to Husserl's thinking of presence, he throws into sharp relief the *passive* aspects of that synthesis, which already in Husserl oppose the unifying power of the I.[18] Levinas emphasizes, furthermore, the experiences of patience and aging (*OB* 43 / 48), which burst apart the structure of intentional consciousness, its making itself present, its will, and its freedom (*OB* 53 / 69). He is concerned with processes "beyond [or on this side of, *en-deçà*] consciousness" (*OB* 57 / 73). In patience and in suffering for the other, the subject denies that the goal of its actions need be *contemporary:* "to act without entering into the Promised Land . . . eschatology without hope for oneself or liberation with regard to my time" (*HAH* 42; *TI* 237–38 / 216–17; *OB* 52 ff. / 68 ff.).

Time derails the subject: "In self-consciousness there is no longer a *presence* of self to self, but senescence" (*OB* 52 / 67). Upon closer examination, subjectivity therefore must be thought not as a "for oneself" but as "putting into question all affirmation 'for oneself'" (*OB* 111 / 141–42), as "for the other [*pour l'autre*]." Allusions to corporeality, vulnerability, and obsession, if we use them in an ethical sense, better express subjectivity than any reference to reflection, reason, belief, action, disposition, or habit.

15. Löwith, *From Hegel to Nietzsche*, 209 / 228, trans. modified.
16. Hegel, *Encyclopedia*, par. 259, supp.; cited in Löwith, *From Hegel to Nietzsche*, 209 / 227.
17. See, on this topic, Strasser, *Jenseits von Sein und Zeit*, 179, 280.
18. See Husserl, *Cartesian Meditations*, 77 ff. / 79 ff.

These and similar alternative idioms induce Levinas, especially in *Otherwise than Being,* to question more critically than heretofore the autonomy and identity of the I, especially because *esse* is of itself an *interesse,* an invested self-interestedness. This late work concentrates on the question of whether the Being of the I itself, the *conatus essendi,* the perseverance of the self in its own being, must not be seen as the prime motor for all reduction of other(s) to sameness. Does not the uniqueness of the I become possible through a "disinterestedness, without compensation, without eternal life, without the pleasingness of happiness, complete gratuity" (*OB* 6 / 6)? In other words, is not the uniqueness of the I first enabled by its involuntary offering of itself to the Other in "a reverse *conatus*" (*OB* 70 / 89) — and, hence, a substitution of the same for the other — of sorts? But, then, how could an inversion of the ontological ever enable us to escape its grip? A *conatus* turned against and into itself: would this inaugurate ontology's cessation, its sublation, its hypostatization? Is Levinas's perspective other than ontological, more ontological than the ontological, or different still?

I will turn to these questions in the following chapter. It is clear that the exteriority of the infinite now gains a further dimension of "interiority" (*OB* 147 / 187) in the inspiration of psychism, in the sincerity of prophetic witness, in the exposure of the posited subject in its becoming hostage and subjected to the Other, to the other within, to the self as other. The terminology is to a certain degree misleading, given that, in *Totality and Infinity,* interiority stands for the realm of the self-same, the *idem*-identity (as Ricoeur says). But the terms of the analysis essentially change in Levinas's late work. There he ties the question of transcendence (of the In-finite, God) to the irreducible secret of subjectivity understood as passivity and passion (see *OB* 16 / 20), the *ipse*-identity (to cite Ricoeur once more). But this motif is accompanied by a stronger emphasis on the ambiguity — indeed, the "anarchy" — of transcendence, whose characteristics the earlier work describes as exteriority and directness, that is to say, as the *primum intelligibile* and *archē* of meaning, truth, judgment, and action. The later work considers transcendence, now interior and immanent, in light of its counterweight, the *il y a,* the contrasting experience of which modifies the earlier unequivocal statues of the ethical. This results in renewed emphasis on the dimension of horror and absurdity, the surplus of non-sense over meaning, as a risk that must be run. In the fraught prose of *Otherwise than Being,* at the vanishing point of our experience, not depersonalization (as in the earliest writings) but an emptying out

(*Entkernung*) and de-substantializing of the (presumably) unified subject, with its intentional consciousness and good conscience, comes into
view. The ethical-metaphysical (no longer ontological?) interiority of the
reversed *conatus* indicates a singularity "without interiority" (*HAH* 99),
a constitutive duplication of the subject.[19] Obsession and trauma rather
than schizophrenia, haunting rather than doubling, form the rhythm of
this conversion of the self into its other, into the Other-within-the-Self.

Insofar as the subject involuntarily renounces its sovereignty—in that
it is no longer able to summon up its thoughts and powers, and consequently can no longer identify itself, so that its very substance splits
open—it gains the position of an exception in Being, a transcendence in
immanence. It becomes divided in and against itself, but only thus does it
find its singular uniqueness (philosophically speaking) as well as its election (religiously speaking) and its nontransferable responsibility (ethically speaking). Levinas writes: "Paradoxically it is qua *alienus*—foreigner
and other—that man is not alienated" (*OB* 59 / 76). Not (only) separation
from the order of nature and of history or of culture marks the site of the
individuum ineffabile but a concentration of the burden of the one and
multiple Being on the less than unified subject, persecuted and contracted
to the vanishing point: "subjectivity as a subjection to everything, as a *supporting everything* and *supporting the whole*" (*OB* 164 / 208). One might
see in this motif a full-scale attempt at an almost dialectical overcoming
of the preontological horror as well as the immanent determination of
the order of the self in the direction of the ethical sublime: "Impassively
undergoing the weight of the other, thereby called to uniqueness, subjectivity no longer belongs to the order where the alternative of activity and
passivity retains its meaning. We have to speak here of expiation *as uniting
identity and alterity*" (*OB* 118 / 151, my emph.).

Such being chosen not only opposes itself in advance to common or
available conceptuality, it is beforehand a *concretissimum* that must be
designated as "absolutely inconstructible conceptually" (*GCM* 93 / 147).
Levinas speaks of a "dis-position [*dé-position*]" or "de-situation" (*OB* 46 /
61) of subjectivity, of a dis-qualification "of the unqualifiable *one*, the pure
someone" (*OB* 50 / 65). Along with this consideration of another, ethical
dimension on this side of our freedom, Levinas expands his previous descriptions of the face and of the idea of the infinite. Of course, one might
ask here, with and perhaps against Levinas, whether such a motif does not

---

19. See Goud, "Wat men van zichzelf eist, eist men van een heilige," 83.

inevitably invite the suspicion of being merely a *flatus vocis* or absurdity. As he puts it: "How can transcendence withdraw from *esse* while being signaled in it?" (*OB* 10 / 12).

Derrida poses a similar question in "Violence and Metaphysics," his first reading of *Totality and Infinity*. There he addresses Levinas's attempt to distinguish himself from Kierkegaard's anti-Hegelianism as well as his insistence that it is "not I who do not accept the system, as Kiekegaard thought, it is the other."[20] On Kierkegaard's behalf Derrida counters this reservation with a critique that, though it partly misses Levinas's intention,[21] brings out the question of the eventual systematics of the motif of the Other: "The Other is not myself—and who has ever maintained that it is?—but it is *an* Ego, as Levinas must suppose in order to maintain his own discourse."[22] According to Derrida, Kierkegaard and Levinas can make their idea of the complete irreducibility of the I or the Other *philosophically* valid only by successfully showing how in this an "essential, non-empirical *egoity* of subjective existence *in general*"[23] opposes itself to every concept. If one were to break through this singularity of the subjective toward the *singular pure and simple*—that is to say, to the *totally singular*, which would be completely interior to (and coincide with) itself— then one would de facto break with every philosophical determination of essence (such as subjective existence). One would stop short of concept, structure, argument, and discourse.

Is this what Levinas achieves in his late philosophy or sets before his readers' eyes in its impracticability? Derrida's proximity to and distance from this horizon of questioning opens up the double-sidedness that Levinas's later writings (like Derrida's own) cannot—indeed, do not aim to—avoid. This is the need to defend the issue of the ab-solute other, whether *thematically* or *formally*, from within critical investigation as determined by traditional philosophical conceptuality. One can scarcely, as Derrida's reading of Levinas shows, distinguish the *thematic* concern from the nonphilosophical position of empiricism.[24] Yet, as a detailed reading of Derrida's work would demonstrate, even the most *formal* approach must finally refer to some substantive matter, however much it might remain suspended (micrologically, as *concretissimum* of the trace, etc.). As a con-

---

20. Quoted in Derrida, *Writing and Difference*, 110 / 162; see *TI* 39 / 10, 305 / 282.
21. See *DEHH* 209, 215; as well as the two essays on Kierkegaard in *NP* 66–80 / 99–115).
22. Derrida, *Writing and Difference*, 110 / 162; see also 122 ff. / 180 ff.
23. Ibid., 120 / 163.
24. Ibid., 151 / 224 ff.

sequence of this double binding of the concrete to the structural and vice versa, Derrida writes:

> the attempt to achieve an opening toward the beyond of philosophical dis-
> course, by means of philosophical discourse, which can never be shaken off
> completely, cannot possibly succeed *within language*—and Levinas recog-
> nizes that there is no thought before language and outside of it—except by
> *formally* and *thematically* posing *the question of the relations between belong-
> ing and the opening,* the *question of closure.* Formally—that is by posing it in
> the most effective and most formal, the most formalized, way possible: not in
> a *logic,* in other words in a philosophy, but in an inscribed description, in an
> inscription of the relations between the philosophical and the nonphilosophi-
> cal, in a kind of unheard of *graphics,* within which philosophical conceptuality
> would be no more than a *function.*[25]

My discussion has outlined a shift in Levinas's understanding of subjectivity. I have portrayed the dialectic of his philosophy of the subject by
first attempting to demonstrate a *relative* separation that can be described
among beings within ontology (through contraction, hypostasis, and the
interior and economical realm of atheism and self-possession they open
up). Something similar is true of the tension between these beings and the
categories that philosophies of identity and totality attribute to them. The
movement of thought by which Levinas plays out interiority and economy against neutral objectivism, as well as against the idea of exteriority
and, finally, of an interiority rendered responsible and once again hospitable, tends to reach beyond the initial premises of the analysis. In a
second movement the inner-ontological separation deepens in the direction of the *absolute* difference between the *il y a,* this time *on this side* of
interiority and economy, and ethical transcendence (the face and illeity),
forever *beyond* them.

Various strands thus come together in Levinas's late work. In what
constellation do these counter-poles of the *il y a* and illeity stand? They
are parallel in structure—or, should we say, in their de-structuring function?—and are often described as "the excluded middle," which indicates
their a-logical, indeed, aporetic format. Can we speak of a secret relation
between the amoral or even diabolical *il y a,* on the one hand, and divine
illeity, revealed only in the ethical trace, on the other? Or do the guiding stars of the idea of the singular good and the neutral dimension of

25. Ibid., 110–11 / 163.

"dis-aster" (to use Blanchot's term) gape asunder in an almost gnosti-cally dualistic way?[26] In fact, Levinas's critique of ontology follows a dual trajectory. In Jean Wahl's terms, I might describe this in the figures of thought "trans-descendence" and "trans-ascendence" (*OS* 81 / 119; see also *TI* 35 n. 2 / 5 n. 1). Both are directed toward an open dimension of "ex-perience" which they will never be able to grasp. *Substantively* and *the-matically*, if these terms still have any meaning here, the sphere of horror and the proximity of the good—often described by Levinas as the "mar-velous" and the "sublime"—are fundamentally different. The respective climates or tonalities they evoke are diametrically opposed. Yet, viewed *formally* and *structurally*, from the perspective of philosophical discourse, they become virtually indistinguishable. Moreover, it is always possible to confuse them. This is the very test and *experimentum crucis*—the trial and temptation—of the ethical, and it gives *horror religiosus* (to cite Kierke-gaard's term) an irreducible place not so much in the restricted or general economy of beings in Being as in the invisible drama and divine comedy of human existence, that is to say, of its necessary fatality no less than its singular election and "difficult freedom."

Beyond any affirmation of the history of Being and the beings con-tained within its course and eventhood, an ethical transcendence still re-mains; on this side of any negation of Being and beings there still remains an amoral horror. The negation of thought and action can never be nega-tive enough to escape the weight and shadow of Being. Interestingly, Levi-nas refers to a formulation from Wahl's *Traité de Métaphysique* (*Treatise on Metaphysics*), which at one point speaks of the "negativity beyond Hegel's negativity."[27]

The position of beings (separation from the whole and from their own persistence in care), furthermore, is never positive enough to ensure open-ness to the ethical relation. Indeed, what is here attributed to one realm could immediately be said of the other. In this, the disturbing parallels between *il y a* and illeity come into view—disturbing because here phi-losophy comes to an end (or, more cautiously, reaches its limit) and be-cause finally only that common feature can wake the subject from its slum-ber: wakefulness is produced by the dissolution of the subject within the resonance of the *il y a* (*EE* 58, 60 / 96, 98). Accordingly, speaking again

26. See Kurt Rudolph, *Die Gnosis: Wesen und Geschichte einer spätantiken Religion* (Leipzig: Koehler & Amelang, 1977) / *Gnosis: The Nature and History of Gnosticism*, trans. and ed. Robert McLachlan Wilson (San Francisco: Harper & Row, 1987).

27. Jean Wahl, *Traité de Métaphysique* (Paris: Payot, 1953), 716; quoted in *OS* 81 / 120.

of Wahl's work and certainly also of his own, Levinas refers to a being-unequal-to-oneself: "A disproportion to oneself that concretely signifies subjectivity: desire, quest, dialectic. But a *dialectic without synthesis:* without repose, without totality, without closure, without conclusion" (*OS* 74 / 109, my emph.). The failure and unhappiness of such a consciousness would secretly be its very accomplishment or, more precisely, its moral perfectibility. In such metaphysical experience the guiding stars of the two extremes — the *tertium datur* of *il y a* and illeity — constantly alternate and shimmer in even the most banal decision.

The unthinkable and unsayable of the excluded middle refer to a pre-predicative dimension within which something like affirmation and negation first occur or acquire propositional form. The motif of a descent ("trans-descendence") into the preworldly appears in Levinas's early texts; in the period of *Totality and Infinity* the figure of an ascent (trans-ascendence) toward the good enters in and complicates things. Both modes of "thought" and "experience" (if we still want to retain these words here), modes that, for the sake of simplicity, I will refer to as mutually opposed or as pointing in contrasting metaphysical directions, are taken up and combined during the phase of *Otherwise than Being*.

There, on the one hand, we find the motif of *descent* into the deepest depths of the subject (a movement technically described as "recurrence" [*OB* 102–9 / 130–39]), to the point at which the passivity of the subject produced by the *il y a* is surpassed in the direction of a subjugation of the emptied-out *subjectum,* with the result not of depersonalization but of election: a singular substitution for the Other in which alienation and a uniqueness "without identity" go hand in hand and prevent the dialectical, culturalist, and, more broadly, normativist theories of selfhood and intersubjectivity from coming into their own. Indeed, Levinas writes: "Before belonging to the empire of Nature or to the self-awareness of Spirit, it is in breaking through the border of being that the *logically unjustifiable uniqueness* of the human person is identified" (*OS* 81–82 / 120, my emph.).

On the other hand, Levinas's language during this period moves in the medium of an "iterative-exalting" *ascent.*[28] Ethical saying, he now suggests — "the *ineffable* in which a spoken word deafening our ears falls silent at the very heart of the words we hear" (*OS* 83 / 122) — always already slips away from what is said. Any serious investigation of the aspects of Levinas's late philosophy concerned with linguistic theory and

28. Burggraeve, "Het 'il y a' in het heteronomie-denken van Emmanuel Levinas," 297.

the theory of meaning would need to examine this *via eminentiae* closely. Here we should note that the ethical dimension not only remains at an unattainable distance *beyond* the categories of being and time but also (conversely?) nestles within the likewise irrecuperable proximity *this side of* ontology, of beings and their being. Thus, Levinas's work manifests a complex of thought or experience which he attributes to Wahl: a "transcendence *indifferent* to hierarchy. A bursting toward the heights or a descent toward the depths of the sensible world" (*OS* 81 / 119, my emph.). The divine comedy, which could only *theologically*—and, for Levinas, unacceptably—be established in an unambiguous order (*OS* 82 / 121), gives rise, in other words, to the philosophical *undecidability* of the two "infinities": "Was Pascal then wrong in speaking of two infinities? At either extremity of being, is it not the same ex-cession, the same transcendence, the height beyond all climbing and descent that stand *opposed to one another in the world and its values*? This taste for the abysmal, this happiness of the chasm, the underground, the subhuman that is not animal, that *humanness alone makes possible!*" (*OS* 81 / 119, my emph.). Levinas even speaks of the enduring temptation of a certain "interchangeability of the *beyond* [*au-delà*] and the *hither side* [*en-deça*] of the *very high* [*très haut*] and the *very low* [*très bas*]" (*OS* 74 / 110).

To Levinas's thinking about subjectivity as I have reconstructed it, one might add three marginal comments.

(1) The structure of the I, according to Levinas, is essentially characterized by remaining within the sphere of the same. The contours of the "I" and the "I can [*je peux*]" are essentially those of a thinking, perceiving, and judging that identifies and experiences itself as actual and of a being that works solely for its own self-preservation, self-determination, possession, pleasure, and happiness. This I in itself—and for itself, following the Hegelian-Sartrian distinction of the *an sich*/*en soi* and *für-sich*/*pour soi*—admits no true alterity insofar as in essence and *in actu* it organizes itself and the world on which it reflects according to the model of a finite totality, which it establishes through reduction, deduction, and induction. Derrida suggests that this identification of subjectivity and identity, of the self (selfhood or ipseity) and the identitarian same—that is to say, the amalgamation of *ipse* and *idem*—functions as "a kind of silent axiom" in Levinas's text.[29] In this it assembles a stylized, exaggerated,

29. Derrida, *Writing and Difference*, 109 / 162, 162 / 206.

and merely one-dimensional image of what is, at most, a dominant tenet in the history of Western philosophy as a whole, one whose legitimacy has with good reason been contested on immanent grounds by many authors.[30]

In modifying this premise, one can draw on two thinkers who made the completion or convalescence (*Verwindung*) of the metaphysical tradition the principle task of their philosophies: Hegel and Heidegger. From Hegel's perspective Levinas's characterization of the philosophy of identity might be criticized as follows: is what he has in mind really an essential feature of Western thought, or has he simply fixed his eye on what might be called an "abstract" identity? Is the question at which one arrives in philosophy not at its deepest that of the "determination of this unity in itself"?[31]

Furthermore, Heidegger observes, with some justification, that at least since the epoch of "speculative idealism" "it remains impossible for thought to imagine the unity of identity as a mere commonness [*das blosse Einerlei*] and avoid the mediation that resides within this unity"; wherever that happens, such identity is "only abstractly imagined."[32] Extrapolating an insight from Gadamer, does Levinas's critique of Hegel's reconstruction of the problem of the "recognition [*Anerkennung*]" of the other ever affect him "seriously [*im Ernst*]?"[33] Is there no room here for acknowledging the Hegelian and Heideggerian conception of hermeneutic experience, according to which "the possible right, indeed, the superiority of one's interlocutor ought be recognized in advance"?[34]

These possible points of departure for an incisive critique of Levinas *from without* do not constitute my main concern, however. Suffice it to say that the premises just discussed—the assumption that identity excludes all true alterity, upon which Levinas's considerations concerning the philosophy of the subject are based, just as those about finite totality shape

30. See Paul Ricoeur, *La Métaphore vive* (Paris: Seuil, 1975), 396–97; Ricoeur, *Soi-même comme un autre* (Paris: Seuil, 1990) / *Oneself as Another,* trans. Kathleen Blamey (Chicago: University of Chicago Press, 1992).

31. G. W. F. Hegel, *Vorlesungen über die Philosophie der Religion,* vols. 16–17 of *Theorie-Werkausgabe* (Frankfurt a.M.: Suhrkamp, 1969–71) / 16:1.1000, trans. E. B. Spiers and J. Burdon Sanderson under the title *Lectures on the Philosophy of Religion* (New York: Humanities Press, 1974), 1:99.

32. Martin Heidegger, *Identität und Differenz* (Pfullingen: Neske, 1957), 12.

33. Gadamer, *Truth and Method,* 310 / 329.

34. Gadamer, *Ergänzungen,* 505.

his philosophy of history—find a remarkable parallel in Adorno's stylized characterization of the main features of Western tradition. Coming from another line of questioning, Adorno also offers a *heuristic,* which teaches us to discover a merely apparent identity in the traditional and modern philosophies of the subject and, likewise, a negative totality in the realm of objective spirit and the philosophies of history. As with Adorno, in Levinas only this heuristic value of his presentations should be important to us. In the works of these two authors suggestive and often rhetorically exaggerated descriptions are often more convincing than suppositions that can be couched in simple formulas.

(2) A noteworthy paradox occurs in Levinas's analyses of sociohistorical objectivity, commerce, and discursivity. This is the necessity, in his view, of *using* the sphere of ontology and of conceptuality as a whole—despite their allergy to every true alterity—via the establishment of institutions, distributive justice, science, and technology, not as an end in itself but quasi-instrumentally *for the ulterior good of the Other (and hence alterity) alone.*[35]

This paradox has no counterpart in the observations on subjectivity in the late work. There Levinas stresses how the I is obsessed and traumatized no less than inspired or instructed by the Other. There, however, Levinas conceives of no alternation within the I. There is no pendular movement corresponding to the figure of an ongoing oscillation, which is elsewhere predominant in his work, between the reflexive-practical level—on which one can still maintain a critical distance from (not freely chosen but superimposed) responsibilities—and being held hostage by the Other without reserve.

In his middle period, from *Existence and Existents* to *Totality and Infinity,* Levinas does speak of an autonomous I, but he does so, finally, in the sense of a hypostasis, of an atheistic subject that works, possesses, and takes its pleasure and which effects only an initial and relative onticoontological break with mythic participation and conceptual totality, a break that can be described from *within* phenomenology and its basic terminology. This separate I, however, does not prove to be metaphysically separated—or ab-solute—in the sense of the "being-for-the-other" of the "one-for-the-other" whose implication the later work teases out in all its consequence.

---

35. See Levinas and Kearney, "Dialogue," in Cohen, *Face to Face with Levinas,* 28.

Yet is there not, in the domain of social philosophy and the philosophy of language, an equal necessity for the subject *to hold its own before
the Other for the Other*? More pointedly, does this necessity merely emerge
after a third—another other or *autrui*—appears, as Levinas claims? Although in *Totality and Infinity* he speaks of the possibility that I can experience myself as the other—or even Other—of the other, he does not pursue
this thought further: "if the other can invest me and invest my freedom,
of itself arbitrary, this is in the last analysis because I myself can feel myself to be the other of the other [*l'Autre de l'Autre*]. But this comes about
only across very complex structures" (*TI* 84 / 56). The fact that there can
also be for me something like justice, if not infinite responsibility, is only
accounted for later and with the help of what seems another type of argumentation, namely, that of the appearance (or is it the revelation?) of the
third person and, hence, of the necessity of institutional distribution and
mutual assurance of support of the one for the other(s) and the other(s)
for me.

(3) Levinas wants to show that the ethical-*metaphysical* relation to
the truly other (including the complex question of the third person and,
hence, of the "mediation" of responsibility in distributive justice and the
"love of wisdom") has priority over the relationship one maintains with
oneself (*egology*) and with the world (*cosmology*),[36] but also with history
and culture. Closely tied to both preceding observations is the question
of whether *the I could and must not be truly other not just for the Other but
also for itself.*

Even if we grant to Levinas that the ethical difference leaves its trace
only in sociality or, as he says with Durkheim, in a certain "collectivity,"
the manner in which he describes the heterogeneity into which the depersonalized I deteriorates exhibits an at least *formal* parallel with the words
he uses to sketch the subject as hostage and substitution. We have become
aware of this through his interpretation of the experience of art. On this
realization rests my suspicion that the experience of the ethical-religious
cannot be the sole dimension in which an ab-solute alterity that breaks
or passes through our common categories of experience, time, and space
can be manifest.

At least two other ways of thinking about the subject—each of which
have left traces in *Totality and Infinity* ("Neither Buber nor Gabriel Marcel
is ignored in this text, and Franz Rosenzweig is invoked from the preface

36. Ibid., 21.

onwards")[37] — are problematized by Levinas: the *personalistic* or *dialogical* and, more indirectly, the *psychoanalytic* models of the subject. We have already spoken about Levinas's reservations concerning the symmetry presupposed in the dialogical principle.[38] He has similar reservations concerning the spiritualist personalism of Christian thinkers, with the possible exception of Jean Wahl.

Despite Levinas's multiple use of Freudian metaphors, Lyotard's characterization of his position is correct: it is one of reversal or inversion, getting "Freud backwards."[39] Whatever truth there might be in the assumptions of psychoanalysis, Levinas leaves no doubt that "we do not need this knowledge in the relationship in which the other is the neighbor, and in which before being an individuation of the genus *man*, a *rational animal*, a *free will*, or any essence whatever, he is the persecuted one for whom I am responsible" (*OB* 59 / 75).

Like the "philosophical antihumanism" of the late Heidegger and of "poststructuralism" (see *HAH* 85 ff., 90), Levinas rejects the merely "humanistically free" interpretation of subjectivity and any other conceptual attempts to fix it.[40] The common formalistic attempt to refute the presumed inconsequence of antihumanism — "to contest the subjective is to affirm the value of the subjective that contests" (*CPP* 128 / *HAH* 68), an argument reiterated tirelessly by authors as different as Manfred Frank, in *Die Unhintergehbarkeit von Individualität* (*The Irreducibility of Individuality*), and Paul Ricoeur, in *Soi-même comme un autre* (*Oneself as Another*) — is, from Levinas's perspective, as unconvincing as the classical-modern correction of skepticism (see chap. 12). Yet where structuralism implies an "effacing of the living man behind the mathematical structures that *think themselves out* in him, rather than he by thinking of them" (*OB* 58 / 74; see also 59 / 76), Levinas reveals, by contrast, a *critical* impulse. He sees his work as being a defense of subjectivity not out of an existential pathos (*TI* 26 / xiv) but in the name of the Other, in view of the "humanism of the other human being." Levinas's philosophy is therefore, as Strasser observes, perhaps less one of subjectivity per se than of a thoroughly pluralistic "philosophy of subjects."[41]

37. Levinas, "Preface to the German Edition," *EN* 197 / 249, trans. modified.
38. See Goud, "Über Definition und Infinition," 128, 138 ff.
39. Lyotard, *Differend*, 115 / 170, trans. modified.
40. De Boer, *Tussen filosofie en profetie*, 155, 20.
41. Strasser, "Ethik als erste Philosophie," 259. See also Strasser, "Antiphénoménologie et phénoménologie dans la philosophie d'Emmanuel Levinas," 114–15, 118.

THE POINT OF LEVINAS's philosophical approach and figure of thought lies both *this side of* and *beyond* modern-critical modes of discourse. Seen from within the history of philosophy, it might be called *postcritical;* by contrast, from a systematic perspective it might be described as *ante-critical,* because "metaphysics precedes ontology" (*TI* 42 ff. / 12 ff.). Levinas's investigation and transgression of modern forms of reason is therefore not congruent with the paradigms of methodological distrust of the subject and sociohistorical objectivity prominently offered by Freudian psychoanalysis and Marxist ideology critique. As I recalled earlier, Derrida describes Levinas's procedure as, in general, a "non-Marxist reading of philosophy as ideology": his social philosophy, for example, concerns "a critique of the state's alienation whose anti-Hegelianism would be neither subjectivist, nor Marxist, nor anarchist."[42] The concept of a crystalline, Archimedean point from which the investigation of what is to be critiqued might be posed dissolves entirely in Levinas: "To philosophize is to trace freedom back to what lies before it, to disclose the investiture that liberates freedom from the arbitrary. Knowledge as a critique, as a tracing back to what precedes freedom, can arise only in a being that has an origin prior to its origin — that is created" (*TI* 84–85 / 57).

But what could the term *origin* mean here apart from being a *cipher* (the terms *metaphor* or *image* are out of place) for a dimension that can never be grasped conceptually (or, indeed, poetically, imaginatively, or visually, let alone theologically)? Suffice it to say that the critical intent of the philosophy of ethical-metaphysical difference cannot be expressed simply *theoretically* (see *TI* 42 / 13). The groundlessness of critique implies that the order of the same can only be suspended or temporarily thrown off balance. That is, it is placed in an ephemeral, open dimension that renders groundless every claim to ontological validity but also, conversely, suggests the *secret condition of possibility* for that order. The subject, sociohistorical reality, and language are three closely interconnected realms in whose midst the intrigue and involvement of the other in the same leaves its trace. The task of philosophy, then, is to make us aware of — to retrace — its imprint, its disturbance, and the "curvature" of social space it entails (*TI* 86 / 59). Otherwise, although in reality such traces can never entirely be erased, they fall into oblivion or succumb to violence. With regard to the question of the conditions of possibility for com-

---

42. Derrida, *Writing and Difference*, 97 / 145, 144.

munication, Levinas's thinking thus points toward a way to understand the structural inadequacy of any historicism, psychologism, sociologism, or culturalism—in short, any naturalism—without thereby lapsing into fideism, irrationalism, mysticism, or empathy: "To wish to escape dissolution into the Neuter, to posit knowing as a welcoming of the Other, is not a pious attempt to maintain the spiritualism of a personal God, but is the condition for language, without which philosophical discourse itself is but an abortive act, a pretext for an unintermitting psychoanalysis or philology or sociology, in which the appearance of a discourse vanishes in the Whole [*le Tout*]. Speaking implies a possibility of breaking off and beginning" (*TI* 88 / 60). Only from this perspective does a judgment of history—before all is said and done, indeed, at every single instant— become possible, necessary, imperative.

THE QUESTION OF WHY Levinas repeatedly draws on a specific experience of modernity to orient his description of historical and social objectivity in toto, while seeking to deny history any right to speak *in ethicis,* is both inescapable and, at first glance, somewhat confusing. How can one deny any metaphysical and moral dimension or relevance in the sphere of objective spirit and the spirit's history of formation (*Bildung*) or effective history (*Wirkungsgeschichte*), to use Hegel's and Gadamer's terms, yet also insist upon a subterranean, mutilated tradition of thinking of the other, whose secret effects animate and disturb the Occidental tradition, the tradition of the same? How could one say that this countercurrent makes history or History just as possible as it is impossible, conditioning it in a noncausal, nondeterministic way, as well as interrupting it at every single instant in which genuine experience or a true "event" comes about or, as Levinas says, "comes to mind [*vient à l'idée*]"?

One can do so only by no longer viewing history or History in an undifferentiated manner, as a nonformal tautology, $A = A$, as the unfolding of something always constant, a mythical fatality, neutrality, or totality sprung from the ever self-same, turning in circles or returning to its point of origin as it attains its telos. In spite of his repeated assurance that totality, finite totality, determines history in its very concept, from its outset to its end, Levinas also claims: "In the spiritual history of the West, the moment at which philosophy becomes suspect is not insignificant" (*GCM* 77 / 126); or again: "My critique of the totality has come in fact after a political experience" (*EI* 78–79 / 73). He thereby implies that the historical moment or momentum — albeit at its most critical juncture, indeed, in the instant of its "downfall," its most desolate negativity — is not without some metaphysical weight or consequence.

Do claims of this sort not at least implicitly give rise to a historical, historicized, if not historicist, perspective, however philosophically modified and radicalized, one that Levinas at times rejects but which remains somehow constitutive of his own presentation?[43] On occasion Levinas seems to acknowledge as much. "If, in order to be historical, an analysis must refer in a very precise way to specific situations, account for them, and announce how all this will turn out, be completed in the absolute or be spoiled definitively, then I have no philosophy of history," he pointedly states, but he immediately adds that he nonetheless does believe "that the *unlimited* responsibility for another . . . could have a translation into history's concreteness" (*GCM* 81 / 131). What, then, does Levinas's "displacement"[44] of the concepts of history and historicity — analogous to that of experience and event — look like? What could a nondialectical "concreteness" concretely mean? How could its singularity — its epiphany or revelation and trace, to remain within the idiom — affect the supposedly neutralizing, generalizing, universalizing, and totalizing tendencies upon which, Levinas asserts, the very concept and course of history (not just History but *all* history) is based?

Like the constitution and destitution of selfhood — from the presubjective through subjectivation to substitution (and back) — the historical-philosophical trajectory of the collectivity of selves, their fates and fatalities, their works and institutions, can be divided into three different yet related stages, at least at the level of phenomenological description. First, one must distinguish the *mythical-archaic* and undifferentiated order of magical participation in the primitive collective; second, the *closed dialectics of modern, enlightened sociohistorical action, its economy and institutions;* and, finally, the *alternation or open dialectic of morality and ethical life* (or *Moralität* and *Sittlichkeit,* to cite Kant and Hegel), that is to say, of obligation and the normative (to cite Lyotard). Levinas, like Adorno, must take these into consideration, although there seems little room to do so, given his stylization and rhetorically exaggerated characterization of the realm of objective spirit and history tout court.

43. Vattimo reads Lyotard's work in a similar way in "Das Ende der Geschichte," in Kunneman and de Vries, *Die Aktualität der "Dialektik der Aufklärung,"* 168–82.
44. See Derrida, *Writing and Difference,* 93–94, 88 / 139, 131.

We should not forget that the preface to *Totality and Infinity,* confronting the violence of war, which seems to dominate all articulations of reality, asks whether morality does not rest on an illusion. At least in the form in which it has been conceived in Western ontology, the order of Being displays a dialectical course in which everything and every human being is taken up as a specific—hence, limited or provisional—moment. Human interest, self-preservation, and self-determination realize themselves as politics, negation, negotiation, calculation, exchange, commerce, work, and project. Yet this interpretation of reality, like the Western image of the self in relation to others which accompanies and enables it (community, contract, being-with, recognition, struggle for power, and reciprocity) fails to recognize what, at the deepest level, constitutes intersubjectivity, freedom, truth, justice, expression, and sincerity. The established interpretations reproduce and strengthen impersonal, indeed inhuman, traits against which Western thinking struggled in its striving toward autonomy from the archaic collectivity, mythical consciousness, the sacred, and undifferentiated totality. Without using this terminology, Levinas observes a developmental logic that resembles a genuine *dialectic of myth and enlightenment,* of emancipation and (renewed) enslavement.

True, modern human beings can see scarcely any possibility of refusing to cooperate in the play of forces and are compelled as individuals to "carry out actions that will destroy every possibility for action" (*TI* 21 / ix). But this is not all there is to say. In *Totality and Infinity* Levinas sets himself the goal of illuminating the remaining fragile conditions of possibility for thinking, action, experience, and judgment. In doing so, he appeals both to what is presupposed by commonly accepted philosophical ideas and to forgotten or repressed metaphors borrowed from the religious tradition, notably those of creation, revelation, election, hospitality, eschatology, and messianic peace. The semantic ranges of these terms are adopted in surprisingly modern and even down-to-earth ways; they are both formalized and concretized, generalized and intensified. Thus, he writes, for example, that the "first 'vision' of eschatology (hereby distinguished from the revealed opinions of positive religions) reveals the very possibility of eschatology, that is, the breach of the totality, the possibility of a *signification without a context*" (*TI* 23 / xi–xii). Neither empirical actuality nor material content is important here. Rather, what matters is the mere opening, indeed, the ethical "optics," for an event, a novelty and marvel, to happen: the encounter with (the being addressed and instructed by) not just any other but another human being—the neighbor, the orphan, the widow, in short, the stranger, *Autrui.*

Greek philosophy claimed to be able to replace the mythico-magical *communio* of the spheres of Being with relationships in which all beings maintain their own separate and independent places (*TI* 49 / 19). It thereby made thinkable a metaphysical-religious relation to the other or the infinite which could distance itself from any participation in the divine, any enthusiasm, any incarnation or *unio mystica* (*TI* 77–79, 269 / 49–52, 247). In a sense the intellectualism of Western reason, of Greece and Europe, thus sets an agenda that is still Levinas's own by asking: "How can separate beings be maintained, and not sink into participation, against which the philosophy of the same will have the immortal merit to have protested?" (*CPP* 54 / *DEHH* 172).

In this view "religion for adults" and the philosophical tradition are allied in the struggle against a "violence of the sacred." To "relate to the absolute as an atheist is to welcome the absolute purified of the violence of the sacred," thereby striving to achieve a "humanity without myths" (*TI* 77 / 49, 50). In its best moments the atheistic and autonomous self-assertion of philosophy reveals an elective affinity with the motif of *creatio ex nihilo,* that is to say, with the contraction of God, as handed down in the tradition of Jewish monotheism and mysticism. According to that tradition—as Scholem and, in his footsteps, Habermas document in their studies of the intellectual sources of modern philosophies of history, from Isaac Luria to Schelling and Marx—creation is destined for independence and freedom, and humans have been made responsible for the maintenance and salvation of the universe as whole: "Man redeems creation" (*TI* 104 / 77). This statement nicely resonates with the modern transformation of which I spoke in my first chapter: that of theodicy—the justification of divine omnipotence in light of the evils and negativity of history—into "anthropodicy" (Odo Marquard). But, if this is how reason seeks to ground human freedom in opposition to myth, then the motif of human freedom has its validity within the philosophical tradition *in opposition to an other but not in itself.* It counterbalances and corrects such alternative strands as immanentism, contractualism, naturalism, historicism, secularism, and materialism but cannot claim any ontological primacy per se. Indeed, it can claim primacy only in a circular fashion—to the extent that it displays a certain analogy to the theological motifs of creation out of nothing, the contraction of God, and the progressive redemption this makes possible, necessary, and imperative.

This claim flows from our preceding discussion of Levinas's reservations about the egological, narcissistic, possessive, and power-struck structure of the philosophy of the self-same (in its interiority, economy, and the like). Indeed, Levinas senses a parallel danger in the positions opposed to idealism and subjectivism: "For the philosophical tradition of the West every relation between the same and the other, when it is no longer an affirmation of the supremacy of the same, reduces itself to an impersonal relation within the universal order" (*TI* 87–88 / 60). The relation to ethical-metaphysical transcendence, which, for Levinas as for Rosenzweig, occurs as a particular kind of temporality, must be thought *neither as an immersion of the self in the other nor as an assimilation of the other to the self-same.*

Levinas writes of what exceeds the subject's solitude, that is, of the ethical relation, the "relation without relation" which is termed "religion" (*TI* 80 / 52): "It will not be a knowledge, because through knowledge, whether one wants it or not, the object is absorbed by the subject and duality disappears. It will not be an ecstasis, because in ecstasis the subject is absorbed in the object and recovers itself in its unity" (*TO* 41 / 13). Not only in myth, magic, mysticism, and enthusiasm (*Schwärmerei,* as Kant would say) but also in philosophy from Spinoza to Hegel and, most succinctly, in the late Heidegger's thought of Being, Levinas suspects an undermining of the "supremacy of the same," this time in the direction of "an impersonal relation" of dissolution into a third term, the "Neuter" (*TI* 87–88 / 60): "To posit being as Desire is to decline at the same time the ontology of isolated subjectivity and the ontology of impersonal reason realizing itself in history" (*TI* 305 / 282). Levinas thus distinguishes his position from two opposite ontico-ontological extremes by outflanking them in the direction of a singularity that is *at once* presubjective, thus also post-, a-, or inhuman, *and* more objective than the objective, more ontological than ontology, tending toward a hyper-ontology of sorts.

I will concentrate here on the motif of impersonal reason; in the following chapter I will return to the question of what could be more ontological than the ontological. Levinas directs his criticism of Occidental objectivism, above all, at the *philosophy of the neuter* which he detects in Spinoza's geometrical conception of God as Nature, Hegel's idealist doctrine of Spirit realizing itself beyond human beings, and in Heidegger's understanding of the fateful epochal history (*Geschick*) of Being. All these authors and their respective motifs, he suggests, "exalt the obedience that no face commands" (*TI* 299 / 275). For each of them history "does not belong to us, but we belong to it."[45] He is particularly concerned with a thought that Hegel expresses in his lectures on the philosophy of religion: "Spirit does not arrive at its goal without having followed its path," and this path of religion is "the true theodicy; it shows that all productions of spirit, every form of its self-knowledge, are necessary."[46]

Although the order imposed on things and on people by the course and ruse of reason has autonomy and freedom as its goal, inevitably the reverse, the dialectical opposite, comes into view. The realm of objective spirit, the entirety of the institutions and establishments in which the West believes it has found its highest expression, proves unexpectedly brittle. At critical moments in history, Levinas observes, ethics is forced back into a powerless interiority, even though philosophy, through the mouths of its most prominent advocates, pretends unerringly to see in history progress toward the consciousness and realization of freedom, civil society, and the sovereignty of the state. It feigns that history moves toward a "final peace from the reason that plays out its stakes in ancient and present-day wars" (*TI* 22 / x).

By contrast, Levinas claims that a permanent situation of war, politics by other means, is not the only way in which reality imposes itself upon us, however objectively evident the situation of violence may seem. If war were the status quo, we would have no choice but to endorse it, without any ground on which to criticize, interrupt, or mitigate it. War and the philosophy that, from Heraclitus through Hegel to contemporary theorists of the "struggle for recognition," takes this agonistic view and its resolution to be the paradigm of reality and sociality in general suspend an emphatic (but not therefore necessarily powerless) concept of ethics. The promises with which the West began its intellectual quest — especially its illusion that peace is a logical, dialogical, or dialectical result of war and its analogues — have obstructed a view toward this *other of history,* which resides this side, beyond, and even within or in the intervals and interstices of history as we know it, the other face of the same.

Levinas's philosophy, like Adorno's, arrives at the idea — which could certainly be disputed in various ways — that the totalitarian traits so forcefully manifest in the political and cultural history of the West can be *directly* linked to the theoretical concept of totality which dominates its

---

45. Gadamer, *Truth and Method,* 245 / 261. In his 1932 essay on Heidegger, Levinas already notes: "ontology is not interested in human being for his own sake. The interest of ontology moves toward the sense of *being in general*" (*DEHH* 58–59).

46. Hegel, *Lectures on the Philosophy of Religion,* 1:76 / 16:1.80.

philosophical tradition (*TI* 22 / x). Because he assumes an isomorphy and, indeed, causal relation between the concept of totality and the historical phenomenon of totalitarianism, Levinas believes that the singularity of every individual and the unique meaning of every cultural expression is *in advance* reductively subsumed in a larger whole. Only on the basis of such totalization could the rational tradition conceive of history as the instance of judgment that, in the end, unlocks, justifies, or discards the objective meaning of all phenomena. Reality, in that tradition, is borne by an impersonal and collective subject.

Levinas's critique of the philosophy of totality, like Adorno's, extends beyond a critique of the supposed teleology of history. It concerns more than the suspect postulate of the presence or unfolding of a divine or horizontal totality. The totalizing common denominators to which Occidental self-understanding reduces all beings are nothing less than those of "Being," the "system," and the "concept." They amount to a Procrustean bed upon which the contingent reality and absurd dimension of both ineffable horror and ineffable good—of the worst and of marvels of all sorts—are bound. These extreme poles of our experience are thus accorded a meaning and attributed a functional role that they lack entirely. Moreover, as regards ethics, such totalizing denies humans the ability to think and experience an *ab-solute* signification or "signifyingness [*signifiance*]," whose primacy within and beyond the restricted and general economy of being is what truly matters. Derrida offers one of the strongest formulations of a reservation one might be tempted to raise about this affirmation of an originary nonviolence at the origin of all violence, of History as violence, a reservation that can scarcely be refuted: "*within history*—but is it meaningful elsewhere?—every philosophy of nonviolence can only choose the lesser violence within an *economy of violence*."[47]

In Levinas's reading Western ontology thus ipso facto—indeed, systematically—legitimates and facilitates the order of violence. It can yoke morality only to theology or to the play of forces in Being and in consequence misunderstands the more mysterious, enigmatic, elusive, and, indeed, absolute motifs and motivations in the composition of the universe, on the grounds that they are irrational, purely "emotional," or incomprehensible (see *TI* 102 / 75). Nonetheless, the "fact" of the emergence of ethical relations and of sociality—a "fact of reason," as Kant would say—in which beings address one another or, rather, are addressed by an Other (a

---

47. Derrida, *Writing and Difference*, 313 n. 21 / 136 n. 1.

neighbor; the stranger; a poor, proletarian, widowed, or orphaned human being), in ways that are not necessarily reciprocal, allows us to suspect that such relations are not meaningless ruses within the whole of a divine or impersonal reason that cunningly unfolds throughout history and "justifies" everything, including what cannot and ought not to be justified. The experience, event, and unprecedented "novelty" and "marvel" of the ethical relation makes plausible a "disengagement" from the objective order of violence, its practices, and its institutions, and confirms in that moment, as in every "now," a *judgment about history*. This and nothing else is what the formulation of eschatology in Levinas's middle period means: quite literally, an ab-solution not *of* but *from* history or History (as we know it, as it alone can be *known*) in the direction and "in view" of an invisible other whose revelation comes to us out of a dimension of height and of ontological poverty at once: "What is above all invisible is the offense universal history inflicts upon particulars" (*TI* 247 / 225). On this *minimal morality* with *maximum effect* hinges the fate of the universe, of the sacred history that runs, as Rosenzweig knew, parallel to — or in the interstices, the *entretemps* of — the other and whose dimensionality escapes the leveling horizon of History's linear course. The judgment passed on history therefore restores beings to their separation, uniqueness, and election, and here alone the drama of responsibility and justice finds its ground: "Judgment no longer alienates the subjectivity, for it does not make it enter into and dissolve in the order of an objective morality, but leaves it a dimension whereby it deepens in itself" (*TI* 245 / 223).

As Derrida explains, Levinas's thinking about history and society, like his observations on the philosophy of subjectivity, is based on a presupposition that is difficult to maintain: "totality, for Levinas, means a finite totality. This functions as a silent axiom."[48] Levinas thus seems almost to reverse the Hegelian perspective and to turn its critique of Kantian "formalism" and "understanding [*Verstand*, as opposed to *Vernunft*]" against itself; that is to say, he dialecticizes the dialectic: "Extreme audacity here would be to turn the accusation of formalism against Hegel, and to denounce speculative reflection as a logic of understanding, as tautological."[49] As I have argued earlier, this is exactly what Adorno, in *Negative Dialectics*, dares to do.

The Western philosophy of totality, in Levinas's account, a priori al-

48. Ibid., 107 / 158.
49. Ibid., 313 n. 20 / 135 n. 1.

lows no irreducible alterity because it can think historical reality only as a *finite* totality.[50] In other words: "for Levinas coherence is always finite (totality, in the meaning he gives to the word, rejecting any possible meaning for the notion of infinite totality)."[51] There could be no history outside totality.[52] But, Derrida asks, if one foists on history such a concept of finite, negative totality—or, conversely, the idea of an actual, positive infinity— is it not completely impossible to understand any event, action, gesture, or judgment, whether moral or amoral? Doesn't history, in its infinite variability, play itself out precisely as the difference, so heavily emphasized by Levinas, between totality and infinity, between the order of the self-same and that of the other? Shouldn't history, rather, be thought "as the very movement of transcendence, of the excess over the totality without which no totality would appear as such"?[53] The conceptual reasons for this seem clear: "in a world where the face would be fully respected (as that which is not of this world), there no longer would be war. In a world where the face no longer would be absolutely respected, where there no longer would be a face, there would be no more cause for war."[54] In Derrida's eyes history is precisely what metaphysics, ethical metaphysics in Levinas's sense, re-serves for eschatology. As such, it is a movement of transcendence, neither closed—that is to say, finite—nor positively infinite: "A *structural totality* escapes this alternative in its functioning [or play, *jeu*]. It escapes the ar-chaeological and the eschatological, and inscribes them in itself."[55]

De Boer raises questions about Derrida's interpretation of Levinas on this point. In his reading Levinas does not understand totality to be a finite category. Totality, he stresses, "encompasses history, because this concept is taken in the Kantian sense. It is the totality of an infinite process, a *pro-gressio ad infinitum*. This is a *horizontal* concept of infinity, which Husserl introduces in *Ideas I* when he analyzes the experience of things. The per-ception of the many-sided things moves to the limit of complete knowl-edge without ever arriving there."[56] By contrast to this concept of a hori-zontally infinite and therefore immanent totality, de Boer argues, Levinas employs an idea of the *vertical* infinite, that is to say, of the infinite as *trans-*

50. See ibid., 107, 119 / 158, 176.
51. Ibid., 315 n. 42 / 172 n. 1.
52. Ibid., 122 / 180.
53. Ibid., 117 / 173.
54. Ibid., 107 / 158.
55. Ibid., 123 / 180, my emph.
56. De Boer, "Ethical Transcendental Philosophy," in Cohen, *Face to Face with Levinas*, 90.

finite. It concerns a quasi-transcendental—at once excessively formalized and de-formalized—dimension or *concretissimum* of experience which, in a sense, is "not of this world." Its revelation strikes us *perpendicularly,* from above (or below), independently of the progressions or regressions of our internal or interior worldly experience. In other words, it affects us only fleetingly, invisibly. In de Boer's words: "this concept of infinity is related to the infinity of the ontological proof for God's existence; it is an infinity that is presupposed by every finite link in the endless chain of horizontal infinity, inasmuch as it can only be recognized *as finite* in relation to vertical infinity."[57] This is an important correction, and, if we set aside for a moment the fact that in both *Totality and Infinity* and "God and Philosophy" Levinas explicitly denounces the ontological proofs for the existence of God (see *TI* 87 / 59), it reminds us of a further parallel with Adorno. For Adorno the very task of philosophical critique revolves around the formal structure and formal equivalents of this particular proof, which retains its minimal features and, indeed, its truth content in the very moment and movement of its downfall, as does metaphysics, with its ideas of transcendence.

Nevertheless, one might object to de Boer that in *Totality and Infinity* there is still a discrepancy—and, perhaps, a philosophical contradiction?—between the *formal,* asymmetrical structure of the idea of the infinite and the simultaneous *substantive* characterization of that idea in terms of an infinite Being. In other words, Levinas's claim that eschatology is a "relation with *a surplus always exterior to the totality,* as though the objective totality did not fill out the true measure of being" is ambiguous in more than one respect (*TI* 22 / xi): it could be interpreted as the proclamation of an ethical philosophy of origins in the name of an infinite Being, but it could with equal justification be seen as a critique of any thinking of Being as such. Moreover, this ambiguity could also secretly or confusingly hint at an implication whose full consequences only the later work, especially *Otherwise than Being,* will spell out in detail: namely, the disturbing fact that the other or otherwise than Being could just as well be described by a "no more Being (a Being no more)" as by a "more (and the surplus) of Being," in all the ambiguity of the *plus d'être* that Derrida has analyzed in his discussion of negative theology.

57. Ibid.; see also 94 and de Boer's comments on the Dutch translation of *Totality and Infinity* (*De plaatsvervanging*), 19 n. 12, 22 n. 16.

TWO RESPONSES TO THIS problem can be found in Levinas's oeuvre.

(1) Levinas first seeks to correct the apparent inconsistency by increasingly emphasizing the *incongruence* or even *incommensurability* of Being, whether thought as finite or infinite, on the one hand, and the other or otherwise than Being, the transfinite beyond essence, on the other. He thus first embarks on the difficult path of a philosophy of the *ambiguity* of any other, including the Other called *Autrui* in whose face the totally other, the third person named God—or, better, illeity—leaves his trace, absolving himself "to the point of absence." In this view the original disparity or discrepancy between the self-same and the other came about only because in the "magnum opus,"[58] *Totality and Infinity,* Levinas still presupposed a common measure for these opposed poles in ontology. One need only push these poles to their respective extremes in order to realize that they have no common denominator, no shared criterion.

Interpreters have often stressed that in his middle period Levinas, like Bataille, contrasts the concept of a *restricted economy* to that of a *general economy.* Whereas the former term, in the etymological sense of the word *economy,* refers to the subject's being at home with itself in the tripartite articulation of the self (in *theoria, praxis,* and *technē*),[59] the latter term presents a more open horizon: "A relation whose terms do not form a totality can hence be produced within the general economy of being only as proceeding from the I to the other" (*TI* 39 / 9).

Yet the thesis that Levinas fundamentally criticizes a horizontal concept of (finitely infinite or infinitely finite) totality through a vertical concept of the transfinite infinite—and thereby corrects his earlier adoption of the distinction between the restrictive and general economy of beings and Being—hardly renders Derrida's questions superfluous. Derrida's reservation might be interpreted as asking whether the concept of an entirely *homogeneous* (finite *or* infinite) horizontal totality, in which only an "other" that is different *in degree* but never an other that is *qualitatively* different, can come into play must not remain philosophically meaningless. It would be just as unthinkable, unexperienceable, and inexpressible

58. De Boer, "Ethical Transcendental Philosophy," in Cohen, *Face to Face with Levinas,* 89. De Boer reads *Totality and Infinity* retrospectively in light of the self-correction Levinas later undertook in response to Derrida's essay. He moves, as we shall see, toward the figure of the trace.

59. See de Boer, *Tussen filosofie en profetie,* 13; Strasser, "Ethik als Erste Philosophie," 227, 263 n. 2.

as the idea of an *entirely* transcendent or vertical (i.e., positive) infinity, which is supposedly opposed to it.

This reservation concerns two complementary axiomatic biases that Levinas's texts — often contrary to their express intention — constantly retract. It is impossible to avoid the impression that the explicit statements of these motifs figure merely as rhetorical exaggerations. Yet at decisive moments Levinas offers an important suggestion about how to "mediate" between these extreme poles of our experience in a postclassical and modern (negative?) metaphysical way. These moments can be found in sections in his later work which elaborate the modality of the ab-solute through the metaphor of the trace.

Derrida's question concerns, above all, Levinas's somewhat misleading assumption of a total "transhistoricity" or "anhistoricity"[60] of ab-solute meaning: "Is not the beyond-history of eschatology the other name of the transition to a more profound history, to History itself? But to a history which, unable any longer to be *itself* in any original or final *presence,* would have to change its name?"[61] These questions are certainly justified. But does not Levinas himself, in the context of his discussion of fecundity, speak of such a modified idea of history, when he insists that "in the form of the son [*sous les espèces du fils*] being *is* infinitely and discontinuously, historical without fate" (*TI* 278 / 255)?

In the apparently dualistic perspective that de Boer's interpretation opens up, the question concerning history and its alternative are only shifted around. Indeed, if the considerations that Derrida brings to bear against the appearance of a simple antithesis of finite totality and infinite Being are at all convincing (as I think they are), they apply a fortiori to the transcendental founding relationship of horizontal-infinite immanence and vertical-infinite transcendence.

(2) At numerous points, however, Levinas's texts suggest another, more ambivalent interpretation, to which I alluded earlier. This interpretation emphasizes not the pure separation of the same and the other but, rather, a singular, inextricable intertwining and imbrication of those realms. The incongruence of the self-same and the other, Being and the otherwise than Being, now comes only from viewing the ethical relation — indeed, substitution — from one particular perspective (whether of philosophical discourse, aesthetics, theology, etc.) and is no longer affirmed

60. Derrida, *Writing and Difference,* 148 / 220.
61. Ibid., 149 / 222; see also 144 / 213.

"in itself." It makes no sense to speak of incongruence or incommensurability in which ethico-metaphysical passivity is remarked as being, above all, a phenomenon of interference (*Interferenzphänomen*), that is to say, in which the more of Being—more ontological than the ontological—substitutes for the other or otherwise than Being (and, hence, for "substitution") itself.

I will limit myself to one brief passage that illustrates the alternative reading proposed here. Speaking of Rosenzweig's *Star of Redemption,* Levinas refers to the decisive point at which Rosenzweig's "new thinking of existence" and the tradition of philosophical idealism from Parmenides to Hegel and Husserl part company. In Rosenzweig's work, Levinas says, "the challenge to the totality is based on man's mortality, on a 'content,' a content that is an exceptional one and not, as in Kant's transcendental dialectic, on the base of the idea of the totality itself and its inadequation to experience."[62] A similar strategy might govern Levinas's engagements with the concept and the philosophies of history. The negative or finite totality of history can be rescinded only on the basis of a certain positivity, better, of a trace of infinity *within* historical reality: "This 'beyond' the totality and objective experience is, however, not to be described in purely negative fashion. It is reflected [*se reflète*] *within* the totality and history, *within* experience" (*TI* 23 / xi). Again: "The absolutely other, whose alterity is overcome in the philosophy of immanence on *the allegedly common plane of history,* maintains his transcendence *in the midst* of history" (*TI* 40 / 10, my emph.). Precisely this third dimension—*tertium datur*—between immanence and abstract alterity might be illuminated by the "trace of the other," a figureless figure that no longer relies on the concept of reflection (*se reflète*), a concept that easily leads to misunderstanding unless one reads it as meaning a subtle form of dialectical speculation.

Robert Bernasconi seems to suggest such an interpretation when he notes that "the terms of the title *Totality and Infinity* are not related to each other antithetically . . . totality in Levinas is not simply the finite totality, for it bears the infinite *within* it. The opposition of 'inside' and 'outside,' 'within' and 'beyond,' is displaced by Levinas, although we shall have to investigate . . . whether the manner of doing so does not introduce a *speculative* idea of infinity that rejoins Hegel, albeit another Hegel

62. Levinas, preface to Mosès, *System and Revelation,* 19 / 13.

from that from which Levinas seeks to separate himself."[63] Levinas's phenomenological critique of the idealist, representationalist, and ontological presuppositions of phenomenology thus touches upon a dialectical extension and reversal of dialectic which Hegel's thought both enables and frustrates. And this was Adorno's project. Following my earlier interpretation of Adorno's dialectics, we might be justified in suspecting that Levinas's figure of thought here touches profoundly on that of an open, that is to say, negative dialectical speculation: micrologically encircling a transcendence in immanence or immanence in transcendence that is, at the same time, a transcendence of transcendence and, hence, an immanence thought and experienced *otherwise*. Seen from this perspective, both Adorno and Levinas are thinkers of the same as much as they are philosophers of the other; deconstructors of transcendence as much as innovators of immanence. A more extensive consideration of Levinas's concept of the infinite, which would refute the misleading suggestion of a postulated *positive* finitude at the origin and beyond the completion of history as we know it, would confirm this view. Suffice it to note here that, for both authors, the "trace left by the infinite is not the residue of a presence; its very glow is ambiguous. Otherwise, its positivity would not preserve the infinity of the infinite any more than negativity would" (*OB* 12 / 15).

THE CENTRAL CONCEPTS OF homogeneous "totality" and "identity" discussed in the preceding section thus name two characteristics of a general picture of the Western history of Being and the Western tradition as reconstructed, constructed, and, we should add, somewhat stylized or rhetorically exaggerated in Levinas's middle period, culminating in *Totality and Infinity*. In his late work the *terminus technicus* he uses for the understanding of history qua totalized History, with which he amalgamates several additional aspects (some of them nonhistorical, i.e., ontological, psychobiological, and semantic) into a single syndrome, is the concept of "essence" or even "essance" (*OB* xlvi, 179 / ix, 207–8; or *GCM* 195 n. 1, 112 / 78 n. 1, 175). This concept does not refer to the Greek *eidos*, "idea," or the Latin *essentia*,[64] "essence" (though in an early essay, Levinas had used the concept *essence* to translate Husserl's term *Wesen*, by which he

---

63. Robert Bernasconi, "Levinas and Derrida: The Question of the Closure of Metaphysics," in Cohen, *Face to Face with Levinas*, 194.

64. See Marc Faessler, "L'Intrigue du Tout-Autre: Dieu dans la pensée d'Emmanuel Levinas," in *Emmanuel Levinas*, ed. Jacques Rolland, *Les Cahiers de "La Nuit surveilée,"* vol. 3 (Lagrasse: Verdier, 1984), 119 n. 1.

means "the ideal condition of existence for the individual object" [*DEHH* 35]). It refers to Being as distinguished from beings and, in this characterization, follows Heidegger in his departure from ancient and modern metaphysics as well as from his own Husserlian beginnings. Levinas's neologism *essance* aims at "the process or event of being" (*OB* 187 n. 1 / 3 n. 1) or, in Heidegger's terms, the "event in itself of Being [*Sich-Ereignen des Seins*]," what Jacques Rolland terms its "*energy of being.*"[65]

Thus construed, the concept includes various traits that Levinas maintains dominate the entire tradition of philosophical thinking: Spinoza's conviction that beings have the natural tendency to persevere in their being (*conatus essendi*);[66] Kant's conception that phenomenal reality falls into line with a priori spatio-temporal forms of sensible intuition and the categories of understanding; Heidegger's explanation of Being as time; and, finally, the insight from the philosophy of language that our forms of life are linguistically and pragmatically structured, that is, that they are language games and modes of coping with the natural history of our species (as Wittgenstein, never cited by Levinas, suggests in *Philosophical Investigations*).[67] In all these different determinations, in Levinas's opinion, the philosophical discourse of the West fails to utter the final word about reality. It would befit philosophy to reach farther and deeper, to dig for what manifests itself *beyond* (*au-delà*) or *beneath* (*en-deça*) this "essence" or "essance," whose fundamental features are consistently presupposed by the tradition of ancient and modern thought, regardless of its different idioms, argumentative strategies, and existential concerns.

In close parallel with and contradistinction to Levinas's emphatic characterization of the *essance* of the Western history of Being and his generalized Spinozic notion of the *conatus essendi*, Adorno, as we have seen, likewise speaks of an "essence [*Wesen*]" that is first of all "the fatal mischief [*Unwesen*] of a world so arranged as to degrade men to means of their *sese conservare*, a world that curtails and threatens their life by reproducing it and making them believe that it has this character so as to satisfy their needs" (*ND* 167 / 169). According to Adorno, other — and no longer false — needs should be hoped for, even though, like Levinas, he is suspicious of

<hr />

65. Rolland, "Getting Out of Being by a New Path," *OE* 11 / 19.

66. Spinoza, *Ethics*, pt. 3, prop. 6: "Unaquaeque res, quantum in se est, in suo esse perseverare conatur": "Each thing, as far as it can by its own power, strives to persevere in its being" (*A Spinoza Reader: The "Ethics" and Other Works*, ed. and trans. Edwin Curley [Princeton: Princeton University Press, 1994], 159).

67. See Strasser, *Jenseits von Sein und Zeit*, 376–77.

the spontaneity of life and the living as such. In Levinas the very concept of need — that is, of *besoin* as opposed to *désir*, desire — and of the *sese conservare* ontologically collapse into each other. But for both thinkers the actual historical necessity that thus unfolds must be ultimately conceived as metaphysically contingent and, hence, can be critically judged at each single instant along the way. For this to be possible its modality — and, hence, the trace of the nonidentical and other or Other — must be conceived or, rather, materialized and concretized as well as infinitized and absolved in a radically different way.

An epiphany or testimony of the Other ought not to be interpreted in terms of an ontological disclosure or even a religious revelation (although Levinas uses the latter concept repeatedly for the "emergence" of the other): the passivity imposed by the Other and others is not only a rejoinder — or response — to the transcendence of the ethical commandment but also the very witness to this infinity. Neither the traditional concept of truth as manifestation nor the modern understanding of communication as the intersubjective transfer of identifiable messages or meanings between a sender and a receiver, let alone normative theories of interaction in terms of social contract, rational choice, communitarian association, and discursive deliberation, is capable of capturing the minimal (i.e., formal and nearly contentless) and momentary (i.e., fleeting and evanescent) quality of the relation between self and other, which Levinas expresses in increasingly radical terms.

Nevertheless, the history of Being and its effective articulation in tradition and modernity must always *nolens volens* run up against two critical points that set limits to the reduction of the other to the self-same, just as they undermine the primitive absorption of the same into some other. First, as we have already seen, according to Levinas the *passivity of the subject* breaks through the homogeneous structure of the I's identity postulated by the Western tradition, the equation or nonformal tautology of the self (or ipseity) and the same or self-same (i.e., the *idem*). This happens *in a double movement, from two opposed directions*. The *heterogeneity* that the experience of the *il y a* inflicts upon the subject, even in its hypostasis and striving for autonomy, and the *heteronomy* that characterizes the statute of the I made responsible and "invested" with its freedom by the Other imply a sense of disgust, a desire for escape, and, subsequently, a longing for the other beyond any possible satisfaction. In its own way each of the extreme poles of our experience of these absolutes (of *il y a* and illeity) stands in a tense relationship to the teleological-harmonistic image of the self in the Western philosophy of the subject. They are vanishing points, structurally analogous yet profoundly different in "substance," in their minimal "content" as seemingly opposed instances of a *tertium datur* and its contrasting *concretissimum* — instances that Levinas, at least at first glance, appears not to weight equally. Yet upon closer examination the sphere of the *il y a* and the ethical situation in which illeity leaves its trace do not appear to be unambiguously or conclusively separate in his thought.

Second is the *idea of the infinite*. The subtitle of *Totality and Infinity* reads, famously, *An Essay on Exteriority*. The ethical relation to the other person points, even if indirectly, toward an exteriority that in principle exceeds every totality. This idea, Levinas insists, has not gone unremarked in the history of thought: "during some flashes [*à quelques instants d'éclair*]" (*OB* 8 / 10; see also *HAH* 94), above all in Plato's idea of the good "beyond being and beingness [*epekeina tes ousias*]," as well as Descartes's idea of the infinite, the West has granted an appropriate place for a metaphysical hint pointing beyond Being and its essences. This also happens in the motif of the One (*to hen*) in Plotinus's *Enneads*, in Augustine's distinction between an exhortative truth (*veritas redarguens*) and an ontological, illuminating truth (*veritas lucens*), in Pseudo-Dionysius' doctrine of the *via eminentiae*,[68] and in Kant, "who finds a meaning to the human without measuring it by ontology" (*OB* 129 / 166). The list is far from complete.

Levinas's undertaking would hardly be thinkable without this subterranean and intermittent history or, rather, counter-history. As he himself acknowledges: "we would not have ventured to recall the *beyond essence* if this history of the West did not bear, in its margins, the trace of events carrying another signification, and if the victims of the triumphs which entitle the eras of History could be separate from its meaning. Here we have the boldness to think that even the Stoic nobility of resignation to the logos already owes its energy to the openness to the *beyond essence*" (*OB* 178 / 224- 25, trans. modified). Such formulations would justify reinscribing Levinas's project in a long intellectual history — that of spiritual exercises and their modern extensions, transformations, and substitutes, from antiquity up to Wittgenstein and the later Foucault — from which he so often seems to set himself apart.[69]

68. Levinas and Kearney, "Dialogue," in Cohen, *Face to Face with Levinas*, 25.
69. Bernasconi, "Levinas and Derrida," in Cohen, *Face to Face with Levinas*, 195–96. See Derrida, *Writing and Difference*, 148, 149 / 220, 222.

Indeed, Levinas writes, "The philosophy that has been handed down to us could not fail to name the paradox of this non-ontological significance; even though, immediately, it turned back to being as to the ultimate foundation of the reason it named" (*GCM* 119 / 184–85). But does such an admission not have repercussions for the radicality of the nominalism and actualism manifest throughout Levinas's work? How can this "history of the face"[70] be reconciled with the *indifference* of the ethical to the power

---

70. Yet another motif would be Levinas's transformation of the Stoic aspiration to "cosmic consciousness" (to cite Pierre Hadot's term, in *La Citadelle intérieure* [*The Inner Citadel*]) into a singular universalism, that is, into the thought, experience, or testimony of a "*Sub-jectum,*" supporting the weight of the whole *universe* on its shoulders. Claiming no place on earth for itself, ethical subjectivity would thus give a meaning to Being and "welcome its gravity." Only from this extraterrestrial view is Being "assembled into a unity of the universe and essence . . . assembled into an event." It is with this motif in mind, Levinas suggests, that even the modern thought experiments that analyze identities as they travel through "interstellar spaces"—one thinks of examples introduced by Derek Parfitt's *Reasons and Persons* and critically evaluated by Ricoeur in *Oneself as Another,* examples that Levinas himself had toyed with in the early essay "Heidegger, Gagarin et nous" ("Heidegger, Gagarin, and Us")—are not so much a "fiction of science-fiction" but the very expression of the "passivity as a self" (*OB* 116 / 147–48). As in Adorno, a radically modified view of totality—here nothing less than a universe justified from within and without, in the interstices of stars and beings—comes to reconfigure an age-old constellation of Western enlightened, that is to say, postmythical thought. Not simply another totality but totality conceived (i.e., rearticulated, resituated, and also displaced) completely—that is, totally—*otherwise*. As Levinas suggests, the unity of the universe is not to be seen as the result of my encompassing theoretical or contemplative gaze (*regard*), in what Kant and Husserl define as the "unity of apperception," but as "what regards me in the two senses of the term, accuses me, is my affair" (ibid.). Totally otherwise, the traditional motif of totality is now guarded as that of a *supporting* of—and substituting for—everything and everyone (*pour tous* [*OB* 116, cf. 196 n. 21 / 148–49, cf. 150 n. 21]), that is, of the whole. My responsibility for the Other would always include being responsible even for the responsibility the Other—albeit the other, namely, God—has for me, meaning that the oneself (*Moi, Soi, soi-même*), in this spiraling "iteration" of responsibilities, has always "one movement more [*un mouvement de plus*]" to make: "always to have one degree of responsibility more," indeed, "suffering 'for God' who suffers from my suffering" (ibid., 196 n. 21, 117, 196 n. 21 / 150 n. 21, 149–50, 150 n. 21). But then, as we will see, even this is not stated as a general theoretical claim that would somehow metaphysically or transcendentally (let alone empirically) concern *all* in the *same* way. Could it be said to regard the singularity of everyone and only thus virtually all? As Levinas sees it: "We cannot speak of every human being, especially not of all human beings as every human being. 'Every human being' is not 'all human beings.' I mean, the 'all-inclusive' is not at the beginning. Perhaps the all-inclusive is at the end, as an open unity or totality" (Levinas, *Is It Righteous to Be?* 47; Poirié, *Emmanuel Levinas,* 91). Tradition in its quest for totality (nature, cosmos, universe, universality, the world, society, the state) is thus both undermined, indeed, disavowed, and reaffirmed in one and the same gesture. Neither repetition of the same (the nonformal tautology of *das Immergleiche*) nor the postulation of a merely theoretical idea of otherness (the heterology of *das ganz Andere*) but a far more subtle deconstruction and rethinking of the history of metaphysics, from its earliest Greek beginnings to its downfall, "after Auschwitz," is at issue in Levinas's philosophy, as in Adorno's.

of tradition and history, which is no less essential to his thought? In his studies of Blanchot, Levinas remarks at one point, "The meaning of the story is lost: what happens does not succeed in happening, does not go into a story" (OMB 169 / 73). Would this insight not hold true of the ethical intrigue and, if so, block all access to its rendering and, hence, intelligibility in historiographical or biographical terms, whether literal or fictive, without which no narratological account of identity (as in, say, McIntyre or Ricoeur) would be possible?

I will leave these questions open for the moment and merely recall that, according to Levinas, tradition and modernity are *hypocritical* (see *TI* 24 / xii), in that they direct their gaze toward the "true" and the "good" and listen both to philosophers and, occasionally, also to prophets. Levinas denounces this global "disorientation" (*HAH* 33; see also 36 / 40; and *TI* 215 / 190), this forgetfulness of the Orient in the West, and insists, provocatively, on a certain primacy of Jerusalem over Athens, of the other over the same, of metaphysics over ontology.

In *Totality and Infinity* Levinas presents his critique of tradition in the form of an *ethical philosophy of origin.* As he explains in the preface to the German translation, the basic intuition of this book is to challenge "the synthesis of knowledge, the totality of being that is embraced by the *transcendental ego,* presence grasped in the representation and the concept, and questioning concerning the semantics of the verbal form of to be—inevitable stations of Reason—as the ultimate instances [*instances*] of *sense* [*du sensé*]."[71] One should break through the Western philosophy of totality from the Archimedean point of the idea of infinity, "the final secret of being, . . . the ultimate structure" (*TI* 80 / 53). This idea of a *primum intelligibile* becomes apparent in the epiphany of the face, "the origin of exteriority" (*TI* 262 / 239). Levinas thus understands ethics to be the ethical transformation of the *prima philosophia* or, as de Boer puts it, an *ethical transcendental philosophy:*[72] "The ethical . . . delineates the structure of exteriority as such. Morality is not a branch of philosophy, but first philosophy" (*TI* 304 / 283).

These characterizations, however, are less appropriate after the radical shift in Levinas's thinking which occurs with *Otherwise than Being.*[73]

71. Levinas, "Preface to the German Edition, *EN* 198 / 250 / 9, trans. modified.

72. See de Boer, "Ethical Transcendental Philosophy," in Cohen, *Face to Face with Levinas;* and Hendrik Johan Adriaanse, "Het rationale karakter van de wijsbegeerte van Levinas," *Nederlands Theologisch Tijdschrift* 29 (1975): 255–63.

73. The concept of a turn, a *Wende* (see Strasser, "Ethik als erste Philosophie," in Walden-

Again, in Levinas's own characterization: "*Otherwise than Being or Be-yond Essence* already avoids the ontological—or more exactly, *eidetic*—language which *Totality and Infinity* resorts to in order to keep its analyses, which challenge the *conatus essendi* of being, from being considered as dependent upon the empiricism of a psychology."[74] In *Humanisme de l'autre homme* (*Humanism of the Other*), *Otherwise than Being*, and *Of God Who Comes to Mind*, Levinas is increasingly concerned with an "an-archeology" (*OB* 7 / 8), rather than a philosophy of origin starting out from a *primum intelligibile*. He writes, "the idea of priority is a Greek idea—it is the idea of principle" (*GCM* 85 / 136). The resulting intensi-fication of the critique of ontology thus affects the concept of principle as foundation and beginning. It likewise undermines the very notion of identity and thereby a further premise of the ethical transcendental phi-losophy, because whoever receives the ethical appeal forms, according to *Totality and Infinity*, an autonomous (a separate and atheist) pole of iden-tity and in this guise constitutes a condition of possibility for the ethical relation. If the relationship between self and Other must be described as one in which the Other "orients" the same,[75] then what, exactly, could *orientation* mean if what orients is never unambiguously communicated? How might the relation of the other to the same be articulated if we avoid concepts such as "foundation" and "orientation" because they so strongly invoke spatial metaphors or the architecture of the tradition? Thinking, as I have already established, ought to be *groundless*. And in its firmament only the stars still shimmer (see *OS* 83 / 121).

In Levinas's late work the very "transcendentality"[76] of Being as such is undermined. Modern allusions to a transformation of classical philo-sophical tasks, however they might be conceived after the linguistic, her-meneutic, and pragmatic paradigm shifts that have punctuated twentieth-

---

fels, *Phänomenologie im Frankreich,* 239) or *Kehre* (see Strasser, *Jenseits von Sein und Zeit,* 223), would certainly be too strong. Goud rightly observes that the development from *Totality and Infinity* to *Otherwise than Being* does not involve an altogether new approach (see Goud, "Über Definition und Infinition," 128–29, 140). At most we might use the term *Kehre* in the sense one finds in Heidegger's late work. Levinas's *Kehre* is, as Goud remarks, "a *deconstruction,* so to speak, of his earlier thought" (141). Elsewhere, however, Goud dismisses the applicability of the term *deconstruction* to Levinas's thought (see Goud, "Joodse filosofie en haar relatie tot de westerse wijsgerige traditie: Het voorbeeld van Emmanuel Levinas," *Wijsgerig Perspektief* 25 [1984–85]: 99).

74. Levinas, "Preface to the German Edition," *EN* 197–98 / 249 / 8.

75. Peperzak, "Introduction à la lecture de *Totalité et Infini*," 216.

76. Strasser, "Ethik als erste Philosophie," 239.

century philosophy, therefore become, if not obsolete—we can never really claim to have completely different categories of thought and experience at our disposal—at least restricted in their validity. This insight is already prepared in *Totality and Infinity,* as becomes clear from Levinas's discussion of Descartes's thought experiment invoking the "evil genius [*malin génie*]" (who could mislead us by presenting the world from a consistently false perspective), as well as from his early emphasis on the impossible auto-foundation of epistemological, moral, and aesthetic critique. But what breaks through the potential and, indeed, principal anarchy of the world of impressions, ideas, signs, and representation is only the *primum intelligibile* of the other, whose grounding and almost criteriological function puts an end to possible delusion, uncertainty, and ambiguity.

The allusion to ethical transcendental philosophy undoubtedly constitutes one of the strongest conceivable interpretations of the middle phase of Levinas's work.[77] This designation highlights the *descriptive* (i.e., denotative) features of the task Levinas attributes to philosophy within and, especially, *at the limits of* theoretical reason and phenomenology. Yet more recent Levinas scholarship is beginning to react against this traditional-modern interpretation, turning toward the performative aspects of his writing and their implications for questions of a more pragmatic, pragmatist, and moral-perfectionist nature. This runs more or less parallel to the shifts of interest within the tradition of Critical Theory and its re-elaboration in "discourse ethics" and the theory of recognition (see chaps. 2 and 11). This parallel enables some connections that will help lead back to the opening questions of my investigation.

The difficulty of theoretically grasping Levinas's work in the form of concepts or arguments that would not be reductive causes many interpreters to see it primarily is an *exerzitium*—as Adorno would say, an *experimentum crucis*—of practical reason and thus as being concerned less with a set of prescriptions, norms, and virtues than with the performative nature of prescriptivity, normativity, ethnicity, and even moral perfectibility as such. Not that these formal features—the phenomenality of the phenomenon of the religious, of the relation to the Other—are *described* from without or within (i.e., hermeneutically or emphatically), but they

77. In addition to the article by de Boer in Cohen, *Face to Face with Levinas;* see also C. W. Reed, "Levinas's Question," in the same volume. Reed speaks of a "diachronic transcendentalism" (74).

are *enacted* or *exercised,* in an exemplary yet singular way. Philosophy itself thus becomes a kind of moral "gesture," a form of testimony: "Levinas's deductions are themselves moral events."[78] The reader of such interpretations often has the sense that Levinas's philosophy is being forced into a moralistic milieu that he takes great pains to avoid, but the arguments in such alternative readings are worthy of consideration.

At first glance the turn toward the pragmatic and the performative seems to provide a cure for the paradoxes and aporias in Levinas's writing. A pragmatic and performative interpretation of the alternation and oscillation between the other and the same, between Saying and the Said, according to a skeptical model that would remove the theoretical, self-referential character from Levinas's claims might seem to avoid the contradictoriness of his thought. In one scholar's words, "the performative does not *represent* what it accomplishes, but . . . *presents* it."[79] In this reading not the propositional content of the "skeptical" utterance—the interruption of the Said—but only the "act" of its speaking is essential for Levinas.

According to Lyotard, Levinas's "deontic logic" attempts, above all, to present the moral law independently of the question of its supposed truth or untruth: "Hence it follows that the 'well-formed' expressions that concern Levinas do not need to be well-formed in the terms required by propositional logic. . . . In their deep structure . . . , properly Levinasian statements are 'imperatives.' "[80] According to Lyotard, Levinas describes this incommensurability of prescriptive language with the descriptive or ontological in the idea of "an-archy," a notion that entails a critical—and perhaps polemical, agonistic, or inspirational?—relationship to the order of the normative.[81] Levinas's manner of expression thus displays *a dimension beyond the statements of yes or no* which is often overlooked in the linguistic-pragmatic considerations of authors such as Apel and Habermas. Indeed, "Levinas's 'doing before understanding' perhaps requires us to extend the notion of the pragmatic, to situate it in a larger context than

78. Smith, "Reason as One for Another: Moral and Theoretical Argument," in Cohen, *Face to Face with Levinas;* see also 57 and 67.

79. Greef, "Skepticism and Reason," in Cohen, *Face to Face with Levinas,* 172.

80. Jean-François Lyotard, "Levinas's Logic," in Cohen, *Face to Face with Levinas,* 124; see also 128–29. A shorter version of this essay was published in Laruelle, *Textes pour Emmanuel Levinas,* 127–50.

81. Ibid., 129. See Lyotard, *The Differend,* 3 ff., 118–19, 133, 142 ff. /16 ff., 174, 193, 206 ff. For a reading of Lyotard's *The Differend* and related texts, see my essays "On Obligation: Lyotard and Levinas" and "*Sei gerecht!* Lyotard over de verplichting," in *Lyotard lezen: Ethiek, onmenselijkheid en sensibiliteit,* ed. R. Brons and H. Kunneman (Amsterdam: Boom, 1995), 32–49.

that of the conversational."[82] This being said, Levinas neither fits his observations on ethical philosophy into the mold of a moralism or virtue ethics (to be distinguished from the tradition of moral perfectionism, to which he comes close) nor expands them into a Kantian determination of pure practical reason, with its distinction between hypothetical maxims and categorical imperatives. As Lyotard elegantly summarizes, "what is at stake in the discourse of Levinas is the power to speak of obligation without ever transforming it into a norm."[83] Levinas neither has in mind a generalizable and ultimately universal moral law, nor does he understand the asymmetrical structure of responsibility as a being obligated to engage upon an endless approach toward an intelligible realm, the Kantian kingdom of ends. Indeed, as Levinas himself clearly states: "This is not a *Sollen* commanding the infinite pursuit of an ideal. The infinity of the infinite lives in going backwards [*à rebours*]" (*OB* 12 / 14). In consequence, emphasis on the renewal of the Kantian primacy of practical reason and the explanatory tools provided by the formal pragmatic turn, though they can provide important insights into Levinas's work, are not the most fruitful approach. Even characterization of the philosophy of the Other as a transformed, ethical *prima philosophia* or transcendental philosophy cannot ignore the fact that Levinas's hardly fits the better-known descriptions of the "human condition."

Derrida's understanding of the question of the relationship between description (*in* discourse) and performance (*with* discourse) seems relevant here. He points out that in Levinas's presentations there appears to be a kind of alternation and oscillation — or, as he says, a "seriality [*sériature*]" — which requires a more complex type of analysis: "The words there describe (constate) and produce (perform) undecidably."[84] Thus, Levinas's thinking can be classified neither purely as a specimen of theoretical philosophy nor as a meditation on practical reason. Rather, he attempts — "at the risk of appearing to confuse theory and practice" (*TI* 29 / xvii) — to understand both sides of this classical-modern opposition as *modes* of metaphysical transcendence. Yet this should not blind us to the fact that Levinas's mode of thinking claims, above all, to be *philosophical*. As pri-

82. Greef, "Skepticism and Reason," in Cohen, *Face to Face with Levinas,* 175.

83. Lyotard, "Levinas's Logic," in Cohen, *Face to Face with Levinas,* 143.

84. Derrida, "En ce moment même dans cet ouvrage me voici," *Psyché: Inventions de l'autre* (Paris: Galilée, 1987), 173; see also 174, 175, 183, 187, 188 / "At this very moment in this work here I am," trans. Ruben Berezdivin, in *Re-Reading Levinas,* ed. Robert Bernasconi and Simon Critchley (Bloomington: Indiana University Press, 1991), 22; see also 23, 24, 30–31, 34–35, 36.

marily a moral gesture, it would be of merely "existential," rather than "systematic," interest.

But how, then, can one account for the circumstance that Levinas's particular kind of construction of the other within the same finally concerns a *quasi*-transcendental "*in*condition"? In his critique of pure reason Kant tried to show that a concurrence of the disparate material imposed upon our senses and a scientifically ordered knowledge of nature is possible only via the existence of formal structures of reason (forms of perception and categories of understanding). By analogy to this transcendental mode of grounding, I will venture to interpret Levinas's figure of thought as follows: from the mere fact that self-critique and sociality are possible, despite the undeniable fact of human egoism, one can deduce that the epiphany of the Other *may* inspire selflessness, disinterestedness, and disengagement in theoretical and practical spheres, though it does not necessarily or by its nature do so.[85] A decision or, better, a preparedness, openness, awareness, and wakefulness is required at each single instant to protect reason from evil or just indifference. In order to account for intelligibility, meaning, cooperation, and uprightness, we must postulate *a reason before reason,*[86] *a reason within and beyond reason,* a *communication of communication,* as we know it.

This ethical condition of possibility for a knowledge striving toward objectivity and for various — more or less peaceful, more or less sincere — forms of community cannot be reconstructed out of phenomena as an impersonal, universal, necessary, formal structure. In this sense it cannot, as de Boer correctly maintains, be compared to Kantian transcendental apperception or even to Heideggerian "clearing [*Lichtung*]."[87] Its very singularity, each time other and absolute, forbids the common ground that all transcendental modes of reasoning — whether classical, modern, idealist, or hermeneutic — must necessarily assume. The reason before, within, and beyond reason is thus "rather an unrecoverable contingent or ontic incidence that intersects the ontological order."[88] Without this *dimension of depth,* which should not be misunderstood as coming from a classical-metaphysical netherworld (*Hinterwelt*), ontology (to cite Kant once again) would be "blind." Nevertheless, as de Boer shows, the reverse

85. See de Boer, "Ethical Transcendental Philosophy," in Cohen, *Face to Face with Levinas,* 108.

86. See ibid., 101.

87. Ibid., 100; see also 97.

88. Ibid., 108.

is no less true: without ontological embeddedness — that is to say, incarnation or, as Levinas has it, deformalization — metaphysics would be ethereal and "empty."[89]

In the middle period of his work Levinas's phenomenology and his use of the transcendental figure of thought run up against a limit, in good Kantian fashion. The ethical condition of possibility, which can urge goodness and may undo the ossification of the divide between theory and practice, though also their dynamic, is itself *not a phenomenon.* In a different way from Husserlian phenomenology, the condition of possibility for experience is not experience itself.[90] As one commentator on the "neostructuralist" engagement with certain transcendental arguments remarks: "What makes an other enter into a particular order is not itself a part of that order. One of the meanings of 'transcendental' indicates precisely this: the condition of possibility of an other's mode of being, without itself belonging to the mode of being of what is established."[91] The "transcendental" thus understood might best be regarded, I would venture, as an experience in a metaphorical or sublime — in any case, a displaced — sense. This experience is unavoidably betrayed when it enters into reflective consciousness, history, action, or language.

Derrida states as much when he analyzes in what sense

> it is true that Ethics, in Levinas's sense, is an Ethics without law and without concept, which maintains its non-violent purity only before being determined as concepts and laws. This is not an objection: let us not forget that Levinas does not seek to propose laws or moral rules, does not seek to determine *a* morality, but rather the essence of the ethical relation in general. But as this determination does not offer itself as a *theory* of Ethics, in question then, is an Ethics of Ethics. In this case, it is perhaps serious that this Ethics of Ethics can occasion neither a determinate ethics nor determined laws without negating and forgetting itself.[92]

Needless to say, the differing positions in the debate about the transcendental-philosophical, pragmatic, or performative status of Levinas's thought imply different valuations of the relative weight of his descriptive and prescriptive procedures in *Totality and Infinity* and *Otherwise*

89. Ibid., 110; see also 103.

90. Ibid., 105. That might also be why Levinas uses the Kantian term *deduction* rather than the Husserlian term *reduction* (108).

91. Frank, *Was ist Neostrukturalismus?* 171.

92. Derrida, *Writing and Difference*, 111 / 164.

than Being. The two major works suggest differently accented models of interpretation. The ethical philosophy of origin can certainly be interpreted in terms of transcendental philosophy, but this is scarcely true of the anarchic figure of thought in the later work. The latter can be analyzed only in terms of an entirely hypothetical (in Kant's sense) and at best quasi-transcendental thinking; in addition, it can only be grasped by recognizing its performative, that is to say, poetic structure and rhetorical strategy. And yet, *just as it would be inappropriate to aestheticize (or moralize) Adorno's late work, so it would be misguided to moralize (or aestheticize) Levinas's late work.* Its figure of thought is *philosophical* to the extent that it takes up the appealing excesses of discourse only as critical moments, as opposing poles, in an alternating, oscillating, open dialectic of thinking and experience.

The claim of *Totality and Infinity* to outline an ethical philosophy of origin with the help of phenomenological and transcendental method (intentional analysis, transcendental reduction or deduction) thus founders on Levinas's own radicality, as well as on the capacity of Western discourse to resist oversimplification. As with Horkheimer and Adorno's *Dialectic of Enlightenment,* we might see this failure as in fact a success. *Totality and Infinity* suggests a structure of argumentation parallel to that of *Dialectic of Enlightenment* insofar as here, too, the autonomy of the I and philosophical contemplation, on the one hand, and nature or the sociality of dialogue, on the other, are not consistently deprived of their ontological status. In the face of the negativity of history—a history to which actual alterity must be denied—both books carry within them an *analogous* promise: in one, the formulation of a—*postponed*—positive, normative concept of enlightenment; in the other, the promise to establish *already now* an ethical *prima philosophia.* These promises, however, cannot be redeemed, for reasons that can be taken as the pièce de résistance of both authors' subsequent work, in *Negative Dialectics* and *Otherwise than Being.* The increasing radicalization of their figures of thought supports this claim. The late works of both Adorno and Levinas, reaching back to earlier motifs, practice a less affirmative and more ambiguous kind of philosophizing, which might be grasped as the interplay of a negative, alternating dialectic and a phenomenological concretization or even materialization. This constellation of a dianoetic and "noetic" aspect in thinking and experience gives form to their version of a philosophy of the trace: "noetic," in quotation marks because it concerns an almost corporeal and fundamentally traumatic dimension of depth, which takes the place of "ideas" in classical-modern idealism and of "affects" in modern empiricism, thus dramatically shifting their original meaning. In the center of philosophical observation now stands an intrigue of meaning, "other than that of re-presentation and empirical experience," indeed, an idea that "in its passivity beyond all receptivity is *no longer an idea*" (*GCM* 66 / 110, my emph.).

Precisely this ambivalence makes possible the seeming—and complementary—excessiveness of a stylization of the self and the other that reaches "diabolical" or "messianic" proportions: that is, the description of the self in terms of a hypothesis forever drawn to the element of mythical-anonymous being as well as in terms of a forever negative, finite historical totality; but also the evocation of the other in terms of an intermittent and always revocable utopian-eschatological escape from these orders. The account of these extremes can only be redeemed by interpreting them *rhetorically:* as expressions of an *exaggeration,* born of solidarity with "damaged life," in remembrance of the horrors of history and the presentiment of horrors yet to come. Adorno and Levinas both employ this procedure of a description carried to the extreme—a semantic and figural overdrive that claims validity not per se but against other alternatives—and pursue it in two directions: down into the depths of distress and outward to the marvels of desire. Only in this way, apparently, can omnipresent meaninglessness and the scattered remains—the traces—of the other and Other be named.

Chapter Ten

Loosening Logocentrism

Language and Skepticism

🐍 THE RELATION TO the Other cannot be grasped directly, whether in any intentional act of conscious representation or imagination or within the negativity of sociohistorical experience or within the framework of the grammatical structures of language and the pragmatic structures of speech acts. In Levinas's attempts to reconstruct, experience, and express this dilemma nothing less than the *rational,* even the *discursive,* character of his philosophical undertaking is at stake. Like Adorno, and without reference to the famous final proposition of Wittgenstein's *Tractatus Logico-Philosophicus,* Levinas repeatedly emphasizes that "one must not be silent," that we "are not before an ineffable mystery" (*GCM* 99 / 157). Yet, despite this courageous assurance, he, like Adorno, confronts the paradox and aporia of wanting to describe and express *philosophically* an ethical-metaphysical dimension that—*by definition,* through its very *infinition*—resists every thematization, possibly even all of language, whether conceptual or poetic, just as it eludes image, sound, touch, and taste. Can the confrontation with the face of the other person and the trace of the infinite within it be articulated *reasonably,* that is, with untiring recourse to the universal plane of the Greek philosophical tradition and its subsequent transformations in medieval and modern thought? Can the ethical relation find suitable expression within it, or is it from the beginning necessarily overwhelmed by the very coherence of discourse, in which Levinas, being a philosopher and inhabiting the spiritual element of the European West, must participate? Does the attempt to think and to put into words an ab-solute alterity not also end in the performative contradiction that Adorno so often announces? Put otherwise, can Levinas's writings offer a way out of the dilemma of the—admittedly, rhetorically exaggerated—characterization of thought, discourse, and experience in terms of identity and totality, on the one hand, and the total immediacy of an actual alterity, on the other? Might Levinas's figure of thought not stand on its head—and, hence, finally escape—the complementarity of a historical-philosophical negativism (or ahistoricism) and its resulting messianism — a constellation that, as we have seen, is unmistakable in Adorno's work?

Levinas's undertaking, like the Platonic tradition of dialectic, modern philosophies of dialogue, and the linguistic and pragmatic turns, is above all a philosophy of language. For all his emphasis on rethinking subjectivity and judging history, his method is primarily that of discourse and writing. In Blanchot's words: "The revelation of *autrui* that does not come about in the lighted space of forms belongs wholly to the domain of speech. *Autrui* expresses himself, and in this speaking proposes himself as other. If there is a relation wherein the other and the same, even while holding themselves in relation, *absolve themselves* of it (being terms that thus remain *absolute* within the relation itself, as Levinas firmly states), this relation is language."[1] Levinas himself writes of "the language of the inaudible, the language of the unheard of, the language of the non-said. Writing!"[2]

In his thinking about the philosophy of language, as in his views of subjectivity and history, Levinas focuses on three stages. First, like Rosenzweig, he describes how language — more precisely, asymmetrical dialogue (*le Discours*) — *breaks through mythical silence*. Here Levinas writes: "The inverse of language is like a laughter that seeks to destroy language, a laughter infinitely reverberated where mystification interlocks in mystification without ever resting on a real speech, without ever commencing. The spectacle of the silent world of facts is bewitched: every phenomenon masks, mystifies ad infinitum, making actuality impossible" (*TI* 91–92 / 64). Second, he explicates the *closed dialectics of discourse* as it articulates and sediments itself in semantically and propositionally ordered sentences, that is to say, in argumentation and prose, system and theory. Third, he directs his attention to the problem of the *alternation of the Said (le Dit) and the Saying (le Dire)*. The latter two steps address the dilemma outlined earlier, the aporia that results from the characterization of thought in terms of identity and totality, on one side, and the immediacy of alterity, on the other.

In Levinas's strategy for avoiding sheer aporia or for rendering it productive, one can distinguish three corresponding aspects or levels of meaning, which must be assessed if we are to approach the question con-

1. Blanchot, *Infinite Conversation*, 55 / 79.
2. Levinas, "Preface to the German Edition," *EN* 199 / 250 / 9, trans. modified.

cerning the rational—if not necessarily discursive or argumentative—character of his philosophy.

Like Adorno's idea of the nonidentical, Levinas's leitmotif of the idea of the infinite, which thinking can brokenly intuit but can never grasp or recognize via theoretical or practical modalities, takes up the old distinctions between discursive and intuitive, *ratio* and *intellectus,* understanding (*Verstand*) and reason (*Vernunft*), though decisively transforming them.[3] Not only does he represent access to infinity and the absolute in a way different from the idealist tradition, but he increasingly blurs the demarcations between discourse and interpellation, speech and address. Indeed, Blanchot argues that he does away with them: "Before all else, speech is this address, this invocation in which the one invoked is beyond reach, in which . . . he is called to the presence of speech."[4] Nonetheless, one can find in Levinas's texts at least two historically and systematically distinct modes of writing designed to help put into words the trace of the ab-solute this side of and beyond onto-theology. They can be roughly designated as a philosophical or *reductive* way and as a rhetorical or *productive* way—that is to say, as *via negationis*[5] and *via eminentiae,* respectively. One can hardly avoid the impression that, viewed from an analytical perspective, these procedures turn out to be paths that lead nowhere in particular but, of necessity, constantly err: *Holzwege,* as Heidegger would have said. In Levinas's work the metaphor of the trace, which cannot be reconstructed conceptually or argumentatively in full rigor and defies any phenomenological description because of its paradox, aporia, and status as *tertium datur,* negotiates (or should we say alternates and oscillates?) between these two modes, approaches that are both ultra-traditional and, in their redeployment, extremely modern, even modernist. Without the subtle "hermeneutics" of the trace, the paths of Levinas's thinking might be blocked entirely in advance, so that no escape (ethically or otherwise, via horror or sublimity) could be intuited, let alone expressed. The invocation of the "hermeneutics" of the trace, at the intersection of the negative, affirmative, and superlative heterodox theological ways, forms the *via regia* of mindfulness (*Eingedenken*) or remembrance (*Andenken*) of the other or Other which punctuates and marks Levinas's writing. Given the resistance of this central theme of the trace to being grasped through discourse—

3. See Peperzak, "Introduction à la lecture de *Totalité et Infini,*" 208.

4. Blanchot, *Infinite Conversation,* 55 / 79.

5. See de Boer, *Tussen filosofie en profetie,* 55, 108. By contrast, see Goud, *Levinas en Barth,* 97.

that is to say, by way of conceptual analysis or reconstructive argument —
we should hardly be surprised that, when Levinas's writing pushes to its
limit, this hermeneutics necessarily risks appearing to be, rather, a her-
meticism, of sorts. Indeed, the trace of the ab-solute resists more than the
grasp of conceptual analysis: it is in the end immune to even the most persistent deconstruction, touching upon something *undeconstructible,* from
within and without.

Via Negationis

Adorno draws on dialectics to free himself from the power of dialectics, using concepts to reach beyond them while inevitably still identifying
the nonidentical. One could say that Levinas's relation to phenomenological method is similarly paradoxical. But that claim would be too weak
because it fails to do justice to the radicality of the undertaking and the
extent of its repercussions.

In his late writings Levinas deepens the critique of ontology in general into a critique of phenomenological method and, above all, of the
transcendental turn within it. He no longer views philosophy as an act
or reconstruction of *founding* moments, premised upon a Greek structure of hierarchization and possibilization, but, rather, as an *alternating* movement, as a gesture of affirmation and revocation which deepens
and reorients the intentionality of the Husserlian understanding of originary donation (and passive synthesis), on the one hand, and of epochē
(and transcendental reduction), on the other. Although Levinas repeatedly confirms the importance of phenomenological procedure for his own
undertaking, in his work the precise relation to Husserl's intentions and
actual observations remains ambiguous: as we have seen, much more than
a "conversion" of the phenomenological gaze and a break with the natural
disposition (*die natürliche Einstellung*), with its naturalist interpretation
of things, the life-world, consciousness, and others, is at stake. Yet Levinas
pursues this "much more" via the phenomenological method and in its
idiom, if not its ontology, whose insufficiency and deconstructability he
increasingly exposes.

Derrida tellingly speaks of a "constant oscillation between the letter
and the spirit of Husserlianism."[6] The latter is found, above all, in the
methods of phenomenological concretion or intentional analysis, which

___

6. Derrida, *Writing and Difference,* 86 / 128. See also *DEHH* 111, 112, 115, 121, 135; *OB* 182–83 /
230–31; *GCM* 11, 87–88 / 11, 139–40.

Levinas believes should be employed to conceptualize the implicit and unexpected horizons of abstract thinking, goal-oriented action, and judgment based on criteria. He writes:

> Intentional analysis is the search for the concrete. Notions held under the direct gaze of the thought that defines them are nevertheless, unbeknown to this naive thought, revealed to be implanted in horizons unsuspected by this thought; these horizons endow them with a meaning—such is the essential teaching of Husserl. What does it matter if in the Husserlian phenomenology taken literally these unsuspected horizons are in their turn interpreted as thoughts aiming at objects! What counts is the idea of the overflowing of objectifying thought by a forgotten experience from which it lives. The break-up of the formal structure of thought (the noema of a noesis) into events which this structure dissimulates, but which sustain it and restore its concrete significance, constitutes a *deduction*—necessary and yet non-analytical. (*TI* 28 / xvi–xvii)

Culture and the body are preconditions for conscious (and practical) life, thought it must always forget these corporeal and life-worldly conditions and, in consequence, can never be in total harmony with them.[7] Heidegger converted this thought into an immanent delineation of an ontology forming the condition for culture and the world of things. But Husserl's method, in Levinas's view, makes it possible to think beyond representation to "an ethical *Sinngebung*," that is to say, "a *Sinngebung* essentially respectful of the Other." Where Husserl lays out the axiological dimensions of phenomenology yet renews the model of *theoria* based on intentional acts of the transcendental ego, he misses the implications of his own discovery, how in it "social relations, irreducible to the objectifying constitution that meant to cradle them in its rhythm, are abruptly awakened" (*DEH* 121 / *DEHH* 135).

"A *Sinngebung* essentially respectful of the Other" undermines both Idealism's basic assumption concerning the sovereignty—the purity, self-presence, and self-sufficiency—of consciousness and the counter-position of naturalistic or historicist objectivism. The ethical *Sinngebung* hints at a dimension of heteronomy whose contours require another mode of description: "A deep-seated *passion* is thus revealed in thought. A passion which no longer has anything in common with the passivity of sensation,

---

7. See de Boer, "Ethical Transcendental Philosophy," in Cohen, *Face to Face with Levinas*, 104–5; *DL* 291 / 406; *DEHH* 134.

of the given — which was starting point for empiricism and realism." (*DEH* 116 / *DEHH* 131).

Although it is not entirely foreign to something in Hegelian ways of thinking, the reflexive discovery, so to speak, of these forgotten levels of meaning ought not be regarded in analytic, synthetic, or dialectical ways. Indeed, Levinas writes: "Is there not reason to distinguish between the *envelopment* of the particular in a concept, the *implication* [sous-entendement] of what is presupposed in a notion, the *potentiality* of the possible in a horizon, on the one hand, and the *intimacy* of the non-intentional in prereflective consciousness, on the other hand?" (*GCM* 173 / 260)? Phenomenological description thus betrays a "resolutely dialectical allure" (*DEH* 94 / *DEHH* 114, trans. modified). In a different way from Hegel, however, phenomenology exhibits a movement of transcendence that has been turned inside out, a "retrogressive transcendence [*en arrière*] . . . a retro-cendence" (*DEH* 98 / *DEHH* 119). Is that a negative or negative dialectical procedure of sorts, operating, as Adorno would say, by way of "determinate [*bestimmte*] negation"?

True, Levinas does speak of the "negativity" — that is, the "denial opposed to the present" (*OB* 12 / 14) — which characterizes the anarchy of responsibility. And in the earliest writings we have encountered a dialectics of intersubjective and temporal relations (*EE* 93 / 160; and *TO* 79 / 74). He seems to espouse a *non-Hegelian* kind of dialectical thinking which is "not a matter of traversing a series of contradictions, or of reconciling them while stopping History," but aims at "a pluralism that does not merely merge into unity" (*TO* 42 / 20).

Derrida emphasizes that Levinas's text progresses "by negations, and by negation against negation. Its proper route is not that of an 'either this . . . or that,' but of a 'neither this . . . nor that.'"[8] Referring to Jean Wahl, Levinas refers to the possibility of a "*credo* followed by a *dubito* that leaves room for a second or third equally possible *credo*. It is an alternance on the model of the '*aut* . . . *aut*.' . . . that succession of *yes's, no's, but's, or's,* those disjunctives that change neither into conjunctions nor convergences" (*OS* 73 / 108). Again, is this motif of a *via negationis* — if we can thus generally designate the model of skepticism to which he refers — comparable to Adorno's conception of a *negative dialectics*? Does it constitute a tenable view of the reduced capacities or knowledge claims of philosophy in (post)modernity? Does it suffer, as Adorno's figure of thought supposedly

8. Derrida, *Writing and Difference*, 90 / 134–35.

does, from what Habermas criticizes as performative contradiction? Or
might Levinas's conception confirm the fruitfulness of Adorno's model?
Further, what is the relationship between "reduction [*réduction*]" and "determinate negation [*bestimmte Negation*]"?

Occasionally, Levinas refers to a "recurrence, which one can, to be
sure, call negativity (but a negativity antecedent to discourse, the unex-
ceptionable homeland of dialectical negativity)" (*OB* 108 / 138–39). Invoking the terminology of his earliest writings, notably "Reality and Its
Shadow," he compares this "recurrence" with the null site—what is inconclusive and cannot be included—upon which the dialectic breaks but
from which it must also take its lead: "without any dialectical germination,
quite sterile and pure, completely cut off from adventure and reminiscence. No grounds [*non-lieu*], meanwhile or contra-tempo time (or bad
times [*malheur*]), it is on the hither side of being and of the nothingness
which is thematizable like being" (*OB* 109 / 138).

At another point, however, he opposes the yes of ethical "submission"
to negativity (*OB* 122 / 156). Does that make him an antidialectical thinker?
Is dialectics here turned against itself in an almost negative dialectical
mode? Or is the medium and method of dialectic, with its implied but
immanently deconstructible ontology—not unlike phenomenology—in
the final analysis indifferent, substitutable, a useful but, in this particular
form, not necessarily indispensable conceptual and strategic tool? Might
a postanalytic, say, Wittgensteinian and "grammatical" account of things
in principle have been just as feasible? Or does Levinas remain steeped in
the tradition of transcendental thought, however formally and infinitely
as well as concretely and intersubjectively transformed?

The transcendental turn in phenomenology presupposes a specific ontology that can be traced back to Descartes.[9] Levinas at one point states
that he is working in a way that resembles the transcendental method but
need not necessarily constitute transcendental idealism (see *TI* 25 / xiii).
The lines of demarcation are drawn more sharply in his late work. The
question concerning the foundations of knowledge and action, he emphasizes there, finally involves a Greek optics and concerns an interest in the
architectonics of reality. The question of the unmoving, of the absolute
ground of Being, concerns "rest *par excellence*" (*GCM* 88 / 141). Indeed,
Levinas claims, "the very idea of ultimate or primary sense . . . is onto-

---

9. See Herman Philipse, *De fundering van de logica in Husserls "Logische Untersuchungen"*
(Leiden: H. Philipse, 1983), 153 ff.

logical" (*OB* 68 / 86), and skepticism "contests the thesis that between the saying and the said the relationship that connects in synchrony a condition with the conditioned is repeated" (*OB* 168 / 213).

For Levinas's purposes, then, the term *transcendental* can be maintained only if it signifies nothing more than a "certain priority," only that "ethics is *before* ontology" (*GCM* 90 / 143, my emph.). In other words, it concerns "a transcendentalism that begins with ethics" (*GCM* 90 / 143). But is the idea of the transcendental not thereby condemned to "death by a thousand qualifications," stripped of its historical meaning and of all conceptual determination?[10] If one accepts this objection, the same holds for all other concepts that Levinas takes from the tradition and attempts from within to release from their boundaries: the subject, intentionality, discourse, saying, and so on. Ontological concepts dissolve in a process of interpretation in which they are forced to refer to "metaphysics" or to "ethics" (terms whose "Greek" connotations he treats with increasing suspicion). But the reason for this need for immanent critique and internal displacement of concepts is easy to understand: it is simply that no other criteria for transcendent, external critique are readily available for any thinking worthy of the name: "There is nothing to be done: philosophy is spoken in Greek" (*GCM* 85 / 137).

This must also be Levinas's answer to Derrida's question "Why is it necessary still to use the word 'exteriority' (which, if it has a meaning, if it is not an algebraic *X*, obstinately beckons toward space and light) in order to signify a nonspatial relationship?"[11] Levinas's use of the word *exteriority*, Derrida suggests, "tears apart, by the superlative excess, the spatial literality of the metaphor."[12] According to him, we are not confronted here with an incidental or avoidable *inconsequence* but, rather, with a philosophical necessity, namely, philosophy's need "of installing itself in traditional conceptuality in order to destroy it."[13] Nevertheless, it becomes clear at the same time that Levinas's re-founding or, better, de-limitation of Western metaphysics, of its ontology no less than its onto-theology, of its dialectic and its transcendentalism, thus comes, *at least in part*, from an "indestructible and unforeseeable resource of the Greek logos" itself.[14]

10. Goud, *Levinas en Barth*, 186. See Anthony Flew, "Theology and Falsification," in *The Philosophy of Religion*, ed. Basil Mitchell (Oxford: Oxford University Press, 1979), 13–15.

11. Derrida, *Writing and Difference*, 112 / 165.

12. Ibid., 93 / 139.

13. Ibid., 112 / 165.

14. Ibid.

Indiscretion with regard to the other is unavoidable in philosophy, given that philosophy begins with a "treacherous" thematization: "Everything shows itself at the price of this betrayal, even the unsayable. In this betrayal the indiscretion with regard to the unsayable, which is probably the very task of philosophy, becomes possible" (*OB* 7 / 8). At the same time, Levinas sees dormant in the medium of philosophical leveling, which can never be conclusive or definitive, a possibility of turning the fixation on coherent discourse — and thereby all reification, idolatry, and blasphemy — back toward ethical saying: "in a said everything is conveyed before us, even the ineffable, at the price of a betrayal which philosophy is called upon to reduce" (*OB* 162 / 206). He legitimates this conception of philosophy — a *pendular movement between thematization and de-thematization* — by referring to the model of skepticism, which follows the philosophical tradition like its shadow: "The said has to be reduced to the signification of saying, giving it over to the philosophical said, which also has to be reduced. Truth is in several times, here again like breathing, a diachrony without synthesis which the fate of skepticism refuted and returning, a bastard child of philosophical research, suggests, and which it encourages" (*OB* 183 / 231). Skepticism — including its scandal, the aporia of its performative contradiction — is thus unavoidable, even though it cannot and should not have the last word. Its interruption is interrupted in turn, by the pluralism of a truth that resonates "in several times," in the alternation of the saying and the said, indeed, in the interstices and *entretemps* of their diametrical opposition: *tertium datur*.

The entire Western rational tradition, Levinas claims, is characterized by the attempt to refute skepticism, along with any true transcendence (*OB* 168 / 214). Thus, for example, in *Logical Investigations* Husserl reproaches skepticism for *in actu* confirming what it *in thesi* seeks to refute.[15] Similarly, like skepticism of any provenance, Levinas's paradoxical figure of thought gives the vertiginous impression that his philosophizing brings

---

15. De Boer, *Tussen filosofie en profetie*, 109. See *TIH* 46–49, 58, 144–45, 197–98, 220, in which Levinas accepts Husserl's refutation of skepticism, notably in the first volume of the *Logical Investigations* and in the second part of "Philosophie als strenge Wissenschaft" ("Philosophy as a Rigorous Science"). But the refutation, Levinas makes clear, triumphs over a dogmatic Cartesian conception of being: "for if one admits that that existing means to exist as things do [*à la manière de la chose*], then one is forced to admit that such existence is always problematic" (58). Levinas also points out that skepticism is not necessarily "anti-intellectualist" (220 n. 2). As Husserl had shown in his rebuttal of psychologism, skepticism is "the absurd" as it becomes total: "absolute scepticism is contradictory" (144–45). But Husserl's refutation also remains "formal" (197).

out about "*in actu exercito*" precisely what, "according to his theses, ought to be impossible."[16] This is what the accusation of performative contradiction, so often leveled at Adorno by Habermas and his students, entails.

Levinas responds by referring to the alternation and oscillation that plays itself out between the saying and the said. These modes — prediscursive address or expression, on the one hand, and conceptual or argumentative articulation, on the other — are temporally and linguistically distinct moments in a dialectic that cannot be concluded or yield any result, a dialectic that escapes and undoes all closure and, in that sense, remains "negative" just as much as it continues to "affirm" (or, as Derrida would say, "af-firm") the other in a nonthetic way. Neither negative or affirmative (or, what comes down to the same, at once negative and affirmative) in the limited — that is, traditional, modern, logical, or propositional — sense of these terms, Levinas's writing proceeds by way of apposition, parataxis, substitution, and seriature. In this it echoes or mimics the rhythm of skepticism, without adopting any of its supposedly inescapable ontological, epistemological, or axiological conclusions:

> Skepticism, which traverses the rationality or logic of knowledge, is a refusal to synchronize the implicit affirmation contained in saying and the negation which this affirmation states in the said. The contradiction is visible to reflection, which refutes it, but skepticism is insensitive to the refutation, as though the affirmation and negation did not resound in the same time . . . since for Western philosophy the saying is exhausted in things said. But skepticism in fact makes a difference, and puts an interval between saying and the said. Skepticism is *refutable,* but it returns [*Le Scepticisme est le* réfutable, *mais aussi le revenant*]. (*OB* 167–68 / 213)

The ghost (*le revenant*) of skepticism thus accompanies philosophical discourse as an inescapable shadow, as its excluded third, defying the principle of identity or noncontradiction and, hence, the logic of argumentation:

> Skepticism . . . does not hesitate to affirm the impossibility of statement while venturing to *realize* this impossibility by the very statement of this impossibility. If, after the innumerable "irrefutable" refutations which logical thought sets against it, skepticism has the gall to return (and it always returns as philosophy's illegitimate child), it is because in the contradiction which logic sees in it the "at the same time" of the contradictories is missing, because a

16. Strasser, "Ethik als Erste Philosophie," 252.

secret diachrony commands this ambiguous or enigmatic way of speaking, and because in general signification signifies beyond synchrony, beyond essence. (*OB* 7 / 9)

The way in which Levinas evokes the motif of "substitution" in the central chapter of *Otherwise than Being* can serve as an example to illustrate this point. In this motif Levinas does not provide an alternative theory of subjectivity, not even of the *sub-jectum,* but instead offers a more paradoxical, indeed aporetic, gesture toward an "in-condition" whose "modality" can no longer be given within — or be protected from — the categories handed down by tradition, starting with the notion of "being": "One could be tempted to take substitution to be the being of the entity that is the ego. And, to be sure, the hither side of the ego lends itself to our speaking only by referring to being, from which it withdraws and which it undoes. The said of language always says being. But in the moment of an enigma language also breaks with its own conditions, as in a skeptical saying, and says a signification before the event, a before-being" (*OB* 196 n. 20 / 149 n. 20).

If one restricts language to its traditional semantic or modern semiotic — that is, differential — organization, if one bases it on its formal-pragmatic structures, an aporia clearly results. Such an aporia is inevitable in theoretical discourse, which can never entirely escape its logocentric heritage. One might, of course, object that Levinas could have simply avoided this predicament had he expressed his observations outside of the mediating organon of philosophical discourse, perhaps in the peaceful medium of a fully immediate — a heterological, purely expressive, or appellative — ethical language. But where the consonance between the other and the same is concerned, we are dealing with a "peace between planes which, as soon as they are thematized, make an irreparable cleavage" (*OB* 70 / 88). In consequence Levinas's core problem poses itself in different terms: "There is, it is true, no Saying that is not the Saying of a *Said.* But does the *Saying* signify nothing but the *Said*?" (*OS* 141 / 210)? In other words, Levinas does "not deny that philosophy is a knowledge, insofar as it names even what is not nameable, and thematizes what is not thematizable. But in thus giving to what breaks with the categories of discourse the form of the *said,* perhaps it impresses onto the said the traces of this rupture" (*EI* 107–8 / 104).

Skepticism bears witness to "the rupture, failure, impotence or impossibility of discourse" (*OB* 168 / 214), that is to say, of the said. But this intrinsic limitation — or, conversely, infinition — of linguistic expression is not a peculiar feature that emerges in matters of epistemology or axiology. It is the structure of the everyday and the ordinary as such: "Language is already skepticism" (*OB* 170 / 216). Already in *Totality and Infinity* Levinas speaks of the "essence of language, which consists in continually undoing its phrase by the foreword or the exegesis, in unsaying the said, in attempting to restate without ceremonies what has *already* been ill understood in the *inevitable* ceremonial in which the said delights" (*TI* 30 / xviii, my emph.). Language, including even prophetic speech, is incapable of comprehending in its own terms its own origin and goal, that is to say, of presenting them without revoking and contradicting them at the same time. This failure is no accident but belongs to the structure and possibility of language, communication, and expression as such: "The return of skepticism, despite the refutation that puts its thesis into contradiction with the conditions for any thesis, would be pure nonsense if everything in time were recallable" (*OB* 171 / 217).

This does not amount to advocating the *theoretical* position, if there is one, of skepticism, because Levinas agrees only with its implied *gesture* of questioning: "Skepticism is not an arbitrary contestation, it is a doctrine of trial and examination, although irreducible to the scientific type of examination" (*GCM* 197–98 n. 8 / 102 n. 3).[17] This primacy of the question, to cite a motif that Gadamer's philosophical hermeneutics develops in an exemplary fashion, can scarcely be classified as an affirmative-dialectical relation to an answer, on the model of the Platonic dialogue between the soul and itself.[18] If, by contrast, we understand that the question can no longer be interpreted as a modality of the theoretical, we can see why it must forever defer any definitive result. In Levinas's words: "'God *found*' is still expressed [*se dit*] as God *sought*" (*GCM* 85 / 136; see also 11–12, 119–20 / 174, 185–86). The question has the final word (see *EI* 23 / 13).

To interpret skepticism by referring to the temporal and modal difference between the saying and the said and by emphasizing the interrogative gesture within discourse offers a possible solution to the problem, the perceived scandal, of performative contradiction. More precisely, it helps to correct its one-sided — indeed, one-dimensional — interpretation of performative contradiction as a failure within philosophical discourse that

17. See also Avital Ronell, *The Test Drive* (Urbana: University of Illinois Press), 2004.

18. See *GCM* 107 / 168; and Gadamer's comments on the priority of the question and on the dialectics of question and answer in *Truth and Method*, 325 ff. / 344 ff.

could be avoided. It confirms, moreover, the basic intuition of Adorno's negative dialectics: that only confrontation with the nonidentical, which it cannot appropriate without violence, can motivate thinking. This thinking is dialectical because in it the prediscursive *and* the discursive play constitutive roles in rational thought, action, judgment, and expression. From the perspective of theoretical discourse such a figure of thought — alternating or in permanent oscillation between two perspectives, which both presuppose (or solicit) and exclude (or undo) each other — necessarily remains aporetic. But this aporetics permeates the entire corpus of the Western tradition: "The philosophy that has been handed down to us could not fail to name the paradox of this non-ontological significance; even though, immediately, it turned back to being as to the ultimate foundation of the reason it named" (*GCM* 119 / 184–85).

ALTHOUGH HERE AND THERE Levinas appears to use terms such as *dialectics* and *negativity* in a positive sense, in general he denies these categories any orientation toward genuine transcendence: "Exteriority is not negation, but a wonder" (*TI* 292 / 269; see also *TI* 41–42 / 11- 12). "In spite of its restlessness" (*GCM* 32 / 61), dialectics finally does not escape the realm of the self-same: "The negation that claims to deny being is still, in its opposition, a position on a terrain upon which it is based. Negation carries with it the dust of being that it rejects. This reference of the negation to the positive in the contradiction is the great discovery of Hegel, who would be the philosopher of the positivity that is stronger than negativity" (*GCM* 113 / 177; see also 138–40 / 215–16; and *OB* 8–9 / 9–10).

We might nevertheless ask whether, between the order of the self-same and the disorder — the being out of order, *hors sujet* — of the trace of the other, a similar dialectical relation, one that is, in a sense, both positive and negative, may not reside. Levinas writes of the ethical event: "It is the breaking point, but also the binding place" (*OB* 12 / 15). How, then, should we interpret the knotting or linking together of these two orders and the perspectives they imply? The transition between them can never be mastered conceptually, but it is not therefore merely intuitive, that is to say, irrational.

It is difficult to resist the impression that in Levinas's work the two extremes of the *tertium datur* — the *il y a* and the ab-solute transcendence of the other, horror and the sublime — are two poles in an open mode of thinking, experiencing, and expression which resists the common concept of dialectics simply because it can never come to rest in any conceptual synthesis. Yet the supposed or intended result of any idealistically or materialistically conceivable sublation—in Derrida's words: "*the* concept of history and of teleology,"[19] which ought, according to Levinas, to be avoided—is not necessarily inherent in the idea of dialectics itself. Not only do Adorno's complex determinations of *negative* dialectics reveal the possibility of retrieving this method in light of a perceived "ontology of the false state of affairs [*Ontologie des falschen Zustandes*]," but the beginnings of an open dialectics can be found in nonconceptual experiences such as those conveyed by modern literature and poetics: "Proust's most profound teaching—if indeed poetry teaches—consists in situating the real in relation with what for ever remains other—with the other as absence and mystery. It consists in rediscovering this relation also within the very intimacy of the *I* and in inaugurating *a dialectic that breaks definitively with Parmenides*" (*NP* 104–5 / 155–56, my emph.). This break already announces itself in the first attempts to think the idea of the infinite in its full rigor, in the Cartesian notion of perfection, in the thinking that thinks more than it can contain: "To affirm the presence in us of the idea of infinity is to deem purely abstract and formal the contradiction the idea of metaphysics is said to harbor, which Plato brings up in the *Parmenides*— that the relation with the Absolute would render the Absolute relative" (*TI* 50 / 21).

Via Eminentiae

In addition to the phenomenological (or perhaps Kantian) reduction of ontology, leading it back to an other or Other (*its* other) which would ground it, Levinas allows for a second, even more remarkable manner of proceeding which would justify ideas with the help of other ideas: "to pass from one idea to its superlative. . . . You see that a new idea—in no way implicated in the first—flows, or emanates, from the overbid. The new idea finds itself justified not on the *basis* of the first, but by its sublimation" (*GCM* 88–89 / 141–42). Not only the revocation and intermittent suspension of ontological categories, therefore, but also their exaggeration can now be brought into play. As de Boer rightly notes, "in the later writings of Levinas, . . . there is also a 'way up'—not a reductive way or method but a productive one. Here the metaphysical relation to the other (which is the terminus of the first way) is the point of departure."[20] In Levinas's own

19. Derrida, *Of Grammatology,* 25 / 40.

20. See de Boer, "Ethical Transcendental Philosophy," in Cohen, *Face to Face with Levinas,* 102.

terms: "It is the superlative, more than the negation of categories, which interrupts systems, as though the logical order and the being it succeeds in espousing retained the superlative which exceeds them. In subjectivity the superlative is the exorbitance of a null-site, in caresses and in sexuality the 'excess' of tangency—as though tangency admitted a gradation—up to contact with the entrails, a skin going under another skin" (*OB* 187 n. 5 / 8 n. 4).[21]

Ethics is thus not a superstructure that one layers onto ontology and thus places above it; ethics is, so to speak, "more ontological than ontology; more *sublime* than ontology" (*GCM* 90 / 143). The reverse movement of "sublimation" and hyperbole appears as well. Thus, the "ill at ease in one's own skin" of the self made responsible to the point of substitution is described in terms of "a materiality more material than all matter—a materiality such that irritability, susceptibility or exposedness to wounds and outrage characterizes its passivity, more passive still than the passivity of effects" (*OB* 108 / 137). De Boer sees in such motifs a kind of "ontodicy," though it remains doubtful whether or to what extent this second, alternative way would avoid the aporias of the first. If it does, that can be only at the cost of yet another *petitio principii*.

In *Otherwise than Being* Levinas investigates the possibilities of an ethical language. In this text he takes up the classical *via eminentiae* (also mentioned in *GCM* 89 / 142). Thus, he speaks of the procedure of "emphasis [*emphase*]," of a nonargumentative, rhetorical figure, of a possibility for language to push to excess its potential for meaning and thus express itself exorbitantly, in what could be called an "exaltation of language" (*OB* 181 / 228). As I have repeatedly remarked, Levinas constantly employs metaphors and rhetorical figures of speech,[22] although at times (notably in *Totality and Infinity*) he condemns rhetoric as a whole. Not until the late work, however, does he speak directly of an undoing of the bounds of the said "by a rhetoric which is not only a linguistic mirage, but a surplus of meaning of which consciousness all by itself would be incapable" (*OB* 152 / 194). There Levinas uses the metaphor of "hyperbole," in which ontological notions can be transformed into ethical ones: "Emphasis signifies at the same time a figure of rhetoric, an excess of expression, a manner of

21. The metaphorics of the erotic is worth noting here. From *Time and the Other* to *Totality and Infinity*, in Levinas's work erotics and fecundity are a privileged model for the movement of transcendence. In his later writings he increasingly abandons this mediation via naturalness and the metaphysical.

22. See Derrida, *Writing and Difference*, 312 n. 7 / 124 n. 1; and *TI* 70–72, 180 / 42–44, 155.

overstating oneself, and a manner of showing oneself. . . . there are hyper-
boles whereby notions are transmuted. To describe this mutation is also
to do phenomenology. Exasperation as a method of philosophy!" (*GCM*
89 / 142; see also *OB* 183 / 231).

In this attempt at a nearly "baroque" style,[23] might one not discern
a parallel to the role that rhetoric and the speculative element play in
Adorno's writings? As in the chapters I have devoted to negative dialectics and its micrological devices, I might reiterate the question that has
occupied me throughout: what, exactly, is the philosophical status of a
thinking that wants to express (itself) through "overdetermination [*sur-
détermination*]" (*OB* 115 / 146; see also 193 n. 35, 120 / 120 n. 35, 154–55), that
is to say, through motifs and significations that do not allow themselves to
be said discursively and which thus offer no alternative than to, quite literally, *circum*scribe them? Should we regard this path as an alternative to
philosophical discourse? If not, how does its procedure relate to the path
of conceptual analysis and argumentative demonstration? If it concerns
a more singular, if not necessarily idiosyncratic, course, can an ethical-
rhetorical language travel along that route? Does such an approach admit
the expression of ab-solute alterity, or does it simply gesture toward an
impossible revolt against the conceptuality inherent in all language and,
perhaps, in all experience, in every "given"?

Levinas is aware of the difficulties of the undertaking that these questions suggest. As in the earlier reference to the writing of Proust, he observes that one can take prose one step farther: "One should have to go all
the way to the nihilism of Nietzsche's poetic writing, reversing irreversible
time in vortices, to the laughter which refuses language" (*OB* 8 / 10). Such
a poetic language might very well be the best instance of the prophetic,
not least because, for all its seeming arbitrariness, it stems from sincerity
(see *HAH* 100).

Because Levinas views the moral-religious relation to the other as a
privileged situation in which what presents itself from the ontological
perspective as being completely heterogeneous, speculative, or fictitious
occurs instead in an effortless "unity," the "tropes" of ethical language,
toward which the *via eminentiae* moves, might seem "closer to the adequate language" (*GCM* 89 / 143; see also *OB* 121 / 155). Indeed, Levinas
writes, it is "in the ethical situation that . . . a certain unity is achieved. This
is the unity of what remains disparate, or seems constructed or dialectical,

---

23. Strasser, *Jensseits von Sein und Zeit*, 219.

in the ontological statement which, moreover, must struggle against the ontic forms of all language" (*GCM* 88 / 140). But things are more complicated, and Levinas's view is not Ricoeur's. The "unity" in question is not the "discordant concordance" of which Ricoeur speaks in writing of "narrative identity" and "ipseity" or "attestation" in *Temps et récit* (*Time and Narrative*) and *Oneself as Another*.

Insofar as the language of exaltation, emphasis, and the superlative involves a certain reduction of onto-theological language, like philosophical discourse it must continually be revoked, because here, too, there can be no definitive formulations, no fully appropriate evocations and appellations. The supposedly more direct method of the *via eminentiae* — ethical language, in a word — remains dependent upon a *via negationis* and, in consequence, cannot on its own initiative lead the way out of aporia, out of the alternation or oscillation between the saying and the said. In Levinas's words it remains contingent upon the ontological correction of ontic reification as well as upon the reduction of its *epochē*: "the range [*portée*] . . . or the context of this language is inseparable from this progression [*marche*] starting out from [*à partir de*] ontology" (*GCM* 88 / 141). If it is correct that the rhetorical path concerns the attempt "to *bend* the founding and examination of ontology into a transcending thinking" in order to make possible the "uncovering of a more genuine ground or abyss,"[24] then the rhetorician/philosopher cannot help but undertake a *determinate negation* of the conceptuality of the tradition. In its very logic of excess and hyperbole, however, the rhetorical path must travel back through the sedimentations and genealogies of historical terminology, of categories and modalities, forms of perception and argumentation, and so on. Here, too, the transascendence and transdescendence of thinking and (its) experience go hand in hand.

This being said, it remains revealing that Levinas attempts to explain the inconclusive character of the classical refutation of skepticism through an in-depth investigation of poetic language. He claims, in a short essay with the title "Façon de parler" ("Manner of Speaking"), that poetic thinking is a kind of "negation" of the Logos, which, because of its indissoluble connection with the immediacy of saying, no distanced reflection can grasp. One must ask, Levinas says, "whether poetic thinking and speaking, notably, are not precisely strong enough or devoted enough

---

24. Adriaan Peperzak, review of Levinas's *Otherwise than Being*, in *Philosophische Rundschau* 24 (1977): 116.

to their kerygma, and sufficiently unimpeachable to prevent this turning back of reflection or to refuse to listen to its contradiction; whether poetry is not defined precisely by this perfect uprightness [*droiture*] and by this urgency" (*GCM* 179 / 267).[25] With differing intentions prophetic *and* poetic forms of speaking make it plausible that language as such can be the revocation of the said and at the same time — and in spite of this quasi-skeptical gesture or, more precisely, thanks to it — in its saying make perceptible a "positive," or an "affirmative," ethical gesture: "Language would exceed the limits of what is thought, by suggesting, letting be understood without ever making understandable, an implication of a meaning distinct from that which comes to signs from the simultaneity of systems of the logical definition of concepts. This possibility is laid bare in the poetic said, and the interpretation it calls for ad infinitum. It is shown in the prophetic said, scorning its conditions in a sort of levitation" (*OB* 169–70 / 215–16).

Of course, poetry cannot simply remove the aporias of philosophical discourse, because poetic speech itself produces a particular diachrony that conceptual analysis, argumentative reconstruction, and, in short, reflection can render only surreptitiously.[26] Poetry, too, must "recount how infinity is produced" (*TI* 26 / xiv), must constantly tell anew an unsayable, an infinite that is at the same time constituted as untellable (i.e., "unnarratable [*inénarrable*]" [*OB* 166 / 211]).

But in Levinas's eyes the question of whether poetry can *reduce* rhetoric, as philosophy does in the order of the said, remains open: "does poetry succeed in reducing the rhetoric?" (*OB* 182 / 230). How can truth (and the ethical uprightness that motivates the quest for truth) shield one against eloquence (see *OS* 137 / 206)? If I understand correctly, these concerns interfere with Levinas's willingness to engage art and aesthetics critically and give rise to three conclusions that underlie his evaluation of art and the aesthetic (which I have analyzed in chap. 8).

First, as we have seen, Levinas opposes to the magic of poetic rhythm the unambiguousness and prosaicism of ethical language (see *TI* 138 / 177). Second, in a late essay, "Langage quotidien et rhétorique sans éloquence" ("Everyday Language and Rhetoric without Eloquence"), he situates the connection between the beautiful and the good in the everyday language

25. See also Goud, "Wat men van zichzelf eist," 84 ff. He recalls that Levinas at times appropriates Nietzsche's writing style.

26. See Jean Greisch, "*Zeitgehöft* und *Anwesen:* La Dia-chronie du poème," in *Contre-jour: Etudes sur Paul Celan*, ed. Martine Broda, Colloque de Cérisy (Paris: Cerf, 1986), 171, 176 ff.

of the life-world, which, though it feeds on a *metaphora continua* of ordinary language, can set bounds to eloquence, which is always distinct from it (*OS* 142 / 211). Third, every poetically or, more broadly, aesthetically inflected expression remains — as in Adorno — dependent upon a critical, philosophical interpretation or upon unending exegesis.[27] This is because all rhetoric or, more generally, all art always carries within it the possibilities of both utopia and myth. In rhetoric and art there "is a *possibility both of ideology and of sacred delirium:* ideology to be circumvented by linguistics, sociology and psychology, delirium to be reduced by philosophy" (*OB* 152 / 194, my emph.). Philosophy and rhetoric, ethics and art, are thus, in Levinas, the mirror image antipodes of a broken and risky but nonetheless complementary relation. They revolve around each other in an open-ended, mutually corrective movement whose alternation or oscillation we could describe in various vocabularies: from a negative metaphysics or negative dialectics, though also, with reference to hidden implications of phenomenology and intentional analysis, to the performative contradiction of skepticism, which formal pragmatics can lay bare yet unavoidably reiterates in its own refutations, and, last but not least, to deconstruction, in the sense Derrida has given to this term.

Herme(neu)tics of the Trace

Verbal expression of the dimension this side of and beyond ontology need not, according to Levinas, be completely contained in the conditions for the said. It can profit from a structural ambiguity, an enigmatic quality, which pertains to every truly absolute (in Levinas's view, ethical) meaning: "the saying, in its power of equivocation, that is, in the enigma whose secret it keeps, escapes the epos of essence that includes it and signifies beyond in a signification that *hesitates* between this beyond and the return to the epos of essence" (*OB* 9–10 / 11, my emph.). We are dealing with a "new modality which is expressed by that 'if one likes' and that 'perhaps,' which one must not reduce to the possibility, reality, and necessity of formal logic, to which skepticism itself refers" (*CPP* 67/ *DEHH* 209). Yet, even if the moral dimension is thus withdrawn from the rational sequence of meanings, it does not become meaningless. Transcendence appears only as an enigma, as a trace.

This figure suggests means of (formal) indication and (rigid) designa-

---

27. This is suggested primarily by the early essay "Reality and Its Shadow" (RS 13–14 / 142 / 788). See also Wiemer, *Passion des Sagens*, 430.

tion other than the *referential*, whereby a sign refers to a state of affairs, or the *differential*, whereby a sign is determined by its place value within a system of mutual relations between phonemes and graphemes.[28] The trace cannot be thought within a semantic or semiotic theory of meaning — and perhaps cannot be thought and said (experienced, expressed, acted upon) at all.

For Levinas the trace, enigma, and ambiguity all hint at a modality of transcendence which is essential in a world that has come to know good reasons for atheism and therefore can no longer believe in any single form of the presence of the absolute: "This truth is irreducible to phenomena, and is hence essential in a world which can no longer believe that the books about God attest to transcendence as a phenomenon and to the Absolute as an apparition. And without good reasons atheism brings forth, there would have been no Enigma" (*CPP* 67 / *DEHH* 209).

With this notion ("Enigma") Levinas clarifies the in principle ambiguous modality of the infinite, which maintains itself in the middle between the traditional determinations of presence and absence: "The infinite then cannot be tracked down like game by a hunter. The trace left by the infinite is not the residue of a presence; its very glow is ambiguous. Otherwise, its positivity would not preserve the infinity of the infinite any more than negativity would" (*OB* 12 / 15). The Other (or other) gives himself only *incognito*. The other is a "disturbance" that "insinuates itself [or slips in, *s'insinue*], withdraws before entering. It remains only for whoever wishes to take it up. Otherwise, it has already restored the order it troubled" (*CPP* 66 / *DEHH* 208). Thus, the call and enigma of the Other always appeals to our *judgment*. It is up to us to decide, even though no such decision finds its origin — or initiative — in us:

> Someone rang, and there is no one at the door: did anyone ring? Language is the possibility of an enigmatic equivocation *for better and for worse*, which men abuse. One diplomat makes an exorbitant proposition to another diplomat, but this proposition is put in terms such that, if one likes, nothing has been said. The audacity withdraws and is extinguished in the very words that bear and inflame it. . . . A lover makes an advance, but the provocative or seductive gesture has, if one likes, not interrupted the decency of the conversation and attitudes; it withdraws as lightly as it had slipped in. A God was revealed on a mountain or in a burning bush, or was attested to in Scriptures.

---

28. See *TI* 91–92 / 64–65; and de Boer, *Tussen Filosofie en Profetie*, 103.

And what if it were a storm! And what if the Scriptures came to us from dream-
ers! Dismiss the illusory call from our minds! The insinuation itself invites us
to do so. It is up to us, or, more exactly, it is up to *me* to retain or to repel
this God without boldness, exiled because allied with the conquered, hunted
down and hence absolute, thus disarticulating the very moment in which he
is presented and proclaimed, un-representable. (*CPP* 66 / *DEHH* 208, trans.
modified; my emph.)

With the poststructuralist critique of "logocentrism" (especially the
thinking of Derrida and, more indirectly, Lacan) Levinas shares the insight that the trace does not point toward a sphere lying available somewhere and only awaiting the illumination of a concept. The trace betrays
an unsublatable, unbridgeable, and permanent difference between any
discourse, any poetics, and the "reality" it attempts to grasp or express.

Echo is the modality of this transcendence; we are dealing with the
"metaphor of a sound that would be audible only in its echo" (*OB* 106 /
134), or, more precisely, with "the echo of a sound that would precede
the resonance of this sound" (*OB* 111 / 141). That this transcendence can
"adequately" or "appropriately" be put into words only in an indirect or
surreptitious way ought not to be misunderstood as a weakness of thought
(*OB* 156 / 199). Levinas never draws the consequence that philosophical
thinking—like any other discourse, whether argumentative, rhetorical, or
poetic—can therefore only be idolatrous and blasphemous. The trace, in
his view, is not an irrational or absurdist motif, yet, as Derrida notes, "the
word [*trace*] can emerge only as a *metaphor whose philosophical elucidation
will ceaselessly call upon 'contradictions.'*"[29]

IN TAKING PHENOMENOLOGY as his methodological starting point, and
in taking it beyond its bounds, Levinas not only attempts to avert the
dangers of psychologism, historicism, or naturalism (of which logocentrism is at times a variety). He also aims to explore and express "a third
condition or the unconditionality of an excluded middle" (*OB* 183–84 /
231). The figure or "metaphor" of the trace does not belong to phenomenology properly speaking, nor can it be reified in any image that would

29. Derrida, *Writing and Difference,* 129 / 190, my emph. In Levinas's view the trace is,
nevertheless, not a metaphor (see *DEHH* 210; *HAH* 21 ff.; *OB* 57 / 73). Conversely, he speaks of
"atomic metaphors" (*GCM* 72 / 119) and claims "the 'movement' beyond is the metaphor and
emphasis themselves" (*GCM* 105 / 166). For Levinas's critique of the symbol, see *TI* 176, 181 /
151, 156.

exceed the parameters of its theory of intuition. In this sense the trace is finally incommensurable with thinking and experience, both as phenomenologically and, perhaps, as more broadly defined (*OB* 99–100 / 126). Only in its alternating and oscillating movement of intermittent interference can it in any way be perceived or sensed, in ways that are indirect, whether negative or superlative: as the performative contradiction of all words and categories, all sayings and saids by which thought, experience, action, and judgment can articulate and express themselves. The trace would thus signal itself *in obliquo* or *in excess:* that is to say, either minimally or maximally, hyperbolically, superlatively — or both at once. Either way, its *tertium datur* cannot be rendered conceptually, argumentatively, or coherently.

Do the ideas of the trace, enigma, and ambiguity offer Levinas the possibility of escaping or loosening up a more or less one-dimensional — a logocentric — conception of language? As we have seen, many scholars believe that such a modification of the linguistic apparatus of philosophy cannot be detected in most of Adorno's observations on language (despite the equally undeniable fact that his work grants the figure of the trace a decisive role, although one that emerges far more episodically than is the case in Levinas). Does the figure of the trace, which, in his late work, seems to help Levinas avoid the methodological bottlenecks of the tradition — with its binarisms of presence and absence, the said and the unsaid, semantics (or semiotics) and rhetoric (or poetics) — actually offer the desired way out?

In *Totality and Infinity* Levinas had spoken of an "anarchy essential to multiplicity" (*TI* 294 / 270). The coherence of language in general and of discourse in particular is owing, Levinas claims in his later writings (again, in surprising proximity to the Marxist tradition as well as to Foucault, the two instances of cultural critique which now seem to him most pertinent), to an alliance between the state, the clinic, and instances of discipline, which must exclude any subversion (see *OB* 170 / 216). Skepticism as a figure of thinking rebels against this in a subtle way, in a seemingly anarchical, if not necessarily anarchist, politics of language of its own: "The permanent return of skepticism does not so much signify the possible breakup of structures as the fact that they are not the ultimate framework of meaning, that for their accord repression can already be necessary. It reminds us of the, in a very broad sense, political character of all logical rationalism, the alliance of logic with politics" (*OB* 171 / 217). In a remarkable Adornian twist, the violence of identification, indeed, of all conceptualization, categorization, classification, and archivization, is not so much (or not simply) attributed to the workings of language—that is to say, to the imposed correspondence or supposed attunement of words and things or object—as such but to the way in which, in determinate socio-historical or politico-juridical contexts, these linguistic and experiential structures may become repressed and, hence, end up being repressive in turn. This is not to say that the pragmatics of linguistic communication is in principle neutral—or that such neutrality would be without violence—but only that it is predisposed toward its own abuse. An elective affinity, as Max Weber knew—an isomorphy, Adorno might add—governs the rapport between (the use of) words and the most totalizing and normativizing orders of the said, between our everyday coping with things and the most alienating aspects of reification. This correspondence becomes fatal only under certain empirically induced conditions.

Nevertheless, this violence that is historically always possible—even some violent nonviolence—is necessary for mediating and negotiating the relationship to the third and, hence, for distributing justice: "That the *saying* must bear a *said* is a necessity of the same order as that which imposes a society with laws, institutions, and social relations" (*EI* 88 / 82). In other words, with one and the same gesture "philosophy justifies and criticizes the laws of being and of the city" (*OB* 165 / 210). Moreover, Levinas suggests, the order of discourse (science, state, system, etc.) and light protects us from falling back into even worse conditions, namely, the diffuse power of silence and the night. Derrida thus aptly summarizes a view that, at least in the later writings, is fundamentally Levinas's own: "If light is the element of violence, one must combat light with a certain other light, in order to avoid the worst violence of the night which precedes or represses discourse"; thus, metaphysics is thinkable and effective only as a kind of "economy," that of "violence against violence."[30]

Levinas finds himself compelled to take part in a discourse that seems in advance to contradict or betray his appeal (*OB* 156–57 / 198–99), or is at least predisposed to do so, depending on historical and empirical context. Yet precisely in this inevitable or likely discursive "foundering" resides a secret "success," because, where discourse names the unnamable, the unsayable leaves its indelible trace—precisely in being said, rendered, and betrayed. Levinas suggests as much when he writes: "Does not the

---

30. Derrida, *Writing and Difference*, 117 / 172. For a more extensive analysis, see my book *Religion and Violence*, chap. 2.

discourse that suppresses the interruptions of discourse by relating them maintain the discontinuity under the *knots* with which the thread is tied again?" (*OB* 170 / 216, my emph.).

In his late work Levinas "grounds" this view with reference to a motif he had already discussed in *Totality and Infinity,* namely, that a speaker or author already breaks through discourse by the simple fact that he must turn that discourse over to a listener or reader, to another whose yes or no, whose judgment and interpretation, remains external to and unanticipated by even the most comprehensive and imaginative text (albeit the most encyclopedic and adequate philosophical expression, once and for all, of Absolute Knowledge as such): "This reference to an interlocutor permanently breaks through the text that the discourse claims to weave in thematizing and enveloping all things. In totalizing being, discourse qua discourse thus belies the very claim to totalize" (*OB* 170 / 217).

Finally, the concepts of tradition and of infinite interpretation allow Levinas to "found" the continued renewal of meaning and the incessant relation to the other, respectively, in (his own) philosophical writing. As he puts it: "this account is itself without end and without continuity, that is, goes from the one to the other, is a tradition. It thereby renews itself. New meanings arise in its meaning, and their exegesis is an unfolding, or *History* before all historiography" (*OB* 169 / 215, my emph.).

Here, at least, the ethical intonation or coloring of the motif of the trace in Levinas seems to touch on the—at first—profane or historical understanding of this motif in other authors, Derrida and Ricoeur among them. Yet one can only agree with the cautious judgment Ricoeur makes at the end of his comments on Levinas's discussion of this motif. He writes that one should "hold open in reserve the open possibility that there is, in the final analysis, only a relative other [*Autre rélatif*], a historical other, if, in whatever manner, the past that is recollected as meaningful is so from an immemorial past. Perhaps it is this possibility that literature holds open when some 'tale [or fable, *fable*] of time' points toward whatever eternity. Who knows what subterranean developments attach this eternity to the infinity of the absolutely other, according to Levinas—the absolutely other of which the face of the Other person bears the trace?"[31]

In this, Levinas's primary engagement with Husserl's phenomenological method, for which—as he had already shown in his doctoral thesis—

---

31. Ricoeur, *Temps et récit,* vol. 3 (Paris: Seuil, 1985), 183 / *Time and Narrative,* vol. 3, trans. Kathleen McLaughlin and David Pellauer (Chicago: University of Chicago Press, 1988), 125.

a theory of immediate intuition is absolutely essential, makes place for a hermeneutical method of sorts: "It is of no little importance to glimpse and sense in hermeneutics with all its audacities religious life and liturgy itself" (*EI* 23 / 13–14, trans. modified). Even if the method of intentional analysis can still be put to use in moral situations, it can no longer offer any evidence beyond *my* affirmation of the description that has been provided of that "indescribable relation" (*OB* 166 / 211).[32] To the extent that there can be any narrative identity or ipseity, as Ricoeur proposes in *Oneself as Another,* it hinges on an unique gesture of "attestation," an "ici, je me tiens," whose singular instance (and temporal instant) escape phenomenological description just as they elude argumentative reconstruction and, indeed, all narratology, its imaginative variations, and the like. Within the hermeneutic a minimal hermetic thus makes us halt, pause, and — intermittently, surreptitiously — move on again.

WE CAN CONCLUDE THAT the question of the rationality of Adorno's and Levinas's philosophies can, in a certain sense, be traced back to a problem of language. The way in which, in his later texts, Levinas increasingly focuses the question concerning the relationship between ontology and metaphysics on the connection between the *said* (the objectified) and the *saying* (the initial readiness to serve or gesture toward the Other) could be interpreted not just as his contribution to the general "linguistic turn" in twentieth-century philosophy but, in particular, to the shift of thematic and methodological interest in postwar French philosophy. In its radical critique of the central concerns of existential phenomenology, all of which focused on the perceiving consciousness as it represents or imagines the world and alter egos, "poststructuralist" philosophy has brought the problems of language and meaning, speech and writing, ever more into the foreground. This reorientation of the philosophical landscape — a paradigm shift that would have been unthinkable without the influence of the very phenomenology and hermeneutics whose place it would take — involves questions of textuality, in which consciousness and conscience must be thought not primarily in terms of intentionality and agency but, rather, as an effect, as constituted rather than constitutive. Insofar as Levinas shares some of the presuppositions of poststructuralist philosophy and its skepticism about the transparency of discourse, about the subjects, predicates, and semantics of discourse, as well as its diacritical or differen-

---

32. See Goud, "Wat men van zichzelf eist," 51.

tial determination of the sign and the signified, he distances himself not only from the tradition of the dialogical philosophy of Buber and Rosenzweig but also from the French personalists and Ricoeur.

Indeed, in his later work Levinas widens the abyss between the ontological and the metaphysical-ethical dimension in that he no longer holds the intersubjectivity that establishes itself through language to be of unique validity as the unambiguous — the intelligible, transparent, principled, and sincere — realm of the Other. In the period after *Totality and Infinity* Levinas distinguishes — this time *within* the very same language or discourse, which had previously (despite his warning about the danger of rhetoric) been the "medium" of the immediacy of the Other — between the discursivity of ontology, on the one hand, and the ethical "foreword [*avant-propos*] preceding languages," on the other (*OB* 5 / 6). That enables him partially to rehabilitate rhetoric, which in the earlier work counts as strategic action in the realm of war, the pursuit of self-interest, and self-absorbed embellishment at best, while assuming a greater reserve about the order of dialogue. In other words, from now on the "ethical quality of language is no longer given with the dialogical situation as such."[33]

Only in part can this shift in emphasis be compared to the figures of thought espoused in Adorno's late work, which, as we have seen, makes explicit that the truly other cannot be brought within the order of the concept and that thus no positive concept of "enlightenment" can be formulated with the help of philosophical argument, strictly defined, but only "speculatively," in "spiritual experience," and, finally, "rhetorically," through excessive expression or "exaggeration [*Übertreibung*]."

Despite the multilayered critique of discursivity which Levinas's later philosophy shares with poststructuralism, his interests are not simply compatible with the fundamental traits of this style of thinking. Yet this claim cannot easily be substantiated with respect to an author whose work is often — and, I would claim, somewhat unjustly — associated with this phase in French thought. Derrida is in accord with Levinas's critique of Western logocentrism, even if, in "Violence and Metaphysics," he puts a much stronger emphasis on the inescapability of the horizon of metaphysics — "our language" — and the order of both empirical and transcendental violence it entails. Further, in Derrida's view the ethical concretization that gives Levinas's thought of difference its particular cast or tonality

---

33. Goud, "Über Definition und Infinition," 128; see also 138; and Goud, *Levinas en Barth*, 321 n. 228.

should be regarded only as making more precise a general philosophy of the trace of the other whose implications cannot be limited to the domain of ethics, intersubjectivity, the human, the living, and so on. As I have suggested — and as Derrida himself has indicated in later readings — Levinas's writings contain *in nuce* all the conceptual, argumentative, and rhetorical elements to push the analysis in this direction, albeit at the price of having to pit the letter against the spirit of his text.

According to de Greef, Derrida's motif of differance — "a *diachronizing* or *deferring* difference" — might help clarify the difference between the saying and the said, to which skepticism continually bears witness.[34] Here the proximity *and* distance between Levinas's and Derrida's philosophies is unmistakable. A few examples can illustrate this. Concerning passion and patience, Levinas speaks of "a waiting that awaits nothing, or hope where nothing hoped for comes to incarnate this Infinite"; a little farther, he writes: "In the deferral or the incessant differance of this pure indication, we suspect time itself, but as an incessant dia-chrony: proximity of the Infinite, this is the *forever* and the *never* of a dis-inter-estedness and of the unto-God [*l'à-Dieu*]" (*GCM* 118 / 184).

It is no accident that in his early essay Derrida holds against Levinas's work not any skeptical traits (as Habermas did with Adorno) but a minimal and perhaps absolute form of "empiricism." What does this mean? It does not escape Derrida that the emphasis on empiricism and, hence, experience in the context of Levinas's thought can easily lead one astray. Indeed, referring to how Rosenzweig — in view of the "experience" of death — turns the thinking of totality on its head, Levinas speaks of an "empiricism" that "has nothing of positivism" (*DF* 260 / 263). Although he does not rely on concepts of subjective or objective experience as they have been historically, scientifically, and culturally or aesthetically defined, he every now and again asserts that the moral relation to the wholly other can be seen as an experience "par excellence" (*TI* 25 / xiii), as a "concrete moral experience" (*TI* 53 / 24). Being absolute, this "experience" cannot be understood in the sense of a disclosure of something present or hidden: it is, rather, a "revelation" (*TI* 66 / 37, trans. modified). Moral consciousness, the event of restless conscience, Levinas writes, is an "experience that is not commensurate with any a priori framework — a conceptless experience" (*TI* 101 / 74). Does Levinas thereby reinstate the "myth of the Given"

---

34. Greef, "Skepticism and Reason," 162. See Derrida, *Writing and Difference:* "the pre-opening of the ontic-ontological difference" (198 / 295).

which in twentieth-century postanalytic philosophy was so effectively deconstructed by authors such as Sellars, Rorty, McDowell, and Brandom? Or is something else at stake here? Does Levinas answer these questions when he observes that characterizations such as the "self without concept," the identity "*in diastasis*," forgetful of itself, devouring itself with "remorse," do not rest on psychological insights? He writes: "These are not events that happen to an empirical ego, that is, to an ego already posited and fully identified, as a trial that would lead it to being more conscious of itself, and make it more apt to put itself in the place of others. What we are here calling oneself, or the other in the same, where inspiration arouses respiration, the very pneuma of the psyche, precedes this empirical order, which is a part of being, of the universe, of the State, and is already conditioned in a system" (*OB* 115–16 / 147).

As Derrida observes, "'Experience' has always designated the relationship with a presence, whether that relationship had the form of consciousness or not."[35] With regard to presence, Levinas speaks of a "welcome of the Other where, *absolutely present*, in his face, the Other—without any metaphor—faces me" (*DEHH* 186). He describes this relation without relation—that is to say, without mediation, conceptual or other, being an end to all ambiguity—as "the end of equivocation or confusion. . . . The presence of the Other dispels the anarchic sorcery of the facts" (*TI* 99 / 72). To highlight that the face or the trace does not thereby imply any correlation between meaning and what carries or enables that meaning (semantically, propositionally, dialectically, or even differentially), Levinas calls it "*irrectitude* itself" (*HAH* 59). It could be characterized as an originary donation at best, nothing more, nothing less. But would this not count as a mythical "Given" of sorts?

By introducing the term *empiricism*, Derrida aims to refer merely to Levinas's desire for a *pure access to* (and *pure expression of*) the other, whereas in his view such access (or such expression) must operate via some conceptual or even argumentative mediation of the order of the same—not least for the sake of the Other. In the terminology of Levinas's later work (not addressed in "Violence and Metaphysics") the order of saying cannot signify—and thereby betray—itself elsewhere than in the realm of the said, whose sedimentations and codification of meaning the saying reveals to be principally and structurally insufficient and whose completion or totality it declares to be unjust, blind, deaf, and insensitive to the Other.

---

35. Derrida, *Of Grammatology,* 60 / 89.

Regarding the circle in which Levinas's thinking continually threatens to be caught anew, Derrida stresses, writing of the early period: "But the true name of this inclination of thought to the Other, of this resigned acceptance of incoherent incoherence inspired by a truth more profound than the 'logic' of philosophical discourse, the true name of this renunciation of the concept, of the a prioris and transcendental horizons of language, is *empiricism*. . . . It is the *dream* of a purely *heterological* thought at its source. A *pure* thought of *pure* difference. Empiricism is its philosophical name, its metaphysical pretension or modesty. We say the *dream* because it must vanish *at daybreak,* as soon as language awakens."[36]

Does Levinas's thought thereby forfeit its philosophical character, as Derrida suggests in his early essay? If empiricism is, as Derrida says somewhat earlier, "thinking *by* metaphor without thinking the metaphor *as such*,"[37] should one not recall Levinas's claim that in welcoming the Other as a face—and, as he will come to say, as trace—we are at a loss for metaphor, just as concepts and categories, intuitions and images, fall short of its signification or, rather, signifyingness? A more cautious claim would be that Levinas's *elliptical* figure of thought does not exhaust itself in the discursive process, premised on the semantic identity of its words and terms, the propositional meaningfulness of its statements, but also on its supposed intent and persuasive purposefulness. The Levinasian model, furthermore, wishes, if not to terminate an open dialectics or a dissemination of meaning, then at least to call them back to the narrow "memory trace" of a conceptless ethical appeal (see *GCM* 13, 77–78 / 32, 127).

Upon closer examination, however, Derrida's deconstructive undertaking makes—or underlies, in its turn—a similar move, even though it initially seeks in a more formal (more consistent and, hence, more rigorous) manner to get around onto-theology, that is to say, to do so without devoting itself in advance or uncritically to a particular, possibly ethical or religious, guiding star. Yet precisely because deconstruction admittedly remains stamped by the models of metaphysical thought which it seeks to break apart, because it heeds no false expectations concerning the overcoming or closure of logocentrism and its implied onto-theology, it likewise "betrays" a moral—and, hence, even minimal theological—impulse. It must inhabit an enlightenment metaphor that it says lies "in ruins" until the moment, which may very well never come, that this heliotropic figure

36. Derrida, *Writing and Difference*, 151 / 224.
37. Ibid., 139 / 204.

can be revoked.[38] The moment deconstruction admits motifs that are historically overdetermined and singularly concrete, the questions that can be put to Levinas from Derrida's work prove to be pertinent — indeed, irrefutable — for himself as well. What Levinas writes elsewhere in his essay of Derrida, "Tout autrement" ("Wholly Otherwise"), thus seems pertinent to the two philosophical projects for which they stand: "One might be tempted to draw an argument from this recourse to logocentric language in opposing that very language, in order to question the validity of the deconstruction thus produced. That is a course that has frequently been followed in refuting skepticism; but the latter, thrown to the ground and trampled on at first, would right itself and return as philosophy's legitimate child. It is a course Derrida himself, perhaps, has not always disdained to follow in his polemics" (*NP* 58 / 85).

Of course, Derrida is correct in pointing out that the motif of the trace counteracts and corrects the "phonocentric" traits in Levinas's analyses. In *Totality and Infinity* Levinas stresses, with explicit reference to Plato's *Phaedrus* (whose central thesis forms an important point of departure for *Of Grammatology* and *Dissemination*), that only living, spoken expression — in contrast to fixed, written language — can, in principle, break through the "anarchism" of the world of appearance, premised, as it seems to be, on the diacritical function and the arbitrariness of signs but also on the enabling role of contexts, language games, and life forms, all of which render the notion of a "signification without context" unintelligible and meaningless, without effect: "in language there is accomplished the unintermittent afflux of a presence that rends the inevitable veil of its own apparition, which is plastic like every apparition. Apparition reveals and conceals; speech consists in surmounting, in a total frankness ever renewed, the dissimulation inevitable in every apparition. Thereby a sense — an orientation — is given to every phenomenon" (*TI* 98 / 71).

Something similar might be true for the saying without the said in *Otherwise than Being* because, as Levinas asserts, it should be "antecedent to the verbal signs it conjugates, to the linguistic systems and the semantic glimmerings" (*OB* 5 / 6). One might ask to what extent any sincerely moral "presence" can be assumed *before, beyond,* or in the *interstices* of the violence of articulation, of writing, and whether such "presence" can actually put an end to ambiguity without becoming entangled in its differential movement and its drift toward the an-archical. And can one still

38. Ibid., 112 / 165.

meaningfully designate that almost wordless gesture *language*?[39] Levinas suggests as much: "One enters into language as a system of signs only out of an already spoken language, which in turn cannot consist in a system of signs" (*OB* 199 n. 9 / 183 n. 9).

But is the motif of the trace not much closer to a complex intrigue of the other in the same that cannot arrive at an unambiguous foundation of meaning?[40] Did not Levinas himself once pertinently describe it as "language of the unheard, language of the unprecedented, language of the unsaid, *writing*"?[41] Is the trace not, by Levinas's own account, concerned with an "unpronounceable inscription" (*OB* 185 / 233)?[42]

The further "critique" of *Totality and Infinity*'s ethical transcendental philosophy made possible by Derrida's deconstructive thinking seems to stem from an overall theoretical interest diametrically opposed to Habermas's "overcoming" of negative dialectics by means of a proposed paradigm switch from the philosophy of consciousness to a formal-pragmatically defined concept of communicative action. Derrida holds up to Levinas not the anchor of reason in the sea of skepticism but, rather, the *groundlessness* of thought and experience, to which even ethics, including its transformation in discourse ethics (*Diskursethik*), can set no bounds. Yet Derrida shares with Habermas a seemingly *formal* optics, which moves in a different direction from the remarkable commonality that we observed between the thought of Adorno and Levinas. By contrast, the latter revolve around the experience and expression of an emphatic — now horrific, then sublime or superlative — content or *concretissimum*. Of course, Derrida's deconstruction shares only part of Habermas's concerns, that is to say, not a formal-*pragmatic* mode of thinking but merely a *quasi-transcendental* one. Not a reconstruction of communicative structures and their respective speech acts stands at the midpoint of Derrida's work but nearly the opposite: a philosophy of the trace. The lines sketched out here may help us along our way, although we should not forget that the relationship between the figures of thought of Levinas and Derrida is no

39. See ibid., 147, 114 / 219, 169.

40. "The limit between violence and nonviolence is perhaps not between speech and writing but within each of them. *The thematic of the trace . . . should lead to a certain rehabilitation of writing*" (ibid., 102 / 151, my emph.; see also 96–97, 99 / 147–48, 150).

41. Levinas, "Preface to the German Edition," *EN* 199 / 12.

42. The trace is thus, as it were, an "*avant-propos*," a "Pre-Script [*Vor-Schrift*]," as Celan puts it in the poem "Wirk nicht voraus," *Gesammelte Werke* 2:328 / "Do Not Work Ahead," in *Selected Poems and Prose of Paul Celan*, trans. John Felstiner [New York: W. W. Norton, 2001], 325).

less complicated, and attests to a proximity as rich and tense, as that between the figures of thought of Adorno and Habermas (and, increasingly, Derrida as well). In all these forms of thought a "reason before thematization . . . , a pre-original reason . . . , an anarchic reason" must be assumed (*OB* 167 / 212). It is to this motif, addressed in the opening chapter of this book, that I will now turn.

PART FOUR

Hermeneutica Sacra sive Profana

Chapter Eleven

From Unhappy Consciousness

to Bad Conscience

WHAT AT THIS HISTORICAL MOMENT — "after Auschwitz" — still remains of the questions traditionally asked by the disciplines of classical historical, biblical, dogmatic, and philosophical theology? What now is "theology's" minimal degree as it demarcates itself from the modern scholarly empirical and comparative study of religion as a merely cultural phenomenon and social fact? In my extended comparison of the writings of Adorno and Levinas, I have explored remnants and echoes of religious forms and figures of thought in these thinkers' critiques of secular reason, finding in the work of both a "theology in pianissimo" constituted by the trace of a transcendent — now natural, then metaphysical or ethical — other/Other. I have sought to analyze, systematize, and formalize this at once negative and superlative idea of an other of (and with respect to) reason, whose contours become visible only in what I have termed a minimal and rhetorical interpretation. In addition, I have framed these thinkers' innovative projects within the arguments of their intellectual heirs, Habermas and Derrida, defending their work against accusations of "performative contradiction" (by the later Habermas) or "empiricism" (by the early Derrida). In the process I have tried to cast some light on those writers and their respective views on pragmatics and deconstruction, as well. Attentive to rational and figural features of Adorno's and Levinas's texts, my investigation of the concepts of history, subjectivity, and language in their writings has attempted to provide a radical interpretation of their paradoxical modes of thought and to reveal remarkable and hitherto unsuspected parallels between their philosophical methods, parallels that amount to a plausible way of overcoming certain impasses in contemporary philosophical thinking, in which the critique of idolatry, both conceptual and political, is of undiminished and, perhaps, increasing urgency. In Adorno, I have argued, this takes the form of a dialectical critique of dialectics; in Levinas, that of a phenomenological critique of phenomenology, each of which sheds new light on ancient and modern questions of metaphysics, ethics, and aesthetics and has repercussions for a rethinking of the political, as well. Not the least important aspect of their thinking, I have suggested, is the paradoxical, indeed aporetic, pairing in their analyses of nonformal tautology (strategically reducing the deployment of Western thought to a repetition of the same, *das Immergleiche, le Même*) and of nonabstract heterology (insisting on the irreducibility of a negatively determinate nonidentical, an ab-solute, in-finite Other). But, as we have seen, they also contrast bad and good totality, good and bad conscience, a radical thinking of the singular and the evocation of near-cosmic consciousness. Ultimately, I concluded, the difference in their respective writings between anti- (or, more precisely, infra-, non-, or an-)ontology, on the one hand, and hyper- (i.e., supra-, meta-, more-than-)ontology, on the other, go hand in hand, leaving their relationship to tradition and its overcoming undecided. This and nothing else is what "solidarity with metaphysics in the moment of its downfall" and "alternation between the Said, Unsaid, and Unsaying" seek to signal. Adorno and Levinas elaborate different parallel and complementary ways of engaging an inherited vocabulary, set of concepts, and problems in light of "experiences" that challenge the very possibility of meaning and sense as it articulates itself historically, subjectively, and linguistically. In so doing, this metaphysical and ontological — indeed, onto-theological — legacy is brought back to its barest minimum, whose negative yet determinate, that is to say, singular and de-formalized, contours are reaffirmed and, as it were, set free. What does this mean?

The interpretation of Levinas offered in the previous chapters in no way involves a claim that his undertaking can inconsiderately be subsumed under the play of ontology.[1] Rather, it seeks to understand his description of the ethical dimension as an attempt to produce a specific or singular idiom — an intonation or curvature — of the general dimension of the trace. What Derrida at one point observes about theology — that it is a determinate moment in the total movement of the trace[2] — also holds true, mutatis mutandis, for ethics as Levinas seeks to think it. Moreover,

---

1. Only at first glance might that be understood to be the tenor of Derrida's "Violence and Metaphysics." Bernasconi correctly points out that Derrida's essay should be viewed not as an attempt to refute Levinas but, rather, as "an illustration of the only way his text can work" (Robert Bernasconi, "Deconstruction and the Possibility of Ethics," in *Deconstruction and Philosophy*, ed. John Sallis [Chicago: University of Chicago Press, 1987], 130). See, in this context, Derrida's comment: "We are wondering about the meaning of a *necessity:* the necessity of lodging oneself within traditional conceptuality in order to destroy it" (*Writing and Difference*, 111 / 165, my emph.).

2. Derrida, *Of Grammatology*, 47 / 69.

it holds for metaphysical and spiritual experience as well as for aesthetics, so that this conclusion involves an analogous interpretation of Adorno's work.

In order to draw together the various strands in my investigation, I will first need to establish explicit commonalities and differences between the lines of questioning and figures of thought in Adorno and Levinas. Then I must attempt to render concrete the preliminary results of this investigation by once again taking up the question of the relation of philosophy to ethics and aesthetics. In this I will distinguish the approaches of Levinas and Adorno, first from "formal pragmatics" and its "discourse ethics," then from the poetics of Paul Celan. Finally, I will examine the extent to which the approaches of these authors overlap, albeit only in part (and largely inexpressively) with Derrida's deconstructive philosophy. Only after I have addressed and clarified this parallel can I determine the theoretical and practical range of minimal theology and sum up its formal and, more broadly, material features.

From Consciousness and Conscience to Wakefulness

To name a series of obvious differences between Adorno and Levinas, one might begin by emphasizing that Levinas is a religious thinker — or, better, a philosopher who indefatigably deals with a religious motif stemming from time immemorial. For Adorno, as we have seen, the modern, profane experience of art is constitutive of salvation or at least the naming of what could be other than whatever presently is. At first glance this is not true for Levinas — not to the same extent. The true relation to the other is, in his opinion, above all moral and thus religious, although this designation cannot be taken in the sense of a substantive-dogmatic confession of faith or any other mythological or ideological bias. Religion, as Derrida rightly notes, means for Levinas not "*a* religion, but *the* religion, the religiosity of the religious."[3] The central questions of positive (affirmative or kataphatic) and negative (mystical or apophatic) theologies in their attempt either to solidify or to undermine the truth of divine existence and its essential attributes (or divine names) would be secondary — if not totally indifferent (but how, exactly?) — with respect to this at once formalizing and deformalizing analysis of and emphasis on "religiosity" in terms of the relationship between self and other, an "ethical" or "eschatological" relationship in which both terms absolve themselves from

3. Derrida, *Writing and Difference*, 96 / 142.

the very relation, retaining and deepening their separation or becoming virtually interchangeable to the point of the substitution of the one for the other. This relationship, Levinas states, "is religion, exceeding the psychology of faith and of the loss of faith" (*OB* 168 / 214).

This concern with the "religiosity of the religious" seems nowhere to be found in Adorno, intent as he is on always spelling out the temporal "truth-content" in historical and contemporary concepts, tropes, and gestures, reducing all "saying" to a (determinate negation of a) said, of sorts. But already the borders start to blur. Levinas wants to graft modern-critical, philosophical discourse onto the Jewish religious tradition—or, more cautiously, to bring the two into a *constellation* (to use one of Adorno's privileged terms), so that the former can be enriched in light of the latter and can be evaluated in novel ways. Analogously, Adorno attempts to saturate a modern-subjective, formally articulated philosophy with contents that the tradition had long excluded. According to him, bodily, moral, aesthetic, and even mythical-religious motifs must—if reason itself is to become reasonable and remain true to itself—be moved to the center of a self-consciously dialectical enlightenment. We must return to the salvific mode of thinking (*rettende Denkweise*), which not only engages these traditional motifs and expressions but permeates them with a strong, sober, and profane point of view.

A hesitation about apprehending and reifying transcendence—in other words, an *epochē* in relation to the promise inherent in the idea of redemption—seems to set the fundamental tone in Adorno. His "negativism" lets redemption dwindle into the critical but necessarily somewhat powerless idea of a negative metaphysics, whose contours I have delineated in the first chapter as well as in part 2. His discussion of the traces of the other certainly plays an important role in his late work, yet it betrays a tone in his thinking which is all too easy to miss. This minimal role of the idea of transcendence can scarcely be justified in the conceptual framework of negative dialectics without admitting into dialectics the possibility of thinking, experiencing, and respecting the other of reason in an encircling and aporetic, alternating or oscillating, mode, that is to say, simultaneously in performative contradiction and in a superlative-rhetorical movement. But Adorno never succeeded in bringing the erratic or surreptitious significance of redemption and its momentary temporality, inspired by the writings of Kafka, Benjamin, Beckett, and Celan, into harmony with the infinitizing structure of metaphysical experience which Levinas—and even Adorno—associated with the Proustian *Recherche*.

By contrast, Levinas's late work consistently explores a modality of transcendence which can dispense with the complementary false affirmatives of a complete negativity of the same (and hence absence of the other) or an unambiguous positivity (and hence presence) of the other. The trace makes plausible the diminishing but still remaining intelligibility of the discourse concerning transcendence in general and God in particular without once again burdening philosophy with a questionable ontotheology, the metaphysics of presence or absence to which theism and its analogues, yet likewise atheism with its naturalisms and humanisms, fall prey. A far more complicated relationship between infinity and fulfillment holds among all these historical, traditional and modern, dogmatic and enlightened, doctrines. In Levinas's words: "Prophecy and ethics in no way exclude the consolations of religion; but . . . only a humanity which can do without these consolations perhaps may be worthy of them" (*EI* 188 / 117, trans. modified).

A corresponding motif can be found in the famous closing aphorism of Adorno's *Minima Moralia*. There he says that, in view of the "imperative" or "demand [*Forderung*]" to bring about or deliver the almost (or completely?) impossible, "the question of the reality or unreality of redemption itself hardly matters." In this moral task (notably, of thought) Adorno envisions the construction of a *critical perspectivism* that will reveal the world "as indigent and distorted as it will appear one day in the messianic light" (*MM* 247 / 281).

A formal and material comparison between Adorno's and Levinas's writings ought first to be concerned with their common investigation—and, I would add, deconstruction—of the philosophy of the subject, of historicism, and of logocentrism. All three come down to a dismantling of naturalism and immanentism, while steering clear of naive, enthusiastic, intuitive, or mystical affirmations of the totally other as present to itself, simple and pure. Their perspective on transcendence, I have argued throughout, is more paradoxical—indeed, is surreptitious—and permanently runs the risk of idolatry and blasphemy. This is not due to a lack of consistency or rigor in their philosophical projects: rather, of the *tertium datur* there can be neither truth or falsity, since this dimension is at once indestructible or irrepressible and undecidable or aporetic. It can only be "said" through "unsaying" and cannot be "unsaid" without entangling it — once again — in the "said" that the "unsaying" interrupts, only immediately to betray itself in turn, ad infinitum.

Nonetheless, such a perspective, at once critical and skeptical, signals an intervention in and perhaps also modification of the *transcendental* orientation of classical-modern and contemporary thought. From all of these points of view Adorno's and Levinas's shift from a philosophy of unhappy consciousness [*unglückliches Bewußtsein*] to one of bad conscience [*mauvaise conscience*] may prove to be the most significant change in orientation which a sustained confrontation of their respective figures of thought brings to light.

At the same time we should differentiate and judge with restraint. The desire for the other, as Levinas sketches it, is neither longing — *Sehnsucht nach dem ganz Anderen,* as Horkheimer had it — nor melancholy. In no way does it involve a temporary unhappiness that might somehow be overcome in a distant and possible future. Derrida accurately summarizes these basic traits in Levinas's thinking: "The metaphysics of desire is a metaphysics of infinite separation. Not a consciousness of separation as a Judaic consciousness, as an unhappy consciousness: in the Hegelian Odyssey Abraham's unhappiness is an expediency [*déterminé comme provision*], the provisional necessity of a figure and a transition [*passage*] within a horizon of a reconciliation, of a return to self and of absolute knowledge. Here there is no return. For desire is not unhappy. It is opening and freedom."[4] Because desire cannot, in principle, be satisfied, there clings to consciousness (which is primarily involved with conscience and in that sense is already conscientious, not unhappy) a trace of despair. As Derrida admits: "this eschatology which awaits *nothing* sometimes appears infinitely hopeless. Truthfully, in *La Trace de l'autre* eschatology does not only 'appear' hopeless. It gives itself as such, and renunciation belongs to its essential meaning."[5]

But does not Levinas himself say, in relation to the unavoidable election, the unchosen chosenness, "that election is indeed a hardship [or unhappiness, *malheur*]" (*NP* 123 / 182)? Does the ontological *malaise* that he has analyzed in all its moral and modernist modalities, from *On Escape* onward, not touch upon the conceptless, musical thinking that Hegel (and later Adorno) identifies as "unhappy consciousness"? Perhaps, but Levinas's insight into the "difficult" — the unchosen and invested — "freedom"

4. Ibid., 92 / 138, trans. modified.
5. Ibid., 95 / 141, trans. modified.

of election in no way diminishes the distance he takes from the pathos of the "beautiful soul" (see *TI* 26, 301, 305 / xiv, 277, 282; *OB* 48 / 61). His increasing avoidance of eschatology and messianism (see *OB* 169 / 215) only strengthens this impression. Neither the difficulty of providing an existential foothold for the vanishing point of meaning nor the impossibility, in thinking or writing (as the comparison with Blanchot made clear), of setting bounds, whether in advance or in the end, to the withdrawal of all axiological validity speaks, according to Levinas, against the necessity of reorienting philosophy in the direction of the Other: "Ethics has a meaning, even without the promises of the Messiah" (*EI* 114 / 112). Or, as he puts it elsewhere: "The term *eschaton* implies that there might exist a finality, an end (*fin*) to the historical relation of difference between man and the absolutely other, a reduction of the gap that safeguards the alterity of the transcendent to a totality of sameness. To realize the *eschaton* would therefore mean that we could seize or appropriate God as a *telos* and degrade the infinite relation with the other to a finite fusion. This is what Hegelian dialectics amounts to." And a little farther: "I could not accept a form of messianism that would end the need for discussion, that would end our watchfulness."[6] One might go still farther and venture the suspicion that ethical meaning can find an echo (*Widerhall*) only by abandoning itself to the absurd (*Widersinn*).

Philosophical Antisubjectivism

One can demonstrate numerous parallels in how Adorno and Levinas determine the relationship between moral or religious concerns, on the one hand, and philosophical discourse, on the other. An important difference, however, lies in their valuation of nature in general (see *OB* 68 / 86) or, in particular, of the subjective, erotic naturalness of the ego. The relation to the Other, according to Levinas's "humanism of the other" (more precisely, "humanism of the other human being [*humanisme de l'autre homme*]"), is not anchored in some psycho-biological, instinctual, or altruistic disposition toward the good, nor does it testify primarily to a promise of happiness in self-seeking bodily pleasure (see *HAH* 71, 80, 92), whereas these seem to inform the epistemological and moral *reductio hominis* (*ND* 186–87; cf. 191 / 187; cf. 192) and the aesthetic "inhumanity" (*AT* 197 / 293) of Adorno's fundamentally materialist-sensualist utopianism. But we should not be too quickly blinded by these variations in em-

---

6. See Levinas and Kearney, "Dialogue," in Cohen, *Face to Face with Levinas*, 30 and 31.

phasis. As we have seen, even in Adorno the good life and sensual fulfill-ment are not on the same footing. He is more interested in a desire without nostalgia, thus a longing without melancholia, than in a need that could be satisfied (as hunger, thirst, or any other privation or deprivation can). Conversely, it is easy to show that not by chance do Levinas's descriptions of the relation to the truly other use an erotic no less than sensualist and at times even materialist metaphorics.

Both Adorno and Levinas take critical distance from the idea of a subjective, homogeneous identity—in Ricoeur's term, *idem*-identity— around which the modern philosophies of consciousness and of reflec-tion finally revolve, whether they seek to establish its ontological fun-dament (from Descartes to analytic philosophies of mind) or try to put such grounding into question (from Hume to Nietzsche and from Rorty to Derek Parfitt).[7]

Adorno and Levinas vehemently protest modernity's dominant image of the autonomous subject and especially *the subordination of language to thought and of the body to language.*[8] They both maintain a deep respect for the experiences of pleasure and pain as well as for the horrifying or sub-lime dimensions bound up with them, whose evocation eludes description in simple positive or ontic, affirmative, and negative terms. In this they profoundly modify the classical concept of experience which continues to govern the post-dialectical and post-phenomenological understanding of this notion in "philosophical" hermeneutics.[9] They do not simply fail to recognize the strong aspects of the modern doctrine of constitutive sub-jectivity—in comparison, for example, with an "I" immersed in magic and myth or an "I" lacking strength (*Ichstärke*), as Adorno says with Freud— nor do they gesture toward the vague new form of a subjectivity which would scarcely be worth mentioning. No redefinition of the subject is pro-posed: merely that even the "smallest excess of the non-identical [*kleinsten Überschuss des Nichtidentischen*]"—something "minimal [*Minimalen*]" (*ND* 183 / 184)—threatens the subject absolutely, precisely because the latter deems itself (the) absolute. Hence, Adorno captures the motifs of a dialectical "negative anthropology" (see the reference to Ulrich Sonne-

---

7. Even references to thought experiments inspired by science fiction—familiar from con-temporary philosophies of mind and decried by Ricoeur, in *Oneself as Another*, as far from helpful—are not absent in Adorno and Levinas (see, e.g., *OB* 113 / 148).

8. See Derrida, *Writing and Difference*, 103 / 153.

9. For a hermeneutic appropriation of the classical concept of experience, see Gadamer, *Truth and Method*, 310–24 / 329–44.

mann's book, *ND* 11, missing in the English translation) in terms that seem applicable to Levinas's engagement with phenomenology: "The path to freedom from anthropomorphism, which first philosophy enters under the standard of demythologization, leads to the apotheosis of ανθρωπος as a second mythology. Not least because it was reminiscent of psychology, did proud philosophy since Husserl reject psychology."[10] At best, one might use the figure of *passivity* as a provisional name for the ethos Adorno and Levinas have in mind—a nearly anti-Heideggerian notion of "releasement," or *Gelassenheit.* Thus Levinas remarks, "ipseity is graceful" (*TI* 301 / 278). Grace, mercy, gentleness, and especially patience are all entwined there with unremitting watchfulness and an intellectual zeal for unending interpretation.

Whether this middle way between a dogmatic moralism, on the one hand, and an all too tolerant and powerless relativism or a doggedly immoral cynicism, on the other, actually overcomes the weakness of the "philosophy of the subject" remains, of course, an open question. From the perspective of Habermas's modern theory of communicative action, as well as the perspective of Derrida's deconstructive philosophy, one must judge that Adorno and Levinas finally remain under the spell of the philosophy of the subject that they seek to undermine, displace, and resituate. However that may be, such a conclusion does not diminish the heuristic power of their thought.

Antihistoricism

Both Adorno and Levinas place a critique of the historical- and social-philosophical concept of totality at the forefront in their work. They seek to defend morality—that is, singular instances and instants, events and encounters, in a morality deprived of principles, norms, virtues, utility, deliberation, and rational choice—against the ethical life forms of Hegelian objective spirit and play those life forms off against its conception of struggle and recognition, terror and freedom, family and civil society, custom and law, nation (or people) and State. Our authors deny any normalizing and normativizing, progressive or regressive, liberating or redeeming power to history, seeing it, rather, as a deeply contingent series of occurrences which, for all its necessities, remains metaphysically arbitrary, perhaps even intrinsically flawed, interpretable only through the metaphor of originary catastrophe or the contraction (*Zimzum*) of God.

10. *Against Epistemology,* 16 / GS 5:24.

In that, Adorno and Levinas contradict one of the central presuppositions of all modern historicizing directions in thinking, which finally assume a rational course in the progress of history, regardless of its moments of rise and fall, stagnation or revolution.[11]

In a first move against the modern idealist philosophies of consciousness and of the subject, Adorno's philosophy emphasizes, as we have seen, the mediations and dialectical contradictions with which, within history, a thinking that is hostile to nature and seeks to float free necessarily finds itself entangled in the thick of things (*in Geschichte verstrickt*). In a second move, however, opposing any positive, idealist, or materialist philosophy of history and totality (i.e., in opposition to both Hegel *and* Marx), he moves toward an open, negative dialectics, which "in its final movement" turns "against itself" (*ND* 403 / 395). Negative dialectics is, therefore, a project both of ideology critique and of self-critique in philosophical reflection. This paradox makes the reading of Adorno's texts a dizzying experience. What could it be that would motivate reason to investigate its own critical standards, turning it "in its final movement," as Adorno says, "against itself"? Furthermore, can such a figure of thought still be designated "reflection," or does it concern a kind of "experience"—perhaps a "metaphysical" or "spiritual [*geistige*]" experience—which finally departs from traditional ontological or onto-theological categories and determinations? If that is so, how can such a figure of thought still be delineated conceptually, in and through philosophical argument? Can the paradox and aporia—indeed, the performative contradiction—of negative dialectics be consistently or convincingly theorized, practiced, judged, or expressed?

In Levinas the figure of argumentation regarding traditional metaphysical and modern-critical philosophy seems to be accented differently. First, in opposition to all the mediations posited by the dominant idealist and materialist tradition and in contrast to Adorno's original course in the critique of ideology, with its dualisms between nature and culture, mind and world, subject and object, Levinas insists primarily on ontological pluralism and the radical *separation* between beings. As I have shown, concepts such as "position," "instant," "hypostasis," "contraction," "atheism," "solitude," "monad," "diachrony," and "recurrence" are so many expressions hinting at this motif, which, as in Adorno, forms only a first step in the genealogy of responsibility. Second, following in Rosenzweig's foot-

---

11. See Löwith, *From Hegel to Nietzsche*, 216–21 / 236–40.

steps, he asks how isolated beings can enter into relation with one another in a way that would not reduce the absolute difference of the terms but, rather, inspire self-critique — and ultimately destitution and election — in one of them (namely, in the self, the ego). Levinas leaves no doubt about "who" or "what" makes the dimension of that *primum intelligibile* — or, later, of metaphysical *an-archy* — reveal itself in all its sublimity, marvel, and enigma (the face of the other person and, in its trace, that of the infinite). Yet for him the question of how to think a modality of transcendence — "to the point of absence" and in possible confusion, interchangeability, indeed substitutability, with violence and horror — which could burst open any subjective identity and historical totality remains in the end fundamentally open.

Can such a figure of thought still be approached with the help of philosophical "reflection"? If not, how could one philosophically name and circumscribe the paradox and aporetics of Levinas's phenomenological procedures? Can Derrida's thinking of an unsublatable barricading of the scope of reflection in any genuine interpretation, irrepressible by the conceptual means of traditional metaphysics and its modern successor forms, offer any further help here? Even for Derrida, it is true that his thinking, "rather than being a philosophy of reflection, is engaged in the systematic exploration of that dull surface without which no reflection and no specular and speculative activity would be possible, but which at the same time has no place and no part in reflection's scintillating play."[12] Can Levinas's (like Adorno's) figure of thought be compared to deconstructive hermeneutics or, better, practice as a mode of philosophical interpretation or rhetorical reading in which the subject, as well as the series of its objectifying sedimentations (in nature, culture, history, and politics), is always turned back on itself, without ever arriving at a reconstitution or realization of its supposed origin and telos, intentionality or motivational drive? Could their projects be seen as parallel attempts to name, figure, explore, and excavate the different folds and fault lines that run through the terrain of Western philosophical thought and which represent as many blind spots, excluded thirds: traces of Nature, of the ethical Other, as well as of their analogues? This question brings us to the third point in a possible comparison between these two authors.

12. Rodolphe Gasché, *The Tain of the Mirror: Derrida and the Philosophy of Reflection* (Cambridge: Harvard University Press, 1986), 6.

Antilogocentrism

Both Adorno and Levinas distance themselves, *linguistically* speaking, from philosophical discourse insofar as it is conceived as an *adequate* or *definitive* representation of a nonlinguistic other or of the nonidentical via conceptual, argumentative, metaphorical, rhetorical, or visual (even acoustical) means. Both authors oppose, above all, the *ontological* privileging of the world of things, whether in existence or becoming, whether material or ideal, past or future. They cast doubt, furthermore, on the *epistemological* primacy of the world of facts and states of affairs and question the *semantic* priority of assertive linguistic utterances and propositional truths, with their supposition of fixed reference, translatability, and so on.[13]

Levinas explains as follows the influential logocentric horizons of understanding which have conferred upon thought a certain security from the Greeks to Heidegger: Western tradition equates the idea of truth with intelligible presence. What is true is fitted within the framework of an ordered cosmos. Even Heidegger's radical attempt at rethinking "presence [or presencing, *Anwesen*]," which is supposed to resist the understanding of Being in terms of the being of "beings ready at hand [*Vorhandenheit*]," is bound to this tradition: "while Heidegger heralds the end of the metaphysics of presence, he continues to think of being as a coming-into-presence."[14] But then, as we have seen, Levinas's understanding of the existent and of exteriority, of the infinite and the other, of the otherwise than Being—a no more as well as more than Being (whether this Being is thought as presence or presencing, as *Sein, Seyn,* or *Ereignis;* the difference, for Levinas, matters little)—does not result in a simple reversal of ontology's central presupposition. The dimensions of the other, of illeity and *il y a,* are not thought as mere abstractions, as simple and purely formal alterities—as abstract negations and bad infinities, as the language of dialectics would have it—but as many instances of the *tertium datur.* And the latter can be philosophically, rhetorically, or poetically expressed only through intermittent interruption, surreption, in the permanent risk of idolatry and blasphemy, that is to say, of confusing the best and the worst. Instead of ascribing to Levinas the ambition of inventing a heterology (or, for that matter, absolute empiricism), we must assume that his

---

13. On this three-part definition of *logocentrism,* see Habermas, "Questions and Counter-questions," in Bernstein, *Habermas and Modernity,* 197; Levinas uses the term in his conversation with Kearney in Cohen, *Face to Face with Levinas,* 33.

14. Levinas and Kearney, "Dialogue," in Cohen, *Face to Face with Levinas,* 20.

discourse operates via a principle and logic of contamination. This, and nothing else, is what its paradox and aporia suggest.

By the same token, because negative dialectics does not want to uncover anew an ontological or transcendental-philosophical "supporting structure" (*ND* 136 / 140) which would underlie all further conceptual edifices and determine or hierarchize their categories, criteria, and norms, Adorno can claim: "In criticizing ontology we do not aim at another ontology, not even at one of being nonontological [*des Nichtontologischen*]. If that were our purpose we would be merely positing another downright first [or something merely different from the purely first, *bloss ein Anderes als das schlechthin Erste*] — not absolute identity, this time, not Being, not the concept, but nonidentity, whatever exists [*das Seiende*], facticity. We would be hypostasizing the concept of non-conceptuality and thus acting counter to its meaning" (*ND* 136 / 140, trans. modified).

Negative dialectics preserves a unifying moment, but not by relying on abstractions or syntheses, or by a "step-by-step progression [*Stufengang*] from concepts to a more general super-concept [*Oberbegriff*]." Instead, it redeems "the specific" in its objects by bringing them into micrological constellations: "Only constellations represent from without what the concept has cut away within" (*ND* 162 / 164, trans. modified). Only in this way can concepts "potentially" determine what is interior to something and interpret what *per definitionem* must be denied to thinking wherever it is seen as a procedure of "classification."

Adorno's idea of unlocking reality with the help of a procedure of constellation takes as its model the "procedure [*Verfahren*]" of language, whose internal structure should not be interpreted as a "mere system of signs for cognitive functions": "Where it appears really [*wirklich*] as a language, where it becomes a form of presentation [*Darstellung*], it does not define its concepts. It lends objectivity to them by the relation into which it puts the concepts, centered about a thing [*Sache*]" (*ND* 162 / 164, trans. modified). Hegel's use of the term *concrete,* that is, his conceptual grasp of a thing via a determination that grows together with it, instead of relying on a "pure selfhood" (*ND* 162 / 165), might be what Adorno has in mind here. Yet Hegelian dialectics remains "without language," and Hegel understands even what finds no language as a determinable moment of Spirit in its unfolding. According to Adorno, such a "supposition [*Supposition*]" must be subject to critique (*ND* 163 / 165), although one can also detect in him a speculative notion in that the indissoluble and the nonidentical are presented as *of themselves* transcending their "closedness" and releasing themselves, precisely by reaching for sound and language, "from the spell [*Bann*] of their selfhood" (*ND* 163 / 165, trans. modified). A movement of things themselves conceptualized in this way can hardly be equated with speculative idealism. Although Adorno opposes naive, pre-Kantian realism, an *asymmetry* in the mediation of subjectivity and objectivity, of the self and the other, of the concept and the nonidentical, seems unavoidable to him: "Not even as an idea can we conceive of a subject without thinking of an object; but we can conceive an object without thinking of a subject. To be an object also is part of the meaning of subjectivity; but it is not equally part of the meaning of objectivity to be a subject" (*ND* 183 / 184, trans. modified).

Quasi-transcendentalia

The three aspects I have named here reveal, in both Adorno and Levinas, grave reservations concerning the transcendental-philosophical tradition. True, in both one encounters an anticipation or echo of the "linguistic turn" in philosophy, whose innovations and repercussions were not exclusively a matter of the twentieth-century analytical tradition. Yet one might suspect that transcendental-philosophical — more precisely, formal-pragmatic — interpretations of our authors' concerns and figures of thought do not press to the core of what they actually express in their writings. Such interpretations at best appeal to a limited aspect of that work, one subsequently rectified by these authors themselves: to claims made in the period during which Adorno, in close collaboration with Horkheimer, dedicated himself to the program of interdisciplinary Critical Theory and contributed central insights to *Dialectic of Enlightenment;* or to *Totality and Infinity,* wherein Levinas attempted to ground an ethical *prima philosophia* in the language of phenomenology and ontology.

What is appealing and praiseworthy in the attempts (by Habermas, Wellmer, Honneth, de Boer, and others) to reformulate Adorno's and Levinas's methods and concerns in terms of a formal-pragmatic or ethical transcendental philosophy, respectively, is that certain of their most challenging motifs — which vain attempts at systematicity tend to submerge, yet a complete lack of system or systematic tends to render esoteric — can thus become fruitful in reconstructing a more compelling conception of undivided rationality. The only stumbling block to this interpretation would seem to be that in Adorno and Levinas, respectively, there seems to be an unsublatable *skepticism* (as in Habermas's "accusation" directed at Adorno) and an unavoidable *empiricism* (as in Derrida's first "critique" of Levinas). In a theoretical discourse, it seems, those moments can never entirely be recuperated, evaluated, or expressed. The rational status of the pre-philosophical experiences from which they stem—and to which even the most refined reconstruction and formalization must inevitably lead us back—is therefore, at best, *quasi*-transcendental. This motif concerns, as I have said, a singular materialization (Adorno) and deformalization (Levinas)—indeed, a *concretissimum*—of what Derrida has designated *différance,* the trace, the supplement. The diminishing yet still-remaining reference to and relevance of the religious—in Adorno, as in Levinas and Derrida—is hardly accidental here. It determines the dialectical, formal-pragmatic, phenomenological, and deconstructive approaches to "transcendence" from within and without. As we found earlier in Derrida's *Of Grammatology,* "The theological is a determinate moment in the total movement of the trace."

The term *transcendental* can signify a philosophical procedure that seeks a third way between scientistic or, more broadly, naturalist discourse, on the one hand, and classical-metaphysical speculation concerning transcendence or doctrines of revelation, on the other.[15] Yet in Levinas (and no less in Adorno) this philosophical movement between two extremes—between the order of the self-same and that of the other, thought this time not as another self or sameness, that is, an identity or a totality in which my self is absorbed, but, on the contrary, in its absolute separation, as an in-finite—finally knows no formally describable premise or end term. It finds no rest, no point to return to.

The phenomenological critique of phenomenology which models itself on the fatal return of skepticism (and its no less fatal refutation, time and again) and the negative-dialectical mode of thinking which indefatigably confronts concepts with what has no concept to begin or end, signify something entirely different from Heidegger's "formally indicative hermeneutics."[16] Their far more singular—some would say rigid—designation of the nonidentical and the singular concerns, rather, a concrete philosophizing in the trace of the other of reason (in both the subjective

15. See O. Duintjer, *De vraag naar het transcendentale: Vooral in verband met Heidegger en Kant* (Leiden: Universitaire Pers, 1966).

16. T. C. W. Oudemanns, "Heideggers formeel aanwijzende hermeneutica," *Algemeen Nederlands Tijdschrift voor Wijsbegeerte* 80, no. 1 (1988): 18-40.

and objective genitive). More specifically, in each case it implies a kind of "thinking," "experiencing," "judging," and even "writing" both *this side of* and *beyond* any form or transformation of transcendental critique. And yet, lest we forget, if these authors offer a *critique of secular reason,* as the subtitle of my study claims, this also means a "critique" in the precise sense Kant attributes to this term. In other words, their endeavors are not merely negative or derogatory and destructive but also positive and, as it were, affirmative: their writings spell out which formal and metaphysical as well as which material or concrete conditions — or, rather, inconditions — make secular and enlightened reason, if one can still say so, *possible.* Put otherwise, they analyze, not unlike Kant, the enabling "experience" of the intelligible and absolute that lies (hidden, forgotten) in experience, that is, both in the knowledge gathered from experimental science and the more elusive experiential nature of the ordinary and the everyday.[17]

A *quasi*-transcendental status is probably the furthest consequence of any thinking that would seek to free itself from becoming caught up in the traditional and modern philosophies of origin (i.e., of *prima philosophia* or of ultimate foundation [*Letztbegründung*]). To do so is the most important stake in the earliest and latest texts of Adorno and Levinas. For this reason, in them one cannot speak of a transcendental philosophy in the narrower sense of the term. The addition of the prefix *quasi*- makes this clear.

Nevertheless, the concept "transcendental" can clarify an important finding: that different paradoxical structures of argumentation and rhetorical figures of speech may enable these thinkers' philosophy to reach to the bounds of rationality and at times beyond them. The problem of form for philosophy is perhaps itself one of rhetoric more than of philosophical system.[18] Without exaggeration one can demonstrate a rhetorical trait in our authors' philosophy and thus a relativizing — though hardly the sublation! — of the difference between philosophy and the more aesthetic modes of presentation which the tradition up to Kant sought to dismiss or render secondary in the order of giving reasons. Their refusal to endorse this hierarchy between concept and figure, argument and hyperbole, measure and excess explains the almost literary, poetic quality of various texts by Adorno and Levinas and, further, the fact that at decisive

17. See Derrida, *Of Grammatology,* 61 / 90.

18. "The problem of form for philosophy is a rhetorical problem" (S. IJsseling, *Retoriek en Filosofie* [Bitthoven: Ambo, 1975], 10 / *Rhetoric and Philosophy in Conflict: An Historical Survey* [The Hague: Martinus Nijhoff, 1976], 4).

places in their work they rely on the expressive power of great writers and lyrical poets.

Before and beyond Discourse Ethics

One problem central to this investigation is the question: is an immanent critique of the philosophical tradition possible without secretly relying on an "outside" and "exteriority" — or, what comes down to the same, a deep-down "inside" and "interiority" — that is, on a nondiscursive element or ferment that surrounds and pervades, enables and threatens the life of words and concepts, arguments and style? Does not such an appeal to nonconceptual and extra-argumentative dimensions disqualify the properly philosophical undertaking and favor, instead, a poetic, literary, or, more broadly, rhetorical procedure, which can bring the other of reason into language only via lyric, narrative, or persuasive appeal: in short, a musical thinking that does not come to the point or cannot make this point clear? Does not the paradoxical figure of a philosophy that by its own account would break with itself lead to what has been termed, in the refutation of classical skepticism, a performative contradiction, to an aporia that inaugurates the demise — or, at least, the impasse and weakness — of philosophical thinking?

At stake in this rebuke — if, indeed, it is one — is the claim of Adorno's and Levinas's work to be philosophical or, more broadly, rational and hence, in a sense, responsible. True, what Adorno insightfully observes applies to both of them: "the self-criticism of reason is its truest morality" (*MM* 126 / 141). But does a critique that sets its own foundations at stake not undermine the statute of any philosophical rationality, indeed, its very ability to give reasons and thus be held accountable? Perhaps this question cannot be answered a priori, in the abstract. It all depends. Let me seek to formulate it more precisely, therefore, by explicating once again the core problem of discourse ethics (see chap. 1).

Wellmer points out that one ought to take the problem of moral-philosophical skepticism — whose consequences, as we have seen, Horkheimer and Adorno attempt to escape at significant moments in their work — both seriously and not seriously at all. As a "moral posture," ethical skepticism lacks any power of conviction. That can be gained only via a "putting into question of rationalist and fundamentalist epistemological claims" in moral philosophy. Not directly but only if its assertions can be transformed and salvaged in a "ferment of enlightenment" could a defense of the rational within ethics — one informed and enriched by philosophical skepticism—be neither "rational nor skeptical, but perhaps . . . reasonable."[19]

Adorno's and Levinas's constructions of morality crystallize, as we have seen, in an unfounded, undemonstrable, and hence, at least in part, unintelligible or even senseless responsibility [*uneinsichtige Verbindlichkeit*], whose contours and consequences cannot be articulated within the framework of "discourse ethics." These implications escape the premises, methods, and aims developed in the *Diskursethik* of Habermas and Apel (and further amplified and refined by Wellmer, Honneth, Benhabib, Fraser, Young, and others). They may, perhaps, have some valence with the "ethics of discussion" as Derrida conceives it in his discussion with Searle's speech act theory and formal pragmatics of the "Frankfurt" variety in the afterword to *Limited Inc.*[20] By the same token, Adorno's and Levinas's views elude the concepts of "virtue" or "narrative" ethics from Alisdair McIntyre to Charles Taylor and Paul Ricoeur,[21] to say nothing of the contractarian, utilitarian, and rational choice normative theories that still abound.

Is there a lack of foundation [*Begründungsdefizit*] here? The theory of communicative action in general and discourse ethics in particular seem no less incapable than Adorno's moral philosophy of distinguishing how one might envision, let alone materialize, a "postmetaphysical" mediation (as Habermas would have it) between formal-pragmatic and, hence, universal structures of cognition, speech, and action, on the one hand, and those of concrete historical life forms and institutions, on the other. Much more than a problem of "application" is at stake here: the mutual implication of normative "validity" and juridico-political "facticity" demands a far more paradoxical—indeed, an aporetic—model of analysis and negotiation than can be provided by a formal pragmatics alone. The reasons for this are clear. Insofar as it shifts the question of the moral point of view, the categorical imperative, duty, virtue, responsibility, and laws—in other words, justice, fairness, solidarity, and the public good—to an open, practical process of argumentation, that is, to the procedure of a discursive

---

19. Wellmer, *Ethik und Dialog*, 12–13. See also Hent de Vries, "Westerse rationaliteit en cynisme, sceptische argumenten voor het politieke realisme," in *Het neorealisme in de politiek: Theologisch beschouwd*, ed. Meerten B. ter Borg and Lammert Leertouwer (Baarn: Ambo, 1987), 109–27.

20. See my book *Philosophy and the Turn to Religion*, 404 ff.

21. See, with explicit reference to Levinas, also Adam Zachary Newton, *Narrative Ethics* (Cambridge: Harvard University Press, 1995).

resolution (*Einlösung*) of normative validity claims, the theory of communicative action and its discourse ethics necessarily lose sight of important problems. If, for the sake of simplicity, we ignore the complicated circumstance that every "struggle for norms . . . , even when carried out with discursive means, remains rooted in the 'struggle for recognition'"[22] — an insight elaborated in considerable detail in the work of Honneth and others — one might still question whether the rationalization of ethics can *primarily* be described as an intersubjective transformation of dispositions in which, as Habermas has it, the "*devout* [pietätvolle] *attachment* to *concrete orders of life* secured in tradition can be superseded in favor of a free orientation to universal principles."[23] One might, first of all, ask whether it is advisable or even possible to articulate general moral perspectives "independently of the *vision of the good life*"[24] and to connect them to the question of "what *everyone* might want."[25] Habermas bases the "capacity for abstraction" of a "differentiation within the practical,"[26] which distinguishes discourse ethics from substantial or narrativist interpretations of the moral perspective and which, according to him, constitutes its "gain in rationality," on an expressly modern insight: "*moral questions,* which can fundamentally be decided in a rational way under the aspect of the capacity for generalization of interests or of *justice,* are now distinguished from *evaluative questions,* which are presented under the general aspect of questions concerning the *good life* (or self-realization) and which are accessible to rational discussion only *within* the unproblematic horizon of a historically concrete life form or of an individual life experience."[27]

But this is not all. It might certainly be reasonable to emphasize, as Habermas does, explicitly borrowing from Adorno, that moral philosophy must *in principle* "be related negatively [*negatorisch*] to the damaged life, instead of affirmatively to the good."[28] If, however, one is not to repeat on a different conceptual level, now transformed in terms of linguistic pragmatism, the complementary biases of negativism and utopianism in

22. Habermas, *Moralbewußtsein und kommunikatives Handeln,* 116.

23. Habermas, *Theory of Communicative Action,* 1:213 / 1:294; see also 1:171–72 / 1:243–44, 1:229 ff / 1:315 ff.

24. Habermas, "Moralität und Sittlichkeit: Treffen Hegels Einwände gegen Kant auch auf die Diskursethik zu?" in Kuhlmann, *Moralität und Sittlichkeit,* 26.

25. Habermas, *Die neue Unübersichtlichkeit,* 237.

26. Habermas, *Moralbewußtsein und kommunikatives Handeln,* 118.

27. Ibid. See also Seyla Benhabib and Fred Dallmayr, eds., *The Communicative Ethics Controversy* (Cambridge: MIT Press, 1990).

28. Habermas, *Die neue Unübersichtlichkeit,* 237.

the philosophy of history which are attributed to Adorno, one cannot be content with this "restrictive" interpretation of the tasks of philosophical ethics.[29] In consequence, Habermas's thinking cannot be seen as having dispensed in advance with the "resulting problems [*Folgeprobleme*]" that the moral perspective must also face,[30] which hardly let themselves be reduced to those of practical wisdom, reflective judgment, hermeneutic application, jurisprudence, and political action. True, the *Theory of Communicative Action* attempts "to provide an equivalent for what was once intended by the idea of the good life."[31] But at the same time it claims that under modern conditions this idea can be grasped only *indirectly* or formally, hypothetically, and fallibilistically, that is, without recourse to the classical conceptuality of substantial (mythical, dogmatic, or totalitarian) worldviews. The concept of a fully rationalized life-world, if it can be consistently thought at all, no longer covers what was once meant by the — no less aporetic — idea of reconciliation.[32] If ever there was an infinite hope for redemption, this is no longer an option for us.

Of course, in Habermas's eyes universalist, justified morality remains bound to an *"application"*[33] in concrete cases and must thus rely upon *"complementary,"*[34] "structurally analogous"[35] life forms. Yet the prohibition on images hangs over the latter, and he scarcely comments on the former — *"reflective judgment."*[36] Let me begin with this sore point in any formalist, universalist, and ultimately cognitivist and normativist philosophical ethics. Like the reflexively broken theoretical observation of reality in relation to daily praxis and like avant-garde art in relation to experience that is customarily subjective, so too abstract morality should be mediated by concrete forms of ethical life (*Sittlichkeit*). How might this be accomplished *without* getting caught up in false sublations, in ideology and, indeed, idolatry — that is, in violating the *Bilderverbot*? The "balance [or negotiation, *Ausgleich*] among non-self-sufficient moments in need of a complement [*ergänzungsbedürftigen Momenten*]"[37] could, it would

29. Ibid., 225; see also 226.

30. Habermas, "Moralität und Sittlichkeit," 31.

31. Habermas, *Theory of Communicative Action*, 1:73 / 1:112.

32. See Habermas, "Entgegnung," *Kommunikatives Handeln*, 341–42.

33. Habermas, "Moralität und Sittlichkeit," 28.

34. Ibid. See Habermas, *Theory of Communicative Action*, 1:186, 189 / 1:264, 267.

35. Habermas, "Entgegnung," 335. See Habermas, *Moralbewußtsein und kommunikatives Handeln*, 115 ff., 187 ff.

36. Habermas, "Moralität und Sittlichkeit," 27; see also 26.

37. Habermas, *Theory of Communicative Action*, 1:73 / 1:112, trans. modified.

seem, only be achieved in a sort of alternation or oscillation, that is to say, within the apparently simultaneous and, in the final analysis, contradictory demands of a particular historical horizon or situation, on the one hand, *and* of a "claim [an appeal, *Anspruch*] transcending all locally shared agreements," on the other.[38] The learning processes within this open dialectics of a universally oriented and, in Habermas's words, postconventional moral consciousness, on the one hand, and the particular "coloring [*Färbung*]" of sociohistorical or personal conditions of life,[39] on the other, cannot obey a logic of discourse or discussion, however conceived. If no single norm contains the rules of its own use,[40] the reasonable or responsible application of rules requires, as Habermas must admit, "a practical intelligence [*Klugheit*] that *precedes* [vorgeordnet] the interpretation of practical reason through discourse ethics, or at least is not subordinate to rules of discourse."[41] To insist that "universal laws of practical reason" — that is, the "topoi" of jurisprudence, which are paradigmatic for every philosophical ethics[42] — also become effective in this intelligent, even "impartial,"[43] application of norms is of no help whatsoever.

This brings me to another important point. Even the concrete conception of the *idea* of complete, universal justice underlies limitations, as we have already encountered in the problem of the paradox of recollective (or anamnestic) solidarity and in the question of our relation to nature in itself. One might, therefore, first ask how we can ever "satisfy the constitutive thesis [*Grundsatz*] of discourse ethics, which always demands *everyone's* agreement, if we are not in a position to redress the pain and injustice suffered for our sake by previous generations — or at least to hold out the prospect for an equivalent to the redemptive power of the last judgment [*erlösende Kraft des jüngsten Gericht*]?"[44] Put otherwise, is the happiness of individuals in later generations gained only at the expense of individual and collective amnesia? There is an indissoluble tension between the *commandment* to recollect the historical sacrifices to which we all too often owe our improved chances of existence and the *need* actually to grasp or to realize these possibilities of being. The idea of universal justice is essen-

---

38. Habermas, *Moralbewußtsein und kommunikatives Handeln*, 114.
39. Ibid., 119.
40. Habermas, "Moralität und Sittlichkeit," 27. See MacIntyre, *After Virtue*, 141.
41. Habermas, *Moralbewußtsein und kommunikatives Handeln*, 114.
42. Habermas, "Moralität und Sittlichkeit," 27.
43. Ibid., 28.
44. Ibid., 32.

tially irredeemable not because it runs counter to the "logic" of practical discourse but because the counterfactual "posthumous consent of the victims" must, in Habermas's words, remain "abstract." It lacks the "power of *redemption*."[45] Peukert draws the full consequence of this observation: "One's own existence turns from solidarity, to which it is owed, into self-contradiction. The condition of its possibility becomes its destruction."[46] Only the "anamnestic power of recollection [*Eingedenken*],"[47] of a memory of the dead, could "compensate,"[48] to some degree, for this lapse or omission in discourse and, hence, counterbalance this "blemish" on the idea of complete justice.

Such anamnestic recollection, actualized in the "sympathetic solidarity with the past despair of the slaughtered,"[49] must thus become an unavoidable postulate of discourse ethics. Its concrete application, however, lies "*beyond* moral-practical *insights*."[50] Nevertheless, it remains doubtful whether there has ever been—or could ever be—a plausible, classical-modern, theological exploration of this obscure, prediscursive, and, hence, nonnormative responsibility. Only the negative metaphysical sketches that constitute the core of minimal theologies can simultaneously respect this aporetics and make it fruitful. We are not so far removed here from an interpretation in one of the most enigmatic notes in Benjamin's *Arcades Project*, in which he claims "that history is not simply a science, but also and not least a form of remembrance [*Eingedenken*]. What science has 'determined [or fixated, *festgestellt*],' remembrance can modify. Such mindfulness can make the incomplete (happiness) into something complete, and the complete (suffering) into something incomplete. That is theology; but in remembrance we have an experience that forbids us to conceive of history as fundamentally atheological, little as it may be granted us to try to write it with immediately theological concepts."[51]

45. Habermas, *Vorstudien und Ergänzungen*, 516.

46. Peukert, *Wissenschaftstheorie, Handlungstheorie, Fundamentale Theologie*, 309. See also Jürgen Habermas, "Israel oder Athen: Wem gehört die anamnetische Vernunft? Johann Baptist Metz zur Einheit in der multikulturellen Vielfalt," *Vom sinnlichen Eindruck zum symbolischen Ausdruck*, 98–111; "Israel or Athens: Where Does Anamnestic Reason Belong? Johann Baptist Metz on Unity amidst Multicultural Plurality," *Religion and Rationality*, 129–38.

47. Habermas, *Vorstudien und Ergänzungen*, 517.

48. Ibid., 516. Elsewhere Habermas speaks of a *virtual* reconciliation of what cannot be redressed. See Habermas, *Philosophical Discourse of Modernity*, 16 / 26.

49. Habermas, *Vorstudien und Ergänzungen*, 517.

50. Ibid., my emph.

51. Benjamin, *Arcades Project*, 471 / 1:589.

Unlike Benjamin (and with him Adorno), however, in his formulation of ethical universalism Habermas restricts moral action to what must be in principle present and explicitly presentable interpersonal relationships, indeed, to relationships between subjects capable of speech and competent in their actions. Given this anthropocentric approach, there can be no plausible, rational "moral access to nature in itself,"[52] as an earlier ethics of sympathy and more recent ecological approaches to a cosmological ethics have proposed. As Habermas observes, "the moralizing of our dealings with external nature, just like a nonobjectifying knowledge of nature, cannot be carried out *on the same level* that Kant achieved in moralizing societal relationships and Newton achieved in objectifying the knowledge of nature."[53] Such a mode of observation, according to Habermas, "stretches the circle of neighbors beyond the potential participants in an already counter-factually conceived community of communication to all *concerned* living beings, in whose suffering we can sympathize: all those salvaged by Noah's Ark *ought* to enjoy the protection of the status of subjects with whom we interact at eye level."[54] The imprecise ethical "intuitions" or "sensations analogous to morality" forced upon us when we observe the "vulnerability of dumb creatures [*stummen Kreatur*]" cannot become *theoretically* fruitful without falling back on substantialistic or mythological worldviews. One can at best assume a heuristic role for them or transfer them to the realm of *"artistic production."*[55]

However that may be, one might suspect that an emphatic and critical moral consciousness, which ought not to be limited to the circle of mature fellow human beings, neither *needs* to progress in a procedural fashion nor *can* be explicitly presented in argument. On the contrary, it involves a finally incomprehensible obligation to what is morally commanded, one that Adorno compellingly phrases as follows: "What will one day be imposed and bestowed upon a better practice can here and now — according to the warning against utopianism — be no more visualized [or anticipated, *absehen*] by thought than practice, under its own concept, will ever be completely exhausted by knowledge" (*ND* 245 / 243, trans. modified). Even an uncanny claim of Benjamin that Adorno mentions somewhat later — "the execution of the death penalty might be

52. Habermas, *Vorstudien und Ergänzungen*, 518.
53. Ibid., 520.
54. Ibid., 518.
55. Ibid., 519.

moral, never its legitimation" (*ND* 286 / 282) — confirms this understanding of the limits of theory in practice.[56] This way of detaching morality from the thought of (ultimate) foundations might nonetheless become the leitmotif of a universalistic ethics because, finally, this "*groundlessness* of ethical life forms, however good they may be, provides the best *ground* for the recognition of other life forms."[57] According to Habermas,

56. See Benjamin, *Einbahnstraße, Gesammelte Schriften,* 4.1:138.

57. Seel, "Plädoyer für die zweite Moderne," in Kunnemann and de Vries, *Die Aktualität der "Dialektik der Aufklärung,"* 54, my emph. What Seel argues here, as I do throughout the present study, comes close to what J. M. Bernstein calls Adorno's "ethical modernism," by which he means the claim that "*all the rational authority of modern norms and principles derives from fugitive ethical action and experience*" (*Adorno: Disenchantment and Ethics* [Cambridge: Cambridge University Press, 2001], 38; see also his *The Fate of Art: Aesthetic Alienation from Kant to Derrida and Adorno* [University Park: Pennsylvania State University Press, 1992]). But what, in this view, would it mean that such ethical modernism "in its fugitive appearances provides both the normative authority of secular norms and principles, and the promise of a form of life in which these norms and principles would be fully instantiated" (*Adorno,* 38)? First, is the authority of norms — and secular norms at that — Adorno's deepest concern? Are not both authority and normativity, like the very concept and experience of the secular, peculiarly refracted and diffused in Adorno's decidedly modern, resolutely actualizing, but far from "presentist" or immanent account? Bernstein rightly points out the specific quality of otherness and othering which marks Adorno's texts: "that we live our relation to present and future in the mode of a *promise* is . . . Adorno's deepest discovery about the modal status of our ethical ideals and norms" (Ibid., 38–39). He also makes clear that Adorno's naturalism means nothing more than that. But these two claims do not conflict with the minimally theological, maximally rhetorical, and even aporetic interpretation that I propose.

What would it mean, as Bernstein's reference to a "form of life" further suggests, to view "living nature as the presupposition of ethical life" (*Adorno,* 38–39) or "life" as "the natural basis of the normative" (J. M. Bernstein, "Re-Enchanting Nature," in *Reading McDowell: On "Mind and World,"* ed. Nicholas H. Smith [London: Routledge, 2002], 217–45), and how does this view relate to the distinct antinaturalism, if not transcendentalism, at work in Adorno — which, on closer scrutiny, corresponds to a Levinasian view of "ethics" rather than to the desire for a "re-enchantment" of nature? No call for *Wiederverzauberung* is to be found in Adorno. Speaking of life as a presupposition or natural basis, then, would at most capture a general insight into the human and intuitive use of "material a priori predicates," enabling us to understand why the meaning of certain notions and concepts (not least that of living nature or natural life) "outruns" their "discursive employment." In Bernstein's words: "If normativity is more than the thin notion of having a reason for a belief this is because there are kinds of objects in the world, the living ones, that demand to be responded to differently than others, the mere ones and the dead ones; if all our reactions are not different, then we will treat the animate as if inanimate, doing it incalculable harm thereby" (ibid., 238).

But for Adorno this — fundamentally Wittgensteinian — reading goes only so far. Can we be certain, for example, that for him, as for the utopian messianism and materialism of Benjamin and Bloch, the realms of the inanimate (i.e., of minerals, stones, plants, mere objects, and "things") and also of the dead or, more precisely, the no longer, not yet, or not quite living (nonpresent past and future generations, ghosts, and angels) are ultimately excluded from the prepredicative responsiveness and responsibility that Wittgenstein, Gadamer, Haber-

morals are *universalistic* "when they permit only those norms to count that might always achieve the well-considered and uncoerced agreement of all concerned."[58] But, then, having to do something truly without any restrictions might, in the end, amount to having no discursively justified "*grounds* for doing something."[59] This insight should not be confused with "neo-Aristotelian" attempts to circumvent the Kantian-Hegelian or formal-pragmatic and pragmatist opposition between the appeal to abstract principles and embodied ethos. That philosophical position views practical reason as "bound to a context of an implicit understanding of the good, whether that be mediated by a practice in which this good is immanent, or by modes of action that are causally related to and constitutive of the good, or by the relation to paradigmatic models of a real or fictional kind."[60] The implications of Habermas's formulations lie elsewhere.

In Levinas we learn that moral obligation does not take place on the basis of empirical or counterfactual conditions of symmetry in interaction, nor can it be understood as an asymptotic approach to ideal limit values. Rather, it plays itself out, thanks to an inversion of reciprocity and intentionality, in a converse direction, so to speak: in its sense of "indescribable duty" (*HAH* 16), "an increasing of the debt beyond the *Sollen*" is revealed (*OB* 55 / 71). The answer to such a "meta-ethical" indebtedness is therefore unlikely to be a communicative action or a verbal dialogue

---

mas, McDowell, and, in their footsteps, Bernstein reserve for a conception of re-enchanted, that is to say, second nature conceived of as exclusively human?

By contrast, is the overall intuition of both Adorno and Levinas not precisely that we are answerable to what is *less* and, at the same time, *larger* and *better* than natural or biological "life," hence (explicitly in the case of Levinas) conceivable only in terms of "spiritual life"? As we have seen, for both living on (after "Auschwitz," in the day and age of "torture"), as well as the very force of life, seem to be characterized by "guilt." Bernstein is thus partly at odds with both Adorno and Levinas when he proclaims the "deep intertwining of the normative and the natural" and—with an antinaturalist twist—adds that "the natural is already in itself normatively constituted" (ibid., 239). Reason, he concludes, "lives off that if it lives at all; hence, the disenchantment of nature is brought about by the subsumption of circumambient, living nature by the system of law-like nature, and that work of subsumption (or supervenience) can generate a transcendental anxiety because it, in fact, destroys a necessary condition for normativity" (ibid.). By contrast, both Adorno and Levinas, in a decidedly anti-Heidegger invective, view the systematic imposition of law on nature by way of science and technology—demythologization and, indeed, disenchantment—as a constitutive possibility of responsibility and justice.

58. Habermas, *Die neue Unübersichtlichkeit*, 50.

59. Habermas, *Moralbewußtsein und kommunikatives Handeln*, 59.

60. Charles Taylor, "Die Motive einer Verfahrensethik," in Kuhlmann, *Moralität und Sittlichkeit*, 130. See also Taylor, "Sprache und Gesellschaft," in Honneth and Joas, *Kommunikatives Handeln*, 38–39, 45–46.

(alone). (See *HAH* 75, 77.) When Levinas nonetheless interprets the central figure of "substitution" in light of the concept of "communication," the inflection of this notion — and, hence, Levinas's distance from the theory of communicative action, from the central presupposition of formal pragmatics, which is the symmetry between agents — is equally clear: "Substitution is a communication from the one to the other and from the other to the one without the two relations having the same sense. It is not like the reversibility of the two way road open to the circulation of information, where the direction is indifferent" (*OB* 106 n. 22 / 152 n. 22).

Furthermore, in Levinas the idea of the infinite is not a critical *postulate* of thinking, as initially appears to be the case in Adorno. For the former it concerns less a theoretical idea than the moral experience (see *TI* 40, 53, 58 / 10, 24, 29) of a metaphysical-eschatological longing for what surpasses totality (*TI* 113 / 86), awakened by the other person in an asymmetrical ethical relation whose exteriority corrects and inflects the realm of the self and the same, of interiority and economy. Formally, however, the manner in which Levinas appropriates and extensively modifies Descartes's ontological proof of God's existence reveals parallels with the negative metaphysical aspect of Adorno's thinking and its similar claim that all philosophy revolves around the central insight upon which the ontological proof is based. Their paths diverge in Levinas's deformalization of this idea, which he takes to be exclusively (or is it primarily?) ethical. Does this conceal a marked difference in optics?

That conclusion would perhaps be too hasty because the negative metaphysical idea of transcendence is concretized, even in Adorno (see pt. 2), in some traces of otherness (*Spuren des Anderen*), in an anamnestic relating to our "nature" and its "transience [*Vergängnis*]," in "spiritual experience," in childhood memories, in the appellation of certain place names, in the minimal moral intuition of how to live as a good "animal," and so on.

By contrast, one must recall that in Levinas the idea of the infinite remains, in an important sense, empty of content. The modality of how it comes into the realm of appearance, the world of phenomena, can be described as that of a trace, an enigma, a marvel, an event, but *what* this unique yet exemplary experience communicates in its appeal can "only" be summed up in the commandment to stand at the other's disposal — to the point of substitution, becoming hostage — and to banish suffering (or even to suffer for the suffering that the other inflicts upon me or suffers for me). Such a core characterization of morality does not annul the necessity—a need (*Bedürfnis*) of reason, as Kant knew—to develop kinds of practical wisdom, judgment, and intelligence (*Klugheit*), that is to say, forms of habit and ethos, even of skills, competence, and mastery. Yet Levinas's quasi-transcendental direction of questioning and its ensuing redescription of responsibility cannot instruct us in the art of weighing up morality versus normalizing forms of ethical life (i.e., *Sittlichkeit*, in Hegel's sense), nor can it provide us with context-specific guidelines. Such criteria and forms of the good life lie outside his meta-ethical perspective: in Derrida's words, his "not (yet) practical ethics."[61] This insight into the ungroundability, asymmetries, and passivity of the moral relation allows the question concerning the hermeneutical—if not necessarily practical— supplement of philosophical reason as well as the role of judgment (see pt. 1) to come more pointedly to the fore. It sharpens our awareness of the necessary failure and structural insufficiency—perhaps, quite literally, *irrelevance*—of merely abstract, categorical, universal, even intelligible ideas of normativity which assume their commensurability with the particular parameters of practical situations and thereby ignore their discrepancy with (and hence intolerance of) the singular good. This, and nothing else, is Adorno's central insight in *Minima Moralia*: "Unrestricted goodness [*Güte*] becomes confirmation of all the bad that exists, in that it downplays its difference from the trace of the good [*Spur des Guten*]" (*MM* 77 / 85, trans. modified). Thinking in unrestricted generalities and thinking concretely—that is to say, micrologically, minimally, and, in precisely this sense, infinitely, indeed ab-solutely—constitute two different approaches to philosophy, to practical reason, and to aesthetic experience. Both Adorno's negative dialectics, in its dialectical critique of dialectics, and Levinas's antiphenomenology, in its phenomenological delimitation of phenomenology, are remarkable instances of the second approach. But in what, exactly, does their relation consist?

The Cross-Pollination of Dialectics and Phenomenology

The suspicion that the figures of thought in Adorno and Levinas might illuminate each other has guided my attempt to compare and contrast their texts. Such an effort can be justified, however, only to the extent that Adorno's mode of thinking can, at least in some part, be described as phe-

61. Derrida, *Writing and Difference*, 135 / 199, my emph.

nomenological (in the sense Levinas gives to this method and its possible innovation) and Levinas's way of thinking be described as dialectical (in Adorno's most consistent, i.e., negative, sense of the term). As we have seen, it is in fact possible to push the interpretation of their texts to a point at which Adorno's (negative) dialectics turns into "phenomenology" and Levinas's phenomenology suddenly reveals a "dialectical" horizon of experience.

In addition, by contrasting their figures of thought, we can see that the critique of phenomenology carried out by Adorno and the critique of dialectics undertaken by Levinas are often flawed or simply dependent upon quite undifferentiated images of these forms of thought in their most influential historical expressions. Adorno's critique of Husserlian thinking, in other words, of its subjective idealism, hardly measures up to the interpretation of phenomenological method—of its "technique," implicit horizons, and intentional analysis—which Levinas gives; and Levinas's critique of Hegelian objective or absolute idealism does not affect the contours of dialectics as negative which Adorno maintains.

Adorno's work becomes phenomenological where it thinks dialectics to the end and turns into a description—which finally remains aporetic—of the moral, metaphysical, and aesthetic traces of the good life (not the good life itself, whose image is prohibited, but its metaphysical hints and remnants, which shine out only in the "very moment of its downfall"). As catchwords for his procedure, one could mention: the Husserlian term *passive synthesis,* of which Levinas makes so much and of which Adorno speaks in his Hegel studies; *dialectics at a standstill,* which he borrows from Benjamin; and *micrology,* which he uses as a concept for gathering together his physiognomic concretizations.[62]

Levinas's work appears dialectical where history, the subject, and linguistic structures are broken through not only by the absolute alterity of the Other (*Autrui* and *illeity* as the privileged instances of the nonidentical) but also by the extreme negative counterpole to this dimension of sense—another and, it would seem, far more risky, diametrically opposite or at least contrary "curvature of social space." I am referring to the absurd *il y a,* which shows certain structural parallels with Adorno's notion of horror (*Grauen*) and which seems to fulfill a comparable role in the general economy of Being, as that which precedes, traverses, exceeds, or es-

---

62. On the concept of micrology, see also *TI* 288 / 265.

capes it. As in Adorno, in Levinas the conceptual, moral, criteriological, as well as expressive inadequacy of the order of the self-same and the longing for the other result in part from an *antagonism internal to ontology* itself. Most important in this connection, however, is the resulting insight, common to both thinkers, that ontology itself never sufficed; more pertinent than the question of Being's limitation or existence's finitude is the insight that even the fullest, most totalized, and most reconciled form of Being falls short of its other, indeed, of its deepest aspiration, its inspiration and orientation, in all the emphatic senses Levinas has given to these words.

A nontrivial comparison and contrast between these authors' modes of thinking stands or falls with the possibility of a *cross-pollination* and *cross-fertilization* of these thematic and methodological aspects of negative dialectics and anti-phenomenology. The structural or formal parallels between Adorno's and Levinas's paradoxical figures of thought, however individually inflected, suggest at the very least that the intricacies and difficulties in which they are caught up cannot be attributed simply to sterile idiosyncrasy on their part. The problem presented by their figures of thought is not a function of their respective intellectual biographies but is, instead, a general philosophical one. Thus, it is not, in principle, tied to exercises in dialectical or phenomenological ways of thinking, casting a doubtful light on these particular schools of thought or on the peculiar adoption of their aims and procedures by these authors. But such an assertion can be made plausible only if we do not limit ourselves to interpreting these thinkers as they at times understood themselves. In any event it seems fruitful to return (negative) dialectical and (anti-) phenomenological figures of thought, driven to their extreme by Adorno and Levinas, back to a temperate and, if one will, skeptical or deconstructive hermeneutics, of sorts.[63] Rationality, as I have said, cannot rely on the risk of a negative metaphysical idea of transcendence alone. It also appeals to a peculiar modality of our judgment (a judgment passed on history, on singular cases, on others, etc.). Can we, once again, think both these things together?

---

63. On the relationship between dialectics and hermeneutics, see Gadamer, *Das Erbe Hegels*, 77. On phenomenology and hermeneutics, see Ricoeur, *Du texte à l'action: Essais d'herméneutique II* (Paris: Seuil, 1986) / *From Text to Action,* trans. Kathleen Blarney and John B. Thompson (Evanston, Ill.: Northwestern University Press, 1991). On the convergences and differences between hermeneutics and deconstruction, see Jean Greisch, *Herméneutique et grammatologie* (Paris: Editions du Centre National de la Recherche Scientifique, 1977).

The Elliptical Construction of the Rational:
On a Motif in Paul Ricoeur

At the end of *La Métaphore vive* (*The Rule of Metaphor*) Paul Ricoeur distinguishes between speculative discourse, which concerns conceptual analysis, and metaphorical discourse, which does not reveal its meanings in that determinate and, in a sense, limited way. Referring to Kant's *Critique of Judgment,* he suggests relating the two alternatives within a "mixed discourse," one that would constitute a hermeneutics. In the alternation between the conceptual and the metaphoric (or, more broadly, poetics, rhetoric, and narrative) we can see that this hermeneutic "mixed discourse" concerns, as Ricoeur puts it, the "presentation of the Idea by the imagination that forces conceptual thought to *think more.*"[64] The speculative and metaphoric dimensions of thought and experience might help to express, respectively, the moment of *differentiation* between distinguishable elements and domains (of thought, action, and judgment) which enables critical distance and, hence, the possibility of decision—the very condition of responsibility—*and* the moment of a less articulate, if not necessarily participatory or mythically diffuse, *belonging.* Both moments, Ricoeur claims, pertain, in good Kantian fashion, to rational or reasonable discourse in its emphatic definition; both moments reveal, in good Hegelian fashion, their truth in their—this time, open-ended—dialectic alone.

It might not be too farfetched to supplement this framework with the elliptical construction of the two foci of the rational which I have analyzed in the writings of both Adorno and Levinas. Their work shows precisely what terms such as "*fundament, systematic, condition of possibility,* and the like can still mean when the speculative is transposed into an open horizon and the dynamic of the metaphorical formation of meaning is suspended."[65] They thereby provide an analysis that resonates with Ricoeur's, whose radical consequences he will address only in his later writings, *Temps et récit* (*Time and Narrative*) and *Soi-même comme un autre* (*Oneself as Another*) in particular, often with explicit reference to Benjamin (though not to Adorno) and, more extensively, to Levinas.[66]

---

64. Ricoeur, *Rule of Metaphor,* 303 / 383–84; see also 318 / 398.

65. This I take to be Adorno's and Levinas's way of responding to the question Bernhard Waldenfels asks Ricoeur in *Phänomenologie in Frankreich,* 323.

66. See, for a more expanded discussion, my essay "Attestation du temps et de l'autre: De *Temps et récit* à *Soi-même comme un autre,*" in *Paul Ricoeur: L'Herméneutique à l'école de la phé-*

"They express together what neither could express alone"

Does Levinas's philosophy offer a persuasive answer to the vacilla-tion between conceptual philosophy and nonconceptual mimesis found throughout Adorno's writing? Especially in his late work, and with far greater consequence than Adorno (who, as we have seen, mentions this motif only incidentally), Levinas tries to present the modality of transcen-dence as an ab-solute, a *trace*. The trace of what "is" other or otherwise than being can be thought neither as the limit of coming into presence nor as an absence that only awaits disclosing nor as a symbol linking absence and presence in a substantialist, dialectical, or hermeneutic way (see *OB* 86–87 / 126–27; *DEHH* 197). And yet, while closer to allegory, the trace nonetheless retains a "relation without relation" to whatever is given or addressed, that is to say, to the realm of the self and the same, as well as to that of the other.

Although the metaphor of the trace (*die Spur des Anderen*) is impor-tant in Adorno's work, one has no trouble also finding even stronger remi-niscences of the pathos of the West. In my view the ambiguity and even contradictoriness in Adorno's work can be attributed in part to the cir-cumstance that, now and again, motifs of utopian redemption seem to hold sway over his more promising exploration of the modalities of the "idea of transcendence" and "spiritual experience." These materialistically and sensually defined utopian motifs should not be confused with the reinterpretation of our metaphysical—and, more importantly, theologi-cal—legacy, in the very moment of its "downfall." Nor could even good-will salvage them entirely as merely critical and polemical interjections whose meaning should be taken rhetorically, strategically. Especially in his discussions of art and aesthetics (though also in various passages on moral and religio-philosophical themes), this irreparable "remainder of bad metaphysics" in Adorno's thinking can be attributed to his tendency to continue to stylize "traces of the other" as silent witnesses and her-alds of an emphatic truth that is either past or yet to come and which lies waiting for us, just around the corner of the present.

Yet Adorno's thinking, for all its lack of consequence and rigor in the pursuit and formal analysis of the figure of the "trace of the other," when

---

noménologie, ed. Jean Greisch (Paris: Beauchesne, 1995), 21–42. I will return to these matters at length in my forthcoming book *Instances*.

compared with Levinas does seem to escape the latter's explicit—and, in this regard, somewhat implausible—*fixation on ethics,* however radically redefined and stripped of its traditional moralism and its ancient and modern humanism (whose residues, as we have seen, are not absent either). To this one might object that Levinas's philosophy stands or falls by the privileged place it grants to morality and the "humanism of the other person"—more precisely, by the attempt to link genuine alterity exclusively to the realm of intersubjective and asymmetrical responsibility. Indeed, he writes, "it is only man who could be absolutely foreign to me—refractory to every typology, to every genus, to every characterology, to every classification—and consequently the term of a 'knowledge' finally penetrating beyond the object" (*TI* 73 / 46).

Nevertheless, one might ask whether Levinas can actually provide *philosophical* plausibility for this "existential" intuition and insight. Do the phenomenological descriptions he presents enable us to consider the transcendence of ethical-metaphysical longing (*Désir*) to be something exclusive and reserved to the human realm—to "discourse," to "saying," to the "curvature of social space," rather than to nature, history, and culture—alone? One can show, on the basis of his texts, that they do not. His detailed descriptions of the experience of art in "Reality and Its Shadow" and "On Maurice Blanchot," as well as his phenomenology of the erotic and (more incidentally) of materiality, "betray" the moral-philosophical intentions upon which his work claims to be grounded.

I have concentrated on Levinas's writings about art because this aspect of his work can best be contrasted with Adorno and because the meaning of the erotic in his philosophy has already been the subject of detailed investigations,[67] whereas the interpretation of materiality finds only a relatively slim (but nonetheless significant) textual basis.

67. See Stephan Strasser, "Erotiek en vruchtbaarheid in de filosofie van Emmanuel Levinas," *Tijdschrift voor Filosofie* 37 (1975): 3–51; Catherine Chalier, *Figures du féminin: Lecture d'Emmanuel Levinas* (Paris: La Nuit Surveillée, 1982); and Luce Irigaray, "Fécondité de la caresse: Lecture de Levinas, *Totalité et Infini*, section IV, B, 'Phénoménologie de l'Eros,'" in *Éthique de la différence sexuelle* (Paris: Minuit, 1984), 173–99 / "The Fecundity of the Caress: A Reading of Levinas, *Totality and Infinity*, 'Phenomenology of Eros,'" trans. Carolyn Burke and Gillian C. Gill, in Luce Irigaray, *An Ethics of Sexual Difference* (Ithaca: Cornell University Press, 1993), 184–217. See also Tina Chanter, *Ethics of Eros: Irigaray's Rewriting of the Philosophers* (New York: Routledge, 1995), chap. 5; Paulette Kayser, *Emmanuel Levinas: La Trace du féminin* (Paris: Presses Universitaires de France, 2000); and, for a further reflection on the "intentionality of love" and the phenomenology of eros, Jean-Luc Marion, *Prolegomènes à la charité* (Paris: La Différence, 1986)/*Prolegomena to Charity*, trans. Stephen Lewis (New York: Fordham Univer-

All these (different, alternative?) areas might, however, give rise to a single question that Levinas's thinking — at least at a superficial or prima facie level — leaves, in my view, unresolved: does a philosophy of ab-solute difference not stand or fall precisely by its ability to investigate *all* dimensions of actual, potential, and virtual difference, to which philosophical thinking, on closer inspection, can never fully catch up, both in the relation of the same to the other and in the relation of the self to its own and to surrounding — nonhuman, animal, and inanimate — nature? Such dimensions pervade and qualify remembrance of the self's own individual and collective past, its tireless dealings with the endless exegesis of traditional texts, and the relationship to its own body; finally, they caution us against identifying the ipseity of "the self" with the (Cartesian or transcendental) ego and "the Other" exclusively with the (human and divine) other.[68]

In Adorno's work all the areas I have named as regions and dimensions in which genuine alterity — whether actual, potential, or virtual — can begin to emerge are more or less explicitly explored without being immediately reduced to realms of morality and intersubjectivity. Aesthetic experience seems, indeed, paradigmatic for the relation to the nonidentical in Adorno, but this does not mean that it is the exclusive model. In his writings one can come across the trace of the other just as easily in moral, metaphysical, and "spiritual [*geistige*]" experience. References to the sensations of the erotic — and, a fortiori, of materiality — are not absent either.

If these observations have some pertinence, then what one of Adorno's most formidable interpreters claims about the relationship between philosophy and art in this author's work might equally apply to the relation between his thinking and that of Levinas as a whole: "They express together what neither could express alone."[69] Referring to a motif that we encountered earlier in *Aesthetic Theory* (see *AT* 191 / 183), Wellmer notes:

> Just as a moment of blindness adheres to the immediacy of aesthetic experience, so does a moment of emptiness adhere to the "mediacy" of philosophical thought. Only in combination are they capable of circumscribing a truth

---

sity Press, 2002), esp. chap. 4 (dedicated to Levinas); and *Le Phénomène érotique* (Paris: Grasset, 2003).

68. See Derrida, *Writing and Difference*, 105, 110 / 155, 161–62.

69. See Wellmer, "Wahrheit, Schein und Versöhnung," in von Friedeburg and Habermas, *Adorno-Konferenz 1983*, 143; see also Wellmer, *Zur Dialektik von Moderne und Postmoderne*, 14.

which neither alone is able to articulate. . . . . In his "Fragment on Music and
Language," Adorno describes this mutual insufficiency of aesthetic and discursive knowledge like this: "Discursive language [*Die meinende Sprache*] wishes
to express the absolute in a mediated way, but the absolute eludes its grasp at
every turn [or in each, even the best, single intention, *in jeder einzelnen Intention*], leaving each attempt behind in its finiteness. Music expresses the absolute directly, but the very moment [*Augenblick*] it does so, the absolute is obscured [*verdunkelt*], just as excessively strong light dazzles [or, rather, blinds,
blendet] the eye so that it can no longer register what is clearly visible [*das
ganz Sichtbare*]." The language of music and discursive language appear as the
separated halves of "true language." . . . The idea of this "true language" is the
"figure of the divine name [*Gestalt des göttlichen Namens*]." In the aporetic relationship between art and philosophy, a theological perspective is sublated:
art and philosophy combine to form the two halves of a negative theology.[70]

Mutatis mutandis, in the complementary yet aporetic relationship between the philosophical projects of Adorno and Levinas a certain theological perspective is, if not "sublated," then at least suggested. The dialectical critique of dialectics presented by Adorno's negative metaphysics
and the phenomenological critique of phenomenology pursued by Levinas's early and later thinking toward the other (*penser-à-l'Autre*) constitute two halves (more precisely, two among many relevant elements) of
the minimal theology whose contours have interested us here. This theology *in pianissimo*, exemplified by and exercised in their writings, is in
some ways reminiscent of the "musical thinking" Hegel identifies as the
unhappy consciousness; I will demonstrate later that, furthermore, it resembles some conceptual and rhetorical strategies of negative theology
or apophatics (see the appendix). By adopting this formula—"They express together what neither could express alone"—I implicitly assert that
the figures of thought which characterize the work of these authors *internally*—the logic of negative dialectics and the skeptical model of alternating reflection—must also be seen as decisive *externally*, as I differentiate their respective approaches from one another. These authors offer
supplementary—and deeply aporetic—accounts of the philosophical relationship between the self, the same, and the other, their mutual implica-

---

70. Ibid., cited after the English translation in Albrecht Wellmer, *The Persistence of Moder-
nity: Essays on Aesthetics, Ethics, and Postmodernism,* trans. David Midgley (Cambridge: MIT
Press, 1993), 7. Adorno quotations from *GS* 16:254, 252 / *Quasi una Fantasia. Essays on Modern
Music,* trans. Rodney Livingstone (London: Verso, 1998), 5, 2.

tion and their indelible tension. They do so in parallel or, more precisely, complementary ways, relying on a strategy that is alternatively rhetorical (based upon a principle of relentless exaggeration and dramatization) and argumentative, at the risk of performative contradiction. One might be tempted to call this model "poetic" or "deconstructive," depending on the motifs, contexts, or procedures from which the analysis starts out. In this chapter's final two sections let me briefly sketch out the elements of these two characterizations.

Adorno and Levinas as Readers of Paul Celan

"Substitution," the central chapter of *Otherwise than Being*, bears an epigraph from Paul Celan's poem "Lob der Ferne" ("Praise of Distance"), which offers in a nutshell the thematic Levinas addresses in his book: "Ich bin du, wenn/ich ich bin [I am you, when/I am I]."[71] According to this poem, the "I" achieves its ipseity not out of itself but only via its identification with—or, more precisely, virtual substitution for—the other, the "you." Because elements of dialogical thinking and Jewish mysticism transmitted via Buber, Benjamin, and Scholem are sprinkled throughout Celan's poetics and lyric art, it is worth asking what sort of refraction (*Brechung*) these rays out of the tradition (which are also themes addressed by Adorno and Levinas) experience as they enter into his texts.

Poetry, Celan observes, is the "majesty of the absurd that bespeaks the presence of human beings."[72] He advocates not a modernist, hermetic, or aestheticizing enlargement of art but, rather, that art be driven into its "innermost narrowness"[73] and thus set free the split and besieged I. In this attempt at contraction the poem balances "at the margin of itself."[74] Art thus brings about an "estranged I [*Ich-Ferne*]."[75] By turning toward "what

71. This poem, which appears as an epigraph in *OB* 99 / 125, was published in the early collection *Mohn und Gedächtnis* (*Poppy and Memory*). It is cited from Paul Celan, *Gesammelte Werke*, 1:33 / "Praise of Distance," trans. John Felstiner, in *Selected Poems and Prose of Paul Celan*, 25. For a more extensive discussion of Celan's poetics, see my essay "Le Schibboleth de l'éthique: Derrida avec Celan," in *L'Ethique du don: Jacques Derrida et la pensée du don*, ed. J. M. Rabaté and M. Wetzel, Colloque de Royaumont, December 1990 (Paris: Métailié, Transition, 1992), 212–38. See also the chapter on Celan in my forthcoming book *Instances*.

72. Celan, "Der Meridian," *Gesammelte Werke*, 3:190 / "The Meridian," in Paul Celan, *Collected Prose*, trans. Rosmarie Waldrop (Riverdale-on-Hudson, N.Y.: Sheep Meadow Press, 1986), 40. The translations from this volume have at times been modified to reflect more closely the German original.

73. Ibid., 52 / 200.

74. Ibid., 29 / 197.

75. Ibid., 46 / 193.

is uncanny and strange,"[76] in a "straitening [*Engführung*]" of its language, art arrives at a "turning of breath [*Atemwende*]"[77] in the I, whose lost and forgotten self can thus find its way back to itself.

Celan wishes to understand this as a kind of "homecoming [*Heimkehr*],"[78] an idea that Levinas lays out in light of his notion that the substitution enacted by the poem is a kind of "statelessness [*apatridie*]" (*NP* 44 / 64).[79] In his essay "Paul Celan: De l'être à l'autre" ("Paul Celan: From Being to the Other") Levinas characterizes Celan's poems as conveying "an unheard-of modality of the *otherwise than being*" (*NP* 46 / 66). Levinas bases this thesis not on specific poems but, above all, on an interpretation of Celan's poetics as presented in the famous address "Der Meridian" ("The Meridian"), given when Celan received the Georg Büchner Prize in 1960. In addition, he takes into consideration a short prose piece that will be important for the present discussion, "Gespräch im Gebirg" ("Conversation in the Mountains").

In Levinas's view Celan's poetic language, which condenses itself, in its increasing tendency toward silence, into the minimal gesture of a hand-shake[80]—of "a saying without a said" (*NP* 43 / 63)—situates itself at a presyntactical and prelogical level of thinking and addressing the other. Levinas characterizes it as "pre-disclosing [*pré-dévoilant*]" (*NP* 41 / 60)—which is to say, escaping the language of ontology, of the thought of Being (as in Heidegger) and the Neuter (as in Blanchot). Levinas later writes more cautiously: "Beyond the mere strangeness of art and the openness of beings on being, *the poem takes yet another step:* strangeness is the stranger, the neighbor" (*NP* 44 / 64, my emph.). The poetic word is neither "language as such" nor the semantic-hermeneutic-differential "corresponding [*Entsprechung*]" of something unspoken to a pregiven (monological) language: it is, rather, an actualized and individualized speech.[81] Implicitly referring to Heidegger's late philosophy, Levinas reads Celan's demarcations as an indirect critique of the "radiance [or outburst,

76. Ibid.

77. Ibid., 47 / 195.

78. Ibid., 53 / 201.

79. Celan's poem "Shibboleth," from the collection *Von Schwelle zu Schwelle*, speaks of an "alien homeland [*Fremde der Heimat*]" (Celan, *Gesammelte Werke*, 1:131 / *Poems of Paul Celan*, trans. Michael Hamburger [New York: Persea Books, 1988], 97) or "homeland strangeness" (trans. John Felstiner, *Selected Poems and Prose of Paul Celan*, 75).

80. Celan, "Brief an Hans Bender," *Gesammelte Werke*, 3:177 / *Collected Prose*, 26.

81. Celan, "Meridian," 29 / 197. See Pöggeler, *Spur des Worts: Zur Lyrik Paul Celans* (Freiburg: Karl Alber, 1986), 149–50.

éclat] of the *physis* of the pre-Socratics" (*NP* 41 / 60).[82] Levinas draws
Celan's seeming "insensibility" (*NP* 45 / 65) to nature from a formulation in "Conversation in the Mountains": "for the Jew and nature are two,
have always been two [*zweierlei*], even today."[83] It can be shown, however,
that Celan did not write down this thought with reference to Heidegger
(or at least not primarily), however much that reference might apply to
the central insights of "The Meridian."[84] By contrast, "Conversation in
the Mountains" brings out points of interest which drop out of sight in
Levinas's interpretation of the Büchner Prize address.

"Conversation in the Mountains" in fact commemorates a planned
encounter with Adorno in Sils-Maria in 1959 — an appointment that was
missed, though "not by chance," as Celan remarks in a letter.[85] According to Pöggeler, this short prose piece should therefore "actually be read
as a conversation with Adorno, whom Celan wanted to meet in the Swiss
Alps."[86]

In the imaginary dialogue between the Jew Klein (Celan) and the Jew
Gross (Adorno) — "around a quarter of a Jew's life older"[87] — which takes
place one evening when "the sun, and not only it,"[88] had been obscured
and had sunk from the sky, the question of the relation between language
and nature plays a key role. According to the narrative, in the Jewish view
everything real is veiled or blemished, the mark of an old wound, and
so the two interlocutors cannot observe the calm and splendor of surrounding nature without inhibition. Jewish consciousness, Pöggeler comments, knows "no embeddedness in a sheltering nature and landscape."[89]
Is the language of natural beauty one for humans? Can its encoded references to a wholly — perhaps divine — other be borrowed by us, or is it
rather, in words that Celan puts into Adorno's mouth, "without *I* and

---

82. See also Stéphane Mosès, "Quand le langage se fait voix: Paul Celan, *Entretien dans le montagne*," in *Contre-jour: Études sur Paul Celan,* ed. Martine Broda, Colloque de Cérisy (Paris: Cerf, 1986), 120.

83. Celan, "Gespräch im Gebirg," *Gesammelte Werke,* 3:169 / "Conversation in the Moun-tains," *Collected Prose,* 18. Quoted in *NP* 45 / 65.

84. See Pöggeler, *Spur des Worts,* 149 ff.

85. Ibid., 157.

86. Ibid., 155; see also 104, 148, 154–57, 247–48, 251–59, 271. Cf. Celan, "Meridian," 53 / 201. The reference to Adorno is missing in Mosès's interpretation mentioned earlier, as it is in J. E. Jackson, "Die Du-Anrede bei Paul Celan: Anmerkungen zu seinem 'Gespräch im Gebirg,'" in H. L. Arnold, ed., *Text + Kritik* 53–54 (1977): 62–68.

87. Celan, "Conversation in the Mountains," 18 / 169.

88. Ibid., 17 / 169.

89. Pöggeler, *Spur des Worts,* 253.

without *You,* nothing but *He,* nothing but *It . . .* , nothing but *She,* and that's all"?[90] Whom does this petrified reality address? Does it say "Do you hear?" into a void? Does it voice its sorrowful cry independently, so that—perhaps—no one can hear it, "nobody and Nobody"?[91] Adorno, Pöggeler believes, owes us an answer to such questions. Consequentially, he would later point out Celan to Gershom Scholem as "the real 'Jew Gross.'"[92]

Nevertheless, Pöggeler concludes, "The conversation, which remains a fiction, still establishes a measure for a possible encounter."[93] How, for example, can one account for the fact, so often emphasized by other interpreters, that the two interlocutors—Jew Klein and Jew Gross—can scarcely be distinguished from each other during the course of their conversation?[94] However correct the evidence of two contrasting motifs may be, equally undeniable seems the dialectic and the absence of difference between its bearers, a difference so slight that it almost disappears: "The speech of one constantly reflects the speech of the other, and an entire chain of echoic effects concludes by canceling the difference between the two interlocutors."[95] How are we to understand the threads entangled in the weave of this most enigmatic of Celan's narratives?

Adorno attributes to natural reality both more and less than Celan does. More, insofar as nature (and art, which takes its paradigm from natural beauty) is supposed to be accompanied by a *weak* messianic power, in accordance with Benjamin. Less, insofar as these traces fall philosophically (and poetically?) under the prohibition against images which forbids us to depict and, hence, to affirm the concrete substantial and material circumstances that make up the good life.

Must, accordingly, Celan's assurance that every "thing, every person is, to the poem, which heads for the other, a form [*Gestalt*] of this other" be subject to Adorno's critique?[96] Does Celan not also say that images

90. Celan, "Conversation in the Mountains," 19–20 / 171; quoted in *NP* 41 / 60.

91. Ibid., 20 / 171.

92. Pöggeler, *Spur des Worts,* 157; see also 271 ff.

93. Ibid., 257.

94. Werner Hamacher speaks of an "alternation of the subject in the dialogue" (Werner Hamacher, "La Seconde de l'inversion: Mouvement d'une figure à travers les poèmes de Celan," in *Contre-jour: Études sur Paul Celan,* ed. Martine Broda, Colloque de Cérisy [Paris: Cerf, 1986], 185–221/ *Premises: Essays on Philosophy and Literature from Kant to Celan,* trans. Peter Fenves (Cambridge: Harvard University Press, 1996), 337–87.

95. Mosès, "Quand le langage se fait voix," 125.

96. Celan, "Meridian," 49 / 198.

of reality here and now dissolve in poetry because the poem is the place "where all tropes and metaphors should be driven *ad absurdum*"?[97]

Yet the works of Adorno and Celan hold in common a paradoxical relation of conceptual or poetic language to truth. This paradoxicality converges with the prohibition on images in the need not to subject the relation to an always concrete other to a quasi-mystical "*secret of encounter* [Geheimnis der Begegnung]"[98] or—more prosaically—to human relations of communication, whether actual or possible, discursive or otherwise. Philosophy and art, according to Adorno, find their truth content and their integrity only where they are not decreed by the standards of what can be immediately communicated (see *ND* 41 / 51; *AT* 321 / 476). They are, rather, always already altered and distorted by a personal dialogic whose harmonizing and sentimental premises Adorno suspects just as much as Levinas does.

Celan, by contrast, is concerned with "*conversation* [Gespräch] as the (perhaps only) possibility of remembering humans' being-to-each-other (and only then to the poet), . . . the 'apprehensive and governed' going-with-the-words, the 'detours' in the encounter with self (an old mystical motif . . .), as well as the dialogical, the 'taking of bearings' as the 'nowhere' and always actual 'place.'"[99] Celan hoped, Pöggeler explains, up to the very end that Adorno would write an essay on his work, although he scarcely recognized himself in the scattered claims about his poems in Adorno's writings on aesthetics. In contrast to how Celan understood his work, Adorno praises him as "the most important contemporary representative of German *hermetic* poetry," adding that his poetry attempts, paradoxically, to "speak of the most extreme horror through silence." Thus, Celan's poems contradict Adorno's own earlier, somewhat overhasty statement that no poetry could be written "after Auschwitz."[100]

97. Ibid., 51 / 199.

98. Ibid., 49 / 198.

99. Quoted from a letter in Pöggeler, *Spur des Worts,* 162. See also Celan, "Meridian," 49 / 198.

100. See Adorno, "Kulturkritik und Gesellschaft," *GS* 10.1:11–30 / "Cultural Criticism and Society," in Theodor W. Adorno, *Prisms,* trans. Samuel and Shierry Weber (Cambridge: MIT Press, 1981), 177–33; and his self-correction in *Negative Dialectics:* "Perennial suffering has as much right to expression as a tortured man has to scream; hence it may have been wrong to say that after Auschwitz you could no longer write poems" (*ND* 362 / 355). This is already true, e.g., for Celan's "Todesfuge" ("Deathfugue"), from his first collection of poems, *Mohn und Gedächtnis (Poppy and Memory) (Gesammelte Werke,* 3:63–64), as well as for "Engführung," from the collection *Sprachgitter (Speech-Grille)* (1:197–204), to which Adorno later paid particular attention (see *NL* 2:xii n. / 700 n. 1). These poems have been translated as "Death Fugue"

They "imitate," as Adorno puts it, "a language beneath the helpless language of human beings, indeed beneath all organic language." And a little farther: "The language of the lifeless becomes the last possible comfort for a death that is deprived of all meaning" (*AT* 322 / 477, my emph.). In this respect, Adorno concludes, Celan's work reminds us of that of Kafka, Beckett (see *AT* 218 / 325), Mallarmé, Valéry, and especially Baudelaire, whose poetry, Benjamin had already claimed, is a poetry "without aura" (*AT* 322 / 477).[101]

Yet Pöggeler and others have rightly shown how distinct from the tradition of modern or hermetic lyric Celan's poetry is. In Adorno's negative aesthetics only art's character as semblance or appearance can counter "second nature" by evoking some otherness. This semblance, paradoxically, both lays claim to truth and "reduces it to a point of virtually nothing [*Nullpunkt*]."[102] That is completely to miss Celan's intention. This, Pöggeler sums up, is unmistakable in "Conversation in the Mountains." Whereas Benjamin still tries to glean concrete insights from Baudelaire's *Fleurs du mal* (*Flowers of Evil*), Adorno, Pöggeler suggests, merely "trivializes" Celan's work as being that of a modernist.[103] In Celan's view, by contrast, instead of following up on Mallarmé's poetry and its supposed modernity, art should be attuned to the slightest quiverings of naturalness or, better, of *creatureliness*.[104]

Celan's undeniable proximity to Adorno—Pöggeler refers to their common admiration of Benjamin's essay on Kafka, in which Benjamin writes, "Attention is the natural prayer of the soul," and "The Meridian" echoes this in its evocation of "a kind of concentration mindful of all our dates"[105]—should therefore not obscure the essential distance of Celan's work from the formalist and thematic features of the modernist aesthetics of negativity. In Celan the broken, (an)organic world is, on the contrary, "directed [*hingeführt*] to the human and more-than-human [*Mehr-als-Menschlichen*], to You and I."[106] There is, moreover, in Celan's eyes

---

or "Deathfugue" and "The Straitening" or "Stretto," in *Poems of Paul Celan,* 61 and 137, and *Selected Poems and Prose of Paul Celan,* 31–32 and 119–31.

101. See Benjamin, "Das Paris des Second Empire bei Baudelaire" and "Über einige Motive bei Baudelaire," in *Gesammelte Schriften,* 1.2.

102. Pöggeler, *Spur des Worts,* 155.

103. Ibid., 258.

104. See Celan, "Meridian," 42 / 191–93.

105. See Benjamin, *Gesammelte Schriften,* 2.2:432. See also Adorno, *Über Walter Benjamin,* letter of 1934; and Celan, "Meridian," 50, 48 / 198, 196.

106. Pöggeler, *Spur des Worts,* 156, my emph.

no possibility of consolation in the utterly lifeless, as Adorno's comments misleadingly suggest, whereas conversely, Pöggeler suggests, "even death in mass annihilation does not simply forfeit all meaning": indeed, what is "untouchable [*das Unantastbare*]" and "immortal [*das Unsterbliche*]" in the murdered shines through in Celan's poetry, and even a new "aura" thereby emerges from their deaths.[107] Unlike Adorno's, Pöggeler claims, Levinas's philosophy makes it possible to articulate such an understanding of reality in its most destructive and indestructible dimensions.[108]

Of course, one might ask whether and to what extent Levinas's philosophy of the infinite can be reduced to a common denominator with Celan's attempt at "infinitely speaking [*Unendlichkeitssprechung*] of nothing but mortality and in vain."[109] Celan's poetry needs "to distinguish" step by step "the strange from the strange,"[110] that is, to distinguish the uncanniness into which the experience of art thrusts us from an other, given that the hope of poetry is finally "to speak *on behalf of an other*—who knows, perhaps of a *wholly other* [in eines Anderen *Sache zu sprechen—wer weiß, vielleicht in eines* ganz *Anderen Sache*]."[111]

The modality of transcendence being discussed here merits our attention. For Celan, it would seem, indecision or even undecidability—punctuated by the "who knows" and the "perhaps"—takes the place of a former theological certainty. What can it mean when Celan continues, in the passage I have just cited: "perhaps an *encounter* [or clash, *Zusammentreffen*] is conceivable between this 'wholly other' . . . and a not so very distant, a quite close 'other'—conceivable, perhaps, again and again"?[112] Does Celan's poetics thus confirm the central thesis of our investigation: that the religious, moral, or aesthetic relation to the other is always a particular coloring or tonality of the trace of the ab-solute? Does he poetically put into words, if not Adorno's perspective, then at least that of Levinas (as Pöggeler insists)?

When Celan describes poems as "detours from you to you [*Umwege von dir zu dir*]," in which language "becomes voice," or as creaturely "encounters [*Begegnungen*], paths from a voice to a listening You,"[113] then the

107. Ibid., 258.
108. See ibid., 11, 405 n. 10; and Wiemer, *Passion des Sagens*, 406–13.
109. Celan, "Meridian," 52 / 200.
110. Ibid., 47 / 196; see also 52 / 200.
111. Ibid., 48 / 196
112. Ibid., 48 / 197.
113. Ibid., 53 / 201.

implicit agreement with Levinas's central philosophical intuitions might appear unmistakable. Yet, when he adds that this involves "outlines for existence [*Daseinsentwürfe*] perhaps, for projecting ourselves into the search for ourselves [*Sichvorausschicken zu sich selbst, auf der Suche nach sich selbst*],"[114] then, in the adoption of this almost Heideggerian terminology, the difference from Levinas also becomes clear. The conceptuality or metaphorics used by Celan in his poetological statements produces, so to speak, a pendular movement between a dialogic enriched by Jewish and mystic sources and the Heideggerian thinking of Being.[115] And this is not all there is to it: not only the secret of the encounter with the You (an eminently Levinasian topos) but also an encounter with the self is somehow constitutive for Celan's poetic remembrance of the suffering that has taken place. In the "The Meridian" he states as much: "Enlarge art? // No. On the contrary, take art with you into your innermost narrowness. And set yourself free."[116] For this motif, we have seen, there is no strict Levinasian equivalent, at least not in the period of writing in which the Western *conatus essendi* forms the main target of his critique.

Could Levinas concur, then, with Celan's claim that the poem itself heads toward an other "which it considers it can reach and set free, which is perhaps vacant and at the same time . . . turned toward it, toward the poem"?[117] Celan contests the possibility of an *absolute* poem—in the sense of modernist aestheticism—yet in his opinion even the "least ambitious [*anspruchloseste*]" poem paradoxically lodges that "exorbitant" claim.[118] In other words, every poem answers in a unique and inimitable way an "'open' question 'without resolution,' which points toward the open, empty, and free."[119] Research into the topoi of the creaturely and human should thus be undertaken only "in a u-topian light."[120]

Celan famously designates this light in a metaphor that (taken literally) makes it possible to pass through tropes and tropics. He speaks of a "meridian": that is, "something—like language—immaterial yet earthly, terrestrial, in the shape of a circle that, via both poles, rejoins itself."[121]

114. Ibid.
115. See intro., Paul Celan, *Gedichten*, trans. F. Roumen, selected with a commentary by Paul Sars (Baarn: Ambo, 1988), 32.
116. Celan, "Meridian," 52 / 200.
117. Ibid., 48 / 197.
118. Ibid., 51 / 199.
119. Ibid., 50 / 199.
120. Ibid., 51 / 199; see also 52, 54 / 200, 202.
121. Ibid., 55 / 202.

The sum of all meridians, as Pöggeler explains, forms the globe and stands for the complete, the absolute: "The complete globe, whose places are all equidistant from the middle point, becomes the wholly other, which must remain utopia."[122] Where does this leave us?

The structure of the modern lyric, it has been argued, was from the outset marked by an "attention to style" which in it breaks out and "forces signs and what is signified as far apart as possible."[123] In this view the poetry of modernity, which wants "to resound [*tönen*] more than to speak,"[124] circles like a "de-romanticized romanticism" around "empty transcendence."[125] In contrast to this sort of autonomy artistic, Celan's poems show that art still "stands in the trace of what withdraws in its absence yet still gives measure to our lives."[126] In closest proximity to Levinas and at a remove from modern authors such as Kafka, Benjamin, Beckett, and Adorno, Celan thus resists the temptation of a historical and textual dissemination of meaning that ventures toward the impersonal and the Neuter:

> The traces that Celan's poems make visible do . . . not refer, like baroque allegories, to an absent meaning [*Sinn*] that can be decoded [*entschlüsseln*] in ways that have become bound to — and persuasive in — history. They pertain, rather, to the risk run by a singular person [*Einzelner*] in a time of transition. Boundary experiences — up to the obsessions of schizophrenia — enter into the poems, and yet Celan does not follow an allegorical mode of speaking that in the manner of Kafka's work, leaves reference to an other so far up in the air that the path back to the simple traces of life [*Spuren des Lebens*] can scarcely be found.[127]

Presumably, only in a concentrated experience of reading poems and texts can one trace the particular (natural historical or personal and interpersonal) substance and contours of this other and its more or less encoded modality. Perhaps only thus can the — *philosophically* ultimately undecidable — question of "attention to what is possible [*Aufmerksamkeit für das Mögliche*]" and the "quest for balance, at least the *minimum* [im Minimalen] that would make survival possible"[128] occasionally and tentatively

122. Pöggeler, *Spur des Worts*, 17; see also 162.
123. Friedrich, *Die Struktur der modernen Lyrik*, 17.
124. Ibid., 50.
125. Ibid., 30.
126. Pöggeler, *Spur des Worts*, 29.
127. Ibid., 34.
128. Ibid., 18.

be answered. For thought, action, and judgment always risk becoming abstract when they are directed in advance toward just one utopia, a single an-archy, in short, *a* meridian.[129]

Rationality and Deconstruction: Habermas, Derrida, and the Other of Reason

The formal-pragmatic theory of communicative action, I have shown, can never really accommodate the legacy of Adorno's and Levinas's most unruly motifs. It denies in advance—and, I have claimed throughout, somewhat overhastily—the necessity, let alone fruitfulness, of adopting a paradoxical model of argumentation which borders upon (and crosses into) the aporetic and does not shun rhetorical procedures in addressing the most challenging problems in practical and theoretical philosophy.

Although in *Postmetaphysical Thinking* Habermas seems to broach the perspective I have developed through attention to the *lectio difficilior* of Adorno's and Levinas's texts, when dealing with the transformation of metaphysical questions—including his assessment of negative metaphysics—the difference remains decisive. In this work Habermas writes: "The moment of unconditionality preserved in the discursive concepts of fallible truth and morality is not an absolute, at best, *an absolute liquefied by critical procedures.* Only with this remainder of metaphysics can we cope with the transfiguration of the world by metaphysical truths—the final trace of a *Nihil contra Deum nisi Deus ipse.*"[130]

But is "an absolute" that has been "liquefied" into critical procedure— by which Habermas means something in principle decidable and determining—ultimately not false coin? Might one not counter that, if such an "absolute" is to have any "critical" meaning, it will more readily give itself to a mode of "understanding" which establishes itself only *micrologically, in pianissimo,* that is to say, through an in principle infinite—and hence undecidable—exegesis and hermeneutics of sorts?

The "wavering shell" of communicative reason is, according to Habermas, not "stable" enough to serve as a new "foundation" for metaphysics, however negatively construed. The contemporary "outsider's perspective" that the latter opens "still offers an equivalent for the *extramundane* perspective of divine vision."[131] As we have seen, however, the mode of

129. See ibid., 13.
130. Habermas, *Nachmetaphysisches Denken,* 184–85, my emph.
131. Ibid., 185, my emph.

analysis which both Adorno and Levinas exemplify is premised not upon an "outsider's perspective" that is "extramundane" but, on the contrary, on an *extra-* and *transdiscursive* experience and expression that cannot be given without constant reference back to the discourse it exceeds. The alternative (leaving discourse behind altogether and adopting the extramundane view as a tenable, independent, prediscursive quasi-divine position based upon "intellectual intuition [*intellektuelle Anschauung*]," as the Romantics said) would amount to *either* regression into myth, with its absorption into diffuse totalities of otherness, *or* forgetting about the extra- and transdiscursive altogether (and hence adopting a one-dimensional, indeed bisected, conception of rationality).

Habermas is correct, in opposition to Schnädelbach (see chap. 2), insofar as the point of his remark in *Postmetaphysical Thinking* is that the contours of negative metaphysics cannot be sought in theoretical discourse as formal pragmatics conceives it. It in no way follows, however, that such negative metaphysics has thereby become obsolete in a more general sense—rather, merely that it might be illuminated along different lines of reasoning, for example, in the performative contradictions and strategic exaggerations of the methods and themes of dialectics and phenomenology as Adorno and Levinas develop them. Such reasoning can, as we have said, receive no other or better proof than *our* agreement with its proposed descriptions.[132] It is not by deduction or demonstration, nor by induction or empirical warrant, that these authors establish their philosophical claims but only through a mode of analysis which is at once conceptual and historical, cultural and existential, and which appeals to *our* acknowledgment of the appropriateness of its figures of thought (its idiom and arguments, systematic and rhetoric) to singular situations in which we happen to find ourselves.

Within the limited framework of this investigation, I can only tentatively sketch a figure of thought which might correct biases from which the work of Adorno and Levinas suffers as well. This final step will at the same time allow us to think through a bit farther the as yet scarcely articulated elective affinity between, on the one hand, the bursting apart of the order of the same and the other which Adorno and Levinas pursue in a similar movement of thought, from within and without, and, on the other, its projected *restitution*.

132. Goud, "Wat men van zichzelf eist," 51.

As my earlier remarks have no doubt indicated, I find Derrida's deconstructive and rhetorical "hermeneutics"[133] to be a treasure trove from which minimal theologies can draw, so long as it dares to practice a certain eclecticism like that employed in my discussion of Habermas's theory of rationality. Such a procedure, by accepting the risk of making new interconnections, can, I believe, uncover important points of reference both in the course of the development of Derrida's own texts and in the history of their reception in Continental and analytical Anglo-American philosophy, as well as in literary, visual, and more broadly defined cultural modes of study.

I have argued throughout that a figure of thought modeled on Adorno's and Levinas's approaches keeps itself *beyond* (but in a certain sense also this side of) the modern theory of communicative action, yet at the same time *this side of* (though in a certain sense also beyond) deconstructive hermeneutics. I have already outlined the strengths and weaknesses of the former in part 1; I must now briefly address the latter.[134]

In this context the points of contact and lines of demarcation between the formal features of Adorno's negative dialectics and Levinas's skeptical model of alternation, on the one hand, and those of the strategy of deconstruction, on the other, are of particular importance. Derrida's deconstructive philosophy, I will claim, offers a conceptual, argumentative, and rhetorical matrix in which Adorno's and Levinas's approaches can be both interrogated and more thoroughly worked out. His formal and quasi-transcendental idea of *différance* upholds, no less attentively than Adorno's discussion of the nonidentical and Levinas's idea of the infinite, the insight that reason does not find its raison d'être in itself, even (or especially) where it seems to carry out its most relentless identifications and totalizations, but is, instead, driven, haunted, or inspired into open dimensions and folds of Being and beings. In all three thinkers an alterity insinuates itself, traversing not only the categories and conceptual schemes of cognition but also the principles and rules of practical reason. When one interprets these three different articulations of—quite literally—the

133. Waldenfels's designation of Derrida's thinking as an "anti-hermeneutics" does not seem fully adequate. See Waldenfels, *Phänomenologie in Frankreich*, 546. The predicates *deconstructive* (see Frank, *What Is Neostructuralism?* 216, 222 / 281, 287) and even *rhetorical* (see T. C. W. Oudemans, "Hermeneutiek: Metaforisch spel van binnen en buiten," *Nederlands Theologisch Tijdschrift* [1984]: 179–96) seem more appropriate.

134. For a more extensive discussion of Derrida's work, see my books *Philosophy and the Turn to Religion* and *Religion and Violence*. See also the appendix to this volume, "The Theology of the Sign and the Sign of Theology."

pièces de résistance of all theorizing, acting, and judging, it is impossible not to notice that this alterity concerns something at once singular and unutterable. To borrow Derrida's terms, the differences in question are a priori "undecidable" and, accordingly, cannot be mastered by any discourse, however sophisticated and formalized; they remain to be decided, acted upon, and judged by singular instances (subjects, events, works) in no less singular situations. But what does the circumstance that they remain—at least theoretically, practically, and aesthetically—undecidable mean? Derrida writes, "An undecidable proposition, as Gödel demonstrated in 1931, is a proposition which, given a system of axioms governing a multiplicity, is neither an analytical nor deductive consequence of those axioms, nor in contradiction with them, neither true nor false with respect to those axioms. *Tertium datur,* without synthesis."[135]

Its modality is that of an unsublatable ambiguity that—being the condition of possibility for every difference and for difference as such, that is to say, the "difference between the same and the other"[136]—can never be wholly reconstructed or conceptually and argumentatively contained in discourse, however extended and open. By the same token, it could not show itself ethically nor be expressed through any aesthetic genre, albeit the most singular of gestures. Levinas, it would seem, indicates as much in the motto taken from Ionesco's *La Cantatrice chauve* (*The Bald Soprano*) which inaugurates and qualifies his discussion of the "trace of the other": "All in all, we never know, when someone knocks at the door, whether anyone is there or not" (*DEHH* 203).

This does not mean simply that Levinas (or, for that matter, Adorno and Derrida) sets out his idea of the ab-solute in such a manner that it merely—or abstractly—transcends its own description.[137] The structural undecidability implies, rather, that an actual and possible loss of meaning accompanies every (speaking about a) meaning fed by singular and concrete experiences. Arnold Burms and Herman de Dijn identify this expo-

135. Derrida, *La Dissémination* (Paris: Seuil, 1972), 248–49 / *Dissemination,* trans. Barbara Johnson (Chicago: University of Chicago Press, 1981), 219. See also *Positions* (Paris: Minuit, 1972), 58 / *Positions,* trans. Alan Bass (Chicago: University of Chicago Press, 1981), 42–43. See also, on Gödel's theorem, Ernest Nagel and James R. Newman, *Gödel's Proof* (New York: New York University Press, 1958).

136. Derrida, *Writing and Difference,* 128 / 189.

137. This is also how Carlos Steel describes Anselm's "ontological argument" in Anselm, *Proslogion gevolgd door de discussie met Gaunilo,* trans. and intro. Carlos Steel (Bussum: Het Wereldvenster, 1981), 48 n. 19. For an alternative account, see M. B. Pranger, *Consequente Theologie: Een studie over het denken van Anselmus van Canterbury* (Assen: Van Gorcum, 1975).

sure to an indelible exteriority and, as they say, "incarnation" of meaning as the most important characteristic of the deconstructive concept of transcendence and of the trace. With reference to Heidegger, Levinas, and Derrida, they explain that the transcendent (the trace, the ab-solute) cannot be attributed to a free design, that is to say, a project or projection sprung from reflection or from any other modality of our self-realizing existence. What arouses horror, inspires us sublimely, or awakens our deepest desires escapes our power and slips away from our cognitive-instrumental and practical categories of experience, just as it eludes even our most sober or sophisticated aesthetic expressions. The experience of such exteriority and "incarnation" is therefore always marked by an "unsublatable fissure or foreignness": "All that has sense or meaning inherits an essential ambiguity or internal dividedness that at once constitutes both meaning and the possibility of its loss."[138] Accordingly, there can be "no enchantment without a loss of splendor, no sense without nonsense, no construction without deconstruction."[139] From such a perspective the explicit or hidden assumption of a supposedly "all-encompassing meaning" must appear simply "illusory." Its logical implication is that transcendence can no longer be spoken of in "positive terms"—as if it concerned ultimately "an inexhaustible wealth," albeit one that "always in part escapes human experience." Consequently, transcendence could at best be discussed in "negative terms"; the source of all meaning, it remains simultaneously "that which can put an end to any experience of meaning."[140]

Yet might this ungraspable character of any genuine transcendence —which constantly withdraws itself from all cognitive, axiological, and other evaluative registers—not in turn be regarded as merely the "negative" side of an experience that may in the end reveal itself to be "positive" in nature?[141] This would be plausible only on the condition that one also affirm that no hidden information can ever be encoded in experiences of transcendence, exteriority, and incarnation. The model of cognition and experience, practice and judgment, which understands reality above all as a *code to be cracked*—whether semantically, referentially, semiotically, differentially, or even via the formally and pragmatically defined dis-

138. Burms and de Dijn, *De rationaliteit en haar grenzen,* 33; see also 28.
139. Ibid., 36.
140. Ibid., 29.
141. See Carlos Steel's review of the study by Burms and De Dijn, "Inzicht en zingeving," *Tijdschrift voor Filosofie* 49 (1987): 305.

course upon which the theory of communicative action is based — fails to measure up to this challenge of thinking through the implication of transcendence in light of its principle — and hence perpetual — loss: "Everything that is strongly desired is a symbol or 'beautiful appearance [*schöne schijn*]'; it is evocative, thus having a meaning not entirely comprised within itself, although it also does not refer to a content independent of this 'beautiful appearance,' that is, of its concretely embodied meaning."[142] Paradoxically, the very incarnation — or, in a different idiom, the "materialization," "concretion," "deformalization," and "inscription" of all meaningful words, things, gestures, and experiences — eludes all definitive description that would rely on preestablished frames of reference, conceptual schemes, predetermined contexts, historical genealogies, etymologies, and so on and so forth. The most singular and the most evasive — indeed, ab-solute — are two sides of the same coin, tossed up into the air for us to catch, in a *coup de dès* whose outcome is never certain, without therefore being simply aleatory, let alone indifferent.

To the extent that the motif of the trace in Adorno and Levinas comprehends such a concept of transcendence, transcendence can indeed be thought, acted upon, expressed, and, last but not least, *lived*. In order to further support this interpretation, let me briefly return to an enigmatic motif in Levinas to which I have already alluded (see chap. 7).

IN AN ESSAY DEVOTED TO the work of Levinas, Blanchot emphasizes what is proper to this author's thinking in light of any form of irrational, romantic, nihilistic, theological, or religious thinking. He observes that the motif of the meaningless *il y a,* of the absolutely indeterminate Neuter and Night — the realm of the untruth and very "error" of Being — manifests itself only as a permanent temptation, that is to say, as the flipside of ethical transcendence. One cannot separate the two. The ambiguity of all genuine transcendence, Blanchot claims, stands or falls by its possible confusion and entanglement with what would seem to be its opposite extreme, the *il y a*.[143] Levinas himself states as much when he writes that there is "ambiguity of sense and non-sense in being, sense turning into non-sense," and immediately adds that this ambiguity "cannot be taken

---

142. Burns and de Dijm, *De rationaliteit en haar grenzen,* 98; see also 100. On the idea of "cracking a code," see Marquard, *Abschied vom Prinzipiellen,* 135.

143. See Blanchot, "Notre Compagne clandestine," in Laruelle, *Textes pour Emmanuel Levinas,* 79–88.

lightly" (*OB* 163 / 208). And again: "To support without compensation, the excessive or disheartening hubbub and encumberment of the *there is* is needed" (*OB* 164 / 209).

If we are to understand Blanchot correctly, however, we must recognize that the dimension of the *there is* has more weight than a mere trial and temptation of the subject now rendered responsible. It plays a constitutive and deeply troubling role in the intrigue of the "divine comedy," although it would be incorrect to see it as a positive-dialectical moment, which could in principle be sublated in the general — this time divine — economy of Being. True, Levinas does not offer us a theodicy in disguise, nor is the Blanchotian motif of the *il y a* in his later writings simply "moralized" or "ethicized," as some interpreters have suggested. Nevertheless, he does qualify it as "a *condition* in the intrigue of subjectivity"[144] and as nothing less than a modality of "the-one-for-the-other" (*OB* 163 / 208–9). The otherwise-than-Being is even characterized as a "comedy taking place in the ambiguity between temple and theater, but wherein the laughter sticks in your throat at the approach of the neighbor" (*GCM* 69–70 / 115; see also 66–67 / 111; and *NP* 8 / 12).

But, one might object to this interpretation, is evil not always unambiguous, whereas the good (or goodness, even *la petite bonté*) — both because of its momentary, transitory nature and because of its constant revocation through subjective and objective, linguistic and, more broadly, ontological structures — remains hopelessly afflicted with an ambiguity that cannot be expunged, for reasons I have set out above? This question cannot hastily be answered either yes or no. An initial approach to an answer might be to introduce an important distinction. Of course, from the perspective of *existential* and personal self-description or narrative, good and evil concern the particular, singular experience of an absolute sense in spite of its possible revocation into non-sense, that is to say, into its nonoppositional perversion — into its image and mask, untruth and untruthfulness, which is the standing risk of idolatry and blasphemy. From the universalist (i.e., general and, at least partly, formal) perspec-

---

144. Rolland, "Getting Out of Being by a New Path," *OE* 46 / 51. Rolland's interpretation of how the disgust with pure Being in *Of Escape* and later the depersonalization of the *il y a* refer to a flight that is at *first indeterminate then ethically qualified* and effect a comparable passivity, especially in *Otherwise than Being,* confirms my hypotheses. Levinas writes: "Signification, as the one-for-the-other in passivity . . . *presupposes the possibility of pure non-sense* invading and threatening signification. . . . folly at the confines of reason" (*OB* 50 / 64, my emph.).

tive of *philosophical* discourse, however, the directness of "horror"—like its counterpart, namely, the (more than) categorical imperative to prevent it, the impulse to do good which cannot be further grounded by reason—can never be grasped, let alone expressed, in its immediacy and full intensity. That philosophy must resort here to paradoxical or aporetic arguments, to the enigmatic notion of the trace as well as to rhetorical exaggeration, marks its—perhaps—inhuman distance from all singular things, a distance to which philosophy also owes its force and freedom. Because philosophical thought produces and analyzes at most *necessary* (albeit not necessarily a priori) conditions for singular things, events, and experiences—and, in so doing, establishes conditions that are, in themselves, never sufficient for their full explanation or understanding—it cannot itself be seen as an actual or possible instantiation of any particular worldview, morality, or aesthetic.

Both Levinas's and Adorno's programs—even in the complementary and supplementary relationship and oblique dialogue that their writings, I have argued, entertain with each other—express precisely these two perspectives in the dual demand that philosophy put into words "the other of reason" (in both senses of the genitive, namely, the *genitivus objectivus,* or "the other or otherness with respect to it," and the *genitivus subjectivus,* or "the other or otherness that is internal to it").

One cannot and should not try to form an image of it. One can at most say that, whereas in Adorno's work the burden of the negativity of a metaphysically contingent history under which critical consciousness labors functions like a photographic negative of this dual other or otherness, in Levinas this experience of contrast has its counterpart in the role played by the weight of Being and its history as a whole. Yet both also think transcendence in positive, if not affirmative, terms, indeed, as a trace of the other, an idea of the good. Whereas this materialization of difference happens for Adorno primarily, if not exclusively, with reference to elements and fragments of happiness and the good life, in Levinas, by contrast, it is concretized in the maddening sense of a just life or, more precisely, of the singular lives of some singular just (as in the novel *Le Dernier des justes,* by Schwarz-Bart). That, in any event, is the intention upon which their work is based. Yet can these negative and positive shadings of the other and of otherness manage without each other? Do they not mutually implicate—that is to say, imbricate and contaminate—each other? Does the positive not remain irrevocably bound to its opposite, to horror and to mourning, just as the minimally material and concrete retains a minimal trait of abstraction and even formalism?

DERRIDA'S THINKING OFFERS A starting point for articulating *philosophically* the various different motifs — including the alternative materializations, concretizations, intonations, and so on — of the figure of the trace of the ab-solute which has guided me throughout this discussion. But, then, could I simply adopt Derrida's figure of thought? Is the deconstructive "relativization" of the human, all too human tradition of reason — if these terms indeed capture his undertaking (which is far from certain) — not itself in need of relativization, as I surmised earlier, following our discussion of Habermas (see chap. 2)? If deconstruction is to maintain its critical counterpoint — for example, with respect to the modern theory of rationality — is the thinking of difference not then also, paradoxically, in need of yet further differentiation, that is to say, de-formalization, materialization, and concretization along lines that Adorno and Levinas have explored in exemplary ways?

Up to this point I have employed the concept of deconstruction in the relatively trivial sense in which deconstructive "hermeneutics" equals a metaphysical-critical unmasking of the onto-theological tradition that makes use of insights derived from rhetorical method and literary criticism, in addition to visual and conceptual analysis. Habermas, for his part, lays out this "minimal interpretation" by claiming that Derrida "calls his procedure deconstruction because it is supposed to *clear away* [abräumen] the ontological *scaffolding* erected by philosophy in the course of its subject-centered history of reason. However, in his business of deconstruction, Derrida does not proceed analytically, in the sense of identifying hidden presuppositions or implications. . . . Instead, Derrida proceeds by a critique of style, in that he finds something like indirect communications, by which the text itself denies its manifest content, in the rhetorical surplus of meaning inherent in the literary strata of texts that present themselves as nonliterary."[145] I must question this brief characterization because it does not adequately account for the "philosophical" and "ethical" points in Derrida's work.

Derrida neither speaks about *transforming* philosophy in a linguistically oriented transcendental- or formal-pragmatic direction (in the pre-

---

145. Habermas, *Philosophical Discourse of Modernity,* 189 / 223. See also Frank, *Was ist Neostrukturalismus?* 11, 281.

cise sense Habermas, Apel, and their pupils have given to these terms), nor does he harbor illusions about conclusively *overcoming* it (in the Heideggerian, Gadamerian, let alone neopositivist, especially Carnapian, understanding of the idea of *Überwindung*).[146] Nor is his work about offering a genealogy of—or carefully marking off—the normative sources and features of the moral point of view. It has often been suggested that Derrida's thinking opposes both objectivism and naive relativism and, in a highly qualified sense, tries to account for the *relative* validity of the transcendental perspective of philosophical thinking.[147] In his work there is no question of the need for restoring the philosophical system in its idealist, let alone positivist, guise, nor should deconstruction be considered a destruction of all meaning and sense: "Rather, it is a question of determining the possibility of *meaning* [*sens*] on the basis of a 'formal' organization which in itself has no meaning, which does not mean that it is either the non-sense or the anguishing absurdity which haunt metaphysical humanism."[148]

In a certain sense the motifs of *archē*-writing, *différance*, the supplement, and, indeed, the trace take the place of timeless transcendental consciousness or of a priori, all too statically defined linguistic and anthropological, psychological and societal, structures. They seek to present something that might initially seem to be "a short-of and a beyond [*un en-deça et un au-delà*] of transcendental criticism" or even an "ultratranscendental text"[149] but, upon closer examination, can better be described as something that is *unthinkable* in theoretical terms alone. Within the framework of the "logic of identity"—and, for our authors, there is no rational alternative to the law(s) of thought—a consistent thinking of the trace, and hence a "logic" of supplementarity, must reveal itself in the final analysis as contradictory, that is to say, not just paradoxical but, in a more emphatic sense, aporetic, punctuated by performative contradictions that are unavoidable and whose recurrence, like the problem of skepticism, follows philosophy as (and in) its shadow. Thinking through

146. On these alternatives, see the essays in Baynes, Bohman, and McCarthy, *After Philosophy;* and also Rudolph Carnap, "Überwindung der Metaphysik durch logische Analyse der Sprache," *Erkenntnis* 2 (1932): 219–41.

147. See Peter Dews, *Logics of Disintegration: Post-structuralist Thought and the Claims of Critical Theory* (London: Routledge, 1987), 7, 19; and Derrida, *Positions,* 104–5 n. 32 / 79–80 n. 23.

148. Derrida, *Margins of Philosophy,* 134 / 161.

149. Derrida, *Of Grammatology,* 61 / 90.

the implication of the concept or, rather, figure of the trace already makes
that clear:

> The trace is not only the disappearance of origin — within the discourse that
> we sustain and according to the path that we follow it means that the origin
> did not even disappear, that it was never constituted except reciprocally by a
> non-origin, the trace, which thus becomes the origin of the origin. From then
> on, to wrench the concept of the trace from the classical scheme, which would
> derive it from a presence or from an originary non-trace and which would
> make of it an empirical mark, one must indeed speak of an originary trace or
> arche-trace. Yet we know that that concept destroys its name and that, if all
> begins with the trace, there is above all no originary trace.[150]

Various critics have wanted to see in this vertiginous perspective a relapse into the old mistake of the self-referential thinking of identity.[151] The
relentless "metaphorization" of language and thinking which would seem
to accompany Derrida's "anticoncept" of the trace (as of *différance,* the
supplement, etc.) is thus said simply to self-destruct on the grounds that "a
naked concept of *différance* is a contradiction, because difference cannot
not be specified,"[152] but also, conversely, because "no philosophical discourse would be possible, not even deconstruction, if we ceased to assume
what Derrida justly holds to be 'the sole thesis of philosophy,' namely,
'that the meaning aimed at through these figures is an essence rigorously
independent of that which carries it over.'"[153]

These objections touch on a difficult problem, which Derrida claims
neither to be able to avoid nor to resolve in a single stroke. In fact, no
philosophy can. From this "logical" dead end, however, Derrida draws a
simple consequence: looking back on the traditional mode of transcendental thinking which forms the point of departure for his own philosophical itinerary, he concludes that "a thought of the trace can no more
break with transcendental phenomenology than be reduced to it."[154] Transcendental questions, here the ones first articulated by Husserl and then
radicalized by Heidegger, are thus neither obsolete nor adequate or sufficient per se.

150. Ibid.

151. See Dews, *Logics of Disintegration,* 26–27, 41–42.

152. Jean Wahl, *Philosophie: La Philosophie entre l'avant et l'après du structuralisme,* vol. 5 of
Qu'est-ce que le structuralisme? (Paris: Seuil, 1973), 186; cited in Dews, *Logics of Disintegration,*
248 n. 65; also 25 ff., 231. See also Frank, *What Is Neostructuralism?* 355 / 550.

153. Ricoeur, *Rule of Metaphor,* 293 / 372.

154. Derrida, *Of Grammatology,* 62 / 91.

Something similar results from my interpretation, in the preceding chapters, of the different figures of thought in Adorno, Benjamin, Blanchot, and Levinas, all of whom teach us that the traditional and modern philosophies of the subject, of history, and of language — in their systematic and rhetorical articulations, in metaphysics, ontology, dialectics, and phenomenology — can be neither simply affirmed nor simply negated in uncritical or abstract ways but need to be infinitely reworked (if not necessarily "worked through," in Freud's sense of the term). Both a command to burst apart the tradition and the impossibility of doing so, let alone an unwillingness ever fully to carry this out, inform all their texts.

Yet in the failure of the attempt definitively to elude the subject-centered and ontological tradition of reason (including its naturalism, emerging historicism, and "transcendental lingualism") there is, as we have seen, a secret success. In the (un)spoken "betrayal" of the tradition its perspective is invisibly, inaudibly, and belatedly continued, deferred, and even expanded. In Derrida's words: "The passage beyond philosophy does not consist in turning the page of philosophy (which usually amounts to philosophizing badly) but in continuing to read the philosophers *in a certain way.*"[155]

The difference between "end [*fin*]" and "closure [*clôture*]" in Derrida and between "overcoming [*Überwindung*]" and "convalescence [*Verwindung*]" in Heidegger makes the consequences of this paradoxical relation clear. As Gadamer notes: "When one convalesces from something, this something does not simply lie behind one as overcome or sublated; rather, it continues to determine one further. [*Was man verwindet, liegt nich einfach hinter einem, als überwunden oder aufgehoven, sondern bestimmt einen fort*]."[156] In Derrida's words: "one does not leave the epoch whose closure one can outline."[157] Only the undeniably recurring, even if fleeting, interruption of discourse authorizes one to discuss the much decried "end" of philosophy (see also *OB* 20 / 24).

In their striving to articulate the nonavailability of meaning (with nature, history, morals, language, and aesthetic experience) in the face of the reductions of the tradition and the modern dialectics of its enlight-

---

155. Derrida, *Writing and Difference*, 288 / 421–22; also 83 / 119; and *Positions*, 6 / 14. From a different perspective, in *Blindness and Insight* de Man writes: "Criticism is a metaphor for the act of reading, and this act is itself inexhaustible" (107).

156. Gadamer, *Das Erbe Hegels*, 94 n. 15; see also Gadamer, "Destruktion und Dekonstruktion," *Gesammelte Werke*, 2:361–72.

157. Derrida, *Of Grammatology*, 12 / 24.

enments, Adorno's and Levinas's writings—at least viewed formally—approach the "double movement" of deconstructive thinking.[158] Their thinking constantly moves from the conceptual framework to the nonidentical, the other of reason, yet never is free of the former, to whose semantics and conceptual schemes, discursive arguments, and rhetorical devices it must always let itself be referred, even in the most radical of its own evasions.

As Adorno observes in his critique of the Kantian "block" or "*ignoramus*," deferral (and, we might add, "infinition" and "absolution," in Levinas's sense of these terms, as well) need not—indeed, cannot—itself be total. To once and for all affirm and hence ontologize the nonavailability of the other (or of all otherness and every othering) would simply mean to turn First Philosophy on its head, abstractly to negate—and thereby to continue—it. As Stanley Cavell notes in a different context: "even if you say that some meaning is always deferred, all meaning is not always deferred forever (to say that total meaning is deferred forever is apt to say nothing, since nothing is apt to count as total meaning; that phrase is apt to mean nothing). It is no more characteristic of the chains of significance to be theoretically open than it is, at each link, for them to close."[159] In consequence, we can conclude that Adorno's (and Horkheimer's) error in *Dialectic of Enlightenment* is to attempt to "prepare" an *in principle possible* "positive concept of enlightenment." Any such genuine event of thinking (as well as its metaphysical, practical, and aesthetic analogues) must instead be considered, approached, and respected as fundamentally *impossible:* that is to say, not only as deeply paradoxical or, what comes down to the same, aporetic, under specific historical, societal, and existential conditions but also as initially creating and instituting the very basis or element—indeed, the possibility or condition of possibility—of this positivity. After all, dialectically and phenomenologically speaking, we do not yet know what future possibilities past and present impossibilities might still make possible, nor should we aspire to such knowledge. This is why not only positive metaphysics but also negative metaphysics—which, in its relentless negativity, becomes once again, well, too affirmative—must remain a problematic concept: "Metaphysics cannot be a positive doctrine about any ontological content which might be proclaimed as meta-

---

158. Derrida speaks in *Dissemination* of a "double session [*séance*]."

159. Stanley Cavell, *Disowning Knowledge in Six Plays of Shakespeare* (Cambridge: Cambridge University Press, 1987), 191.

physical; it consists of the *questions* relating to such entities. . . . To put it trenchantly: negative metaphysics is metaphysics no less than positive metaphysics."[160]

Conversely, Levinas's error, in the middle phase of his writing, to insist on the nonepistemic but, as it were, practical availability of the *primum intelligibile* of the idea of the infinite, the face of the Other, and its "signification without context." Only later, like Adorno, does he correct and complicate this correlative positivity of the other (Other/other). Nonavailability and availability, negativity and positivity, are no longer presented as given—whether provisionally or once and for all, historically or metaphysically—but as deeply paradoxical, indeed, aporetic in themselves, revealing an indecision or hesitation between absence and presence which uproots the very premises of traditional thought and forces one to take a perspective at once from within and without.

By and large, Derrida's deconstruction accounts for this doubled basic feature of Adorno's negative dialectics as well as for the quasi-skeptical and alternating-oscillating reflection whose model Levinas espouses in his late work. Like these apparently circular figures of thought, it, too, has the character of a *spiral*, which does not just oscillate between two stationary poles but moves from one extreme to its counter—*en-deçà* and *au-delà*—and then back again in an open direction, ad infinitum.[161]

Because of this open-endedness, the philosophy of difference, of the trace of the other, can never arrive at an exhaustive analysis, a synthesizing sublation, or a clear and well-differentiated conceptual determination of its premises and end term(s). The quasi-inductive procedures of "configuration," "constellation," and "micrology" in Adorno's and Levinas's phenomenological concretizations or conceptual "ex-positions" encircle a singularity to which we have too often been blinded by the "evidence" of classical-modern thinking, with its metaphorics of light and the intuited image, its ideal of linear progression according to the deductive order of reasons, axioms, presupposition, possibilization, the approximation to the ideal, and so on and so forth.

Adorno and Levinas, like Derrida, philosophize beyond any nostalgia

---

160. Adorno, *Philosophische Terminologie*, 2:166; cited after the "Editor's Afterword," in Adorno, *Metaphysics*, 195–96 / 300.

161. As I have argued in the final chapter of my book *Philosophy and the Turn to Religion*, one might also redescribe this movement of thinking with the help of the—mathematical rather than rhetorical—figure of the *ellipse*. See also the concluding text in Derrida's *Writing and Difference*.

and this side of any well-grounded expectation—that is, they look beyond the traditional and modern metaphysical pillars of "archē" and "eschaton." In this lies hidden a remarkable agreement between their concrete philosophies of difference and the formal thinking of *différance*, whose "theoretical matrix" (to cite the terminology of *Of Grammatology*) allows other—and not necessarily (or exclusively) materialist, sensualist, or ethical—tones to be heard.

One obvious difference between the figures of thought of Adorno and Levinas, on the one hand, and Derrida, on the other, is that Derrida's deconstruction at first appears to be directed toward "an always other other of reason [*ein jeweils anderes Anderes der Vernunft*],"[162] whereas Adorno and Levinas seek to materialize or concretize their particular motifs of the nonidentical and of ab-solute alterity, respectively. In that, the matter or *proprium* of their thinking lies hidden. Or so it seems. They never go as far as Derrida in their attempt to denaturalize and, indeed, singularize the other. Derrida, it would seem, does not let himself get drawn into the materialization and concretization of an always-particular difference but, rather, restricts himself to the more formal and abstract question of the one *quasi*-transcendental condition of possibility of any such particular other, that is to say, to *différance*.[163] This in itself, Derrida seems to think, neither involves nor promises any particular interpretation and intonation of the trace. Indeed, in *Margins of Philosophy* Derrida writes: "the thought of the letter *a* in *différance* is not the primary prescription or the prophetic annunciation of an imminent and as yet unheard-of nomination."[164] Does this imply that Derrida's deconstruction would be unsuited for thinking as truly ab-solute the different traces followed by minimal theologies? Can it capture their modality of transcendence—that is, their "in-finition" *in pianissimo*—while respecting or expressing its *concretissimum*?

Of course, the deconstructive figure of thought should not, cannot—and, indeed, does not—content itself with the more abstract and seemingly merely formal quasi-transcendental understanding of *différance*. If it did, the idea of rationality in Derrida's thinking would, in turn, be bisected, in almost the same way we earlier observed in Habermas. But "rationality" is a designation that Derrida would not assume for

162. The term is taken from Wellmer, *Zur Dialektik von Moderne und Postmoderne;* see also chapter 2.

163. See Derrida, *Writing and Difference,* 105 / 155.

164. Derrida, *Margins of Philosophy,* 27 / 29.

his project without some hesitation: "The 'rationality' — but perhaps that word should be abandoned . . . — which governs a writing thus enlarged and radicalized [i.e., the 'archē-writing' of the trace or of 'différance'], no longer issues from a logos."[165] What conclusion should we draw from this observation?

As I postulated in chapter 2, the concept of a postmetaphysical and nonetheless emphatic rationality can bear weight only if it succeeds in bringing together a formally discursive, explicitly *dianoetic* strategy of argumentation with a concretely intelligible and *noetic* ferment in a unique constellation or configuration. Philosophy, I said, must seek to oscillate back and forth between the poles of thinking (i.e., of ideas, concepts, arguments) and experience (i.e., of intuition and sensation), without any hope of mediation or resolution. How does this alternation between the dianoetic and the noetic present itself in Derrida?

The motif of *différance,* we learn from him, should always leave the figure of the trace open to an in principle infinite range of possible singular interpretations. The ideas of natural history and its transience and of spiritual experience (in Adorno), as well as those of the face of the Other, responsibility to the point of substitution, and the surplus of non-sense over sense (in Levinas), do not exhaust the past, present, and future *instantiations* of the trace, whose structural capacity for opening up and deepening our most emphatic experiences we cannot and should not systematize in merely formal (ontological, transcendental) terms alone. Indeed, no thinking can take even a single step forward or backward without already being imbued, whether implicitly or explicitly, with the coloring and intonation imparted by the particular historical forms of articulation which it deconstructs. It is no accident, then, that Derrida's deconstructive philosophy is from the outset — and, indeed, increasingly — enriched with the deformalizing motifs in contemporary philosophizing brought forward by Levinas. "Violence and Metaphysics" amply testifies to this reception, but *Adieu to Emmanuel Levinas* does so even more. Nor is it an accident that Derrida eventually picks up on comparable motifs, first in Benjamin, in "Force of Law," then in Adorno, in *Fichus.*

But other — un-Adornian and un-Levinasian — motifs in Derrida's texts allude, if often obliquely, to specific interpretations, intonations, and instantiations of the "theoretical matrix" in which the notion of a generalized difference (or *différance*) plays a key role. These supplements tes-

---

165. Derrida, *Of Grammatology,* 10 / 21.

tify, interestingly, to the heritage of the Enlightenment, in the form of an
(ethical?) appeal whose structural contours and concrete features can now,
under the conditions of modernity, be thought or expressed only with
the greatest difficulty. Numerous examples of this difficulty can be given:
for example, in "On a Newly Arisen Apocalyptic Tone in Philosophy."[166]
There Derrida centers his exegesis of Kant on a question that sums up
the central difficulty that has guided my discussion throughout: "wouldn't
the apocalyptic be a transcendental condition of all discourse, of all experience even, of every mark or every trace? And the genre of writings
called 'apocalyptic' in the strict sense, then, would be only an example, an
exemplary revelation of this transcendental structure."[167] Even the most
self-critical and self-referential turn in philosophical thinking is thus still
motivated or borne by an appeal, a command, and a gift of which it can
no longer say in *positive* terms *what* they are, where they come from, or
to whom they are addressed, and whose *normative* status therefore lies
in the dark. To designate them as "moral imperative" ("desire," "prayer,"
"command") would already be to miss the mark, because the appeal in
question—and in even the most critical question—concerns what Derrida calls an "*affirmative* tone" or, in particular, "the gesture in speaking
[*parole*], that gesture that does not let itself be recovered by the analysis—
linguistic, semantic, or rhetorical—of speaking."[168]

Derrida's invocation of such an indeterminate "appeal" does not give
in to the ineradicable tendency in ancient and modern philosophy (decried in Kant's essay) toward "enthusiasm [*Schwärmerei*]" or irrationalism. Of this appeal, this "Come [*viens*]," he acknowledges: "I do not know
what *it is,* not because I yield to obscurantism, but because the question
'what is' belongs to a space (ontology, and from it the knowledge of grammar, linguistics, semantics, and so on) opened by a 'come' come from
the other."[169] The appeal in question merely eludes any *dianoetic* (discursive, argumentative, conceptual, even linguistic) grasp and articula-

166. See the final chapter of my book *Philosophy and the Turn to Religion*.

167. Derrida, "On a Newly Arisen Apocalyptic Tone in Philosophy," 117–71 / 445–79. See
also Joseph Simon, "Vornehme und apokalyptische Töne in der Philosophie," *Zeitschrift für
philosophische Forschung* (1986): 489–519.

168. Derrida, "On a Newly Arisen Apocalyptic Tone in Philosophy," 165, 166 / 476, 477.

169. Ibid., 166 / 476. See also Derrida, *Writing and Difference*, 133 / 195–96; and *Éperons:
Les Styles de Nietzsche,* bilingual ed. (Chicago: University of Chicago Press, 1979): "Just as there
is no being or essence of woman or of sexual difference, there is no essence of the *es gibt* in the
es gibt Sein, no essence of the gift and of the donation of being" (120). See also ibid., 106, 126,
132.

tion and signals the merely *noetic* remainder of Enlightenment brought down to its minimal meaning, its *concretissimum,* as it were. The appeal evokes a speechless wakefulness imposed on us no less as command than as fate.[170]

Derrida thus does not avoid alluding—however cryptically, indirectly, hypothetically, and provisionally—to what he calls a "concrete condition of rationality [*condition concrète de la rationalité*]."[171] But he does not delude himself by assuming that the various (free or forced, active or passive, moral or aesthetic) engagements with this "condition" or this "rationality" can ever be decided within the framework of disengaged theoretical discourse, for a simple reason: in the final analysis the difference between such singular engagements is only "*tonal.*"[172]

But does this claim not also betray a certain—unsatisfactory, even questionable—indifference, whose nature is at once theoretical and practical, even ethical? Perhaps. Yet such in-difference—the very art of *living in* (i.e., with, among, for, before, beyond, from, in spite of, etc.) "differences"—is an at once historical and conceptual, linguistic and affective, *necessity* of sorts.

Levinas seems to object to this consequence when he writes: "The concreteness of the Good is the worth [*le valoir*] of the other man. It is only to some *formalization* that the ambivalence of worth appears, as *undecidable,* at equal distance between Good and Evil" (*GCM* 147 / 225, my emph.). But if the ethical appeal were the *only* unmistakable ab-solute, the sole singular *concretissimum,* which can touch us—cutting across all the models that we impose on experience in general—then it would hardly be evidence of our morality to pay attention to it, to say nothing of actually obeying it. Therefore, Levinas can also claim that the *primum intelligibile* of the ethical appeal needs its temptation—the very contestation of its "evidence"—for intrinsic reasons, both analytical and moral: "Evil claims to be the contemporary, the equal, the twin, of the Good. This is an irrefutable lie, a Luciferian lie. It is the very egoism of the ego that posits itself as its own origin, an uncreated, sovereign principle, a prince. Without the impossibility of humbling this pride, the anarchical submission to the Good would no longer be an-archical and would be equivalent to the demonstration of God, the theology which treats God as though he belonged to being or to

170. Derrida, "On a Newly Arisen Apocalyptic Tone in Philosophy," 153, 157 / 466, 470.
171. Derrida, *Writing and Difference,* 127 / 187.
172. Derrida, "On a Newly Arisen Apocalyptic Tone in Philosophy," 166 / 477, my emph.

perception. It would be equivalent to the optimism a theology can teach and religion must hope in, but which philosophy is silent about" (*CPP* 138 / *HAH* 81; see also 132–33, 73).

The ethical-metaphysical transcendence that has from time immemorial been addressed with the word *God* can, accordingly, be given only as an in principle disputed and controversial "reality," and hence, as Max Weber knew (see chap. 1), always only *in pianissimo*, as a *minima moralia* of sorts. Again, in Levinas's words: "The transcendent cannot — *qua* transcendent — have come unless its coming is contested. Its epiphany is ambiguity or enigma, and may be just a word [*Elle n'est peut-être qu'un mot*]." Just this word reveals the very structure and meaning of speech and writing as such, for Levinas immediately adds: "Language is the fact that always one sole word is proffered: God" (*NP* 93 / 137). Minimal theology would mean just this: the theological, materialized and concretized in the name and the concept of "God," stands for "just a word," which is at the same time "the sole word" of language. The word *God* would thus signal itself *nowhere* and *everywhere*: almost nothing, it is at the same time the very heart of — at least all linguistic — meaning. But this meaning absolves itself from whatever *criteria* one would want to measure it against, whether semantically, epistemologically, normatively, pragmatically, or aesthetically. And this insight is not only the fruit of a modernist sensibility but lies at the very heart of the Scriptures: "the God of the Bible signifies in an unlikely manner the beyond of being, or transcendence. That is, the God of the Bible signifies without analogy to an idea subject to *criteria*, without analogy to an idea exposed to the summons to show itself true or false" (*GCM* 56 / 95).

Revelation through Interpretation

Habermas believes that Derrida, by maintaining a consequent *epochē* of meaning, establishes an unholy alliance between Heidegger's "temporalized philosophy of origins," on the one hand, and the tradition of Jewish mysticism (from the Kabbalah to Kafka), on the other. For him Derrida finally conjures up an "indeterminate" authority, even if not that of a "Being that has been distorted by beings, but the authority of a no longer holy scripture, of a scripture that is in exile, wandering about, estranged from its own meaning, a scripture that testamentarily documents the absence of the holy."[173] Like the Kabbalists, as reported by Scholem, in *dif-*

---

173. Habermas, *Philosophical Discourse of Modernity*, 181 / 214.

férance Derrida seems to reduce revelation to the opening up (or *anacrusis, Auftakt*) of all commandments: to the first letter, the *aleph*.

The "turning of the breath [*Atemwende*]" of this minimized revelation is "in itself infinite and full of meaning [*sinnerfüllt*], but *without* any *specific* meaning [*Sinn*]."[174] This remarkable connection supports an interpretation different from the one Habermas follows. According to this mystical tradition, the translation of the law into human language both first establishes the authority of the religious and, by the same gesture, withholds it. In consequence, "every statement on which authority is grounded would become a human interpretation, however valid and exalted, of something that transcends it."[175] Deformalization, that is to say, materialization and concretization, is the very method of revelation, but one that leaves the ultimate meaning of revelation open, indeterminate, undecided.

We can leave aside the question of to what extent Derrida actually develops his "heretical" hermeneutics in connection with the rabbinical tradition. Perhaps his own, somewhat laconic, comments might suffice. Derrida remarks: "Some people may spend their time asking how a person can be influenced by what he doesn't know. I don't say that it's impossible. If my ignorance of the Talmud, for example, is a fact I deeply regret, it may be that the Talmud knows me, or knows itself in me. A kind of unconscious, you might say; and that would open up paradoxical pathways."[176]

What is important here is the formal parallel evident in the ambivalent relation to tradition or in the concept of a *revelation through interpretation*. Of both it is true that "the paradox is the return to tradition by way of heresy."[177] In other words, the divine does not approach humanity in a singular incarnation, that is to say, in a single stroke; its dispersed traces can only be "collected [*eingesammelt*]" in the process of an unending, sometimes profane or even antinomian work of interpretation.[178] This trait is

174. Gershom Scholem, *Zur Kabbala und ihrer Symbolik* (Frankfurt a.M.: Suhrkamp, 1973), 47; cited in Habermas, *Philosophical Discourse of Modernity*, 183 / 216.

175. Scholem, *Zur Kabbala und ihrer Symbolik,* 47.

176. Derrida, *Philosophies,* vol. 1 of *Entretiens avec 'Le Monde,'* intro. C. Delacampagne (Paris:, Éditions de la Découverte / Le Monde, 1984), 80.

177. Susan Handelman, "Jacques Derrida and the Heretic Hermeneutic," in *Displacement: Derrida and After,* ed. Mark Krupnick (Bloomington: Indiana University Press, 1983), 119. Handelman speaks of "a re-emergence of Rabbinic hermeneutics in a displaced way" and of "an unacknowledged displaced theology" (111, 113).

178. See ibid., 104. Handelman further comments: "Derrida's notion of the trace sounds strangely similar to Scholem's description of the Kabbalistic 'Name of God'" (120). See also Derrida, *Writing and Difference,* 136 / 201.

particularly apparent in Derrida's studies of Edmond Jabès and Walter Benjamin.[179] Thus, in the essay "Des tours de Babel" Derrida describes, with the help of Benjamin's discussion of translation, how the narrative of the dispersion or "dissemination" of languages[180] — as if by analogy to the idea of the contraction of God — explains both the *duty* of interpretation and its *impossibility*. Because no meaning can be attributed to the law and to the name of God outside the work of commentary, interpretation becomes a kind of *irredeemable guilt,* which stands as a model for the work of interpretation in modern institutions of higher learning as well. Thus, with reference to Schelling, in "Theologie de la traduction" ("Theology of Translation") Derrida notes: "By his very activity, man is to develop (*entwickeln*) that which is lacking in God's total revelation (*was nur zur Totalität der Offenbarung Gottes fehlt*). . . . // That is what is called translation; it is also what is called the destination of the university."[181]

In such a view the meaning embodied in language — in the letters and literality of the texts themselves, as it were — gains a power of signification without ever directly, let alone communicatively, transmitting a determinate spiritual authority. This explains why the hermeneutics of the divine is folded into that of the profane or the literal and thereby into the very concept of all interpretation, whether semantic or semiotic, pragmatic or juridical, aesthetic or theological: "What comes to pass in a sacred text is the occurrence of a *pas de sens*. And this event is also the one starting from which it is possible to think the poetic or literary text which tries to redeem the lost sacred and there translates itself as in its model. *Pas de sens* — that does not signify poverty of meaning but no meaning that would be itself, meaning, beyond any 'literality.'"[182]

Hermeneutica sacra sive profana, a hermeneutic of the sacred (or the holy, as Levinas would have preferred) which is at the same time a hermeneutic of the profane: it is not too farfetched to see a certain commonality between the works of Adorno, Levinas, Habermas, and Derrida in this programmatic statement of an unending decipherment of the ab-solute.[183] Let me explain, in concluding, what that formula entails.

179. Derrida, "Edmond Jabès and the Question of the Book," *Writing and Difference,* 64–78 / 99–116, esp. 76–77 / 114–15.
180. Derrida, "Des tours de Babel," *Psyché,* 206 / "Des tours de Babel," trans. Joseph F. Graham; Derrida, *Acts of Religion,* 106.
181. Derrida, "Théologie de la traduction," 184 / "Theology of Translation," 152.
182. Derrida, "Des tours de Babel," *Acts of Religion,* 235 / *Psyché,* 133.
183. On this issue in Levinas, see Greisch, "Du vouloir-dire au pouvoir-dire," 218, 220.

Philosophies of Infinity

Neither Adorno nor Levinas presents a philosophy of transience or finitude in the narrow sense of these words.[184] Rather, they develop a thinking of the infinite, an infinitizing thought (*Unendlichkeitsdenken*), even if not in the sense of the classical-modern or metaphysical doctrine of the infinity of God, Being, mathematical or logical objects, and so on. Thus, they are concerned neither with "the imitation substantiality of a metaphysics renewed one more time"[185] nor with "encircling that which metaphysics had always intended and had always failed to achieve."[186] For them, the thinking of the infinite does not secretly thirst after the hidden sources of an earlier philosophy of origins. Rather, paradoxically, it uses the conceptual means prepared by the tradition to articulate what is almost never or only tangentially intended in the history of thought.

In his second major essay devoted to Levinas, "At This Very Moment in This Work Here I Am," Derrida therefore rightly comments: "It is not, then, a thought of the limit. . . . The passage beyond language requires language or rather a text as a place for the trace of a step that is not (present) elsewhere. That is why the movement of that trace, passing beyond language, is not classical nor does it render the *logos* either secondary or instrumental. *Logos* remains . . . indispensable."[187] The passage recalls the observation in "Violence and Metaphysics" of "the necessity of lodging oneself within traditional conceptuality in order to destroy it."[188] Mutatis mutandis, the same holds true for Adorno in his at once consistent re-

184. On this problematic, see Marquard, *Abschied vom Prinzipiellen,* and his understanding of hermeneutics as a "reply to human finitude" (119). He defines *finitude* simply as "being-among-others" (121). In explicit opposition to Heidegger's grounding of understanding in the future, Marquard believes that hermeneutics is "primarily a relation to the past" (19; see also 139 n. 7). The memory of what is past in Adorno (cf. the concept of natural history and the importance of childhood memories, place names, etc.) and the exegetical relation to history, the biblical tradition, and the national literatures in Levinas (see Wiemer, *Passion des Sagens,* 150) correspond to a specific, metaphysical-moral "experience" of historicity, not to pastness or historicity as such (whether defined in formal indicative terms, as in Heidegger, or narratively and anthropologically construed, as in Marquard).

185. Habermas, *Postmetaphysical Thinking,* 9 / 17.

186. Ibid., 28 / 35. For this characterization, which identifies the core of both Heidegger's and Adorno's thought as "radical contextualism," see 116 / 154.

187. Derrida, "En ce moment même dans cet ouvrage me voici," *Psyché,* 170 / "At This Very Moment in This Work Here I Am," trans. Ruben Berezdivin, in Bernasconi and Critchley, *Re-Reading Levinas,* 20.

188. Derrida, *Writing and Difference,* 111 / 165.

fusal of the pathos of the ever-proclaimed end of philosophy in its supposed overcoming (from Nietzsche and Heidegger to Carnap and pragmatism) and in his—in part strategic—solidarity with metaphysics in the
very moment of its downfall. Here, it would seem, a certain precedence
of philosophical terminology and, hence, of language or even Logos remains "indispensable" for the step that leads neither beyond immanence
nor into the free realm of transcendence but walks the thin line between—
and does so ad infinitum.

In precisely this sense Adorno's and Levinas's figure of thought, for
all their negative-metaphysical critiques of the presuppositions and central theorems of First Philosophy, ontology, and onto-theology, is *in its
conceptual and rhetorical movement* neither negativistic nor skeptical of
reason per se. The point of their thinking of the infinite lies, rather, in *encircling the intentionless (Umkreisen des Intensionlosen)* as it reveals itself
in the always new experiences and attestations of the trace of the other,
whether horrific or sublime, the worst or the best. Indeed, in complex and
often uncanny and lurid ways, for Adorno and Levinas these two extremes
seem to shadow each other, to the point of becoming virtually indistinguishable. Which is yet another reason why these authors do not so easily
give up on the historical and systematic weight of tradition and modernity, Logos and Enlightenment, mediation and measure. Left to itself the
idea of the Good resembles its opposite; it is a stroke of luck, therefore,
that it gives itself only *in obliquo,* ab-solutely, and hence impurely, always
already past and contaminated, indecidably, that is to say, in ways that
permit no good conscience and border upon the idolatrous, blasphemy,
frivolity, and play—as a "divine comedy," of sorts.

SUCH A *hermeneutica sacra sive profana* can no longer be reconciled with a
positive or negative theology, however carefully—and philosophically—
construed. We do not need to recall here in what sense, according to Derrida, the concept of negative theology, like its counterpart, is still mired
in classical thinking (even though there is yet another implication of the
apophatic genre which allows it not only to escape some of metaphysics'
most questionable presuppositions but also to resemble—more precisely,
to initiate, echo, or, at least, strategically exemplify—the most rigorous
steps beyond proposed by deconstruction).[189] The concept of a *minimal
theology,* by contrast, not unlike that of "a/theology," can avert the onto-

---

189. See appendix; and the opening chapters of *Philosophy and the Turn to Religion.*

theological misunderstanding or fixation of the other of reason. But it can only do so, as I have said, at the price of becoming concrete, of minimally materializing, instantiating, intoning, or coloring itself, nothing more, nothing less. Let me therefore briefly revisit the perspectives in the work of Adorno and Levinas which suggest a new way out of the classical and modern alternatives—namely, dogmatics, the theologies of the genitive, and the science of religion—which have been proposed thus far.

As Adorno vehemently insists, "taking literally what theology promises would be . . . barbarian." He grounds this view in the philosophy of history, for "historically accumulated respect" protects the judgment of modern people from taking religious ideas "à la lettre" (*ND* 399 / 391). This circumstance inevitably calls up "the antinomy of theological consciousness today" (*ND* 399 / 392). In what does this antinomy—which, Adorno suggests, did not always have its present form—consist? Adorno sets it up as a straightforward dilemma. If, that is, all theological means of speaking were to be "cleansed of subject matter [more precisely, of 'all possible determinations of content'], if their sublimation were complete," then one could hardly "say what they stand for. If every symbol symbolizes nothing but another symbol, another conceptuality, their core remains empty—and so does religion" (*ND* 399 / 392, trans. modified). Religion nowadays, Adorno suggests, must for reasons of historical decency shun virtually all its purported content and yet, at the same time, espouse some solidity—that is to say, material determination—if it is not to evaporate into thin air.

In the open end of Goethe's *Faust,* Adorno believes he can already hear the echo of this modern aporia: "The dramatic poem leaves unsettled whether its gradual progress refutes the skepticism of mature thinking [*des mündig Denkenden*], or whether its last word is yet again a symbol—'only a parabel [*nur ein Gleichnis*]'" (*ND* 400 / 392, trans. modified). What Adorno presents here as sheer antagonism, he interprets more subtly in his short remarks "Zur Schlusszene des *Faust*" ("On the Final Scene in *Faust*"), in *Notes to Literature,* with which I can aptly draw together my observations in the preceding chapters about the minimal concept of theology. There he writes of an inevitable difference between what is discovered in the "interpretive immersion in traditional texts," on the one hand, and "metaphysical intentions," on the other, which might be betrayed if they were to be immediately expressed in summary argumentation: "The negative, the impossibility, is expressed in that difference, an 'if only it were so [*Ach wär' es doch*],' as far from the assurance that it is so as from the assurance that it is not. Interpretation does not seize upon what it finds as valid truth, and yet it knows that without the light it tracks [or traces, *das Licht, dessen Spur . . . sie folgt*] in the texts there would be no truth. This tinges interpretation with a sorrow [*Trauer*] wholly unsuspected by the assertion [or affirmation, *Behauptung*] of meaning and frantically denied by an insistence on what the case is [*was der Fall sei*]" (*NL* 1:111 / 129).

Such a third way between, on the one hand, traditional metaphysics and positivism (here associated with the early Wittgenstein) and, on the other, full-fledged, say, Schopenhauerian negativism should not be confused with "mere skepticism" — not even in its mitigated or, as Hume would say, "academic" variety — because it redeems a minimal semantic potential in the former theological world of symbols. With a gesture of thought which unmistakably recalls Benjamin's figure of allegory, Adorno's quasi-hermeneutical mode, at least seen from this perspective and undoubtedly without his fully intending it, provides a compelling answer to the question concerning the philosophical adoption of the religious heritage that has guided us all along. As Adorno formulates it programmatically, in a way that is still inimitable: "the authority of great texts is a secularized form of the unattainable authority that philosophy, as teaching [*Lehre*], envisions. To regard profane texts as sacred texts — that is the answer to the fact that all transcendence has migrated into the profane sphere [more precisely, "into profanity," *Profanität*] and survives only where it conceals itself" (ibid.).

Adorno's philosophy can therefore hardly be described as a "running amok to God."[190] And, although consistent yet determinate negation undeniably forms the trademark of his thought, the reverse tendency seems to be present as well. Indeed, according to the conclusion of *Negative Dialectics*, the "possibility represented by the divine name is maintained, rather, by the one who does not believe" (*ND* 402 / 394), or, apodictically, a little earlier in the text: "one who believes in God can therefore not believe in God [*Wer an Gott glaubt, kann deshalb nicht an ihn glauben*]" (*ND* 401 / 394, trans. modified). This insight into the paradox, the aporia, or the performative contradiction of the genuine act of faith nonetheless in no way refers to a *theologia occulta* of sorts.[191] Rather, Adorno agrees

190. As Scheler says of Bloch, cited in a letter from Siegfried Kracauer, in Richard Löwenthal, *Mitmachen wollte ich nie: Ein autobiographisches Gespräch mit H. Dubiel* (Frankfurt a.M.: Suhrkamp, 1980), 245.

191. See W. Ries, "'Die Rettung des Hoffnungslosen': Zur 'theologia occulta' in der Spätphilosophie Horkheimers und Adornos," *Zeitschrift für philosophische Forschung* 30 (1978): 69–

with Kafka in that the latter's work remains centered on an ab-solute in which it can never take part directly or symbolically. Adorno writes, "Nowhere in Kafka does there glimmer [*verdämmert*] the aura of the infinite idea; nowhere does the horizon open." Kafka's prose is, on the contrary, "a parabolic system the key to which has been stolen: yet any effort to make this fact itself the key is bound to go astray."[192]

UP TO A CERTAIN POINT, in his writings Levinas follows a similar path: for example, when he states that "theological language destroys the religious situation of transcendence" and immediately adds that language "about God rings false or becomes a myth, that is, *can never be taken literally*" (*OB* 197 n. 25 / 155 n. 25, my emph.). The method of the phenomenological description of the experience of the other, the exegesis of both religious and profane traditions, and the rhetorical exaggeration of their common semantic potential promise a new, third way of thought, action, and judgment, which places in doubt various established suppositions. The most salient is probably the antithesis between knowledge (or science) and faith, with which I began my investigation in chapter 2. And, lest one mistake Levinas's thinking and its critique of onto-theology as being motivated by an alternative theological or confessional ambition, we would do well to keep his skepticism about this *apparent* "alternative" in mind, given that "nothing is less opposed to ontology than the opinion of faith. To ask oneself, as we are attempting to do here, whether God cannot be uttered in a reasonable discourse that would be neither ontology nor faith, is implicitly to doubt the formal opposition, established by Yehuda Halevy and taken up by Pascal, between, on the one hand, the God of Abraham, Isaac, and Jacob, invoked without philosophy in faith, and on the other the god of the philosophers. It is to doubt that this opposition constitutes an alternative" (*GCM* 57 / 96–97; see 61–62 / 103).

The ethical testimony in which, according to Levinas, the trace of the wholly other, that is, of the divinely infinite or infinitely divine, emerges should not be misunderstood as being a dogmatic content or proposition of faith. It does not depend upon a perception or representation, and its revelation "*gives* us nothing" (*EI* 107 / 103). Levinas claims, with his

---

81; P. Steinacker, "Verborgenheit als theologisches Motiv in der Ästhetik," *Neue Zeitschrift für systematische Theologie und Religionsphilosophie* 23 (1981): 254–71.

192. Adorno, "Aufzeichnungen zu Kafka," *GS* 10.1:255 / "Notes on Kafka," trans. Samuel and Shierry Weber, in Theodor W. Adorno, *Prisms* (Cambridge: MIT Press, 1981), 246.

characteristic reprise of Platonic terminology, that the relationship between self and other cannot be defined in terms of a cognitive gain for
the self. Moreover, one should not think it simply in terms of a unilateral
"revelation" of the other to the self, even where this revelation would already be drastically distinguished from a phenomenological "disclosure."
If Nietzsche's term *drama* were not so ambiguous, Levinas declares in the
opening pages of *Totality and Infinity,* it might best describe the modality
of the relation that ethics characterizes or supports (*TI* 28 n. 2 / xvi n. 1;
see *DEHH* 204). That would imply, if I might put it this way, a *rational-
mystical* motif, namely, that of a multifaceted *intrigue of the other in the
self,* to be distinguished from the false totalities of absorption in which
the self separates itself from separation and becomes identical with the
other, however sublime. The ethical intrigue, Levinas insists, resides elsewhere and leaves its mark otherwise, as language — more precisely, as the
mere gesturing, or saying, of discourse. In Derrida's apt summary we are
dealing here with "Discourse with God, and not in God as *participation.*
Discourse with God, and not discourse on God and his attributes as *theology.*"[193] In Levinas's own words, this — and nothing else — can teach us
the minimally appropriate theological meaning of the phrase "word of
God": "The word of God. A theology which does not proceed from any
speculation on the beyond of worlds-behind-the-world, from any knowledge transcending knowledge. A phenomenology of the face: a necessary
ascent to God, which will allow for a recognition or a denial of the voice
that, in positive religions, speaks to children or to the childhood in each
one of us, already readers of the Books and interpreters of Scripture" (*EN*
199 / 251).

By thus circumscribing a transcendence that is virtually empty of content and cannot be contained by the very discourse that addresses it, Levinas also avoids succumbing to negative theology, at least in its classical
articulation.[194] As he says, "the non-presence of the infinite is not a figure
of negative theology. All the negative attributes which state what is beyond the essence become positive in responsibility" (*OB* 11–12 / 14). Or
again: "The transcendence of the Infinite is not recovered in propositions,
though they were negative ones" (*TO* 91 n. 1/ 91 n. 1; and *GCM* 120 / 186).

193. Derrida, *Writing and Difference,* 108 / 159.
194. On this thematic, see Derrida, "Comment ne pas parler: Dénégations," in *Psyché,* 535–
95 / "How to Avoid Speaking: Denials," trans. Ken Frieden, in *Languages of the Unsayable: The
Play of Negativity in Literature and Literary Theory,* ed. Sanford Budick and Wolfgang Iser (New
York: Columbia University Press, 1987), 3–70.

But, then, as I have verified throughout, the term *positive* is hardly used without reservation or at least qualification. Thus, Levinas writes of the ethical relation that it is "premature and in any case insufficient to qualify it, by opposition to negativity, as positive. It would be false to qualify it as theological. It is prior to the negative or affirmative proposition" (*TI* 42 / 12). What, then, is its distinctive modality, if any?

Levinas sometimes speaks of the possibility of thinking "a God not contaminated by Being" (*OB* xlviii / x), which should also be thought as "transcendence to the point of absence" (*GCM* 69 / 115). I have sought to describe, interpret, formalize, and expand upon the concrete features — indeed, the *concretissimum* — which this *tertium datur* assumes in Levinas's writing. I have also found in it a possible mode of the "trace of the other" of which Adorno speaks in his musings concerning nature, natural history, transience, and so on, suggesting that his negative metaphysical ideas, while not limiting themselves to the realm of the ethical or intersubjectivity, lack a certain rigor in thinking through the figure of the trace, by contrast to the earliest and late Levinas. Of this motif Derrida rightly notes that "its presence (*is*) [(est)] a certain absence. Not pure and simple absence, for there logic could make its claim, but a *certain* absence." Explaining what such circumvention, indeed, deconstruction of the principle of the excluded third (either *p* or not-*p*) must entail, Derrida explains that this formulation ("a *certain* absence") "shows clearly that within this experience of the other the logic of noncontradiction, that is, everything which Levinas designates as 'formal logic,' is contested in its root. This root would be not only the root of our language, but the root of all of Western philosophy, particularly phenomenology and ontology. This naïveté would prevent them from thinking the other (that is from thinking; and reason, although Levinas doesn't say so, would in this way [*ainsi*] be 'the enemy of thought'), and from aligning their discourse with the other."[195]

The thought that we might be in a position — "after the death of a certain god inhabiting the world behind the scenes" (*OB* 185 / 233) — to come across the trace of the infinite other would be no less compelling *and* risky than Heidegger's attempt to work against the forgetting of Being (including the forgetting of this forgetting) effected by metaphysics and ontotheology (see *OB* xlviii / x). But its ambition would be far more radical: "One cannot describe meaning on the basis of a still economical idea of God" (*HAH* 39; see also 38).

---

195. Derrida, *Writing and Difference*, 91 / 135, trans. modified.

In consequence, Levinas's texts seem to marked by a strategy that is neither thetic nor, as it were, sympathetic and emotive. They can be characterized as a singular sample of "memorial writing."[196] In other words, they testify to the "constitution in and of writing [*Schriftkonstitution*]"[197] of everything human and demonstrate why both holy and profane scripture can inadvertently become the *"scene of the other."*[198] *Hermeneutica sacra sive profana*, once again. The reality named by the word *God,* in this view, would have no meaning outside of the quest for this reality (see *GCM* 94 / 150). Irrespective of diffuse feelings and transparent voices, *independent also of any religious experience whatsoever,* the tonality of the "otherwise than Being" would perhaps still be audible in the "resonance of silence [*Geläut der Stille*]" (see *GCM* 72 / 118; HAH 74) of which Heidegger at times speaks. In other words, where God appears, as if for the first time, in our linguistic gesture, the explicit mention and use of the word *God* might very well still (have to?) be absent. Metaphysical-moral language thus need not necessarily or primarily articulate itself in a confession of faith, in the utterance of a belief: "To bear witness to God is precisely not to state this extraordinary word" (*OB* 149 / 190).

196. Wiemer, *Passion des Sagens,* 145.
197. Ibid., 434 ff.
198. Ibid., 436.

Chapter Twelve

"The Other Theology"

Conceptual, Historical, and Political Idolatry

MY TOPIC IN THIS final chapter will be some puzzling yet revealing formulations by Adorno, which shed light on the intrinsic relationship between the question of negative theology and the complex phenomenon of idolatry, in particular the prohibition of images, the *Bilderverbot*. Any analysis of the contribution of "Western neo-Marxist Critical Theory" — and eventually, for Adorno, negative dialectics — to the understanding of religion and the "negative theological" discourses (apophatic as well as mystical ones) needs to pass through a discussion of this older concern, which dates back to biblical times. Indeed, Adorno's entire philosophy of history, language, and art — the ultimate "solidarity" between his thinking and "metaphysics in the very moment of its downfall" — hinges on a peculiar understanding of the original meaning and modern transformation of the critique of false representation of the divine, the condemnation of uttering its name(s), the destruction of magic and myth, and the enlightened critique of ideology, fetishism, commodification, and reification, as well as their functional equivalents — equivalency in the most general sense being precisely the problem, as opposed to the "universal equivalent," money, of which Marx makes so much in *Capital*. Idolatry and blasphemy are recurrent themes throughout Adorno's work; these motifs, I will argue, resonate with those of the negative way, the *via negativa* or *negationis*, including its intrinsic link with "positive," kataphatic theologies, the rhetorical superlatives of the *via eminentiae*, and so on, though these might seem absent from his central concerns.

As Moshe Halbertal and Avishai Margalit have demonstrated in *Idolatry*, the critique of idolatry — from the Greek terms *eidolon* (image) and *latreia* (adoration) — can take many different forms, including the *prohibition of images* (historically its dominant meaning), a call to avoid unlawful, impious speech (the inappropriate use of the name or names of God, i.e., *blasphemy*), and the condemnation of *particular loyalties* (be they individual, existential, familial, sexual, communal, or political).[1] The last, Halbertal and Margalit demonstrate, constitutes the original horizon of the critique of idolatry. It gained new prominence in twentieth-century political thought, in which questions of identity and recognition — and their many pitfalls — are increasingly reformulated in religious and theologico-political terms. To give just three examples (none of them mentioned in Halbertal and Margalit's *Idolatry,* though their final chapter is entitled "Idolatry and Political Authority"), one thinks of: (1) the problematics of "negative political theology" pursued by Jakob Taubes in the wake of Carl Schmitt and especially Walter Benjamin; (2) the "negative politology," "messianicity without messianism," and "spirit of Marxism" (stripped of its ontological, historicist, and economic claims) invoked on occasion by Derrida;[2] and (3) the internal connection Levinas construes between the "prohibition against representation and 'the rights of man.' "[3]

These motifs form part of a larger, collective, interdisciplinary project on "political theologies"; here I mention them only in passing.[4] Philosophy and cultural analysis face the challenge of asking to what extent traditional and modern concepts of the ban on graven images and blasphemy, together with their meanings — including the views on religion, violence, imagery, and language they entail — can still (or once again) shed light on contemporary debates concerning the relationship between self and

1. See Moshe Halbertal and Avishai Margalit, *Idolatry,* trans. Naomi Goldblum (Cambridge: Harvard University Press, 1992).

2. On Taubes and Derrida, see my *Religion and Violence,* chaps. 3–4. See also my *Philosophy and the Turn to Religion,* 187–88 n. 28.

3. See Emmanuel Levinas, *Altérité et Transcendence* (Montpellier: Fata Morgana, 1995) / *Alterity and Transcendence,* trans. Michael B. Smith (New York: Columbia University Press, 1999), chap. 8. To situate this argument adequately, one would need to examine a preliminary consideration Levinas put forward in his earliest writings, notably "Reality and Its Shadow." There Levinas implicitly debates the existential phenomenology of Sartre and, more indirectly, the ideas of Merleau-Ponty, proposing a view of art as a realm of evasion and shadow rather than a variety of truth and engagement. The theses of this essay provide a corrective to the reduction of his thought to a moralistic relation to the Other by showing that for him art, ethics, aesthetic experience, and philosophical criticism intersect and become interchangeable in the extreme of nontruth. Art forms the foil against which philosophy takes on its distinctive profile while remaining an intrinsic presupposition and possibility of the philosophical. See chap. 8 of the present book.

4. The Political Theologies project, sponsored by the Netherlands Organization for Scientific Research (NWO) and the Amsterdam School for Cultural Analysis (ASCA), in cooperation with the Harvard Center for the Study of World Religions, found its first articulation in an international conference at the University of Amsterdam in June 2001. The project builds on four earlier conferences and workshops, which formed the basis for de Vries and Weber, *Violence, Identity, and Self-Determination;* and *Religion and Media.*

other in increasingly mediatized, global, and multicultural forms of communality and conflict. In other words, to what extent can the notion of idolatry (and is it a concept, strictly speaking?) be "extended" (to borrow a term from Halbertal and Margalit) to include posttraditional and postclassical, if not necessarily postmetaphysical, meanings and uses?

One of the most significant features of the current interest in "religion," especially in nontheological disciplines, seems to be the growing insight that categories taken from the religious and theological tradition — and categories such as idolatry, blasphemy, and their analogues are eminently religious and theological, given that they are introduced and justified in scriptural, doctrinal, ritual, and ecclesial texts and contexts — offer great promise in addressing some of the most pressing intellectual and political issues of our time. They contain conceptual, argumentative, rhetorical, and pragmatically relevant intellectual resources whose potential has far from been exhausted and whose methodological and strategic use may (at least for some time to come) prove more promising in analyzing the theoretical and practical problems of modernity than, say, the traditional categories of metaphysics or the leading concepts of Enlightenment.

All modalities of the critique of idolatry — whether they address false or improper imagery, misnomers, or traitorous conduct — imply an emphasis on and a determination of the conceptual and, hence, circumscribe (albeit negatively) *the very concept of the concept,* the properties and the propriety of certain concepts, indeed, of any concept. That becomes most evident, Halbertal and Margalit demonstrate, in the *philosophical* varieties of this critique, which have increasingly abstracted, formalized, and idealized the original familial and societal meaning of idolatry and intellectualized it almost beyond recognition.[5] Indeed, throughout the history of

---

5. Most firmly and strictly, the concept of idolatry, the prohibition on making images of God in visible, plastic form, seems to be introduced in the Decalogue at Exodus 20:4–5; 20:23–25; and 34:17 (see also Deuteronomy 4:14–15, 23, 28; 5:7–9; 27:15). The second commandment, concerning the prohibition of graven images, is followed by the prohibition on illicit speech concerning the divine name(s): "You shall not make wrongful use of the name of the Lord your God" (Exodus 20:7; see Deuteronomy 5:11 and Leviticus 19:11: "You shall not swear falsely by my name, profaning the name of your God").

The notion of blasphemy is no less fluid than that of idolatry. In the words of French historian Alain Cabantous: "Blasphemy eludes the historian, with its shifting definitions and approaches, with the multifarious perceptions imposed on it by political, legal, and, of course, religious thinking. An evolving object of inquiry, beset by distortions and modulations, it has never failed to generate commentary and investigation, at least up to the end of the nineteenth century" (*Histoire du blasphème en Occident: Fin XVIe–milieu XIXe siècle* [Paris: Albin Michel,

thought, Halbertal and Margalit suggest, "the central effort of philosophical religion" has been "the attempt to attain a proper metaphysical conception of God. This conception is not only a necessary condition for the
worship of God but also constitutes the high point of religious life. Philosophical religion, which attempts to purify the divinity of anthropomorphism, considers the crux of the problem of idolatry to be the problem of
error. Idolatry is perceived first and foremost as an improper conception
of God in the mind of the worshipper, thereby internalizing the sin."[6]

1998] / *Blasphemy: Impious Speech in the West from the Seventeenth to the Nineteenth Century,*
trans. Eric Rauth [New York: Columbia University Press, 2002], 9). As a tentative definition,
the following emerges: *blasphemy* is "human beings' willful breaking away and falling out in the
expression of their relationship to the divine" (9). Cabantous notes that most Church Fathers
regarded blasphemy as "the act of refusing that which belonged or amounted to God Himself
or attributing to God that which was not of Him." He gives the following examples from clerical
handbooks: "To blaspheme . . . is to deny the existence of the divine perfections by attributing
to God a deficiency He is incapable of having, such as that he is unjust"; inversely, "blasphemy
attributes to the devil what is God's" (11).

    What the relationship between idolatry and blasphemy has meant historically, concep-
tually, and politically remains to be established. While the problem of blasphemy becomes a
central issue at a later historical date (in theological treatises and, institutionally, in the complex
dealings between civil and ecclesiastical authorities), the distinction between the prohibition on
impious speech and that on graven images is not so easy to uphold. They become increasingly
intertwined in the history of thought, not least as a result of the process of "internalization"
which occurs between the biblical period and the time of Maimonides, who is, in Halbertal's
and Margalit's reading, the prime witness to that development (see *Idolatry,* 239). Throughout
the Hebrew Bible, they point out, idolatry is conceived in an almost anthropomorphic sense,
being viewed as the betrayal of (sexual and political) loyalty. By contrast, the process of internalization is clear from the treatises on negative theology which have been most influential
in the Western tradition: Pseudo-Dionysius the Aereopagite's *The Divine Names* (fifth or sixth
century) and the first part of Maimonides' *The Guide of the Perplexed* (late twelfth century).
Their approaches can be interpreted in parallel ways (*Idolatry,* 282 n. 21).

    A further question is why the biblical prohibition on images — that is to say, on picto-
rial representation — seems severer than that directed at linguistic imagery, say, metaphorical
representation or evocation.

    As Halbertal and Margalit make clear, in biblical and later times idolatry concerned the
problem of both the pictorial and the linguistic representation of God. See also Alain Besançon,
L'Image interdite: Une histoire intellectuelle de l'iconoclasme (1994; rpt., Paris: Gallimard, 2000) /
The Forbidden Image: An Intellectual History of Iconoclasm, trans. Jane Marie Todd (Chicago:
University of Chicago Press, 2001).

    6. Halbertal and Margalit, *Idolatry,* 2. On internalization as being both societal and men-
tal, see 109: "When socially internalized, idolatry is no longer a form of worship that takes
place within other nations, with the Israelites following after them, but becomes something
occurring within the monotheistic society itself." Interestingly, Halbertal and Margalit stress
a certain dependency of this societal internalization on the mental internalization that precedes and enables it, for this "social internalization within the community is made possible by
the mental internalization whose essence is the shift from external worship to internal belief."
Thus, given Maimonides' view of idolatry as "metaphysical error," it can "be performed in the

As Halbertal and Margalit point out, idolatry, when internalized, is viewed as an "error" to the extent that there is an error "in the longing for gods that are 'no-gods' (Jeremiah 2:11), which may be compared to 'broken cisterns' (Jeremiah 2:13)."[7] Nonetheless, they argue, at least in biblical times and in the main tradition of Rabbinic Judaism metaphysical, epistemological error is not the primary aspect of idolatry. More central—again, at least historically and perhaps also systematically—is the aspect of "attitude," of a "disloyalty" that has political connotations: "The error in the worship of idols adds to the sin, but it is not the sin itself."[8] Rather, the sin of idolatry lies in the critique constituted by "others'" erroneous view of the divine, to which some fall prey. Indeed, Halbertal and Margalit understand their book as an "attempt to understand a community's self-definition through its idea of what is excluded and through its notion of 'the other.' The prohibition against idolatry is the thick wall that separates the pagans from the non-pagans. It is supposed to be the wall that constitutes the city of God, leaving the strange gods outside and marking the community of the faithful."[9] The historical and systematic "fluidity" of the concept of idolatry—and, hence, of self and other—explains why and how this demarcation is never fully successful, why and how the "thick wall" is ruined from the ground up. Halbertal and Margalit conclude, therefore, that "the location of that dividing wall is not fixed, and that opposing conceptions of idolatry define the outskirts of the city of God differently. . . . It is essential for the self-definition of nonpagans to share the general concept of idolatry, but they do not share a specific definition of what is idolatry and what is wrong with it. Changing conceptions of God create

---

synagogue while praying to the God of Israel. Idolatry is thus internalized; it is an event that happens in the mind and in the midst of the community. The criticism of idolatry is the criticism of superstition and its allegedly damaging effects on human life and society. Uprooting idolatry is chaining the imaginative faculty, and eradicating its role in the formation of the metaphysical picture of the world and its impact on the political behavior of the multitudes" (238).

7. Ibid., 108–9.

8. Ibid., 109. Perhaps for the authors of *Idolatry* this is not just historically but also systematically so. For all their insistence on the ethico-political or theologico-political features of idolatry and its critique, they ultimately take their philosophical distance from the pragmatist view (which they ascribe to Richard Rorty) that the "vertical semantics" of the critique of idolatry—that is to say, its insistence on a certain referent, for example, God, and its denial of another, namely, that of the idol or nongod—could simply be replaced by a "horizontal" semantics. They believe this would amount to providing a mere "sociology of solidarity" (160–61).

9. Ibid., 237.

606 Hermeneutica Sacra sive Profana

different ideas about what is idolatry. The converse holds true too: the notion of the alien, of false gods, shapes the concept of God."[10] The aim of their book, the authors write, is nothing less than "to capture the mutual effect of these concepts on each other."[11]

The discursive strategy of mysticism and of negative, apophatic philosophical theology—and does its entire method not boil down to a certain strategy concerning the "discursive," reducing its supposed reductionism in view of a more originary (albeit it nonmythical) given or mode of donation and givenness?—likewise revolves around the problem of how to avoid idolatry, more specifically, the pitfall of *conceptual* idolatry. Such idolatry and its political resonance (and this motivates, in part, my interest in Adorno in relation to the negative way) is often presented as being at once inevitable—historically, linguistically, semantically, indeed, conceptually—*and* to be avoided. Idolatry thus belongs to the nature of the labor of thought and of propositional utterance *as such*. Hence, the need for supplementary and, as it were, performative devices in order to say anything *at all* (or *after* all)—that is to say, for rhetorical substitutes, for a plurality, indeed, a postulated infinity and nonsynonymous substitution of divine *names* (not concepts), and for a *via eminentiae* that works (or does things) not by abstraction and subtraction but by adding on, by excess, by hyperbole, exaggeration, hymn, prayer, and praise.

But what, exactly, is the conceptual nature and, I am tempted to say, the truth—or truth content (the *Wahrheitsgehalt*, as Adorno would have it)—of idolatry thus conceived? What is conceptual in idolatry, what is the idol in the concept, indeed, in *any* concept, not just those that are worn-out, reified, and dead but also those that are deemed to be living and new or which have yet to be invented? Moreover, what can the fundamentally religious concept of idolatry (and the whole theological archive that it has enabled and made necessary) teach us about the nature and truth of the concept, and hence about thought, or even experience, in general?

To sketch out a possible answer to these questions, let me recall the basic argument—the silent axiom or intuition—of Adorno's "dialectic of nonidentity." The dialectic of negativity, as he formulates it early on, starts out from a simple premise: the need to express the nonidentical by way of a necessary *identification* (a *generalization,* meaning an *idealization* and *reification,* indeed, *idolatry* and *blasphemy*). This presupposition is never

10. Ibid.
11. Ibid.

justified or questioned as such. It finds one of its most forceful formulations in "Reason and Revelation," in which Adorno spells out the paradoxes and aporias of theism and atheism and concludes by seeing "no other possibility than an extreme ascesis toward any type of revealed faith, an extreme loyalty to the prohibition of images [*äusserste Treue zum Bilderverbot*], far beyond what this once originally meant."[12]

What interests me in this text (and especially in its final words) is its apparent inconclusiveness (its aporetics, as it were), plus the enigmatic and promising way in which it eludes the alternatives of fideism and secularism, even though Adorno defends a "secularization" (*Säkularisierung*), of sorts.[13] This formulation condenses and radicalizes the repeated invocation of the ban on graven images in the opening section of *Dialectic of Enlightenment,* "The Concept of Enlightenment," which speaks in unmistakable terms about the "paradox of faith" and the intrinsic relationship to violence it entails—including the transcendental violence of the conceptual, of any concept.[14]

As Adorno puts it in "Reason and Revelation," ascesis toward "any type of revealed faith" implies no simple denial, no denegation, no negation, of any faith as such. Conceptually, ascesis, even "extreme ascesis," toward some revelation and some faith leaves some revelation and some faith, some of that revelation, some of that faith, intact, to be affirmed, to be believed. Moreover, the "extreme loyalty to the prohibition of images, far beyond what this once originally meant" (to recall the second half of Adorno's formulation) echoes, in turn, a theological source and archive— and not just of "any type of revealed religion"—whose integrity it seeks to protect and whose apparently as yet unredeemed possibilities it seeks to set free. That this "loyalty" extends "far beyond" what the prohibition "once originally meant" can mean at least two things.

On the one hand, it entails that loyalty to the second commandment of revealed—that is to say, positive—religion finds its motive in a "commandment" that precedes the religion it calls into being and whose sanctity it prescribes and guards. The sole possibility of religion is thus, for Adorno, not religion itself but a pre- and an-ethical—indeed, pre- and apolitical—possibility, whose constitutive role is not (or not yet) of the

---

12. Adorno, "Reason and Revelation," 142 / 10.2:616.

13. Adorno, "Reason and Revelation," 138 / 611.

14. *DE* 17–18 / 46. For a discussion, see Gertrud Koch, "Mimesis and the Ban on Graven Images," in de Vries and Weber, *Religion and Media,* 151–62. On the "paradox of faith," see *DE* 14–15 / 42.

order of the religious. This possibility must lack any religious determination, conceptual or otherwise, and hence is a negativity of sorts.

On the other hand, the "extreme loyalty" reminds us of a past or future of a religion which has not (yet) come into its own, that is not (yet) itself, in other words, a religion that is more religious than what religion "once" or "originally" meant (to be): at once the surplus, the superlative, the supplement—and the surreption, surrender, or even superfluousness—of religion.

These two mutually exclusive, yet somehow also mutually constitutive, readings of "extreme loyalty" enable one to see how the *via negativa* and the *via eminentiae*—ascesis and excess, saying less (or the least) and saying more (the most or too much), negative and positive theologies— touch upon each other, solicit each other, collapse or dialectically revert into each other, and thus become virtually indistinguishable from each other. Indeed, if one allows a slight but pertinent modification of Adorno's expression of "extreme loyalty to the prohibition of images," it becomes clear that *loyalty to the extreme* (whose image remains likewise prohibited) implies also that an openness to extreme negativity, to the negativity of extremes—here the more negative than negative reversal of quantity into quality, into the horror of the worst (*das Grauen*)—go hand in hand with the "joy [*Glück*]" of a no less excessive "elevation" or "sublimity" of "thought" and even imply each other reciprocally. And do so for good and for ill.

To understand this complicity—or at least structural resemblance— between the worst and the best (that of the better rather than the good life, whose image, like that of the worst, is prohibited), it is necessary to examine a notion that Adorno, despite his reservation (or extreme ascesis) concerning the very concept of a revealed religion and its theology (its dogmatics and the like), introduced in an early letter to Walter Benjamin: namely, that of the "other theology [*die andere Theologie*]." This "theology"—a postsecularist or, rather, materialist and, as Adorno will say, "inverse" theology—for which Franz Kafka (and much later Samuel Beckett) is at once the major protagonist and primary antagonist, is neither the positive nor the negative, the orthodox nor the heterodox theology of tradition, nor does it let itself be reduced to the historico-empirical and literary criteria adopted by the "science of religion." Neither biblical nor systematic, let alone dogmatic, in its orientation, it proffers no "loyalty"—let alone "extreme loyalty"—to the onto-theological legacy as it stands or as it is traditionally or normally conceived. And yet, as the final words of Adorno's *Negative Dialectics* make clear, "thought [*Denken*]" — or what amounts to the same, the "other theology" — entertains a certain "solidarity" with metaphysics in its downfall. What, exactly, does that mean?

Before answering that question, let me briefly sketch (1) the aporetics of the nonidentical and (2) the apophatic reading of it which will always be possible, if not necessary, but which can illustrate a formal argument in light of some of its historical antecedents. This analysis and its illustration will prepare the ground for thinking these two modes of thinking together: more precisely, for comprehending the impossibility of thinking them together in full rigor, consistently, or coherently. The "inverse" or other — I would say minimal — theology for which Adorno stands must be seen as (3) the very expression of this insight, if it is one.[15]

15. Recent attempts to read Adorno from what could be called a Wittgensteinian perspective offer another possibility for understanding these motifs. This can be seen in the work of Albrecht Wellmer and Rolf Wiggershaus and also, more indirectly, in Stanley Cavell's recent engagement with Benjamin. Needless to say, this reading must work around Adorno's dismissive characterizations of Wittgenstein's *Tractatus*. See Albrecht Wellmer, "Ludwig Wittgenstein: Über die Schwierigkeiten einer Rezeption seiner Philosophie und ihre Stellung zur Philosophie Adornos," in Brian McGuinness and others, *"Der Löwe spricht . . . und wir können ihn nicht verstehen": Ein Symposium an der Universität Frankfurt anlässlich des hundertsten Geburtstages von Ludwig Wittgenstein* (Frankfurt a.M.: Suhrkamp, 1991), 138–48; also in Albrecht Wellmer, *Endspiele: Die unversöhnliche Moderne, Essays und Vorträge* (Frankfurt a.M.: Suhrkamp, 1993), 239–49; Rolf Wiggershaus, *Wittgenstein und Adorno: Zwei Spielarten modernen Philosophierens* (Göttingen: Wallstein, 2000). See also Stanley Cavell, "Benjamin and Wittgenstein: Signals and Affinities," in *Philosophie in synthetischer Absicht / Synthesis in Mind*, ed. Marcelo Stamm (Stuttgart: Klett-Cotta, 1998), 565–82.

Halbertal and Margalit cite Wittgenstein's dictum "All that philosophy can do is to destroy idols. And that means not making new ones — say out of the 'absence of idols'" (cited in *Idolatry*, 244). Halbertal and Margalit rightly note: "The metaphor of idolatry that Wittgenstein uses in describing his stand against foundationalism points to the possibility of the extension of idolatry to its opposites." This "metaphorical extension," they continue,

> has some similarity to the Maimonidean view of negative theology. According to Maimonides, any linguistic positive description of God will constitute a belief in a false god. Since Maimonides considers language inherently limited, the predication of meaningful attributes to God will portray the world and God under the same categories and will necessarily make God into a thing of the world. The strict Maimonidean demands for total linguistic constraint exclude any possibility of articulation of what stands in opposition to the false god. At the moment such a formulation will be suggested it will mean replacing one false god with another. Maimonides, through his approach to the limits of language, extended the category of idolatry to any positive description of God. (244–45)

The Dialectic and Aporetic of the Nonidentical

As we have seen, the unquestioned premise of dialectics (of dialectics *tout court* or of dialectics dialectically, i.e., consistently and hence negatively *thought* [and what, exactly, would it mean to *practice* or to *live* it?]) is the assumption that thinking requires concepts in order to grasp the singular (the *Besonderes:* not the particular, *Besonderheit,* or the individual), but also that any concept (albeit the concept of the singular, i.e., of singularity) already betrays—by generalizing, abstracting, idealizing, formalizing, neutralizing, and hence violating—what it seeks to convey (and to which alone it, and it alone! must and should, nonetheless, give voice). The antinomy reaches farther when transposed onto the question of the theological, of the singular of the absolute: not merely the totally other but the One, the Infinite, which absolves itself—as trace—from all finite, and hence necessarily limiting, determination. Adorno will draw a dramatic, paradoxical, and, indeed, aporetic consequence from this, which will come to stand for the difficulty of thinking the singular *in general,* as it were. Reiterating his radicalization of the ban on graven images, he writes, in *Negative Dialectics:* "one who believes in God therefore cannot believe in Him. The possibility for which the divine name stands is maintained by whoever does not believe. Although at one time the prohibition of images extended to the pronunciation of the name, it has, in this form, itself become suspicious of superstition. Things have gotten worse: even to think hope forsakes hope and works against it" (*ND* 402 / 394, trans. modified).

The passage echoes—or, rather, mirrors—similar reasoning in *Dialectic of Enlightenment,* in which Horkheimer and Adorno explain that the *act* and *utterance* of faith rest upon an internal antinomy. Premised on a propositional content, however minimal, they cannot be reduced to a *mere* gesture or *pure* performative, whose emptied intentional act—the "power of the word," which one "*only* believes"—could never be fulfilled or whose absolute, forever absolved "Referent" could never be ascertained once and for all. Hence, the essential privation and deprivation, the neither-nor of faith—hence also the violence, fanaticism, and horrors to which it inevitably gives rise. "Faith," Horkheimer and Adorno write, is

> a privative concept: it is abolished as faith if it does not continuously assert either its opposition to knowledge or its agreement with it. In being dependent on the limits set to knowledge, it is itself limited. The attempt made by faith under Protestantism to locate the principle of truth, which transcends

faith and without which faith cannot exist, directly in the word itself, as in primeval times, and to restore the symbolic power of the word, was paid for by obedience to the word, but not in its sacred form. Because faith is unavoidably tied to knowledge as its friend or its foe, faith perpetuates the split in the struggle to overcome knowledge: its fanaticism is the mark of its untruth, the objective admission that anyone who *only* believes for that reason no longer believes. Bad conscience is second nature to it. The secret awareness of this necessary, inherent flaw, the immanent contradiction that lies in making a profession of reconciliation, is the reason why honesty in believers has always been a sensitive and dangerous affair. The horrors of fire and sword, of counter-Reformation and Reformation, were perpetrated not as an exaggeration but as a realization of the principle of faith. Faith repeatedly shows itself of the same stamp as the world history it would like to command; indeed, in the modern period it has become that history's preferred means, its special ruse. Not only is the Enlightenment of the eighteenth century inexorable, as Hegel confirmed; so, too, as none knew better than he, is the movement of thought itself. The lowest insight, like the highest, contains the knowledge of the distance from the truth, which makes the apologist a liar. The paradox of faith degenerates finally into fraud, the myth of the twentieth century and faith's irrationality into rational organization in the hands of the utterly enlightened as they steer society toward barbarism. (*DE* 14–15 / 42–43)

Again, what is said of faith and its paradox here—of its structural untruth or "distance from the truth"—holds true for the course of "world history" in general, for "the movement of thought itself," *including* the dialectic (or, for Adorno, the negative dialectic) which seeks to spell out and dispel its inexorable logic. What is remarkable, however, is the fact that Adorno and Horkheimer seek to analyze this general law—indeed, the law of the general, of all generalization, abstraction, reduction, and reification—with the help of unmistakenly *religious* figures of thought, as if the whole task of critical thinking revolved in the end (no, from the very outset!) around an "extreme loyalty to the prohibition of images, far beyond what this once originally meant," as if "religion" (or at least some of its most challenging commands and pivotal doctrines) spoke the truth of the concept, the labor of thought, knowledge, responsibility, judgment, in short: the philosophical, the secular, and so on.

Faith would have no hope of positively stating (or, for that matter, of avoiding stating and thus merely silently gesturing toward) what it stands for, what it aims at, in an always partial and limited—and, hence, ipso facto idolatrous and blasphemous—way. If extreme ascesis toward the pronunciation of the divine name—whose "possibility" is everything that matters, the fundamental possibility and ultimate impossibility of thinking, action, and judging—is imperative (being required by the prereligious *Bilderverbot* of which I spoke earlier and intensified by the ongoing process of history), then mere thought, even the metaphysical (philosophical, theological) *idea* of a divinity purified of all anthropomorphism, will not help. Not even silence does the trick.[16] Only "extreme" (rather than, say, consistent or radical) ascesis does.

The Two Times of the Negative: Negative Metaphysics and Negative Theology

Dialectically and materialistically seen, the intrinsic conceptual idolatry thus detected—the sin or guilt involved in even thinking hope (and there can be no thought without or beyond the concept)—does not stem from an epistemological difficulty alone. Nor is it the result of sharpened insight into the semantics and formal pragmatics (say, the performative contradiction) of religious language and its singular (and singularizing, say, ethical and existential, aesthetic and expressive) features as such. All of these difficulties—the "crisis of the concept and of meaning," of which Adorno speaks in "Reason and Revelation"—are contingent upon a reflection on the philosophy of history and on the transience (*Vergänglichkeit*) and, indeed, the natural history (*Naturgeschichte*) which it conveys.

Speaking about "the possible status of what might be called *metaphysical experience* today," in the informal parlance of the lecture course given while he was completing *Negative Dialectics,* recently published as *Metaphysics: Concept and Problems,* Adorno formulates this insight as follows:

> I will not be giving away a big secret—and perhaps will just provoke a laugh—if I tell you that, for me, there seems to be no possible treatment of the question of metaphysics other than the dialectical one. Now, a dialectical treatment cannot suppose—and I come here to the specific nature of the experience I want to talk about—that the immutable is true and substantial while the transient is inferior and despicable, a mere mode or deception of the senses, as which it has been tirelessly denounced by philosophers since Plato. If we start from an awareness that, for us, the equation of the immutable with the good, the true and the beautiful has simply been refuted, then the content of metaphysics is changed. . . . In the light of what we have experienced in our time—

16. In fact, historically only magic (*Magie, Zauberei*) does.

and I am aware that, in the face of these experiences, the form of a lecture, and the attempt even to touch upon such things in the language of philosophy and the vantage point of a lectern, has something unseemly, ridiculous, even shameless about it (yet one cannot get away from it) — these experiences, I say, change the content of metaphysics. The mutual indifference of the temporal world and ideas, which has been asserted throughout metaphysics, can no longer be maintained [but, then, was the "temporal," the very concept or form of perception of time, not itself a metaphysical notion of sorts, and could Adorno himself do away completely with a notion of, say, the "atemporal"?]. There are isolated motifs scattered in the history of ideas which hint at this [but, then, how could they be isolated and scattered if the movement and intrinsic articulation of ideas follows — or corresponds to — that of history at large? And, finally, what would it mean to "hint" without resorting to some "immediacy," that *proton pseudos* of all nondialectical thought?]. And, curiously enough, they are to be found less in the history of philosophy, if you leave aside certain elements in Hegel, than in heretical theology — that is to say, mystical speculation, which has always been essentially heretical and has always occupied a precarious position within institutional religions. I am thinking here of the mystical doctrine — which is common to the Cabbala and to Christian mysticism such as that of Angelus Silesius — of the infinite relevance of the intra-mundane, and thus the historical, to transcendence, and to any possible conception of transcendence. The supposition of a radical separation, *chorismos*, between the intra-mundane realm and the transcendental is highly problematic, since it is constantly confronted with evidence showing that it has picked out its eternal values, its immutabilities, from the mutable and from experience, and has then abstracted them. And if a metaphysics were consistent, it would refrain from using apologetics to keep such evidence at bay. A thinking which is defensive, which attempts to cling to something in the face of compelling objections, is always doomed. The only way a fruitful thinking can save itself is by following the injunction: "Cast away, that you may gain [*Wirf weg, damit du gewinnst*]."[17]

A reminder of the world and words of Angelus Silesius's *Cherubinischer Wandersmann* (*Cherubinic Wanderer*), this dictum epitomizes both the *via negativa* and the final gesture of *Negative Dialectics*. It is the sole form hope is allowed to retain. Even to think hope — positively, affirmatively — would be to sin against it. Only a kenosis and ascesis of discourse, to the point of unbelief, atheism — in short, "extreme loyalty to the pro-

17. Adorno, *Metaphysics*, 58–59 / 100–101.

hibition of images, far beyond what this once originally meant"—holds open the "possibility for which the divine name stands."

Of course, one can always try to turn the tables and take the most stringent (and seemingly heterodox, heretic, mystic, iconoclastic, and antinomian) negation to be the paradoxical expression of the most consequent (and, perhaps, most orthodox, faithful, devout, and even iconic) affirmation. An "extreme ascesis toward any type of revealed faith, an extreme loyalty to the prohibition of images, far beyond what this once originally meant"—the last and seemingly least of the gestures of faith under the sign of the times (namely, of the worst)—just might amount to the sole "possibility" for faith to retain (or establish) its integrity for the last (or, perhaps, first) time.

Mikel Dufrenne and Jacques Derrida have given alternative readings of this possibility: Dufrenne in "Toward a Non-Theological Philosophy," the preface to the second edition of *La Poétique* (*Poetics*); Derrida in "How to Avoid Speaking: Denials" and in the concluding pages of *De l'esprit* (*Of Spirit*). More indirectly, we find a version of this reading in the convolutions of "Circumfession," which plays throughout on the reversal of *last* in the sense of the "latest," the "least," and the "best" ("The last of the Jews which I am, the last of the eschatologists; *le dernier des juifs que je suis, le dernier des eschatologistes*"), and, last but not least, in the recent lecture entitled "La Langue de l'étranger" ("The Foreigner's Language"), with which Derrida accepted the Adorno Prize in Frankfurt in 2001.[18] Let me limit myself to a single formalization of the argument—or "hint"— which should make this turning clear:

> for essential reasons one is never certain of being able to attribute to anyone a project of negative theology *as such.*
>
> . . .
>
> once the apophatic discourse is analyzed in its logical-grammatical form, if it is not merely sterile, repetitive, obscurantist, mechanical, it perhaps leads us to consider the becoming-theological of all discourse. From the moment a proposition takes a negative form, the negativity that manifests itself need only be pushed to the limit, and it at least resembles an apophatic theology. Every time I say: X is neither this nor that, neither the contrary of this nor

18. Jacques Derrida, "La Langue de l'étranger: Discours de réception du prix Adorno à Francfort," *Le Monde Diplomatique*, no. 574 (January 2002): 24–27; rpt. as *Fichus: Discours de Francfort* (Paris: Galilée, 2002).

of that, neither the simple neutralization of this nor of that with which it *has nothing in common,* being absolutely heterogeneous to or incommensurable with them, I would start to speak of God, under this name or another. God's name would then be the hyperbolic effect of that negativity or all negativity that is consistent in its discourse. God's name would suit everything that may not be broached, approached, or designated, except in an indirect and negative manner. Every negative sentence would already be haunted by God or by the name of God, the distinction between God and God's name opening up the very space of this enigma. If there is a work of negativity in discourse and predication, it will produce divinity. It would then suffice to change a sign (or rather to show, something easy and classical enough, that this inversion has *always already* taken place, that it is the essential movement of thought) in order to say that divinity is not produced but productive. Infinitely productive, Hegel would say, for example. God would be not merely the end, but the origin of this work of the negative. Not only would atheism not be the truth of negative theology; rather, God would be the truth of all negativity. One would thus arrive at a kind of proof of God—not a proof of the *existence* of God, but a proof of God *by His effects,* or more precisely a proof of what one calls God, or of the name of God, by effects without [determining] cause. . . . "God" would name *that without which* one would not know how to account for any negativity: grammatical or logical negation, illness, evil, and finally neurosis which, far from permitting psychoanalysis to reduce religion to a symptom, would obligate it to recognize in the symptom the negative manifestation to God. Without saying that there must be at least as much "reality" in the cause as in the effect, and that the "existence" of God has no need of any proof other than the religious symptomatics, one would see on the contrary—in the negation or suspension of the predicate, even of the thesis of "existence"— the first mark of respect for a divine cause which does not even need to "be." And those who would like to consider "deconstruction" a symptom of modern or postmodern nihilism could indeed, if they wished, recognize in it the last testimony—not to say martyrdom—of faith in the present *fin de siècle.* This reading will always be possible.[19]

This is one way to affirm the continuing—and, perhaps, ever more prominent and promising—conceptual, imaginative, argumentative, and rhetorical resources of the religious and theological tradition, of its ar-

19. Jacques Derrida, "How to Avoid Speaking: Denials," trans. Ken Frieden, in *Languages of the Unsayable: The Play of Negativity in Literature and Literary Theory,* ed. Sanford Budick and Wolfgang Iser (New York: Columbia University Press, 1989), 6–7.

chive and its acts, its judgments and imaginings.[20] Seen from this perspective, the sole possibility for responsible thought — again, "an extreme
ascesis toward any type of revealed faith, an extreme loyalty to the prohibition of images, far beyond what this once originally meant" — while preceding and pointing "far beyond" (or "way back before") tradition, would
thus still draw on its critical potential for critique and (as Kant would say)
"reflective faith," that is to say, for the very possibility of extreme ascesis
to the point of atheism. Reason is conditioned by revelation in the very
act of negating it, and the reverse holds true as well: revelation is conditioned by reason in the very act of suspending or supplementing it. That
contradiction and nothing else — no single thesis, no single concept, no
dogma, spirituality, or icon — constitutes reason's minimal theology *and*
revelation's inevitable idolatry, the blasphemy of its very first word, its
unavoidable "admixture of paganism," as Kant already knew.[21]

Adorno, however, hesitates to speak of theology. He is willing, rather,
to speak of "the other theology," of an "inverse theology," of a theology
whose intentions, vocabularies, and imagery are profanized or have wan-
dered into the realm of the secular — and he therefore chooses instead
the idiom of a metaphysics, a metaphysical experience, experiment, and
exercise whose minimal contours he elaborates in the final part of *Negative Dialectics*, entitled "Meditations on Metaphysics." The reasons for this
reservation with respect to the theological are simple and are formulated
in almost simplistic, linear, and progressivist terms: "Vis-à-vis theology,
metaphysics is not just a historically later stage, as it is according to positivistic doctrine. It is not just the secularization of theology into concept.
It preserves theology in the very critique of it, by uncovering the possibility of what theology imposes on humans and thus desecrates" (*ND* 397 /
389).

Whereas theology remains caught in an insurpassable antinomy, meta-

---

20. See Derrida, *Acts of Religion.* Along similar lines, in his essay "The Deconstruction
of Christianity" (the pilot essay for a larger project), Jean-Luc Nancy suggests: "In what way
and up to what point do we want *to hold onto* Christianity? How, exactly, through the whole of
our tradition, have we been *held by* it?" In Nancy's view these questions entail two correlative
claims. He borrows one from the Italian philosopher Luigi Pareysson, who notes, "The only
current Christianity is one that contemplates the present possibility of its negation," and he
formulates the other in the complementary insight: "The only current atheism is one that contemplates the reality of its Christian roots" ("La Déconstruction du christianisme," *Les Études
Philosophiques*, no. 4 [1998]: 504 / "The Deconstruction of Christianity," trans. Simon Sparks,
in de Vries and Weber, *Religion and Media*, 113).

21. See my book *Religion and Violence,* chap. 1.

physics — though only in its downfall — has a chance of saving the critical possibility for which it once historically and systematically stood. It can do so, however, only by transforming itself into what, traditionally speaking, formed its opposite: by becoming a *micrology* (instead of a discourse of generalities, of the universal and the essential), by becoming *materialist* (instead of remaining idealist, spiritualist, dualistic), by *inverting* and *reversing* the premises and direction from which it once set out. All these opposites are prefigured and anticipated in the other theology, whose isolated *instances*, Adorno assumes, punctuate the history of religion even more than the history of philosophical thought and whose legacy needs to be reclaimed and redeemed (i.e., brought about and into its own).

Seen in this light, the antinomy of theological consciousness is — analytically and structurally speaking — none other than that of metaphysics or even negative dialectics *in its downfall*. The possibility for which the theological stands here is that of a negative metaphysics — the negative, the virtual counterimage, of metaphysics as we knew it — whose hope lies in extreme ascesis alone. The theological prefigures the metaphysical; the latter echoes the former, remaining captivated by its most vulnerable presuppositions and destined to liberate its most formidable potential (both semantic and metaphorical, argumentative and rhetorical). The metaphysical is the legacy and the promise of the theological, which metaphysics must negate in order to bring that legacy — and *itself!* — into its "own."

Inverse Theology

With the rhetorical exaggeration that forms his trademark — being the reverse (the inverse and the other) of the apophatic and ascetic trait that characterizes negative dialectics in its final moment — Adorno states that "within the constellations which now define our experience all the traditional [or, rather, historically transmitted, *tradierten*] affirmative or positive theses of metaphysics . . . simply become blasphemies [*Blasphemie*]."[22] What is other than whatever exists thus comes to occupy a different space or, rather, comes to inflect our space differently, less frontally and more tangentially, in any case *ever more minimally*. It transcends, though neither as a Platonic or a regulative — Kantian — idea nor as the abstract otherness of the totally other (*das ganz Andere*), which Adorno sees as the *proprium* and the *proton pseudos* of "dialectical theology" or "theology of the crisis"

22. Adorno, *Metaphysics*, 121 / 189.

from Kierkegaard to Barth, Brunner, Ebner, and Gogarten and which he explicitly criticizes in *Metaphysics* and elsewhere. Their conception of a revealed religion (of the Word) takes "religious paradox" in a fateful direction, namely, that of a *negative positivity* or *positive negativity,* whose dialectics (as in dialectical theology) is not thought dialectically—and, hence, negatively—enough. In "Reason and Revelation" Adorno states:

> The irrationalism of revealed religion [*Offenbarungsreligion*] today is expressed in the central status of the concept of religious paradox. It is enough here merely to recall dialectical theology. Even it is not a theological invariant but has its historical status. What the apostle in the age of the Hellenistic enlightenment called a folly for the Greeks and what now demands the abdication of reason was not always so. At its medieval height Christian revealed religion defended itself powerfully against the doctrine of the two types of truth by claiming that the doctrine was self-destructive. High Scholasticism, and especially the *Summa* of St. Thomas, have their force and dignity in the fact that, without absolutizing the concept of reason, they never condemned it: theology went so far only in the age of nominalism, particularly with Luther. ... [O]nce faith no longer accords with knowledge, or at least no longer exists in productive tension with it, it forfeits the quality of binding power, that character of "necessitation [*Nötigung*]" Kant subsequently set out to save in the moral law as a secularization of the authority of faith. Why one should adopt *that* particular faith and not another: nowadays consciousness can find no other justification than simply its own need, which does not warrant truth. In order that I be able to adopt the revealed faith, it must acquire an authority in relation to my reason that would already presuppose that I have adopted the faith—an inescapable circle![23]

In consequence, Adorno suggests, the philosophical tradition of metaphysics and religion can no longer rely on an a priori of sorts; its truth content is endowed with a spatiotemporal index whose materiality (historical situatedness or contextuality) it can no longer ignore or gloss over (and, perhaps, never could). A little earlier he writes:

> Certainly a *ratio* that does not wantonly absolutize itself as a rigid means of domination requires self-reflection, some of which is expressed in the need for religion today. But this self-reflection cannot stop at the mere negation of thought by thought itself, a kind of mythical sacrifice, and cannot realize itself through a "leap": that would all too closely resemble the politics of catastro-

23. Adorno, "Reason and Revelation," 139–40 / 613–14, trans. modified.

phe. On the contrary, reason must attempt to define rationality itself, not as an absolute, but rather as a moment within the totality, though admittedly this moment has also become independent in relation to that totality. Rationality must become cognizant [*innewerden*] of its own nature-like essence [*naturhaften Wesens*]. Although not unknown to the great religions, precisely this theme requires "secularization" today if, isolated and inflated, it is not to further that very darkening of the world it wants to exorcize.[24]

As we saw earlier, the possibility (not the name, let alone the concept, of the divine, but the possibility for which it stands) is not a mere abstraction, an emptiness, empty signifier, or purely intelligible — and purely purifying — idea, free from all "admixture of paganism," as Kant would say. On the contrary, for it to be what it is, the theological must *cast away, so that it may gain*. Where it does not, it risks a dangerous "irrationalism," the troubling fact that the "paradox of faith degenerates finally into fraud, the myth of the twentieth century and faith's irrationality into rational organization in the hands of the utterly enlightened as they steer society toward barbarism." This indictment may seem unfair and irresponsible (one is reminded of Levinas's equally harsh characterizations of Kierkegaard in the opening lines of the essay on this thinker in *Proper Names*), but Adorno is developing a consistent line of reasoning which is in tune with the central argument he and Horkheimer had formulated in the opening chapter of *Dialectic of Enlightenment*. Mere abstraction, insistence on the "totally other" (to cite Rudolf Otto's phrase) *pure and simple* is, literally, hopeless, and it leaves everything — the forces that be — as is:

Nothing of theological content will persist without being transformed; every content will have to put itself to the test of migrating into the realm of the secular, the profane. In contrast to the richly and concretely developed religious imagination of old, the currently prevailing opinion, which claims that the life and experience of people, their immanence, is a kind of glass case, through whose walls one can gaze upon the eternally immutable ontological stock of a *philosophia* or *religio perennis,* is itself an expression of a state of affairs in which the belief in revelation is no longer substantially present in people and in the organization of their relationships and can be maintained only through a desperate abstraction. What counts in the endeavors of ontology today, its attempt to leap without mediation out of the ongoing nominalistic situation into realism, the world of ideas in themselves, which then for its part is ren-

24. Ibid., 138 / 611, trans. modified.

dered into a product of mere subjectivity, of so-called decision, namely, an arbitrary act—all this is also in large measure valid for the closely related turn toward positive religion.[25]

The conceptual (formal or structural) difference between the dogmatic and merely abstract affirmation of the totally other, on the one hand, and Adorno's own repeated invocation of the nonidentical, on the other, is crucial here, but it is difficult—indeed, almost impossible—to determine. The difference between *das ganz Andere* and the "trace of the other [*Spur des Anderen*]" is a near in-difference and yet, somehow, all that matters. The latter's intelligibility—standing in what is supposedly a "productive tension" of "determinate negation" to knowledge while retaining a certain heteronomy of its own—is affirmed only negatively, paradoxically, indeed, aporetically, as various formulations testify. We have discovered and cited some of them before: "The concept of the intelligible realm would be [i.e., we cannot even assume that it somehow, somewhere, at some time 'is'] the concept of something which is not, and yet not only is not [*Der Begriff des intelligibelen Bereichs wäre der von etwas, was nicht ist und doch nicht nur nicht ist*]"; or "The concept of the intelligible is not one of a reality, nor is it a concept of something imaginary. It is aporetical, rather [i.e., not even this would be certain]. [*Der Begriff des Intelligibelen ist weder einer von Realem noch einer von Imaginärem. Vielmehr aporetisch*]" (*ND* 393 / 385, trans. modified, and 391 / 384). It can only be affirmed in solidarity with its "downfall," in awareness of its necessary conceptual idolatry. The extreme ascesis, the "extreme loyalty to the prohibition of images, far beyond what this once originally meant," neither negates what is "said [*le Dit*]" nor indulges in a "saying without being said [*le Dire sans Dit*]," nor does it admit their unproblematic—that is to say, nonaporetic—alternation, oscillation, let alone mediation. Rather, idolatrous blasphemy is inevitable, and bad conscience is the sole figure of its hope.

By contrast, the abstract transcendence—the totally or, rather, otherwise other—of dialectical theology and its existentialist or fundamental-existential precursors and substitutes merely mimics the realm of immanence: "The turn toward transcendence functions as a screen-image [or distortion and idol, *Deckbild*] for immanent, societal hopelessness."[26] If

---

25. Ibid., 136 / 608–9.
26. Ibid., 139 / 612.

religion is based on the contents of its positive theologies, it conflicts with reason. But the moment it reverts to the other extreme and "abandons its factual content [*Sachgehalt*], it threatens to vanish into mere symbolism and that imperils the very existence of its truth claim [*Wahrheitsanspruch*]."[27] On this—now productive, then unproductive—tension the life of the spirit (or, more precisely, "spiritual experience," *geistige Erfahrung*) is built. Its internal contradictions—that is, its conceptual idolatry, its being either too concrete or too abstract, or both—comes with a historical index, whose singularly dual composition varies depending on changing societal (economic, technological) determinants and cultural tendencies but never resolves itself, so long as history has not come to a close.

There is no escape from this dialectic: *deification and reification, divine speech and blasphemy, go hand in hand.* Adorno concludes, "in the name of a paradoxical purity revealed religion would dissolve into something completely indeterminate, a nothingness that could hardly be distinguished from religion's liquidation. Anything more than this nothingness would lead immediately to the insoluble [*zum Unlösbaren*], and it would be a mere ruse of imprisoned consciousness to transfigure into a religious category this very insolubility itself, the failure of finite man, whereas it instead attests to the present impotence of religious categories."[28] Either too substantial or too formal, the impossible possibility—and always possible impossibility—of "religion," its theologies, and its substitutes would thus play itself off against two extremes, each of which mirrors the other.

Adorno 's best examples are the literary works of Kafka and Beckett, whose "theological" universes subtract themselves from both "natural and supranatural interpretation," without thereby falling into some form of existentialist or dialectical theology. In Adorno's view they confront the tradition and its late-nineteenth- and early-twentieth-century overcoming with a dialectical counterimage (a virtual mirror image), whose contours evoke in absentia and hence *ex negativo* the other—here the other of the totally (abstract) other, hence, a figure of hope:

> Kafka's theology—if one can speak of such a thing at all—is antinomian towards the same God whose concept Lessing has championed against orthodoxy, the God of the Enlightenment. But that is a *deus absconditus*. Kafka

27. Ibid., 141 /615.
28. Ibid., 142 / 616.

becomes an accuser of dialectical theology, which he is mistakenly believed to support. Its absolutely Other converges with the mythical powers. The entirely abstract, indeterminate God, cleansed of all anthropomorphic and mytho-logical qualities, is transformed into the fateful, ambivalent and threatening God who instills nothing but fear and trembling. In the terror in face of the radically unknown, his "purity," modeled after the spirit [*dem Geiste nach-geschaffen*], which the expressionist inwardness in Kafka sets up as absolute, reinstates the ancient humanity entrapped in nature. Kafka's work records the striking of the hour when purified faith reveals itself as impure, demytholo-gization as demonology.[29]

Wiggershaus aptly disengages Adorno's interpretation of Beckett's *End-game*—with its more than phenomenological reduction or "subtraction [*Subtraktion*]" of the latest, barest "minimal existence [*Existenzmini-mum*]" (*NL* 243, 246 / 284, 287)—from its supposed metaphysical pes-simism by claiming that he "read Beckett's dark writings as representing the construction of a point of indifference at which the distinction be-tween hell, where there is no longer any possibility of change, and the messianic condition, in which everything is in its correct place, disap-peared."[30] As Adorno adds, the final absurdity Beckett evokes is that the "peace of the nothing [*Ruhe des Nichts*]"—in which the world has become absolute and time, history, and transience have been banned by space—and the peace of "redemption [*Versöhung*]," in which everything has been set aright, can no longer be kept apart by any criteriological means (*NL* 273-74 / 320-21). Metaphysically distinct, their difference is no longer decidable epistemologically, normatively, aesthetically: which is another way of saying that the maximal importance of the minimally other no longer finds any ontological—or, for that matter, theological—halt in the world as we know it but signals itself in more elusive, ab-solute ways. Such indifference between two extremes whose—negative metaphysical—dif-ference nonetheless makes all the difference in the world should not be seen as a mere generalization of "unsymbolic" situations of the worst, nor should it be seen as a simple trivialization of the chances and significance of the best, of "what is other than is so": in it we find a certain *intensifica-*

29. Adorno, "Aufzeichnungen zu Kafka," *GS* 10.1:283 / *Metaphysics*, 181 n. 4 / 280 n. 213, trans. modified. See on this topic also chapter 5, devoted to the *theologia negativa* and the *utopia negativa* in Kafka, in Michael Löwy, *Rédemption et utopie: Le Judaïsme en Europe centrale* (Paris: Presses Universitaires de France, 1988) / *Redemption and Utopia: Jewish Libertarian Thought in Central Europe, A Study in Elective Affinity,* trans. Hope Heaney (London: Athlone Press, 1992).

30. Wiggershaus, *Frankfurt School,* 529 / 540.

tion of experience in general in light and view of its most singular instances according to the logic of the *horror religiosus* and the *adieu, à dieu, a-dieu,* which I have analyzed in *Philosophy and the Turn to Religion* and *Religion and Violence.* Uncannily, this negativity, the mere *thought* or *spiritual exercise* of negativity, somehow—dialectically but in an anti-Hegelian, that is to say, negative, ascetic way—conjures up the possibility of what is other than what exists. The idol gives way to an icon of the possible (or possibly) other. As Adorno writes in his lecture course on metaphysics:

> If there is any way out of the hellish circle . . . it is probably the ability of the mind to assimilate, to think the last extreme of horror and, in face of this spiritual experience, to gain mastery over it. That is little enough. For obviously, such an imagination, such an ability to think extreme negativity, is not comparable to what one undergoes if one is oneself caught up in such situations. Nevertheless, I would think that in the ability not to feel manipulated, but to feel that one has gone relentlessly to the furthest extreme, there lies the only respect which is fitting: a respect for the possibility of the mind, despite everything, to raise itself however slightly above that which is.[31]

What critical good could this do? With reference to these two "inverse theological" authors, Adorno notes two crucial spiritual experiences that their work provokes: through the intensive reading of Kafka's novels, "vigilant experience [*wache Erfahrung*]" tends to discern their singularly described situations "everywhere [*allerorten*]," whereas the language of Beckett's plays and novels effects a "salutary sickening of the patient [*eine heilsame Erkrankung des Erkrankten*]": "whoever listens to himself fears that he might speak likewise" (*NL* 262 / 306, trans. modified).

Other than What Is So

The "neutralization" of religion to a mere element of "culture"—or, for that matter, the reduction of the theological to the demand to abstract from all propositions (*Glaubenssätze*) and merely to live according to the law (as in "the theology of Judaism" or, perhaps, in Tolstoy's "primitive Christianity [*Urchristentum*]")—would not resolve the contradictions that we have sought to understand in their historical and systematic complexity: "Even if this allows the antinomy of knowledge and faith to be circumvented . . . the contradiction continues to operate implicitly. For the question of where the authority of doctrine comes from was not re-

---

31. Adorno, *Metaphysics*, 125 / 196.

solved but rather cut off [*abgeschnitten*] as soon as the Haggadah element had dissociated itself completely from the halachah element."[32]

What remains of metaphysical or spiritual (*geistige*) experience—or what is now possible only in its terms—is at best a paradoxical "joy of thought [*Glück des Gedankens*], which motivates us to think on metaphysical matters in the first place," the "joy of elevation [*Glück der Elevation*]," the "joy of rising beyond what merely is [*Glück der Erhebung; das Glück, über das was bloss ist hinauszugehen*]," a "sublime [*sublime*]" as opposed to "trivial" consciousness.[33] This sublimity is supported and expressed by a materially defined sensuosity whose mirror image is utter revulsion for the physical suffering of other human beings, for "torture [*Tortur*]" and everything for which it stands: the "sign"—not the "symbol"!—of "Auschwitz": (as Adorno says: "the word symbol would be wretchedly inadequate, since we are concerned with the most unsymbolic [*Allerunsymbolischeste*] of all"),[34] but also, as the lecture course *Metaphysics* testifies, and as if this metonymy of the uniqueness of the worst, of a more than radical evil and expansion of evil in general, were unproblematic, also Vietnam, the anticolonial wars, South Africa, mass unemployment, and so forth. Indeed, Adorno suggests, the two sublimities resemble each other in their very structure, to the point of being virtually indistinguishable or at least mutually constitutive. Hence, the codependence of the inverse and the other theology, of redemption and the demonic, of religion and *horror religiosus,* of the resurrection of the body and the mythical and seemingly immobile world of a Kafka and a Beckett.

Secularization, rationalization, modernization, and differentiation are distant and fundamentally inadequate indications of the reversals analyzed here. *Inverse theology,* the *andere Theologie,* obeys a far more complex logic, which touches upon and is prefigured by the theology (and, indeed, myth) which it is supposed to replace with a figure, the very possibility, of hope. As it does so, one can no longer tell whether it becomes the other of revealed theology (its opposite or alternative), theology stripped of its "admixtures" of idolatry and blasphemy (hence, the *surplus* of theology), or, as it were, the *same* (i.e., more of the same) theology *otherwise.* The difference matters little.

Mutatis mutandis, Adorno suggests elsewhere, the same holds for the

---

32. Adorno, "Reason and Revelation," 140 / 614, trans. modified.
33. Adorno, *Metaphysics,* 114–15 / 179.
34. Adorno, *Metaphysics,* 101 / 160, trans. modified.

relationship between this "otherwise" and the scientific establishment of matters of fact, determinant causes, and rules: "Metaphysics confronts the totality of facts with which we are dealing in the sciences with something that is other in principle [*ein prinzipiell Anderes*] without, however, asserting that this other exists, as theologies tend to do with regard to their divinities.... This explains the image of metaphysics as a sort of no-man's-land ..., that is to say, a land in which things take on a nebulous quality. That which is, for this thought, is not enough; but of that which is more than what merely exists, it does not, in turn, affirm that it exists."[35]

In *Die politische Theologie des Paulus* (*The Political Theology of Paul*) Jakob Taubes criticizes this perspective and that of the final aphorism of *Minima Moralia*, "Zum Ende" (translated as "Finale" or "About/Toward the End"), as being a *comme-si-Sache*, merely a matter of a perspective *Als-ob* (as if). Taubes considers messianism in Adorno to be "inflected in an aesthetic way [*ins Ästhetische abgebogen*]," with the result that it would be "totally indifferent whether it is real [*ganz gleichgültig, ob es wirklich ist*]."[36] Adorno's "aestheticized messianism" would thus sharply contrast with Benjamin's conception of "nihilism as world politics," expressed in the *Theologico-Political Fragment*, as well as with Bloch's *Spirit of Utopia*. Adorno, however, literally says that it is "almost indifferent [*fast gleichgültig*]" and, hence, escapes the critique leveled at him by Taubes and, in somewhat more cautious terms, by Giorgio Agamben.[37]

At stake here is neither some fictionalization nor a pragmatist appeal to what it is better for us to believe. Adorno draws on a completely different tradition — or on a completely different possibility within the same tradition — and says so explicitly: "What would be other, the no longer perverted essence, refuses a language that bears the stigmata of existence — there was a time when theology spoke of the mystical name."[38]

---

35. Adorno, *Philosophische Terminologie*.

36. Taubes, *Die politische Theologie des Paulus*, 103-4.

37. Giorgio Agamben, in *Le Temps qui reste: Un Commentaire de l'Épître aux Romains* (Paris: Payot & Rivages, 2000), 60-61, 64-65, 70, takes issue with Taubes's accusation of the aestheticization of the messianic in Adorno's "Zum Ende" ("Finale"). Agamben mistranslates a formulation from Adorno's *Aesthetic Theory* which echoes the considerations I have been studying here, "der Bann der Bann." This expression does not identify art with the "enchantment of enchantment" but reiterates the doubling and exaggeration of the ban on graven images on which *Dialectic of Enlightenment*, "Reason and Revelation," and *Negative Dialectics* insist so much.

38. *ND*, 297-98 / 292-93, trans. modified. See also the contrasting formulation, in the opening section of *Dialectic of Enlightenment*, of the "principle of immanence," "myth," "repetition," "regularity [*Gesetzlichkeit*]," and the "sanction of fate": "Whatever might be different is made

the same [*Was anders wäre, wird gleichgemacht*]" (*DE* 8 / 34). Enlightenment, Horkheimer and Adorno write, "amputates the incommensurable [*schneidet das Inkommensurable weg*]" (*DE* 9 / 35). Interestingly, the only exception to the general rule that supposedly governs the dialectic of Western mythology and its enlightened demythologization is, in their view, "magic [*Magie, Zauberei*]" (see *DE* 6–7, 13 / 31–33, 41). "Magic implies specific representation" (6 / 32), just as, for the "primitive," *mana* "fixes the transcendence of the unknown in relation to the known, permanently linking horror [*Schauder*] to holiness" (10 / 37).

Horkheimer and Adorno's perspective differs from Freud's *Totem and Taboo*, which they explicitly criticize, and from Lévy-Bruehl — or, in his wake, Levinas — who considers magic, like myth, in terms of "participation." Instead, they cite Henri Hubert and Marcel Mauss, who, in "Théorie générale de la magie," published in *L'Année Sociologique* in 1902–3, define *magic* and *mimetic "sympathy"* as "L'un est le tout, tout est dans l'un" (cited after *DE*, 256 n. 20 / 37 n. 20; see also Marcel Mauss, *A General Theory of Magic*, trans. Robert Brain [London: Routledge, 1972], which reproduces the essay as it appeared in Mauss, *Sociologie et anthropologie: Précédé d'une introduction à l'oeuvre de Marcel Mauss par Claude Lévi-Strauss* [Paris: Presses Universitaires de France, 1950, 2001], 3–141).

The "mimesis" that Adorno and Horkheimer grant to shamanic identification with the feared or desired object retains a difference — indeed, a transcendence — of sorts, though this transcendent difference at the same time condenses and echoes a totality. Although it is not a "projection," its image is "imaginary": "the echo of the real preponderance of nature in the weak psyches of primitive people" (*DE* 10–11 / 37). The "specific representation" of magic is echoed in the most advanced and accomplished works of autonomous art, which, in their pursuit of an image of otherness, differ from the historical forms of both philosophy and religion:

> The making of images was proscribed by Plato as it was by the Jews. Both reason and reli-
> gion outlaw the principle of magic. . . . Nature is no longer to be influenced by likeness
> but mastered through work [*Arbeit*]. Art has in common with magic the postulation of
> a special, self-contained sphere removed from the context of profane existence. Within
> it special laws prevail. Just as the sorcerer begins the ceremony by marking out from all
> its surroundings the place in which the sacred forces are to come into play, each work of
> art [*Kunstwerk*] is closed off from reality by its own circumference. The very renunciation
> of external effects by which art is distinguished from magical sympathy binds art only
> more deeply to the heritage of magic. This renunciation places the pure image in oppo-
> sition to corporeal existence, the elements of which the image sublates within itself. It is
> in the nature of the work of art, of aesthetic illusion, to be what was experienced as a new
> and terrible event in the magic of primitiveness: the appearance of the whole in the par-
> ticular. The work of art constantly reenacts the duplicity by which the thing appeared as
> something spiritual, a manifestation of *mana*. That constitutes its aura. As an expression
> of totality art claims the dignity of the absolute. This has occasionally led philosophy to
> rank it higher than conceptual knowledge." (13–14 / 41)

Adorno does not follow this path. It is not implied, as has often been suggested, by the development of his thought from *Dialectic of Enlightenment* through *Negative Dialectics* to *Aesthetic Theory*.

Horkheimer and Adorno spell out the transcendent — imaginary — difference between magic and religion in the opening section of *Dialectic of Enlightenment*:

> Enlightenment as a nominalist tendency stops short before the *nomen*, the non-extensive
> [*umfanglosen*], restricted [*punktuellen*] concept, the proper name. Although it cannot be
> established with certainty whether proper names were originally generic names, as some
> maintain, the former have not yet shared the fate of the latter. . . . In the Jewish religion, in

Metaphysics, thus conceived, stands "against scientism, for example, Wittgenstein's position that fundamentally consciousness has to do only with that which is the case." Adorno suggests that this intuition "might call forth another definition: metaphysics is the form of consciousness in which it attempts to know what is more than the case, or not merely the case, and yet must be thought, because that which, as one says, is the case [e.g., science and the world as it is or as we see it] compels us to do so."[39]

What compels us most, however—and, perhaps, more than ever or even for the first time, this time without further condition, not even that of the general form of pure obligation but as a new and singular categorical imperative—is a sign whose horrific contours and moral, let alone political, consequences escape all conceptual determination. As we have seen, this unintelligibility (*Unausdenkbarkeit*) does not call for an apophatics, *strictly speaking*. The negativity, the "extreme ascesis toward any type of revealed faith, an extreme loyalty to the prohibition of images, far beyond what this once originally meant," does not exhaust itself in the recitation of a totally other, albeit the totally other of this totally other. On the con-

---

which the idea of the patriarchy is heightened to the point of annihilating myth, the link between name and essence is still acknowledged in the prohibition of uttering the name of God. The disenchanted world of Judaism propitiates [or "redeems," *versöhnt*] magic by negating it in the idea of God. The Jewish religion brooks no word which might bring solace to the despair of all mortality. It places all hope in the prohibition of invoking falsity as God, the finite as the infinite, the lie as truth. The pledge of salvation lies in the rejection of any faith which claims to depict it, knowledge in the denunciation of illusion. Negation, however, is not abstract. The indiscriminate denial of anything positive, the stereotyped formula of nothingness as used by Buddhism, ignores the ban on calling the absolute by its name no less than its opposite, pantheism, or the latter's caricature, bourgeois skepticism. Explanations of the world as nothingness or as the entire cosmos [or "as nothing or all," *als des Nichts oder Alles*] are mythologies and the guaranteed paths to redemption sublimated magical practices. The self-satisfaction of knowing in advance, and the transfiguration of negativity as redemption, are untrue forms of the resistance to deception. The right of the image is rescued in the faithful observance of its prohibition. Such observance, "determinate negation," is not exempted from the enticements of intuition by the sovereignty of the abstract concept, as is skepticism, for which falsehood and truth are equally void. Unlike rigorism, determinate negation does not simply reject imperfect representations of the absolute, idols, confronting them with an idea that they are unable to match. Rather, dialectic discloses each image as script [*Schrift*]. It teaches us to read from its features the admission of falseness that cancels its power and hands it over to truth. Language thereby becomes more than a systems of signs. (*DE* 17–18 / 45–47)

Here, more clearly than elsewhere, *Dialectic of Enlightenment* testifies to some of its Benjaminian motifs and motivations.

39. Adorno, *Philosophische Terminologie*, 2:167; cited after Adorno, *Metaphysics*, "Editor's Afterword," 196.

trary, it thinks this other *conceptually* "in its downfall," that is to say, not *as such* but paradoxically, aporetically, in its absolution and its trace, its impurity and, hence, its *idolatry*. This, and nothing else, forces us to think again, to think better, without possible complacency.

Put Otherwise

There is, Halbertal and Margalit conclude, "an astonishing fluidity to 'idolatry': a category that is supposed to be the firmest and strictest of all,"[40] given that idolatry concerns the *indirect* definition of the divine (that which exists most eminently; the immutable, the eternally true, good, and beautiful, the Being to which all "perfections," i.e., all the attributes of perfection we humans can discern, can be ascribed without restriction). Idolatry gives this definition *indirectly* because it circumscribes the divine — godly existence and essence — by demarcating it from what it is not. In that sense the traditional discourses on idolatry and blasphemy, as well as their modern or contemporary analogues, are theologies — *negative* theologies, indeed, *other* theologies — in disguise. They spell out the nonnaturalness or, as it were, nonpositivity of all meaning or meaningfulness.

Any attempt to define or determine something divine or infinite must, in a sense, adopt such a conceptual strategy. Take, for example, Spinoza's *omnis determinatio negatio est* or Saussure's argument that there are no positive signs, but every sign acquires its meaning or value by differentiating itself from others. In idolatry, blasphemy, and their historical analogues this principle is carried to its extreme, as it were, in the way the divine is protected from *everything* it is not. Hence, the parallels between the avoidance and condemnation of idolatrous blasphemy and the conceptual, argumentative, and rhetorical strategies of negative theology.

Hence, also, the parallels between the avoidance of idolatry and the recent discourses concerning "difference," the culturally and politically other, and so on. As Halbertal and Margalit insist, the historical and systematical articulations of what constitutes idolatry and blasphemy concern the self-definition of religious traditions, practices, and communities, insofar as they are processes of defining — and excluding — the other. Rethinking the historical concept and present forms of the prohibition on idolatry and blasphemy might help us, therefore, better to understand the emotional investment involved in any relationship between self and other,

---

40. Halbertal and Margalit, *Idolatry,* 250.

not least because it would allow us to draw on one of the most elaborate and profound archives and imaginaries still with us — at least for some time yet to come.

In one sense, Halbertal and Margalit observe, the concept of idolatry has also come to stand for a general philosophical problem. The different "modern extensions" they identify (from Bacon to Marx, Nietzsche to Wittgenstein) all testify in their own ways to the "fluidity" of the concept from its earliest formulation in the biblical ban on graven images to recent phenomenological projects that deconstruct the tradition of representational thought or disentangle the idol from its opposite, the icon. Along the way, the original theological impetus and referent grows ever dimmer. Or so it seems.

> What distinguishes some instances of modern rhetoric of idolatry is, on the one hand, its use of terminology from the religious critique of idolatry and, on other hand, its attitude to what stands against the idols and what is supposed to complement them. The complementary concept to idolatry is no longer a proper God but something else. Thus the category of idolatry is maintained, while what it is in opposition to changes. A second, more radical modern use of idolatry occurs when the category of idolatry is extended to include any competing opposite, even what was supposedly conceived as the right God himself. According to this view any candidate for opposing the idol is by definition an erection of a new idol. A third way in which the rhetoric of idolatry is applied in modern use is to accept the basic oppositions between pagans and nonpagans but to invert the value assigned to them, namely, to attach the positive value to the pagans and the negative to the nonpagans.[41]

Conversely, the concept of idolatry could be "formulated in a kind of general rule," which could be formalized as: "any nonabsolute value that is made absolute and demands to be the center of dedicated life is idolatry."[42] Of course, Halbertal and Margalit continue, this formulation, "although extending the sphere of idolatry, leaves room for some values that are absolute."[43] Moreover: "Stronger formulations can be extended to include any value: 'any human value should not be made absolute.'"[44] Yet the authors of *Idolatry* do not hesitate to draw out the radical consequences of such an assumption. This consequence captures the central feature of

41. Ibid., 241–42.
42. Ibid., 246.
43. Ibid.
44. Ibid.

Adorno's project as I have reconstructed it: "The internal logic of this general formulation 'nothing human can be made absolute,' as the core understanding of idolatry, threatens to include all complements of idolatry as idolatry, even the worthy God. If the knowledge of the worthy God is ultimately channeled through humans, then it cannot itself be made absolute. . . . What will stand in opposition to idolatry will not be any sense of absolute but the freedom from absolutes and the denial of ultimates; extension reaches its extreme limit."[45]

Seeing, with Adorno, "no other possibility than an extreme ascesis toward any type of revealed faith, an extreme loyalty to the prohibition of images, far beyond what this once originally meant," would be just this: the critique of idolatry — and of idolatry itself — at "its extreme limit." A freedom of, and from, hope.

45. Ibid.

Appendix

The Theology of the Sign and
the Sign of Theology

The Apophatics of Deconstruction

The sign and divinity have the same place and time of
birth. The epoch of the sign is essentially theological.
Perhaps it will never *end*. Its historical *closure* is, however,
outlined.

one does not leave the epoch whose closure one can
outline. The movements of belonging or not belonging are
too subtle, the illusions in that regard are too easy, for us
to make a definite judgment here.
—JACQUES DERRIDA, *Of Grammatology*

IT HAS BECOME COMMON to introduce Derrida's thinking by paraphrasing
its supposedly "neo- (if not post-) structuralist" character. Manfred Frank's
Was ist Neostrukturalismus? (What Is Neostructuralism?) is the best-known
example of this trend.[1] The classification "neostructuralist" suggests that
Derrida's work is immediately linked to the classical structuralism of Ferdinand de Saussure, Claude Lévi-Strauss, and others and preserves, as Frank
asserts, an "*inner* continuity" with them: "Put differently, neostructuralism
is not only — as the title 'post-structuralist' suggests — a line of thinking that
appears *after* structuralism; it is also one that is critically linked to structuralism, without which its origin cannot be understood."[2] Whereas classical structuralism had been understood as a consequent continuation of a
renewed *linguistic* method in the human sciences, specifically ethnology, political economy, and literary criticism, neostructuralism, according to Frank,

1. In *Logics of Disintegration,* a no less critical book, Dews chooses the adjective *poststructuralist.*
2. Frank, *What Is Neostructuralism?* 21 / 31–32.

must be understood as a *philosophically* inspired revolution in the history of reception. The novelty of neostructuralism, so Frank's argument goes, consists first of all in the fact that in its transformation of the structuralist method it let itself be inspired by Nietzsche but also by Freud, Heidegger, Bataille, and Levinas.

Neostructuralism?

The attempt to understand Derrida's work against the backdrop of the "structuralist controversy" easily results in a warped image.[3] This widespread interpretation, I would claim, is disputable not only in that it overlooks that the structuralist insight into the arbitrary character or differentiality of the sign is merely one of many possible entries for clarifying the "point" of deconstruction — supposing that there is one or is just one. What is particularly striking in this reduction of Derrida's writings to a variant of neostructuralism is that it *neutralizes beforehand* the ethical effort and implications of deconstructive practice. The very circumstance that the term *structuralism* has become a well-known term has undoubtedly contributed to the association of the term *deconstruction* with a "negative" operation — the dismantling or destruction of structures. If we disregard terminological details and skip over subtle reinterpretations of the Heideggerian notions of *Destruktion* (destruction) and *Abbau* (dismantling), we easily forget that deconstruction involves in the first place an *affirmative* act. To demonstrate this we must not only keep sight of the line of argument in Derrida's texts, particularly his much-discussed analyses of Saussure and Lévi-Strauss; equally important are the diverse occasional references to the appeal of the *Viens!* (Come!), to the original, even preoriginal, *gift*, and to the response of the *Oui, oui* (Yes, yes), in short, to motifs that have little in common with a prolongation of structuralism or with its supposed Nietzschean or Heideggerian transformations.

3. The term *structuralist controversy* is the revised title of the proceedings of the famous symposium held at the Johns Hopkins University in 1966, which initiated the reception of Derrida's work in the United States. See Richard Macksey and Eugenio Donato, eds., *The Structuralist Controversy: The Languages of Criticism and the Sciences of Man* (Baltimore: Johns Hopkins University Press, 1972). There Derrida delivered the lecture "La Structure, le signe et le jeu dans le discours des sciences humaines" ("Structure, Sign, and Play in the Human Sciences"), which was later included in *Writing and Difference*. See also François Dosse, *Histoire du structuralisme*, vol. 1: *Le Champ du signe, 1945–1966*; vol. 2: *Le Chant du cygne, 1967 à nos jours* (Paris: Éditions La Découverte, 1992) / *History of Structuralism*, vol. 1: *The Rising Sign, 1945–1966*; vol. 2: *The Sign Sets, 1967–Present*, trans. Deborah Glassman (Minneapolis: University of Minnesota Press, 1997), who speaks of Derrida's works in terms of "ultra-structuralism."

Why does Frank's *What Is Neostructuralism?*—one of the most frequently cited works in recent French philosophy—repeatedly lose sight of this complexity? What is it that makes him link the criticism of *logocentrism,* a term Derrida, Lyotard, and Deleuze have used, with nothing less than Bäumler's, Spengler's, and Klages's *pre-fascism*?[4] Is this comparison a "slip of the pen"? Or is it a symptom of a widespread inability *to read* what is written, combined with total inattention to elementary premises of academic ethics? To answer this question we must turn to several ostensibly abstract problems of interpretation. That much is at risk here should be obvious by now.

I noted that, according to Frank, Derrida's thinking about writing and difference must first of all be understood as a critical analysis and further development of the *differential interpretation of the sign* in Ferdinand de Saussure's semiology (*semeion* is the Greek word for "sign"), most pregnantly formulated in his *Cours de linguistique générale* (*Course in General Linguistics*).[5] Derrida is said to have found in this theoretical matrix of later struc-

4. Manfred Frank, "Kleiner (Tübinger) Programmentwurf," *Frankfurter Rundschau,* 5 March 1988.

5. Ferdinand de Saussure, *Cours de linguistique generale,* ed. Charles Bailly and Albert Sechehaye, with the collaboration of Albert Riedlinger, critical edition prepared by Tullio de Mauro, postface by Louis-Jean Calvet (Paris: Payot & Rivages, 1995) / *Course in General Linguistics,* trans. Roy Harris (La Salle: Open Court, 1986). Since my present essay first appeared, the publication of a recently discovered manuscript by Saussure, *Écrits de linguistique générale,* ed. Simon Bouquet and Rudolf Engler (Paris: Gallimard, 2002), has rekindled a long-standing debate concerning the legacy and original intentions of Saussure's work, which heretofore had been transmitted only through the heavily edited *Course in General Linguistics,* originally published in 1916. A reading of this manuscript helps us newly understand how a seemingly technical and formalist program could come to be viewed as the "theoretical matrix" (to use Derrida's expression in *Of Grammatology* and *Positions*) of a whole intellectual movement, as diverse as it may otherwise have been. The double stature of Saussure's work as the foundational text of particular disciplines (phonetics, comparative linguistics, etc.) and the main source of a general cultural episteme was enabled by a certain ambiguity in his project. As the editors of the newly discovered manuscript point out, Saussure appears there at once as the epistemologist of a scholarly discipline and as the philosopher of language which he also wanted to be. The thinker who now emerges both provides the categories and conditions of possibility of any future science of language and treats these categories in terms of their temporality. Indeed, the question of the relationship between the system of language (and signification in general), on the one hand, and history, on the other, is one of his most pressing concerns. The fact that Saussure distinguishes between the actual usage of language (*la parole*) and the abstract system of language (*le système de la langue*) in itself had already touched upon a preeminently philosophical insight into the condition of possibility of all signification: namely, that the system of language—though never tangibly present—is a prerequisite for every linguistic utterance that could be identified and thereby understood or iterated. Without the presupposition of this "deep" structure, every use of language, all ability to understand and communicate, would be inexplicable. Yet he also saw that this does not mean that the use of language is merely a deriva-

turalism the argumentation, central to his own thinking of *différance*, that every linguistic sign is *essentially arbitrary*. What does this mean?

Saussure's use of the term *arbitrary* reflects a simple, yet abyssal, insight into how language and meaning work. He summarizes it in three closely related propositions:[6]

1. Neither the linguistic sign (the signifier, the *signifiant*) nor the concept or notion that it represents, and to which it refers (the signified, the *signifié*), are ever given "positively," that is, as endowed with intrinsic "meaning."

2. There is no natural, that is, immediately evident, link between written and acoustic signs (graphemes and phonemes) and the concepts to which they refer.

3. Linguistic signs derive their meaning solely from the endlessly expanded tissue or network of mutual references or differential relations. In Derrida's words: "in language there are only differences *without positive terms*. Whether we take the signified or signifier, language has neither ideas nor sounds that existed before the linguistic system, but only conceptual and phonic differences that have issued from the system. The idea or phonic substance that a sign contains is of less importance than the other signs that surround it."[7]

Derrida notes that this differential, structuralist semiotics breaks *to a certain extent* with traditional (and modern) semantics. Saussure shows clearly that the signified is inseparably bound to the signifier and is incomprehensible without it. They are two sides of the same coin, of the same effort to "produce" meaning.[8] Linguistic signs are never a purely sensible reflection of an intelligible meaning "beyond meaning," nor are they the ultimate expression of any preceding inner (psychic, intentional) process.

If there is no "meaning" or "idea" that can exist *independently of* the linguistic signifier or differential articulation of this meaning or idea, then a *transcendental signified* is from the start, that is, structurally or a priori, impossible. A "first cause," "idea," or "purpose" in any metaphysical sense which is not itself a link in an endless chain of finite mutual references but,

---

tive realization of the linguistic system. Each presupposes or implies the other. Although no *parole*, no repetition of meaning, can be imagined without accepting the silent basis of the *système de la langue*, the reverse is equally true: the linguistic system is present only in reiterated linguistic usage. Put more forcefully, "historically the fact of speech always comes first."

6. See also Egide Berns, Samuel IJsseling, and Paul Moyaert, *Denken in Parijs: Taal en Lacan, Foucault, Althusser, Derrida* (Alphen: Samson, 1981), 141–69.

7. Saussure, cited after Derrida, *Margins of Philosophy*, 11 / 11.

8. See Derrida, *Positions*, 18 / 28.

rather, *grounds, orients,* or *terminates* this chain would not only be unthinkable and unspeakable but would remain without any physical, semantic, practical, or historico-political "effect."[9] In consequence, the "effects" of linguistic differences are effects in an unusual sense of the word: "Since language . . . has not fallen from the sky, its differences have been produced, are produced effects, but they are effects which do not find their cause in a subject or a substance, in a thing in general, a being that is somewhere present, thereby eluding the play of *différance*."[10] Metaphysics stands or falls by the postulation of such a *transcendent* and *transcendental* being. It is borne by the conviction that the world of transitory phenomena is a more or less accurate reflection of a deeper, more original, unchangeable, and permanent reality. Derrida points out that we could understand the history of Western thinking as a sequence of different names for this meaning — conferring foundation, center, and goal, which pretend to be unique and which must guarantee the cohesion of reality, "*eidos, archē, telos, energeia, ousia* (essence, existence, substance, subject), *aletheia,* transcendentality, consciousness, God, man, and so forth." Their common denominator, Derrida assures us, following Heidegger, is "the definition of Being as *presence*."[11]

By reducing the "structural character" of all experience to a "something" that is not part of any "structure," metaphysics both constitutes and effaces itself. It puts itself *out of bounds,* literally and figuratively. If metaphysics claims to be meaningful, then its concepts must be defined to a certain extent. But, as Saussure shows, every sign in a spoken or written discourse — every phoneme and grapheme — always refers to something other than itself. It can only be understood, thought, read, spoken, and discussed insofar as it is delimited from other linguistic elements. The centrality the sign claims is thus an "illusion." No metaphysical postulate can be proclaimed or claim validity without betraying itself, without becoming something other than it means or pretends to be. Nothing has meaning and sense *in, of,* or *as itself.* There is no meaning without context, that is to say, without difference.

Derrida notes that even the theoretical-systematic distinction between signifier and signified remains in debt to the binary opposition between the intelligible and the sensible, which it had made it its purpose to compli-

9. See Derrida, *Of Grammatology,* 49 / 71–72.

10. Derrida, *Margins of Philosophy,* 11 / 12. On the notion of "play," see *Of Grammatology,* 50 / 73, in which Derrida also defines *writing* as "the play in language" (trans. modified).

11. Derrida, *Writing and Difference,* 279–80 / 411.

cate and undercut. Nor does Saussure fully escape the Stoic and scholastic distinction between the *signans* and the *signatum*. Although he concedes that signifier and signified can never de facto act separately, he nonetheless believes that they differ de jure. But, if every signifier in its turn takes on the role of signified, then this analytical distinction, Derrida notes, loses its foundation from the very outset.

Yet this conclusion should not lead us to forsake the distinction between signifier and signified altogether. Use of this opposition is even, within certain limits, unavoidable. As Derrida rightly observes: "Without it *translation,* for example, would be impossible. It is within the horizon of an absolutely pure, transparent and unequivocal ability to translate that the theme of transcendental signifier has been constituted. To the extent that it is possible, or *appears* possible, translation puts into practice the differentiation between signified and signifier. But if the differentiation is never pure, the translation cannot be. The notion translation will have to be replaced by *transformation.*"[12] Translation can thus no longer be thought as if it were a "transportation" of pure meaning between two languages or linguistic systems in which the "vehicle" is irrelevant. Similarly, *communication* is no longer imaginable as the transposition of a content in or by a neutral, homogeneous medium that does not change the shape of the message sent.

According to Derrida, the teaching on the differentiality of meaning and sense also has repercussions for the *concept of system* used by classical structuralism. The metaphysical-critical potential of the (re)discovery of the sign's arbitrary character itself returns to a certain degree to semiotics. Saussure distinguished between the actual usage of language (*la parole*) and the abstract system of language (*le système de la langue*). The latter—though never tangibly present—is a prerequisite for every linguistic utterance that can be identified and thereby understood or iterated. Without the presupposition of this deeper structure, every use of language, any ability to understand and communicate, would be inexplicable. This does not mean that the use of language is merely a derivative or realization of the linguistic system. Each presupposes or implies the other. Although no *parole*, no *repetition* of meaning, is imaginable without accepting the silent basis of the *système de la langue,* the reverse is equally true: the linguistic system is present only in reiterated linguistic usage. Put more forcefully, "historically the fact of speech always comes first."[13]

12. Derrida, *Positions*, 20 / 31, trans. modified.
13. Cited after Derrida, *Margins of Philosophy,* 12 / 12.

Derrida does not reject without further ado that the linguistic system is the (quasi-, simili-, or crypto-transcendental) condition of possibility of any linguistic utterance. But he leaves no doubt that a consequent reflection on the differentiality of all meaning is hardly compatible with the assumption of synchronicity, taxonomics, and the supposed ahistoricity of the concept of the structure or the system of language. This does not mean that the principle of differentiality "has no structure [or is 'astructural']."[14] It should be described as a "moving structure," to which we can scarcely apply the customary contrasts used to define concepts such as "movement"—dynamic and static, present and absent. The "structural character" at risk here *precedes and destabilizes* every system, every real or virtual structure of *langue* or *parole* (or of code and message, schema and usage), even the constitution and structure of all experience, and is thus in a certain way their "foundation." This should not be understood in a logical or chronological sense. Furthermore, the principle of differentiality is *nowhere else* a separate—intelligible—area of being. Nor is it Being. It is "revealed" only in the meaning it effects. Alone it "is nothing" and not even that: it withdraws not only from the Hegelian dialectical logic of negativity but also from the movement Heidegger attributes to the *Nichts*. This differentiality meshes with the more complex working of the *sans* (without) and the *pas* (not) which play such an important role in the writings of Maurice Blanchot and which also permeate the tradition of *negative theology*.[15] (In "How to Avoid Speaking: Denials," Derrida cites Eckhart, who in turn cites Augustine: "God is wise without being wise, good without being good," etc.). I will return to this.

Interestingly, the *circular* relationship or mutual implication that Saussure ascribes to *la langue* and *le parole* resurfaces in Derrida on another plane and, I would claim, in a far more differentiated way. Saussure thought that, when we pause at one of these two necessary postulates of (linguistic) communication, we can never explain how meaning is created or transmitted. Only their interaction makes them comprehensible. Compared to this interaction, linguistic system and usage are, in a certain sense, secondary and abstract. In a certain sense, because the principle of differentiation is located nowhere as such. From the start it differs from "itself"; that *système* and *parole* are secondary to both this interplay and their "own" interaction must not be taken in any logical or chronological sense. The interplay of differentiation "marks" the *paroles* in language and the relationship of these *paroles*

14. Derrida, *Positions*, 28 / 39.
15. See Derrida's essay "Pas," in *Parages*.

to language. It is the "detour" we must take if we are to speak, but then again it is also *"the silent promise* [or pledge, *gage silencieux*] *I must make."*[16]

In his early writings Derrida calls this differentiality "Différence" (with a capital *D*),[17] whereas later he speaks of "difference in general,"[18] and finally *différance*. This neologism—or better, "neographism"[19]—is, like so many other of Derrida's key terms, untranslatable, neither a word nor a concept. But the inability to translate it by no means excludes precision and rigor in describing it. More than once Derrida typifies *différance* as "the product of a system of differences,"[20] "the movement . . . in which the linguistic system, *like every code, every system of references,* is 'historically' constituted as a tissue of differences."[21] Seen in this way, *différance* stands for another "order" (a "law," necessity, fate, or fatality but always an order, command, or imperative) than the one delimited by our traditional ontological or deontological concepts. This explains why Derrida puts immediately after the sentence cited here the warning: "'Is constituted,' 'is produced,' 'is created,' 'movement,' 'historically,' etc., necessarily being understood beyond the metaphysical language in which they are retained, along with all their implications."[22] The customary distinction between a diachronical-generative and a synchronic-structuralist reflection is no longer applicable to the differential movement or production of *différance* "as such." *Différance* is "no more static than dynamic, no more structural than historical. But also no less." Put differently, "the differend, the *différence,* between Dionysus and Apollo, between ardor and structure, cannot be erased in history, for it is not in history. It too, in an unexpected sense, is an original structure: the opening of history, historicity itself. Difference does not simply belong either to history or to structure."[23] It is certainly no preoriginal "cause" or (supreme) being whose purely "phenomenal" reality gives only signals.[24]

The introduction of the silent but legible *a* in the French word for "difference"—with unmistakable reference to the active connotations of the present participle of *différer* (i.e., *différant*)—not only draws attention to the

16. Derrida, *Margins of Philosophy,* 15 / 16.

17. See Edmund Husserl, *L'Origine de la géometrie,* trans. and intro. Jacques Derrida (1962; rpt. Paris: Presses Universitaires de France, 1974), 171.

18. Derrida, *Of Grammatology,* 18 / 31.

19. Derrida, *Margins of Philosophy,* 3 / 3.

20. Derrida, *Positions,* 28 / 40.

21. Derrida, *Margins of Philosophy,* 37 / 40, my emph.

22. Ibid., 12 / 12–13.

23. Derrida, *Writing and Difference,* 28 / 47.

24. Derrida, *Positions,* 106–7 n. 42 / 109 n. 31.

"production" and movement of temporal and spatial displacement; it marks the "conflict" side of this process. Long before the publication of Lyotard's *The Differend* and anticipating the interpretation of Heidegger's "Herakleitos" lecture, this *différance* (*différante* and *différend*) evokes the connotation of controversy, conflict, and *polemos*.[25]

Against this backdrop we can now bring together several lines in our argument. Derrida uses the motif of the "arbitrary sign" and that of "differential structure" to refer indirectly to a production or movement that permits meaning (without itself having any meaning, strictly speaking). The concepts "sign" and "structure" are not simply adopted or rejected but are grafted onto "something else": onto the "otherness," the difference par excellence, the *grammè* (or, better, the *marque*), or, in still other words, onto *différance*. The last figure, if that's the right word, is a *grapheme*, not a word, concept, idea, substance, or material. It represents a "configuration," "bundling," or "graph" of various transformational and transgressive motifs.[26] The semiological formulation of the principle of differentiation is only one of these, and certainly not the most *striking*. Derrida leaves no doubt that writing (about) *différance* "develops the most legitimate, fundamental demands of structuralism."[27] But it should be noted that this does not turn *différance* into, say, a neostructuralist motif.

Farther along in *Margins of Philosophy*, Derrida therefore explains that a relentless reflection on the "structural nature" of linguistic experience "consists neither a) in restoring the classical motif of the system, which can always be shown to be ordered by *telos, aletheia,* and *ousia*, all of which are values reassembled in the concepts 'essence' or of 'meaning'; nor b) in erasing or destroying meaning. Rather, it is a question of determining possibility of meaning on the basis of a 'formal' organization which in itself has no meaning, which does not mean that it is either the non-sense or the anguishing absurdity which haunt metaphysical humanism."[28]

As a "formal" organization, the interplay of differences is stripped of every specific content; as the prerequisite for the functioning of every sign and thus of all meaning, it is itself "silent." It remains noncommittal and "exceeds the order of truth at a certain precise point, but without dissimulating itself as something, as a mysterious being, in the occult of a non-knowledge

25. In ibid., 8 / 16, Derrida speaks of the (silent) graphic and grammatical "aggression" of the *a* in *différance*.

26. Ibid., 9 / 17.

27. Ibid., 28 / 39.

28. Derrida, *Margins of Philosophy*, 134 / 161.

or in a hole with indeterminable borders (for example, in a topology of cas-
tration)."[29] This means, again, that *différance* goes beyond the psychoana-
lytical frame of mind (from, say, Freud to Lacan). Nor can it be envisioned
simply as the hidden object of a negative theology, even though Derrida recognizes that various formulations could very well lead us to this conclusion.
Différance is neither this nor that, no essence or existence, and, while it is
nothing specific, it is therefore not merely "nothing." All this allows us to
conclude only that it is sufficient to remember that *insofar as* psychoanalysis or negative theology rests on the—intolerable—premise that ultimate
reality must be pictured as self-satisfied Being present to itself, or felt only as
a lack or absence, it is not immune to deconstructive reservations. Nothing
more and nothing less is claimed here.

Metaphysics stands or falls by the misjudgment of the "principle of difference," which states that no single linguistic or other element of meaning
can function—or have meaning—without referring to others, without invoking something other than itself. What does this mean? Metaphysically
speaking, every attempt to snatch a privileged concept away from the differential chain in which everything refers to something else—and does so,
infinitely, in an infinite way, ad infinitum—is to be avoided: "every time
people pretend to cut free or isolate an area or layer of pure meaning or pure
signified [in the play of signifiers], they make the same gesture."[30]

In this corrosion of the supremacy of meaning above the sign and the
unity of the concept, of the sign above the play of *marks,* we find the deconstruction of an at-bottom theological motif: "The sign and divinity have the
same place and time of birth. The age of the sign is essentially theological."[31]
The deconstruction of the sign ipso facto disrupts the ontotheological presuppositions and ramifications linked to the Western Logos. And, while this
theology of the sign may never *end,* it has already demarcated its historical
limit.

It would be incorrect to think we could just abandon the metaphysical gesture of wanting to reach beyond differentiality. The metaphysical hypostasis of a single signifier is a *transcendental illusion* or a *longing in reason,* to use Kant's terms, which is given with thinking, speaking, and judging or acting "as such."[32] When we read in the essay on Lévi-Strauss found
in *Writing and Difference* that "even today the notion of a structure lack-

29. Ibid., 6 / 6.
30. Derrida, *Positions,* 32 / 44.
31. Derrida, *Of Grammatology,* 14 / 25.
32. Derrida, *Positions,* 32; see also 22 and 60 / 45; see also 33 and 82.

ing any center represents the unthinkable itself,"[33] the reason for this is not so much an empirical-psychological secondary *condition humaine* (a desire for firm footing or cherishing of a presupposed certainty that makes fear of the unmanageable manageable). Instead, Derrida means that we cannot simply put behind us the structural distortion of reality by claiming some supposedly Archimedean vantage point. Western metaphysics is only the best-known and most dominant expression of this need to posit a foundation. If "postmetaphysical" thinking were possible, it would still have to obey the same "law." And deconstruction is no exception to this rule, which explains, perhaps, why traditional—ethical and theological—images and motifs continue to play a crucial role in Derrida's analyses. We cannot simply push aside this heritage (and the accompanying concept pairs of spirit and letter, "pneumatology" and "Scripture," symbol and allegory), as if a totally other, more adequate, nonmetaphysical conceptual apparatus were somewhere available. Without concepts, Derrida insists no less than Kant, thought would be impossible.

If we deduce from the arbitrary character of the sign that *everything is merely a signifier* and that every theoretical initiative is based solely on a random collection of arbitrary perspectives, then every attribution of meaning becomes obsolete and thinking loses its *critical* potential. At the risk of returning to a "regressive" stage, we must therefore try to set traditional concepts in motion to the point where they begin to betray their own internal and external limits. Through this narrow opening in language, Derrida writes, we can, perhaps, perceive the "yet unnameable glimmer" of the other.[34] The repetition (*Wiederholung*) of "the same," of the inherited fundamental structure of metaphysics, is thus never a repetition in the strict or even Heideggerian and Kierkegaardian sense of the word. It always causes a certain minimal, yet critical, shift and thereby displaces the borders of possible experience.

Seen against this backdrop, a certain indelible distance from linguistic structuralism seems to dominate Derrida's reading of Saussure within the "theoretical matrix" of his own work, that is, in the first part of *Of Grammatology*, in *Margins of Philosophy* (notably "Différance"), and in the opening interviews of *Positions*. What is more, Saussure's text is presented only as a "privileged example" of the question of the sign.[35] No more and no less. The "particularity of the example," Derrida writes, does not "interfere" with

33. Derrida, *Writing and Difference,* 279 / 409.
34. Derrida, *Of Grammatology,* 14 / 25.
35. Ibid., 29 /44; see also *Positions,* 18 / 28, which refers to it as "only one example."

the "generality" of his "argument."[36] There is no question of any affinity in content or method, let alone any natural alliance between deconstruction and semiotics or semiology. Derrida's exposition of the differentiality of the sign fits with Saussure's linguistics because the latter is the backbone of the "dominant discourse,"[37] one that in truth prolongs metaphysics, although it pretended to have superseded it once and for all. Derrida's assertion that he draws only extreme consequences from the legitimate—metaphysical-critical—aspiration of structuralism does not contradict this conclusion.[38] Saussure's linguistics and the structuralist sciences that espouse his methodological principles have "reminded" us again of the arbitrary character of the sign,[39] but deconstruction does not halt at this insight. It aims at nothing less than "the transformation of general semiology into grammatology."[40] But then, the term *grammatology* also falls short as a description of the effort and process of deconstruction. Its concern cannot be encapsulated in any term ending in *-ology* and does not even coincide with the *gramma*, the written sign, which easily leads to misunderstanding, for example, as a limited interpretation of the *written* text.

Deconstructions rather obey, and bear witness to, a paradoxical *pas d'écriture* (step of [not] writing)—a "step" and also a crossing out—which can probably best be expressed as a "practice" (*pratique*),[41] at least insofar as this term is removed from the traditional Aristotelian opposition between *theoria* and *praxis* and delimited by the Hegelian, dialectical (i.e., "negative") "labor of the concept."

The argumentative pattern in which Derrida approaches Saussure—playing the text's letter against the spirit, exposing the "tension between gesture [*geste*] and statement [*propos*]"[42]—does not differ in effort and result from that of his accompanying deconstructive readings of Hegel, Freud, Heidegger, Levinas, or, for that matter, anyone else. The ambiguity uncovered in Saussure is also found in Hegel's semiology, in Freud's psychoanalysis, in Heidegger's fundamental ontology, and in Levinas's thinking of the Other. Yet one would hesitate to call the deconstructive readings neo-

36. Derrida, *Of Grammatology,* 29 / 44.
37. Ibid., 99 / 147; and *Positions,* 8 / 109.
38. See Derrida, *Positions,* 27–28 and 36 / 39 and 49.
39. Ibid., 9 / 17.
40. Derrida, *Margins of Philosophy,* 15 / 16.
41. Derrida, *Positions,* 90 / 124.
42. Derrida, *Of Grammatology,* 30 / 45. He also writes: "my quarry is not primarily Ferdinand de Saussure's intention or motivation, but rather the entire uncritical tradition which he inherits here" (45–46 / 67, trans. modified).

Hegelian, neo-Freudian, neo-Heideggerian, or neo-Levinasian. Why, then, insist on the adjective *neostructuralist*?

Frank's assertion that Derrida both "radicalizes" and "refutes" Saussure's theory of signs and system of concepts — from a Nietzschean perspective or, rather, perspectivism — can only with great difficulty be seen as an adequate response to this question.[43] Neither the repertory of radicalization nor that of radical refutation and decisive breaks — of a *coupure épistémologique,* to use Louis Althusser's terminology — characterizes the gesture or practice called "deconstruction." All characterizations of deconstruction in terms of some iconoclasm are of little help in clarifying its "point" — if there is one (or only one). They put Derrida's enterprise in a certain — suspect, adventuristic, and at bottom irresponsible — light.

Derrida and the Jewish Tradition: Habermas's Critique

If Derrida's notions of Scripture and trace should be understood neither as neostructuralist nor as Heideggerian, Nietzschean, Freudian, or even Levinasian, against what backdrop should they be understood? Is it useful and justifiable to carry them back to a Jewish or negative theological and mystical heritage? Or does this hermeneutical search for the most appropriate context neutralize the purpose of Derrida's work from the start? In other words, does such a maneuver block the ability to observe his particular use of, for example, religious idiom?

In a cultural climate in which deconstructive thinking is often accused of "indifferentism," its surprising links with the religious-theological tradition can offer an important counterweight. Yet here, too, care should be taken. We meet here a theme in Derrida's work which until recently has appeared marginal in several respects. Except for one crucial lecture devoted to his preoccupation with negative theology, the theme announced itself mainly in marginal notes to texts by Kafka, Benjamin, Celan, Jabès, Blanchot, and Levinas, in which ethical-religious motifs were traced and varied. The undeniable involvement of these and other writings with the Jewish heritage can only with difficulty, if at all, be traced back to religious sources (Tenach, Talmud, let alone Kabbalah) and is only obliquely observable in a continuous process of translation and reinscription. At the same time, it seems to involve no more than occasionally inserted *quotations*. But a quotation is never "merely" a quotation: it summons, shakes awake, spurs on,[44] even (or

43. Frank, *What Is Neostructuralism?* 22 / 32, trans. modified.

44. A quotation, says Derrida, referring to the Latin connotation of the term, is an "incitement," a "solicitation" (see *Parages,* 10).

especially) where it is cited out of context. This does not deny that for de-construction all supposedly "original" motifs are always already subject to a ceaseless process of shifting meanings. The "origin" that Derrida's text more or less expressly "reflects" and to which it reacts was in a certain sense never there in its integrity or as such.

It does not help to remind Derrida of the — unconscious or unplanned — Jewish signature of his work.[45] Although he signs the final essay in *Writing and Difference* "Reb Dérissa,"[46] Derrida reacts with unconcealed irony to the suggestion that he may be under the latent influence of the Jewish tradition of commentary and midrash. In an interview, he admitted that he regrets being unfamiliar with the Talmud. The supposed echo of Jewish themes in his writings cannot be explained by a thorough familiarity with Hebrew or by religious education. The most that could be suspected, he suggests, is that the Talmud, in some puzzling way, knows *him* — or perhaps *itself in him*.[47]

To further analyze the scope of Derrida's use of religious tradition, we may perhaps best turn to the interpretation, equally intriguing and moot, that Habermas has given to his work. In a polemical treatment of several alleged characteristics of Derrida's thinking, in his *Philosophical Discourse of Modernity* Habermas defends two apparently contradictory theses. First, he asserts that, all things considered, Derrida has been unable to free himself from the "subject-philosophical" premises in Heidegger's "temporalized philosophy of origins." Second, he stresses that the *tenor* of these thinkers' writings nevertheless exhibits a remarkable difference. According to Habermas, Derrida's work, like Heidegger's, is obsessed by the — as it were exponentially — increasing volatility of meaning in the modern epoch. Both would agree that this "withdrawal" of what was once unified in the true, the good, and the beautiful is no longer comprehensible in classical, metaphysical, or substantialist referential — or even differential — terms. What we are left with is no longer the feeble silhouette of an original divine revelation and the reason reflected in and on it: in principle and, if we might say so, in fact the trace of the other "is" at once much less and, paradoxically, far more than what traditional ontology and onto-theology, including the late Heideggerian thinking of Being, aim at.

Yet Derrida is supposed to (want to) give a more radically different turn

45. See François Laruelle, *Les Philosophies de la différence: Introduction critique* (Paris: Presses Universitaires de France, 1986), 125.

46. Derrida, *Writing and Difference*, 300 / 436.

47. See Delacampagne, intro., *Philosophies*, vol. 1 of *Entretiens avec "Le Monde,"* 80–81.

to this diagnosis than does Heidegger. This other orientation finds its foundation, according to Habermas, in the numerous themes or quotations taken from Jewish messianism and from mysticism. But various characteristics of rabbinical and kabbalistic *hermeneutics* are also said to have left their traces in Derrida's reading. His rehabilitation of Scripture is said to have drawn on religious sources without being theological or confessional in the customary sense. What is more, Derrida owes to this thematic and methodological heritage his resistance to the political-moral insensitivity of the "paganism purified by Hölderlin" which, Habermas believes, ultimately characterizes Heidegger's work.[48] Unlike Heidegger, Derrida is said to have been on his guard against discovering a diffuse ontological "fluid" in what withdraws in or from modern experience.[49] A *labyrinthine* mirror of texts is thus found to have replaced the epochal history of Being. These texts—and the commentary attached to them—refer to a primeval scripture that as such can never be discovered by any text, concept, or poetic word.

Yet Habermas thinks that, in the final analysis, this different tone leaves a fundamental agreement between the two authors intact. And that is ultimately his point. Both Heidegger and Derrida are thought to abandon the task of critical reflection, preferring to invoke an *indefinable* authority. To be sure, Derrida is said no longer to fixate on a thought of "Being that being lacks" but, rather, turns to deciphering a "no longer holy Scripture, wandering in exile, alienated from its own meaning and witnessing to the absence of the holy testament."[50] Undermining the hierarchy of living word and dead writing, of spirit and letter, as well as the contrast between pneumatology and grammatology, reveals in essence a radically transformed rabbinical hermeneutic.[51] It is no longer a reflection on the unique incarnation of a divine act of will, creation, or recreation, for from now on only an interminable process of revelation that takes place in the indefatigable interpretation of texts is deemed to bring about the redemption of humanity and the world. Even the most secular translation of the holy continues this revelation.[52] Derrida drastically modifies the traditional way of commenting on texts because he includes nonreligiously inspired texts in his considerations and gives no text absolute authority. But this procedure nonetheless guarantees him a place in the tradition of what is called the "heretical hermeneutic,"

48. Habermas, *Philosophical Discourse of Modernity,* 165 / 197.
49. Ibid., 164 / 196.
50. Ibid., 182 / 214.
51. See Handelman, "Jacques Derrida and the Heretic Hermeneutic," 111, 113.
52. Ibid., 104, 120.

which Gershom Scholem's historical studies on Jewish mysticism, especially on Kabbalah, have recalled from oblivion. Derrida's work is thus likewise said to return to orthodox tradition via a heretical way of thinking.[53] His Kafkaesque vision of the documentary value of modern experience is said to renew a Jewish tradition that, in contrast to Christian teaching, cannot be incorporated in the one book that seals the canon but seeks traces where totality or ultimate meaning no longer shines through. For the same reason his work is said to show no archaic or fatalistic traits. On the contrary, the bent toward subversive, anarchistic revolt dominates.[54]

According to Habermas, this difference in intention is linked to a difference in frame of reference. Not Hölderlin and the romantic Dionysus reception but monotheistic tradition ultimately determines the horizon of deconstruction. Whereas Heidegger turns against the ontotheological heritage, even against all of modernity, Derrida "luckily"[55]—that is to say, less radically than Heidegger—falls back on the critical point where monotheism and mysticism turned into Enlightenment. Seen in this way, the main point of Derrida's work is not the destruction of all traditional dogmatic content but the renewal of a "discourse with God," albeit this time under postmetaphysical and, perhaps, postmodern conditions.[56] What makes Derrida's undertaking more responsible but—philosophically speaking—no less problematic, in Habermas's opinion, is a melody whose timbre, while not excluding certain perilous dissonances, does, in the end, temper and eventually silence them.

How are we to understand this minimal but crucial and indelible distinction between Heidegger and Derrida? Must we examine biographical and historical elements, *data,* in the emphatic sense Derrida gives to these notions, in the wake of Celan?[57] Or does a more meticulous reading provide us with additional information on the undeniable differences between Heidegger and Derrida? Does not Habermas's polemical essay unwittingly provide the best proof of Derrida's thesis that the decisive difference between philosophical discussions ultimately lies in their different *tonality*? What is decisive seems thus not an argumentative, reconstructible difference in the way thought is structured but a distinction in tact and judgment. The "thinking of Being," or *Andenken,* unlike deconstructive thinking, responds to an

53. Ibid., 119.
54. Habermas, *Philosophical Discourse of Modernity,* 182 / 214.
55. Ibid., 183 / 216.
56. Ibid., 184 / 218.
57. See de Vries, "Le Schibboleth de l'éthique: Derrida avec Celan."

indefinable sending of Being, or *Seinsgeschick.* Nevertheless, Habermas is suspicious, even in the subversive Derridian thinking about difference, of a merely formal pattern of thought, which is poor in concrete political content and must be filled in, as the historical-social situation requires, in an arbitrary and therefore ultimately *decisionist* manner.[58] Needless to say, this is not Derrida's own view.

Derrida notes that his thinking is marked by

> what is more at home in literature than in philosophy, . . . an *idiomatic* writing . . . , a character that you cannot appropriate [because] it characterizes you without belonging to you. You never notice it, only others do, except in fits of madness that fuse life and death. It is ruinous to dream of creating a language or song that would be yours—not as the attributes of an "ego," but rather the accented timbre, I mean, the musical timbre of your own most illegible history . . . ; not a *style* but an intersection of singularities, life styles, voices, writing, the baggage you carry with you and cannot leave behind.[59]

In this sense there is in Derrida a certain participation in a manner in which a community—the Jewish—deciphers its forcefully uprooted existence in writings and, in this way, lives out its restlessness.[60]

It is not in any religious *content* or *substance,* therefore, that we should seek the common element that links deconstruction to the Jewish hermeneutical tradition. Habermas again shows this in a comment as involuntary as it is apt. He refers to Scholem's analysis of a kabbalistic tradition according to which only the *aleph* (as first letter of all commandments) really belongs to revelation in the strict sense of the word. This revelation would then become a mystical concept that "while itself being infinitely filled with meaning is yet without *specific* meaning. It is something that—to ground religious authority—would have to be translated into human languages. . . . Every utterance that grounds authority [in this way], however valid and eminent it may be, is still a human interpretation of something that transcends this explanation."[61]

58. Habermas, *Philosophical Discourse of Modernity,* 140–41 / 168–69. See for this and the following analysis also Habermas, "Comment répondre à la question éthique?" in Cohen and Zagury-Orly, *Judéités,* 181–96.

59. Derrida, "An Interview with Derrida," in *Derrida and Différance,* ed. David Wood and Robert Bernasconi (Evanston, Ill.: Northwestern University Press, 1988), 73.

60. Didier Cahen, "Entretien avec Jacques Derrida," *Digraphe* 42 (1987): 14–27, see esp. 20–21.

61. Gershom Scholem, *Zur Kabbala und ihrer Symbolik* (Frankfurt a.M.; Suhrkamp, 1973), 47; cited after Habermas, *Philosophical Discourse of Modernity,* 183 / 216. See also Habermas's

In this kabbalistic, mystical concept of a revelation that precedes every articulation of content, being its prerequisite without being its possession, Habermas sees an analogy with the *a* of Derrida's *différance*. Is this analogy plausible? Does it bring us any farther? My closing considerations center on the inevitability and limited value of such a parallelism.

Derrida and Negative Theology

There is a good deal of confusion about the ethical-theological purport of Derrida's work. Some authors accuse Derrida of a suspect revival of mysticism and negative theology; others do just the reverse, accusing him of being insensitive to religious and ethical questions. At the basis of both interpretations lies a widespread incomprehension that, in concluding I would like to try to clarify. My hypothesis is, once again, treacherously simple, almost trivial. In tune with my insistence on the diminishing and abiding intelligibility of the discourse on (and of) God, in part 1 of this study, and in line with my overall argumentation in *Philosophy and the Turn to Religion,* I wish to show that Derrida neither writes off the core questions of negative theology nor naively repeats them. His position is best summarized in an early quotation from *Of Grammatology:* "The 'theological' is a determined moment in the total movement of the trace."[62] What does "the theological" mean here? In what sense is it a "well-determined," *inevitable,* and even perhaps *constitutive* "moment within the total movement of the trace"?

Peter Kemp has noted that there is a deep abyss between deconstructive thinking and eighteenth- and nineteenth-century humanism and materialism. The latter, in his view, only reverse the hierarchy of metaphysical oppositions, specifically theology and anthropology, without putting them into question, as deconstruction does. But, Kemp continues, the deconstruction of these oppositions also overshoots its goal because it loses sight of the *ethical impetus* of modern religious criticism. By contrast, Kemp concludes, Derrida's work, all things considered, leads to the defense of an *amoral atheism.*[63]

Various motifs in Derrida's post-1972 work after the "turn," or *Kehre,* apparent in the publication of *Dissemination* (Kemp refers to *Glas* and *Spurs*)

essays on Scholem in *Philosophisch-politische Profile* and in *Vom sinnlichen Eindruck zum symbolischer Ausdruck,* trans. in *Religion and Rationality,* ed. Mendieta. For an interpretation of the so-called mystical postulate, see my *Religion and Violence,* chap. 3.

62. Derrida, *Of Grammatology,* 47 / 69.

63. Peter Kemp, "L'Éthique au lendemain des victoires des athéismes: Réflexions sur la philosophie de Jacques Derrida," *Revue de Théologie et de Philosophie* 111 (1979): 112–13.

contradict this interpretation on virtually each and every page. They are all linked to the notion of a *gift*, which is said to precede Being, its truth, and, it should be added, also the very figure of the *es gibt*, and is thus no longer thinkable or utterable in ontological terms, in terms of the thought of Being, of *Seyn* or *Sein,* crossed out or otherwise. But even this new timbre in Derrida's work does not, in Kemp's opinion, undo the ethical lacuna.

At the other end of the spectrum of interpretation, Mikel Dufrenne pleads for a philosophy that is no longer overdetermined ethically or theologically.[64] Dufrenne contends that Derrida's work should not be understood as amoral or atheistic but, rather, as a resumption of the very tradition of theology—especially negative theology—from which it seeks to set itself apart. In negative theology we encounter the secret core of truth in *every* theology, which says that above all we must avoid giving names to God that do not do Him justice. Since every determination (*determinatio*) of the divine essence is at once a *negation* (a denial of other determinations, i.e., other negations), only a permanent "negating" of all feasible negations could, in this view, guarantee respect for the name called. Only by traversing the *via negationis* might the idolatry of anthropomorphism be put aside indefinitely. Or so it seems.

Dufrenne believes we find a similar idea in the thought of *différance.* Like negative theology, deconstructive reading affirms the effectiveness of a "non-presence." It endorses the absence of the origin, the "originary" supplementarity, of all meaning. Such a notion is incompatible with affirmation of a highest Being, an absolute telos, or, for that matter, a creation out of nothing. If anything, we are dealing here with a "*nihil* that creates, a determining indeterminateness."[65] In Derrida's analyses of the differential play that precedes Being and beings (and both permits and precludes them from coming into existence), Dufrenne thus sees "a sort of pre-God," meaning "not the negation of God, but the negative of a God."[66]

I see at least two different argumentative strategies in Derrida's work which require an analysis of the relationship between deconstruction and negative theology more nuanced than those Kemp and Dufrenne give. I will analyze them more closely using two texts: the early, programmatic "Différance," published in 1968, and "Comment ne pas parler: Dénégations" ("How to Avoid Speaking: Denials"), delivered as a lecture in Jerusalem in

---

64. In the introduction to the second edition of Mikel Dufrenne, *Le Poétique* (Paris: Presses Universitaires de France, 1973), 4–57.

65. Ibid., 20.

66. Ibid.

1986. Both texts contain a subtle resumption of the destruction of onto-theology in the line of (and in discussion with) Heidegger. They also antici-pate and reiterate certain central arguments and motifs we have analyzed in Adorno and Levinas.

In the first essay Derrida emphasizes that *différance* is preeminently the "inexpressible." But being the interplay of temporal and spatial differences, the "production" of difference, it "is" in no way "the primary prescription or the prophetic annunciation of an imminent and as yet unheard-of nomi-nation."[67] It includes no *"ineffable Being which no name could approach: God, for example."*[68] *Différance* cannot be classified in any category of being and must be not only distinguished from a religious doctrine and impera-tive but also withdrawn from the jurisdiction of any ontology or any other semantic system: "yet aspects which are thereby delineated are not theologi-cal, not even in the order of the most negative of negative theologies, which are always concerned with disengaging a superessentiality beyond the finite categories of essence and existence, that is, of presence, and always hasten-ing to recall that God is refused the predicate of existence, only in order to acknowledge his superior, inconceivable, and ineffable mode of being."[69]

In "How to Avoid Speaking" Derrida's goal is to demonstrate this propo-sition using citations from Pseudo-Dionysius the Areopagite and Meister Eckhart. His later "Sauf le nom" (originally published as the postscript to a book entitled *Derrida and Negative Theology*) further explicates this analysis in a few ostensibly poly-voiced comments on work by Angelus Silesius.[70]

Certainly, some mystics withhold every ontic characteristic, sometimes even the predicate "existence," from the superior, divine, existing. Speaking about God's "perfection" amounts to referring to a reality on the far side of being, or even to more than all that. Derrida tellingly sets out this condi-tion. He writes that, in the tradition of negative theology, the *hyper-* of the *hyperousios* attributed to God indicates both "no more being" and "being more than being," that is, a "being more" beyond all negative and positive predication. The prefix *hyper-* refers to more than a removal in a spatial or temporal sense. It evokes more than a reality that precedes space and time, surpasses, encompasses, or permeates them. The *hyper-* also evokes a notion

67. Derrida, *Margins of Philosophy,* 27 / 29.
68. Ibid., 26 / 26, my emph.
69. Ibid., 6 / 6.
70. See Jacques Derrida, *Sauf le nom (Post Scriptum)* (Paris: Galilée, 1993); trans. under the title *On the Name,* ed. Thomas Dutoit (Stanford: Stanford University Press, 1993). See also the section devoted to Angelus Silesius in my *Philosophy and the Turn to Religion.*

of hierarchy. Derrida summarizes this pluriform meaning in the expression "plus (être) que l'être: *no more being and being more than Being.*"[71] Negative theology's hyperbolic imagery thus doubly outdoes the thought of presence. Its project stands or falls by this strategy, for, however much it succeeds with a given form of presence, the *deus absconditus,* the *theos agnostos* — about which it is said that He surpasses all intellectual, discursive knowledge — *is not Himself nothing.* The antithesis between theism and atheism and the question of God's *existence* has lost most of its relevance here. But this does not deny that the *plus d'être* of His essence includes not only a negation but above all a superlative modifying Being. Even more, the most negative theology "is" a *super-ontology.*[72]

The negative theological thinking that Derrida studies here is marked by an "unusual alliance," a *double bind* of "*two powers*" and "*two voices*": first, a "hyper-critique" that leaves nothing intact and, all things considered, undermines every philosophy, theology, science, ethics, aesthetics, and *common sense;* and, second, an affirmation that withdraws from every discussion and every critique and which in the tradition sometimes can adopt an extremely dogmatic tone.

By way of clarification Derrida cites Meister Eckhart's sermon "Quasi stella matutina." There Eckhart states that the assertion that God proceeds above Being (*über wesen*) in no way implies that He should be denied all Being. The expression stresses that Being is "heightened [*gehöhet*]." Thus, the negative predications that Eckhart adopts from Augustine — "God is wise without wisdom, good without goodness, powerful without power" — are, all things considered, *denials without negativity.* Formulations in the pattern of "God is *X* without *X*" not only liberate God from all generalities; they are *hyper-affirmative.* They shed light on a "grammatical anthropomorphism" inherent in the vernacular that can only express an inner worldly — finite — negativity. Above all, they evoke a transcendent instance that, as Derrida suggests in "How to Avoid Speaking," is at once "nothing else" and "totally other" than whatever it is that is transcended. It is this process of *reiteration without strict or simple repetition* (without mimesis, analogy, or specula-

71. Jacques Derrida, "Comment ne pas parler: Dénégations," *Psyché: Inventions de l'autre* (Paris: Galilée, 1987); "How to Avoid Speaking: Denials," trans. Ken Frieden in *Languages of the Unsayable: The Play of Negativity in Literature and Literary Theory,* ed. Sanford Buddick and Wolfgang Iser (New York: Columbia University Press, 1989), 20 / *Psyché,* 552.

72. Levinas, too, makes no secret of this hyperbolic double bind. In his deployment of the *via eminentiae,* the *plus* has, above all, the meaning of being *better than Being.* But this is not to deny that the way of the superlative consists less in devaluing ontology than in attempting to outdo it: the "other-than-being" is more ontological than ontology.

tive reflection) which permits negative theology to augment finite language "ad infinitum." Thus, according to Eckhart, all being can be considered as a "gateway" to the divine space (temple) or, put differently, as a threshold that must be crossed on the way to God's atopia, but one that also separates us from it. And, according to Pseudo-Dionysius, all anthropomorphic words and images can assume the function of "holy allegories" when they are used and taught in the right way.[73]

The *hyperbole* of the "*X* 'is' above/beyond all that is," Derrida writes. It witnesses to this transcendence and announces it. It does this in more than one sense: it not only displays it as one possibility; it also evokes it. It "provokes" and "produces" the structure that it describes: it is a postscript and an introduction simultaneously.

Derrida's deconstruction of theology therefore takes aim at both its classical and its nonclassical concepts. Theology here means the hard core of the thought of *presence* (i.e., of the *parousia,* the logocentrism at the heart of every ontotheology), as well as the ontologizing or hypostasizing of an *absence* or lack. Every theology continues to be borne by the biblical assurance "someday we will see in the light." On closer analysis this eschato-apocalyptic prospect of removing the veil in a divine manifestation makes of every theology a "positive" argument, even when it is presented as a *via analogiae,* a *via negativa,* a *via eminentiae,* or takes the silent form of some inexpressible mysticism. Where one has no conceivable prospect of *visio dei,* one has forsaken the realm of theology.

Measured against such a conception of theology, deconstruction can only be called "atheological." It calls into question every postulation of a center that gives meaning—although it does not disclaim the desire for one —and so it examines classical and modern variants of the *via analogiae, via negationis,* and *via eminentiae* against the light of a more original "event": a differential "interplay" without beginning or end which literally thwarts the *existence* of every spiritual secret through its writing—through the *grammē* or, more precisely still, the seriature of marks.

This procedure has an unmistakably *negative* aspect. Deconstruction brings about a certain corrosion of the authority of tradition and more: it disrupts the theological investment as well as the emotional charge of *every* sign. When it is correct that "the sign" and "the divinity," as Derrida writes, have "the same time and place of birth," when the "epoch of the sign" is

---

73. The same logic of denial also explains why, according to Derrida, mystical theology is in a certain sense coextensive with the symbolical.

"essentially theological," there follows an unavoidable conclusion. Deconstruction of the linguistic sign shakes the foundations of nothing less than the central theological premise of Western Logos — "even when it professes to be atheistic."[74] Outside the generalized matrix, conception, and practice of "writing" there is no question of a theological notion, and "within it" or, better, *as* "writing" it becomes extremely problematic.

Is that the only, or even the most decisive, conclusion to be drawn from Derrida's argument? Or does this merely blur the line that demarcates the religious and isolates the profane? Does Derrida's analysis stipulate without further ado that theological difference can only be found in extreme asceticism, or does he also betray a singular inscription of theology? Is it perhaps even possible to interpret his reading as a revival of the discursive strategy and the central motif of negative theology?

In "How to Avoid Speaking," this question is not answered with a mere denial. This extremely difficult and subtle text promises a more detailed development of what Derrida admits is thus far a brief, elliptical answer to the problem of how the paths of deconstruction and negative theology cross only to diverge again. "How to Avoid Speaking" gives nuance to the delimiting line drawn in "Différance": insofar as negative theology postulates, or at least accepts as possible, a hyperessentiality and an intuitive assessment prepared by the *via negativa,* it rests on premises that can indeed be deconstructed.

Yet is it so easy to speak of *the* tradition of negative theology, as if we knew what that means? Supposing, furthermore, that this negative theology can be identified as a more or less homogeneous corpus of texts with its own theme and rhetoric, how is one to speak of it? Is not the *via negativa* the only suitable approach to negative theology? In other words: "Is there ever anything other than a 'negative theology' of 'negative theology'?"[75] If this is the case, the intention to enumerate the agreements and differences between deconstruction and negative theology once and for all is a *promise* that can never be fulfilled. Derrida's intention, expressed in Jerusalem, to take up this subject without further delay indicates an almost impossible task. Perhaps, he suggests, this circumstance is the sought-for "answer" to the fact that one "can never decide whether deferring, as such, brings about precisely that which it defers and alters."[76]

---

74. Derrida, *Of Grammatology,* 323 n. 3 / 13 n. 3.
75. Derrida, "How to Avoid Speaking," 13 / *Psyché,* 546.
76. Ibid.

The text that "keeps" an old promise has itself the character of a promise. There is more to be said on the complex structure of this *Versprechen,* as analyzed by Heidegger and Paul de Man. It will suffice here to note that Derrida's lecture not only, or not primarily, tries to provide a theoretical essay *about* negative theology. Rather, it consciously adopts—as always—the contours of what it describes. But this "performative interpretation" is, in all seriousness, also a parody. Derrida does not speak of a fable—a "mystic fable," as Michel de Certeau would have said—without reason.

"How to Avoid Speaking" is, in Derrida's own words, the most "autobiographical" text he has written thus far (except, perhaps, for "Circonfession"). Yet here Derrida does not directly pursue what we would expect. There is no explanation of a Jewish (and Arabic) heritage. These resound only indirectly. That this lecture lets the way of arguing—the *via negativa*—speak for itself has repercussions for the contours that this text's "author" adopts: this "autobiographical" lecture follows or performs the figure it describes. The question "How to Avoid Speaking?" touches more than theology; it touches the author, the self in question. How is one to avoid speaking of oneself? How can one, in an explanation of oneself, be it arbitrary or not, also find or discover the other, perhaps even oneself *as* another (*Soi-même comme un autre,* as Ricoeur's title suggests)?

Thus, in the present text Derrida speaks about himself *in obliquo,* in the nearly casual reference to a negative-theological or quasi-mystical figure of thought that is neither Greek nor Christian but, rather, Jewish or Arabic. As he says himself, he constructs his reading of three different paradigms, which he borrows successively from Plato, Christian mystics (particularly Pseudo-Dionysius and Eckhart), and finally Heidegger, into an open space—an emptiness or *desert,* the most consistent apophasis—in which the vague echo of these alternative traditions concerning the absolute otherness of the other can resonate.

What permits Derrida to link his indirectly discussed "heritage" to the tradition of negative theology? He gives the following reason. Wherever (philosophical, ethical-political, or literary) assertions or presentations appear in a negative guise—and deconstructive reading is compelled to use a similar mode of speaking and writing—a first step on the path of negative theology has already been taken and the argumentative procedure becomes in a certain sense "theological." Adorno's dialectical critique of dialectics and Levinas's phenomenological critique of phenomenology—the two main examples of negative metaphysics whose contours we have been exploring—would be no exception to this general rule and hence, like Derrida's own oeuvre, resemble the apophatic path *up to a certain point*. Indeed, in Derrida's words, "Every time I say: *X* is neither this nor that, neither the contrary of this nor of that, neither the simple neutralization of this nor of that with which it has *nothing in common,* being absolutely heterogeneous to or incommensurable with them, I would start to speak of God, under this name or another."[77] The name (not the concept) of God, seen this way, represents all that cannot be named directly: "'God' would name *that without which* one would not know to account for any negativity."[78] Even in denying or suspending God's existence, a certain *respect* can be heard, a "respect for a divine cause which does not even need to 'be.'"[79] According to Derrida, it is here that those who want to brand deconstruction a symptom of (post)modern nihilism (or the last convulsion of faith) find their primary argument. Nothing forbids such a reading. One can always with reason assert that the hyperessence of which negative theology speaks has "the same" referent as the term *différance,* that it expresses an "event" that does not use the terminology of Being in giving to understand all that is or all that matters, that is to say, signifies or counts in the end. It is true that such a theological annexation of deconstruction, as well as of all its negative dialectical or phenomenological analogues, backfires and is successful only when the theological reading empties itself and the name *God* is—unsuccessfully— stripped of every proposition and reference and thereby becomes a virtual abstraction or emptied *X* and is hence divided in and against itself. But this does not deny that this annexation always remains possible, even inevitable, as the inescapable horizon of idolatry and blasphemy, of fidelity by way of betrayal. Such betrayal always remains the "opportunity" (and the risk) of an "incomparable" structure of "limitless ability to translate," which has nothing to do with a "universal language," with an "ecumenism" or a "consensus," but with a future-oriented speaking and writing that in a much more radical sense can be shared and on whose basis the Greek, Christian, and European *apophasis* permits, or requires, numerous other instantiations. The real question then becomes how not to speak, now that theological speaking has become unavoidable and silence impossible.

For these reasons alone, Derrida believes that the well-known last sentence in Wittgenstein's *Tractatus Logico-Philosophicus*—"Whereof one cannot speak, thereof one must be silent"—cannot be the last word, giving way to a mere wordless showing of what matters and, if not signals, then at least

77. Ibid., 6 / 538.
78. Ibid., 7 / 538.
79. Ibid.

appeals to us most. Like Adorno, whose explicit reversals of Wittgenstein's proposition we have studied in part 3, Derrida turns this logical inference from "transcendental lingualism" upside down: whereof one cannot speak, thereof one must speak. There can, therefore, be no question of God's death *in language*. In Derrida this "obligation" to speak of (or from) "God" is not a moral obligation. It is, as in Wittgenstein, a *must*, not (or not primarily) an ought. Every moral obligation that one adopts with regard to this having to "name what cannot be named" is always borne by a special structure that makes this injunction a troublesome necessity. For Derrida, this necessity differs from the necessity to keep silent which Wittgenstein analyses in his *Tractatus:* it has less to do with the propositional structure of language than with the unavoidable risk of a *defilement* (or *contamination*) of every mark.

This structure fares poorly with the express affirmation that, not accidentally, is the converse of Wittgenstein's well-known dictum "There are, indeed, things that cannot be put into words [*Es gibt allerdings Unaussprechliches*]. They make themselves manifest. They are what is mystical" (*Tractatus* 6.522). According to Derrida, this assurance should make clear that Wittgenstein's radical imperative to be silent, like the circumscribing movement of negative theology, nonetheless prepares for the manifestation of an emphatic (or apophatic) reality. By contrast, this is a promise that the thought of the trace can never keep. Can a totally other "discourse," an articulation that precedes and exceeds every enunciation of speaking and writing—indeed, every gesture of doing and judging—possibly respect the alterity of this trace?

Sometimes it seems as if Derrida sees this respect guaranteed in pre-predicative *prayer*. But a closer analysis shows that when negative theologies begin or end with prayer, this does not turn them into a *purely* performative genre. They are never protected from the accusation of secretly postulating or implying metaphysical or ontological truths. Although prayer may be ante-predicative in the way it addresses the other, Derrida leaves no doubt that it owes its very existence to a possible contamination. Praise is never purely performative (or never simply "neither true nor untrue," to use Aristotle's words). It always contains a constitutive component, however implicit. If prayer did not contain the risk of being lost (in predication, citation, mechanical repetition, Scripture, code, or parody) and thus of missing its mark, no theology, positive or negative, would be necessary or, for that matter, possible. In a certain sense it is only prayer's failure that calls theology into existence. Yet this "negativity" also presupposes an indelible "affirmation"—an "acquiescence" or "originary affirmation," as Derrida says in *De l'esprit* (*Of Spirit*) — lest the trace's lapse become inexperienceable "as such," that is to say, in its barely dialectizable structure and even less phenomenologizable givenness or event.

This signaling of and appeal to the other (or others, or Other), which, says Derrida, "always already preceded the speech to which it has never been present a first time, announces itself in advance as a *recall* [a reminder and warning, *rappel*]. . . . Prior to every proposition and even before all discourse in general — whether a promise, prayer, praise, celebration. The most negative discourse, even beyond all nihilisms and negative dialectics, preserves a trace of the other."[80] As Derrida remarks elsewhere, in the original affirmation given with (and through) the introduction of language (or any other system of signification), we are linked via a faith that cannot be eliminated by any erasure in any discourse and by any narrative. A text in which such erasure would be complete would be, precisely, a "figure of evil [*figure du mal*],"[81] the very specter of the worst, of violence become absolute.

80. Ibid., 28 / 560.
81. Jacques Derrida, *De l'esprit: Heidegger et la question* (Paris: Galilée, 1987), 153n / *Of Spirit: Heidegger and the Question,* trans. Geoffrey Bennington and Rachel Bowlby (Chicago: University of Chicago Press, 1989), 134n.

Bibliography

Aboulafia, Mitchell, Myra Bookman, and Catherine Kemp, eds. *Habermas and Pragmatism*. London: Routledge, 2002.

Adorno Archiv (Theodor W.), Gabriel Ewenz, Christoph Gödde, Henri Lonitiz, and Michael Schwartz, eds. *Adorno: Eine Bildmonographie* (Frankfurt a.M.: Suhrkamp, 2003).

Adorno, Theodor W. *Gesammelte Schriften*. Ed. Rolf Tiedemann. Frankfurt a.M.: Suhrkamp, 1970–86. (Abbreviated *GS* hereafter.)

———. "Die Aktualität der Philosophie." *GS* 1, *Philosophische Frühschriften* (1973): 325–44. Trans. Benjamin Snow under the title "The Actuality of Philosophy." *Telos*, no. 31 (Spring 1977): 120–33.

———. *Ästhetische Theorie. GS* 7 (1972). Trans. Robert Hullot-Kentor under the title *Aesthetic Theory* (Minneapolis: University of Minnesota Press, 1997).

———. "Aufzeichnung zu Kafka." *GS* 10.1 (1977): 254–87. Trans. Samuel and Shierry Weber under the title "Notes on Kafka," in Adorno, *Prisms* (Cambridge: MIT Press, 1981), 243–71.

———. *Drei Studien zu Hegel. GS* 5 (1970): 247–375.

———. "Fortschritt." In *Stichworte, GS* 10.2 (1977): 617–38. Trans. Henry W. Pickford under the title "Progress," in Adorno, *Critical Models: Interventions and Catchwords* (New York: Columbia University Press, 1998), 143–60.

———. "Die Idee der Naturgeschichte." *GS* 1, *Philosophische Frühschriften* (1973): 345–65.

———. *Kants "Kritik der reinen Vernunft."* Ed. Rolf Tiedemann. Frankfurt a.M.: Suhrkamp, 1995. Trans. Rodney Livingstone under the title *Kant's "Critique of Pure Reason"* (Stanford: Stanford University Press, 2001).

———. *Kierkegaard: Konstruktion des Ästhetischen. GS* 2 (1997). Trans. Robert Hullot-Kentor under the title *Kierkegaard: Construction of the Aesthetic* (Minneapolis: University of Minnesota Press, 1989).

———. "Kulturkritik und Gesellschaft." *GS* 10.1 (1977): 11–21. Trans. Samuel and Shierry Weber under the title "Cultural Criticism and Society," in Adorno, *Prisms* (Cambridge: MIT Press, 1981), 17–34.

———. *Metaphysik: Begriff und Probleme*. Ed. Rolf Tiedemann. Frankfurt a.M.:

Suhrkamp, 1998. Trans. Edmund Jephcott under the title *Metaphysics: Concept and Problems* (Stanford: Stanford University Press, 2000).

———. *Minima Moralia: Reflexionen aus dem beschädigten Leben. GS* 4 (1980). Trans. E. F. N. Jephcott under the title *Minima Moralia: Reflections from Damaged Life* (London: Verso, 1974).

———. *Negative Dialektik. GS* 6 (1973): 9–412. Trans. E. B. Ashton under the title *Negative Dialectics* (London: Routledge and Kegan Paul, 1973).

———. *Noten zur Literatur. GS* 11 (1974). Trans. Shierry Weber Nicholsen under the title *Notes to Literature,* 2 vols. (New York: Columbia University Press, 1991–92).

———. *Ontologie und Dialektik.* Ed. Rolf Tiedemann. Frankfurt a.M.: Suhrkamp, 2002.

———. *Philosophie der neuen Musik. GS* 12 (1975).

———. *Philosophische Terminologie.* Ed. R. zur Lippe. 2 vols. Frankfurt a.M.: Suhrkamp, 1974.

———. *Prisms.* Trans. Samuel and Shierry Weber. Cambridge: MIT Press, 1981.

———. *Probleme der Moralphilosophie.* Ed. Thomas Schröder. Frankfurt a.M.: Suhrkamp, 1996. Trans. Rodney Livingstone under the title *Problems of Moral Philosophy.* (Stanford: Stanford University Press, 2000).

———. *Quasi una fantasia. GS* 16 (1997): 249–540. Trans. Rodney Livingstone under the title *Quasi una Fantasia: Essays on Modern Music* (London: Verso, 1998).

———. *Über Walter Benjamin.* Ed. Rolf Tiedemann. Frankfurt a.M.: Suhrkamp, 1970.

———. "Vernunft und Offenbarung." *GS* 10.2 (1977): 608–16. Trans. Henry W. Pickford under the title "Reason and Revelation," in Adorno, *Critical Models: Interventions and Catchwords* (New York: Columbia University Press, 1998), 135–42.

———. "Wissenschaftliche Erfahrungen in Amerika," *GS* 10.2:702–38.

———. *Zur Lehre von der Geschichte und von der Freiheit.* Ed. Rolf Tiedemann. Frankfurt a.M.: Suhrkamp, 2001.

———. *Zur Metakritik der Erkenntnistheorie: Studien über Husserl und die phänomenologische Antinomien. GS* 5 (1970): 9–245. Trans. Willis Domingo under the title *Against Epistemology: A Metacritique, Studies in Husserl and the Phenomenological Antinomies.* Cambridge: MIT Press, 1983.

Adorno, Theodor W., and Walter Benjamin. *The Complete Correspondence, 1928–1940.* Ed. Henri Lonitz. Trans. Nicholas Walker. Cambridge: Harvard University Press, 1999.

Adorno, Theodor W., and Thomas Mann. *Briefwechsel 1943–1955*. Ed. Christoph Gödde and Thomas Sprecher. Frankfurt a.M.: Suhrkamp, 2003.

Adriaanse, Hendrik Johan. "After Theism." In *Posttheism: Reframing the Judeo-Christian Tradition*, ed. Henri Krop, Arie L. Molendijk, and Hent de Vries, 33–61. Leuven: Peeters, 2000.

———. "Het rationale karakter van de wijsbegeerte van Levinas," *Nederlands Theologisch Tijdschrift* 29 (1975): 255–63.

———. *Het specifiek theologische aan een rijksuniversiteit: De verborgenheid der godgeleerdheid*. The Hague: Universitaire Pers Leiden, 1979.

———. *Zu den Sachen selbst: Versuch einer Konfrontation der Theologie Karl Barths mit der phänomenologischen Philosophie Edmund Husserls*. The Hague: Mouton, 1974.

Adriaanse, Hendrik Johan, and Henry A. Krop, eds. *Theologie en Rationaliteit: Godsdienstwijsgerige bijdragen*. Kampen, Neth.: Kok, 1988.

Adriaanse, Hendrik Johan, Henry A. Krop, and Lammert Leertouwer. *Het verschijnsel theologie: Over de wetenschappelijke status van de theologie*. Amsterdam: Boom, 1987.

Agamben, Giorgio. *Le Temps qui reste: Un Commentaire de l'Épître aux Romains*. Paris: Payot & Rivages, 2000.

Altwicker, Norbert, and Alfred Schmidt, eds. *Max Horkheimer heute: Werk und Wirkung*. Frankfurt a.M.: Fischer Tauschenbuch, 1986.

Anscombe, G. E. M. *Intention*. 2d ed. 1957. Rpt. Cambridge: Harvard University Press, 2000.

Anselm. *Proslogion gevolgd door de discussie met Gaunilo*. Trans. and intro. Carlos Steel. Bussum: Het Wereldvenster, 1981.

Apel, Karl-Otto. *Diskurs und Verantwortung: Das Problem des Übergangs zur postkonventionellen Moral*. Frankfurt a.M.: Suhrkamp, 1988.

———. *Transformation der Philosophie*. 2 vols. Frankfurt a.M.: Suhrkamp, 19–76.

———."Types of Rationality Today: The Continuum of Reason between Science and Ethics." In *Rationality Today*, ed. Thomas Geraets (Ottawa: University of Ottawa Press, 1979), 307–40.

Apel, Karl-Otto, et al., eds. *Hermeneutik und Ideologiekritik*. Frankfurt a.M.: Suhrkamp, 1971.

Arlt, G. "Erkenntnistheorie und Gesellschaftskritik: Zur Möglichkeit einer transzendentalpsychologischen Analyse des Begriffs des Unbewußten in den Frühschriften Theodor W. Adornos." *Philosophisches Jahrbuch* 90 (1983): 129–45.

Arnold, Heinz Ludwig, ed. *Theodor W. Adorno: Text und Kritik*. Munich: Edition Text + Kritik, 1977.

Aron, Raymond. Preface to Max Weber, *Le Savant et le politique,* trans. Julien Freund, rev. E. Fleischmann and Éric de Dampierre, 9–69. Paris: Plon, 1959.

Baars, Jan. *De mythe van de totale beheersing: Adorno, Horkheimer en de dialectiek van de vooruitgang.* Amsterdam: SUA, 1987.

Badiou, Alain. *L'Éthique: Essai sur la conscience du Mal.* Paris: Éditions Hatier, 1998. Trans. Peter Hallward under the title *Ethics: An Essay on the Understanding of Evil.* London: Verso, 2002.

Barth, Karl. *Die Lehre vom Wort Gottes: Prolegomena zur kirchlichen Dogmatik.* Vol. 1 of *Die kirchliche Dogmatik.* Zurich: EVZ, 1964.

Bataille, Georges. "De l'existentialisme au primat de l'économie." *Critique* 21 (1948): 127–41. Trans. Jill Robbins under the title "From Existentialism to the Primacy of Economy," *Altered Reading: Levinas and Literature* (Chicago: University of Chicago Press, 1999), 155–80.

———. *L'Expérience intérieure.* Paris: Gallimard, 1954. Trans. Leslie Boldt under the title *Inner Experience* (Albany: State University of New York Press, 1988).

Baudelaire, Charles. *Les Fleurs du mal.* Vol. 1 of *Oeuvres complètes.* Ed. Claude Pichois. Paris: Gallimard 1975.

Baumeister, Thomas, and Jens Kulenkampff. "Geschichtsphilosophie und philosophische Ästhetik." *Neue Hefte für Philosophie* 5 (1973): 74–104.

Baynes, Kenneth, James Bohman, and Thomas McCarthy, eds. *After Philosophy: End or Transformation?* Cambridge: MIT Press, 1987.

Behrens, Roger. *Adorno-ABC.* Leipzig: Reklam, 2003.

Beier, Christel. *Zum Verhältnis von Gesellschaftstheorie und Erkenntnistheorie: Untersuchungen zum Totalitätsbegriff in der kritischen Theorie Adornos.* Frankfurt a.M.: Surkamp, 1977.

Beierwaltes, Werner. *Identität und Differenz.* Frankfurt a.M.: Klostermann, 1980.

Benhabib, Seyla. *Critique, Norm, and Utopia: A Study of the Foundations of Critical Theory.* New York: Columbia University Press, 1986.

Benhabib, Seyla, Wolfgang Bonss, and John McCole, eds. *On Max Horkheimer: New Perspectives.* Cambridge: MIT Press, 1993.

Benhabib, Seyla, and Fred Dallmayr, eds. *The Communicative Ethics Controversy.* Cambridge: MIT Press, 1990.

Benjamin, Walter. *Gesammelte Schriften.* Ed. Rolf Tiedemann and H. Schweppenhäuser, with the assistance of Theodor W. Adorno and Gershom Scholem. Frankfurt a.M.: Suhrkamp, 1972–82.

———. *1913–1926.* Ed. Marcus Bullock and Michael Jennings. Vol. 1 of *Selected Writings,* ed. Michael Jennings. Cambridge: Harvard University Press, 1996.

———. *1927–1934.* Ed. Michael W. Jennings, Howard Eiland, and Gary Smith.

Trans. Rodney Livingstone et al. Vol. 2 of *Selected Writings,* ed. Michael Jennings Cambridge: Harvard University Press, 1999.

———. *Briefe.* Ed. Gershom Scholem and Theodor W. Adorno. 2 vols. Frankfurt a.M.: Suhrkamp, 1978.

———. *Illuminations.* Trans. Harry Zohn. Ed. and intro. Hannah Arendt. New York: Schocken, 1969.

———. *Das Passagenwerk.* Ed. Rolf Tiedemann. 2 vols. Frankfurt a.M.: Suhrkamp, 1983. Trans. Howard Eiland and Kevin McLaughlin as *The Arcades Project* (Cambridge: Harvard University Press, 1999).

———. "Über den Begriff der Geschichte." In *Gesammelte Schriften,* vol. 1.2. Frankfurt a.M.: Suhrkamp, 1980. Trans. Harry Zohn under the title "Theses on the Philosophy of History," in *Illuminations,* ed. Hannah Arendt (New York: Harcourt, Brace and World, 1955), 253–64.

Bergo, Bettina, and Diane Perpich, eds. *Levinas's Contribution to Contemporary Philosophy.* Special issue of *Graduate Faculty Philosophy Journal* 20, no. 2, and 21, no. 1 (1998).

Berkhof, Hendrikus. *Christelijk Geloof: Een inleiding tot de geloofsleer.* Nijkerk: Callenbach, 1975.

Bernasconi, Robert. "Deconstruction and the Possibility of Ethics." In *Deconstruction and Philosophy,* ed. John Sallis, 122–39. Chicago: University of Chicago Press, 1987.

———. "Levinas and Derrida: The Question of the Closure of Metaphysics." In *Face to Face with Levinas,* ed. R. Cohen, 181–202. Albany: State University of New York Press, 1986.

Bernasconi, Robert, and Simon Critchley, eds. *Re-Reading Levinas.* Bloomington: Indiana University Press, 1991.

Berns, Egide, Samuel IJsseling, and Paul Moyaert. *Denken in Parijs: Taal en Lacan, Foucault, Althusser, Derrida.* Alphen: Samson, 1981.

Bernstein, J. M. *Adorno: Disenchantment and Ethics.* Cambridge: Cambridge University Press, 2001.

———. *The Fate of Art: Aesthetic Alienation from Kant to Derrida and Adorno.* University Park: Pennsylvania State University Press, 1992.

———. "Mimetic Rationality and Material Inference: Adorno and Brandom." *Revue Internationale de Philosophie,* no. 1 (2004): 7–23.

———. "Re-enchanting Nature." In *Reading McDowell: On Mind and World,* ed. Nicholas H. Smith, 217–45. London: Routledge, 2002.

Bernstein, Richard J., ed. *Habermas and Modernity.* Cambridge: MIT Press, 1985.

Bertens, H. "Die Postmoderne und ihr Verhältnis zum Modernismus: Ein Überblick." In *Die unvollendete Vernunft: Moderne versus Postmoderne,* ed. D. Kamper and W. van Reijen, 46–98. Frankfurt a.M.: Suhrkamp, 1987.

Besançon, Alain. *L'Image interdite: Une Histoire intellectuelle de l'iconoclasme.* Paris: Fayard, 1994; Gallimard, 2000. Trans. Jane Marie Todd under the title *The Forbidden Image: An Intellectual History of Iconoclasm* (Chicago: University of Chicago Press, 2001).

Blanchot, Maurice. *L'Écriture du désastre.* Paris: Gallimard, 1980. Trans. Ann Smock under the title *The Writing of the Disaster* (Lincoln: University of Nebraska Press, 1986).

———. *L'Entretien infini.* Paris: Gallimard, 1969. Trans. Susan Hanson under the title *The Infinite Conversation* (Minneapolis: University of Minnesota Press, 1992).

———. "La Littérature et le droit à la mort." In *La Part du feu,* 294–331. Paris: Gallimard, 1949. Trans. Lydia Davis as "Literature and the Right to Death," in Blanchot, *The Work of Fire,* trans. Charlotte Mandell (Stanford: Stanford University Press, 1995), 300–344.

———. *Michel Foucault tel que je l'imagine.* Montpellier: Fata Morgana, 1986.

———. "Notre Compagne clandestine." In *Textes pour Emmanuel Levinas,* ed. François Laruelle, 79–87. Paris: Jean-Michel Place, 1980.

Boer, Theodore de. "An Ethical Transcendental Philosophy." In *Face to Face with Levinas,* ed. R. Cohen, 83–115. Albany: State University of New York Press, 1986.

———. Introduction to Emmanuel Levinas, *De plaatsvervanging,* 9–33. Trans. and intro. Theodore de Boer. Baarn: Ambo, 1977.

———. *Tussen filosofie en profetie: De wijsbegeerte van Emmanuel Levinas.* Baarn: Ambo, 1976.

Böhme, Gernot, and Hartmut Böhme. *Das Andere der Vernunft: Zur Entwicklung von Rationalitätsstrukturen am Beispiel Kants.* Frankfurt a.M.: Suhrkamp, 1983.

Böhme, Gernot, and Gregor Schiemann, eds. *Phänomenologie der Natur.* Frankfurt a.M.: Suhrkamp, 1997.

Bohrer, Karl Heinz, ed. *Mythos und Moderne: Begriff und Bild einer Rekonstruktion.* Frankfurt a.M.: Suhrkamp, 1983.

Bonss, W. "Empirie und Dechiffrierung von Wirklichkeit: Zur Methodologie bei Adorno." In *Adorno-Konferenz 1983,* ed. L. von Friedeburg and J. Habermas, 201–25. Frankfurt a.M.: Suhrkamp, 1983.

Brändle, Werner. *Rettung des Hoffnungslosen: Die theologischen Implikationen der Philosophie Theodor W. Adornos.* Göttingen: Vandenhoeck and Ruprecht, 1984.

Brandom, Robert B. *Making It Explicit.* Cambridge: Harvard University Press, 1994.

———, ed. *Rorty and His Critics.* Malden, Oxford: Blackwell, 2000.

———. *Tales of the Mighty Dead: Historical Essays in the Metaphysics of Intentionality.* Cambridge: Harvard University Press, 2002.

Broda, Martine, ed. *Contre-jour: Études sur Paul Celan.* Colloque de Cérisy. Paris: Cerf, 1986.

Bubner, Rüdiger. "Adornos negative Dialektik." In *Adorno-Konferenz 1983,* ed. Ludwig von Friedeburg and Jürgen Habermas, 35–40. Frankfurt a.M.: Suhrkamp, 1983.

———. "Kann Theorie ästhetisch werden? Zum Hauptmotiv der Philosophie Adornos." In *Materialien zur ästhetischen Theorie Th. W. Adornos: Konstruktion der Moderne,* ed. B. Lindner and W. M. Lüdke, 108–37. Frankfurt a.M.: Suhrkamp, 1980.

Buck-Morss, Susan. *The Origin of Negative Dialectics: Th. W. Adorno, Walter Benjamin, and the Frankfurt Institute.* New York: Free Press, 1979.

Budick, Sanford, and Wolfgang Iser, eds. *Languages of the Unsayable: The Play of Negativity in Literature and Literary Theory.* New York: Columbia University Press, 1987.

Bulthaup, Peter, ed. *Materialien zu Benjamins Thesen "Über den Begriff der Geschichte."* Frankfurt a.M.: Suhrkamp, 1975.

Burggraeve, Roger. "E. Levinas' metafysisch-ethische herdefiniëring van het subject vanuit joodse en filosofische achtergronden." Vol. 1 of "De hermeneutische context van het levinasiaanse denken." Ph.D. diss., Löwen, 1980.

———. *Emmanuel Levinas: Une Bibliographie primaire et secondaire (1929–1985).* Leuven: Peeters, 1986.

———. "Het 'il y a' in het heteronomie-denken van Levinas." *Bijdragen* 44 (1983): 266–300.

———. *Mens en medemens, verantwoordelijkheid en God: De metafysische ethiek van Emmanuel Levinas.* Leuven: Acco, 1986.

Burms, Arnold, and Herman de Dijn. *De rationaliteit en haar grenzen.* Assen: Van Gorcum, 1986.

Butler, Judith. *Giving an Account of Oneself: A Critique of Ethical Violence.* Assen: Van Gorcum, 2003.

———. *Subjects of Desire: Hegelian Reflections in Twentieth-Century France.* New York: Columbia University Press, 1987.

———. "Values of Difficulty." In *Just Being Difficult? Academic Writing in the Public Arena,* ed. Jonathan Culler and Kevin Lamb, 199–215. Stanford: Stanford University Press, 2003.

———. "Vorbemerkung." In J. Butler, *Kritik der ethischen Gewalt: Adorno-Vorle-sungen 2002*, 7–11. Trans. Reiner Ansén. Frankfurt a.M.: Suhrkamp, 2003.

Cabantous, Alain. *Histoire du blasphème en Occident: Fin XVIe–milieu XIXe siècle.* Paris: Albin Michel, 1998. Trans. Eric Rauth as *Blasphemy: Impious Speech in the West from the Seventeenth to the Nineteenth Century* (New York: Columbia University Press, 2002).

Cahen, Didier. "Entretien avec Jacques Derrida." *Digraphe* 42 (1987): 14–27.

Carnap, Rudolf. "Überwindung der Metaphysik durch logische Analyse der Sprache." *Erkenntnis* 2 (1932): 219–41.

Casanova, Jose. *Public Religions in the Modern World.* Chicago: University of Chicago Press, 1994.

Cavell, Stanley. "Benjamin and Wittgenstein: Signals and Affinities." In *Philosophie in synthetischer Absicht / Synthesis in Mind,* ed. Marcelo Stamm, 565–82. Stuttgart: Klett-Cotta, 1998.

———. *Disowning Knowledge in Six Plays of Shakespeare.* Cambridge: Cambridge University Press, 1987.

———. "What Is the Scandal of Skepticism?" In *ASCA Report 2000,* 22–47, and *Skepticism in Context,* ed. James Conant and Andrea Kern, forthcoming.

Caygill, Howard. *Art of Judgement.* Oxford: Blackwell, 1989.

———. *Levinas and the Political.* London: Routledge, 2002.

———. "Levinas's Political Judgment: The Esprit Articles 1934–1983." *Radical Philosophy* 104 (November–December 2000).

Celan, Paul. *Collected Prose.* Trans. Rosmarie Waldrop. Riverdale-on-Hudson, N.Y.: Sheep Meadow Press, 1986.

———. *Gedichten.* Trans. F. Roumen. Selected with commentary by Paul Sars. Baarn: Ambo, 1988.

———. *Gesammelte Werke.* Ed. B. Allemann and S. Reichert. 5 vols. Frankfurt a.M.: Suhrkamp, 1983.

———. *Poems of Paul Celan.* Trans. Michael Hamburger. New York: Persea Books, 1988.

———. *Selected Poems and Prose of Paul Celan.* Trans. John Felstiner. New York: W. W. Norton, 2001.

Chalier, Cathérine. *Figures du féminin: Lecture d'Emmanuel Levinas.* Paris: La Nuit Surveillée, 1982.

Chalier, Cathérine, and Miguel Abensour, eds. *Emmanuel Levinas. Cahier de l'Herne.* Paris: L'Herne, 1991.

Chanter, Tina. *Ethics of Eros: Irigaray's Rewriting of the Philosophers.* New York: Routledge, 1995.

Ciaramelli, Fabio. "L'Appel infini à l'interprétation: Remarques sur Levinas et l'art." *Revue Philosophique de Louvain* 1 (1994): 32–52.

———. "De l'évasion à l'exode: Subjectivité et existence chez le jeune Levinas." *Revue Philosophique de Louvain* 80 (1982): 553–78.

Clausen, Detlev. *Theodor W. Adorno: Ein Letztes Genie.* Frankfurt a.M.: S. Fischer, 2003.

Cohen, Joseph, and Raphael Zagury-Orly, eds. *Judéités:* Questions pour Jacques Derrida. Paris: Galilée, 2003.

Cohen, R. A., ed. *Face to Face with Levinas.* Albany: State University of New York Press, 1986.

Cohen-Solal, Annie. *Sartre: 1905–1980.* Paris: Gallimard, 1985.

Collin, Françoise. *Maurice Blanchot et la question de l'écriture.* Paris: Gallimard, 1986.

———. "La Peur: Emmanuel Levinas et Maurice Blanchot." In *Emmanuel Levinas,* ed. Catherine Chalier and Miguel Abensour, 334–56. *Cahier de l'Herne.* Paris: L'Herne, 1991.

Cornelius, Hans. *Transcendentale Systematik: Untersuchungen zur Begründung der Erkenntnistheorie.* Munich: E. Reinhardt, 1916.

Critchley, Simon. *Ethics, Politics, Subjectivity: Essays on Derrida, Levinas, and Contemporary French Thought.* London: Verso, 1999.

Critchley, Simon, and Robert Bernasconi, eds. *The Cambridge Companion to Levinas.* Cambridge: Cambridge University Press, 2002.

Dahms, Hans-Joachim. *Positivismusstreit: Die Auseinandersetzungen der Frankfurter Schule mit dem logischen Positivismus, dem amerikanischen Pragmatismus und den kritischen Rationalismus.* Frankfurt a.M.: Suhrkamp, 1994.

Dallmayr, Fred R. "Phenomenology and Critical Theory: Adorno." *Cultural Hermeneutics* 3 (1976): 367–405.

Davidson, Donald. *Subjective, Intersubjective, Objective.* Oxford: Oxford University Press, 2001.

Debray, Régis. *Dieu: Un Itinéraire.* Paris: Odile Jacob, 2001.

———. *L'Enseignement du fait religieux dans l'école laïque.* Intro. Jack Lang. Paris: Odile Jacob, 2002.

De Cauter, Lieven. *De dwerg in de schaakautomaat: Benjamins verborgen leer.* Nijmegen: Uitgeverij SUN, 1999.

Delacampagne, Christian, ed. *Philosophies.* Vol. 1 of *Entretiens avec 'Le Monde,'* intro. Christian Delacampagne. Paris: Éditions de la Découverte / Le Monde, 1984.

Demirović, Alex. *Der nonkonformistische Intellektuelle: Die Entwicklung der Kritischen Theorie zur Frankfurter Schule.* Frankfurt a.M.: Suhrkamp, 1999.

Derrida, Jacques. *Acts of Religion*. Ed. Gil Anidjar. New York: Routledge, 2002.

———. *Adieu à Emmanuel Levinas*. Paris: Galilée, 1997. Trans. Pascale-Anne Brault and Michael Naas under the title *Adieu to Emmanuel Levinas* (Stanford: Stanford University Press, 1999).

———. "L'Animal que donc je suis (à suivre)." In *L'Animal autobiographique: Autour de Jacques Derrida*, ed. Marie-Louise Mallet, 251–301. Paris: Galilée, 1999.

———. *La Carte postale: De Socrate à Freud et au-delà*. Paris: Flammarion, 1980. Trans. Alan Bass under the title *The Postcard: From Socrates to Freud and Beyond* (Chicago: University of Chicago Press, 1987).

———. *De l'esprit: Heidegger et la question*. Paris: Galilée, 1987. Trans. Geoffrey Bennington and Rachel Bowlby under the title *Of Spirit* (Chicago: University of Chicago Press, 1989).

———. *De la grammatologie*. Paris: Minuit, 1967. Trans. Gayatri Chakravorty Spivak under the title *Of Grammatology* (Baltimore: Johns Hopkins University Press, 1976; corrected ed., 1998).

———. *La Dissémination*. Paris: Seuil, 1972. Trans. and intro. Barbara Johnson under the title *Dissemination* (Chicago: University of Chicago Press, 1981).

———. "Donner la mort." In *L'Éthique du don: Jacques Derrida et la pensée du don*, ed. Jean-Michel Rabaté and Michael Wenzel, 11–108. Paris: Métailié, Transition, 1992. Trans. David Wills under the title *The Gift of Death* (Chicago: University of Chicago Press, 1995).

———. "D'un ton apocalyptique adopté naguère en philosophie." In *Les Fins de l'homme: À partir du travail de Jacques Derrida*, ed. Philippe Lacoue-Labarthe and Jean-Luc Nancy, 445–79. Paris: Galilée, 1981. Trans. John P. Leavey Jr., under the title "On a Newly Arisen Apocalyptic Tone in Philosophy," in *Raising the Tone of Philosophy: Late Essays by Immanuel Kant, Transformative Critique by Jacques Derrida*, ed. Peter Fenves (Baltimore: Johns Hopkins University Press, 1993), 117–71.

———. *L'Écriture et la différence*. Paris: Seuil, 1967. Trans. Alan Bass under the title *Writing and Difference*. Chicago: University of Chicago Press, 1978.

———. *Éperons: Les Styles de Nietzsche*. Bilingual edition. Chicago: University of Chicago Press, 1979.

———. *Fichus: Discours de Francfort*. Paris: Galilée, 2002.

———. "How to Avoid Speaking: Denials." Trans. Ken Frieden. In *Languages of the Unsayable: The Play of Negativity in Literature and Literary Theory*, ed. Sanford Budick and Wolfgang Iser, 3–70. New York: Columbia University Press, 1989.

———. "An Interview with Derrida." In *Derrida and Différance*, ed. David Wood and Robert Bernasconi, 71–82. Evanston, Ill.: Northwestern University Press, 1988.

———. "Languages and Institutions of Philosophy." Trans. Joseph Adamson. *Recherches Sémiotiques / Semiotic Inquiry* 4, no. 2 (1984): 152.

———. "La Langue de l'étranger: Discours de réception du prix Adorno à Francfort." *Le Monde diplomatique,* no. 574 (January 2002): 24–27. Republished as *Fichus: Discours de Francfort* (Paris: Galilée, 2002).

———. *Limited Inc.* Ed. and trans. Elisabeth Weber. Paris: Galilée, 1990. Trans. Samuel Weber under the title *Limited Inc* (Evanston, Ill.: Northwestern University Press, 1988).

———. "Limited Inc a b c. . . ." *Glyph,* no. 2 (1977): 162–254.

———. *Marges de la philosophie.* Paris: Minuit, 1972. Trans. Alan Bass under the title *Margins of Philosophy* (Chicago: University of Chicago Press, 1982).

———. *Negotiations: Interventions and Interviews, 1971–2001.* Ed., trans., and intro. Elizabeth Rottenberg. Stanford: Stanford University Press, 2002.

———. *Papier machine.* Paris: Galilée, 2001.

———. *Positions.* Paris: Minuit, 1972. Trans. Alan Bass under the title *Positions* (Chicago: University of Chicago Press, 1981).

———. *Psyché: Inventions de l'autre.* Paris: Galilée, 1987.

———. "Théologie de la traduction." In *Qu'est-ce que Dieu? Philosophie-Théologie, hommage à l'abbé Daniel Coppieters de Gibson,* 163–84. Brussels, 1985. Trans. Joseph Adamson under the title "Theology of Translation," in "Languages and Institutions of Philosophy," *Recherches Sémiotiques / Semiotic Inquiry* 4, no. 2 (1984): 139–52.

Descombes, Vincent. *Le Même et l'autre: Quarante-cinq ans de philosophie française (1933- 1978).* Paris: Minuit, 1979. Trans. L. Scott-Fox and J. M. Harding under the title *Modern French Philosophy* (Cambridge: Cambridge University Press, 1982).

Deuser, Hermann. *Dialektische Theologie: Studien zu Adornos Metaphysik und zum Spätwerk Kierkegaards.* Munich: Kaiser, 1980.

———. "Kierkegaard in der Kritischen Theorie." In *Die Rezeption S. Kierkegaards in der deutschen und dänischen Philosophie und Theologie,* ed. Heinrich Anz, Poul Lübke, and Friedrich Schmöe, 101–13. Copenhagen: Fink, 1983.

Dews, Peter, *Logics of Disintegration: Post-Structuralist Thought and the Claims of Critical Theory.* London: Verso, 1987.

Dijksterhuis, E. J. *De mechanisering van het wereldbeeld.* Amsterdam: H. M. Meulenhoff, 1950. Trans. C. Dikshoorn under the title *The Mechanization of the World Picture* (Oxford: Oxford University Press, 1961).

Dilthey, Wilhelm. "Die Entstehung der Hermeneutik." *Gesammelte Schriften,* 5:317–31. Stuttgart: B. G. Teubner, 1964.

Dorschel, A., et al., eds. *Transzendentalpragmatik.* Frankfurt a.M.: Suhrkamp, 1993.

Dosse, François. *Histoire du structuralisme,* vol. 1: *Le Champ du signe, 1945–1966;* vol. 2: *Le Chant du cygne, 1967 à nos jours.* Paris: Éditions la Découverte, 1992. Trans. Deborah Glassman as *History of Structuralism,* vol. 1: *The Rising Sign, 1945–1966;* vol. 2: *The Sign Sets, 1967–Present* (Minneapolis: University of Minnesota Press, 1997).

Dubiel, Helmut. "Die Aktualität der Gesellschaftstheorie Adornos." In *Adorno-Konferenz 1983,* ed. L. von Friedeburg and J. Habermas, 293–313. Frankfurt a.M.: Suhrkamp, 1983.

———. *Wissenschaftsorganisation und politische Erfahrung: Studien zur frühen Kritischen Theorie.* Frankfurt a.M.: Suhrkamp, 1978. Trans. Benjamin Gregg under the title *Theory and Politics: Studies in the Development of Critical Theory* (Cambridge: MIT Press, 1985).

Dufrenne, Mikel. *Le Poétique.* 2d ed. Paris: Presses Universitaires de France, 1973.

Duintjer, Otto D. *De vraag naar het transcendentale: Vooral in verband met Heidegger en Kant.* Leiden: Universitaire Pers, 1966.

Duvenage, Pieter. *Habermas and Aesthetics: The Limits of Communicative Rationality.* Cambridge: Polity Press, 2003.

Ebeling, H. "Adornos Heidegger und die Zeit der Schuldlosen." *Philosophische Rundschau* 29 (1982): 188–96.

Escoubas, Éliane. "Adorno, Benjamin et Kierkegaard." In Theodor W. Adorno, *Kierkegaard: Construction de l'esthétique,* trans. Éliane Escoubas, i–xvii. Paris: Payot & Rivages, 1995.

Faessler, Marc. "L'Intrigue de Tout-Autre: Dieu dans la pensée d'Emmanuel Levinas." In "Emmanuel Levinas," ed. J. Rolland, 119–45. *Les Cahiers de "La Nuit Surveilée,"* vol. 3. Lagrasse: Verdier, 1984.

Fenves, Peter. *"Chatter": Language and History in Kierkegaard.* Stanford: Stanford University Press, 1993.

Fisher, Philip. *Wonder, The Rainbow, and the Aesthetics of Rare Experiences.* Cambridge: Harvard University Press, 1998.

Flew, Anthony. "Theology and Falsification." In *The Philosophy of Religion,* ed. Basil Mitchell, 13–15. Oxford: Oxford University Press, 1979.

Fontanier, Pierre. *Les Figures du discours.* Intro. Gérard Genette. Paris: Flammarion, 1977.

Frank, Manfred. "Kleiner (Tübinger) Programmentwurf." *Frankfurter Rundschau,* 5 March 1988.

————. *Das Sagbare und das Unsagbare: Studien zur neuesten französischen Hermeneutik und Texttheorie*. Frankfurt a.M.: Suhrkamp, 1980. Trans. Helen Atkins under the title *The Subject and the Text: Essays on Literary Theory and Philosophy*, ed. and intro. Andrew Bowie (Cambridge: Cambridge University Press, 1997).

————. *Die Unhintergehbarkeit von Individualität: Reflexionen über Subjekt, Person und Individuum aus Anlass ihrer "postmodernen" Toterklärung*. Frankfurt a.M.: Suhrkamp, 1986.

————. *Was ist Neostrukturalismus?* Frankfurt a.M.: Suhrkamp, 1984. Trans. Sabine Wilke and Richard Gray under the title *What Is Neostructuralism?* (Minneapolis: University of Minnesota Press, 1989).

Frankenberry, Nancy K. *Radical Interpretation in Religion*. Cambridge: Cambridge University Press, 2002.

Freud, Sigmund. "Das Unbehagen in der Kultur." In *Kulturtheoretische Schriften*, 197- 270. Frankfurt a.M.: S. Fischer Verlag, 1974. Trans. under the title *Civilization and Its Discontents* (New York: W. W. Norton, 1961).

Friedeburg, Ludwig von, and Jürgen Habermas, eds., *Adorno-Konferenz 1983*. Frankfurt a.M.: Suhrkamp, 1983.

Friedrich, Hugo. *Die Struktur der modernen Lyrik: Vor der Mitte des 19. bis zur Mitte des 20. Jahrhunderts*. Reibeck bes Hamburg: Rowohlt, 1973. Trans. Joachim Neugroschel under the title *The Structure of Modern Poetry: From the Mid-Nineteenth to the Mid-Twentieth Century*. Evanston, Ill.: Northwestern University Press, 1974.

Früchtl, Josef. *Mimesis: Konstellation eines Zentralbegriffs bei Adorno*. Würzberg: Königshausen & Neumann, 1986.

Früchtl, Josef, and Maria Calloni, eds. *Gegen den Zeitgeist: Erinnern an Adorno*. Frankfurt a.M.: Suhrkamp, 1991.

Gadamer, Hans-Georg. *Hermeneutik II. Wahrheit und Methode, Ergänzungen. Gesammelte Werke*, vol. 2. Tübingen: J. C. B. Mohr, 1986.

————. *Wahrheit und Methode: Gründzuge einer philosophischen Hermeneutik*. Tübingen: J. C. B. Mohr, 1965. Trans. under the title *Truth and Method* rev. Joel Weinsheimer and Donald G. Marshall (New York: Crossroad, 1982).

Gadamer, Hans-Georg, and Jürgen Habermas. *Das Erbe Hegels: Zwei Reden*. Frankfurt a.M.: Suhrkamp, 1979.

Gasché, Rodolphe. *The Idea of Form: Rethinking Kant's Aesthetics*. Stanford: Stanford University Press, 2003.

————. *Of Minimal Things: Studies on the Notion of Relation*. Stanford: Stanford University Press, 1999.

———. *The Tain of the Mirror: Derrida and the Philosophy of Reflection.* Cambridge: Harvard University Press, 1986.

———. *The Wild Card of Reading: On Paul de Man.* Cambridge: Harvard University Press, 1998.

Geyer, Carl-Friedrich. *Aporien des Metaphysik- und Geschichtsbegriff der Kritischen Theorie.* Darmstadt: Wissenschaftsliche Buchgesellschaft, 1980.

Gibson, Nigel, and Andrew Rubin, eds. *Adorno: A Critical Reader.* Oxford: Blackwell, 2002.

Goud, Johan F. "Joodse filosofie en haar relatie tot de westerse wijsgerige traditie: Het voorbeeld van Emmanuel Levinas." *Wijsgerig Perspectief* 25 (1984–85): 98–102.

———. *Levinas en Barth: Een godsdienstwijsgerige en ethische vergelijking.* Amsterdam: Rodopi, 1984.

———. "Über Definition und Infinition: Probleme bei der Interpretation des Denkens des Emmanuel Levinas." *Nederlands Theologisch Tijdschrift* 36 (1982): 126–44.

———. "'Wat men van zichzelf eist, eist men van een heilige': Een gesprek met Emmanuel Levinas." *Ter Herkenning* (1983): 19–25, 49–57, 82–88, 147–54.

Granger, Gilles Gaston. *L'Irrationnel.* Paris: Odile Jacob, 1998.

Gray, John. *Enlightenment's Wake: Politics and Culture at the Close of the Modern Age.* London: Routledge, 1995.

Greef, J. de. "Skepticism and Reason." In *Face to Face with Levinas,* ed. Richard A. Cohen, 159–70. Albany: State University of New York Press, 1986.

Greisch, Jean. *Le Buisson ardent et les lumières de la raison: L'Invention de la philosophie de la religion.* Vol. 1 of *Héritages et héritiers du XIXe siècle.* Paris: Cerf, 2002.

———. "Du vouloir-dire au pouvoir-dire." In *Emmanuel Levinas,* ed. J. Rolland, 211–21. *Les Cahiers de "La Nuit Surveilée,"* vol. 3. Paris, 1984.

———. *Herméneutique et grammatologie.* Paris: Editions du Centre National de la Recherche Scientifique, 1977.

———. "*Zeitgehöft* und *Anwesen:* La Dia-chronie du poème." In *Contre-jour: Études sur Paul Celan,* ed. Martine Broda, 167–83. Colloque de Cérisy. Paris: Cerf, 1986.

Grenz, Friedemann. *Adornos Philosophie in Grundbegriffen: Auflösung einiger Deutungsprobleme.* Frankfurt a.M.: Suhrkamp, 1974.

———. "'Die Idee der Naturgeschichte': Zu einem frühen, unbekannten Text Adornos." In *Natur und Geschichte,* ed. Kurt Hübner and Albert Menne, 344–50. Hamburg: Meiner, 1973.

Gripp, Helga. *Theodor W. Adorno: Erkenntnisdimensionen negativer Dialektik.* Paderborn: F. Schöningh, 1986.

Günther, Klaus, *Der Sinn für Angemessenheit: Anwendungsdiskurse in Moral und Recht.* Frankfurt a.M.: Suhrkamp, 1988. Trans. under the title *The Sense of Appropriateness: Application Discourses in Morality and Law.* Albany: State University of New York Press, 1993.

Guzzoni, Ute. "Hegels 'Unwahrheit': Zu Adornos Hegelkritik." In *Hegel-Jahrbuch 1975,* 242–46. Cologne, 1976.

Habermas, Jürgen. "Das Absolute in der Geschichte: Von der Zwiespältigkeit in Schellings Denken." Ph.D. diss., Bonn, 1954.

―――. Afterword. In Max Horkheimer and Theodor W. Adorno, *Dialektik der Aufklärung: Philosophische Fragmente,* 277–94. Frankfurt a.M.: S. Fischer, 1986.

―――. *Autonomy and Solidarity: Interviews.* Ed. and intro. Peter Dews. London: Verso, 1986.

―――. "Bermerkungen zur Entwicklungsgeschichte des Horkheimerschen Werkes." In *Max Horkheimer heute: Werk und Wirkung,* ed. Norbert Altwicker and Alfred Schmidt, 163- 79. Frankfurt a.M.: Fischer, 1986.

―――. "Comment répondre à la question éthique?" In *Judéités: Questions pour Jacques Derrida,* ed. Joseph Cohen and Raphaël Zagury-Orly, 181–96. Paris: Galilée, 2003.

―――. "Drei Thesen zur Wirkungsgeschichte der Frankfurter Schule." In *Die Frankfurter Schule und die Folgen,* ed. Axel Honneth and Albrecht Wellmer, 8-12. Berlin: Walter de Gruyter, 1986.

―――. *Die Einbeziehung des Anderen: Studien zur politischen Theorie.* Frankfurt a.M.: Suhrkamp, 1996. Trans. Ciaran Cronin under the title *The Inclusion of the Other: Studies in Political Theory,* ed. Ciaran Cronin and Pablo de Greiff (Cambridge: MIT Press, 1998).

―――. "Entgegnung." In *Kommunikatives Handeln: Beiträge zu Jürgen Habermas' 'Theorie des kommunikativen Handelns,'* ed. Axel Honneth and H. Joas, 327–405. Frankfurt a.M.: Suhrkamp, 1986. Trans. Jeremy Gaines and Doris L. Jones under the title "Reply," in *Communicative Action: Essays on Jürgen Habermas's "The Theory of Communicative Action,"* ed. Axel Honneth and Hans Joas, 214–64. (Cambridge: MIT Press, 1991).

―――. *Erläuterungen zur Diskursethik.* Frankfurt a.M.: Suhrkamp, 1991.

―――. *Faktizität und Geltung: Beiträge zur Diskurstheorie des Rechts und des demokratischen Rechtsstaats.* Frankfurt a.M.: Suhrkamp, 1992. Trans. William Rehg under the title *Between Facts and Norms: Contributions to a Discourse Theory of Law and Denocracy* (Cambridge: MIT Press, 1996).

———. "Gegen einen positivistisch halbierten Rationalismus." In Theodor W. Adorno et al., *Der Positivismusstreit in der deutschen Soziologie*, 235–66. Darmstadt: Luchterhand, 1972. Trans. under the title "A Positivistically Bisected Rationalism." In Theodor W. Adorno et al., *The Positivist Dispute in German Sociology*, 198–225 (New York: Harper & Row, 1976).

———. *Glauben und Wissen: Friedenspreis des deutschen Buchhandels 2001*. Frankfurt a.M.: Suhrkamp, 2001.

———. *Kommunikatives Handeln und detranszendentalisierte Vernunft*. Stuttgart: Reclam, 2001.

———. "Die Moderne—ein unvollendetes Projekt." *Kleine politische Schriften, I–IV*, 444–64. Frankfurt a.M.: Suhrkamp, 1981.

———. *Moralbewusstsein und kommunikatives Handeln*. Frankfurt a.M.: Suhrkamp, 1983. Trans. Christian Lenhardt and Shierry Weber Nicholsen under the title *Moral Consciousness and Communicative Action* (Cambridge: MIT Press, 1991).

———. "Moralität und Sittlichkeit: Treffen Hegels Einwände gegen Kant auch auf die Diskursethik zu?" In *Moralität und Sittlichkeit: Das Problem Hegels und die Diskursethik*, ed. Wolfgang Kuhlmann, 16–37. Frankfurt a.M.: Suhrkamp, 1986.

———. *Nachmetaphysisches Denken: Philosophische Aufsätze*. Frankfurt a.M.: Suhrkamp, 1988. Trans. William Mark Hohengarten under the title *Postmetaphysical Thinking: Philosophical Essays* (Cambridge: MIT Press, 1993).

———. *Die neue Unübersichtlichkeit: Kleine Politische Schriften V*. Frankfurt a.M.: Suhrkamp, 1985.

———. *Die Normalität einer Berliner Republik: Kleine Politische Schriften VIII*. Frankfurt a.M.: Suhrkamp, 1995.

———. *Der philosophische Diskurs der Moderne: Zwölf Vorlesungen*. Frankfurt a.M.: Suhrkamp, 1985. Trans. Frederick G. Lawrence under the title *The Philosophical Discourse of Modernity: Twelve Lectures* (Cambridge: MIT Press, 1987).

———. *Philosophisch-politische Profile*. Expanded ed. Frankfurt a.M.: Suhrkamp, 1984.

———. *Die postnationale Konstellation: Politische Essays*. Frankfurt a.M.: Suhrkamp, 1998.

———. "Questions and Counterquestions." In *Habermas and Modernity*, ed. R. J. Bernstein, 192–216. Cambridge: MIT Press, 1985.

———. *Religion and Rationality: Essays on Reason, God, and Modernity*. Ed. and intro. Eduardo Mendieta. Cambridge: Polity Press, 2002.

———. *Texte und Kontexte*. Frankfurt a.M.: Surhkamp, 1991.

———. *Theorie des kommunikativen Handelns*. 2 vols. Frankfurt a.M: Suhrkamp,

1981. Trans. Thomas McCarthy under the title *The Theory of Communicative Action*, 2 vols. (Boston: Beacon Press, 1984).

———. *Theorie und Praxis: Sozialphilosophische Studien*. Frankfurt a.M.: Suhrkamp, 1978.

———. *Vergangenheit als Zukunft*. Zurich: Pendo, 1990. Trans. and ed. Max Pensky under the title *The Past as Future* (Lincoln: University of Nebraska Press, 1994).

———. "Die Verschlingung von Mythos und Aufklärung: Bermerkungen zur 'Dialektik der Aufklärung' nach einer erneutern Lektüre." In *Mythos und Moderne: Begriff und Bild einer Rekonstruktion*, ed. Karl-Heinz Bohrer (Frankfurt a.M.: Suhrkamp, 1983), 405–31. Rpt. in *The Philosophical Discourse of Modernity*, 130–57.

———. *Vom sinnlichen Eindruck zum symbolischer Ausdruck: Philosophische Essays*. Frankfurt a.M.: Suhrkamp, 1997.

———. *Vorstudien und Ergänzungen zur Theorie des kommunikativen Handelns*. Frankfurt a.M.: Suhrkamp, 1984. Partially Trans. Barbara Fultner under the title *On the Pragmatics of Social Interaction: Preliminary Studies in the Theory of Communicative Action*. Cambridge: MIT Press, 2001.

———. *Wahrheit und Rechtfertigung: Philosophische Aufsätze*. Frankfurt a.M.: Suhrkamp, 1999.

———. "Werte und Normen: Ein Kommentar zu Hilary Putnams Kantischen Pragmatismus." In *Hilary Putnam und die Tradition des Pragmatismus*, ed. Marie-Luise Raters and Marcus Willaschek, 280–305. Frankfurt a.M.: Suhrkamp, 2002.

———. *Zeit der Übergänge*. Frankfurt a.M.: Suhrkamp, 2001.

———. *Die Zukunft der menschlichen Natur: Auf dem Weg zu einer liberalen Eugenik?* Frankfurt a.M.: Suhrkamp, 2001.

———. *Zur Rekonstruktion des historischen Materialismus*. Frankfurt a.M.: Suhrkamp, 1976.

Hackett, J., and J. Wallulis, eds. *Philosophy of Religion for a New Century: Essays in Honor of Eugene Thomas Long*. Dordrecht: Kluwer Academic Publishers, 2004.

Hadot, Pierre. *Exercices spirituels et philosophie antique*. 2d ed. Paris: Études Augustiniennes, 1987. Trans. Michael Chase under the title *Philosophy as a Way of Life*, ed. Arnold I. Davidson (Oxford: Blackwell, 1995).

Halbertal, Moshe, and Avishai Margalit. *Idolatry*. Trans. Naomi Goldblum. Cambridge: Harvard University Press, 1992.

Hallward, Peter. *Badiou: A Subject to Truth*. Minneapolis: University of Minnesota Press, 2003.

Hamacher, Werner. *Erntferntes Verstehen: Studien zu Philosophie und Literatur von Kant bis Celan.* Frankfurt a.M.: Suhrkamp, 1998.

―――. *Premises: Essays on Philosophy and Literature from Kant to Celan.* Trans. Peter Fenves. Cambridge: Harvard University Press, 1996.

―――. "La Seconde de l'inversion: Mouvement d'une figure à travers les poèmes de Celan." In *Contre-jour: Études sur Paul Celan,* ed. M. Broda, 185–221. Colloque de Cérisy. Paris: Cerf, 1986.

Handelman, Susan. "Jacques Derrida and the Heretic Hermeneutic." In *Displacement: Derrida and After,* ed. Mark Krupnick, 98–129. Bloomington: Indiana University Press, 1983.

Harnack, Adolph von. *Lehrbuch der Dogmengeschichte.* 3 vols. Tübingen: J. C. B. Mohr, 1909.

Haselberg, Peter von. "Wiesengrund-Adorno." In *Theodor W. Adorno: Text und Kritik,* ed. Heinz Ludwig Arnold, 7–21. Munich: Edition Text + Kritik, 1977.

Heering, H. J. "Die Idee der Schöpfung im Werk Levinas." *Nederlands Theologisch Tijdschrift* 38 (1984): 298–309.

―――. *Inleiding tot de godsdienstwijsbegeerte.* Amsterdam: Boom, 1976.

Hegel, Georg Wilhelm Friedrich. *Grundlinien der Philosophie des Rechts.* Ed. J. von Hoffmeister. Hamburg: F. Meiner, 1955. Trans. H. B. Nisbet under the title *Elements of the Philosophy of Rights,* ed. Allan Wood (Cambridge: Cambridge University Press, 1991).

―――. *Phänomenologie des Geistes.* Vol. 3 of *Theorie-Werkausgabe.* Frankfurt a.M.: Suhrkamp, 1969–71. Trans. A. V. Miller under the title *Phenomenology of Spirit,* with analysis of the text and foreword by J. N. Findlay (Oxford: Oxford University Press, 1977).

―――. *Die Vernunft in der Geschichte.* Hamburg: F. Meiner, 1955.

―――. *Vorlesungen über die Philosophie der Religion,* Vols. 16–17 of *Theorie-Werkausgabe.* Frankfurt a.M.: Suhrkamp, 1969–71. Trans. E. B. Speirs and J. Burdon Sanderson under the title *Lectures on the Philosophy of Religion,* 3 vols. (New York: Humanities Press, 1974).

Heidegger, Martin. "Brief über den Humanismus." *Wegmarken,* 311–60. Frankfurt a.M.: V. Klostermann, 1967. Trans. under the title "Letters on Humanism" in 236–76 / *Pathmarks,* ed. William McNeill (Cambridge: Cambridge University Press, 1998).

―――. *Identität und Differenz,* Pfullingen: G. Neske, 1957. Trans. Joan Stambaugh under the title *Identity and Difference* (New York: Harper & Row, 1969).

―――. *Sein und Zeit.* Tübingen: Neomarius, 1979. Trans. John MacQuarrie and Edward Robinson under the title *Being and Time* (New York: Harper & Row, 1962).

————. *Der Ursprung des Kunstwerkes.* Stuttgart: Reclam, 1988. Trans. Albert Hofstadter under the title "The Origin of the Work of Art," in Heidegger, *Poetry, Language, Thought* (New York: Harper & Row, 1975).

————. *Was ist Metaphysik?* Frankfurt a.M.: V. Klostermann, 1969.

————. *Wegmarken.* Frankfurt a.M.: Vittorio Klostermann, 1967. Trans. under the title *Pathmarks,* ed. William McNeill (Cambridge: Cambridge University Press, 1998).

Heimann, B. "Thomas Manns *Doktor Faustus* und die Musikphilosophie Adornos." *Deutsche Vierteljahrschrift für Literaturwissenschaft und Geistesgeschichte* 38 (1964): 248–66.

Henrich, Dieter. *Hegel im Kontext.* Frankfurt a.M.: Suhrkamp, 1981.

Hölderlin, Friedrich. *Poems and Fragments.* Trans. Michael Hamburger. Cambridge: Cambridge University Press, 1980.

Honneth, Axel. *Das Andere der Gerechtigkeit: Aufsätze zur praktischen Philosophie.* Frankfurt a.M.: Suhrkamp, 2000.

————. *Kampf um Anerkennung: Zur moralischen Grammatik sozialer Konflikte.* Frankfurt a.M.: Suhrkamp, 1992.

————. *Kritik der Macht: Reflexionsstufen einer kritischen Gesellschaftstheorie.* Frankfurt a.M.: Suhrkamp, 1985.

————. "The Other of Justice: Habermas and the Ethical Challenge of Postmodernism." In *The Cambridge Companion to Habermas,* ed. Stephen K. White, 289–323. Cambridge: Cambridge University Press, 1995.

————. *Die zerissene Welt des Sozialen: Sozialphilosophische Aufsätze. Erweiterte Neuausgabe.* Frankfurt a.M.: Suhrkamp, 1999.

Honneth, Axel, and Hans Joas, eds. *Kommunikatives Handeln: Beiträge zu Jürgen Habermas's "Theorie des kommunikativen Handelns,"* Frankfurt a.M.: Suhrkamp, 1986. Trans. Jeremy Gaines and Doris L. Jones under the title *Communicative Action: Essays on Jürgen Habermas's "The Theory of Communicative Action"* (Cambridge: MIT Press, 1991).

Honneth, Axel, and Albrecht Wellmer, eds. *Die Frankfurter Schule und die Folgen.* Berlin: Walter de Gruyter, 1986.

Hörisch, Jochen, "Herrscherwort, Geld und geltende Sätze: Adornos Aktualisierung der Frühromantik und ihre Affinität zur poststrukturalistischen Kritik des Subjeckts." In *Materialien zur ästhetischen Theorie Th. W. Adornos: Konstruktion der Moderne,* ed. B. Lindner and W. M. Lüdke, 397–414. Frankfurt a.M.: Suhrkamp, 1980.

Horkheimer, Max. "Die Sehnsucht nach dem ganz Anderen." In *Gesammelte Schriften,* ed. Gunzelin Schmid Noerr, 7:385–404. Frankfurt a.M.: S. Fischer, 1985.

———. "Traditionelle und kritische Theorie." In *Gesammelte Schriften,* ed. Alfred Schmidt and Gunzelin Schmid Noerr, 4:162–216. Frankfurt a.M.: S. Fischer, 1988.

Horkheimer, Max, and Theodor W. Adorno. *Dialektik der Aufklärung: Philosophische Fragmente. GS* 3 (1981). Trans. Edmund Jephcott as *Dialectic of Enlightenment* (Stanford: Stanford University Press, 2002).

Hornsby, Jennifer. *Simple Mindedness: In Defense of Naive Naturalism in the Philosophy of Mind.* Cambridge: Harvard University Press, 1997.

Hortian, Ulrich, "Zeit und Geschichte bei Franz Rosenzweig und Walter Benjamin." In *Der Philosoph Franz Rosenzweig (1886–1929): Internationaler Kongreß —Kassel 1986,* ed. Wolfdietrich Schmied-Kowarzik, 2:815–27. Freiburg: K. Alber, 1988.

Hösle, Vittorio. *Hegels System: Der Idealismus der Subjektivität.* Hamburg: F. Meiner, 1987.

Hudson, W. "Zur Frage postmoderner Philosophie." In *Die unvollendete Vernunft: Moderne versus Postmoderne,* ed. Dietmar Kamper and Willem van Reijen, 122–56. Frankfurt a.M.:Suhrkamp, 1987.

Huizinga, Johan. "Het aesthetisch bestanddeel von geschiedkundige voorstellingen." *Verzamelde Werken,* 7:3–28. Haarlem: H. D. Tjeenk Willink, 1948–53.

Hume, David. *Enquiries concerning Human Understanding and concerning the Principles of Morals.* Ed. L. A. Selby-Bigge and P. H. Nidditch. Oxford: Oxford University Press, 1975.

Husserl, Edmund. *Cartesianische Meditationen: Eine Einleitung in die Phänomenologie.* Ed. and intro. Elisabeth Ströker. Hamburg: F. Meiner, 1977. Trans. Dorion Cairns under the title *Cartesian Meditations: An Introduction to Phenomenology* (Dordrecht: Martinus Mijhoff, 1960).

———. *L'Origine de la géométrie.* Trans. and intro. Jacques Derrida. 1962. Rpt. Paris: Presses Universitaires de France, 1974.

Huyssen, Andreas. "Of Mice and Mimesis: Reading Spiegelman with Adorno." *Present Pasts: Urban Palimpsests and the Politics of Memory,* 122–37. Stanford: Stanford University Press, 2003.

IJsseling, Samuel. *Retoriek en Filosofie.* Bitthoven: Ambo, 1975. Trans. under the title *Rhetoric and Philosophy in Conflict: An Historical Survey* (The Hague: Martinus Nijhoff, 1976).

Irigaray, Luce. "Fécondité de la caresse: Lecture de Levinas, *Totalité et Infini,* sec. 4, B, Phénoménologie de l'Eros." *Éthique de la différence sexuelle,* 173–99. Paris: Minuit, 1984. Trans. Carolyn Burke and Gillian C. Gill under the title "The Fecundity of the Caress: A Reading of Levinas, *Totality and Infinity,* 'Phenomenology of Eros,'" in Irigaray, *An Ethics of Sexual Difference* (Ithaca, N.Y.: Cornell University Press, 1993), 184–217.

Jackson, J. E. "Die Du-Anrede bei Paul Celan: Anmerkungen zu seinem 'Gespräch im Gebirg.'" In H. L. Arnold, ed., *Text + Kritik* 53–54 (1977): 62–68.

Jameson, Fredric. *Late Marxism: Adorno, or The Persistence of the Dialectic.* 1990. Rpt. London: Verso, 2000.

Janicaud, Dominique. *Heidegger en France.* Vol. 1: *Récit.* Vol. 2: *Entretiens.* Paris: Albin Michel, 2001.

Jarvis, Simon. *Adorno: A Critical Introduction.* Cambridge: Polity Press, 1998.

———. "What Is Speculative Thinking?" *Revue Internationale de Philosophie,* no. 1 (2004): 69–83.

Jauss, H. R. "Der literarische Prozess des Modernismus von Rousseau bis Adorno." In *Adorno-Konferenz 1983,* ed. Ludwig von Friedeburg and Jürgen Habermas, 95–130. Frankfurt a.M.: Suhrkamp, 1983.

Jay, Martin. *Adorno.* Cambridge: Harvard University Press, 1984.

———. "Adorno in Amerika." In *Adorno-Konferenz 1983,* ed. Ludwig von Friedeburg and Jürgen Habermas, 354–87. Frankfurt a.M.: Suhrkamp, 1983.

———. "The Debate over Performative Contradiction: Habermas vs. the Post-Structuralists." In *Zwischenbetrachtungen: Im Prozess der Aufklärung, Jürgen Habermas zum 60. Geburtstag,* ed. Axel Honneth, Thomas McCarthy, Claus Offe, and Albrecht Wellmer, 171–89. Frankfurt a.M.: Suhrkamp, 1989.

———. *The Dialectical Imagination: A History of the Frankfurt School and the Institute of Social Research, 1923–1950.* Berkeley: University of California, 1973.

———. *Downcast Eyes: The Denigration of Vision in Twentieth-Century French Thought.* Berkeley: University of California Press, 1993.

———. "Frankfurter Schule und Judentum: Die Antisemitismusanalyse der Kritischen Theorie." *Geschichte und Gesellschaft* 5 (1979): 439–54.

———. *Marxism and Totality: The Adventures of a Concept from Lukács to Habermas.* Berkeley: University of California Press, 1984.

———. *Permanent Exiles: Essays on the Intellectual Migration from Germany to America.* New York: Columbia University Press, 1986.

———. *Refractions of Violence.* New York: Routledge, 2003.

Jimenez, Marc. *Vers un esthétique négative: Adorno et la modernité.* Paris: Le Sycomore, 1983.

Kafka, Franz. *Das Schloss. Gesammelte Werke.* Ed. Max Brod. Frankfurt a.M.: Suhrkamp, 1983. Trans. Willa and Edwin Muir under the title *The Castle* (New York: Modern Library, 1969).

Kamper, Dietmar, and Willem van Reijen, eds. *Die unvollendete Vernunft: Moderne versus Postmoderne.* Frankfurt a.M.: Suhrkamp, 1987.

Kant, Immanuel. *Kritik der reinen Vernunft.* Vols. 3–4 of *Werke,* ed. Wilhelm Weischedel. Darmstadt: Wissenschaftliche Buchgesellschaft, 1983. Trans. Norman Kemp Smith under the title *Critique of Pure Reason* (New York: St. Martin's Press, 1965).

―――. *Prolegomena.* In *Werke,* ed. Weischedel, 5:109–264. Trans. P. Carus under the title Kant, *Prolegomena to Any Future Metaphysics,* rev. and intro. Lewis White Beck (Indianapolis: Bobbs-Merrill, 1950).

―――. "Was ist Aufklärung?" In *Werke,* ed. Weischedel, 9:53–61. Trans. Lewis White Beck under the title "What Is Enlightenment?" in *Philosophical Writings,* ed. Ernst Behler (New York: Continuum, 1986), 263–64.

Kayser, Paulette. *Emmanuel Levinas: La Trace du féminin.* Paris: Presses Universitaires de France, 2000.

Kearny, Richard. *The God Who May Be: A Hermeneutics of Religion.* Bloomington: Indiana University Press, 2001.

Kearney, Richard, and Emmanuel Levinas. "Dialogue with Levinas." In *Face to Face with Levinas,* ed. R. Cohen, 13–33. Albany: State University of New York Press, 1986.

Kemp, Peter. "L'Éthique au lendemain des victoires des athéismes: Réflexions sur la philosophie de Jacques Derrida." *Revue de Théologie et de Philosophie* 111 (1979): 105–21.

Koch, Traugott, Klaus-M. Kodalle, and Hermann Schweppenhäuser. *Negative Dialektik und die Idee der Versöhnung.* Stuttgart: W. Kohlhammer, 1973.

Kodalle, Klaus-M. "Adornos Kierkegaard—Ein kritischer Kommentar." In *Die Rezeption S. Kierkegaards in der deutschen und dänischen Philosophie und Theologie: Vorträge des Kolloquiums am 22. und 23 März 1982,* ed. Heinrich Anz, Poul Lübke, and Friedrich Schmöe, 70–100. Copenhagen: W. Fink, 1983.

―――. *Die Eroberung des Nutzlosen: Kritik des Wunschdenkens und der Zweckrationalität im Anschluss an Kierkegaard.* Paderborn: F. Schöningh, 1988,

―――. "Gott." In *Philosophie: Ein Grundkurs,* ed. E. Matens and H. Schnädelbach, 395–439. Reinbeck bei Hamburg: Rowohlt, 1985.

―――. "Versprachlichung des Sakralen? Zur religionsphilosophischen Auseinandersetzung mit Jürgen Habermas' Theorie des kommunikativen Handelns." *Allgemeine Zeitschrift für Philosophie* 12 (1987): 39–66.

―――. "Walter Benjamins politischer Dezisionismus im theologischen Kontext: Der 'Kierkegaard' unter den spekulativen Materialisten." In *Spiegel und Gleichnis: Festschrift für Jacob Taubes,* ed. Norbert W. Bolz and Wolfgang Hübner, 301–17. Würzburg: Königshausen & Neumann, 1983.

Köhler, M. "'Postmodernismus': Ein begriffsgeschichtlicher Überblick." *Amerikastudien* 22 (1977): 8–18.

Kolakowski, L. *Main Currents of Marxism: Its Rise, Growth and Dissolution.* 3 vols. Oxford: Oxford University Press, 1978.

Korsgaard, Christine. *The Sources of Normativity,* with G. A. Cohen, Raymond Geuss, Thomas Nagel, and Bernard Williams, ed. Onora O'Neill. Cambridge: Cambridge University Press, 1996.

Koselleck, Reinhart. *The Practice of Conceptual History: Timing History, Spacing Concepts.* Trans. Todd Samuel Presner et al. Foreword by Hayden White. Stanford: Stanford University Press, 2002.

Krop, Henri. "Abraham en Odysseus: Een confrontatie van Levinas en Hegel." *Tijdschrift voor Filosofie* 46 (1984): 92–135.

Krop, Henri, Arie L. Molendijk, and Hent de Vries, eds. *Posttheism: Reframing the Judeo-Christian Tradition.* Leuven: Peeters, 2000.

Krupnick, Mark., ed. *Displacement: Derrida and After.* Bloomington: Indiana University Press, 1983.

Kuhlmann, Wolfgang., ed. *Moralität und Sittlichkeit: Das Problem Hegels und die Diskursethik.* Frankfurt a.M.: Suhrkamp, 1986.

Kuitert, Harry M. *Wat heet geloven? Structuur en herkomst van de christelijke geloofsuitspraken.* Baarn: Ten Have, 1977.

Kundera, Milan. *The Art of the Novel.* Trans. Linda Asher. New York: Grove Press, 1986.

———. *The Unbearable Lightness of Being.* Trans. Michael Henry Heim. New York: Harper & Row, 1984.

Kunneman, Harry. *De waarheidstrechter: Een communicatietheoretisch perspectief op wetenschap en samenleving.* Amsterdam: Boom, 1986.

Kunneman, Harry, and Hent de Vries, eds. *Die Aktualität der "Dialektik der Aufklärung": Zwischen Moderne und Postmoderne.* Frankfurt a.M.: Campus, 1989.

———, eds. *Enlightenments: Encounters between Critical Theory and Contemporary French Thought.* Kampen, Neth.: Kok Pharos, 1993.

Lacan, Jacques. "Le Séminaire sur 'La Lettre volée.'" *Écrits,* 11–61. Paris: Seuil, 1966.

Lacoue-Labarthe, Philippe, and Jean-Luc Nancy, eds. *Les Fins de l'homme: À partir du travail de Jacques Derrida.* Paris: Galilée, 1981.

Lafont, Cristina. *The Linguistic Turn in Hermeneutic Philosophy.* Trans. José Medina. Cambridge: MIT Press, 1999.

Laruelle, François. *Les Philosophies de la différence: Introduction critique.* Paris: Presses Universitaires de France, 1986.

———, ed. *Textes pour Emmanuel Levinas.* Paris: Jean-Michel Place, 1980.

Legendre, Pierre. *Sur la question dogmatique en Occident: Aspect théoriques.* Paris: Fayard, 1999.

Lehmann, H-T. "Das Subjekt als Schrift: Hinweise zur französischen Texttheorie." *Merkur* 347 (1979): 665–77.

Lescourret, Marie-Anne. *Emmanuel Levinas*. Paris: Flammarion, 1994.

Levinas, Emmanuel. *Altérité et transcendence*. Montpellier: Fata Morgana, 1995. Trans. Michael B. Smith under the title *Alterity and Transcendence* (New York: Columbia University Press, 1999).

———. *Autrement qu'être ou au-delà de l'essence*. The Hague: Martinus Nijhoff, 1974. Trans. Alphonso Lingis under the title *Otherwise than Being, or Beyond Essence* (The Hague: Martinus Nijhoff, 1981).

———. *Collected Philosophical Papers*. Trans. Alphonso Lingis. Dordrecht: M. Nijhoff, 1987.

———. *De Dieu qui vient à l'idée*. Paris: Vrin, 1982. Trans. Bettina Bergo under the title *Of God Who Comes to Mind* (Stanford: Stanford University Press, 1998).

———. *De l'évasion*. Intro. and ed. Jacques Rolland. Montepellier: Fata Morgana, 1982. Trans. Bettina Bergo under the title *On Escape* (Palo Alto: Stanford University Press, 2003).

———. *De l'existence à l'existant*. Paris: Vrin, 1978. Trans. Alphonso Lingis under the title *Existence and Existents* (Dordrecht: Kluwer, 1988).

———. *Dieu, la mort et le temps*. Paris: Grasset & Fasquelle, 1993. Trans. Bettina Bergo under the title *God, Death, and Time* (Stanford: Stanford University Press, 2000).

———. *Difficile liberté: Essais sur le Judaïsme*. Paris: Albin Michel, 1976. Trans. Seán Hand under the title *Difficult Freedom: Essays on Judaism* (Baltimore: Johns Hopkins University Press, 1990).

———. *Discovering Existence with Husserl*. Trans. Richard A. Cohen and Michael B. Smith. Evanston, Ill.: Northwestern University Press, 1998.

———. *Emmanuel Levinas: Basic Philosophical Writings*. Ed. Adriaan T. Peperzak, Simon Critchley, and Robert Bernasconi. Bloomington: Indiana University Press, 1996.

———. *En découvrant l'existence avec Husserl et Heidegger*. 2d ed. Paris: Vrin, 1967.

———. *Entre nous: Essais sur le penser-à-l'autre*. Paris: Grasset & Fasquelle, 1991. Trans. Michael B. Smith and Barbara Harshav under the title *Entre Nous: Thinking-of-the-Other* (New York: Columbia University Press, 1998).

———. *Ethique et Infini: Dialogues avec Philippe Nemo*. Paris: Arthème Fayard and Radio France, 1982. Trans. Richard A. Cohen under the title *Ethics and Infinity: Conversations with Philippe Nemo* (Pittsburgh: Duquesne University Press, 1985).

———. "Être juif." *Confluences* 7, nos. 15–17 (1947): 253–64. Rpt. *Cahiers d'Études Lévinassiennes*, no. 1 (2002): 99–106.

————. *Hors sujet.* Montpellier: Fata Morgana, 1987. Trans. Michael B. Smith under the title *Outside the Subject* (Stanford: Stanford University Press, 1994).

————. *Humanisme de l'autre homme.* Montepellier: Fata Morgana, 1972.

————. *Les Imprévus de l'histoire.* Montpellier: Fata Morgana, 1994

————. "Infini." In *Encyclopaedia Universalis,* 8:991–94. Paris: Presses Universitaires de France, 1976.

————. Interview with Christian Decamps. In *Entretiens avec "Le Monde,"* ed. Christian Delacampagne, vol. 1 of *Philosophies,* 138–47. Paris: Découverte / Le Monde, 1984. Trans. Alin Christian and Bettina Bergo under the title "Reality Has Weight." In *Is It Righteous to Be?* Ed. and intro. Jill Robbins (Stanford: Stanford University Press, 2001), 158–64.

————. "Intervention dans *Petite histoire de l'existentialisme* de Jean Wahl." In Jean Wahl, *Petite histoire de "l'existentialisme,"* 81–87. Paris: Club Maintenant.

————. *Is It Righteous to Be? Interviews with Emmanuel Levinas.* Ed. Jill Robbins. Stanford: Stanford University Press, 2001.

————. "Lévy-Bruhl et la philosophie contemporaine." *Revue Philosophique* 147 (1957): 556–69.

————. "Le Moi et la totalité." *Revue de Métaphysique et de Morale* 59 (1954): 353–73.

————. *Noms propres.* Montpellier: Fata Morgana, 1976. Trans. Michael B. Smith under the title "Proper Names," *Proper Names* (Stanford: Stanford University Press, 1996), 1–123.

————. "L'Ontologie est-elle fondamentale?" *Revue de Métaphysique et de Morale* 56 (1951): 88- 98.

————. *Positivité et transcendance.* Ed. Jean-Luc Marion. Paris: Presses Universitaires de France, 2000.

————. Preface to T. F. Geraets, *Vers une nouvelle philosophie transcendentale: La Genèse de la philosophie de Merleau-Ponty jusqu'à la 'Phénoménologie de la perception,'* xi–xv. The Hague: Martinus Nijhoff, 1971.

————. Preface to Rabbi Hayyim de Volozhyn, *L'Âme de la vie (nefesh hahayyim),* vii–x. Trans. Benjamin Gross. Paris: Verdier, 1986.

————. Preface to Stéphane Mosès, *Système et révélation: La Philosophie de Franz Rosenzweig,* 7–24. Paris: Seuil, 1982. Trans. Catherine Tihanyi as foreword to Stéphane Mosès, *System and Revelation: The Philosophy of Franz Rosenzweig* (Detroit: Wayne State University Press, 1992).

————. *Quatre lectures talmudiques.* Paris: Minuit, 1968. Trans. Anne Aronowicz under the title *Nine Talmudic Readings* (Bloomington: Indiana University Press, 1990).

————. "La Réalité et son ombre." *Les Temps Modernes* 38 (1948): 771–89. Trans.

Alphonso Lingis under the title "Reality and Its Shadow," *Collected Philosophical Papers* (Dordrecht: M. Nijhoff, 1987), 1–13. Rpt. in Seán Hand, ed., *The Levinas Reader* (Oxford: Basil Blackwell, 1989), 129–43.

———. *Sur Maurice Blanchot.* Montpellier: Fata Morgana, 1975. Trans. Michael B. Smith under the title "On Maurice Blanchot," *Proper Names* (Stanford: Stanford University Press, 1996), 125–70.

———. *Le Temps et l'autre.* Paris: Presses Universitaires de France, 1979. Trans. Richard A. Cohen under the title *Time and the Other and Additional Essays* (Pittsburgh: Dusquesne University Press, 1987).

———. *Théorie de l'intuition dans la phénoménologie de Husserl.* 1930. Rpt. Paris: Vrin, 1978. Trans. Andre Orianne under the title *The Theory of Intuition in Husserl's Phenomenology* (1973; rpt., Evanston, Ill.: Northwestern University Press, 1995).

———. *Totalité et infini: Essai sur l'extériorité.* The Hague: Martinus Nijhoff, 1961. Trans. Alphonso Lingis under the title *Totality and Infinity: An Essay on Exteriority* (Pittsburgh: Duquesne University Press, 1969).

———. "Totalité et totalisation." In *Encyclopaedia Universalis,* 16:192–94. Paris: Presses Universitaires de France, 1973.

———. "La Trace de l'autre." *Tijdschrift voor Filosofie,* no. 3 (1963): 605–23. Rpt. in *En découvrant l'existence avec Husserl et Heidegger,* 2d ed. (Paris: Vrin, 1967), 187–202. Trans. Alphonso Lingis under the title "The Trace of the Other," in *Deconstruction in Context,* ed. Mark Taylor (Chicago: University of Chicago Press, 1986), 345–59.

———. "La Transcendence des mots." *Les Temps Modernes* 44 (1949): 1090–95.

———. *Transcendance et intelligibilité.* Geneva: Labor & Fides, 1984.

———. "Vorwort zur deutschen Übersetzung." *Totalität und Unendlichkeit,* 7–12. Trans. W. N. Krewani. Freiburg: Alber, 1987.

Lévi-Strauss, Claude, and Didier Éribon. *De près et de loin.* Paris: Odile Jacob, 2001.

Lindner, B., and W. M. Lüdke, eds. *Materialien zur ästhetischen Theorie Th. W. Adornos: Konstruktion der Moderne.* Frankfurt a.M.: Suhrkamp, 1980.

Lovejoy, Arthur O., and George Boas. *Primitivism and Related Ideas in Antiquity,* with supplementary essays by W. F. Albright and P.-E. Dumont. 1935. Rpt. Baltimore: Johns Hopkins University Press, 1997.

Lovibond, Sabina. *Ethical Formation.* Cambridge: Harvard University Press, 2002.

Löwenthal, Richard. *Mitmachen wollte ich nie: Ein autobiographisches Gespräch mit H. Dubiel.* Frankfurt a.M.: Suhrkamp, 1980.

Löwith, Karl. *Heidegger: Denker in dürftiger Zeit.* Frankfurt a.M.: S. Fischer, 1953.

———. *Mein Leben in Deutschland vor und nach 1933: Ein Bericht.* Stuttgart: J. B. Metzler, 1986.

———. *Von Hegel zu Nietzsche: Der revolutionäre Bruch im Denken des 19. Jahrhunderts.* Hamburg: Meiner, 1981. Trans. David E. Green under the title *From Hegel to Nietzsche: The Revolution in Nineteenth-Century Thought,* trans. David E. Green (New York: Holt, Rinehart and Winston, 1964).

Löwy, Michael. *Rédemption et utopie: Le judïsme en Europe centrale.* Paris: Presses Universitaires de France, 1988. Trans. Hope Heaney under the title *Redemption and Utopia: Jewish Libertarian Thought in Central Europe, A Study in Elective Affinity* (London: Athlone Press, 1992).

———. *Walter Benjamin: Avertissement d'incendie — Une Lecture des thèses "Sur le concept d'histoire."* Paris: Presses Universitaires de France, 2001.

Lüdke, Werner Martin. *Anmerkungen zu einer "Logik des Zerfalls": Adorno-Beckett.* Frankfurt a.M.: Suhrkamp, 1981.

Lukàcs, Georg. *Geschichte und Klassenbewußtsein: Studien zur marxistischen Dialektik.* Darmstadt: Luchterhand, 1968. Trans. Rodney Livingstone under the title *History and Class Consciousness: Studies in Marxist Dialectics* (Cambridge: MIT Press, 1972).

———. *Die Theorie des Romans: Ein geschichtsphilosophischer Versuch über die Formen der grossen Epik.* Darmstadt: Luchterhand, 1971. Trans. Anna Bostock under the title *The Theory of the Novel: A Historico-Philosophical Essay on the Forms of Great Epic Literature* (London: Merlin, 1971).

Lyotard, Jean-François. "Adorno come diavolo." *Des dispositifs pulsionnels,* 115–33. Paris: Union Générale d'Éditions, 1973.

———. *La Condition postmoderne: Rapport sur le savoir.* Paris: Minuit, 1979. Trans. Geoffrey Bennington and Brian Massumi under the title *The Postmodern Condition: A Report on Knowledge* (Minneapolis: University of Minnesota Press, 1984).

———. *Le Différend.* Paris: Minuit, 1983. Trans. Georges Van Den Abbeele under the title *The Differend: Phrases in Dispute* (Minneapolis: University of Minnesota Press, 1988).

———. "Discussions, ou, Phraser 'après Auschwitz.'" In *Les Fins de l'homme: À partir du travail de Jacques Derrida,* ed. Philippe Lacoue-Labarthe and Jean-Luc Nancy, 283–315. Paris: Galilée, 1981.

———. "Levinas' Logic." In *Face to Face with Levinas,* ed. R. A. Cohen, 117–58. Albany: State University of New York Press, 1986.

———. *Le Postmoderne expliqué aux enfants.* Paris: Galilée, 1988. Trans. Julian Pefanis and Morgan Thomas under the title *The Postmodern Explained* (Minneapolis: University of Minnesota Press, 1993).

————. *Tombeau de l'intellectuel et autres papiers*. Paris: Galilée, 1984.

MacIntyre, Alasdair. *After Virtue: A Study in Moral Theory*. London: Duckworth, 1981.

————. *A Short History of Ethics: A History of Moral Philosophy from the Homeric Age to the Twentieth Century*. Notre Dame, Ind.: University of Notre Dame Press, 1998.

Macksey, Richard, and Eugenio Donato, eds. *The Structuralist Controversy: The Languages of Criticism and the Sciences of Man*. Baltimore: Johns Hopkins University Press, 1972.

Malka, Salomon. *Emmanuel Lévinas: La Vie et la trace*. Paris: Jean-Claude Lattès, 2002.

Man, Paul de. *Blindness and Insight: Essays in the Rhetoric of Contemporary Criticism*. 2d ed. Intro. Wlad Godzich. Minneapolis: University of Minnesota Press, 1983.

Mann, Thomas. *Doktor Faustus: Das Leben des deutschen Tonsetzers Adrian Leverkühn erzählt von einem Freunde*. Frankfurt a.M.: S Fischer, 1982. Trans. H. T. Lowe-Porter under the title *Doctor Faustus: The Life of the German Composer Adrian Leverkühn as Told by a Friend* (New York: Alfred A. Knopf, 1948).

————. *Die Entstehung des Doktor Faustus: Roman eines Romans*. Frankfurt a.M.: S. Fischer, 1949.

Marcuse, Herbert. *Eros and Civilization: A Philosophical Inquiry into Freud*. Boston: Beacon Press, 1966.

————. "Neue Quellen zur Gundlegung des Historischen Materialismus." In Marcuse, *Ideen zu einer kritischen Theorie der Gesellschaft*, 7–54. Frankfurt a.M.: Suhrkamp, 1969.

Marion, Jean-Luc. *L'Idole et la distance: Cinq études*. Paris: Grasset, 1977. Trans. Thomas A. Carlson under the title *The Idol and Distance: Five Studies* (New York: Fordham University Press, 2001).

————. *Le Phénomène érotique*. Paris: Grasset, 2003.

————. *Prolegomènes à la charité*. Paris: La Différence, 1986. Trans. Stephen Lewis under the title *Prolegomena to Charity* (New York: Fordham University Press, 2002).

Marquard, Odo. *Abschied vom Prinzipiellen: Philosophische Studien*. Stuttgart: Reklam, 1981.

————. *Apologie des Zufälligen: Philosophische Studien*. Stuttgart: Reklam, 1986.

————. *Schwierigkeiten mit der Geschichtsphilosophie: Aufsätze*. Frankfurt a.M.: Suhrkamp, 1973.

————. *Skepsis und Zustimmung: Philosophische Studien*. Stuttgart: Reklam, 1994.

Marrati, Paola. "'The Catholicism of Cinema': Gilles Deleuze on Image and Belief." In *Religion and Media,* ed. Hent de Vries and Samuel Weber, 227–40. (Stanford: Stanford University Press, 2001).

———. "Derrida et Lévinas. Ethique, écriture et historicité." *Les Cahiers Philosophiques de Strasbourg* (1996): 257–79.

———. *La Genèse et la trace: Derrida lecteur de Husserl et Heidegger.* Dordrecht: Kluwer, 1998. Trans. Simon Sparks under the title *Genesis and Trace: Derrida Reading Husserl and Heidegger* (Stanford: Stanford University Press, 2004).

———. *Gilles Deleuze: Philosophie et cinéma.* Paris: Presses Universitaires de France, 2003.

Marx, Karl. *Die Frühschriften.* Ed. Siegfried von Landshut. Stuttgart: A. Kröner, 1971.

McDowell, John. *Mind and World: With a New Introduction.* 1994. Rpt. Cambridge: Harvard University Press, 1996.

Menke, Christoph. *Die Souveränität der Kunst: Ästhetische Erfahrung nach Adorno und Derrida.* Frankfurt a.M.: Suhrkamp, 1991.

Mensching, G. *L'Expression au-delà de la représentation: Sur l'aisthêsis et l'esthétique chez Merleau-Ponty.* Louvain: Peeters, 2003.

———. "Zeit und Fortschritt in den geschichtsphilosophischen Thesen Walter Benjamins." In *Materialien zu Benjamins Thesen "Über den Begriff der Geschichte,"* ed. Peter Bulthaup, 170–92. Frankfurt a.M.: Suhrkamp, 1975.

Merleau-Ponty, Maurice. *Parcours, 1935–1951.* Lagrasse: Éditions Verdier, 1997.

Michaud, Éric. *Un art d'éternité: L'Image et le temps du national-socialisme.* Paris: Gallimard, 1996.

Molendijk, Arie L., and Peter Pels, eds. *Religion in the Making: The Emergence of the Sciences of Religion.* Leiden: Brill, 1998.

Moore, A. W. *The Infinite.* London: Routledge, 1990.

Mörchen, Hermann. *Adorno und Heidegger: Untersuchung einer philosophischen Kommunikationsverweigerung.* Stuttgart: Klett-Cotta, 1981.

———. *Macht und Herrschaft im Denken von Heidegger und Adorno.* Stuttgart: Klett-Cotta, 1980.

Mosès, Stéphane. *L'Ange de l'histoire: Rosenzweig, Benjamin, Scholem.* Paris: Éditions du Seuil, 1992.

———. *Au-delà de la guerre: Trois études sur Levinas.* Paris: Éditions de l'Éclat, 2004.

———. "Hegel beim Wort genommen: Geschichtskritik bei Franz Rosenzweig." In *Zeitgewinn: Messianisches Denken nach Franz Rosenzweig,* ed. G. Fuchs and H. H. Henrix, 67–89. Frankfurt a.M.: J. Knecht, 1987.

———. "Quand le langage se fait voix: Paul Celan: 'Entretien dan le montagne.'"

In *Contre-jour: Études sur Paul Celan,* ed. M. Broda, 117–31. Colloque de Cérisy. Paris: Cerf, 1986.

———. *Système et Révélation: La Philosophie de Franz Rosenzweig.* Paris: Seuil, 1982. Trans. Catherine Tihanyi under the title *System and Revelation: The Philosophy of Franz Rosenzweig* (Detroit: Wayne State University Press, 1992).

———. "Walter Benjamin und Franz Rosenzweig." *Deutsche Vierteljahrschrift für Literaturwissenschaft und Geistesgeschichte* 56, no. 4 (1982): 622–40.

Müller-Doohm, Stefan. *Adorno: Eine Biographie.* Frankfurt a.M.: Suhrkamp, 2003.

Münster, Arno. *Le Principe dialogique: De la réflexion monologique vers la proflexion intersubjective: Essais sur M. Buber, E. Lévinas, F. Rosenzweig, G. Scholem et E. Bloch.* Paris: Kimé, 1997.

———. *Utopie, Messianismus und Apokalypse im Frühwerk von Ernst Bloch.* Frankfurt a.M.: Suhrkamp, 1982.

Musil, Robert. *Der Mann ohne Eigenschaften.* ed. A. Frisé. Reibeck bei Hamburg: Rowohlt, 1978. Trans. Sophie Wilkins under the title *The Man without Qualities,* 2 vols. (New York: Alfred A. Knopf, 1995).

Nadler, Allan. *The Faith of the Mithnagdim: Rabbinic Responses to Hasidic Rapture.* Baltimore: Johns Hopkins University Press, 1997.

Nagel, Ernest, and James R. Newman. *Gödel's Proof.* New York: New York University Press, 1958.

Nägele, Rainer. "The Scene of the Other: Theodor W. Adorno's Negative Dialectic in the Context of Poststructuralism." In *Postmodernism and Politics,* ed. Jonathan Arac, 91–111. Minneapolis: University of Minnesota Press, 1986.

Nagl, Ludwig, and Chantal Mouffe, eds. *The Legacy of Wittgenstein: Pragmatism or Deconstruction.* Frankfurt a.M.: Peter Lang, 2001.

Negt, Oskar, ed. *Aktualität und Folgen der Philosophie Hegels.* Frankfurt a.M.: Suhrkamp, 1970.

Neiman, Susan. *Evil in Modern Thought: An Alternative History of Philosophy.* Princeton: Princeton University Press, 2002.

Newton, Adam Zachary. *Narrative Ethics.* Cambridge: Harvard University Press, 1995.

Ottmann, H. *Individuum und Gemeinschaft bei Hegel.* Vol. 1 of *Hegel im Spiegel der Interpretation.* Berlin: Walter de Gruyter, 1977.

Oudemanns, T. C. W. "Heideggers formeel aanwijzende hermeneutica." *Algemeen Nederlands Tijdschrift voor Wijsbegeerte* 80, no. 1 (1988): 18–40.

———. "Hermeneutiek: Metaforisch spel van binnen en buiten." *Nederlands Theologisch Tijdschrift* (1984): 179–96.

Painter, G. D. *Marcel Proust: A Biography.* 2 vols. Harmondsworth, Middlesex: Penguin, 1977.

Pangritz, Andreas. *Vom Kleiner- und Unsichtbarwerden der Theologie: Ein Versuch über das Projekt einer "impliziten Theologie" bei Barth, Tillich, Bonhoeffer, Horkheimer und Adorno.* Tübingen: Theologischer Verlag, 1996.

Pannenberg, Wolfhart. *Wissenschaftstheorie und Theologie.* Frankfurt a.M.: Suhrkamp, 1977.

Pauer-Studer, Herlinde, ed. *Konstruktionen praktischer Vernunft: Philosophie im Gespräch.* Frankfurt a.M.: Suhrkamp, 2000. Trans. under the title *Constructions of Practical Reason: Interviews on Moral and Political Philosophy* (Stanford: Stanford University Press, 2003).

Peperzak, Adriaan. "Une introduction à la lecture de *Totalité et Infini,* commentaire de 'La Philosophie et l'idée de l'infini.'" *Revue des Sciences Philosophiques et Théologiques* 71 (1987): 191–218.

———. "Rezension von E. Levinas, *Autrement qu'être ou au-delà de l'essence.*" *Philosophische Rundschau* 24 (1977): 91–116.

———. "Some Remarks on Hegel, Kant, and Levinas." In *Face to Face with Levinas,* ed. R. A. Cohen, 205–17. Albany: State University of New York Press, 1986.

———. *To the Other: An Introduction to the Philosophy of Emmanuel Levinas.* West Lafayette, Ind.: Purdue University Press, 1993.

Perloff, Marjorie. *Wittgenstein's Ladder: Poetic Language and the Strangeness of the Ordinary.* Chicago: University of Chicago Press, 1996.

Petazzi, C. "Studien zu Leben und Werk Adornos bis 1938." In *Theodor W. Adorno: Text und Kritik,* ed. Heinz Ludwig Arnold, 22–43. Munich: Edition Text + Kritik, 1977.

Petrosino, Silvano. *La Vérité nomade: Introduction à Emmanuel Lévinas.* Paris: Découverte, 1984. Trans. of *La Verità nomade* (Milan: Editoriale Jaca Book, 1984).

Peukert, Helmut. *Wissenschaftstheorie, Handlungstheorie, Fundamentale Theologie: Analysen zu Ansatz und Status theologischer Theoriebildung.* Dusseldorf: Patmos, 1978. Trans. James Bohman under the title *Science, Action, and Fundamental Theology: Toward a Theology of Communicative Action* (Cambridge: MIT Press, 1984).

Philipse, Herman. *De fundering van de logica in Husserls "Logische Untersuchungen."* Leiden: H. Philipse, 1983.

———. "Theologie: Een wetenschap? Beschouwingen naar aanleiding van drie redes gehouden aan de Theologische Faculteit van de Rijksuniversiteit te Leiden." *Nederlands Theologisch Tijdschrift* 38 (1984): 45–66.

Pippin, Robert. "*Critical Inquiry* and Critical Theory: A Short History of Nonbeing." *Critical Inquiry* 30 (Winter 2004): 424–28.

Poe, Edgar Allan. "The Purloined Letter." *The Fall of the House of Usher and Other*

Writings, ed. and intro. D. Galloway, 330–49. Harmondsworth, Middlesex: Penguin, 1986.

Pöggeler, Otto. *Der Denkweg Martin Heideggers.* Pfullingen: Neske, 1983. Trans. Daniel Magurshak and Sigmund Barber under the title *Martin Heidegger's Path of Thinking* (Atlantic Highlands, N.J.: Humanities Press, 1987).

———. *Spur des Wortes: Zur Lyrik Paul Celans.* Freiburg: Karl Alber, 1986.

Post, Werner. *Kritische Theorie und metaphysischer Pessimismus: Zum Spätwerk Max Horkheimers.* Munich: Kösel, 1971.

Poster, Mark. *Existential Marxism in Postwar France: From Sartre to Althusser.* Princeton: Princeton University Press, 1975.

Pothast, U. *Die eigentlich metaphysische Tätigkeit: Über Schopenhauers Ästhetik und ihre Anwendung durch Samuel Beckett.* Frankfurt a.M.: Suhrkamp, 1982.

Pranger, M. B. *Consequente theologie: Een studie over het denken van Anselmus van Canterbury.* Assen: Van Gorcum, 1975.

Putnam, Hilary. "Antwort auf Habermas." In *Hilary Putnam und die Tradition des Pragmatismus,* ed. Marie-Luise Raters and Marcus Willaschek, 306–32. Frankfurt a.M.: Suhrkamp, 2002.

———. *The Collapse of the Fact/Value Dichotomy and Other Essays.* Cambridge: Harvard University Press, 2002.

———. *Ethics without Ontology.* Cambridge: Harvard University Press, 2004.

———. "Introduction." in Franz Rosenzweig, *Understanding the Sick and the Healthy: A View of World, Man, and God,* trans. and intro. Nahum Glatzer. Cambridge: Harvard University Press, 1999.

———. "Levinas and Judaism." In *The Cambridge Companion to Levinas,* ed. Simon Critichley and Robert Bernasconi, 33–62. Cambridge: Cambridge University Press, 2002.

———. *Realism and Reason.* Vol. 3 of *Philosophical Papers.* Cambridge: Cambridge University Press, 1983.

———. *Renewing Philosophy.* Cambridge: Harvard University Press, 1992.

Pütz, P. "Nietzsche im Lichte der Kritischen Theorie." *Nietzsche-Studien* 3 (1974): 175–91.

Rabinbach, Anson. *In the Shadow of Catastrophe: German Intellectuals between Apocalypse and Enlightenment.* Berkeley: University of California Press, 1997.

Raters, Marie-Luise, and Marcus Willaschek, eds. *Hilary Putnam und die Tradition des Pragmatismus.* Frankfurt a.M.: Suhrkamp, 2002.

Rath, N. "Zur Nietzsche-Rezeption Horkheimers und Adornos." In *Vierzig Jahre Flaschenpost, 'Dialektik der Aufklärung': 1947 bis 1987,* ed. Willem van Reijen and Gunzelin Schmid Noerr, 73–110. Frankfurt a.M.: Fischer, 1987.

Reed, C. W. "Levinas' Question." In *Face to Face with Levinas*, ed. R. A. Cohen, 73–82. Albany: State University of New York Press, 1986.

Reijen, Willem van, and Gunzelin Schmid Noerr, eds. *Vierzig Jahre Flaschenpost, 'Dialektik der Aufklärung': 1947 bis 1987.* Frankfurt a.M.: Fischer, 1987.

Ricoeur, Paul. *De l'interprétation: Essai sur Freud.* Paris: Seuil, 1965.

———. *Du texte à l'action: Essais d'herméneutique II.* Paris: Seuil, 1986. Trans. Kathleen Blamey and John B. Thompson under the title *From Text to Action* (Evanston, Ill.: Northwestern University Press, 1991).

———. *La Métaphore vive.* Paris: Seuil, 1975. Trans. Robert Czerny, with Kathleen McLaughlin and John Costello, under the title *The Rule of Metaphor:* Multidisciplinary studies of the Creation of Meaning (Toronto: University of Toronto Press, 1981).

———. *Soi-même comme un autre.* Paris: Seuil, 1990. Trans. Kathleen Blamey under the title *Oneself as Another* (Chicago: University of Chicago Press, 1992).

———. *Temps et récit.* Vol. 3. Paris: Seuil, 1985. Trans. Kathleen McLaughlin and David Pellauer under the title *Time and Narrative* (Chicago: University of Chicago Press, 1988).

Riedel, Manfred. *Norm und Werturteil: Grundprobleme der Ethik.* Stuttgart: Reklam, 1979.

Ries, W. "'Die Rettung des Hoffnungslosen': Zur 'theologia occulta' in der Spätphilosophie Horkheimers und Adornos." *Zeitschrift für philosophische Forschung* 30 (1978): 69–81.

Ritter, Joachim. *Metaphysik und Politik: Studien zu Aristoteles und Hegel.* Frankfurt a.M.: Suhrkamp, 1977.

Robbins, Jill. *Altered Reading: Levinas and Literature.* Chicago: University of Chicago Press, 1999.

Rohrmoser, Günter. *Das Elend der kritischen Theorie: Theodor W. Adorno, Herbert Marcuse, Jürgen Habermas.* Freiburg i.B.: Rombach, 1970.

Rolland, Jacques. "Sortie d'être par une nouvelle voie." In Emmanual Levinas, *De l'évasion*, 11–64. Montpellier: Fata Morgana, 1982. Trans. Bettina Bergo under the title "Getting Out of Being by a New Path," in Levinas, *On Escape* (Palo Alto: Stanford University Press, 2003), 3–48.

———, ed. *Emmanuel Levinas.* Vol. 3 of *Les Cahiers de "La Nuit surveilée."* Lagrasse: Verdier, 1984.

Ronell, Avital. *The Test Drive.* Urbana: University of Illinois Press, 2004.

Rorty, Richard. "Cultural Politics and the Question of the Existence of God." In *Radical Interpretation in Religion*, ed. Nancy K. Frankenberry, 53–77. Cambridge: Cambridge University Press, 2002.

————. "Habermas and Lyotard on Postmodernity." In *Habermas and Modernity,* ed. Richard J. Bernstein, 161–75. Cambridge: MIT Press, 1985.

————. *Philosophy and Social Hope.* Harmondsworth, Middlesex: Penguin, 1999.

————. *Philosophy and the Mirror of Nature.* Oxford: Blackwell, 1980.

————. "Universality and Truth." In *Rorty and His Critics,* ed. Robert Brandom, 1–30. Malden: Blackwell, 2000.

————, ed. *The Linguistic Turn.* 2d enlarged ed. 1967. Rpt. Chicago: University of Chicago Press, 1992.

Rudolph, Kurt. *Die Gnosis: Wesen und Geschichte einer spätantiken Religion.* Leipzig: Koehler & Amelang, 1977. Trans. and ed. Robert McLachlan under the title *Gnosis: The Nature and History of Gnosticism* (San Francisco: Harper & Row, 1987).

Russell, Bertrand. *The History of Western Philosophy and Its Connection with Political and Social Circumstances from the Earliest Times to the Present Day.* London: George Allen & Unwin, 1975.

Ryan, Michael. *Marxism and Deconstruction: A Critical Articulation.* Baltimore: Johns Hopkins University Press, 1982.

Ryle, Gilbert. *The Concept of Mind.* Harmondsworth, Middlesex: Penguin, 1978.

Said, Edward. "Adorno as Lateness Itself." In *Apocalypse Theory and the Ends of the World,* ed. Malcolm Bull, 264–81. Oxford: Blackwell, 1995.

Santner, Eric L. *On the Psychotheology of Everyday Life: Reflections on Freud and Rosenzweig.* Chicago: University of Chicago Press, 2001.

Sartre, Jean-Paul. *L'Imaginaire: Psychologie phénoménologique de l'imagination.* 1940. Rpt. Paris: Gallimard, 1986. Trans. and intro. Jonathan Webber as *The Imaginary: A Phenomenological Psychology of the Imagination,* rev. Arlette Elkaim-Sartre (London: Routledge, 2004).

————. *L'Imagination.* Paris: Presses Universitaires de France, 1936.

————. *La Nausée.* Paris: Gallimard, 1938.

————. "Qu'est-ce que la littérature?" Published in six installments in *Les Temps Modernes* 17–22 (February–July 1947). Reissued in Sartre, *Situations, II* (Paris: Gallimard, 1948). Trans. under the title *"What Is Literature?" and Other Essays,* ed. Steven Ungar (Cambridge: Harvard University Press, 1988), 23–245.

————. *La Transcendence de l'ego: Esquisse d'une description phénoménologique.* Paris: Vrin, 1978. Trans. Forrest Williams and Robert Kirkpatrick under the title *The Transcendence of the Ego: An Existentialist Theory of Consciousness,* trans. (New York: Hill & Wang, 2001).

Saussure, Ferdinand de. *Cours de linguistique generale.* Ed. Charles Bailly and Albert Sechehaye, with the collaboration of Albert Riedlinger. Critical Edition prepared by Tullio de Mauro. Postface by Louis-Jean Calvet. Paris: Payot

& Rivages, 1995. Trans. Roy Harris under the title *Course in General Linguistics* (La Salle: Open Court, 1986).

———. *Écrits de linguistique générale,* ed. Simon Bouquet and Rudolf Engler. Paris: Gallimard, 2002.

Scheible, Hartmut. *Theodor W. Adorno.* Reibeck bei Hamburg: Rowohlt, 1989.

Schlick, M. "Die Wende der Philosophie." In *Logischer Empirismus—Der Wiener Kreis: Ausgewählte Texte mit einer Einleitung,* ed. H. Schliechert, 12–19. Munich: Wilhelm Fink, 1975.

Schmid Noerr, Gunzelin. Editor's afterword. In Max Horkheimer, *Gesammelte Schriften,* ed. Alfred Schmidt and Gunzelin Schmid Noerr, 5:432–34. Frankfurt a.M.: S. Fischer, 1985.

Schmidt, Alfred. *Der Begriff der Natur in der Lehre von Marx: Überarbeitete, ergänzte und mit einem Postscriptum versehene Neuausgabe.* Frankfurt a.M.: Europäische Verlagsanstalt, 1971.

———. "Begriff des Materialismus bei Adorno." In *Adorno-Konferenz 1983,* ed. Ludwig von Friedeburg and Jürgen Habermas, 14–31. Frankfurt a.M.: Suhrkamp, 1983.

———. *Zur Idee der kritischen Theorie.* Regensburg: Carl Hanser, 1974.

Schmidt, F. W. "Hegel in der kritischen Theorie der Frankfurter Schule." In *Aktualität und Folgen der Philosophie Hegels,* ed. Oskar Negt, 17–57. Frankfurt a.M.: Suhrkamp, 1970.

Schmidt, T. M. "Immanente Transzendenz." In *Im Netz der Begriffe: Religionsphilosophische Analysen,* ed. Linus Hauser and Eckhard Nordhofen, 78–96. Freiburg: Oros, 1994.

Schmied-Kowarzik, Wolfdietrich, ed. *Der Philosoph Franz Rosenzweig (1886–1929).* Freiburg: Karl Alber, 1988.

Schmucker, Joseph F. *Adorno: Logik des Zerfalls.* Stuttgart: Frommann-Holzboog, 1977.

Schnädelbach, Herbert. *Philosophie in Deutschland, 1831–1933.* Frankfurt a.M. Suhrkamp, 1983.

———. "Sartre und die Frankfurter Schule." In *Sartre: Ein Kongreß,* ed. Traugott König. Reibeck bei Hamburg: Rowohlt, 1988.

———. *Vernunft und Geschichte: Vorträge und Abhandlungen.* Frankfurt a.M.: Suhrkamp, 1987.

———. "Was ist Neoaristotelismus?" In *Moralität und Sittlichkeit: Das Problem Hegels und die Diskursethik,* ed. W. Kuhlmann, 38–63. Frankfurt a.M.: Suhrkamp, 1986.

Scholem, Gershom. *Über einige Grundbegriffe des Judentums.* Frankfurt a.M.: Suhrkamp, 1970.

————. "Walter Benjamin." in Scholem, *Judaica 2*. Frankfurt a.M.: Suhrkamp, 1970.

————. *Zur Kabbala und ihrer Symbolik*. Frankfurt a.M.: Suhrkamp, 1973.

Schulte Nordholt, Annelies. "Langage et négativité: La Poetique de Maurice Blanchot dans son rapport à le pensée hégelienne." MS, Amsterdam, 1987.

————. *Maurice Blanchot: L'Écriture comme expérience du dehors*. Geneva: Droz, 1995.

Schütte, Wolfram, ed. *Adorno in Frankfurt: Ein Kaleidoskop mit Texten und Bildern*. Frankfurt a.M.: Suhrkamp, 2003.

Schweppenhäuser, Hermann. "Negativität und Intransigenz: Wider eine Reidealisierung Adornos." In T. Koch, Klaus-M. Kodalle, and Hermann Schweppenhäuser, *Negative Dialektik und die Idee der Versöhnung*. Stuttgart: W. Kohlhammer, 1973.

————. "Spekulative und negative Dialektik." In *Aktualität und Folgen der Philosophie Hegels*, ed. Oskar Negt, 81–93. Frankfurt a.M.: Suhrkamp, 1970.

Searle, John. "Reiterating the Differences: A Reply to Derrida." *Glyph*, no. 1 (1977): 198–208.

————. "The Word Upside Down." *New York Review of Books*, 27 October 1983, 74–77.

Sebbah, François-David. *L'Épreuve de la limite: Derrida, Henry, Levinas et la phénoménologie*. Paris: Presses Universitaires de France, 2001.

Seel, Martin. *Ästhetik des Erscheinens*. Munich: Carl Hanser, 2000.

————. *Die Kunst der Entzweiung: Zum Begriff der ästhetischen Rationalität*. Frankfurt a.M.: Suhrkamp, 1985.

————. "Plädoyer für die zweite Moderne." In *Die Aktualität der "Dialektik der Aufklärung,"* ed. Harry Kunneman and Hent de Vries, 36–66. Frankfurt a.M.: Campus, 1989.

————. "Die zwei Bedeutungen 'kommunikativer Rationalität': Bermerkungen zu Habermas' Kritik der pluralen Vernunft." In *Kommunikatives Handeln: Beiträge zu Jürgen Habermas' 'Theorie des kommunikativen Handelns,'* ed. Axel Honneth and Hans Joas, 53–72. Frankfurt a.M.: Suhrkamp, 1986. Trans. Jeremy Gaines and Doris L. Jones under the title "The Two Meanings of 'Communicative' Rationality: Remarks on Habermas's Critique of a Plural Concept of Reason," in *Communicative Action: Essays on Jürgen Habermas's "The Theory of Communicative Action,"* ed. Axel Honneth and Hans Joas (Cambridge: MIT Press, 1991), 36–48.

Siebert, R. J. *The Critical Theory of Religion: The Frankfurt School, from Universal Pragmatic to Political Theology*. Berlin: Mouton, 1985.

Simon, Josef. "Vornehme und apokalyptische Töne in der Philosophie." *Zeitschrift für philosophische Forschung* (1986): 489–519.

Slatman, Jenny. *L'Expression au-delà de la représentation: Sur l'aisthêsis et l'esthetique chez Merleau-Ponty* (Louvain: Vrin, Peeters, 2003).

Sloterdijk, Peter. *Kritik der zynischen Vernunft.* 2 vols. Frankfurt a.M.: Suhrkamp, 1983. Trans. Michael Eldred under the title *Critique of Cynical Reason* (Minneapolis: University of Minnesota Press, 1987).

———. "Was ist Solidarität mit Metaphysik im Augenblick ihres Sturzes: Notiz über kritische und übertriebene Theorie." *Nicht gerettet,* 235–74. Frankfurt a.M.: Suhrkamp, 2001.

Smith, S. "Reason as One for Another: Moral and Theoretical Argument in the Philosophy of Levinas." In *Face to Face with Levinas,* ed. R. A. Cohen, 53–71. Albany: State University of New York Press, 1986.

Söllner, A. "Angst und Politik: Zur Aktualität Adornos im Spannungsfeld von Politikwissenschaft und Sozialpsychologie." In *Adorno-Konferenz 1983,* ed. Ludwig von Friedeburg and Jürgen Habermas, 338–49. Frankfurt a.M.: Suhrkamp, 1983.

Spinoza, Benedict de. *A Spinoza Reader: The "Ethics" and Other Works.* Ed. and trans. Edwin Curley. Princeton: Princeton University Press, 1994.

Steel, Carlos. "Inzicht en zingeving." *Tijdschrift voor Filosofie* 49 (1987): 297–307.

Steinacker, P. "Verborgenheit als theologisches Motiv in der Ästhetik." *Neue Zeitschrift für systematische Theologie und Religionsphilosophie* 23 (1981): 254–71.

Stone, Martin. "Wittgenstein on Deconstruction." In *The New Wittgenstein,* ed. Alice Crary and Rupert Read, 83–117. London: Routledge, 2000.

Strasser, Stephan. "Antiphénoménologie et phénoménologie dans la philosophie d'Emmanuel Levinas." *Revue Philosophique de Louvain* 75 (1977): 101–25.

———. "Erotiek en vruchtbaarheid in de filosofie van Emmanuel Levinas." *Tijdschrift voor Filosofie* 37 (1975): 3–51.

———. "Ethik als Erste Philosophie." In *Phänomenologie in Frankreich,* ed. Bernhard Waldenfels, 218–265. Frankfurt a.M.: Suhrkamp, 1987.

———. *Jenseits von Sein und Zeit: Eine Einführung in Emmanuel Levinas' Philosophie.* The Hague: Martinus Nijhoff, 1978.

Strauss, Leo. *Persecution and the Art of Writing.* Chicago: University of Chicago Press, 1952.

Taminiaux, Jacques. "The Origin of 'The Origin of the Work of Art.'" In *Reading Heidegger: Commemorations,* 392–404. Bloomington: Indiana University Press, 1993.

Taubes, Jakob. *Die politische Theologie des Paulus.* Ed. Aleida Assmann and Jan Assmann, in conjunction with Horst Folkers, Wolf-Daniel Hartwich, and

Christoph Schulte. Munich: Wilhelm Fink Verlag, 1993. Trans. Dana Hollander under the title *The Political Theology of Paul* (Stanford: Stanford University Press, 2004).

———. *Vom Kult zur Kultur: Bausteine zu einer Kritik der historischen Vernunft, gesammelte Aufsätze zur Religions- und Geistesgeschichte.* Ed. Aleida and Jan Assmann, Wolf-Daniel Hartwich, and Winfried Menninghaus. Munich: Wilhelm Fink, 1996.

Taussig, Michael. *Defacement: Public Secrecy and the Labor of the Negative.* Stanford: Stanford University Press, 1999.

Taylor, Charles. "Die Motive einere Verfahrensethik." In *Moralität und Sittlichkeit: Das Problem Hegels und die Diskursethik,* ed. W. Kuhlmann, 101–35. Frankfurt a.M.: Suhrkamp, 1986.

———. "Sprache und Gesellschaft." In *Kommunikatives Handeln: Beiträge zu Jürgen Habermas' "Theorie des kommunikativen Handelns,"* ed. Axel Honneth and Hans Joas, 35–52. Frankfurt a.M.: Suhrkamp, 1986. Trans. under the title *Communicative Action* (Cambridge: MIT Press, 1991).

Tenbruck, Friedrich. Afterword to Max Weber, *Wissenschaft als Beruf,* 47–77. Stuttgart: Reklam, 1995.

Theunissen, Michael. *Der Andere: Studien zur Sozialontologie der Gegenwart.* Berlin: Walter de Gruyter, 1965. Trans. Christopher MacCann under the title *The Other* (Cambridge: MIT Press, 1984).

———. *Negative Theologie der Zeit.* Frankfurt a.M.: Suhrkamp, 1991.

———. "Negativität bei Adorno." In *Adorno-Konferenz 1983,* ed. Ludwig von Friedenburg and Jürgen Habermas, 41–65. Frankfurt a.M.: Suhrkamp, 1983.

———. *Selbstverwirklichung und Allgemeinheit: Zur Kritik des gegenwärtigen Bewußtseins.* Berlin: Walter de Gruyter, 1982.

Thyen, Anke. *Negative Dialektik und Erfahrung: Zur Rationalität des Nichtidentischen bei Adorno.* Frankfurt a.M.: Suhrkamp, 1989.

Tiedemann, Rolf. "Begriff Bild Name: Über Adornos Utopie von Erkenntnis." In *Hamburger Adorno-Symposion,* ed. Michael Löbig and Gerhard Schweppenhäuser, 67–78. Lüneburg: D. zu Klampen, 1984.

———. "Historischer Materialismus oder politischer Messianismus? Politische Gehalte der Geschichtsphilosophie Walter Benjamins." In *Materialien zu Benjamins Thesen "Über den Begriff der Geschichte,"* ed. Peter Bulthaup, 77–121. Frankfurt a.M.: Suhrkamp, 1975.

———. "Nicht die Erste Philosophie sondern eine letzte." In Theodor W. Adorno, *"Ob nach Auschwitz noch sich leben lässe": Ein philosophisches Lesebuch,* ed. Rolf Tiedemann, 7–27. Leipzig: Suhrkamp, 1997. Trans. Rodney Livingstone under the title "Introduction: Not the First Philosophy but a Last One," *Can*

One Live after Auschwitz?: A Philosophical Reader, trans. Rodney Livingstone et al. (Stanford: Stanford University Press, 2003), xi–xxvii.

Tillich, Paul. "Das Frankfurter Gespräch." In *Briefwechsel und Streitschriften: Theologische, philosophische und politische Stellungnahmen und Gespräche,* ed. Renate Albrecht and Rene Tautmann, 314–69. Frankfurt a.M.: Evangelisches Verlagswerk, 1983.

Travis, Charles. *Unshadowed Thought: Representation in Thought and Language.* Cambridge: Harvard University Press, 2000.

Vattimo, Gianni. "Das Ende der Geschichte." In *Die Aktualität der "Dialektik der Aufklärung": Zwischen Moderne und Postmoderne,* ed. Harry Kunneman and Hent de Vries, 168–82. Frankfurt a.M.: Campus, 1989.

Vernant, Jean-Pierre. "La Religion objet de science." *Entre mythe et politique,* 94–105. Paris: Seuil, 1996.

Vries, Hent de. "Adieu, à dieu, a-Dieu." In *Ethics as First Philosophy: The Significance of Emmanuel Levinas for Philosophy, Literature, and Religion,* ed. and intro. Adriaan T. Peperzak, 211–20. New York: Routledge, 1995.

———. "Attestation du temps et de l'autre: De *Temps et récit* à *Soi-même comme un autre.*" In *Paul Ricoeur: L'Herméneutique à l'école de la phénoménologie,* ed. Jean Greisch, 21–42. Paris: Beauchesne, 1995.

———. "Die *Dialektik der Aufklärung* und die Tugenden der 'Vernunftskepsis': Versuch einer dekonstruktiven Lektüre ihrer subjektphilosophischen Züge." In *Die Aktualität der "Dialektik der Aufklärung": Zwischen Moderne und Postmoderne,* ed. Harry Kunneman and Hent de Vries, 183–209. Frankfurt a.M.: Campus, 1989.

———. "De godsdienstwijsgerige relevantie van Adorno's 'Meditationen zur Metaphysik': Prolegomena voor een confrontatie met het werk van Levinas." In *Praesidium libertatis: Lezingen op de Filosofiedag 1985 te Leiden,* ed. Caroline van Eck and Hermann Philipse, 92–98. *Filosofische Reeks,* no. 12. Delft, Eburon, 1985.

———. "'Lapsus absolu': Some Remarks on Maurice Blanchot's *L'Instant de ma mort.*" *Yale French Studies* 93 (1998): 30–59.

———. "Moralität und Sittlichkeit: Zu Adornos Hegelkritik." In *Hegel-Jahrbuch 1988,* ed. H. Kimmerle, R. W. Meyer, and W. Lefèvre, 300–307.

———. "On Obligation: Lyotard and Levinas." *Graduate Faculty Philosophy Journal* 20–21, nos. 1–2 (1998): 83–112.

———. *Philosophy and the Turn to Religion.* Baltimore: Johns Hopkins University Press, 1999.

———. *Religion and Violence: Philosophical Perspectives from Kant to Derrida.* Baltimore: Johns Hopkins University Press, 2001.

————. Review of Cohen, *Face to Face with Levinas. Bijdragen* 3 (1988): 348–50.

————. Review of Siebert, *The Critical Theory of Religion. Bijdragen* 4 (1988): 468–70.

————. "Le Schibboleth de l'éthique: Derrida avec Celan." In *L'Ethique du don: Jacques Derrida et la pensée du don,* ed. J. M. Rabaté and M. Wetzel, Colloque de Royaumont, December 1990, 212–38. Paris: Métailié-Transition, 1992.

————. "*Sei gerecht!* Lyotard over de verplichting." In *Lyotard lezen: Ethiek, onmenselijkheid en sensibiliteit,* ed. R. Brons and H. Kunneman, 32–49. Amsterdam: Boom, 1995.

————. "Theologie als allegorie: Over de status van de joodse gedachtenmotieven in het werk van Walter Benjamin." In *Vier joodse denkers in de twintigste eeuw: Rosenzweig, Benjamin, Levinas, Fackenheim,* ed. H. J. Heering et al., 22–51. Kampen, Neth.: J. H. Kok, 1987.

————. "Theologie en moderniteit, rationaliteit en skepsis." *Nederlands Theologisch Tijdschrift* 42 (1988): 21–41.

————. *Theologie im pianissimo: Zur Aktualität der Denkfiguren Adornos und Levinas.* Kampen, Neth.: J. H. Kok, 1989.

————. "Theologie in pianissimo: De afnemende en de blijvende verstaanbaarheid van het spreken over God." In *Theologie en rationaliteit,* ed. H. J. Adriaanse and H. A. Krop, 260–302. Kampen, Neth.: J. H. Kok, 1988.

————. "The Theology of the Sign and the Sign of Theology." In *Flight of the Gods: Philosophical Perspectives on Negative Theology,* ed. Ilse N. Bulhof and Laurens ten Kate, 166–94. New York: Fordham University Press, 2000.

————. "Westerse rationaliteit en cynisme, sceptische argumenten voor het politieke realisme." In *Het neorealisme in de politiek: Theologisch beschouwed,* ed. Meerten B. ter Borg and Lammert Leertouwer, 109–27. Baarn: Ambo, 1987.

————. "Zum Begriff der Allegorie in Schopenhauers Religionsphilosphie." In *Schopenhauer, Nietzsche und die Kunst,* ed. Wolfgang Schirmacher, 187–97. Schopenhauer-Studien 4. Vienna: Passagen, 1991.

Vries, Hent de, and Samuel Weber, eds. *Religion and Media.* Stanford: Stanford University Press, 2001.

————. *Violence, Identity, and Self-Determination.* Stanford: Stanford University Press, 1997.

Wahl, Jean. *Qu'est-ce que le structuralisme?* Vol. 5 of *Philosophie: La Philosophie entre l'avant et l'après du structuralisme.* Paris: Seuil, 1968.

————. *Traité de Métaphysique.* Paris: Payot, 1953.

Waldenfels, Bernhard. *Deutsch-Französische Gedankengänge.* Frankfurt a.M.: Suhrkamp, 1995.

————. "Gespräch mit Bernhard Waldenfels: '. . . jeder philosophische Satz ist eigentlich in Unordnung, in Bewegung.'" In *Vernunft im Zeichen des Fremden: Zur Philosophie Bernhard Waldenfels*, ed. Matthias Fischer, Hans-Dieter Gondek, and Burkhard Liebsch, 408–59. Frankfurt a.M: Suhrkamp, 2001.

———. *Im den Netzen der Lebenswelt.* Frankfurt a.M.: Suhrkamp, 1985.

———. *Phänomenologie des Fremden.* 4 vols. Frankfurt a.M.: Suhrkamp, 1997–99.

———. *Phänomenologie in Frankreich.* Frankfurt a.M.: Suhrkamp, 1987.

Walravens, E., ed., *Dialectiek van de Verlichting.* Special issue of *Tijdschrift voor de studie van de Verlichting en van het wrije denken* 12 (1984): 1–2.

Weber, Elisabeth. Verfolgung and Trauma: Zu Emmanuel Levinas' 'Autrement qu'être ou au-delà de l'essence' (Vienna: Passagen, 1990).

Weber, Max. "Wissenschaft als Beruf." *Gesammelte Aufsätze zur Wissenschaftslehre,* 524–55. Tübingen: J. C. B. Mohr, 1973. Trans. under the title "Science as a Vocation," in *From Max Weber: Essays in Sociology,* ed. and trans. H. H. Gerth and C. Wright Mills (New York: Oxford University Press, 1946), 129–56.

Wellmer, Albrecht. *Endspiele: Die unversöhnliche Moderne: Essays und Vorträge.* Frankfurt a.M.: Suhrkamp, 1993. Trans. David Midgley as *Endgames: The Irreconcilable Nature of Modernity: Essays and Lectures.* Cambridge: MIT Press, 1998.

———. *Ethik und Dialog: Elemente des moralischen Urteils bei Kant und in der Diskursethik.* Frankfurt a.M.: Surhkamp, 1986. Trans. David Midgley as the final chapter in Albrecht Wellmer, *The Persistence of Modernity: Essays on Aesthetics, Ethics, and Postmodernism* (Cambridge: MIT Press, 1991), 168–70.

———. "Ludwig Wittgenstein: Über die Schwierigkeiten einer Rezeption seiner Philosophie und ihre Stellung zur Philosophie Adornos." In Brian McGuinness et al., *"Der Löwe spricht . . . und wir können ihn nicht verstehen": Ein Symposium an der Universität Frankfurt anlässlich des hundersten Geburtstages von Ludwig Wittgenstein,* 138–48. Frankfurt a.M.: Suhrkamp, 1991.

———. "Wahrkheit, Schein, *Versöhnung: Adornos ästhetischer Rettung der Modernität.* In *Adorno-Konferenz 1983,* ed. Ludwig von Friedenburg and Jürgen Habermas, 183–76. Frankfurt a.M.: Suhrkamp, 1983.

———. *Zur Dialektik von Moderne und Postmoderne: Vernunfkritik nach Adorno.* Frankfurt a.M.: Suhrkamp, 1985.

Welsch, Wolfgang. "Heterogenität, Widerstreit und Vernunft: Zu Jean-François Lyotards philosophischer Konzeption von Postmoderne." *Philosophische Rundschau* (1987).

———. *Unsere postmoderne Moderne.* 2d ed. Weinheim: VCH, 1988.

———. "Vielheit ohne Einheit? Zum gegenwärtigen Spektrum der philosophischen Diskussion um die 'Postmoderne': Französische, italienische, amerikanische, deutsche Aspekte." *Philosophisches Jahrbuch* 1 (1987): 111–41.

Welten, Ruud. *Fenomenologie en beeldverbod bij Emmanuel Levinas en Jean-Luc Marion.* Budel: Damon, 2001.

Wheeler, Samuel C., III. *Deconstruction as Analytic Philosophy.* Stanford: Stanford University Press, 2000.

Wiemer, Thomas. *Die Passion des Sagens: Zur Deutung der Sprache bei Emmanuel Levinas und ihrer Realisierung im philosophischen Diskurs.* Freibrug: Karl Alber, 1988.

Wiggershaus, Rolf. *Die Frankfurter Schule: Geschichte, theoretische Entwicklung, politische Bedeutung.* Munich: Carl Hanser, 1986. Trans. Michael Robertson under the title *The Frankfurt School: Its History, Theories, and Political Significance* (Cambridge: MIT Press, 1994).

—————. *Wittgenstein und Adorno: Zwei Spielarten modernen Philosophierens.* Göttingen: Wallstein, 2000.

Wilke, Sabine. "Adornos und Derridas Husserllektüre: Ein Annäherungsversuch." *Husserl Studies* 5 (1988): 41–68.

Wingert, Lutz, and Klaus Günther, eds. *Die Öffentlichkeit der Vernunft und die Vernunft der Öffentlichkeit: Festschrift für Jürgen Habermas.* Frankfurt a.M.: Suhrkamp, 2001.

Wohlmuth, Josef, ed. *Emmanuel Levinas—eine Herausforderung für die christliche Theologie.* Paderborn: Ferdinand Schöningh, 1998.

Wood, David, and Robert Bernasconi, eds. *Derrida and Différance.* Evanston, Ill.: Northwestern University Press, 1988.

Zarader, Marlène. *L'Être et le neutre: À partir de Maurice Blanchot.* Lagrasse: Verdier, 2001.

Zielinski, Agata. *Lecture de Merleau-Ponty et Levinas: Le Corps, le monde, l'autre.* Paris: Presses Universitaires de France, 2002.

Zmegac, V. "Adorno und die Wiener Moderne der Jahrhundertwende." In *Die Frankfurter Schule und die Folgen,* ed. Axel Honneth and Albrecht Wellmer, 321–38. Berlin: Walter de Gruyter, 1986.

Index